2019 NATIONAL REPAIR & REMODELING ESTIMATOR

by Albert S. Paxton

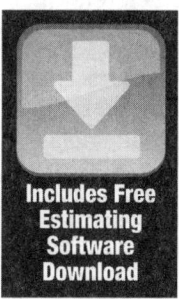

Includes Free Estimating Software Download

Includes inside the back cover:

Inside the back cover of this book you'll find a software download certificate. To access the download, follow the instructions printed there. The download includes the National Estimator, an easy-to-use estimating program with all the cost estimates in this book. The software will run on PCs using Windows XP, Vista, 7, 8, or 10 operating systems.

Quarterly price updates on the Web are free and automatic all during 2019. You'll be prompted when it's time to collect the next update. A connection to the Web is required.

Download all of Craftsman's most popular costbooks for one low price with the Craftsman Site License. http://www.CraftsmanSiteLicense.com

- Turn your estimate into a bid.
- Turn your bid into a contract.
- ConstructionContractWriter.com

Craftsman Book Company
6058 Corte del Cedro, Carlsbad, CA 92011

Preface

The author has corresponded with manufacturers and wholesalers of building material supplies and surveyed retail pricing services. From these sources, he has developed Average Material Unit Costs which should apply in most parts of the country.

Wherever possible, the author has listed Average Labor Unit Costs which are derived from the Average Manhours per Unit, the Crew Size, and the Wage Rates used in this book. Please read How to Use This Book for a more in-depth explanation of the arithmetic.

If you prefer, you can develop your own local labor unit costs. You can do this by simply multiplying the Average Manhours per Unit by your local crew wage rates per hour. Using your actual local labor wage rates for the trades will make your estimate more accurate.

What is a realistic labor unit cost to one reader may well be low or high to another reader, because of variations in labor efficiency. The Average Manhours per Unit figures were developed by time studies at job sites around the country. To determine the daily production rate for the crew, divide the total crew manhours per day by the Average Manhours per Unit.

The subject topics in this book are arranged in alphabetical order, A to Z. To help you find specific construction items, there is a complete alphabetical index at the end of the book, and a main subject index at the beginning of the book.

This manual shows crew, manhours, material, labor and equipment cost estimates based on Large or Small Volume work, then a total cost and a total including overhead and profit. No single price fits all repair and remodeling jobs. Generally, work done on smaller jobs costs more per unit installed and work on larger jobs costs less. The estimates in this book reflect that simple fact. The two estimates you find for each work item show the author's opinion of the likely range of costs for most contractors and for most jobs. So, which cost do you use, High Volume or Low Volume?

The only right price is the one that gets the job and earns a reasonable profit. Finding that price always requires estimating judgment. Use Small Volume cost estimates when some or most of the following conditions are likely:

- The crews won't work more than a few days on site.
- Better quality work is required.
- Productivity will probably be below average.
- Volume discounts on materials aren't available.
- Bidding is less competitive.
- Your overhead is higher than most contractors.

When few or none of those conditions apply, use Large Volume cost estimates.

Credits and Acknowledgments

This book has over 12,000 cost estimates for 2019. To develop these estimates, the author and editors relied on information supplied by hundreds of construction cost authorities. We offer our sincere thanks to the contractors, engineers, design professionals, construction estimators, material suppliers and manufacturers who, in the spirit of cooperation, have assisted in the preparation of this 39th edition of the National Repair & Remodeling Estimator. Our appreciation is extended to those listed below.

American Standard Products
DAP Products
Outwater Plastic Industries
Con-Rock Concrete
Georgia Pacific Products

Kohler Products
Wood Mode Cabinets
Transit Mixed Concrete
U.S. Gypsum Products
Henry Roofing Products

Special thanks to: **Dal-Tile Corporation** 1713 Stewart, Santa Monica, California

About the Author

Albert Paxton is a Project Director at *Unified Building Sciences, Inc. (UBS)* (www.UnifiedGroup.com), located in Dallas, Texas.

Mr. Paxton (ALP@UnifiedGroup.com) is a California licensed General Contractor (B1-425946) and a Certified Professional Estimator with the *American Society of Professional Estimators*. The *UBS* staff is comprised of estimators, engineers and project managers who are also expert witnesses, building appraisers and arbitrators operating throughout the United States.

UBS clients include property insurance carriers, financial institutions, self-insureds, and private individuals.

The expertise of UBS is in both new and repair/remodel work, for both residential and commercial construction. In addition to daily claims involving individual structures, UBS assignments have included natural disasters such as the 1994 Northridge earthquake in California, the 2004 Hurricanes Charley, Frances, Ivan and Jeanne, striking Florida and the southeastern states, the catastrophic Hurricane Katrina (2005), the Texas Hurricanes Dolly (2008) and Ike (2008), the cleanup, repair and rebuilding of the massive destruction of Superstorms Sandy (2012), and, more recently, Hurricanes Matthew (2016), Harvey (2017), Irma (2017) and Michael (2018).

©2019 Craftsman Book Company ISBN 978-1-57218-349-0

Cover design by *Jennifer Johnson*

Main Subject Index

How to Use This Book

1	2	3	4	5	6	7	8	9	10	11	12
Description	Oper	Unit	Vol	Crew Size	Man-hours per Unit	Crew Output per Day	Avg Mat'l Unit Cost	Avg Labor Unit Cost	Avg Equip Unit Cost	Avg Total Unit Cost	Avg Price Incl O&P

The descriptions and cost data in this book are arranged in a series of columns, which are described below. The cost data is divided into two categories: Costs Based On Large Volume and Costs Based On Small Volume. These two categories provide the estimator with a pricing range for each construction topic.

The Description column (1) contains the pertinent, specific information necessary to make the pricing information relevant and accurate.

The Operation column (2) contains a description of the construction repair or remodeling operation being performed. Generally the operations are Demolition, Install, and Reset.

The Unit column (3) contains the unit of measurement or quantity which applies to the item described.

The Volume column (4) breaks jobs into Large and Small categories. Based on the information given regarding volume (on page 2), select your job size.

The Crew Size column (5) contains a description of the trade that usually installs or labors on the specified item. It includes information on the labor trade that installs the material and the typical crew size. Letters and numbers are used in the abbreviations in the crew size column. Full descriptions of these abbreviations are in the Crew Compositions and Wage Rates table, beginning on page 15.

The Manhours per Unit column (6) is for the listed operation and listed crew.

The units per day in this book don't take into consideration unusually large or small quantities. But items such as travel, accessibility to work, experience of workers, and protection of undamaged property, which can favorably or adversely affect productivity, have been considered in developing Average Manhours per Unit. For further information about labor, see "Notes — Labor" in the Notes Section of some specific items.

Crew Output per Day (7) is based on how many units, on average, a crew can install or demo in one 8-hour day.

Crew Output per Day and Average Material Unit (8) Cost should assist the estimator in:

1. Checking prices quoted by others.

2. Developing local prices.

The Average Material Unit Cost column contains an average material cost for products (including, in many cases, the by-products used in installing the products) for both large and small volume. It doesn't include an allowance for sales tax, delivery charges, overhead and profit. Percentages for waste, shrinkage, or coverage have been taken into consideration unless indicated. For other information, see "Dimensions" or "Installation" in the Notes Section.

If the item described has many or very unusual by-products which are essential to determining the Average Material Unit Cost, the author has provided examples of material pricing. These examples are placed throughout the book in the Notes Section.

You should verify labor rates and material prices locally. Though the prices in this book are average material prices, prices vary from locality to locality. A local hourly wage rate should normally include taxes, benefits, and insurance. Some contractors may also include overhead and profit in the hourly rate.

The Average Labor Unit Cost column (9) contains an average labor cost based on the Average Manhours per Unit and the Crew Compositions and Wage Rates table. The average labor unit cost equals the Average Manhours per Unit multiplied by the Average Crew Rate per hour. The rates include fringe benefits, taxes, and insurance. Examples that show how to determine the average labor unit cost are provided in the Notes Section.

The Average Equipment Unit Cost column (10) contains an average equipment cost, based on both the average daily rental and the cost per day if owned and depreciated. The costs of daily maintenance and the operator are included.

The Average Total Unit Cost column (11) includes the sum of the Material, Equipment, and Labor Cost columns. It doesn't include an allowance for overhead and profit.

The Average (Total) Price Including Overhead and Profit column (12) results from adding an overhead and profit allowance to Total Cost. This allowance reflects the author's interpretation of average fixed and variable overhead expenses and the labor intensiveness of the operation vs. the costs of materials for the operation. This allowance factor varies throughout the book, depending on the operation. Each contractor interprets O&P differently. The range can be from 15 percent to 80 percent of the Average Total Unit Cost.

Estimating Techniques

Estimating Repair/Remodeling Jobs: The unforeseen, unpredictable, or unexpected can ruin you.

Each year, the residential repair and remodeling industry grows. It's currently outpacing residential new construction due to increases in land costs, labor wage rates, interest rates, material costs, and economic uncertainty. When people can't afford a new home, they tend to remodel their old one. And there are always houses that need repair, from natural disasters or accidents like fire. The professional repair and remodeling contractor is moving to the forefront of the industry.

Repair and remodeling spawns three occupations: the contractor and his workers, the insurance company property claims adjuster, and the property damage appraiser. Each of these professionals shares common functions, including estimating the cost of the repair or remodeling work.

Estimating isn't an exact science. Yet the estimate determines the profit or loss for the contractor, the fairness of the claim payout by the adjuster, and the amount of grant or loan by the appraiser. Quality estimating must be uppermost in the mind of each of these professionals. And accurate estimates are possible only when you know exactly what materials are needed and the number of manhours required for demolition, removal, and installation. Remember, profits follow the professional. To be profitable you must control costs — and cost control is directly related to accurate, professional estimates.

There are four general types of estimates, each with a different purpose and a corresponding degree of accuracy:

- The guess method: "All bathrooms cost $5,000." or "It looks like an $8,000 job to me."

- The per measure method: (I like to call it the surprise package.) "Remodeling costs $60 per SF, the job is 500 SF, so the price is $30,000."

These two methods are the least accurate and accomplish little for the adjuster or the appraiser. The contractor might use the methods for qualifying customers (e.g., "I thought a bathroom would only cost $2,000."), but never as the basis for bidding or negotiating a price.

- The piece estimate or stick-by-stick method.

- The unit cost estimate method.

These two methods yield a detailed estimate itemizing all of the material quantities and costs, the labor manhours and wage rates, the subcontract costs, and the allowance for overhead and profit.

Though time-consuming, the detailed estimate is the most accurate and predictable. It's a very satisfactory tool for negotiating either the contract price or the adjustment of a building loss. The piece estimate and the unit cost estimate rely on historical data, such as manhours per specific job operation and recent material costs. The successful repair and remodeling contractor, or insurance/appraisal company, maintains records of previous jobs detailing allocation of crew manhours per day and materials expended.

While new estimators don't have historical data records, they can rely on reference books, magazines, and newsletters to estimate manhours and material costs. It is important to remember that **the reference must pertain to repair and remodeling**. This book is designed *specifically* to meet this requirement.

The reference material must specialize in repair and remodeling work because there's a large cost difference between new construction and repair and remodeling. Material and labor construction costs vary radically with the size of the job or project. Economies of scale come into play. The larger the quantity of materials, the better the purchase price should be. The larger the number of units to be installed, the greater the labor efficiency.

Repair and remodeling work, compared to new construction, is more expensive due to a normally smaller volume of work. Typical repair work involves only two or three rooms of a house, or one roof. In new construction, the job size may be three to five complete homes or an entire development. And there's another factor: a lot of repair and remodeling is done with the house occupied, forcing the crew to work around the normal, daily activities of the occupants. In new construction, the approach is systematic and logical — work proceeds from the ground up to the roof and to the inside of the structure.

Since the jobs are small, the repair and remodeling contractor doesn't employ trade specialists. Repairers employ the "jack-of-all-trades" who is less specialized and therefore less efficient. This isn't to say the repairer is less professional than the trade specialist. On the contrary, the repairer must know about many more facets of construction: not just framing, but painting, finish carpentry, roofing, and electrical as well. But because the repairer has to spread his expertise over a greater area, he will be less efficient than the specialist who repeats the same operation all day long.

Another factor reducing worker efficiency is poor access to the work area. With new construction, where building is an orderly "from the ground up" approach, workers have easy access to the work area for any given operation. The workers can spread out as much as needed, which facilitates efficiency and minimizes the manhours required to perform a given operation.

The opposite situation exists with repair and remodeling construction. Consider an example where the work area involves fire damage on the second floor. Materials either go up through the interior stairs or through a second story window. Neither is easy when the exterior and interior walls have a finished covering such as siding and drywall. That results in greater labor costs with repair and remodeling because it takes more manhours to perform many of the same tasks.

If, as a professional estimator, you want to start collecting historical data, the place to begin is with daily worker time sheets that detail:

1. total hours worked by each worker per day

2. what specific operations each worker performed that day

3. how many hours (to the nearest tenth) each worker used in each operation performed that day.

Second, you must catalog all material invoices daily, being sure that quantities and unit costs per item are clearly indicated.

Third, maintain a record of overhead expenses attributable to the particular project. Then, after a number of jobs, you'll be able to calculate an average percentage of the job's gross amount that's attributable to overhead. Many contractors add 45% for overhead and profit to their total direct costs (direct labor, direct material, and direct subcontract costs). But that figure may not be right for your jobs.

Finally, each week you should reconcile in a job summary file the actual costs versus the estimated costs, and determine why there is any difference. This information can't immediately help you on this job since the contract has been signed, but it will be invaluable to you on your next job.

Up to now I've been talking about general estimating theory. Now let's be more specific. On page 8 is a Building Repair Estimate form. Each line is keyed to an explanation. A filled-out copy of the form is also provided, and on page 10, a blank, full-size copy that you can reproduce for your own use.

You can adapt the Building Repair Estimate form, whether you're a contractor, adjuster, or appraiser. Use of the form will yield a detailed estimate that will identify:

- The room or area involved, including sizes, dimensions and measurements.

- The kind and quality of material to be used.

- The quantities of materials to be used and verification of their prices.

- The type of work to be performed (demolish, remove, install, remove and reset) by what type of crew.

- The crew manhours per job operation and verification of the hourly wage scale.

- All arithmetical calculations that can be verified.

- Areas of difference between your estimate and others.

- Areas that will be a basis for negotiation and discussion of details.

Each job estimate begins with a visual inspection of the work site. If it's a repair job, you've got to see the damage. Without a visual inspection, you can't select a method of repair and you can't properly evaluate the opinions of others regarding repair or replacement. With either repair or remodeling work, the visual inspection is essential to uncover the "hiders" — the unpredictable, unforeseen, and unexpected problems that can turn profit into loss, or simplicity into nightmare. You're looking for the many variables and unknowns that exist behind an exterior or interior wall covering.

Along with the Building Repair Estimate form, use this checklist to make sure you're not forgetting anything.

Checklist

- Site accessibility: Will you store materials and tools in the garage? Is it secure? You can save a half hour to an hour each day by storing tools in the garage. Will the landscaping prevent trucks from reaching the work site? Are wheelbarrows or concrete pumpers going to be required?

- Soil: What type and how much water content? Will the soil change your excavation estimate?

- Utility lines: What's under the soil and where? Should you schedule the utilities to stake their lines?

- Soundness of the structure: If you're going to remodel, repair or add on, how sound is that portion of the house that you're going to have to work around? Where are the load-bearing walls? Are you going to remove and reset any walls? Do the floor joists sag?

- Roof strength: Can the roof support the weight of another layer of shingles. (Is four layers of composition shingles already too much?)

- Electrical: Is another breaker box required for the additional load?

This checklist is by no means complete, but it is a start. Take pictures! A digital camera will quickly pay for itself. When you're back at the office, the picture helps reconstruct the scene. Before and after pictures are also a sales tool representing your professional expertise.

During the visual inspection always be asking yourself "what if" this or that happened. Be looking for potential problem areas that would be extremely labor intensive or expensive in material to repair or replace.

Also spend some time getting to know your clients and their attitudes. Most of repair and remodeling work occurs while the house is occupied. If the work will be messy, let the homeowners know in advance. Their satisfaction is your ultimate goal — and their satisfaction will provide you a pleasant working atmosphere. You're there to communicate with them. At the end of an estimate and visual inspection, the homeowner should have a clear idea of what you can or can't do, how it will be done, and approximately how long it will take. Don't discuss costs now! Save the estimating for your quiet office with a print-out calculator and your cost files or reference books.

What you create on your estimate form during a visual inspection is a set of rough notes and diagrams that make the estimate speak. To avoid duplications and omissions, estimate in a *systematic sequence of inspection*. There are two questions to consider. First, where do you start the estimate? Second, in what order will you list the damaged or replaced items? It's customary to start in the room having either the most damage or requiring the most extensive remodeling. The sequence of listing is important. Start with either the floor or the ceiling. When starting with the floor, you might list items in the following sequence: Joists, subfloor, finish floor, base — listing from bottom to top. When starting with the ceiling, you reverse, and list from top to bottom. The important thing is to be consistent as you go from room to room! It's a good idea to figure the roof and foundation separately, instead of by the room.

After completing your visual inspection, go back to your office to cost out the items. Talk to your material supply houses and get unit costs for the quantity involved. Consult your job files or reference books and assign crew manhours to the different job operations.

There's one more reason for creating detailed estimates. Besides an estimate, what else have your notes given you? A material take-off sheet, a lumber list, a plan and specification sheet — the basis for writing a job summary for comparing estimated costs and profit versus actual costs and profit — and a project schedule that minimizes down time.

Here's the last step: Enter an amount for overhead and profit. No matter how small or large your work volume is, be realistic — everyone has overhead and every business entity works to make a fair and reasonable profit. An office, even in your home, costs money to operate. If family members help out, pay them. Everyone's time is valuable!

If you expect there will be a supervising general contractor on the job, and the overhead and profit is computed as a percentage of the job, then overhead and profit dollars automatically adjust to the job size and the job complexity.

Don't forget to charge for performing your estimate. A professional expects to be paid. You'll render a better product if you know you're being paid for your time. If you want to soften the blow to the owner, say the first hour is free or that the cost of the estimate will be deducted from the job price if you get the job.

In conclusion, whether you're a contractor, adjuster, or appraiser, you're selling your personal service, your ideas, and your reputation. To be successful you must:

- Know yourself and your capabilities.

- Know what the job will require by ferreting out the "hiders."

- Know your products and your work crew.

- Know your productivity and be able to deliver in a reasonable manner and within a reasonable time frame.

- Know your client and make it clear that all change orders, no matter how large or small, will cost money.

Inside the back cover of this book you'll find a software download certificate. To access the download, follow the instructions printed there. The download includes the *National Estimator*, an easy-to-use estimating program with all the cost estimates in this book. The software will run on PCs using Windows XP, Vista, 7, 8, or 10 operating systems. When the *National Estimator* program has been installed, click Help on the menu bar to see a list of topics that will get you up and running. Or, go online to www.craftsman-book.com, click on "Support," then "Tutorials" to view an interactive video for *National Estimator*.

Building Repair Estimate

Filled Example (Page 1 of 2)

Insured	John Q. Smith	Claim or Policy No.	DP 0029	Page 1 of 2
Loss Address	123 A. Main St.	Home Ph. 555-1241		Cause of Loss Fire
City	Anywhere, Anystate 00010	Bus. Ph. 555-1438		Other Ins. Y (N)
Bldg. R.C.V. 100,000	Bldg. A.C.V. 80,000	Insurance Amount $100,000		

Insurance Required R.C.V. (80%) A.C.V.(80%)

Description of Item	Unit Cost or Material Price Only			Labor Price Only		
	Unit	Unit Price	Total (Col. A)	Hours	Rate	Total Col. B
Install 1/2" sheetrock (standard,) on walls, including tape and finish 400 (page 164)	400	0.56	224.00	9.6	50.48	484.61
Paint walls, roller, smooth finish						
1 coat sealer 600 (page 330)	600	0.08	48.00	4.2	52.95	222.39
2 coats latex flat 600 (page 333)	600	0.24	144.00	7.2	52.95	381.24
TOTALS			416.00			1088.24

THIS IS NOT AN ORDER TO REPAIR

The undersigned agrees to complete and guarantee repairs at a total of $

Total Column A	416.00
Repairer ABC Construction	Total Column A 1504.24
Street 316 E. 2nd Street	6% Tax 90.25
City Anywhere Phone	1594.49
By Jack Williams	10% Overhead 159.45
Adjuster Stan Jones Date of A/P N/A	10% Profit 159.45
Adj. License No. (If Any) 561-84	**Grand Total 1913.39**
Service Office Name Phoenix	

Note: This form does not replace the need for field notes, sketches and measurements.

Building Repair Estimate

Blank Template (numbered fields)

Date (33)

Insured (1)	Claim or Policy No. (2)	Page of (3)
Loss Address (4)	Home Ph.	Cause of Loss (5)
City	Bus. Ph.	Other Ins. Y N (6)
Bldg. R.C.V. (7)	Bldg. A.C.V. (8)	Insurance Amount (9)

Insurance Required R.C.V. ((10) %) A.C.V.((11))%

Description of Item	Unit Cost or Material Price Only			Labor Price Only		
	Unit	Unit Price	Total (Col. A)	Hours	Rate	Total Col. B
(20)	(13)	(14)	(15)	(17)	(18)	(19)
TOTALS	(21)					(22)

THIS IS NOT AN ORDER TO REPAIR

The undersigned agrees to complete and guarantee repairs at a total of $ (29)

Total Column A	
Repairer (30)	Total Column A (23)
Street (31) Phone	6% Tax (24)
City (32)	(25)
By (33) [sic]	10% Overhead (26)
Adjuster (34) Date of A/P (35)	10% Profit (27)
Adj. License No. (If Any)	**Grand Total (28)**
Service Office Name (36)	

Note: This form does not replace the need for field notes, sketches and measurements.

Keyed Explanations of the Building Repair Estimate Form

1. Insert name of insured(s).

2. Insert claim number or, if claim number is not available, insert policy number or binder number.

3. Insert the page number and the total number of pages.

4. Insert street address, city and state where loss or damage occurred.

5. Insert type of loss (wind, hail, fire, water, etc.)

6. Check YES if there is other insurance, whether collectible or not. Check NO if there's only one insurer.

7. Insert the present replacement cost of the building. What would it cost to build the structure today?

8. Insert present actual cash value of the building.

9. Insert the amount of insurance applicable. If there is more than one insurer, insert the total amount of applicable insurance provided by all insurers.

10. If the amount of insurance required is based on replacement cost value, circle RCV and insert the percent required by the policy, if any.

11. If the amount of insurance required is based on actual cash value, circle ACV and insert the percent required by the policy, if any.

   Note: (regarding 10 and 11) if there is a non-concurrency, i.e., one insurer requires insurance to 90% of value while another requires insurance to 80% of value, make a note here. Comment on the non-concurrency in the settlement report.

12. The installed price and/or material price only, as expressed in columns 13 through 15, may include any of the following (expressed in units and unit prices):

   Material only (no labor)

   Material and labor to replace

   Material and labor to remove and replace

   Unit Cost is determined by dividing dollar cost by quantity. The term cost, as used in unit cost, is not intended to include any allowance, percentage or otherwise, for overhead or profit. Usually, overhead and profit are expressed as a percentage of cost. Cost must be determined first. Insert a line or dash in a space(s) in columns 13, 14, 15, 17, 18 or 19 if the space is not to be used.

13. The units column includes both the quantity and the unit of measure, i.e., 100 SF, 100 BF, 200 CF, 100 CY, 20 ea., etc.

14. The unit price may be expressed in dollars, cents or both. If the units column has 100 SF and if the unit price column has $.10, this would indicate the price to be $.10 per SF.

15. The total column is merely the dollar product of the quantity (in column 13) times the price per unit measure (in column 14).

16. 16-19. These columns are normally used to express labor as follows: hours times rate per hour. However, it is possible to express labor as a unit price, i.e., 100 SF in column 13, a dash in column 17, $.05 in column 18 and $5.00 in column 19.

20. Under description of item, the following may be included:

   Description of item to be repaired or replaced (studs 2" x 4" 8'0" #2 Fir, Sheetrock 1/2", etc.)

   Quantities or dimensions (20 pcs., 8'0" x 14'0", etc.)

   Location within a room or area (north wall, ceiling, etc.)

   Method of correcting damage (paint - 1 coat; sand, fill and finish; R&R; remove only; replace; resize; etc.)

21-22. Dollar totals of columns A and B respectively.

23-27. Spaces provided for items not included in the body of the estimate (subtotals, overhead, profit, sales tax, etc.)

28. Total cost of repair.

29. Insert the agreed amount here. The agreement may be between the claim representative and the insured or between the claim rep and the repairer. If the agreed price is different from the grand total, the reason(s) for the difference should be itemized on the estimate sheet. If there is no room, attach an additional estimate sheet.

30. PRINT the name of the insured or the repairer so that it is legible.

31. PRINT the address of the insured or repairer legibly. Include phone number.

32. The insured or a representative of the repairer should sign here indicating agreement with the claim rep's estimate.

33. Insured or representative of the repairer should insert date here.

34. Claim rep should sign here.

35. Claim rep should insert date here.

36. Insert name of service office here.

Building Repair Estimate

Date

Insured	Claim or Policy No.	Page of
Loss Address	Home Ph.	Cause of Loss
City	Bus. Ph.	Other Ins. Y N
Building. R.C.V. Bldg. A.C.V.	Insurance Amount	

Insurance Required R.C.V.(%) A.C.V.(%)	Unit Cost or Material Price Only			Labor Price Only		
Description of Item	Unit	Unit Price	Total (Col. A)	Hours	Rate	Total Col. B
THIS IS NOT AN ORDER TO REPAIR TOTALS	▮			▮		

The undersigned agrees to complete and guarantee repairs at a total of $	Total Column A
Repairer	
Street	
City Phone	
By	
Adjuster Date of A/P	
Adj. License No. (If Any)	Grand Total
Service Office Name	

Note: This form does not replace the need for field notes, sketches and measurements.

Wage Rates Used in This Book

Wage rates listed here and used in this book were compiled in the fall of 2018 and projected to mid-2019. Wage rates are in dollars per hour.

"Base Wage Per Hour" (Col. 1) includes items such as vacation pay and sick leave which are normally taxed as wages. Nationally, these benefits average 5.48% of the Base Wage Per Hour. This amount is paid by the Employer in addition to the Base Wage Per Hour.

"Liability Insurance and Employer Taxes" (Cols. 3 & 4) include national averages for state unemployment insurance (4.00%), federal unemployment insurance (0.60%), Social Security and Medicare tax (7.65%), lia-

bility insurance (2.29%), and Workers' Compensation Insurance which varies by trade. This total percentage (Col. 3) is applied to the sum of Base Wage Per Hour and Taxable Fringe Benefits (Col. 1 + Col. 2) and is listed in Dollars (Col. 4). This amount is paid by the Employer in addition to the Base Wage Per Hour and the Taxable Fringe Benefits.

"Non-Taxable Fringe Benefits" (Col. 5) include employer-sponsored medical insurance and other benefits, which nationally average 4.84% of the Base Wage Per Hour.

"Total Hourly Cost Used In This Book" is the sum of Columns 1, 2, 4, & 5.

	1	2	3	4	5	6
Trade	Base Wage Per Hour	Taxable Fringe Benefits (5.48% of Base Wage)	Liability Insurance & Employer Taxes %	Liability Insurance & Employer Taxes $	Non-Taxable Fringe Benefits (4.84% of Base Wage)	Total Hourly Cost Used in This Book
Air Tool Operator	$31.69	$1.74	25.95%	$8.68	$1.54	$43.65
Bricklayer or Stone Mason	$27.48	$1.51	25.06%	$7.26	$1.33	$37.58
Bricktender	$20.36	$1.12	25.06%	$5.38	$0.99	$27.85
Carpenter	$25.85	$1.42	31.17%	$8.50	$1.25	$37.02
Cement Mason	$26.13	$1.43	22.97%	$6.33	$1.27	$35.16
Drywall Installer	$26.74	$1.47	23.32%	$6.58	$1.30	$36.09
Drywall Taper	$26.69	$1.47	23.32%	$6.57	$1.29	$36.02
Electrician, Journeyman Wireman	$30.65	$1.68	19.71%	$6.37	$1.49	$40.19
Equipment Operator	$30.93	$1.70	24.95%	$8.14	$1.50	$42.27
Fence Erector	$27.91	$1.53	25.74%	$7.58	$1.35	$38.37
Floor Layer: Carpet, Linoleum, Soft Tile	$25.08	$1.38	23.61%	$6.25	$1.22	$33.93
Floor Layer: Hardwood	$26.33	$1.45	23.61%	$6.56	$1.28	$35.62
Glazier	$26.08	$1.43	25.47%	$7.01	$1.26	$35.78
Laborer, General Construction	$20.78	$1.14	32.27%	$7.07	$1.01	$30.00
Lather	$26.83	$1.47	21.12%	$5.98	$1.30	$35.58
Marble Setter	$24.80	$1.36	21.20%	$5.55	$1.20	$32.91
Millwright / Finish Carpenter	$26.29	$1.44	21.09%	$5.85	$1.28	$34.86
Mosaic & Terrazzo Setter	$26.35	$1.45	21.20%	$5.89	$1.28	$34.97
Mosaic & Terrazzo Setter Helper	$20.16	$1.11	21.20%	$4.51	$0.98	$26.76
Painter, Brush	$27.74	$1.52	24.65%	$7.21	$1.35	$37.82
Painter, Spray-Gun	$28.57	$1.57	24.65%	$7.43	$1.39	$38.96
Paperhanger	$29.13	$1.60	24.65%	$7.57	$1.41	$39.71
Plasterer	$26.46	$1.45	28.21%	$7.87	$1.28	$37.06
Plasterer Helper	$20.76	$1.14	28.21%	$6.18	$1.01	$29.09
Plumber	$31.69	$1.74	24.08%	$8.05	$1.54	$43.02
Reinforcing Ironworker	$27.78	$1.53	28.27%	$8.29	$1.35	$38.95
Roofer, Foreman	$29.10	$1.60	43.34%	$13.30	$1.41	$45.41
Roofer, Journeyman	$26.45	$1.45	43.34%	$12.09	$1.28	$41.27
Roofer, Hot Mop Pitch	$27.24	$1.50	43.34%	$12.46	$1.32	$42.52
Roofer, Wood Shingles	$27.77	$1.52	43.34%	$12.70	$1.35	$43.34
Sheet Metal Worker	$30.34	$1.67	25.74%	$8.24	$1.47	$41.72
Tile Setter	$26.59	$1.46	21.20%	$5.95	$1.29	$35.29
Tile Setter's Helper	$20.16	$1.11	21.20%	$4.51	$0.98	$26.76
Truck Driver	$22.37	$1.23	25.95%	$6.12	$1.08	$30.80

Area Modification Factors

Construction costs are higher in some areas than in other areas. Add or deduct the percentages shown on the following pages to adapt the costs in this book to your job site. Adjust your cost estimate by the appropriate percentages in this table to find the estimated cost for the site selected. Where 0% is shown, it means no modification is required.

Modification factors are listed alphabetically by state and province. Areas within each state are listed by the first three digits of the postal zip code. For convenience, one representative city is identified in each three-digit zip or range of zips. Percentages are based on the average of all data points in the table.

Factors listed for each state and province are the average of all data points in that state or province. Figures for three-digit zips are the average of all five-digit zips in that area, and are the weighted average of factors for labor, material and equipment.

The National Estimator program will apply an area modification factor for any five-digit zip you select. Click Utilities. Click Options. Then select the Area Modification Factors tab.

These percentages are composites of many costs and will not necessarily be accurate when estimating the cost of any particular part of a building. But when used to modify costs for an entire structure, they should improve the accuracy of your estimates

Alabama Average		-4%
Anniston	362	-8%
Auburn	368	-4%
Bellamy	369	5%
Birmingham	350-352	2%
Dothan	363	-7%
Evergreen	364	-10%
Gadsden	359	-9%
Huntsville	358	-1%
Jasper	355	-8%
Mobile	365-366	-2%
Montgomery	360-361	-2%
Scottsboro	357	-4%
Selma	367	-5%
Sheffield	356	0%
Tuscaloosa	354	-4%

Alaska Average		23%
Anchorage	995	26%
Fairbanks	997	27%
Juneau	998	19%
Ketchikan	999	18%
King Salmon	996	23%

Arizona Average		-4%
Chambers	865	-8%
Douglas	855	-8%
Flagstaff	860	-7%
Kingman	864	-5%
Mesa	852	3%
Phoenix	850	3%
Prescott	863	-6%
Show Low	859	-7%
Tucson	856-857	-5%
Yuma	853	2%

Arkansas Average		-7%
Batesville	725	-9%
Camden	717	-2%
Fayetteville	727	-4%
Fort Smith	729	-7%
Harrison	726	-12%
Hope	718	-8%
Hot Springs	719	-13%
Jonesboro	724	-9%
Little Rock	720-722	-3%
Pine Bluff	716	-11%
Russellville	728	-4%
West Memphis	723	-2%

California Average		9%
Alhambra	917-918	8%
Bakersfield	932-933	2%
El Centro	922	0%
Eureka	955	20%
Fresno	936-938	-2%
Herlong	961	22%
Inglewood	902-905	9%
Irvine	926-927	13%
Lompoc	934	3%
Long Beach	907-908	9%
Los Angeles	900-901	8%
Marysville	959	22%
Modesto	953	1%
Mojave	935	5%
Novato	949	26%
Oakland	945-947	32%
Orange	928	12%
Oxnard	930	2%
Pasadena	910-912	9%
Rancho Cordova	956-957	4%
Redding	960	-3%
Richmond	948	17%
Riverside	925	4%
Sacramento	958	3%
Salinas	939	1%
San Bernardino	923-924	2%
San Diego	919-921	8%
San Francisco	941	27%
San Jose	950-951	17%
San Mateo	943-944	21%
Santa Barbara	931	7%
Santa Rosa	954	5%
Stockton	952	4%
Sunnyvale	940	20%
Van Nuys	913-916	8%
Whittier	906	8%

Colorado Average		1%
Aurora	800-801	7%
Boulder	803-804	4%
Colorado Springs	808-809	0%
Denver	802	8%
Durango	813	-1%
Fort Morgan	807	-2%
Glenwood Springs	816	4%
Grand Junction	814-815	0%
Greeley	806	5%
Longmont	805	2%
Pagosa Springs	811	-4%
Pueblo	810	0%
Salida	812	-6%

Connecticut Average		8%
Bridgeport	66	6%
Bristol	60	12%
Fairfield	64	9%
Hartford	61	11%
New Haven	65	7%
Norwich	63	3%
Stamford	068-069	12%
Waterbury	67	6%
West Hartford	62	5%

Delaware Average		2%
Dover	199	-4%
Newark	197	6%
Wilmington	198	4%

District of Columbia		
Washington	200-205	12%

Florida Average		-5%
Altamonte Springs	327	-3%
Bradenton	342	-6%
Brooksville	346	-7%
Daytona Beach	321	-9%
Fort Lauderdale	333	2%
Fort Myers	339	-6%
Fort Pierce	349	-10%
Gainesville	326	-9%
Jacksonville	322	-2%
Lakeland	338	-8%
Melbourne	329	-8%
Miami	330-332	1%
Naples	341	-2%
Ocala	344	-12%
Orlando	328	1%
Panama City	324	-11%
Pensacola	325	-8%
Saint Augustine	320	-2%
Saint Cloud	347	-2%
St Petersburg	337	-6%
Tallahassee	323	-6%
Tampa	335-336	-1%
W. Palm Beach	334	-2%

Georgia Average		-4%
Albany	317	-6%
Athens	306	-5%
Atlanta	303	12%
Augusta	308-309	-2%
Buford	305	-2%
Calhoun	307	-9%
Columbus	318-319	-3%
Dublin/Fort Valley	310	-8%
Hinesville	313	-6%
Kings Bay	315	-10%
Macon	312	-4%
Marietta	300-302	4%
Savannah	314	-4%
Statesboro	304	-11%
Valdosta	316	-1%

Hawaii Average		20%
Aliamanu	968	22%
Ewa	967	20%
Halawa Heights	967	20%
Hilo	967	20%
Honolulu	968	22%
Kailua	968	22%
Lualualei	967	20%
Mililani Town	967	20%
Pearl City	967	20%
Wahiawa	967	20%
Waianae	967	20%
Wailuku (Maui)	967	20%

Idaho Average		-9%
Boise	837	-5%
Coeur d'Alene	838	-10%
Idaho Falls	834	-9%
Lewiston	835	-11%
Meridian	836	-9%
Pocatello	832	-10%
Sun Valley	833	-8%

Illinois Average		4%
Arlington Heights	600	14%
Aurora	605	14%
Belleville	622	0%
Bloomington	617	-1%
Carbondale	629	-4%
Carol Stream	601	14%
Centralia	628	-3%
Champaign	618	-2%
Chicago	606-608	15%
Decatur	623	-7%
Galesburg	614	-4%
Granite City	620	3%
Green River	612	5%
Joliet	604	13%
Kankakee	609	-3%
Lawrenceville	624	-6%
Oak Park	603	18%
Peoria	615-616	6%
Peru	613	2%
Quincy	602	16%
Rockford	610-611	3%
Springfield	625-627	0%
Urbana	619	-4%

Indiana Average		-3%
Aurora	470	-5%
Bloomington	474	-2%
Columbus	472	-4%
Elkhart	465	-4%
Evansville	476-477	4%

Fort Wayne 467-468 ....-1%
Gary 463-464 ....8%
Indianapolis 460-462 ....4%
Jasper 475................-8%
Jeffersonville 471.............-5%
Kokomo 469................-8%
Lafayette 479.............-5%
Muncie 473................-8%
South Bend 466.............-2%
Terre Haute 478.............-3%

Iowa Average -3%
Burlington 526.............1%
Carroll 514............-11%
Cedar Falls 506............-4%
Cedar Rapids 522-524 ....2%
Cherokee 510.............1%
Council Bluffs 515.............-1%
Creston 508.............1%
Davenport 527-528 ....1%
Decorah 521.............-8%
Des Moines 500-503 ....5%
Dubuque 520.............-4%
Fort Dodge 505.............-3%
Mason City 504.............-3%
Ottumwa 525.............-6%
Sheldon 512.............-7%
Shenandoah 516............-14%
Sioux City 511.............5%
Spencer 513.............-7%
Waterloo 507.............-3%

Kansas Average 0%
Colby 677.............-8%
Concordia 669............-12%
Dodge City 678.............-4%
Emporia 668.............8%
Fort Scott 667.............-6%
Hays 676............-13%
Hutchinson 675.............-6%
Independence 673............29%
Kansas City 660-662 ....5%
Liberal 679............14%
Salina 674.............-7%
Topeka 664-666 ......-1%
Wichita 670-672 ......-4%

Kentucky Average -4%
Ashland 411-412 ....-4%
Bowling Green 421.............-5%
Campton 413-414 .....-11%
Covington 410.............2%
Elizabethtown 427............-10%
Frankfort 406.............7%
Hazard 417-418 .....-10%
Hopkinsville 422.............-5%
Lexington 403-405 ....1%
London 407-409 ....-7%
Louisville 400-402 ....2%
Owensboro 423.............-4%
Paducah 420.............0%
Pikeville 415-416 ......-8%
Somerset 425-426 .....-11%
White Plains 424.............-4%

Louisiana Average 2%
Alexandria 713-714 ...-2%
Baton Rouge 707-708 ......10%
Houma 703.............4%
Lafayette 705.............16%
Lake Charles 706.............21%
Mandeville 704.............-3%
Minden 710.............-5%
Monroe 712.............-8%
New Orleans 700-701 ....2%
Shreveport 711.............-4%

Maine Average -5%
Auburn 42................-4%
Augusta 43................-5%
Bangor 44................-6%
Bath 45................-6%
Brunswick 039-040 ....-1%
Camden 48................-10%
Cutler 46................-7%
Dexter 49................-4%
Northern Area 47................-8%
Portland 41................2%

Maryland Average 2%
Annapolis 214.............8%
Baltimore 210-212 ....7%
Bethesda 208-209 ......13%
Church Hill 216.............-4%
Cumberland 215.............-8%
Elkton 219.............-5%
Frederick 217.............7%
Laurel 206-207 ....8%
Salisbury 218.............-6%

Massachusetts Average 12%
Ayer 015-016 ....6%
Bedford 17................15%
Boston 021-022 ......37%
Brockton 023-024 ......20%
Cape Cod 26.............4%
Chicopee 10................7%
Dedham 19................18%
Fitchburg 14................11%
Hingham 20................19%
Lawrence 18................14%
Nantucket 25.............9%
New Bedford 27.............6%
Northfield 13................2%
Pittsfield 12................1%
Springfield 11................8%

Michigan Average 1%
Battle Creek 490-491 ....-1%
Detroit 481-482 ......7%
Flint 484-485 ....-4%
Grand Rapids 493-495 ....1%
Grayling 497.............-7%
Jackson 492.............-1%
Lansing 488-489 ....0%
Marquette 498-499 ....3%
Pontiac 483.............12%
Royal Oak 480.............7%
Saginaw 486-487 ....-5%
Traverse City 496.............-2%

Minnesota Average -1%
Bemidji 566.............-6%
Brainerd 564.............-3%
Duluth 556-558 ....2%
Fergus Falls 565............-10%
Magnolia 561.............-8%
Mankato 560.............-4%
Minneapolis 553-555 ......13%
Rochester 559.............-1%
St Cloud 563.............2%
St Paul 550-551 ......12%
Thief River Falls 567.............-2%
Willmar 562.............-6%

Mississippi Average -6%
Clarksdale 386.............-9%
Columbus 397.............0%
Greenville 387............-14%
Greenwood 389............-10%
Gulfport 395.............-6%
Jackson 390-392 ....-3%
Laurel 394.............-7%
McComb 396............-11%

Meridian 393................3%
Tupelo 388................-7%

Missouri Average -3%
Cape Girardeau 637.............-5%
Caruthersville 638.............-7%
Chillicothe 646.............-4%
Columbia 652.............-4%
East Lynne 647.............4%
Farmington 636.............-8%
Hannibal 634.............-2%
Independence 640.............5%
Jefferson City 650-651 ......-5%
Joplin 648.............-6%
Kansas City 641.............6%
Kirksville 635.............-15%
Knob Noster 653.............3%
Lebanon 654-655 .....-12%
Poplar Bluff 639.............-10%
Saint Charles 633.............1%
Saint Joseph 644-645 ......-1%
Springfield 656-658 ......-8%
St Louis 630-631 ......8%

Montana Average -3%
Billings 590-591 ......-2%
Butte 597.............-3%
Fairview 592.............12%
Great Falls 594.............-6%
Havre 595.............-9%
Helena 596.............-2%
Kalispell 599.............-6%
Miles City 593.............-7%
Missoula 598.............-6%

Nebraska Average -8%
Alliance 693.............-10%
Columbus 686.............-7%
Grand Island 688.............-8%
Hastings 689.............-9%
Lincoln 683-685 ......-4%
McCook 690.............-9%
Norfolk 687.............-10%
North Platte 691.............-6%
Omaha 680-681 ....0%
Valentine 692.............-15%

Nevada Average 1%
Carson City 897.............-4%
Elko 898.............9%
Ely 893.............-3%
Fallon 894.............0%
Las Vegas 889-891 ....3%
Reno 895.............-1%

New Hampshire Average -1%
Charlestown 36................-5%
Concord 34................-3%
Dover 38................1%
Lebanon 37................-3%
Littleton 35................-6%
Manchester 032-033 ....2%
New Boston 030-031 ....3%

New Jersey Average 9%
Atlantic City 080-084 ....4%
Brick 87................2%
Dover 78................9%
Edison 088-089 ......13%
Hackensack 76................10%
Monmouth 77................12%
Newark 071-073 ......11%
Passaic 70................12%
Paterson 074-075 ....7%
Princeton 85................10%
Summit 79................16%
Trenton 86................7%

New Mexico Average -8%
Alamogordo 883.............-11%
Albuquerque 870-871 ....-3%
Clovis 881.............-11%
Farmington 874.............-1%
Fort Sumner 882.............-2%
Gallup 873.............-7%
Holman 877.............-10%
Las Cruces 880.............-8%
Santa Fe 875.............-8%
Socorro 878.............-14%
Truth or
Consequences 879.............-8%
Tucumcari 884.............-8%

New York Average 6%
Albany 120-123 ....7%
Amityville 117.............9%
Batavia 140.............1%
Binghamton 137-139 ....-2%
Bronx 104.............10%
Brooklyn 112.............7%
Buffalo 142.............2%
Elmira 149.............-3%
Flushing 113.............15%
Garden City 115.............15%
Hicksville 118.............14%
Ithaca 148.............-5%
Jamaica 114.............14%
Jamestown 147.............-7%
Kingston 124.............-4%
Long Island 111.............30%
Montauk 119.............7%
New York
(Manhattan) 100-102 ......31%
New York City 100-102 ......31%
Newcomb 128.............0%
Niagara Falls 143.............-6%
Plattsburgh 129.............-1%
Poughkeepsie 125-126 ....1%
Queens 110.............17%
Rochester 144-146 ....2%
Rockaway 116.............10%
Rome 133-134 ....-4%
Staten Island 103.............8%
Stewart 127.............-5%
Syracuse 130-132 ....2%
Tonawanda 141.............-1%
Utica 135.............-6%
Watertown 136.............-1%
West Point 109.............6%
White Plains 105-108 ......14%

North Carolina Average 2%
Asheville 287-289 ....-7%
Charlotte 280-282 ....7%
Durham 277.............0%
Elizabeth City 279.............0%
Fayetteville 283.............2%
Goldsboro 275.............8%
Greensboro 274.............5%
Hickory 286.............0%
Kinston 285.............-1%
Raleigh 276.............2%
Rocky Mount 278.............1%
Wilmington 284.............2%
Winston-Salem 270-273 ....4%

North Dakota Average 4%
Bismarck 585.............3%
Dickinson 586.............15%
Fargo 580-581 ....0%
Grand Forks 582.............-1%

Jamestown 584.............-4%
Minot 587.............9%
Nekoma 583.............-10%
Williston 588.............21%

Ohio Average 0%
Akron 442-443 ....1%
Canton 446-447 ....-2%
Chillicothe 456.............-2%
Cincinnati 450-452 ....3%
Cleveland 440-441 ....3%
Columbus 432.............5%
Dayton 453-455 ....1%
Lima 458.............-5%
Marietta 457.............-5%
Marion 433.............-6%
Newark 430-431 ....3%
Sandusky 448-449 ....-3%
Steubenville 439.............1%
Toledo 434-436 ....7%
Warren 444.............-5%
Youngstown 445.............-3%
Zanesville 437-438 ....-1%

Oklahoma Average -5%
Adams 739.............-10%
Ardmore 734.............-1%
Clinton 736.............-3%
Durant 747.............-11%
Enid 737.............-4%
Lawton 735.............-8%
McAlester 745.............-7%
Muskogee 744.............-8%
Norman 730.............-4%
Oklahoma City 731.............-3%
Ponca City 746.............-1%
Poteau 749.............-7%
Pryor 743.............-6%
Shawnee 748.............-8%
Tulsa 740-741 ....0%
Woodward 738.............5%

Oregon Average -3%
Adrian 979.............-12%
Bend 977.............-5%
Eugene 974.............-3%
Grants Pass 975.............-5%
Klamath Falls 976.............-8%
Pendleton 978.............-3%
Portland 970-972 ......10%
Salem 973.............-2%

Pennsylvania Average -1%
Allentown 181.............3%
Altoona 166.............-8%
Beaver Springs 178.............-5%
Bethlehem 180.............4%
Bradford 167.............-8%
Butler 160.............-2%
Chambersburg 172.............-7%
Clearfield 168.............-3%
DuBois 158.............-10%
East Stroudsburg 183.............-5%
Erie 164-165 ....-6%
Genesee 169.............-4%
Greensburg 156.............-4%
Harrisburg 170-171 ....3%
Hazleton 182.............-3%
Johnstown 159.............-9%
Kittanning 162.............-6%
Lancaster 175-176 ....-1%
Meadville 163.............-9%
Montrose 188.............-4%

New Castle 161.............-3%
Philadelphia 190-191 ......11%
Pittsburgh 152.............6%
Pottsville 179.............-8%
Punxsutawney 157.............-3%
Reading 195-196 ....2%
Scranton 184-185 ....1%
Somerset 155.............-9%
Southeastern 193.............8%
Uniontown 154.............-6%
Valley Forge 194.............11%
Warminster 189.............11%
Warrendale 150-151 ....5%
Washington 153.............8%
Wilkes Barre 186-187 ....-1%
Williamsport 177.............-2%
York 173-174 ....-1%

Rhode Island Average 5%
Bristol 28.................5%
Coventry 28.................5%
Cranston 29.................6%
Davisville 28.................5%
Narragansett 28.................5%
Newport 28.................5%
Providence 29.................6%
Warwick 28.................5%

South Carolina Average 3%
Aiken 298.................4%
Beaufort 299.................-2%
Charleston 294.................7%
Columbia 290-292 ....6%
Greenville 296.................5%
Myrtle Beach 295.................0%
Rock Hill 297.................3%
Spartanburg 293.................-3%

South Dakota Average -6%
Aberdeen 574.............-7%
Mitchell 573.............-6%
Mobridge 576.............-9%
Pierre 575.............-10%
Rapid City 577.............-8%
Sioux Falls 570-571 ......-1%
Watertown 572.............-4%

Tennessee Average -2%
Chattanooga 374.................2%
Clarksville 370.................1%
Cleveland 373.................-1%
Columbia 384.................-7%
Cookeville 385.................-8%
Jackson 383.................-2%
Kingsport 376.................-5%
Knoxville 377-379 ....-2%
McKenzie 382.................-8%
Memphis 380-381 ....1%
Nashville 371-372 ....2%

Texas Average 11%
Abilene 795-796 ......-2%
Amarillo 790-791 ......-2%
Arlington 760.............1%
Austin 786-787 ......20%
Bay City 774.............52%
Beaumont 776-777 ......31%
Brownwood 768.............-8%
Bryan 778.............21%
Childress 792.............-14%
Corpus Christi 783-784 ......31%
Dallas 751-753 ....6%
Del Rio 788.............0%
El Paso 798-799 ....1%
Fort Worth 761-762 ....2%
Galveston 775.............37%
Giddings 789.............0%
Greenville 754.............3%

Houston 770-772 ......39%
Huntsville 773.............39%
Longview 756.............1%
Lubbock 793-794 ......-7%
Lufkin 759.............21%
McAllen 785.............-6%
Midland 797.............10%
Palestine 758.............2%
Plano 750.............7%
San Angelo 769.............-6%
San Antonio 780-782 ......16%
Texarkana 755.............-8%
Tyler 757.............-7%
Victoria 779.............25%
Waco 765-767 ......-3%
Wichita Falls 763.............-9%
Woodson 764.............-3%

Utah Average -3%
Clearfield 840.............0%
Green River 845.............-3%
Ogden 843-844 ....-9%
Provo 846-847 ....-6%
Salt Lake City 841.............1%

Vermont Average -5%
Albany 58.............-7%
Battleboro 53.............-4%
Beecher Falls 59.............-8%
Bennington 52.............-6%
Burlington 54.............4%
Montpelier 56.............-4%
Rutland 57.............-7%
Springfield 51.............-6%
White River Junction 50.............-5%

Virginia Average -4%
Abingdon 242.............-9%
Alexandria 220-223 ......10%
Charlottesville 229.............-6%
Chesapeake 233.............-4%
Culpeper 227.............-5%
Farmville 239.............-12%
Fredericksburg 224-225 ......-5%
Galax 243.............-10%
Harrisonburg 228.............-6%
Lynchburg 245.............-9%
Norfolk 235-237 ......-2%
Petersburg 238.............-3%
Radford 241.............-9%
Reston 201.............7%
Richmond 232.............2%
Roanoke 240.............-9%
Staunton 244.............-7%
Tazewell 246.............-6%
Virginia Beach 234.............-2%
Williamsburg 230-231 ......-3%
Winchester 226.............4%

Washington Average 0%
Clarkston 994.............-8%
Everett 982.............2%
Olympia 985.............-2%
Pasco 993.............1%
Seattle 980-981 ......11%
Spokane 990-992 ......-3%
Tacoma 983-984 ....2%
Vancouver 986.............3%
Wenatchee 988.............-6%
Yakima 989.............-5%

West Virginia Average -5%
Beckley 258-259 ......-5%
Bluefield 247-248 ....0%
Charleston 250-253 ....4%
Clarksburg 263-264 ......-7%
Fairmont 266.............-11%

Huntington 255-257 ....-4%
Lewisburg 249.............-14%
Martinsburg 254.............-5%
Morgantown 265.............-4%
New Martinsville 262.............-9%
Parkersburg 261.............1%
Romney 267.............-7%
Sugar Grove 268.............-8%
Wheeling 260.............5%

Wisconsin Average 0%
Amery 540.............-1%
Beloit 535.............5%
Clam Lake 545.............-8%
Eau Claire 547.............-2%
Green Bay 541-543 ....3%
La Crosse 546.............0%
Ladysmith 548.............-2%
Madison 537.............8%
Milwaukee 530-534 ....6%
Oshkosh 549.............4%
Portage 539.............0%
Prairie du Chien 538.............-7%
Wausau 544.............-3%

Wyoming Average -1%
Casper 826.............1%
Cheyenne/Laramie 820.............-2%
Gillette 827.............3%
Powell 824.............-3%
Rawlins 823.............8%
Riverton 825.............-6%
Rock Springs 829-831 ......1%
Sheridan 828.............-3%
Wheatland 822.............-3%

CANADIAN AREA MODIFIERS
These figures assume an exchange rate of $1.00 Canadian to $0.76 U.S.

Alberta 13%
Calgary 14%
Edmonton 14%
Fort McMurray 12%

British Columbia 7%
Fraser Valley 6%
Okanagan 6%
Vancouver 9%

Manitoba 0%
North Manitoba 0%
South Manitoba 0%
Selkirk 0%
Winnipeg 0%

New Brunswick -13%
Moncton ....-13%

Nova Scotia -8%
Amherst ....-8%
Nova Scotia ....-7%
Sydney ....-8%

Newfoundland/Labrador -3%

Ontario 7%
London 7%
Thunder Bay 6%
Toronto 7%

Quebec -1%
Montreal ....-1%
Quebec City ....-1%

Saskatchewan 4%
La Ronge 3%
Prince Albert 2%
Saskatoon 5%

Crew Compositions & Wage Rates

Crew Code		Manhours per day	Total costs $/Hr.	$/Day	Average Crew Rate (ACR) per Hour	Average Crew Rate (ACROP) per Hour w/O&P
AB	1 Air tool operator	8.00	$43.65	$349.20		
	1 Laborer	8.00	$30.00	$240.00		
	TOTAL	**16.00**		**$589.20**	**$36.83**	**$51.56**
AD	2 Air tool operators	16.00	$43.65	$698.40		
	1 Laborer	8.00	$30.00	$240.00		
	TOTAL	**24.00**		**$938.40**	**$39.10**	**$54.74**
BD	3 Bricklayers	24.00	$37.58	$901.92		
	2 Bricktenders	16.00	$27.85	$445.60		
	TOTAL	**40.00**		**$1,347.52**	**$33.69**	**$47.84**
BK	1 Bricklayer	8.00	$37.58	$300.64		
	1 Bricktender	8.00	$27.85	$222.80		
	TOTAL	**16.00**		**$523.44**	**$32.72**	**$46.46**
BO	2 Bricklayers	16.00	$37.58	$601.28		
	2 Bricktenders	16.00	$27.85	$445.60		
	TOTAL	**32.00**		**$1,046.88**	**$32.72**	**$46.46**
2C	2 Carpenters	16.00	$37.02	$592.32	$37.02	$51.83
CA	1 Carpenter	8.00	$37.02	$296.16	$37.02	$51.83
CH	1 Carpenter	8.00	$37.02	$296.16		
	1/2 Laborer	4.00	$30.00	$120.00		
	TOTAL	**12.00**		**$416.16**	**$34.68**	**$48.55**
CJ	1 Carpenter	8.00	$37.02	$296.16		
	1 Laborer	8.00	$30.00	$240.00		
	TOTAL	**16.00**		**$536.16**	**$33.51**	**$46.91**
CN	2 Carpenters	16.00	$37.02	$592.32		
	1/2 Laborer	4.00	$30.00	$120.00		
	TOTAL	**20.00**		**$712.32**	**$35.62**	**$49.86**
CS	2 Carpenters	16.00	$37.02	$592.32		
	1 Laborer	8.00	$30.00	$240.00		
	TOTAL	**24.00**		**$832.32**	**$34.68**	**$48.55**
CT	1 Mosaic & terrazzo setter	8.00	$34.97	$279.76	$34.97	$49.66
CU	4 Carpenters	32.00	$37.02	$1,184.64		
	1 Laborer	8.00	$30.00	$240.00		
	TOTAL	**40.00**		**$1,424.64**	**$35.62**	**$49.86**
CW	2 Carpenters	16.00	$37.02	$592.32		
	2 Laborers	16.00	$30.00	$480.00		
	TOTAL	**32.00**		**$1,072.32**	**$33.51**	**$46.91**
CX	4 Carpenters	32.00	$37.02	$1,184.64	$37.02	$51.83

Crew Code		Manhours per day	Total costs $/Hr.	$/Day	Average Crew Rate (ACR) per Hour	Average Crew Rate (ACROP) per Hour w/O&P
CY	3 Carpenters	24.00	$37.02	$888.48		
	2 Laborers	16.00	$30.00	$480.00		
	1 Equipment operator	8.00	$42.27	$338.16		
	1 Laborer	8.00	$30.00	$240.00		
	TOTAL	**56.00**		**$1,946.64**	**$34.76**	**$48.67**
CZ	4 Carpenters	32.00	$37.02	$1,184.64		
	3 Laborers	24.00	$30.00	$720.00		
	1 Equipment operator	8.00	$42.27	$338.16		
	1 Laborer	8.00	$30.00	$240.00		
	TOTAL	**72.00**		**$2,482.80**	**$34.48**	**$48.28**
DD	2 Cement masons	16.00	$35.16	$562.56		
	1 Laborer	8.00	$30.00	$240.00		
	TOTAL	**24.00**		**$802.56**	**$33.44**	**$47.48**
DF	3 Cement masons	24.00	$35.16	$843.84		
	5 Laborers	40.00	$30.00	$1,200.00		
	TOTAL	**64.00**		**$2,043.84**	**$31.94**	**$45.35**
DI	1 Drywall installer	8.00	$36.09	$288.72	$36.09	$50.53
DJ	1 Drywall installer	8.00	$36.09	$288.72		
	1 Laborer	8.00	$30.00	$240.00		
	TOTAL	**16.00**		**$528.72**	**$33.05**	**$46.26**
DK	1 Drywall installer	8.00	$36.09	$288.72		
	1 Drywall taper	8.00	$36.02	$288.16		
	TOTAL	**16.00**		**$576.88**	**$36.06**	**$50.48**
DL	2 Drywall installers	16.00	$36.09	$577.44		
	1 Drywall taper	8.00	$36.02	$288.16		
	TOTAL	**24.00**		**$865.60**	**$36.07**	**$50.49**
DM	2 Drywall installers	16.00	$36.09	$577.44	$36.09	$50.53
DT	1 Drywall taper	8.00	$36.02	$288.16	$36.02	$50.43
DU	2 Drywall tapers	16.00	$36.02	$576.32	$36.02	$50.43
EA	1 Electrician	8.00	$40.19	$321.52	$40.19	$58.28
EB	2 Electricians	16.00	$40.19	$643.04	$40.19	$58.28
ED	1 Electrician	8.00	$40.19	$321.52		
	1 Carpenter	8.00	$37.02	$296.16		
	TOTAL	**16.00**		**$617.68**	**$38.61**	**$55.98**
FA	1 Floorlayer	8.00	$33.93	$271.44	$33.93	$47.50
FB	2 Floorlayers	16.00	$33.93	$542.88		
	1/4 Laborer	2.00	$30.00	$60.00		
	TOTAL	**18.00**		**$602.88**	**$33.49**	**$46.89**
FC	1 Floorlayer (hardwood)	8.00	$35.62	$284.99	$35.62	$50.59

Crew Code		Manhours per day	Total costs $/Hr.	$/Day	Average Crew Rate (ACR) per Hour	Average Crew Rate (ACROP) per Hour w/O&P
FD	2 Floorlayers (hardwood)	16.00	$35.62	$569.98		
	1/4 Laborer	2.00	$30.00	$60.00		
	TOTAL	**18.00**		**$629.98**	**$35.00**	**$49.70**
GA	1 Glazier	8.00	$35.78	$286.24	$35.78	$50.81
GB	2 Glaziers	16.00	$35.78	$572.48	$35.78	$50.81
GC	3 Glaziers	24.00	$35.78	$858.72	$35.78	$50.81
HA	1 Fence erector	8.00	$38.37	$306.98	$38.37	$54.49
HB	1 Fence erector	8.00	$38.37	$306.98		
	1 Laborer	8.00	$30.00	$240.00		
	TOTAL	**16.00**		**$546.98**	**$34.19**	**$48.54**
HD	2 Fence erectors	16.00	$38.37	$613.96		
	1 Laborer	8.00	$30.00	$240.00		
	TOTAL	**24.00**		**$853.96**	**$35.58**	**$50.53**
1L	1 Laborer	8.00	$30.00	$240.00	$30.00	$42.00
LB	2 Laborers	16.00	$30.00	$480.00	$30.00	$42.00
LC	2 Laborers	16.00	$30.00	$480.00		
	1 Carpenter	8.00	$37.02	$296.16		
	TOTAL	**24.00**		**$776.16**	**$32.34**	**$45.28**
LD	2 Laborers	16.00	$30.00	$480.00		
	2 Carpenters	16.00	$37.02	$592.32		
	TOTAL	**32.00**		**$1,072.32**	**$33.51**	**$46.91**
LG	5 Laborers	40.00	$30.00	$1,200.00		
	1 Carpenter	8.00	$37.02	$296.16		
	TOTAL	**48.00**		**$1,496.16**	**$31.17**	**$43.64**
LH	3 Laborers	24.00	$30.00	$720.00	$30.00	$42.00
LJ	4 Laborers	32.00	$30.00	$960.00	$30.00	$42.00
LK	2 Laborers	16.00	$30.00	$480.00		
	2 Carpenters	16.00	$37.02	$592.32		
	1 Equipment operator	8.00	$42.27	$338.16		
	1 Laborer	8.00	$30.00	$240.00		
	TOTAL	**48.00**		**$1,650.48**	**$34.39**	**$48.14**
LL	3 Laborers	24.00	$30.00	$720.00		
	1 Carpenter	8.00	$37.02	$296.16		
	1 Equipment operator	8.00	$42.27	$338.16		
	1 Laborer	8.00	$30.00	$240.00		
	TOTAL	**48.00**		**$1,594.32**	**$33.22**	**$46.50**
LR	1 Lather	8.00	$35.58	$284.64	$35.58	$50.52
MB	1 Millwright finish carpenter	8.00	$34.86	$278.88	$34.86	$49.50
	1 Laborer	8.00	$30.00	$240.00		
	TOTAL	**16.00**		**$518.88**	**$32.43**	**$46.05**

Crew Code		Manhours per day	Total costs $/Hr.	$/Day	Average Crew Rate (ACR) per Hour	Average Crew Rate (ACROP) per Hour w/O&P
ML	2 Bricklayers	16.00	$37.58	$601.28		
	1 Bricktender	8.00	$27.85	$222.80		
	TOTAL	24.00		$824.08	$34.34	$48.76
MR	1 Millwright finish carpenter	8.00	$34.86	$278.88	$34.86	$49.50
NA	1 Painter (brush)	8.00	$37.82	$302.56	$37.82	$52.95
NC	1 Painter (spray)	8.00	$38.96	$311.70	$38.96	$54.55
PD	2 Plasterers	16.00	$37.06	$592.96		
	1 Plasterer helper	8.00	$29.09	$232.72		
	TOTAL	24.00		$825.68	$34.40	$48.85
PE	3 Plasterers	24.00	$37.06	$889.44		
	2 Plasterer helpers	16.00	$29.09	$465.44		
	TOTAL	40.00		$1,354.88	$33.87	$48.10
QA	1 Paperhanger	8.00	$39.71	$317.66	$39.71	$57.58
2R	2 Roofers (journeyman)	16.00	$41.27	$660.32	$41.27	$60.67
RG	2 Roofers (journeyman)	16.00	$41.27	$660.32		
	1 Laborer	8.00	$30.00	$240.00		
	TOTAL	24.00		$900.32	$37.51	$55.14
RJ	2 Roofers (wood shingles)	16.00	$43.34	$693.48	$43.34	$63.71
RL	2 Roofers (journeyman)	16.00	$41.27	$660.32		
	1/2 Laborer	4.00	$30.00	$120.00		
	TOTAL	20.00		$780.32	$39.02	$57.35
RM	2 Roofers (wood shingles)	16.00	$43.34	$693.48		
	1/2 Laborer	4.00	$30.00	$120.00		
	TOTAL	20.00		$813.48	$40.67	$59.79
RQ	2 Roofers (wood shingles)	16.00	$43.34	$693.48		
	7/8 Laborer	7.00	$30.00	$210.00		
	TOTAL	23.00		$903.48	$39.28	$57.74
RS	1 Roofer (foreman)	8.00	$45.41	$363.24		
	3 Roofers (pitch)	24.00	$42.52	$1,020.56		
	2 Laborers	16.00	$30.00	$480.00		
	TOTAL	48.00		$1,863.80	$38.83	$57.08
RT	2 Roofers (pitch)	16.00	$42.52	$680.38		
	1 Laborer	8.00	$30.00	$240.00		
	TOTAL	24.00		$920.38	$38.35	$56.37
SA	1 Plumber	8.00	$43.02	$344.16	$43.02	$62.38
SB	1 Plumber	8.00	$43.02	$344.16		
	1 Laborer	8.00	$30.00	$240.00		
	TOTAL	16.00		$584.16	$36.51	$52.94

Crew Code		Manhours per day	Total costs $/Hr.	$/Day	Average Crew Rate (ACR) per Hour	Average Crew Rate (ACROP) per Hour w/O&P
SC	1 Plumber	8.00	$43.02	$344.16		
	1 Electrician	8.00	$40.19	$321.52		
	TOTAL	16.00		$665.68	$41.61	$60.33
SD	1 Plumber	8.00	$43.02	$344.16		
	1 Laborer	8.00	$30.00	$240.00		
	1 Electrician	8.00	$40.19	$321.52		
	TOTAL	24.00		$905.68	$37.74	$54.72
SE	2 Plumbers	16.00	$43.02	$688.32		
	1 Laborer	8.00	$30.00	$240.00		
	1 Electrician	8.00	$40.19	$321.52		
	TOTAL	32.00		$1,249.84	$39.06	$56.63
SF	2 Plumbers	16.00	$43.02	$688.32		
	1 Laborer	8.00	$30.00	$240.00		
	TOTAL	24.00		$928.32	$38.68	$56.09
SG	3 Plumbers	24.00	$43.02	$1,032.48		
	1 Laborer	8.00	$30.00	$240.00		
	TOTAL	32.00		$1,272.48	$39.77	$57.66
TB	1 Tile setter (ceramic)	8.00	$35.29	$282.32		
	1 Tile setter helper (ceramic)	8.00	$26.76	$214.05		
	TOTAL	16.00		$496.37	$31.02	$44.05
UA	1 Sheet metal worker	8.00	$41.72	$333.76	$41.72	$59.24
UB	2 Sheet metal workers	16.00	$41.72	$667.52	$41.72	$59.24
UC	2 Sheet metal workers	16.00	$41.72	$667.52		
	2 Laborers	16.00	$30.00	$480.00		
	TOTAL	32.00		$1,147.52	$35.86	$50.92
UD	1 Sheet metal worker	8.00	$41.72	$333.76		
	1 Laborer	8.00	$30.00	$240.00		
	TOTAL	16.00		$573.76	$35.86	$50.92
UE	1 Sheet metal worker	8.00	$41.72	$333.76		
	1 Laborer	8.00	$30.00	$240.00		
	1/2 Electrician	4.00	$40.19	$160.76		
	TOTAL	20.00		$734.52	$36.73	$52.15
UF	2 Sheet metal workers	16.00	$41.72	$667.52		
	1 Laborer	8.00	$30.00	$240.00		
	TOTAL	24.00		$907.52	$37.81	$53.69
VB	1 Equipment operator	8.00	$42.27	$338.16		
	1 Laborer	8.00	$30.00	$240.00		
	TOTAL	16.00		$578.16	$36.14	$50.59

Abbreviations Used in This Book

ABS	acrylonitrile butadiene styrene
ACR	average crew rate
AGA	American Gas Association
AMP	ampere
Approx.	approximately
ASME	American Society of Mechanical Engineers
auto.	automatic
Avg.	average
Bdle.	bundle
BTU	British thermal unit
BTUH	British thermal unit per hour
C	100
cc	center to center or cubic centimeter
CF	cubic foot
CFM	cubic foot per minute
CLF	100 linear feet
Const.	construction
Corr.	corrugated
CSF	100 square feet
CSY	100 square yards
Ctn	carton
CWT	100 pounds
CY	cubic yard
Cu.	cubic
d	penny
D	deep or depth
Demo	demolish
dia.	diameter
D.S.A.	double strength, A grade
D.S.B.	double strength, B grade
Ea	each
e.g.	for example
etc.	et cetera
exp.	exposure
FAS	First and Select grade

F.H.A.	Federal Housing Administration
fl. oz.	fluid ounce
flt	flight
ft.	foot
ga.	gauge
gal	gallon
galv.	galvanized
GFI	ground fault interrupter
GPH	gallons per hour
GPM	gallons per minute
H	height or high
HP, hp	horsepower
Hr.	hour
HVAC	heating, ventilating, air conditioning
i.d.	inside diameter
i.e.	that is
Inst	install
I.P.S.	iron pipe size
KD	knocked down
KW, kw	kilowatts
L	length or long
lb, lbs.	pound(s)
LF	linear feet
LS	lump sum
M	1000
Mat'l	material
Max.	maximum
MBF	1000 board feet
MBHP	1000 boiler horsepower
Mi	miles
Min.	minimum
MSF	1000 square feet
O.B.	opposed blade
oc	on center
o.d.	outside dimension
oz.	ounce
pcs.	pieces
pkg.	package

PSI	per square inch
PVC	polyvinyl chloride
Qt.	quart
R.E.	rounded edge
R/L	random length
RS	rapid start (lamps)
R/W/L	random width and length
S4S	surfaced-four-sides
SF	square foot
SL	slimline (lamps)
Sq.	1 square or 100 square feet
S.S.B.	single strength, B quality
std.	standard
SY	square yard
T	thick
T&G	tongue and groove
U	thermal conductivity
U.I.	united inches
UL	Underwriters Laboratories
U.S.G.	United States Gypsum
VLF	vertical linear feet
W	width or wide
yr.	year

Symbols

/	per
%	percent
"	inches
'	foot or feet
x	by
o	degree
#	number or pounds
$	dollar
+/-	plus or minus

For crew abbreviations, please see Crew Compositions & Wage Rates chart, pages 15 to 19.

Acoustical and insulating tile

1. **Dimensions**

   a. Acoustical tile. $\frac{1}{2}$" thick x 12" x 12", 24".

   b. Insulating tile, decorative. $\frac{1}{2}$" thick x 12" x 12", 24"; $\frac{1}{2}$" thick x 16" x 16", 32".

2. **Installation.** Tile may be applied to existing plaster (if joist spacing is suitable) or to wood furring strips. Tile may have a square edge or flange. Depending on the type and shape of the tile, you can use adhesive, staples, nails or clips to attach the tile.

3. **Estimating Technique.** Determine area and add 5 percent to 10 percent for waste.

4. **Notes on Material Pricing.** A material price of $20.00 a gallon for adhesive was used to compile the Average Material Cost/Unit on the following pages. Here are the coverage rates:

12" x 12"	1.25 Gal/CSF
12" x 24"	0.95 Gal/CSF
16" x 16"	0.75 Gal/CSF
16" x 32"	0.55 Gal/CSF

Description	Oper	Unit	Vol	Crew Size	Man-hours per Unit	Crew Output per Day	Avg Mat'l Unit Cost	Avg Labor Unit Cost	Avg Equip Unit Cost	Avg Total Unit Cost	Avg Price Incl O&P

Acoustical treatment
See also Suspended ceiling systems, page 439

Ceiling and wall tile
Adhesive set

Tile only, no grid system

	Oper	Unit	Vol	Crew Size	MH/Unit	Output/Day	Mat'l	Labor	Equip	Total	Price O&P
	Demo	SF	Lg	LB	.012	1300	---	.36	---	.36	.50
	Demo	SF	Sm	LB	.018	910.0	---	.54	---	.54	.76

Tile on furring strips

| | Demo | SF | Lg | LB | .009 | 1710 | --- | .27 | --- | .27 | .38 |
| | Demo | SF | Sm | LB | .013 | 1197 | --- | .39 | --- | .39 | .55 |

Mineral fiber, vinyl coated, tile only
Applied in square pattern by adhesive to solid backing; 5% tile waste
1/2" thick, 12" x 12" or 12" x 24"

Description	Oper	Unit	Vol	Crew Size	MH/Unit	Output/Day	Mat'l	Labor	Equip	Total	Price O&P
Economy, mini perforated	Inst	SF	Lg	2C	.018	880.0	.95	.67	---	1.62	2.03
	Inst	SF	Sm	2C	.026	616.0	1.04	.96	---	2.00	2.54
Standard, random perforated	Inst	SF	Lg	2C	.018	880.0	1.58	.67	---	2.25	2.75
	Inst	SF	Sm	2C	.026	616.0	1.73	.96	---	2.69	3.34
Designer, swirl perforation	Inst	SF	Lg	2C	.018	880.0	2.18	.67	---	2.85	3.44
	Inst	SF	Sm	2C	.026	616.0	2.39	.96	---	3.35	4.10
Deluxe, sculptured face	Inst	SF	Lg	2C	.018	880.0	2.96	.67	---	3.63	4.34
	Inst	SF	Sm	2C	.026	616.0	3.24	.96	---	4.20	5.07

5/8" thick, 12" x 12" or 12" x 24"

Description	Oper	Unit	Vol	Crew Size	MH/Unit	Output/Day	Mat'l	Labor	Equip	Total	Price O&P
Economy, mini perforated	Inst	SF	Lg	2C	.018	880.0	1.14	.67	---	1.81	2.24
	Inst	SF	Sm	2C	.026	616.0	1.25	.96	---	2.21	2.79
Standard, random perforated	Inst	SF	Lg	2C	.018	880.0	1.93	.67	---	2.60	3.15
	Inst	SF	Sm	2C	.026	616.0	2.12	.96	---	3.08	3.79
Designer, swirl perforation	Inst	SF	Lg	2C	.018	880.0	2.69	.67	---	3.36	4.03
	Inst	SF	Sm	2C	.026	616.0	2.94	.96	---	3.90	4.73
Deluxe, sculptured face	Inst	SF	Lg	2C	.018	880.0	3.66	.67	---	4.33	5.14
	Inst	SF	Sm	2C	.026	616.0	4.01	.96	---	4.97	5.96

3/4" thick, 12" x 12" or 12" x 24"

Description	Oper	Unit	Vol	Crew Size	MH/Unit	Output/Day	Mat'l	Labor	Equip	Total	Price O&P
Economy, mini perforated	Inst	SF	Lg	2C	.018	880.0	1.26	.67	---	1.93	2.38
	Inst	SF	Sm	2C	.026	616.0	1.38	.96	---	2.34	2.93
Standard, random perforated	Inst	SF	Lg	2C	.018	880.0	2.14	.67	---	2.81	3.39
	Inst	SF	Sm	2C	.026	616.0	2.35	.96	---	3.31	4.05
Designer, swirl perforation	Inst	SF	Lg	2C	.018	880.0	2.99	.67	---	3.66	4.37
	Inst	SF	Sm	2C	.026	616.0	3.28	.96	---	4.24	5.12
Deluxe, sculptured face	Inst	SF	Lg	2C	.018	880.0	4.08	.67	---	4.75	5.62
	Inst	SF	Sm	2C	.026	616.0	4.47	.96	---	5.43	6.49

Applied by adhesive to furring strips ADD

| | Inst | SF | Lg | 2C | .002 | --- | --- | .07 | --- | .07 | .10 |
| | Inst | SF | Sm | 2C | .002 | --- | --- | .07 | --- | .07 | .10 |

Description	Oper	Unit	Vol	Crew Size	Man-hours per Unit	Crew Output per Day	Avg Mat'l Unit Cost	Avg Labor Unit Cost	Avg Equip Unit Cost	Avg Total Unit Cost	Avg Price Incl O&P

Stapled

Description	Oper	Unit	Vol	Crew Size	Man-hours per Unit	Crew Output per Day	Avg Mat'l Unit Cost	Avg Labor Unit Cost	Avg Equip Unit Cost	Avg Total Unit Cost	Avg Price Incl O&P
Tile only, no grid system	Demo	SF	Lg	LB	.014	1170	---	.42	---	.42	**.59**
	Demo	SF	Sm	LB	.020	819	---	.60	---	.60	**.84**
Tile on furring strips	Demo	SF	Lg	LB	.010	1540	---	.30	---	.30	**.42**
	Demo	SF	Sm	LB	.015	1078	---	.45	---	.45	**.63**

Mineral fiber, vinyl coated, tile only

Applied in square pattern by staples, nails, or clips; 5% tile waste

1/2" thick, 12" x 12" or 12" x 24"

Description	Oper	Unit	Vol	Crew Size	Man-hours per Unit	Crew Output per Day	Avg Mat'l Unit Cost	Avg Labor Unit Cost	Avg Equip Unit Cost	Avg Total Unit Cost	Avg Price Incl O&P
Economy, mini perforated	Inst	SF	Lg	2C	.017	960.0	.86	.63	---	1.49	**1.87**
	Inst	SF	Sm	2C	.024	672.0	.94	.89	---	1.83	**2.32**
Standard, random perforated	Inst	SF	Lg	2C	.017	960.0	1.49	.63	---	2.12	**2.59**
	Inst	SF	Sm	2C	.024	672.0	1.63	.89	---	2.52	**3.12**
Designer, swirl perforation	Inst	SF	Lg	2C	.017	960.0	2.10	.63	---	2.73	**3.30**
	Inst	SF	Sm	2C	.024	672.0	2.30	.89	---	3.19	**3.89**
Deluxe, sculptured face	Inst	SF	Lg	2C	.017	960.0	2.88	.63	---	3.51	**4.19**
	Inst	SF	Sm	2C	.024	672.0	3.15	.89	---	4.04	**4.87**

5/8" thick, 12" x 12" or 12" x 24"

Description	Oper	Unit	Vol	Crew Size	Man-hours per Unit	Crew Output per Day	Avg Mat'l Unit Cost	Avg Labor Unit Cost	Avg Equip Unit Cost	Avg Total Unit Cost	Avg Price Incl O&P
Economy, mini perforated	Inst	SF	Lg	2C	.017	960.0	1.06	.63	---	1.69	**2.10**
	Inst	SF	Sm	2C	.024	672.0	1.16	.89	---	2.05	**2.58**
Standard, random perforated	Inst	SF	Lg	2C	.017	960.0	1.85	.63	---	2.48	**3.01**
	Inst	SF	Sm	2C	.024	672.0	2.02	.89	---	2.91	**3.57**
Designer, swirl perforation	Inst	SF	Lg	2C	.017	960.0	2.60	.63	---	3.23	**3.87**
	Inst	SF	Sm	2C	.024	672.0	2.85	.89	---	3.74	**4.52**
Deluxe, sculptured face	Inst	SF	Lg	2C	.017	960.0	3.58	.63	---	4.21	**5.00**
	Inst	SF	Sm	2C	.024	672.0	3.92	.89	---	4.81	**5.75**

3/4" thick, 12" x 12" or 12" x 24"

Description	Oper	Unit	Vol	Crew Size	Man-hours per Unit	Crew Output per Day	Avg Mat'l Unit Cost	Avg Labor Unit Cost	Avg Equip Unit Cost	Avg Total Unit Cost	Avg Price Incl O&P
Economy, mini perforated	Inst	SF	Lg	2C	.017	960.0	1.18	.63	---	1.81	**2.24**
	Inst	SF	Sm	2C	.024	672.0	1.29	.89	---	2.18	**2.73**
Standard, random perforated	Inst	SF	Lg	2C	.017	960.0	2.06	.63	---	2.69	**3.25**
	Inst	SF	Sm	2C	.024	672.0	2.25	.89	---	3.14	**3.83**
Designer, swirl perforation	Inst	SF	Lg	2C	.017	960.0	2.91	.63	---	3.54	**4.23**
	Inst	SF	Sm	2C	.024	672.0	3.19	.89	---	4.08	**4.91**
Deluxe, sculptured face	Inst	SF	Lg	2C	.017	960.0	4.00	.63	---	4.63	**5.48**
	Inst	SF	Sm	2C	.024	672.0	4.38	.89	---	5.27	**6.28**

Applied by staples, nails or clips to furring strips ADD

Description	Oper	Unit	Vol	Crew Size	Man-hours per Unit	Crew Output per Day	Avg Mat'l Unit Cost	Avg Labor Unit Cost	Avg Equip Unit Cost	Avg Total Unit Cost	Avg Price Incl O&P
	Inst	SF	Lg	2C	.017	960.0	---	.63	---	.63	**.88**
	Inst	SF	Sm	2C	.024	672.0	---	.89	---	.89	**1.24**

Tile patterns, effect on labor

Description	Oper	Unit	Vol	Crew Size	Man-hours per Unit	Crew Output per Day	Avg Mat'l Unit Cost	Avg Labor Unit Cost	Avg Equip Unit Cost	Avg Total Unit Cost	Avg Price Incl O&P
Herringbone, Increase manhours	Inst	%	Lg	2C	25.0	---	---	---	---	---	---
	Inst	%	Sm	2C	25.0	---	---	---	---	---	---
Diagonal, Increase manhours	Inst	%	Lg	2C	20.0	---	---	---	---	---	---
	Inst	%	Sm	2C	20.0	---	---	---	---	---	---
Ashlar, Increase manhours	Inst	%	Lg	2C	30.0	---	---	---	---	---	---

Description	Oper	Unit	Vol	Crew Size	Man-hours per Unit	Crew Output per Day	Avg Mat'l Unit Cost	Avg Labor Unit Cost	Avg Equip Unit Cost	Avg Total Unit Cost	Avg Price Incl O&P

Furring strips, 8% waste included

Over wood

Description	Oper	Unit	Vol	Crew Size	Man-hours per Unit	Crew Output per Day	Avg Mat'l Unit Cost	Avg Labor Unit Cost	Avg Equip Unit Cost	Avg Total Unit Cost	Avg Price Incl O&P
1" x 4", 12" oc	Inst	SF	Lg	2C	.010	1600	.29	.37	---	.66	.85
	Inst	SF	Sm	2C	.014	1120	.32	.52	---	.84	1.09
1" x 4", 16" oc	Inst	SF	Lg	2C	.008	1920	.25	.30	---	.55	.70
	Inst	SF	Sm	2C	.012	1344	.28	.44	---	.72	.94

Over plaster

Description	Oper	Unit	Vol	Crew Size	Man-hours per Unit	Crew Output per Day	Avg Mat'l Unit Cost	Avg Labor Unit Cost	Avg Equip Unit Cost	Avg Total Unit Cost	Avg Price Incl O&P
1" x 4", 12" oc	Inst	SF	Lg	2C	.013	1280	.29	.48	---	.77	1.01
	Inst	SF	Sm	2C	.018	896	.32	.67	---	.99	1.30
1" x 4", 16" oc	Inst	SF	Lg	2C	.010	1600	.25	.37	---	.62	.81
	Inst	SF	Sm	2C	.014	1120	.28	.52	---	.80	1.05

Adhesives

Better quality, gun-applied in continuous bead to wood or metal framing or furring members.
Per 100 SF of surface area including 6% waste.

Panel adhesives

Subfloor adhesives, on floors

12" oc members

Description	Oper	Unit	Vol	Crew Size	Man-hours per Unit	Crew Output per Day	Avg Mat'l Unit Cost	Avg Labor Unit Cost	Avg Equip Unit Cost	Avg Total Unit Cost	Avg Price Incl O&P
1/8" diameter (11 fl.oz./CSF)	Inst	CSF	Lg	CA	.075	106.0	3.92	2.78	---	6.70	8.28
	Inst	CSF	Sm	CA	.101	79.50	4.30	3.74	---	8.04	10.10
1/4" diameter (43 fl.oz./CSF)	Inst	CSF	Lg	CA	.075	106.0	15.60	2.78	---	18.38	21.40
	Inst	CSF	Sm	CA	.101	79.50	17.20	3.74	---	20.94	24.40
3/8" diameter (97 fl.oz./CSF)	Inst	CSF	Lg	CA	.075	106.0	35.30	2.78	---	38.08	43.40
	Inst	CSF	Sm	CA	.101	79.50	38.70	3.74	---	42.44	48.60
1/2" diameter (172 fl.oz./CSF)	Inst	CSF	Lg	CA	.075	106.0	62.40	2.78	---	65.18	73.80
	Inst	CSF	Sm	CA	.101	79.50	68.40	3.74	---	72.14	81.90

16" oc members

Description	Oper	Unit	Vol	Crew Size	Man-hours per Unit	Crew Output per Day	Avg Mat'l Unit Cost	Avg Labor Unit Cost	Avg Equip Unit Cost	Avg Total Unit Cost	Avg Price Incl O&P
1/8" diameter (9 fl.oz./CSF)	Inst	CSF	Lg	CA	.056	143.0	3.14	2.07	---	5.21	6.42
	Inst	CSF	Sm	CA	.075	107.3	3.44	2.78	---	6.22	7.74
1/4" diameter (34 fl.oz./CSF)	Inst	CSF	Lg	CA	.056	143.0	12.50	2.07	---	14.57	16.90
	Inst	CSF	Sm	CA	.075	107.3	13.70	2.78	---	16.48	19.20
3/8" diameter (78 fl.oz./CSF)	Inst	CSF	Lg	CA	.056	143.0	28.20	2.07	---	30.27	34.50
	Inst	CSF	Sm	CA	.075	107.3	30.90	2.78	---	33.68	38.50
1/2" diameter (137 fl.oz./CSF)	Inst	CSF	Lg	CA	.056	143.0	49.90	2.07	---	51.97	58.80
	Inst	CSF	Sm	CA	.075	107.3	54.70	2.78	---	57.48	65.20

24" oc members

Description	Oper	Unit	Vol	Crew Size	Man-hours per Unit	Crew Output per Day	Avg Mat'l Unit Cost	Avg Labor Unit Cost	Avg Equip Unit Cost	Avg Total Unit Cost	Avg Price Incl O&P
1/8" diameter (7 fl.oz./CSF)	Inst	CSF	Lg	CA	.052	154.0	2.35	1.93	---	4.28	5.33
	Inst	CSF	Sm	CA	.069	115.5	2.58	2.55	---	5.13	6.47
1/4" diameter (26 fl.oz./CSF)	Inst	CSF	Lg	CA	.052	154.0	9.38	1.93	---	11.31	13.20
	Inst	CSF	Sm	CA	.069	115.5	10.30	2.55	---	12.85	15.10
3/8" diameter (58 fl.oz./CSF)	Inst	CSF	Lg	CA	.052	154.0	21.20	1.93	---	23.13	26.40
	Inst	CSF	Sm	CA	.069	115.5	23.20	2.55	---	25.75	29.60
1/2" diameter (103 fl.oz./CSF)	Inst	CSF	Lg	CA	.052	154.0	37.50	1.93	---	39.43	44.60
	Inst	CSF	Sm	CA	.069	115.5	41.10	2.55	---	43.65	49.60

Description	Oper	Unit	Vol	Crew Size	Man-hours per Unit	Crew Output per Day	Avg Mat'l Unit Cost	Avg Labor Unit Cost	Avg Equip Unit Cost	Avg Total Unit Cost	Avg Price Incl O&P

Wall sheathing or shear panel wall adhesive on walls, floors or ceilings
12" oc members

Description	Oper	Unit	Vol	Crew Size	Man-hours per Unit	Crew Output per Day	Avg Mat'l Unit Cost	Avg Labor Unit Cost	Avg Equip Unit Cost	Avg Total Unit Cost	Avg Price Incl O&P
1/8" diameter (11 fl.oz./CSF)	Inst	CSF	Lg	CA	.100	80.00	2.81	3.70	---	6.51	**8.33**
	Inst	CSF	Sm	CA	.133	60.00	3.08	4.92	---	8.00	**10.30**
1/4" diameter (43 fl.oz./CSF)	Inst	CSF	Lg	CA	.100	80.00	11.20	3.70	---	14.90	**17.70**
	Inst	CSF	Sm	CA	.133	60.00	12.20	4.92	---	17.12	**20.60**
3/8" diameter (97 fl.oz./CSF)	Inst	CSF	Lg	CA	.100	80.00	25.20	3.70	---	28.90	**33.40**
	Inst	CSF	Sm	CA	.133	60.00	27.60	4.92	---	32.52	**37.80**
1/2" diameter (172 fl.oz./CSF)	Inst	CSF	Lg	CA	.100	80.00	44.60	3.70	---	48.30	**55.10**
	Inst	CSF	Sm	CA	.133	60.00	48.90	4.92	---	53.82	**61.60**

16" oc members

Description	Oper	Unit	Vol	Crew Size	Man-hours per Unit	Crew Output per Day	Avg Mat'l Unit Cost	Avg Labor Unit Cost	Avg Equip Unit Cost	Avg Total Unit Cost	Avg Price Incl O&P
1/8" diameter (9 fl.oz./CSF)	Inst	CSF	Lg	CA	.091	88.00	2.25	3.37	---	5.62	**7.24**
	Inst	CSF	Sm	CA	.121	66.00	2.46	4.48	---	6.94	**9.03**
1/4" diameter (34 fl.oz./CSF)	Inst	CSF	Lg	CA	.091	88.00	8.93	3.37	---	12.30	**14.70**
	Inst	CSF	Sm	CA	.121	66.00	9.79	4.48	---	14.27	**17.20**
3/8" diameter (78 fl.oz./CSF)	Inst	CSF	Lg	CA	.091	88.00	20.20	3.37	---	23.57	**27.30**
	Inst	CSF	Sm	CA	.121	66.00	22.10	4.48	---	26.58	**31.00**
1/2" diameter (137 fl.oz./CSF)	Inst	CSF	Lg	CA	.091	88.00	35.70	3.37	---	39.07	**44.70**
	Inst	CSF	Sm	CA	.121	66.00	39.10	4.48	---	43.58	**50.10**

24" oc members

Description	Oper	Unit	Vol	Crew Size	Man-hours per Unit	Crew Output per Day	Avg Mat'l Unit Cost	Avg Labor Unit Cost	Avg Equip Unit Cost	Avg Total Unit Cost	Avg Price Incl O&P
1/8" diameter (7 fl.oz./CSF)	Inst	CSF	Lg	CA	.084	95.00	1.68	3.11	---	4.79	**6.24**
	Inst	CSF	Sm	CA	.112	71.25	1.85	4.15	---	6.00	**7.88**
1/4" diameter (26 fl.oz./CSF)	Inst	CSF	Lg	CA	.084	95.00	6.70	3.11	---	9.81	**11.90**
	Inst	CSF	Sm	CA	.112	71.25	7.34	4.15	---	11.49	**14.00**
3/8" diameter (58 fl.oz./CSF)	Inst	CSF	Lg	CA	.084	95.00	15.10	3.11	---	18.21	**21.30**
	Inst	CSF	Sm	CA	.112	71.25	16.60	4.15	---	20.75	**24.40**
1/2" diameter (103 fl.oz./CSF)	Inst	CSF	Lg	CA	.084	95.00	26.80	3.11	---	29.91	**34.30**
	Inst	CSF	Sm	CA	.112	71.25	29.30	4.15	---	33.45	**38.60**

Polystyrene or polyurethane foam panel adhesive, on walls
12" oc members

Description	Oper	Unit	Vol	Crew Size	Man-hours per Unit	Crew Output per Day	Avg Mat'l Unit Cost	Avg Labor Unit Cost	Avg Equip Unit Cost	Avg Total Unit Cost	Avg Price Incl O&P
1/8" diameter (11 fl.oz./CSF)	Inst	CSF	Lg	CA	.100	80.00	4.04	3.70	---	7.74	**9.71**
	Inst	CSF	Sm	CA	.133	60.00	4.42	4.92	---	9.34	**11.80**
1/4" diameter (43 fl.oz./CSF)	Inst	CSF	Lg	CA	.100	80.00	16.10	3.70	---	19.80	**23.20**
	Inst	CSF	Sm	CA	.133	60.00	17.60	4.92	---	22.52	**26.70**
3/8" diameter (97 fl.oz./CSF)	Inst	CSF	Lg	CA	.100	80.00	36.30	3.70	---	40.00	**45.80**
	Inst	CSF	Sm	CA	.133	60.00	39.80	4.92	---	44.72	**51.40**
1/2" diameter (172 fl.oz./CSF)	Inst	CSF	Lg	CA	.100	80.00	64.20	3.70	---	67.90	**77.10**
	Inst	CSF	Sm	CA	.133	60.00	70.40	4.92	---	75.32	**85.70**

16" oc members

Description	Oper	Unit	Vol	Crew Size	Man-hours per Unit	Crew Output per Day	Avg Mat'l Unit Cost	Avg Labor Unit Cost	Avg Equip Unit Cost	Avg Total Unit Cost	Avg Price Incl O&P
1/8" diameter (9 fl.oz./CSF)	Inst	CSF	Lg	CA	.091	88.00	3.22	3.37	---	6.59	**8.32**
	Inst	CSF	Sm	CA	.121	66.00	3.53	4.48	---	8.01	**10.20**
1/4" diameter (34 fl.oz./CSF)	Inst	CSF	Lg	CA	.091	88.00	12.90	3.37	---	16.27	**19.10**
	Inst	CSF	Sm	CA	.121	66.00	14.10	4.48	---	18.58	**22.10**
3/8" diameter (78 fl.oz./CSF)	Inst	CSF	Lg	CA	.091	88.00	29.00	3.37	---	32.37	**37.20**
	Inst	CSF	Sm	CA	.121	66.00	31.80	4.48	---	36.28	**41.90**
1/2" diameter (137 fl.oz./CSF)	Inst	CSF	Lg	CA	.091	88.00	51.40	3.37	---	54.77	**62.20**
	Inst	CSF	Sm	CA	.121	66.00	56.30	4.48	---	60.78	**69.30**

Description	Oper	Unit	Vol	Crew Size	Man-hours per Unit	Crew Output per Day	Avg Mat'l Unit Cost	Avg Labor Unit Cost	Avg Equip Unit Cost	Avg Total Unit Cost	Avg Price Incl O&P
24" oc members											
1/8" diameter (7 fl.oz./CSF)	Inst	CSF	Lg	CA	.084	95.00	2.42	3.11	---	5.53	**7.06**
	Inst	CSF	Sm	CA	.129	62.00	2.66	4.78	---	7.44	**9.67**
1/4" diameter (26 fl.oz./CSF)	Inst	CSF	Lg	CA	.084	95.00	9.65	3.11	---	12.76	**15.20**
	Inst	CSF	Sm	CA	.129	62.00	10.60	4.78	---	15.38	**18.50**
3/8" diameter (58 fl.oz./CSF)	Inst	CSF	Lg	CA	.084	95.00	21.80	3.11	---	24.91	**28.70**
	Inst	CSF	Sm	CA	.129	62.00	23.90	4.78	---	28.68	**33.40**
1/2" diameter (103 fl.oz./CSF)	Inst	CSF	Lg	CA	.084	95.00	38.50	3.11	---	41.61	**47.50**
	Inst	CSF	Sm	CA	.129	62.00	42.20	4.78	---	46.98	**54.00**

Gypsum drywall adhesive, on ceilings

Description	Oper	Unit	Vol	Crew Size	Man-hours per Unit	Crew Output per Day	Avg Mat'l Unit Cost	Avg Labor Unit Cost	Avg Equip Unit Cost	Avg Total Unit Cost	Avg Price Incl O&P
12" oc members											
1/8" diameter (11 fl.oz./CSF)	Inst	CSF	Lg	CA	.100	80.00	2.46	3.70	---	6.16	**7.94**
	Inst	CSF	Sm	CA	.133	60.00	2.70	4.92	---	7.62	**9.92**
1/4" diameter (43 fl.oz./CSF)	Inst	CSF	Lg	CA	.100	80.00	9.83	3.70	---	13.53	**16.20**
	Inst	CSF	Sm	CA	.133	60.00	10.80	4.92	---	15.72	**19.00**
3/8" diameter (97 fl.oz./CSF)	Inst	CSF	Lg	CA	.100	80.00	22.20	3.70	---	25.90	**30.00**
	Inst	CSF	Sm	CA	.133	60.00	24.30	4.92	---	29.22	**34.10**
1/2" diameter (172 fl.oz./CSF)	Inst	CSF	Lg	CA	.100	80.00	39.20	3.70	---	42.90	**49.10**
	Inst	CSF	Sm	CA	.133	60.00	43.00	4.92	---	47.92	**55.10**
16" oc members											
1/8" diameter (9 fl.oz./CSF)	Inst	CSF	Lg	CA	.091	88.00	1.98	3.37	---	5.35	**6.93**
	Inst	CSF	Sm	CA	.121	66.00	2.17	4.48	---	6.65	**8.70**
1/4" diameter (34 fl.oz./CSF)	Inst	CSF	Lg	CA	.091	88.00	7.86	3.37	---	11.23	**13.50**
	Inst	CSF	Sm	CA	.121	66.00	8.62	4.48	---	13.10	**15.90**
3/8" diameter (78 fl.oz./CSF)	Inst	CSF	Lg	CA	.091	88.00	17.70	3.37	---	21.07	**24.60**
	Inst	CSF	Sm	CA	.121	66.00	19.40	4.48	---	23.88	**28.00**
1/2" diameter (137 fl.oz./CSF)	Inst	CSF	Lg	CA	.091	88.00	31.40	3.37	---	34.77	**39.90**
	Inst	CSF	Sm	CA	.121	66.00	34.40	4.48	---	38.88	**44.80**
24" oc members											
1/8" diameter (7 fl.oz./CSF)	Inst	CSF	Lg	CA	.084	95.00	1.48	3.11	---	4.59	**6.01**
	Inst	CSF	Sm	CA	.112	71.25	1.62	4.15	---	5.77	**7.62**
1/4" diameter (26 fl.oz./CSF)	Inst	CSF	Lg	CA	.084	95.00	5.90	3.11	---	9.01	**11.00**
	Inst	CSF	Sm	CA	.112	71.25	6.46	4.15	---	10.61	**13.00**
3/8" diameter (58 fl.oz./CSF)	Inst	CSF	Lg	CA	.084	95.00	13.30	3.11	---	16.41	**19.30**
	Inst	CSF	Sm	CA	.112	71.25	14.60	4.15	---	18.75	**22.10**
1/2" diameter (103 fl.oz./CSF)	Inst	CSF	Lg	CA	.084	95.00	23.50	3.11	---	26.61	**30.70**
	Inst	CSF	Sm	CA	.112	71.25	25.80	4.15	---	29.95	**34.70**

Gypsum drywall adhesive, on walls

Description	Oper	Unit	Vol	Crew Size	Man-hours per Unit	Crew Output per Day	Avg Mat'l Unit Cost	Avg Labor Unit Cost	Avg Equip Unit Cost	Avg Total Unit Cost	Avg Price Incl O&P
12" oc members											
1/8" diameter (11 fl.oz./CSF)	Inst	CSF	Lg	CA	.100	80.00	2.46	3.70	---	6.16	**7.94**
	Inst	CSF	Sm	CA	.133	60.00	2.70	4.92	---	7.62	**9.92**
1/4" diameter (43 fl.oz./CSF)	Inst	CSF	Lg	CA	.100	80.00	9.83	3.70	---	13.53	**16.20**
	Inst	CSF	Sm	CA	.133	60.00	10.80	4.92	---	15.72	**19.00**
3/8" diameter (97 fl.oz./CSF)	Inst	CSF	Lg	CA	.100	80.00	22.20	3.70	---	25.90	**30.00**
	Inst	CSF	Sm	CA	.133	60.00	24.30	4.92	---	29.22	**34.10**
1/2" diameter (172 fl.oz./CSF)	Inst	CSF	Lg	CA	.100	80.00	39.20	3.70	---	42.90	**49.10**
	Inst	CSF	Sm	CA	.133	60.00	43.00	4.92	---	47.92	**55.10**

Description	Oper	Unit	Vol	Crew Size	Man-hours per Unit	Crew Output per Day	Avg Mat'l Unit Cost	Avg Labor Unit Cost	Avg Equip Unit Cost	Avg Total Unit Cost	Avg Price Incl O&P
16" oc members											
1/8" diameter (9 fl.oz./CSF)	Inst	CSF	Lg	CA	.091	88.00	1.98	3.37	---	5.35	**6.93**
	Inst	CSF	Sm	CA	.121	66.00	2.17	4.48	---	6.65	**8.70**
1/4" diameter (34 fl.oz./CSF)	Inst	CSF	Lg	CA	.091	88.00	7.86	3.37	---	11.23	**13.50**
	Inst	CSF	Sm	CA	.121	66.00	8.62	4.48	---	13.10	**15.90**
3/8" diameter (78 fl.oz./CSF)	Inst	CSF	Lg	CA	.091	88.00	17.70	3.37	---	21.07	**24.60**
	Inst	CSF	Sm	CA	.121	66.00	19.40	4.48	---	23.88	**28.00**
1/2" diameter (137 fl.oz./CSF)	Inst	CSF	Lg	CA	.091	88.00	31.40	3.37	---	34.77	**39.90**
	Inst	CSF	Sm	CA	.121	66.00	34.40	4.48	---	38.88	**44.80**
24" oc members											
1/8" diameter (7 fl.oz./CSF)	Inst	CSF	Lg	CA	.084	95.00	1.48	3.11	---	4.59	**6.01**
	Inst	CSF	Sm	CA	.112	71.25	1.62	4.15	---	5.77	**7.62**
1/4" diameter (26 fl.oz./CSF)	Inst	CSF	Lg	CA	.084	95.00	5.90	3.11	---	9.01	**11.00**
	Inst	CSF	Sm	CA	.112	71.25	6.46	4.15	---	10.61	**13.00**
3/8" diameter (58 fl.oz./CSF)	Inst	CSF	Lg	CA	.084	95.00	13.30	3.11	---	16.41	**19.30**
	Inst	CSF	Sm	CA	.112	71.25	14.60	4.15	---	18.75	**22.10**
1/2" diameter (103 fl.oz./CSF)	Inst	CSF	Lg	CA	.084	95.00	23.50	3.11	---	26.61	**30.70**
	Inst	CSF	Sm	CA	.112	71.25	25.80	4.15	---	29.95	**34.70**

Hardboard or plastic panel adhesive, on walls

Description	Oper	Unit	Vol	Crew Size	Man-hours per Unit	Crew Output per Day	Avg Mat'l Unit Cost	Avg Labor Unit Cost	Avg Equip Unit Cost	Avg Total Unit Cost	Avg Price Incl O&P
12" oc members											
1/8" diameter (11 fl.oz./CSF)	Inst	CSF	Lg	CA	.100	80.00	4.04	3.70	---	7.74	**9.71**
	Inst	CSF	Sm	CA	.133	60.00	4.42	4.92	---	9.34	**11.80**
1/4" diameter (43 fl.oz./CSF)	Inst	CSF	Lg	CA	.100	80.00	16.10	3.70	---	19.80	**23.20**
	Inst	CSF	Sm	CA	.133	60.00	17.60	4.92	---	22.52	**26.70**
3/8" diameter (97 fl.oz./CSF)	Inst	CSF	Lg	CA	.100	80.00	36.30	3.70	---	40.00	**45.80**
	Inst	CSF	Sm	CA	.133	60.00	39.80	4.92	---	44.72	**51.40**
1/2" diameter (172 fl.oz./CSF)	Inst	CSF	Lg	CA	.100	80.00	64.20	3.70	---	67.90	**77.10**
	Inst	CSF	Sm	CA	.133	60.00	70.40	4.92	---	75.32	**85.70**
16" oc members											
1/8" diameter (9 fl.oz./CSF)	Inst	CSF	Lg	CA	.091	88.00	3.22	3.37	---	6.59	**8.32**
	Inst	CSF	Sm	CA	.121	66.00	3.53	4.48	---	8.01	**10.20**
1/4" diameter (34 fl.oz./CSF)	Inst	CSF	Lg	CA	.091	88.00	12.90	3.37	---	16.27	**19.10**
	Inst	CSF	Sm	CA	.121	66.00	14.10	4.48	---	18.58	**22.10**
3/8" diameter (78 fl.oz./CSF)	Inst	CSF	Lg	CA	.091	88.00	29.00	3.37	---	32.37	**37.20**
	Inst	CSF	Sm	CA	.121	66.00	31.80	4.48	---	36.28	**41.90**
1/2" diameter (137 fl.oz./CSF)	Inst	CSF	Lg	CA	.091	88.00	51.40	3.37	---	54.77	**62.20**
	Inst	CSF	Sm	CA	.121	66.00	56.30	4.48	---	60.78	**69.30**
24" oc members											
1/8" diameter (7 fl.oz./CSF)	Inst	CSF	Lg	CA	.084	95.00	2.42	3.11	---	5.53	**7.06**
	Inst	CSF	Sm	CA	.112	71.25	2.66	4.15	---	6.81	**8.78**
1/4" diameter (26 fl.oz./CSF)	Inst	CSF	Lg	CA	.084	95.00	9.65	3.11	---	12.76	**15.20**
	Inst	CSF	Sm	CA	.112	71.25	10.60	4.15	---	14.75	**17.70**
3/8" diameter (58 fl.oz./CSF)	Inst	CSF	Lg	CA	.084	95.00	21.80	3.11	---	24.91	**28.70**
	Inst	CSF	Sm	CA	.112	71.25	23.90	4.15	---	28.05	**32.50**
1/2" diameter (103 fl.oz./CSF)	Inst	CSF	Lg	CA	.084	95.00	38.50	3.11	---	41.61	**47.50**
	Inst	CSF	Sm	CA	.112	71.25	42.20	4.15	---	46.35	**53.10**

Description	Oper	Unit	Vol	Crew Size	Man-hours per Unit	Crew Output per Day	Avg Mat'l Unit Cost	Avg Labor Unit Cost	Avg Equip Unit Cost	Avg Total Unit Cost	Avg Price Incl O&P

Air conditioning and ventilating systems

System components

Condensing units

Air cooled, compressor, standard controls

Description	Oper	Unit	Vol	Crew Size	Man-hours per Unit	Crew Output per Day	Avg Mat'l Unit Cost	Avg Labor Unit Cost	Avg Equip Unit Cost	Avg Total Unit Cost	Avg Price Incl O&P
1.0 ton	Inst	Ea	Lg	SB	8.00	2.00	678.00	292.00	---	970.00	**1200.00**
	Inst	Ea	Sm	SB	10.0	1.60	742.00	365.00	---	1107.00	**1270.00**
1.5 ton	Inst	Ea	Lg	SB	9.14	1.75	832.00	334.00	---	1166.00	**1440.00**
	Inst	Ea	Sm	SB	11.4	1.40	911.00	416.00	---	1327.00	**1510.00**
2.0 ton	Inst	Ea	Lg	SB	10.7	1.50	954.00	391.00	---	1345.00	**1660.00**
	Inst	Ea	Sm	SB	13.3	1.20	1040.00	486.00	---	1526.00	**1750.00**
2.5 ton	Inst	Ea	Lg	SB	12.8	1.25	1140.00	467.00	---	1607.00	**1990.00**
	Inst	Ea	Sm	SB	16.0	1.00	1250.00	584.00	---	1834.00	**2090.00**
3.0 ton	Inst	Ea	Lg	SB	16.0	1.00	1350.00	584.00	---	1934.00	**2400.00**
	Inst	Ea	Sm	SB	20.0	0.80	1480.00	730.00	---	2210.00	**2540.00**
4.0 ton	Inst	Ea	Lg	SB	21.3	0.75	1780.00	778.00	---	2558.00	**3170.00**
	Inst	Ea	Sm	SB	26.7	0.60	1940.00	975.00	---	2915.00	**3360.00**
5.0 ton	Inst	Ea	Lg	SB	32.0	0.50	2170.00	1170.00	---	3340.00	**4190.00**
	Inst	Ea	Sm	SB	40.0	0.40	2380.00	1460.00	---	3840.00	**4500.00**
Minimum Job Charge											
	Inst	Job	Lg	SB	5.33	3.00	---	195.00	---	195.00	**282.00**
	Inst	Job	Sm	SB	6.67	2.40	---	244.00	---	244.00	**353.00**

Diffusers

Aluminum, opposed blade damper, unless otherwise noted

Ceiling or sidewall, linear

Description	Oper	Unit	Vol	Crew Size	Man-hours per Unit	Crew Output per Day	Avg Mat'l Unit Cost	Avg Labor Unit Cost	Avg Equip Unit Cost	Avg Total Unit Cost	Avg Price Incl O&P
2" wide	Inst	LF	Lg	UA	.267	30.00	24.90	11.10	---	36.00	**44.50**
	Inst	LF	Sm	UA	.333	24.00	27.30	13.90	---	41.20	**47.00**
4" wide	Inst	LF	Lg	UA	.296	27.00	33.40	12.40	---	45.80	**55.90**
	Inst	LF	Sm	UA	.370	21.60	36.50	15.40	---	51.90	**58.50**
6" wide	Inst	LF	Lg	UA	.333	24.00	41.30	13.90	---	55.20	**67.30**
	Inst	LF	Sm	UA	.417	19.20	45.20	17.40	---	62.60	**69.90**
8" wide	Inst	LF	Lg	UA	.400	20.00	48.20	16.70	---	64.90	**79.20**
	Inst	LF	Sm	UA	.500	16.00	52.80	20.90	---	73.70	**82.40**

Perforated, 24" x 24" panel size

Description	Oper	Unit	Vol	Crew Size	Man-hours per Unit	Crew Output per Day	Avg Mat'l Unit Cost	Avg Labor Unit Cost	Avg Equip Unit Cost	Avg Total Unit Cost	Avg Price Incl O&P
6" x 6"	Inst	Ea	Lg	UA	.500	16.00	67.80	20.90	---	88.70	**108.00**
	Inst	Ea	Sm	UA	.625	12.80	74.20	26.10	---	100.30	**111.00**
8" x 8"	Inst	Ea	Lg	UA	.571	14.00	70.00	23.80	---	93.80	**114.00**
	Inst	Ea	Sm	UA	.714	11.20	76.60	29.80	---	106.40	**119.00**
10" x 10"	Inst	Ea	Lg	UA	.667	12.00	71.00	27.80	---	98.80	**121.00**
	Inst	Ea	Sm	UA	.833	9.60	77.70	34.80	---	112.50	**127.00**
12" x 12"	Inst	Ea	Lg	UA	.800	10.00	73.70	33.40	---	107.10	**132.00**
	Inst	Ea	Sm	UA	1.00	8.00	80.60	41.70	---	122.30	**140.00**
18" x 18"	Inst	Ea	Lg	UA	1.00	8.00	98.10	41.70	---	139.80	**172.00**
	Inst	Ea	Sm	UA	1.25	6.40	107.00	52.20	---	159.20	**181.00**

Description	Oper	Unit	Vol	Crew Size	Man-hours per Unit	Crew Output per Day	Avg Mat'l Unit Cost	Avg Labor Unit Cost	Avg Equip Unit Cost	Avg Total Unit Cost	Avg Price Incl O&P
Rectangular, one- to four-way blow											
6" x 6"	Inst	Ea	Lg	UA	.500	16.00	39.80	20.90	---	60.70	**75.30**
	Inst	Ea	Sm	UA	.625	12.80	43.50	26.10	---	69.60	**80.50**
12" x 6"	Inst	Ea	Lg	UA	.571	14.00	50.90	23.80	---	74.70	**92.30**
	Inst	Ea	Sm	UA	.714	11.20	55.70	29.80	---	85.50	**98.00**
12" x 9"	Inst	Ea	Lg	UA	.667	12.00	59.90	27.80	---	87.70	**108.00**
	Inst	Ea	Sm	UA	.833	9.60	65.50	34.80	---	100.30	**115.00**
12" x 12"	Inst	Ea	Lg	UA	.800	10.00	70.00	33.40	---	103.40	**128.00**
	Inst	Ea	Sm	UA	1.00	8.00	76.60	41.70	---	118.30	**136.00**
24" x 12"	Inst	Ea	Lg	UA	1.00	8.00	119.00	41.70	---	160.70	**196.00**
	Inst	Ea	Sm	UA	1.25	6.40	130.00	52.20	---	182.20	**204.00**
T-bar mounting, 24" x 24" lay in frame											
6" x 6"	Inst	Ea	Lg	UA	.500	16.00	64.10	20.90	---	85.00	**103.00**
	Inst	Ea	Sm	UA	.625	12.80	70.20	26.10	---	96.30	**107.00**
9" x 9"	Inst	Ea	Lg	UA	.571	14.00	71.60	23.80	---	95.40	**116.00**
	Inst	Ea	Sm	UA	.714	11.20	78.30	29.80	---	108.10	**121.00**
12" x 12"	Inst	Ea	Lg	UA	.667	12.00	93.80	27.80	---	121.60	**147.00**
	Inst	Ea	Sm	UA	.833	9.60	103.00	34.80	---	137.80	**152.00**
15" x 15"	Inst	Ea	Lg	UA	.800	10.00	97.50	33.40	---	130.90	**160.00**
	Inst	Ea	Sm	UA	1.00	8.00	107.00	41.70	---	148.70	**166.00**
18" x 18"	Inst	Ea	Lg	UA	1.00	8.00	128.00	41.70	---	169.70	**207.00**
	Inst	Ea	Sm	UA	1.25	6.40	140.00	52.20	---	192.20	**214.00**
Minimum Job Charge											
	Inst	Job	Lg	UA	2.29	3.50	---	95.50	---	95.50	**136.00**
	Inst	Job	Sm	UA	2.86	2.80	---	119.00	---	119.00	**169.00**

Ductwork

Fabricated rectangular, includes fittings, joints, supports

Description	Oper	Unit	Vol	Crew Size	Man-hours per Unit	Crew Output per Day	Avg Mat'l Unit Cost	Avg Labor Unit Cost	Avg Equip Unit Cost	Avg Total Unit Cost	Avg Price Incl O&P
Aluminum alloy											
Under 100 lbs	Inst	Lb	Lg	UF	.343	70.00	3.71	13.00	---	16.71	**22.70**
	Inst	Lb	Sm	UF	.429	56.00	4.06	16.20	---	20.26	**27.10**
100 to 500 lbs	Inst	Lb	Lg	UF	.267	90.00	2.68	10.10	---	12.78	**17.40**
	Inst	Lb	Sm	UF	.333	72.00	2.93	12.60	---	15.53	**20.80**
500 to 1,000 lbs	Inst	Lb	Lg	UF	.218	110.0	1.93	8.24	---	10.17	**13.90**
	Inst	Lb	Sm	UF	.273	88.00	2.11	10.30	---	12.41	**16.80**
Over 1,000 lbs	Inst	Lb	Lg	UF	.185	130.0	1.43	6.99	---	8.42	**11.60**
	Inst	Lb	Sm	UF	.231	104.0	1.57	8.73	---	10.30	**14.00**
Galvanized steel											
Under 400 lbs	Inst	Lb	Lg	UF	.120	200.0	1.11	4.54	---	5.65	**7.72**
	Inst	Lb	Sm	UF	.150	160.0	1.22	5.67	---	6.89	**9.27**
400 to 1,000 lbs	Inst	Lb	Lg	UF	.112	215.0	.71	4.23	---	4.94	**6.83**
	Inst	Lb	Sm	UF	.140	172.0	.78	5.29	---	6.07	**8.30**
1,000 to 2,000 lbs	Inst	Lb	Lg	UF	.104	230.0	.53	3.93	---	4.46	**6.19**
	Inst	Lb	Sm	UF	.130	184.0	.58	4.92	---	5.50	**7.56**
2,000 to 5,000 lbs	Inst	Lb	Lg	UF	.100	240.0	.42	3.78	---	4.20	**5.85**
	Inst	Lb	Sm	UF	.125	192.0	.46	4.73	---	5.19	**7.17**
Over 10,000 lbs	Inst	Lb	Lg	UF	.096	250.0	.37	3.63	---	4.00	**5.58**
	Inst	Lb	Sm	UF	.120	200.0	.41	4.54	---	4.95	**6.85**

Description	Oper	Unit	Vol	Crew Size	Man-hours per Unit	Crew Output per Day	Avg Mat'l Unit Cost	Avg Labor Unit Cost	Avg Equip Unit Cost	Avg Total Unit Cost	Avg Price Incl O&P
Flexible, coated fabric on spring steel, aluminum, or corrosion-resistant metal											
Non-insulated											
3" diameter	Inst	LF	Lg	UD	.058	275.0	.83	2.08	---	2.91	**3.91**
	Inst	LF	Sm	UD	.073	220.0	.90	2.62	---	3.52	**4.62**
5" diameter	Inst	LF	Lg	UD	.071	225.0	.96	2.55	---	3.51	**4.72**
	Inst	LF	Sm	UD	.089	180.0	1.06	3.19	---	4.25	**5.59**
6" diameter	Inst	LF	Lg	UD	.080	200.0	1.08	2.87	---	3.95	**5.32**
	Inst	LF	Sm	UD	.100	160.0	1.18	3.59	---	4.77	**6.27**
7" diameter	Inst	LF	Lg	UD	.091	175.0	1.42	3.26	---	4.68	**6.27**
	Inst	LF	Sm	UD	.114	140.0	1.55	4.09	---	5.64	**7.35**
8" diameter	Inst	LF	Lg	UD	.107	150.0	1.47	3.84	---	5.31	**7.14**
	Inst	LF	Sm	UD	.133	120.0	1.61	4.77	---	6.38	**8.38**
10" diameter	Inst	LF	Lg	UD	.128	125.0	1.89	4.59	---	6.48	**8.69**
	Inst	LF	Sm	UD	.160	100.0	2.06	5.74	---	7.80	**10.20**
12" diameter	Inst	LF	Lg	UD	.160	100.0	2.24	5.74	---	7.98	**10.70**
	Inst	LF	Sm	UD	.200	80.0	2.45	7.17	---	9.62	**12.60**
Insulated											
3" diameter	Inst	LF	Lg	UD	.064	250.0	1.42	2.30	---	3.72	**4.89**
	Inst	LF	Sm	UD	.080	200.0	1.55	2.87	---	4.42	**5.62**
4" diameter	Inst	LF	Lg	UD	.071	225.0	1.42	2.55	---	3.97	**5.25**
	Inst	LF	Sm	UD	.089	180.0	1.55	3.19	---	4.74	**6.08**
5" diameter	Inst	LF	Lg	UD	.080	200.0	1.66	2.87	---	4.53	**5.98**
	Inst	LF	Sm	UD	.100	160.0	1.82	3.59	---	5.41	**6.91**
6" diameter	Inst	LF	Lg	UD	.091	175.0	1.83	3.26	---	5.09	**6.74**
	Inst	LF	Sm	UD	.114	140.0	2.01	4.09	---	6.10	**7.81**
7" diameter	Inst	LF	Lg	UD	.107	150.0	2.24	3.84	---	6.08	**8.02**
	Inst	LF	Sm	UD	.133	120.0	2.45	4.77	---	7.22	**9.22**
8" diameter	Inst	LF	Lg	UD	.128	125.0	2.29	4.59	---	6.88	**9.15**
	Inst	LF	Sm	UD	.160	100.0	2.51	5.74	---	8.25	**10.70**
10" diameter	Inst	LF	Lg	UD	.160	100.0	2.98	5.74	---	8.72	**11.60**
	Inst	LF	Sm	UD	.200	80.00	3.26	7.17	---	10.43	**13.40**
12" diameter	Inst	LF	Lg	UD	.213	75.00	3.47	7.64	---	11.11	**14.80**
	Inst	LF	Sm	UD	.267	60.00	3.79	9.57	---	13.36	**17.40**
14" diameter	Inst	LF	Lg	UD	.320	50.00	4.20	11.50	---	15.70	**21.10**
	Inst	LF	Sm	UD	.400	40.00	4.59	14.30	---	18.89	**25.00**

Duct accessories

Air extractors

Description	Oper	Unit	Vol	Crew Size	Man-hours per Unit	Crew Output per Day	Avg Mat'l Unit Cost	Avg Labor Unit Cost	Avg Equip Unit Cost	Avg Total Unit Cost	Avg Price Incl O&P
12" x 4"	Inst	Ea	Lg	UA	.333	24.00	13.00	13.90	---	26.90	**34.70**
	Inst	Ea	Sm	UA	.417	19.20	14.20	17.40	---	31.60	**38.90**
8" x 6"	Inst	Ea	Lg	UA	.400	20.00	13.00	16.70	---	29.70	**38.60**
	Inst	Ea	Sm	UA	.500	16.00	14.20	20.90	---	35.10	**43.80**
20" x 8"	Inst	Ea	Lg	UA	.500	16.00	29.20	20.90	---	50.10	**63.10**
	Inst	Ea	Sm	UA	.625	12.80	31.90	26.10	---	58.00	**68.90**
18" x 10"	Inst	Ea	Lg	UA	.571	14.00	28.60	23.80	---	52.40	**66.70**
	Inst	Ea	Sm	UA	.714	11.20	31.30	29.80	---	61.10	**73.60**
24" x 12"	Inst	Ea	Lg	UA	.800	10.00	39.80	33.40	---	73.20	**93.10**
	Inst	Ea	Sm	UA	1.00	8.00	43.50	41.70	---	85.20	**103.00**

Description	Oper	Unit	Vol	Crew Size	Man-hours per Unit	Crew Output per Day	Avg Mat'l Unit Cost	Avg Labor Unit Cost	Avg Equip Unit Cost	Avg Total Unit Cost	Avg Price Incl O&P
Dampers, fire, curtain-type, vertical											
8" x 4"	Inst	Ea	Lg	UA	.333	24.00	17.70	13.90	---	31.60	**40.00**
	Inst	Ea	Sm	UA	.417	19.20	19.30	17.40	---	36.70	**44.00**
12" x 4"	Inst	Ea	Lg	UA	.364	22.00	17.70	15.20	---	32.90	**41.90**
	Inst	Ea	Sm	UA	.455	17.60	19.30	19.00	---	38.30	**46.30**
16" x 14"	Inst	Ea	Lg	UA	.667	12.00	28.10	27.80	---	55.90	**71.80**
	Inst	Ea	Sm	UA	.833	9.60	30.70	34.80	---	65.50	**80.10**
24" x 20"	Inst	Ea	Lg	UA	1.00	8.00	35.50	41.70	---	77.20	**100.00**
	Inst	Ea	Sm	UA	1.25	6.40	38.90	52.20	---	91.10	**113.00**
Dampers, multi-blade, opposed blade											
12" x 12"	Inst	Ea	Lg	UA	.500	16.00	26.00	20.90	---	46.90	**59.50**
	Inst	Ea	Sm	UA	.625	12.80	28.40	26.10	---	54.50	**65.50**
12" x 18"	Inst	Ea	Lg	UA	.667	12.00	34.50	27.80	---	62.30	**79.10**
	Inst	Ea	Sm	UA	.833	9.60	37.70	34.80	---	72.50	**87.10**
24" x 24"	Inst	Ea	Lg	UA	1.00	8.00	73.10	41.70	---	114.80	**143.00**
	Inst	Ea	Sm	UA	1.25	6.40	80.00	52.20	---	132.20	**154.00**
48" x 36"	Inst	Ea	Lg	UD	2.67	6.00	222.00	95.80	---	317.80	**391.00**
	Inst	Ea	Sm	UD	3.33	4.80	242.00	119.00	---	361.00	**412.00**
Dampers, variable volume modulating, motorized											
12" x 12"	Inst	Ea	Lg	UA	0.80	10.00	134.00	33.40	---	167.40	**201.00**
	Inst	Ea	Sm	UA	1.00	8.00	146.00	41.70	---	187.70	**205.00**
24" x 12"	Inst	Ea	Lg	UA	1.33	6.00	160.00	55.50	---	215.50	**263.00**
	Inst	Ea	Sm	UA	1.67	4.80	175.00	69.70	---	244.70	**274.00**
30" x 18"	Inst	Ea	Lg	UA	2.00	4.00	297.00	83.40	---	380.40	**460.00**
	Inst	Ea	Sm	UA	2.50	3.20	325.00	104.00	---	429.00	**473.00**
Thermostat, ADD	Inst	Ea	Lg	UA	1.33	6.00	31.80	55.50	---	87.30	**115.00**
	Inst	Ea	Sm	UA	1.67	4.80	34.80	69.70	---	104.50	**134.00**
Dampers, multi-blade, parallel blade											
8" x 8"	Inst	Ea	Lg	UA	.400	20.00	54.10	16.70	---	70.80	**85.90**
	Inst	Ea	Sm	UA	.500	16.00	59.20	20.90	---	80.10	**88.80**
16" x 10"	Inst	Ea	Lg	UA	.500	16.00	56.70	20.90	---	77.60	**94.80**
	Inst	Ea	Sm	UA	.625	12.80	62.10	26.10	---	88.20	**99.10**
18" x 12"	Inst	Ea	Lg	UA	.667	12.00	58.30	27.80	---	86.10	**107.00**
	Inst	Ea	Sm	UA	.833	9.60	63.80	34.80	---	98.60	**113.00**
28" x 16"	Inst	Ea	Lg	UA	1.00	8.00	79.00	41.70	---	120.70	**150.00**
	Inst	Ea	Sm	UA	1.25	6.40	86.40	52.20	---	138.60	**160.00**
Mixing box, with electric or pneumatic motor, with silencer											
150 to 250 CFM	Inst	Ea	Lg	UD	1.60	10.00	482.00	57.40	---	539.40	**636.00**
	Inst	Ea	Sm	UD	2.00	8.00	528.00	71.70	---	599.70	**630.00**
270 to 600 CFM	Inst	Ea	Lg	UD	2.00	8.00	498.00	71.70	---	569.70	**675.00**
	Inst	Ea	Sm	UD	2.50	6.40	545.00	89.70	---	634.70	**673.00**

Description	Oper	Unit	Vol	Crew Size	Man-hours per Unit	Crew Output per Day	Avg Mat'l Unit Cost	Avg Labor Unit Cost	Avg Equip Unit Cost	Avg Total Unit Cost	Avg Price Incl O&P
Fans											
Air conditioning or processed air handling											
Axial flow, compact, low sound 2.5" self-propelled											
3,800 CFM, 5 HP	Inst	Ea	Lg	UE	6.67	3.00	3520.00	245.00	---	3765.00	**4400.00**
	Inst	Ea	Sm	UE	8.33	2.40	3860.00	306.00	---	4166.00	**4290.00**
15,600 CFM, 10 HP	Inst	Ea	Lg	UE	13.3	1.50	6150.00	489.00	---	6639.00	**7760.00**
	Inst	Ea	Sm	UE	16.7	1.20	6730.00	613.00	---	7343.00	**7600.00**
In-line centrifugal, supply/exhaust booster, aluminum wheel/hub, disconnect switch, 1/4" self-propelled											
500 CFM, 10" dia. connect	Inst	Ea	Lg	UE	6.67	3.00	742.00	245.00	---	987.00	**1200.00**
	Inst	Ea	Sm	UE	8.33	2.40	812.00	306.00	---	1118.00	**1250.00**
1,520 CFM, 16" dia. connect	Inst	Ea	Lg	UE	10.0	2.00	970.00	367.00	---	1337.00	**1640.00**
	Inst	Ea	Sm	UE	12.5	1.60	1060.00	459.00	---	1519.00	**1710.00**
3,480 CFM, 20" dia. connect	Inst	Ea	Lg	UE	20.0	1.00	1270.00	735.00	---	2005.00	**2510.00**
	Inst	Ea	Sm	UE	25.0	0.80	1390.00	918.00	---	2308.00	**2700.00**
Ceiling fan, right angle, extra quiet 0.10" self-propelled											
200 CFM	Inst	Ea	Lg	UE	1.25	16.00	158.00	45.90	---	203.90	**247.00**
	Inst	Ea	Sm	UE	1.56	12.80	173.00	57.30	---	230.30	**254.00**
900 CFM	Inst	Ea	Lg	UE	1.67	12.00	376.00	61.30	---	437.30	**520.00**
	Inst	Ea	Sm	UE	2.08	9.60	412.00	76.40	---	488.40	**520.00**
3,000 CFM	Inst	Ea	Lg	UE	2.50	8.00	716.00	91.80	---	807.80	**953.00**
	Inst	Ea	Sm	UE	3.13	6.40	783.00	115.00	---	898.00	**946.00**
Exterior wall or roof cap	Inst	Ea	Lg	UA	.667	12.00	104.00	27.80	---	131.80	**160.00**
	Inst	Ea	Sm	UA	.833	9.60	114.00	34.80	---	148.80	**164.00**
Roof ventilators, corrosive fume resistant, plastic blades											
Roof ventilator, centrifugal V belt drive motor, 1/4" self-propelled											
250 CFM, 1/4 HP	Inst	Ea	Lg	UE	5.00	4.00	2200.00	184.00	---	2384.00	**2790.00**
	Inst	Ea	Sm	UE	6.25	3.20	2410.00	230.00	---	2640.00	**2730.00**
900 CFM, 1/3 HP	Inst	Ea	Lg	UE	6.67	3.00	2390.00	245.00	---	2635.00	**3090.00**
	Inst	Ea	Sm	UE	8.33	2.40	2610.00	306.00	---	2916.00	**3040.00**
1,650 CFM, 1/2 HP	Inst	Ea	Lg	UE	8.00	2.50	2840.00	294.00	---	3134.00	**3680.00**
	Inst	Ea	Sm	UE	10.0	2.00	3100.00	367.00	---	3467.00	**3620.00**
2,250 CFM, 1 HP	Inst	Ea	Lg	UE	10.0	2.00	2970.00	367.00	---	3337.00	**3930.00**
	Inst	Ea	Sm	UE	12.5	1.60	3250.00	459.00	---	3709.00	**3900.00**
Utility set centrifugal V belt drive motor, 1/4" self-propelled											
1,200 CFM, 1/4 HP	Inst	Ea	Lg	UE	5.00	4.00	2200.00	184.00	---	2384.00	**2790.00**
	Inst	Ea	Sm	UE	6.25	3.20	2410.00	230.00	---	2640.00	**2730.00**
1,500 CFM, 1/3 HP	Inst	Ea	Lg	UE	6.67	3.00	2230.00	245.00	---	2475.00	**2910.00**
	Inst	Ea	Sm	UE	8.33	2.40	2440.00	306.00	---	2746.00	**2870.00**
1,850 CFM, 1/2 HP	Inst	Ea	Lg	UE	8.00	2.50	2230.00	294.00	---	2524.00	**2980.00**
	Inst	Ea	Sm	UE	10.0	2.00	2440.00	367.00	---	2807.00	**2960.00**
2,200 CFM, 3/4 HP	Inst	Ea	Lg	UE	10.0	2.00	2250.00	367.00	---	2617.00	**3110.00**
	Inst	Ea	Sm	UE	12.5	1.60	2470.00	459.00	---	2929.00	**3120.00**
Direct drive											
320 CFM, 11" x 11" damper	Inst	Ea	Lg	UE	5.00	4.00	266.00	184.00	---	450.00	**567.00**
	Inst	Ea	Sm	UE	6.25	3.20	291.00	230.00	---	521.00	**617.00**
600 CFM, 11" x 11" damper	Inst	Ea	Lg	UE	5.00	4.00	293.00	184.00	---	477.00	**597.00**
	Inst	Ea	Sm	UE	6.25	3.20	320.00	230.00	---	550.00	**646.00**

Description	Oper	Unit	Vol	Crew Size	Man-hours per Unit	Crew Output per Day	Avg Mat'l Unit Cost	Avg Labor Unit Cost	Avg Equip Unit Cost	Avg Total Unit Cost	Avg Price Incl O&P
Ventilation, residential											
Attic											
Roof-type ventilators											
Aluminum dome, damper and curb											
6" diameter, 300 CFM	Inst	Ea	Lg	EA	.667	12.00	223.00	26.80	---	249.80	**295.00**
	Inst	Ea	Sm	EA	.833	9.60	244.00	33.50	---	277.50	**292.00**
7" diameter, 450 CFM	Inst	Ea	Lg	EA	.727	11.00	243.00	29.20	---	272.20	**322.00**
	Inst	Ea	Sm	EA	.909	8.80	266.00	36.50	---	302.50	**319.00**
9" diameter, 900 CFM	Inst	Ea	Lg	EA	.800	10.00	392.00	32.20	---	424.20	**498.00**
	Inst	Ea	Sm	EA	1.00	8.00	429.00	40.20	---	469.20	**487.00**
12" diameter, 1,000 CFM	Inst	Ea	Lg	EA	1.00	8.00	241.00	40.20	---	281.20	**335.00**
	Inst	Ea	Sm	EA	1.25	6.40	263.00	50.20	---	313.20	**336.00**
16" diameter, 1,500 CFM	Inst	Ea	Lg	EA	1.14	7.00	290.00	45.80	---	335.80	**400.00**
	Inst	Ea	Sm	EA	1.43	5.60	318.00	57.50	---	375.50	**401.00**
20" diameter, 2,500 CFM	Inst	Ea	Lg	EA	1.33	6.00	355.00	53.50	---	408.50	**486.00**
	Inst	Ea	Sm	EA	1.67	4.80	389.00	67.10	---	456.10	**486.00**
26" diameter, 4,000 CFM	Inst	Ea	Lg	EA	1.60	5.00	429.00	64.30	---	493.30	**587.00**
	Inst	Ea	Sm	EA	2.00	4.00	470.00	80.40	---	550.40	**586.00**
32" diameter, 6,500 CFM	Inst	Ea	Lg	EA	2.00	4.00	594.00	80.40	---	674.40	**799.00**
	Inst	Ea	Sm	EA	2.50	3.20	650.00	100.00	---	750.00	**795.00**
38" diameter, 8,000 CFM	Inst	Ea	Lg	EA	2.67	3.00	880.00	107.00	---	987.00	**1170.00**
	Inst	Ea	Sm	EA	3.33	2.40	963.00	134.00	---	1097.00	**1160.00**
50" diameter, 13,000 CFM	Inst	Ea	Lg	EA	4.00	2.00	1270.00	161.00	---	1431.00	**1700.00**
	Inst	Ea	Sm	EA	5.00	1.60	1390.00	201.00	---	1591.00	**1680.00**
Plastic ABS dome											
900 CFM	Inst	Ea	Lg	EA	.667	12.00	71.00	26.80	---	97.80	**121.00**
	Inst	Ea	Sm	EA	.833	9.60	77.70	33.50	---	111.20	**126.00**
1,600 CFM	Inst	Ea	Lg	EA	.800	10.00	106.00	32.20	---	138.20	**169.00**
	Inst	Ea	Sm	EA	1.00	8.00	116.00	40.20	---	156.20	**174.00**
Wall-type ventilators, one speed, with shutter											
12" diameter, 1,000 CFM	Inst	Ea	Lg	EA	.667	12.00	131.00	26.80	---	157.80	**190.00**
	Inst	Ea	Sm	EA	.833	9.60	144.00	33.50	---	177.50	**192.00**
14" diameter, 1,500 CFM	Inst	Ea	Lg	EA	.800	10.00	160.00	32.20	---	192.20	**231.00**
	Inst	Ea	Sm	EA	1.00	8.00	175.00	40.20	---	215.20	**233.00**
16" diameter, 2,000 CFM	Inst	Ea	Lg	EA	1.00	8.00	241.00	40.20	---	281.20	**335.00**
	Inst	Ea	Sm	EA	1.25	6.40	263.00	50.20	---	313.20	**336.00**
Entire structure, wall-type, one speed, with shutter											
30" diameter, 4,800 CFM	Inst	Ea	Lg	EA	1.60	5.00	413.00	64.30	---	477.30	**569.00**
	Inst	Ea	Sm	EA	2.00	4.00	452.00	80.40	---	532.40	**569.00**
36" diameter, 7,000 CFM	Inst	Ea	Lg	EA	2.00	4.00	451.00	80.40	---	531.40	**635.00**
	Inst	Ea	Sm	EA	2.50	3.20	493.00	100.00	---	593.00	**639.00**
42" diameter, 10,000 CFM	Inst	Ea	Lg	EA	2.67	3.00	551.00	107.00	---	658.00	**789.00**
	Inst	Ea	Sm	EA	3.33	2.40	603.00	134.00	---	737.00	**797.00**
48" diameter, 16,000 CFM	Inst	Ea	Lg	EA	4.00	2.00	721.00	161.00	---	882.00	**1060.00**
	Inst	Ea	Sm	EA	5.00	1.60	789.00	201.00	---	990.00	**1080.00**
Two speeds, ADD	Inst	Ea	Lg	---	---	---	51.40	---	---	51.40	**59.10**
	Inst	Ea	Sm	---	---	---	56.30	---	---	56.30	**64.70**

Description	Oper	Unit	Vol	Crew Size	Man-hours per Unit	Crew Output per Day	Avg Mat'l Unit Cost	Avg Labor Unit Cost	Avg Equip Unit Cost	Avg Total Unit Cost	Avg Price Incl O&P
Entire structure, lay-down type, one speed, with shutter											
30" diameter, 4,500 CFM	Inst	Ea	Lg	EA	1.33	6.00	451.00	53.50	---	504.50	**596.00**
	Inst	Ea	Sm	EA	1.67	4.80	493.00	67.10	---	560.10	**590.00**
36" diameter, 6,500 CFM	Inst	Ea	Lg	EA	1.60	5.00	493.00	64.30	---	557.30	**660.00**
	Inst	Ea	Sm	EA	2.00	4.00	539.00	80.40	---	619.40	**656.00**
42" diameter, 9,000 CFM	Inst	Ea	Lg	EA	2.00	4.00	583.00	80.40	---	663.40	**787.00**
	Inst	Ea	Sm	EA	2.50	3.20	638.00	100.00	---	738.00	**784.00**
48" diameter, 12,000 CFM	Inst	Ea	Lg	EA	2.67	3.00	769.00	107.00	---	876.00	**1040.00**
	Inst	Ea	Sm	EA	3.33	2.40	841.00	134.00	---	975.00	**1040.00**
Two speeds, ADD	Inst	Ea	Lg	---	---	---	12.60	---	---	12.60	**14.50**
	Inst	Ea	Sm	---	---	---	13.80	---	---	13.80	**15.90**
12-hour timer, ADD	Inst	Ea	Lg	EA	.500	16.00	22.80	20.10	---	42.90	**55.40**
	Inst	Ea	Sm	EA	.625	12.80	24.90	25.10	---	50.00	**61.40**
Minimum Job Charge											
	Inst	Job	Lg	EA	2.29	3.50	---	92.00	---	92.00	**133.00**
	Inst	Job	Sm	EA	2.86	2.80	---	115.00	---	115.00	**167.00**

Grilles

Aluminum
Air return

Description	Oper	Unit	Vol	Crew Size	Man-hours per Unit	Crew Output per Day	Avg Mat'l Unit Cost	Avg Labor Unit Cost	Avg Equip Unit Cost	Avg Total Unit Cost	Avg Price Incl O&P
6" x 6"	Inst	Ea	Lg	UA	.333	24.00	10.50	13.90	---	24.40	**31.80**
	Inst	Ea	Sm	UA	.417	19.20	11.50	17.40	---	28.90	**36.20**
10" x 6"	Inst	Ea	Lg	UA	.364	22.00	12.80	15.20	---	28.00	**36.30**
	Inst	Ea	Sm	UA	.455	17.60	14.00	19.00	---	33.00	**41.00**
16" x 8"	Inst	Ea	Lg	UA	.400	20.00	18.70	16.70	---	35.40	**45.20**
	Inst	Ea	Sm	UA	.500	16.00	20.40	20.90	---	41.30	**50.00**
12" x 12"	Inst	Ea	Lg	UA	.500	16.00	18.70	20.90	---	39.60	**51.10**
	Inst	Ea	Sm	UA	.625	12.80	20.40	26.10	---	46.50	**57.50**
24" x 12"	Inst	Ea	Lg	UA	.571	14.00	33.40	23.80	---	57.20	**72.20**
	Inst	Ea	Sm	UA	.714	11.20	36.50	29.80	---	66.30	**78.80**
48" x 24"	Inst	Ea	Lg	UA	.800	10.00	128.00	33.40	---	161.40	**195.00**
	Inst	Ea	Sm	UA	1.00	8.00	140.00	41.70	---	181.70	**200.00**
Minimum Job Charge											
	Inst	Job	Lg	UA	2.29	3.50	---	95.50	---	95.50	**136.00**
	Inst	Job	Sm	UA	2.86	2.80	---	119.00	---	119.00	**169.00**

Registers, air supply

Ceiling/wall, O.B. damper, anodized aluminum
One- or two-way deflection, adjustable curved face bars

Description	Oper	Unit	Vol	Crew Size	Man-hours per Unit	Crew Output per Day	Avg Mat'l Unit Cost	Avg Labor Unit Cost	Avg Equip Unit Cost	Avg Total Unit Cost	Avg Price Incl O&P
14" x 8"	Inst	Ea	Lg	UA	.500	16.00	22.30	20.90	---	43.20	**55.20**
	Inst	Ea	Sm	UA	.625	12.80	24.40	26.10	---	50.50	**61.40**

Description	Oper	Unit	Vol	Crew Size	Man-hours per Unit	Crew Output per Day	Avg Mat'l Unit Cost	Avg Labor Unit Cost	Avg Equip Unit Cost	Avg Total Unit Cost	Avg Price Incl O&P
Baseboard, adjustable damper, enameled steel											
10" x 6"	Inst	Ea	Lg	UA	.333	24.00	9.65	13.90	---	23.55	**30.80**
	Inst	Ea	Sm	UA	.417	19.20	10.60	17.40	---	28.00	**35.30**
12" x 5"	Inst	Ea	Lg	UA	.364	22.00	10.50	15.20	---	25.70	**33.60**
	Inst	Ea	Sm	UA	.455	17.60	11.50	19.00	---	30.50	**38.40**
12" x 6"	Inst	Ea	Lg	UA	.364	22.00	9.65	15.20	---	24.85	**32.70**
	Inst	Ea	Sm	UA	.455	17.60	10.60	19.00	---	29.60	**37.50**
12" x 8"	Inst	Ea	Lg	UA	.400	20.00	14.10	16.70	---	30.80	**39.90**
	Inst	Ea	Sm	UA	.500	16.00	15.40	20.90	---	36.30	**45.00**
14" x 6"	Inst	Ea	Lg	UA	.444	18.00	10.50	18.50	---	29.00	**38.40**
	Inst	Ea	Sm	UA	.556	14.40	11.50	23.20	---	34.70	**44.40**
Minimum Job Charge											
	Inst	Job	Lg	UA	2.29	3.50	---	95.50	---	95.50	**136.00**
	Inst	Job	Sm	UA	2.86	2.80	---	119.00	---	119.00	**169.00**

Ventilators
Base, damper, screen; 8" neck diameter

Description	Oper	Unit	Vol	Crew Size	Man-hours per Unit	Crew Output per Day	Avg Mat'l Unit Cost	Avg Labor Unit Cost	Avg Equip Unit Cost	Avg Total Unit Cost	Avg Price Incl O&P
215 CFM @ 5 MPH wind	Inst	Ea	Lg	UD	2.67	6.00	58.80	95.80	---	154.60	**204.00**
	Inst	Ea	Sm	UD	3.33	4.80	64.40	119.00	---	183.40	**234.00**

System units complete
Fan coil air conditioning
Cabinet mounted, with filters
Chilled water

Description	Oper	Unit	Vol	Crew Size	Man-hours per Unit	Crew Output per Day	Avg Mat'l Unit Cost	Avg Labor Unit Cost	Avg Equip Unit Cost	Avg Total Unit Cost	Avg Price Incl O&P
0.5 ton cooling	Inst	Ea	Lg	SB	4.00	4.00	763.00	146.00	---	909.00	**1090.00**
	Inst	Ea	Sm	SB	5.00	3.20	835.00	183.00	---	1018.00	**1100.00**
1 ton cooling	Inst	Ea	Lg	SB	5.33	3.00	864.00	195.00	---	1059.00	**1280.00**
	Inst	Ea	Sm	SB	6.67	2.40	945.00	244.00	---	1189.00	**1300.00**
2.5 ton cooling	Inst	Ea	Lg	SB	8.00	2.00	1560.00	292.00	---	1852.00	**2220.00**
	Inst	Ea	Sm	SB	10.0	1.60	1710.00	365.00	---	2075.00	**2240.00**
3 ton cooling	Inst	Ea	Lg	SB	16.0	1.00	1720.00	584.00	---	2304.00	**2830.00**
	Inst	Ea	Sm	SB	20.0	0.80	1890.00	730.00	---	2620.00	**2940.00**
10 ton cooling	Inst	Ea	Lg	SF	12.0	2.00	2490.00	464.00	---	2954.00	**3540.00**
	Inst	Ea	Sm	SF	15.0	1.60	2730.00	580.00	---	3310.00	**3570.00**
15 ton cooling	Inst	Ea	Lg	SF	16.0	1.50	3470.00	619.00	---	4089.00	**4890.00**
	Inst	Ea	Sm	SF	20.0	1.20	3800.00	774.00	---	4574.00	**4920.00**
20 ton cooling	Inst	Ea	Lg	SF	32.0	0.75	4450.00	1240.00	---	5690.00	**6910.00**
	Inst	Ea	Sm	SF	40.0	0.60	4870.00	1550.00	---	6420.00	**7120.00**
30 ton cooling	Inst	Ea	Lg	SF	48.0	0.50	6600.00	1860.00	---	8460.00	**10300.00**
	Inst	Ea	Sm	SF	60.0	0.40	7220.00	2320.00	---	9540.00	**10600.00**
Minimum Job Charge											
	Inst	Job	Lg	SB	5.33	3.00	---	195.00	---	195.00	**282.00**
	Inst	Job	Sm	SB	6.67	2.40	---	244.00	---	244.00	**353.00**

Description	Oper	Unit	Vol	Crew Size	Man-hours per Unit	Crew Output per Day	Avg Mat'l Unit Cost	Avg Labor Unit Cost	Avg Equip Unit Cost	Avg Total Unit Cost	Avg Price Incl O&P

Heat pumps

Air to air, split system, not including curbs or pads

Description	Oper	Unit	Vol	Crew Size	Man-hours per Unit	Crew Output per Day	Avg Mat'l Unit Cost	Avg Labor Unit Cost	Avg Equip Unit Cost	Avg Total Unit Cost	Avg Price Incl O&P
2 ton cool, 8.5 MBHP heat	Inst	Ea	Lg	SB	16.0	1.00	2170.00	584.00	---	2754.00	**3350.00**
	Inst	Ea	Sm	SB	20.0	0.80	2380.00	730.00	---	3110.00	**3440.00**
3 ton cool, 13 MBHP heat	Inst	Ea	Lg	SB	32.0	0.50	2810.00	1170.00	---	3980.00	**4920.00**
	Inst	Ea	Sm	SB	40.0	0.40	3070.00	1460.00	---	4530.00	**5190.00**
7.5 ton cool, 33 MBHP heat	Inst	Ea	Lg	SB	48.5	0.33	6810.00	1770.00	---	8580.00	**10400.00**
	Inst	Ea	Sm	SB	61.5	0.26	7450.00	2250.00	---	9700.00	**10700.00**
15 ton cool, 64 MBHP heat	Inst	Ea	Lg	SB	64.0	0.25	12200.00	2340.00	---	14540.00	**17400.00**
	Inst	Ea	Sm	SB	80.0	0.20	13300.00	2920.00	---	16220.00	**17600.00**

Air to air, single package, not including curbs, pads, or plenums

Description	Oper	Unit	Vol	Crew Size	Man-hours per Unit	Crew Output per Day	Avg Mat'l Unit Cost	Avg Labor Unit Cost	Avg Equip Unit Cost	Avg Total Unit Cost	Avg Price Incl O&P
2 ton cool, 6.5 MBHP heat	Inst	Ea	Lg	SB	12.8	1.25	2620.00	467.00	---	3087.00	**3690.00**
	Inst	Ea	Sm	SB	16.0	1.00	2870.00	584.00	---	3454.00	**3720.00**
3 ton cool, 10 MBHP heat	Inst	Ea	Lg	SB	21.3	0.75	3150.00	778.00	---	3928.00	**4750.00**
	Inst	Ea	Sm	SB	26.7	0.60	3450.00	975.00	---	4425.00	**4860.00**

Water source to air, single package

Description	Oper	Unit	Vol	Crew Size	Man-hours per Unit	Crew Output per Day	Avg Mat'l Unit Cost	Avg Labor Unit Cost	Avg Equip Unit Cost	Avg Total Unit Cost	Avg Price Incl O&P
1 ton cool, 13 MBHP heat	Inst	Ea	Lg	SB	9.14	1.75	1010.00	334.00	---	1344.00	**1640.00**
	Inst	Ea	Sm	SB	11.4	1.40	1100.00	416.00	---	1516.00	**1710.00**
2 ton cool, 19 MBHP heat	Inst	Ea	Lg	SB	10.7	1.50	1270.00	391.00	---	1661.00	**2030.00**
	Inst	Ea	Sm	SB	13.3	1.20	1390.00	486.00	---	1876.00	**2100.00**
5 ton cool, 29 MBHP heat	Inst	Ea	Lg	SB	21.3	0.75	2230.00	778.00	---	3008.00	**3690.00**
	Inst	Ea	Sm	SB	26.7	0.60	2440.00	975.00	---	3415.00	**3850.00**

Minimum Job Charge

Description	Oper	Unit	Vol	Crew Size	Man-hours per Unit	Crew Output per Day	Avg Mat'l Unit Cost	Avg Labor Unit Cost	Avg Equip Unit Cost	Avg Total Unit Cost	Avg Price Incl O&P
	Inst	Job	Lg	SB	8.00	2.00	---	292.00	---	292.00	**424.00**
	Inst	Job	Sm	SB	10.0	1.60	---	365.00	---	365.00	**529.00**

Roof top air conditioners

Standard controls, curb, energy economizer

Single zone, electric-fired cooling, gas-fired heating

Description	Oper	Unit	Vol	Crew Size	Man-hours per Unit	Crew Output per Day	Avg Mat'l Unit Cost	Avg Labor Unit Cost	Avg Equip Unit Cost	Avg Total Unit Cost	Avg Price Incl O&P
3 ton cool, 60 MBHP heat	Inst	Ea	Lg	SB	13.3	1.20	4210.00	486.00	---	4696.00	**5550.00**
	Inst	Ea	Sm	SB	16.7	0.96	4610.00	610.00	---	5220.00	**5500.00**
4 ton cool, 95 MBHP heat	Inst	Ea	Lg	SB	16.0	1.00	4370.00	584.00	---	4954.00	**5880.00**
	Inst	Ea	Sm	SB	20.0	0.80	4790.00	730.00	---	5520.00	**5840.00**
10 ton cool, 200 MBHP heat	Inst	Ea	Lg	SF	60.0	0.40	9860.00	2320.00	---	12180.00	**14700.00**
	Inst	Ea	Sm	SF	75.0	0.32	10800.00	2900.00	---	13700.00	**15000.00**
30 ton cool, 540 MBHP heat	Inst	Ea	Lg	SG	160	0.20	30300.00	6360.00	---	36660.00	**44100.00**
	Inst	Ea	Sm	SG	200	0.16	33200.00	7950.00	---	41150.00	**44700.00**
40 ton cool, 675 MBHP heat	Inst	Ea	Lg	SG	200	0.16	39400.00	7950.00	---	47350.00	**56900.00**
	Inst	Ea	Sm	SG	246	0.13	43200.00	9780.00	---	52980.00	**57300.00**
50 ton cool, 810 MBHP heat	Inst	Ea	Lg	SG	267	0.12	47800.00	10600.00	---	58400.00	**70400.00**
	Inst	Ea	Sm	SG	320	0.10	52300.00	12700.00	---	65000.00	**70800.00**

Single zone, gas-fired cooling and heating

Description	Oper	Unit	Vol	Crew Size	Man-hours per Unit	Crew Output per Day	Avg Mat'l Unit Cost	Avg Labor Unit Cost	Avg Equip Unit Cost	Avg Total Unit Cost	Avg Price Incl O&P
3 ton cool, 90 MBHP heat	Inst	Ea	Lg	SB	16.0	1.00	5250.00	584.00	---	5834.00	**6880.00**
	Inst	Ea	Sm	SB	20.0	0.80	5740.00	730.00	---	6470.00	**6800.00**

Description	Oper	Unit	Vol	Crew Size	Man-hours per Unit	Crew Output per Day	Avg Mat'l Unit Cost	Avg Labor Unit Cost	Avg Equip Unit Cost	Avg Total Unit Cost	Avg Price Incl O&P
Multizone, electric-fired cooling, gas-fired cooling											
20 ton cool, 360 MBHP heat	Inst	Ea	Lg	SG	160	0.20	47400.00	6360.00	---	53760.00	**63700.00**
	Inst	Ea	Sm	SG	200	0.16	51900.00	7950.00	---	59850.00	**63400.00**
30 ton cool, 540 MBHP heat	Inst	Ea	Lg	SG	229	0.14	59400.00	9110.00	---	68510.00	**81500.00**
	Inst	Ea	Sm	SG	291	0.11	65000.00	11600.00	---	76600.00	**81700.00**
70 ton cool, 1,500 MBHP heat	Inst	Ea	Lg	SG	400	0.08	111000.00	15900.00	---	126900.00	**151000.00**
	Inst	Ea	Sm	SG	533	0.06	122000.00	21200.00	---	143200.00	**153000.00**
80 ton cool, 1,500 MBHP heat	Inst	Ea	Lg	SG	457	0.07	127000.00	18200.00	---	145200.00	**173000.00**
	Inst	Ea	Sm	SG	533	0.06	139000.00	21200.00	---	160200.00	**170000.00**
105 ton cool, 1,500 MBHP heat	Inst	Ea	Lg	SG	640	0.05	167000.00	25500.00	---	192500.00	**229000.00**
	Inst	Ea	Sm	SG	800	0.04	183000.00	31800.00	---	214800.00	**229000.00**
Minimum Job Charge											
	Inst	Job	Lg	SB	5.00	3.20	---	183.00	---	183.00	**265.00**
	Inst	Job	Sm	SB	6.25	2.56	---	228.00	---	228.00	**331.00**

Window unit air conditioners

Semi-permanent installation, 3-speed fan, 125-volt GFI receptacle, energy-efficient models

Description	Oper	Unit	Vol	Crew Size	Man-hours per Unit	Crew Output per Day	Avg Mat'l Unit Cost	Avg Labor Unit Cost	Avg Equip Unit Cost	Avg Total Unit Cost	Avg Price Incl O&P
6,000 BTUH (0.5 ton cool)	Inst	Ea	Lg	EB	4.00	4.00	551.00	161.00	---	712.00	**867.00**
	Inst	Ea	Sm	EB	5.00	3.20	603.00	201.00	---	804.00	**895.00**
9,000 BTUH (0.75 ton cool)	Inst	Ea	Lg	EB	4.00	4.00	567.00	161.00	---	728.00	**885.00**
	Inst	Ea	Sm	EB	5.00	3.20	621.00	201.00	---	822.00	**912.00**
12,000 BTUH (1.0 ton cool)	Inst	Ea	Lg	EB	4.00	4.00	705.00	161.00	---	866.00	**1040.00**
	Inst	Ea	Sm	EB	5.00	3.20	771.00	201.00	---	972.00	**1060.00**
18,000 BTUH (1.5 ton cool)	Inst	Ea	Lg	EB	5.33	3.00	938.00	214.00	---	1152.00	**1390.00**
	Inst	Ea	Sm	EB	6.67	2.40	1030.00	268.00	---	1298.00	**1420.00**
24,000 BTUH (2.0 ton cool)	Inst	Ea	Lg	EB	5.33	3.00	1060.00	214.00	---	1274.00	**1530.00**
	Inst	Ea	Sm	EB	6.67	2.40	1160.00	268.00	---	1428.00	**1550.00**
36,000 BTUH (3.0 ton cool)	Inst	Ea	Lg	EB	5.33	3.00	1380.00	214.00	---	1594.00	**1900.00**
	Inst	Ea	Sm	EB	6.67	2.40	1510.00	268.00	---	1778.00	**1900.00**
Minimum Job Charge											
	Inst	Job	Lg	EA	2.67	3.00	---	107.00	---	107.00	**156.00**
	Inst	Job	Sm	EA	3.33	2.40	---	134.00	---	134.00	**194.00**

Awnings. See Canopies, page 75

Backfill. See Excavation, page 161

Bath accessories.
For plumbing fixtures, see individual items.

The material cost of an item includes the fixture, water supply, and trim (includes fittings and faucets). The labor cost of an item includes installation of the fixture and connection of water supply and/or electricity, but no demolition or clean-up is included. Average rough-in of pipe, waste, and vent is an "add" item shown below each major grouping of fixtures, unless noted otherwise.

Detail of pop-up drain

From: *Basic Plumbing with Illustrations* Craftsman Book Company

Description	Oper	Unit	Vol	Crew Size	Man-hours per Unit	Crew Output per Day	Avg Mat'l Unit Cost	Avg Labor Unit Cost	Avg Equip Unit Cost	Avg Total Unit Cost	Avg Price Incl O&P

Bath accessories

Average quality

Cup holder, surface mounted

Description	Oper	Unit	Vol	Crew Size	Man-hours per Unit	Crew Output per Day	Avg Mat'l Unit Cost	Avg Labor Unit Cost	Avg Equip Unit Cost	Avg Total Unit Cost	Avg Price Incl O&P
Chrome	Inst	Ea	Lg	MR	.333	24.00	6.72	11.60	---	18.32	**24.20**
	Inst	Ea	Sm	MR	.444	18.00	7.79	15.50	---	23.29	**30.90**
Cup and toothbrush holder											
Brass	Inst	Ea	Lg	MR	.333	24.00	9.40	11.60	---	21.00	**27.30**
	Inst	Ea	Sm	MR	.444	18.00	10.90	15.50	---	26.40	**34.50**
Chrome	Inst	Ea	Lg	MR	.333	24.00	7.52	11.60	---	19.12	**25.10**
	Inst	Ea	Sm	MR	.444	18.00	8.72	15.50	---	24.22	**32.00**
Cup, toothbrush and soapholder, recessed											
Chrome	Inst	Ea	Lg	MR	.500	16.00	15.20	17.40	---	32.60	**42.20**
	Inst	Ea	Sm	MR	.667	12.00	17.60	23.30	---	40.90	**53.30**
Glass shelf, chrome											
18" long	Inst	Ea	Lg	MR	.400	20.00	45.10	13.90	---	59.00	**71.60**
	Inst	Ea	Sm	MR	.533	15.00	52.30	18.60	---	70.90	**86.50**
24" long	Inst	Ea	Lg	MR	.400	20.00	47.00	13.90	---	60.90	**73.80**
	Inst	Ea	Sm	MR	.533	15.00	54.50	18.60	---	73.10	**89.00**
Grab bars, concealed mounting											
Satin stainless steel											
12" long	Inst	Ea	Lg	MR	.400	20.00	25.70	13.90	---	39.60	**49.30**
	Inst	Ea	Sm	MR	.533	15.00	29.80	18.60	---	48.40	**60.60**
18" long	Inst	Ea	Lg	MR	.400	20.00	25.70	13.90	---	39.60	**49.30**
	Inst	Ea	Sm	MR	.533	15.00	29.80	18.60	---	48.40	**60.60**
24" long	Inst	Ea	Lg	MR	.400	20.00	25.70	13.90	---	39.60	**49.30**
	Inst	Ea	Sm	MR	.533	15.00	29.80	18.60	---	48.40	**60.60**
30" long	Inst	Ea	Lg	MR	.400	20.00	27.60	13.90	---	41.50	**51.60**
	Inst	Ea	Sm	MR	.533	15.00	32.10	18.60	---	50.70	**63.20**
36" long	Inst	Ea	Lg	MR	.400	20.00	27.90	13.90	---	41.80	**51.90**
	Inst	Ea	Sm	MR	.533	15.00	32.40	18.60	---	51.00	**63.60**
42" long	Inst	Ea	Lg	MR	.400	20.00	30.20	13.90	---	44.10	**54.50**
	Inst	Ea	Sm	MR	.533	15.00	35.00	18.60	---	53.60	**66.60**
48" long	Inst	Ea	Lg	MR	.400	20.00	33.00	13.90	---	46.90	**57.70**
	Inst	Ea	Sm	MR	.533	15.00	38.30	18.60	---	56.90	**70.40**
Angle bar, 16" L x 32" H	Inst	Ea	Lg	MR	.400	20.00	61.10	13.90	---	75.00	**90.10**
	Inst	Ea	Sm	MR	.533	15.00	70.90	18.60	---	89.50	**108.00**
Tub-shower bar, 36" L x 54" H	Inst	Ea	Lg	MR	.400	20.00	95.90	13.90	---	109.80	**130.00**
	Inst	Ea	Sm	MR	.533	15.00	111.00	18.60	---	129.60	**154.00**
Robe hooks, single or double	Inst	Ea	Lg	MR	.250	32.00	4.37	8.72	---	13.09	**17.40**
	Inst	Ea	Sm	MR	.333	24.00	5.07	11.60	---	16.67	**22.30**
Shower curtain rod, 1" dia x 5' 5" L with adjacent rod holder											
	Inst	Ea	Lg	MR	.250	32.00	14.00	8.72	---	22.72	**28.50**
	Inst	Ea	Sm	MR	.333	24.00	16.20	11.60	---	27.80	**35.20**
Soap dish, chrome											
Surface	Inst	Ea	Lg	MR	.250	32.00	6.72	8.72	---	15.44	**20.10**
	Inst	Ea	Sm	MR	.333	24.00	7.79	11.60	---	19.39	**25.40**
Recessed	Inst	Ea	Lg	MR	.250	32.00	12.70	8.72	---	21.42	**27.00**
	Inst	Ea	Sm	MR	.333	24.00	14.80	11.60	---	26.40	**33.50**
Soap holder with bar											
Surface	Inst	Ea	Lg	MR	.250	32.00	7.52	8.72	---	16.24	**21.00**
	Inst	Ea	Sm	MR	.333	24.00	8.72	11.60	---	20.32	**26.50**
Recessed	Inst	Ea	Lg	MR	.250	32.00	17.70	8.72	---	26.42	**32.70**
	Inst	Ea	Sm	MR	.333	24.00	20.50	11.60	---	32.10	**40.10**

Description	Oper	Unit	Vol	Crew Size	Man-hours per Unit	Crew Output per Day	Avg Mat'l Unit Cost	Avg Labor Unit Cost	Avg Equip Unit Cost	Avg Total Unit Cost	Avg Price Incl O&P
Toilet roll holder											
Surface	Inst	Ea	Lg	MR	.250	32.00	11.30	8.72	---	20.02	**25.40**
	Inst	Ea	Sm	MR	.333	24.00	13.10	11.60	---	24.70	**31.50**
Recessed	Inst	Ea	Lg	MR	.250	32.00	22.10	8.72	---	30.82	**37.80**
	Inst	Ea	Sm	MR	.333	24.00	25.70	11.60	---	37.30	**46.00**
Toilet roll holder with hood, recessed											
Surface	Inst	Ea	Lg	MR	.333	24.00	23.50	11.60	---	35.10	**43.50**
	Inst	Ea	Sm	MR	.444	18.00	27.30	15.50	---	42.80	**53.30**
Recessed	Inst	Ea	Lg	MR	.333	24.00	37.60	11.60	---	49.20	**59.70**
	Inst	Ea	Sm	MR	.444	18.00	43.60	15.50	---	59.10	**72.10**
Towel bars, square or round											
Stainless steel											
18"	Inst	Ea	Lg	MR	.250	32.00	11.30	8.72	---	20.02	**25.40**
	Inst	Ea	Sm	MR	.333	24.00	13.10	11.60	---	24.70	**31.60**
24"	Inst	Ea	Lg	MR	.250	32.00	12.40	8.72	---	21.12	**26.70**
	Inst	Ea	Sm	MR	.333	24.00	14.40	11.60	---	26.00	**33.00**
30"	Inst	Ea	Lg	MR	.250	32.00	13.40	8.72	---	22.12	**27.80**
	Inst	Ea	Sm	MR	.333	24.00	15.60	11.60	---	27.20	**34.40**
36"	Inst	Ea	Lg	MR	.250	32.00	14.50	8.72	---	23.22	**29.10**
	Inst	Ea	Sm	MR	.333	24.00	16.80	11.60	---	28.40	**35.90**
Aluminum											
18"	Inst	Ea	Lg	MR	.250	32.00	10.40	8.72	---	19.12	**24.30**
	Inst	Ea	Sm	MR	.333	24.00	12.00	11.60	---	23.60	**30.30**
24"	Inst	Ea	Lg	MR	.250	32.00	11.20	8.72	---	19.92	**25.20**
	Inst	Ea	Sm	MR	.333	24.00	13.00	11.60	---	24.60	**31.40**
30"	Inst	Ea	Lg	MR	.250	32.00	12.00	8.72	---	20.72	**26.20**
	Inst	Ea	Sm	MR	.333	24.00	13.90	11.60	---	25.50	**32.50**
36"	Inst	Ea	Lg	MR	.250	32.00	12.90	8.72	---	21.62	**27.20**
	Inst	Ea	Sm	MR	.333	24.00	14.90	11.60	---	26.50	**33.70**
Towel pin, chrome											
	Inst	Ea	Lg	MR	.222	36.00	6.72	7.74	---	14.46	**18.70**
	Inst	Ea	Sm	MR	.296	27.00	7.79	10.30	---	18.09	**23.60**
Towel ring											
Chrome	Inst	Ea	Lg	MR	.222	36.00	9.21	7.74	---	16.95	**21.60**
	Inst	Ea	Sm	MR	.296	27.00	10.70	10.30	---	21.00	**26.90**
Antique brass	Inst	Ea	Lg	MR	.222	36.00	9.64	7.74	---	17.38	**22.10**
	Inst	Ea	Sm	MR	.296	27.00	11.20	10.30	---	21.50	**27.50**
Towel ladder, 4 arms											
Antique brass	Inst	Ea	Lg	MR	.333	24.00	55.50	11.60	---	67.10	**80.30**
	Inst	Ea	Sm	MR	.444	18.00	64.30	15.50	---	79.80	**95.90**
Polished chrome	Inst	Ea	Lg	MR	.333	24.00	44.50	11.60	---	56.10	**67.70**
	Inst	Ea	Sm	MR	.444	18.00	51.60	15.50	---	67.10	**81.30**
Towel supply shelf, with towel bar											
18" long	Inst	Ea	Lg	MR	.250	32.00	75.70	8.72	---	84.42	**99.40**
	Inst	Ea	Sm	MR	.333	24.00	87.70	11.60	---	99.30	**117.00**
24" long	Inst	Ea	Lg	MR	.250	32.00	135.00	8.72	---	143.72	**167.00**
	Inst	Ea	Sm	MR	.333	24.00	156.00	11.60	---	167.60	**196.00**
Wall-to-floor angle bar with flange, bolt, washer and screws											
	Inst	Ea	Lg	MR	.444	18.00	108.00	15.50	---	123.50	**146.00**
	Inst	Ea	Sm	MR	.593	13.50	125.00	20.70	---	145.70	**174.00**

Description	Oper	Unit	Vol	Crew Size	Man-hours per Unit	Crew Output per Day	Avg Mat'l Unit Cost	Avg Labor Unit Cost	Avg Equip Unit Cost	Avg Total Unit Cost	Avg Price Incl O&P

Medicine cabinets

No electrical work included; for wall outlet cost, see Electrical, page 156

Surface mounting, no wall opening

Swing door cabinets with reversible mirror door

Description	Oper	Unit	Vol	Crew Size	Man-hours per Unit	Crew Output per Day	Avg Mat'l Unit Cost	Avg Labor Unit Cost	Avg Equip Unit Cost	Avg Total Unit Cost	Avg Price Incl O&P
16" x 22"	Inst	Ea	Lg	MR	.800	10.00	55.90	27.90	---	83.80	**104.00**
	Inst	Ea	Sm	MR	1.07	7.50	64.80	37.30	---	102.10	**128.00**
16" x 26"	Inst	Ea	Lg	MR	.800	10.00	74.80	27.90	---	102.70	**126.00**
	Inst	Ea	Sm	MR	1.07	7.50	86.70	37.30	---	124.00	**153.00**

Swing door, corner cabinets with reversible mirror door

Description	Oper	Unit	Vol	Crew Size	Man-hours per Unit	Crew Output per Day	Avg Mat'l Unit Cost	Avg Labor Unit Cost	Avg Equip Unit Cost	Avg Total Unit Cost	Avg Price Incl O&P
16" x 36"	Inst	Ea	Lg	MR	.800	10.00	98.20	27.90	---	126.10	**153.00**
	Inst	Ea	Sm	MR	1.07	7.50	114.00	37.30	---	151.30	**184.00**

Sliding door cabinets, bypassing mirror doors
Toplighted, stainless steel

Description	Oper	Unit	Vol	Crew Size	Man-hours per Unit	Crew Output per Day	Avg Mat'l Unit Cost	Avg Labor Unit Cost	Avg Equip Unit Cost	Avg Total Unit Cost	Avg Price Incl O&P
20" x 20"	Inst	Ea	Lg	MR	.800	10.00	118.00	27.90	---	145.90	**175.00**
	Inst	Ea	Sm	MR	1.07	7.50	136.00	37.30	---	173.30	**210.00**
24" x 20"	Inst	Ea	Lg	MR	.800	10.00	141.00	27.90	---	168.90	**202.00**
	Inst	Ea	Sm	MR	1.07	7.50	164.00	37.30	---	201.30	**241.00**
28" x 20"	Inst	Ea	Lg	MR	.800	10.00	155.00	27.90	---	182.90	**218.00**
	Inst	Ea	Sm	MR	1.07	7.50	180.00	37.30	---	217.30	**260.00**

Cosmetic box with framed mirror stainless steel, Builders series

Description	Oper	Unit	Vol	Crew Size	Man-hours per Unit	Crew Output per Day	Avg Mat'l Unit Cost	Avg Labor Unit Cost	Avg Equip Unit Cost	Avg Total Unit Cost	Avg Price Incl O&P
18" x 26"	Inst	Ea	Lg	MR	.800	10.00	77.80	27.90	---	105.70	**129.00**
	Inst	Ea	Sm	MR	1.07	7.50	90.20	37.30	---	127.50	**157.00**
24" x 32"	Inst	Ea	Lg	MR	.800	10.00	82.20	27.90	---	110.10	**134.00**
	Inst	Ea	Sm	MR	1.07	7.50	95.30	37.30	---	132.60	**163.00**
30" x 32"	Inst	Ea	Lg	MR	.800	10.00	89.80	27.90	---	117.70	**143.00**
	Inst	Ea	Sm	MR	1.07	7.50	104.00	37.30	---	141.30	**173.00**
36" x 32"	Inst	Ea	Lg	MR	.800	10.00	95.00	27.90	---	122.90	**149.00**
	Inst	Ea	Sm	MR	1.07	7.50	110.00	37.30	---	147.30	**180.00**
48" x 32"	Inst	Ea	Lg	MR	.800	10.00	108.00	27.90	---	135.90	**164.00**
	Inst	Ea	Sm	MR	1.07	7.50	125.00	37.30	---	162.30	**197.00**

3-way mirror, tri-view
30" x 30"

Description	Oper	Unit	Vol	Crew Size	Man-hours per Unit	Crew Output per Day	Avg Mat'l Unit Cost	Avg Labor Unit Cost	Avg Equip Unit Cost	Avg Total Unit Cost	Avg Price Incl O&P
Frameless, beveled mirror	Inst	Ea	Lg	MR	.889	9.00	248.00	31.00	---	279.00	**330.00**
	Inst	Ea	Sm	MR	1.19	6.75	288.00	41.50	---	329.50	**390.00**
Natural oak	Inst	Ea	Lg	MR	.889	9.00	286.00	31.00	---	317.00	**373.00**
	Inst	Ea	Sm	MR	1.19	6.75	331.00	41.50	---	372.50	**440.00**
White finish	Inst	Ea	Lg	MR	.889	9.00	267.00	31.00	---	298.00	**351.00**
	Inst	Ea	Sm	MR	1.19	6.75	310.00	41.50	---	351.50	**415.00**

36" x 30"

Description	Oper	Unit	Vol	Crew Size	Man-hours per Unit	Crew Output per Day	Avg Mat'l Unit Cost	Avg Labor Unit Cost	Avg Equip Unit Cost	Avg Total Unit Cost	Avg Price Incl O&P
Frameless, beveled mirror	Inst	Ea	Lg	MR	.889	9.00	283.00	31.00	---	314.00	**369.00**
	Inst	Ea	Sm	MR	1.19	6.75	328.00	41.50	---	369.50	**436.00**
Natural oak	Inst	Ea	Lg	MR	.889	9.00	320.00	31.00	---	351.00	**412.00**
	Inst	Ea	Sm	MR	1.19	6.75	371.00	41.50	---	412.50	**485.00**
White finish	Inst	Ea	Lg	MR	.889	9.00	301.00	31.00	---	332.00	**390.00**
	Inst	Ea	Sm	MR	1.19	6.75	349.00	41.50	---	390.50	**460.00**

Description	Oper	Unit	Vol	Crew Size	Man-hours per Unit	Crew Output per Day	Avg Mat'l Unit Cost	Avg Labor Unit Cost	Avg Equip Unit Cost	Avg Total Unit Cost	Avg Price Incl O&P
48" x 30"											
Frameless, beveled mirror	Inst	Ea	Lg	MR	1.00	8.00	366.00	34.90	---	400.90	**470.00**
	Inst	Ea	Sm	MR	1.33	6.00	424.00	46.40	---	470.40	**553.00**
Natural oak	Inst	Ea	Lg	MR	1.00	8.00	393.00	34.90	---	427.90	**501.00**
	Inst	Ea	Sm	MR	1.33	6.00	456.00	46.40	---	502.40	**590.00**
White finish	Inst	Ea	Lg	MR	1.00	8.00	384.00	34.90	---	418.90	**491.00**
	Inst	Ea	Sm	MR	1.33	6.00	445.00	46.40	---	491.40	**577.00**
With matching light fixture											
with 2 lights	Inst	Ea	Lg	EA	2.00	4.00	65.80	80.40	---	146.20	**192.00**
	Inst	Ea	Sm	EA	2.67	3.00	76.30	107.00	---	183.30	**243.00**
with 3 lights	Inst	Ea	Lg	EA	2.00	4.00	98.70	80.40	---	179.10	**230.00**
	Inst	Ea	Sm	EA	2.67	3.00	114.00	107.00	---	221.00	**287.00**
with 4 lights	Inst	Ea	Lg	EA	2.00	4.00	108.00	80.40	---	188.40	**241.00**
	Inst	Ea	Sm	EA	2.67	3.00	125.00	107.00	---	232.00	**300.00**
with 6 lights	Inst	Ea	Lg	EA	2.00	4.00	132.00	80.40	---	212.40	**268.00**
	Inst	Ea	Sm	EA	2.67	3.00	153.00	107.00	---	260.00	**331.00**
With matching light fixture for beveled mirror cabinets only											
with 2 lights	Inst	Ea	Lg	EA	2.00	4.00	89.30	80.40	---	169.70	**219.00**
	Inst	Ea	Sm	EA	2.67	3.00	104.00	107.00	---	211.00	**275.00**
with 3 lights	Inst	Ea	Lg	EA	2.00	4.00	108.00	80.40	---	188.40	**241.00**
	Inst	Ea	Sm	EA	2.67	3.00	125.00	107.00	---	232.00	**300.00**
with 4 lights	Inst	Ea	Lg	EA	2.00	4.00	141.00	80.40	---	221.40	**279.00**
	Inst	Ea	Sm	EA	2.67	3.00	164.00	107.00	---	271.00	**344.00**
with 6 lights	Inst	Ea	Lg	EA	2.00	4.00	165.00	80.40	---	245.40	**306.00**
	Inst	Ea	Sm	EA	2.67	3.00	191.00	107.00	---	298.00	**375.00**

Recessed mounting, overall sizes

Swing door with mirror

Builders series

Description	Oper	Unit	Vol	Crew Size	Man-hours per Unit	Crew Output per Day	Avg Mat'l Unit Cost	Avg Labor Unit Cost	Avg Equip Unit Cost	Avg Total Unit Cost	Avg Price Incl O&P
14" x 18"											
Polished brass strip	Inst	Ea	Lg	MR	1.00	8.00	57.30	34.90	---	92.20	**115.00**
	Inst	Ea	Sm	MR	1.33	6.00	66.50	46.40	---	112.90	**142.00**
Polished edge strip	Inst	Ea	Lg	MR	1.00	8.00	81.80	34.90	---	116.70	**144.00**
	Inst	Ea	Sm	MR	1.33	6.00	94.80	46.40	---	141.20	**175.00**
Stainless steel strip	Inst	Ea	Lg	MR	1.00	8.00	68.60	34.90	---	103.50	**128.00**
	Inst	Ea	Sm	MR	1.33	6.00	79.60	46.40	---	126.00	**157.00**
14" x 24"											
Polished brass strip	Inst	Ea	Lg	MR	1.00	8.00	63.00	34.90	---	97.90	**122.00**
	Inst	Ea	Sm	MR	1.33	6.00	73.00	46.40	---	119.40	**150.00**
Polished edge strip	Inst	Ea	Lg	MR	1.00	8.00	87.40	34.90	---	122.30	**150.00**
	Inst	Ea	Sm	MR	1.33	6.00	101.00	46.40	---	147.40	**182.00**
Stainless steel strip	Inst	Ea	Lg	MR	1.00	8.00	75.20	34.90	---	110.10	**136.00**
	Inst	Ea	Sm	MR	1.33	6.00	87.20	46.40	---	133.60	**166.00**

Description	Oper	Unit	Vol	Crew Size	Man-hours per Unit	Crew Output per Day	Avg Mat'l Unit Cost	Avg Labor Unit Cost	Avg Equip Unit Cost	Avg Total Unit Cost	Avg Price Incl O&P
Decorator series											
14" x 18"											
Frameless bevel mirror	Inst	Ea	Lg	MR	1.00	8.00	93.10	34.90	---	128.00	**157.00**
	Inst	Ea	Sm	MR	1.33	6.00	108.00	46.40	---	154.40	**190.00**
Natural oak	Inst	Ea	Lg	MR	1.00	8.00	126.00	34.90	---	160.90	**194.00**
	Inst	Ea	Sm	MR	1.33	6.00	146.00	46.40	---	192.40	**234.00**
White birch	Inst	Ea	Lg	MR	1.00	8.00	122.00	34.90	---	156.90	**190.00**
	Inst	Ea	Sm	MR	1.33	6.00	142.00	46.40	---	188.40	**229.00**
White finish	Inst	Ea	Lg	MR	1.00	8.00	150.00	34.90	---	184.90	**222.00**
	Inst	Ea	Sm	MR	1.33	6.00	174.00	46.40	---	220.40	**266.00**
14" x 24"											
Frameless bevel mirror	Inst	Ea	Lg	MR	1.00	8.00	94.00	34.90	---	128.90	**158.00**
	Inst	Ea	Sm	MR	1.33	6.00	109.00	46.40	---	155.40	**191.00**
Natural oak	Inst	Ea	Lg	MR	1.00	8.00	127.00	34.90	---	161.90	**195.00**
	Inst	Ea	Sm	MR	1.33	6.00	147.00	46.40	---	193.40	**235.00**
White birch	Inst	Ea	Lg	MR	1.00	8.00	123.00	34.90	---	157.90	**191.00**
	Inst	Ea	Sm	MR	1.33	6.00	143.00	46.40	---	189.40	**230.00**
White finish	Inst	Ea	Lg	MR	1.00	8.00	155.00	34.90	---	189.90	**228.00**
	Inst	Ea	Sm	MR	1.33	6.00	180.00	46.40	---	226.40	**273.00**
Oak framed cabinet with oval mirror											
20" x 36"											
	Inst	Ea	Lg	MR	1.00	8.00	188.00	34.90	---	222.90	**266.00**
	Inst	Ea	Sm	MR	1.33	6.00	218.00	46.40	---	264.40	**317.00**

Mirrors

Decorator oval mirrors, antique gold

Description	Oper	Unit	Vol	Crew Size	Man-hours per Unit	Crew Output per Day	Avg Mat'l Unit Cost	Avg Labor Unit Cost	Avg Equip Unit Cost	Avg Total Unit Cost	Avg Price Incl O&P
16" x 24"	Inst	Ea	Lg	MR	.160	50.00	61.10	5.58	---	66.68	**78.20**
	Inst	Ea	Sm	MR	.213	37.50	70.90	7.43	---	78.33	**92.00**
16" x 32"	Inst	Ea	Lg	MR	.160	50.00	75.20	5.58	---	80.78	**94.40**
	Inst	Ea	Sm	MR	.213	37.50	87.20	7.43	---	94.63	**111.00**

Shower equipment. See Shower stalls, page 383
Vanity cabinets. See Cabinets, page 72

Description	Oper	Unit	Vol	Crew Size	Man-hours per Unit	Crew Output per Day	Avg Mat'l Unit Cost	Avg Labor Unit Cost	Avg Equip Unit Cost	Avg Total Unit Cost	Avg Price Incl O&P

Bathtubs (includes whirlpools)

Plumbing fixtures with good quality supply fittings and faucets included in material cost. Labor cost for installation only of fixture, supply fittings, and faucets. For rough-in, see Adjustments in this bathtub section

Frequently encountered applications

Detach & reset operations

Description	Oper	Unit	Vol	Crew Size	Man-hours per Unit	Crew Output per Day	Avg Mat'l Unit Cost	Avg Labor Unit Cost	Avg Equip Unit Cost	Avg Total Unit Cost	Avg Price Incl O&P
Free-standing tub	Reset	Ea	Lg	SB	3.20	5.00	51.70	117.00	---	168.70	**229.00**
	Reset	Ea	Sm	SB	4.27	3.75	60.00	156.00	---	216.00	**295.00**
Recessed tub	Reset	Ea	Lg	SB	4.00	4.00	51.70	146.00	---	197.70	**271.00**
	Reset	Ea	Sm	SB	5.33	3.00	60.00	195.00	---	255.00	**351.00**
Sunken tub	Reset	Ea	Lg	SB	5.33	3.00	51.70	195.00	---	246.70	**342.00**
	Reset	Ea	Sm	SB	7.11	2.25	60.00	260.00	---	320.00	**445.00**

Remove operations

Description	Oper	Unit	Vol	Crew Size	Man-hours per Unit	Crew Output per Day	Avg Mat'l Unit Cost	Avg Labor Unit Cost	Avg Equip Unit Cost	Avg Total Unit Cost	Avg Price Incl O&P
Free-standing tub	Demo	Ea	Lg	SB	1.33	12.00	14.10	48.60	---	62.70	**86.60**
	Demo	Ea	Sm	SB	1.78	9.00	16.40	65.00	---	81.40	**113.00**
Recessed tub	Demo	Ea	Lg	SB	2.00	8.00	28.20	73.00	---	101.20	**138.00**
	Demo	Ea	Sm	SB	2.67	6.00	32.70	97.50	---	130.20	**179.00**
Sunken tub	Demo	Ea	Lg	SB	2.67	6.00	42.30	97.50	---	139.80	**190.00**
	Demo	Ea	Sm	SB	3.56	4.50	49.10	130.00	---	179.10	**245.00**

Replace operations

Recessed into wall (above floor installation)

Enameled cast iron, colors
60" L x 30" W x 14" H

Description	Oper	Unit	Vol	Crew Size	Man-hours per Unit	Crew Output per Day	Avg Mat'l Unit Cost	Avg Labor Unit Cost	Avg Equip Unit Cost	Avg Total Unit Cost	Avg Price Incl O&P
	Inst	Ea	Lg	SB	6.67	2.40	1070.00	244.00	---	1314.00	**1580.00**
	Inst	Ea	Sm	SB	8.89	1.80	1240.00	325.00	---	1565.00	**1890.00**

66" L x 32" W x 16-1/4" H

Description	Oper	Unit	Vol	Crew Size	Man-hours per Unit	Crew Output per Day	Avg Mat'l Unit Cost	Avg Labor Unit Cost	Avg Equip Unit Cost	Avg Total Unit Cost	Avg Price Incl O&P
	Inst	Ea	Lg	SB	6.67	2.40	2450.00	244.00	---	2694.00	**3170.00**
	Inst	Ea	Sm	SB	8.89	1.80	2840.00	325.00	---	3165.00	**3740.00**

Enameled steel, colors
60" L x 30" W x 17-1/2" H

Description	Oper	Unit	Vol	Crew Size	Man-hours per Unit	Crew Output per Day	Avg Mat'l Unit Cost	Avg Labor Unit Cost	Avg Equip Unit Cost	Avg Total Unit Cost	Avg Price Incl O&P
	Inst	Ea	Lg	SB	6.67	2.40	548.00	244.00	---	792.00	**983.00**
	Inst	Ea	Sm	SB	8.89	1.80	635.00	325.00	---	960.00	**1200.00**

Sunken (below floor installation) or full frame support with full sidewall finish

Enameled cast iron, colors
60" L x 32" W x 18-1/4" H

Description	Oper	Unit	Vol	Crew Size	Man-hours per Unit	Crew Output per Day	Avg Mat'l Unit Cost	Avg Labor Unit Cost	Avg Equip Unit Cost	Avg Total Unit Cost	Avg Price Incl O&P
	Inst	Ea	Lg	SB	6.67	2.40	2710.00	244.00	---	2954.00	**3470.00**
	Inst	Ea	Sm	SB	8.89	1.80	3140.00	325.00	---	3465.00	**4090.00**
Bathtub with whirlpool											
Plumbing installation	Inst	Ea	Lg	SB	13.3	1.20	4210.00	486.00	---	4696.00	**5550.00**
	Inst	Ea	Sm	SB	17.8	0.90	4890.00	650.00	---	5540.00	**6560.00**
Electrical installation	Inst	Ea	Lg	EA	6.15	1.30	188.00	247.00	---	435.00	**575.00**
	Inst	Ea	Sm	EA	8.16	0.98	218.00	328.00	---	546.00	**726.00**

Description	Oper	Unit	Vol	Crew Size	Man-hours per Unit	Crew Output per Day	Avg Mat'l Unit Cost	Avg Labor Unit Cost	Avg Equip Unit Cost	Avg Total Unit Cost	Avg Price Incl O&P

Frequently encountered applications (continued)

71-3/4" L x 36" W x 20-7/8" H

Description	Oper	Unit	Vol	Crew Size	Man-hours per Unit	Crew Output per Day	Avg Mat'l Unit Cost	Avg Labor Unit Cost	Avg Equip Unit Cost	Avg Total Unit Cost	Avg Price Incl O&P
	Inst	Ea	Lg	SB	6.67	2.40	4760.00	244.00	---	5004.00	5820.00
	Inst	Ea	Sm	SB	8.89	1.80	5510.00	325.00	---	5835.00	6810.00
Bathtub with whirlpool											
Plumbing installation	Inst	Ea	Lg	SB	13.3	1.20	6570.00	486.00	---	7056.00	8260.00
	Inst	Ea	Sm	SB	17.8	0.90	7620.00	650.00	---	8270.00	9710.00
Electrical installation	Inst	Ea	Lg	EA	6.15	1.30	188.00	247.00	---	435.00	575.00
	Inst	Ea	Sm	EA	8.16	0.98	218.00	328.00	---	546.00	726.00

Fiberglass, colors

60" L x 42" W x 20" H

Description	Oper	Unit	Vol	Crew Size	Man-hours per Unit	Crew Output per Day	Avg Mat'l Unit Cost	Avg Labor Unit Cost	Avg Equip Unit Cost	Avg Total Unit Cost	Avg Price Incl O&P
	Inst	Ea	Lg	SB	6.67	2.40	1420.00	244.00	---	1664.00	1990.00
	Inst	Ea	Sm	SB	8.89	1.80	1650.00	325.00	---	1975.00	2370.00
Bathtub with whirlpool											
Plumbing installation	Inst	Ea	Lg	SB	13.3	1.20	2520.00	486.00	---	3006.00	3610.00
	Inst	Ea	Sm	SB	17.8	0.90	2930.00	650.00	---	3580.00	4310.00
Electrical installation	Inst	Ea	Lg	EA	6.15	1.30	188.00	247.00	---	435.00	575.00
	Inst	Ea	Sm	EA	8.16	0.98	218.00	328.00	---	546.00	726.00

72" L x 42" W x 20" H

Description	Oper	Unit	Vol	Crew Size	Man-hours per Unit	Crew Output per Day	Avg Mat'l Unit Cost	Avg Labor Unit Cost	Avg Equip Unit Cost	Avg Total Unit Cost	Avg Price Incl O&P
	Inst	Ea	Lg	SB	6.67	2.40	1460.00	244.00	---	1704.00	2030.00
	Inst	Ea	Sm	SB	8.89	1.80	1690.00	325.00	---	2015.00	2420.00
Bathtub with whirlpool											
Plumbing installation	Inst	Ea	Lg	SB	13.3	1.20	2990.00	486.00	---	3476.00	4140.00
	Inst	Ea	Sm	SB	17.8	0.90	3470.00	650.00	---	4120.00	4930.00
Electrical installation	Inst	Ea	Lg	EA	6.15	1.30	188.00	247.00	---	435.00	575.00
	Inst	Ea	Sm	EA	8.16	0.98	218.00	328.00	---	546.00	726.00

60" L x 60" W x 21" H, corner

Description	Oper	Unit	Vol	Crew Size	Man-hours per Unit	Crew Output per Day	Avg Mat'l Unit Cost	Avg Labor Unit Cost	Avg Equip Unit Cost	Avg Total Unit Cost	Avg Price Incl O&P
	Inst	Ea	Lg	SB	6.67	2.40	1750.00	244.00	---	1994.00	2370.00
	Inst	Ea	Sm	SB	8.89	1.80	2030.00	325.00	---	2355.00	2810.00
Bathtub with whirlpool											
Plumbing installation	Inst	Ea	Lg	SB	13.3	1.20	3340.00	486.00	---	3826.00	4550.00
	Inst	Ea	Sm	SB	17.8	0.90	3880.00	650.00	---	4530.00	5400.00
Electrical installation	Inst	Ea	Lg	EA	6.15	1.30	188.00	247.00	---	435.00	575.00
	Inst	Ea	Sm	EA	8.16	0.98	218.00	328.00	---	546.00	726.00

Adjustments

Install rough-In

Description	Oper	Unit	Vol	Crew Size	Man-hours per Unit	Crew Output per Day	Avg Mat'l Unit Cost	Avg Labor Unit Cost	Avg Equip Unit Cost	Avg Total Unit Cost	Avg Price Incl O&P
	Inst	Ea	Lg	SB	10.0	1.60	79.90	365.00	---	444.90	621.00
	Inst	Ea	Sm	SB	13.3	1.20	92.70	486.00	---	578.70	811.00

Install shower head with mixer valve over tub

Description	Oper	Unit	Vol	Crew Size	Man-hours per Unit	Crew Output per Day	Avg Mat'l Unit Cost	Avg Labor Unit Cost	Avg Equip Unit Cost	Avg Total Unit Cost	Avg Price Incl O&P
Open wall, ADD	Inst	Ea	Lg	SA	2.00	4.00	108.00	86.00	---	194.00	249.00
	Inst	Ea	Sm	SA	2.67	3.00	125.00	115.00	---	240.00	311.00
Closed wall, ADD	Inst	Ea	Lg	SA	4.00	2.00	169.00	172.00	---	341.00	444.00
	Inst	Ea	Sm	SA	5.33	1.50	196.00	229.00	---	425.00	558.00

Description	Oper	Unit	Vol	Crew Size	Man-hours per Unit	Crew Output per Day	Avg Mat'l Unit Cost	Avg Labor Unit Cost	Avg Equip Unit Cost	Avg Total Unit Cost	Avg Price Incl O&P

Free-standing

American Standard Products, enameled steel

Reminiscence Slipper Soaking Bathtub, white or black textured exterior
72-1/8" L x 37-1/2" W x 28-3/4" H

Description	Oper	Unit	Vol	Crew Size	Man-hours per Unit	Crew Output per Day	Avg Mat'l Unit Cost	Avg Labor Unit Cost	Avg Equip Unit Cost	Avg Total Unit Cost	Avg Price Incl O&P
White	Inst	Ea	Lg	SB	8.00	2.00	3720.00	292.00	---	4012.00	**4700.00**
	Inst	Ea	Sm	SB	10.7	1.50	4310.00	391.00	---	4701.00	**5530.00**
Colors	Inst	Ea	Lg	SB	8.00	2.00	3800.00	292.00	---	4092.00	**4790.00**
	Inst	Ea	Sm	SB	10.7	1.50	4410.00	391.00	---	4801.00	**5640.00**
Premium Colors	Inst	Ea	Lg	SB	8.00	2.00	3880.00	292.00	---	4172.00	**4880.00**
	Inst	Ea	Sm	SB	10.7	1.50	4490.00	391.00	---	4881.00	**5740.00**
Required accessories											
Ball-and-claw legs (four)	Inst	Set	Lg	SB	---	---	595.00	---	---	595.00	**684.00**
	Inst	Set	Sm	SB	---	---	690.00	---	---	690.00	**793.00**
Filler w/Shower, brass	Inst	Ea	Lg	SB	---	---	919.00	---	---	919.00	**1060.00**
	Inst	Ea	Sm	SB	---	---	1070.00	---	---	1070.00	**1230.00**
Drain, chain & stopper	Inst	Set	Lg	SB	---	---	226.00	---	---	226.00	**259.00**
	Inst	Set	Sm	SB	---	---	262.00	---	---	262.00	**301.00**
Supply valves, brass	Inst	Set	Lg	SB	---	---	554.00	---	---	554.00	**637.00**
	Inst	Set	Sm	SB	---	---	642.00	---	---	642.00	**738.00**

Kohler Products, enameled cast iron

Birthday Bath
72" L x 37-1/2" W x 21-1/2" H

Description	Oper	Unit	Vol	Crew Size	Man-hours per Unit	Crew Output per Day	Avg Mat'l Unit Cost	Avg Labor Unit Cost	Avg Equip Unit Cost	Avg Total Unit Cost	Avg Price Incl O&P
White	Inst	Ea	Lg	SB	8.00	2.00	7400.00	292.00	---	7692.00	**8930.00**
	Inst	Ea	Sm	SB	10.7	1.50	8580.00	391.00	---	8971.00	**10400.00**
Colors	Inst	Ea	Lg	SB	8.00	2.00	8800.00	292.00	---	9092.00	**10500.00**
	Inst	Ea	Sm	SB	10.7	1.50	10200.00	391.00	---	10591.00	**12300.00**
Premium Colors	Inst	Ea	Lg	SB	8.00	2.00	9840.00	292.00	---	10132.00	**11700.00**
	Inst	Ea	Sm	SB	10.7	1.50	11400.00	391.00	---	11791.00	**13700.00**
Required accessories											
Ball-and-claw legs (four)	Inst	Set	Lg	SB	---	---	1400.00	---	---	1400.00	**1610.00**
	Inst	Set	Sm	SB	---	---	1620.00	---	---	1620.00	**1860.00**
Filler w/Shower, brass	Inst	Ea	Lg	SB	---	---	752.00	---	---	752.00	**865.00**
	Inst	Ea	Sm	SB	---	---	872.00	---	---	872.00	**1000.00**
Drain, chain & stopper	Inst	Set	Lg	SB	---	---	416.00	---	---	416.00	**479.00**
	Inst	Set	Sm	SB	---	---	483.00	---	---	483.00	**555.00**
Supply valves, brass	Inst	Set	Lg	SB	---	---	191.00	---	---	191.00	**220.00**
	Inst	Set	Sm	SB	---	---	222.00	---	---	222.00	**255.00**

Description	Oper	Unit	Vol	Crew Size	Man-hours per Unit	Crew Output per Day	Avg Mat'l Unit Cost	Avg Labor Unit Cost	Avg Equip Unit Cost	Avg Total Unit Cost	Avg Price Incl O&P
Vintage Bath											
72" L x 42" W x 22" H											
White	Inst	Ea	Lg	SB	8.00	2.00	7020.00	292.00	---	7312.00	**8500.00**
	Inst	Ea	Sm	SB	10.7	1.50	8140.00	391.00	---	8531.00	**9930.00**
Colors	Inst	Ea	Lg	SB	8.00	2.00	8330.00	292.00	---	8622.00	**10000.00**
	Inst	Ea	Sm	SB	10.7	1.50	9660.00	391.00	---	10051.00	**11700.00**
Premium Colors	Inst	Ea	Lg	SB	8.00	2.00	9310.00	292.00	---	9602.00	**11100.00**
	Inst	Ea	Sm	SB	10.7	1.50	10800.00	391.00	---	11191.00	**13000.00**
Required accessories											
Wood base	Inst	Ea	Lg	SB	---	---	3030.00	---	---	3030.00	**3490.00**
	Inst	Ea	Sm	SB	---	---	3520.00	---	---	3520.00	**4040.00**
Ceramic base	Inst	Ea	Lg	SB	---	---	1250.00	---	---	1250.00	**1440.00**
	Inst	Ea	Sm	SB	---	---	1450.00	---	---	1450.00	**1670.00**
Adjustable feet	Inst	Set	Lg	SB	---	---	70.30	---	---	70.30	**80.90**
	Inst	Set	Sm	SB	---	---	81.50	---	---	81.50	**93.80**

Recessed

American Standard Products, Americast

Description	Oper	Unit	Vol	Crew Size	Man-hours per Unit	Crew Output per Day	Avg Mat'l Unit Cost	Avg Labor Unit Cost	Avg Equip Unit Cost	Avg Total Unit Cost	Avg Price Incl O&P
60" L x 32" W x 17-3/4" H, w/ grab bar (Cambridge)											
White	Inst	Ea	Lg	SB	6.67	2.40	1020.00	244.00	---	1264.00	**1520.00**
	Inst	Ea	Sm	SB	8.89	1.80	1180.00	325.00	---	1505.00	**1830.00**
Colors	Inst	Ea	Lg	SB	6.67	2.40	1170.00	244.00	---	1414.00	**1700.00**
	Inst	Ea	Sm	SB	8.89	1.80	1330.00	325.00	---	1655.00	**2000.00**
Premium Colors	Inst	Ea	Lg	SB	6.67	2.40	1270.00	244.00	---	1514.00	**1810.00**
	Inst	Ea	Sm	SB	8.89	1.80	1440.00	325.00	---	1765.00	**2130.00**
Bathtub with whirlpool (System-I)											
Plumbing installation											
White	Inst	Ea	Lg	SB	13.3	1.20	3320.00	486.00	---	3806.00	**4520.00**
	Inst	Ea	Sm	SB	17.8	0.90	3850.00	650.00	---	4500.00	**5360.00**
Colors	Inst	Ea	Lg	SB	13.3	1.20	3480.00	486.00	---	3966.00	**4710.00**
	Inst	Ea	Sm	SB	17.8	0.90	4040.00	650.00	---	4690.00	**5590.00**
Premium Colors	Inst	Ea	Lg	SB	13.3	1.20	3610.00	486.00	---	4096.00	**4850.00**
	Inst	Ea	Sm	SB	17.8	0.90	4180.00	650.00	---	4830.00	**5750.00**
Electrical installation											
	Inst	Ea	Lg	EA	6.15	1.30	188.00	247.00	---	435.00	**575.00**
	Inst	Ea	Sm	EA	8.16	0.98	218.00	328.00	---	546.00	**726.00**
60" L x 34" W x 17-1/2" H, w/ luxury ledge (Princeton)											
White	Inst	Ea	Lg	SB	6.67	2.40	1070.00	244.00	---	1314.00	**1580.00**
	Inst	Ea	Sm	SB	8.89	1.80	1240.00	325.00	---	1565.00	**1900.00**
Colors	Inst	Ea	Lg	SB	6.67	2.40	1160.00	244.00	---	1404.00	**1680.00**
	Inst	Ea	Sm	SB	8.89	1.80	1340.00	325.00	---	1665.00	**2010.00**
Premium Colors	Inst	Ea	Lg	SB	6.67	2.40	1220.00	244.00	---	1464.00	**1760.00**
	Inst	Ea	Sm	SB	8.89	1.80	1420.00	325.00	---	1745.00	**2100.00**

Description	Oper	Unit	Vol	Crew Size	Man-hours per Unit	Crew Output per Day	Avg Mat'l Unit Cost	Avg Labor Unit Cost	Avg Equip Unit Cost	Avg Total Unit Cost	Avg Price Incl O&P
66" L x 32" W x 20" H (Stratford)											
White	Inst	Ea	Lg	SB	6.67	2.40	1620.00	244.00	---	1864.00	**2220.00**
	Inst	Ea	Sm	SB	8.89	1.80	1880.00	325.00	---	2205.00	**2640.00**
Colors	Inst	Ea	Lg	SB	6.67	2.40	1890.00	244.00	---	2134.00	**2530.00**
	Inst	Ea	Sm	SB	8.89	1.80	2190.00	325.00	---	2515.00	**2990.00**
Bathtub with whirlpool											
Plumbing installation											
White	Inst	Ea	Lg	SB	13.3	1.20	3930.00	486.00	---	4416.00	**5230.00**
	Inst	Ea	Sm	SB	17.8	0.90	4560.00	650.00	---	5210.00	**6190.00**
Colors	Inst	Ea	Lg	SB	13.3	1.20	4180.00	486.00	---	4666.00	**5510.00**
	Inst	Ea	Sm	SB	17.8	0.90	4840.00	650.00	---	5490.00	**6510.00**
Electrical installation											
	Inst	Ea	Lg	EA	6.15	1.30	188.00	247.00	---	435.00	**575.00**
	Inst	Ea	Sm	EA	8.16	0.98	218.00	328.00	---	546.00	**726.00**
Options											
Grab bar kit											
Chrome	Inst	Ea	Lg	SB	---	---	186.00	---	---	186.00	**214.00**
	Inst	Ea	Sm	SB	---	---	216.00	---	---	216.00	**248.00**
Brass	Inst	Ea	Lg	SB	---	---	305.00	---	---	305.00	**350.00**
	Inst	Ea	Sm	SB	---	---	353.00	---	---	353.00	**406.00**
White	Inst	Ea	Lg	SB	---	---	186.00	---	---	186.00	**214.00**
	Inst	Ea	Sm	SB	---	---	216.00	---	---	216.00	**248.00**
Satin	Inst	Ea	Lg	SB	---	---	305.00	---	---	305.00	**350.00**
	Inst	Ea	Sm	SB	---	---	353.00	---	---	353.00	**406.00**
Drain kit											
Chrome	Inst	Ea	Lg	SB	---	---	132.00	---	---	132.00	**151.00**
	Inst	Ea	Sm	SB	---	---	153.00	---	---	153.00	**175.00**
Brass	Inst	Ea	Lg	SB	---	---	224.00	---	---	224.00	**257.00**
	Inst	Ea	Sm	SB	---	---	259.00	---	---	259.00	**298.00**
White	Inst	Ea	Lg	SB	---	---	224.00	---	---	224.00	**257.00**
	Inst	Ea	Sm	SB	---	---	259.00	---	---	259.00	**298.00**
Satin	Inst	Ea	Lg	SB	---	---	224.00	---	---	224.00	**257.00**
	Inst	Ea	Sm	SB	---	---	259.00	---	---	259.00	**298.00**

American Standard Products, enameled steel

Description	Oper	Unit	Vol	Crew Size	Man-hours per Unit	Crew Output per Day	Avg Mat'l Unit Cost	Avg Labor Unit Cost	Avg Equip Unit Cost	Avg Total Unit Cost	Avg Price Incl O&P
60" L x 30" W x 14" H (Salem)											
White, slip resistant	Inst	Ea	Lg	SB	6.67	2.40	498.00	244.00	---	742.00	**926.00**
	Inst	Ea	Sm	SB	8.89	1.80	578.00	325.00	---	903.00	**1130.00**
Colors, slip resistant	Inst	Ea	Lg	SB	6.67	2.40	527.00	244.00	---	771.00	**960.00**
	Inst	Ea	Sm	SB	8.89	1.80	611.00	325.00	---	936.00	**1170.00**
60" L x 30" W x 17-1/2" H (Solar)											
White, slip resistant	Inst	Ea	Lg	SB	6.67	2.40	517.00	244.00	---	761.00	**948.00**
	Inst	Ea	Sm	SB	8.89	1.80	600.00	325.00	---	925.00	**1160.00**
Colors, slip resistant	Inst	Ea	Lg	SB	6.67	2.40	548.00	244.00	---	792.00	**983.00**
	Inst	Ea	Sm	SB	8.89	1.80	635.00	325.00	---	960.00	**1200.00**

Description	Oper	Unit	Vol	Crew Size	Man-hours per Unit	Crew Output per Day	Avg Mat'l Unit Cost	Avg Labor Unit Cost	Avg Equip Unit Cost	Avg Total Unit Cost	Avg Price Incl O&P

Kohler Products, enameled cast iron

48" L x 44" W x 14" H, corner (Mayflower)

Description	Oper	Unit	Vol	Crew Size	Man-hours per Unit	Crew Output per Day	Avg Mat'l Unit Cost	Avg Labor Unit Cost	Avg Equip Unit Cost	Avg Total Unit Cost	Avg Price Incl O&P
White	Inst	Ea	Lg	SB	6.67	2.40	2940.00	244.00	---	3184.00	**3730.00**
	Inst	Ea	Sm	SB	8.89	1.80	3410.00	325.00	---	3735.00	**4390.00**
Colors	Inst	Ea	Lg	SB	6.67	2.40	3580.00	244.00	---	3824.00	**4470.00**
	Inst	Ea	Sm	SB	8.89	1.80	4160.00	325.00	---	4485.00	**5250.00**

54" L x 30-1/4" W x 14" H (Seaforth)

Description	Oper	Unit	Vol	Crew Size	Man-hours per Unit	Crew Output per Day	Avg Mat'l Unit Cost	Avg Labor Unit Cost	Avg Equip Unit Cost	Avg Total Unit Cost	Avg Price Incl O&P
White	Inst	Ea	Lg	SB	6.67	2.40	1470.00	244.00	---	1714.00	**2040.00**
	Inst	Ea	Sm	SB	8.89	1.80	1700.00	325.00	---	2025.00	**2430.00**
Colors	Inst	Ea	Lg	SB	6.67	2.40	1760.00	244.00	---	2004.00	**2380.00**
	Inst	Ea	Sm	SB	8.89	1.80	2040.00	325.00	---	2365.00	**2820.00**

60" L x 32" W x 16-1/4" H (Mendota)

Description	Oper	Unit	Vol	Crew Size	Man-hours per Unit	Crew Output per Day	Avg Mat'l Unit Cost	Avg Labor Unit Cost	Avg Equip Unit Cost	Avg Total Unit Cost	Avg Price Incl O&P
White	Inst	Ea	Lg	SB	6.67	2.40	1280.00	244.00	---	1524.00	**1830.00**
	Inst	Ea	Sm	SB	8.89	1.80	1490.00	325.00	---	1815.00	**2180.00**
Colors	Inst	Ea	Lg	SB	6.67	2.40	1580.00	244.00	---	1824.00	**2170.00**
	Inst	Ea	Sm	SB	8.89	1.80	1830.00	325.00	---	2155.00	**2580.00**
Premium Colors	Inst	Ea	Lg	SB	6.67	2.40	1770.00	244.00	---	2014.00	**2390.00**
	Inst	Ea	Sm	SB	8.89	1.80	2050.00	325.00	---	2375.00	**2830.00**

60" L x 34-1/4" W x 14" H (Villager, w/ 4" ledge)

Description	Oper	Unit	Vol	Crew Size	Man-hours per Unit	Crew Output per Day	Avg Mat'l Unit Cost	Avg Labor Unit Cost	Avg Equip Unit Cost	Avg Total Unit Cost	Avg Price Incl O&P
White	Inst	Ea	Lg	SB	6.67	2.40	889.00	244.00	---	1133.00	**1380.00**
	Inst	Ea	Sm	SB	8.89	1.80	1030.00	325.00	---	1355.00	**1660.00**
Colors	Inst	Ea	Lg	SB	6.67	2.40	1070.00	244.00	---	1314.00	**1580.00**
	Inst	Ea	Sm	SB	8.89	1.80	1240.00	325.00	---	1565.00	**1890.00**

66" L x 32" W x 16-1/4" H (Dynametric)

Description	Oper	Unit	Vol	Crew Size	Man-hours per Unit	Crew Output per Day	Avg Mat'l Unit Cost	Avg Labor Unit Cost	Avg Equip Unit Cost	Avg Total Unit Cost	Avg Price Incl O&P
White	Inst	Ea	Lg	SB	6.67	2.40	2020.00	244.00	---	2264.00	**2670.00**
	Inst	Ea	Sm	SB	8.89	1.80	2340.00	325.00	---	2665.00	**3160.00**
Colors	Inst	Ea	Lg	SB	6.67	2.40	2450.00	244.00	---	2694.00	**3170.00**
	Inst	Ea	Sm	SB	8.89	1.80	2840.00	325.00	---	3165.00	**3740.00**

Sunken

American Standard Products, acrylic

58-1/4" L x 58-1/4" W x 22-1/2" H, corner, with grab bar drilling (Savona)

Bathtub with whirlpool (System-II)

Plumbing installation

Description	Oper	Unit	Vol	Crew Size	Man-hours per Unit	Crew Output per Day	Avg Mat'l Unit Cost	Avg Labor Unit Cost	Avg Equip Unit Cost	Avg Total Unit Cost	Avg Price Incl O&P
White	Inst	Ea	Lg	SB	13.3	1.20	3840.00	486.00	---	4326.00	**5120.00**
	Inst	Ea	Sm	SB	17.8	0.90	4450.00	650.00	---	5100.00	**6060.00**
Colors	Inst	Ea	Lg	SB	13.3	1.20	3900.00	486.00	---	4386.00	**5190.00**
	Inst	Ea	Sm	SB	17.8	0.90	4520.00	650.00	---	5170.00	**6150.00**
Premium Colors	Inst	Ea	Lg	SB	13.3	1.20	3970.00	486.00	---	4456.00	**5270.00**
	Inst	Ea	Sm	SB	17.8	0.90	4610.00	650.00	---	5260.00	**6240.00**

Electrical installation

Description	Oper	Unit	Vol	Crew Size	Man-hours per Unit	Crew Output per Day	Avg Mat'l Unit Cost	Avg Labor Unit Cost	Avg Equip Unit Cost	Avg Total Unit Cost	Avg Price Incl O&P
	Inst	Ea	Lg	EA	6.15	1.30	188.00	247.00	---	435.00	**575.00**
	Inst	Ea	Sm	EA	8.16	0.98	218.00	328.00	---	546.00	**726.00**

Description	Oper	Unit	Vol	Crew Size	Man-hours per Unit	Crew Output per Day	Avg Mat'l Unit Cost	Avg Labor Unit Cost	Avg Equip Unit Cost	Avg Total Unit Cost	Avg Price Incl O&P
Options											
Grab bar kit											
Chrome	Inst	Ea	Lg	SB	---	---	110.00	---	---	110.00	**126.00**
	Inst	Ea	Sm	SB	---	---	128.00	---	---	128.00	**147.00**
Brass	Inst	Ea	Lg	SB	---	---	153.00	---	---	153.00	**176.00**
	Inst	Ea	Sm	SB	---	---	178.00	---	---	178.00	**204.00**
White	Inst	Ea	Lg	SB	---	---	137.00	---	---	137.00	**158.00**
	Inst	Ea	Sm	SB	---	---	159.00	---	---	159.00	**183.00**
Satin	Inst	Ea	Lg	SB	---	---	153.00	---	---	153.00	**176.00**
	Inst	Ea	Sm	SB	---	---	178.00	---	---	178.00	**204.00**
Drain kit											
Chrome	Inst	Ea	Lg	SB	---	---	132.00	---	---	132.00	**151.00**
	Inst	Ea	Sm	SB	---	---	153.00	---	---	153.00	**175.00**
Brass	Inst	Ea	Lg	SB	---	---	224.00	---	---	224.00	**257.00**
	Inst	Ea	Sm	SB	---	---	259.00	---	---	259.00	**298.00**
White	Inst	Ea	Lg	SB	---	---	224.00	---	---	224.00	**257.00**
	Inst	Ea	Sm	SB	---	---	259.00	---	---	259.00	**298.00**
Satin	Inst	Ea	Lg	SB	---	---	224.00	---	---	224.00	**257.00**
	Inst	Ea	Sm	SB	---	---	259.00	---	---	259.00	**298.00**
59-1/2" L x 42-1/4" W x 21-1/4" H, oval (Savona)											
White	Inst	Ea	Lg	SB	6.67	2.40	1150.00	244.00	---	1394.00	**1670.00**
	Inst	Ea	Sm	SB	8.89	1.80	1330.00	325.00	---	1655.00	**2000.00**
Colors	Inst	Ea	Lg	SB	6.67	2.40	1200.00	244.00	---	1444.00	**1730.00**
	Inst	Ea	Sm	SB	8.89	1.80	1390.00	325.00	---	1715.00	**2070.00**
Premium Colors	Inst	Ea	Lg	SB	6.67	2.40	1260.00	244.00	---	1504.00	**1800.00**
	Inst	Ea	Sm	SB	8.89	1.80	1460.00	325.00	---	1785.00	**2150.00**
Bathtub with whirlpool (System-II)											
Plumbing installation											
White	Inst	Ea	Lg	SB	13.3	1.20	2230.00	486.00	---	2716.00	**3270.00**
	Inst	Ea	Sm	SB	17.8	0.90	2580.00	650.00	---	3230.00	**3910.00**
Colors	Inst	Ea	Lg	SB	13.3	1.20	2300.00	486.00	---	2786.00	**3340.00**
	Inst	Ea	Sm	SB	17.8	0.90	2660.00	650.00	---	3310.00	**4000.00**
Premium Colors	Inst	Ea	Lg	SB	13.3	1.20	2380.00	486.00	---	2866.00	**3450.00**
	Inst	Ea	Sm	SB	17.8	0.90	2760.00	650.00	---	3410.00	**4120.00**
Electrical installation											
	Inst	Ea	Lg	EA	6.15	1.30	188.00	247.00	---	435.00	**575.00**
	Inst	Ea	Sm	EA	8.16	0.98	218.00	328.00	---	546.00	**726.00**
Drain kit											
Chrome	Inst	Ea	Lg	SB	---	---	132.00	---	---	132.00	**151.00**
	Inst	Ea	Sm	SB	---	---	153.00	---	---	153.00	**175.00**
Brass	Inst	Ea	Lg	SB	---	---	224.00	---	---	224.00	**257.00**
	Inst	Ea	Sm	SB	---	---	259.00	---	---	259.00	**298.00**
White	Inst	Ea	Lg	SB	---	---	224.00	---	---	224.00	**257.00**
	Inst	Ea	Sm	SB	---	---	259.00	---	---	259.00	**298.00**
Satin	Inst	Ea	Lg	SB	---	---	224.00	---	---	224.00	**257.00**
	Inst	Ea	Sm	SB	---	---	259.00	---	---	259.00	**298.00**

Description	Oper	Unit	Vol	Crew Size	Man-hours per Unit	Crew Output per Day	Avg Mat'l Unit Cost	Avg Labor Unit Cost	Avg Equip Unit Cost	Avg Total Unit Cost	Avg Price Incl O&P
60" L x 32" W x 21-1/2" H (Hampton Drop-In)											
Bathtub with Hydro Massage (System-I)											
Plumbing installation											
White	Inst	Ea	Lg	SB	13.3	1.20	2150.00	486.00	---	2636.00	**3170.00**
	Inst	Ea	Sm	SB	17.8	0.90	2490.00	650.00	---	3140.00	**3810.00**
Colors	Inst	Ea	Lg	SB	13.3	1.20	2210.00	486.00	---	2696.00	**3250.00**
	Inst	Ea	Sm	SB	17.8	0.90	2560.00	650.00	---	3210.00	**3890.00**
Electrical installation											
	Inst	Ea	Lg	EA	6.15	1.30	188.00	247.00	---	435.00	**575.00**
	Inst	Ea	Sm	EA	8.16	0.98	218.00	328.00	---	546.00	**726.00**
60" L x 32" W x 21-1/2" H (Ellisse Built-In)											
Bathtub with whirlpool (System-II)											
Plumbing installation											
White	Inst	Ea	Lg	SB	13.3	1.20	3500.00	486.00	---	3986.00	**4730.00**
	Inst	Ea	Sm	SB	17.8	0.90	4060.00	650.00	---	4710.00	**5610.00**
Colors	Inst	Ea	Lg	SB	13.3	1.20	3570.00	486.00	---	4056.00	**4810.00**
	Inst	Ea	Sm	SB	17.8	0.90	4140.00	650.00	---	4790.00	**5700.00**
Premium Colors	Inst	Ea	Lg	SB	13.3	1.20	3620.00	486.00	---	4106.00	**4870.00**
	Inst	Ea	Sm	SB	17.8	0.90	4200.00	650.00	---	4850.00	**5770.00**
Electrical installation											
	Inst	Ea	Lg	EA	6.15	1.30	188.00	247.00	---	435.00	**575.00**
	Inst	Ea	Sm	EA	8.16	0.98	218.00	328.00	---	546.00	**726.00**
Options											
Grab bar kit											
Chrome	Inst	Ea	Lg	SB	---	---	186.00	---	---	186.00	**214.00**
	Inst	Ea	Sm	SB	---	---	216.00	---	---	216.00	**248.00**
Brass	Inst	Ea	Lg	SB	---	---	280.00	---	---	280.00	**322.00**
	Inst	Ea	Sm	SB	---	---	325.00	---	---	325.00	**374.00**
White	Inst	Ea	Lg	SB	---	---	280.00	---	---	280.00	**322.00**
	Inst	Ea	Sm	SB	---	---	325.00	---	---	325.00	**374.00**
Drain kit											
Chrome	Inst	Ea	Lg	SB	---	---	132.00	---	---	132.00	**151.00**
	Inst	Ea	Sm	SB	---	---	153.00	---	---	153.00	**175.00**
Brass	Inst	Ea	Lg	SB	---	---	224.00	---	---	224.00	**257.00**
	Inst	Ea	Sm	SB	---	---	259.00	---	---	259.00	**298.00**
White	Inst	Ea	Lg	SB	---	---	224.00	---	---	224.00	**257.00**
	Inst	Ea	Sm	SB	---	---	259.00	---	---	259.00	**298.00**
72" L x 42" W x 21" H (Green Tea)											
Bathtub with whirlpool (System-I)											
Plumbing installation											
White	Inst	Ea	Lg	SB	13.3	1.20	3020.00	486.00	---	3506.00	**4180.00**
	Inst	Ea	Sm	SB	17.8	0.90	3510.00	650.00	---	4160.00	**4970.00**
Colors	Inst	Ea	Lg	SB	13.3	1.20	3130.00	486.00	---	3616.00	**4300.00**
	Inst	Ea	Sm	SB	17.8	0.90	3630.00	650.00	---	4280.00	**5110.00**
Premium Colors	Inst	Ea	Lg	SB	13.3	1.20	3130.00	486.00	---	3616.00	**4300.00**
	Inst	Ea	Sm	SB	17.8	0.90	3630.00	650.00	---	4280.00	**5110.00**
Electrical installation											
	Inst	Ea	Lg	EA	6.15	1.30	188.00	247.00	---	435.00	**575.00**
	Inst	Ea	Sm	EA	8.16	0.98	218.00	328.00	---	546.00	**726.00**

Description	Oper	Unit	Vol	Crew Size	Man-hours per Unit	Crew Output per Day	Avg Mat'l Unit Cost	Avg Labor Unit Cost	Avg Equip Unit Cost	Avg Total Unit Cost	Avg Price Incl O&P
Options											
Grab bar kit											
Chrome	Inst	Ea	Lg	SB	---	---	186.00	---	---	186.00	**214.00**
	Inst	Ea	Sm	SB	---	---	216.00	---	---	216.00	**248.00**
Brass	Inst	Ea	Lg	SB	---	---	280.00	---	---	280.00	**322.00**
	Inst	Ea	Sm	SB	---	---	325.00	---	---	325.00	**374.00**
White	Inst	Ea	Lg	SB	---	---	280.00	---	---	280.00	**322.00**
	Inst	Ea	Sm	SB	---	---	325.00	---	---	325.00	**374.00**
Satin	Inst	Ea	Lg	SB	---	---	280.00	---	---	280.00	**322.00**
	Inst	Ea	Sm	SB	---	---	325.00	---	---	325.00	**374.00**
Drain kit											
Chrome	Inst	Ea	Lg	SB	---	---	132.00	---	---	132.00	**151.00**
	Inst	Ea	Sm	SB	---	---	153.00	---	---	153.00	**175.00**
Brass	Inst	Ea	Lg	SB	---	---	224.00	---	---	224.00	**257.00**
	Inst	Ea	Sm	SB	---	---	259.00	---	---	259.00	**298.00**
White	Inst	Ea	Lg	SB	---	---	224.00	---	---	224.00	**257.00**
	Inst	Ea	Sm	SB	---	---	259.00	---	---	259.00	**298.00**
Satin	Inst	Ea	Lg	SB	---	---	224.00	---	---	224.00	**257.00**
	Inst	Ea	Sm	SB	---	---	259.00	---	---	259.00	**298.00**

72" L x 48" W x 21-1/2" H (Ellisse)

Bathtub with whirlpool
Plumbing installation

Description	Oper	Unit	Vol	Crew Size	Man-hours per Unit	Crew Output per Day	Avg Mat'l Unit Cost	Avg Labor Unit Cost	Avg Equip Unit Cost	Avg Total Unit Cost	Avg Price Incl O&P
White	Inst	Ea	Lg	SB	13.3	1.20	4060.00	486.00	---	4546.00	**5370.00**
	Inst	Ea	Sm	SB	17.8	0.90	4710.00	650.00	---	5360.00	**6350.00**
Colors	Inst	Ea	Lg	SB	13.3	1.20	4120.00	486.00	---	4606.00	**5440.00**
	Inst	Ea	Sm	SB	17.8	0.90	4780.00	650.00	---	5430.00	**6430.00**
Premium Colors	Inst	Ea	Lg	SB	13.3	1.20	4180.00	486.00	---	4666.00	**5510.00**
	Inst	Ea	Sm	SB	17.8	0.90	4840.00	650.00	---	5490.00	**6510.00**
Electrical installation											
	Inst	Ea	Lg	EA	6.15	1.30	188.00	247.00	---	435.00	**575.00**
	Inst	Ea	Sm	EA	8.16	0.98	218.00	328.00	---	546.00	**726.00**
Options											
Grab bar kit											
Chrome	Inst	Ea	Lg	SB	---	---	110.00	---	---	110.00	**126.00**
	Inst	Ea	Sm	SB	---	---	128.00	---	---	128.00	**147.00**
Brass	Inst	Ea	Lg	SB	---	---	153.00	---	---	153.00	**176.00**
	Inst	Ea	Sm	SB	---	---	178.00	---	---	178.00	**204.00**
White	Inst	Ea	Lg	SB	---	---	137.00	---	---	137.00	**158.00**
	Inst	Ea	Sm	SB	---	---	159.00	---	---	159.00	**183.00**
Satin	Inst	Ea	Lg	SB	---	---	153.00	---	---	153.00	**176.00**
	Inst	Ea	Sm	SB	---	---	178.00	---	---	178.00	**204.00**
Drain kit											
Chrome	Inst	Ea	Lg	SB	---	---	132.00	---	---	132.00	**151.00**
	Inst	Ea	Sm	SB	---	---	153.00	---	---	153.00	**175.00**
Brass	Inst	Ea	Lg	SB	---	---	224.00	---	---	224.00	**257.00**
	Inst	Ea	Sm	SB	---	---	259.00	---	---	259.00	**298.00**
White	Inst	Ea	Lg	SB	---	---	224.00	---	---	224.00	**257.00**
	Inst	Ea	Sm	SB	---	---	259.00	---	---	259.00	**298.00**
Satin	Inst	Ea	Lg	SB	---	---	224.00	---	---	224.00	**257.00**
	Inst	Ea	Sm	SB	---	---	259.00	---	---	259.00	**298.00**

Description	Oper	Unit	Vol	Crew Size	Man-hours per Unit	Crew Output per Day	Avg Mat'l Unit Cost	Avg Labor Unit Cost	Avg Equip Unit Cost	Avg Total Unit Cost	Avg Price Incl O&P

Kohler Products, enameled cast iron

60" L x 36" W x 20-3/8" H (Steeping Bath)

Description	Oper	Unit	Vol	Crew Size	Man-hours per Unit	Crew Output per Day	Avg Mat'l Unit Cost	Avg Labor Unit Cost	Avg Equip Unit Cost	Avg Total Unit Cost	Avg Price Incl O&P
White	Inst	Ea	Lg	SB	6.67	2.40	3040.00	244.00	---	3284.00	**3850.00**
	Inst	Ea	Sm	SB	8.89	1.80	3520.00	325.00	---	3845.00	**4520.00**
Colors	Inst	Ea	Lg	SB	6.67	2.40	3710.00	244.00	---	3954.00	**4610.00**
	Inst	Ea	Sm	SB	8.89	1.80	4300.00	325.00	---	4625.00	**5410.00**
Premium Colors	Inst	Ea	Lg	SB	6.67	2.40	4200.00	244.00	---	4444.00	**5190.00**
	Inst	Ea	Sm	SB	8.89	1.80	4880.00	325.00	---	5205.00	**6080.00**

Bathtub with whirlpool (System-III)
Plumbing installation

Description	Oper	Unit	Vol	Crew Size	Man-hours per Unit	Crew Output per Day	Avg Mat'l Unit Cost	Avg Labor Unit Cost	Avg Equip Unit Cost	Avg Total Unit Cost	Avg Price Incl O&P
White	Inst	Ea	Lg	SB	13.3	1.20	7020.00	486.00	---	7506.00	**8770.00**
	Inst	Ea	Sm	SB	17.8	0.90	8140.00	650.00	---	8790.00	**10300.00**
Colors	Inst	Ea	Lg	SB	13.3	1.20	7640.00	486.00	---	8126.00	**9490.00**
	Inst	Ea	Sm	SB	17.8	0.90	8860.00	650.00	---	9510.00	**11100.00**
Premium Colors	Inst	Ea	Lg	SB	13.3	1.20	7980.00	486.00	---	8466.00	**9880.00**
	Inst	Ea	Sm	SB	17.8	0.90	9250.00	650.00	---	9900.00	**11600.00**

Electrical installation

Description	Oper	Unit	Vol	Crew Size	Man-hours per Unit	Crew Output per Day	Avg Mat'l Unit Cost	Avg Labor Unit Cost	Avg Equip Unit Cost	Avg Total Unit Cost	Avg Price Incl O&P
	Inst	Ea	Lg	EA	6.15	1.30	188.00	247.00	---	435.00	**575.00**
	Inst	Ea	Sm	EA	8.16	0.98	218.00	328.00	---	546.00	**726.00**

60" L x 32" W x 18-1/4" H (Tea-for-Two)

Description	Oper	Unit	Vol	Crew Size	Man-hours per Unit	Crew Output per Day	Avg Mat'l Unit Cost	Avg Labor Unit Cost	Avg Equip Unit Cost	Avg Total Unit Cost	Avg Price Incl O&P
White	Inst	Ea	Lg	SB	6.67	2.40	2260.00	244.00	---	2504.00	**2960.00**
	Inst	Ea	Sm	SB	8.89	1.80	2620.00	325.00	---	2945.00	**3490.00**
Colors	Inst	Ea	Lg	SB	6.67	2.40	2710.00	244.00	---	2954.00	**3470.00**
	Inst	Ea	Sm	SB	8.89	1.80	3140.00	325.00	---	3465.00	**4090.00**
Premium Colors	Inst	Ea	Lg	SB	6.67	2.40	3050.00	244.00	---	3294.00	**3860.00**
	Inst	Ea	Sm	SB	8.89	1.80	3530.00	325.00	---	3855.00	**4530.00**

Bathtub with whirlpool (System-II)
Plumbing installation

Description	Oper	Unit	Vol	Crew Size	Man-hours per Unit	Crew Output per Day	Avg Mat'l Unit Cost	Avg Labor Unit Cost	Avg Equip Unit Cost	Avg Total Unit Cost	Avg Price Incl O&P
White	Inst	Ea	Lg	SB	13.3	1.20	3910.00	486.00	---	4396.00	**5200.00**
	Inst	Ea	Sm	SB	17.8	0.90	4530.00	650.00	---	5180.00	**6150.00**
Colors	Inst	Ea	Lg	SB	13.3	1.20	4210.00	486.00	---	4696.00	**5550.00**
	Inst	Ea	Sm	SB	17.8	0.90	4890.00	650.00	---	5540.00	**6560.00**
Premium Colors	Inst	Ea	Lg	SB	13.3	1.20	4380.00	486.00	---	4866.00	**5750.00**
	Inst	Ea	Sm	SB	17.8	0.90	5080.00	650.00	---	5730.00	**6790.00**

Electrical installation

Description	Oper	Unit	Vol	Crew Size	Man-hours per Unit	Crew Output per Day	Avg Mat'l Unit Cost	Avg Labor Unit Cost	Avg Equip Unit Cost	Avg Total Unit Cost	Avg Price Incl O&P
	Inst	Ea	Lg	EA	6.15	1.30	188.00	247.00	---	435.00	**575.00**
	Inst	Ea	Sm	EA	8.16	0.98	218.00	328.00	---	546.00	**726.00**

66" L x 32" W x 18-1/4" H (Maestro)

Description	Oper	Unit	Vol	Crew Size	Man-hours per Unit	Crew Output per Day	Avg Mat'l Unit Cost	Avg Labor Unit Cost	Avg Equip Unit Cost	Avg Total Unit Cost	Avg Price Incl O&P
White	Inst	Ea	Lg	SB	6.67	2.40	1770.00	244.00	---	2014.00	**2390.00**
	Inst	Ea	Sm	SB	8.89	1.80	2050.00	325.00	---	2375.00	**2830.00**
Colors	Inst	Ea	Lg	SB	6.67	2.40	2100.00	244.00	---	2344.00	**2770.00**
	Inst	Ea	Sm	SB	8.89	1.80	2440.00	325.00	---	2765.00	**3280.00**
Premium Colors	Inst	Ea	Lg	SB	6.67	2.40	2350.00	244.00	---	2594.00	**3060.00**
	Inst	Ea	Sm	SB	8.89	1.80	2730.00	325.00	---	3055.00	**3610.00**

Description	Oper	Unit	Vol	Crew Size	Man-hours per Unit	Crew Output per Day	Avg Mat'l Unit Cost	Avg Labor Unit Cost	Avg Equip Unit Cost	Avg Total Unit Cost	Avg Price Incl O&P
Bathtub with whirlpool (System-II)											
Plumbing installation											
White	Inst	Ea	Lg	SB	13.3	1.20	4920.00	486.00	---	5406.00	**6360.00**
	Inst	Ea	Sm	SB	17.8	0.90	5700.00	650.00	---	6350.00	**7500.00**
Colors	Inst	Ea	Lg	SB	13.3	1.20	5340.00	486.00	---	5826.00	**6850.00**
	Inst	Ea	Sm	SB	17.8	0.90	6190.00	650.00	---	6840.00	**8070.00**
Premium Colors	Inst	Ea	Lg	SB	13.3	1.20	5570.00	486.00	---	6056.00	**7120.00**
	Inst	Ea	Sm	SB	17.8	0.90	6460.00	650.00	---	7110.00	**8380.00**
Electrical installation											
	Inst	Ea	Lg	EA	6.15	1.30	188.00	247.00	---	435.00	**575.00**
	Inst	Ea	Sm	EA	8.16	0.98	218.00	328.00	---	546.00	**726.00**
66" L x 32" W x 18" H (Tea-for-Two)											
White	Inst	Ea	Lg	SB	6.67	2.40	2620.00	244.00	---	2864.00	**3370.00**
	Inst	Ea	Sm	SB	8.89	1.80	3040.00	325.00	---	3365.00	**3970.00**
Colors	Inst	Ea	Lg	SB	6.67	2.40	3050.00	244.00	---	3294.00	**3860.00**
	Inst	Ea	Sm	SB	8.89	1.80	3540.00	325.00	---	3865.00	**4540.00**
Premium Colors	Inst	Ea	Lg	SB	6.67	2.40	3370.00	244.00	---	3614.00	**4230.00**
	Inst	Ea	Sm	SB	8.89	1.80	3910.00	325.00	---	4235.00	**4970.00**
Bathtub with whirlpool (System-II)											
Plumbing installation											
White	Inst	Ea	Lg	SB	13.3	1.20	5250.00	486.00	---	5736.00	**6740.00**
	Inst	Ea	Sm	SB	17.8	0.90	6090.00	650.00	---	6740.00	**7940.00**
Colors	Inst	Ea	Lg	SB	13.3	1.20	5670.00	486.00	---	6156.00	**7220.00**
	Inst	Ea	Sm	SB	17.8	0.90	6570.00	650.00	---	7220.00	**8500.00**
Premium Colors	Inst	Ea	Lg	SB	13.3	1.20	5980.00	486.00	---	6466.00	**7580.00**
	Inst	Ea	Sm	SB	17.8	0.90	6930.00	650.00	---	7580.00	**8910.00**
Electrical installation											
	Inst	Ea	Lg	EA	6.15	1.30	188.00	247.00	---	435.00	**575.00**
	Inst	Ea	Sm	EA	8.16	0.98	218.00	328.00	---	546.00	**726.00**
71-3/4" L x 36" W x 20-7/8" H (Tea-for-Two)											
White	Inst	Ea	Lg	SB	6.67	2.40	3900.00	244.00	---	4144.00	**4840.00**
	Inst	Ea	Sm	SB	8.89	1.80	4520.00	325.00	---	4845.00	**5670.00**
Colors	Inst	Ea	Lg	SB	6.67	2.40	4760.00	244.00	---	5004.00	**5820.00**
	Inst	Ea	Sm	SB	8.89	1.80	5510.00	325.00	---	5835.00	**6810.00**
Premium Colors	Inst	Ea	Lg	SB	6.67	2.40	5400.00	244.00	---	5644.00	**6560.00**
	Inst	Ea	Sm	SB	8.89	1.80	6260.00	325.00	---	6585.00	**7670.00**
Bathtub with whirlpool (System-III)											
Plumbing installation											
White	Inst	Ea	Lg	SB	13.3	1.20	6050.00	486.00	---	6536.00	**7660.00**
	Inst	Ea	Sm	SB	17.8	0.90	7010.00	650.00	---	7660.00	**9010.00**
Colors	Inst	Ea	Lg	SB	13.3	1.20	6570.00	486.00	---	7056.00	**8260.00**
	Inst	Ea	Sm	SB	17.8	0.90	7620.00	650.00	---	8270.00	**9710.00**
Premium Colors	Inst	Ea	Lg	SB	13.3	1.20	6860.00	486.00	---	7346.00	**8590.00**
	Inst	Ea	Sm	SB	17.8	0.90	7950.00	650.00	---	8600.00	**10100.00**
Electrical installation											
	Inst	Ea	Lg	EA	6.15	1.30	188.00	247.00	---	435.00	**575.00**
	Inst	Ea	Sm	EA	8.16	0.98	218.00	328.00	---	546.00	**726.00**

Description	Oper	Unit	Vol	Crew Size	Man-hours per Unit	Crew Output per Day	Avg Mat'l Unit Cost	Avg Labor Unit Cost	Avg Equip Unit Cost	Avg Total Unit Cost	Avg Price Incl O&P
72" L x 36" W x 18-1/4" H (Caribbean)											
White	Inst	Ea	Lg	SB	6.67	2.40	3290.00	244.00	---	3534.00	**4130.00**
	Inst	Ea	Sm	SB	8.89	1.80	3810.00	325.00	---	4135.00	**4850.00**
Colors	Inst	Ea	Lg	SB	6.67	2.40	3950.00	244.00	---	4194.00	**4900.00**
	Inst	Ea	Sm	SB	8.89	1.80	4580.00	325.00	---	4905.00	**5740.00**
Premium Colors	Inst	Ea	Lg	SB	6.67	2.40	4450.00	244.00	---	4694.00	**5470.00**
	Inst	Ea	Sm	SB	8.89	1.80	5160.00	325.00	---	5485.00	**6410.00**
Bathtub with whirlpool (System-III)											
Plumbing installation											
White	Inst	Ea	Lg	SB	13.3	1.20	7010.00	486.00	---	7496.00	**8760.00**
	Inst	Ea	Sm	SB	17.8	0.90	8130.00	650.00	---	8780.00	**10300.00**
Colors	Inst	Ea	Lg	SB	13.3	1.20	7630.00	486.00	---	8116.00	**9480.00**
	Inst	Ea	Sm	SB	17.8	0.90	8850.00	650.00	---	9500.00	**11100.00**
Premium Colors	Inst	Ea	Lg	SB	13.3	1.20	7970.00	486.00	---	8456.00	**9870.00**
	Inst	Ea	Sm	SB	17.8	0.90	9240.00	650.00	---	9890.00	**11600.00**
Electrical installation											
	Inst	Ea	Lg	EA	6.15	1.30	188.00	247.00	---	435.00	**575.00**
	Inst	Ea	Sm	EA	8.16	0.98	218.00	328.00	---	546.00	**726.00**
72" L x 42" W x 22" H (Seawall Bath) with personal shower system											
White	Inst	Ea	Lg	SB	6.67	2.40	4480.00	244.00	---	4724.00	**5500.00**
	Inst	Ea	Sm	SB	8.89	1.80	5190.00	325.00	---	5515.00	**6440.00**
Colors	Inst	Ea	Lg	SB	6.67	2.40	5540.00	244.00	---	5784.00	**6730.00**
	Inst	Ea	Sm	SB	8.89	1.80	6430.00	325.00	---	6755.00	**7860.00**
Premium Colors	Inst	Ea	Lg	SB	6.67	2.40	6350.00	244.00	---	6594.00	**7650.00**
	Inst	Ea	Sm	SB	8.89	1.80	7360.00	325.00	---	7685.00	**8930.00**
Bathtub with whirlpool (System-III)											
Plumbing installation											
White	Inst	Ea	Lg	SB	13.3	1.20	7940.00	486.00	---	8426.00	**9830.00**
	Inst	Ea	Sm	SB	17.8	0.90	9200.00	650.00	---	9850.00	**11500.00**
Colors	Inst	Ea	Lg	SB	13.3	1.20	8440.00	486.00	---	8926.00	**10400.00**
	Inst	Ea	Sm	SB	17.8	0.90	9790.00	650.00	---	10440.00	**12200.00**
Premium Colors	Inst	Ea	Lg	SB	13.3	1.20	8840.00	486.00	---	9326.00	**10900.00**
	Inst	Ea	Sm	SB	17.8	0.90	10200.00	650.00	---	10850.00	**12700.00**
Electrical installation											
	Inst	Ea	Lg	EA	6.15	1.30	188.00	247.00	---	435.00	**575.00**
	Inst	Ea	Sm	EA	8.16	0.98	218.00	328.00	---	546.00	**726.00**
Options											
Grab bar kit											
Chrome	Inst	Ea	Lg	SB	---	---	240.00	---	---	240.00	**276.00**
	Inst	Ea	Sm	SB	---	---	279.00	---	---	279.00	**321.00**
Brass	Inst	Ea	Lg	SB	---	---	423.00	---	---	423.00	**487.00**
	Inst	Ea	Sm	SB	---	---	491.00	---	---	491.00	**564.00**
Nickel	Inst	Ea	Lg	SB	---	---	554.00	---	---	554.00	**638.00**
	Inst	Ea	Sm	SB	---	---	643.00	---	---	643.00	**739.00**

Description	Oper	Unit	Vol	Crew Size	Man-hours per Unit	Crew Output per Day	Avg Mat'l Unit Cost	Avg Labor Unit Cost	Avg Equip Unit Cost	Avg Total Unit Cost	Avg Price Incl O&P
Drain kit											
Chrome	Inst	Ea	Lg	SB	---	---	345.00	---	---	345.00	**397.00**
	Inst	Ea	Sm	SB	---	---	400.00	---	---	400.00	**460.00**
Brass	Inst	Ea	Lg	SB	---	---	361.00	---	---	361.00	**415.00**
	Inst	Ea	Sm	SB	---	---	419.00	---	---	419.00	**482.00**
Nickel	Inst	Ea	Lg	SB	---	---	456.00	---	---	456.00	**524.00**
	Inst	Ea	Sm	SB	---	---	529.00	---	---	529.00	**608.00**

Kohler Products, fiberglass

60" L x 36" W x 20" H (Mariposa)

Description	Oper	Unit	Vol	Crew Size	Man-hours per Unit	Crew Output per Day	Avg Mat'l Unit Cost	Avg Labor Unit Cost	Avg Equip Unit Cost	Avg Total Unit Cost	Avg Price Incl O&P
White	Inst	Ea	Lg	SB	6.67	2.40	1230.00	244.00	---	1474.00	**1770.00**
	Inst	Ea	Sm	SB	8.89	1.80	1430.00	325.00	---	1755.00	**2120.00**
Colors	Inst	Ea	Lg	SB	6.67	2.40	1270.00	244.00	---	1514.00	**1820.00**
	Inst	Ea	Sm	SB	8.89	1.80	1470.00	325.00	---	1795.00	**2170.00**

Bathtub with whirlpool (System-I)
Plumbing installation

Description	Oper	Unit	Vol	Crew Size	Man-hours per Unit	Crew Output per Day	Avg Mat'l Unit Cost	Avg Labor Unit Cost	Avg Equip Unit Cost	Avg Total Unit Cost	Avg Price Incl O&P
White	Inst	Ea	Lg	SB	13.3	1.20	2610.00	486.00	---	3096.00	**3710.00**
	Inst	Ea	Sm	SB	17.8	0.90	3030.00	650.00	---	3680.00	**4420.00**
Colors	Inst	Ea	Lg	SB	13.3	1.20	2950.00	486.00	---	3436.00	**4100.00**
	Inst	Ea	Sm	SB	17.8	0.90	3420.00	650.00	---	4070.00	**4880.00**

Electrical installation

Description	Oper	Unit	Vol	Crew Size	Man-hours per Unit	Crew Output per Day	Avg Mat'l Unit Cost	Avg Labor Unit Cost	Avg Equip Unit Cost	Avg Total Unit Cost	Avg Price Incl O&P
	Inst	Ea	Lg	EA	6.15	1.30	188.00	247.00	---	435.00	**575.00**
	Inst	Ea	Sm	EA	8.16	0.98	218.00	328.00	---	546.00	**726.00**

60" L x 42" W x 20" H (Hourglass)

Description	Oper	Unit	Vol	Crew Size	Man-hours per Unit	Crew Output per Day	Avg Mat'l Unit Cost	Avg Labor Unit Cost	Avg Equip Unit Cost	Avg Total Unit Cost	Avg Price Incl O&P
White	Inst	Ea	Lg	SB	6.67	2.40	1170.00	244.00	---	1414.00	**1700.00**
	Inst	Ea	Sm	SB	8.89	1.80	1360.00	325.00	---	1685.00	**2030.00**
Colors	Inst	Ea	Lg	SB	6.67	2.40	1250.00	244.00	---	1494.00	**1790.00**
	Inst	Ea	Sm	SB	8.89	1.80	1450.00	325.00	---	1775.00	**2130.00**

Bathtub with whirlpool (System-I)
Plumbing installation

Description	Oper	Unit	Vol	Crew Size	Man-hours per Unit	Crew Output per Day	Avg Mat'l Unit Cost	Avg Labor Unit Cost	Avg Equip Unit Cost	Avg Total Unit Cost	Avg Price Incl O&P
White	Inst	Ea	Lg	SB	13.3	1.20	2430.00	486.00	---	2916.00	**3500.00**
	Inst	Ea	Sm	SB	17.8	0.90	2820.00	650.00	---	3470.00	**4180.00**
Colors	Inst	Ea	Lg	SB	13.3	1.20	2490.00	486.00	---	2976.00	**3570.00**
	Inst	Ea	Sm	SB	17.8	0.90	2890.00	650.00	---	3540.00	**4260.00**

Electrical installation

Description	Oper	Unit	Vol	Crew Size	Man-hours per Unit	Crew Output per Day	Avg Mat'l Unit Cost	Avg Labor Unit Cost	Avg Equip Unit Cost	Avg Total Unit Cost	Avg Price Incl O&P
	Inst	Ea	Lg	EA	6.15	1.30	188.00	247.00	---	435.00	**575.00**
	Inst	Ea	Sm	EA	8.16	0.98	218.00	328.00	---	546.00	**726.00**

60" L x 42" W x 20" H (Seaside)

Description	Oper	Unit	Vol	Crew Size	Man-hours per Unit	Crew Output per Day	Avg Mat'l Unit Cost	Avg Labor Unit Cost	Avg Equip Unit Cost	Avg Total Unit Cost	Avg Price Incl O&P
White	Inst	Ea	Lg	SB	6.67	2.40	1420.00	244.00	---	1664.00	**1990.00**
	Inst	Ea	Sm	SB	8.89	1.80	1650.00	325.00	---	1975.00	**2360.00**
Colors	Inst	Ea	Lg	SB	6.67	2.40	1470.00	244.00	---	1714.00	**2040.00**
	Inst	Ea	Sm	SB	8.89	1.80	1700.00	325.00	---	2025.00	**2430.00**

Bathtub with whirlpool (System-I)
Plumbing installation

Description	Oper	Unit	Vol	Crew Size	Man-hours per Unit	Crew Output per Day	Avg Mat'l Unit Cost	Avg Labor Unit Cost	Avg Equip Unit Cost	Avg Total Unit Cost	Avg Price Incl O&P
White	Inst	Ea	Lg	SB	13.3	1.20	2670.00	486.00	---	3156.00	**3780.00**
	Inst	Ea	Sm	SB	17.8	0.90	3100.00	650.00	---	3750.00	**4510.00**
Colors	Inst	Ea	Lg	SB	13.3	1.20	2810.00	486.00	---	3296.00	**3930.00**
	Inst	Ea	Sm	SB	17.8	0.90	3260.00	650.00	---	3910.00	**4690.00**

Description	Oper	Unit	Vol	Crew Size	Man-hours per Unit	Crew Output per Day	Avg Mat'l Unit Cost	Avg Labor Unit Cost	Avg Equip Unit Cost	Avg Total Unit Cost	Avg Price Incl O&P
Electrical installation											
	Inst	Ea	Lg	EA	6.15	1.30	188.00	247.00	---	435.00	**575.00**
	Inst	Ea	Sm	EA	8.16	0.98	218.00	328.00	---	546.00	**726.00**
60" L x 42" W x 20" H (Synchrony)											
White	Inst	Ea	Lg	SB	6.67	2.40	1400.00	244.00	---	1644.00	**1960.00**
	Inst	Ea	Sm	SB	8.89	1.80	1620.00	325.00	---	1945.00	**2330.00**
Colors	Inst	Ea	Lg	SB	6.67	2.40	1420.00	244.00	---	1664.00	**1990.00**
	Inst	Ea	Sm	SB	8.89	1.80	1650.00	325.00	---	1975.00	**2370.00**
Bathtub with whirlpool (System-I)											
Plumbing installation											
White	Inst	Ea	Lg	SB	13.3	1.20	2510.00	486.00	---	2996.00	**3590.00**
	Inst	Ea	Sm	SB	17.8	0.90	2910.00	650.00	---	3560.00	**4290.00**
Colors	Inst	Ea	Lg	SB	13.3	1.20	2520.00	486.00	---	3006.00	**3610.00**
	Inst	Ea	Sm	SB	17.8	0.90	2930.00	650.00	---	3580.00	**4310.00**
Electrical installation											
	Inst	Ea	Lg	EA	6.15	1.30	188.00	247.00	---	435.00	**575.00**
	Inst	Ea	Sm	EA	8.16	0.98	218.00	328.00	---	546.00	**726.00**
60" L x 42-1/4" W x 18" H (Dockside)											
White	Inst	Ea	Lg	SB	6.67	2.40	1410.00	244.00	---	1654.00	**1980.00**
	Inst	Ea	Sm	SB	8.89	1.80	1640.00	325.00	---	1965.00	**2350.00**
Colors	Inst	Ea	Lg	SB	6.67	2.40	1460.00	244.00	---	1704.00	**2030.00**
	Inst	Ea	Sm	SB	8.89	1.80	1690.00	325.00	---	2015.00	**2420.00**
Bathtub with whirlpool (System-I)											
Plumbing installation											
White	Inst	Ea	Lg	SB	13.3	1.20	2630.00	486.00	---	3116.00	**3730.00**
	Inst	Ea	Sm	SB	17.8	0.90	3050.00	650.00	---	3700.00	**4450.00**
Colors	Inst	Ea	Lg	SB	13.3	1.20	2720.00	486.00	---	3206.00	**3830.00**
	Inst	Ea	Sm	SB	17.8	0.90	3150.00	650.00	---	3800.00	**4570.00**
Electrical installation											
	Inst	Ea	Lg	EA	6.15	1.30	188.00	247.00	---	435.00	**575.00**
	Inst	Ea	Sm	EA	8.16	0.98	218.00	328.00	---	546.00	**726.00**
60" L x 60" W x 21" H, corner (Sojourn)											
White	Inst	Ea	Lg	SB	6.67	2.40	1690.00	244.00	---	1934.00	**2300.00**
	Inst	Ea	Sm	SB	8.89	1.80	1960.00	325.00	---	2285.00	**2730.00**
Colors	Inst	Ea	Lg	SB	6.67	2.40	1750.00	244.00	---	1994.00	**2370.00**
	Inst	Ea	Sm	SB	8.89	1.80	2030.00	325.00	---	2355.00	**2810.00**
Bathtub with whirlpool (System-I)											
Plumbing installation											
White	Inst	Ea	Lg	SB	13.3	1.20	3220.00	486.00	---	3706.00	**4410.00**
	Inst	Ea	Sm	SB	17.8	0.90	3740.00	650.00	---	4390.00	**5240.00**
Colors	Inst	Ea	Lg	SB	13.3	1.20	3340.00	486.00	---	3826.00	**4550.00**
	Inst	Ea	Sm	SB	17.8	0.90	3880.00	650.00	---	4530.00	**5400.00**
Electrical installation											
	Inst	Ea	Lg	EA	6.15	1.30	188.00	247.00	---	435.00	**575.00**
	Inst	Ea	Sm	EA	8.16	0.98	218.00	328.00	---	546.00	**726.00**

Description	Oper	Unit	Vol	Crew Size	Man-hours per Unit	Crew Output per Day	Avg Mat'l Unit Cost	Avg Labor Unit Cost	Avg Equip Unit Cost	Avg Total Unit Cost	Avg Price Incl O&P
66" L x 35-7/8" W x 20" H (Mariposa)											
White	Inst	Ea	Lg	SB	6.67	2.40	1240.00	244.00	---	1484.00	**1780.00**
	Inst	Ea	Sm	SB	8.89	1.80	1440.00	325.00	---	1765.00	**2120.00**
Colors	Inst	Ea	Lg	SB	6.67	2.40	1280.00	244.00	---	1524.00	**1820.00**
	Inst	Ea	Sm	SB	8.89	1.80	1480.00	325.00	---	1805.00	**2180.00**
Bathtub with whirlpool (System-I)											
Plumbing installation											
White	Inst	Ea	Lg	SB	13.3	1.20	2740.00	486.00	---	3226.00	**3850.00**
	Inst	Ea	Sm	SB	17.8	0.90	3170.00	650.00	---	3820.00	**4590.00**
Colors	Inst	Ea	Lg	SB	13.3	1.20	2830.00	486.00	---	3316.00	**3960.00**
	Inst	Ea	Sm	SB	17.8	0.90	3280.00	650.00	---	3930.00	**4720.00**
Electrical installation											
	Inst	Ea	Lg	EA	6.15	1.30	188.00	247.00	---	435.00	**575.00**
	Inst	Ea	Sm	EA	8.16	0.98	218.00	328.00	---	546.00	**726.00**
66" L x 42" W x 22-5/8" H (Folio)											
White	Inst	Ea	Lg	SB	6.67	2.40	1430.00	244.00	---	1674.00	**2000.00**
	Inst	Ea	Sm	SB	8.89	1.80	1660.00	325.00	---	1985.00	**2380.00**
Colors	Inst	Ea	Lg	SB	6.67	2.40	1480.00	244.00	---	1724.00	**2050.00**
	Inst	Ea	Sm	SB	8.89	1.80	1710.00	325.00	---	2035.00	**2440.00**
Bathtub with whirlpool (System-I)											
Plumbing installation											
White	Inst	Ea	Lg	SB	13.3	1.20	2710.00	486.00	---	3196.00	**3830.00**
	Inst	Ea	Sm	SB	17.8	0.90	3150.00	650.00	---	3800.00	**4560.00**
Colors	Inst	Ea	Lg	SB	13.3	1.20	2810.00	486.00	---	3296.00	**3930.00**
	Inst	Ea	Sm	SB	17.8	0.90	3260.00	650.00	---	3910.00	**4690.00**
Electrical installation											
	Inst	Ea	Lg	EA	6.15	1.30	188.00	247.00	---	435.00	**575.00**
	Inst	Ea	Sm	EA	8.16	0.98	218.00	328.00	---	546.00	**726.00**
72" L x 36" W x 20" H (Mariposa)											
White	Inst	Ea	Lg	SB	6.67	2.40	1250.00	244.00	---	1494.00	**1790.00**
	Inst	Ea	Sm	SB	8.89	1.80	1440.00	325.00	---	1765.00	**2130.00**
Colors	Inst	Ea	Lg	SB	6.67	2.40	1280.00	244.00	---	1524.00	**1830.00**
	Inst	Ea	Sm	SB	8.89	1.80	1490.00	325.00	---	1815.00	**2180.00**
Bathtub with whirlpool (System-I)											
Plumbing installation											
White	Inst	Ea	Lg	SB	13.3	1.20	2750.00	486.00	---	3236.00	**3860.00**
	Inst	Ea	Sm	SB	17.8	0.90	3190.00	650.00	---	3840.00	**4610.00**
Colors	Inst	Ea	Lg	SB	13.3	1.20	2840.00	486.00	---	3326.00	**3980.00**
	Inst	Ea	Sm	SB	17.8	0.90	3300.00	650.00	---	3950.00	**4740.00**
Electrical installation											
	Inst	Ea	Lg	EA	6.15	1.30	188.00	247.00	---	435.00	**575.00**
	Inst	Ea	Sm	EA	8.16	0.98	218.00	328.00	---	546.00	**726.00**

Description	Oper	Unit	Vol	Crew Size	Man-hours per Unit	Crew Output per Day	Avg Mat'l Unit Cost	Avg Labor Unit Cost	Avg Equip Unit Cost	Avg Total Unit Cost	Avg Price Incl O&P
72" L x 42" W x 20" H (Synchrony)											
White	Inst	Ea	Lg	SB	6.67	2.40	1410.00	244.00	---	1654.00	**1980.00**
	Inst	Ea	Sm	SB	8.89	1.80	1640.00	325.00	---	1965.00	**2350.00**
Colors	Inst	Ea	Lg	SB	6.67	2.40	1460.00	244.00	---	1704.00	**2030.00**
	Inst	Ea	Sm	SB	8.89	1.80	1690.00	325.00	---	2015.00	**2420.00**
Bathtub with whirlpool (System-I)											
Plumbing installation											
White	Inst	Ea	Lg	SB	13.3	1.20	2880.00	486.00	---	3366.00	**4020.00**
	Inst	Ea	Sm	SB	17.8	0.90	3350.00	650.00	---	4000.00	**4790.00**
Colors	Inst	Ea	Lg	SB	13.3	1.20	2990.00	486.00	---	3476.00	**4140.00**
	Inst	Ea	Sm	SB	17.8	0.90	3470.00	650.00	---	4120.00	**4930.00**
Electrical installation											
	Inst	Ea	Lg	EA	6.15	1.30	188.00	247.00	---	435.00	**575.00**
	Inst	Ea	Sm	EA	8.16	0.98	218.00	328.00	---	546.00	**726.00**

Adjustments

Detach & Reset Tub

Description	Oper	Unit	Vol	Crew Size	Man-hours per Unit	Crew Output per Day	Avg Mat'l Unit Cost	Avg Labor Unit Cost	Avg Equip Unit Cost	Avg Total Unit Cost	Avg Price Incl O&P
Free-standing tub	Reset	Ea	Lg	SB	3.20	5.00	51.70	117.00	---	168.70	**229.00**
	Reset	Ea	Sm	SB	4.27	3.75	60.00	156.00	---	216.00	**295.00**
Recessed tub	Reset	Ea	Lg	SB	4.00	4.00	51.70	146.00	---	197.70	**271.00**
	Reset	Ea	Sm	SB	5.33	3.00	60.00	195.00	---	255.00	**351.00**
Sunken tub	Reset	Ea	Lg	SB	5.33	3.00	51.70	195.00	---	246.70	**342.00**
	Reset	Ea	Sm	SB	7.11	2.25	60.00	260.00	---	320.00	**445.00**

Remove Tub

Description	Oper	Unit	Vol	Crew Size	Man-hours per Unit	Crew Output per Day	Avg Mat'l Unit Cost	Avg Labor Unit Cost	Avg Equip Unit Cost	Avg Total Unit Cost	Avg Price Incl O&P
Free-standing tub	Demo	Ea	Lg	SB	1.33	12.00	14.10	48.60	---	62.70	**86.60**
	Demo	Ea	Sm	SB	1.78	9.00	16.40	65.00	---	81.40	**113.00**
Recessed tub	Demo	Ea	Lg	SB	2.00	8.00	28.20	73.00	---	101.20	**138.00**
	Demo	Ea	Sm	SB	2.67	6.00	32.70	97.50	---	130.20	**179.00**
Sunken tub	Demo	Ea	Lg	SB	2.67	6.00	42.30	97.50	---	139.80	**190.00**
	Demo	Ea	Sm	SB	3.56	4.50	49.10	130.00	---	179.10	**245.00**

Install Rough-In

Description	Oper	Unit	Vol	Crew Size	Man-hours per Unit	Crew Output per Day	Avg Mat'l Unit Cost	Avg Labor Unit Cost	Avg Equip Unit Cost	Avg Total Unit Cost	Avg Price Incl O&P
	Inst	Ea	Lg	SB	10.0	1.60	79.90	365.00	---	444.90	**621.00**
	Inst	Ea	Sm	SB	13.3	1.20	92.70	486.00	---	578.70	**811.00**

Install shower head w/mixer valve over tub

Description	Oper	Unit	Vol	Crew Size	Man-hours per Unit	Crew Output per Day	Avg Mat'l Unit Cost	Avg Labor Unit Cost	Avg Equip Unit Cost	Avg Total Unit Cost	Avg Price Incl O&P
Open wall, ADD	Inst	Ea	Lg	SA	2.00	4.00	108.00	86.00	---	194.00	**249.00**
	Inst	Ea	Sm	SA	2.67	3.00	125.00	115.00	---	240.00	**311.00**
Closed wall, ADD	Inst	Ea	Lg	SA	4.00	2.00	169.00	172.00	---	341.00	**444.00**
	Inst	Ea	Sm	SA	5.33	1.50	196.00	229.00	---	425.00	**558.00**

Block, concrete. See Masonry, page 290
Brick. See Masonry, page 284

Cabinets

Top quality cabinets are built with the structural stability of fine furniture. Framing stock is kiln dried and a full 1" thick. Cabinets have backs, usually 5-ply $3/16$"-thick plywood, with all backs and interiors finished. Frames should be constructed of hardwood with mortise and tenon joints; corner blocks should be used on all four corners of all base cabinets. Doors are usually of select $7/16$" thick solid core construction using semi-concealed hinges. End panels are $1/2$" thick and attached to frames with mortise and tenon joints, glued and pinned under pressure. Panels should also be dadoed to receive the tops and bottoms of wall cabinets. Shelves are adjustable with veneer faces and front edges. The hardware includes magnetic catches, heavy duty die cast pulls and hinges, and ball-bearing suspension system. The finish is scratch and stain resistant, including a first coat of hand-wiped stain, a sealer coat, and a synthetic varnish with plastic laminate characteristics.

Average quality cabinets feature hardwood frame construction with plywood backs and veneered plywood end panels. Joints are glued mortise and tenon. Doors are solid core attached with exposed self-closing hinges. Shelves are adjustable, and drawers ride on a ball-bearing side suspension glide system. The finish is usually three coats including stain, sealer, and a mar-resistant top coat for easy cleaning.

Economy quality cabinets feature pine construction with joints glued under pressure. Doors, drawer fronts, and side or end panels are constructed of either $1/2$"-thick wood composition board or $1/2$"-thick veneered pine. Face frames are $3/4$"-thick wood composition board or $3/4$"-thick pine. Features include adjustable shelves, hinge straps, and a three-point suspension system on drawers (using nylon rollers). The finish consists of a filler coat, base coat, and final polyester top coat.

Kitchen Cabinet Installation Procedure

To develop a layout plan, measure and write down the following:

1. Floor space.

2. Height and width of all walls.

3. Location of electrical outlets.

4. Size and position of doors, windows, and vents.

5. Location of any posts or pillars. Walls must be prepared if chair rails or baseboards are located where cabinets will be installed.

6. Common height and depth of base cabinets (including 1" for countertops) and wall cabinets.

When you plan the cabinet placement, consider this Rule of Thumb:

Allow between $4^1/2'$ and $5^1/2'$ of counter surface between the refrigerator and sink. Allow between 3' and 4' between the sink and range.

1. What do you have to fit into the available space?

2. Is there enough counter space on both sides of all appliances and sinks? The kitchen has three work centers, each with a major appliance as its hub, and each needing adequate counter space. They are:

    a. Fresh and frozen food center — Refrigerator-freezer

    b. Clean-up center — Sink with disposal-dishwasher

    c. Cooking center — Range-oven

3. Will the sink workspace fit neatly in front of a window?

4. The kitchen triangle is the most efficient kitchen design; it means placing each major center at approximately equidistant triangle points. The ideal triangle is 22 feet total. It should never be less than 13 feet or more than 25 feet.

5. Where are the centers located? A logical working and walking pattern is from refrigerator to sink to range. The refrigerator should be at a triangle point near a door, to minimize the distance to bring in groceries and reduce traffic that could interfere with food preparation. The range should be at a triangle point near the serving and dining area. The sink is located between the two. The refrigerator should be located far enough from the range so that the heat will not affect the refrigerator's cooling efficiency.

6. Does the plan allow for lighting the range and sink work centers and for ventilating the range center?

7. Make sure that open doors (such as cabinet doors or entrance/exit doors) won't interfere with access to an appliance. To clear appliances and cabinets, a door opening should not be less than 30" from the corner, since such equipment is 24" to 28" in depth. A clearance of 48" is necessary when a range is next to a door.

8. Next locate the wall studs with a stud finder or hammer, since all cabinets attach to walls with screws, never nails. Also remove chair rails or baseboards where they conflict with cabinets.

Wall Cabinets: From the highest point on the floor, measure up approximately 84" to determine the top of wall cabinets. Using two #10 x $2^1/2$" wood screws, drill through hanging strips built into the cabinet backs at top and bottom. Use a level to assure that cabinets and doors are aligned, then tighten the screws.

Base Cabinets: Start with a corner unit and a base unit on each side of the corner unit. Place this combination in the corner and work out from both sides. Use "C" clamps when connecting cabinets to draw adjoining units into alignment. With the front face plumb and the unit level from front to back and across the front edge, attach the unit to wall studs by screwing through the hanging strips. To attach adjoining cabinets, drill two holes in the vertical side of one cabinet, inside the door (near top and bottom), and just into the stile of the adjoining cabinet.

Island

Oven cabinet

Base

Vanity

Sink front

Base

Description	Oper	Unit	Vol	Crew Size	Man-hours per Unit	Crew Output per Day	Avg Mat'l Unit Cost	Avg Labor Unit Cost	Avg Equip Unit Cost	Avg Total Unit Cost	Avg Price Incl O&P

Cabinets

Labor costs include hanging and fitting of cabinets

Kitchen

3' x 4', wood; base, wall, or peninsula

Description	Oper	Unit	Vol	Crew Size	Man-hours per Unit	Crew Output per Day	Avg Mat'l Unit Cost	Avg Labor Unit Cost	Avg Equip Unit Cost	Avg Total Unit Cost	Avg Price Incl O&P
	Demo	Ea	Lg	LB	.640	25.00	---	19.20	---	19.20	**26.90**
	Demo	Ea	Sm	LB	1.07	15.00	---	32.10	---	32.10	**44.90**

Kitchen; all hardware included

Base cabinets, 35" H, 24" D; no tops

12" W, 1 door, 1 drawer

Description	Oper	Unit	Vol	Crew Size	Man-hours per Unit	Crew Output per Day	Avg Mat'l Unit Cost	Avg Labor Unit Cost	Avg Equip Unit Cost	Avg Total Unit Cost	Avg Price Incl O&P
High quality workmanship	Inst	Ea	Lg	MB	1.00	16.00	131.00	32.40	---	163.40	**203.00**
	Inst	Ea	Sm	MB	1.67	9.60	147.00	54.20	---	201.20	**253.00**
Good quality workmanship	Inst	Ea	Lg	MB	.667	24.00	107.00	21.60	---	128.60	**159.00**
	Inst	Ea	Sm	MB	1.11	14.40	120.00	36.00	---	156.00	**195.00**
Average quality workmanship	Inst	Ea	Lg	MB	.667	24.00	81.60	21.60	---	103.20	**129.00**
	Inst	Ea	Sm	MB	1.11	14.40	91.80	36.00	---	127.80	**161.00**

15" W, 1 door, 1 drawer

Description	Oper	Unit	Vol	Crew Size	Man-hours per Unit	Crew Output per Day	Avg Mat'l Unit Cost	Avg Labor Unit Cost	Avg Equip Unit Cost	Avg Total Unit Cost	Avg Price Incl O&P
High quality workmanship	Inst	Ea	Lg	MB	1.00	16.00	138.00	32.40	---	170.40	**212.00**
	Inst	Ea	Sm	MB	1.67	9.60	155.00	54.20	---	209.20	**263.00**
Good quality workmanship	Inst	Ea	Lg	MB	.667	24.00	114.00	21.60	---	135.60	**168.00**
	Inst	Ea	Sm	MB	1.11	14.40	128.00	36.00	---	164.00	**205.00**
Average quality workmanship	Inst	Ea	Lg	MB	.667	24.00	86.40	21.60	---	108.00	**134.00**
	Inst	Ea	Sm	MB	1.11	14.40	97.20	36.00	---	133.20	**168.00**

18" W, 1 door, 1 drawer

Description	Oper	Unit	Vol	Crew Size	Man-hours per Unit	Crew Output per Day	Avg Mat'l Unit Cost	Avg Labor Unit Cost	Avg Equip Unit Cost	Avg Total Unit Cost	Avg Price Incl O&P
High quality workmanship	Inst	Ea	Lg	MB	1.00	16.00	143.00	32.40	---	175.40	**217.00**
	Inst	Ea	Sm	MB	1.67	9.60	161.00	54.20	---	215.20	**270.00**
Good quality workmanship	Inst	Ea	Lg	MB	.667	24.00	118.00	21.60	---	139.60	**172.00**
	Inst	Ea	Sm	MB	1.11	14.40	132.00	36.00	---	168.00	**210.00**
Average quality workmanship	Inst	Ea	Lg	MB	.667	24.00	90.00	21.60	---	111.60	**139.00**
	Inst	Ea	Sm	MB	1.11	14.40	101.00	36.00	---	137.00	**173.00**

21" W, 1 door, 1 drawer

Description	Oper	Unit	Vol	Crew Size	Man-hours per Unit	Crew Output per Day	Avg Mat'l Unit Cost	Avg Labor Unit Cost	Avg Equip Unit Cost	Avg Total Unit Cost	Avg Price Incl O&P
High quality workmanship	Inst	Ea	Lg	MB	1.16	13.80	158.00	37.60	---	195.60	**244.00**
	Inst	Ea	Sm	MB	1.93	8.28	178.00	62.60	---	240.60	**303.00**
Good quality workmanship	Inst	Ea	Lg	MB	.741	21.60	131.00	24.00	---	155.00	**191.00**
	Inst	Ea	Sm	MB	1.23	12.96	147.00	39.90	---	186.90	**233.00**
Average quality workmanship	Inst	Ea	Lg	MB	.741	21.60	101.00	24.00	---	125.00	**155.00**
	Inst	Ea	Sm	MB	1.23	12.96	113.00	39.90	---	152.90	**193.00**

Description	Oper	Unit	Vol	Crew Size	Man-hours per Unit	Crew Output per Day	Avg Mat'l Unit Cost	Avg Labor Unit Cost	Avg Equip Unit Cost	Avg Total Unit Cost	Avg Price Incl O&P
24" W, 1 door, 1 drawer											
High quality workmanship	Inst	Ea	Lg	MB	1.16	13.80	174.00	37.60	---	211.60	**262.00**
	Inst	Ea	Sm	MB	1.93	8.28	196.00	62.60	---	258.60	**324.00**
Good quality workmanship	Inst	Ea	Lg	MB	.741	21.60	143.00	24.00	---	167.00	**205.00**
	Inst	Ea	Sm	MB	1.23	12.96	161.00	39.90	---	200.90	**249.00**
Average quality workmanship	Inst	Ea	Lg	MB	.741	21.60	126.00	24.00	---	150.00	**185.00**
	Inst	Ea	Sm	MB	1.23	12.96	142.00	39.90	---	181.90	**227.00**
30" W, 2 doors, 2 drawers											
High quality workmanship	Inst	Ea	Lg	MB	1.54	10.40	222.00	49.90	---	271.90	**337.00**
	Inst	Ea	Sm	MB	2.56	6.24	250.00	83.00	---	333.00	**418.00**
Good quality workmanship	Inst	Ea	Lg	MB	1.04	15.40	192.00	33.70	---	225.70	**278.00**
	Inst	Ea	Sm	MB	1.73	9.24	216.00	56.10	---	272.10	**339.00**
Average quality workmanship	Inst	Ea	Lg	MB	1.04	15.40	145.00	33.70	---	178.70	**222.00**
	Inst	Ea	Sm	MB	1.73	9.24	163.00	56.10	---	219.10	**276.00**
36" W, 2 doors, 2 drawers											
High quality workmanship	Inst	Ea	Lg	MB	1.54	10.40	256.00	49.90	---	305.90	**378.00**
	Inst	Ea	Sm	MB	2.56	6.24	288.00	83.00	---	371.00	**463.00**
Good quality workmanship	Inst	Ea	Lg	MB	1.04	15.40	211.00	33.70	---	244.70	**301.00**
	Inst	Ea	Sm	MB	1.73	9.24	238.00	56.10	---	294.10	**365.00**
Average quality workmanship	Inst	Ea	Lg	MB	1.04	15.40	161.00	33.70	---	194.70	**241.00**
	Inst	Ea	Sm	MB	1.73	9.24	181.00	56.10	---	237.10	**297.00**
42" W, 2 doors, 2 drawers											
High quality workmanship	Inst	Ea	Lg	MB	2.00	8.00	295.00	64.90	---	359.90	**446.00**
	Inst	Ea	Sm	MB	3.33	4.80	332.00	108.00	---	440.00	**552.00**
Good quality workmanship	Inst	Ea	Lg	MB	1.33	12.00	245.00	43.10	---	288.10	**355.00**
	Inst	Ea	Sm	MB	2.22	7.20	275.00	72.00	---	347.00	**433.00**
Average quality workmanship	Inst	Ea	Lg	MB	1.33	12.00	186.00	43.10	---	229.10	**284.00**
	Inst	Ea	Sm	MB	2.22	7.20	209.00	72.00	---	281.00	**353.00**
48" W, 4 doors, 2 drawers											
High quality workmanship	Inst	Ea	Lg	MB	2.00	8.00	284.00	64.90	---	348.90	**433.00**
	Inst	Ea	Sm	MB	3.33	4.80	320.00	108.00	---	428.00	**537.00**
Good quality workmanship	Inst	Ea	Lg	MB	1.33	12.00	235.00	43.10	---	278.10	**343.00**
	Inst	Ea	Sm	MB	2.22	7.20	265.00	72.00	---	337.00	**420.00**
Average quality workmanship	Inst	Ea	Lg	MB	1.33	12.00	178.00	43.10	---	221.10	**274.00**
	Inst	Ea	Sm	MB	2.22	7.20	200.00	72.00	---	272.00	**342.00**

Base corner cabinet, blind, 35" H, 24" D, no tops

Description	Oper	Unit	Vol	Crew Size	Man-hours per Unit	Crew Output per Day	Avg Mat'l Unit Cost	Avg Labor Unit Cost	Avg Equip Unit Cost	Avg Total Unit Cost	Avg Price Incl O&P
36" W, 1 door, 1 drawer											
High quality workmanship	Inst	Ea	Lg	MB	1.43	11.20	186.00	46.40	---	232.40	**289.00**
	Inst	Ea	Sm	MB	2.38	6.72	209.00	77.20	---	286.20	**361.00**
Good quality workmanship	Inst	Ea	Lg	MB	.988	16.20	149.00	32.00	---	181.00	**224.00**
	Inst	Ea	Sm	MB	1.65	9.72	167.00	53.50	---	220.50	**277.00**
Average quality workmanship	Inst	Ea	Lg	MB	.988	16.20	119.00	32.00	---	151.00	**188.00**
	Inst	Ea	Sm	MB	1.65	9.72	134.00	53.50	---	187.50	**236.00**

Description	Oper	Unit	Vol	Crew Size	Man-hours per Unit	Crew Output per Day	Avg Mat'l Unit Cost	Avg Labor Unit Cost	Avg Equip Unit Cost	Avg Total Unit Cost	Avg Price Incl O&P
42" W, 1 door, 1 drawer											
High quality workmanship	Inst	Ea	Lg	MB	1.82	8.80	205.00	59.00	---	264.00	**330.00**
	Inst	Ea	Sm	MB	3.03	5.28	231.00	98.30	---	329.30	**417.00**
Good quality workmanship	Inst	Ea	Lg	MB	1.16	13.80	169.00	37.60	---	206.60	**256.00**
	Inst	Ea	Sm	MB	1.93	8.28	190.00	62.60	---	252.60	**317.00**
Average quality workmanship	Inst	Ea	Lg	MB	1.16	13.80	128.00	37.60	---	165.60	**208.00**
	Inst	Ea	Sm	MB	1.93	8.28	144.00	62.60	---	206.60	**262.00**
36" x 36" (Lazy Susan)											
High quality workmanship	Inst	Ea	Lg	MB	1.43	11.20	277.00	46.40	---	323.40	**398.00**
	Inst	Ea	Sm	MB	2.38	6.72	312.00	77.20	---	389.20	**484.00**
Good quality workmanship	Inst	Ea	Lg	MB	.988	16.20	229.00	32.00	---	261.00	**321.00**
	Inst	Ea	Sm	MB	1.65	9.72	258.00	53.50	---	311.50	**385.00**
Average quality workmanship	Inst	Ea	Lg	MB	.988	16.20	175.00	32.00	---	207.00	**256.00**
	Inst	Ea	Sm	MB	1.65	9.72	197.00	53.50	---	250.50	**313.00**

Utility closets, 81" to 85" H, 24" W, 24" D

Description	Oper	Unit	Vol	Crew Size	Man-hours per Unit	Crew Output per Day	Avg Mat'l Unit Cost	Avg Labor Unit Cost	Avg Equip Unit Cost	Avg Total Unit Cost	Avg Price Incl O&P
High quality workmanship	Inst	Ea	Lg	MB	2.00	8.00	425.00	64.90	---	489.90	**602.00**
	Inst	Ea	Sm	MB	3.33	4.80	478.00	108.00	---	586.00	**727.00**
Good quality workmanship	Inst	Ea	Lg	MB	1.33	12.00	331.00	43.10	---	374.10	**459.00**
	Inst	Ea	Sm	MB	2.22	7.20	373.00	72.00	---	445.00	**549.00**
Average quality workmanship	Inst	Ea	Lg	MB	1.33	12.00	252.00	43.10	---	295.10	**364.00**
	Inst	Ea	Sm	MB	2.22	7.20	284.00	72.00	---	356.00	**442.00**

Drawer base cabinets, 35" H, 24" D

4 drawers, no tops

18" W

Description	Oper	Unit	Vol	Crew Size	Man-hours per Unit	Crew Output per Day	Avg Mat'l Unit Cost	Avg Labor Unit Cost	Avg Equip Unit Cost	Avg Total Unit Cost	Avg Price Incl O&P
High quality workmanship	Inst	Ea	Lg	MB	1.00	16.00	213.00	32.40	---	245.40	**302.00**
	Inst	Ea	Sm	MB	1.67	9.60	240.00	54.20	---	294.20	**365.00**
Good quality workmanship	Inst	Ea	Lg	MB	.667	24.00	183.00	21.60	---	204.60	**250.00**
	Inst	Ea	Sm	MB	1.11	14.40	206.00	36.00	---	242.00	**298.00**
Average quality workmanship	Inst	Ea	Lg	MB	.667	24.00	140.00	21.60	---	161.60	**198.00**
	Inst	Ea	Sm	MB	1.11	14.40	157.00	36.00	---	193.00	**240.00**
24" W											
High quality workmanship	Inst	Ea	Lg	MB	1.16	13.80	239.00	37.60	---	276.60	**340.00**
	Inst	Ea	Sm	MB	1.93	8.28	269.00	62.60	---	331.60	**412.00**
Good quality workmanship	Inst	Ea	Lg	MB	.741	21.60	197.00	24.00	---	221.00	**271.00**
	Inst	Ea	Sm	MB	1.23	12.96	222.00	39.90	---	261.90	**323.00**
Average quality workmanship	Inst	Ea	Lg	MB	.741	21.60	151.00	24.00	---	175.00	**216.00**
	Inst	Ea	Sm	MB	1.23	12.96	170.00	39.90	---	209.90	**261.00**

Description	Oper	Unit	Vol	Crew Size	Man-hours per Unit	Crew Output per Day	Avg Mat'l Unit Cost	Avg Labor Unit Cost	Avg Equip Unit Cost	Avg Total Unit Cost	Avg Price Incl O&P

Island cabinets

Island base cabinets, 35" H, 24" D

24" W, 1 door both sides

Description	Oper	Unit	Vol	Crew Size	Man-hours per Unit	Crew Output per Day	Avg Mat'l Unit Cost	Avg Labor Unit Cost	Avg Equip Unit Cost	Avg Total Unit Cost	Avg Price Incl O&P
High quality workmanship	Inst	Ea	Lg	MB	1.23	13.00	310.00	39.90	---	349.90	**428.00**
	Inst	Ea	Sm	MB	2.05	7.80	348.00	66.50	---	414.50	**512.00**
Good quality workmanship	Inst	Ea	Lg	MB	.821	19.50	254.00	26.60	---	280.60	**343.00**
	Inst	Ea	Sm	MB	1.37	11.70	286.00	44.40	---	330.40	**407.00**
Average quality workmanship	Inst	Ea	Lg	MB	.821	19.50	196.00	26.60	---	222.60	**273.00**
	Inst	Ea	Sm	MB	1.37	11.70	220.00	44.40	---	264.40	**327.00**

30" W, 2 doors both sides

Description	Oper	Unit	Vol	Crew Size	Man-hours per Unit	Crew Output per Day	Avg Mat'l Unit Cost	Avg Labor Unit Cost	Avg Equip Unit Cost	Avg Total Unit Cost	Avg Price Incl O&P
High quality workmanship	Inst	Ea	Lg	MB	1.60	10.00	328.00	51.90	---	379.90	**467.00**
	Inst	Ea	Sm	MB	2.67	6.00	369.00	86.60	---	455.60	**565.00**
Good quality workmanship	Inst	Ea	Lg	MB	1.07	15.00	270.00	34.70	---	304.70	**373.00**
	Inst	Ea	Sm	MB	1.78	9.00	304.00	57.70	---	361.70	**446.00**
Average quality workmanship	Inst	Ea	Lg	MB	1.07	15.00	205.00	34.70	---	239.70	**296.00**
	Inst	Ea	Sm	MB	1.78	9.00	231.00	57.70	---	288.70	**359.00**

36" W, 2 doors both sides

Description	Oper	Unit	Vol	Crew Size	Man-hours per Unit	Crew Output per Day	Avg Mat'l Unit Cost	Avg Labor Unit Cost	Avg Equip Unit Cost	Avg Total Unit Cost	Avg Price Incl O&P
High quality workmanship	Inst	Ea	Lg	MB	1.60	10.00	344.00	51.90	---	395.90	**487.00**
	Inst	Ea	Sm	MB	2.67	6.00	387.00	86.60	---	473.60	**588.00**
Good quality workmanship	Inst	Ea	Lg	MB	1.07	15.00	284.00	34.70	---	318.70	**391.00**
	Inst	Ea	Sm	MB	1.78	9.00	320.00	57.70	---	377.70	**466.00**
Average quality workmanship	Inst	Ea	Lg	MB	1.07	15.00	216.00	34.70	---	250.70	**308.00**
	Inst	Ea	Sm	MB	1.78	9.00	243.00	57.70	---	300.70	**374.00**

48" W, 4 doors both sides

Description	Oper	Unit	Vol	Crew Size	Man-hours per Unit	Crew Output per Day	Avg Mat'l Unit Cost	Avg Labor Unit Cost	Avg Equip Unit Cost	Avg Total Unit Cost	Avg Price Incl O&P
High quality workmanship	Inst	Ea	Lg	MB	2.13	7.50	370.00	69.10	---	439.10	**542.00**
	Inst	Ea	Sm	MB	3.56	4.50	416.00	115.00	---	531.00	**663.00**
Good quality workmanship	Inst	Ea	Lg	MB	1.39	11.50	305.00	45.10	---	350.10	**430.00**
	Inst	Ea	Sm	MB	2.32	6.90	343.00	75.20	---	418.20	**518.00**
Average quality workmanship	Inst	Ea	Lg	MB	1.39	11.50	232.00	45.10	---	277.10	**342.00**
	Inst	Ea	Sm	MB	2.32	6.90	261.00	75.20	---	336.20	**420.00**

Corner island base cabinets, 35" H, 24" D

42" W, 4 doors, 2 drawers

Description	Oper	Unit	Vol	Crew Size	Man-hours per Unit	Crew Output per Day	Avg Mat'l Unit Cost	Avg Labor Unit Cost	Avg Equip Unit Cost	Avg Total Unit Cost	Avg Price Incl O&P
High quality workmanship	Inst	Ea	Lg	MB	2.13	7.50	328.00	69.10	---	397.10	**491.00**
	Inst	Ea	Sm	MB	3.56	4.50	369.00	115.00	---	484.00	**606.00**
Good quality workmanship	Inst	Ea	Lg	MB	1.39	11.50	268.00	45.10	---	313.10	**385.00**
	Inst	Ea	Sm	MB	2.32	6.90	301.00	75.20	---	376.20	**468.00**
Average quality workmanship	Inst	Ea	Lg	MB	1.39	11.50	202.00	45.10	---	247.10	**306.00**
	Inst	Ea	Sm	MB	2.32	6.90	227.00	75.20	---	302.20	**379.00**

48" W, 6 doors, 2 drawers

Description	Oper	Unit	Vol	Crew Size	Man-hours per Unit	Crew Output per Day	Avg Mat'l Unit Cost	Avg Labor Unit Cost	Avg Equip Unit Cost	Avg Total Unit Cost	Avg Price Incl O&P
High quality workmanship	Inst	Ea	Lg	MB	2.67	6.00	343.00	86.60	---	429.60	**535.00**
	Inst	Ea	Sm	MB	4.44	3.60	386.00	144.00	---	530.00	**668.00**
Good quality workmanship	Inst	Ea	Lg	MB	1.78	9.00	283.00	57.70	---	340.70	**422.00**
	Inst	Ea	Sm	MB	2.96	5.40	319.00	96.00	---	415.00	**519.00**
Average quality workmanship	Inst	Ea	Lg	MB	1.78	9.00	215.00	57.70	---	272.70	**340.00**
	Inst	Ea	Sm	MB	2.96	5.40	242.00	96.00	---	338.00	**426.00**

Description	Oper	Unit	Vol	Crew Size	Man-hours per Unit	Crew Output per Day	Avg Mat'l Unit Cost	Avg Labor Unit Cost	Avg Equip Unit Cost	Avg Total Unit Cost	Avg Price Incl O&P
Hanging corner island wall cabinets, 18" H, 24" D											
18" W, 3 doors											
High quality workmanship	Inst	Ea	Lg	MB	1.45	11.00	238.00	47.00	---	285.00	**352.00**
	Inst	Ea	Sm	MB	2.42	6.60	267.00	78.50	---	345.50	**432.00**
Good quality workmanship	Inst	Ea	Lg	MB	.970	16.50	174.00	31.50	---	205.50	**253.00**
	Inst	Ea	Sm	MB	1.62	9.90	196.00	52.50	---	248.50	**310.00**
Average quality workmanship	Inst	Ea	Lg	MB	.970	16.50	133.00	31.50	---	164.50	**205.00**
	Inst	Ea	Sm	MB	1.62	9.90	150.00	52.50	---	202.50	**254.00**
24" W, 3 doors											
High quality workmanship	Inst	Ea	Lg	MB	1.45	11.00	245.00	47.00	---	292.00	**361.00**
	Inst	Ea	Sm	MB	2.42	6.60	275.00	78.50	---	353.50	**442.00**
Good quality workmanship	Inst	Ea	Lg	MB	.970	16.50	181.00	31.50	---	212.50	**262.00**
	Inst	Ea	Sm	MB	1.62	9.90	204.00	52.50	---	256.50	**319.00**
Average quality workmanship	Inst	Ea	Lg	MB	.970	16.50	137.00	31.50	---	168.50	**209.00**
	Inst	Ea	Sm	MB	1.62	9.90	154.00	52.50	---	206.50	**259.00**
30" W, 3 doors											
High quality workmanship	Inst	Ea	Lg	MB	1.88	8.50	252.00	61.00	---	313.00	**389.00**
	Inst	Ea	Sm	MB	3.14	5.10	284.00	102.00	---	386.00	**485.00**
Good quality workmanship	Inst	Ea	Lg	MB	1.26	12.70	188.00	40.90	---	228.90	**284.00**
	Inst	Ea	Sm	MB	2.10	7.62	212.00	68.10	---	280.10	**351.00**
Average quality workmanship	Inst	Ea	Lg	MB	1.26	12.70	144.00	40.90	---	184.90	**231.00**
	Inst	Ea	Sm	MB	2.10	7.62	162.00	68.10	---	230.10	**291.00**
Hanging island cabinets, 18" H, 12" D											
30" W, 2 doors both sides											
High quality workmanship	Inst	Ea	Lg	MB	1.70	9.40	252.00	55.10	---	307.10	**381.00**
	Inst	Ea	Sm	MB	2.84	5.64	284.00	92.10	---	376.10	**471.00**
Good quality workmanship	Inst	Ea	Lg	MB	1.14	14.00	185.00	37.00	---	222.00	**274.00**
	Inst	Ea	Sm	MB	1.90	8.40	208.00	61.60	---	269.60	**337.00**
Average quality workmanship	Inst	Ea	Lg	MB	1.14	14.00	140.00	37.00	---	177.00	**221.00**
	Inst	Ea	Sm	MB	1.90	8.40	158.00	61.60	---	219.60	**277.00**
36" W, 2 doors both sides											
High quality workmanship	Inst	Ea	Lg	MB	1.70	9.40	259.00	55.10	---	314.10	**389.00**
	Inst	Ea	Sm	MB	2.84	5.64	292.00	92.10	---	384.10	**481.00**
Good quality workmanship	Inst	Ea	Lg	MB	1.14	14.00	191.00	37.00	---	228.00	**281.00**
	Inst	Ea	Sm	MB	1.90	8.40	215.00	61.60	---	276.60	**345.00**
Average quality workmanship	Inst	Ea	Lg	MB	1.14	14.00	145.00	37.00	---	182.00	**227.00**
	Inst	Ea	Sm	MB	1.90	8.40	163.00	61.60	---	224.60	**284.00**
Hanging island cabinets, 24" H, 12" D											
24" W, 2 doors both sides											
High quality workmanship	Inst	Ea	Lg	MB	1.45	11.00	238.00	47.00	---	285.00	**352.00**
	Inst	Ea	Sm	MB	2.42	6.60	267.00	78.50	---	345.50	**432.00**
Good quality workmanship	Inst	Ea	Lg	MB	.970	16.50	166.00	31.50	---	197.50	**243.00**
	Inst	Ea	Sm	MB	1.62	9.90	186.00	52.50	---	238.50	**298.00**
Average quality workmanship	Inst	Ea	Lg	MB	.970	16.50	122.00	31.50	---	153.50	**192.00**
	Inst	Ea	Sm	MB	1.62	9.90	138.00	52.50	---	190.50	**240.00**

Description	Oper	Unit	Vol	Crew Size	Man-hours per Unit	Crew Output per Day	Avg Mat'l Unit Cost	Avg Labor Unit Cost	Avg Equip Unit Cost	Avg Total Unit Cost	Avg Price Incl O&P
30" W, 2 doors both sides											
High quality workmanship	Inst	Ea	Lg	MB	1.88	8.50	247.00	61.00	---	308.00	**383.00**
	Inst	Ea	Sm	MB	3.14	5.10	278.00	102.00	---	380.00	**478.00**
Good quality workmanship	Inst	Ea	Lg	MB	1.26	12.70	179.00	40.90	---	219.90	**273.00**
	Inst	Ea	Sm	MB	2.10	7.62	201.00	68.10	---	269.10	**338.00**
Average quality workmanship	Inst	Ea	Lg	MB	1.26	12.70	132.00	40.90	---	172.90	**216.00**
	Inst	Ea	Sm	MB	2.10	7.62	149.00	68.10	---	217.10	**275.00**
36" W, 2 doors both sides											
High quality workmanship	Inst	Ea	Lg	MB	1.88	8.50	259.00	61.00	---	320.00	**398.00**
	Inst	Ea	Sm	MB	3.14	5.10	292.00	102.00	---	394.00	**495.00**
Good quality workmanship	Inst	Ea	Lg	MB	1.26	12.70	191.00	40.90	---	231.90	**287.00**
	Inst	Ea	Sm	MB	2.10	7.62	215.00	68.10	---	283.10	**354.00**
Average quality workmanship	Inst	Ea	Lg	MB	1.26	12.70	145.00	40.90	---	185.90	**232.00**
	Inst	Ea	Sm	MB	2.10	7.62	163.00	68.10	---	231.10	**293.00**
42" W, 2 doors both sides											
High quality workmanship	Inst	Ea	Lg	MB	2.46	6.50	313.00	79.80	---	392.80	**489.00**
	Inst	Ea	Sm	MB	4.10	3.90	352.00	133.00	---	485.00	**612.00**
Good quality workmanship	Inst	Ea	Lg	MB	1.63	9.80	230.00	52.90	---	282.90	**352.00**
	Inst	Ea	Sm	MB	2.72	5.88	259.00	88.20	---	347.20	**436.00**
Average quality workmanship	Inst	Ea	Lg	MB	1.63	9.80	176.00	52.90	---	228.90	**287.00**
	Inst	Ea	Sm	MB	2.72	5.88	198.00	88.20	---	286.20	**363.00**
48" W, 4 doors both sides											
High quality workmanship	Inst	Ea	Lg	MB	2.46	6.50	376.00	79.80	---	455.80	**564.00**
	Inst	Ea	Sm	MB	4.10	3.90	423.00	133.00	---	556.00	**696.00**
Good quality workmanship	Inst	Ea	Lg	MB	1.63	9.80	277.00	52.90	---	329.90	**408.00**
	Inst	Ea	Sm	MB	2.72	5.88	312.00	88.20	---	400.20	**499.00**
Average quality workmanship	Inst	Ea	Lg	MB	1.63	9.80	211.00	52.90	---	263.90	**329.00**
	Inst	Ea	Sm	MB	2.72	5.88	238.00	88.20	---	326.20	**410.00**

Oven cabinets

81" to 85" H, 24" D, 27" W

Description	Oper	Unit	Vol	Crew Size	Man-hours per Unit	Crew Output per Day	Avg Mat'l Unit Cost	Avg Labor Unit Cost	Avg Equip Unit Cost	Avg Total Unit Cost	Avg Price Incl O&P
High quality workmanship	Inst	Ea	Lg	MB	2.00	8.00	454.00	64.90	---	518.90	**636.00**
	Inst	Ea	Sm	MB	3.33	4.80	510.00	108.00	---	618.00	**766.00**
Good quality workmanship	Inst	Ea	Lg	MB	1.33	12.00	353.00	43.10	---	396.10	**485.00**
	Inst	Ea	Sm	MB	2.22	7.20	397.00	72.00	---	469.00	**579.00**
Average quality workmanship	Inst	Ea	Lg	MB	1.33	12.00	270.00	43.10	---	313.10	**385.00**
	Inst	Ea	Sm	MB	2.22	7.20	304.00	72.00	---	376.00	**467.00**

Sink/range

Base cabinets, 35" H, 24" D, 2 doors, no tops included

30" W

Description	Oper	Unit	Vol	Crew Size	Man-hours per Unit	Crew Output per Day	Avg Mat'l Unit Cost	Avg Labor Unit Cost	Avg Equip Unit Cost	Avg Total Unit Cost	Avg Price Incl O&P
High quality workmanship	Inst	Ea	Lg	MB	1.33	12.00	177.00	43.10	---	220.10	**274.00**
	Inst	Ea	Sm	MB	2.22	7.20	199.00	72.00	---	271.00	**341.00**
Good quality workmanship	Inst	Ea	Lg	MB	.889	18.00	145.00	28.80	---	173.80	**215.00**
	Inst	Ea	Sm	MB	1.48	10.80	164.00	48.00	---	212.00	**265.00**
Average quality workmanship	Inst	Ea	Lg	MB	.889	18.00	111.00	28.80	---	139.80	**174.00**
	Inst	Ea	Sm	MB	1.48	10.80	125.00	48.00	---	173.00	**218.00**

Description	Oper	Unit	Vol	Crew Size	Man-hours per Unit	Crew Output per Day	Avg Mat'l Unit Cost	Avg Labor Unit Cost	Avg Equip Unit Cost	Avg Total Unit Cost	Avg Price Incl O&P
36" W											
High quality workmanship	Inst	Ea	Lg	MB	1.33	12.00	226.00	43.10	---	269.10	**333.00**
	Inst	Ea	Sm	MB	2.22	7.20	254.00	72.00	---	326.00	**407.00**
Good quality workmanship	Inst	Ea	Lg	MB	.889	18.00	187.00	28.80	---	215.80	**266.00**
	Inst	Ea	Sm	MB	1.48	10.80	211.00	48.00	---	259.00	**321.00**
Average quality workmanship	Inst	Ea	Lg	MB	.889	18.00	143.00	28.80	---	171.80	**212.00**
	Inst	Ea	Sm	MB	1.48	10.80	160.00	48.00	---	208.00	**261.00**
42" W											
High quality workmanship	Inst	Ea	Lg	MB	1.74	9.20	251.00	56.40	---	307.40	**381.00**
	Inst	Ea	Sm	MB	2.90	5.52	282.00	94.10	---	376.10	**472.00**
Good quality workmanship	Inst	Ea	Lg	MB	1.16	13.80	207.00	37.60	---	244.60	**302.00**
	Inst	Ea	Sm	MB	1.93	8.28	233.00	62.60	---	295.60	**369.00**
Average quality workmanship	Inst	Ea	Lg	MB	1.16	13.80	157.00	37.60	---	194.60	**242.00**
	Inst	Ea	Sm	MB	1.93	8.28	177.00	62.60	---	239.60	**301.00**
48" W											
High quality workmanship	Inst	Ea	Lg	MB	1.74	9.20	284.00	56.40	---	340.40	**421.00**
	Inst	Ea	Sm	MB	2.90	5.52	319.00	94.10	---	413.10	**517.00**
Good quality workmanship	Inst	Ea	Lg	MB	1.16	13.80	233.00	37.60	---	270.60	**333.00**
	Inst	Ea	Sm	MB	1.93	8.28	262.00	62.60	---	324.60	**404.00**
Average quality workmanship	Inst	Ea	Lg	MB	1.16	13.80	179.00	37.60	---	216.60	**268.00**
	Inst	Ea	Sm	MB	1.93	8.28	201.00	62.60	---	263.60	**330.00**

Sink/range front cabinets, 35" H, 2 doors

Description	Oper	Unit	Vol	Crew Size	Man-hours per Unit	Crew Output per Day	Avg Mat'l Unit Cost	Avg Labor Unit Cost	Avg Equip Unit Cost	Avg Total Unit Cost	Avg Price Incl O&P
30" W											
High quality workmanship	Inst	Ea	Lg	MB	1.16	13.80	111.00	37.60	---	148.60	**186.00**
	Inst	Ea	Sm	MB	1.93	8.28	125.00	62.60	---	187.60	**239.00**
Good quality workmanship	Inst	Ea	Lg	MB	.800	20.00	92.20	25.90	---	118.10	**147.00**
	Inst	Ea	Sm	MB	1.33	12.00	104.00	43.10	---	147.10	**186.00**
Average quality workmanship	Inst	Ea	Lg	MB	.800	20.00	70.60	25.90	---	96.50	**122.00**
	Inst	Ea	Sm	MB	1.33	12.00	79.40	43.10	---	122.50	**157.00**
36" W											
High quality workmanship	Inst	Ea	Lg	MB	1.16	13.80	150.00	37.60	---	187.60	**233.00**
	Inst	Ea	Sm	MB	1.93	8.28	168.00	62.60	---	230.60	**291.00**
Good quality workmanship	Inst	Ea	Lg	MB	.800	20.00	124.00	25.90	---	149.90	**185.00**
	Inst	Ea	Sm	MB	1.33	12.00	139.00	43.10	---	182.10	**228.00**
Average quality workmanship	Inst	Ea	Lg	MB	.800	20.00	96.50	25.90	---	122.40	**153.00**
	Inst	Ea	Sm	MB	1.33	12.00	109.00	43.10	---	152.10	**191.00**
42" W											
High quality workmanship	Inst	Ea	Lg	MB	1.51	10.60	164.00	49.00	---	213.00	**267.00**
	Inst	Ea	Sm	MB	2.52	6.36	185.00	81.70	---	266.70	**338.00**
Good quality workmanship	Inst	Ea	Lg	MB	1.00	16.00	137.00	32.40	---	169.40	**210.00**
	Inst	Ea	Sm	MB	1.67	9.60	154.00	54.20	---	208.20	**262.00**
Average quality workmanship	Inst	Ea	Lg	MB	1.00	16.00	104.00	32.40	---	136.40	**170.00**
	Inst	Ea	Sm	MB	1.67	9.60	117.00	54.20	---	171.20	**217.00**
48" W											
High quality workmanship	Inst	Ea	Lg	MB	1.51	10.60	173.00	49.00	---	222.00	**277.00**
	Inst	Ea	Sm	MB	2.52	6.36	194.00	81.70	---	275.70	**349.00**
Good quality workmanship	Inst	Ea	Lg	MB	1.00	16.00	148.00	32.40	---	180.40	**224.00**
	Inst	Ea	Sm	MB	1.67	9.60	167.00	54.20	---	221.20	**277.00**
Average quality workmanship	Inst	Ea	Lg	MB	1.00	16.00	112.00	32.40	---	144.40	**181.00**
	Inst	Ea	Sm	MB	1.67	9.60	126.00	54.20	---	180.20	**229.00**

Description	Oper	Unit	Vol	Crew Size	Man-hours per Unit	Crew Output per Day	Avg Mat'l Unit Cost	Avg Labor Unit Cost	Avg Equip Unit Cost	Avg Total Unit Cost	Avg Price Incl O&P

Wall cabinets

Refrigerator cabinets, 15" H, 12" D, 2 doors

30" W

Description	Oper	Unit	Vol	Crew Size	Man-hours	Crew Output	Mat'l	Labor	Equip	Total	Price O&P
High quality workmanship	Inst	Ea	Lg	MB	1.54	10.40	125.00	49.90	---	174.90	**221.00**
	Inst	Ea	Sm	MB	2.56	6.24	140.00	83.00	---	223.00	**286.00**
Good quality workmanship	Inst	Ea	Lg	MB	1.03	15.60	92.40	33.40	---	125.80	**158.00**
	Inst	Ea	Sm	MB	1.71	9.36	104.00	55.50	---	159.50	**203.00**
Average quality workmanship	Inst	Ea	Lg	MB	1.03	15.60	70.80	33.40	---	104.20	**132.00**
	Inst	Ea	Sm	MB	1.71	9.36	79.70	55.50	---	135.20	**174.00**

33" W

Description	Oper	Unit	Vol	Crew Size	Man-hours	Crew Output	Mat'l	Labor	Equip	Total	Price O&P
High quality workmanship	Inst	Ea	Lg	MB	1.54	10.40	130.00	49.90	---	179.90	**226.00**
	Inst	Ea	Sm	MB	2.56	6.24	146.00	83.00	---	229.00	**293.00**
Good quality workmanship	Inst	Ea	Lg	MB	1.03	15.60	94.80	33.40	---	128.20	**161.00**
	Inst	Ea	Sm	MB	1.71	9.36	107.00	55.50	---	162.50	**207.00**
Average quality workmanship	Inst	Ea	Lg	MB	1.03	15.60	72.00	33.40	---	105.40	**134.00**
	Inst	Ea	Sm	MB	1.71	9.36	81.00	55.50	---	136.50	**176.00**

36" W

Description	Oper	Unit	Vol	Crew Size	Man-hours	Crew Output	Mat'l	Labor	Equip	Total	Price O&P
High quality workmanship	Inst	Ea	Lg	MB	1.54	10.40	137.00	49.90	---	186.90	**235.00**
	Inst	Ea	Sm	MB	2.56	6.24	154.00	83.00	---	237.00	**303.00**
Good quality workmanship	Inst	Ea	Lg	MB	1.03	15.60	101.00	33.40	---	134.40	**168.00**
	Inst	Ea	Sm	MB	1.71	9.36	113.00	55.50	---	168.50	**215.00**
Average quality workmanship	Inst	Ea	Lg	MB	1.03	15.60	76.80	33.40	---	110.20	**140.00**
	Inst	Ea	Sm	MB	1.71	9.36	86.40	55.50	---	141.90	**182.00**

Range cabinets, 21" H, 12" D

24" W, 1 door

Description	Oper	Unit	Vol	Crew Size	Man-hours	Crew Output	Mat'l	Labor	Equip	Total	Price O&P
High quality workmanship	Inst	Ea	Lg	MB	1.51	10.60	107.00	49.00	---	156.00	**198.00**
	Inst	Ea	Sm	MB	2.52	6.36	120.00	81.70	---	201.70	**260.00**
Good quality workmanship	Inst	Ea	Lg	MB	1.01	15.80	79.20	32.80	---	112.00	**142.00**
	Inst	Ea	Sm	MB	1.69	9.48	89.10	54.80	---	143.90	**185.00**
Average quality workmanship	Inst	Ea	Lg	MB	1.01	15.80	60.00	32.80	---	92.80	**119.00**
	Inst	Ea	Sm	MB	1.69	9.48	67.50	54.80	---	122.30	**159.00**

30" W, 2 doors

Description	Oper	Unit	Vol	Crew Size	Man-hours	Crew Output	Mat'l	Labor	Equip	Total	Price O&P
High quality workmanship	Inst	Ea	Lg	MB	1.51	10.60	119.00	49.00	---	168.00	**212.00**
	Inst	Ea	Sm	MB	2.52	6.36	134.00	81.70	---	215.70	**276.00**
Good quality workmanship	Inst	Ea	Lg	MB	1.01	15.80	87.60	32.80	---	120.40	**152.00**
	Inst	Ea	Sm	MB	1.69	9.48	98.60	54.80	---	153.40	**196.00**
Average quality workmanship	Inst	Ea	Lg	MB	1.01	15.80	67.20	32.80	---	100.00	**127.00**
	Inst	Ea	Sm	MB	1.69	9.48	75.60	54.80	---	130.40	**169.00**

33" W, 2 doors

Description	Oper	Unit	Vol	Crew Size	Man-hours	Crew Output	Mat'l	Labor	Equip	Total	Price O&P
High quality workmanship	Inst	Ea	Lg	MB	1.60	10.00	124.00	51.90	---	175.90	**222.00**
	Inst	Ea	Sm	MB	2.67	6.00	139.00	86.60	---	225.60	**290.00**
Good quality workmanship	Inst	Ea	Lg	MB	1.07	15.00	91.20	34.70	---	125.90	**159.00**
	Inst	Ea	Sm	MB	1.78	9.00	103.00	57.70	---	160.70	**205.00**
Average quality workmanship	Inst	Ea	Lg	MB	1.07	15.00	69.60	34.70	---	104.30	**133.00**
	Inst	Ea	Sm	MB	1.78	9.00	78.30	57.70	---	136.00	**176.00**

Description	Oper	Unit	Vol	Crew Size	Man-hours per Unit	Crew Output per Day	Avg Mat'l Unit Cost	Avg Labor Unit Cost	Avg Equip Unit Cost	Avg Total Unit Cost	Avg Price Incl O&P
36" W, 2 doors											
High quality workmanship	Inst	Ea	Lg	MB	1.60	10.00	132.00	51.90	---	183.90	**232.00**
	Inst	Ea	Sm	MB	2.67	6.00	149.00	86.60	---	235.60	**301.00**
Good quality workmanship	Inst	Ea	Lg	MB	1.07	15.00	96.00	34.70	---	130.70	**164.00**
	Inst	Ea	Sm	MB	1.78	9.00	108.00	57.70	---	165.70	**212.00**
Average quality workmanship	Inst	Ea	Lg	MB	1.07	15.00	73.20	34.70	---	107.90	**137.00**
	Inst	Ea	Sm	MB	1.78	9.00	82.40	57.70	---	140.10	**181.00**
42" W, 2 doors											
High quality workmanship	Inst	Ea	Lg	MB	1.60	10.00	144.00	51.90	---	195.90	**246.00**
	Inst	Ea	Sm	MB	2.67	6.00	162.00	86.60	---	248.60	**317.00**
Good quality workmanship	Inst	Ea	Lg	MB	1.07	15.00	107.00	34.70	---	141.70	**177.00**
	Inst	Ea	Sm	MB	1.78	9.00	120.00	57.70	---	177.70	**226.00**
Average quality workmanship	Inst	Ea	Lg	MB	1.07	15.00	81.60	34.70	---	116.30	**147.00**
	Inst	Ea	Sm	MB	1.78	9.00	91.80	57.70	---	149.50	**192.00**
48" W, 2 doors											
High quality workmanship	Inst	Ea	Lg	MB	2.00	8.00	163.00	64.90	---	227.90	**288.00**
	Inst	Ea	Sm	MB	3.33	4.80	184.00	108.00	---	292.00	**374.00**
Good quality workmanship	Inst	Ea	Lg	MB	1.33	12.00	121.00	43.10	---	164.10	**207.00**
	Inst	Ea	Sm	MB	2.22	7.20	136.00	72.00	---	208.00	**266.00**
Average quality workmanship	Inst	Ea	Lg	MB	1.33	12.00	92.40	43.10	---	135.50	**172.00**
	Inst	Ea	Sm	MB	2.22	7.20	104.00	72.00	---	176.00	**227.00**

Range cabinets, 30" H, 12" D

Description	Oper	Unit	Vol	Crew Size	Man-hours per Unit	Crew Output per Day	Avg Mat'l Unit Cost	Avg Labor Unit Cost	Avg Equip Unit Cost	Avg Total Unit Cost	Avg Price Incl O&P
12" W, 1 door											
High quality workmanship	Inst	Ea	Lg	MB	1.18	13.60	93.60	38.30	---	131.90	**167.00**
	Inst	Ea	Sm	MB	1.96	8.16	105.00	63.60	---	168.60	**217.00**
Good quality workmanship	Inst	Ea	Lg	MB	.780	20.50	68.40	25.30	---	93.70	**118.00**
	Inst	Ea	Sm	MB	1.30	12.30	77.00	42.20	---	119.20	**152.00**
Average quality workmanship	Inst	Ea	Lg	MB	.780	20.50	51.60	25.30	---	76.90	**97.80**
	Inst	Ea	Sm	MB	1.30	12.30	58.10	42.20	---	100.30	**130.00**
15" W, 1 door											
High quality workmanship	Inst	Ea	Lg	MB	1.18	13.60	103.00	38.30	---	141.30	**178.00**
	Inst	Ea	Sm	MB	1.96	8.16	116.00	63.60	---	179.60	**230.00**
Good quality workmanship	Inst	Ea	Lg	MB	.780	20.50	75.60	25.30	---	100.90	**127.00**
	Inst	Ea	Sm	MB	1.30	12.30	85.10	42.20	---	127.30	**162.00**
Average quality workmanship	Inst	Ea	Lg	MB	.780	20.50	57.60	25.30	---	82.90	**105.00**
	Inst	Ea	Sm	MB	1.30	12.30	64.80	42.20	---	107.00	**138.00**
18" W, 1 door											
High quality workmanship	Inst	Ea	Lg	MB	1.18	13.60	108.00	38.30	---	146.30	**184.00**
	Inst	Ea	Sm	MB	1.96	8.16	122.00	63.60	---	185.60	**236.00**
Good quality workmanship	Inst	Ea	Lg	MB	.780	20.50	79.20	25.30	---	104.50	**131.00**
	Inst	Ea	Sm	MB	1.30	12.30	89.10	42.20	---	131.30	**167.00**
Average quality workmanship	Inst	Ea	Lg	MB	.780	20.50	60.00	25.30	---	85.30	**108.00**
	Inst	Ea	Sm	MB	1.30	12.30	67.50	42.20	---	109.70	**141.00**

Description	Oper	Unit	Vol	Crew Size	Man-hours per Unit	Crew Output per Day	Avg Mat'l Unit Cost	Avg Labor Unit Cost	Avg Equip Unit Cost	Avg Total Unit Cost	Avg Price Incl O&P
21" W, 1 door											
High quality workmanship	Inst	Ea	Lg	MB	1.33	12.00	114.00	43.10	---	157.10	**198.00**
	Inst	Ea	Sm	MB	2.22	7.20	128.00	72.00	---	200.00	**256.00**
Good quality workmanship	Inst	Ea	Lg	MB	.889	18.00	84.00	28.80	---	112.80	**142.00**
	Inst	Ea	Sm	MB	1.48	10.80	94.50	48.00	---	142.50	**182.00**
Average quality workmanship	Inst	Ea	Lg	MB	.889	18.00	63.60	28.80	---	92.40	**117.00**
	Inst	Ea	Sm	MB	1.48	10.80	71.60	48.00	---	119.60	**154.00**
24" W, 1 door											
High quality workmanship	Inst	Ea	Lg	MB	1.33	12.00	127.00	43.10	---	170.10	**214.00**
	Inst	Ea	Sm	MB	2.22	7.20	143.00	72.00	---	215.00	**274.00**
Good quality workmanship	Inst	Ea	Lg	MB	.889	18.00	93.60	28.80	---	122.40	**153.00**
	Inst	Ea	Sm	MB	1.48	10.80	105.00	48.00	---	153.00	**195.00**
Average quality workmanship	Inst	Ea	Lg	MB	.889	18.00	70.80	28.80	---	99.60	**126.00**
	Inst	Ea	Sm	MB	1.48	10.80	79.70	48.00	---	127.70	**164.00**
27" W, 2 doors											
High quality workmanship	Inst	Ea	Lg	MB	1.33	12.00	140.00	43.10	---	183.10	**230.00**
	Inst	Ea	Sm	MB	2.22	7.20	158.00	72.00	---	230.00	**292.00**
Good quality workmanship	Inst	Ea	Lg	MB	.889	18.00	103.00	28.80	---	131.80	**165.00**
	Inst	Ea	Sm	MB	1.48	10.80	116.00	48.00	---	164.00	**207.00**
Average quality workmanship	Inst	Ea	Lg	MB	.889	18.00	79.20	28.80	---	108.00	**136.00**
	Inst	Ea	Sm	MB	1.48	10.80	89.10	48.00	---	137.10	**175.00**
30" W, 2 doors											
High quality workmanship	Inst	Ea	Lg	MB	1.78	9.00	149.00	57.70	---	206.70	**261.00**
	Inst	Ea	Sm	MB	2.96	5.40	167.00	96.00	---	263.00	**337.00**
Good quality workmanship	Inst	Ea	Lg	MB	1.19	13.50	110.00	38.60	---	148.60	**187.00**
	Inst	Ea	Sm	MB	1.98	8.10	124.00	64.20	---	188.20	**240.00**
Average quality workmanship	Inst	Ea	Lg	MB	1.19	13.50	82.80	38.60	---	121.40	**154.00**
	Inst	Ea	Sm	MB	1.98	8.10	93.20	64.20	---	157.40	**203.00**
33" W, 2 doors											
High quality workmanship	Inst	Ea	Lg	MB	1.78	9.00	157.00	57.70	---	214.70	**271.00**
	Inst	Ea	Sm	MB	2.96	5.40	177.00	96.00	---	273.00	**349.00**
Good quality workmanship	Inst	Ea	Lg	MB	1.19	13.50	116.00	38.60	---	154.60	**194.00**
	Inst	Ea	Sm	MB	1.98	8.10	131.00	64.20	---	195.20	**248.00**
Average quality workmanship	Inst	Ea	Lg	MB	1.19	13.50	88.80	38.60	---	127.40	**161.00**
	Inst	Ea	Sm	MB	1.98	8.10	99.90	64.20	---	164.10	**211.00**
36" W, 2 doors											
High quality workmanship	Inst	Ea	Lg	MB	1.78	9.00	163.00	57.70	---	220.70	**278.00**
	Inst	Ea	Sm	MB	2.96	5.40	184.00	96.00	---	280.00	**357.00**
Good quality workmanship	Inst	Ea	Lg	MB	1.19	13.50	121.00	38.60	---	159.60	**200.00**
	Inst	Ea	Sm	MB	1.98	8.10	136.00	64.20	---	200.20	**255.00**
Average quality workmanship	Inst	Ea	Lg	MB	1.19	13.50	92.40	38.60	---	131.00	**166.00**
	Inst	Ea	Sm	MB	1.98	8.10	104.00	64.20	---	168.20	**216.00**

Description	Oper	Unit	Vol	Crew Size	Man-hours per Unit	Crew Output per Day	Avg Mat'l Unit Cost	Avg Labor Unit Cost	Avg Equip Unit Cost	Avg Total Unit Cost	Avg Price Incl O&P
42" W, 2 doors											
High quality workmanship	Inst	Ea	Lg	MB	2.29	7.00	178.00	74.30	---	252.30	**319.00**
	Inst	Ea	Sm	MB	3.81	4.20	200.00	124.00	---	324.00	**415.00**
Good quality workmanship	Inst	Ea	Lg	MB	1.52	10.50	131.00	49.30	---	180.30	**227.00**
	Inst	Ea	Sm	MB	2.54	6.30	147.00	82.40	---	229.40	**294.00**
Average quality workmanship	Inst	Ea	Lg	MB	1.52	10.50	99.60	49.30	---	148.90	**190.00**
	Inst	Ea	Sm	MB	2.54	6.30	112.00	82.40	---	194.40	**251.00**
48" W, 2 doors											
High quality workmanship	Inst	Ea	Lg	MB	2.29	7.00	210.00	74.30	---	284.30	**357.00**
	Inst	Ea	Sm	MB	3.81	4.20	236.00	124.00	---	360.00	**459.00**
Good quality workmanship	Inst	Ea	Lg	MB	1.52	10.50	155.00	49.30	---	204.30	**256.00**
	Inst	Ea	Sm	MB	2.54	6.30	174.00	82.40	---	256.40	**326.00**
Average quality workmanship	Inst	Ea	Lg	MB	1.52	10.50	118.00	49.30	---	167.30	**211.00**
	Inst	Ea	Sm	MB	2.54	6.30	132.00	82.40	---	214.40	**276.00**
24" W, blind corner unit, 1 door											
High quality workmanship	Inst	Ea	Lg	MB	1.68	9.50	114.00	54.50	---	168.50	**214.00**
	Inst	Ea	Sm	MB	2.81	5.70	128.00	91.10	---	219.10	**283.00**
Good quality workmanship	Inst	Ea	Lg	MB	1.14	14.00	90.00	37.00	---	127.00	**161.00**
	Inst	Ea	Sm	MB	1.90	8.40	101.00	61.60	---	162.60	**209.00**
Average quality workmanship	Inst	Ea	Lg	MB	1.14	14.00	87.60	37.00	---	124.60	**158.00**
	Inst	Ea	Sm	MB	1.90	8.40	98.60	61.60	---	160.20	**206.00**
24" x 24" angle corner unit, stationary											
High quality workmanship	Inst	Ea	Lg	MB	1.68	9.50	163.00	54.50	---	217.50	**273.00**
	Inst	Ea	Sm	MB	2.81	5.70	184.00	91.10	---	275.10	**350.00**
Good quality workmanship	Inst	Ea	Lg	MB	1.14	14.00	120.00	37.00	---	157.00	**197.00**
	Inst	Ea	Sm	MB	1.90	8.40	135.00	61.60	---	196.60	**250.00**
Average quality workmanship	Inst	Ea	Lg	MB	1.14	14.00	93.60	37.00	---	130.60	**165.00**
	Inst	Ea	Sm	MB	1.90	8.40	105.00	61.60	---	166.60	**214.00**
24" x 24" angle corner unit, Lazy Susan											
High quality workmanship	Inst	Ea	Lg	MB	1.68	9.50	242.00	54.50	---	296.50	**368.00**
	Inst	Ea	Sm	MB	2.81	5.70	273.00	91.10	---	364.10	**457.00**
Good quality workmanship	Inst	Ea	Lg	MB	1.14	14.00	197.00	37.00	---	234.00	**289.00**
	Inst	Ea	Sm	MB	1.90	8.40	221.00	61.60	---	282.60	**353.00**
Average quality workmanship	Inst	Ea	Lg	MB	1.14	14.00	134.00	37.00	---	171.00	**214.00**
	Inst	Ea	Sm	MB	1.90	8.40	151.00	61.60	---	212.60	**269.00**

Vanity cabinets and sink top

Description	Oper	Unit	Vol	Crew Size	Man-hours per Unit	Crew Output per Day	Avg Mat'l Unit Cost	Avg Labor Unit Cost	Avg Equip Unit Cost	Avg Total Unit Cost	Avg Price Incl O&P
Disconnect plumbing and remove to dumpster											
	Demo	Ea	Lg	LB	1.00	16.00	---	30.00	---	30.00	**42.00**
	Demo	Ea	Sm	LB	1.67	9.60	---	50.10	---	50.10	**70.10**
Remove old unit, replace with new unit, reconnect plumbing											
	Reset	Ea	Lg	SB	2.29	7.00	---	83.60	---	83.60	**121.00**
	Reset	Ea	Sm	SB	3.81	4.20	---	139.00	---	139.00	**202.00**

Description	Oper	Unit	Vol	Crew Size	Man-hours per Unit	Crew Output per Day	Avg Mat'l Unit Cost	Avg Labor Unit Cost	Avg Equip Unit Cost	Avg Total Unit Cost	Avg Price Incl O&P

Vanity units, with marble tops, good quality fittings and faucets; hardware, deluxe, finished models

Stained ash and birch primed composition construction Labor costs include fitting and hanging only of vanity units For rough-in costs, see Adjustments in this cabinets section, page 74

2-door units
20" x 16"

Description	Oper	Unit	Vol	Crew Size	Man-hours per Unit	Crew Output per Day	Avg Mat'l Unit Cost	Avg Labor Unit Cost	Avg Equip Unit Cost	Avg Total Unit Cost	Avg Price Incl O&P
Ash	Inst	Ea	Lg	SB	5.00	3.20	271.00	183.00	---	454.00	**590.00**
	Inst	Ea	Sm	SB	8.33	1.92	305.00	304.00	---	609.00	**807.00**
Birch	Inst	Ea	Lg	SB	5.00	3.20	247.00	183.00	---	430.00	**561.00**
	Inst	Ea	Sm	SB	8.33	1.92	278.00	304.00	---	582.00	**775.00**
Composition construction	Inst	Ea	Lg	SB	5.00	3.20	187.00	183.00	---	370.00	**489.00**
	Inst	Ea	Sm	SB	8.33	1.92	211.00	304.00	---	515.00	**694.00**

25" x 19"

Description	Oper	Unit	Vol	Crew Size	Man-hours per Unit	Crew Output per Day	Avg Mat'l Unit Cost	Avg Labor Unit Cost	Avg Equip Unit Cost	Avg Total Unit Cost	Avg Price Incl O&P
Ash	Inst	Ea	Lg	SB	5.00	3.20	316.00	183.00	---	499.00	**643.00**
	Inst	Ea	Sm	SB	8.33	1.92	355.00	304.00	---	659.00	**867.00**
Birch	Inst	Ea	Lg	SB	5.00	3.20	288.00	183.00	---	471.00	**610.00**
	Inst	Ea	Sm	SB	8.33	1.92	324.00	304.00	---	628.00	**830.00**
Composition construction	Inst	Ea	Lg	SB	5.00	3.20	205.00	183.00	---	388.00	**511.00**
	Inst	Ea	Sm	SB	8.33	1.92	231.00	304.00	---	535.00	**718.00**

31" x 19"

Description	Oper	Unit	Vol	Crew Size	Man-hours per Unit	Crew Output per Day	Avg Mat'l Unit Cost	Avg Labor Unit Cost	Avg Equip Unit Cost	Avg Total Unit Cost	Avg Price Incl O&P
Ash	Inst	Ea	Lg	SB	5.00	3.20	376.00	183.00	---	559.00	**715.00**
	Inst	Ea	Sm	SB	8.33	1.92	423.00	304.00	---	727.00	**948.00**
Birch	Inst	Ea	Lg	SB	5.00	3.20	341.00	183.00	---	524.00	**674.00**
	Inst	Ea	Sm	SB	8.33	1.92	383.00	304.00	---	687.00	**901.00**
Composition construction	Inst	Ea	Lg	SB	5.00	3.20	244.00	183.00	---	427.00	**557.00**
	Inst	Ea	Sm	SB	8.33	1.92	274.00	304.00	---	578.00	**770.00**

35" x 19"

Description	Oper	Unit	Vol	Crew Size	Man-hours per Unit	Crew Output per Day	Avg Mat'l Unit Cost	Avg Labor Unit Cost	Avg Equip Unit Cost	Avg Total Unit Cost	Avg Price Incl O&P
Ash	Inst	Ea	Lg	SB	5.33	3.00	406.00	195.00	---	601.00	**769.00**
	Inst	Ea	Sm	SB	8.89	1.80	456.00	325.00	---	781.00	**1020.00**
Birch	Inst	Ea	Lg	SB	5.33	3.00	367.00	195.00	---	562.00	**723.00**
	Inst	Ea	Sm	SB	8.89	1.80	413.00	325.00	---	738.00	**966.00**
Composition construction	Inst	Ea	Lg	SB	5.33	3.00	265.00	195.00	---	460.00	**600.00**
	Inst	Ea	Sm	SB	8.89	1.80	298.00	325.00	---	623.00	**829.00**

For drawers in any above unit, ADD per drawer

Description	Oper	Unit	Vol	Crew Size	Man-hours per Unit	Crew Output per Day	Avg Mat'l Unit Cost	Avg Labor Unit Cost	Avg Equip Unit Cost	Avg Total Unit Cost	Avg Price Incl O&P
	Inst	Ea	Lg	SB	---	---	36.00	---	---	36.00	**43.20**
	Inst	Ea	Sm	SB	---	---	40.50	---	---	40.50	**48.60**

2-door cutback units with 3 drawers
36" x 19"

Description	Oper	Unit	Vol	Crew Size	Man-hours per Unit	Crew Output per Day	Avg Mat'l Unit Cost	Avg Labor Unit Cost	Avg Equip Unit Cost	Avg Total Unit Cost	Avg Price Incl O&P
Ash	Inst	Ea	Lg	SB	5.33	3.00	470.00	195.00	---	665.00	**847.00**
	Inst	Ea	Sm	SB	8.89	1.80	529.00	325.00	---	854.00	**1110.00**
Birch	Inst	Ea	Lg	SB	5.33	3.00	422.00	195.00	---	617.00	**789.00**
	Inst	Ea	Sm	SB	8.89	1.80	475.00	325.00	---	800.00	**1040.00**
Composition construction	Inst	Ea	Lg	SB	5.33	3.00	316.00	195.00	---	511.00	**661.00**
	Inst	Ea	Sm	SB	8.89	1.80	355.00	325.00	---	680.00	**897.00**

Description	Oper	Unit	Vol	Crew Size	Man-hours per Unit	Crew Output per Day	Avg Mat'l Unit Cost	Avg Labor Unit Cost	Avg Equip Unit Cost	Avg Total Unit Cost	Avg Price Incl O&P
49" x 19											
Ash	Inst	Ea	Lg	SB	5.33	3.00	588.00	195.00	---	783.00	**988.00**
	Inst	Ea	Sm	SB	8.89	1.80	662.00	325.00	---	987.00	**1260.00**
Birch	Inst	Ea	Lg	SB	5.33	3.00	509.00	195.00	---	704.00	**893.00**
	Inst	Ea	Sm	SB	8.89	1.80	572.00	325.00	---	897.00	**1160.00**
Composition construction	Inst	Ea	Lg	SB	5.33	3.00	380.00	195.00	---	575.00	**739.00**
	Inst	Ea	Sm	SB	8.89	1.80	428.00	325.00	---	753.00	**984.00**
60" x 19"											
Ash	Inst	Ea	Lg	SB	6.67	2.40	742.00	244.00	---	986.00	**1240.00**
	Inst	Ea	Sm	SB	11.1	1.44	834.00	405.00	---	1239.00	**1590.00**
Birch	Inst	Ea	Lg	SB	6.67	2.40	616.00	244.00	---	860.00	**1090.00**
	Inst	Ea	Sm	SB	11.1	1.44	693.00	405.00	---	1098.00	**1420.00**
Composition construction	Inst	Ea	Lg	SB	6.67	2.40	479.00	244.00	---	723.00	**928.00**
	Inst	Ea	Sm	SB	11.1	1.44	539.00	405.00	---	944.00	**1230.00**

Corner unit, 1 door

Description	Oper	Unit	Vol	Crew Size	Man-hours per Unit	Crew Output per Day	Avg Mat'l Unit Cost	Avg Labor Unit Cost	Avg Equip Unit Cost	Avg Total Unit Cost	Avg Price Incl O&P
22" x 22"											
Ash	Inst	Ea	Lg	SB	5.00	3.20	349.00	183.00	---	532.00	**684.00**
	Inst	Ea	Sm	SB	8.33	1.92	393.00	304.00	---	697.00	**912.00**
Birch	Inst	Ea	Lg	SB	5.00	3.20	330.00	183.00	---	513.00	**661.00**
	Inst	Ea	Sm	SB	8.33	1.92	371.00	304.00	---	675.00	**886.00**
Composition construction	Inst	Ea	Lg	SB	5.00	3.20	269.00	183.00	---	452.00	**587.00**
	Inst	Ea	Sm	SB	8.33	1.92	302.00	304.00	---	606.00	**804.00**

Adjustments
To remove and reset

Description	Oper	Unit	Vol	Crew Size	Man-hours per Unit	Crew Output per Day	Avg Mat'l Unit Cost	Avg Labor Unit Cost	Avg Equip Unit Cost	Avg Total Unit Cost	Avg Price Incl O&P
Vanity units with tops	Reset	Ea	Lg	SA	3.33	2.40	---	143.00	---	143.00	**208.00**
	Reset	Ea	Sm	SA	5.56	1.44	---	239.00	---	239.00	**347.00**
Top only	Reset	Ea	Lg	SA	2.00	4.00	---	86.00	---	86.00	**125.00**
	Reset	Ea	Sm	SA	3.33	2.40	---	143.00	---	143.00	**208.00**

To install rough-in

Description	Oper	Unit	Vol	Crew Size	Man-hours per Unit	Crew Output per Day	Avg Mat'l Unit Cost	Avg Labor Unit Cost	Avg Equip Unit Cost	Avg Total Unit Cost	Avg Price Incl O&P
	Inst	Ea	Lg	SB	4.00	4.00	---	146.00	---	146.00	**212.00**
	Inst	Ea	Sm	SB	6.67	2.40	---	244.00	---	244.00	**353.00**

Description	Oper	Unit	Vol	Crew Size	Man-hours per Unit	Crew Output per Day	Avg Mat'l Unit Cost	Avg Labor Unit Cost	Avg Equip Unit Cost	Avg Total Unit Cost	Avg Price Incl O&P

Canopies
Costs for awnings include all hardware

Residential prefabricated
Aluminum

Carport, freestanding

Description	Oper	Unit	Vol	Crew Size	Man-hours per Unit	Crew Output per Day	Avg Mat'l Unit Cost	Avg Labor Unit Cost	Avg Equip Unit Cost	Avg Total Unit Cost	Avg Price Incl O&P
16' x 8'	Inst	Ea	Lg	2C	5.33	3.00	1180.00	197.00	---	1377.00	1630.00
	Inst	Ea	Sm	2C	7.11	2.25	1350.00	263.00	---	1613.00	1920.00
20' x 10'	Inst	Ea	Lg	2C	8.00	2.00	1250.00	296.00	---	1546.00	1850.00
	Inst	Ea	Sm	2C	10.7	1.50	1420.00	396.00	---	1816.00	2190.00

Door canopies, 36" projection

Description	Oper	Unit	Vol	Crew Size	Man-hours per Unit	Crew Output per Day	Avg Mat'l Unit Cost	Avg Labor Unit Cost	Avg Equip Unit Cost	Avg Total Unit Cost	Avg Price Incl O&P
4' wide	Inst	Ea	Lg	CA	1.00	8.00	197.00	37.00	---	234.00	278.00
	Inst	Ea	Sm	CA	1.33	6.00	225.00	49.20	---	274.20	328.00
5' wide	Inst	Ea	Lg	CA	1.33	6.00	221.00	49.20	---	270.20	323.00
	Inst	Ea	Sm	CA	1.78	4.50	252.00	65.90	---	317.90	382.00
6' wide	Inst	Ea	Lg	CA	2.00	4.00	238.00	74.00	---	312.00	378.00
	Inst	Ea	Sm	CA	2.67	3.00	272.00	98.80	---	370.80	452.00
8' wide	Inst	Ea	Lg	2C	3.20	5.00	326.00	118.00	---	444.00	540.00
	Inst	Ea	Sm	2C	4.27	3.75	372.00	158.00	---	530.00	649.00
10' wide	Inst	Ea	Lg	2C	5.33	3.00	373.00	197.00	---	570.00	705.00
	Inst	Ea	Sm	2C	7.11	2.25	426.00	263.00	---	689.00	858.00
12' wide	Inst	Ea	Lg	2C	8.00	2.00	443.00	296.00	---	739.00	924.00
	Inst	Ea	Sm	2C	10.7	1.50	506.00	396.00	---	902.00	1140.00

Door canopies, 42" projection

Description	Oper	Unit	Vol	Crew Size	Man-hours per Unit	Crew Output per Day	Avg Mat'l Unit Cost	Avg Labor Unit Cost	Avg Equip Unit Cost	Avg Total Unit Cost	Avg Price Incl O&P
4' wide	Inst	Ea	Lg	CA	1.00	8.00	226.00	37.00	---	263.00	311.00
	Inst	Ea	Sm	CA	1.33	6.00	258.00	49.20	---	307.20	366.00
5' wide	Inst	Ea	Lg	CA	1.33	6.00	247.00	49.20	---	296.20	353.00
	Inst	Ea	Sm	CA	1.78	4.50	282.00	65.90	---	347.90	417.00
6' wide	Inst	Ea	Lg	CA	2.00	4.00	312.00	74.00	---	386.00	462.00
	Inst	Ea	Sm	CA	2.67	3.00	356.00	98.80	---	454.80	548.00
8' wide	Inst	Ea	Lg	2C	3.20	5.00	364.00	118.00	---	482.00	585.00
	Inst	Ea	Sm	2C	4.27	3.75	416.00	158.00	---	574.00	700.00
10' wide	Inst	Ea	Lg	2C	5.33	3.00	422.00	197.00	---	619.00	762.00
	Inst	Ea	Sm	2C	7.11	2.25	482.00	263.00	---	745.00	923.00
12' wide	Inst	Ea	Lg	2C	8.00	2.00	496.00	296.00	---	792.00	985.00
	Inst	Ea	Sm	2C	10.7	1.50	566.00	396.00	---	962.00	1210.00

Door canopies, 48" projection

Description	Oper	Unit	Vol	Crew Size	Man-hours per Unit	Crew Output per Day	Avg Mat'l Unit Cost	Avg Labor Unit Cost	Avg Equip Unit Cost	Avg Total Unit Cost	Avg Price Incl O&P
4' wide	Inst	Ea	Lg	CA	1.00	8.00	247.00	37.00	---	284.00	336.00
	Inst	Ea	Sm	CA	1.33	6.00	282.00	49.20	---	331.20	393.00
5' wide	Inst	Ea	Lg	CA	1.33	6.00	289.00	49.20	---	338.20	401.00
	Inst	Ea	Sm	CA	1.78	4.50	330.00	65.90	---	395.90	472.00
6' wide	Inst	Ea	Lg	CA	2.00	4.00	328.00	74.00	---	402.00	480.00
	Inst	Ea	Sm	CA	2.67	3.00	374.00	98.80	---	472.80	569.00
8' wide	Inst	Ea	Lg	2C	3.20	5.00	446.00	118.00	---	564.00	679.00
	Inst	Ea	Sm	2C	4.27	3.75	510.00	158.00	---	668.00	808.00
10' wide	Inst	Ea	Lg	2C	5.33	3.00	499.00	197.00	---	696.00	850.00
	Inst	Ea	Sm	2C	7.11	2.25	570.00	263.00	---	833.00	1020.00
12' wide	Inst	Ea	Lg	2C	8.00	2.00	562.00	296.00	---	858.00	1060.00
	Inst	Ea	Sm	2C	10.7	1.50	642.00	396.00	---	1038.00	1290.00

Description	Oper	Unit	Vol	Crew Size	Man-hours per Unit	Crew Output per Day	Avg Mat'l Unit Cost	Avg Labor Unit Cost	Avg Equip Unit Cost	Avg Total Unit Cost	Avg Price Incl O&P
Door canopies, 54" projection											
4' wide	Inst	Ea	Lg	CA	1.00	8.00	284.00	37.00	---	321.00	**378.00**
	Inst	Ea	Sm	CA	1.33	6.00	324.00	49.20	---	373.20	**442.00**
5' wide	Inst	Ea	Lg	CA	1.33	6.00	301.00	49.20	---	350.20	**415.00**
	Inst	Ea	Sm	CA	1.78	4.50	344.00	65.90	---	409.90	**488.00**
6' wide	Inst	Ea	Lg	CA	2.00	4.00	375.00	74.00	---	449.00	**535.00**
	Inst	Ea	Sm	CA	2.67	3.00	428.00	98.80	---	526.80	**631.00**
8' wide	Inst	Ea	Lg	2C	3.20	5.00	511.00	118.00	---	629.00	**754.00**
	Inst	Ea	Sm	2C	4.27	3.75	584.00	158.00	---	742.00	**893.00**
10' wide	Inst	Ea	Lg	2C	5.33	3.00	578.00	197.00	---	775.00	**940.00**
	Inst	Ea	Sm	2C	7.11	2.25	660.00	263.00	---	923.00	**1130.00**
12' wide	Inst	Ea	Lg	2C	8.00	2.00	656.00	296.00	---	952.00	**1170.00**
	Inst	Ea	Sm	2C	10.7	1.50	750.00	396.00	---	1146.00	**1420.00**
Patio cover											
16' x 8'	Inst	Ea	Lg	2C	5.33	3.00	630.00	197.00	---	827.00	**1000.00**
	Inst	Ea	Sm	2C	7.11	2.25	720.00	263.00	---	983.00	**1200.00**
20' x 10'	Inst	Ea	Lg	2C	8.00	2.00	853.00	296.00	---	1149.00	**1400.00**
	Inst	Ea	Sm	2C	10.7	1.50	974.00	396.00	---	1370.00	**1680.00**
Window awnings, 3' high											
4' wide	Inst	Ea	Lg	CA	1.14	7.00	65.60	42.20	---	107.80	**135.00**
	Inst	Ea	Sm	CA	1.52	5.25	75.00	56.30	---	131.30	**165.00**
6' wide	Inst	Ea	Lg	CA	1.60	5.00	79.30	59.20	---	138.50	**174.00**
	Inst	Ea	Sm	CA	2.13	3.75	90.60	78.90	---	169.50	**215.00**
9' wide	Inst	Ea	Lg	2C	2.67	6.00	109.00	98.80	---	207.80	**263.00**
	Inst	Ea	Sm	2C	3.56	4.50	124.00	132.00	---	256.00	**327.00**
12' wide	Inst	Ea	Lg	2C	4.00	4.00	137.00	148.00	---	285.00	**364.00**
	Inst	Ea	Sm	2C	5.33	3.00	156.00	197.00	---	353.00	**456.00**
Window awnings, 4' high											
4' wide	Inst	Ea	Lg	CA	1.14	7.00	75.60	42.20	---	117.80	**146.00**
	Inst	Ea	Sm	CA	1.52	5.25	86.40	56.30	---	142.70	**178.00**
6' wide	Inst	Ea	Lg	CA	1.60	5.00	99.80	59.20	---	159.00	**198.00**
	Inst	Ea	Sm	CA	2.13	3.75	114.00	78.90	---	192.90	**242.00**
9' wide	Inst	Ea	Lg	2C	2.67	6.00	137.00	98.80	---	235.80	**295.00**
	Inst	Ea	Sm	2C	3.56	4.50	156.00	132.00	---	288.00	**364.00**
12' wide	Inst	Ea	Lg	2C	4.00	4.00	179.00	148.00	---	327.00	**413.00**
	Inst	Ea	Sm	2C	5.33	3.00	204.00	197.00	---	401.00	**511.00**
Window awnings, 6' high											
4' wide	Inst	Ea	Lg	CA	1.14	7.00	124.00	42.20	---	166.20	**202.00**
	Inst	Ea	Sm	CA	1.52	5.25	142.00	56.30	---	198.30	**242.00**
6' wide	Inst	Ea	Lg	CA	1.60	5.00	168.00	59.20	---	227.20	**276.00**
	Inst	Ea	Sm	CA	2.13	3.75	192.00	78.90	---	270.90	**331.00**
9' wide	Inst	Ea	Lg	2C	2.67	6.00	210.00	98.80	---	308.80	**380.00**
	Inst	Ea	Sm	2C	3.56	4.50	240.00	132.00	---	372.00	**461.00**
12' wide	Inst	Ea	Lg	2C	4.00	4.00	236.00	148.00	---	384.00	**479.00**
	Inst	Ea	Sm	2C	5.33	3.00	270.00	197.00	---	467.00	**587.00**

Description	Oper	Unit	Vol	Crew Size	Man-hours per Unit	Crew Output per Day	Avg Mat'l Unit Cost	Avg Labor Unit Cost	Avg Equip Unit Cost	Avg Total Unit Cost	Avg Price Incl O&P
Roll-up											
3' wide	Inst	Ea	Lg	CA	1.00	8.00	51.50	37.00	---	88.50	**111.00**
	Inst	Ea	Sm	CA	1.33	6.00	58.80	49.20	---	108.00	**137.00**
4' wide	Inst	Ea	Lg	CA	1.14	7.00	66.20	42.20	---	108.40	**135.00**
	Inst	Ea	Sm	CA	1.52	5.25	75.60	56.30	---	131.90	**166.00**
6' wide	Inst	Ea	Lg	CA	1.60	5.00	81.90	59.20	---	141.10	**177.00**
	Inst	Ea	Sm	CA	2.13	3.75	93.60	78.90	---	172.50	**218.00**
9' wide	Inst	Ea	Lg	2C	2.67	6.00	119.00	98.80	---	217.80	**275.00**
	Inst	Ea	Sm	2C	3.56	4.50	136.00	132.00	---	268.00	**340.00**
12' wide	Inst	Ea	Lg	2C	4.00	4.00	145.00	148.00	---	293.00	**374.00**
	Inst	Ea	Sm	2C	5.33	3.00	166.00	197.00	---	363.00	**467.00**

Canvas

Traditional fabric awning, with waterproof, colorfast acrylic duck, double-stitched seams, tubular metal framing and all hardware included

Description	Oper	Unit	Vol	Crew Size	Man-hours per Unit	Crew Output per Day	Avg Mat'l Unit Cost	Avg Labor Unit Cost	Avg Equip Unit Cost	Avg Total Unit Cost	Avg Price Incl O&P
Window awning, 24" drop											
3' wide	Inst	Ea	Lg	CA	1.00	8.00	168.00	37.00	---	205.00	**245.00**
	Inst	Ea	Sm	CA	1.33	6.00	192.00	49.20	---	241.20	**290.00**
4' wide	Inst	Ea	Lg	CA	1.14	7.00	206.00	42.20	---	248.20	**296.00**
	Inst	Ea	Sm	CA	1.52	5.25	235.00	56.30	---	291.30	**349.00**
Window awning, 30" drop											
3' wide	Inst	Ea	Lg	CA	1.00	8.00	192.00	37.00	---	229.00	**273.00**
	Inst	Ea	Sm	CA	1.33	6.00	220.00	49.20	---	269.20	**321.00**
4' wide	Inst	Ea	Lg	CA	1.14	7.00	231.00	42.20	---	273.20	**325.00**
	Inst	Ea	Sm	CA	1.52	5.25	264.00	56.30	---	320.30	**382.00**
5' wide	Inst	Ea	Lg	CA	1.33	6.00	263.00	49.20	---	312.20	**371.00**
	Inst	Ea	Sm	CA	1.78	4.50	300.00	65.90	---	365.90	**437.00**
6' wide	Inst	Ea	Lg	CA	1.60	5.00	294.00	59.20	---	353.20	**421.00**
	Inst	Ea	Sm	CA	2.13	3.75	336.00	78.90	---	414.90	**497.00**
8' wide	Inst	Ea	Lg	2C	3.20	5.00	328.00	118.00	---	446.00	**543.00**
	Inst	Ea	Sm	2C	4.27	3.75	374.00	158.00	---	532.00	**652.00**
10' wide	Inst	Ea	Lg	2C	4.00	4.00	373.00	148.00	---	521.00	**636.00**
	Inst	Ea	Sm	2C	5.33	3.00	426.00	197.00	---	623.00	**766.00**
Minimum Job Charge											
	Inst	Ea	Lg	CA	2.00	4.00	---	74.00	---	74.00	**104.00**
	Inst	Ea	Sm	CA	2.67	3.00	---	98.80	---	98.80	**138.00**

Description	Oper	Unit	Vol	Crew Size	Man-hours per Unit	Crew Output per Day	Avg Mat'l Unit Cost	Avg Labor Unit Cost	Avg Equip Unit Cost	Avg Total Unit Cost	Avg Price Incl O&P

Carpet

Detach & reset operations

Detach and re-lay

Existing carpet only	Reset	SY	Lg	FA	.095	84.00	---	3.22	.14	3.36	**4.65**
	Reset	SY	Sm	FA	.159	50.40	---	5.39	.24	5.63	**7.79**
Existing carpet w/ new pad	Reset	SY	Lg	FA	.111	72.00	3.96	3.77	---	7.73	**9.83**
	Reset	SY	Sm	FA	.185	43.20	4.50	6.28	---	10.78	**14.00**

Remove operations

Carpet only, tacked	Demo	SY	Lg	FA	.035	228.0	---	1.19	---	1.19	**1.66**
	Demo	SY	Sm	FA	.058	136.8	---	1.97	---	1.97	**2.76**
Pad, minimal glue	Demo	SY	Lg	FA	.018	456.0	---	.61	---	.61	**.86**
	Demo	SY	Sm	FA	.029	273.6	---	.98	---	.98	**1.38**
Scrape up backing residue	Demo	SY	Lg	FA	.083	96.00	---	2.82	---	2.82	**3.94**
	Demo	SY	Sm	FA	.139	57.60	---	4.72	---	4.72	**6.60**

Replace operations

Price includes consultation, measurement, pad separate, carpet separate, installation using tack strips and hot melt tape on seams

Standard quality

Poly, thin pile density	Inst	SY	Lg	FA	.083	96.00	15.00	2.82	.13	17.95	**21.30**
	Inst	SY	Sm	FA	.139	57.60	17.00	4.72	.21	21.93	**26.40**
Loop pile, 20 oz.	Inst	SY	Lg	FA	.083	96.00	9.92	2.82	.13	12.87	**15.50**
	Inst	SY	Sm	FA	.139	57.60	11.30	4.72	.21	16.23	**19.80**
Cut pile, 24 oz.	Inst	SY	Lg	FA	.083	96.00	11.50	2.82	.13	14.45	**17.30**
	Inst	SY	Sm	FA	.139	57.60	13.10	4.72	.21	18.03	**21.90**
Pad	Inst	SY	Lg	FA	.018	456.0	2.74	.61	---	3.35	**4.01**
	Inst	SY	Sm	FA	.029	273.6	3.11	.98	---	4.09	**4.95**

Average quality

Poly, medium pile density	Inst	SY	Lg	FA	.083	96.00	21.40	2.82	.13	24.35	**28.70**
	Inst	SY	Sm	FA	.139	57.60	24.30	4.72	.21	29.23	**34.80**
Loop pile, 26 oz.	Inst	SY	Lg	FA	.083	96.00	15.00	2.82	.13	17.95	**21.30**
	Inst	SY	Sm	FA	.139	57.60	17.00	4.72	.21	21.93	**26.40**
Cut pile, 36 oz.	Inst	SY	Lg	FA	.083	96.00	21.00	2.82	.13	23.95	**28.20**
	Inst	SY	Sm	FA	.139	57.60	23.90	4.72	.21	28.83	**34.30**
Wool	Inst	SY	Lg	FA	.083	96.00	26.80	2.82	.13	29.75	**34.90**
	Inst	SY	Sm	FA	.139	57.60	30.40	4.72	.21	35.33	**41.80**
Pad	Inst	SY	Lg	FA	.018	456.0	3.96	.61	---	4.57	**5.41**
	Inst	SY	Sm	FA	.029	273.6	4.50	.98	---	5.48	**6.55**

Description	Oper	Unit	Vol	Crew Size	Man-hours per Unit	Crew Output per Day	Avg Mat'l Unit Cost	Avg Labor Unit Cost	Avg Equip Unit Cost	Avg Total Unit Cost	Avg Price Incl O&P
High quality											
Nylon, medium pile density	Inst	SY	Lg	FA	.083	96.00	33.70	2.82	.13	36.65	**42.80**
	Inst	SY	Sm	FA	.139	57.60	38.30	4.72	.21	43.23	**50.80**
Loop pile, 36 oz.	Inst	SY	Lg	FA	.083	96.00	22.70	2.82	.13	25.65	**30.20**
	Inst	SY	Sm	FA	.139	57.60	25.80	4.72	.21	30.73	**36.50**
Cut pile, 46 oz.	Inst	SY	Lg	FA	.083	96.00	27.10	2.82	.13	30.05	**35.30**
	Inst	SY	Sm	FA	.139	57.60	30.80	4.72	.21	35.73	**42.30**
Wool	Inst	SY	Lg	FA	.083	96.00	54.30	2.82	.13	57.25	**66.50**
	Inst	SY	Sm	FA	.139	57.60	61.70	4.72	.21	66.63	**77.80**
Pad	Inst	SY	Lg	FA	.018	456.0	5.26	.61	---	5.87	**6.90**
	Inst	SY	Sm	FA	.029	273.6	5.98	.98	---	6.96	**8.25**
Premium quality											
Nylon, thick pile density	Inst	SY	Lg	FA	.083	96.00	48.10	2.82	.13	51.05	**59.40**
	Inst	SY	Sm	FA	.139	57.60	54.70	4.72	.21	59.63	**69.70**
Cut pile, 54 oz.	Inst	SY	Lg	FA	.083	96.00	40.90	2.82	.13	43.85	**51.10**
	Inst	SY	Sm	FA	.139	57.60	46.50	4.72	.21	51.43	**60.30**
Wool	Inst	SY	Lg	FA	.083	96.00	103.00	2.82	.13	105.95	**123.00**
	Inst	SY	Sm	FA	.139	57.60	117.00	4.72	.21	121.93	**142.00**
Decorator, floral or design	Inst	SY	Lg	FA	.160	50.00	124.00	5.43	.24	129.67	**150.00**
	Inst	SY	Sm	FA	.267	30.00	140.00	9.06	.40	149.46	**175.00**
Pad	Inst	SY	Lg	FA	.018	456.0	8.06	.61	---	8.67	**10.10**
	Inst	SY	Sm	FA	.029	273.6	9.16	.98	---	10.14	**11.90**
Steps											
Waterfall (wrap over nose)	Inst	Ea	Lg	FA	.100	80.00	5.70	3.39	---	9.09	**11.30**
	Inst	Ea	Sm	FA	.167	48.00	6.48	5.67	---	12.15	**15.40**
Tucked (under tread nose)	Inst	Ea	Lg	FA	.160	50.00	8.55	5.43	---	13.98	**17.40**
	Inst	Ea	Sm	FA	.267	30.00	9.72	9.06	---	18.78	**23.90**
Open Riser	Inst	Ea	Lg	FA	.267	30.00	15.20	9.06	---	24.26	**30.20**
	Inst	Ea	Sm	FA	.444	18.00	17.30	15.10	---	32.40	**41.00**
Cove or wall wrap											
4" high	Inst	LF	Lg	FA	.062	130.0	5.37	2.10	---	7.47	**9.12**
	Inst	LF	Sm	FA	.103	78.00	6.10	3.49	---	9.59	**11.90**
6" high	Inst	LF	Lg	FA	.067	120.0	6.18	2.27	---	8.45	**10.30**
	Inst	LF	Sm	FA	.111	72.00	7.02	3.77	---	10.79	**13.40**
8" high	Inst	LF	Lg	FA	.073	110.0	6.98	2.48	---	9.46	**11.50**
	Inst	LF	Sm	FA	.121	66.00	7.94	4.11	---	12.05	**14.90**

Description	Oper	Unit	Vol	Crew Size	Man-hours per Unit	Crew Output per Day	Avg Mat'l Unit Cost	Avg Labor Unit Cost	Avg Equip Unit Cost	Avg Total Unit Cost	Avg Price Incl O&P

Caulking

Material costs are typical costs for the listed bead diameters. Figures in parentheses, following bead diameter, indicate approximate coverage including 5% waste. Labor costs are per LF of bead length and assume good quality application on smooth to slightly irregular surfaces

Multi-purpose caulk, good quality

Description	Oper	Unit	Vol	Crew Size	Man-hours per Unit	Crew Output per Day	Avg Mat'l Unit Cost	Avg Labor Unit Cost	Avg Equip Unit Cost	Avg Total Unit Cost	Avg Price Incl O&P
1/8" (11.6 LF/fluid oz.)	Inst	LF	Lg	CA	.018	445.0	.02	.67	---	.69	.96
	Inst	LF	Sm	CA	.024	333.8	.02	.89	---	.91	1.27
1/4" (2.91 LF/fluid oz.)	Inst	LF	Lg	CA	.025	320.0	.07	.93	---	1.00	1.38
	Inst	LF	Sm	CA	.033	240.0	.08	1.22	---	1.30	1.80
3/8" (1.29 LF/fluid oz.)	Inst	LF	Lg	CA	.030	265.0	.16	1.11	---	1.27	1.74
	Inst	LF	Sm	CA	.040	198.8	.18	1.48	---	1.66	2.28
1/2" (.729 LF/fluid oz.)	Inst	LF	Lg	CA	.033	240.0	.28	1.22	---	1.50	2.03
	Inst	LF	Sm	CA	.044	180.0	.30	1.63	---	1.93	2.63

Butyl flex caulk, premium quality

Description	Oper	Unit	Vol	Crew Size	Man-hours per Unit	Crew Output per Day	Avg Mat'l Unit Cost	Avg Labor Unit Cost	Avg Equip Unit Cost	Avg Total Unit Cost	Avg Price Incl O&P
1/8" (11.6 LF/fluid oz.)	Inst	LF	Lg	CA	.018	445.0	.07	.67	---	.74	1.01
	Inst	LF	Sm	CA	.024	333.8	.08	.89	---	.97	1.34
1/4" (2.91 LF/fluid oz.)	Inst	LF	Lg	CA	.025	320.0	.28	.93	---	1.21	1.62
	Inst	LF	Sm	CA	.033	240.0	.30	1.22	---	1.52	2.06
3/8" (1.29 LF/fluid oz.)	Inst	LF	Lg	CA	.030	265.0	.62	1.11	---	1.73	2.27
	Inst	LF	Sm	CA	.040	198.8	.68	1.48	---	2.16	2.86
1/2" (.729 LF/fluid oz.)	Inst	LF	Lg	CA	.033	240.0	1.10	1.22	---	2.32	2.98
	Inst	LF	Sm	CA	.044	180.0	1.21	1.63	---	2.84	3.67

Latex, premium quality

Description	Oper	Unit	Vol	Crew Size	Man-hours per Unit	Crew Output per Day	Avg Mat'l Unit Cost	Avg Labor Unit Cost	Avg Equip Unit Cost	Avg Total Unit Cost	Avg Price Incl O&P
1/8" (11.6 LF/fluid oz.)	Inst	LF	Lg	CA	.018	445.0	.04	.67	---	.71	.98
	Inst	LF	Sm	CA	.024	333.8	.04	.89	---	.93	1.29
1/4" (2.91 LF/fluid oz.)	Inst	LF	Lg	CA	.025	320.0	.14	.93	---	1.07	1.46
	Inst	LF	Sm	CA	.033	240.0	.16	1.22	---	1.38	1.89
3/8" (1.29 LF/fluid oz.)	Inst	LF	Lg	CA	.030	265.0	.33	1.11	---	1.44	1.93
	Inst	LF	Sm	CA	.040	198.8	.36	1.48	---	1.84	2.49
1/2" (.729 LF/fluid oz.)	Inst	LF	Lg	CA	.033	240.0	.57	1.22	---	1.79	2.37
	Inst	LF	Sm	CA	.044	180.0	.63	1.63	---	2.26	3.01

Latex caulk, good quality

Description	Oper	Unit	Vol	Crew Size	Man-hours per Unit	Crew Output per Day	Avg Mat'l Unit Cost	Avg Labor Unit Cost	Avg Equip Unit Cost	Avg Total Unit Cost	Avg Price Incl O&P
1/8" (11.6 LF/fluid oz.)	Inst	LF	Lg	CA	.018	445.0	.02	.67	---	.69	.96
	Inst	LF	Sm	CA	.024	333.8	.02	.89	---	.91	1.27
1/4" (2.91 LF/fluid oz.)	Inst	LF	Lg	CA	.025	320.0	.08	.93	---	1.01	1.39
	Inst	LF	Sm	CA	.033	240.0	.09	1.22	---	1.31	1.81
3/8" (1.29 LF/fluid oz.)	Inst	LF	Lg	CA	.030	265.0	.18	1.11	---	1.29	1.76
	Inst	LF	Sm	CA	.040	198.8	.20	1.48	---	1.68	2.30
1/2" (.729 LF/fluid oz.)	Inst	LF	Lg	CA	.033	240.0	.33	1.22	---	1.55	2.09
	Inst	LF	Sm	CA	.044	180.0	.36	1.63	---	1.99	2.69

Description	Oper	Unit	Vol	Crew Size	Man-hours per Unit	Crew Output per Day	Avg Mat'l Unit Cost	Avg Labor Unit Cost	Avg Equip Unit Cost	Avg Total Unit Cost	Avg Price Incl O&P
Oil base caulk, good quality											
1/8" (11.6 LF/fluid oz.)	Inst	LF	Lg	CA	.018	445.0	.04	.67	---	.71	.98
	Inst	LF	Sm	CA	.024	333.8	.04	.89	---	.93	1.29
1/4" (2.91 LF/fluid oz.)	Inst	LF	Lg	CA	.025	320.0	.17	.93	---	1.10	1.49
	Inst	LF	Sm	CA	.033	240.0	.19	1.22	---	1.41	1.93
3/8" (1.29 LF/fluid oz.)	Inst	LF	Lg	CA	.030	265.0	.40	1.11	---	1.51	2.01
	Inst	LF	Sm	CA	.040	198.8	.44	1.48	---	1.92	2.58
1/2" (.729 LF/fluid oz.)	Inst	LF	Lg	CA	.033	240.0	.69	1.22	---	1.91	2.50
	Inst	LF	Sm	CA	.044	180.0	.76	1.63	---	2.39	3.15
Oil base caulk, economy quality											
1/8" (11.6 LF/fluid oz.)	Inst	LF	Lg	CA	.018	445.0	.02	.67	---	.69	.96
	Inst	LF	Sm	CA	.024	333.8	.02	.89	---	.91	1.27
1/4" (2.91 LF/fluid oz.)	Inst	LF	Lg	CA	.025	320.0	.09	.93	---	1.02	1.40
	Inst	LF	Sm	CA	.033	240.0	.10	1.22	---	1.32	1.83
3/8" (1.29 LF/fluid oz.)	Inst	LF	Lg	CA	.030	265.0	.19	1.11	---	1.30	1.77
	Inst	LF	Sm	CA	.040	198.8	.21	1.48	---	1.69	2.31
1/2" (.729 LF/fluid oz.)	Inst	LF	Lg	CA	.033	240.0	.35	1.22	---	1.57	2.11
	Inst	LF	Sm	CA	.044	180.0	.38	1.63	---	2.01	2.72
Silicone caulk, good quality											
1/8" (11.6 LF/fluid oz.)	Inst	LF	Lg	CA	.018	445.0	.05	.67	---	.72	.99
	Inst	LF	Sm	CA	.024	333.8	.06	.89	---	.95	1.31
1/4" (2.91 LF/fluid oz.)	Inst	LF	Lg	CA	.025	320.0	.21	.93	---	1.14	1.54
	Inst	LF	Sm	CA	.033	240.0	.24	1.22	---	1.46	1.99
3/8" (1.29 LF/fluid oz.)	Inst	LF	Lg	CA	.030	265.0	.49	1.11	---	1.60	2.12
	Inst	LF	Sm	CA	.040	198.8	.54	1.48	---	2.02	2.69
1/2" (.729 LF/fluid oz.)	Inst	LF	Lg	CA	.033	240.0	.87	1.22	---	2.09	2.71
	Inst	LF	Sm	CA	.044	180.0	.95	1.63	---	2.58	3.37
Silicone caulk, premium quality											
1/8" (11.6 LF/fluid oz.)	Inst	LF	Lg	CA	.018	445.0	.07	.67	---	.74	1.01
	Inst	LF	Sm	CA	.024	333.8	.08	.89	---	.97	1.34
1/4" (2.91 LF/fluid oz.)	Inst	LF	Lg	CA	.025	320.0	.29	.93	---	1.22	1.63
	Inst	LF	Sm	CA	.033	240.0	.31	1.22	---	1.53	2.07
3/8" (1.29 LF/fluid oz.)	Inst	LF	Lg	CA	.030	265.0	.64	1.11	---	1.75	2.29
	Inst	LF	Sm	CA	.040	198.8	.71	1.48	---	2.19	2.89
1/2" (.729 LF/fluid oz.)	Inst	LF	Lg	CA	.033	240.0	1.13	1.22	---	2.35	3.01
	Inst	LF	Sm	CA	.044	180.0	1.24	1.63	---	2.87	3.71
Tub caulk, white siliconized											
1/8" (11.6 LF/fluid oz.)	Inst	LF	Lg	CA	.018	445.0	.04	.67	---	.71	.98
	Inst	LF	Sm	CA	.024	333.8	.04	.89	---	.93	1.29
1/4" (2.91 LF/fluid oz.)	Inst	LF	Lg	CA	.025	320.0	.18	.93	---	1.11	1.50
	Inst	LF	Sm	CA	.033	240.0	.20	1.22	---	1.42	1.94
3/8" (1.29 LF/fluid oz.)	Inst	LF	Lg	CA	.030	265.0	.41	1.11	---	1.52	2.03
	Inst	LF	Sm	CA	.040	198.8	.45	1.48	---	1.93	2.59
1/2" (.729 LF/fluid oz.)	Inst	LF	Lg	CA	.033	240.0	.72	1.22	---	1.94	2.54
	Inst	LF	Sm	CA	.044	180.0	.80	1.63	---	2.43	3.20

Description	Oper	Unit	Vol	Crew Size	Man-hours per Unit	Crew Output per Day	Avg Mat'l Unit Cost	Avg Labor Unit Cost	Avg Equip Unit Cost	Avg Total Unit Cost	Avg Price Incl O&P
Anti-algae and mildew-resistant tub caulk, premium quality white or clear silicone											
1/8" (11.6 LF/fluid oz.)	Inst	LF	Lg	CA	.018	445.0	.07	.67	---	.74	**1.01**
	Inst	LF	Sm	CA	.024	333.8	.08	.89	---	.97	**1.34**
1/4" (2.91 LF/fluid oz.)	Inst	LF	Lg	CA	.025	320.0	.29	.93	---	1.22	**1.63**
	Inst	LF	Sm	CA	.033	240.0	.31	1.22	---	1.53	**2.07**
3/8" (1.29 LF/fluid oz.)	Inst	LF	Lg	CA	.030	265.0	.64	1.11	---	1.75	**2.29**
	Inst	LF	Sm	CA	.040	198.8	.71	1.48	---	2.19	**2.89**
1/2" (.729 LF/fluid oz.)	Inst	LF	Lg	CA	.033	240.0	1.13	1.22	---	2.35	**3.01**
	Inst	LF	Sm	CA	.044	180.0	1.24	1.63	---	2.87	**3.71**
Elastomeric caulk, premium quality											
1/8" (11.6 LF/fluid oz.)	Inst	LF	Lg	CA	.018	445.0	.07	.67	---	.74	**1.01**
	Inst	LF	Sm	CA	.024	333.8	.08	.89	---	.97	**1.34**
1/4" (2.91 LF/fluid oz.)	Inst	LF	Lg	CA	.025	320.0	.28	.93	---	1.21	**1.62**
	Inst	LF	Sm	CA	.033	240.0	.30	1.22	---	1.52	**2.06**
3/8" (1.29 LF/fluid oz.)	Inst	LF	Lg	CA	.030	265.0	.62	1.11	---	1.73	**2.27**
	Inst	LF	Sm	CA	.040	198.8	.68	1.48	---	2.16	**2.86**
1/2" (.729 LF/fluid oz.)	Inst	LF	Lg	CA	.033	240.0	1.10	1.22	---	2.32	**2.98**
	Inst	LF	Sm	CA	.044	180.0	1.21	1.63	---	2.84	**3.67**
Add for irregular surfaces such as vertical masonry or lap siding											
	Inst	%	Lg	CA	---	---	5.0	---	---	5.0	---
	Inst	%	Sm	CA	---	---	5.0	---	---	5.0	---
Caulking gun, contractor grade, heavy duty, battery operated											
	Inst	Ea	Lg	CA	---	---	40.80	---	---	40.80	**46.90**
	Inst	Ea	Sm	CA	---	---	44.80	---	---	44.80	**51.50**
Caulking gun, heavy duty											
	Inst	Ea	Lg	CA	---	---	14.30	---	---	14.30	**16.40**
	Inst	Ea	Sm	CA	---	---	15.70	---	---	15.70	**18.00**
Caulking gun, economy grade											
	Inst	Ea	Lg	CA	---	---	6.71	---	---	6.71	**7.72**
	Inst	Ea	Sm	CA	---	---	7.37	---	---	7.37	**8.48**

Ceramic tile

1. **Dimensions.** There are many sizes of ceramic tile. Only 4¹⁄₄" x 4¹⁄₄" and 1" x 1" will be discussed here.

    a. 4¹⁄₄" x 4¹⁄₄" tile is furnished both unmounted and back-mounted. Back-mounted tile are usually furnished in sheets of 12 tile.

    b. 1" x 1" mosaic tile is furnished face-mounted and back-mounted in sheets; normally, 2'-0" x 1'-0".

2. **Installation.** There are three methods:

    a. Conventional, which uses portland cement, sand and wet tile grout.

    b. Dry-set, which uses dry-set mix and dry tile grout mix.

    c. Organic adhesive, which uses adhesive and dry tile grout mix.

    The conventional method is the most expensive and is used less frequently than the other methods.

3. **Estimating Technique.** For tile, determine the area and add 5% to 10% for waste. For cove, base or trim, determine the length in linear feet and add 5% to 10% for waste.

*This installation would be similar if wall finish above tile wainscot were of other material such as wallboard, plywood, etc.

Wood or steel construction with plaster above tile wainscot

Courtesy: *Ceramic Tile Institute of America* 700 N. Virgil Ave., Ste 300, Los Angeles, CA 90029

Cross section of bathtub wall using cement mortar

Wood or steel construction with solid covered backing

Description	Oper	Unit	Vol	Crew Size	Man-hours per Unit	Crew Output per Day	Avg Mat'l Unit Cost	Avg Labor Unit Cost	Avg Equip Unit Cost	Avg Total Unit Cost	Avg Price Incl O&P

Ceramic tile

Countertop/backsplash

Adhesive set with backmounted tile

Description	Oper	Unit	Vol	Crew Size	Man-hours per Unit	Crew Output per Day	Avg Mat'l Unit Cost	Avg Labor Unit Cost	Avg Equip Unit Cost	Avg Total Unit Cost	Avg Price Incl O&P
1" x 1"	Inst	SF	Lg	TB	.229	70.00	6.91	7.10	---	14.01	**18.00**
	Inst	SF	Sm	TB	.381	42.00	7.58	11.80	---	19.38	**25.50**
4-1/4" x 4-1/4"	Inst	SF	Lg	TB	.200	80.00	5.52	6.20	---	11.72	**15.20**
	Inst	SF	Sm	TB	.333	48.00	6.05	10.30	---	16.35	**21.60**

Cove/base

Adhesive set with unmounted tile

Description	Oper	Unit	Vol	Crew Size	Man-hours per Unit	Crew Output per Day	Avg Mat'l Unit Cost	Avg Labor Unit Cost	Avg Equip Unit Cost	Avg Total Unit Cost	Avg Price Incl O&P
4-1/4" x 4-1/4"	Inst	LF	Lg	TB	.200	80.00	5.31	6.20	---	11.51	**14.90**
	Inst	LF	Sm	TB	.333	48.00	5.82	10.30	---	16.12	**21.40**
6" x 4-1/4"	Inst	LF	Lg	TB	.168	95.00	5.18	5.21	---	10.39	**13.40**
	Inst	LF	Sm	TB	.281	57.00	5.68	8.72	---	14.40	**18.90**

Conventional mortar set with unmounted tile

Description	Oper	Unit	Vol	Crew Size	Man-hours per Unit	Crew Output per Day	Avg Mat'l Unit Cost	Avg Labor Unit Cost	Avg Equip Unit Cost	Avg Total Unit Cost	Avg Price Incl O&P
4-1/4" x 4-1/4"	Inst	LF	Lg	TB	.356	45.00	5.21	11.00	---	16.21	**21.70**
	Inst	LF	Sm	TB	.593	27.00	5.71	18.40	---	24.11	**32.70**
6" x 4-1/4"	Inst	LF	Lg	TB	.320	50.00	5.03	9.93	---	14.96	**19.90**
	Inst	LF	Sm	TB	.533	30.00	5.52	16.50	---	22.02	**29.80**

Dry-set mortar with unmounted tile

Description	Oper	Unit	Vol	Crew Size	Man-hours per Unit	Crew Output per Day	Avg Mat'l Unit Cost	Avg Labor Unit Cost	Avg Equip Unit Cost	Avg Total Unit Cost	Avg Price Incl O&P
4-1/4" x 4-1/4"	Inst	LF	Lg	TB	.246	65.00	5.22	7.63	---	12.85	**16.80**
	Inst	LF	Sm	TB	.410	39.00	5.73	12.70	---	18.43	**24.70**
6" x 4-1/4"	Inst	LF	Lg	TB	.213	75.00	5.06	6.61	---	11.67	**15.20**
	Inst	LF	Sm	TB	.356	45.00	5.55	11.00	---	16.55	**22.10**

Floors

1-1/2" x 1-1/2"

Description	Oper	Unit	Vol	Crew Size	Man-hours per Unit	Crew Output per Day	Avg Mat'l Unit Cost	Avg Labor Unit Cost	Avg Equip Unit Cost	Avg Total Unit Cost	Avg Price Incl O&P
Adhesive or dry-set base	Demo	SF	Lg	LB	.029	550.0	---	.87	---	.87	**1.22**
	Demo	SF	Sm	LB	.048	330.0	---	1.44	---	1.44	**2.02**
Conventional mortar base	Demo	SF	Lg	LB	.034	475.0	---	1.02	---	1.02	**1.43**
	Demo	SF	Sm	LB	.056	285.0	---	1.68	---	1.68	**2.35**

Adhesive set with backmounted tile

Description	Oper	Unit	Vol	Crew Size	Man-hours per Unit	Crew Output per Day	Avg Mat'l Unit Cost	Avg Labor Unit Cost	Avg Equip Unit Cost	Avg Total Unit Cost	Avg Price Incl O&P
1-1/2" x 1-1/2"	Inst	SF	Lg	TB	.133	120.0	6.91	4.13	---	11.04	**13.80**
	Inst	SF	Sm	TB	.222	72.00	7.58	6.89	---	14.47	**18.50**
4-1/4" x 4-1/4"	Inst	SF	Lg	TB	.123	130.0	5.52	3.82	---	9.34	**11.80**
	Inst	SF	Sm	TB	.205	78.00	6.05	6.36	---	12.41	**16.00**

Conventional mortar set with backmounted tile

Description	Oper	Unit	Vol	Crew Size	Man-hours per Unit	Crew Output per Day	Avg Mat'l Unit Cost	Avg Labor Unit Cost	Avg Equip Unit Cost	Avg Total Unit Cost	Avg Price Incl O&P
1-1/2" x 1-1/2"	Inst	SF	Lg	TB	.267	60.00	6.60	8.28	---	14.88	**19.40**
	Inst	SF	Sm	TB	.444	36.00	7.24	13.80	---	21.04	**27.90**
4-1/4" x 4-1/4"	Inst	SF	Lg	TB	.229	70.00	5.23	7.10	---	12.33	**16.10**
	Inst	SF	Sm	TB	.381	42.00	5.74	11.80	---	17.54	**23.40**

Dry-set mortar with backmounted tile

Description	Oper	Unit	Vol	Crew Size	Man-hours per Unit	Crew Output per Day	Avg Mat'l Unit Cost	Avg Labor Unit Cost	Avg Equip Unit Cost	Avg Total Unit Cost	Avg Price Incl O&P
1-1/2" x 1-1/2"	Inst	SF	Lg	TB	.168	95.00	6.66	5.21	---	11.87	**15.10**
	Inst	SF	Sm	TB	.281	57.00	7.30	8.72	---	16.02	**20.80**
4-1/4" x 4-1/4"	Inst	SF	Lg	TB	.152	105.0	5.27	4.72	---	9.99	**12.80**
	Inst	SF	Sm	TB	.254	63.00	5.78	7.88	---	13.66	**17.80**

Description	Oper	Unit	Vol	Crew Size	Man-hours per Unit	Crew Output per Day	Avg Mat'l Unit Cost	Avg Labor Unit Cost	Avg Equip Unit Cost	Avg Total Unit Cost	Avg Price Incl O&P

Wainscot cap

Adhesive set with unmounted tile

2" x 6"	Inst	LF	Lg	TB	.133	120.0	2.70	4.13	---	6.83	**8.96**
	Inst	LF	Sm	TB	.222	72.00	2.96	6.89	---	9.85	**13.20**

Conventional mortar set with unmounted tile

2" x 6"	Inst	LF	Lg	TB	.213	75.00	2.65	6.61	---	9.26	**12.40**
	Inst	LF	Sm	TB	.356	45.00	2.91	11.00	---	13.91	**19.00**

Dry-set mortar with unmounted tile

2" x 6"	Inst	LF	Lg	TB	.160	100.0	2.65	4.96	---	7.61	**10.10**
	Inst	LF	Sm	TB	.267	60.00	2.91	8.28	---	11.19	**15.10**

Walls, 1-1/2" x 1-1/2" or 4-1/4" x 4-1/4"

Adhesive or dry-set base

	Demo	SF	Lg	LB	.033	480.0	---	.99	---	.99	**1.39**
	Demo	SF	Sm	LB	.056	288.0	---	1.68	---	1.68	**2.35**

Conventional mortar base

	Demo	SF	Lg	LB	.040	400.0	---	1.20	---	1.20	**1.68**
	Demo	SF	Sm	LB	.067	240.0	---	2.01	---	2.01	**2.81**

Adhesive set with backmounted tile

1-1/2" x 1-1/2"	Inst	SF	Lg	TB	.160	100.0	6.91	4.96	---	11.87	**15.00**
	Inst	SF	Sm	TB	.267	60.00	7.58	8.28	---	15.86	**20.50**
4-1/4" x 4-1/4"	Inst	SF	Lg	TB	.145	110.0	5.52	4.50	---	10.02	**12.70**
	Inst	SF	Sm	TB	.242	66.00	6.05	7.51	---	13.56	**17.60**

Conventional mortar set with backmounted tile

1-1/2" x 1-1/2"	Inst	SF	Lg	TB	.320	50.00	6.60	9.93	---	16.53	**21.70**
	Inst	SF	Sm	TB	.533	30.00	7.24	16.50	---	23.74	**31.80**
4-1/4" x 4-1/4"	Inst	SF	Lg	TB	.267	60.00	5.23	8.28	---	13.51	**17.80**
	Inst	SF	Sm	TB	.444	36.00	5.74	13.80	---	19.54	**26.20**

Dry-set mortar with backmounted tile

1-1/2" x 1-1/2"	Inst	SF	Lg	TB	.200	80.00	6.66	6.20	---	12.86	**16.50**
	Inst	SF	Sm	TB	.333	48.00	7.30	10.30	---	17.60	**23.10**
4-1/4" x 4-1/4"	Inst	SF	Lg	TB	.178	90.00	5.27	5.52	---	10.79	**13.90**
	Inst	SF	Sm	TB	.296	54.00	5.78	9.18	---	14.96	**19.70**

Related Materials

Cement backer board

1/4" thick	Inst	SF	Lg	TB	.017	960.0	.76	.53	---	1.29	**1.62**
	Inst	SF	Sm	TB	.028	576.0	.82	.87	---	1.69	**2.18**
1/2" thick	Inst	SF	Lg	TB	.019	864.0	.83	.59	---	1.42	**1.79**
	Inst	SF	Sm	TB	.031	518.4	.86	.96	---	1.82	**2.35**

Description	Oper	Unit	Vol	Crew Size	Man-hours per Unit	Crew Output per Day	Avg Mat'l Unit Cost	Avg Labor Unit Cost	Avg Equip Unit Cost	Avg Total Unit Cost	Avg Price Incl O&P

Closet door systems

Labor costs include hanging and fitting of doors and hardware

Bi-folding units

Includes hardware and pine fascia trim

Unfinished

Birch, flush face, 1-3/8" T, hollow core

Description	Oper	Unit	Vol	Crew Size	Man-hours per Unit	Crew Output per Day	Avg Mat'l Unit Cost	Avg Labor Unit Cost	Avg Equip Unit Cost	Avg Total Unit Cost	Avg Price Incl O&P
2'-0" x 6'-8", 2 doors	Inst	Set	Lg	2C	1.60	10.00	50.00	59.20	---	109.20	**140.00**
	Inst	Set	Sm	2C	2.46	6.50	57.20	91.10	---	148.30	**193.00**
2'-6" x 6'-8", 2 doors	Inst	Set	Lg	2C	1.60	10.00	55.60	59.20	---	114.80	**147.00**
	Inst	Set	Sm	2C	2.46	6.50	63.50	91.10	---	154.60	**201.00**
3'-0" x 6'-8", 2 doors	Inst	Set	Lg	2C	1.60	10.00	65.60	59.20	---	124.80	**158.00**
	Inst	Set	Sm	2C	2.46	6.50	75.00	91.10	---	166.10	**214.00**
4'-0" x 6'-8", 4 doors	Inst	Set	Lg	2C	2.00	8.00	100.00	74.00	---	174.00	**219.00**
	Inst	Set	Sm	2C	3.08	5.20	114.00	114.00	---	228.00	**291.00**
6'-0" x 6'-8", 4 doors	Inst	Set	Lg	2C	2.00	8.00	111.00	74.00	---	185.00	**231.00**
	Inst	Set	Sm	2C	3.08	5.20	127.00	114.00	---	241.00	**306.00**
8'-0" x 6'-8", 4 doors	Inst	Set	Lg	2C	2.00	8.00	131.00	74.00	---	205.00	**255.00**
	Inst	Set	Sm	2C	3.08	5.20	150.00	114.00	---	264.00	**332.00**
4'-0" x 8'-0", 4 doors	Inst	Set	Lg	2C	2.00	8.00	120.00	74.00	---	194.00	**242.00**
	Inst	Set	Sm	2C	3.08	5.20	137.00	114.00	---	251.00	**317.00**
6'-0" x 8'-0", 4 doors	Inst	Set	Lg	2C	2.00	8.00	133.00	74.00	---	207.00	**257.00**
	Inst	Set	Sm	2C	3.08	5.20	152.00	114.00	---	266.00	**335.00**
8'-0" x 8'-0", 4 doors	Inst	Set	Lg	2C	2.00	8.00	157.00	74.00	---	231.00	**285.00**
	Inst	Set	Sm	2C	3.08	5.20	180.00	114.00	---	294.00	**367.00**

Lauan, flush face, 1-3/8" T, hollow core

Description	Oper	Unit	Vol	Crew Size	Man-hours per Unit	Crew Output per Day	Avg Mat'l Unit Cost	Avg Labor Unit Cost	Avg Equip Unit Cost	Avg Total Unit Cost	Avg Price Incl O&P
2'-0" x 6'-8", 2 doors	Inst	Set	Lg	2C	1.60	10.00	38.30	59.20	---	97.50	**127.00**
	Inst	Set	Sm	2C	2.46	6.50	43.70	91.10	---	134.80	**178.00**
2'-6" x 6'-8", 2 doors	Inst	Set	Lg	2C	1.60	10.00	42.50	59.20	---	101.70	**132.00**
	Inst	Set	Sm	2C	2.46	6.50	48.60	91.10	---	139.70	**183.00**
3'-0" x 6'-8", 2 doors	Inst	Set	Lg	2C	1.60	10.00	50.20	59.20	---	109.40	**141.00**
	Inst	Set	Sm	2C	2.46	6.50	57.40	91.10	---	148.50	**193.00**
4'-0" x 6'-8", 4 doors	Inst	Set	Lg	2C	2.00	8.00	76.60	74.00	---	150.60	**192.00**
	Inst	Set	Sm	2C	3.08	5.20	87.50	114.00	---	201.50	**260.00**
6'-0" x 6'-8", 4 doors	Inst	Set	Lg	2C	2.00	8.00	85.10	74.00	---	159.10	**201.00**
	Inst	Set	Sm	2C	3.08	5.20	97.20	114.00	---	211.20	**271.00**
8'-0" x 6'-8", 4 doors	Inst	Set	Lg	2C	2.00	8.00	100.00	74.00	---	174.00	**219.00**
	Inst	Set	Sm	2C	3.08	5.20	115.00	114.00	---	229.00	**292.00**
4'-0" x 8'-0", 4 doors	Inst	Set	Lg	2C	2.00	8.00	91.90	74.00	---	165.90	**209.00**
	Inst	Set	Sm	2C	3.08	5.20	105.00	114.00	---	219.00	**280.00**
6'-0" x 8'-0", 4 doors	Inst	Set	Lg	2C	2.00	8.00	102.00	74.00	---	176.00	**221.00**
	Inst	Set	Sm	2C	3.08	5.20	117.00	114.00	---	231.00	**294.00**
8'-0" x 8'-0", 4 doors	Inst	Set	Lg	2C	2.00	8.00	120.00	74.00	---	194.00	**242.00**
	Inst	Set	Sm	2C	3.08	5.20	138.00	114.00	---	252.00	**318.00**

Description	Oper	Unit	Vol	Crew Size	Man-hours per Unit	Crew Output per Day	Avg Mat'l Unit Cost	Avg Labor Unit Cost	Avg Equip Unit Cost	Avg Total Unit Cost	Avg Price Incl O&P
Ponderosa pine, colonial raised panel (2/door), 1-3/8" T, solid core											
2'-0" x 6'-8", 2 doors	Inst	Set	Lg	2C	1.60	10.00	159.00	59.20	---	218.20	**265.00**
	Inst	Set	Sm	2C	2.46	6.50	181.00	91.10	---	272.10	**336.00**
4'-0" x 6'-8", 4 doors	Inst	Set	Lg	2C	2.00	8.00	318.00	74.00	---	392.00	**470.00**
	Inst	Set	Sm	2C	3.08	5.20	364.00	114.00	---	478.00	**578.00**
6'-0" x 6'-8", 4 doors	Inst	Set	Lg	2C	2.00	8.00	375.00	74.00	---	449.00	**535.00**
	Inst	Set	Sm	2C	3.08	5.20	429.00	114.00	---	543.00	**653.00**
8'-0" x 6'-8", 4 doors	Inst	Set	Lg	2C	2.00	8.00	443.00	74.00	---	517.00	**613.00**
	Inst	Set	Sm	2C	3.08	5.20	506.00	114.00	---	620.00	**742.00**
Ponderosa pine, raised panel louver, 1-3/8" T, solid core											
2'-0" x 6'-8", 2 doors	Inst	Set	Lg	2C	1.60	10.00	92.40	59.20	---	151.60	**189.00**
	Inst	Set	Sm	2C	2.46	6.50	106.00	91.10	---	197.10	**249.00**
4'-0" x 6'-8", 4 doors	Inst	Set	Lg	2C	2.00	8.00	185.00	74.00	---	259.00	**316.00**
	Inst	Set	Sm	2C	3.08	5.20	211.00	114.00	---	325.00	**403.00**
6'-0" x 6'-8", 4 doors	Inst	Set	Lg	2C	2.00	8.00	218.00	74.00	---	292.00	**354.00**
	Inst	Set	Sm	2C	3.08	5.20	249.00	114.00	---	363.00	**446.00**
Colonist style, raised panel, 1-3/8" T, hollow core											
2'-0" x 6'-8", 2 doors	Inst	Set	Lg	2C	1.60	10.00	46.00	59.20	---	105.20	**136.00**
	Inst	Set	Sm	2C	2.46	6.50	52.60	91.10	---	143.70	**188.00**
2'-6" x 6'-8", 2 doors	Inst	Set	Lg	2C	1.60	10.00	51.20	59.20	---	110.40	**142.00**
	Inst	Set	Sm	2C	2.46	6.50	58.50	91.10	---	149.60	**195.00**
3'-0" x 6'-8", 2 doors	Inst	Set	Lg	2C	1.60	10.00	60.40	59.20	---	119.60	**152.00**
	Inst	Set	Sm	2C	2.46	6.50	69.00	91.10	---	160.10	**207.00**
4'-0" x 6'-8", 4 doors	Inst	Set	Lg	2C	2.00	8.00	92.10	74.00	---	166.10	**210.00**
	Inst	Set	Sm	2C	3.08	5.20	105.00	114.00	---	219.00	**281.00**
6'-0" x 6'-8", 4 doors	Inst	Set	Lg	2C	2.00	8.00	102.00	74.00	---	176.00	**221.00**
	Inst	Set	Sm	2C	3.08	5.20	117.00	114.00	---	231.00	**294.00**
8'-0" x 6'-8", 4 doors	Inst	Set	Lg	2C	2.00	8.00	121.00	74.00	---	195.00	**243.00**
	Inst	Set	Sm	2C	3.08	5.20	138.00	114.00	---	252.00	**318.00**
4'-0" x 8'-0", 4 doors	Inst	Set	Lg	2C	2.00	8.00	111.00	74.00	---	185.00	**231.00**
	Inst	Set	Sm	2C	3.08	5.20	126.00	114.00	---	240.00	**305.00**
6'-0" x 8'-0", 4 doors	Inst	Set	Lg	2C	2.00	8.00	123.00	74.00	---	197.00	**245.00**
	Inst	Set	Sm	2C	3.08	5.20	140.00	114.00	---	254.00	**321.00**
8'-0" x 8'-0", 4 doors	Inst	Set	Lg	2C	2.00	8.00	145.00	74.00	---	219.00	**270.00**
	Inst	Set	Sm	2C	3.08	5.20	166.00	114.00	---	280.00	**350.00**
Ash, flush face, 1-3/8" T, hollow core											
2'-0" x 6'-8", 2 doors	Inst	Set	Lg	2C	1.60	10.00	94.50	59.20	---	153.70	**192.00**
	Inst	Set	Sm	2C	2.46	6.50	108.00	91.10	---	199.10	**252.00**
2'-6" x 6'-8", 2 doors	Inst	Set	Lg	2C	1.60	10.00	105.00	59.20	---	164.20	**204.00**
	Inst	Set	Sm	2C	2.46	6.50	120.00	91.10	---	211.10	**266.00**
3'-0" x 6'-8", 2 doors	Inst	Set	Lg	2C	1.60	10.00	124.00	59.20	---	183.20	**225.00**
	Inst	Set	Sm	2C	2.46	6.50	142.00	91.10	---	233.10	**290.00**
4'-0" x 6'-8", 4 doors	Inst	Set	Lg	2C	2.00	8.00	189.00	74.00	---	263.00	**321.00**
	Inst	Set	Sm	2C	3.08	5.20	216.00	114.00	---	330.00	**408.00**

Description	Oper	Unit	Vol	Crew Size	Man-hours per Unit	Crew Output per Day	Avg Mat'l Unit Cost	Avg Labor Unit Cost	Avg Equip Unit Cost	Avg Total Unit Cost	Avg Price Incl O&P
6'-0" x 6'-8", 4 doors	Inst	Set	Lg	2C	2.00	8.00	210.00	74.00	---	284.00	**345.00**
	Inst	Set	Sm	2C	3.08	5.20	240.00	114.00	---	354.00	**436.00**
8'-0" x 6'-8", 4 doors	Inst	Set	Lg	2C	2.00	8.00	248.00	74.00	---	322.00	**389.00**
	Inst	Set	Sm	2C	3.08	5.20	283.00	114.00	---	397.00	**485.00**
4'-0" x 8'-0", 4 doors	Inst	Set	Lg	2C	2.00	8.00	227.00	74.00	---	301.00	**364.00**
	Inst	Set	Sm	2C	3.08	5.20	259.00	114.00	---	373.00	**458.00**
6'-0" x 8'-0", 4 doors	Inst	Set	Lg	2C	2.00	8.00	252.00	74.00	---	326.00	**393.00**
	Inst	Set	Sm	2C	3.08	5.20	288.00	114.00	---	402.00	**491.00**
8'-0" x 8'-0", 4 doors	Inst	Set	Lg	2C	2.00	8.00	297.00	74.00	---	371.00	**446.00**
	Inst	Set	Sm	2C	3.08	5.20	340.00	114.00	---	454.00	**550.00**

Prefinished

Walnut tone, mar-resistant finish

Embossed (distressed wood appearance) lauan, flush face, 1-3/8" T, hollow core

Description	Oper	Unit	Vol	Crew Size	Man-hours per Unit	Crew Output per Day	Avg Mat'l Unit Cost	Avg Labor Unit Cost	Avg Equip Unit Cost	Avg Total Unit Cost	Avg Price Incl O&P
2'-0" x 6'-8", 2 doors	Inst	Set	Lg	2C	1.60	10.00	62.00	59.20	---	121.20	**154.00**
	Inst	Set	Sm	2C	2.46	6.50	70.80	91.10	---	161.90	**209.00**
4'-0" x 6'-8", 4 doors	Inst	Set	Lg	2C	2.00	8.00	124.00	74.00	---	198.00	**246.00**
	Inst	Set	Sm	2C	3.08	5.20	142.00	114.00	---	256.00	**322.00**
6'-0" x 6'-8", 4 doors	Inst	Set	Lg	2C	2.00	8.00	163.00	74.00	---	237.00	**291.00**
	Inst	Set	Sm	2C	3.08	5.20	186.00	114.00	---	300.00	**374.00**

Lauan, flush face, 1-3/8" T, hollow core

Description	Oper	Unit	Vol	Crew Size	Man-hours per Unit	Crew Output per Day	Avg Mat'l Unit Cost	Avg Labor Unit Cost	Avg Equip Unit Cost	Avg Total Unit Cost	Avg Price Incl O&P
2'-0" x 6'-8", 2 doors	Inst	Set	Lg	2C	1.60	10.00	69.30	59.20	---	128.50	**163.00**
	Inst	Set	Sm	2C	2.46	6.50	79.20	91.10	---	170.30	**219.00**
4'-0" x 6'-8", 4 doors	Inst	Set	Lg	2C	2.00	8.00	138.00	74.00	---	212.00	**262.00**
	Inst	Set	Sm	2C	3.08	5.20	157.00	114.00	---	271.00	**340.00**
6'-0" x 6'-8", 4 doors	Inst	Set	Lg	2C	2.00	8.00	185.00	74.00	---	259.00	**316.00**
	Inst	Set	Sm	2C	3.08	5.20	211.00	114.00	---	325.00	**403.00**

Ponderosa pine, full louver, 1-3/8" T, hollow core

Description	Oper	Unit	Vol	Crew Size	Man-hours per Unit	Crew Output per Day	Avg Mat'l Unit Cost	Avg Labor Unit Cost	Avg Equip Unit Cost	Avg Total Unit Cost	Avg Price Incl O&P
2'-0" x 6'-8", 2 doors	Inst	Set	Lg	2C	1.60	10.00	144.00	59.20	---	203.20	**248.00**
	Inst	Set	Sm	2C	2.46	6.50	164.00	91.10	---	255.10	**317.00**
4'-0" x 6'-8", 4 doors	Inst	Set	Lg	2C	2.00	8.00	281.00	74.00	---	355.00	**427.00**
	Inst	Set	Sm	2C	3.08	5.20	322.00	114.00	---	436.00	**529.00**
6'-0" x 6'-8", 4 doors	Inst	Set	Lg	2C	2.00	8.00	358.00	74.00	---	432.00	**515.00**
	Inst	Set	Sm	2C	3.08	5.20	409.00	114.00	---	523.00	**630.00**

Ponderosa pine, raised louver, 1-3/8" T, hollow core

Description	Oper	Unit	Vol	Crew Size	Man-hours per Unit	Crew Output per Day	Avg Mat'l Unit Cost	Avg Labor Unit Cost	Avg Equip Unit Cost	Avg Total Unit Cost	Avg Price Incl O&P
2'-0" x 6'-8", 2 doors	Inst	Set	Lg	2C	1.60	10.00	152.00	59.20	---	211.20	**258.00**
	Inst	Set	Sm	2C	2.46	6.50	174.00	91.10	---	265.10	**328.00**
4'-0" x 6'-8", 4 doors	Inst	Set	Lg	2C	2.00	8.00	297.00	74.00	---	371.00	**445.00**
	Inst	Set	Sm	2C	3.08	5.20	340.00	114.00	---	454.00	**550.00**
6'-0" x 6'-8", 4 doors	Inst	Set	Lg	2C	2.00	8.00	358.00	74.00	---	432.00	**515.00**
	Inst	Set	Sm	2C	3.08	5.20	409.00	114.00	---	523.00	**630.00**

Description	Oper	Unit	Vol	Crew Size	Man-hours per Unit	Crew Output per Day	Avg Mat'l Unit Cost	Avg Labor Unit Cost	Avg Equip Unit Cost	Avg Total Unit Cost	Avg Price Incl O&P

Sliding or bypassing units

Includes hardware, 4-5/8" jambs, header, and fascia

Wood inserts, 1-3/8" T, hollow core

Unfinished birch

Description	Oper	Unit	Vol	Crew Size	Man-hours per Unit	Crew Output per Day	Avg Mat'l Unit Cost	Avg Labor Unit Cost	Avg Equip Unit Cost	Avg Total Unit Cost	Avg Price Incl O&P
4'-0" x 6'-8", 2 doors	Inst	Set	Lg	2C	2.29	7.00	100.00	84.80	---	184.80	**234.00**
	Inst	Set	Sm	2C	3.52	4.55	115.00	130.00	---	245.00	**314.00**
6'-0" x 6'-8", 2 doors	Inst	Set	Lg	2C	2.29	7.00	111.00	84.80	---	195.80	**247.00**
	Inst	Set	Sm	2C	3.52	4.55	127.00	130.00	---	257.00	**329.00**
8'-0" x 6'-8", 2 doors	Inst	Set	Lg	2C	2.29	7.00	131.00	84.80	---	215.80	**270.00**
	Inst	Set	Sm	2C	3.52	4.55	150.00	130.00	---	280.00	**355.00**
4'-0" x 8'-0", 2 doors	Inst	Set	Lg	2C	2.29	7.00	120.00	84.80	---	204.80	**257.00**
	Inst	Set	Sm	2C	3.52	4.55	138.00	130.00	---	268.00	**341.00**
6'-0" x 8'-0", 2 doors	Inst	Set	Lg	2C	2.29	7.00	134.00	84.80	---	218.80	**272.00**
	Inst	Set	Sm	2C	3.52	4.55	153.00	130.00	---	283.00	**358.00**
8'-0" x 8'-0", 2 doors	Inst	Set	Lg	2C	2.29	7.00	158.00	84.80	---	242.80	**300.00**
	Inst	Set	Sm	2C	3.52	4.55	180.00	130.00	---	310.00	**390.00**
10'-0" x 6'-8", 3 doors	Inst	Set	Lg	2C	3.20	5.00	201.00	118.00	---	319.00	**396.00**
	Inst	Set	Sm	2C	4.92	3.25	229.00	182.00	---	411.00	**519.00**
12'-0" x 6'-8", 3 doors	Inst	Set	Lg	2C	3.20	5.00	223.00	118.00	---	341.00	**422.00**
	Inst	Set	Sm	2C	4.92	3.25	255.00	182.00	---	437.00	**548.00**
10'-0" x 8'-0", 3 doors	Inst	Set	Lg	2C	3.20	5.00	232.00	118.00	---	350.00	**432.00**
	Inst	Set	Sm	2C	4.92	3.25	265.00	182.00	---	447.00	**560.00**
12'-0" x 8'-0", 3 doors	Inst	Set	Lg	2C	3.20	5.00	241.00	118.00	---	359.00	**443.00**
	Inst	Set	Sm	2C	4.92	3.25	275.00	182.00	---	457.00	**571.00**

Unfinished hardboard

Description	Oper	Unit	Vol	Crew Size	Man-hours per Unit	Crew Output per Day	Avg Mat'l Unit Cost	Avg Labor Unit Cost	Avg Equip Unit Cost	Avg Total Unit Cost	Avg Price Incl O&P
4'-0" x 6'-8", 2 doors	Inst	Set	Lg	2C	2.29	7.00	74.50	84.80	---	159.30	**204.00**
	Inst	Set	Sm	2C	3.52	4.55	85.10	130.00	---	215.10	**280.00**
6'-0" x 6'-8", 2 doors	Inst	Set	Lg	2C	2.29	7.00	82.80	84.80	---	167.60	**214.00**
	Inst	Set	Sm	2C	3.52	4.55	94.60	130.00	---	224.60	**291.00**
8'-0" x 6'-8", 2 doors	Inst	Set	Lg	2C	2.29	7.00	97.70	84.80	---	182.50	**231.00**
	Inst	Set	Sm	2C	3.52	4.55	112.00	130.00	---	242.00	**311.00**
4'-0" x 8'-0", 2 doors	Inst	Set	Lg	2C	2.29	7.00	89.40	84.80	---	174.20	**222.00**
	Inst	Set	Sm	2C	3.52	4.55	102.00	130.00	---	232.00	**300.00**
6'-0" x 8'-0", 2 doors	Inst	Set	Lg	2C	2.29	7.00	99.30	84.80	---	184.10	**233.00**
	Inst	Set	Sm	2C	3.52	4.55	114.00	130.00	---	244.00	**313.00**
8'-0" x 8'-0", 2 doors	Inst	Set	Lg	2C	2.29	7.00	117.00	84.80	---	201.80	**253.00**
	Inst	Set	Sm	2C	3.52	4.55	134.00	130.00	---	264.00	**336.00**
10'-0" x 6'-8", 3 doors	Inst	Set	Lg	2C	3.20	5.00	149.00	118.00	---	267.00	**337.00**
	Inst	Set	Sm	2C	4.92	3.25	170.00	182.00	---	352.00	**451.00**
12'-0" x 6'-8", 3 doors	Inst	Set	Lg	2C	3.20	5.00	166.00	118.00	---	284.00	**356.00**
	Inst	Set	Sm	2C	4.92	3.25	189.00	182.00	---	371.00	**473.00**
10'-0" x 8'-0", 3 doors	Inst	Set	Lg	2C	3.20	5.00	172.00	118.00	---	290.00	**364.00**
	Inst	Set	Sm	2C	4.92	3.25	197.00	182.00	---	379.00	**481.00**
12'-0" x 8'-0", 3 doors	Inst	Set	Lg	2C	3.20	5.00	179.00	118.00	---	297.00	**371.00**
	Inst	Set	Sm	2C	4.92	3.25	204.00	182.00	---	386.00	**490.00**

Description	Oper	Unit	Vol	Crew Size	Man-hours per Unit	Crew Output per Day	Avg Mat'l Unit Cost	Avg Labor Unit Cost	Avg Equip Unit Cost	Avg Total Unit Cost	Avg Price Incl O&P
Unfinished lauan											
4'-0" x 6'-8", 2 doors	Inst	Set	Lg	2C	2.29	7.00	71.20	84.80	---	156.00	**201.00**
	Inst	Set	Sm	2C	3.52	4.55	81.30	130.00	---	211.30	**276.00**
6'-0" x 6'-8", 2 doors	Inst	Set	Lg	2C	2.29	7.00	79.10	84.80	---	163.90	**210.00**
	Inst	Set	Sm	2C	3.52	4.55	90.40	130.00	---	220.40	**286.00**
8'-0" x 6'-8", 2 doors	Inst	Set	Lg	2C	2.29	7.00	93.30	84.80	---	178.10	**226.00**
	Inst	Set	Sm	2C	3.52	4.55	107.00	130.00	---	237.00	**305.00**
4'-0" x 8'-0", 2 doors	Inst	Set	Lg	2C	2.29	7.00	85.40	84.80	---	170.20	**217.00**
	Inst	Set	Sm	2C	3.52	4.55	97.60	130.00	---	227.60	**295.00**
6'-0" x 8'-0", 2 doors	Inst	Set	Lg	2C	2.29	7.00	94.90	84.80	---	179.70	**228.00**
	Inst	Set	Sm	2C	3.52	4.55	108.00	130.00	---	238.00	**307.00**
8'-0" x 8'-0", 2 doors	Inst	Set	Lg	2C	2.29	7.00	112.00	84.80	---	196.80	**247.00**
	Inst	Set	Sm	2C	3.52	4.55	128.00	130.00	---	258.00	**330.00**
10'-0" x 6'-8", 3 doors	Inst	Set	Lg	2C	3.20	5.00	142.00	118.00	---	260.00	**330.00**
	Inst	Set	Sm	2C	4.92	3.25	163.00	182.00	---	345.00	**442.00**
12'-0" x 6'-8", 3 doors	Inst	Set	Lg	2C	3.20	5.00	158.00	118.00	---	276.00	**348.00**
	Inst	Set	Sm	2C	4.92	3.25	181.00	182.00	---	363.00	**463.00**
10'-0" x 8'-0", 3 doors	Inst	Set	Lg	2C	3.20	5.00	164.00	118.00	---	282.00	**355.00**
	Inst	Set	Sm	2C	4.92	3.25	188.00	182.00	---	370.00	**471.00**
12'-0" x 8'-0", 3 doors	Inst	Set	Lg	2C	3.20	5.00	171.00	118.00	---	289.00	**362.00**
	Inst	Set	Sm	2C	4.92	3.25	195.00	182.00	---	377.00	**479.00**
Unfinished red oak											
4'-0" x 6'-8", 2 doors	Inst	Set	Lg	2C	2.29	7.00	142.00	84.80	---	226.80	**282.00**
	Inst	Set	Sm	2C	3.52	4.55	162.00	130.00	---	292.00	**369.00**
6'-0" x 6'-8", 2 doors	Inst	Set	Lg	2C	2.29	7.00	158.00	84.80	---	242.80	**300.00**
	Inst	Set	Sm	2C	3.52	4.55	180.00	130.00	---	310.00	**389.00**
8'-0" x 6'-8", 2 doors	Inst	Set	Lg	2C	2.29	7.00	186.00	84.80	---	270.80	**332.00**
	Inst	Set	Sm	2C	3.52	4.55	212.00	130.00	---	342.00	**427.00**
4'-0" x 8'-0", 2 doors	Inst	Set	Lg	2C	2.29	7.00	170.00	84.80	---	254.80	**314.00**
	Inst	Set	Sm	2C	3.52	4.55	194.00	130.00	---	324.00	**406.00**
6'-0" x 8'-0", 2 doors	Inst	Set	Lg	2C	2.29	7.00	189.00	84.80	---	273.80	**336.00**
	Inst	Set	Sm	2C	3.52	4.55	216.00	130.00	---	346.00	**431.00**
8'-0" x 8'-0", 2 doors	Inst	Set	Lg	2C	2.29	7.00	223.00	84.80	---	307.80	**375.00**
	Inst	Set	Sm	2C	3.52	4.55	255.00	130.00	---	385.00	**476.00**
10'-0" x 6'-8", 3 doors	Inst	Set	Lg	2C	3.20	5.00	284.00	118.00	---	402.00	**492.00**
	Inst	Set	Sm	2C	4.92	3.25	324.00	182.00	---	506.00	**628.00**
12'-0" x 6'-8", 3 doors	Inst	Set	Lg	2C	3.20	5.00	315.00	118.00	---	433.00	**528.00**
	Inst	Set	Sm	2C	4.92	3.25	360.00	182.00	---	542.00	**669.00**
10'-0" x 8'-0", 3 doors	Inst	Set	Lg	2C	3.20	5.00	328.00	118.00	---	446.00	**543.00**
	Inst	Set	Sm	2C	4.92	3.25	374.00	182.00	---	556.00	**686.00**
12'-0" x 8'-0", 3 doors	Inst	Set	Lg	2C	3.20	5.00	340.00	118.00	---	458.00	**557.00**
	Inst	Set	Sm	2C	4.92	3.25	389.00	182.00	---	571.00	**702.00**

Description	Oper	Unit	Vol	Crew Size	Man-hours per Unit	Crew Output per Day	Avg Mat'l Unit Cost	Avg Labor Unit Cost	Avg Equip Unit Cost	Avg Total Unit Cost	Avg Price Incl O&P
Mirror bypass units											
Frameless unit with 1/2" beveled mirror edges											
4'-0" x 6'-8", 2 doors	Inst	Set	Lg	2C	2.67	6.00	223.00	98.80	---	321.80	**394.00**
	Inst	Set	Sm	2C	4.10	3.90	254.00	152.00	---	406.00	**505.00**
6'-0" x 6'-8", 2 doors	Inst	Set	Lg	2C	2.67	6.00	287.00	98.80	---	385.80	**468.00**
	Inst	Set	Sm	2C	4.10	3.90	328.00	152.00	---	480.00	**589.00**
8'-0" x 6'-8", 2 doors	Inst	Set	Lg	2C	2.67	6.00	398.00	98.80	---	496.80	**596.00**
	Inst	Set	Sm	2C	4.10	3.90	455.00	152.00	---	607.00	**736.00**
4'-0" x 8'-0", 2 doors	Inst	Set	Lg	2C	2.67	6.00	272.00	98.80	---	370.80	**451.00**
	Inst	Set	Sm	2C	4.10	3.90	311.00	152.00	---	463.00	**570.00**
6'-0" x 8'-0", 2 doors	Inst	Set	Lg	2C	2.67	6.00	322.00	98.80	---	420.80	**509.00**
	Inst	Set	Sm	2C	4.10	3.90	368.00	152.00	---	520.00	**636.00**
8'-0" x 8'-0", 2 doors	Inst	Set	Lg	2C	2.67	6.00	422.00	98.80	---	520.80	**624.00**
	Inst	Set	Sm	2C	4.10	3.90	482.00	152.00	---	634.00	**767.00**
10'-0" x 6'-8", 3 doors	Inst	Set	Lg	2C	3.20	5.00	536.00	118.00	---	654.00	**782.00**
	Inst	Set	Sm	2C	4.92	3.25	612.00	182.00	---	794.00	**959.00**
12'-0" x 6'-8", 3 doors	Inst	Set	Lg	2C	3.20	5.00	580.00	118.00	---	698.00	**832.00**
	Inst	Set	Sm	2C	4.92	3.25	662.00	182.00	---	844.00	**1020.00**
10'-0" x 8'-0", 3 doors	Inst	Set	Lg	2C	3.20	5.00	611.00	118.00	---	729.00	**869.00**
	Inst	Set	Sm	2C	4.92	3.25	698.00	182.00	---	880.00	**1060.00**
12'-0" x 8'-0", 3 doors	Inst	Set	Lg	2C	3.20	5.00	669.00	118.00	---	787.00	**935.00**
	Inst	Set	Sm	2C	4.92	3.25	764.00	182.00	---	946.00	**1130.00**
Aluminum frame unit											
4'-0" x 6'-8", 2 doors	Inst	Set	Lg	2C	2.67	6.00	212.00	98.80	---	310.80	**382.00**
	Inst	Set	Sm	2C	4.10	3.90	242.00	152.00	---	394.00	**491.00**
6'-0" x 6'-8", 2 doors	Inst	Set	Lg	2C	2.67	6.00	249.00	98.80	---	347.80	**425.00**
	Inst	Set	Sm	2C	4.10	3.90	285.00	152.00	---	437.00	**540.00**
8'-0" x 6'-8", 2 doors	Inst	Set	Lg	2C	2.67	6.00	357.00	98.80	---	455.80	**549.00**
	Inst	Set	Sm	2C	4.10	3.90	408.00	152.00	---	560.00	**682.00**
4'-0" x 8'-0", 2 doors	Inst	Set	Lg	2C	2.67	6.00	254.00	98.80	---	352.80	**431.00**
	Inst	Set	Sm	2C	4.10	3.90	291.00	152.00	---	443.00	**547.00**
6'-0" x 8'-0", 2 doors	Inst	Set	Lg	2C	2.67	6.00	299.00	98.80	---	397.80	**482.00**
	Inst	Set	Sm	2C	4.10	3.90	342.00	152.00	---	494.00	**606.00**
8'-0" x 8'-0", 2 doors	Inst	Set	Lg	2C	2.67	6.00	428.00	98.80	---	526.80	**631.00**
	Inst	Set	Sm	2C	4.10	3.90	490.00	152.00	---	642.00	**776.00**
10'-0" x 6'-8", 3 doors	Inst	Set	Lg	2C	3.20	5.00	508.00	118.00	---	626.00	**751.00**
	Inst	Set	Sm	2C	4.92	3.25	581.00	182.00	---	763.00	**923.00**
12'-0" x 6'-8", 3 doors	Inst	Set	Lg	2C	3.20	5.00	598.00	118.00	---	716.00	**854.00**
	Inst	Set	Sm	2C	4.92	3.25	684.00	182.00	---	866.00	**1040.00**
10'-0" x 8'-0", 3 doors	Inst	Set	Lg	2C	3.20	5.00	610.00	118.00	---	728.00	**867.00**
	Inst	Set	Sm	2C	4.92	3.25	697.00	182.00	---	879.00	**1060.00**
12'-0" x 8'-0", 3 doors	Inst	Set	Lg	2C	3.20	5.00	718.00	118.00	---	836.00	**991.00**
	Inst	Set	Sm	2C	4.92	3.25	820.00	182.00	---	1002.00	**1200.00**

Description	Oper	Unit	Vol	Crew Size	Man-hours per Unit	Crew Output per Day	Avg Mat'l Unit Cost	Avg Labor Unit Cost	Avg Equip Unit Cost	Avg Total Unit Cost	Avg Price Incl O&P
Golden oak frame unit											
4'-0" x 6'-8", 2 doors	Inst	Set	Lg	2C	2.67	6.00	318.00	98.80	---	416.80	**504.00**
	Inst	Set	Sm	2C	4.10	3.90	363.00	152.00	---	515.00	**630.00**
6'-0" x 6'-8", 2 doors	Inst	Set	Lg	2C	2.67	6.00	374.00	98.80	---	472.80	**568.00**
	Inst	Set	Sm	2C	4.10	3.90	427.00	152.00	---	579.00	**704.00**
8'-0" x 6'-8", 2 doors	Inst	Set	Lg	2C	2.67	6.00	535.00	98.80	---	633.80	**754.00**
	Inst	Set	Sm	2C	4.10	3.90	612.00	152.00	---	764.00	**916.00**
4'-0" x 8'-0", 2 doors	Inst	Set	Lg	2C	2.67	6.00	381.00	98.80	---	479.80	**577.00**
	Inst	Set	Sm	2C	4.10	3.90	436.00	152.00	---	588.00	**714.00**
6'-0" x 8'-0", 2 doors	Inst	Set	Lg	2C	2.67	6.00	449.00	98.80	---	547.80	**654.00**
	Inst	Set	Sm	2C	4.10	3.90	513.00	152.00	---	665.00	**802.00**
8'-0" x 8'-0", 2 doors	Inst	Set	Lg	2C	2.67	6.00	643.00	98.80	---	741.80	**877.00**
	Inst	Set	Sm	2C	4.10	3.90	734.00	152.00	---	886.00	**1060.00**
10'-0" x 6'-8", 3 doors	Inst	Set	Lg	2C	3.20	5.00	763.00	118.00	---	881.00	**1040.00**
	Inst	Set	Sm	2C	4.92	3.25	872.00	182.00	---	1054.00	**1260.00**
12'-0" x 6'-8", 3 doors	Inst	Set	Lg	2C	3.20	5.00	897.00	118.00	---	1015.00	**1200.00**
	Inst	Set	Sm	2C	4.92	3.25	1030.00	182.00	---	1212.00	**1430.00**
10'-0" x 8'-0", 3 doors	Inst	Set	Lg	2C	3.20	5.00	915.00	118.00	---	1033.00	**1220.00**
	Inst	Set	Sm	2C	4.92	3.25	1050.00	182.00	---	1232.00	**1460.00**
12'-0" x 8'-0", 3 doors	Inst	Set	Lg	2C	3.20	5.00	1080.00	118.00	---	1198.00	**1400.00**
	Inst	Set	Sm	2C	4.92	3.25	1230.00	182.00	---	1412.00	**1670.00**
Steel frame unit											
4'-0" x 6'-8", 2 doors	Inst	Set	Lg	2C	2.67	6.00	169.00	98.80	---	267.80	**333.00**
	Inst	Set	Sm	2C	4.10	3.90	194.00	152.00	---	346.00	**435.00**
6'-0" x 6'-8", 2 doors	Inst	Set	Lg	2C	2.67	6.00	199.00	98.80	---	297.80	**368.00**
	Inst	Set	Sm	2C	4.10	3.90	228.00	152.00	---	380.00	**475.00**
8'-0" x 6'-8", 2 doors	Inst	Set	Lg	2C	2.67	6.00	286.00	98.80	---	384.80	**467.00**
	Inst	Set	Sm	2C	4.10	3.90	326.00	152.00	---	478.00	**588.00**
4'-0" x 8'-0", 2 doors	Inst	Set	Lg	2C	2.67	6.00	203.00	98.80	---	301.80	**372.00**
	Inst	Set	Sm	2C	4.10	3.90	232.00	152.00	---	384.00	**480.00**
6'-0" x 8'-0", 2 doors	Inst	Set	Lg	2C	2.67	6.00	239.00	98.80	---	337.80	**414.00**
	Inst	Set	Sm	2C	4.10	3.90	273.00	152.00	---	425.00	**527.00**
8'-0" x 8'-0", 2 doors	Inst	Set	Lg	2C	2.67	6.00	343.00	98.80	---	441.80	**533.00**
	Inst	Set	Sm	2C	4.10	3.90	392.00	152.00	---	544.00	**663.00**
10'-0" x 6'-8", 3 doors	Inst	Set	Lg	2C	3.20	5.00	407.00	118.00	---	525.00	**634.00**
	Inst	Set	Sm	2C	4.92	3.25	465.00	182.00	---	647.00	**790.00**
12'-0" x 6'-8", 3 doors	Inst	Set	Lg	2C	3.20	5.00	478.00	118.00	---	596.00	**716.00**
	Inst	Set	Sm	2C	4.92	3.25	547.00	182.00	---	729.00	**884.00**
10'-0" x 8'-0", 3 doors	Inst	Set	Lg	2C	3.20	5.00	488.00	118.00	---	606.00	**727.00**
	Inst	Set	Sm	2C	4.92	3.25	558.00	182.00	---	740.00	**896.00**
12'-0" x 8'-0", 3 doors	Inst	Set	Lg	2C	3.20	5.00	574.00	118.00	---	692.00	**826.00**
	Inst	Set	Sm	2C	4.92	3.25	656.00	182.00	---	838.00	**1010.00**

Description	Oper	Unit	Vol	Crew Size	Man-hours per Unit	Crew Output per Day	Avg Mat'l Unit Cost	Avg Labor Unit Cost	Avg Equip Unit Cost	Avg Total Unit Cost	Avg Price Incl O&P
Accordion doors											
Custom prefinished woodgrain print											
2'-0" x 6'-8"	Inst	Set	Lg	2C	1.60	10.00	257.00	59.20	---	316.20	**379.00**
	Inst	Set	Sm	2C	2.46	6.50	294.00	91.10	---	385.10	**466.00**
3'-0" x 6'-8"	Inst	Set	Lg	2C	1.60	10.00	349.00	59.20	---	408.20	**484.00**
	Inst	Set	Sm	2C	2.46	6.50	398.00	91.10	---	489.10	**586.00**
4'-0" x 6'-8"	Inst	Set	Lg	2C	1.60	10.00	452.00	59.20	---	511.20	**602.00**
	Inst	Set	Sm	2C	2.46	6.50	516.00	91.10	---	607.10	**721.00**
5'-0" x 6'-8"	Inst	Set	Lg	2C	1.60	10.00	522.00	59.20	---	581.20	**683.00**
	Inst	Set	Sm	2C	2.46	6.50	596.00	91.10	---	687.10	**813.00**
6'-0" x 6'-8"	Inst	Set	Lg	2C	1.60	10.00	637.00	59.20	---	696.20	**816.00**
	Inst	Set	Sm	2C	2.46	6.50	728.00	91.10	---	819.10	**965.00**
7'-0" x 6'-8"	Inst	Set	Lg	2C	2.00	8.00	758.00	74.00	---	832.00	**975.00**
	Inst	Set	Sm	2C	3.08	5.20	866.00	114.00	---	980.00	**1160.00**
8'-0" x 6'-8"	Inst	Set	Lg	2C	2.00	8.00	826.00	74.00	---	900.00	**1050.00**
	Inst	Set	Sm	2C	3.08	5.20	944.00	114.00	---	1058.00	**1250.00**
9'-0" x 6'-8"	Inst	Set	Lg	2C	2.00	8.00	925.00	74.00	---	999.00	**1170.00**
	Inst	Set	Sm	2C	3.08	5.20	1060.00	114.00	---	1174.00	**1380.00**
10'-0" x 6'-8"	Inst	Set	Lg	2C	2.00	8.00	1060.00	74.00	---	1134.00	**1330.00**
	Inst	Set	Sm	2C	3.08	5.20	1220.00	114.00	---	1334.00	**1560.00**
For 8'-0"H, ADD	Inst	%	Lg	2C	---	---	12.0	---	---	12.0	---
	Inst	%	Sm	2C	---	---	12.0	---	---	12.0	---
Heritage prefinished real wood veneer											
2'-0" x 6'-8"	Inst	Set	Lg	2C	1.60	10.00	502.00	59.20	---	561.20	**660.00**
	Inst	Set	Sm	2C	2.46	6.50	574.00	91.10	---	665.10	**787.00**
3'-0" x 6'-8"	Inst	Set	Lg	2C	1.60	10.00	706.00	59.20	---	765.20	**894.00**
	Inst	Set	Sm	2C	2.46	6.50	806.00	91.10	---	897.10	**1050.00**
4'-0" x 6'-8"	Inst	Set	Lg	2C	1.60	10.00	915.00	59.20	---	974.20	**1130.00**
	Inst	Set	Sm	2C	2.46	6.50	1050.00	91.10	---	1141.10	**1330.00**
5'-0" x 6'-8"	Inst	Set	Lg	2C	1.60	10.00	1050.00	59.20	---	1109.20	**1290.00**
	Inst	Set	Sm	2C	2.46	6.50	1200.00	91.10	---	1291.10	**1510.00**
6'-0" x 6'-8"	Inst	Set	Lg	2C	1.60	10.00	1270.00	59.20	---	1329.20	**1540.00**
	Inst	Set	Sm	2C	2.46	6.50	1450.00	91.10	---	1541.10	**1790.00**
7'-0" x 6'-8"	Inst	Set	Lg	2C	2.00	8.00	1470.00	74.00	---	1544.00	**1800.00**
	Inst	Set	Sm	2C	3.08	5.20	1680.00	114.00	---	1794.00	**2090.00**
8'-0" x 6'-8"	Inst	Set	Lg	2C	2.00	8.00	1610.00	74.00	---	1684.00	**1960.00**
	Inst	Set	Sm	2C	3.08	5.20	1840.00	114.00	---	1954.00	**2280.00**
9'-0" x 6'-8"	Inst	Set	Lg	2C	2.00	8.00	1820.00	74.00	---	1894.00	**2200.00**
	Inst	Set	Sm	2C	3.08	5.20	2080.00	114.00	---	2194.00	**2560.00**
10'-0" x 6'-8"	Inst	Set	Lg	2C	2.00	8.00	2030.00	74.00	---	2104.00	**2440.00**
	Inst	Set	Sm	2C	3.08	5.20	2320.00	114.00	---	2434.00	**2830.00**
For 8'-0"H, ADD	Inst	%	Lg	2C	---	---	20.0	---	---	20.0	---
	Inst	%	Sm	2C	---	---	20.0	---	---	20.0	---

Description	Oper	Unit	Vol	Crew Size	Man-hours per Unit	Crew Output per Day	Avg Mat'l Unit Cost	Avg Labor Unit Cost	Avg Equip Unit Cost	Avg Total Unit Cost	Avg Price Incl O&P

Track and hardware only

Description	Oper	Unit	Vol	Crew Size	Man-hours per Unit	Crew Output per Day	Avg Mat'l Unit Cost	Avg Labor Unit Cost	Avg Equip Unit Cost	Avg Total Unit Cost	Avg Price Incl O&P
4'-0" x 6'-8", 2 doors	Inst	Set	Lg	---	---	---	18.90	---	---	18.90	**21.70**
	Inst	Set	Sm	---	---	---	21.60	---	---	21.60	**24.80**
6'-0" x 6'-8", 2 doors	Inst	Set	Lg	---	---	---	25.20	---	---	25.20	**29.00**
	Inst	Set	Sm	---	---	---	28.80	---	---	28.80	**33.10**
8'-0" x 6'-8", 2 doors	Inst	Set	Lg	---	---	---	31.50	---	---	31.50	**36.20**
	Inst	Set	Sm	---	---	---	36.00	---	---	36.00	**41.40**
4'-0" x 8'-0", 2 doors	Inst	Set	Lg	---	---	---	18.90	---	---	18.90	**21.70**
	Inst	Set	Sm	---	---	---	21.60	---	---	21.60	**24.80**
6'-0" x 8'-0", 2 doors	Inst	Set	Lg	---	---	---	24.20	---	---	24.20	**27.80**
	Inst	Set	Sm	---	---	---	27.60	---	---	27.60	**31.70**
8'-0" x 8'-0", 2 doors	Inst	Set	Lg	---	---	---	31.50	---	---	31.50	**36.20**
	Inst	Set	Sm	---	---	---	36.00	---	---	36.00	**41.40**
10'-0" x 6'-8", 3 doors	Inst	Set	Lg	---	---	---	43.10	---	---	43.10	**49.50**
	Inst	Set	Sm	---	---	---	49.20	---	---	49.20	**56.60**
12'-0" x 6'-8", 3 doors	Inst	Set	Lg	---	---	---	53.60	---	---	53.60	**61.60**
	Inst	Set	Sm	---	---	---	61.20	---	---	61.20	**70.40**
10'-0" x 8'-0", 3 doors	Inst	Set	Lg	---	---	---	43.10	---	---	43.10	**49.50**
	Inst	Set	Sm	---	---	---	49.20	---	---	49.20	**56.60**
12'-0" x 8'-0", 3 doors	Inst	Set	Lg	---	---	---	53.60	---	---	53.60	**61.60**
	Inst	Set	Sm	---	---	---	61.20	---	---	61.20	**70.40**

Columns

See also Framing, page 183

Aluminum, extruded; self supporting

Designed as decorative, loadbearing elements for porches, entrances, colonnades, etc.; primed, knocked-down, and carton packed complete with cap and base

Column with standard cap and base

Description	Oper	Unit	Vol	Crew Size	Man-hours per Unit	Crew Output per Day	Avg Mat'l Unit Cost	Avg Labor Unit Cost	Avg Equip Unit Cost	Avg Total Unit Cost	Avg Price Incl O&P
8" dia. x 8' to 12' H	Inst	Ea	Lg	CS	4.00	6.00	162.00	139.00	101.00	402.00	**489.00**
	Inst	Ea	Sm	CS	6.15	3.90	184.00	213.00	156.00	553.00	**675.00**
10" dia. x 8' to 12' H	Inst	Ea	Lg	CS	4.00	6.00	216.00	139.00	101.00	456.00	**554.00**
	Inst	Ea	Sm	CS	6.15	3.90	245.00	213.00	156.00	614.00	**748.00**
10" dia. x 16' to 20' H	Inst	Ea	Lg	CS	5.33	4.50	244.00	185.00	135.00	564.00	**686.00**
	Inst	Ea	Sm	CS	8.19	2.93	277.00	284.00	207.00	768.00	**937.00**
12" dia. x 9' to 12' H	Inst	Ea	Lg	CS	4.00	6.00	391.00	139.00	101.00	631.00	**764.00**
	Inst	Ea	Sm	CS	6.15	3.90	444.00	213.00	156.00	813.00	**987.00**
12" dia. x 16' to 24' H	Inst	Ea	Lg	CS	5.33	4.50	450.00	185.00	135.00	770.00	**933.00**
	Inst	Ea	Sm	CS	8.19	2.93	511.00	284.00	207.00	1002.00	**1220.00**

Column with Corinthian cap and decorative base

Description	Oper	Unit	Vol	Crew Size	Man-hours per Unit	Crew Output per Day	Avg Mat'l Unit Cost	Avg Labor Unit Cost	Avg Equip Unit Cost	Avg Total Unit Cost	Avg Price Incl O&P
8" dia. x 8' to 12' H	Inst	Ea	Lg	CS	4.00	6.00	281.00	139.00	101.00	521.00	**632.00**
	Inst	Ea	Sm	CS	6.15	3.90	319.00	213.00	156.00	688.00	**837.00**
10" dia. x 8' to 12' H	Inst	Ea	Lg	CS	4.00	6.00	352.00	139.00	101.00	592.00	**718.00**
	Inst	Ea	Sm	CS	6.15	3.90	400.00	213.00	156.00	769.00	**934.00**
10" dia. x 16' to 20' H	Inst	Ea	Lg	CS	5.33	4.50	385.00	185.00	135.00	705.00	**856.00**
	Inst	Ea	Sm	CS	8.19	2.93	438.00	284.00	207.00	929.00	**1130.00**
12" dia. x 9' to 12' H	Inst	Ea	Lg	CS	4.00	6.00	576.00	139.00	101.00	816.00	**987.00**
	Inst	Ea	Sm	CS	6.15	3.90	655.00	213.00	156.00	1024.00	**1240.00**
12" dia. x 16' to 24' H	Inst	Ea	Lg	CS	5.33	4.50	647.00	185.00	135.00	967.00	**1170.00**
	Inst	Ea	Sm	CS	8.19	2.93	735.00	284.00	207.00	1226.00	**1490.00**

Description	Oper	Unit	Vol	Crew Size	Man-hours per Unit	Crew Output per Day	Avg Mat'l Unit Cost	Avg Labor Unit Cost	Avg Equip Unit Cost	Avg Total Unit Cost	Avg Price Incl O&P

Brick columns. See Masonry, page 285

Wood, treated, No. 1 common and better white pine, T&G construction

Designed as decorative, loadbearing elements for porches, entrances, colonnades, etc.; primed, knocked-down, and carton packed complete with cap and base

Plain column with standard cap and base

Description	Oper	Unit	Vol	Crew Size	Man-hours per Unit	Crew Output per Day	Avg Mat'l Unit Cost	Avg Labor Unit Cost	Avg Equip Unit Cost	Avg Total Unit Cost	Avg Price Incl O&P
8" dia. x 8' to 12' H	Inst	Ea	Lg	CS	4.80	5.00	250.00	166.00	121.00	537.00	654.00
	Inst	Ea	Sm	CS	7.38	3.25	284.00	256.00	187.00	727.00	885.00
10" dia. x 8' to 12' H	Inst	Ea	Lg	CS	4.80	5.00	299.00	166.00	121.00	586.00	713.00
	Inst	Ea	Sm	CS	7.38	3.25	340.00	256.00	187.00	783.00	953.00
12" dia. x 8' to 12' H	Inst	Ea	Lg	CS	5.33	4.50	347.00	185.00	135.00	667.00	809.00
	Inst	Ea	Sm	CS	8.19	2.93	394.00	284.00	207.00	885.00	1080.00
14" dia. x 12' to 16' H	Inst	Ea	Lg	CS	6.86	3.50	565.00	238.00	173.00	976.00	1180.00
	Inst	Ea	Sm	CS	10.5	2.28	643.00	364.00	266.00	1273.00	1550.00
16" dia. x 18' to 20' H	Inst	Ea	Lg	CS	7.50	3.20	831.00	260.00	190.00	1281.00	1550.00
	Inst	Ea	Sm	CS	11.5	2.08	944.00	399.00	292.00	1635.00	1980.00

Plain column with Corinthian cap and decorative base

Description	Oper	Unit	Vol	Crew Size	Man-hours per Unit	Crew Output per Day	Avg Mat'l Unit Cost	Avg Labor Unit Cost	Avg Equip Unit Cost	Avg Total Unit Cost	Avg Price Incl O&P
8" dia. x 8' to 12' H	Inst	Ea	Lg	CS	4.80	5.00	286.00	166.00	121.00	573.00	698.00
	Inst	Ea	Sm	CS	7.38	3.25	325.00	256.00	187.00	768.00	935.00
10" dia. x 8' to 12' H	Inst	Ea	Lg	CS	4.80	5.00	371.00	166.00	121.00	658.00	799.00
	Inst	Ea	Sm	CS	7.38	3.25	421.00	256.00	187.00	864.00	1050.00
12" dia. x 8' to 12' H	Inst	Ea	Lg	CS	5.33	4.50	418.00	185.00	135.00	738.00	895.00
	Inst	Ea	Sm	CS	8.19	2.93	475.00	284.00	207.00	966.00	1170.00
14" dia. x 12' to 16' H	Inst	Ea	Lg	CS	6.86	3.50	629.00	238.00	173.00	1040.00	1260.00
	Inst	Ea	Sm	CS	10.5	2.28	715.00	364.00	266.00	1345.00	1630.00
16" dia. x 18' to 20' H	Inst	Ea	Lg	CS	7.50	3.20	886.00	260.00	190.00	1336.00	1620.00
	Inst	Ea	Sm	CS	11.5	2.08	1010.00	399.00	292.00	1701.00	2060.00

Concrete

Concrete Footings

1. **Dimensions.** 6" T, 8" T, 12" T x 12" W, 16" W, 20" W; 12" T x 24" W.

2. **Installation**

   a. Forms. 2" side forms equal in height to the thickness of the footing. 2" x 4" stakes 4'-0" oc, no less than the thickness of the footing. 2" x 4" bracing for stakes 8'-0" oc for 6" and 8" thick footings and 4'-0" oc for 12" thick footings. 1" x 2" or 1" x 3" spreaders 4'-0" oc

   b. Concrete. 1-2-4 mix is used in this section.

   c. Reinforcing steel. Various sizes, but usually only #3, #4, or #5 straight rods with end ties are used.

3. **Notes on Labor**

   a. Forming. Output based on a crew of two carpenters and one laborer.

   b. Grading, finish. Output based on what one laborer can do in one day.

   c. Reinforcing steel. Output based on what one laborer or one ironworker can do in one day.

   d. Concrete. Output based on a crew of two laborers and one carpenter.

   e. Forms, wrecking and cleaning. Output based on what one laborer can do in one day.

4. **Estimating Technique.** Determine the linear feet of footing.

Concrete Foundations

1. **Dimensions.** 8" T, 12" T x 4' H, 8' H, or 12' H.

2. **Installation**

   a. Forms. 4' x 8' panels made of ¾" form grade plywood backed with 2" x 4" studs and sills (studs approximately 16" oc), three sets and six sets of 2" x 4" wales for 4', 8' and 12' high walls. 2" x 4" wales for 4', 8' and 12' high walls. 2" x 4" diagonal braces (with stakes) 12'-0" oc one side. Snap ties spaced 22" oc, 20" oc and 17" oc along each wale for 4', 8' and 12' high walls. Paraffin oil coating for forms. Twelve uses are estimated for panels; twenty uses for wales and braces; snap ties are used only once.

   b. Concrete. 1-2-4 mix.

   c. Reinforcing steel. Sizes #3 to #7. Bars are straight except dowels which may on occasion be bent rods.

3. **Notes on Labor**

   a. Concrete, placing. Output based on a crew of one carpenter and five laborers.

   b. Forming. Output based on a crew of four carpenters and one laborer.

   c. Reinforcing steel rods. Output based on what two laborers or two ironworkers can do in one day.

   d. Wrecking and cleaning forms. Output based on what two laborers can do in one day.

4. **Estimating Technique**

   a. Determine linear feet of wall if wall is 8" or 12" x 4', 8' or 12', or determine square feet of wall. Then calculate and add the linear feet of rods.

Concrete Interior Floor Finishes

1. **Dimensions.** 3½", 4", 5", 6" thick x various areas.

2. **Installation**

   a. Forms. A wood form may or may not be required. A foundation wall may serve as a form for both basement and first floor slabs. In this section, only 2" x 4" and 2" x 6" side forms with stakes 4'-0" oc are considered.

   b. Finish grading. Dirt or gravel.

   c. Screeds (wood strips placed in area where concrete is to be placed). The concrete when placed will be finished even with top of the screeds. Screeds must be pulled before concrete sets up and the voids filled with concrete. 2" x 2" and 2" x 4" screeds with 2" x 2" stakes 6'-0" oc will be covered in this section.

   d. Steel reinforcing. Items to be covered are: #3, #4, #5 rods; 6 x 6/10-10 and 6 x 6/6-6 welded wire mesh.

   e. Concrete. 1-2-4 mix.

3. Notes on Labor

a. Forms and screeds. Output based on a crew of two masons and one laborer.

b. Finish grading. Output based on what one laborer can do in one day.

c. Reinforcing. Output based on what two laborers or two ironworkers can do in one day.

d. Concrete, place and finish. Output based on three cement masons and five laborers as a crew.

e. Wrecking and cleaning forms. Output based on what one laborer can do in one day.

4. Estimating Technique

a. Finish grading, mesh, and concrete. Determine the area and add waste.

b. Forms, screeds and rods. Determine the linear feet.

Spacer for anchor bolt

1" boards

2" x 4" tie

Braces

2" x 4"

Removable spreader

2" x 4"

2" x 4" braces

2" x 4" stakes

Footing

Description	Oper	Unit	Vol	Crew Size	Man-hours per Unit	Crew Output per Day	Avg Mat'l Unit Cost	Avg Labor Unit Cost	Avg Equip Unit Cost	Avg Total Unit Cost	Avg Price Incl O&P

Concrete, cast-in-place
Footings
Demo with air tools, reinforced

Description	Oper	Unit	Vol	Crew Size	Man-hours per Unit	Crew Output per Day	Avg Mat'l Unit Cost	Avg Labor Unit Cost	Avg Equip Unit Cost	Avg Total Unit Cost	Avg Price Incl O&P
8" T x 12" W	Demo	LF	Lg	AD	.171	140.0	---	6.69	1.73	8.42	**11.10**
	Demo	LF	Sm	AD	.214	112.0	---	8.37	2.17	10.54	**13.90**
8" T x 16" W	Demo	LF	Lg	AD	.182	132.0	---	7.12	1.84	8.96	**11.80**
	Demo	LF	Sm	AD	.214	112.0	---	8.37	2.17	10.54	**13.90**
8" T x 20" W	Demo	LF	Lg	AD	.194	124.0	---	7.59	1.96	9.55	**12.60**
	Demo	LF	Sm	AD	.229	105.0	---	8.95	2.31	11.26	**14.90**
12" T x 12" W	Demo	LF	Lg	AD	.190	126.0	---	7.43	1.93	9.36	**12.30**
	Demo	LF	Sm	AD	.224	107.0	---	8.76	2.27	11.03	**14.50**
12" T x 16" W	Demo	LF	Lg	AD	.200	120.0	---	7.82	2.02	9.84	**13.00**
	Demo	LF	Sm	AD	.235	102.0	---	9.19	2.38	11.57	**15.20**
12" T x 20" W	Demo	LF	Lg	AD	.211	114.0	---	8.25	2.13	10.38	**13.70**
	Demo	LF	Sm	AD	.247	97.00	---	9.66	2.50	12.16	**16.00**
12" T x 24" W	Demo	LF	Lg	AD	.222	108.0	---	8.68	2.25	10.93	**14.40**
	Demo	LF	Sm	AD	.261	92.00	---	10.20	2.64	12.84	**16.90**

Place per LF poured footing
Forming, 4 uses

Description	Oper	Unit	Vol	Crew Size	Man-hours per Unit	Crew Output per Day	Avg Mat'l Unit Cost	Avg Labor Unit Cost	Avg Equip Unit Cost	Avg Total Unit Cost	Avg Price Incl O&P
2" x 6"	Inst	LF	Lg	CS	.107	225.0	.59	3.71	---	4.30	**5.78**
	Inst	LF	Sm	CS	.116	207.0	.64	4.02	---	4.66	**6.27**
2" x 8"	Inst	LF	Lg	CS	.120	200.0	.62	4.16	---	4.78	**6.45**
	Inst	LF	Sm	CS	.130	184.0	.67	4.51	---	5.18	**6.98**
2" x 12"	Inst	LF	Lg	CS	.133	180.0	.73	4.61	---	5.34	**7.19**
	Inst	LF	Sm	CS	.145	166.0	.90	5.03	---	5.93	**7.94**

Grading, finish by hand

Description	Oper	Unit	Vol	Crew Size	Man-hours per Unit	Crew Output per Day	Avg Mat'l Unit Cost	Avg Labor Unit Cost	Avg Equip Unit Cost	Avg Total Unit Cost	Avg Price Incl O&P
6", 8", 12" T x 12" W	Inst	LF	Lg	1L	.023	345.0	---	.69	---	.69	**.97**
	Inst	LF	Sm	1L	.026	311.0	---	.78	---	.78	**1.09**
6", 8", 12" T x 16" W	Inst	LF	Lg	1L	.027	295.0	---	.81	---	.81	**1.13**
	Inst	LF	Sm	1L	.030	266.0	---	.90	---	.90	**1.26**
6", 8", 12" T x 20" W	Inst	LF	Lg	1L	.031	260.0	---	.93	---	.93	**1.30**
	Inst	LF	Sm	1L	.034	234.0	---	1.02	---	1.02	**1.43**
12" T x 24" W	Inst	LF	Lg	1L	.035	230.0	---	1.05	---	1.05	**1.47**
	Inst	LF	Sm	1L	.039	207.0	---	1.17	---	1.17	**1.64**

Description	Oper	Unit	Vol	Crew Size	Man-hours per Unit	Crew Output per Day	Avg Mat'l Unit Cost	Avg Labor Unit Cost	Avg Equip Unit Cost	Avg Total Unit Cost	Avg Price Incl O&P
Reinforcing steel in place, material costs include lap, waste, and tie wire											
Two (No. 3) 3/8" rods	Inst	LF	Lg	1L	.014	590.0	.72	.42	---	1.14	**1.31**
	Inst	LF	Sm	1L	.015	531.0	.79	.45	---	1.24	**1.42**
Two (No. 4) 1/2" rods	Inst	LF	Lg	1L	.014	560.0	1.02	.42	---	1.44	**1.61**
	Inst	LF	Sm	1L	.016	504.0	1.11	.48	---	1.59	**1.78**
Two (No. 5) 5/8" rods	Inst	LF	Lg	1L	.015	540.0	1.19	.45	---	1.64	**1.82**
	Inst	LF	Sm	1L	.016	486.0	1.28	.48	---	1.76	**1.95**
Three (No. 3) 3/8" rods	Inst	LF	Lg	1L	.017	460.0	1.08	.51	---	1.59	**1.79**
	Inst	LF	Sm	1L	.019	414.0	1.18	.57	---	1.75	**1.98**
Three (No. 4) 1/2" rods	Inst	LF	Lg	1L	.018	440.0	1.53	.54	---	2.07	**2.29**
	Inst	LF	Sm	1L	.020	396.0	1.66	.60	---	2.26	**2.50**
Three (No. 5) 5/8" rods	Inst	LF	Lg	1L	.019	420.0	1.78	.57	---	2.35	**2.58**
	Inst	LF	Sm	1L	.021	378.0	1.92	.63	---	2.55	**2.80**
Concrete, pour from truck into forms, material cost includes 5% waste and assumes use of 3,000 PSI, 1-1/2" aggregate, 5.7 sack mix											
6" T x 12" W (54.0 LF/CY)	Inst	LF	Lg	LC	.039	615.0	2.14	1.26	---	3.40	**3.91**
	Inst	LF	Sm	LC	.043	554.0	2.16	1.39	---	3.55	**4.11**
6" T x 16" W (40.5 LF/CY)	Inst	LF	Lg	LC	.043	560.0	2.14	1.39	---	3.53	**4.09**
	Inst	LF	Sm	LC	.048	504.0	2.88	1.55	---	4.43	**5.05**
6" T x 20" W (32.3 LF/CY)	Inst	LF	Lg	LC	.044	545.0	3.21	1.42	---	4.63	**5.20**
	Inst	LF	Sm	LC	.049	491.0	3.61	1.58	---	5.19	**5.83**
8" T x 12" W (40.5 LF/CY)	Inst	LF	Lg	LC	.043	560.0	2.14	1.39	---	3.53	**4.09**
	Inst	LF	Sm	LC	.048	504.0	2.88	1.55	---	4.43	**5.05**
8" T x 16" W (30.4 LF/CY)	Inst	LF	Lg	LC	.047	510.0	3.21	1.52	---	4.73	**5.34**
	Inst	LF	Sm	LC	.052	459.0	3.83	1.68	---	5.51	**6.18**
8" T x 20" W (24.3 LF/CY)	Inst	LF	Lg	LC	.049	485.0	4.29	1.58	---	5.87	**6.51**
	Inst	LF	Sm	LC	.055	437.0	4.80	1.78	---	6.58	**7.29**
12" T x 12" W (27.0 LF/CY)	Inst	LF	Lg	LC	.045	535.0	4.29	1.46	---	5.75	**6.33**
	Inst	LF	Sm	LC	.050	482.0	4.31	1.62	---	5.93	**6.57**
12" T x 16" W (20.3 LF/CY)	Inst	LF	Lg	LC	.052	460.0	5.36	1.68	---	7.04	**7.71**
	Inst	LF	Sm	LC	.058	414.0	5.74	1.88	---	7.62	**8.37**
12" T x 20" W (16.2 LF/CY)	Inst	LF	Lg	LC	.057	420.0	6.43	1.84	---	8.27	**9.01**
	Inst	LF	Sm	LC	.063	378.0	7.19	2.04	---	9.23	**10.00**
12" T x 24" W (13.5 LF/CY)	Inst	LF	Lg	LC	.049	485.0	7.50	1.58	---	9.08	**9.72**
	Inst	LF	Sm	LC	.055	437.0	8.63	1.78	---	10.41	**11.10**
Forms, wreck, remove and clean											
2" x 6"	Inst	LF	Lg	1L	.046	175.0	---	1.38	---	1.38	**1.93**
	Inst	LF	Sm	1L	.051	158.0	---	1.53	---	1.53	**2.14**
2" x 8"	Inst	LF	Lg	1L	.050	160.0	---	1.50	---	1.50	**2.10**
	Inst	LF	Sm	1L	.056	144.0	---	1.68	---	1.68	**2.35**
2" x 12"	Inst	LF	Lg	1L	.055	145.0	---	1.65	---	1.65	**2.31**
	Inst	LF	Sm	1L	.061	131.0	---	1.83	---	1.83	**2.56**

Description	Oper	Unit	Vol	Crew Size	Man-hours per Unit	Crew Output per Day	Avg Mat'l Unit Cost	Avg Labor Unit Cost	Avg Equip Unit Cost	Avg Total Unit Cost	Avg Price Incl O&P

Foundations and retaining walls, demo with air tools, per LF wall

Demo with air tools

With reinforcing
4'-0" H

Description	Oper	Unit	Vol	Crew Size	Man-hours per Unit	Crew Output per Day	Avg Mat'l Unit Cost	Avg Labor Unit Cost	Avg Equip Unit Cost	Avg Total Unit Cost	Avg Price Incl O&P
8" T	Demo	LF	Lg	AD	.300	80.00	---	11.70	3.03	14.73	**19.50**
	Demo	LF	Sm	AD	.353	68.00	---	13.80	3.57	17.37	**22.90**
12" T	Demo	LF	Lg	AD	.414	58.00	---	16.20	4.18	20.38	**26.80**
	Demo	LF	Sm	AD	.490	49.00	---	19.20	4.95	24.15	**31.80**

8'-0" H

Description	Oper	Unit	Vol	Crew Size	Man-hours per Unit	Crew Output per Day	Avg Mat'l Unit Cost	Avg Labor Unit Cost	Avg Equip Unit Cost	Avg Total Unit Cost	Avg Price Incl O&P
8" T	Demo	LF	Lg	AD	.324	74.00	---	12.70	3.28	15.98	**21.00**
	Demo	LF	Sm	AD	.381	63.00	---	14.90	3.85	18.75	**24.70**
12" T	Demo	LF	Lg	AD	.462	52.00	---	18.10	4.67	22.77	**30.00**
	Demo	LF	Sm	AD	.545	44.00	---	21.30	5.52	26.82	**35.40**

12"-0" H

Description	Oper	Unit	Vol	Crew Size	Man-hours per Unit	Crew Output per Day	Avg Mat'l Unit Cost	Avg Labor Unit Cost	Avg Equip Unit Cost	Avg Total Unit Cost	Avg Price Incl O&P
8" T	Demo	LF	Lg	AD	.353	68.00	---	13.80	3.57	17.37	**22.90**
	Demo	LF	Sm	AD	.414	58.00	---	16.20	4.18	20.38	**26.80**
12" T	Demo	LF	Lg	AD	.545	44.00	---	21.30	5.52	26.82	**35.40**
	Demo	LF	Sm	AD	.649	37.00	---	25.40	6.56	31.96	**42.10**

Without reinforcing
4'-0" H

Description	Oper	Unit	Vol	Crew Size	Man-hours per Unit	Crew Output per Day	Avg Mat'l Unit Cost	Avg Labor Unit Cost	Avg Equip Unit Cost	Avg Total Unit Cost	Avg Price Incl O&P
8" T	Demo	LF	Lg	AD	.261	92.00	---	10.20	2.64	12.84	**16.90**
	Demo	LF	Sm	AD	.308	78.00	---	12.00	3.11	15.11	**20.00**
12" T	Demo	LF	Lg	AD	.353	68.00	---	13.80	3.57	17.37	**22.90**
	Demo	LF	Sm	AD	.414	58.00	---	16.20	4.18	20.38	**26.80**

8'-0" H

Description	Oper	Unit	Vol	Crew Size	Man-hours per Unit	Crew Output per Day	Avg Mat'l Unit Cost	Avg Labor Unit Cost	Avg Equip Unit Cost	Avg Total Unit Cost	Avg Price Incl O&P
8" T	Demo	LF	Lg	AD	.286	84.00	---	11.20	2.89	14.09	**18.60**
	Demo	LF	Sm	AD	.338	71.00	---	13.20	3.42	16.62	**21.90**
12" T	Demo	LF	Lg	AD	.400	60.00	---	15.60	4.04	19.64	**25.90**
	Demo	LF	Sm	AD	.471	51.00	---	18.40	4.76	23.16	**30.50**

12"-0" H

Description	Oper	Unit	Vol	Crew Size	Man-hours per Unit	Crew Output per Day	Avg Mat'l Unit Cost	Avg Labor Unit Cost	Avg Equip Unit Cost	Avg Total Unit Cost	Avg Price Incl O&P
8" T	Demo	LF	Lg	AD	.316	76.00	---	12.40	3.19	15.59	**20.50**
	Demo	LF	Sm	AD	.369	65.00	---	14.40	3.73	18.13	**23.90**
12" T	Demo	LF	Lg	AD	.462	52.00	---	18.10	4.67	22.77	**30.00**
	Demo	LF	Sm	AD	.545	44.00	---	21.30	5.52	26.82	**35.40**

Place foundations and retaining walls

Forming only. Material price includes panel forms, wales, braces, snap ties, paraffin oil and nails
8" or 12" T x 4'-0" H

Description	Oper	Unit	Vol	Crew Size	Man-hours per Unit	Crew Output per Day	Avg Mat'l Unit Cost	Avg Labor Unit Cost	Avg Equip Unit Cost	Avg Total Unit Cost	Avg Price Incl O&P
Make (@ 12 uses)	Inst	SF	Lg	CU	.058	685.0	1.06	2.07	---	3.13	**3.95**
	Inst	SF	Sm	CU	.063	630.0	1.15	2.24	---	3.39	**4.29**
Erect and coat	Inst	SF	Lg	CU	.098	410.0	.05	3.49	---	3.54	**4.94**
	Inst	SF	Sm	CU	.106	377.0	.05	3.78	---	3.83	**5.34**
Wreck and clean	Inst	SF	Lg	LB	.043	370.0	---	1.29	---	1.29	**1.81**
	Inst	SF	Sm	LB	.048	333.0	---	1.44	---	1.44	**2.02**

Description	Oper	Unit	Vol	Crew Size	Man-hours per Unit	Crew Output per Day	Avg Mat'l Unit Cost	Avg Labor Unit Cost	Avg Equip Unit Cost	Avg Total Unit Cost	Avg Price Incl O&P
8" or 12" T x 8'-0" H											
Make (@ 12 uses)	Inst	SF	Lg	CU	.061	655.0	.98	2.17	---	3.15	**4.02**
	Inst	SF	Sm	CU	.066	603.0	1.06	2.35	---	3.41	**4.35**
Erect and coat	Inst	SF	Lg	CU	.118	340.0	.05	4.20	---	4.25	**5.93**
	Inst	SF	Sm	CU	.128	313.0	.05	4.56	---	4.61	**6.43**
Wreck and clean	Inst	SF	Lg	LB	.052	305.0	---	1.56	---	1.56	**2.18**
	Inst	SF	Sm	LB	.058	275.0	---	1.74	---	1.74	**2.44**
8" or 12" T x 12'-0" H											
Make (@ 12 uses)	Inst	SF	Lg	CU	.060	670.0	1.02	2.14	---	3.16	**4.01**
	Inst	SF	Sm	CU	.065	616.0	1.11	2.32	---	3.43	**4.35**
Erect and coat	Inst	SF	Lg	CU	.138	290.0	.05	4.92	---	4.97	**6.93**
	Inst	SF	Sm	CU	.150	267.0	.05	5.34	---	5.39	**7.53**
Wreck and clean	Inst	SF	Lg	LB	.062	260.0	---	1.86	---	1.86	**2.60**
	Inst	SF	Sm	LB	.068	234.0	---	2.04	---	2.04	**2.86**

Reinforcing steel rods. 5% waste included, pricing based on LF of rod

Description	Oper	Unit	Vol	Crew Size	Man-hours per Unit	Crew Output per Day	Avg Mat'l Unit Cost	Avg Labor Unit Cost	Avg Equip Unit Cost	Avg Total Unit Cost	Avg Price Incl O&P
No. 3 (3/8" rod)	Inst	LF	Lg	LB	.012	1390	.34	.36	---	.70	**.84**
	Inst	LF	Sm	LB	.013	1251	.38	.39	---	.77	**.93**
No. 4 (1/2" rod)	Inst	LF	Lg	LB	.012	1330	.49	.36	---	.85	**.99**
	Inst	LF	Sm	LB	.013	1197	.53	.39	---	.92	**1.08**
No. 5 (5/8" rod)	Inst	LF	Lg	LB	.013	1260	.57	.39	---	.96	**1.12**
	Inst	LF	Sm	LB	.014	1134	.61	.42	---	1.03	**1.20**
No. 6 (3/4" rod)	Inst	LF	Lg	LB	.014	1130	.82	.42	---	1.24	**1.41**
	Inst	LF	Sm	LB	.016	1017	.88	.48	---	1.36	**1.55**
No. 7 (7/8" rod)	Inst	LF	Lg	LB	.016	1000	1.09	.48	---	1.57	**1.76**
	Inst	LF	Sm	LB	.018	900.0	1.18	.54	---	1.72	**1.94**

Concrete, placed from trucks into forms, material cost includes 5% waste and assumes use of 3,000 PSI, 1-1/2" aggregate, 5.7 sack mix

Description	Oper	Unit	Vol	Crew Size	Man-hours per Unit	Crew Output per Day	Avg Mat'l Unit Cost	Avg Labor Unit Cost	Avg Equip Unit Cost	Avg Total Unit Cost	Avg Price Incl O&P
8" T x 4'-0" H (10.12 LF/CY)	Inst	LF	Lg	LG	.070	690.0	10.70	2.18	---	12.88	**13.80**
	Inst	LF	Sm	LG	.077	621.0	11.50	2.40	---	13.90	**14.90**
8" T x 4'-0" H (40.5 SF/CY)	Inst	SF	Lg	LG	.017	2760	2.14	.53	---	2.67	**2.88**
	Inst	SF	Sm	LG	.019	2484	2.88	.59	---	3.47	**3.71**
8" T x 8'-0" H (5.06 LF/CY)	Inst	LF	Lg	LG	.139	345.0	21.40	4.33	---	25.73	**27.50**
	Inst	LF	Sm	LG	.154	311.0	23.00	4.80	---	27.80	**29.70**
8" T x 8'-0" H (40.5 SF/CY)	Inst	SF	Lg	LG	.017	2760	2.14	.53	---	2.67	**2.88**
	Inst	SF	Sm	LG	.019	2484	2.88	.59	---	3.47	**3.71**
8" T x 12'-0" H (3.37 LF/CY)	Inst	LF	Lg	LG	.209	230.0	32.20	6.51	---	38.71	**41.30**
	Inst	LF	Sm	LG	.232	207.0	34.60	7.23	---	41.83	**44.70**
8" T x 12'-0" H (40.5 SF/CY)	Inst	SF	Lg	LG	.017	2760	2.14	.53	---	2.67	**2.88**
	Inst	SF	Sm	LG	.019	2484	2.88	.59	---	3.47	**3.71**
12' T x 4'-0" H (6.75 LF/CY)	Inst	LF	Lg	LG	.104	463.0	16.10	3.24	---	19.34	**20.60**
	Inst	LF	Sm	LG	.115	417.0	17.30	3.58	---	20.88	**22.30**

Description	Oper	Unit	Vol	Crew Size	Man-hours per Unit	Crew Output per Day	Avg Mat'l Unit Cost	Avg Labor Unit Cost	Avg Equip Unit Cost	Avg Total Unit Cost	Avg Price Incl O&P
12" T x 4'-0" H (27.0 LF/CY)	Inst	SF	Lg	LG	.026	1850	4.29	.81	---	5.10	**5.42**
	Inst	SF	Sm	LG	.029	1665	4.31	.90	---	5.21	**5.58**
12" T x 8'-0" H (3.38 LF/CY)	Inst	LF	Lg	LG	.208	231.0	32.20	6.48	---	38.68	**41.20**
	Inst	LF	Sm	LG	.231	208.0	34.50	7.20	---	41.70	**44.60**
12" T x 8'-0" H (27.0 SF/CY)	Inst	SF	Lg	LG	.026	1850	4.29	.81	---	5.10	**5.42**
	Inst	SF	Sm	LG	.026	1850	4.31	.81	---	5.12	**5.44**
12" T x 12'-0" H (2.25 LF/CY)	Inst	LF	Lg	LG	.312	154.0	47.20	9.73	---	56.93	**60.80**
	Inst	LF	Sm	LG	.312	154.0	51.80	9.73	---	61.53	**65.40**
12" T x 12'-0" H (27.0 SF/CY)	Inst	SF	Lg	LG	.026	1850	4.29	.81	---	5.10	**5.42**
	Inst	SF	Sm	LG	.026	1850	4.31	.81	---	5.12	**5.44**

Slabs, sidewalks and driveways, demo with air tools

Demo with air tools

With reinforcing (6 x 6 / 10 x 10)

Description	Oper	Unit	Vol	Crew Size	Man-hours per Unit	Crew Output per Day	Avg Mat'l Unit Cost	Avg Labor Unit Cost	Avg Equip Unit Cost	Avg Total Unit Cost	Avg Price Incl O&P
4" T	Demo	SF	Lg	AD	.063	380.0	---	2.46	.55	3.01	**4.00**
	Demo	SF	Sm	AD	.074	323.0	---	2.89	.64	3.53	**4.69**
5" T	Demo	SF	Lg	AD	.073	330.0	---	2.85	.63	3.48	**4.63**
	Demo	SF	Sm	AD	.085	281.0	---	3.32	.74	4.06	**5.39**
6" T	Demo	SF	Lg	AD	.083	290.0	---	3.25	.72	3.97	**5.26**
	Demo	SF	Sm	AD	.097	247.0	---	3.79	.84	4.63	**6.15**

Without reinforcing

Description	Oper	Unit	Vol	Crew Size	Man-hours per Unit	Crew Output per Day	Avg Mat'l Unit Cost	Avg Labor Unit Cost	Avg Equip Unit Cost	Avg Total Unit Cost	Avg Price Incl O&P
4" T	Demo	SF	Lg	AD	.044	550.0	---	1.72	.38	2.10	**2.79**
	Demo	SF	Sm	AD	.051	468.0	---	1.99	.44	2.43	**3.23**
5" T	Demo	SF	Lg	AD	.051	475.0	---	1.99	.44	2.43	**3.23**
	Demo	SF	Sm	AD	.059	404.0	---	2.31	.51	2.82	**3.74**
6" T	Demo	SF	Lg	AD	.057	420.0	---	2.23	.50	2.73	**3.62**
	Demo	SF	Sm	AD	.067	357.0	---	2.62	.58	3.20	**4.25**

Place concrete

Forming, 4 uses

Description	Oper	Unit	Vol	Crew Size	Man-hours per Unit	Crew Output per Day	Avg Mat'l Unit Cost	Avg Labor Unit Cost	Avg Equip Unit Cost	Avg Total Unit Cost	Avg Price Incl O&P
2" x 4" (4" T slab)	Inst	LF	Lg	DD	.041	580.0	.21	1.37	---	1.58	**2.16**
	Inst	LF	Sm	DD	.045	534.0	.23	1.50	---	1.73	**2.37**
2" x 6" (5" T and 6" T slab)	Inst	LF	Lg	DD	.041	580.0	.24	1.37	---	1.61	**2.19**
	Inst	LF	Sm	DD	.045	534.0	.26	1.50	---	1.76	**2.40**

Grading

Description	Oper	Unit	Vol	Crew Size	Man-hours per Unit	Crew Output per Day	Avg Mat'l Unit Cost	Avg Labor Unit Cost	Avg Equip Unit Cost	Avg Total Unit Cost	Avg Price Incl O&P
Dirt, cut and fill, +/- 1/10 ft	Inst	SF	Lg	1L	.010	800.0	---	.30	---	.30	**.42**
	Inst	SF	Sm	1L	.011	720.0	---	.33	---	.33	**.46**
Gravel, 3/4" to 1-1/2" stone	Inst	SF	Lg	1L	.011	750.0	.48	.33	---	.81	**.94**
	Inst	SF	Sm	1L	.012	675.0	.53	.36	---	.89	**1.03**

Screeds, 3 uses

Description	Oper	Unit	Vol	Crew Size	Man-hours per Unit	Crew Output per Day	Avg Mat'l Unit Cost	Avg Labor Unit Cost	Avg Equip Unit Cost	Avg Total Unit Cost	Avg Price Incl O&P
2" x 2"	Inst	LF	Lg	DD	.029	835.0	.08	.97	---	1.05	**1.46**
	Inst	LF	Sm	DD	.031	768.0	.09	1.04	---	1.13	**1.56**
2" x 4"	Inst	LF	Lg	DD	.032	760.0	.16	1.07	---	1.23	**1.68**
	Inst	LF	Sm	DD	.034	699.0	.17	1.14	---	1.31	**1.78**

Description	Oper	Unit	Vol	Crew Size	Man-hours per Unit	Crew Output per Day	Avg Mat'l Unit Cost	Avg Labor Unit Cost	Avg Equip Unit Cost	Avg Total Unit Cost	Avg Price Incl O&P
Reinforcing steel rods, includes 5% waste, costs are per LF of rod or SF of mesh											
No. 3 (3/8" rod)	Inst	LF	Lg	LB	.011	1480	.34	.33	---	.67	**.80**
	Inst	LF	Sm	LB	.012	1332	.38	.36	---	.74	**.88**
No. 4 (1/2" rod)	Inst	LF	Lg	LB	.011	1410	.49	.33	---	.82	**.95**
	Inst	LF	Sm	LB	.013	1269	.53	.39	---	.92	**1.08**
No. 5 (5/8" rod)	Inst	LF	Lg	LB	.012	1340	.57	.36	---	.93	**1.07**
	Inst	LF	Sm	LB	.013	1206	.61	.39	---	1.00	**1.16**
6 x 6 / 10-10 @ 21 lbs/CSF	Inst	SF	Lg	LB	.003	5250	.19	.09	---	.28	**.32**
	Inst	SF	Sm	LB	.003	4725	.20	.09	---	.29	**.33**
6 x 6 / 6-6 @ 42 lbs/CSF	Inst	SF	Lg	LB	.004	4500	.25	.12	---	.37	**.42**
	Inst	SF	Sm	LB	.004	4050	.28	.12	---	.40	**.45**
Concrete, pour and finish (steel trowel), material cost includes 5% waste and assumes use of 2500 PSI, 1" aggregate, 5.5 sack mix											
3-1/2" T (92.57 SF/CY)	Inst	SF	Lg	DF	.023	2805	1.16	.73	---	1.89	**2.20**
	Inst	SF	Sm	DF	.025	2581	1.26	.80	---	2.06	**2.39**
4" T (81.00 SF/CY)	Inst	SF	Lg	DF	.024	2720	1.32	.77	---	2.09	**2.41**
	Inst	SF	Sm	DF	.026	2502	1.43	.83	---	2.26	**2.61**
5" T (64.80 SF/CY)	Inst	SF	Lg	DF	.025	2590	1.65	.80	---	2.45	**2.78**
	Inst	SF	Sm	DF	.027	2383	1.79	.86	---	2.65	**3.01**
6" T (54.00 SF/CY)	Inst	SF	Lg	DF	.026	2460	1.98	.83	---	2.81	**3.16**
	Inst	SF	Sm	DF	.028	2263	2.16	.89	---	3.05	**3.43**
Forms, wreck and clean											
2" x 4"	Inst	LF	Lg	1L	.022	360.0	---	.66	---	.66	**.92**
	Inst	LF	Sm	1L	.025	324.0	---	.75	---	.75	**1.05**
2" x 6"	Inst	LF	Lg	1L	.024	340.0	---	.72	---	.72	**1.01**
	Inst	LF	Sm	1L	.026	306.0	---	.78	---	.78	**1.09**

Material information

Ready mix delivered by truck

Material costs only, prices are typical for most cities and assumes delivery up to 20 miles for 10 CY or more, 3" to 4" slump

Footing and foundation, using 1-1/2" aggregate

Description	Oper	Unit	Vol	Crew Size	Man-hours per Unit	Crew Output per Day	Avg Mat'l Unit Cost	Avg Labor Unit Cost	Avg Equip Unit Cost	Avg Total Unit Cost	Avg Price Incl O&P
2000 PSI, 4.8 sack mix	Inst	CY	Lg	---	---	---	94.90	---	---	94.90	**94.90**
	Inst	CY	Sm	---	---	---	103.00	---	---	103.00	**103.00**
2500 PSI, 5.2 sack mix	Inst	CY	Lg	---	---	---	98.00	---	---	98.00	**98.00**
	Inst	CY	Sm	---	---	---	107.00	---	---	107.00	**107.00**
3000 PSI, 5.7 sack mix	Inst	CY	Lg	---	---	---	102.00	---	---	102.00	**102.00**
	Inst	CY	Sm	---	---	---	111.00	---	---	111.00	**111.00**
3500 PSI, 6.3 sack mix	Inst	CY	Lg	---	---	---	104.00	---	---	104.00	**104.00**
	Inst	CY	Sm	---	---	---	113.00	---	---	113.00	**113.00**
4000 PSI, 6.9 sack mix	Inst	CY	Lg	---	---	---	111.00	---	---	111.00	**111.00**
	Inst	CY	Sm	---	---	---	121.00	---	---	121.00	**121.00**

Description	Oper	Unit	Vol	Crew Size	Man-hours per Unit	Crew Output per Day	Avg Mat'l Unit Cost	Avg Labor Unit Cost	Avg Equip Unit Cost	Avg Total Unit Cost	Avg Price Incl O&P

Slab, sidewalk and driveway, using 1" aggregate

Description	Oper	Unit	Vol	Crew	MH	Out	Mat'l	Labor	Equip	Total	Price
2000 PSI, 5.0 sack mix	Inst	CY	Lg	---	---	---	97.00	---	---	97.00	**97.00**
	Inst	CY	Sm	---	---	---	105.00	---	---	105.00	**105.00**
2500 PSI, 5.5 sack mix	Inst	CY	Lg	---	---	---	101.00	---	---	101.00	**101.00**
	Inst	CY	Sm	---	---	---	110.00	---	---	110.00	**110.00**
3000 PSI, 6.0 sack mix	Inst	CY	Lg	---	---	---	104.00	---	---	104.00	**104.00**
	Inst	CY	Sm	---	---	---	113.00	---	---	113.00	**113.00**
3500 PSI, 6.6 sack mix	Inst	CY	Lg	---	---	---	109.00	---	---	109.00	**109.00**
	Inst	CY	Sm	---	---	---	119.00	---	---	119.00	**119.00**
4000 PSI, 7.1 sack mix	Inst	CY	Lg	---	---	---	112.00	---	---	112.00	**112.00**
	Inst	CY	Sm	---	---	---	122.00	---	---	122.00	**122.00**

Pump & grout mix, using pea gravel, 3/8" aggregate

Description	Oper	Unit	Vol	Crew	MH	Out	Mat'l	Labor	Equip	Total	Price
2000 PSI, 6.0 sack mix	Inst	CY	Lg	---	---	---	104.00	---	---	104.00	**104.00**
	Inst	CY	Sm	---	---	---	113.00	---	---	113.00	**113.00**
2500 PSI, 6.5 sack mix	Inst	CY	Lg	---	---	---	108.00	---	---	108.00	**108.00**
	Inst	CY	Sm	---	---	---	118.00	---	---	118.00	**118.00**
3000 PSI, 7.2 sack mix	Inst	CY	Lg	---	---	---	113.00	---	---	113.00	**113.00**
	Inst	CY	Sm	---	---	---	123.00	---	---	123.00	**123.00**
3500 PSI, 7.9 sack mix	Inst	CY	Lg	---	---	---	118.00	---	---	118.00	**118.00**
	Inst	CY	Sm	---	---	---	129.00	---	---	129.00	**129.00**
4000 PSI, 8.5 sack mix	Inst	CY	Lg	---	---	---	126.00	---	---	126.00	**126.00**
	Inst	CY	Sm	---	---	---	136.00	---	---	136.00	**136.00**

Adjustments

Extra delivery costs for ready-mix concrete

Delivery over 20 miles, ADD

Description	Oper	Unit	Vol	Crew	MH	Out	Mat'l	Labor	Equip	Total	Price
	Inst	Mi	Lg	---	---	---	8.96	---	---	8.96	**8.96**
	Inst	Mi	Sm	---	---	---	8.96	---	---	8.96	**8.96**

Standby charge in excess of 5 minutes per CY delivered per minute extra time, ADD

Description	Oper	Unit	Vol	Crew	MH	Out	Mat'l	Labor	Equip	Total	Price
	Inst	Min	Lg	---	---	---	1.68	---	---	1.68	**1.68**
	Inst	Min	Sm	---	---	---	1.68	---	---	1.68	**1.68**

Loads 7.25 CY or less, ADD

Description	Oper	Unit	Vol	Crew	MH	Out	Mat'l	Labor	Equip	Total	Price
7.25 CY	Inst	LS	Lg	---	---	---	8.00	---	---	8.00	**8.00**
	Inst	LS	Sm	---	---	---	8.00	---	---	8.00	**8.00**
6.0 CY	Inst	LS	Lg	---	---	---	28.60	---	---	28.60	**28.60**
	Inst	LS	Sm	---	---	---	28.60	---	---	28.60	**28.60**
5.0 CY	Inst	LS	Lg	---	---	---	45.70	---	---	45.70	**45.70**
	Inst	LS	Sm	---	---	---	45.70	---	---	45.70	**45.70**
4.0 CY	Inst	LS	Lg	---	---	---	62.90	---	---	62.90	**62.90**
	Inst	LS	Sm	---	---	---	62.90	---	---	62.90	**62.90**
3.0 CY	Inst	LS	Lg	---	---	---	80.00	---	---	80.00	**80.00**
	Inst	LS	Sm	---	---	---	80.00	---	---	80.00	**80.00**
2.0 CY	Inst	LS	Lg	---	---	---	97.20	---	---	97.20	**97.20**
	Inst	LS	Sm	---	---	---	97.20	---	---	97.20	**97.20**
1.0 CY	Inst	LS	Lg	---	---	---	114.00	---	---	114.00	**114.00**
	Inst	LS	Sm	---	---	---	114.00	---	---	114.00	**114.00**

Description	Oper	Unit	Vol	Crew Size	Man-hours per Unit	Crew Output per Day	Avg Mat'l Unit Cost	Avg Labor Unit Cost	Avg Equip Unit Cost	Avg Total Unit Cost	Avg Price Incl O&P

Extra costs for non-standard mix additives
High early strength

Description	Oper	Unit	Vol	Crew	Man	Crew	Mat'l	Labor	Equip	Total	O&P
5.0 sack mix	Inst	CY	Lg	---	---	---	14.00	---	---	14.00	**14.00**
	Inst	CY	Sm	---	---	---	14.00	---	---	14.00	**14.00**
6.0 sack mix	Inst	CY	Lg	---	---	---	18.50	---	---	18.50	**18.50**
	Inst	CY	Sm	---	---	---	18.50	---	---	18.50	**18.50**

White cement (architectural)

Description	Oper	Unit	Vol	Crew	Man	Crew	Mat'l	Labor	Equip	Total	O&P
	Inst	CY	Lg	---	---	---	63.80	---	---	63.80	**63.80**
	Inst	CY	Sm	---	---	---	63.80	---	---	63.80	**63.80**
For 1% calcium chloride	Inst	CY	Lg	---	---	---	1.79	---	---	1.79	**1.79**
	Inst	CY	Sm	---	---	---	1.79	---	---	1.79	**1.79**
For 2% calcium chloride	Inst	CY	Lg	---	---	---	2.80	---	---	2.80	**2.80**
	Inst	CY	Sm	---	---	---	2.80	---	---	2.80	**2.80**

Chemical compensated shrinkage (WRDA Admix)

Description	Oper	Unit	Vol	Crew	Man	Crew	Mat'l	Labor	Equip	Total	O&P
	Inst	CY	Lg	---	---	---	23.50	---	---	23.50	**23.50**
	Inst	CY	Sm	---	---	---	23.50	---	---	23.50	**23.50**

Super plasticized mix, with 7"-8" slump

Description	Oper	Unit	Vol	Crew	Man	Crew	Mat'l	Labor	Equip	Total	O&P
	Inst	%	Lg	---	---	---	8.0	---	---	8.0	**8.0**
	Inst	%	Sm	---	---	---	8.0	---	---	8.0	**8.0**

Coloring of concrete, ADD

Description	Oper	Unit	Vol	Crew	Man	Crew	Mat'l	Labor	Equip	Total	O&P
Light or sand colors	Inst	CY	Lg	---	---	---	20.20	---	---	20.20	**20.20**
	Inst	CY	Sm	---	---	---	20.20	---	---	20.20	**20.20**
Medium or buff colors	Inst	CY	Lg	---	---	---	26.90	---	---	26.90	**26.90**
	Inst	CY	Sm	---	---	---	26.90	---	---	26.90	**26.90**
Dark colors	Inst	CY	Lg	---	---	---	40.30	---	---	40.30	**40.30**
	Inst	CY	Sm	---	---	---	40.30	---	---	40.30	**40.30**
Green	Inst	CY	Lg	---	---	---	44.80	---	---	44.80	**44.80**
	Inst	CY	Sm	---	---	---	44.80	---	---	44.80	**44.80**

Extra costs for non-standard aggregates
Lightweight aggregate, ADD

Description	Oper	Unit	Vol	Crew	Man	Crew	Mat'l	Labor	Equip	Total	O&P
Mix from truck to forms	Inst	CY	Lg	---	---	---	52.00	---	---	52.00	**52.00**
	Inst	CY	Sm	---	---	---	52.00	---	---	52.00	**52.00**
Pump mix	Inst	CY	Lg	---	---	---	55.60	---	---	55.60	**55.60**
	Inst	CY	Sm	---	---	---	55.60	---	---	55.60	**55.60**

Granite aggregate, ADD

Description	Oper	Unit	Vol	Crew	Man	Crew	Mat'l	Labor	Equip	Total	O&P
	Inst	CY	Lg	---	---	---	7.73	---	---	7.73	**7.73**
	Inst	CY	Sm	---	---	---	7.73	---	---	7.73	**7.73**

Concrete block. See Masonry, page 290

Description	Oper	Unit	Vol	Crew Size	Man-hours per Unit	Crew Output per Day	Avg Mat'l Unit Cost	Avg Labor Unit Cost	Avg Equip Unit Cost	Avg Total Unit Cost	Avg Price Incl O&P

Countertops

Ceramic tile

Countertop/backsplash
Adhesive set with backmounted tile

Description	Oper	Unit	Vol	Crew Size	Man-hours per Unit	Crew Output per Day	Avg Mat'l Unit Cost	Avg Labor Unit Cost	Avg Equip Unit Cost	Avg Total Unit Cost	Avg Price Incl O&P
1" x 1"	Inst	SF	Lg	TB	.229	70.00	6.91	7.10	---	14.01	**18.00**
	Inst	SF	Sm	TB	.381	42.00	7.58	11.80	---	19.38	**25.50**
4-1/4" x 4-1/4"	Inst	SF	Lg	TB	.200	80.00	5.52	6.20	---	11.72	**15.20**
	Inst	SF	Sm	TB	.333	48.00	6.05	10.30	---	16.35	**21.60**

Concrete

One-piece tops; straight, "L", or "U" shapes; minimal sanding, grinding, or polishing; cemented to particleboard base

25" W, 1-1/2" H front edge, with integral coved 4" H backsplash

Description	Oper	Unit	Vol	Crew Size	Man-hours per Unit	Crew Output per Day	Avg Mat'l Unit Cost	Avg Labor Unit Cost	Avg Equip Unit Cost	Avg Total Unit Cost	Avg Price Incl O&P
Standard grade, solid color	Inst	SF	Lg	2C	.107	150.00	50.00	3.96	---	53.96	**63.10**
	Inst	SF	Sm	2C	.152	105.00	55.00	5.63	---	60.63	**71.10**
Average grade, solid and mixed color											
	Inst	SF	Lg	2C	.107	150.00	70.00	3.96	---	73.96	**86.10**
	Inst	SF	Sm	2C	.152	105.00	77.00	5.63	---	82.63	**96.40**
High grade, specialty mixed colors or finish patterns											
	Inst	SF	Lg	2C	.107	150.00	85.00	3.96	---	88.96	**103.00**
	Inst	SF	Sm	2C	.152	105.00	93.50	5.63	---	99.13	**115.00**

Adjustments, ADD
For edge treatment, ADD
Standard and Average grade

Description	Oper	Unit	Vol	Crew Size	Man-hours per Unit	Crew Output per Day	Avg Mat'l Unit Cost	Avg Labor Unit Cost	Avg Equip Unit Cost	Avg Total Unit Cost	Avg Price Incl O&P
	Inst	LF	Lg	2C	.213	75.00	---	7.89	---	7.89	**11.00**
	Inst	LF	Sm	2C	.305	52.50	---	11.30	---	11.30	**15.80**
High grade	Inst	LF	Lg	2C	.291	55.00	---	10.80	---	10.80	**15.10**
	Inst	LF	Sm	2C	.416	38.50	---	15.40	---	15.40	**21.60**

For buff and polish, ADD
Any grade

Description	Oper	Unit	Vol	Crew Size	Man-hours per Unit	Crew Output per Day	Avg Mat'l Unit Cost	Avg Labor Unit Cost	Avg Equip Unit Cost	Avg Total Unit Cost	Avg Price Incl O&P
	Inst	SF	Lg	2C	.114	140.00	.45	4.22	---	4.67	**6.43**
	Inst	SF	Sm	2C	.163	98.00	.50	6.03	---	6.53	**9.02**

Formica

One-piece tops; straight, "L", or "U" shapes; surfaced with laminated plastic cemented to particleboard base

Post formed countertop with raised front drip edge
25" W, 1-1/2" H front edge, with integral coved 4" H backsplash

Description	Oper	Unit	Vol	Crew Size	Man-hours per Unit	Crew Output per Day	Avg Mat'l Unit Cost	Avg Labor Unit Cost	Avg Equip Unit Cost	Avg Total Unit Cost	Avg Price Incl O&P
Standard grade, solid pattern	Inst	LF	Lg	2C	.080	200.00	16.50	2.96	---	19.46	**23.10**
	Inst	LF	Sm	2C	.114	140.00	18.20	4.22	---	22.42	**26.80**
Average grade, simple patterns											
	Inst	LF	Lg	2C	.080	200.00	33.00	2.96	---	35.96	**42.10**
	Inst	LF	Sm	2C	.114	140.00	36.30	4.22	---	40.52	**47.70**

Description	Oper	Unit	Vol	Crew Size	Man-hours per Unit	Crew Output per Day	Avg Mat'l Unit Cost	Avg Labor Unit Cost	Avg Equip Unit Cost	Avg Total Unit Cost	Avg Price Incl O&P
High grade, specialty finish patterns											
	Inst	LF	Lg	2C	.080	200.00	42.00	2.96	---	44.96	**52.50**
	Inst	LF	Sm	2C	.114	140.00	46.20	4.22	---	50.42	**59.00**
Premium grade, stone and wood tone patterns											
	Inst	LF	Lg	2C	.080	200.00	50.00	2.96	---	52.96	**61.70**
	Inst	LF	Sm	2C	.114	140.00	55.00	4.22	---	59.22	**69.20**

Double roll top, 1-1/2" H front and back edges, no backsplash
25" W

Description	Oper	Unit	Vol	Crew Size	Man-hours per Unit	Crew Output per Day	Avg Mat'l Unit Cost	Avg Labor Unit Cost	Avg Equip Unit Cost	Avg Total Unit Cost	Avg Price Incl O&P
Standard grade, solid pattern											
	Inst	LF	Lg	2C	.071	225.00	18.20	2.63	---	20.83	**24.60**
	Inst	LF	Sm	2C	.102	157.50	20.00	3.78	---	23.78	**28.30**
Average grade, simple patterns											
	Inst	LF	Lg	2C	.071	225.00	26.30	2.63	---	28.93	**33.90**
	Inst	LF	Sm	2C	.102	157.50	28.90	3.78	---	32.68	**38.50**
High grade, specialty finish patterns											
	Inst	LF	Lg	2C	.071	225.00	30.50	2.63	---	33.13	**38.80**
	Inst	LF	Sm	2C	.102	157.50	33.60	3.78	---	37.38	**43.90**
Premium grade, stone and wood tone patterns											
	Inst	LF	Lg	2C	.071	225.00	41.30	2.63	---	43.93	**51.10**
	Inst	LF	Sm	2C	.102	157.50	45.40	3.78	---	49.18	**57.50**

36" W

Description	Oper	Unit	Vol	Crew Size	Man-hours per Unit	Crew Output per Day	Avg Mat'l Unit Cost	Avg Labor Unit Cost	Avg Equip Unit Cost	Avg Total Unit Cost	Avg Price Incl O&P
Standard grade, solid pattern											
	Inst	LF	Lg	2C	.058	275.00	22.50	2.15	---	24.65	**28.90**
	Inst	LF	Sm	2C	.083	192.50	24.80	3.07	---	27.87	**32.80**
Average grade, simple patterns											
	Inst	LF	Lg	2C	.058	275.00	32.50	2.15	---	34.65	**40.40**
	Inst	LF	Sm	2C	.083	192.50	35.80	3.07	---	38.87	**45.40**
High grade, specialty finish patterns											
	Inst	LF	Lg	2C	.058	275.00	38.00	2.15	---	40.15	**46.70**
	Inst	LF	Sm	2C	.083	192.50	41.80	3.07	---	44.87	**52.40**
Premium grade, stone and wood tone patterns											
	Inst	LF	Lg	2C	.058	275.00	51.00	2.15	---	53.15	**61.70**
	Inst	LF	Sm	2C	.083	192.50	56.10	3.07	---	59.17	**68.80**

Post formed countertop with square edge veneer front
25" W, 1-1/2" H front edge, 4" H coved backsplash

Description	Oper	Unit	Vol	Crew Size	Man-hours per Unit	Crew Output per Day	Avg Mat'l Unit Cost	Avg Labor Unit Cost	Avg Equip Unit Cost	Avg Total Unit Cost	Avg Price Incl O&P
Standard grade, solid pattern											
	Inst	LF	Lg	2C	.080	200.00	21.30	2.96	---	24.26	**28.60**
	Inst	LF	Sm	2C	.114	140.00	23.40	4.22	---	27.62	**32.80**
Average grade, simple patterns											
	Inst	LF	Lg	2C	.080	200.00	31.00	2.96	---	33.96	**39.80**
	Inst	LF	Sm	2C	.114	140.00	34.10	4.22	---	38.32	**45.10**

Description	Oper	Unit	Vol	Crew Size	Man-hours per Unit	Crew Output per Day	Avg Mat'l Unit Cost	Avg Labor Unit Cost	Avg Equip Unit Cost	Avg Total Unit Cost	Avg Price Incl O&P
High grade, specialty finish patterns											
	Inst	LF	Lg	2C	.080	200.00	36.00	2.96	---	38.96	**45.60**
	Inst	LF	Sm	2C	.114	140.00	39.60	4.22	---	43.82	**51.50**
Premium grade, stone and wood tone patterns											
	Inst	LF	Lg	2C	.080	200.00	49.00	2.96	---	51.96	**60.50**
	Inst	LF	Sm	2C	.114	140.00	53.90	4.22	---	58.12	**67.90**

Self-edge countertop with square edge veneer front
25" W, 1-1/2" H front edge, 4" H coved backsplash (@ 90-degree angle to deck)

Description	Oper	Unit	Vol	Crew Size	Man-hours per Unit	Crew Output per Day	Avg Mat'l Unit Cost	Avg Labor Unit Cost	Avg Equip Unit Cost	Avg Total Unit Cost	Avg Price Incl O&P
Standard grade, solid pattern											
	Inst	LF	Lg	2C	.080	200.00	23.50	2.96	---	26.46	**31.20**
	Inst	LF	Sm	2C	.114	140.00	25.90	4.22	---	30.12	**35.60**
Average grade, simple patterns											
	Inst	LF	Lg	2C	.080	200.00	34.00	2.96	---	36.96	**43.30**
	Inst	LF	Sm	2C	.114	140.00	37.40	4.22	---	41.62	**48.90**
High grade, specialty finish patterns											
	Inst	LF	Lg	2C	.080	200.00	39.50	2.96	---	42.46	**49.60**
	Inst	LF	Sm	2C	.114	140.00	43.50	4.22	---	47.72	**55.90**
Premium grade, stone and wood tone patterns											
	Inst	LF	Lg	2C	.080	200.00	53.50	2.96	---	56.46	**65.70**
	Inst	LF	Sm	2C	.114	140.00	58.90	4.22	---	63.12	**73.60**

Adjustments, ADD
Countertop edge treatment

Description	Oper	Unit	Vol	Crew Size	Man-hours per Unit	Crew Output per Day	Avg Mat'l Unit Cost	Avg Labor Unit Cost	Avg Equip Unit Cost	Avg Total Unit Cost	Avg Price Incl O&P
Plastic laminate	Inst	Ea	Lg	2C	.040	400.00	.65	1.48	---	2.13	**2.82**
	Inst	Ea	Sm	2C	.057	280.00	.72	2.11	---	2.83	**3.78**
Wood	Inst	Ea	Lg	2C	.064	250.00	1.25	2.37	---	3.62	**4.75**
	Inst	Ea	Sm	2C	.091	175.00	1.38	3.37	---	4.75	**6.30**

Diagonal corner cut

Description	Oper	Unit	Vol	Crew Size	Man-hours per Unit	Crew Output per Day	Avg Mat'l Unit Cost	Avg Labor Unit Cost	Avg Equip Unit Cost	Avg Total Unit Cost	Avg Price Incl O&P
Standard	Inst	Ea	Lg	---	---	---	18.00	---	---	18.00	**18.00**
	Inst	Ea	Sm	---	---	---	19.80	---	---	19.80	**19.80**
With plateau shelf	Inst	Ea	Lg	---	---	---	85.00	---	---	85.00	**85.00**
	Inst	Ea	Sm	---	---	---	93.50	---	---	93.50	**93.50**

Radius corner cut

Description	Oper	Unit	Vol	Crew Size	Man-hours per Unit	Crew Output per Day	Avg Mat'l Unit Cost	Avg Labor Unit Cost	Avg Equip Unit Cost	Avg Total Unit Cost	Avg Price Incl O&P
3" or 6"	Inst	Ea	Lg	---	---	---	12.00	---	---	12.00	**12.00**
	Inst	Ea	Sm	---	---	---	13.20	---	---	13.20	**13.20**
12"	Inst	Ea	Lg	---	---	---	12.00	---	---	12.00	**12.00**
	Inst	Ea	Sm	---	---	---	13.20	---	---	13.20	**13.20**
Quarter radius end	Inst	Ea	Lg	---	---	---	12.00	---	---	12.00	**12.00**
	Inst	Ea	Sm	---	---	---	13.20	---	---	13.20	**13.20**
Half radius end	Inst	Ea	Lg	---	---	---	22.00	---	---	22.00	**22.00**
	Inst	Ea	Sm	---	---	---	24.20	---	---	24.20	**24.20**

Description	Oper	Unit	Vol	Crew Size	Man-hours per Unit	Crew Output per Day	Avg Mat'l Unit Cost	Avg Labor Unit Cost	Avg Equip Unit Cost	Avg Total Unit Cost	Avg Price Incl O&P
Miter corner, shop assembled											
	Inst	Ea	Lg	---	---	---	70.00	---	---	70.00	**70.00**
	Inst	Ea	Sm	---	---	---	77.00	---	---	77.00	**77.00**
Splicing any top or leg 12' or longer, shop assembled											
	Inst	Ea	Lg	---	---	---	21.00	---	---	21.00	**21.00**
	Inst	Ea	Sm	---	---	---	23.10	---	---	23.10	**23.10**
Endsplash with finished sides and edges											
	Inst	Ea	Lg	---	---	---	16.00	---	---	16.00	**16.00**
	Inst	Ea	Sm	---	---	---	17.60	---	---	17.60	**17.60**
Sink or range cutout	Inst	Ea	Lg	---	---	---	7.00	---	---	7.00	**7.00**
	Inst	Ea	Sm	---	---	---	7.70	---	---	7.70	**7.70**

Granite or Marble

One-piece tops; straight, "L", or "U" shapes; cemented to particleboard base

25" W, 1-1/2" H front edge, additional for 4" H backsplash

Description	Oper	Unit	Vol	Crew Size	Man-hours per Unit	Crew Output per Day	Avg Mat'l Unit Cost	Avg Labor Unit Cost	Avg Equip Unit Cost	Avg Total Unit Cost	Avg Price Incl O&P
Standard grade, light to neutral colors, small stone patterns											
	Inst	SF	Lg	2C	.229	70.00	14.00	8.48	---	22.48	**28.00**
	Inst	SF	Sm	2C	.327	49.00	15.40	12.10	---	27.50	**34.70**
Average grade, dark colors, small to medium stone patterns											
	Inst	SF	Lg	2C	.229	70.00	27.50	8.48	---	35.98	**43.50**
	Inst	SF	Sm	2C	.327	49.00	30.30	12.10	---	42.40	**51.70**
High grade, specialty colors	Inst	SF	Lg	2C	.229	70.00	41.00	8.48	---	49.48	**59.00**
	Inst	SF	Sm	2C	.327	49.00	45.10	12.10	---	57.20	**68.80**
Premium grade, intense primary colors, intricate or matched patterns											
	Inst	SF	Lg	2C	.229	70.00	71.00	8.48	---	79.48	**93.50**
	Inst	SF	Sm	2C	.327	49.00	78.10	12.10	---	90.20	**107.00**

Adjustments, ADD

For undermount sink cutout and polish, ADD

Description	Oper	Unit	Vol	Crew Size	Man-hours per Unit	Crew Output per Day	Avg Mat'l Unit Cost	Avg Labor Unit Cost	Avg Equip Unit Cost	Avg Total Unit Cost	Avg Price Incl O&P
Single sink	Inst	Ea	Lg	2C	1.067	15.00	---	39.50	---	39.50	**55.30**
	Inst	Ea	Sm	2C	1.524	10.50	---	56.40	---	56.40	**79.00**
Double sink	Inst	Ea	Lg	2C	2.133	7.50	---	79.00	---	79.00	**111.00**
	Inst	Ea	Sm	2C	3.048	5.25	---	113.00	---	113.00	**158.00**

For edge treatment, ADD

Description	Oper	Unit	Vol	Crew Size	Man-hours per Unit	Crew Output per Day	Avg Mat'l Unit Cost	Avg Labor Unit Cost	Avg Equip Unit Cost	Avg Total Unit Cost	Avg Price Incl O&P
Standard grade	Inst	LF	Lg	2C	.178	90.00	---	6.59	---	6.59	**9.23**
	Inst	LF	Sm	2C	.254	63.00	---	9.40	---	9.40	**13.20**
Average grade	Inst	LF	Lg	2C	.320	50.00	---	11.90	---	11.90	**16.60**
	Inst	LF	Sm	2C	.457	35.00	---	16.90	---	16.90	**23.70**
High grade	Inst	LF	Lg	2C	.457	35.00	---	16.90	---	16.90	**23.70**
	Inst	LF	Sm	2C	.653	24.50	---	24.20	---	24.20	**33.80**
Premium grade	Inst	LF	Lg	2C	.800	20.00	---	29.60	---	29.60	**41.50**
	Inst	LF	Sm	2C	1.143	14.00	---	42.30	---	42.30	**59.20**

Description	Oper	Unit	Vol	Crew Size	Man-hours per Unit	Crew Output per Day	Avg Mat'l Unit Cost	Avg Labor Unit Cost	Avg Equip Unit Cost	Avg Total Unit Cost	Avg Price Incl O&P
For backsplash, ADD											
Coved, seamless, permanently joined											
	Inst	LF	Lg	2C	.400	40.00	15.00	14.80	---	29.80	**38.00**
	Inst	LF	Sm	2C	.571	28.00	16.50	21.10	---	37.60	**48.60**
Unattached, then butt joint @ 90 degree angle											
	Inst	LF	Lg	2C	.027	600.00	10.10	1.00	---	11.10	**13.00**
	Inst	LF	Sm	2C	.038	420.00	11.10	1.41	---	12.51	**14.80**
For buff and polish, ADD											
Any grade											
	Inst	SF	Lg	2C	.114	140.00	.45	4.22	---	4.67	**6.43**
	Inst	SF	Sm	2C	.163	98.00	.50	6.03	---	6.53	**9.02**

Quartz

One-piece tops; straight, "L", or "U" shapes; cemented to particleboard base

25" W, 1-1/2" H front edge, additional for 4" H backsplash

Description	Oper	Unit	Vol	Crew Size	Man-hours per Unit	Crew Output per Day	Avg Mat'l Unit Cost	Avg Labor Unit Cost	Avg Equip Unit Cost	Avg Total Unit Cost	Avg Price Incl O&P
High grade, specialty colors	Inst	SF	Lg	2C	.229	70.00	57.00	8.48	---	65.48	**77.40**
	Inst	SF	Sm	2C	.327	49.00	62.70	12.10	---	74.80	**89.10**
Premium grade, intense primary colors, intricate or matched patterns											
	Inst	SF	Lg	2C	.229	70.00	69.00	8.48	---	77.48	**91.20**
	Inst	SF	Sm	2C	.327	49.00	75.90	12.10	---	88.00	**104.00**

Adjustments, ADD

For undermount sink cutout and polish, ADD

Description	Oper	Unit	Vol	Crew Size	Man-hours per Unit	Crew Output per Day	Avg Mat'l Unit Cost	Avg Labor Unit Cost	Avg Equip Unit Cost	Avg Total Unit Cost	Avg Price Incl O&P
Single sink	Inst	Ea	Lg	2C	1.067	15.00	---	39.50	---	39.50	**55.30**
	Inst	Ea	Sm	2C	1.524	10.50	---	56.40	---	56.40	**79.00**
Double sink	Inst	Ea	Lg	2C	2.133	7.50	---	79.00	---	79.00	**111.00**
	Inst	Ea	Sm	2C	3.048	5.25	---	113.00	---	113.00	**158.00**
For edge treatment, ADD											
High grade	Inst	LF	Lg	2C	.457	35.00	---	16.90	---	16.90	**23.70**
	Inst	LF	Sm	2C	.653	24.50	---	24.20	---	24.20	**33.80**
Premium grade	Inst	LF	Lg	2C	.800	20.00	---	29.60	---	29.60	**41.50**
	Inst	LF	Sm	2C	1.143	14.00	---	42.30	---	42.30	**59.20**
For backsplash, ADD											
Coved, seamless, permanently joined											
	Inst	LF	Lg	2C	.400	40.00	15.00	14.80	---	29.80	**38.00**
	Inst	LF	Sm	2C	.571	28.00	16.50	21.10	---	37.60	**48.60**
Unattached, then butt joint @ 90 degree angle											
	Inst	LF	Lg	2C	.027	600.00	10.10	1.00	---	11.10	**13.00**
	Inst	LF	Sm	2C	.038	420.00	11.10	1.41	---	12.51	**14.80**
For buff and polish, ADD											
Any grade	Inst	SF	Lg	2C	.114	140.00	.45	4.22	---	4.67	**6.43**
	Inst	SF	Sm	2C	.163	98.00	.50	6.03	---	6.53	**9.02**

Description	Oper	Unit	Vol	Crew Size	Man-hours per Unit	Crew Output per Day	Avg Mat'l Unit Cost	Avg Labor Unit Cost	Avg Equip Unit Cost	Avg Total Unit Cost	Avg Price Incl O&P

Engineered Stone (e.g., imitation granite / marble / Silestone)

One-piece tops; straight, "L", or "U" shapes; cemented to particleboard base, matte finish

25" W, 1-1/2" H front edge, additional for 4" H backsplash

Description	Oper	Unit	Vol	Crew Size	Man-hours per Unit	Crew Output per Day	Avg Mat'l Unit Cost	Avg Labor Unit Cost	Avg Equip Unit Cost	Avg Total Unit Cost	Avg Price Incl O&P
Standard grade, light to neutral colors, small stone patterns											
	Inst	SF	Lg	2C	.091	175.00	33.50	3.37	---	36.87	**43.20**
	Inst	SF	Sm	2C	.131	122.50	36.90	4.85	---	41.75	**49.20**
Average grade, dark colors, small to medium stone patterns											
	Inst	SF	Lg	2C	.091	175.00	42.50	3.37	---	45.87	**53.60**
	Inst	SF	Sm	2C	.131	122.50	46.80	4.85	---	51.65	**60.60**
High grade, specialty colors	Inst	SF	Lg	2C	.091	175.00	56.50	3.37	---	59.87	**69.70**
	Inst	SF	Sm	2C	.131	122.50	62.20	4.85	---	67.05	**78.30**
Premium grade, intense primary colors, intricate or matched patterns											
	Inst	SF	Lg	2C	.091	175.00	69.00	3.37	---	72.37	**84.10**
	Inst	SF	Sm	2C	.131	122.50	75.90	4.85	---	80.75	**94.10**

Adjustments, ADD

For undermount sink cutout and polish, includes material for a solid surface sink with seaming kit, and installation labor, ADD

Description	Oper	Unit	Vol	Crew Size	Man-hours per Unit	Crew Output per Day	Avg Mat'l Unit Cost	Avg Labor Unit Cost	Avg Equip Unit Cost	Avg Total Unit Cost	Avg Price Incl O&P
Bar sink	Inst	Ea	Lg	2C	.444	36.00	347.00	16.40	---	363.40	**422.00**
	Inst	Ea	Sm	2C	.635	25.20	382.00	23.50	---	405.50	**472.00**
Single sink	Inst	Ea	Lg	2C	.667	24.00	495.00	24.70	---	519.70	**604.00**
	Inst	Ea	Sm	2C	.952	16.80	545.00	35.20	---	580.20	**676.00**
Double sink	Inst	Ea	Lg	2C	.889	18.00	587.00	32.90	---	619.90	**721.00**
	Inst	Ea	Sm	2C	1.270	12.60	645.00	47.00	---	692.00	**808.00**
For edge treatment, ADD											
Standard grade	Inst	LF	Lg	2C	.178	90.00	---	6.59	---	6.59	**9.23**
	Inst	LF	Sm	2C	.254	63.00	---	9.40	---	9.40	**13.20**
Average grade	Inst	LF	Lg	2C	.320	50.00	---	11.90	---	11.90	**16.60**
	Inst	LF	Sm	2C	.457	35.00	---	16.90	---	16.90	**23.70**
High grade	Inst	LF	Lg	2C	.457	35.00	---	16.90	---	16.90	**23.70**
	Inst	LF	Sm	2C	.653	24.50	---	24.20	---	24.20	**33.80**
Premium grade	Inst	LF	Lg	2C	.800	20.00	---	29.60	---	29.60	**41.50**
	Inst	LF	Sm	2C	1.143	14.00	---	42.30	---	42.30	**59.20**
For backsplash, ADD											
Coved, seamless, permanently joined											
	Inst	LF	Lg	2C	.400	40.00	15.00	14.80	---	29.80	**38.00**
	Inst	LF	Sm	2C	.571	28.00	16.50	21.10	---	37.60	**48.60**
Unattached, then butt joint @ 90 degree angle											
	Inst	LF	Lg	2C	.027	600.00	10.10	1.00	---	11.10	**13.00**
	Inst	LF	Sm	2C	.038	420.00	11.10	1.41	---	12.51	**14.80**
For inlays, ADD											
Any grade	Inst	LF	Lg	2C	.200	80.00	3.10	7.40	---	10.50	**13.90**
	Inst	LF	Sm	2C	.286	56.00	3.41	10.60	---	14.01	**18.70**
For gloss finish, ADD											
Any grade	Inst	SF	Lg	2C	.178	90.00	---	6.59	---	6.59	**9.23**
	Inst	SF	Sm	2C	.254	63.00	---	9.40	---	9.40	**13.20**

Description	Oper	Unit	Vol	Crew Size	Man-hours per Unit	Crew Output per Day	Avg Mat'l Unit Cost	Avg Labor Unit Cost	Avg Equip Unit Cost	Avg Total Unit Cost	Avg Price Incl O&P

Stainless Steel

One-piece tops; straight, "L", or "U" shapes; cemented to particleboard base

25" W, 1-1/2" H front edge, with integral coved 4" H backsplash

Description	Oper	Unit	Vol	Crew Size	Man-hours per Unit	Crew Output per Day	Avg Mat'l Unit Cost	Avg Labor Unit Cost	Avg Equip Unit Cost	Avg Total Unit Cost	Avg Price Incl O&P
Square edges eased	Inst	LF	Lg	2C	.457	35.00	167.00	16.90	---	183.90	**216.00**
	Inst	LF	Sm	2C	.653	24.50	184.00	24.20	---	208.20	**245.00**

Terrazzo

One-piece tops; straight, "L", or "U" shapes; material and labor to form, pour, and polish highly

25" W, 1-1/2" H front edge, no backsplash

Description	Oper	Unit	Vol	Crew Size	Man-hours per Unit	Crew Output per Day	Avg Mat'l Unit Cost	Avg Labor Unit Cost	Avg Equip Unit Cost	Avg Total Unit Cost	Avg Price Incl O&P
Square edges eased	Inst	SF	Lg	2C	.800	20.00	3.25	29.60	---	32.85	**45.20**
	Inst	SF	Sm	2C	1.143	14.00	3.58	42.30	---	45.88	**63.40**

Wood

Butcher block construction (hard rock maple) throughout top; custom, straight, "L", or "U" shapes

Self-edge top; 26" W, with 4" H backsplash, 1-1/2" H front and back edges

Description	Oper	Unit	Vol	Crew Size	Man-hours per Unit	Crew Output per Day	Avg Mat'l Unit Cost	Avg Labor Unit Cost	Avg Equip Unit Cost	Avg Total Unit Cost	Avg Price Incl O&P
	Inst	LF	Lg	2C	.267	60.00	26.00	9.88	---	35.88	**43.70**
	Inst	LF	Sm	2C	.381	42.00	28.60	14.10	---	42.70	**52.60**
Adjustments, ADD											
Miter corner	Inst	Ea	Lg	---	---	---	10.00	---	---	10.00	**10.00**
	Inst	Ea	Sm	---	---	---	11.00	---	---	11.00	**11.00**
Sink or surface saver cutout	Inst	Ea	Lg	---	---	---	30.00	---	---	30.00	**30.00**
	Inst	Ea	Sm	---	---	---	33.00	---	---	33.00	**33.00**
45-degree plateau corner	Inst	Ea	Lg	---	---	---	150.00	---	---	150.00	**150.00**
	Inst	Ea	Sm	---	---	---	165.00	---	---	165.00	**165.00**
End splash	Inst	Ea	Lg	---	---	---	35.00	---	---	35.00	**35.00**
	Inst	Ea	Sm	---	---	---	38.50	---	---	38.50	**38.50**

Cupolas

Wood, cedar / redwood or comparable, natural finish.

Description	Oper	Unit	Vol	Crew Size	Man-hours per Unit	Crew Output per Day	Avg Mat'l Unit Cost	Avg Labor Unit Cost	Avg Equip Unit Cost	Avg Total Unit Cost	Avg Price Incl O&P
24" x 24" x 32" H	Inst	Ea	Lg	CA	1.33	6.00	448.00	49.20	---	497.20	**629.00**
	Inst	Ea	Sm	CA	1.78	4.50	492.00	65.90	---	557.90	**707.00**
30" x 30" x 40" H	Inst	Ea	Lg	CA	1.60	5.00	850.00	59.20	---	909.20	**1150.00**
	Inst	Ea	Sm	CA	2.13	3.75	932.00	78.90	---	1010.90	**1280.00**
36" x 36" x 48" H	Inst	Ea	Lg	CA	2.00	4.00	1480.00	74.00	---	1554.00	**1960.00**
	Inst	Ea	Sm	CA	2.67	3.00	1630.00	98.80	---	1728.80	**2170.00**

Vinyl, pre-finished.

Description	Oper	Unit	Vol	Crew Size	Man-hours per Unit	Crew Output per Day	Avg Mat'l Unit Cost	Avg Labor Unit Cost	Avg Equip Unit Cost	Avg Total Unit Cost	Avg Price Incl O&P
24" x 24" x 32" H	Inst	Ea	Lg	CA	1.33	6.00	577.00	49.20	---	626.20	**790.00**
	Inst	Ea	Sm	CA	1.78	4.50	633.00	65.90	---	698.90	**883.00**
30" x 30" x 40" H	Inst	Ea	Lg	CA	1.60	5.00	1110.00	59.20	---	1169.20	**1470.00**
	Inst	Ea	Sm	CA	2.13	3.75	1210.00	78.90	---	1288.90	**1630.00**
36" x 36" x 48" H	Inst	Ea	Lg	CA	2.00	4.00	1750.00	74.00	---	1824.00	**2290.00**
	Inst	Ea	Sm	CA	2.67	3.00	1920.00	98.80	---	2018.80	**2540.00**

Description	Oper	Unit	Vol	Crew Size	Man-hours per Unit	Crew Output per Day	Avg Mat'l Unit Cost	Avg Labor Unit Cost	Avg Equip Unit Cost	Avg Total Unit Cost	Avg Price Incl O&P
Copper.											
24" x 24" x 32" H	Inst	Ea	Lg	CA	1.60	5.00	2940.00	59.20	---	2999.20	**3750.00**
	Inst	Ea	Sm	CA	2.13	3.75	3220.00	78.90	---	3298.90	**4140.00**
30" x 30" x 40" H	Inst	Ea	Lg	CA	2.00	4.00	4220.00	74.00	---	4294.00	**5380.00**
	Inst	Ea	Sm	CA	2.67	3.00	4630.00	98.80	---	4728.80	**5930.00**
36" x 36" x 48" H	Inst	Ea	Lg	CA	2.67	3.00	7060.00	98.80	---	7158.80	**8960.00**
	Inst	Ea	Sm	CA	3.56	2.25	7740.00	132.00	---	7872.00	**9860.00**
Weathervanes for above, aluminum											
18" H, black finish	Inst	Ea	Lg	---	---	---	103.00	---	---	103.00	**103.00**
	Inst	Ea	Sm	---	---	---	113.00	---	---	113.00	**113.00**
24" H, black finish	Inst	Ea	Lg	---	---	---	155.00	---	---	155.00	**155.00**
	Inst	Ea	Sm	---	---	---	170.00	---	---	170.00	**170.00**
36" H, black and gold finish	Inst	Ea	Lg	---	---	---	232.00	---	---	232.00	**232.00**
	Inst	Ea	Sm	---	---	---	254.00	---	---	254.00	**254.00**
24" H, copper	Inst	Ea	Lg	---	---	---	309.00	---	---	309.00	**309.00**
	Inst	Ea	Sm	---	---	---	339.00	---	---	339.00	**339.00**
36" H, copper	Inst	Ea	Lg	---	---	---	464.00	---	---	464.00	**464.00**
	Inst	Ea	Sm	---	---	---	509.00	---	---	509.00	**509.00**

Demolition

Average Manhours per Unit is based on what the designated crew can do in one day. In this section, the crew might be a laborer, a carpenter, a floor layer, etc. Who does the wrecking depends on the quantity of wrecking to be done.

A contractor might use laborers exclusively on a large volume job, but use a carpenter or a carpenter and a laborer on a small volume job.

The choice of tools and equipment greatly affects the quantity of work that a worker can accomplish in a day. A person can remove more brick with a compressor and pneumatic tool than with a sledgehammer or pry bar. In this section, the phrase "by hand" includes the use of hand tools, i.e., sledgehammers, wrecking bars, claw hammers, etc. When the Average Manhours per Unit is based on the use of equipment (not hand tools), a description of the equipment is provided.

The Average Manhours per Unit is not based on the use of "heavy" equipment such as bulldozers, cranes with wrecking balls, etc. The Average Manhours per Unit does include the labor involved in hauling wrecked material or debris to a dumpster located at the site. Average rental costs for dumpsters are: $590.00 for 40 CY (20' x 8' x 8' H); $530.00 for 30 CY (20' x 8' x 6' H). Rental period includes delivery and pickup when full.

Description	Oper	Unit	Vol	Crew Size	Man-hours per Unit	Crew Output per Day	Avg Mat'l Unit Cost	Avg Labor Unit Cost	Avg Equip Unit Cost	Avg Total Unit Cost	Avg Price Incl O&P

Demolition
Wreck and remove to dumpster

Concrete

Footings, with air tools; reinforced

Description	Oper	Unit	Vol	Crew	MH	Output	Mat'l	Labor	Equip	Total	O&P
8" T x 12" W (.67 CF/LF)	Demo	LF	Lg	AB	.133	120.0	---	4.90	2.02	6.92	**8.88**
	Demo	LF	Sm	AB	.205	78.00	---	7.55	3.11	10.66	**13.70**
8" T x 16" W (.89 CF/LF)	Demo	LF	Lg	AB	.160	100.0	---	5.89	2.43	8.32	**10.70**
	Demo	LF	Sm	AB	.246	65.00	---	9.06	3.73	12.79	**16.40**
8" T x 20" W (1.11 CF/LF)	Demo	LF	Lg	AB	.178	90.00	---	6.56	2.70	9.26	**11.90**
	Demo	LF	Sm	AB	.274	58.50	---	10.10	4.15	14.25	**18.30**
12" T x 12" W (1.00 CF/LF)	Demo	LF	Lg	AB	.229	70.00	---	8.43	3.47	11.90	**15.30**
	Demo	LF	Sm	AB	.352	45.50	---	13.00	5.33	18.33	**23.50**
12" T x 16" W (1.33 CF/LF)	Demo	LF	Lg	AB	.267	60.00	---	9.83	4.04	13.87	**17.80**
	Demo	LF	Sm	AB	.410	39.00	---	15.10	6.22	21.32	**27.40**
12" T x 20" W (1.67 CF/LF)	Demo	LF	Lg	AB	.291	55.00	---	10.70	4.41	15.11	**19.40**
	Demo	LF	Sm	AB	.448	35.75	---	16.50	6.79	23.29	**29.90**
12" T x 24" W (2.00 CF/LF)	Demo	LF	Lg	AB	.320	50.00	---	11.80	4.85	16.65	**21.40**
	Demo	LF	Sm	AB	.492	32.50	---	18.10	7.47	25.57	**32.80**

Foundations and retaining walls, with air tools, per LF wall

With reinforcing
4'-0" H

Description	Oper	Unit	Vol	Crew	MH	Output	Mat'l	Labor	Equip	Total	O&P
8" T (2.67 CF/LF)	Demo	SF	Lg	AB	.267	60.00	---	9.83	4.04	13.87	**17.80**
	Demo	SF	Sm	AB	.410	39.00	---	15.10	6.22	21.32	**27.40**
12" T (4.00 CF/LF)	Demo	SF	Lg	AB	.356	45.00	---	13.10	5.39	18.49	**23.80**
	Demo	SF	Sm	AB	.547	29.25	---	20.20	8.30	28.50	**36.50**

8'-0" H

Description	Oper	Unit	Vol	Crew	MH	Output	Mat'l	Labor	Equip	Total	O&P
8" T (5.33 CF/LF)	Demo	SF	Lg	AB	.291	55.00	---	10.70	4.41	15.11	**19.40**
	Demo	SF	Sm	AB	.448	35.75	---	16.50	6.79	23.29	**29.90**
12" T (8.00 CF/LF)	Demo	SF	Lg	AB	.400	40.00	---	14.70	6.07	20.77	**26.70**
	Demo	SF	Sm	AB	.615	26.00	---	22.70	9.33	32.03	**41.00**

12'-0" H

Description	Oper	Unit	Vol	Crew	MH	Output	Mat'l	Labor	Equip	Total	O&P
8" T (8.00 CF/LF)	Demo	SF	Lg	AB	.320	50.00	---	11.80	4.85	16.65	**21.40**
	Demo	SF	Sm	AB	.492	32.50	---	18.10	7.47	25.57	**32.80**
12" T (12.00 CF/LF)	Demo	SF	Lg	AB	.457	35.00	---	16.80	6.93	23.73	**30.50**
	Demo	SF	Sm	AB	.703	22.75	---	25.90	10.70	36.60	**46.90**

Without reinforcing
4'-0" H

Description	Oper	Unit	Vol	Crew	MH	Output	Mat'l	Labor	Equip	Total	O&P
8" T (2.67 CF/LF)	Demo	SF	Lg	AB	.200	80.00	---	7.37	3.03	10.40	**13.30**
	Demo	SF	Sm	AB	.308	52.00	---	11.30	4.67	15.97	**20.60**
12" T (4.00 CF/LF)	Demo	SF	Lg	AB	.267	60.00	---	9.83	4.04	13.87	**17.80**
	Demo	SF	Sm	AB	.410	39.00	---	15.10	6.22	21.32	**27.40**

Description	Oper	Unit	Vol	Crew Size	Man-hours per Unit	Crew Output per Day	Avg Mat'l Unit Cost	Avg Labor Unit Cost	Avg Equip Unit Cost	Avg Total Unit Cost	Avg Price Incl O&P
8'-0" H											
8" T (5.33 CF/LF)	Demo	SF	Lg	AB	.229	70.00	---	8.43	3.47	11.90	**15.30**
	Demo	SF	Sm	AB	.352	45.50	---	13.00	5.33	18.33	**23.50**
12" T (8.00 CF/LF)	Demo	SF	Lg	AB	.320	50.00	---	11.80	4.85	16.65	**21.40**
	Demo	SF	Sm	AB	.492	32.50	---	18.10	7.47	25.57	**32.80**
12'-0" H											
8" T (8.00 CF/LF)	Demo	SF	Lg	AB	.267	60.00	---	9.83	4.04	13.87	**17.80**
	Demo	SF	Sm	AB	.410	39.00	---	15.10	6.22	21.32	**27.40**
12" T (12.00 CF/LF)	Demo	SF	Lg	AB	.400	40.00	---	14.70	6.07	20.77	**26.70**
	Demo	SF	Sm	AB	.615	26.00	---	22.70	9.33	32.03	**41.00**

Slabs with air tools
With reinforcing

Description	Oper	Unit	Vol	Crew Size	Man-hours per Unit	Crew Output per Day	Avg Mat'l Unit Cost	Avg Labor Unit Cost	Avg Equip Unit Cost	Avg Total Unit Cost	Avg Price Incl O&P
4" T	Demo	SF	Lg	AB	.038	425.0	---	1.40	.57	1.97	**2.53**
	Demo	SF	Sm	AB	.058	276.3	---	2.14	.88	3.02	**3.87**
5" T	Demo	SF	Lg	AB	.043	370.0	---	1.58	.66	2.24	**2.88**
	Demo	SF	Sm	AB	.067	240.5	---	2.47	1.01	3.48	**4.46**
6" T	Demo	SF	Lg	AB	.046	350.0	---	1.69	.69	2.38	**3.06**
	Demo	SF	Sm	AB	.070	227.5	---	2.58	1.07	3.65	**4.68**

Without reinforcing

Description	Oper	Unit	Vol	Crew Size	Man-hours per Unit	Crew Output per Day	Avg Mat'l Unit Cost	Avg Labor Unit Cost	Avg Equip Unit Cost	Avg Total Unit Cost	Avg Price Incl O&P
4" T	Demo	SF	Lg	AB	.032	500.0	---	1.18	.49	1.67	**2.14**
	Demo	SF	Sm	AB	.049	325.0	---	1.80	.75	2.55	**3.28**
5" T	Demo	SF	Lg	AB	.038	425.0	---	1.40	.57	1.97	**2.53**
	Demo	SF	Sm	AB	.058	276.3	---	2.14	.88	3.02	**3.87**
6" T	Demo	SF	Lg	AB	.043	370.0	---	1.58	.66	2.24	**2.88**
	Demo	SF	Sm	AB	.067	240.5	---	2.47	1.01	3.48	**4.46**

Masonry
Brick
Chimneys

Description	Oper	Unit	Vol	Crew Size	Man-hours per Unit	Crew Output per Day	Avg Mat'l Unit Cost	Avg Labor Unit Cost	Avg Equip Unit Cost	Avg Total Unit Cost	Avg Price Incl O&P
4" T wall	Demo	VLF	Lg	LB	.640	25.00	---	19.20	---	19.20	**26.90**
	Demo	VLF	Sm	LB	.985	16.25	---	29.60	---	29.60	**41.40**
8" T wall	Demo	VLF	Lg	LB	1.60	10.00	---	48.00	---	48.00	**67.20**
	Demo	VLF	Sm	LB	2.46	6.50	---	73.80	---	73.80	**103.00**
Columns, 12" x 12" o.d.											
	Demo	VLF	Lg	LB	.320	50.00	---	9.60	---	9.60	**13.40**
	Demo	VLF	Sm	LB	.492	32.50	---	14.80	---	14.80	**20.70**
Veneer, 4" T, with air tools	Demo	SF	Lg	AB	.059	270.0	---	2.17	.90	3.07	**3.94**
	Demo	SF	Sm	AB	.091	175.5	---	3.35	1.38	4.73	**6.07**
Walls, with air tools											
8" T wall	Demo	SF	Lg	AB	.119	135.0	---	4.38	1.80	6.18	**7.94**
	Demo	SF	Sm	AB	.182	87.75	---	6.70	2.77	9.47	**12.20**
12" T wall	Demo	SF	Lg	AB	.168	95.00	---	6.19	2.55	8.74	**11.20**
	Demo	SF	Sm	AB	.259	61.75	---	9.54	3.93	13.47	**17.30**

Description	Oper	Unit	Vol	Crew Size	Man-hours per Unit	Crew Output per Day	Avg Mat'l Unit Cost	Avg Labor Unit Cost	Avg Equip Unit Cost	Avg Total Unit Cost	Avg Price Incl O&P

Concrete block; lightweight (haydite), standard or heavyweight

Foundations and retaining walls; no excavation included
Without reinforcing or with only lateral reinforcing
With air tools

Description	Oper	Unit	Vol	Crew Size	Man-hours per Unit	Crew Output per Day	Avg Mat'l Unit Cost	Avg Labor Unit Cost	Avg Equip Unit Cost	Avg Total Unit Cost	Avg Price Incl O&P
8" W x 8" H x 16" L	Demo	SF	Lg	AB	.057	280.0	---	2.10	.87	2.97	**3.81**
	Demo	SF	Sm	AB	.088	182.0	---	3.24	1.33	4.57	**5.87**
12" W x 8" H x 16" L	Demo	SF	Lg	AB	.067	240.0	---	2.47	1.01	3.48	**4.46**
	Demo	SF	Sm	AB	.103	156.0	---	3.79	1.56	5.35	**6.87**

Without air tools

Description	Oper	Unit	Vol	Crew Size	Man-hours per Unit	Crew Output per Day	Avg Mat'l Unit Cost	Avg Labor Unit Cost	Avg Equip Unit Cost	Avg Total Unit Cost	Avg Price Incl O&P
8" W x 8" H x 16" L	Demo	SF	Lg	LB	.071	225.0	---	2.13	---	2.13	**2.98**
	Demo	SF	Sm	LB	.109	146.3	---	3.27	---	3.27	**4.58**
12" W x 8" H x 16" L	Demo	SF	Lg	LB	.084	190.0	---	2.52	---	2.52	**3.53**
	Demo	SF	Sm	LB	.130	123.5	---	3.90	---	3.90	**5.46**

With vertical reinforcing in every other core (2 cores per block) with cores filled
With air tools

Description	Oper	Unit	Vol	Crew Size	Man-hours per Unit	Crew Output per Day	Avg Mat'l Unit Cost	Avg Labor Unit Cost	Avg Equip Unit Cost	Avg Total Unit Cost	Avg Price Incl O&P
8" W x 8" H x 16" L	Demo	SF	Lg	AB	.094	170.0	---	3.46	1.43	4.89	**6.28**
	Demo	SF	Sm	AB	.145	110.5	---	5.34	2.20	7.54	**9.68**
12" W x 8" H x 16" L	Demo	SF	Lg	AB	.110	145.0	---	4.05	1.67	5.72	**7.34**
	Demo	SF	Sm	AB	.170	94.25	---	6.26	2.57	8.83	**11.30**

Exterior walls (above grade) and partitions, no shoring included

Without reinforcing or with only lateral reinforcing
With air tools

Description	Oper	Unit	Vol	Crew Size	Man-hours per Unit	Crew Output per Day	Avg Mat'l Unit Cost	Avg Labor Unit Cost	Avg Equip Unit Cost	Avg Total Unit Cost	Avg Price Incl O&P
8" W x 8" H x 16" L	Demo	SF	Lg	AB	.046	350.0	---	1.69	.69	2.38	**3.06**
	Demo	SF	Sm	AB	.070	227.5	---	2.58	1.07	3.65	**4.68**
12" W x 8" H x 16" L	Demo	SF	Lg	AB	.053	300.0	---	1.95	.81	2.76	**3.54**
	Demo	SF	Sm	AB	.082	195.0	---	3.02	1.24	4.26	**5.47**

Without air tools

Description	Oper	Unit	Vol	Crew Size	Man-hours per Unit	Crew Output per Day	Avg Mat'l Unit Cost	Avg Labor Unit Cost	Avg Equip Unit Cost	Avg Total Unit Cost	Avg Price Incl O&P
8" W x 8" H x 16" L	Demo	SF	Lg	LB	.057	280.0	---	1.71	---	1.71	**2.39**
	Demo	SF	Sm	LB	.088	182.0	---	2.64	---	2.64	**3.70**
12" W x 8" H x 16" L	Demo	SF	Lg	LB	.067	240.0	---	2.01	---	2.01	**2.81**
	Demo	SF	Sm	LB	.103	156.0	---	3.09	---	3.09	**4.33**

Fences

Without reinforcing or with only lateral reinforcing
With air tools

Description	Oper	Unit	Vol	Crew Size	Man-hours per Unit	Crew Output per Day	Avg Mat'l Unit Cost	Avg Labor Unit Cost	Avg Equip Unit Cost	Avg Total Unit Cost	Avg Price Incl O&P
6" W x 4" H x 16" L	Demo	SF	Lg	AB	.041	390.0	---	1.51	.62	2.13	**2.73**
	Demo	SF	Sm	AB	.063	253.5	---	2.32	.96	3.28	**4.21**
6" W x 6" H x 16" L	Demo	SF	Lg	AB	.043	370.0	---	1.58	.66	2.24	**2.88**
	Demo	SF	Sm	AB	.067	240.5	---	2.47	1.01	3.48	**4.46**
8" W x 8" H x 16" L	Demo	SF	Lg	AB	.046	350.0	---	1.69	.69	2.38	**3.06**
	Demo	SF	Sm	AB	.070	227.5	---	2.58	1.07	3.65	**4.68**
12" W x 8" H x 16" L	Demo	SF	Lg	AB	.053	300.0	---	1.95	.81	2.76	**3.54**
	Demo	SF	Sm	AB	.082	195.0	---	3.02	1.24	4.26	**5.47**

Without air tools

Description	Oper	Unit	Vol	Crew Size	Man-hours per Unit	Crew Output per Day	Avg Mat'l Unit Cost	Avg Labor Unit Cost	Avg Equip Unit Cost	Avg Total Unit Cost	Avg Price Incl O&P
6" W x 4" H x 16" L	Demo	SF	Lg	LB	.052	310.0	---	1.56	---	1.56	**2.18**
	Demo	SF	Sm	LB	.079	201.5	---	2.37	---	2.37	**3.32**
6" W x 6" H x 16" L	Demo	SF	Lg	LB	.054	295.0	---	1.62	---	1.62	**2.27**
	Demo	SF	Sm	LB	.083	191.8	---	2.49	---	2.49	**3.49**
8" W x 8" H x 16" L	Demo	SF	Lg	LB	.057	280.0	---	1.71	---	1.71	**2.39**
	Demo	SF	Sm	LB	.088	182.0	---	2.64	---	2.64	**3.70**
12" W x 8" H x 16" L	Demo	SF	Lg	LB	.067	240.0	---	2.01	---	2.01	**2.81**
	Demo	SF	Sm	LB	.103	156.0	---	3.09	---	3.09	**4.33**

Description	Oper	Unit	Vol	Crew Size	Man-hours per Unit	Crew Output per Day	Avg Mat'l Unit Cost	Avg Labor Unit Cost	Avg Equip Unit Cost	Avg Total Unit Cost	Avg Price Incl O&P

Quarry tile, 6" or 9" squares

Floors

Description	Oper	Unit	Vol	Crew Size	Man-hours per Unit	Crew Output per Day	Avg Mat'l Unit Cost	Avg Labor Unit Cost	Avg Equip Unit Cost	Avg Total Unit Cost	Avg Price Incl O&P
Conventional mortar set	Demo	SF	Lg	LB	.036	445.0	---	1.08	---	1.08	**1.51**
	Demo	SF	Sm	LB	.055	289.3	---	1.65	---	1.65	**2.31**
Dry-set mortar	Demo	SF	Lg	LB	.031	515.0	---	.93	---	.93	**1.30**
	Demo	SF	Sm	LB	.048	334.8	---	1.44	---	1.44	**2.02**

Rough carpentry (framing)

Dimension lumber

Beams, set on steel columns

Built-up from 2" lumber

Description	Oper	Unit	Vol	Crew Size	Man-hours per Unit	Crew Output per Day	Avg Mat'l Unit Cost	Avg Labor Unit Cost	Avg Equip Unit Cost	Avg Total Unit Cost	Avg Price Incl O&P
4" T x 10" W - 10' L (2 pcs)	Demo	LF	Lg	LB	.019	855.0	---	.57	---	.57	**.80**
	Demo	LF	Sm	LB	.029	555.8	---	.87	---	.87	**1.22**
4" T x 12" W - 12' L (2 pcs)	Demo	LF	Lg	LB	.016	1025	---	.48	---	.48	**.67**
	Demo	LF	Sm	LB	.024	666.3	---	.72	---	.72	**1.01**
6" T x 10" W - 10' L (3 pcs)	Demo	LF	Lg	LB	.019	855.0	---	.57	---	.57	**.80**
	Demo	LF	Sm	LB	.029	555.8	---	.87	---	.87	**1.22**
6" T x 12" W - 12' L (3 pcs)	Demo	LF	Lg	LB	.016	1025	---	.48	---	.48	**.67**
	Demo	LF	Sm	LB	.024	666.3	---	.72	---	.72	**1.01**

Single member (solid lumber)

Description	Oper	Unit	Vol	Crew Size	Man-hours per Unit	Crew Output per Day	Avg Mat'l Unit Cost	Avg Labor Unit Cost	Avg Equip Unit Cost	Avg Total Unit Cost	Avg Price Incl O&P
3" T x 12" W - 12' L	Demo	LF	Lg	LB	.016	1025	---	.48	---	.48	**.67**
	Demo	LF	Sm	LB	.024	666.3	---	.72	---	.72	**1.01**
4" T x 12" W - 12' L	Demo	LF	Lg	LB	.016	1025	---	.48	---	.48	**.67**
	Demo	LF	Sm	LB	.024	666.3	---	.72	---	.72	**1.01**

Bracing, diagonal, notched-in, studs oc

Description	Oper	Unit	Vol	Crew Size	Man-hours per Unit	Crew Output per Day	Avg Mat'l Unit Cost	Avg Labor Unit Cost	Avg Equip Unit Cost	Avg Total Unit Cost	Avg Price Incl O&P
1" x 6" - 10' L	Demo	LF	Lg	LB	.026	605.0	---	.78	---	.78	**1.09**
	Demo	LF	Sm	LB	.041	393.3	---	1.23	---	1.23	**1.72**

Bridging, "X" type, 1" x 3", (8", 10", 12" T)

Description	Oper	Unit	Vol	Crew Size	Man-hours per Unit	Crew Output per Day	Avg Mat'l Unit Cost	Avg Labor Unit Cost	Avg Equip Unit Cost	Avg Total Unit Cost	Avg Price Incl O&P
16" oc	Demo	LF	Lg	LB	.046	350.0	---	1.38	---	1.38	**1.93**
	Demo	LF	Sm	LB	.070	227.5	---	2.10	---	2.10	**2.94**

Columns or posts

Description	Oper	Unit	Vol	Crew Size	Man-hours per Unit	Crew Output per Day	Avg Mat'l Unit Cost	Avg Labor Unit Cost	Avg Equip Unit Cost	Avg Total Unit Cost	Avg Price Incl O&P
4" x 4" -8' L	Demo	LF	Lg	LB	.021	770.0	---	.63	---	.63	**.88**
	Demo	LF	Sm	LB	.032	500.5	---	.96	---	.96	**1.34**
6" x 6" -8' L	Demo	LF	Lg	LB	.021	770.0	---	.63	---	.63	**.88**
	Demo	LF	Sm	LB	.032	500.5	---	.96	---	.96	**1.34**
6" x 8" -8' L	Demo	LF	Lg	LB	.025	650.0	---	.75	---	.75	**1.05**
	Demo	LF	Sm	LB	.038	422.5	---	1.14	---	1.14	**1.60**
8" x 8" -8' L	Demo	LF	Lg	LB	.026	615.0	---	.78	---	.78	**1.09**
	Demo	LF	Sm	LB	.040	399.8	---	1.20	---	1.20	**1.68**

Fascia

Description	Oper	Unit	Vol	Crew Size	Man-hours per Unit	Crew Output per Day	Avg Mat'l Unit Cost	Avg Labor Unit Cost	Avg Equip Unit Cost	Avg Total Unit Cost	Avg Price Incl O&P
1" x 4" - 12" L	Demo	LF	Lg	LB	.012	1315	---	.36	---	.36	**.50**
	Demo	LF	Sm	LB	.019	854.8	---	.57	---	.57	**.80**

Description	Oper	Unit	Vol	Crew Size	Man-hours per Unit	Crew Output per Day	Avg Mat'l Unit Cost	Avg Labor Unit Cost	Avg Equip Unit Cost	Avg Total Unit Cost	Avg Price Incl O&P
Firestops or stiffeners											
2" x 4" - 16"	Demo	LF	Lg	LB	.034	475.0	---	1.02	---	1.02	**1.43**
	Demo	LF	Sm	LB	.052	308.8	---	1.56	---	1.56	**2.18**
2" x 6" - 16"	Demo	LF	Lg	LB	.034	475.0	---	1.02	---	1.02	**1.43**
	Demo	LF	Sm	LB	.052	308.8	---	1.56	---	1.56	**2.18**
Furring strips, 1" x 4" - 8' L											
Walls; strips 12" oc											
Studs 16" oc	Demo	SF	Lg	LB	.013	1215	---	.39	---	.39	**.55**
	Demo	SF	Sm	LB	.020	789.8	---	.60	---	.60	**.84**
Studs 24" oc	Demo	SF	Lg	LB	.012	1365	---	.36	---	.36	**.50**
	Demo	SF	Sm	LB	.018	887.3	---	.54	---	.54	**.76**
Masonry (concrete blocks)	Demo	SF	Lg	LB	.015	1095	---	.45	---	.45	**.63**
	Demo	SF	Sm	LB	.022	711.8	---	.66	---	.66	**.92**
Concrete	Demo	SF	Lg	LB	.025	645.0	---	.75	---	.75	**1.05**
	Demo	SF	Sm	LB	.038	419.3	---	1.14	---	1.14	**1.60**
Ceiling; joists 16" oc											
Strips 12" oc	Demo	SF	Lg	LB	.019	840.0	---	.57	---	.57	**.80**
	Demo	SF	Sm	LB	.029	546.0	---	.87	---	.87	**1.22**
Strips 16" oc	Demo	SF	Lg	LB	.015	1075	---	.45	---	.45	**.63**
	Demo	SF	Sm	LB	.023	698.8	---	.69	---	.69	**.97**
Headers or lintels, over openings											
Built-up or single member											
4" T x 6" W - 4' L	Demo	LF	Lg	LB	.029	560.0	---	.87	---	.87	**1.22**
	Demo	LF	Sm	LB	.044	364.0	---	1.32	---	1.32	**1.85**
4" T x 8" W - 8' L	Demo	LF	Lg	LB	.022	720.0	---	.66	---	.66	**.92**
	Demo	LF	Sm	LB	.034	468.0	---	1.02	---	1.02	**1.43**
4" T x 10" W - 10' L	Demo	LF	Lg	LB	.019	855.0	---	.57	---	.57	**.80**
	Demo	LF	Sm	LB	.029	555.8	---	.87	---	.87	**1.22**
4" T x 12" W - 12' L	Demo	LF	Lg	LB	.016	1025	---	.48	---	.48	**.67**
	Demo	LF	Sm	LB	.024	666.3	---	.72	---	.72	**1.01**
4" T x 14" W - 14' L	Demo	LF	Lg	LB	.016	1025	---	.48	---	.48	**.67**
	Demo	LF	Sm	LB	.024	666.3	---	.72	---	.72	**1.01**
Joists											
Ceiling											
2" x 4" - 8' L	Demo	LF	Lg	LB	.013	1230	---	.39	---	.39	**.55**
	Demo	LF	Sm	LB	.020	799.5	---	.60	---	.60	**.84**
2" x 4" - 10' L	Demo	LF	Lg	LB	.011	1395	---	.33	---	.33	**.46**
	Demo	LF	Sm	LB	.018	906.8	---	.54	---	.54	**.76**
2" x 8" - 12' L	Demo	LF	Lg	LB	.011	1420	---	.33	---	.33	**.46**
	Demo	LF	Sm	LB	.017	923.0	---	.51	---	.51	**.71**
2" x 10" - 14' L	Demo	LF	Lg	LB	.010	1535	---	.30	---	.30	**.42**
	Demo	LF	Sm	LB	.016	997.8	---	.48	---	.48	**.67**
2" x 12" - 16' L	Demo	LF	Lg	LB	.010	1585	---	.30	---	.30	**.42**
	Demo	LF	Sm	LB	.016	1030	---	.48	---	.48	**.67**
Floor; seated on sill plate											
2" x 8" - 12' L	Demo	LF	Lg	LB	.010	1600	---	.30	---	.30	**.42**
	Demo	LF	Sm	LB	.015	1040	---	.45	---	.45	**.63**
2" x 10" - 14' L	Demo	LF	Lg	LB	.009	1725	---	.27	---	.27	**.38**
	Demo	LF	Sm	LB	.014	1121	---	.42	---	.42	**.59**
2" x 12" - 16' L	Demo	LF	Lg	LB	.009	1755	---	.27	---	.27	**.38**
	Demo	LF	Sm	LB	.014	1141	---	.42	---	.42	**.59**

Description	Oper	Unit	Vol	Crew Size	Man-hours per Unit	Crew Output per Day	Avg Mat'l Unit Cost	Avg Labor Unit Cost	Avg Equip Unit Cost	Avg Total Unit Cost	Avg Price Incl O&P
Ledgers											
Nailed, 2" x 6" - 12' L	Demo	LF	Lg	LB	.023	710.0	---	.69	---	.69	**.97**
	Demo	LF	Sm	LB	.035	461.5	---	1.05	---	1.05	**1.47**
Bolted, 3" x 8" - 12' L	Demo	LF	Lg	LB	.016	970.0	---	.48	---	.48	**.67**
	Demo	LF	Sm	LB	.025	630.5	---	.75	---	.75	**1.05**
Plates; 2" x 4" or 2" x 6"											
Double top nailed	Demo	LF	Lg	LB	.020	820.0	---	.60	---	.60	**.84**
	Demo	LF	Sm	LB	.030	533.0	---	.90	---	.90	**1.26**
Sill, nailed	Demo	LF	Lg	LB	.012	1360	---	.36	---	.36	**.50**
	Demo	LF	Sm	LB	.018	884.0	---	.54	---	.54	**.76**
Sill or bottom, bolted	Demo	LF	Lg	LB	.023	685.0	---	.69	---	.69	**.97**
	Demo	LF	Sm	LB	.036	445.3	---	1.08	---	1.08	**1.51**
Rafters											
Common											
2" x 4" - 14' L	Demo	LF	Lg	LB	.009	1795	---	.27	---	.27	**.38**
	Demo	LF	Sm	LB	.014	1167	---	.42	---	.42	**.59**
2" x 6" - 14' L	Demo	LF	Lg	LB	.010	1660	---	.30	---	.30	**.42**
	Demo	LF	Sm	LB	.015	1079	---	.45	---	.45	**.63**
2" x 8" - 14' L	Demo	LF	Lg	LB	.011	1435	---	.33	---	.33	**.46**
	Demo	LF	Sm	LB	.017	932.8	---	.51	---	.51	**.71**
2" x 10" - 14' L	Demo	LF	Lg	LB	.013	1195	---	.39	---	.39	**.55**
	Demo	LF	Sm	LB	.021	776.8	---	.63	---	.63	**.88**
Hip and/or valley											
2" x 4" - 16' L	Demo	LF	Lg	LB	.008	2050	---	.24	---	.24	**.34**
	Demo	LF	Sm	LB	.012	1333	---	.36	---	.36	**.50**
2" x 6" - 16' L	Demo	LF	Lg	LB	.008	1895	---	.24	---	.24	**.34**
	Demo	LF	Sm	LB	.013	1232	---	.39	---	.39	**.55**
2" x 8" - 16' L	Demo	LF	Lg	LB	.010	1640	---	.30	---	.30	**.42**
	Demo	LF	Sm	LB	.015	1066	---	.45	---	.45	**.63**
2" x 10" - 16' L	Demo	LF	Lg	LB	.012	1360	---	.36	---	.36	**.50**
	Demo	LF	Sm	LB	.018	884.0	---	.54	---	.54	**.76**
Jack											
2" x 4" - 6' L	Demo	LF	Lg	LB	.020	805.0	---	.60	---	.60	**.84**
	Demo	LF	Sm	LB	.031	523.3	---	.93	---	.93	**1.30**
2" x 6" - 6' L	Demo	LF	Lg	LB	.022	740.0	---	.66	---	.66	**.92**
	Demo	LF	Sm	LB	.033	481.0	---	.99	---	.99	**1.39**
2" x 8" - 6' L	Demo	LF	Lg	LB	.024	655.0	---	.72	---	.72	**1.01**
	Demo	LF	Sm	LB	.038	425.8	---	1.14	---	1.14	**1.60**
2" x 10" - 6' L	Demo	LF	Lg	LB	.030	540.0	---	.90	---	.90	**1.26**
	Demo	LF	Sm	LB	.046	351.0	---	1.38	---	1.38	**1.93**

Description	Oper	Unit	Vol	Crew Size	Man-hours per Unit	Crew Output per Day	Avg Mat'l Unit Cost	Avg Labor Unit Cost	Avg Equip Unit Cost	Avg Total Unit Cost	Avg Price Incl O&P
Roof decking, solid T&G											
2" x 6" - 12' L	Demo	LF	Lg	LB	.025	645.0	---	.75	---	.75	**1.05**
	Demo	LF	Sm	LB	.038	419.3	---	1.14	---	1.14	**1.60**
2" x 8" - 12' L	Demo	LF	Lg	LB	.018	900.0	---	.54	---	.54	**.76**
	Demo	LF	Sm	LB	.027	585.0	---	.81	---	.81	**1.13**
Studs											
2" x 4" - 8' L	Demo	LF	Lg	LB	.012	1360	---	.36	---	.36	**.50**
	Demo	LF	Sm	LB	.018	884.0	---	.54	---	.54	**.76**
2" x 6" - 8' L	Demo	LF	Lg	LB	.012	1360	---	.36	---	.36	**.50**
	Demo	LF	Sm	LB	.018	884.0	---	.54	---	.54	**.76**
Stud partitions, studs 16" oc with bottom plate and double top plates and firestops; per LF partition											
2" x 4" - 8' L	Demo	LF	Lg	LB	.160	100.0	---	4.80	---	4.80	**6.72**
	Demo	LF	Sm	LB	.246	65.00	---	7.38	---	7.38	**10.30**
2" x 6" - 8' L	Demo	LF	Lg	LB	.160	100.0	---	4.80	---	4.80	**6.72**
	Demo	LF	Sm	LB	.246	65.00	---	7.38	---	7.38	**10.30**

Boards

Sheathing, regular or diagonal
1" x 8"

Description	Oper	Unit	Vol	Crew Size	Man-hours per Unit	Crew Output per Day	Avg Mat'l Unit Cost	Avg Labor Unit Cost	Avg Equip Unit Cost	Avg Total Unit Cost	Avg Price Incl O&P
Roof	Demo	SF	Lg	LB	.012	1340	---	.36	---	.36	**.50**
	Demo	SF	Sm	LB	.018	871.0	---	.54	---	.54	**.76**
Sidewall	Demo	SF	Lg	LB	.010	1615	---	.30	---	.30	**.42**
	Demo	SF	Sm	LB	.015	1050	---	.45	---	.45	**.63**

Subflooring, regular or diagonal

Description	Oper	Unit	Vol	Crew Size	Man-hours per Unit	Crew Output per Day	Avg Mat'l Unit Cost	Avg Labor Unit Cost	Avg Equip Unit Cost	Avg Total Unit Cost	Avg Price Incl O&P
1" x 8" - 16' L	Demo	SF	Lg	LB	.010	1525	---	.30	---	.30	**.42**
	Demo	SF	Sm	LB	.016	991.3	---	.48	---	.48	**.67**
1" x 10" - 16' L	Demo	SF	Lg	LB	.008	1930	---	.24	---	.24	**.34**
	Demo	SF	Sm	LB	.013	1255	---	.39	---	.39	**.55**

Plywood

Sheathing
Roof

Description	Oper	Unit	Vol	Crew Size	Man-hours per Unit	Crew Output per Day	Avg Mat'l Unit Cost	Avg Labor Unit Cost	Avg Equip Unit Cost	Avg Total Unit Cost	Avg Price Incl O&P
1/2" T, CDX	Demo	SF	Lg	LB	.008	1970	---	.24	---	.24	**.34**
	Demo	SF	Sm	LB	.012	1281	---	.36	---	.36	**.50**
5/8" T, CDX	Demo	SF	Lg	LB	.008	1935	---	.24	---	.24	**.34**
	Demo	SF	Sm	LB	.013	1258	---	.39	---	.39	**.55**

Wall

Description	Oper	Unit	Vol	Crew Size	Man-hours per Unit	Crew Output per Day	Avg Mat'l Unit Cost	Avg Labor Unit Cost	Avg Equip Unit Cost	Avg Total Unit Cost	Avg Price Incl O&P
3/8" or 1/2" T, CDX	Demo	SF	Lg	LB	.006	2520	---	.18	---	.18	**.25**
	Demo	SF	Sm	LB	.010	1638	---	.30	---	.30	**.42**
5/8" T, CDX	Demo	SF	Lg	LB	.007	2460	---	.21	---	.21	**.29**
	Demo	SF	Sm	LB	.010	1599	---	.30	---	.30	**.42**

Description	Oper	Unit	Vol	Crew Size	Man-hours per Unit	Crew Output per Day	Avg Mat'l Unit Cost	Avg Labor Unit Cost	Avg Equip Unit Cost	Avg Total Unit Cost	Avg Price Incl O&P
Subflooring											
5/8", 3/4" T, CDX	Demo	SF	Lg	LB	.007	2305	---	.21	---	.21	.29
	Demo	SF	Sm	LB	.011	1498	---	.33	---	.33	.46
1-1/8" T, 2-4-1, T&G long edges											
	Demo	SF	Lg	LB	.010	1615	---	.30	---	.30	.42
	Demo	SF	Sm	LB	.015	1050	---	.45	---	.45	.63
Trusses, "W" pattern with gin pole, 24' to 30' spans											
3 - in - 12 slope	Demo	Ea	Lg	LB	.615	26.00	---	18.50	---	18.50	25.80
	Demo	Ea	Sm	LB	.947	16.90	---	28.40	---	28.40	39.80
5 - in - 12 slope	Demo	Ea	Lg	LB	.615	26.00	---	18.50	---	18.50	25.80
	Demo	Ea	Sm	LB	.947	16.90	---	28.40	---	28.40	39.80

Finish carpentry

Description	Oper	Unit	Vol	Crew Size	Man-hours per Unit	Crew Output per Day	Avg Mat'l Unit Cost	Avg Labor Unit Cost	Avg Equip Unit Cost	Avg Total Unit Cost	Avg Price Incl O&P
Bath accessories, screwed											
	Demo	Ea	Lg	LB	.128	125.0	---	3.84	---	3.84	5.38
	Demo	Ea	Sm	LB	.197	81.25	---	5.91	---	5.91	8.27
Cabinets											
Kitchen, to 3' x 4', wood; base, wall, or peninsula											
	Demo	Ea	Lg	LB	.640	25.00	---	19.20	---	19.20	26.90
	Demo	Ea	Sm	LB	.985	16.25	---	29.60	---	29.60	41.40
Medicine, metal											
	Demo	Ea	Lg	LB	.533	30.00	---	16.00	---	16.00	22.40
	Demo	Ea	Sm	LB	.821	19.50	---	24.60	---	24.60	34.50
Vanity, cabinet and sink top											
Disconnect plumbing and remove to dumpster											
	Demo	Ea	Lg	LB	1.00	16.00	---	30.00	---	30.00	42.00
	Demo	Ea	Sm	LB	1.54	10.40	---	46.20	---	46.20	64.70
Remove old unit, replace with new unit, reconnect plumbing											
	Demo	Ea	Lg	SB	2.29	7.00	---	83.60	---	83.60	121.00
	Demo	Ea	Sm	SB	3.52	4.55	---	129.00	---	129.00	186.00
Hardwood flooring (over wood subfloors)											
Block, set in mastic	Demo	SF	Lg	LB	.013	1200	---	.39	---	.39	.55
	Demo	SF	Sm	LB	.021	780.0	---	.63	---	.63	.88
Strip, nailed	Demo	SF	Lg	LB	.018	900.0	---	.54	---	.54	.76
	Demo	SF	Sm	LB	.027	585.0	---	.81	---	.81	1.13
Marlite panels, 4' x 8',											
adhesive set	Demo	SF	Lg	LB	.019	850.0	---	.57	---	.57	.80
	Demo	SF	Sm	LB	.029	552.5	---	.87	---	.87	1.22
Molding and trim											
At base (floor)	Demo	LF	Lg	LB	.015	1060	---	.45	---	.45	.63
	Demo	LF	Sm	LB	.023	689.0	---	.69	---	.69	.97
At ceiling	Demo	LF	Lg	LB	.013	1200	---	.39	---	.39	.55
	Demo	LF	Sm	LB	.021	780.0	---	.63	---	.63	.88
On walls or cabinets	Demo	LF	Lg	LB	.010	1600	---	.30	---	.30	.42
	Demo	LF	Sm	LB	.015	1040	---	.45	---	.45	.63
Paneling											
Plywood, prefinished	Demo	SF	Lg	LB	.009	1850	---	.27	---	.27	.38
	Demo	SF	Sm	LB	.013	1203	---	.39	---	.39	.55
Wood	Demo	SF	Lg	LB	.010	1650	---	.30	---	.30	.42
	Demo	SF	Sm	LB	.015	1073	---	.45	---	.45	.63

Description	Oper	Unit	Vol	Crew Size	Man-hours per Unit	Crew Output per Day	Avg Mat'l Unit Cost	Avg Labor Unit Cost	Avg Equip Unit Cost	Avg Total Unit Cost	Avg Price Incl O&P

Weather protection
Insulation
Batt/roll, with wall or ceiling finish already removed

Description	Oper	Unit	Vol	Crew Size	Man-hours per Unit	Crew Output per Day	Avg Mat'l Unit Cost	Avg Labor Unit Cost	Avg Equip Unit Cost	Avg Total Unit Cost	Avg Price Incl O&P
Joists, 16" or 24" oc	Demo	SF	Lg	LB	.005	2935	---	.15	---	.15	.21
	Demo	SF	Sm	LB	.008	1908	---	.24	---	.24	.34
Rafters, 16" or 24" oc	Demo	SF	Lg	LB	.006	2560	---	.18	---	.18	.25
	Demo	SF	Sm	LB	.010	1664	---	.30	---	.30	.42
Studs, 16" or 24" oc	Demo	SF	Lg	LB	.005	3285	---	.15	---	.15	.21
	Demo	SF	Sm	LB	.007	2135	---	.21	---	.21	.29

Loose, with ceiling finish already removed
Joists, 16" or 24" oc

Description	Oper	Unit	Vol	Crew Size	Man-hours per Unit	Crew Output per Day	Avg Mat'l Unit Cost	Avg Labor Unit Cost	Avg Equip Unit Cost	Avg Total Unit Cost	Avg Price Incl O&P
4" T	Demo	SF	Lg	LB	.004	3900	---	.12	---	.12	.17
	Demo	SF	Sm	LB	.006	2535	---	.18	---	.18	.25
6" T	Demo	SF	Lg	LB	.007	2340	---	.21	---	.21	.29
	Demo	SF	Sm	LB	.011	1521	---	.33	---	.33	.46

Rigid
Roofs

Description	Oper	Unit	Vol	Crew Size	Man-hours per Unit	Crew Output per Day	Avg Mat'l Unit Cost	Avg Labor Unit Cost	Avg Equip Unit Cost	Avg Total Unit Cost	Avg Price Incl O&P
1/2" T	Demo	Sq	Lg	LB	.941	17.00	---	28.20	---	28.20	39.50
	Demo	Sq	Sm	LB	1.45	11.05	---	43.50	---	43.50	60.90
1" T	Demo	Sq	Lg	LB	1.07	15.00	---	32.10	---	32.10	44.90
	Demo	Sq	Sm	LB	1.64	9.75	---	49.20	---	49.20	68.90
Walls, 1/2" T	Demo	SF	Lg	LB	.007	2140	---	.21	---	.21	.29
	Demo	SF	Sm	LB	.012	1391	---	.36	---	.36	.50

Sheet metal
Gutter and downspouts

Description	Oper	Unit	Vol	Crew Size	Man-hours per Unit	Crew Output per Day	Avg Mat'l Unit Cost	Avg Labor Unit Cost	Avg Equip Unit Cost	Avg Total Unit Cost	Avg Price Incl O&P
Aluminum	Demo	LF	Lg	LB	.019	850.0	---	.57	---	.57	.80
	Demo	LF	Sm	LB	.029	552.5	---	.87	---	.87	1.22
Galvanized	Demo	LF	Lg	LB	.025	640.0	---	.75	---	.75	1.05
	Demo	LF	Sm	LB	.038	416.0	---	1.14	---	1.14	1.60

Roofing and siding
Aluminum
Roofing, nailed to wood
Corrugated (2-1/2"), 26" W with 3-3/4" side lap and 6" end lap

Description	Oper	Unit	Vol	Crew Size	Man-hours per Unit	Crew Output per Day	Avg Mat'l Unit Cost	Avg Labor Unit Cost	Avg Equip Unit Cost	Avg Total Unit Cost	Avg Price Incl O&P
	Demo	Sq	Lg	LB	1.60	10.00	---	48.00	---	48.00	67.20
	Demo	Sq	Sm	LB	2.46	6.50	---	73.80	---	73.80	103.00

Siding, nailed to wood
Clapboard (i.e., lap drop)

Description	Oper	Unit	Vol	Crew Size	Man-hours per Unit	Crew Output per Day	Avg Mat'l Unit Cost	Avg Labor Unit Cost	Avg Equip Unit Cost	Avg Total Unit Cost	Avg Price Incl O&P
8" exposure	Demo	SF	Lg	LB	.016	1025	---	.48	---	.48	.67
	Demo	SF	Sm	LB	.024	666.3	---	.72	---	.72	1.01
10" exposure	Demo	SF	Lg	LB	.013	1280	---	.39	---	.39	.55
	Demo	SF	Sm	LB	.019	832.0	---	.57	---	.57	.80

Corrugated (2-1/2"), 26" W with 2-1/2" side lap and 4" end lap

Description	Oper	Unit	Vol	Crew Size	Man-hours per Unit	Crew Output per Day	Avg Mat'l Unit Cost	Avg Labor Unit Cost	Avg Equip Unit Cost	Avg Total Unit Cost	Avg Price Incl O&P
	Demo	SF	Lg	LB	.013	1200	---	.39	---	.39	.55
	Demo	SF	Sm	LB	.021	780.0	---	.63	---	.63	.88
Panels, 4' x 8'	Demo	SF	Lg	LB	.007	2400	---	.21	---	.21	.29
	Demo	SF	Sm	LB	.010	1560	---	.30	---	.30	.42

Shingle, 24" L with 12" exposure

Description	Oper	Unit	Vol	Crew Size	Man-hours per Unit	Crew Output per Day	Avg Mat'l Unit Cost	Avg Labor Unit Cost	Avg Equip Unit Cost	Avg Total Unit Cost	Avg Price Incl O&P
	Demo	SF	Lg	LB	.011	1450	---	.33	---	.33	.46
	Demo	SF	Sm	LB	.017	942.5	---	.51	---	.51	.71

Description	Oper	Unit	Vol	Crew Size	Man-hours per Unit	Crew Output per Day	Avg Mat'l Unit Cost	Avg Labor Unit Cost	Avg Equip Unit Cost	Avg Total Unit Cost	Avg Price Incl O&P
Asphalt shingle roofing											
240 lb/sq, strip, 3 tab 5" exposure											
	Demo	Sq	Lg	LB	1.00	16.00	---	30.00	---	30.00	**42.00**
	Demo	Sq	Sm	LB	1.54	10.40	---	46.20	---	46.20	**64.70**
Built-up/hot roofing (to wood deck)											
3 ply											
With gravel	Demo	Sq	Lg	LB	1.45	11.00	---	43.50	---	43.50	**60.90**
	Demo	Sq	Sm	LB	2.24	7.15	---	67.20	---	67.20	**94.10**
Without gravel	Demo	Sq	Lg	LB	1.14	14.00	---	34.20	---	34.20	**47.90**
	Demo	Sq	Sm	LB	1.76	9.10	---	52.80	---	52.80	**73.90**
5 ply											
With gravel	Demo	Sq	Lg	LB	1.60	10.00	---	48.00	---	48.00	**67.20**
	Demo	Sq	Sm	LB	2.46	6.50	---	73.80	---	73.80	**103.00**
Without gravel	Demo	Sq	Lg	LB	1.23	13.00	---	36.90	---	36.90	**51.70**
	Demo	Sq	Sm	LB	1.89	8.45	---	56.70	---	56.70	**79.40**
Clay tile roofing											
2 piece interlocking	Demo	Sq	Lg	LB	1.60	10.00	---	48.00	---	48.00	**67.20**
	Demo	Sq	Sm	LB	2.46	6.50	---	73.80	---	73.80	**103.00**
1 piece	Demo	Sq	Lg	LB	1.45	11.00	---	43.50	---	43.50	**60.90**
	Demo	Sq	Sm	LB	2.24	7.15	---	67.20	---	67.20	**94.10**
Hardboard siding											
Lap, 1/2" T x 12" W x 16' L, with 11" exposure											
	Demo	SF	Lg	LB	.012	1345	---	.36	---	.36	**.50**
	Demo	SF	Sm	LB	.018	874.3	---	.54	---	.54	**.76**
Panels, 7/16" T x 4' W x 8' H											
	Demo	SF	Lg	LB	.006	2520	---	.18	---	.18	**.25**
	Demo	SF	Sm	LB	.010	1638	---	.30	---	.30	**.42**
Mineral surfaced roll roofing											
Single coverage 90 lb/sq roll with 6" end lap and 2" headlap											
	Demo	Sq	Lg	LB	.500	32.00	---	15.00	---	15.00	**21.00**
	Demo	Sq	Sm	LB	.769	20.80	---	23.10	---	23.10	**32.30**
Double coverage selvage roll, with 6" end lap and 17" exposure											
	Demo	Sq	Lg	LB	.727	22.00	---	21.80	---	21.80	**30.50**
	Demo	Sq	Sm	LB	1.12	14.30	---	33.60	---	33.60	**47.00**
Wood											
Roofing											
Shakes											
24" L with 10" exposure											
1/2" to 3/4" T	Demo	Sq	Lg	LB	.640	25.00	---	19.20	---	19.20	**26.90**
	Demo	Sq	Sm	LB	.985	16.25	---	29.60	---	29.60	**41.40**
3/4" to 5/4" T	Demo	Sq	Lg	LB	.696	23.00	---	20.90	---	20.90	**29.20**
	Demo	Sq	Sm	LB	1.07	14.95	---	32.10	---	32.10	**44.90**
Shingles											
16" L with 5" exposure	Demo	Sq	Lg	LB	1.33	12.00	---	39.90	---	39.90	**55.90**
	Demo	Sq	Sm	LB	2.05	7.80	---	61.50	---	61.50	**86.10**
18" L with 5-1/2" exposure	Demo	Sq	Lg	LB	1.23	13.00	---	36.90	---	36.90	**51.70**
	Demo	Sq	Sm	LB	1.89	8.45	---	56.70	---	56.70	**79.40**
24" L with 7-1/2" exposure	Demo	Sq	Lg	LB	.889	18.00	---	26.70	---	26.70	**37.30**
	Demo	Sq	Sm	LB	1.37	11.70	---	41.10	---	41.10	**57.50**

Description	Oper	Unit	Vol	Crew Size	Man-hours per Unit	Crew Output per Day	Avg Mat'l Unit Cost	Avg Labor Unit Cost	Avg Equip Unit Cost	Avg Total Unit Cost	Avg Price Incl O&P
Siding											
Bevel											
1/2" x 8" with 6-3/4" exposure	Demo	SF	Lg	LB	.018	910.0	---	.54	---	.54	.76
	Demo	SF	Sm	LB	.027	591.5	---	.81	---	.81	**1.13**
5/8" x 10" with 8-3/4" exposure											
	Demo	SF	Lg	LB	.014	1180	---	.42	---	.42	.59
	Demo	SF	Sm	LB	.021	767.0	---	.63	---	.63	.88
3/4" x 12" with 10-3/4" exposure											
	Demo	SF	Lg	LB	.011	1450	---	.33	---	.33	.46
	Demo	SF	Sm	LB	.017	942.5	---	.51	---	.51	.71
Drop (horizontal), 1/4" T&G											
1" x 8" with 7" exposure	Demo	SF	Lg	LB	.017	945.0	---	.51	---	.51	.71
	Demo	SF	Sm	LB	.026	614.3	---	.78	---	.78	**1.09**
1" x 10" with 9" exposure	Demo	SF	Lg	LB	.013	1215	---	.39	---	.39	.55
	Demo	SF	Sm	LB	.020	789.8	---	.60	---	.60	.84
Board (1" x 12") and batten (1" x 2") @ 12" oc											
Horizontal	Demo	SF	Lg	LB	.013	1280	---	.39	---	.39	.55
	Demo	SF	Sm	LB	.019	832.0	---	.57	---	.57	.80
Vertical											
Standard	Demo	SF	Lg	LB	.016	1025	---	.48	---	.48	.67
	Demo	SF	Sm	LB	.024	666.3	---	.72	---	.72	**1.01**
Reverse	Demo	SF	Lg	LB	.015	1065	---	.45	---	.45	.63
	Demo	SF	Sm	LB	.023	692.3	---	.69	---	.69	.97
Board on board (1" x 12" with 1-1/2" overlap), vertical											
	Demo	SF	Lg	LB	.017	950.0	---	.51	---	.51	.71
	Demo	SF	Sm	LB	.026	617.5	---	.78	---	.78	**1.09**
Plywood (1/2" T) with battens (1" x 2")											
16" oc battens	Demo	SF	Lg	LB	.007	2255	---	.21	---	.21	.29
	Demo	SF	Sm	LB	.011	1466	---	.33	---	.33	.46
24" oc battens	Demo	SF	Lg	LB	.007	2365	---	.21	---	.21	.29
	Demo	SF	Sm	LB	.010	1537	---	.30	---	.30	.42
Shakes											
24" L with 11-1/2" exposure											
1/2" to 3/4" T	Demo	SF	Lg	LB	.010	1600	---	.30	---	.30	.42
	Demo	SF	Sm	LB	.015	1040	---	.45	---	.45	.63
3/4" to 5/4" T	Demo	SF	Lg	LB	.011	1440	---	.33	---	.33	.46
	Demo	SF	Sm	LB	.017	936.0	---	.51	---	.51	.71
Shingles											
16" L with 7-1/2" exposure	Demo	SF	Lg	LB	.016	1000	---	.48	---	.48	.67
	Demo	SF	Sm	LB	.025	650.0	---	.75	---	.75	**1.05**
18" L with 8-1/2" exposure	Demo	SF	Lg	LB	.014	1130	---	.42	---	.42	.59
	Demo	SF	Sm	LB	.022	734.5	---	.66	---	.66	.92
24" L with 11-1/2" exposure	Demo	SF	Lg	LB	.010	1530	---	.30	---	.30	.42
	Demo	SF	Sm	LB	.016	994.5	---	.48	---	.48	.67

Description	Oper	Unit	Vol	Crew Size	Man-hours per Unit	Crew Output per Day	Avg Mat'l Unit Cost	Avg Labor Unit Cost	Avg Equip Unit Cost	Avg Total Unit Cost	Avg Price Incl O&P

Doors, windows and glazing
Doors with related trim and frame

Closet, with track

Description	Oper	Unit	Vol	Crew Size	Man-hours per Unit	Crew Output per Day	Avg Mat'l Unit Cost	Avg Labor Unit Cost	Avg Equip Unit Cost	Avg Total Unit Cost	Avg Price Incl O&P
Folding, 4 doors	Demo	Set	Lg	LB	1.33	12.00	---	39.90	---	39.90	**55.90**
	Demo	Set	Sm	LB	2.05	7.80	---	61.50	---	61.50	**86.10**
Sliding, 2 or 3 doors	Demo	Set	Lg	LB	1.33	12.00	---	39.90	---	39.90	**55.90**
	Demo	Set	Sm	LB	2.05	7.80	---	61.50	---	61.50	**86.10**

Entry, 3' x 7'

Description	Oper	Unit	Vol	Crew Size	Man-hours per Unit	Crew Output per Day	Avg Mat'l Unit Cost	Avg Labor Unit Cost	Avg Equip Unit Cost	Avg Total Unit Cost	Avg Price Incl O&P
	Demo	Ea	Lg	LB	1.14	14.00	---	34.20	---	34.20	**47.90**
	Demo	Ea	Sm	LB	1.76	9.10	---	52.80	---	52.80	**73.90**

Fire, 3' x 7'

Description	Oper	Unit	Vol	Crew Size	Man-hours per Unit	Crew Output per Day	Avg Mat'l Unit Cost	Avg Labor Unit Cost	Avg Equip Unit Cost	Avg Total Unit Cost	Avg Price Incl O&P
	Demo	Ea	Lg	LB	1.14	14.00	---	34.20	---	34.20	**47.90**
	Demo	Ea	Sm	LB	1.76	9.10	---	52.80	---	52.80	**73.90**

Garage

Wood, aluminum, or hardboard

Description	Oper	Unit	Vol	Crew Size	Man-hours per Unit	Crew Output per Day	Avg Mat'l Unit Cost	Avg Labor Unit Cost	Avg Equip Unit Cost	Avg Total Unit Cost	Avg Price Incl O&P
Single	Demo	Ea	Lg	LB	2.00	8.00	---	60.00	---	60.00	**84.00**
	Demo	Ea	Sm	LB	3.08	5.20	---	92.40	---	92.40	**129.00**
Double	Demo	Ea	Lg	LB	2.67	6.00	---	80.10	---	80.10	**112.00**
	Demo	Ea	Sm	LB	4.10	3.90	---	123.00	---	123.00	**172.00**

Steel

Description	Oper	Unit	Vol	Crew Size	Man-hours per Unit	Crew Output per Day	Avg Mat'l Unit Cost	Avg Labor Unit Cost	Avg Equip Unit Cost	Avg Total Unit Cost	Avg Price Incl O&P
Single	Demo	Ea	Lg	LB	2.29	7.00	---	68.70	---	68.70	**96.20**
	Demo	Ea	Sm	LB	3.52	4.55	---	106.00	---	106.00	**148.00**
Double	Demo	Ea	Lg	LB	3.20	5.00	---	96.00	---	96.00	**134.00**
	Demo	Ea	Sm	LB	4.92	3.25	---	148.00	---	148.00	**207.00**

Glass sliding, with track

Description	Oper	Unit	Vol	Crew Size	Man-hours per Unit	Crew Output per Day	Avg Mat'l Unit Cost	Avg Labor Unit Cost	Avg Equip Unit Cost	Avg Total Unit Cost	Avg Price Incl O&P
2 lites wide	Demo	Set	Lg	LB	2.00	8.00	---	60.00	---	60.00	**84.00**
	Demo	Set	Sm	LB	3.08	5.20	---	92.40	---	92.40	**129.00**
3 lites wide	Demo	Set	Lg	LB	2.67	6.00	---	80.10	---	80.10	**112.00**
	Demo	Set	Sm	LB	4.10	3.90	---	123.00	---	123.00	**172.00**
4 lites wide	Demo	Set	Lg	LB	4.00	4.00	---	120.00	---	120.00	**168.00**
	Demo	Set	Sm	LB	6.15	2.60	---	185.00	---	185.00	**258.00**

Interior, 3' x 7'

Description	Oper	Unit	Vol	Crew Size	Man-hours per Unit	Crew Output per Day	Avg Mat'l Unit Cost	Avg Labor Unit Cost	Avg Equip Unit Cost	Avg Total Unit Cost	Avg Price Incl O&P
	Demo	Ea	Lg	LB	1.00	16.00	---	30.00	---	30.00	**42.00**
	Demo	Ea	Sm	LB	1.54	10.40	---	46.20	---	46.20	**64.70**

Screen, 3' x 7'

Description	Oper	Unit	Vol	Crew Size	Man-hours per Unit	Crew Output per Day	Avg Mat'l Unit Cost	Avg Labor Unit Cost	Avg Equip Unit Cost	Avg Total Unit Cost	Avg Price Incl O&P
	Demo	Ea	Lg	LB	.800	20.00	---	24.00	---	24.00	**33.60**
	Demo	Ea	Sm	LB	1.23	13.00	---	36.90	---	36.90	**51.70**

Storm combination, 3' x 7'

Description	Oper	Unit	Vol	Crew Size	Man-hours per Unit	Crew Output per Day	Avg Mat'l Unit Cost	Avg Labor Unit Cost	Avg Equip Unit Cost	Avg Total Unit Cost	Avg Price Incl O&P
	Demo	Ea	Lg	LB	.800	20.00	---	24.00	---	24.00	**33.60**
	Demo	Ea	Sm	LB	1.23	13.00	---	36.90	---	36.90	**51.70**

Windows, with related trim and frame

To 12 SF

Description	Oper	Unit	Vol	Crew Size	Man-hours per Unit	Crew Output per Day	Avg Mat'l Unit Cost	Avg Labor Unit Cost	Avg Equip Unit Cost	Avg Total Unit Cost	Avg Price Incl O&P
Aluminum	Demo	Ea	Lg	LB	.762	21.00	---	22.90	---	22.90	**32.00**
	Demo	Ea	Sm	LB	1.17	13.65	---	35.10	---	35.10	**49.10**
Wood	Demo	Ea	Lg	LB	1.00	16.00	---	30.00	---	30.00	**42.00**
	Demo	Ea	Sm	LB	1.54	10.40	---	46.20	---	46.20	**64.70**

13 SF to 50 SF

Description	Oper	Unit	Vol	Crew Size	Man-hours per Unit	Crew Output per Day	Avg Mat'l Unit Cost	Avg Labor Unit Cost	Avg Equip Unit Cost	Avg Total Unit Cost	Avg Price Incl O&P
Aluminum	Demo	Ea	Lg	LB	1.23	13.00	---	36.90	---	36.90	**51.70**
	Demo	Ea	Sm	LB	1.89	8.45	---	56.70	---	56.70	**79.40**
Wood	Demo	Ea	Lg	LB	1.60	10.00	---	48.00	---	48.00	**67.20**
	Demo	Ea	Sm	LB	2.46	6.50	---	73.80	---	73.80	**103.00**

Description	Oper	Unit	Vol	Crew Size	Man-hours per Unit	Crew Output per Day	Avg Mat'l Unit Cost	Avg Labor Unit Cost	Avg Equip Unit Cost	Avg Total Unit Cost	Avg Price Incl O&P
Glazing, clean sash and remove old putty or rubber											
3/32" T float, putty or rubber											
8" x 12" (0.667 SF)	Demo	SF	Lg	GA	.320	25.00	---	11.50	---	11.50	**16.30**
	Demo	SF	Sm	GA	.492	16.25	---	17.60	---	17.60	**25.00**
12" x 16" (1.333 SF)	Demo	SF	Lg	GA	.178	45.00	---	6.37	---	6.37	**9.04**
	Demo	SF	Sm	GA	.274	29.25	---	9.80	---	9.80	**13.90**
14" x 20" (1.944 SF)	Demo	SF	Lg	GA	.145	55.00	---	5.19	---	5.19	**7.37**
	Demo	SF	Sm	GA	.224	35.75	---	8.01	---	8.01	**11.40**
16" x 24" (2.667 SF)	Demo	SF	Lg	GA	.114	70.00	---	4.08	---	4.08	**5.79**
	Demo	SF	Sm	GA	.176	45.50	---	6.30	---	6.30	**8.94**
24" x 26" (4.333 SF)	Demo	SF	Lg	GA	.084	95.00	---	3.01	---	3.01	**4.27**
	Demo	SF	Sm	GA	.130	61.75	---	4.65	---	4.65	**6.61**
36" x 24" (6.000 SF)	Demo	SF	Lg	GA	.064	125.0	---	2.29	---	2.29	**3.25**
	Demo	SF	Sm	GA	.098	81.25	---	3.51	---	3.51	**4.98**
1/8" T float, putty, steel sash											
12" x 16" (1.333 SF)	Demo	SF	Lg	GA	.178	45.00	---	6.37	---	6.37	**9.04**
	Demo	SF	Sm	GA	.274	29.25	---	9.80	---	9.80	**13.90**
16" x 20" (2.222 SF)	Demo	SF	Lg	GA	.123	65.00	---	4.40	---	4.40	**6.25**
	Demo	SF	Sm	GA	.189	42.25	---	6.76	---	6.76	**9.60**
16" x 24" (2.667 SF)	Demo	SF	Lg	GA	.114	70.00	---	4.08	---	4.08	**5.79**
	Demo	SF	Sm	GA	.176	45.50	---	6.30	---	6.30	**8.94**
24" x 26" (4.333 SF)	Demo	SF	Lg	GA	.084	95.00	---	3.01	---	3.01	**4.27**
	Demo	SF	Sm	GA	.130	61.75	---	4.65	---	4.65	**6.61**
28" x 32" (6.222 SF)	Demo	SF	Lg	GA	.062	130.0	---	2.22	---	2.22	**3.15**
	Demo	SF	Sm	GA	.095	84.50	---	3.40	---	3.40	**4.83**
36" x 36" (9.000 SF)	Demo	SF	Lg	GA	.050	160.0	---	1.79	---	1.79	**2.54**
	Demo	SF	Sm	GA	.077	104.0	---	2.76	---	2.76	**3.91**
36" x 48" (12.000 SF)	Demo	SF	Lg	GA	.042	190.0	---	1.50	---	1.50	**2.13**
	Demo	SF	Sm	GA	.065	123.5	---	2.33	---	2.33	**3.30**
1/4" T float											
Wood sash with putty											
72" x 48" (24.0 SF)	Demo	SF	Lg	GA	.043	185.0	---	1.54	---	1.54	**2.18**
	Demo	SF	Sm	GA	.067	120.3	---	2.40	---	2.40	**3.40**
Aluminum sash with aluminum channel and rigid neoprene rubber											
48" x 96" (32.0 SF)	Demo	SF	Lg	GA	.046	175.0	---	1.65	---	1.65	**2.34**
	Demo	SF	Sm	GA	.070	113.8	---	2.50	---	2.50	**3.56**
96" x 96" (64.0 SF)	Demo	SF	Lg	GA	.044	180.0	---	1.57	---	1.57	**2.24**
	Demo	SF	Sm	GA	.068	117.0	---	2.43	---	2.43	**3.46**
1" T insulating glass; with 2 pieces 1/4" float and 1/2" air space											
To 6.0 SF	Demo	SF	Lg	GA	.160	50.00	---	5.72	---	5.72	**8.13**
	Demo	SF	Sm	GA	.246	32.50	---	8.80	---	8.80	**12.50**
6.1 to 12.0 SF	Demo	SF	Lg	GA	.073	110.0	---	2.61	---	2.61	**3.71**
	Demo	SF	Sm	GA	.112	71.50	---	4.01	---	4.01	**5.69**
12.1 to 18.0 SF	Demo	SF	Lg	GA	.055	145.0	---	1.97	---	1.97	**2.79**
	Demo	SF	Sm	GA	.085	94.25	---	3.04	---	3.04	**4.32**
18.1 to 24.0 SF	Demo	SF	Lg	GA	.053	150.0	---	1.90	---	1.90	**2.69**
	Demo	SF	Sm	GA	.082	97.50	---	2.93	---	2.93	**4.17**

Description	Oper	Unit	Vol	Crew Size	Man-hours per Unit	Crew Output per Day	Avg Mat'l Unit Cost	Avg Labor Unit Cost	Avg Equip Unit Cost	Avg Total Unit Cost	Avg Price Incl O&P

Aluminum sliding door glass with aluminum channel and rigid neoprene rubber

34" x 76" (17.944 SF)

5/8" T insulating glass with 2 pieces 5/32" T (tempered with 1-1/4" air space)

Description	Oper	Unit	Vol	Crew Size	Man-hours per Unit	Crew Output per Day	Avg Mat'l Unit Cost	Avg Labor Unit Cost	Avg Equip Unit Cost	Avg Total Unit Cost	Avg Price Incl O&P
	Demo	SF	Lg	GA	.047	170.0	---	1.68	---	1.68	**2.39**
	Demo	SF	Sm	GA	.072	110.5	---	2.58	---	2.58	**3.66**
5/32" T tempered	Demo	SF	Lg	GA	.041	195.0	---	1.47	---	1.47	**2.08**
	Demo	SF	Sm	GA	.063	126.8	---	2.25	---	2.25	**3.20**

46" x 76" (24.278 SF)

5/8" T insulating glass with 2 pieces 5/32" T (tempered with 1-1/4" air space)

Description	Oper	Unit	Vol	Crew Size	Man-hours per Unit	Crew Output per Day	Avg Mat'l Unit Cost	Avg Labor Unit Cost	Avg Equip Unit Cost	Avg Total Unit Cost	Avg Price Incl O&P
	Demo	SF	Lg	GA	.037	215.0	---	1.32	---	1.32	**1.88**
	Demo	SF	Sm	GA	.057	139.8	---	2.04	---	2.04	**2.90**
5/32" T tempered	Demo	SF	Lg	GA	.033	245.0	---	1.18	---	1.18	**1.68**
	Demo	SF	Sm	GA	.050	159.3	---	1.79	---	1.79	**2.54**

Finishes

Exterior and interior, with hand tools; no insulation removal included

Plaster and stucco; remove to studs or sheathing

Lath (wood or metal) and plaster, walls and ceiling

Description	Oper	Unit	Vol	Crew Size	Man-hours per Unit	Crew Output per Day	Avg Mat'l Unit Cost	Avg Labor Unit Cost	Avg Equip Unit Cost	Avg Total Unit Cost	Avg Price Incl O&P
2 coats	Demo	SY	Lg	LB	.123	130.0	---	3.69	---	3.69	**5.17**
	Demo	SY	Sm	LB	.189	84.50	---	5.67	---	5.67	**7.94**
3 coats	Demo	SY	Lg	LB	.133	120.0	---	3.99	---	3.99	**5.59**
	Demo	SY	Sm	LB	.205	78.00	---	6.15	---	6.15	**8.61**

Stucco and metal netting

Description	Oper	Unit	Vol	Crew Size	Man-hours per Unit	Crew Output per Day	Avg Mat'l Unit Cost	Avg Labor Unit Cost	Avg Equip Unit Cost	Avg Total Unit Cost	Avg Price Incl O&P
2 coats	Demo	SY	Lg	LB	.168	95.00	---	5.04	---	5.04	**7.06**
	Demo	SY	Sm	LB	.259	61.75	---	7.77	---	7.77	**10.90**
3 coats	Demo	SY	Lg	LB	.200	80.00	---	6.00	---	6.00	**8.40**
	Demo	SY	Sm	LB	.308	52.00	---	9.24	---	9.24	**12.90**

Wallboard, gypsum (drywall)

Description	Oper	Unit	Vol	Crew Size	Man-hours per Unit	Crew Output per Day	Avg Mat'l Unit Cost	Avg Labor Unit Cost	Avg Equip Unit Cost	Avg Total Unit Cost	Avg Price Incl O&P
Walls and ceilings	Demo	SF	Lg	LB	.010	1540	---	.30	---	.30	**.42**
	Demo	SF	Sm	LB	.016	1001	---	.48	---	.48	**.67**

Ceramic, metal, plastic tile

Floors, 1" x 1"

Description	Oper	Unit	Vol	Crew Size	Man-hours per Unit	Crew Output per Day	Avg Mat'l Unit Cost	Avg Labor Unit Cost	Avg Equip Unit Cost	Avg Total Unit Cost	Avg Price Incl O&P
Adhesive or dry-set base	Demo	SF	Lg	LB	.029	550.0	---	.87	---	.87	**1.22**
	Demo	SF	Sm	LB	.045	357.5	---	1.35	---	1.35	**1.89**
Conventional mortar base	Demo	SF	Lg	LB	.034	475.0	---	1.02	---	1.02	**1.43**
	Demo	SF	Sm	LB	.052	308.8	---	1.56	---	1.56	**2.18**

Walls, 1" x 1" or 4-1/4" x 4-1/4"

Description	Oper	Unit	Vol	Crew Size	Man-hours per Unit	Crew Output per Day	Avg Mat'l Unit Cost	Avg Labor Unit Cost	Avg Equip Unit Cost	Avg Total Unit Cost	Avg Price Incl O&P
Adhesive or dry-set base	Demo	SF	Lg	LB	.033	480.0	---	.99	---	.99	**1.39**
	Demo	SF	Sm	LB	.051	312.0	---	1.53	---	1.53	**2.14**
Conventional mortar base	Demo	SF	Lg	LB	.040	400.0	---	1.20	---	1.20	**1.68**
	Demo	SF	Sm	LB	.062	260.0	---	1.86	---	1.86	**2.60**

Description	Oper	Unit	Vol	Crew Size	Man-hours per Unit	Crew Output per Day	Avg Mat'l Unit Cost	Avg Labor Unit Cost	Avg Equip Unit Cost	Avg Total Unit Cost	Avg Price Incl O&P
Acoustical or insulating ceiling tile											
Adhesive set, tile only	Demo	SF	Lg	LB	.012	1300	---	.36	---	.36	.50
	Demo	SF	Sm	LB	.019	845.0	---	.57	---	.57	.80
Stapled, tile only	Demo	SF	Lg	LB	.014	1170	---	.42	---	.42	.59
	Demo	SF	Sm	LB	.021	760.5	---	.63	---	.63	.88
Stapled, tile and furring strips	Demo	SF	Lg	LB	.010	1540	---	.30	---	.30	.42
	Demo	SF	Sm	LB	.016	1001	---	.48	---	.48	.67
Suspended ceiling system											
Panels and grid system	Demo	SF	Lg	LB	.009	1780	---	.27	---	.27	.38
	Demo	SF	Sm	LB	.014	1157	---	.42	---	.42	.59
Resilient flooring, adhesive set											
Sheet products	Demo	SY	Lg	LB	.100	160.0	---	3.00	---	3.00	4.20
	Demo	SY	Sm	LB	.154	104.0	---	4.62	---	4.62	6.47
Tile products	Demo	SF	Lg	LB	.011	1500	---	.33	---	.33	.46
	Demo	SF	Sm	LB	.016	975.0	---	.48	---	.48	.67

Wallpaper

Average output is expressed in rolls (36.0 SF/single roll)

Single layer of paper from plaster with steaming equipment

	Demo	Roll	Lg	1L	.400	20.00	---	12.00	---	12.00	16.80
	Demo	Roll	Sm	1L	.615	13.00	---	18.50	---	18.50	25.80

Several layers of paper from plaster with steaming equipment

	Demo	Roll	Lg	1L	.667	12.00	---	20.00	---	20.00	28.00
	Demo	Roll	Sm	1L	1.03	7.80	---	30.90	---	30.90	43.30

Vinyls (with non-woven, woven, or synthetic fiber backings) from plaster with steaming equipment

	Demo	Roll	Lg	1L	.267	30.00	---	8.01	---	8.01	11.20
	Demo	Roll	Sm	1L	.410	19.50	---	12.30	---	12.30	17.20

Single layer of paper from drywall with steaming equipment

	Demo	Roll	Lg	1L	.400	20.00	---	12.00	---	12.00	16.80
	Demo	Roll	Sm	1L	.615	13.00	---	18.50	---	18.50	25.80

Several layers of paper from drywall with steaming equipment

	Demo	Roll	Lg	1L	.667	12.00	---	20.00	---	20.00	28.00
	Demo	Roll	Sm	1L	1.03	7.80	---	30.90	---	30.90	43.30

Vinyls (with synthetic fiber backing) from drywall with steaming equipment

	Demo	Roll	Lg	1L	.267	30.00	---	8.01	---	8.01	11.20
	Demo	Roll	Sm	1L	.410	19.50	---	12.30	---	12.30	17.20

Vinyls (with other backings) from drywall with steaming equipment

	Demo	Roll	Lg	1L	.400	20.00	---	12.00	---	12.00	16.80
	Demo	Roll	Sm	1L	.615	13.00	---	18.50	---	18.50	25.80

Description	Oper	Unit	Vol	Crew Size	Man-hours per Unit	Crew Output per Day	Avg Mat'l Unit Cost	Avg Labor Unit Cost	Avg Equip Unit Cost	Avg Total Unit Cost	Avg Price Incl O&P

Dishwashers

High quality units. Labor cost includes rough-in

Frequently encountered applications

Description	Oper	Unit	Vol	Crew Size	Man-hours per Unit	Crew Output per Day	Avg Mat'l Unit Cost	Avg Labor Unit Cost	Avg Equip Unit Cost	Avg Total Unit Cost	Avg Price Incl O&P
Detach & reset unit	Reset	Ea	Lg	SA	1.33	6.00	---	57.20	---	57.20	**83.00**
	Reset	Ea	Sm	SA	1.78	4.50	---	76.60	---	76.60	**111.00**
Remove unit	Demo	Ea	Lg	SA	0.80	10.00	---	34.40	---	34.40	**49.90**
	Demo	Ea	Sm	SA	1.07	7.50	---	46.00	---	46.00	**66.80**
Install unit											
Standard											
	Inst	Ea	Lg	SC	6.67	2.40	634.00	278.00	---	912.00	**1130.00**
	Inst	Ea	Sm	SC	8.89	1.80	737.00	370.00	---	1107.00	**1380.00**
Average											
	Inst	Ea	Lg	SC	6.67	2.40	763.00	278.00	---	1041.00	**1280.00**
	Inst	Ea	Sm	SC	8.89	1.80	887.00	370.00	---	1257.00	**1560.00**
High											
	Inst	Ea	Lg	SC	6.67	2.40	947.00	278.00	---	1225.00	**1490.00**
	Inst	Ea	Sm	SC	8.89	1.80	1100.00	370.00	---	1470.00	**1800.00**
Premium											
	Inst	Ea	Lg	SC	6.67	2.40	1130.00	278.00	---	1408.00	**1700.00**
	Inst	Ea	Sm	SC	8.89	1.80	1320.00	370.00	---	1690.00	**2050.00**

Built-in front loading

Description	Oper	Unit	Vol	Crew Size	Man-hours per Unit	Crew Output per Day	Avg Mat'l Unit Cost	Avg Labor Unit Cost	Avg Equip Unit Cost	Avg Total Unit Cost	Avg Price Incl O&P
Six cycles	Inst	Ea	Lg	SC	6.67	2.40	1130.00	278.00	---	1408.00	**1700.00**
	Inst	Ea	Sm	SC	8.89	1.80	1320.00	370.00	---	1690.00	**2050.00**
Five cycles	Inst	Ea	Lg	SC	6.67	2.40	947.00	278.00	---	1225.00	**1490.00**
	Inst	Ea	Sm	SC	8.89	1.80	1100.00	370.00	---	1470.00	**1800.00**
Four cycles	Inst	Ea	Lg	SC	6.67	2.40	763.00	278.00	---	1041.00	**1280.00**
	Inst	Ea	Sm	SC	8.89	1.80	887.00	370.00	---	1257.00	**1560.00**
Three cycles	Inst	Ea	Lg	SC	6.67	2.40	634.00	278.00	---	912.00	**1130.00**
	Inst	Ea	Sm	SC	8.89	1.80	737.00	370.00	---	1107.00	**1380.00**
Two cycles	Inst	Ea	Lg	SC	6.67	2.40	367.00	278.00	---	645.00	**825.00**
	Inst	Ea	Sm	SC	8.89	1.80	427.00	370.00	---	797.00	**1030.00**

Adjustments

Description	Oper	Unit	Vol	Crew Size	Man-hours per Unit	Crew Output per Day	Avg Mat'l Unit Cost	Avg Labor Unit Cost	Avg Equip Unit Cost	Avg Total Unit Cost	Avg Price Incl O&P
Remove and reset dishwasher only											
	Reset	Ea	Lg	SA	1.33	6.00	---	57.20	---	57.20	**83.00**
	Reset	Ea	Sm	SA	1.78	4.50	---	76.60	---	76.60	**111.00**
Remove dishwasher											
	Demo	Ea	Lg	SA	0.80	10.00	---	34.40	---	34.40	**49.90**
	Demo	Ea	Sm	SA	1.07	7.50	---	46.00	---	46.00	**66.80**
Front and side panel kits											
White or prime finish	Inst	Ea	Lg	---	---	---	47.80	---	---	47.80	**47.80**
	Inst	Ea	Sm	---	---	---	55.60	---	---	55.60	**55.60**
Regular color finish	Inst	Ea	Lg	---	---	---	47.80	---	---	47.80	**47.80**
	Inst	Ea	Sm	---	---	---	55.60	---	---	55.60	**55.60**
Brushed chrome finish	Inst	Ea	Lg	---	---	---	58.00	---	---	58.00	**58.00**
	Inst	Ea	Sm	---	---	---	67.40	---	---	67.40	**67.40**
Stainless steel finish	Inst	Ea	Lg	---	---	---	71.80	---	---	71.80	**71.80**
	Inst	Ea	Sm	---	---	---	83.50	---	---	83.50	**83.50**
Black-glass acrylic finish with trim kit											
	Inst	Ea	Lg	---	---	---	96.60	---	---	96.60	**96.60**
	Inst	Ea	Sm	---	---	---	112.00	---	---	112.00	**112.00**
Stainless steel trim kit	Inst	Ea	Lg	---	---	---	44.20	---	---	44.20	**44.20**
	Inst	Ea	Sm	---	---	---	51.40	---	---	51.40	**51.40**

Description	Oper	Unit	Vol	Crew Size	Man-hours per Unit	Crew Output per Day	Avg Mat'l Unit Cost	Avg Labor Unit Cost	Avg Equip Unit Cost	Avg Total Unit Cost	Avg Price Incl O&P

Portable front loading

Convertible, front loading, portable dishwashers; hardwood top, front & side panels

Six cycles

White	Inst	Ea	Lg	SC	4.00	4.00	689.00	166.00	---	855.00	**1030.00**
	Inst	Ea	Sm	SC	5.33	3.00	801.00	222.00	---	1023.00	**1240.00**
Colors	Inst	Ea	Lg	SC	4.00	4.00	736.00	166.00	---	902.00	**1090.00**
	Inst	Ea	Sm	SC	5.33	3.00	856.00	222.00	---	1078.00	**1310.00**

Four cycles

White	Inst	Ea	Lg	SC	4.00	4.00	606.00	166.00	---	772.00	**939.00**
	Inst	Ea	Sm	SC	5.33	3.00	705.00	222.00	---	927.00	**1130.00**
Colors	Inst	Ea	Lg	SC	4.00	4.00	671.00	166.00	---	837.00	**1010.00**
	Inst	Ea	Sm	SC	5.33	3.00	780.00	222.00	---	1002.00	**1220.00**

Three cycles

White	Inst	Ea	Lg	SC	4.00	4.00	514.00	166.00	---	680.00	**833.00**
	Inst	Ea	Sm	SC	5.33	3.00	598.00	222.00	---	820.00	**1010.00**
Colors	Inst	Ea	Lg	SC	4.00	4.00	547.00	166.00	---	713.00	**871.00**
	Inst	Ea	Sm	SC	5.33	3.00	637.00	222.00	---	859.00	**1050.00**

Front loading portables

Three cycles with hardwood top

White	Inst	Ea	Lg	SC	4.00	4.00	514.00	166.00	---	680.00	**833.00**
	Inst	Ea	Sm	SC	5.33	3.00	598.00	222.00	---	820.00	**1010.00**
Colors	Inst	Ea	Lg	SC	4.00	4.00	547.00	166.00	---	713.00	**871.00**
	Inst	Ea	Sm	SC	5.33	3.00	637.00	222.00	---	859.00	**1050.00**

Two cycles with porcelain top

White	Inst	Ea	Lg	SC	4.00	4.00	459.00	166.00	---	625.00	**769.00**
	Inst	Ea	Sm	SC	5.33	3.00	534.00	222.00	---	756.00	**936.00**
Colors	Inst	Ea	Lg	SC	4.00	4.00	523.00	166.00	---	689.00	**843.00**
	Inst	Ea	Sm	SC	5.33	3.00	609.00	222.00	---	831.00	**1020.00**

Dishwasher - sink combination, includes good quality fittings, 36"-42" cabinet, faucets and water supply kit

Six cycles

White	Inst	Ea	Lg	SC	10.7	1.50	1680.00	445.00	---	2125.00	**2580.00**
	Inst	Ea	Sm	SC	14.2	1.13	1960.00	591.00	---	2551.00	**3110.00**
Colors	Inst	Ea	Lg	SC	10.7	1.50	1770.00	445.00	---	2215.00	**2680.00**
	Inst	Ea	Sm	SC	14.2	1.13	2060.00	591.00	---	2651.00	**3230.00**

Three cycles

White	Inst	Ea	Lg	SC	10.7	1.50	1400.00	445.00	---	1845.00	**2250.00**
	Inst	Ea	Sm	SC	14.2	1.13	1630.00	591.00	---	2221.00	**2730.00**

Remove and reset combination dishwasher - sink only

	Reset	Ea	Lg	SA	2.22	3.60	---	95.50	---	95.50	**138.00**
	Reset	Ea	Sm	SA	2.96	2.70	---	127.00	---	127.00	**185.00**

Remove only, d/w - sink combo

	Demo	Ea	Lg	SA	1.33	6.00	---	57.20	---	57.20	**83.00**
	Demo	Ea	Sm	SA	1.78	4.50	---	76.60	---	76.60	**111.00**

Material adjustments

For standard quality, DEDUCT	Inst	%	Lg	---	---	---	-20.0	---	---	---	---
	Inst	%	Sm	---	---	---	-20.0	---	---	---	---
For economy quality, DEDUCT	Inst	%	Lg	---	---	---	-30.0	---	---	---	---
	Inst	%	Sm	---	---	---	-30.0	---	---	---	---

Description	Oper	Unit	Vol	Crew Size	Man-hours per Unit	Crew Output per Day	Avg Mat'l Unit Cost	Avg Labor Unit Cost	Avg Equip Unit Cost	Avg Total Unit Cost	Avg Price Incl O&P

Door frames

Exterior wood door frames

Exterior frame with exterior trim

5/4 x 4-9/16" deep

Description	Oper	Unit	Vol	Crew Size	Man-hours per Unit	Crew Output per Day	Avg Mat'l Unit Cost	Avg Labor Unit Cost	Avg Equip Unit Cost	Avg Total Unit Cost	Avg Price Incl O&P
Pine	Inst	LF	Lg	2C	.046	350.0	3.86	1.70	---	5.56	**6.82**
	Inst	LF	Sm	2C	.070	227.5	4.15	2.59	---	6.74	**8.40**
Oak	Inst	LF	Lg	2C	.049	325.0	6.60	1.81	---	8.41	**10.10**
	Inst	LF	Sm	2C	.076	211.3	7.09	2.81	---	9.90	**12.10**
Walnut	Inst	LF	Lg	2C	.053	300.0	8.25	1.96	---	10.21	**12.20**
	Inst	LF	Sm	2C	.082	195.0	8.87	3.04	---	11.91	**14.50**

5/4 x 5-3/16" deep

Description	Oper	Unit	Vol	Crew Size	Man-hours per Unit	Crew Output per Day	Avg Mat'l Unit Cost	Avg Labor Unit Cost	Avg Equip Unit Cost	Avg Total Unit Cost	Avg Price Incl O&P
Pine	Inst	LF	Lg	2C	.046	350.0	4.19	1.70	---	5.89	**7.20**
	Inst	LF	Sm	2C	.070	227.5	4.50	2.59	---	7.09	**8.80**
Oak	Inst	LF	Lg	2C	.049	325.0	7.12	1.81	---	8.93	**10.70**
	Inst	LF	Sm	2C	.076	211.3	7.65	2.81	---	10.46	**12.70**
Walnut	Inst	LF	Lg	2C	.053	300.0	10.70	1.96	---	12.66	**15.10**
	Inst	LF	Sm	2C	.082	195.0	11.50	3.04	---	14.54	**17.50**

5/4 x 6-9/16" deep

Description	Oper	Unit	Vol	Crew Size	Man-hours per Unit	Crew Output per Day	Avg Mat'l Unit Cost	Avg Labor Unit Cost	Avg Equip Unit Cost	Avg Total Unit Cost	Avg Price Incl O&P
Pine	Inst	LF	Lg	2C	.046	350.0	4.89	1.70	---	6.59	**8.01**
	Inst	LF	Sm	2C	.070	227.5	5.26	2.59	---	7.85	**9.68**
Oak	Inst	LF	Lg	2C	.049	325.0	8.38	1.81	---	10.19	**12.20**
	Inst	LF	Sm	2C	.076	211.3	9.01	2.81	---	11.82	**14.30**
Walnut	Inst	LF	Lg	2C	.053	300.0	12.60	1.96	---	14.56	**17.20**
	Inst	LF	Sm	2C	.082	195.0	13.50	3.04	---	16.54	**19.80**

Exterior sills

8/4 x 8" deep

Description	Oper	Unit	Vol	Crew Size	Man-hours per Unit	Crew Output per Day	Avg Mat'l Unit Cost	Avg Labor Unit Cost	Avg Equip Unit Cost	Avg Total Unit Cost	Avg Price Incl O&P
No horns	Inst	LF	Lg	2C	.200	80.00	11.00	7.40	---	18.40	**23.00**
	Inst	LF	Sm	2C	.308	52.00	11.80	11.40	---	23.20	**29.50**
2" horns	Inst	LF	Lg	2C	.200	80.00	11.80	7.40	---	19.20	**23.90**
	Inst	LF	Sm	2C	.308	52.00	12.70	11.40	---	24.10	**30.50**
3" horns	Inst	LF	Lg	2C	.200	80.00	12.80	7.40	---	20.20	**25.10**
	Inst	LF	Sm	2C	.308	52.00	13.70	11.40	---	25.10	**31.80**

8/4 x 10" deep

Description	Oper	Unit	Vol	Crew Size	Man-hours per Unit	Crew Output per Day	Avg Mat'l Unit Cost	Avg Labor Unit Cost	Avg Equip Unit Cost	Avg Total Unit Cost	Avg Price Incl O&P
No horns	Inst	LF	Lg	2C	.267	60.00	14.20	9.88	---	24.08	**30.20**
	Inst	LF	Sm	2C	.410	39.00	15.30	15.20	---	30.50	**38.90**
2" horns	Inst	LF	Lg	2C	.267	60.00	15.60	9.88	---	25.48	**31.80**
	Inst	LF	Sm	2C	.410	39.00	16.80	15.20	---	32.00	**40.60**
3" horns	Inst	LF	Lg	2C	.267	60.00	17.10	9.88	---	26.98	**33.50**
	Inst	LF	Sm	2C	.410	39.00	18.40	15.20	---	33.60	**42.40**

Exterior, colonial frame and trim

Description	Oper	Unit	Vol	Crew Size	Man-hours per Unit	Crew Output per Day	Avg Mat'l Unit Cost	Avg Labor Unit Cost	Avg Equip Unit Cost	Avg Total Unit Cost	Avg Price Incl O&P
3' opening, in swing	Inst	Ea	Lg	2C	.800	20.00	552.00	29.60	---	581.60	**676.00**
	Inst	Ea	Sm	2C	1.23	13.00	593.00	45.50	---	638.50	**746.00**
5' 4" opening, in/out swing	Inst	Ea	Lg	2C	1.07	15.00	891.00	39.60	---	930.60	**1080.00**
	Inst	Ea	Sm	2C	1.64	9.75	958.00	60.70	---	1018.70	**1190.00**
6' opening, in/out swing	Inst	Ea	Lg	2C	1.60	10.00	1100.00	59.20	---	1159.20	**1350.00**
	Inst	Ea	Sm	2C	2.46	6.50	1190.00	91.10	---	1281.10	**1490.00**

Description	Oper	Unit	Vol	Crew Size	Man- hours per Unit	Crew Output per Day	Avg Mat'l Unit Cost	Avg Labor Unit Cost	Avg Equip Unit Cost	Avg Total Unit Cost	Avg Price Incl O&P
Interior wood door frames											
Interior frame											
11/16" x 3-5/8" deep											
Pine	Inst	LF	Lg	2C	.046	350.0	3.90	1.70	---	5.60	**6.87**
	Inst	LF	Sm	2C	.070	227.5	4.19	2.59	---	6.78	**8.45**
Oak	Inst	LF	Lg	2C	.049	325.0	4.79	1.81	---	6.60	**8.05**
	Inst	LF	Sm	2C	.076	211.3	5.15	2.81	---	7.96	**9.86**
Walnut	Inst	LF	Lg	2C	.053	300.0	7.18	1.96	---	9.14	**11.00**
	Inst	LF	Sm	2C	.082	195.0	7.72	3.04	---	10.76	**13.10**
11/16" x 4-9/16" deep											
Pine	Inst	LF	Lg	2C	.046	350.0	4.02	1.70	---	5.72	**7.01**
	Inst	LF	Sm	2C	.070	227.5	4.32	2.59	---	6.91	**8.60**
Oak	Inst	LF	Lg	2C	.049	325.0	4.79	1.81	---	6.60	**8.05**
	Inst	LF	Sm	2C	.076	211.3	5.15	2.81	---	7.96	**9.86**
Walnut	Inst	LF	Lg	2C	.053	300.0	7.18	1.96	---	9.14	**11.00**
	Inst	LF	Sm	2C	.082	195.0	7.72	3.04	---	10.76	**13.10**
11/16" x 5-3/16" deep											
Pine	Inst	LF	Lg	2C	.046	350.0	4.55	1.70	---	6.25	**7.62**
	Inst	LF	Sm	2C	.070	227.5	4.89	2.59	---	7.48	**9.25**
Oak	Inst	LF	Lg	2C	.049	325.0	4.92	1.81	---	6.73	**8.20**
	Inst	LF	Sm	2C	.076	211.3	5.29	2.81	---	8.10	**10.00**
Walnut	Inst	LF	Lg	2C	.053	300.0	7.45	1.96	---	9.41	**11.30**
	Inst	LF	Sm	2C	.082	195.0	8.01	3.04	---	11.05	**13.50**
Pocket door frame											
2'-0" to 3'-0" x 6'-8"	Inst	Ea	Lg	2C	1.33	12.00	99.80	49.20	---	149.00	**184.00**
	Inst	Ea	Sm	2C	2.05	7.80	107.00	75.90	---	182.90	**230.00**
3'-6" x 6'-8"	Inst	Ea	Lg	2C	1.33	12.00	184.00	49.20	---	233.20	**280.00**
	Inst	Ea	Sm	2C	2.05	7.80	197.00	75.90	---	272.90	**333.00**
4'-0" x 6'-8"	Inst	Ea	Lg	2C	1.33	12.00	186.00	49.20	---	235.20	**283.00**
	Inst	Ea	Sm	2C	2.05	7.80	200.00	75.90	---	275.90	**336.00**
Threshold, oak											
5/8" x 3-5/8" deep	Inst	LF	Lg	2C	.100	160.0	2.61	3.70	---	6.31	**8.18**
	Inst	LF	Sm	2C	.154	104.0	2.80	5.70	---	8.50	**11.20**
5/8" x 4-5/8" deep	Inst	LF	Lg	2C	.107	150.0	3.39	3.96	---	7.35	**9.44**
	Inst	LF	Sm	2C	.164	97.50	3.65	6.07	---	9.72	**12.70**
5/8" x 5-5/8" deep	Inst	LF	Lg	2C	.114	140.0	4.04	4.22	---	8.26	**10.60**
	Inst	LF	Sm	2C	.176	91.00	4.35	6.52	---	10.87	**14.10**

Description	Oper	Unit	Vol	Crew Size	Man-hours per Unit	Crew Output per Day	Avg Mat'l Unit Cost	Avg Labor Unit Cost	Avg Equip Unit Cost	Avg Total Unit Cost	Avg Price Incl O&P

Door hardware

Locksets

Outside locks
Knobs (pin tumbler)

Description	Oper	Unit	Vol	Crew Size	Man-hours per Unit	Crew Output per Day	Avg Mat'l Unit Cost	Avg Labor Unit Cost	Avg Equip Unit Cost	Avg Total Unit Cost	Avg Price Incl O&P
Excellent quality	Inst	Ea	Lg	CA	.667	12.00	162.00	24.70	---	186.70	**221.00**
	Inst	Ea	Sm	CA	1.03	7.80	182.00	38.10	---	220.10	**263.00**
Good quality	Inst	Ea	Lg	CA	.500	16.00	120.00	18.50	---	138.50	**164.00**
	Inst	Ea	Sm	CA	.769	10.40	135.00	28.50	---	163.50	**195.00**
Average quality	Inst	Ea	Lg	CA	.500	16.00	84.00	18.50	---	102.50	**123.00**
	Inst	Ea	Sm	CA	.769	10.40	94.50	28.50	---	123.00	**149.00**

Handlesets

Description	Oper	Unit	Vol	Crew Size	Man-hours per Unit	Crew Output per Day	Avg Mat'l Unit Cost	Avg Labor Unit Cost	Avg Equip Unit Cost	Avg Total Unit Cost	Avg Price Incl O&P
Excellent quality	Inst	Ea	Lg	CA	.667	12.00	210.00	24.70	---	234.70	**276.00**
	Inst	Ea	Sm	CA	1.03	7.80	236.00	38.10	---	274.10	**325.00**
Good quality	Inst	Ea	Lg	CA	.500	16.00	132.00	18.50	---	150.50	**178.00**
	Inst	Ea	Sm	CA	.769	10.40	149.00	28.50	---	177.50	**211.00**
Average quality	Inst	Ea	Lg	CA	.500	16.00	96.00	18.50	---	114.50	**136.00**
	Inst	Ea	Sm	CA	.769	10.40	108.00	28.50	---	136.50	**164.00**

Bath or bedroom locks

Description	Oper	Unit	Vol	Crew Size	Man-hours per Unit	Crew Output per Day	Avg Mat'l Unit Cost	Avg Labor Unit Cost	Avg Equip Unit Cost	Avg Total Unit Cost	Avg Price Incl O&P
Excellent quality	Inst	Ea	Lg	CA	.533	15.00	120.00	19.70	---	139.70	**166.00**
	Inst	Ea	Sm	CA	.821	9.75	135.00	30.40	---	165.40	**198.00**
Good quality	Inst	Ea	Lg	CA	.400	20.00	102.00	14.80	---	116.80	**138.00**
	Inst	Ea	Sm	CA	.615	13.00	115.00	22.80	---	137.80	**164.00**
Average quality	Inst	Ea	Lg	CA	.400	20.00	78.00	14.80	---	92.80	**110.00**
	Inst	Ea	Sm	CA	.615	13.00	87.80	22.80	---	110.60	**133.00**

Passage latches

Description	Oper	Unit	Vol	Crew Size	Man-hours per Unit	Crew Output per Day	Avg Mat'l Unit Cost	Avg Labor Unit Cost	Avg Equip Unit Cost	Avg Total Unit Cost	Avg Price Incl O&P
Excellent quality	Inst	Ea	Lg	CA	.400	20.00	138.00	14.80	---	152.80	**179.00**
	Inst	Ea	Sm	CA	.615	13.00	155.00	22.80	---	177.80	**210.00**
Good quality	Inst	Ea	Lg	CA	.308	26.00	103.00	11.40	---	114.40	**135.00**
	Inst	Ea	Sm	CA	.473	16.90	116.00	17.50	---	133.50	**158.00**
Average quality	Inst	Ea	Lg	CA	.308	26.00	72.00	11.40	---	83.40	**98.80**
	Inst	Ea	Sm	CA	.473	16.90	81.00	17.50	---	98.50	**118.00**

Dead locks (double key)

Description	Oper	Unit	Vol	Crew Size	Man-hours per Unit	Crew Output per Day	Avg Mat'l Unit Cost	Avg Labor Unit Cost	Avg Equip Unit Cost	Avg Total Unit Cost	Avg Price Incl O&P
Excellent quality	Inst	Ea	Lg	CA	.533	15.00	138.00	19.70	---	157.70	**186.00**
	Inst	Ea	Sm	CA	.821	9.75	155.00	30.40	---	185.40	**221.00**
Good quality	Inst	Ea	Lg	CA	.400	20.00	108.00	14.80	---	122.80	**145.00**
	Inst	Ea	Sm	CA	.615	13.00	122.00	22.80	---	144.80	**172.00**
Average quality	Inst	Ea	Lg	CA	.400	20.00	73.20	14.80	---	88.00	**105.00**
	Inst	Ea	Sm	CA	.615	13.00	82.40	22.80	---	105.20	**127.00**

Kickplates, 8" x 30"

Description	Oper	Unit	Vol	Crew Size	Man-hours per Unit	Crew Output per Day	Avg Mat'l Unit Cost	Avg Labor Unit Cost	Avg Equip Unit Cost	Avg Total Unit Cost	Avg Price Incl O&P
Aluminum	Inst	Ea	Lg	CA	.308	26.00	18.80	11.40	---	30.20	**37.60**
	Inst	Ea	Sm	CA	.473	16.90	21.20	17.50	---	38.70	**48.90**
Brass or bronze	Inst	Ea	Lg	CA	.308	26.00	26.90	11.40	---	38.30	**46.90**
	Inst	Ea	Sm	CA	.473	16.90	30.20	17.50	---	47.70	**59.30**

Description	Oper	Unit	Vol	Crew Size	Man-hours per Unit	Crew Output per Day	Avg Mat'l Unit Cost	Avg Labor Unit Cost	Avg Equip Unit Cost	Avg Total Unit Cost	Avg Price Incl O&P
Thresholds											
Aluminum, pre-notched, draft-proof, standard											
3/4" high											
32" long	Inst	Ea	Lg	CA	.250	32.00	12.40	9.26	---	21.66	**27.20**
	Inst	Ea	Sm	CA	.385	20.80	13.90	14.30	---	28.20	**36.00**
36" long	Inst	Ea	Lg	CA	.250	32.00	14.20	9.26	---	23.46	**29.20**
	Inst	Ea	Sm	CA	.385	20.80	15.90	14.30	---	30.20	**38.30**
42" long	Inst	Ea	Lg	CA	.250	32.00	16.90	9.26	---	26.16	**32.40**
	Inst	Ea	Sm	CA	.385	20.80	19.00	14.30	---	33.30	**41.80**
48" long	Inst	Ea	Lg	CA	.250	32.00	19.30	9.26	---	28.56	**35.20**
	Inst	Ea	Sm	CA	.385	20.80	21.70	14.30	---	36.00	**45.00**
60" long	Inst	Ea	Lg	CA	.250	32.00	24.00	9.26	---	33.26	**40.60**
	Inst	Ea	Sm	CA	.385	20.80	27.00	14.30	---	41.30	**51.00**
72" long	Inst	Ea	Lg	CA	.250	32.00	28.40	9.26	---	37.66	**45.70**
	Inst	Ea	Sm	CA	.385	20.80	32.00	14.30	---	46.30	**56.80**
For high rug-type, 1-1/8"											
ADD	Inst	%	Lg	CA	---	---	25.0	---	---	25.0	---
	Inst	%	Sm	CA	---	---	25.0	---	---	25.0	---
Wood, oak threshold with vinyl weather seal											
5/8" x 3-1/2"											
33" long	Inst	Ea	Lg	CA	.250	32.00	14.40	9.26	---	23.66	**29.50**
	Inst	Ea	Sm	CA	.385	20.80	16.20	14.30	---	30.50	**38.60**
37" long	Inst	Ea	Lg	CA	.250	32.00	16.20	9.26	---	25.46	**31.60**
	Inst	Ea	Sm	CA	.385	20.80	18.30	14.30	---	32.60	**40.90**
43" long	Inst	Ea	Lg	CA	.250	32.00	17.50	9.26	---	26.76	**33.10**
	Inst	Ea	Sm	CA	.385	20.80	19.70	14.30	---	34.00	**42.60**
49" long	Inst	Ea	Lg	CA	.250	32.00	20.00	9.26	---	29.26	**35.90**
	Inst	Ea	Sm	CA	.385	20.80	22.50	14.30	---	36.80	**45.80**
61" long	Inst	Ea	Lg	CA	.250	32.00	25.40	9.26	---	34.66	**42.10**
	Inst	Ea	Sm	CA	.385	20.80	28.50	14.30	---	42.80	**52.80**
73" long	Inst	Ea	Lg	CA	.250	32.00	30.40	9.26	---	39.66	**47.90**
	Inst	Ea	Sm	CA	.385	20.80	34.20	14.30	---	48.50	**59.20**
3/4" x 3-1/2"											
33" long	Inst	Ea	Lg	CA	.250	32.00	15.30	9.26	---	24.56	**30.50**
	Inst	Ea	Sm	CA	.385	20.80	17.20	14.30	---	31.50	**39.70**
37" long	Inst	Ea	Lg	CA	.250	32.00	17.10	9.26	---	26.36	**32.70**
	Inst	Ea	Sm	CA	.385	20.80	19.30	14.30	---	33.60	**42.10**

Doors

Interior Door Systems

| Two panel | Colonial six panel | Full louver | Raised panel louver | 10 lite | 15 lite |

- Nails
- Framing studs
- Plaster ground
- Shingle wedge
- Jamb
- Stop
- Casing
- Nail
- 3/16"
- Bevel cut

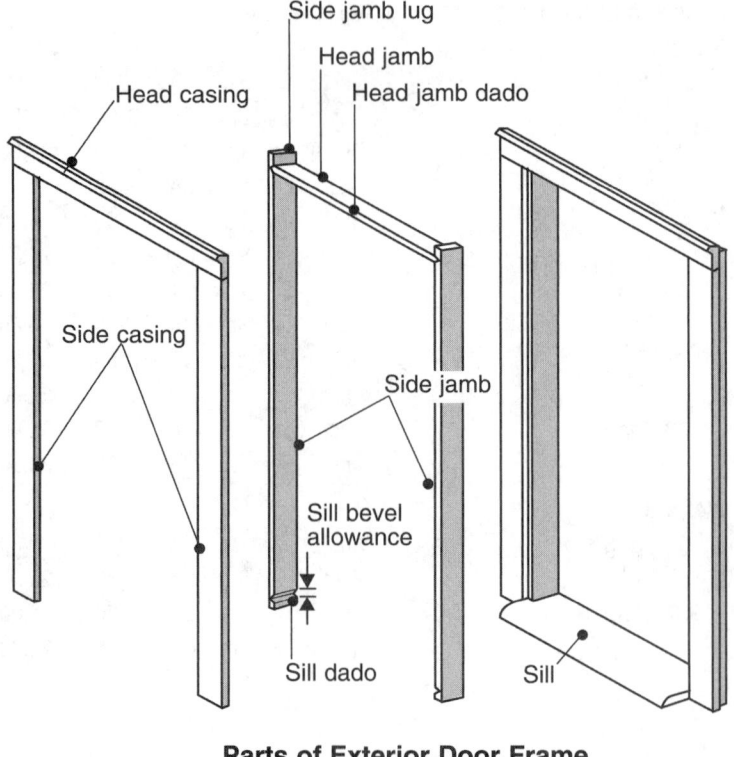

- Side jamb lug
- Head jamb
- Head jamb dado
- Head casing
- Side casing
- Side jamb
- Sill bevel allowance
- Sill dado
- Sill

Parts of Exterior Door Frame

Assembled Package Door Units (Interior)

Door Clearances

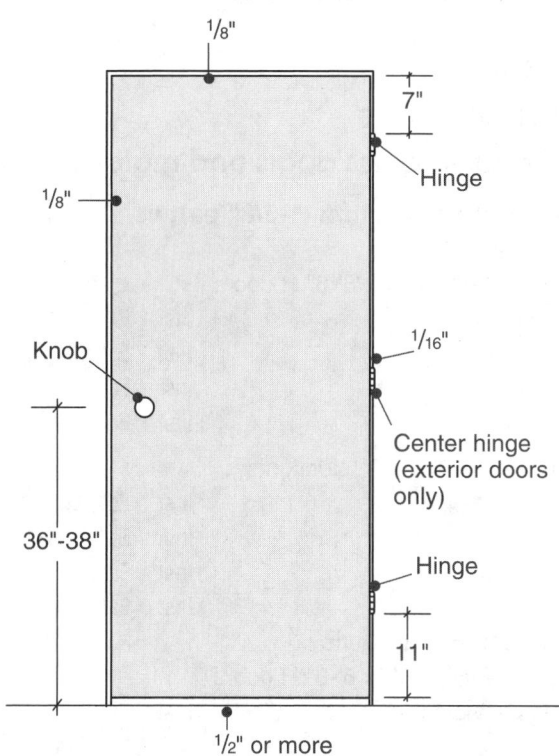

Unit Includes:

Jamb: 4⁹/₁₆" finger joint pine w/ stops applied.

Butts: 1 pair 3¹/₂" x 3¹/₂" applied to door and jamb.

Door: 3 degree bevel one side ³/₁₆" under std. width - net 80"
H center bored - 2¹/₈" bore
2³/₈" backset - 1" edge bore

Head jamb   **Side jamb**   **Sill**

Description	Oper	Unit	Vol	Crew Size	Man-hours per Unit	Crew Output per Day	Avg Mat'l Unit Cost	Avg Labor Unit Cost	Avg Equip Unit Cost	Avg Total Unit Cost	Avg Price Incl O&P

Doors

Entrance doors

Decorative glass doors and matching sidelights

Lafayette collection, 1-3/8" panels

Astoria style
2'-6", 2'-8", 3' W x 6'-8" H doors

Fir & pine	Inst	Ea	Lg	2C	1.33	12.00	1390.00	49.20	---	1439.20	**1670.00**
	Inst	Ea	Sm	2C	2.05	7.80	1560.00	75.90	---	1635.90	**1900.00**
Oak	Inst	Ea	Lg	2C	1.33	12.00	1820.00	49.20	---	1869.20	**2160.00**
	Inst	Ea	Sm	2C	2.05	7.80	2050.00	75.90	---	2125.90	**2460.00**

1', 1'-2" x 6'-8-1/2" sidelights

Fir & pine	Inst	Ea	Lg	2C	1.00	16.00	614.00	37.00	---	651.00	**758.00**
	Inst	Ea	Sm	2C	1.54	10.40	691.00	57.00	---	748.00	**875.00**
Oak	Inst	Ea	Lg	2C	1.00	16.00	781.00	37.00	---	818.00	**950.00**
	Inst	Ea	Sm	2C	1.54	10.40	879.00	57.00	---	936.00	**1090.00**

Bourbon Royale style
2'-6", 2'-8", 3' W x 6'-8" H doors

Fir & pine	Inst	Ea	Lg	2C	1.33	12.00	1360.00	49.20	---	1409.20	**1640.00**
	Inst	Ea	Sm	2C	2.05	7.80	1530.00	75.90	---	1605.90	**1870.00**
Oak	Inst	Ea	Lg	2C	1.33	12.00	1800.00	49.20	---	1849.20	**2140.00**
	Inst	Ea	Sm	2C	2.05	7.80	2030.00	75.90	---	2105.90	**2440.00**

1', 1'-2" x 6'-8-1/2" sidelights

Fir & pine	Inst	Ea	Lg	2C	1.00	16.00	647.00	37.00	---	684.00	**796.00**
	Inst	Ea	Sm	2C	1.54	10.40	728.00	57.00	---	785.00	**917.00**
Oak	Inst	Ea	Lg	2C	1.00	16.00	802.00	37.00	---	839.00	**974.00**
	Inst	Ea	Sm	2C	1.54	10.40	902.00	57.00	---	959.00	**1120.00**

Jubilee style
2'-6", 2'-8", 3' W x 6'-8" H doors

Fir & pine	Inst	Ea	Lg	2C	1.33	12.00	1440.00	49.20	---	1489.20	**1720.00**
	Inst	Ea	Sm	2C	2.05	7.80	1620.00	75.90	---	1695.90	**1960.00**
Oak	Inst	Ea	Lg	2C	1.33	12.00	1870.00	49.20	---	1919.20	**2220.00**
	Inst	Ea	Sm	2C	2.05	7.80	2110.00	75.90	---	2185.90	**2530.00**

1', 1'-2" x 6'-8-1/2" sidelights

Fir & pine	Inst	Ea	Lg	2C	1.00	16.00	602.00	37.00	---	639.00	**745.00**
	Inst	Ea	Sm	2C	1.54	10.40	678.00	57.00	---	735.00	**859.00**
Oak	Inst	Ea	Lg	2C	1.00	16.00	916.00	37.00	---	953.00	**1100.00**
	Inst	Ea	Sm	2C	1.54	10.40	1030.00	57.00	---	1087.00	**1260.00**

Lexington style
2'-6", 2'-8", 3' W x 6'-8" H doors

Fir & pine	Inst	Ea	Lg	2C	1.33	12.00	1430.00	49.20	---	1479.20	**1720.00**
	Inst	Ea	Sm	2C	2.05	7.80	1610.00	75.90	---	1685.90	**1960.00**
Oak	Inst	Ea	Lg	2C	1.33	12.00	1870.00	49.20	---	1919.20	**2220.00**
	Inst	Ea	Sm	2C	2.05	7.80	2100.00	75.90	---	2175.90	**2520.00**

Description	Oper	Unit	Vol	Crew Size	Man-hours per Unit	Crew Output per Day	Avg Mat'l Unit Cost	Avg Labor Unit Cost	Avg Equip Unit Cost	Avg Total Unit Cost	Avg Price Incl O&P
1', 1'-2" x 6'-8-1/2" sidelights											
Fir & pine	Inst	Ea	Lg	2C	1.00	16.00	642.00	37.00	---	679.00	**790.00**
	Inst	Ea	Sm	2C	1.54	10.40	722.00	57.00	---	779.00	**910.00**
Oak	Inst	Ea	Lg	2C	1.00	16.00	797.00	37.00	---	834.00	**968.00**
	Inst	Ea	Sm	2C	1.54	10.40	896.00	57.00	---	953.00	**1110.00**
Marquis style											
2'-6", 2'-8", 3' W x 6'-8" H doors											
Fir & pine	Inst	Ea	Lg	2C	1.33	12.00	1500.00	49.20	---	1549.20	**1790.00**
	Inst	Ea	Sm	2C	2.05	7.80	1680.00	75.90	---	1755.90	**2040.00**
Oak	Inst	Ea	Lg	2C	1.33	12.00	1940.00	49.20	---	1989.20	**2290.00**
	Inst	Ea	Sm	2C	2.05	7.80	2180.00	75.90	---	2255.90	**2610.00**
1', 1'-2" x 6'-8-1/2" sidelights											
Fir & pine	Inst	Ea	Lg	2C	1.00	16.00	676.00	37.00	---	713.00	**829.00**
	Inst	Ea	Sm	2C	1.54	10.40	760.00	57.00	---	817.00	**954.00**
Oak	Inst	Ea	Lg	2C	1.00	16.00	752.00	37.00	---	789.00	**917.00**
	Inst	Ea	Sm	2C	1.54	10.40	846.00	57.00	---	903.00	**1050.00**
Monaco style											
2'-6", 2'-8", 3'-0" W x 6'-8" H doors											
Fir & pine	Inst	Ea	Lg	2C	1.33	12.00	1760.00	49.20	---	1809.20	**2090.00**
	Inst	Ea	Sm	2C	2.05	7.80	1980.00	75.90	---	2055.90	**2380.00**
Oak	Inst	Ea	Lg	2C	1.33	12.00	2180.00	49.20	---	2229.20	**2580.00**
	Inst	Ea	Sm	2C	2.05	7.80	2450.00	75.90	---	2525.90	**2930.00**
1', 1'-2" x 6'-8-1/2" sidelights											
Fir & pine	Inst	Ea	Lg	2C	1.00	16.00	805.00	37.00	---	842.00	**978.00**
	Inst	Ea	Sm	2C	1.54	10.40	906.00	57.00	---	963.00	**1120.00**
Oak	Inst	Ea	Lg	2C	1.00	16.00	960.00	37.00	---	997.00	**1160.00**
	Inst	Ea	Sm	2C	1.54	10.40	1080.00	57.00	---	1137.00	**1320.00**
Windsor style											
2'-6", 2'-8", 3' W x 6'-8" H doors											
Fir & pine	Inst	Ea	Lg	2C	1.33	12.00	1480.00	49.20	---	1529.20	**1770.00**
	Inst	Ea	Sm	2C	2.05	7.80	1660.00	75.90	---	1735.90	**2020.00**
Oak	Inst	Ea	Lg	2C	1.33	12.00	1910.00	49.20	---	1959.20	**2270.00**
	Inst	Ea	Sm	2C	2.05	7.80	2150.00	75.90	---	2225.90	**2580.00**
1', 1'-2" x 6'-8-1/2" sidelights											
Fir & pine	Inst	Ea	Lg	2C	1.00	16.00	635.00	37.00	---	672.00	**782.00**
	Inst	Ea	Sm	2C	1.54	10.40	714.00	57.00	---	771.00	**901.00**
Oak	Inst	Ea	Lg	2C	1.00	16.00	793.00	37.00	---	830.00	**964.00**
	Inst	Ea	Sm	2C	1.54	10.40	892.00	57.00	---	949.00	**1110.00**

Description	Oper	Unit	Vol	Crew Size	Man-hours per Unit	Crew Output per Day	Avg Mat'l Unit Cost	Avg Labor Unit Cost	Avg Equip Unit Cost	Avg Total Unit Cost	Avg Price Incl O&P

Stile and rail raised panels

No lites
2 raised panels

Description	Oper	Unit	Vol	Crew Size	Man-hours per Unit	Crew Output per Day	Avg Mat'l Unit Cost	Avg Labor Unit Cost	Avg Equip Unit Cost	Avg Total Unit Cost	Avg Price Incl O&P
2'-6" to 3' x 6'-8" x 1-3/4" T	Inst	Ea	Lg	2C	1.33	12.00	389.00	49.20	---	438.20	**516.00**
	Inst	Ea	Sm	2C	2.05	7.80	437.00	75.90	---	512.90	**609.00**
3'-6" x 6'-8" x 1-3/4" T	Inst	Ea	Lg	2C	1.45	11.00	389.00	53.70	---	442.70	**522.00**
	Inst	Ea	Sm	2C	2.24	7.15	437.00	82.90	---	519.90	**619.00**

4 raised panels

Description	Oper	Unit	Vol	Crew Size	Man-hours per Unit	Crew Output per Day	Avg Mat'l Unit Cost	Avg Labor Unit Cost	Avg Equip Unit Cost	Avg Total Unit Cost	Avg Price Incl O&P
2'-6" to 3' x 6'-8" x 1-3/4" T	Inst	Ea	Lg	2C	1.33	12.00	354.00	49.20	---	403.20	**476.00**
	Inst	Ea	Sm	2C	2.05	7.80	398.00	75.90	---	473.90	**564.00**
3'-6" x 6'-8" x 1-3/4" T	Inst	Ea	Lg	2C	1.45	11.00	520.00	53.70	---	573.70	**673.00**
	Inst	Ea	Sm	2C	2.24	7.15	585.00	82.90	---	667.90	**788.00**

6 raised panels

Description	Oper	Unit	Vol	Crew Size	Man-hours per Unit	Crew Output per Day	Avg Mat'l Unit Cost	Avg Labor Unit Cost	Avg Equip Unit Cost	Avg Total Unit Cost	Avg Price Incl O&P
2' to 2'-8" x 6'-8" x 1-3/4" T	Inst	Ea	Lg	2C	1.33	12.00	342.00	49.20	---	391.20	**462.00**
	Inst	Ea	Sm	2C	2.05	7.80	385.00	75.90	---	460.90	**549.00**
3' x 6'-8" x 1-3/4" T	Inst	Ea	Lg	2C	1.45	11.00	352.00	53.70	---	405.70	**479.00**
	Inst	Ea	Sm	2C	2.24	7.15	396.00	82.90	---	478.90	**571.00**
3'-6" x 6'-8" x 1-3/4" T	Inst	Ea	Lg	2C	1.60	10.00	515.00	59.20	---	574.20	**675.00**
	Inst	Ea	Sm	2C	2.46	6.50	579.00	91.10	---	670.10	**794.00**

8 raised panels

Description	Oper	Unit	Vol	Crew Size	Man-hours per Unit	Crew Output per Day	Avg Mat'l Unit Cost	Avg Labor Unit Cost	Avg Equip Unit Cost	Avg Total Unit Cost	Avg Price Incl O&P
2'-6" to 2'-8" x 6'-8" x 1-3/4" T	Inst	Ea	Lg	2C	1.33	12.00	343.00	49.20	---	392.20	**464.00**
	Inst	Ea	Sm	2C	2.05	7.80	386.00	75.90	---	461.90	**550.00**
3' x 6'-8" x 1-3/4" T	Inst	Ea	Lg	2C	1.45	11.00	352.00	53.70	---	405.70	**479.00**
	Inst	Ea	Sm	2C	2.24	7.15	396.00	82.90	---	478.90	**571.00**
3'-6" x 6'-8" x 1-3/4" T	Inst	Ea	Lg	2C	1.60	10.00	515.00	59.20	---	574.20	**675.00**
	Inst	Ea	Sm	2C	2.46	6.50	579.00	91.10	---	670.10	**794.00**
2'-6" to 2'-8" x 7' x 1-3/4" T	Inst	Ea	Lg	2C	1.33	12.00	371.00	49.20	---	420.20	**495.00**
	Inst	Ea	Sm	2C	2.05	7.80	417.00	75.90	---	492.90	**586.00**
3' x 7' x 1-3/4" T	Inst	Ea	Lg	2C	1.45	11.00	400.00	53.70	---	453.70	**535.00**
	Inst	Ea	Sm	2C	2.24	7.15	450.00	82.90	---	532.90	**633.00**
3'-6" x 7' x 1-3/4" T	Inst	Ea	Lg	2C	1.60	10.00	541.00	59.20	---	600.20	**705.00**
	Inst	Ea	Sm	2C	2.46	6.50	609.00	91.10	---	700.10	**828.00**

10 raised panels

Description	Oper	Unit	Vol	Crew Size	Man-hours per Unit	Crew Output per Day	Avg Mat'l Unit Cost	Avg Labor Unit Cost	Avg Equip Unit Cost	Avg Total Unit Cost	Avg Price Incl O&P
2'-6" to 2'-8" x 8' x 1-3/4" T	Inst	Ea	Lg	2C	1.45	11.00	450.00	53.70	---	503.70	**593.00**
	Inst	Ea	Sm	2C	2.24	7.15	506.00	82.90	---	588.90	**698.00**
3' x 8' x 1-3/4" T	Inst	Ea	Lg	2C	1.60	10.00	472.00	59.20	---	531.20	**625.00**
	Inst	Ea	Sm	2C	2.46	6.50	531.00	91.10	---	622.10	**738.00**
3'-6" x 8' x 1-3/4" T	Inst	Ea	Lg	2C	1.78	9.00	598.00	65.90	---	663.90	**780.00**
	Inst	Ea	Sm	2C	2.74	5.85	672.00	101.00	---	773.00	**915.00**

Description	Oper	Unit	Vol	Crew Size	Man-hours per Unit	Crew Output per Day	Avg Mat'l Unit Cost	Avg Labor Unit Cost	Avg Equip Unit Cost	Avg Total Unit Cost	Avg Price Incl O&P
Lites											
1 raised panel, 1 lite											
2'-6" to 3' x 6'-8" x 1-3/4" T											
Open w/stops	Inst	Ea	Lg	2C	1.33	12.00	340.00	49.20	---	389.20	**459.00**
	Inst	Ea	Sm	2C	2.05	7.80	382.00	75.90	---	457.90	**546.00**
Tempered clear	Inst	Ea	Lg	2C	1.33	12.00	354.00	49.20	---	403.20	**476.00**
	Inst	Ea	Sm	2C	2.05	7.80	398.00	75.90	---	473.90	**564.00**
Acrylic or tempered amber	Inst	Ea	Lg	2C	1.33	12.00	425.00	49.20	---	474.20	**557.00**
	Inst	Ea	Sm	2C	2.05	7.80	478.00	75.90	---	553.90	**656.00**
1 raised panel, 6 lites											
2'-6" to 3' x 6'-8" x 1-3/4" T											
Open w/stops	Inst	Ea	Lg	2C	1.33	12.00	366.00	49.20	---	415.20	**490.00**
	Inst	Ea	Sm	2C	2.05	7.80	412.00	75.90	---	487.90	**580.00**
Tempered clear	Inst	Ea	Lg	2C	1.33	12.00	391.00	49.20	---	440.20	**519.00**
	Inst	Ea	Sm	2C	2.05	7.80	440.00	75.90	---	515.90	**612.00**
Acrylic or tempered amber	Inst	Ea	Lg	2C	1.33	12.00	444.00	49.20	---	493.20	**580.00**
	Inst	Ea	Sm	2C	2.05	7.80	500.00	75.90	---	575.90	**681.00**
1 raised panel, 9 lites											
2'-6" to 3' x 6'-8" x 1-3/4" T											
Open w/stops	Inst	Ea	Lg	2C	1.33	12.00	372.00	49.20	---	421.20	**497.00**
	Inst	Ea	Sm	2C	2.05	7.80	419.00	75.90	---	494.90	**588.00**
Tempered clear	Inst	Ea	Lg	2C	1.33	12.00	401.00	49.20	---	450.20	**530.00**
	Inst	Ea	Sm	2C	2.05	7.80	451.00	75.90	---	526.90	**625.00**
Acrylic or tempered amber	Inst	Ea	Lg	2C	1.33	12.00	486.00	49.20	---	535.20	**628.00**
	Inst	Ea	Sm	2C	2.05	7.80	547.00	75.90	---	622.90	**735.00**
1 raised panel, 12 diamond lites											
2'-6" to 3' x 6'-8" x 1-3/4" T											
Open w/stops	Inst	Ea	Lg	2C	1.33	12.00	382.00	49.20	---	431.20	**508.00**
	Inst	Ea	Sm	2C	2.05	7.80	429.00	75.90	---	504.90	**600.00**
Tempered clear	Inst	Ea	Lg	2C	1.33	12.00	486.00	49.20	---	535.20	**628.00**
	Inst	Ea	Sm	2C	2.05	7.80	547.00	75.90	---	622.90	**735.00**
Acrylic or tempered amber	Inst	Ea	Lg	2C	1.33	12.00	606.00	49.20	---	655.20	**766.00**
	Inst	Ea	Sm	2C	2.05	7.80	682.00	75.90	---	757.90	**890.00**

Dutch doors, country style, fir, stile and rail

Two raised panels in lower door

1 lite in upper door
2'-6" to 3' x 6'-8" x 1-3/4" T

Description	Oper	Unit	Vol	Crew Size	Man-hours per Unit	Crew Output per Day	Avg Mat'l Unit Cost	Avg Labor Unit Cost	Avg Equip Unit Cost	Avg Total Unit Cost	Avg Price Incl O&P
Empty	Inst	Ea	Lg	2C	1.33	12.00	468.00	49.20	---	517.20	**607.00**
	Inst	Ea	Sm	2C	2.05	7.80	527.00	75.90	---	602.90	**712.00**
Tempered clear	Inst	Ea	Lg	2C	1.33	12.00	486.00	49.20	---	535.20	**628.00**
	Inst	Ea	Sm	2C	2.05	7.80	547.00	75.90	---	622.90	**735.00**
Tempered amber	Inst	Ea	Lg	2C	1.33	12.00	606.00	49.20	---	655.20	**766.00**
	Inst	Ea	Sm	2C	2.05	7.80	682.00	75.90	---	757.90	**890.00**

Description	Oper	Unit	Vol	Crew Size	Man-hours per Unit	Crew Output per Day	Avg Mat'l Unit Cost	Avg Labor Unit Cost	Avg Equip Unit Cost	Avg Total Unit Cost	Avg Price Incl O&P
4 lites in upper door											
2'-6" to 3' x 6'-8" x 1-3/4" T											
Empty	Inst	Ea	Lg	2C	1.33	12.00	479.00	49.20	---	528.20	**620.00**
	Inst	Ea	Sm	2C	2.05	7.80	539.00	75.90	---	614.90	**726.00**
Tempered clear	Inst	Ea	Lg	2C	1.33	12.00	523.00	49.20	---	572.20	**671.00**
	Inst	Ea	Sm	2C	2.05	7.80	589.00	75.90	---	664.90	**783.00**
Tempered amber	Inst	Ea	Lg	2C	1.33	12.00	552.00	49.20	---	601.20	**704.00**
	Inst	Ea	Sm	2C	2.05	7.80	621.00	75.90	---	696.90	**820.00**
9 lites in upper door											
2'-6" to 3' x 6'-8" x 1-3/4" T											
Empty	Inst	Ea	Lg	2C	1.33	12.00	474.00	49.20	---	523.20	**614.00**
	Inst	Ea	Sm	2C	2.05	7.80	533.00	75.90	---	608.90	**719.00**
Tempered clear	Inst	Ea	Lg	2C	1.33	12.00	492.00	49.20	---	541.20	**635.00**
	Inst	Ea	Sm	2C	2.05	7.80	554.00	75.90	---	629.90	**743.00**
Tempered amber	Inst	Ea	Lg	2C	1.33	12.00	611.00	49.20	---	660.20	**771.00**
	Inst	Ea	Sm	2C	2.05	7.80	687.00	75.90	---	762.90	**896.00**
12 diamond lites in upper door											
2'-6" to 3' x 6'-8" x 1-3/4" T											
Empty	Inst	Ea	Lg	2C	1.33	12.00	521.00	49.20	---	570.20	**668.00**
	Inst	Ea	Sm	2C	2.05	7.80	586.00	75.90	---	661.90	**780.00**
Tempered clear	Inst	Ea	Lg	2C	1.33	12.00	559.00	49.20	---	608.20	**712.00**
	Inst	Ea	Sm	2C	2.05	7.80	629.00	75.90	---	704.90	**830.00**
Tempered amber	Inst	Ea	Lg	2C	1.33	12.00	691.00	49.20	---	740.20	**864.00**
	Inst	Ea	Sm	2C	2.05	7.80	778.00	75.90	---	853.90	**1000.00**

Four diamond-shaped raised panels in lower door

Description	Oper	Unit	Vol	Crew Size	Man-hours per Unit	Crew Output per Day	Avg Mat'l Unit Cost	Avg Labor Unit Cost	Avg Equip Unit Cost	Avg Total Unit Cost	Avg Price Incl O&P
1 lite in upper door											
2'-6" to 3' x 6'-8" x 1-3/4" T											
Empty	Inst	Ea	Lg	2C	1.33	12.00	472.00	49.20	---	521.20	**611.00**
	Inst	Ea	Sm	2C	2.05	7.80	531.00	75.90	---	606.90	**716.00**
Tempered clear	Inst	Ea	Lg	2C	1.33	12.00	490.00	49.20	---	539.20	**632.00**
	Inst	Ea	Sm	2C	2.05	7.80	551.00	75.90	---	626.90	**740.00**
Tempered amber	Inst	Ea	Lg	2C	1.33	12.00	610.00	49.20	---	659.20	**770.00**
	Inst	Ea	Sm	2C	2.05	7.80	686.00	75.90	---	761.90	**895.00**
6 lites in upper door											
2'-6" to 3' x 6'-8" x 1-3/4" T											
Empty	Inst	Ea	Lg	2C	1.33	12.00	510.00	49.20	---	559.20	**655.00**
	Inst	Ea	Sm	2C	2.05	7.80	574.00	75.90	---	649.90	**766.00**
Tempered clear	Inst	Ea	Lg	2C	1.33	12.00	529.00	49.20	---	578.20	**678.00**
	Inst	Ea	Sm	2C	2.05	7.80	595.00	75.90	---	670.90	**791.00**
Tempered amber	Inst	Ea	Lg	2C	1.33	12.00	655.00	49.20	---	704.20	**822.00**
	Inst	Ea	Sm	2C	2.05	7.80	737.00	75.90	---	812.90	**954.00**

Description	Oper	Unit	Vol	Crew Size	Man-hours per Unit	Crew Output per Day	Avg Mat'l Unit Cost	Avg Labor Unit Cost	Avg Equip Unit Cost	Avg Total Unit Cost	Avg Price Incl O&P
9 lites in upper door											
2'-6" to 3' x 6'-8" x 1-3/4" T											
Empty	Inst	Ea	Lg	2C	1.33	12.00	475.00	49.20	---	524.20	**615.00**
	Inst	Ea	Sm	2C	2.05	7.80	535.00	75.90	---	610.90	**721.00**
Tempered clear	Inst	Ea	Lg	2C	1.33	12.00	496.00	49.20	---	545.20	**639.00**
	Inst	Ea	Sm	2C	2.05	7.80	558.00	75.90	---	633.90	**747.00**
Tempered amber	Inst	Ea	Lg	2C	1.33	12.00	614.00	49.20	---	663.20	**775.00**
	Inst	Ea	Sm	2C	2.05	7.80	691.00	75.90	---	766.90	**901.00**
12 diamond lites in upper door											
2'-6" to 3' x 6'-8" x 1-3/4" T											
Empty	Inst	Ea	Lg	2C	1.33	12.00	524.00	49.20	---	573.20	**672.00**
	Inst	Ea	Sm	2C	2.05	7.80	590.00	75.90	---	665.90	**785.00**
Tempered clear	Inst	Ea	Lg	2C	1.33	12.00	564.00	49.20	---	613.20	**718.00**
	Inst	Ea	Sm	2C	2.05	7.80	635.00	75.90	---	710.90	**836.00**
Tempered amber	Inst	Ea	Lg	2C	1.33	12.00	696.00	49.20	---	745.20	**869.00**
	Inst	Ea	Sm	2C	2.05	7.80	783.00	75.90	---	858.90	**1010.00**

French doors

Douglas fir or hemlock 4-1/2" stiles and top rail, 9-1/2" bottom rail, tempered glass with stops

Description	Oper	Unit	Vol	Crew Size	Man-hours per Unit	Crew Output per Day	Avg Mat'l Unit Cost	Avg Labor Unit Cost	Avg Equip Unit Cost	Avg Total Unit Cost	Avg Price Incl O&P
1 lite											
1-3/8" T and 1-3/4" T											
2' x 6'-8"	Inst	Ea	Lg	2C	1.14	14.00	256.00	42.20	---	298.20	**353.00**
	Inst	Ea	Sm	2C	1.76	9.10	288.00	65.20	---	353.20	**422.00**
2'-4", 2'-6", 2'-8" x 6'-8"	Inst	Ea	Lg	2C	1.33	12.00	262.00	49.20	---	311.20	**370.00**
	Inst	Ea	Sm	2C	2.05	7.80	294.00	75.90	---	369.90	**445.00**
3' x 6'-8"	Inst	Ea	Lg	2C	1.60	10.00	265.00	59.20	---	324.20	**388.00**
	Inst	Ea	Sm	2C	2.46	6.50	298.00	91.10	---	389.10	**471.00**
5 lites, 5 high											
1-3/8" T and 1-3/4" T											
2' x 6'-8"	Inst	Ea	Lg	2C	1.14	14.00	226.00	42.20	---	268.20	**319.00**
	Inst	Ea	Sm	2C	1.76	9.10	254.00	65.20	---	319.20	**383.00**
2'-4", 2'-6", 2'-8" x 6'-8"	Inst	Ea	Lg	2C	1.33	12.00	228.00	49.20	---	277.20	**331.00**
	Inst	Ea	Sm	2C	2.05	7.80	257.00	75.90	---	332.90	**401.00**
3' x 6'-8"	Inst	Ea	Lg	2C	1.60	10.00	232.00	59.20	---	291.20	**349.00**
	Inst	Ea	Sm	2C	2.46	6.50	261.00	91.10	---	352.10	**427.00**
10 lites, 5 high											
1-3/8" T and 1-3/4" T											
2' x 6'-8"	Inst	Ea	Lg	2C	1.14	14.00	251.00	42.20	---	293.20	**348.00**
	Inst	Ea	Sm	2C	1.76	9.10	282.00	65.20	---	347.20	**416.00**
2'-4", 2'-6", 2'-8" x 6'-8"	Inst	Ea	Lg	2C	1.33	12.00	258.00	49.20	---	307.20	**366.00**
	Inst	Ea	Sm	2C	2.05	7.80	290.00	75.90	---	365.90	**440.00**
3' x 6'-8"	Inst	Ea	Lg	2C	1.60	10.00	264.00	59.20	---	323.20	**387.00**
	Inst	Ea	Sm	2C	2.46	6.50	297.00	91.10	---	388.10	**469.00**
15 lites, 5 high											
1-3/8" T and 1-3/4" T											
2'-6", 2'-8" x 6'-8"	Inst	Ea	Lg	2C	1.33	12.00	288.00	49.20	---	337.20	**400.00**
	Inst	Ea	Sm	2C	2.05	7.80	324.00	75.90	---	399.90	**479.00**
3' x 6'-8"	Inst	Ea	Lg	2C	1.60	10.00	300.00	59.20	---	359.20	**428.00**
	Inst	Ea	Sm	2C	2.46	6.50	338.00	91.10	---	429.10	**516.00**

Description	Oper	Unit	Vol	Crew Size	Man-hours per Unit	Crew Output per Day	Avg Mat'l Unit Cost	Avg Labor Unit Cost	Avg Equip Unit Cost	Avg Total Unit Cost	Avg Price Incl O&P

French sidelites

Douglas fir or hemlock 4-1/2" stiles and top rail, 9-1/2" bottom rail, tempered glass with stops

1 lite
1-3/4" T

Description	Oper	Unit	Vol	Crew Size	Man-hours per Unit	Crew Output per Day	Avg Mat'l Unit Cost	Avg Labor Unit Cost	Avg Equip Unit Cost	Avg Total Unit Cost	Avg Price Incl O&P
1', 1'-2" x 6'-8"	Inst	Ea	Lg	2C	1.00	16.00	174.00	37.00	---	211.00	**252.00**
	Inst	Ea	Sm	2C	1.54	10.40	196.00	57.00	---	253.00	**305.00**
1'-4", 1'-6" x 6'-8"	Inst	Ea	Lg	2C	1.00	16.00	186.00	37.00	---	223.00	**266.00**
	Inst	Ea	Sm	2C	1.54	10.40	209.00	57.00	---	266.00	**320.00**

5 lites, 5 high
1-3/4" T

Description	Oper	Unit	Vol	Crew Size	Man-hours per Unit	Crew Output per Day	Avg Mat'l Unit Cost	Avg Labor Unit Cost	Avg Equip Unit Cost	Avg Total Unit Cost	Avg Price Incl O&P
1', 1'-2" x 6'-8"	Inst	Ea	Lg	2C	1.00	16.00	168.00	37.00	---	205.00	**245.00**
	Inst	Ea	Sm	2C	1.54	10.40	189.00	57.00	---	246.00	**297.00**
1'-4", 1'-6" x 6'-8"	Inst	Ea	Lg	2C	1.00	16.00	182.00	37.00	---	219.00	**262.00**
	Inst	Ea	Sm	2C	1.54	10.40	205.00	57.00	---	262.00	**316.00**

Garden doors

1 door, "X" unit

Description	Oper	Unit	Vol	Crew Size	Man-hours per Unit	Crew Output per Day	Avg Mat'l Unit Cost	Avg Labor Unit Cost	Avg Equip Unit Cost	Avg Total Unit Cost	Avg Price Incl O&P
2'-6" x 6'-8"	Inst	LS	Lg	2C	1.33	12.00	336.00	49.20	---	385.20	**455.00**
	Inst	LS	Sm	2C	2.05	7.80	378.00	75.90	---	453.90	**541.00**
3' x 6'-8"	Inst	LS	Lg	2C	1.60	10.00	360.00	59.20	---	419.20	**497.00**
	Inst	LS	Sm	2C	2.46	6.50	405.00	91.10	---	496.10	**593.00**

2 doors, "XO/OX" unit

Description	Oper	Unit	Vol	Crew Size	Man-hours per Unit	Crew Output per Day	Avg Mat'l Unit Cost	Avg Labor Unit Cost	Avg Equip Unit Cost	Avg Total Unit Cost	Avg Price Incl O&P
5' x 6'-8"	Inst	LS	Lg	2C	2.42	6.60	630.00	89.60	---	719.60	**850.00**
	Inst	LS	Sm	2C	3.73	4.29	709.00	138.00	---	847.00	**1010.00**
6' x 6'-8"	Inst	LS	Lg	2C	2.91	5.50	672.00	108.00	---	780.00	**924.00**
	Inst	LS	Sm	2C	4.47	3.58	756.00	165.00	---	921.00	**1100.00**

3 doors, "XOX" unit

Description	Oper	Unit	Vol	Crew Size	Man-hours per Unit	Crew Output per Day	Avg Mat'l Unit Cost	Avg Labor Unit Cost	Avg Equip Unit Cost	Avg Total Unit Cost	Avg Price Incl O&P
7'-6" x 6'-8"	Inst	LS	Lg	2C	3.64	4.40	894.00	135.00	---	1029.00	**1220.00**
	Inst	LS	Sm	2C	5.59	2.86	1010.00	207.00	---	1217.00	**1450.00**
9' x 6'-8"	Inst	LS	Lg	2C	4.32	3.70	960.00	160.00	---	1120.00	**1330.00**
	Inst	LS	Sm	2C	6.64	2.41	1080.00	246.00	---	1326.00	**1590.00**

Sliding doors

Glass sliding doors, with 5-1/2" anodized aluminum frame, trim, weatherstripping, tempered 3/16" T clear single-glazed glass, with screen

6'-8" H

Description	Oper	Unit	Vol	Crew Size	Man-hours per Unit	Crew Output per Day	Avg Mat'l Unit Cost	Avg Labor Unit Cost	Avg Equip Unit Cost	Avg Total Unit Cost	Avg Price Incl O&P
5' W, 2 lites, 1 sliding	Inst	Set	Lg	2C	4.00	4.00	492.00	148.00	---	640.00	**773.00**
	Inst	Set	Sm	2C	6.15	2.60	554.00	228.00	---	782.00	**955.00**
6' W, 2 lites, 1 sliding	Inst	Set	Lg	2C	4.00	4.00	548.00	148.00	---	696.00	**838.00**
	Inst	Set	Sm	2C	6.15	2.60	617.00	228.00	---	845.00	**1030.00**
7' W, 2 lites, 1 sliding	Inst	Set	Lg	2C	4.00	4.00	589.00	148.00	---	737.00	**885.00**
	Inst	Set	Sm	2C	6.15	2.60	663.00	228.00	---	891.00	**1080.00**
8' W, 2 lites, 1 sliding	Inst	Set	Lg	2C	4.00	4.00	632.00	148.00	---	780.00	**935.00**
	Inst	Set	Sm	2C	6.15	2.60	711.00	228.00	---	939.00	**1140.00**
10' W, 2 lites, 1 sliding	Inst	Set	Lg	2C	4.00	4.00	822.00	148.00	---	970.00	**1150.00**
	Inst	Set	Sm	2C	6.15	2.60	925.00	228.00	---	1153.00	**1380.00**

Description	Oper	Unit	Vol	Crew Size	Man-hours per Unit	Crew Output per Day	Avg Mat'l Unit Cost	Avg Labor Unit Cost	Avg Equip Unit Cost	Avg Total Unit Cost	Avg Price Incl O&P
9' W, 3 lites, 1 sliding	Inst	Set	Lg	2C	5.33	3.00	728.00	197.00	---	925.00	**1110.00**
	Inst	Set	Sm	2C	8.21	1.95	819.00	304.00	---	1123.00	**1370.00**
12' W, 3 lites, 1 sliding	Inst	Set	Lg	2C	5.33	3.00	854.00	197.00	---	1051.00	**1260.00**
	Inst	Set	Sm	2C	8.21	1.95	961.00	304.00	---	1265.00	**1530.00**
15' W, 3 lites, 1 sliding	Inst	Set	Lg	2C	5.33	3.00	1140.00	197.00	---	1337.00	**1590.00**
	Inst	Set	Sm	2C	8.21	1.95	1280.00	304.00	---	1584.00	**1900.00**
8' H											
5' W, 2 lites, 1 sliding	Inst	Set	Lg	2C	4.00	4.00	580.00	148.00	---	728.00	**874.00**
	Inst	Set	Sm	2C	6.15	2.60	652.00	228.00	---	880.00	**1070.00**
6' W, 2 lites, 1 sliding	Inst	Set	Lg	2C	4.00	4.00	623.00	148.00	---	771.00	**924.00**
	Inst	Set	Sm	2C	6.15	2.60	701.00	228.00	---	929.00	**1120.00**
7' W, 2 lites, 1 sliding	Inst	Set	Lg	2C	4.00	4.00	737.00	148.00	---	885.00	**1050.00**
	Inst	Set	Sm	2C	6.15	2.60	829.00	228.00	---	1057.00	**1270.00**
8' W, 2 lites, 1 sliding	Inst	Set	Lg	2C	4.00	4.00	852.00	148.00	---	1000.00	**1190.00**
	Inst	Set	Sm	2C	6.15	2.60	959.00	228.00	---	1187.00	**1420.00**
10' W, 2 lites, 1 sliding	Inst	Set	Lg	2C	4.00	4.00	983.00	148.00	---	1131.00	**1340.00**
	Inst	Set	Sm	2C	6.15	2.60	1110.00	228.00	---	1338.00	**1590.00**
9' W, 3 lites, 1 sliding	Inst	Set	Lg	2C	5.33	3.00	857.00	197.00	---	1054.00	**1260.00**
	Inst	Set	Sm	2C	8.21	1.95	964.00	304.00	---	1268.00	**1530.00**
12' W, 3 lites, 1 sliding	Inst	Set	Lg	2C	5.33	3.00	1150.00	197.00	---	1347.00	**1590.00**
	Inst	Set	Sm	2C	8.21	1.95	1290.00	304.00	---	1594.00	**1910.00**
15' W, 3 lites, 1 sliding	Inst	Set	Lg	2C	5.33	3.00	1330.00	197.00	---	1527.00	**1810.00**
	Inst	Set	Sm	2C	8.21	1.95	1500.00	304.00	---	1804.00	**2150.00**

French sliding door units

Douglas fir doors, solid brass hardware, screen, frames, and exterior molding included

1 lite, 2 panels, single glazed
  1-3/4" T

Description	Oper	Unit	Vol	Crew Size	Man-hours per Unit	Crew Output per Day	Avg Mat'l Unit Cost	Avg Labor Unit Cost	Avg Equip Unit Cost	Avg Total Unit Cost	Avg Price Incl O&P
5' x 6'-8"	Inst	Ea	Lg	2C	5.33	3.00	2640.00	197.00	---	2837.00	**3320.00**
	Inst	Ea	Sm	2C	8.21	1.95	2980.00	304.00	---	3284.00	**3850.00**
6' x 6'-8"	Inst	Ea	Lg	2C	5.33	3.00	2820.00	197.00	---	3017.00	**3520.00**
	Inst	Ea	Sm	2C	8.21	1.95	3170.00	304.00	---	3474.00	**4070.00**
7' x 6'-8"	Inst	Ea	Lg	2C	5.33	3.00	3050.00	197.00	---	3247.00	**3780.00**
	Inst	Ea	Sm	2C	8.21	1.95	3430.00	304.00	---	3734.00	**4370.00**
8' x 6'-8"	Inst	Ea	Lg	2C	5.33	3.00	3210.00	197.00	---	3407.00	**3970.00**
	Inst	Ea	Sm	2C	8.21	1.95	3610.00	304.00	---	3914.00	**4580.00**
5' x 7'	Inst	Ea	Lg	2C	5.33	3.00	2710.00	197.00	---	2907.00	**3390.00**
	Inst	Ea	Sm	2C	8.21	1.95	3040.00	304.00	---	3344.00	**3930.00**
6' x 7'	Inst	Ea	Lg	2C	5.33	3.00	2850.00	197.00	---	3047.00	**3550.00**
	Inst	Ea	Sm	2C	8.21	1.95	3200.00	304.00	---	3504.00	**4110.00**
7' x 7'	Inst	Ea	Lg	2C	5.33	3.00	3140.00	197.00	---	3337.00	**3880.00**
	Inst	Ea	Sm	2C	8.21	1.95	3530.00	304.00	---	3834.00	**4490.00**
8' x 7'	Inst	Ea	Lg	2C	5.33	3.00	3330.00	197.00	---	3527.00	**4110.00**
	Inst	Ea	Sm	2C	8.21	1.95	3750.00	304.00	---	4054.00	**4740.00**
5' x 8'	Inst	Ea	Lg	2C	5.33	3.00	3060.00	197.00	---	3257.00	**3800.00**
	Inst	Ea	Sm	2C	8.21	1.95	3450.00	304.00	---	3754.00	**4390.00**

Description	Oper	Unit	Vol	Crew Size	Man-hours per Unit	Crew Output per Day	Avg Mat'l Unit Cost	Avg Labor Unit Cost	Avg Equip Unit Cost	Avg Total Unit Cost	Avg Price Incl O&P
6' x 8'	Inst	Ea	Lg	2C	5.33	3.00	3280.00	197.00	---	3477.00	**4050.00**
	Inst	Ea	Sm	2C	8.21	1.95	3690.00	304.00	---	3994.00	**4670.00**
7' x 8'	Inst	Ea	Lg	2C	5.33	3.00	3530.00	197.00	---	3727.00	**4330.00**
	Inst	Ea	Sm	2C	8.21	1.95	3970.00	304.00	---	4274.00	**4990.00**
8' x 8'	Inst	Ea	Lg	2C	5.33	3.00	3750.00	197.00	---	3947.00	**4590.00**
	Inst	Ea	Sm	2C	8.21	1.95	4220.00	304.00	---	4524.00	**5280.00**

10 lites, 2 panels, single glazed
1-3/4" T

Description	Oper	Unit	Vol	Crew Size	Man-hours per Unit	Crew Output per Day	Avg Mat'l Unit Cost	Avg Labor Unit Cost	Avg Equip Unit Cost	Avg Total Unit Cost	Avg Price Incl O&P
5' x 6'-8"	Inst	Ea	Lg	2C	5.33	3.00	2860.00	197.00	---	3057.00	**3560.00**
	Inst	Ea	Sm	2C	8.21	1.95	3220.00	304.00	---	3524.00	**4120.00**
6' x 6'-8"	Inst	Ea	Lg	2C	5.33	3.00	2980.00	197.00	---	3177.00	**3710.00**
	Inst	Ea	Sm	2C	8.21	1.95	3360.00	304.00	---	3664.00	**4290.00**
5' x 7'	Inst	Ea	Lg	2C	5.33	3.00	2910.00	197.00	---	3107.00	**3620.00**
	Inst	Ea	Sm	2C	8.21	1.95	3270.00	304.00	---	3574.00	**4180.00**
6' x 7'	Inst	Ea	Lg	2C	5.33	3.00	3060.00	197.00	---	3257.00	**3800.00**
	Inst	Ea	Sm	2C	8.21	1.95	3450.00	304.00	---	3754.00	**4390.00**
5' x 8'	Inst	Ea	Lg	2C	5.33	3.00	3240.00	197.00	---	3437.00	**4000.00**
	Inst	Ea	Sm	2C	8.21	1.95	3640.00	304.00	---	3944.00	**4610.00**
6' x 8'	Inst	Ea	Lg	2C	5.33	3.00	3410.00	197.00	---	3607.00	**4190.00**
	Inst	Ea	Sm	2C	8.21	1.95	3830.00	304.00	---	4134.00	**4830.00**

15 lites, 2 panels, single glazed
1-3/4" T

Description	Oper	Unit	Vol	Crew Size	Man-hours per Unit	Crew Output per Day	Avg Mat'l Unit Cost	Avg Labor Unit Cost	Avg Equip Unit Cost	Avg Total Unit Cost	Avg Price Incl O&P
5' x 6'-8"	Inst	Ea	Lg	2C	5.33	3.00	3000.00	197.00	---	3197.00	**3730.00**
	Inst	Ea	Sm	2C	8.21	1.95	3380.00	304.00	---	3684.00	**4310.00**
6' x 6'-8"	Inst	Ea	Lg	2C	5.33	3.00	3140.00	197.00	---	3337.00	**3890.00**
	Inst	Ea	Sm	2C	8.21	1.95	3530.00	304.00	---	3834.00	**4490.00**
7' x 6'-8"	Inst	Ea	Lg	2C	5.33	3.00	3340.00	197.00	---	3537.00	**4120.00**
	Inst	Ea	Sm	2C	8.21	1.95	3760.00	304.00	---	4064.00	**4750.00**
8' x 6'-8"	Inst	Ea	Lg	2C	5.33	3.00	3490.00	197.00	---	3687.00	**4290.00**
	Inst	Ea	Sm	2C	8.21	1.95	3930.00	304.00	---	4234.00	**4940.00**
5' x 7'	Inst	Ea	Lg	2C	5.33	3.00	3060.00	197.00	---	3257.00	**3800.00**
	Inst	Ea	Sm	2C	8.21	1.95	3450.00	304.00	---	3754.00	**4390.00**
6' x 7'	Inst	Ea	Lg	2C	5.33	3.00	3220.00	197.00	---	3417.00	**3980.00**
	Inst	Ea	Sm	2C	8.21	1.95	3620.00	304.00	---	3924.00	**4590.00**
7' x 7'	Inst	Ea	Lg	2C	5.33	3.00	3430.00	197.00	---	3627.00	**4220.00**
	Inst	Ea	Sm	2C	8.21	1.95	3860.00	304.00	---	4164.00	**4870.00**
8' x 7'	Inst	Ea	Lg	2C	5.33	3.00	3600.00	197.00	---	3797.00	**4420.00**
	Inst	Ea	Sm	2C	8.21	1.95	4050.00	304.00	---	4354.00	**5080.00**
5' x 8'	Inst	Ea	Lg	2C	5.33	3.00	3390.00	197.00	---	3587.00	**4180.00**
	Inst	Ea	Sm	2C	8.21	1.95	3820.00	304.00	---	4124.00	**4820.00**
6' x 8'	Inst	Ea	Lg	2C	5.33	3.00	3560.00	197.00	---	3757.00	**4370.00**
	Inst	Ea	Sm	2C	8.21	1.95	4010.00	304.00	---	4314.00	**5040.00**
7' x 8'	Inst	Ea	Lg	2C	5.33	3.00	3820.00	197.00	---	4017.00	**4670.00**
	Inst	Ea	Sm	2C	8.21	1.95	4300.00	304.00	---	4604.00	**5370.00**
8' x 8'	Inst	Ea	Lg	2C	5.33	3.00	3970.00	197.00	---	4167.00	**4840.00**
	Inst	Ea	Sm	2C	8.21	1.95	4460.00	304.00	---	4764.00	**5560.00**

Description	Oper	Unit	Vol	Crew Size	Man-hours per Unit	Crew Output per Day	Avg Mat'l Unit Cost	Avg Labor Unit Cost	Avg Equip Unit Cost	Avg Total Unit Cost	Avg Price Incl O&P
Fire doors, natural birch											
1 hour rating											
2'-6" x 6'-8" x 1-3/4" T	Inst	Ea	Lg	2C	1.23	13.00	257.00	45.50	---	302.50	**359.00**
	Inst	Ea	Sm	2C	1.89	8.45	289.00	70.00	---	359.00	**430.00**
3'-6" x 6'-8" x 1-3/4" T	Inst	Ea	Lg	2C	1.45	11.00	320.00	53.70	---	373.70	**444.00**
	Inst	Ea	Sm	2C	2.24	7.15	360.00	82.90	---	442.90	**531.00**
2'-6" x 7' x 1-3/4" T	Inst	Ea	Lg	2C	1.23	13.00	269.00	45.50	---	314.50	**373.00**
	Inst	Ea	Sm	2C	1.89	8.45	302.00	70.00	---	372.00	**446.00**
3'-6" x 7' x 1-3/4" T	Inst	Ea	Lg	2C	1.45	11.00	335.00	53.70	---	388.70	**460.00**
	Inst	Ea	Sm	2C	2.24	7.15	377.00	82.90	---	459.90	**549.00**
1.5 hour rating											
2'-6" x 6'-8" x 1-3/4" T	Inst	Ea	Lg	2C	1.23	13.00	365.00	45.50	---	410.50	**483.00**
	Inst	Ea	Sm	2C	1.89	8.45	410.00	70.00	---	480.00	**570.00**
3'-6" x 6'-8" x 1-3/4" T	Inst	Ea	Lg	2C	1.45	11.00	407.00	53.70	---	460.70	**543.00**
	Inst	Ea	Sm	2C	2.24	7.15	458.00	82.90	---	540.90	**642.00**
2'-6" x 7' x 1-3/4" T	Inst	Ea	Lg	2C	1.23	13.00	384.00	45.50	---	429.50	**505.00**
	Inst	Ea	Sm	2C	1.89	8.45	432.00	70.00	---	502.00	**595.00**
3'-6" x 7' x 1-3/4" T	Inst	Ea	Lg	2C	1.45	11.00	480.00	53.70	---	533.70	**627.00**
	Inst	Ea	Sm	2C	2.24	7.15	540.00	82.90	---	622.90	**737.00**

Interior doors

Passage doors, flush face, includes hinge hardware

Hollow core prehung door units

Description	Oper	Unit	Vol	Crew Size	Man-hours per Unit	Crew Output per Day	Avg Mat'l Unit Cost	Avg Labor Unit Cost	Avg Equip Unit Cost	Avg Total Unit Cost	Avg Price Incl O&P
Hardboard											
2'-6" x 6'-8" x 1-3/8" T	Inst	Ea	Lg	2C	1.07	15.00	46.50	39.60	---	86.10	**109.00**
	Inst	Ea	Sm	2C	1.64	9.75	52.30	60.70	---	113.00	**145.00**
2'-8" x 6'-8" x 1-3/8" T	Inst	Ea	Lg	2C	1.14	14.00	49.40	42.20	---	91.60	**116.00**
	Inst	Ea	Sm	2C	1.76	9.10	55.60	65.20	---	120.80	**155.00**
3' x 6'-8" x 1-3/8" T	Inst	Ea	Lg	2C	1.14	14.00	52.20	42.20	---	94.40	**119.00**
	Inst	Ea	Sm	2C	1.76	9.10	58.70	65.20	---	123.90	**159.00**
2'-6" x 7' x 1-3/8" T	Inst	Ea	Lg	2C	1.07	15.00	59.20	39.60	---	98.80	**123.00**
	Inst	Ea	Sm	2C	1.64	9.75	66.60	60.70	---	127.30	**162.00**
2'-8" x 7' x 1-3/8" T	Inst	Ea	Lg	2C	1.14	14.00	62.10	42.20	---	104.30	**131.00**
	Inst	Ea	Sm	2C	1.76	9.10	69.90	65.20	---	135.10	**172.00**
3' x 7' x 1-3/8" T	Inst	Ea	Lg	2C	1.14	14.00	64.90	42.20	---	107.10	**134.00**
	Inst	Ea	Sm	2C	1.76	9.10	73.00	65.20	---	138.20	**175.00**
Lauan											
2'-6" x 6'-8" x 1-3/8" T	Inst	Ea	Lg	2C	1.07	15.00	61.60	39.60	---	101.20	**126.00**
	Inst	Ea	Sm	2C	1.64	9.75	69.30	60.70	---	130.00	**165.00**
2'-8" x 6'-8" x 1-3/8" T	Inst	Ea	Lg	2C	1.14	14.00	64.00	42.20	---	106.20	**133.00**
	Inst	Ea	Sm	2C	1.76	9.10	72.00	65.20	---	137.20	**174.00**
3' x 6'-8" x 1-3/8" T	Inst	Ea	Lg	2C	1.14	14.00	68.60	42.20	---	110.80	**138.00**
	Inst	Ea	Sm	2C	1.76	9.10	77.20	65.20	---	142.40	**180.00**
2'-6" x 7' x 1-3/8" T	Inst	Ea	Lg	2C	1.07	15.00	73.00	39.60	---	112.60	**139.00**
	Inst	Ea	Sm	2C	1.64	9.75	82.10	60.70	---	142.80	**179.00**
2'-8" x 7' x 1-3/8" T	Inst	Ea	Lg	2C	1.14	14.00	75.60	42.20	---	117.80	**146.00**
	Inst	Ea	Sm	2C	1.76	9.10	85.10	65.20	---	150.30	**189.00**
3' x 7' x 1-3/8" T	Inst	Ea	Lg	2C	1.14	14.00	80.30	42.20	---	122.50	**151.00**
	Inst	Ea	Sm	2C	1.76	9.10	90.40	65.20	---	155.60	**195.00**

Description	Oper	Unit	Vol	Crew Size	Man-hours per Unit	Crew Output per Day	Avg Mat'l Unit Cost	Avg Labor Unit Cost	Avg Equip Unit Cost	Avg Total Unit Cost	Avg Price Incl O&P
Birch											
2'-6" x 6'-8" x 1-3/8" T	Inst	Ea	Lg	2C	1.07	15.00	74.50	39.60	---	114.10	**141.00**
	Inst	Ea	Sm	2C	1.64	9.75	83.80	60.70	---	144.50	**181.00**
2'-8" x 6'-8" x 1-3/8" T	Inst	Ea	Lg	2C	1.14	14.00	77.00	42.20	---	119.20	**148.00**
	Inst	Ea	Sm	2C	1.76	9.10	86.70	65.20	---	151.90	**191.00**
3' x 6'-8" x 1-3/8" T	Inst	Ea	Lg	2C	1.14	14.00	81.50	42.20	---	123.70	**153.00**
	Inst	Ea	Sm	2C	1.76	9.10	91.70	65.20	---	156.90	**197.00**
2'-6" x 7' x 1-3/8" T	Inst	Ea	Lg	2C	1.07	15.00	92.60	39.60	---	132.20	**162.00**
	Inst	Ea	Sm	2C	1.64	9.75	104.00	60.70	---	164.70	**205.00**
2'-8" x 7' x 1-3/8" T	Inst	Ea	Lg	2C	1.14	14.00	96.10	42.20	---	138.30	**170.00**
	Inst	Ea	Sm	2C	1.76	9.10	108.00	65.20	---	173.20	**216.00**
3' x 7' x 1-3/8" T	Inst	Ea	Lg	2C	1.14	14.00	101.00	42.20	---	143.20	**176.00**
	Inst	Ea	Sm	2C	1.76	9.10	114.00	65.20	---	179.20	**222.00**

Solid core prehung door units

Description	Oper	Unit	Vol	Crew Size	Man-hours per Unit	Crew Output per Day	Avg Mat'l Unit Cost	Avg Labor Unit Cost	Avg Equip Unit Cost	Avg Total Unit Cost	Avg Price Incl O&P
Hardboard											
2'-6" x 6'-8" x 1-3/8" T	Inst	Ea	Lg	2C	1.14	14.00	94.90	42.20	---	137.10	**168.00**
	Inst	Ea	Sm	2C	1.76	9.10	107.00	65.20	---	172.20	**214.00**
2'-8" x 6'-8" x 1-3/8" T	Inst	Ea	Lg	2C	1.23	13.00	98.40	45.50	---	143.90	**177.00**
	Inst	Ea	Sm	2C	1.89	8.45	111.00	70.00	---	181.00	**225.00**
3' x 6'-8" x 1-3/8" T	Inst	Ea	Lg	2C	1.23	13.00	101.00	45.50	---	146.50	**180.00**
	Inst	Ea	Sm	2C	1.89	8.45	113.00	70.00	---	183.00	**228.00**
2'-6" x 7' x 1-3/8" T	Inst	Ea	Lg	2C	1.14	14.00	105.00	42.20	---	147.20	**180.00**
	Inst	Ea	Sm	2C	1.76	9.10	118.00	65.20	---	183.20	**227.00**
2'-8" x 7' x 1-3/8" T	Inst	Ea	Lg	2C	1.23	13.00	108.00	45.50	---	153.50	**188.00**
	Inst	Ea	Sm	2C	1.89	8.45	122.00	70.00	---	192.00	**238.00**
3' x 7' x 1-3/8" T	Inst	Ea	Lg	2C	1.23	13.00	108.00	45.50	---	153.50	**188.00**
	Inst	Ea	Sm	2C	1.89	8.45	122.00	70.00	---	192.00	**238.00**
Lauan											
2'-6" x 6'-8" x 1-3/8" T	Inst	Ea	Lg	2C	1.14	14.00	108.00	42.20	---	150.20	**184.00**
	Inst	Ea	Sm	2C	1.76	9.10	122.00	65.20	---	187.20	**231.00**
2'-8" x 6'-8" x 1-3/8" T	Inst	Ea	Lg	2C	1.23	13.00	112.00	45.50	---	157.50	**193.00**
	Inst	Ea	Sm	2C	1.89	8.45	126.00	70.00	---	196.00	**243.00**
3' x 6'-8" x 1-3/8" T	Inst	Ea	Lg	2C	1.23	13.00	116.00	45.50	---	161.50	**197.00**
	Inst	Ea	Sm	2C	1.89	8.45	131.00	70.00	---	201.00	**248.00**
2'-6" x 7' x 1-3/8" T	Inst	Ea	Lg	2C	1.14	14.00	119.00	42.20	---	161.20	**196.00**
	Inst	Ea	Sm	2C	1.76	9.10	134.00	65.20	---	199.20	**245.00**
2'-8" x 7' x 1-3/8" T	Inst	Ea	Lg	2C	1.23	13.00	122.00	45.50	---	167.50	**204.00**
	Inst	Ea	Sm	2C	1.89	8.45	137.00	70.00	---	207.00	**255.00**
3' x 7' x 1-3/8" T	Inst	Ea	Lg	2C	1.23	13.00	126.00	45.50	---	171.50	**209.00**
	Inst	Ea	Sm	2C	1.89	8.45	142.00	70.00	---	212.00	**261.00**
Birch											
2'-6" x 6'-8" x 1-3/8" T	Inst	Ea	Lg	2C	1.14	14.00	118.00	42.20	---	160.20	**195.00**
	Inst	Ea	Sm	2C	1.76	9.10	133.00	65.20	---	198.20	**244.00**
2'-8" x 6'-8" x 1-3/8" T	Inst	Ea	Lg	2C	1.23	13.00	121.00	45.50	---	166.50	**203.00**
	Inst	Ea	Sm	2C	1.89	8.45	136.00	70.00	---	206.00	**254.00**
3' x 6'-8" x 1-3/8" T	Inst	Ea	Lg	2C	1.23	13.00	126.00	45.50	---	171.50	**208.00**
	Inst	Ea	Sm	2C	1.89	8.45	141.00	70.00	---	211.00	**261.00**
2'-6" x 7' x 1-3/8" T	Inst	Ea	Lg	2C	1.14	14.00	129.00	42.20	---	171.20	**207.00**
	Inst	Ea	Sm	2C	1.76	9.10	145.00	65.20	---	210.20	**258.00**
2'-8" x 7' x 1-3/8" T	Inst	Ea	Lg	2C	1.23	13.00	131.00	45.50	---	176.50	**215.00**
	Inst	Ea	Sm	2C	1.89	8.45	148.00	70.00	---	218.00	**268.00**
3' x 7' x 1-3/8" T	Inst	Ea	Lg	2C	1.23	13.00	137.00	45.50	---	182.50	**221.00**
	Inst	Ea	Sm	2C	1.89	8.45	154.00	70.00	---	224.00	**275.00**

Description	Oper	Unit	Vol	Crew Size	Man- hours per Unit	Crew Output per Day	Avg Mat'l Unit Cost	Avg Labor Unit Cost	Avg Equip Unit Cost	Avg Total Unit Cost	Avg Price Incl O&P

Prehung package door units

Hollow core, flush face door units

Hardboard

Description	Oper	Unit	Vol	Crew Size	Man-hours per Unit	Crew Output per Day	Avg Mat'l Unit Cost	Avg Labor Unit Cost	Avg Equip Unit Cost	Avg Total Unit Cost	Avg Price Incl O&P
2'-6" x 6'-8" x 1-3/8" T	Inst	Ea	Lg	2C	1.33	12.00	145.00	49.20	---	194.20	**236.00**
	Inst	Ea	Sm	2C	2.05	7.80	164.00	75.90	---	239.90	**294.00**
2'-8" x 6'-8" x 1-3/8" T	Inst	Ea	Lg	2C	1.33	12.00	148.00	49.20	---	197.20	**240.00**
	Inst	Ea	Sm	2C	2.05	7.80	167.00	75.90	---	242.90	**298.00**
3' x 6'-8" x 1-3/8" T	Inst	Ea	Lg	2C	1.33	12.00	151.00	49.20	---	200.20	**243.00**
	Inst	Ea	Sm	2C	2.05	7.80	170.00	75.90	---	245.90	**302.00**

Lauan

Description	Oper	Unit	Vol	Crew Size	Man-hours per Unit	Crew Output per Day	Avg Mat'l Unit Cost	Avg Labor Unit Cost	Avg Equip Unit Cost	Avg Total Unit Cost	Avg Price Incl O&P
2'-6" x 6'-8" x 1-3/8" T	Inst	Ea	Lg	2C	1.33	12.00	161.00	49.20	---	210.20	**254.00**
	Inst	Ea	Sm	2C	2.05	7.80	181.00	75.90	---	256.90	**314.00**
2'-8" x 6'-8" x 1-3/8" T	Inst	Ea	Lg	2C	1.33	12.00	163.00	49.20	---	212.20	**256.00**
	Inst	Ea	Sm	2C	2.05	7.80	183.00	75.90	---	258.90	**317.00**
3' x 6'-8" x 1-3/8" T	Inst	Ea	Lg	2C	1.33	12.00	167.00	49.20	---	216.20	**262.00**
	Inst	Ea	Sm	2C	2.05	7.80	188.00	75.90	---	263.90	**323.00**

Birch

Description	Oper	Unit	Vol	Crew Size	Man-hours per Unit	Crew Output per Day	Avg Mat'l Unit Cost	Avg Labor Unit Cost	Avg Equip Unit Cost	Avg Total Unit Cost	Avg Price Incl O&P
2'-6" x 6'-8" x 1-3/8" T	Inst	Ea	Lg	2C	1.33	12.00	173.00	49.20	---	222.20	**268.00**
	Inst	Ea	Sm	2C	2.05	7.80	195.00	75.90	---	270.90	**331.00**
2'-8" x 6'-8" x 1-3/8" T	Inst	Ea	Lg	2C	1.33	12.00	176.00	49.20	---	225.20	**271.00**
	Inst	Ea	Sm	2C	2.05	7.80	198.00	75.90	---	273.90	**334.00**
3' x 6'-8" x 1-3/8" T	Inst	Ea	Lg	2C	1.33	12.00	180.00	49.20	---	229.20	**276.00**
	Inst	Ea	Sm	2C	2.05	7.80	203.00	75.90	---	278.90	**340.00**

Ash

Description	Oper	Unit	Vol	Crew Size	Man-hours per Unit	Crew Output per Day	Avg Mat'l Unit Cost	Avg Labor Unit Cost	Avg Equip Unit Cost	Avg Total Unit Cost	Avg Price Incl O&P
2'-6" x 6'-8" x 1-3/8" T	Inst	Ea	Lg	2C	1.33	12.00	195.00	49.20	---	244.20	**293.00**
	Inst	Ea	Sm	2C	2.05	7.80	220.00	75.90	---	295.90	**359.00**
2'-8" x 6'-8" x 1-3/8" T	Inst	Ea	Lg	2C	1.33	12.00	205.00	49.20	---	254.20	**304.00**
	Inst	Ea	Sm	2C	2.05	7.80	230.00	75.90	---	305.90	**371.00**
3' x 6'-8" x 1-3/8" T	Inst	Ea	Lg	2C	1.33	12.00	210.00	49.20	---	259.20	**310.00**
	Inst	Ea	Sm	2C	2.05	7.80	236.00	75.90	---	311.90	**377.00**

Solid core, flush face door units

Hardboard

Description	Oper	Unit	Vol	Crew Size	Man-hours per Unit	Crew Output per Day	Avg Mat'l Unit Cost	Avg Labor Unit Cost	Avg Equip Unit Cost	Avg Total Unit Cost	Avg Price Incl O&P
2'-6" x 6'-8" x 1-3/8" T	Inst	Ea	Lg	2C	1.45	11.00	196.00	53.70	---	249.70	**300.00**
	Inst	Ea	Sm	2C	2.24	7.15	220.00	82.90	---	302.90	**369.00**
2'-8" x 6'-8" x 1-3/8" T	Inst	Ea	Lg	2C	1.45	11.00	199.00	53.70	---	252.70	**304.00**
	Inst	Ea	Sm	2C	2.24	7.15	224.00	82.90	---	306.90	**374.00**
3' x 6'-8" x 1-3/8" T	Inst	Ea	Lg	2C	1.45	11.00	202.00	53.70	---	255.70	**307.00**
	Inst	Ea	Sm	2C	2.24	7.15	227.00	82.90	---	309.90	**377.00**

Lauan

Description	Oper	Unit	Vol	Crew Size	Man-hours per Unit	Crew Output per Day	Avg Mat'l Unit Cost	Avg Labor Unit Cost	Avg Equip Unit Cost	Avg Total Unit Cost	Avg Price Incl O&P
2'-6" x 6'-8" x 1-3/8" T	Inst	Ea	Lg	2C	1.45	11.00	209.00	53.70	---	262.70	**316.00**
	Inst	Ea	Sm	2C	2.24	7.15	236.00	82.90	---	318.90	**387.00**
2'-8" x 6'-8" x 1-3/8" T	Inst	Ea	Lg	2C	1.45	11.00	213.00	53.70	---	266.70	**320.00**
	Inst	Ea	Sm	2C	2.24	7.15	240.00	82.90	---	322.90	**392.00**
3' x 6'-8" x 1-3/8" T	Inst	Ea	Lg	2C	1.45	11.00	217.00	53.70	---	270.70	**325.00**
	Inst	Ea	Sm	2C	2.24	7.15	244.00	82.90	---	326.90	**397.00**

Description	Oper	Unit	Vol	Crew Size	Man-hours per Unit	Crew Output per Day	Avg Mat'l Unit Cost	Avg Labor Unit Cost	Avg Equip Unit Cost	Avg Total Unit Cost	Avg Price Incl O&P
Birch											
2'-6" x 6'-8" x 1-3/8" T	Inst	Ea	Lg	2C	1.45	11.00	219.00	53.70	---	272.70	**327.00**
	Inst	Ea	Sm	2C	2.24	7.15	247.00	82.90	---	329.90	**400.00**
2'-8" x 6'-8" x 1-3/8" T	Inst	Ea	Lg	2C	1.45	11.00	222.00	53.70	---	275.70	**330.00**
	Inst	Ea	Sm	2C	2.24	7.15	250.00	82.90	---	332.90	**403.00**
3' x 6'-8" x 1-3/8" T	Inst	Ea	Lg	2C	1.45	11.00	227.00	53.70	---	280.70	**336.00**
	Inst	Ea	Sm	2C	2.24	7.15	255.00	82.90	---	337.90	**409.00**
Ash											
2'-6" x 6'-8" x 1-3/8" T	Inst	Ea	Lg	2C	1.45	11.00	237.00	53.70	---	290.70	**348.00**
	Inst	Ea	Sm	2C	2.24	7.15	267.00	82.90	---	349.90	**423.00**
2'-8" x 6'-8" x 1-3/8" T	Inst	Ea	Lg	2C	1.45	11.00	242.00	53.70	---	295.70	**354.00**
	Inst	Ea	Sm	2C	2.24	7.15	273.00	82.90	---	355.90	**430.00**
3' x 6'-8" x 1-3/8" T	Inst	Ea	Lg	2C	1.45	11.00	251.00	53.70	---	304.70	**363.00**
	Inst	Ea	Sm	2C	2.24	7.15	282.00	82.90	---	364.90	**440.00**

Adjustments

For mitered casing, both sides, supplied but not applied

Description	Oper	Unit	Vol	Crew Size	Man-hours per Unit	Crew Output per Day	Avg Mat'l Unit Cost	Avg Labor Unit Cost	Avg Equip Unit Cost	Avg Total Unit Cost	Avg Price Incl O&P
9/16" x 1-1/2" finger joint,	Inst	Ea	Lg	---	---	---	25.00	---	---	25.00	**28.80**
ADD	Inst	Ea	Sm	---	---	---	33.80	---	---	33.80	**38.80**
9/16" x 2-1/4" solid pine,	Inst	Ea	Lg	---	---	---	42.00	---	---	42.00	**48.30**
ADD	Inst	Ea	Sm	---	---	---	47.30	---	---	47.30	**54.30**
9/16" x 2-1/2" solid pine,	Inst	Ea	Lg	---	---	---	39.60	---	---	39.60	**45.50**
ADD	Inst	Ea	Sm	---	---	---	44.60	---	---	44.60	**51.20**
For solid fir jamb, 4-9/16", ADD											
	Inst	Ea	Lg	---	---	---	38.60	---	---	38.60	**44.40**
	Inst	Ea	Sm	---	---	---	43.50	---	---	43.50	**50.00**

Screen doors

Aluminum frame with fiberglass wire screen, and plain grille, includes hardware, hinges, closer and latch

Description	Oper	Unit	Vol	Crew Size	Man-hours per Unit	Crew Output per Day	Avg Mat'l Unit Cost	Avg Labor Unit Cost	Avg Equip Unit Cost	Avg Total Unit Cost	Avg Price Incl O&P
3' x 7'	Inst	Ea	Lg	2C	1.00	16.00	72.00	37.00	---	109.00	**135.00**
	Inst	Ea	Sm	2C	1.54	10.40	81.00	57.00	---	138.00	**173.00**

Wood screen doors, pine, aluminum wire screen, 1-1/8" T

Description	Oper	Unit	Vol	Crew Size	Man-hours per Unit	Crew Output per Day	Avg Mat'l Unit Cost	Avg Labor Unit Cost	Avg Equip Unit Cost	Avg Total Unit Cost	Avg Price Incl O&P
2'-6" x 6'-9"	Inst	Ea	Lg	2C	1.00	16.00	120.00	37.00	---	157.00	**190.00**
	Inst	Ea	Sm	2C	1.54	10.40	135.00	57.00	---	192.00	**235.00**
2'-8" x 6'-9"	Inst	Ea	Lg	2C	1.00	16.00	120.00	37.00	---	157.00	**190.00**
	Inst	Ea	Sm	2C	1.54	10.40	135.00	57.00	---	192.00	**235.00**
3' x 6'-9"	Inst	Ea	Lg	2C	1.00	16.00	132.00	37.00	---	169.00	**204.00**
	Inst	Ea	Sm	2C	1.54	10.40	149.00	57.00	---	206.00	**251.00**
Half screen											
2'-6" x 6'-9"	Inst	Ea	Lg	2C	1.00	16.00	150.00	37.00	---	187.00	**224.00**
	Inst	Ea	Sm	2C	1.54	10.40	169.00	57.00	---	226.00	**274.00**
2'-8" x 6'-9"	Inst	Ea	Lg	2C	1.00	16.00	150.00	37.00	---	187.00	**224.00**
	Inst	Ea	Sm	2C	1.54	10.40	169.00	57.00	---	226.00	**274.00**
3' x 6'-9"	Inst	Ea	Lg	2C	1.00	16.00	180.00	37.00	---	217.00	**259.00**
	Inst	Ea	Sm	2C	1.54	10.40	203.00	57.00	---	260.00	**313.00**

Description	Oper	Unit	Vol	Crew Size	Man-hours per Unit	Crew Output per Day	Avg Mat'l Unit Cost	Avg Labor Unit Cost	Avg Equip Unit Cost	Avg Total Unit Cost	Avg Price Incl O&P

Steel doors

24-gauge steel faces, fully primed, reversible, prices are for a standard 2-3/8" diameter bore

Decorative doors

Dual glazed, tempered clear

Description	Oper	Unit	Vol	Crew Size	Man-hours per Unit	Crew Output per Day	Avg Mat'l Unit Cost	Avg Labor Unit Cost	Avg Equip Unit Cost	Avg Total Unit Cost	Avg Price Incl O&P
2'-6", 2'-8", 3' x 6'-8" x 1-3/4" T	Inst	Ea	Lg	2C	1.45	11.00	284.00	53.70	---	337.70	**402.00**
	Inst	Ea	Sm	2C	2.24	7.15	320.00	82.90	---	402.90	**484.00**

Dual glazed, tempered clear, two bevel

Description	Oper	Unit	Vol	Crew Size	Man-hours per Unit	Crew Output per Day	Avg Mat'l Unit Cost	Avg Labor Unit Cost	Avg Equip Unit Cost	Avg Total Unit Cost	Avg Price Incl O&P
2'-6", 2'-8", 3' x 6'-8" x 1-3/4" T	Inst	Ea	Lg	2C	1.45	11.00	334.00	53.70	---	387.70	**459.00**
	Inst	Ea	Sm	2C	2.24	7.15	375.00	82.90	---	457.90	**548.00**

Embossed raised panel doors

6 raised panels

Description	Oper	Unit	Vol	Crew Size	Man-hours per Unit	Crew Output per Day	Avg Mat'l Unit Cost	Avg Labor Unit Cost	Avg Equip Unit Cost	Avg Total Unit Cost	Avg Price Incl O&P
2'-6", 2'-8", 3' x 6'-8" x 1-3/4" T	Inst	Ea	Lg	2C	1.45	11.00	160.00	53.70	---	213.70	**259.00**
	Inst	Ea	Sm	2C	2.24	7.15	180.00	82.90	---	262.90	**323.00**
2'-8" x 8' x 1-3/4" T	Inst	Ea	Lg	2C	1.60	10.00	270.00	59.20	---	329.20	**393.00**
	Inst	Ea	Sm	2C	2.46	6.50	304.00	91.10	---	395.10	**477.00**
3' x 8' x 1-3/4" T	Inst	Ea	Lg	2C	1.60	10.00	295.00	59.20	---	354.20	**422.00**
	Inst	Ea	Sm	2C	2.46	6.50	332.00	91.10	---	423.10	**509.00**

6 raised panels, dual glazed, tempered clear

Description	Oper	Unit	Vol	Crew Size	Man-hours per Unit	Crew Output per Day	Avg Mat'l Unit Cost	Avg Labor Unit Cost	Avg Equip Unit Cost	Avg Total Unit Cost	Avg Price Incl O&P
2'-6", 2'-8", 3' x 6'-8" x 1-3/4" T	Inst	Ea	Lg	2C	1.45	11.00	250.00	53.70	---	303.70	**362.00**
	Inst	Ea	Sm	2C	2.24	7.15	281.00	82.90	---	363.90	**439.00**

8 raised panels

Description	Oper	Unit	Vol	Crew Size	Man-hours per Unit	Crew Output per Day	Avg Mat'l Unit Cost	Avg Labor Unit Cost	Avg Equip Unit Cost	Avg Total Unit Cost	Avg Price Incl O&P
2'-8", 3' x 6'-8" x 1-3/4" T	Inst	Ea	Lg	2C	1.45	11.00	163.00	53.70	---	216.70	**263.00**
	Inst	Ea	Sm	2C	2.24	7.15	184.00	82.90	---	266.90	**327.00**

Embossed raised panels and dual glazed tempered clear glass

2 raised panels with 1 lite

Description	Oper	Unit	Vol	Crew Size	Man-hours per Unit	Crew Output per Day	Avg Mat'l Unit Cost	Avg Labor Unit Cost	Avg Equip Unit Cost	Avg Total Unit Cost	Avg Price Incl O&P
2'-6", 2'-8", 3' x 6'-8" x 1-3/4" T	Inst	Ea	Lg	2C	1.45	11.00	269.00	53.70	---	322.70	**385.00**
	Inst	Ea	Sm	2C	2.24	7.15	303.00	82.90	---	385.90	**465.00**

2 raised panels with 9 lites

Description	Oper	Unit	Vol	Crew Size	Man-hours per Unit	Crew Output per Day	Avg Mat'l Unit Cost	Avg Labor Unit Cost	Avg Equip Unit Cost	Avg Total Unit Cost	Avg Price Incl O&P
2'-6", 2'-8", 3' x 6'-8" x 1-3/4" T	Inst	Ea	Lg	2C	1.45	11.00	274.00	53.70	---	327.70	**390.00**
	Inst	Ea	Sm	2C	2.24	7.15	308.00	82.90	---	390.90	**471.00**

2 raised panels with 12 diamond lites

Description	Oper	Unit	Vol	Crew Size	Man-hours per Unit	Crew Output per Day	Avg Mat'l Unit Cost	Avg Labor Unit Cost	Avg Equip Unit Cost	Avg Total Unit Cost	Avg Price Incl O&P
2'-6", 2'-8", 3' x 6'-8" x 1-3/4" T	Inst	Ea	Lg	2C	1.45	11.00	284.00	53.70	---	337.70	**402.00**
	Inst	Ea	Sm	2C	2.24	7.15	320.00	82.90	---	402.90	**484.00**

4 diamond raised panels with 1 lite

Description	Oper	Unit	Vol	Crew Size	Man-hours per Unit	Crew Output per Day	Avg Mat'l Unit Cost	Avg Labor Unit Cost	Avg Equip Unit Cost	Avg Total Unit Cost	Avg Price Incl O&P
2'-6", 2'-8", 3' x 6'-8" x 1-3/4" T	Inst	Ea	Lg	2C	1.45	11.00	269.00	53.70	---	322.70	**385.00**
	Inst	Ea	Sm	2C	2.24	7.15	303.00	82.90	---	385.90	**465.00**

4 diamond raised panels with 9 lites

Description	Oper	Unit	Vol	Crew Size	Man-hours per Unit	Crew Output per Day	Avg Mat'l Unit Cost	Avg Labor Unit Cost	Avg Equip Unit Cost	Avg Total Unit Cost	Avg Price Incl O&P
2'-6", 2'-8", 3' x 6'-8" x 1-3/4" T	Inst	Ea	Lg	2C	1.45	11.00	274.00	53.70	---	327.70	**390.00**
	Inst	Ea	Sm	2C	2.24	7.15	308.00	82.90	---	390.90	**471.00**

4 diamond raised panels with 12 diamond lites

Description	Oper	Unit	Vol	Crew Size	Man-hours per Unit	Crew Output per Day	Avg Mat'l Unit Cost	Avg Labor Unit Cost	Avg Equip Unit Cost	Avg Total Unit Cost	Avg Price Incl O&P
2'-6", 2'-8", 3' x 6'-8" x 1-3/4" T	Inst	Ea	Lg	2C	1.45	11.00	284.00	53.70	---	337.70	**402.00**
	Inst	Ea	Sm	2C	2.24	7.15	320.00	82.90	---	402.90	**484.00**

Description	Oper	Unit	Vol	Crew Size	Man-hours per Unit	Crew Output per Day	Avg Mat'l Unit Cost	Avg Labor Unit Cost	Avg Equip Unit Cost	Avg Total Unit Cost	Avg Price Incl O&P
Flush doors											
2' to 3' x 6'-8" x 1-3/4" T	Inst	Ea	Lg	2C	1.45	11.00	154.00	53.70	---	207.70	**252.00**
	Inst	Ea	Sm	2C	2.24	7.15	173.00	82.90	---	255.90	**315.00**
2' to 3' x 8' x 1-3/4" T	Inst	Ea	Lg	2C	1.33	12.00	278.00	49.20	---	327.20	**389.00**
	Inst	Ea	Sm	2C	2.05	7.80	313.00	75.90	---	388.90	**466.00**
Dual glazed, tempered clear											
2'-6", 2'-8", 3' x 6'-8" x 1-3/4" T	Inst	Ea	Lg	2C	1.45	11.00	235.00	53.70	---	288.70	**346.00**
	Inst	Ea	Sm	2C	2.24	7.15	265.00	82.90	---	347.90	**420.00**
1-1/2 hour fire label											
2' to 3' x 6'-8" x 1-3/4" T	Inst	Ea	Lg	2C	1.45	11.00	168.00	53.70	---	221.70	**268.00**
	Inst	Ea	Sm	2C	2.24	7.15	189.00	82.90	---	271.90	**333.00**
2' to 3' x 7' x 1-3/4" T	Inst	Ea	Lg	2C	1.33	12.00	204.00	49.20	---	253.20	**304.00**
	Inst	Ea	Sm	2C	2.05	7.80	230.00	75.90	---	305.90	**370.00**
French doors, flush face											
1 lite											
2'-6", 2'-8", 3' x 6'-8" x 1-3/4" T	Inst	Ea	Lg	2C	1.45	11.00	306.00	53.70	---	359.70	**427.00**
	Inst	Ea	Sm	2C	2.24	7.15	344.00	82.90	---	426.90	**512.00**
2'-6", 2'-8", 3' x 8' x 1-3/4" T	Inst	Ea	Lg	2C	1.60	10.00	504.00	59.20	---	563.20	**663.00**
	Inst	Ea	Sm	2C	2.46	6.50	567.00	91.10	---	658.10	**780.00**
10 lite											
2'-6", 2'-8", 3' x 6'-8" x 1-3/4" T	Inst	Ea	Lg	2C	1.45	11.00	324.00	53.70	---	377.70	**448.00**
	Inst	Ea	Sm	2C	2.24	7.15	365.00	82.90	---	447.90	**535.00**
2'-6", 2'-8", 3' x 8' x 1-3/4" T	Inst	Ea	Lg	2C	1.60	10.00	534.00	59.20	---	593.20	**697.00**
	Inst	Ea	Sm	2C	2.46	6.50	601.00	91.10	---	692.10	**818.00**
15 lite											
2'-6", 2'-8", 3' x 6'-8" x 1-3/4" T	Inst	Ea	Lg	2C	1.45	11.00	330.00	53.70	---	383.70	**455.00**
	Inst	Ea	Sm	2C	2.24	7.15	371.00	82.90	---	453.90	**543.00**
2'-6", 2'-8", 3' x 8' x 1-3/4" T	Inst	Ea	Lg	2C	1.60	10.00	546.00	59.20	---	605.20	**711.00**
	Inst	Ea	Sm	2C	2.46	6.50	614.00	91.10	---	705.10	**834.00**
French sidelites											
Embossed raised panel											
3 lite											
1', 1'-2" x 6'-8"	Inst	Ea	Lg	2C	1.00	16.00	168.00	37.00	---	205.00	**245.00**
	Inst	Ea	Sm	2C	1.54	10.40	189.00	57.00	---	246.00	**297.00**
Flush face											
1', 1'-2" x 6'-8"	Inst	Ea	Lg	2C	1.00	16.00	82.80	37.00	---	119.80	**147.00**
	Inst	Ea	Sm	2C	1.54	10.40	93.20	57.00	---	150.20	**187.00**
Dual glazed, tempered clear											
1', 1'-2" x 6'-8"	Inst	Ea	Lg	2C	1.00	16.00	174.00	37.00	---	211.00	**252.00**
	Inst	Ea	Sm	2C	1.54	10.40	196.00	57.00	---	253.00	**305.00**
Prehung package door units											
Flush steel door											
2'-6" x 6'-8" x 1-3/8" T	Inst	Ea	Lg	2C	1.33	12.00	286.00	49.20	---	335.20	**397.00**
	Inst	Ea	Sm	2C	2.05	7.80	321.00	75.90	---	396.90	**476.00**

Drywall (Sheetrock or wallboard)

The types of drywall are Standard, Fire Resistant, Water Resistant, and Fire and Water Resistant.

1. **Dimensions.** $1/4$", $3/8$" x 6' to 12'; $1/2$", $5/8$" x 6' to 14'.

2. **Installation**

   a. One ply. Sheets are nailed to studs and joists using $1 1/4$" or $1 3/8$" x .101 type 500 nails. Nails are usually spaced 8" oc on walls and 7" oc on ceilings. The joints between sheets are filled, taped and sanded. Tape and compound are available in kits containing 250 LF of tape and 18 lbs of compound or 75 LF of tape and 5 lbs of compound.

   b. Two plies. Initial ply is nailed to studs or joists. Second ply is laminated to first with taping compounds as the adhesive. Only the joints in the second ply are filled, taped and finished.

3. **Estimating Technique.** Determine area, deduct openings and add approximately 10% for waste.

Ceiling application

Stud — Gypsum board — Tapered edge — Joint cement — Feather

Ceiling joists — Nails 7" oc — Omit nails here — Floating angles — Gypsum wallboard

Wall application

Tapered edge — Gypsum board

Ceiling joists — Omit nails here — Nails 7" oc — Studs — Nails 8" oc — Omit nails here — Gypsum wallboard (horizontal application) — Gypsum wallboard (vertical application)

Description	Oper	Unit	Vol	Crew Size	Man-hours per Unit	Crew Output per Day	Avg Mat'l Unit Cost	Avg Labor Unit Cost	Avg Equip Unit Cost	Avg Total Unit Cost	Avg Price Incl O&P

Drywall

Demo Drywall or Sheetrock, walls and ceilings

Description	Oper	Unit	Vol	Crew Size	Man-hours per Unit	Crew Output per Day	Avg Mat'l Unit Cost	Avg Labor Unit Cost	Avg Equip Unit Cost	Avg Total Unit Cost	Avg Price Incl O&P
	Demo	SF	Lg	LH	.007	3680	---	.21	---	.21	.29
	Demo	SF	Sm	LB	.009	1766	---	.27	---	.27	.38

Install Drywall or Sheetrock (gypsum plasterboard)

Includes tape, finish, nails or screws, and 5% waste
Applied to wood or metal frame

Walls only, 4' x 8', 10', 12'

Description	Oper	Unit	Vol	Crew Size	Man-hours per Unit	Crew Output per Day	Avg Mat'l Unit Cost	Avg Labor Unit Cost	Avg Equip Unit Cost	Avg Total Unit Cost	Avg Price Incl O&P
3/8" T, standard	Inst	SF	Lg	DL	.015	1600.0	.52	.54	---	1.06	1.36
	Inst	SF	Sm	DK	.021	768.0	.56	.76	---	1.32	1.70
1/2" T, standard	Inst	SF	Lg	DL	.015	1600.0	.52	.54	---	1.06	1.36
	Inst	SF	Sm	DK	.021	768.0	.56	.76	---	1.32	1.70
5/8" T, standard	Inst	SF	Lg	DL	.017	1440.0	.56	.61	---	1.17	1.50
	Inst	SF	Sm	DK	.023	691.2	.60	.83	---	1.43	1.85
Laminated 3/8" T sheets, std.	Inst	SF	Lg	DL	.029	840.0	.96	1.05	---	2.01	2.57
	Inst	SF	Sm	DK	.040	403.2	1.06	1.44	---	2.50	3.24

Ceilings only, 4' x 8', 10', 12'

Description	Oper	Unit	Vol	Crew Size	Man-hours per Unit	Crew Output per Day	Avg Mat'l Unit Cost	Avg Labor Unit Cost	Avg Equip Unit Cost	Avg Total Unit Cost	Avg Price Incl O&P
3/8" T, standard	Inst	SF	Lg	DL	.019	1280.0	.52	.69	---	1.21	1.56
	Inst	SF	Sm	DK	.026	614.4	.56	.94	---	1.50	1.96
1/2" T, standard	Inst	SF	Lg	DL	.019	1280.0	.52	.69	---	1.21	1.56
	Inst	SF	Sm	DK	.026	614.4	.56	.94	---	1.50	1.96
5/8" T, standard	Inst	SF	Lg	DL	.021	1152.0	.56	.76	---	1.32	1.70
	Inst	SF	Sm	DK	.029	553.0	.60	1.05	---	1.65	2.15
Laminated 3/8" T sheets, std.	Inst	SF	Lg	DL	.036	672.0	.96	1.30	---	2.26	2.92
	Inst	SF	Sm	DK	.050	322.6	1.06	1.80	---	2.86	3.74

Average for ceilings and walls

Description	Oper	Unit	Vol	Crew Size	Man-hours per Unit	Crew Output per Day	Avg Mat'l Unit Cost	Avg Labor Unit Cost	Avg Equip Unit Cost	Avg Total Unit Cost	Avg Price Incl O&P
3/8" T, standard	Inst	SF	Lg	DL	.016	1536.0	.52	.58	---	1.10	1.41
	Inst	SF	Sm	DK	.022	737.3	.56	.79	---	1.35	1.75
1/2" T, standard	Inst	SF	Lg	DL	.016	1536.0	.52	.58	---	1.10	1.41
	Inst	SF	Sm	DK	.022	737.3	.56	.79	---	1.35	1.75
5/8" T, standard	Inst	SF	Lg	DL	.017	1382.4	.56	.61	---	1.17	1.50
	Inst	SF	Sm	DK	.024	663.6	.60	.87	---	1.47	1.90
Laminated 3/8" T sheets, std.	Inst	SF	Lg	DL	.030	806.4	.96	1.08	---	2.04	2.62
	Inst	SF	Sm	DK	.041	387.1	1.06	1.48	---	2.54	3.29

Tape and bed joints on repaired sheetrock

Description	Oper	Unit	Vol	Crew Size	Man-hours per Unit	Crew Output per Day	Avg Mat'l Unit Cost	Avg Labor Unit Cost	Avg Equip Unit Cost	Avg Total Unit Cost	Avg Price Incl O&P
Walls	Inst	SF	Lg	DU	.022	728.0	.18	.79	---	.97	1.32
	Inst	SF	Sm	DT	.023	349.4	.19	.83	---	1.02	1.38
Ceilings	Inst	SF	Lg	DU	.025	632.0	.18	.90	---	1.08	1.47
	Inst	SF	Sm	DT	.026	303.4	.19	.94	---	1.13	1.53

Thin coat plaster

Description	Oper	Unit	Vol	Crew Size	Man-hours per Unit	Crew Output per Day	Avg Mat'l Unit Cost	Avg Labor Unit Cost	Avg Equip Unit Cost	Avg Total Unit Cost	Avg Price Incl O&P
	Inst	SF	Lg	DU	.014	1125	.35	.50	---	.85	1.11
	Inst	SF	Sm	DT	.015	540.0	.39	.54	---	.93	1.20

Material and labor adjustments

Description	Oper	Unit	Vol	Crew Size	Man-hours per Unit	Crew Output per Day	Avg Mat'l Unit Cost	Avg Labor Unit Cost	Avg Equip Unit Cost	Avg Total Unit Cost	Avg Price Incl O&P
No tape and finish, DEDUCT	Inst	SF	Lg	2C	-.017	-1420	-.18	-.61	---	-.79	---
	Inst	SF	Sm	CA	-.023	-681.6	-.19	-.83	---	-1.02	---

Description	Oper	Unit	Vol	Crew Size	Man-hours per Unit	Crew Output per Day	Avg Mat'l Unit Cost	Avg Labor Unit Cost	Avg Equip Unit Cost	Avg Total Unit Cost	Avg Price Incl O&P
For ceilings 9' H											
Ceiling only, ADD	Inst	SF	Lg	DL	.012	2000	---	.43	---	.43	.61
	Inst	SF	Sm	DK	.017	960	---	.61	---	.61	.86
Walls & ceilings (average), ADD											
	Inst	SF	Lg	DL	.005	5000	---	.18	---	.18	.25
	Inst	SF	Sm	DK	.007	2400	---	.25	---	.25	.35
Material adjustments											
For fire resistant (1/2" and 5/8" T) ADD											
	Inst	SF	Lg	DL	---	---	.06	---	---	.06	.07
	Inst	SF	Sm	DK	---	---	.06	---	---	.06	.07
For water resistant (1/2" and 5/8" T) ADD											
	Inst	SF	Lg	DL	---	---	.12	---	---	.12	.14
	Inst	SF	Sm	DK	---	---	.12	---	---	.12	.14
For fire and water resistant (5/8" T only) ADD											
	Inst	SF	Lg	DL	---	---	.18	---	---	.18	.21
	Inst	SF	Sm	DK	---	---	.18	---	---	.18	.21

Electrical

General work

Residential service, single phase system. Prices given on a cost per each basis for a unit price system which includes a weathercap, service entrance cable, meter socket, entrance disconnect switch, ground rod with clamp, ground cable, EMT, and panelboard

Weathercap

Description	Oper	Unit	Vol	Crew Size	Man-hours per Unit	Crew Output per Day	Avg Mat'l Unit Cost	Avg Labor Unit Cost	Avg Equip Unit Cost	Avg Total Unit Cost	Avg Price Incl O&P
100 AMP service	Inst	Ea	Lg	EA	1.00	8.00	6.65	40.20	---	46.85	**65.90**
	Inst	Ea	Sm	EA	1.43	5.60	7.36	57.50	---	64.86	**91.80**
200 AMP service	Inst	Ea	Lg	EA	1.60	5.00	19.60	64.30	---	83.90	**116.00**
	Inst	Ea	Sm	EA	2.29	3.50	21.70	92.00	---	113.70	**158.00**

Service entrance cable (typical allowance is 20 LF)

Description	Oper	Unit	Vol	Crew Size	Man-hours per Unit	Crew Output per Day	Avg Mat'l Unit Cost	Avg Labor Unit Cost	Avg Equip Unit Cost	Avg Total Unit Cost	Avg Price Incl O&P
100 AMP service	Inst	LF	Lg	EA	.123	65.00	.15	4.94	---	5.09	**7.34**
	Inst	LF	Sm	EA	.176	45.50	.17	7.07	---	7.24	**10.50**
200 AMP service	Inst	LF	Lg	EA	.178	45.00	.34	7.15	---	7.49	**10.80**
	Inst	LF	Sm	EA	.254	31.50	.37	10.20	---	10.57	**15.20**

Meter socket

Description	Oper	Unit	Vol	Crew Size	Man-hours per Unit	Crew Output per Day	Avg Mat'l Unit Cost	Avg Labor Unit Cost	Avg Equip Unit Cost	Avg Total Unit Cost	Avg Price Incl O&P
100 AMP service	Inst	Ea	Lg	EA	4.00	2.00	36.80	161.00	---	197.80	**275.00**
	Inst	Ea	Sm	EA	5.71	1.40	40.70	229.00	---	269.70	**380.00**
200 AMP service	Inst	Ea	Lg	EA	6.40	1.25	57.40	257.00	---	314.40	**439.00**
	Inst	Ea	Sm	EA	9.09	0.88	63.60	365.00	---	428.60	**603.00**

Entrance disconnect switch

Description	Oper	Unit	Vol	Crew Size	Man-hours per Unit	Crew Output per Day	Avg Mat'l Unit Cost	Avg Labor Unit Cost	Avg Equip Unit Cost	Avg Total Unit Cost	Avg Price Incl O&P
100 AMP service	Inst	Ea	Lg	EA	6.40	1.25	182.00	257.00	---	439.00	**582.00**
	Inst	Ea	Sm	EA	9.09	0.88	202.00	365.00	---	567.00	**761.00**
200 AMP service	Inst	Ea	Lg	EA	9.41	0.85	364.00	378.00	---	742.00	**967.00**
	Inst	Ea	Sm	EA	13.3	0.60	403.00	535.00	---	938.00	**1240.00**

Description	Oper	Unit	Vol	Crew Size	Man-hours per Unit	Crew Output per Day	Avg Mat'l Unit Cost	Avg Labor Unit Cost	Avg Equip Unit Cost	Avg Total Unit Cost	Avg Price Incl O&P
Ground rod, with clamp											
100 AMP service	Inst	Ea	Lg	EA	2.67	3.00	19.60	107.00	---	126.60	**178.00**
	Inst	Ea	Sm	EA	3.81	2.10	21.70	153.00	---	174.70	**247.00**
200 AMP service	Inst	Ea	Lg	EA	2.67	3.00	37.80	107.00	---	144.80	**199.00**
	Inst	Ea	Sm	EA	3.81	2.10	41.90	153.00	---	194.90	**270.00**
Ground cable (typical allowance is 10 LF)											
100 AMP service	Inst	LF	Lg	EA	.080	100.0	.18	3.22	---	3.40	**4.87**
	Inst	LF	Sm	EA	.114	70.00	.20	4.58	---	4.78	**6.87**
200 AMP service	Inst	LF	Lg	EA	.100	80.00	.29	4.02	---	4.31	**6.16**
	Inst	LF	Sm	EA	.143	56.00	.33	5.75	---	6.08	**8.71**
3/4" EMT (typical allowance is 10 LF)											
200 AMP service	Inst	LF	Lg	EA	.107	75.00	.73	4.30	---	5.03	**7.08**
	Inst	LF	Sm	EA	.152	52.50	.81	6.11	---	6.92	**9.79**
Panelboard											
100 AMP service - 12-circuit	Inst	Ea	Lg	EA	1.60	5.00	161.00	64.30	---	225.30	**278.00**
	Inst	Ea	Sm	EA	2.29	3.50	178.00	92.00	---	270.00	**338.00**
200 AMP service - 24-circuit	Inst	Ea	Lg	EA	2.29	3.50	385.00	92.00	---	477.00	**576.00**
	Inst	Ea	Sm	EA	3.27	2.45	426.00	131.00	---	557.00	**681.00**
Adjustments for other than normal working situations											
Cut and patch, ADD	Inst	%	Lg	EA	---	---	---	---	---	---	**20.0**
	Inst	%	Sm	EA	---	---	---	---	---	---	**50.0**
Dust protection, ADD	Inst	%	Lg	EA	---	---	---	---	---	---	**10.0**
	Inst	%	Sm	EA	---	---	---	---	---	---	**40.0**
Protect existing work, ADD	Inst	%	Lg	EA	---	---	---	---	---	---	**20.0**
	Inst	%	Sm	EA	---	---	---	---	---	---	**50.0**

Wiring per outlet or switch; wall or ceiling

Romex, non-metallic sheathed cable, 600 volt, copper with ground wire

Description	Oper	Unit	Vol	Crew Size	Man-hours per Unit	Crew Output per Day	Avg Mat'l Unit Cost	Avg Labor Unit Cost	Avg Equip Unit Cost	Avg Total Unit Cost	Avg Price Incl O&P
	Inst	Ea	Lg	EA	.500	16.00	9.45	20.10	---	29.55	**40.00**
	Inst	Ea	Sm	EA	.714	11.20	10.50	28.70	---	39.20	**53.60**
BX, flexible armored cable, 600 volt, copper											
	Inst	Ea	Lg	EA	.667	12.00	15.10	26.80	---	41.90	**56.20**
	Inst	Ea	Sm	EA	.952	8.40	16.70	38.30	---	55.00	**74.60**
EMT with wire, electric metallic thinwall, 1/2"											
	Inst	Ea	Lg	EA	1.33	6.00	20.70	53.50	---	74.20	**101.00**
	Inst	Ea	Sm	EA	1.90	4.20	22.90	76.40	---	99.30	**137.00**
Rigid with wire, 1/2"											
	Inst	Ea	Lg	EA	2.00	4.00	35.00	80.40	---	115.40	**157.00**
	Inst	Ea	Sm	EA	2.86	2.80	38.80	115.00	---	153.80	**211.00**
Wiring, connection, and installation in closed wall structure, ADD											
	Inst	Ea	Lg	EA	1.00	8.00	---	40.20	---	40.20	**58.30**
	Inst	Ea	Sm	EA	1.43	5.60	---	57.50	---	57.50	**83.30**

Lighting. See Lighting fixtures, page 278

Description	Oper	Unit	Vol	Crew Size	Man-hours per Unit	Crew Output per Day	Avg Mat'l Unit Cost	Avg Labor Unit Cost	Avg Equip Unit Cost	Avg Total Unit Cost	Avg Price Incl O&P

Special systems
Burglary detection systems

Description	Oper	Unit	Vol	Crew Size	Man-hours per Unit	Crew Output per Day	Avg Mat'l Unit Cost	Avg Labor Unit Cost	Avg Equip Unit Cost	Avg Total Unit Cost	Avg Price Incl O&P
Alarm bell	Inst	Ea	Lg	EA	2.00	4.00	84.00	80.40	---	164.40	**213.00**
	Inst	Ea	Sm	EA	2.86	2.80	93.00	115.00	---	208.00	**274.00**
Burglar alarm, battery operated											
Mechanical trigger	Inst	Ea	Lg	EA	2.00	4.00	301.00	80.40	---	381.40	**463.00**
	Inst	Ea	Sm	EA	2.86	2.80	333.00	115.00	---	448.00	**550.00**
Electrical trigger	Inst	Ea	Lg	EA	2.00	4.00	364.00	80.40	---	444.40	**535.00**
	Inst	Ea	Sm	EA	2.86	2.80	403.00	115.00	---	518.00	**630.00**
Adjustments, ADD											
Outside key control	Inst	Ea	Lg	---	---	---	84.00	---	---	84.00	**96.60**
	Inst	Ea	Sm	---	---	---	93.00	---	---	93.00	**107.00**
Remote signaling circuitry	Inst	Ea	Lg	---	---	---	136.00	---	---	136.00	**156.00**
	Inst	Ea	Sm	---	---	---	150.00	---	---	150.00	**173.00**
Card reader											
Standard	Inst	Ea	Lg	EA	3.20	2.50	1020.00	129.00	---	1149.00	**1350.00**
	Inst	Ea	Sm	EA	4.57	1.75	1120.00	184.00	---	1304.00	**1560.00**
Multi-code	Inst	Ea	Lg	EA	3.20	2.50	1310.00	129.00	---	1439.00	**1690.00**
	Inst	Ea	Sm	EA	4.57	1.75	1450.00	184.00	---	1634.00	**1930.00**
Detectors											
Motion											
Infrared photoelectric	Inst	Ea	Lg	EA	4.00	2.00	210.00	161.00	---	371.00	**475.00**
	Inst	Ea	Sm	EA	5.71	1.40	233.00	229.00	---	462.00	**600.00**
Passive infrared	Inst	Ea	Lg	EA	4.00	2.00	280.00	161.00	---	441.00	**555.00**
	Inst	Ea	Sm	EA	5.71	1.40	310.00	229.00	---	539.00	**689.00**
Ultrasonic, 12 volt	Inst	Ea	Lg	EA	4.00	2.00	252.00	161.00	---	413.00	**523.00**
	Inst	Ea	Sm	EA	5.71	1.40	279.00	229.00	---	508.00	**654.00**
Microwave											
10' to 200'	Inst	Ea	Lg	EA	4.00	2.00	728.00	161.00	---	889.00	**1070.00**
	Inst	Ea	Sm	EA	5.71	1.40	806.00	229.00	---	1035.00	**1260.00**
10' to 350'	Inst	Ea	Lg	EA	4.00	2.00	2100.00	161.00	---	2261.00	**2650.00**
	Inst	Ea	Sm	EA	5.71	1.40	2330.00	229.00	---	2559.00	**3010.00**
Door switches											
Hinge switch	Inst	Ea	Lg	EA	1.60	5.00	64.40	64.30	---	128.70	**167.00**
	Inst	Ea	Sm	EA	2.29	3.50	71.30	92.00	---	163.30	**215.00**
Magnetic switch	Inst	Ea	Lg	EA	1.60	5.00	77.00	64.30	---	141.30	**182.00**
	Inst	Ea	Sm	EA	2.29	3.50	85.30	92.00	---	177.30	**232.00**
Exit control locks											
Horn alarm	Inst	Ea	Lg	EA	2.00	4.00	378.00	80.40	---	458.40	**551.00**
	Inst	Ea	Sm	EA	2.86	2.80	419.00	115.00	---	534.00	**648.00**
Flashing light alarm	Inst	Ea	Lg	EA	2.00	4.00	427.00	80.40	---	507.40	**608.00**
	Inst	Ea	Sm	EA	2.86	2.80	473.00	115.00	---	588.00	**710.00**
Glass break alarm switch	Inst	Ea	Lg	EA	1.00	8.00	51.80	40.20	---	92.00	**118.00**
	Inst	Ea	Sm	EA	1.43	5.60	57.40	57.50	---	114.90	**149.00**
Indicating panels											
1 channel	Inst	Ea	Lg	EA	3.20	2.50	399.00	129.00	---	528.00	**645.00**
	Inst	Ea	Sm	EA	4.57	1.75	442.00	184.00	---	626.00	**774.00**
10 channel	Inst	Ea	Lg	EA	5.33	1.50	1380.00	214.00	---	1594.00	**1900.00**
	Inst	Ea	Sm	EA	7.62	1.05	1530.00	306.00	---	1836.00	**2200.00**
20 channel	Inst	Ea	Lg	EA	8.00	1.00	2660.00	322.00	---	2982.00	**3530.00**
	Inst	Ea	Sm	EA	11.4	0.70	2950.00	458.00	---	3408.00	**4050.00**
40 channel	Inst	Ea	Lg	EA	16.0	0.50	4900.00	643.00	---	5543.00	**6570.00**
	Inst	Ea	Sm	EA	22.9	0.35	5430.00	920.00	---	6350.00	**7570.00**

Description	Oper	Unit	Vol	Crew Size	Man-hours per Unit	Crew Output per Day	Avg Mat'l Unit Cost	Avg Labor Unit Cost	Avg Equip Unit Cost	Avg Total Unit Cost	Avg Price Incl O&P
Police connect panel											
	Inst	Ea	Lg	EA	2.00	4.00	266.00	80.40	---	346.40	**422.00**
	Inst	Ea	Sm	EA	2.86	2.80	295.00	115.00	---	410.00	**505.00**
Siren											
	Inst	Ea	Lg	EA	2.00	4.00	160.00	80.40	---	240.40	**300.00**
	Inst	Ea	Sm	EA	2.86	2.80	177.00	115.00	---	292.00	**370.00**
Switchmats											
30" x 5'	Inst	Ea	Lg	EA	1.60	5.00	92.40	64.30	---	156.70	**200.00**
	Inst	Ea	Sm	EA	2.29	3.50	102.00	92.00	---	194.00	**251.00**
30" x 25'	Inst	Ea	Lg	EA	2.00	4.00	221.00	80.40	---	301.40	**371.00**
	Inst	Ea	Sm	EA	2.86	2.80	245.00	115.00	---	360.00	**448.00**
Telephone dialer											
	Inst	Ea	Lg	EA	1.60	5.00	420.00	64.30	---	484.30	**576.00**
	Inst	Ea	Sm	EA	2.29	3.50	465.00	92.00	---	557.00	**668.00**

Doorbell systems
Includes transformer, button, bell

Description	Oper	Unit	Vol	Crew Size	Man-hours per Unit	Crew Output per Day	Avg Mat'l Unit Cost	Avg Labor Unit Cost	Avg Equip Unit Cost	Avg Total Unit Cost	Avg Price Incl O&P
Door chimes, 2 notes											
	Inst	Ea	Lg	EA	.800	10.00	84.00	32.20	---	116.20	**143.00**
	Inst	Ea	Sm	EA	1.14	7.00	93.00	45.80	---	138.80	**173.00**
Tube-type chimes	Inst	Ea	Lg	EA	1.00	8.00	210.00	40.20	---	250.20	**300.00**
	Inst	Ea	Sm	EA	1.43	5.60	233.00	57.50	---	290.50	**351.00**
Transformer and button only											
	Inst	Ea	Lg	EA	.667	12.00	49.00	26.80	---	75.80	**95.20**
	Inst	Ea	Sm	EA	.952	8.40	54.30	38.30	---	92.60	**118.00**
Push button only											
	Inst	Ea	Lg	EA	.500	16.00	21.00	20.10	---	41.10	**53.30**
	Inst	Ea	Sm	EA	.714	11.20	23.30	28.70	---	52.00	**68.40**

Fire alarm systems

Description	Oper	Unit	Vol	Crew Size	Man-hours per Unit	Crew Output per Day	Avg Mat'l Unit Cost	Avg Labor Unit Cost	Avg Equip Unit Cost	Avg Total Unit Cost	Avg Price Incl O&P
Battery and rack											
	Inst	Ea	Lg	EA	2.67	3.00	840.00	107.00	---	947.00	**1120.00**
	Inst	Ea	Sm	EA	3.81	2.10	930.00	153.00	---	1083.00	**1290.00**
Automatic charger	Inst	Ea	Lg	EA	1.33	6.00	539.00	53.50	---	592.50	**697.00**
	Inst	Ea	Sm	EA	1.90	4.20	597.00	76.40	---	673.40	**797.00**
Detector											
Fixed temperature	Inst	Ea	Lg	EA	1.33	6.00	33.60	53.50	---	87.10	**116.00**
	Inst	Ea	Sm	EA	1.90	4.20	37.20	76.40	---	113.60	**154.00**
Rate of rise	Inst	Ea	Lg	EA	1.33	6.00	42.00	53.50	---	95.50	**126.00**
	Inst	Ea	Sm	EA	1.90	4.20	46.50	76.40	---	122.90	**164.00**
Door holder											
Electro-magnetic	Inst	Ea	Lg	EA	2.00	4.00	93.80	80.40	---	174.20	**224.00**
	Inst	Ea	Sm	EA	2.86	2.80	104.00	115.00	---	219.00	**286.00**
Combination holder/closer	Inst	Ea	Lg	EA	2.67	3.00	525.00	107.00	---	632.00	**759.00**
	Inst	Ea	Sm	EA	3.81	2.10	581.00	153.00	---	734.00	**890.00**
Fire drill switch	Inst	Ea	Lg	EA	1.33	6.00	105.00	53.50	---	158.50	**198.00**
	Inst	Ea	Sm	EA	1.90	4.20	116.00	76.40	---	192.40	**244.00**
Glass break alarm switch	Inst	Ea	Lg	EA	1.00	8.00	60.20	40.20	---	100.40	**128.00**
	Inst	Ea	Sm	EA	1.43	5.60	66.70	57.50	---	124.20	**160.00**
Signal bell	Inst	Ea	Lg	EA	1.33	6.00	60.20	53.50	---	113.70	**147.00**
	Inst	Ea	Sm	EA	1.90	4.20	66.70	76.40	---	143.10	**187.00**
Smoke detector											
Ceiling type	Inst	Ea	Lg	EA	1.33	6.00	78.40	53.50	---	131.90	**168.00**
	Inst	Ea	Sm	EA	1.90	4.20	86.80	76.40	---	163.20	**211.00**
Duct type	Inst	Ea	Lg	EA	2.67	3.00	308.00	107.00	---	415.00	**510.00**
	Inst	Ea	Sm	EA	3.81	2.10	341.00	153.00	---	494.00	**614.00**

Description	Oper	Unit	Vol	Crew Size	Man-hours per Unit	Crew Output per Day	Avg Mat'l Unit Cost	Avg Labor Unit Cost	Avg Equip Unit Cost	Avg Total Unit Cost	Avg Price Incl O&P

Intercom systems

Master stations, with digital AM/FM receiver, up to 20 remote stations, & telephone interface
Solid state with antenna, with 200' wire, 4 speakers

Description	Oper	Unit	Vol	Crew Size	Man-hours per Unit	Crew Output per Day	Avg Mat'l Unit Cost	Avg Labor Unit Cost	Avg Equip Unit Cost	Avg Total Unit Cost	Avg Price Incl O&P
	Inst	Set	Lg	EA	4.00	2.00	1680.00	161.00	---	1841.00	**2170.00**
	Inst	Set	Sm	EA	5.71	1.40	1860.00	229.00	---	2089.00	**2470.00**

Solid state with antenna, with 1000' wire, 8 speakers

| | Inst | Set | Lg | EA | 8.00 | 1.00 | 2240.00 | 322.00 | --- | 2562.00 | **3040.00** |
| | Inst | Set | Sm | EA | 11.4 | 0.70 | 2480.00 | 458.00 | --- | 2938.00 | **3520.00** |

Room to door intercoms
  Master station, door station, with transformer, wire

	Inst	Set	Lg	EA	2.00	4.00	420.00	80.40	---	500.40	**600.00**
	Inst	Set	Sm	EA	2.86	2.80	465.00	115.00	---	580.00	**701.00**
Second door station, ADD	Inst	Ea	Lg	EA	1.00	8.00	56.00	40.20	---	96.20	**123.00**
	Inst	Ea	Sm	EA	1.43	5.60	62.00	57.50	---	119.50	**155.00**

  Installation, wiring, and transformer, wire ADD

| | Inst | LS | Lg | EA | 1.60 | 5.00 | --- | 64.30 | --- | 64.30 | **93.30** |
| | Inst | LS | Sm | EA | 2.29 | 3.50 | --- | 92.00 | --- | 92.00 | **133.00** |

Telephone, phone-jack wiring

Pre-wiring, per outlet or jack

| | Inst | Ea | Lg | EA | .667 | 12.00 | 28.00 | 26.80 | --- | 54.80 | **71.10** |
| | Inst | Ea | Sm | EA | .952 | 8.40 | 31.00 | 38.30 | --- | 69.30 | **91.10** |

Wiring, connection, and installation in closed wall structure, ADD

| | Inst | Ea | Lg | EA | 1.00 | 8.00 | --- | 40.20 | --- | 40.20 | **58.30** |
| | Inst | Ea | Sm | EA | 1.43 | 5.60 | --- | 57.50 | --- | 57.50 | **83.30** |

Television antenna

Television antenna outlet, with 300 OHM

| | Inst | Ea | Lg | EA | .667 | 12.00 | 16.80 | 26.80 | --- | 43.60 | **58.20** |
| | Inst | Ea | Sm | EA | .952 | 8.40 | 18.60 | 38.30 | --- | 56.90 | **76.90** |

Wiring, connection, and installation in closed wall structure, ADD

| | Inst | Ea | Lg | EA | 1.00 | 8.00 | --- | 40.20 | --- | 40.20 | **58.30** |
| | Inst | Ea | Sm | EA | 1.43 | 5.60 | --- | 57.50 | --- | 57.50 | **83.30** |

Thermostat wiring

For heating units located on the first floor
Thermostat on first floor

| | Inst | Ea | Lg | EA | 1.00 | 8.00 | 28.00 | 40.20 | --- | 68.20 | **90.50** |
| | Inst | Ea | Sm | EA | 1.43 | 5.60 | 31.00 | 57.50 | --- | 88.50 | **119.00** |

  Wiring, connection, and installation in closed wall structure, ADD

| | Inst | Ea | Lg | EA | 1.00 | 8.00 | --- | 40.20 | --- | 40.20 | **58.30** |
| | Inst | Ea | Sm | EA | 1.43 | 5.60 | --- | 57.50 | --- | 57.50 | **83.30** |

Thermostat on second floor

| | Inst | Ea | Lg | EA | 1.60 | 5.00 | 35.00 | 64.30 | --- | 99.30 | **134.00** |
| | Inst | Ea | Sm | EA | 2.29 | 3.50 | 38.80 | 92.00 | --- | 130.80 | **178.00** |

  Wiring, connection, and installation in closed wall structure, ADD

| | Inst | Ea | Lg | EA | 1.33 | 6.00 | --- | 53.50 | --- | 53.50 | **77.50** |
| | Inst | Ea | Sm | EA | 1.90 | 4.20 | --- | 76.40 | --- | 76.40 | **111.00** |

Description	Oper	Unit	Vol	Crew Size	Man-hours per Unit	Crew Output per Day	Avg Mat'l Unit Cost	Avg Labor Unit Cost	Avg Equip Unit Cost	Avg Total Unit Cost	Avg Price Incl O&P

Entrances

Single & double door entrances

| | Demo | Ea | Lg | LB | .640 | 25.00 | --- | 19.20 | --- | 19.20 | **26.90** |
| | Demo | Ea | Sm | LB | .889 | 18.00 | --- | 26.70 | --- | 26.70 | **37.30** |

Colonial design

White pine includes frames, pediments, and pilasters

Plain carved archway

Single door units

| 3'-0" W x 6'-8" H | Inst | Ea | Lg | 2C | 2.00 | 8.00 | 329.00 | 74.00 | --- | 403.00 | **433.00** |
| | Inst | Ea | Sm | 2C | 2.67 | 6.00 | 374.00 | 98.80 | --- | 472.80 | **512.00** |

Double door units

Two - 2'-6" W x 6'-8" H	Inst	Ea	Lg	2C	2.67	6.00	353.00	98.80	---	451.80	**491.00**
	Inst	Ea	Sm	2C	3.56	4.50	401.00	132.00	---	533.00	**586.00**
Two - 2'-8" W x 6'-8" H	Inst	Ea	Lg	2C	2.67	6.00	383.00	98.80	---	481.80	**521.00**
	Inst	Ea	Sm	2C	3.56	4.50	435.00	132.00	---	567.00	**620.00**
Two - 3'-0" W x 6'-8" H	Inst	Ea	Lg	2C	2.67	6.00	501.00	98.80	---	599.80	**639.00**
	Inst	Ea	Sm	2C	3.56	4.50	569.00	132.00	---	701.00	**753.00**

Decorative carved archway

Single door units

| 3'-0" W x 6'-8" H | Inst | Ea | Lg | 2C | 2.00 | 8.00 | 413.00 | 74.00 | --- | 487.00 | **516.00** |
| | Inst | Ea | Sm | 2C | 2.67 | 6.00 | 469.00 | 98.80 | --- | 567.80 | **607.00** |

Double door units

Two - 2'-6" W x 6'-8" H	Inst	Ea	Lg	2C	2.67	6.00	353.00	98.80	---	451.80	**491.00**
	Inst	Ea	Sm	2C	3.56	4.50	401.00	132.00	---	533.00	**586.00**
Two - 2'-8" W x 6'-8" H	Inst	Ea	Lg	2C	2.67	6.00	375.00	98.80	---	473.80	**513.00**
	Inst	Ea	Sm	2C	3.56	4.50	426.00	132.00	---	558.00	**611.00**
Two - 3 -0" W x 6'-8" H	Inst	Ea	Lg	2C	2.67	6.00	391.00	98.80	---	489.80	**529.00**
	Inst	Ea	Sm	2C	3.56	4.50	444.00	132.00	---	576.00	**628.00**

Excavation

Digging out or trenching

| | Demo | CY | Lg | LB | .034 | 475.0 | --- | 1.02 | --- | 1.02 | **1.43** |
| | Demo | CY | Sm | LB | .056 | 285.0 | --- | 1.68 | --- | 1.68 | **2.35** |

Pits, medium earth, piled

With front end loader, track mounted, 1-1/2 CY capacity; 55 CY per hour

| | Demo | CY | Lg | VB | .036 | 440.0 | --- | 1.30 | .98 | 2.28 | **2.80** |
| | Demo | CY | Sm | VB | .061 | 264.0 | --- | 2.20 | 1.64 | 3.84 | **4.73** |

By hand

To 4'-0" D	Demo	CY	Lg	LB	1.07	15.00	---	32.10	---	32.10	**44.90**
	Demo	CY	Sm	LB	1.78	9.00	---	53.40	---	53.40	**74.80**
4'-0" to 6'-0" D	Demo	CY	Lg	LB	1.60	10.00	---	48.00	---	48.00	**67.20**
	Demo	CY	Sm	LB	2.67	6.00	---	80.10	---	80.10	**112.00**
6'-0" to 8'-0" D	Demo	CY	Lg	LB	2.67	6.00	---	80.10	---	80.10	**112.00**
	Demo	CY	Sm	LB	4.00	4.00	---	120.00	---	120.00	**168.00**

Description	Oper	Unit	Vol	Crew Size	Man-hours per Unit	Crew Output per Day	Avg Mat'l Unit Cost	Avg Labor Unit Cost	Avg Equip Unit Cost	Avg Total Unit Cost	Avg Price Incl O&P

Continuous footing or trench, medium earth, piled
With tractor backhoe, 3/8 CY capacity (48 HP); 15 CY per hour

| | Demo | CY | Lg | VB | .133 | 120.0 | --- | 4.81 | 3.61 | 8.42 | **10.30** |
| | Demo | CY | Sm | VB | .222 | 72.00 | --- | 8.02 | 6.02 | 14.04 | **17.30** |

By hand, to 4'-0" D

| | Demo | CY | Lg | LB | 1.07 | 15.00 | --- | 32.10 | --- | 32.10 | **44.90** |
| | Demo | CY | Sm | LB | 1.78 | 9.00 | --- | 53.40 | --- | 53.40 | **74.80** |

Backfilling, by hand, medium soil
Without compaction

| | Demo | CY | Lg | LB | .571 | 28.00 | --- | 17.10 | --- | 17.10 | **24.00** |
| | Demo | CY | Sm | LB | .941 | 17.00 | --- | 28.20 | --- | 28.20 | **39.50** |

With hand compaction

6" layers

| | Demo | CY | Lg | LB | .941 | 17.00 | --- | 28.20 | --- | 28.20 | **39.50** |
| | Demo | CY | Sm | LB | 1.60 | 10.00 | --- | 48.00 | --- | 48.00 | **67.20** |

12" layers

| | Demo | CY | Lg | LB | .727 | 22.00 | --- | 21.80 | --- | 21.80 | **30.50** |
| | Demo | CY | Sm | LB | 1.23 | 13.00 | --- | 36.90 | --- | 36.90 | **51.70** |

With vibrating plate compaction

6" layers

| | Demo | CY | Lg | AB | .800 | 20.00 | --- | 29.50 | 2.17 | 31.67 | **43.40** |
| | Demo | CY | Sm | AB | 1.33 | 12.00 | --- | 49.00 | 3.61 | 52.61 | **72.20** |

12" layers

| | Demo | CY | Lg | AB | .667 | 24.00 | --- | 24.60 | 1.81 | 26.41 | **36.20** |
| | Demo | CY | Sm | AB | 1.14 | 14.00 | --- | 42.00 | 3.10 | 45.10 | **61.90** |

Description	Oper	Unit	Vol	Crew Size	Man-hours per Unit	Crew Output per Day	Avg Mat'l Unit Cost	Avg Labor Unit Cost	Avg Equip Unit Cost	Avg Total Unit Cost	Avg Price Incl O&P

Fences

Basketweave

Redwood, preassembled, 8' L panels, includes 4" x 4" line posts, horizontal or vertical weave

Description	Oper	Unit	Vol	Crew Size	Man-hours per Unit	Crew Output per Day	Avg Mat'l Unit Cost	Avg Labor Unit Cost	Avg Equip Unit Cost	Avg Total Unit Cost	Avg Price Incl O&P
5' H	Inst	LF	Lg	CS	.100	240.0	12.50	3.47	---	15.97	**19.20**
	Inst	LF	Sm	CS	.133	180.0	14.00	4.61	---	18.61	**22.60**
6' H	Inst	LF	Lg	CS	.100	240.0	18.80	3.47	---	22.27	**26.40**
	Inst	LF	Sm	CS	.133	180.0	21.00	4.61	---	25.61	**30.60**

Adjustments

Corner or end posts, 8' H

Description	Oper	Unit	Vol	Crew Size	Man-hours per Unit	Crew Output per Day	Avg Mat'l Unit Cost	Avg Labor Unit Cost	Avg Equip Unit Cost	Avg Total Unit Cost	Avg Price Incl O&P
	Inst	Ea	Lg	CA	.615	13.00	25.00	22.80	---	47.80	**60.60**
	Inst	Ea	Sm	CA	.821	9.75	28.00	30.40	---	58.40	**74.80**

3-1/2' W x 5' H gate, with hardware

Description	Oper	Unit	Vol	Crew Size	Man-hours per Unit	Crew Output per Day	Avg Mat'l Unit Cost	Avg Labor Unit Cost	Avg Equip Unit Cost	Avg Total Unit Cost	Avg Price Incl O&P
	Inst	Ea	Lg	CA	.800	10.00	106.00	29.60	---	135.60	**164.00**
	Inst	Ea	Sm	CA	1.07	7.50	119.00	39.60	---	158.60	**192.00**

Board, per LF complete fence system

6' H boards nailed to wood frame, on 1 side only; 8' L redwood 4" x 4" (milled) posts, set 2' D in concrete filled holes @ 6' oc; frame members 2" x 4" (milled) as 2 rails between posts per 6' L fence section; costs are per LF of fence

Douglas fir frame members with redwood posts

Milled boards, "dog-eared" one end
Cedar

Description	Oper	Unit	Vol	Crew Size	Man-hours per Unit	Crew Output per Day	Avg Mat'l Unit Cost	Avg Labor Unit Cost	Avg Equip Unit Cost	Avg Total Unit Cost	Avg Price Incl O&P
1" x 6" - 6' H	Inst	LF	Lg	CS	.400	60.00	41.50	13.90	---	55.40	**67.20**
	Inst	LF	Sm	CS	.533	45.00	46.50	18.50	---	65.00	**79.40**
1" x 8" - 6' H	Inst	LF	Lg	CS	.343	70.00	42.30	11.90	---	54.20	**65.30**
	Inst	LF	Sm	CS	.457	52.50	47.40	15.90	---	63.30	**76.70**
1" x 10" - 6' H	Inst	LF	Lg	CS	.300	80.00	41.50	10.40	---	51.90	**62.20**
	Inst	LF	Sm	CS	.400	60.00	46.40	13.90	---	60.30	**72.80**

Douglas fir

Description	Oper	Unit	Vol	Crew Size	Man-hours per Unit	Crew Output per Day	Avg Mat'l Unit Cost	Avg Labor Unit Cost	Avg Equip Unit Cost	Avg Total Unit Cost	Avg Price Incl O&P
1" x 6" - 6' H	Inst	LF	Lg	CS	.400	60.00	40.00	13.90	---	53.90	**65.40**
	Inst	LF	Sm	CS	.533	45.00	44.80	18.50	---	63.30	**77.40**
1" x 8" - 6' H	Inst	LF	Lg	CS	.343	70.00	40.30	11.90	---	52.20	**63.00**
	Inst	LF	Sm	CS	.457	52.50	45.20	15.90	---	61.10	**74.10**
1" x 10" - 6' H	Inst	LF	Lg	CS	.300	80.00	40.00	10.40	---	50.40	**60.60**
	Inst	LF	Sm	CS	.400	60.00	44.80	13.90	---	58.70	**70.80**

Redwood

Description	Oper	Unit	Vol	Crew Size	Man-hours per Unit	Crew Output per Day	Avg Mat'l Unit Cost	Avg Labor Unit Cost	Avg Equip Unit Cost	Avg Total Unit Cost	Avg Price Incl O&P
1" x 6" - 6' H	Inst	LF	Lg	CS	.400	60.00	41.50	13.90	---	55.40	**67.20**
	Inst	LF	Sm	CS	.533	45.00	46.50	18.50	---	65.00	**79.40**
1" x 8" - 6' H	Inst	LF	Lg	CS	.343	70.00	42.30	11.90	---	54.20	**65.30**
	Inst	LF	Sm	CS	.457	52.50	47.40	15.90	---	63.30	**76.70**
1" x 10" - 6' H	Inst	LF	Lg	CS	.300	80.00	43.80	10.40	---	54.20	**65.00**
	Inst	LF	Sm	CS	.400	60.00	49.10	13.90	---	63.00	**75.90**

Description	Oper	Unit	Vol	Crew Size	Man-hours per Unit	Crew Output per Day	Avg Mat'l Unit Cost	Avg Labor Unit Cost	Avg Equip Unit Cost	Avg Total Unit Cost	Avg Price Incl O&P

Rough boards, both ends squared
Cedar
Description	Oper	Unit	Vol	Crew Size	Man-hours per Unit	Crew Output per Day	Avg Mat'l Unit Cost	Avg Labor Unit Cost	Avg Equip Unit Cost	Avg Total Unit Cost	Avg Price Incl O&P
1" x 6" - 6' H	Inst	LF	Lg	CS	.369	65.00	40.70	12.80	---	53.50	**64.70**
	Inst	LF	Sm	CS	.492	48.75	45.60	17.10	---	62.70	**76.30**
1" x 8" - 6' H	Inst	LF	Lg	CS	.320	75.00	41.50	11.10	---	52.60	**63.20**
	Inst	LF	Sm	CS	.427	56.25	46.40	14.80	---	61.20	**74.10**
1" x 10" - 6' H	Inst	LF	Lg	CS	.282	85.00	40.60	9.78	---	50.38	**60.40**
	Inst	LF	Sm	CS	.376	63.75	45.50	13.00	---	58.50	**70.50**

Douglas fir
Description	Oper	Unit	Vol	Crew Size	Man-hours per Unit	Crew Output per Day	Avg Mat'l Unit Cost	Avg Labor Unit Cost	Avg Equip Unit Cost	Avg Total Unit Cost	Avg Price Incl O&P
1" x 6" - 6' H	Inst	LF	Lg	CS	.369	65.00	39.40	12.80	---	52.20	**63.20**
	Inst	LF	Sm	CS	.492	48.75	44.10	17.10	---	61.20	**74.60**
1" x 8" - 6' H	Inst	LF	Lg	CS	.320	75.00	39.80	11.10	---	50.90	**61.30**
	Inst	LF	Sm	CS	.427	56.25	44.50	14.80	---	59.30	**71.90**
1" x 10" - 6' H	Inst	LF	Lg	CS	.282	85.00	39.50	9.78	---	49.28	**59.20**
	Inst	LF	Sm	CS	.376	63.75	44.30	13.00	---	57.30	**69.20**

Redwood
Description	Oper	Unit	Vol	Crew Size	Man-hours per Unit	Crew Output per Day	Avg Mat'l Unit Cost	Avg Labor Unit Cost	Avg Equip Unit Cost	Avg Total Unit Cost	Avg Price Incl O&P
1" x 6" - 6' H	Inst	LF	Lg	CS	.369	65.00	40.70	12.80	---	53.50	**64.70**
	Inst	LF	Sm	CS	.492	48.75	45.60	17.10	---	62.70	**76.30**
1" x 8" - 6' H	Inst	LF	Lg	CS	.320	75.00	41.50	11.10	---	52.60	**63.20**
	Inst	LF	Sm	CS	.427	56.25	46.40	14.80	---	61.20	**74.10**
1" x 10" - 6' H	Inst	LF	Lg	CS	.282	85.00	43.00	9.78	---	52.78	**63.10**
	Inst	LF	Sm	CS	.376	63.75	48.10	13.00	---	61.10	**73.60**

Redwood frame members with redwood posts

Milled boards, "dog-eared" one end
Cedar
Description	Oper	Unit	Vol	Crew Size	Man-hours per Unit	Crew Output per Day	Avg Mat'l Unit Cost	Avg Labor Unit Cost	Avg Equip Unit Cost	Avg Total Unit Cost	Avg Price Incl O&P
1" x 6" - 6' H	Inst	LF	Lg	CS	.400	60.00	41.60	13.90	---	55.50	**67.20**
	Inst	LF	Sm	CS	.533	45.00	46.60	18.50	---	65.10	**79.40**
1" x 8" - 6' H	Inst	LF	Lg	CS	.343	70.00	42.40	11.90	---	54.30	**65.40**
	Inst	LF	Sm	CS	.457	52.50	47.40	15.90	---	63.30	**76.70**
1" x 10" - 6' H	Inst	LF	Lg	CS	.300	80.00	41.50	10.40	---	51.90	**62.30**
	Inst	LF	Sm	CS	.400	60.00	46.50	13.90	---	60.40	**72.90**

Douglas fir
Description	Oper	Unit	Vol	Crew Size	Man-hours per Unit	Crew Output per Day	Avg Mat'l Unit Cost	Avg Labor Unit Cost	Avg Equip Unit Cost	Avg Total Unit Cost	Avg Price Incl O&P
1" x 6" - 6' H	Inst	LF	Lg	CS	.400	60.00	40.00	13.90	---	53.90	**65.50**
	Inst	LF	Sm	CS	.533	45.00	44.80	18.50	---	63.30	**77.40**
1" x 8" - 6' H	Inst	LF	Lg	CS	.343	70.00	40.40	11.90	---	52.30	**63.10**
	Inst	LF	Sm	CS	.457	52.50	45.20	15.90	---	61.10	**74.20**
1" x 10" - 6' H	Inst	LF	Lg	CS	.300	80.00	40.10	10.40	---	50.50	**60.60**
	Inst	LF	Sm	CS	.400	60.00	44.90	13.90	---	58.80	**71.00**

Redwood
Description	Oper	Unit	Vol	Crew Size	Man-hours per Unit	Crew Output per Day	Avg Mat'l Unit Cost	Avg Labor Unit Cost	Avg Equip Unit Cost	Avg Total Unit Cost	Avg Price Incl O&P
1" x 6" - 6' H	Inst	LF	Lg	CS	.400	60.00	41.60	13.90	---	55.50	**67.20**
	Inst	LF	Sm	CS	.533	45.00	46.60	18.50	---	65.10	**79.40**
1" x 8" - 6' H	Inst	LF	Lg	CS	.343	70.00	42.40	11.90	---	54.30	**65.40**
	Inst	LF	Sm	CS	.457	52.50	47.40	15.90	---	63.30	**76.70**
1" x 10" - 6' H	Inst	LF	Lg	CS	.300	80.00	43.90	10.40	---	54.30	**65.00**
	Inst	LF	Sm	CS	.400	60.00	49.10	13.90	---	63.00	**75.90**

Description	Oper	Unit	Vol	Crew Size	Man-hours per Unit	Crew Output per Day	Avg Mat'l Unit Cost	Avg Labor Unit Cost	Avg Equip Unit Cost	Avg Total Unit Cost	Avg Price Incl O&P
Rough boards, both ends squared											
Cedar											
1" x 6" - 6' H	Inst	LF	Lg	CS	.369	65.00	40.70	12.80	---	53.50	**64.70**
	Inst	LF	Sm	CS	.492	48.75	45.60	17.10	---	62.70	**76.30**
1" x 8" - 6' H	Inst	LF	Lg	CS	.320	75.00	41.50	11.10	---	52.60	**63.30**
	Inst	LF	Sm	CS	.427	56.25	46.50	14.80	---	61.30	**74.20**
1" x 10" - 6' H	Inst	LF	Lg	CS	.282	85.00	40.60	9.78	---	50.38	**60.40**
	Inst	LF	Sm	CS	.376	63.75	45.50	13.00	---	58.50	**70.60**
Douglas fir											
1" x 6" - 6' H	Inst	LF	Lg	CS	.369	65.00	39.40	12.80	---	52.20	**63.20**
	Inst	LF	Sm	CS	.492	48.75	44.10	17.10	---	61.20	**74.60**
1" x 8" - 6' H	Inst	LF	Lg	CS	.320	75.00	39.80	11.10	---	50.90	**61.30**
	Inst	LF	Sm	CS	.427	56.25	44.60	14.80	---	59.40	**72.00**
1" x 10" - 6' H	Inst	LF	Lg	CS	.282	85.00	39.60	9.78	---	49.38	**59.20**
	Inst	LF	Sm	CS	.376	63.75	44.30	13.00	---	57.30	**69.30**
Redwood											
1" x 6" - 6' H	Inst	LF	Lg	CS	.369	65.00	40.70	12.80	---	53.50	**64.70**
	Inst	LF	Sm	CS	.492	48.75	45.60	17.10	---	62.70	**76.30**
1" x 8" - 6' H	Inst	LF	Lg	CS	.320	75.00	41.50	11.10	---	52.60	**63.30**
	Inst	LF	Sm	CS	.427	56.25	46.50	14.80	---	61.30	**74.20**
1" x 10" - 6' H	Inst	LF	Lg	CS	.282	85.00	43.00	9.78	---	52.78	**63.10**
	Inst	LF	Sm	CS	.376	63.75	48.20	13.00	---	61.20	**73.60**

Chain link

9 gauge galvanized steel, includes top rail (1-5/8" o.d.), line posts (2" o.d.) @ 10' oc and sleeves

Description	Oper	Unit	Vol	Crew Size	Man-hours per Unit	Crew Output per Day	Avg Mat'l Unit Cost	Avg Labor Unit Cost	Avg Equip Unit Cost	Avg Total Unit Cost	Avg Price Incl O&P
36" H	Inst	LF	Lg	HB	.073	220.0	4.60	2.50	---	7.10	**8.83**
	Inst	LF	Sm	HB	.097	165.0	5.15	3.32	---	8.47	**10.60**
42" H	Inst	LF	Lg	HB	.076	210.0	4.93	2.60	---	7.53	**9.36**
	Inst	LF	Sm	HB	.102	157.5	5.52	3.49	---	9.01	**11.30**
48" H	Inst	LF	Lg	HB	.080	200.0	5.16	2.74	---	7.90	**9.82**
	Inst	LF	Sm	HB	.107	150.0	5.78	3.66	---	9.44	**11.80**
60" H	Inst	LF	Lg	HB	.089	180.0	5.95	3.04	---	8.99	**11.20**
	Inst	LF	Sm	HB	.119	135.0	6.66	4.07	---	10.73	**13.40**
72" H	Inst	LF	Lg	HB	.100	160.0	6.75	3.42	---	10.17	**12.60**
	Inst	LF	Sm	HB	.133	120.0	7.56	4.55	---	12.11	**15.20**

Description	Oper	Unit	Vol	Crew Size	Man-hours per Unit	Crew Output per Day	Avg Mat'l Unit Cost	Avg Labor Unit Cost	Avg Equip Unit Cost	Avg Total Unit Cost	Avg Price Incl O&P
Adjustments											
11-1/2"-gauge galvanized steel fabric											
DEDUCT	Inst	%	Lg	---	---		-27.0	---	---	---	---
	Inst	%	Sm	---	---		-27.0	---	---	---	---
12-gauge galvanized steel fabric											
DEDUCT	Inst	%	Lg	---	---		-29.0	---	---	---	---
	Inst	%	Sm	---	---		-29.0	---	---	---	---
9-gauge green vinyl-coated fabric											
DEDUCT	Inst	%	Lg	---	---		-4.0	---	---	---	---
	Inst	%	Sm	---	---		-4.0	---	---	---	---
11-gauge green vinyl-coated fabric											
DEDUCT	Inst	%	Lg	---	---		-3.8	---	---	---	---
	Inst	%	Sm	---	---		-3.8	---	---	---	---
Filler strips, ADD											
Aluminum, baked-on enamel finish											
Diagonal, 1-7/8" W											
48" H	Inst	LF	Lg	LB	.160	100.0	4.23	4.80	---	9.03	**11.60**
	Inst	LF	Sm	LB	.213	75.00	4.73	6.39	---	11.12	**14.40**
60" H	Inst	LF	Lg	LB	.160	100.0	5.13	4.80	---	9.93	**12.60**
	Inst	LF	Sm	LB	.213	75.00	5.74	6.39	---	12.13	**15.60**
72" H	Inst	LF	Lg	LB	.160	100.0	6.00	4.80	---	10.80	**13.60**
	Inst	LF	Sm	LB	.213	75.00	6.72	6.39	---	13.11	**16.70**
Vertical, 1-1/4" W											
48" H	Inst	LF	Lg	LB	.160	100.0	4.23	4.80	---	9.03	**11.60**
	Inst	LF	Sm	LB	.213	75.00	4.73	6.39	---	11.12	**14.40**
60" H	Inst	LF	Lg	LB	.160	100.0	4.98	4.80	---	9.78	**12.50**
	Inst	LF	Sm	LB	.213	75.00	5.57	6.39	---	11.96	**15.40**
72" H	Inst	LF	Lg	LB	.160	100.0	5.85	4.80	---	10.65	**13.50**
	Inst	LF	Sm	LB	.213	75.00	6.55	6.39	---	12.94	**16.50**
Wood, redwood stain											
Vertical, 1-1/4" W											
48" H	Inst	LF	Lg	LB	.160	100.0	4.23	4.80	---	9.03	**11.60**
	Inst	LF	Sm	LB	.213	75.00	4.73	6.39	---	11.12	**14.40**
60" H	Inst	LF	Lg	LB	.160	100.0	5.13	4.80	---	9.93	**12.60**
	Inst	LF	Sm	LB	.213	75.00	5.74	6.39	---	12.13	**15.60**
72" H	Inst	LF	Lg	LB	.160	100.0	6.00	4.80	---	10.80	**13.60**
	Inst	LF	Sm	LB	.213	75.00	6.72	6.39	---	13.11	**16.70**

Description	Oper	Unit	Vol	Crew Size	Man-hours per Unit	Crew Output per Day	Avg Mat'l Unit Cost	Avg Labor Unit Cost	Avg Equip Unit Cost	Avg Total Unit Cost	Avg Price Incl O&P
Corner posts (2-1/2" o.d.), installed, heavyweight											
36" H	Inst	Ea	Lg	HA	.286	28.00	24.40	11.00	---	35.40	**43.60**
	Inst	Ea	Sm	HA	.381	21.00	27.30	14.60	---	41.90	**52.20**
42" H	Inst	Ea	Lg	HA	.296	27.00	27.60	11.40	---	39.00	**47.90**
	Inst	Ea	Sm	HA	.395	20.25	30.90	15.20	---	46.10	**57.10**
48" H	Inst	Ea	Lg	HA	.320	25.00	29.30	12.30	---	41.60	**51.10**
	Inst	Ea	Sm	HA	.427	18.75	32.80	16.40	---	49.20	**60.90**
60" H	Inst	Ea	Lg	HA	.364	22.00	34.90	14.00	---	48.90	**60.00**
	Inst	Ea	Sm	HA	.485	16.50	39.10	18.60	---	57.70	**71.40**
72" H	Inst	Ea	Lg	HA	.400	20.00	40.60	15.40	---	56.00	**68.50**
	Inst	Ea	Sm	HA	.533	15.00	45.50	20.50	---	66.00	**81.40**
End or gate posts (2-1/2" o.d.), installed, heavyweight											
36" H	Inst	Ea	Lg	HA	.286	28.00	18.70	11.00	---	29.70	**37.10**
	Inst	Ea	Sm	HA	.381	21.00	20.90	14.60	---	35.50	**44.80**
42" H	Inst	Ea	Lg	HA	.296	27.00	20.30	11.40	---	31.70	**39.50**
	Inst	Ea	Sm	HA	.395	20.25	22.80	15.20	---	38.00	**47.70**
48" H	Inst	Ea	Lg	HA	.320	25.00	22.80	12.30	---	35.10	**43.60**
	Inst	Ea	Sm	HA	.427	18.75	25.50	16.40	---	41.90	**52.60**
60" H	Inst	Ea	Lg	HA	.364	22.00	26.80	14.00	---	40.80	**50.70**
	Inst	Ea	Sm	HA	.485	16.50	30.00	18.60	---	48.60	**61.00**
72" H	Inst	Ea	Lg	HA	.400	20.00	30.90	15.40	---	46.30	**57.30**
	Inst	Ea	Sm	HA	.533	15.00	34.60	20.50	---	55.10	**68.80**
Gates, square corner frame, 9 gauge wire, installed											
3' W walkway gates											
36" H	Inst	Ea	Lg	HA	.615	13.00	68.30	23.60	---	91.90	**112.00**
	Inst	Ea	Sm	HA	.821	9.75	76.40	31.50	---	107.90	**133.00**
42" H	Inst	Ea	Lg	HA	.615	13.00	71.50	23.60	---	95.10	**116.00**
	Inst	Ea	Sm	HA	.821	9.75	80.10	31.50	---	111.60	**137.00**
48" H	Inst	Ea	Lg	HA	.667	12.00	73.10	25.60	---	98.70	**120.00**
	Inst	Ea	Sm	HA	.889	9.00	81.90	34.10	---	116.00	**143.00**
60" H	Inst	Ea	Lg	HA	.667	12.00	87.80	25.60	---	113.40	**137.00**
	Inst	Ea	Sm	HA	.889	9.00	98.30	34.10	---	132.40	**161.00**
72" H	Inst	Ea	Lg	HA	.727	11.00	102.00	27.90	---	129.90	**157.00**
	Inst	Ea	Sm	HA	0.97	8.25	115.00	37.20	---	152.20	**185.00**
12' W double driveway gates											
36" H	Inst	Ea	Lg	HA	1.33	6.00	180.00	51.00	---	231.00	**280.00**
	Inst	Ea	Sm	HA	1.78	4.50	202.00	68.30	---	270.30	**329.00**
42" H	Inst	Ea	Lg	HA	1.33	6.00	190.00	51.00	---	241.00	**291.00**
	Inst	Ea	Sm	HA	1.78	4.50	213.00	68.30	---	281.30	**342.00**
48" H	Inst	Ea	Lg	HA	1.60	5.00	197.00	61.40	---	258.40	**313.00**
	Inst	Ea	Sm	HA	2.13	3.75	220.00	81.70	---	301.70	**369.00**
60" H	Inst	Ea	Lg	HA	1.60	5.00	236.00	61.40	---	297.40	**358.00**
	Inst	Ea	Sm	HA	2.13	3.75	264.00	81.70	---	345.70	**420.00**
72" H	Inst	Ea	Lg	HA	2.00	4.00	260.00	76.70	---	336.70	**408.00**
	Inst	Ea	Sm	HA	2.67	3.00	291.00	102.00	---	393.00	**480.00**

Description	Oper	Unit	Vol	Crew Size	Man-hours per Unit	Crew Output per Day	Avg Mat'l Unit Cost	Avg Labor Unit Cost	Avg Equip Unit Cost	Avg Total Unit Cost	Avg Price Incl O&P

Split rail

Red cedar, 10' L sectional spans

Rails only

Description	Oper	Unit	Vol	Crew Size	Man-hours per Unit	Crew Output per Day	Avg Mat'l Unit Cost	Avg Labor Unit Cost	Avg Equip Unit Cost	Avg Total Unit Cost	Avg Price Incl O&P
	Inst	Ea	Lg	---	---	---	11.10	---	---	11.10	**11.10**
	Inst	Ea	Sm	---	---	---	12.40	---	---	12.40	**12.40**
Bored 2 rail posts											
5'-6" line or end posts	Inst	Ea	Lg	CA	.615	13.00	13.00	22.80	---	35.80	**46.80**
	Inst	Ea	Sm	CA	.821	9.75	14.60	30.40	---	45.00	**59.30**
5'-6" corner posts	Inst	Ea	Lg	CA	.615	13.00	14.60	22.80	---	37.40	**48.70**
	Inst	Ea	Sm	CA	.821	9.75	16.40	30.40	---	46.80	**61.40**
Bored 3 rail posts											
6'-6" line or end posts	Inst	Ea	Lg	CA	.615	13.00	16.30	22.80	---	39.10	**50.60**
	Inst	Ea	Sm	CA	.821	9.75	18.20	30.40	---	48.60	**63.50**
6'-6" corner posts	Inst	Ea	Lg	CA	.615	13.00	17.90	22.80	---	40.70	**52.40**
	Inst	Ea	Sm	CA	.821	9.75	20.00	30.40	---	50.40	**65.60**

Complete fence estimate (does not include gates)

2 rail

Description	Oper	Unit	Vol	Crew Size	Man-hours per Unit	Crew Output per Day	Avg Mat'l Unit Cost	Avg Labor Unit Cost	Avg Equip Unit Cost	Avg Total Unit Cost	Avg Price Incl O&P
36" H, 5'-6" post	Inst	LF	Lg	CJ	.042	380.0	3.68	1.41	---	5.09	**6.20**
	Inst	LF	Sm	CJ	.056	285.0	4.12	1.88	---	6.00	**7.36**

3 rail

Description	Oper	Unit	Vol	Crew Size	Man-hours per Unit	Crew Output per Day	Avg Mat'l Unit Cost	Avg Labor Unit Cost	Avg Equip Unit Cost	Avg Total Unit Cost	Avg Price Incl O&P
48" H, 6'-6" post	Inst	LF	Lg	CJ	.048	330.0	4.78	1.61	---	6.39	**7.75**
	Inst	LF	Sm	CJ	.065	247.5	5.35	2.18	---	7.53	**9.20**

Gate

2 rails

Description	Oper	Unit	Vol	Crew Size	Man-hours per Unit	Crew Output per Day	Avg Mat'l Unit Cost	Avg Labor Unit Cost	Avg Equip Unit Cost	Avg Total Unit Cost	Avg Price Incl O&P
3-1/2' W	Inst	Ea	Lg	CA	.615	13.00	65.00	22.80	---	87.80	**107.00**
	Inst	Ea	Sm	CA	.821	9.75	72.80	30.40	---	103.20	**126.00**
5' W	Inst	Ea	Lg	CA	.800	10.00	84.50	29.60	---	114.10	**139.00**
	Inst	Ea	Sm	CA	1.07	7.50	94.60	39.60	---	134.20	**164.00**

3 rails

Description	Oper	Unit	Vol	Crew Size	Man-hours per Unit	Crew Output per Day	Avg Mat'l Unit Cost	Avg Labor Unit Cost	Avg Equip Unit Cost	Avg Total Unit Cost	Avg Price Incl O&P
3-1/2' W	Inst	Ea	Lg	CA	.615	13.00	81.30	22.80	---	104.10	**125.00**
	Inst	Ea	Sm	CA	.821	9.75	91.00	30.40	---	121.40	**147.00**
5' W	Inst	Ea	Lg	CA	.800	10.00	94.30	29.60	---	123.90	**150.00**
	Inst	Ea	Sm	CA	1.07	7.50	106.00	39.60	---	145.60	**177.00**

Description	Oper	Unit	Vol	Crew Size	Man-hours per Unit	Crew Output per Day	Avg Mat'l Unit Cost	Avg Labor Unit Cost	Avg Equip Unit Cost	Avg Total Unit Cost	Avg Price Incl O&P

Fiberglass panels

Corrugated; 8', 10', or 12' L panels; 2-1/2" W x 1/2" D corrugation

Nailed on wood frame

Description	Oper	Unit	Vol	Crew Size	Man-hours per Unit	Crew Output per Day	Avg Mat'l Unit Cost	Avg Labor Unit Cost	Avg Equip Unit Cost	Avg Total Unit Cost	Avg Price Incl O&P
4 oz., 0.03" T, 26" W	Inst	SF	Lg	CA	.040	200.0	1.70	1.48	---	3.18	**4.03**
	Inst	SF	Sm	CA	.053	150.0	1.83	1.96	---	3.79	**4.85**
Fire retardant	Inst	SF	Lg	CA	.040	200.0	2.35	1.48	---	3.83	**4.78**
	Inst	SF	Sm	CA	.053	150.0	2.52	1.96	---	4.48	**5.64**
5 oz., 0.037" T, 26" W	Inst	SF	Lg	CA	.040	200.0	2.09	1.48	---	3.57	**4.48**
	Inst	SF	Sm	CA	.053	150.0	2.25	1.96	---	4.21	**5.33**
Fire retardant	Inst	SF	Lg	CA	.040	200.0	2.89	1.48	---	4.37	**5.40**
	Inst	SF	Sm	CA	.053	150.0	3.10	1.96	---	5.06	**6.31**
6 oz., 0.045" T, 26" W	Inst	SF	Lg	CA	.040	200.0	2.48	1.48	---	3.96	**4.93**
	Inst	SF	Sm	CA	.053	150.0	2.67	1.96	---	4.63	**5.82**
Fire retardant	Inst	SF	Lg	CA	.040	200.0	3.43	1.48	---	4.91	**6.02**
	Inst	SF	Sm	CA	.053	150.0	3.68	1.96	---	5.64	**6.98**
8 oz., 0.06" T, 26" W	Inst	SF	Lg	CA	.040	200.0	2.88	1.48	---	4.36	**5.39**
	Inst	SF	Sm	CA	.053	150.0	3.09	1.96	---	5.05	**6.30**
Fire retardant	Inst	SF	Lg	CA	.040	200.0	3.97	1.48	---	5.45	**6.64**
	Inst	SF	Sm	CA	.053	150.0	4.26	1.96	---	6.22	**7.65**

Flat panels; 8', 10', or 12' L panels; clear, green, or white

Description	Oper	Unit	Vol	Crew Size	Man-hours per Unit	Crew Output per Day	Avg Mat'l Unit Cost	Avg Labor Unit Cost	Avg Equip Unit Cost	Avg Total Unit Cost	Avg Price Incl O&P
5 oz., 48" W	Inst	SF	Lg	CA	.040	200.0	1.13	1.48	---	2.61	**3.37**
	Inst	SF	Sm	CA	.053	150.0	1.22	1.96	---	3.18	**4.15**
Fire retardant	Inst	SF	Lg	CA	.040	200.0	1.13	1.48	---	2.61	**3.37**
	Inst	SF	Sm	CA	.053	150.0	1.22	1.96	---	3.18	**4.15**
6 oz., 48" W	Inst	SF	Lg	CA	.040	200.0	2.23	1.48	---	3.71	**4.64**
	Inst	SF	Sm	CA	.053	150.0	2.39	1.96	---	4.35	**5.50**
Fire retardant	Inst	SF	Lg	CA	.040	200.0	3.85	1.48	---	5.33	**6.50**
	Inst	SF	Sm	CA	.053	150.0	4.13	1.96	---	6.09	**7.50**
8 oz., 48" W	Inst	SF	Lg	CA	.040	200.0	2.88	1.48	---	4.36	**5.39**
	Inst	SF	Sm	CA	.053	150.0	3.09	1.96	---	5.05	**6.30**
Fire retardant	Inst	SF	Lg	CA	.040	200.0	4.97	1.48	---	6.45	**7.79**
	Inst	SF	Sm	CA	.053	150.0	5.34	1.96	---	7.30	**8.89**

Solar block; 8', 10', 12' L panels; 2-1/2" W x 1/2" D corrugation; nailed on wood frame

Description	Oper	Unit	Vol	Crew Size	Man-hours per Unit	Crew Output per Day	Avg Mat'l Unit Cost	Avg Labor Unit Cost	Avg Equip Unit Cost	Avg Total Unit Cost	Avg Price Incl O&P
5 oz., 26" W	Inst	SF	Lg	CA	.040	200.0	1.28	1.48	---	2.76	**3.55**
	Inst	SF	Sm	CA	.053	150.0	1.38	1.96	---	3.34	**4.33**

Description	Oper	Unit	Vol	Crew Size	Man-hours per Unit	Crew Output per Day	Avg Mat'l Unit Cost	Avg Labor Unit Cost	Avg Equip Unit Cost	Avg Total Unit Cost	Avg Price Incl O&P
Accessories											
Wood corrugated											
2-1/2" W x 1-1/2" D x 6' L	Inst	Ea	Lg	---	---	---	3.38	---	---	3.38	**3.89**
	Inst	Ea	Sm	---	---	---	3.63	---	---	3.63	**4.17**
2-1/2" W x 1-1/2" D x 8' L	Inst	Ea	Lg	---	---	---	4.10	---	---	4.10	**4.72**
	Inst	Ea	Sm	---	---	---	4.41	---	---	4.41	**5.07**
2-1/2" W x 3/4" D x 6' L	Inst	Ea	Lg	---	---	---	1.55	---	---	1.55	**1.78**
	Inst	Ea	Sm	---	---	---	1.67	---	---	1.67	**1.92**
2-1/2" W x 3/4" D x 8' L	Inst	Ea	Lg	---	---	---	2.00	---	---	2.00	**2.30**
	Inst	Ea	Sm	---	---	---	2.15	---	---	2.15	**2.47**
Rubber corrugated											
1" x 3"	Inst	Ea	Lg	---	---	---	1.55	---	---	1.55	**1.78**
	Inst	Ea	Sm	---	---	---	1.67	---	---	1.67	**1.92**
Polyfoam corrugated											
1" x 3"	Inst	Ea	Lg	---	---	---	1.09	---	---	1.09	**1.25**
	Inst	Ea	Sm	---	---	---	1.17	---	---	1.17	**1.35**
Vertical crown molding											
Wood											
1-1/2" x 6' L	Inst	Ea	Lg	---	---	---	2.82	---	---	2.82	**3.24**
	Inst	Ea	Sm	---	---	---	3.03	---	---	3.03	**3.48**
1-1/2" x 8' L	Inst	Ea	Lg	---	---	---	3.73	---	---	3.73	**4.29**
	Inst	Ea	Sm	---	---	---	4.00	---	---	4.00	**4.60**
Polyfoam											
1" x 1" x 3' L	Inst	Ea	Lg	---	---	---	1.36	---	---	1.36	**1.56**
	Inst	Ea	Sm	---	---	---	1.46	---	---	1.46	**1.68**
Rubber											
1" x 1" x 3' L	Inst	Ea	Lg	---	---	---	2.58	---	---	2.58	**2.97**
	Inst	Ea	Sm	---	---	---	2.77	---	---	2.77	**3.19**

Description	Oper	Unit	Vol	Crew Size	Man-hours per Unit	Crew Output per Day	Avg Mat'l Unit Cost	Avg Labor Unit Cost	Avg Equip Unit Cost	Avg Total Unit Cost	Avg Price Incl O&P

Fireplaces

Woodburning, prefabricated. No masonry support required, installs directly on floor. Ceramic-backed firebox with black vitreous enamel side panels. No finish plastering or brick hearthwork included. Fire screen, 9" (i.d.) factory-built insulated chimneys with flue, lining, damper, and flashing with rain cap included. Chimney height from floor to where chimney exits through roof

36" W fireplace unit with:

Description	Oper	Unit	Vol	Crew Size	Man-hours per Unit	Crew Output per Day	Avg Mat'l Unit Cost	Avg Labor Unit Cost	Avg Equip Unit Cost	Avg Total Unit Cost	Avg Price Incl O&P
Up to 9'-0" chimney height	Inst	LS	Lg	CJ	16.0	1.00	1000.00	536.00	---	1536.00	1900.00
	Inst	LS	Sm	CJ	22.9	0.70	1110.00	767.00	---	1877.00	2350.00
9'-3" to 12'-2" chimney	Inst	LS	Lg	CJ	16.0	1.00	1050.00	536.00	---	1586.00	1960.00
	Inst	LS	Sm	CJ	22.9	0.70	1170.00	767.00	---	1937.00	2410.00
12'-3" to 15'-1" chimney	Inst	LS	Lg	CJ	16.0	1.00	1100.00	536.00	---	1636.00	2020.00
	Inst	LS	Sm	CJ	22.9	0.70	1220.00	767.00	---	1987.00	2480.00
15'-2" to 18'-0" chimney	Inst	LS	Lg	CJ	16.0	1.00	1160.00	536.00	---	1696.00	2080.00
	Inst	LS	Sm	CJ	22.9	0.70	1280.00	767.00	---	2047.00	2550.00
18'-1" to 20'-11" chimney	Inst	LS	Lg	CJ	24.6	0.65	1210.00	824.00	---	2034.00	2540.00
	Inst	LS	Sm	CJ	34.8	0.46	1340.00	1170.00	---	2510.00	3170.00
21'-3" to 23'-10" chimney	Inst	LS	Lg	CJ	24.6	0.65	1260.00	824.00	---	2084.00	2600.00
	Inst	LS	Sm	CJ	34.8	0.46	1390.00	1170.00	---	2560.00	3230.00
23'-11" to 24'-9" chimney	Inst	LS	Lg	CJ	24.6	0.65	1310.00	824.00	---	2134.00	2660.00
	Inst	LS	Sm	CJ	34.8	0.46	1450.00	1170.00	---	2620.00	3300.00

42" W fireplace unit with:

Description	Oper	Unit	Vol	Crew Size	Man-hours per Unit	Crew Output per Day	Avg Mat'l Unit Cost	Avg Labor Unit Cost	Avg Equip Unit Cost	Avg Total Unit Cost	Avg Price Incl O&P
Up to 9'-0" chimney height	Inst	LS	Lg	CJ	16.0	1.00	1130.00	536.00	---	1666.00	2050.00
	Inst	LS	Sm	CJ	22.9	0.70	1250.00	767.00	---	2017.00	2510.00
9'-3" to 12'-2" chimney	Inst	LS	Lg	CJ	16.0	1.00	1190.00	536.00	---	1726.00	2120.00
	Inst	LS	Sm	CJ	22.9	0.70	1320.00	767.00	---	2087.00	2590.00
12'-3" to 15'-1" chimney	Inst	LS	Lg	CJ	16.0	1.00	1250.00	536.00	---	1786.00	2190.00
	Inst	LS	Sm	CJ	22.9	0.70	1380.00	767.00	---	2147.00	2670.00
15'-2" to 18'-0" chimney	Inst	LS	Lg	CJ	16.0	1.00	1310.00	536.00	---	1846.00	2260.00
	Inst	LS	Sm	CJ	22.9	0.70	1450.00	767.00	---	2217.00	2740.00
18'-1" to 20'-11" chimney	Inst	LS	Lg	CJ	24.6	0.65	1370.00	824.00	---	2194.00	2730.00
	Inst	LS	Sm	CJ	34.8	0.46	1510.00	1170.00	---	2680.00	3370.00
21'-3" to 23'-10" chimney	Inst	LS	Lg	CJ	24.6	0.65	1430.00	824.00	---	2254.00	2800.00
	Inst	LS	Sm	CJ	34.8	0.46	1580.00	1170.00	---	2750.00	3450.00
23'-11" to 24'-9" chimney	Inst	LS	Lg	CJ	24.6	0.65	1490.00	824.00	---	2314.00	2860.00
	Inst	LS	Sm	CJ	34.8	0.46	1650.00	1170.00	---	2820.00	3530.00

Description	Oper	Unit	Vol	Crew Size	Man-hours per Unit	Crew Output per Day	Avg Mat'l Unit Cost	Avg Labor Unit Cost	Avg Equip Unit Cost	Avg Total Unit Cost	Avg Price Incl O&P
Accessories											
Log lighter with gas valve (straight or angle pattern)											
	Inst	Ea	Lg	SA	1.33	6.00	33.60	57.20	---	90.80	**122.00**
	Inst	Ea	Sm	SA	1.90	4.20	37.20	81.70	---	118.90	**161.00**
Log lighter, less gas valve (straight, angle, tee pattern)											
	Inst	Ea	Lg	SA	.667	12.00	12.60	28.70	---	41.30	**56.10**
	Inst	Ea	Sm	SA	0.95	8.40	14.00	40.90	---	54.90	**75.30**
Gas valve for log lighter											
	Inst	Ea	Lg	SA	.667	12.00	22.40	28.70	---	51.10	**67.40**
	Inst	Ea	Sm	SA	0.95	8.40	24.80	40.90	---	65.70	**87.80**
Spare parts											
Gas valve key											
	Inst	Ea	Lg	---	---	---	1.54	---	---	1.54	**1.54**
	Inst	Ea	Sm	---	---	---	1.71	---	---	1.71	**1.71**
Stem extender											
	Inst	Ea	Lg	---	---	---	2.80	---	---	2.80	**2.80**
	Inst	Ea	Sm	---	---	---	3.10	---	---	3.10	**3.10**
Extra long											
	Inst	Ea	Lg	---	---	---	3.85	---	---	3.85	**3.85**
	Inst	Ea	Sm	---	---	---	4.26	---	---	4.26	**4.26**
Valve floor plate											
	Inst	Ea	Lg	---	---	---	3.22	---	---	3.22	**3.22**
	Inst	Ea	Sm	---	---	---	3.57	---	---	3.57	**3.57**
Lighter burner tube (12" to 17")											
	Inst	Ea	Lg	---	---	---	6.44	---	---	6.44	**6.44**
	Inst	Ea	Sm	---	---	---	7.13	---	---	7.13	**7.13**

Fireplace mantels. See Mantels, fireplace, page 281

Flashing. See Sheet metal, page 372

Floor finishes. See individual items

Floor joists. See Framing, page 185

Description	Oper	Unit	Vol	Crew Size	Man-hours per Unit	Crew Output per Day	Avg Mat'l Unit Cost	Avg Labor Unit Cost	Avg Equip Unit Cost	Avg Total Unit Cost	Avg Price Incl O&P

Food centers

Includes wiring, connection and installation in exposed drainboard only

Built-in models, 4-1/4" x 6-3/4" x 10" rough cut

600 watt motor, 110 volts, 5 speed, 8.7 sones quiet

Description	Oper	Unit	Vol	Crew Size	Man-hours per Unit	Crew Output per Day	Avg Mat'l Unit Cost	Avg Labor Unit Cost	Avg Equip Unit Cost	Avg Total Unit Cost	Avg Price Incl O&P
	Inst	Ea	Lg	EA	2.67	3.00	297.00	107.00	---	404.00	**497.00**
	Inst	Ea	Sm	EA	3.81	2.10	327.00	153.00	---	480.00	**598.00**
Options											
Blender, glass	Inst	Ea	Lg	---	---	---	64.40	---	---	64.40	**64.40**
	Inst	Ea	Sm	---	---	---	70.90	---	---	70.90	**70.90**
Blender, stainless steel	Inst	Ea	Lg	---	---	---	79.20	---	---	79.20	**79.20**
	Inst	Ea	Sm	---	---	---	87.20	---	---	87.20	**87.20**
Food processor	Inst	Ea	Lg	---	---	---	149.00	---	---	149.00	**149.00**
	Inst	Ea	Sm	---	---	---	164.00	---	---	164.00	**164.00**
Grinder	Inst	Ea	Lg	---	---	---	74.30	---	---	74.30	**74.30**
	Inst	Ea	Sm	---	---	---	81.80	---	---	81.80	**81.80**
Mini-chopper	Inst	Ea	Lg	---	---	---	59.40	---	---	59.40	**59.40**
	Inst	Ea	Sm	---	---	---	65.40	---	---	65.40	**65.40**
Mixer	Inst	Ea	Lg	---	---	---	149.00	---	---	149.00	**149.00**
	Inst	Ea	Sm	---	---	---	164.00	---	---	164.00	**164.00**

Footings. See Concrete, page 98

Formica. See Countertops, page 106

Forming. See Concrete, page 98

Foundations. See Concrete, page 100

Framing

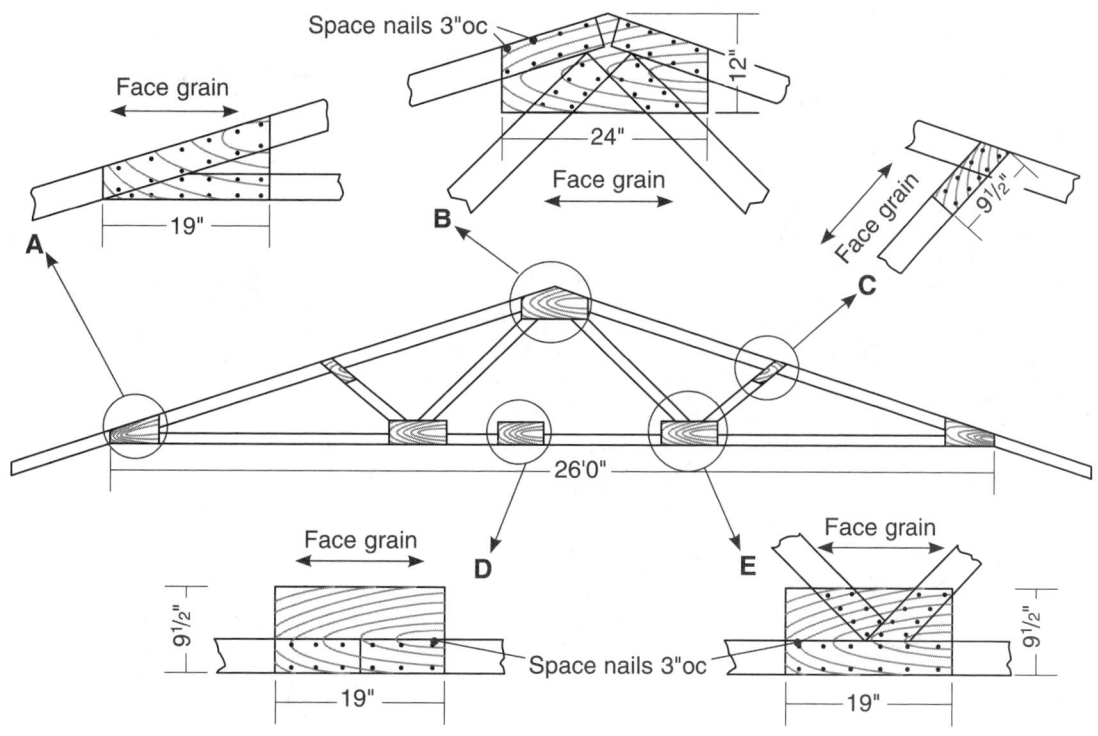

Face grain

Space nails 3"oc

12"

24"

Face grain

Face grain

9 1/2"

A

B

C

26'0"

Face grain

D

E

Face grain

9 1/2"

9 1/2"

Space nails 3"oc

19"

19"

Construction of a 26 foot W truss:

A Bevel-heel gusset
B Peak gusset
C Upper chord intermediate gusset
D Splice of lower chord
E Lower chord intermediate gusset

Metal strap anchor

Rafter

Joist

Nail rafter and joist together

Toenail to plate

Wall

Wood hanger

Nail joists to each other

Toenail to plate

Ceiling joists

Load-bearing partition

Splice cleat

Metal joist hanger

Flush ceiling framing

A

Joint (over stud)

Let-in corner brace

Stud

Joint (over stud)

End matched may fall between studs

45º

Foundation

Horizontal application

Diagonal application

Application of wood sheathing:
A Horizontal and diagonal
B Started at subfloor
C Started at foundation wall

B

Sheathing
Stud
Sole plate
Subfloor
Joist
Sill plate
Anchor bolt
Foundation wall

C

Sheathing
Stud
Sole plate
Subfloor
Joist
Sill plate
Anchor bolt
Foundation wall

Top plates
Lap top plates and nail
Temporary brace
Window header
Stud
Let-in corner brace
Window sill
Header joist
Sole plate
Foundation wall
Subfloor
Stringer joist
Anchored sill plates
Spacer block

Header
Jack rafter
Ridge board
Double rafter
Dormer
Valley rafter
Side stud
Joist

Diagonal subfloor 8" maximum width - square edge

Joint over joists

Double joists under partitions

16" oc

Plywood subfloor

Solid bridging

Header joist

Anchored sill

3/4" space for sheathing

Lap joists over girder
(4" minimum) or
butt and scab

Stringer joist

Floor framing:
1. Nailing bridge to joists
2. Nailing board subfloor to joists
3. Nailing header to joists
4. Toenailing header to sill

Stud arrangements at exterior corners

Description	Oper	Unit	Vol	Crew Size	Man-hours per Unit	Crew Output per Day	Avg Mat'l Unit Cost	Avg Labor Unit Cost	Avg Equip Unit Cost	Avg Total Unit Cost	Avg Price Incl O&P

Framing, rough carpentry
Dimension lumber
Beams; set on steel columns, not wood columns
Built-up (2 pieces)

Description	Oper	Unit	Vol	Crew Size	Man-hours per Unit	Crew Output per Day	Avg Mat'l Unit Cost	Avg Labor Unit Cost	Avg Equip Unit Cost	Avg Total Unit Cost	Avg Price Incl O&P
4" x 6" - 10'	Demo	LF	Lg	LB	.024	661.0	---	.72	---	.72	1.01
	Demo	LF	Sm	LB	.028	561.9	---	.84	---	.84	1.18
4" x 6" - 10'	Inst	LF	Lg	2C	.047	339.0	1.46	1.74	.23	3.43	4.35
	Inst	LF	Sm	2C	.056	288.2	1.60	2.07	.27	3.94	5.01
4" x 8" - 10'	Demo	LF	Lg	LB	.027	595.0	---	.81	---	.81	1.13
	Demo	LF	Sm	LB	.032	505.8	---	.96	---	.96	1.34
4" x 8" - 10'	Inst	LF	Lg	2C	.046	350.0	1.91	1.70	.22	3.83	4.80
	Inst	LF	Sm	2C	.054	297.5	2.09	2.00	.26	4.35	5.46
4" x 10" - 10'	Demo	LF	Lg	LB	.030	540.0	---	.90	---	.90	1.26
	Demo	LF	Sm	LB	.035	459.0	---	1.05	---	1.05	1.47
4" x 10" - 10'	Inst	LF	Lg	2C	.049	325.0	2.58	1.81	.24	4.63	5.75
	Inst	LF	Sm	2C	.058	276.3	2.81	2.15	.28	5.24	6.52
4" x 12" - 12'	Demo	LF	Lg	LB	.032	495.0	---	.96	---	.96	1.34
	Demo	LF	Sm	LB	.038	420.8	---	1.14	---	1.14	1.60
4" x 12" - 12'	Inst	LF	Lg	2C	.053	304.0	3.00	1.96	.26	5.22	6.46
	Inst	LF	Sm	2C	.062	258.4	3.27	2.30	.30	5.87	7.27
6" x 8" - 10'	Demo	LF	Lg	LD	.043	744.0	---	1.44	---	1.44	2.02
	Demo	LF	Sm	LD	.051	632.4	---	1.71	---	1.71	2.39
6" x 8" - 10'	Inst	LF	Lg	CW	.074	435.0	4.81	2.48	.18	7.47	9.18
	Inst	LF	Sm	CW	.087	369.8	5.25	2.92	.21	8.38	10.30
6" x 10" - 10'	Demo	LF	Lg	LD	.047	676.0	---	1.57	---	1.57	2.20
	Demo	LF	Sm	LD	.056	574.6	---	1.88	---	1.88	2.63
6" x 10" - 10'	Inst	LF	Lg	CW	.079	405.0	6.00	2.65	.19	8.84	10.80
	Inst	LF	Sm	CW	.093	344.3	6.50	3.12	.23	9.85	12.10
6" x 12" - 12'	Demo	LF	Lg	LD	.052	619.0	---	1.74	---	1.74	2.44
	Demo	LF	Sm	LD	.061	526.2	---	2.04	---	2.04	2.86
6" x 12" - 12'	Inst	LF	Lg	CW	.084	379.0	6.99	2.81	.21	10.01	12.20
	Inst	LF	Sm	CW	.099	322.2	7.58	3.32	.24	11.14	13.60

Built-up (3 pieces)

Description	Oper	Unit	Vol	Crew Size	Man-hours per Unit	Crew Output per Day	Avg Mat'l Unit Cost	Avg Labor Unit Cost	Avg Equip Unit Cost	Avg Total Unit Cost	Avg Price Incl O&P
6" x 8" - 10'	Demo	LF	Lg	LD	.044	733.0	---	1.47	---	1.47	2.06
	Demo	LF	Sm	LD	.051	623.1	---	1.71	---	1.71	2.39
6" x 8" - 10'	Inst	LF	Lg	CW	.075	425.0	2.88	2.51	.18	5.57	7.01
	Inst	LF	Sm	CW	.089	361.3	3.16	2.98	.22	6.36	8.03
6" x 10" - 10'	Demo	LF	Lg	LD	.048	669.0	---	1.61	---	1.61	2.25
	Demo	LF	Sm	LD	.056	568.7	---	1.88	---	1.88	2.63
6" x 10" - 10'	Inst	LF	Lg	CW	.081	397.0	3.91	2.71	.20	6.82	8.50
	Inst	LF	Sm	CW	.095	337.5	4.25	3.18	.23	7.66	9.57

Description	Oper	Unit	Vol	Crew Size	Man-hours per Unit	Crew Output per Day	Avg Mat'l Unit Cost	Avg Labor Unit Cost	Avg Equip Unit Cost	Avg Total Unit Cost	Avg Price Incl O&P
6" x 12" - 12'	Demo	LF	Lg	LD	.053	609.0	---	1.78	---	1.78	**2.49**
	Demo	LF	Sm	LD	.062	517.7	---	2.08	---	2.08	**2.91**
6" x 12" - 12'	Inst	LF	Lg	CW	.087	368.0	4.53	2.92	.21	7.66	**9.50**
	Inst	LF	Sm	CW	.102	312.8	4.94	3.42	.25	8.61	**10.70**
9" x 10" - 12'	Demo	LF	Lg	LD	.059	541.0	---	1.98	---	1.98	**2.77**
	Demo	LF	Sm	LD	.070	459.9	---	2.35	---	2.35	**3.28**
9" x 10" - 12'	Inst	LF	Lg	CW	.095	338.0	9.02	3.18	.23	12.43	**15.10**
	Inst	LF	Sm	CW	.111	287.3	9.77	3.72	.27	13.76	**16.70**
9" x 12" - 12'	Demo	LF	Lg	LD	.065	493.0	---	2.18	---	2.18	**3.05**
	Demo	LF	Sm	LD	.076	419.1	---	2.55	---	2.55	**3.57**
9" x 12" - 12'	Inst	LF	Lg	CW	.102	315.0	10.50	3.42	.25	14.17	**17.10**
	Inst	LF	Sm	CW	.120	267.8	11.40	4.02	.29	15.71	**19.00**

Single member

Description	Oper	Unit	Vol	Crew Size	Man-hours per Unit	Crew Output per Day	Avg Mat'l Unit Cost	Avg Labor Unit Cost	Avg Equip Unit Cost	Avg Total Unit Cost	Avg Price Incl O&P
2" x 6"	Demo	LF	Lg	LB	.017	947.0	---	.51	---	.51	**.71**
	Demo	LF	Sm	LB	.020	805.0	---	.60	---	.60	**.84**
2" x 6"	Inst	LF	Lg	2C	.031	520.0	.81	1.15	.15	2.11	**2.69**
	Inst	LF	Sm	2C	.036	442.0	.89	1.33	.18	2.40	**3.07**
2" x 8"	Demo	LF	Lg	LB	.018	874.0	---	.54	---	.54	**.76**
	Demo	LF	Sm	LB	.022	742.9	---	.66	---	.66	**.92**
2" x 8"	Inst	LF	Lg	2C	.033	491.0	1.03	1.22	.16	2.41	**3.05**
	Inst	LF	Sm	2C	.038	417.4	1.13	1.41	.19	2.73	**3.46**
2" x 10"	Demo	LF	Lg	LB	.020	811.0	---	.60	---	.60	**.84**
	Demo	LF	Sm	LB	.023	689.4	---	.69	---	.69	**.97**
2" x 10"	Inst	LF	Lg	2C	.034	465.0	1.38	1.26	.17	2.81	**3.52**
	Inst	LF	Sm	2C	.040	395.3	1.50	1.48	.20	3.18	**4.00**
2" x 12"	Demo	LF	Lg	LB	.021	756.0	---	.63	---	.63	**.88**
	Demo	LF	Sm	LB	.025	642.6	---	.75	---	.75	**1.05**
2" x 12"	Inst	LF	Lg	2C	.036	440.0	1.58	1.33	.18	3.09	**3.86**
	Inst	LF	Sm	2C	.043	374.0	1.73	1.59	.21	3.53	**4.43**
3" x 6"	Demo	LF	Lg	LB	.019	832.0	---	.57	---	.57	**.80**
	Demo	LF	Sm	LB	.023	707.2	---	.69	---	.69	**.97**
3" x 6"	Inst	LF	Lg	2C	.034	472.0	1.58	1.26	.17	3.01	**3.75**
	Inst	LF	Sm	2C	.040	401.2	1.72	1.48	.19	3.39	**4.24**
3" x 8"	Demo	LF	Lg	LB	.021	756.0	---	.63	---	.63	**.88**
	Demo	LF	Sm	LB	.025	642.6	---	.75	---	.75	**1.05**
3" x 8"	Inst	LF	Lg	2C	.036	440.0	2.49	1.33	.18	4.00	**4.91**
	Inst	LF	Sm	2C	.043	374.0	2.72	1.59	.21	4.52	**5.57**
3" x 10"	Demo	LF	Lg	LB	.024	680.0	---	.72	---	.72	**1.01**
	Demo	LF	Sm	LB	.028	578.0	---	.84	---	.84	**1.18**
3" x 10"	Inst	LF	Lg	2C	.039	408.0	3.08	1.44	.19	4.71	**5.75**
	Inst	LF	Sm	2C	.046	346.8	3.34	1.70	.22	5.26	**6.45**

Description	Oper	Unit	Vol	Crew Size	Man-hours per Unit	Crew Output per Day	Avg Mat'l Unit Cost	Avg Labor Unit Cost	Avg Equip Unit Cost	Avg Total Unit Cost	Avg Price Incl O&P
3" x 12"	Demo	LF	Lg	LB	.026	623.0	---	.78	---	.78	1.09
	Demo	LF	Sm	LB	.030	529.6	---	.90	---	.90	1.26
3" x 12"	Inst	LF	Lg	2C	.042	381.0	3.58	1.55	.20	5.33	6.49
	Inst	LF	Sm	2C	.049	323.9	3.88	1.81	.24	5.93	7.24
3" x 14"	Demo	LF	Lg	LB	.028	575.0	---	.84	---	.84	1.18
	Demo	LF	Sm	LB	.033	488.8	---	.99	---	.99	1.39
3" x 14"	Inst	LF	Lg	2C	.045	359.0	4.35	1.67	.22	6.24	7.55
	Inst	LF	Sm	2C	.052	305.2	4.74	1.93	.26	6.93	8.41
4" x 6"	Demo	LF	Lg	LB	.021	745.0	---	.63	---	.63	.88
	Demo	LF	Sm	LB	.025	633.3	---	.75	---	.75	1.05
4" x 6"	Inst	LF	Lg	2C	.037	433.0	2.07	1.37	.18	3.62	4.48
	Inst	LF	Sm	2C	.043	368.1	2.25	1.59	.21	4.05	5.03
4" x 8"	Demo	LF	Lg	LB	.025	653.0	---	.75	---	.75	1.05
	Demo	LF	Sm	LB	.029	555.1	---	.87	---	.87	1.22
4" x 8"	Inst	LF	Lg	2C	.041	394.0	3.28	1.52	.20	5.00	6.10
	Inst	LF	Sm	2C	.048	334.9	3.59	1.78	.23	5.60	6.85
4" x 10"	Demo	LF	Lg	LB	.027	586.0	---	.81	---	.81	1.13
	Demo	LF	Sm	LB	.032	498.1	---	.96	---	.96	1.34
4" x 10"	Inst	LF	Lg	2C	.044	363.0	4.07	1.63	.21	5.91	7.17
	Inst	LF	Sm	2C	.052	308.6	4.41	1.93	.25	6.59	8.02
4" x 12"	Demo	LF	Lg	LB	.031	522.0	---	.93	---	.93	1.30
	Demo	LF	Sm	LB	.036	443.7	---	1.08	---	1.08	1.51
4" x 12"	Inst	LF	Lg	2C	.048	333.0	4.73	1.78	.23	6.74	8.16
	Inst	LF	Sm	2C	.057	283.1	5.14	2.11	.28	7.53	9.15
4" x 14"	Demo	LF	Lg	LH	.037	642.0	---	1.11	---	1.11	1.55
	Demo	LF	Sm	LH	.044	545.7	---	1.32	---	1.32	1.85
4" x 14"	Inst	LF	Lg	CS	.059	404.0	5.76	2.05	.19	8.00	9.68
	Inst	LF	Sm	CS	.070	343.4	6.28	2.43	.23	8.94	10.90
4" x 16"	Demo	LF	Lg	LH	.040	594.0	---	1.20	---	1.20	1.68
	Demo	LF	Sm	LH	.048	504.9	---	1.44	---	1.44	2.02
4" x 16"	Inst	LF	Lg	CS	.063	379.0	6.56	2.18	.21	8.95	10.80
	Inst	LF	Sm	CS	.074	322.2	7.16	2.57	.24	9.97	12.10
6" x 8"	Demo	LF	Lg	LJ	.041	782.0	---	1.23	---	1.23	1.72
	Demo	LF	Sm	LJ	.048	664.7	---	1.44	---	1.44	2.02
6" x 8"	Inst	LF	Lg	CW	.069	466.0	5.92	2.31	.17	8.40	10.20
	Inst	LF	Sm	CW	.081	396.1	6.46	2.71	.20	9.37	11.40
6" x 10"	Demo	LF	Lg	LJ	.046	694.0	---	1.38	---	1.38	1.93
	Demo	LF	Sm	LJ	.054	589.9	---	1.62	---	1.62	2.27
6" x 10"	Inst	LF	Lg	CW	.075	427.0	7.37	2.51	.18	10.06	12.20
	Inst	LF	Sm	CW	.088	363.0	8.04	2.95	.21	11.20	13.60
6" x 12"	Demo	LF	Lg	LJ	.051	631.0	---	1.53	---	1.53	2.14
	Demo	LF	Sm	LJ	.060	536.4	---	1.80	---	1.80	2.52
6" x 12"	Inst	LF	Lg	CW	.081	396.0	8.82	2.71	.20	11.73	14.10
	Inst	LF	Sm	CW	.095	336.6	9.62	3.18	.23	13.03	15.80

Description	Oper	Unit	Vol	Crew Size	Man-hours per Unit	Crew Output per Day	Avg Mat'l Unit Cost	Avg Labor Unit Cost	Avg Equip Unit Cost	Avg Total Unit Cost	Avg Price Incl O&P
6" x 14"	Demo	LF	Lg	LJ	.056	567.0	---	1.68	---	1.68	**2.35**
	Demo	LF	Sm	LJ	.066	482.0	---	1.98	---	1.98	**2.77**
6" x 14"	Inst	LF	Lg	CW	.088	365.0	10.30	2.95	.21	13.46	**16.20**
	Inst	LF	Sm	CW	.103	310.3	11.20	3.45	.25	14.90	**18.00**
6" x 16"	Demo	LF	Lg	LJ	.061	523.0	---	1.83	---	1.83	**2.56**
	Demo	LF	Sm	LJ	.072	444.6	---	2.16	---	2.16	**3.02**
6" x 16"	Inst	LF	Lg	CW	.094	342.0	11.70	3.15	.23	15.08	**18.10**
	Inst	LF	Sm	CW	.110	290.7	12.80	3.69	.27	16.76	**20.10**
8" x 8"	Demo	LF	Lg	LJ	.048	668.0	---	1.44	---	1.44	**2.02**
	Demo	LF	Sm	LJ	.056	567.8	---	1.68	---	1.68	**2.35**
8" x 8"	Inst	LF	Lg	CW	.077	413.0	11.70	2.58	.19	14.47	**17.30**
	Inst	LF	Sm	CW	.091	351.1	12.80	3.05	.22	16.07	**19.20**
8" x 10"	Demo	LF	Lg	LJ	.058	556.0	---	1.74	---	1.74	**2.44**
	Demo	LF	Sm	LJ	.068	472.6	---	2.04	---	2.04	**2.86**
8" x 10"	Inst	LF	Lg	CW	.088	363.0	14.60	2.95	.21	17.76	**21.20**
	Inst	LF	Sm	CW	.104	308.6	16.00	3.49	.25	19.74	**23.50**
8" x 12"	Demo	LF	Lg	LJ	.062	515.0	---	1.86	---	1.86	**2.60**
	Demo	LF	Sm	LJ	.073	437.8	---	2.19	---	2.19	**3.07**
8" x 12"	Inst	LF	Lg	CW	.094	341.0	17.50	3.15	.23	20.88	**24.80**
	Inst	LF	Sm	CW	.110	289.9	19.10	3.69	.27	23.06	**27.40**
8" x 14"	Demo	LF	Lg	LJ	.068	468.0	---	2.04	---	2.04	**2.86**
	Demo	LF	Sm	LJ	.080	397.8	---	2.40	---	2.40	**3.36**
8" x 14"	Inst	LF	Lg	CW	.101	316.0	20.40	3.38	.25	24.03	**28.50**
	Inst	LF	Sm	CW	.119	268.6	22.30	3.99	.29	26.58	**31.50**
8" x 16"	Demo	LF	Lg	LJ	.076	423.0	---	2.28	---	2.28	**3.19**
	Demo	LF	Sm	LJ	.089	359.6	---	2.67	---	2.67	**3.74**
8" x 16"	Inst	LF	Lg	CW	.110	292.0	23.40	3.69	.27	27.36	**32.30**
	Inst	LF	Sm	CW	.129	248.2	25.50	4.32	.31	30.13	**35.70**

Blocking, horizontal, for studs

Description	Oper	Unit	Vol	Crew Size	Man-hours per Unit	Crew Output per Day	Avg Mat'l Unit Cost	Avg Labor Unit Cost	Avg Equip Unit Cost	Avg Total Unit Cost	Avg Price Incl O&P
2" x 4" - 12"	Demo	LF	Lg	1L	.011	710.0	---	.33	---	.33	**.46**
	Demo	LF	Sm	1L	.013	603.5	---	.39	---	.39	**.55**
2" x 4" - 12"	Inst	LF	Lg	CA	.036	224.0	.46	1.33	.35	2.14	**2.74**
	Inst	LF	Sm	CA	.042	190.4	.51	1.55	.41	2.47	**3.17**
2" x 4" - 16"	Demo	LF	Lg	1L	.011	761.0	---	.33	---	.33	**.46**
	Demo	LF	Sm	1L	.012	646.9	---	.36	---	.36	**.50**
2" x 4" - 16"	Inst	LF	Lg	CA	.029	274.0	.46	1.07	.28	1.81	**2.31**
	Inst	LF	Sm	CA	.034	232.9	.51	1.26	.33	2.10	**2.68**
2" x 4" - 24"	Demo	LF	Lg	1L	.010	810.0	---	.30	---	.30	**.42**
	Demo	LF	Sm	1L	.012	688.5	---	.36	---	.36	**.50**
2" x 4" - 24"	Inst	LF	Lg	CA	.023	350.0	.46	.85	.22	1.53	**1.94**
	Inst	LF	Sm	CA	.027	297.5	.51	1.00	.26	1.77	**2.25**

Description	Oper	Unit	Vol	Crew Size	Man-hours per Unit	Crew Output per Day	Avg Mat'l Unit Cost	Avg Labor Unit Cost	Avg Equip Unit Cost	Avg Total Unit Cost	Avg Price Incl O&P
2" x 6" - 12"	Demo	LF	Lg	1L	.013	608.0	---	.39	---	.39	**.55**
	Demo	LF	Sm	1L	.015	516.8	---	.45	---	.45	**.63**
2" x 6" - 12"	Inst	LF	Lg	CA	.039	207.0	.72	1.44	.38	2.54	**3.23**
	Inst	LF	Sm	CA	.045	176.0	.78	1.67	.44	2.89	**3.67**
2" x 6" - 16"	Demo	LF	Lg	1L	.012	647.0	---	.36	---	.36	**.50**
	Demo	LF	Sm	1L	.015	550.0	---	.45	---	.45	**.63**
2" x 6" - 16"	Inst	LF	Lg	CA	.032	252.0	.72	1.18	.31	2.21	**2.80**
	Inst	LF	Sm	CA	.037	214.2	.78	1.37	.36	2.51	**3.17**
2" x 6" - 24"	Demo	LF	Lg	1L	.012	683.0	---	.36	---	.36	**.50**
	Demo	LF	Sm	1L	.014	580.6	---	.42	---	.42	**.59**
2" x 6" - 24"	Inst	LF	Lg	CA	.025	323.0	.72	.93	.24	1.89	**2.36**
	Inst	LF	Sm	CA	.029	274.6	.78	1.07	.28	2.13	**2.68**
2" x 8" - 12"	Demo	LF	Lg	1L	.015	532.0	---	.45	---	.45	**.63**
	Demo	LF	Sm	1L	.018	452.2	---	.54	---	.54	**.76**
2" x 8" - 12"	Inst	LF	Lg	CA	.041	193.0	.93	1.52	.40	2.85	**3.59**
	Inst	LF	Sm	CA	.049	164.1	1.02	1.81	.48	3.31	**4.19**
2" x 8" - 16"	Demo	LF	Lg	1L	.014	564.0	---	.42	---	.42	**.59**
	Demo	LF	Sm	1L	.017	479.4	---	.51	---	.51	**.71**
2" x 8" - 16"	Inst	LF	Lg	CA	.034	235.0	.93	1.26	.33	2.52	**3.16**
	Inst	LF	Sm	CA	.040	199.8	1.02	1.48	.39	2.89	**3.64**
2" x 8" - 24"	Demo	LF	Lg	1L	.014	592.0	---	.42	---	.42	**.59**
	Demo	LF	Sm	1L	.016	503.2	---	.48	---	.48	**.67**
2" x 8" - 24"	Inst	LF	Lg	CA	.027	299.0	.93	1.00	.26	2.19	**2.73**
	Inst	LF	Sm	CA	.031	254.2	1.02	1.15	.31	2.48	**3.09**

Bracing, diagonal let-ins

Studs, 12" oc

Description	Oper	Unit	Vol	Crew Size	Man-hours per Unit	Crew Output per Day	Avg Mat'l Unit Cost	Avg Labor Unit Cost	Avg Equip Unit Cost	Avg Total Unit Cost	Avg Price Incl O&P
1" x 6"	Demo	Set	Lg	1L	.011	714.0	---	.33	---	.33	**.46**
	Demo	Set	Sm	1L	.013	606.9	---	.39	---	.39	**.55**
1" x 6"	Inst	Set	Lg	CA	.056	143.0	.89	2.07	.55	3.51	**4.48**
	Inst	Set	Sm	CA	.066	121.6	.97	2.44	.64	4.05	**5.18**

Studs, 16" oc

Description	Oper	Unit	Vol	Crew Size	Man-hours per Unit	Crew Output per Day	Avg Mat'l Unit Cost	Avg Labor Unit Cost	Avg Equip Unit Cost	Avg Total Unit Cost	Avg Price Incl O&P
1" x 6"	Demo	Set	Lg	1L	.010	770.0	---	.30	---	.30	**.42**
	Demo	Set	Sm	1L	.012	654.5	---	.36	---	.36	**.50**
1" x 6"	Inst	Set	Lg	CA	.043	184.0	.89	1.59	.42	2.90	**3.67**
	Inst	Set	Sm	CA	.051	156.4	.97	1.89	.50	3.36	**4.26**

Studs, 24" oc

Description	Oper	Unit	Vol	Crew Size	Man-hours per Unit	Crew Output per Day	Avg Mat'l Unit Cost	Avg Labor Unit Cost	Avg Equip Unit Cost	Avg Total Unit Cost	Avg Price Incl O&P
1" x 6"	Demo	Set	Lg	1L	.010	825.0	---	.30	---	.30	**.42**
	Demo	Set	Sm	1L	.011	701.3	---	.33	---	.33	**.46**
1" x 6"	Inst	Set	Lg	CA	.033	242.0	.89	1.22	.32	2.43	**3.05**
	Inst	Set	Sm	CA	.039	205.7	.97	1.44	.38	2.79	**3.52**

Description	Oper	Unit	Vol	Crew Size	Man-hours per Unit	Crew Output per Day	Avg Mat'l Unit Cost	Avg Labor Unit Cost	Avg Equip Unit Cost	Avg Total Unit Cost	Avg Price Incl O&P
Bridging, "X" type											
For joists 12" oc											
1" x 3"	Demo	Set	Lg	1L	.015	550.0	---	.45	---	.45	**.63**
	Demo	Set	Sm	1L	.017	467.5	---	.51	---	.51	**.71**
1" x 3"	Inst	Set	Lg	CA	.057	140.0	1.90	2.11	.56	4.57	**5.70**
	Inst	Set	Sm	CA	.067	119.0	2.06	2.48	.66	5.20	**6.50**
2" x 2"	Demo	Set	Lg	1L	.015	536.0	---	.45	---	.45	**.63**
	Demo	Set	Sm	1L	.018	455.6	---	.54	---	.54	**.76**
2" x 2"	Inst	Set	Lg	CA	.058	139.0	.74	2.15	.56	3.45	**4.42**
	Inst	Set	Sm	CA	.068	118.2	.81	2.52	.66	3.99	**5.12**
For joists 16" oc											
1" x 3"	Demo	Set	Lg	1L	.015	530.0	---	.45	---	.45	**.63**
	Demo	Set	Sm	1L	.018	450.5	---	.54	---	.54	**.76**
1" x 3"	Inst	Set	Lg	CA	.058	137.0	2.05	2.15	.57	4.77	**5.93**
	Inst	Set	Sm	CA	.069	116.5	2.23	2.55	.67	5.45	**6.81**
2" x 2"	Demo	Set	Lg	1L	.016	515.0	---	.48	---	.48	**.67**
	Demo	Set	Sm	1L	.018	437.8	---	.54	---	.54	**.76**
2" x 2"	Inst	Set	Lg	CA	.059	136.0	.78	2.18	.57	3.53	**4.52**
	Inst	Set	Sm	CA	.069	115.6	.86	2.55	.67	4.08	**5.24**
For joists 24" oc											
1" x 3"	Demo	Set	Lg	1L	.016	507.0	---	.48	---	.48	**.67**
	Demo	Set	Sm	1L	.019	431.0	---	.57	---	.57	**.80**
1" x 3"	Inst	Set	Lg	CA	.016	492.0	2.30	.59	.16	3.05	**3.63**
	Inst	Set	Sm	CA	.019	418.2	2.50	.70	.19	3.39	**4.05**
2" x 2"	Demo	Set	Lg	1L	.060	134.0	---	1.80	---	1.80	**2.52**
	Demo	Set	Sm	1L	.070	113.9	---	2.10	---	2.10	**2.94**
2" x 2"	Inst	Set	Lg	CA	.060	133.0	.87	2.22	.59	3.68	**4.70**
	Inst	Set	Sm	CA	.071	113.1	.96	2.63	.69	4.28	**5.47**
Bridging, solid, between joists											
2" x 6" - 12"	Demo	Set	Lg	1L	.014	590.0	---	.42	---	.42	**.59**
	Demo	Set	Sm	1L	.016	501.5	---	.48	---	.48	**.67**
2" x 6" - 12"	Inst	Set	Lg	CA	.040	199.0	.72	1.48	.39	2.59	**3.29**
	Inst	Set	Sm	CA	.047	169.2	.78	1.74	.46	2.98	**3.79**
2" x 8" - 12"	Demo	Set	Lg	1L	.015	517.0	---	.45	---	.45	**.63**
	Demo	Set	Sm	1L	.018	439.5	---	.54	---	.54	**.76**
2" x 8" - 12"	Inst	Set	Lg	CA	.043	185.0	.93	1.59	.42	2.94	**3.72**
	Inst	Set	Sm	CA	.051	157.3	1.02	1.89	.50	3.41	**4.32**
2" x 10" - 12"	Demo	Set	Lg	1L	.018	455.0	---	.54	---	.54	**.76**
	Demo	Set	Sm	1L	.021	386.8	---	.63	---	.63	**.88**
2" x 10" - 12"	Inst	Set	Lg	CA	.046	174.0	1.28	1.70	.45	3.43	**4.31**
	Inst	Set	Sm	CA	.054	147.9	1.39	2.00	.53	3.92	**4.93**

Description	Oper	Unit	Vol	Crew Size	Man-hours per Unit	Crew Output per Day	Avg Mat'l Unit Cost	Avg Labor Unit Cost	Avg Equip Unit Cost	Avg Total Unit Cost	Avg Price Incl O&P
2" x 12" - 12"	Demo	Set	Lg	1L	.019	412.0	---	.57	---	.57	.80
	Demo	Set	Sm	1L	.023	350.2	---	.69	---	.69	.97
2" x 12" - 12"	Inst	Set	Lg	CA	.049	164.0	1.49	1.81	.48	3.78	4.73
	Inst	Set	Sm	CA	.057	139.4	1.62	2.11	.56	4.29	5.38
2" x 6" - 16"	Demo	Set	Lg	1L	.013	628.0	---	.39	---	.39	.55
	Demo	Set	Sm	1L	.015	533.8	---	.45	---	.45	.63
2" x 6" - 16"	Inst	Set	Lg	CA	.033	243.0	.72	1.22	.32	2.26	2.86
	Inst	Set	Sm	CA	.039	206.6	.78	1.44	.38	2.60	3.30
2" x 8" - 16"	Demo	Set	Lg	1L	.015	548.0	---	.45	---	.45	.63
	Demo	Set	Sm	1L	.017	465.8	---	.51	---	.51	.71
2" x 8" - 16"	Inst	Set	Lg	CA	.035	226.0	.93	1.30	.35	2.58	3.23
	Inst	Set	Sm	CA	.042	192.1	1.02	1.55	.41	2.98	3.76
2" x 10" - 16"	Demo	Set	Lg	1L	.017	481.0	---	.51	---	.51	.71
	Demo	Set	Sm	1L	.020	408.9	---	.60	---	.60	.84
2" x 10" - 16"	Inst	Set	Lg	CA	.038	211.0	1.28	1.41	.37	3.06	3.81
	Inst	Set	Sm	CA	.045	179.4	1.39	1.67	.43	3.49	4.36
2" x 12" - 16"	Demo	Set	Lg	1L	.018	434.0	---	.54	---	.54	.76
	Demo	Set	Sm	1L	.022	368.9	---	.66	---	.66	.92
2" x 12" - 16"	Inst	Set	Lg	CA	.040	198.0	1.49	1.48	.39	3.36	4.18
	Inst	Set	Sm	CA	.048	168.3	1.62	1.78	.46	3.86	4.81
2" x 6" - 24"	Demo	Set	Lg	1L	.012	664.0	---	.36	---	.36	.50
	Demo	Set	Sm	1L	.014	564.4	---	.42	---	.42	.59
2" x 6" - 24"	Inst	Set	Lg	CA	.026	312.0	.72	.96	.25	1.93	2.43
	Inst	Set	Sm	CA	.030	265.2	.78	1.11	.29	2.18	2.74
2" x 8" - 24"	Demo	Set	Lg	1L	.014	577.0	---	.42	---	.42	.59
	Demo	Set	Sm	1L	.016	490.5	---	.48	---	.48	.67
2" x 8" - 24"	Inst	Set	Lg	CA	.028	289.0	.93	1.04	.27	2.24	2.79
	Inst	Set	Sm	CA	.033	245.7	1.02	1.22	.32	2.56	3.20
2" x 10" - 24"	Demo	Set	Lg	1L	.016	504.0	---	.48	---	.48	.67
	Demo	Set	Sm	1L	.019	428.4	---	.57	---	.57	.80
2" x 10" - 24"	Inst	Set	Lg	CA	.030	270.0	1.28	1.11	.29	2.68	3.32
	Inst	Set	Sm	CA	.035	229.5	1.39	1.30	.34	3.03	3.75
2" x 12" - 24"	Demo	Set	Lg	1L	.018	453.0	---	.54	---	.54	.76
	Demo	Set	Sm	1L	.021	385.1	---	.63	---	.63	.88
2" x 12" - 24"	Inst	Set	Lg	CA	.032	252.0	1.49	1.18	.31	2.98	3.68
	Inst	Set	Sm	CA	.037	214.2	1.62	1.37	.36	3.35	4.14

Description	Oper	Unit	Vol	Crew Size	Man-hours per Unit	Crew Output per Day	Avg Mat'l Unit Cost	Avg Labor Unit Cost	Avg Equip Unit Cost	Avg Total Unit Cost	Avg Price Incl O&P
Columns or posts, without base or cap, hardware, or chamfer corners											
4" x 4" - 8'	Demo	LF	Lg	LB	.027	584.0	---	.81	---	.81	1.13
	Demo	LF	Sm	LB	.032	496.4	---	.96	---	.96	1.34
4" x 4" - 8'	Inst	LF	Lg	2C	.051	315.0	1.25	1.89	.25	3.39	4.33
	Inst	LF	Sm	2C	.060	267.8	1.35	2.22	.29	3.86	4.95
4" x 6" - 8'	Demo	LF	Lg	LB	.030	529.0	---	.90	---	.90	1.26
	Demo	LF	Sm	LB	.036	449.7	---	1.08	---	1.08	1.51
4" x 6" - 8'	Inst	LF	Lg	2C	.054	294.0	1.99	2.00	.27	4.26	5.36
	Inst	LF	Sm	2C	.064	249.9	2.17	2.37	.31	4.85	6.12
4" x 8" - 8'	Demo	LF	Lg	LB	.033	479.0	---	.99	---	.99	1.39
	Demo	LF	Sm	LB	.039	407.2	---	1.17	---	1.17	1.64
4" x 8" - 8'	Inst	LF	Lg	2C	.058	274.0	3.20	2.15	.28	5.63	6.97
	Inst	LF	Sm	2C	.069	232.9	3.50	2.55	.33	6.38	7.93
6" x 6" - 8'	Demo	LF	Lg	LB	.037	432.0	---	1.11	---	1.11	1.55
	Demo	LF	Sm	LB	.044	367.2	---	1.32	---	1.32	1.85
6" x 6" - 8'	Inst	LF	Lg	2C	.065	248.0	4.03	2.41	.31	6.75	8.31
	Inst	LF	Sm	2C	.076	210.8	4.39	2.81	.37	7.57	9.36
6" x 8" - 8'	Demo	LF	Lg	LB	.042	385.0	---	1.26	---	1.26	1.76
	Demo	LF	Sm	LB	.049	327.3	---	1.47	---	1.47	2.06
6" x 8" - 8'	Inst	LF	Lg	2C	.070	229.0	5.84	2.59	.34	8.77	10.70
	Inst	LF	Sm	2C	.082	194.7	6.37	3.04	.40	9.81	12.00
6" x 10" - 8'	Demo	LF	Lg	LB	.046	345.0	---	1.38	---	1.38	1.93
	Demo	LF	Sm	LB	.055	293.3	---	1.65	---	1.65	2.31
6" x 10" - 8'	Inst	LF	Lg	2C	.075	212.0	7.29	2.78	.37	10.44	12.60
	Inst	LF	Sm	2C	.089	180.2	7.96	3.29	.43	11.68	14.20
8" x 8" - 8'	Demo	LF	Lg	LB	.050	319.0	---	1.50	---	1.50	2.10
	Demo	LF	Sm	LB	.059	271.2	---	1.77	---	1.77	2.48
8" x 8" - 8'	Inst	LF	Lg	2C	.082	196.0	11.60	3.04	.40	15.04	18.00
	Inst	LF	Sm	2C	.096	166.6	12.70	3.55	.47	16.72	20.10
8" x 10" - 8'	Demo	LF	Lg	LB	.059	269.0	---	1.77	---	1.77	2.48
	Demo	LF	Sm	LB	.070	228.7	---	2.10	---	2.10	2.94
8" x 10" - 8'	Inst	LF	Lg	2C	.092	174.0	14.60	3.41	.45	18.46	22.00
	Inst	LF	Sm	2C	.108	147.9	15.90	4.00	.53	20.43	24.40
Fascia											
1" x 4" - 12'	Demo	LF	Lg	LB	.012	1315	---	.36	---	.36	.50
	Demo	LF	Sm	LB	.014	1118	---	.42	---	.42	.59
1" x 4" - 12'	Inst	LF	Lg	2C	.041	386.0	.71	1.52	.20	2.43	3.14
	Inst	LF	Sm	2C	.049	328.1	.77	1.81	.24	2.82	3.67
Furring strips on ceilings											
1" x 3" on wood	Demo	LF	Lg	LB	.026	625.0	---	.78	---	.78	1.09
	Demo	LF	Sm	LB	.030	531.3	---	.90	---	.90	1.26
1" x 3" on wood	Inst	LF	Lg	2C	.028	574.0	.64	1.04	.14	1.82	2.33
	Inst	LF	Sm	2C	.033	487.9	.70	1.22	.16	2.08	2.68

Description	Oper	Unit	Vol	Crew Size	Man-hours per Unit	Crew Output per Day	Avg Mat'l Unit Cost	Avg Labor Unit Cost	Avg Equip Unit Cost	Avg Total Unit Cost	Avg Price Incl O&P
Furring strips on walls											
1" x 3" on wood	Demo	LF	Lg	LB	.020	805.0	---	.60	---	.60	**.84**
	Demo	LF	Sm	LB	.023	684.3	---	.69	---	.69	**.97**
1" x 3" on wood	Inst	LF	Lg	2C	.022	741.0	.64	.81	.11	1.56	**1.99**
	Inst	LF	Sm	2C	.025	629.9	.70	.93	.12	1.75	**2.22**
1" x 3" on masonry	Demo	LF	Lg	LB	.026	625.0	---	.78	---	.78	**1.09**
	Demo	LF	Sm	LB	.030	531.3	---	.90	---	.90	**1.26**
1" x 3" on masonry	Inst	LF	Lg	2C	.028	574.0	.64	1.04	.14	1.82	**2.33**
	Inst	LF	Sm	2C	.033	487.9	.70	1.22	.16	2.08	**2.68**
1" x 3" on concrete	Demo	LF	Lg	LB	.035	456.0	---	1.05	---	1.05	**1.47**
	Demo	LF	Sm	LB	.041	387.6	---	1.23	---	1.23	**1.72**
1" x 3" on concrete	Inst	LF	Lg	2C	.038	418.0	.64	1.41	.19	2.24	**2.90**
	Inst	LF	Sm	2C	.045	355.3	.70	1.67	.22	2.59	**3.36**
Headers or lintels, over openings											
4 feet wide											
4" x 6"	Demo	LF	Lg	1L	.024	338.0	---	.72	---	.72	**1.01**
	Demo	LF	Sm	1L	.028	287.3	---	.84	---	.84	**1.18**
4" x 6"	Inst	LF	Lg	CA	.040	198.0	1.98	1.48	.39	3.85	**4.74**
	Inst	LF	Sm	CA	.048	168.3	2.16	1.78	.46	4.40	**5.43**
4" x 8"	Demo	LF	Lg	1L	.026	302.0	---	.78	---	.78	**1.09**
	Demo	LF	Sm	1L	.031	256.7	---	.93	---	.93	**1.30**
4" x 8"	Inst	LF	Lg	CA	.043	186.0	3.19	1.59	.42	5.20	**6.32**
	Inst	LF	Sm	CA	.051	158.1	3.49	1.89	.49	5.87	**7.15**
4" x 12"	Demo	LF	Lg	1L	.032	250.0	---	.96	---	.96	**1.34**
	Demo	LF	Sm	1L	.038	212.5	---	1.14	---	1.14	**1.60**
4" x 12"	Inst	LF	Lg	CA	.049	164.0	4.64	1.81	.48	6.93	**8.36**
	Inst	LF	Sm	CA	.057	139.4	5.04	2.11	.56	7.71	**9.31**
4" x 14"	Demo	LF	Lg	1L	.034	236.0	---	1.02	---	1.02	**1.43**
	Demo	LF	Sm	1L	.040	200.6	---	1.20	---	1.20	**1.68**
4" x 14"	Inst	LF	Lg	CA	.051	158.0	5.67	1.89	.49	8.05	**9.65**
	Inst	LF	Sm	CA	.060	134.3	6.19	2.22	.58	8.99	**10.80**
6 feet wide											
4" x 12"	Demo	LF	Lg	LB	.027	583.0	---	.81	---	.81	**1.13**
	Demo	LF	Sm	LB	.032	495.6	---	.96	---	.96	**1.34**
4" x 12"	Inst	LF	Lg	2C	.041	392.0	4.64	1.52	.20	6.36	**7.66**
	Inst	LF	Sm	2C	.048	333.2	5.04	1.78	.23	7.05	**8.51**
8 feet wide											
4" x 12"	Demo	LF	Lg	LB	.024	655.0	---	.72	---	.72	**1.01**
	Demo	LF	Sm	LB	.029	556.8	---	.87	---	.87	**1.22**
4" x 12"	Inst	LF	Lg	2C	.035	453.0	4.64	1.30	.17	6.11	**7.32**
	Inst	LF	Sm	2C	.042	385.1	5.04	1.55	.20	6.79	**8.17**

Description	Oper	Unit	Vol	Crew Size	Man-hours per Unit	Crew Output per Day	Avg Mat'l Unit Cost	Avg Labor Unit Cost	Avg Equip Unit Cost	Avg Total Unit Cost	Avg Price Incl O&P
10 feet wide											
4" x 12"	Demo	LF	Lg	LB	.022	743.0	---	.66	---	.66	.92
	Demo	LF	Sm	LB	.025	631.6	---	.75	---	.75	1.05
4" x 12"	Inst	LF	Lg	2C	.030	535.0	4.64	1.11	.15	5.90	7.04
	Inst	LF	Sm	2C	.035	454.8	5.04	1.30	.17	6.51	7.78
4" x 14"	Demo	LF	Lg	LB	.026	627.0	---	.78	---	.78	1.09
	Demo	LF	Sm	LB	.030	533.0	---	.90	---	.90	1.26
4" x 14"	Inst	LF	Lg	2C	.035	455.0	5.67	1.30	.17	7.14	8.50
	Inst	LF	Sm	2C	.041	386.8	6.19	1.52	.20	7.91	9.44
12 feet wide											
4" x 14"	Demo	LF	Lg	LB	.024	667.0	---	.72	---	.72	1.01
	Demo	LF	Sm	LB	.028	567.0	---	.84	---	.84	1.18
4" x 14"	Inst	LF	Lg	2C	.033	491.0	5.67	1.22	.16	7.05	8.39
	Inst	LF	Sm	2C	.038	417.4	6.19	1.41	.19	7.79	9.28
4" x 16"	Demo	LF	Lg	LB	.028	562.0	---	.84	---	.84	1.18
	Demo	LF	Sm	LB	.033	477.7	---	.99	---	.99	1.39
4" x 16"	Inst	LF	Lg	2C	.037	429.0	6.47	1.37	.18	8.02	9.54
	Inst	LF	Sm	2C	.044	364.7	7.06	1.63	.21	8.90	10.60
14 feet wide											
4" x 16"	Demo	LF	Lg	LB	.027	588.0	---	.81	---	.81	1.13
	Demo	LF	Sm	LB	.032	499.8	---	.96	---	.96	1.34
4" x 16"	Inst	LF	Lg	2C	.035	453.0	6.47	1.30	.17	7.94	9.42
	Inst	LF	Sm	2C	.042	385.1	7.06	1.55	.20	8.81	10.50
16 feet wide											
4" x 16"	Demo	LF	Lg	LB	.026	611.0	---	.78	---	.78	1.09
	Demo	LF	Sm	LB	.031	519.4	---	.93	---	.93	1.30
4" x 16"	Inst	LF	Lg	2C	.034	475.0	6.47	1.26	.16	7.89	9.36
	Inst	LF	Sm	2C	.040	403.8	7.06	1.48	.19	8.73	10.40
18 feet wide											
4" x 16"	Demo	LF	Lg	LB	.025	632.0	---	.75	---	.75	1.05
	Demo	LF	Sm	LB	.030	537.2	---	.90	---	.90	1.26
4" x 16"	Inst	LF	Lg	2C	.032	495.0	6.47	1.18	.16	7.81	9.26
	Inst	LF	Sm	2C	.038	420.8	7.06	1.41	.19	8.66	10.30

Joists, ceiling/floor, per LF of stick

Description	Oper	Unit	Vol	Crew Size	Man-hours per Unit	Crew Output per Day	Avg Mat'l Unit Cost	Avg Labor Unit Cost	Avg Equip Unit Cost	Avg Total Unit Cost	Avg Price Incl O&P
2" x 4" - 6'	Demo	LF	Lg	LB	.016	1024	---	.48	---	.48	.67
	Demo	LF	Sm	LB	.018	870.4	---	.54	---	.54	.76
2" x 4" - 6'	Inst	LF	Lg	2C	.019	844.0	.46	.70	.09	1.25	1.60
	Inst	LF	Sm	2C	.022	717.4	.51	.81	.11	1.43	1.84
2" x 4" - 8'	Demo	LF	Lg	LB	.013	1213	---	.39	---	.39	.55
	Demo	LF	Sm	LB	.016	1031	---	.48	---	.48	.67
2" x 4" - 8'	Inst	LF	Lg	2C	.016	1004	.46	.59	.08	1.13	1.44
	Inst	LF	Sm	2C	.019	853.4	.51	.70	.09	1.30	1.66

Description	Oper	Unit	Vol	Crew Size	Man-hours per Unit	Crew Output per Day	Avg Mat'l Unit Cost	Avg Labor Unit Cost	Avg Equip Unit Cost	Avg Total Unit Cost	Avg Price Incl O&P
2" x 4" - 10'	Demo	LF	Lg	LB	.012	1367	---	.36	---	.36	.50
	Demo	LF	Sm	LB	.014	1162	---	.42	---	.42	.59
2" x 4" - 10'	Inst	LF	Lg	2C	.014	1134	.46	.52	.07	1.05	1.32
	Inst	LF	Sm	2C	.017	963.9	.51	.63	.08	1.22	1.55
2" x 4" - 12'	Demo	LF	Lg	LB	.011	1498	---	.33	---	.33	.46
	Demo	LF	Sm	LB	.013	1273	---	.39	---	.39	.55
2" x 4" - 12'	Inst	LF	Lg	2C	.013	1245	.46	.48	.06	1.00	1.26
	Inst	LF	Sm	2C	.015	1058	.51	.56	.07	1.14	1.43
2" x 6" - 8'	Demo	LF	Lg	LB	.015	1064	---	.45	---	.45	.63
	Demo	LF	Sm	LB	.018	904.4	---	.54	---	.54	.76
2" x 6" - 8'	Inst	LF	Lg	2C	.018	891.0	.72	.67	.09	1.48	1.85
	Inst	LF	Sm	2C	.021	757.4	.78	.78	.10	1.66	2.09
2" x 6" - 10'	Demo	LF	Lg	LB	.013	1195	---	.39	---	.39	.55
	Demo	LF	Sm	LB	.016	1016	---	.48	---	.48	.67
2" x 6" - 10'	Inst	LF	Lg	2C	.016	1005	.72	.59	.08	1.39	1.74
	Inst	LF	Sm	2C	.019	854.3	.78	.70	.09	1.57	1.97
2" x 6" - 12'	Demo	LF	Lg	LB	.012	1307	---	.36	---	.36	.50
	Demo	LF	Sm	LB	.014	1111	---	.42	---	.42	.59
2" x 6" - 12'	Inst	LF	Lg	2C	.015	1102	.72	.56	.07	1.35	1.68
	Inst	LF	Sm	2C	.017	936.7	.78	.63	.08	1.49	1.86
2" x 6" - 14'	Demo	LF	Lg	LB	.011	1405	---	.33	---	.33	.46
	Demo	LF	Sm	LB	.013	1194	---	.39	---	.39	.55
2" x 6" - 14'	Inst	LF	Lg	2C	.013	1187	.72	.48	.07	1.27	1.57
	Inst	LF	Sm	2C	.016	1009	.78	.59	.08	1.45	1.81
2" x 8" - 10'	Demo	LF	Lg	LB	.015	1060	---	.45	---	.45	.63
	Demo	LF	Sm	LB	.018	901.0	---	.54	---	.54	.76
2" x 8" - 10'	Inst	LF	Lg	2C	.018	901.0	.93	.67	.09	1.69	2.09
	Inst	LF	Sm	2C	.021	765.9	1.02	.78	.10	1.90	2.36
2" x 8" - 12'	Demo	LF	Lg	LB	.014	1156	---	.42	---	.42	.59
	Demo	LF	Sm	LB	.016	982.6	---	.48	---	.48	.67
2" x 8" - 12'	Inst	LF	Lg	2C	.016	986.0	.93	.59	.08	1.60	1.98
	Inst	LF	Sm	2C	.019	838.1	1.02	.70	.09	1.81	2.25
2" x 8" - 14'	Demo	LF	Lg	LB	.013	1239	---	.39	---	.39	.55
	Demo	LF	Sm	LB	.015	1053	---	.45	---	.45	.63
2" x 8" - 14'	Inst	LF	Lg	2C	.015	1059	.93	.56	.07	1.56	1.92
	Inst	LF	Sm	2C	.018	900.2	1.02	.67	.09	1.78	2.20
2" x 8" - 16'	Demo	LF	Lg	LB	.012	1313	---	.36	---	.36	.50
	Demo	LF	Sm	LB	.014	1116	---	.42	---	.42	.59
2" x 8" - 16'	Inst	LF	Lg	2C	.014	1124	.93	.52	.07	1.52	1.87
	Inst	LF	Sm	2C	.017	955.4	1.02	.63	.08	1.73	2.13

Description	Oper	Unit	Vol	Crew Size	Man-hours per Unit	Crew Output per Day	Avg Mat'l Unit Cost	Avg Labor Unit Cost	Avg Equip Unit Cost	Avg Total Unit Cost	Avg Price Incl O&P
2" x 10" - 12'	Demo	LF	Lg	LB	.015	1034	---	.45	---	.45	**.63**
	Demo	LF	Sm	LB	.018	878.9	---	.54	---	.54	**.76**
2" x 10" - 12'	Inst	LF	Lg	2C	.018	890.0	1.28	.67	.09	2.04	**2.49**
	Inst	LF	Sm	2C	.021	756.5	1.39	.78	.10	2.27	**2.79**
2" x 10" - 14'	Demo	LF	Lg	LB	.014	1106	---	.42	---	.42	**.59**
	Demo	LF	Sm	LB	.017	940.1	---	.51	---	.51	**.71**
2" x 10" - 14'	Inst	LF	Lg	2C	.017	955.0	1.28	.63	.08	1.99	**2.43**
	Inst	LF	Sm	2C	.020	811.8	1.39	.74	.10	2.23	**2.74**
2" x 10" - 16'	Demo	LF	Lg	LB	.014	1171	---	.42	---	.42	**.59**
	Demo	LF	Sm	LB	.016	995.4	---	.48	---	.48	**.67**
2" x 10" - 16'	Inst	LF	Lg	2C	.016	1013	1.28	.59	.08	1.95	**2.38**
	Inst	LF	Sm	2C	.019	861.1	1.39	.70	.09	2.18	**2.67**
2" x 10" - 18'	Demo	LF	Lg	LB	.013	1229	---	.39	---	.39	**.55**
	Demo	LF	Sm	LB	.015	1045	---	.45	---	.45	**.63**
2" x 10" - 18'	Inst	LF	Lg	2C	.015	1065	1.28	.56	.07	1.91	**2.32**
	Inst	LF	Sm	2C	.018	905.3	1.39	.67	.09	2.15	**2.62**
2" x 12" - 14'	Demo	LF	Lg	LB	.016	998.0	---	.48	---	.48	**.67**
	Demo	LF	Sm	LB	.019	848.3	---	.57	---	.57	**.80**
2" x 12" - 14'	Inst	LF	Lg	2C	.018	869.0	1.49	.67	.09	2.25	**2.74**
	Inst	LF	Sm	2C	.022	738.7	1.62	.81	.11	2.54	**3.11**
2" x 12" - 16'	Demo	LF	Lg	LB	.015	1054	---	.45	---	.45	**.63**
	Demo	LF	Sm	LB	.018	895.9	---	.54	---	.54	**.76**
2" x 12" - 16'	Inst	LF	Lg	2C	.017	920.0	1.49	.63	.08	2.20	**2.67**
	Inst	LF	Sm	2C	.020	782.0	1.62	.74	.10	2.46	**3.00**
2" x 12" - 18'	Demo	LF	Lg	LB	.014	1106	---	.42	---	.42	**.59**
	Demo	LF	Sm	LB	.017	940.1	---	.51	---	.51	**.71**
2" x 12" - 18'	Inst	LF	Lg	2C	.017	967.0	1.49	.63	.08	2.20	**2.67**
	Inst	LF	Sm	2C	.019	822.0	1.62	.70	.09	2.41	**2.94**
2" x 12" - 20'	Demo	LF	Lg	LB	.014	1151	---	.42	---	.42	**.59**
	Demo	LF	Sm	LB	.016	978.4	---	.48	---	.48	**.67**
2" x 12" - 20'	Inst	LF	Lg	2C	.016	1009	1.49	.59	.08	2.16	**2.62**
	Inst	LF	Sm	2C	.019	857.7	1.62	.70	.09	2.41	**2.94**
3" x 8" - 12'	Demo	LF	Lg	LB	.017	942.0	---	.51	---	.51	**.71**
	Demo	LF	Sm	LB	.020	800.7	---	.60	---	.60	**.84**
3" x 8" - 12'	Inst	LF	Lg	2C	.020	816.0	2.39	.74	.10	3.23	**3.89**
	Inst	LF	Sm	2C	.023	693.6	2.61	.85	.11	3.57	**4.30**
3" x 8" - 14'	Demo	LF	Lg	LB	.016	1007	---	.48	---	.48	**.67**
	Demo	LF	Sm	LB	.019	856.0	---	.57	---	.57	**.80**
3" x 8" - 14'	Inst	LF	Lg	2C	.018	876.0	2.39	.67	.09	3.15	**3.77**
	Inst	LF	Sm	2C	.021	744.6	2.61	.78	.10	3.49	**4.19**
3" x 8" - 16'	Demo	LF	Lg	LB	.015	1065	---	.45	---	.45	**.63**
	Demo	LF	Sm	LB	.018	905.3	---	.54	---	.54	**.76**
3" x 8" - 16'	Inst	LF	Lg	2C	.017	929.0	2.39	.63	.08	3.10	**3.71**
	Inst	LF	Sm	2C	.020	789.7	2.61	.74	.10	3.45	**4.14**

Description	Oper	Unit	Vol	Crew Size	Man-hours per Unit	Crew Output per Day	Avg Mat'l Unit Cost	Avg Labor Unit Cost	Avg Equip Unit Cost	Avg Total Unit Cost	Avg Price Incl O&P
3" x 8" - 18'	Demo	LF	Lg	LB	.014	1117	---	.42	---	.42	.59
	Demo	LF	Sm	LB	.017	949.5	---	.51	---	.51	.71
3" x 8" - 18'	Inst	LF	Lg	2C	.016	976.0	2.39	.59	.08	3.06	3.66
	Inst	LF	Sm	2C	.019	829.6	2.61	.70	.09	3.40	4.08
3" x 10" - 16'	Demo	LF	Lg	LB	.017	918.0	---	.51	---	.51	.71
	Demo	LF	Sm	LB	.021	780.3	---	.63	---	.63	.88
3" x 10" - 16'	Inst	LF	Lg	2C	.020	811.0	2.98	.74	.10	3.82	4.56
	Inst	LF	Sm	2C	.023	689.4	3.23	.85	.11	4.19	5.02
3" x 10" - 18'	Demo	LF	Lg	LB	.017	961.0	---	.51	---	.51	.71
	Demo	LF	Sm	LB	.020	816.9	---	.60	---	.60	.84
3" x 10" - 18'	Inst	LF	Lg	2C	.019	851.0	2.98	.70	.09	3.77	4.50
	Inst	LF	Sm	2C	.022	723.4	3.23	.81	.11	4.15	4.96
3" x 10" - 20'	Demo	LF	Lg	LB	.016	1001	---	.48	---	.48	.67
	Demo	LF	Sm	LB	.019	850.9	---	.57	---	.57	.80
3" x 10" - 20'	Inst	LF	Lg	2C	.018	888.0	2.98	.67	.09	3.74	4.45
	Inst	LF	Sm	2C	.021	754.8	3.23	.78	.10	4.11	4.90
3" x 12" - 16'	Demo	LF	Lg	LB	.019	821.0	---	.57	---	.57	.80
	Demo	LF	Sm	LB	.023	697.9	---	.69	---	.69	.97
3" x 12" - 16'	Inst	LF	Lg	2C	.022	732.0	2.90	.81	.11	3.82	4.59
	Inst	LF	Sm	2C	.026	622.2	3.15	.96	.13	4.24	5.10
3" x 12" - 18'	Demo	LF	Lg	LB	.018	873.0	---	.54	---	.54	.76
	Demo	LF	Sm	LB	.022	742.1	---	.66	---	.66	.92
3" x 12" - 18'	Inst	LF	Lg	2C	.020	781.0	3.48	.74	.10	4.32	5.14
	Inst	LF	Sm	2C	.024	663.9	3.77	.89	.12	4.78	5.70
3" x 12" - 20'	Demo	LF	Lg	LB	.018	898.0	---	.54	---	.54	.76
	Demo	LF	Sm	LB	.021	763.3	---	.63	---	.63	.88
3" x 12" - 20'	Inst	LF	Lg	2C	.020	805.0	3.48	.74	.10	4.32	5.14
	Inst	LF	Sm	2C	.023	684.3	3.77	.85	.11	4.73	5.64
3" x 12" - 22'	Demo	LF	Lg	LB	.017	925.0	---	.51	---	.51	.71
	Demo	LF	Sm	LB	.020	786.3	---	.60	---	.60	.84
3" x 12" - 22'	Inst	LF	Lg	2C	.019	830.0	3.48	.70	.09	4.27	5.08
	Inst	LF	Sm	2C	.023	705.5	3.77	.85	.11	4.73	5.64

Joists, ceiling/floor, per SF of area

Description	Oper	Unit	Vol	Crew Size	Man-hours per Unit	Crew Output per Day	Avg Mat'l Unit Cost	Avg Labor Unit Cost	Avg Equip Unit Cost	Avg Total Unit Cost	Avg Price Incl O&P
2" x 4" - 6', 12" oc	Demo	SF	Lg	LB	.016	998.0	---	.48	---	.48	.67
	Demo	SF	Sm	LB	.019	848.3	---	.57	---	.57	.80
2" x 4" - 6', 12" oc	Inst	SF	Lg	2C	.019	823.0	.47	.70	.09	1.26	1.62
	Inst	SF	Sm	2C	.023	699.6	.52	.85	.11	1.48	1.90
2" x 4" - 6', 16" oc	Demo	SF	Lg	LB	.013	1188	---	.39	---	.39	.55
	Demo	SF	Sm	LB	.016	1010	---	.48	---	.48	.67
2" x 4" - 6', 16" oc	Inst	SF	Lg	2C	.016	979.0	.36	.59	.08	1.03	1.32
	Inst	SF	Sm	2C	.019	832.2	.40	.70	.09	1.19	1.53

Description	Oper	Unit	Vol	Crew Size	Man-hours per Unit	Crew Output per Day	Avg Mat'l Unit Cost	Avg Labor Unit Cost	Avg Equip Unit Cost	Avg Total Unit Cost	Avg Price Incl O&P
2" x 4" - 6', 24" oc	Demo	SF	Lg	LB	.010	1559	---	.30	---	.30	.42
	Demo	SF	Sm	LB	.012	1325	---	.36	---	.36	.50
2" x 4" - 6', 24" oc	Inst	SF	Lg	2C	.012	1285	.25	.44	.06	.75	.97
	Inst	SF	Sm	2C	.015	1092	.27	.56	.07	.90	1.16
2" x 6" - 8', 12" oc	Demo	SF	Lg	LB	.015	1037	---	.45	---	.45	.63
	Demo	SF	Sm	LB	.018	881.5	---	.54	---	.54	.76
2" x 6" - 8', 12" oc	Inst	SF	Lg	2C	.018	869.0	.74	.67	.09	1.50	1.87
	Inst	SF	Sm	2C	.022	738.7	.81	.81	.11	1.73	2.18
2" x 6" - 8', 16" oc	Demo	SF	Lg	LB	.013	1235	---	.39	---	.39	.55
	Demo	SF	Sm	LB	.015	1050	---	.45	---	.45	.63
2" x 6" - 8', 16" oc	Inst	SF	Lg	2C	.015	1034	.56	.56	.08	1.20	1.50
	Inst	SF	Sm	2C	.018	878.9	.61	.67	.09	1.37	1.72
2" x 6" - 8', 24" oc	Demo	SF	Lg	LB	.010	1622	---	.30	---	.30	.42
	Demo	SF	Sm	LB	.012	1379	---	.36	---	.36	.50
2" x 6" - 8', 24" oc	Inst	SF	Lg	2C	.012	1359	.38	.44	.06	.88	1.12
	Inst	SF	Sm	2C	.014	1155	.42	.52	.07	1.01	1.28
2" x 8" - 10', 12" oc	Demo	SF	Lg	LB	.015	1033	---	.45	---	.45	.63
	Demo	SF	Sm	LB	.018	878.1	---	.54	---	.54	.76
2" x 8" - 10', 12" oc	Inst	SF	Lg	2C	.018	878.0	.96	.67	.09	1.72	2.13
	Inst	SF	Sm	2C	.021	746.3	1.05	.78	.10	1.93	2.40
2" x 8" - 10', 16" oc	Demo	SF	Lg	LB	.013	1231	---	.39	---	.39	.55
	Demo	SF	Sm	LB	.015	1046	---	.45	---	.45	.63
2" x 8" - 10', 16" oc	Inst	SF	Lg	2C	.015	1046	.72	.56	.07	1.35	1.68
	Inst	SF	Sm	2C	.018	889.1	.79	.67	.09	1.55	1.93
2" x 8" - 10', 24" oc	Demo	SF	Lg	LB	.010	1614	---	.30	---	.30	.42
	Demo	SF	Sm	LB	.012	1372	---	.36	---	.36	.50
2" x 8" - 10', 24" oc	Inst	SF	Lg	2C	.012	1372	.50	.44	.06	1.00	1.26
	Inst	SF	Sm	2C	.014	1166	.54	.52	.07	1.13	1.42
2" x 10" - 12', 12" oc	Demo	SF	Lg	LB	.016	1008	---	.48	---	.48	.67
	Demo	SF	Sm	LB	.019	856.8	---	.57	---	.57	.80
2" x 10" - 12', 12" oc	Inst	SF	Lg	2C	.018	868.0	1.31	.67	.09	2.07	2.53
	Inst	SF	Sm	2C	.022	737.8	1.42	.81	.11	2.34	2.88
2" x 10" - 12', 16" oc	Demo	SF	Lg	LB	.013	1200	---	.39	---	.39	.55
	Demo	SF	Sm	LB	.016	1020	---	.48	---	.48	.67
2" x 10" - 12', 16" oc	Inst	SF	Lg	2C	.015	1033	.99	.56	.08	1.63	2.00
	Inst	SF	Sm	2C	.018	878.1	1.08	.67	.09	1.84	2.26

Description	Oper	Unit	Vol	Crew Size	Man-hours per Unit	Crew Output per Day	Avg Mat'l Unit Cost	Avg Labor Unit Cost	Avg Equip Unit Cost	Avg Total Unit Cost	Avg Price Incl O&P
2" x 10" - 12', 24" oc	Demo	SF	Lg	LB	.010	1575	---	.30	---	.30	.42
	Demo	SF	Sm	LB	.012	1339	---	.36	---	.36	.50
2" x 10" - 12', 24" oc	Inst	SF	Lg	2C	.012	1356	.68	.44	.06	1.18	1.46
	Inst	SF	Sm	2C	.014	1153	.74	.52	.07	1.33	1.65
2" x 12" - 14', 12" oc	Demo	SF	Lg	LB	.016	974.0	---	.48	---	.48	.67
	Demo	SF	Sm	LB	.019	827.9	---	.57	---	.57	.80
2" x 12" - 14', 12" oc	Inst	SF	Lg	2C	.019	848.0	1.52	.70	.09	2.31	2.82
	Inst	SF	Sm	2C	.022	720.8	1.66	.81	.11	2.58	3.16
2" x 12" - 14', 16" oc	Demo	SF	Lg	LB	.014	1159	---	.42	---	.42	.59
	Demo	SF	Sm	LB	.016	985.2	---	.48	---	.48	.67
2" x 12" - 14', 16" oc	Inst	SF	Lg	2C	.016	1009	1.15	.59	.08	1.82	2.23
	Inst	SF	Sm	2C	.019	857.7	1.26	.70	.09	2.05	2.52
2" x 12" - 14', 24" oc	Demo	SF	Lg	LB	.011	1521	---	.33	---	.33	.46
	Demo	SF	Sm	LB	.012	1293	---	.36	---	.36	.50
2" x 12" - 14', 24" oc	Inst	SF	Lg	2C	.012	1324	.78	.44	.06	1.28	1.58
	Inst	SF	Sm	2C	.014	1125	.86	.52	.07	1.45	1.78
3" x 8" - 14', 12" oc	Demo	SF	Lg	LB	.016	983.0	---	.48	---	.48	.67
	Demo	SF	Sm	LB	.019	835.6	---	.57	---	.57	.80
3" x 8" - 14', 12" oc	Inst	SF	Lg	2C	.019	855.0	2.45	.70	.09	3.24	3.89
	Inst	SF	Sm	2C	.022	726.8	2.67	.81	.11	3.59	4.32
3" x 8" - 14', 16" oc	Demo	SF	Lg	LB	.014	1170	---	.42	---	.42	.59
	Demo	SF	Sm	LB	.016	994.5	---	.48	---	.48	.67
3" x 8" - 14', 16" oc	Inst	SF	Lg	2C	.016	1017	1.85	.59	.08	2.52	3.04
	Inst	SF	Sm	2C	.019	864.5	2.02	.70	.09	2.81	3.40
3" x 8" - 14', 24" oc	Demo	SF	Lg	LB	.010	1535	---	.30	---	.30	.42
	Demo	SF	Sm	LB	.012	1305	---	.36	---	.36	.50
3" x 8" - 14', 24" oc	Inst	SF	Lg	2C	.012	1335	1.26	.44	.06	1.76	2.13
	Inst	SF	Sm	2C	.014	1135	1.37	.52	.07	1.96	2.37
3" x 10" - 16', 12" oc	Demo	SF	Lg	LB	.018	896.0	---	.54	---	.54	.76
	Demo	SF	Sm	LB	.021	761.6	---	.63	---	.63	.88
3" x 10" - 16', 12" oc	Inst	SF	Lg	2C	.020	792.0	3.05	.74	.10	3.89	4.64
	Inst	SF	Sm	2C	.024	673.2	3.31	.89	.12	4.32	5.17
3" x 10" - 16', 16" oc	Demo	SF	Lg	LB	.015	1066	---	.45	---	.45	.63
	Demo	SF	Sm	LB	.018	906.1	---	.54	---	.54	.76
3" x 10" - 16', 16" oc	Inst	SF	Lg	2C	.017	943.0	2.32	.63	.08	3.03	3.63
	Inst	SF	Sm	2C	.020	801.6	2.51	.74	.10	3.35	4.02
3" x 10" - 16', 24" oc	Demo	SF	Lg	LB	.011	1399	---	.33	---	.33	.46
	Demo	SF	Sm	LB	.013	1189	---	.39	---	.39	.55
3" x 10" - 16', 24" oc	Inst	SF	Lg	2C	.013	1236	1.57	.48	.06	2.11	2.54
	Inst	SF	Sm	2C	.015	1051	1.70	.56	.07	2.33	2.80

Description	Oper	Unit	Vol	Crew Size	Man-hours per Unit	Crew Output per Day	Avg Mat'l Unit Cost	Avg Labor Unit Cost	Avg Equip Unit Cost	Avg Total Unit Cost	Avg Price Incl O&P
3" x 12" - 18', 12" oc	Demo	SF	Lg	LB	.019	851.0	---	.57	---	.57	.80
	Demo	SF	Sm	LB	.022	723.4	---	.66	---	.66	.92
3" x 12" - 18', 12" oc	Inst	SF	Lg	2C	.021	762.0	3.57	.78	.10	4.45	5.29
	Inst	SF	Sm	2C	.025	647.7	3.87	.93	.12	4.92	5.87
3" x 12" - 18', 16" oc	Demo	SF	Lg	LB	.016	1013	---	.48	---	.48	.67
	Demo	SF	Sm	LB	.019	861.1	---	.57	---	.57	.80
3" x 12" - 18', 16" oc	Inst	SF	Lg	2C	.018	907.0	2.70	.67	.09	3.46	4.13
	Inst	SF	Sm	2C	.021	771.0	2.93	.78	.10	3.81	4.56
3" x 12" - 18', 24" oc	Demo	SF	Lg	LB	.012	1330	---	.36	---	.36	.50
	Demo	SF	Sm	LB	.014	1131	---	.42	---	.42	.59
3" x 12" - 18', 24" oc	Inst	SF	Lg	2C	.013	1190	1.84	.48	.07	2.39	2.86
	Inst	SF	Sm	2C	.016	1012	1.99	.59	.08	2.66	3.20

Ledgers

Nailed

Description	Oper	Unit	Vol	Crew Size	Man-hours per Unit	Crew Output per Day	Avg Mat'l Unit Cost	Avg Labor Unit Cost	Avg Equip Unit Cost	Avg Total Unit Cost	Avg Price Incl O&P
2" x 4" - 12'	Demo	LF	Lg	LB	.013	1220	---	.39	---	.39	.55
	Demo	LF	Sm	LB	.015	1037	---	.45	---	.45	.63
2" x 4" - 12'	Inst	LF	Lg	2C	.019	857.0	.52	.70	.09	1.31	1.67
	Inst	LF	Sm	2C	.022	728.5	.57	.81	.11	1.49	1.91
2" x 6" - 12'	Demo	LF	Lg	LB	.015	1082	---	.45	---	.45	.63
	Demo	LF	Sm	LB	.017	919.7	---	.51	---	.51	.71
2" x 6" - 12'	Inst	LF	Lg	2C	.021	774.0	.77	.78	.10	1.65	2.07
	Inst	LF	Sm	2C	.024	657.9	.84	.89	.12	1.85	2.33
2" x 8" - 12'	Demo	LF	Lg	LB	.016	973.0	---	.48	---	.48	.67
	Demo	LF	Sm	LB	.019	827.1	---	.57	---	.57	.80
2" x 8" - 12'	Inst	LF	Lg	2C	.023	706.0	.99	.85	.11	1.95	2.44
	Inst	LF	Sm	2C	.027	600.1	1.08	1.00	.13	2.21	2.77

Bolted
Labor/material costs are for ledgers with pre-embedded bolts.
Labor costs include securing ledgers

Description	Oper	Unit	Vol	Crew Size	Man-hours per Unit	Crew Output per Day	Avg Mat'l Unit Cost	Avg Labor Unit Cost	Avg Equip Unit Cost	Avg Total Unit Cost	Avg Price Incl O&P
3" x 6" - 12'	Demo	LF	Lg	LB	.022	718.0	---	.66	---	.66	.92
	Demo	LF	Sm	LB	.026	610.3	---	.78	---	.78	1.09
3" x 6" - 12'	Inst	LF	Lg	2C	.031	513.0	1.47	1.15	.15	2.77	3.45
	Inst	LF	Sm	2C	.037	436.1	1.60	1.37	.18	3.15	3.94
3" x 8" - 12'	Demo	LF	Lg	LB	.024	654.0	---	.72	---	.72	1.01
	Demo	LF	Sm	LB	.029	555.9	---	.87	---	.87	1.22
3" x 8" - 12'	Inst	LF	Lg	2C	.034	475.0	2.38	1.26	.16	3.80	4.66
	Inst	LF	Sm	2C	.040	403.8	2.60	1.48	.19	4.27	5.25
3" x 10" - 12'	Demo	LF	Lg	LB	.027	593.0	---	.81	---	.81	1.13
	Demo	LF	Sm	LB	.032	504.1	---	.96	---	.96	1.34
3" x 10" - 12'	Inst	LF	Lg	2C	.037	438.0	2.97	1.37	.18	4.52	5.51
	Inst	LF	Sm	2C	.043	372.3	3.22	1.59	.21	5.02	6.14
3" x 12" - 12'	Demo	LF	Lg	LB	.029	547.0	---	.87	---	.87	1.22
	Demo	LF	Sm	LB	.034	465.0	---	1.02	---	1.02	1.43
3" x 12" - 12'	Inst	LF	Lg	2C	.039	408.0	3.47	1.44	.19	5.10	6.20
	Inst	LF	Sm	2C	.046	346.8	3.76	1.70	.22	5.68	6.93

Description	Oper	Unit	Vol	Crew Size	Man-hours per Unit	Crew Output per Day	Avg Mat'l Unit Cost	Avg Labor Unit Cost	Avg Equip Unit Cost	Avg Total Unit Cost	Avg Price Incl O&P

Patio framing

Wood deck: 4" x 4" rough sawn beams (4'-0" oc) leveled 1/16" to 1/8" and nailed to pre-set concrete piers with woodblock on top; 2" T x 4" W decking (S4S) with 1/2" spacing, double-nailed beam junctures

Description	Oper	Unit	Vol	Crew Size	Man-hours per Unit	Crew Output per Day	Avg Mat'l Unit Cost	Avg Labor Unit Cost	Avg Equip Unit Cost	Avg Total Unit Cost	Avg Price Incl O&P
Fir	Demo	SF	Lg	LB	.042	380.0	---	1.26	---	1.26	1.76
	Demo	SF	Sm	LB	.050	323.0	---	1.50	---	1.50	2.10
Fir	Inst	SF	Lg	CN	.061	330.0	4.62	2.17	.24	7.03	8.59
	Inst	SF	Sm	CN	.071	280.5	5.04	2.53	.28	7.85	9.62
Redwood	Demo	SF	Lg	LB	.042	380.0	---	1.26	---	1.26	1.76
	Demo	SF	Sm	LB	.050	323.0	---	1.50	---	1.50	2.10
Redwood	Inst	SF	Lg	CN	.061	330.0	6.93	2.17	.24	9.34	11.30
	Inst	SF	Sm	CN	.071	280.5	7.56	2.53	.28	10.37	12.50

Wood awning: 4" x 4" columns (10'-0" oc) nailed to wood; 2" x 6" beams nailed horizontally either side of columns; 2" x 6" ledger nailed to wall studs; 2" x 6" joists (4'-0" oc) nailed to ledger and toe-nailed on top of beams; 2" x 2" (4" oc) nailed to joists for sunscreen

Description	Oper	Unit	Vol	Crew Size	Man-hours per Unit	Crew Output per Day	Avg Mat'l Unit Cost	Avg Labor Unit Cost	Avg Equip Unit Cost	Avg Total Unit Cost	Avg Price Incl O&P
Redwood, rough sawn	Demo	SF	Lg	LB	.055	290.0	---	1.65	---	1.65	2.31
	Demo	SF	Sm	LB	.065	246.5	---	1.95	---	1.95	2.73
Redwood, rough sawn	Inst	SF	Lg	CS	.096	250.0	3.40	3.33	.31	7.04	8.88
	Inst	SF	Sm	CS	.113	212.5	3.70	3.92	.37	7.99	10.10

Plates; joined with studs before setting

Double top, nailed

Description	Oper	Unit	Vol	Crew Size	Man-hours per Unit	Crew Output per Day	Avg Mat'l Unit Cost	Avg Labor Unit Cost	Avg Equip Unit Cost	Avg Total Unit Cost	Avg Price Incl O&P
2" x 4" - 8'	Demo	LF	Lg	LB	.020	820.0	---	.60	---	.60	.84
	Demo	LF	Sm	LB	.023	697.0	---	.69	---	.69	.97
2" x 4" - 8'	Inst	LF	Lg	2C	.039	410.0	.96	1.44	.19	2.59	3.32
	Inst	LF	Sm	2C	.046	348.5	1.05	1.70	.22	2.97	3.81
2" x 6" - 8'	Demo	LF	Lg	LB	.020	820.0	---	.60	---	.60	.84
	Demo	LF	Sm	LB	.023	697.0	---	.69	---	.69	.97
2" x 6" - 8'	Inst	LF	Lg	2C	.039	410.0	1.44	1.44	.19	3.07	3.87
	Inst	LF	Sm	2C	.046	348.5	1.58	1.70	.22	3.50	4.42

Single bottom, nailed

Description	Oper	Unit	Vol	Crew Size	Man-hours per Unit	Crew Output per Day	Avg Mat'l Unit Cost	Avg Labor Unit Cost	Avg Equip Unit Cost	Avg Total Unit Cost	Avg Price Incl O&P
2" x 4" - 8'	Demo	LF	Lg	LB	.012	1360	---	.36	---	.36	.50
	Demo	LF	Sm	LB	.014	1156	---	.42	---	.42	.59
2" x 4" - 8'	Inst	LF	Lg	2C	.020	815.0	.47	.74	.10	1.31	1.68
	Inst	LF	Sm	2C	.023	692.8	.52	.85	.11	1.48	1.90
2" x 6" - 8'	Demo	LF	Lg	LB	.012	1360	---	.36	---	.36	.50
	Demo	LF	Sm	LB	.014	1156	---	.42	---	.42	.59
2" x 6" - 8'	Inst	LF	Lg	2C	.020	815.0	.72	.74	.10	1.56	1.96
	Inst	LF	Sm	2C	.023	692.8	.78	.85	.11	1.74	2.20

Sill or bottom, bolted. Labor/material costs are for plates with pre-embedded bolts.
Labor cost includes securing plates

Description	Oper	Unit	Vol	Crew Size	Man-hours per Unit	Crew Output per Day	Avg Mat'l Unit Cost	Avg Labor Unit Cost	Avg Equip Unit Cost	Avg Total Unit Cost	Avg Price Incl O&P
2" x 4" - 8'	Demo	LF	Lg	LB	.023	685.0	---	.69	---	.69	.97
	Demo	LF	Sm	LB	.027	582.3	---	.81	---	.81	1.13
2" x 4" - 8'	Inst	LF	Lg	2C	.029	560.0	.43	1.07	.14	1.64	2.14
	Inst	LF	Sm	2C	.034	476.0	.47	1.26	.16	1.89	2.46
2" x 6" - 8'	Demo	LF	Lg	LB	.023	685.0	---	.69	---	.69	.97
	Demo	LF	Sm	LB	.027	582.3	---	.81	---	.81	1.13
2" x 6" - 8'	Inst	LF	Lg	2C	.029	560.0	.67	1.07	.14	1.88	2.41
	Inst	LF	Sm	2C	.034	476.0	.74	1.26	.16	2.16	2.77

Description	Oper	Unit	Vol	Crew Size	Man-hours per Unit	Crew Output per Day	Avg Mat'l Unit Cost	Avg Labor Unit Cost	Avg Equip Unit Cost	Avg Total Unit Cost	Avg Price Incl O&P

Rafters, per LF of stick

Common, gable or hip, to 1/3 pitch

Description	Oper	Unit	Vol	Crew Size	Man-hours per Unit	Crew Output per Day	Avg Mat'l Unit Cost	Avg Labor Unit Cost	Avg Equip Unit Cost	Avg Total Unit Cost	Avg Price Incl O&P
2" x 4" - 8' Avg.	Demo	LF	Lg	LB	.022	744.0	---	.66	---	.66	.92
	Demo	LF	Sm	LB	.025	632.4	---	.75	---	.75	1.05
2" x 4" - 8' Avg.	Inst	LF	Lg	2C	.023	683.0	.46	.85	.11	1.42	1.83
	Inst	LF	Sm	2C	.028	580.6	.51	1.04	.13	1.68	2.17
2" x 4" - 10' Avg.	Demo	LF	Lg	LB	.019	861.0	---	.57	---	.57	.80
	Demo	LF	Sm	LB	.022	731.9	---	.66	---	.66	.92
2" x 4" - 10' Avg.	Inst	LF	Lg	2C	.020	793.0	.46	.74	.10	1.30	1.67
	Inst	LF	Sm	2C	.024	674.1	.51	.89	.12	1.52	1.95
2" x 4" - 12' Avg.	Demo	LF	Lg	LB	.017	963.0	---	.51	---	.51	.71
	Demo	LF	Sm	LB	.020	818.6	---	.60	---	.60	.84
2" x 4" - 12' Avg.	Inst	LF	Lg	2C	.018	887.0	.46	.67	.09	1.22	1.55
	Inst	LF	Sm	2C	.021	754.0	.51	.78	.10	1.39	1.77
2" x 4" - 14' Avg.	Demo	LF	Lg	LB	.015	1053	---	.45	---	.45	.63
	Demo	LF	Sm	LB	.018	895.1	---	.54	---	.54	.76
2" x 4" - 14' Avg.	Inst	LF	Lg	2C	.016	971.0	.46	.59	.08	1.13	1.44
	Inst	LF	Sm	2C	.019	825.4	.51	.70	.09	1.30	1.66
2" x 4" - 16' Avg.	Demo	LF	Lg	LB	.014	1134	---	.42	---	.42	.59
	Demo	LF	Sm	LB	.017	963.9	---	.51	---	.51	.71
2" x 4" - 16' Avg.	Inst	LF	Lg	2C	.015	1047	.46	.56	.07	1.09	1.38
	Inst	LF	Sm	2C	.018	890.0	.51	.67	.09	1.27	1.61
2" x 6" - 10' Avg.	Demo	LF	Lg	LB	.021	748.0	---	.63	---	.63	.88
	Demo	LF	Sm	LB	.025	635.8	---	.75	---	.75	1.05
2" x 6" - 10' Avg.	Inst	LF	Lg	2C	.023	691.0	.72	.85	.11	1.68	2.13
	Inst	LF	Sm	2C	.027	587.4	.78	1.00	.13	1.91	2.43
2" x 6" - 12' Avg.	Demo	LF	Lg	LB	.019	843.0	---	.57	---	.57	.80
	Demo	LF	Sm	LB	.022	716.6	---	.66	---	.66	.92
2" x 6" - 12' Avg.	Inst	LF	Lg	2C	.021	779.0	.72	.78	.10	1.60	2.02
	Inst	LF	Sm	2C	.024	662.2	.78	.89	.12	1.79	2.26
2" x 6" - 14' Avg.	Demo	LF	Lg	LB	.017	929.0	---	.51	---	.51	.71
	Demo	LF	Sm	LB	.020	789.7	---	.60	---	.60	.84
2" x 6" - 14' Avg.	Inst	LF	Lg	2C	.019	860.0	.72	.70	.09	1.51	1.90
	Inst	LF	Sm	2C	.022	731.0	.78	.81	.11	1.70	2.15
2" x 6" - 16' Avg.	Demo	LF	Lg	LB	.016	1008	---	.48	---	.48	.67
	Demo	LF	Sm	LB	.019	856.8	---	.57	---	.57	.80
2" x 6" - 16' Avg.	Inst	LF	Lg	2C	.017	933.0	.72	.63	.08	1.43	1.79
	Inst	LF	Sm	2C	.020	793.1	.78	.74	.10	1.62	2.03
2" x 6" - 18' Avg.	Demo	LF	Lg	LB	.015	1081	---	.45	---	.45	.63
	Demo	LF	Sm	LB	.017	918.9	---	.51	---	.51	.71
2" x 6" - 18' Avg.	Inst	LF	Lg	2C	.016	1001	.72	.59	.08	1.39	1.74
	Inst	LF	Sm	2C	.019	850.9	.78	.70	.09	1.57	1.97

Description	Oper	Unit	Vol	Crew Size	Man-hours per Unit	Crew Output per Day	Avg Mat'l Unit Cost	Avg Labor Unit Cost	Avg Equip Unit Cost	Avg Total Unit Cost	Avg Price Incl O&P
2" x 8" - 12' Avg.	Demo	LF	Lg	LB	.022	737.0	---	.66	---	.66	**.92**
	Demo	LF	Sm	LB	.026	626.5	---	.78	---	.78	**1.09**
2" x 8" - 12' Avg.	Inst	LF	Lg	2C	.023	684.0	.93	.85	.11	1.89	**2.37**
	Inst	LF	Sm	2C	.028	581.4	1.02	1.04	.13	2.19	**2.75**
2" x 8" - 14' Avg.	Demo	LF	Lg	LB	.020	804.0	---	.60	---	.60	**.84**
	Demo	LF	Sm	LB	.023	683.4	---	.69	---	.69	**.97**
2" x 8" - 14' Avg.	Inst	LF	Lg	2C	.021	748.0	.93	.78	.10	1.81	**2.26**
	Inst	LF	Sm	2C	.025	635.8	1.02	.93	.12	2.07	**2.59**
2" x 8" - 16' Avg.	Demo	LF	Lg	LB	.019	864.0	---	.57	---	.57	**.80**
	Demo	LF	Sm	LB	.022	734.4	---	.66	---	.66	**.92**
2" x 8" - 16' Avg.	Inst	LF	Lg	2C	.020	805.0	.93	.74	.10	1.77	**2.21**
	Inst	LF	Sm	2C	.023	684.3	1.02	.85	.11	1.98	**2.48**
2" x 8" - 18' Avg.	Demo	LF	Lg	LB	.017	918.0	---	.51	---	.51	**.71**
	Demo	LF	Sm	LB	.021	780.3	---	.63	---	.63	**.88**
2" x 8" - 18' Avg.	Inst	LF	Lg	2C	.019	856.0	.93	.70	.09	1.72	**2.14**
	Inst	LF	Sm	2C	.022	727.6	1.02	.81	.11	1.94	**2.42**
2" x 8" - 20' Avg.	Demo	LF	Lg	LB	.017	967.0	---	.51	---	.51	**.71**
	Demo	LF	Sm	LB	.019	822.0	---	.57	---	.57	**.80**
2" x 8" - 20' Avg.	Inst	LF	Lg	2C	.018	902.0	.93	.67	.09	1.69	**2.09**
	Inst	LF	Sm	2C	.021	766.7	1.02	.78	.10	1.90	**2.36**

Common, gable or hip, to 3/8-1/2 pitch

Description	Oper	Unit	Vol	Crew Size	Man-hours per Unit	Crew Output per Day	Avg Mat'l Unit Cost	Avg Labor Unit Cost	Avg Equip Unit Cost	Avg Total Unit Cost	Avg Price Incl O&P
2" x 4" - 8' Avg.	Demo	LF	Lg	LB	.025	632.0	---	.75	---	.75	**1.05**
	Demo	LF	Sm	LB	.030	537.2	---	.90	---	.90	**1.26**
2" x 4" - 8' Avg.	Inst	LF	Lg	2C	.028	580.0	.46	1.04	.13	1.63	**2.11**
	Inst	LF	Sm	2C	.032	493.0	.51	1.18	.16	1.85	**2.41**
2" x 4" - 10' Avg.	Demo	LF	Lg	LB	.022	740.0	---	.66	---	.66	**.92**
	Demo	LF	Sm	LB	.025	629.0	---	.75	---	.75	**1.05**
2" x 4" - 10' Avg.	Inst	LF	Lg	2C	.024	680.0	.46	.89	.11	1.46	**1.88**
	Inst	LF	Sm	2C	.028	578.0	.51	1.04	.13	1.68	**2.17**
2" x 4" - 12' Avg.	Demo	LF	Lg	LB	.019	836.0	---	.57	---	.57	**.80**
	Demo	LF	Sm	LB	.023	710.6	---	.69	---	.69	**.97**
2" x 4" - 12' Avg.	Inst	LF	Lg	2C	.021	769.0	.46	.78	.10	1.34	**1.72**
	Inst	LF	Sm	2C	.024	653.7	.51	.89	.12	1.52	**1.95**
2" x 4" - 14' Avg.	Demo	LF	Lg	LB	.017	922.0	---	.51	---	.51	**.71**
	Demo	LF	Sm	LB	.020	783.7	---	.60	---	.60	**.84**
2" x 4" - 14' Avg.	Inst	LF	Lg	2C	.019	849.0	.46	.70	.09	1.25	**1.60**
	Inst	LF	Sm	2C	.022	721.7	.51	.81	.11	1.43	**1.84**
2" x 4" - 16' Avg.	Demo	LF	Lg	LB	.016	999.0	---	.48	---	.48	**.67**
	Demo	LF	Sm	LB	.019	849.2	---	.57	---	.57	**.80**
2" x 4" - 16' Avg.	Inst	LF	Lg	2C	.017	921.0	.46	.63	.08	1.17	**1.49**
	Inst	LF	Sm	2C	.020	782.9	.51	.74	.10	1.35	**1.72**

Description	Oper	Unit	Vol	Crew Size	Man-hours per Unit	Crew Output per Day	Avg Mat'l Unit Cost	Avg Labor Unit Cost	Avg Equip Unit Cost	Avg Total Unit Cost	Avg Price Incl O&P
2" x 6" - 10' Avg.	Demo	LF	Lg	LB	.024	655.0	---	.72	---	.72	1.01
	Demo	LF	Sm	LB	.029	556.8	---	.87	---	.87	1.22
2" x 6" - 10' Avg.	Inst	LF	Lg	2C	.026	604.0	.72	.96	.13	1.81	2.31
	Inst	LF	Sm	2C	.031	513.4	.78	1.15	.15	2.08	2.65
2" x 6" - 12' Avg.	Demo	LF	Lg	LB	.022	743.0	---	.66	---	.66	.92
	Demo	LF	Sm	LB	.025	631.6	---	.75	---	.75	1.05
2" x 6" - 12' Avg.	Inst	LF	Lg	2C	.023	686.0	.72	.85	.11	1.68	2.13
	Inst	LF	Sm	2C	.027	583.1	.78	1.00	.13	1.91	2.43
2" x 6" - 14' Avg.	Demo	LF	Lg	LB	.019	825.0	---	.57	---	.57	.80
	Demo	LF	Sm	LB	.023	701.3	---	.69	---	.69	.97
2" x 6" - 14' Avg.	Inst	LF	Lg	2C	.021	762.0	.72	.78	.10	1.60	2.02
	Inst	LF	Sm	2C	.025	647.7	.78	.93	.12	1.83	2.31
2" x 6" - 16' Avg.	Demo	LF	Lg	LB	.018	901.0	---	.54	---	.54	.76
	Demo	LF	Sm	LB	.021	765.9	---	.63	---	.63	.88
2" x 6" - 16' Avg.	Inst	LF	Lg	2C	.019	833.0	.72	.70	.09	1.51	1.90
	Inst	LF	Sm	2C	.023	708.1	.78	.85	.11	1.74	2.20
2" x 6" - 18' Avg.	Demo	LF	Lg	LB	.016	971.0	---	.48	---	.48	.67
	Demo	LF	Sm	LB	.019	825.4	---	.57	---	.57	.80
2" x 6" - 18' Avg.	Inst	LF	Lg	2C	.018	898.0	.72	.67	.09	1.48	1.85
	Inst	LF	Sm	2C	.021	763.3	.78	.78	.10	1.66	2.09
2" x 8" - 12' Avg.	Demo	LF	Lg	LB	.024	660.0	---	.72	---	.72	1.01
	Demo	LF	Sm	LB	.029	561.0	---	.87	---	.87	1.22
2" x 8" - 12' Avg.	Inst	LF	Lg	2C	.026	612.0	.93	.96	.13	2.02	2.55
	Inst	LF	Sm	2C	.031	520.2	1.02	1.15	.15	2.32	2.93
2" x 8" - 14' Avg.	Demo	LF	Lg	LB	.022	725.0	---	.66	---	.66	.92
	Demo	LF	Sm	LB	.026	616.3	---	.78	---	.78	1.09
2" x 8" - 14' Avg.	Inst	LF	Lg	2C	.024	673.0	.93	.89	.12	1.94	2.43
	Inst	LF	Sm	2C	.028	572.1	1.02	1.04	.14	2.20	2.76
2" x 8" - 16' Avg.	Demo	LF	Lg	LB	.020	784.0	---	.60	---	.60	.84
	Demo	LF	Sm	LB	.024	666.4	---	.72	---	.72	1.01
2" x 8" - 16' Avg.	Inst	LF	Lg	2C	.022	728.0	.93	.81	.11	1.85	2.32
	Inst	LF	Sm	2C	.026	618.8	1.02	.96	.13	2.11	2.65
2" x 8" - 18' Avg.	Demo	LF	Lg	LB	.019	837.0	---	.57	---	.57	.80
	Demo	LF	Sm	LB	.022	711.5	---	.66	---	.66	.92
2" x 8" - 18' Avg.	Inst	LF	Lg	2C	.021	779.0	.93	.78	.10	1.81	2.26
	Inst	LF	Sm	2C	.024	662.2	1.02	.89	.12	2.03	2.54
2" x 8" - 20' Avg.	Demo	LF	Lg	LB	.018	885.0	---	.54	---	.54	.76
	Demo	LF	Sm	LB	.021	752.3	---	.63	---	.63	.88
2" x 8" - 20' Avg.	Inst	LF	Lg	2C	.019	825.0	.93	.70	.09	1.72	2.14
	Inst	LF	Sm	2C	.023	701.3	1.02	.85	.11	1.98	2.48

Description	Oper	Unit	Vol	Crew Size	Man-hours per Unit	Crew Output per Day	Avg Mat'l Unit Cost	Avg Labor Unit Cost	Avg Equip Unit Cost	Avg Total Unit Cost	Avg Price Incl O&P
Common, cut-up roofs, to 1/3 pitch											
2" x 4" - 8' Avg.	Demo	LF	Lg	LB	.027	588.0	---	.81	---	.81	1.13
	Demo	LF	Sm	LB	.032	499.8	---	.96	---	.96	1.34
2" x 4" - 8' Avg.	Inst	LF	Lg	2C	.030	539.0	.47	1.11	.14	1.72	2.24
	Inst	LF	Sm	2C	.035	458.2	.51	1.30	.17	1.98	2.57
2" x 4" - 10' Avg.	Demo	LF	Lg	LB	.023	692.0	---	.69	---	.69	.97
	Demo	LF	Sm	LB	.027	588.2	---	.81	---	.81	1.13
2" x 4" - 10' Avg.	Inst	LF	Lg	2C	.025	635.0	.47	.93	.12	1.52	1.96
	Inst	LF	Sm	2C	.030	539.8	.51	1.11	.14	1.76	2.28
2" x 4" - 12' Avg.	Demo	LF	Lg	LB	.020	783.0	---	.60	---	.60	.84
	Demo	LF	Sm	LB	.024	665.6	---	.72	---	.72	1.01
2" x 4" - 12' Avg.	Inst	LF	Lg	2C	.022	720.0	.47	.81	.11	1.39	1.79
	Inst	LF	Sm	2C	.026	612.0	.51	.96	.13	1.60	2.06
2" x 4" - 14' Avg.	Demo	LF	Lg	LB	.018	868.0	---	.54	---	.54	.76
	Demo	LF	Sm	LB	.022	737.8	---	.66	---	.66	.92
2" x 4" - 14' Avg.	Inst	LF	Lg	2C	.020	799.0	.47	.74	.10	1.31	1.68
	Inst	LF	Sm	2C	.024	679.2	.51	.89	.11	1.51	1.94
2" x 4" - 16' Avg.	Demo	LF	Lg	LB	.017	945.0	---	.51	---	.51	.71
	Demo	LF	Sm	LB	.020	803.3	---	.60	---	.60	.84
2" x 4" - 16' Avg.	Inst	LF	Lg	2C	.018	870.0	.47	.67	.09	1.23	1.56
	Inst	LF	Sm	2C	.022	739.5	.51	.81	.11	1.43	1.84
2" x 6" - 10' Avg.	Demo	LF	Lg	LB	.026	617.0	---	.78	---	.78	1.09
	Demo	LF	Sm	LB	.031	524.5	---	.93	---	.93	1.30
2" x 6" - 10' Avg.	Inst	LF	Lg	2C	.028	569.0	.73	1.04	.14	1.91	2.43
	Inst	LF	Sm	2C	.033	483.7	.80	1.22	.16	2.18	2.79
2" x 6" - 12' Avg.	Demo	LF	Lg	LB	.023	703.0	---	.69	---	.69	.97
	Demo	LF	Sm	LB	.027	597.6	---	.81	---	.81	1.13
2" x 6" - 12' Avg.	Inst	LF	Lg	2C	.025	648.0	.73	.93	.12	1.78	2.26
	Inst	LF	Sm	2C	.029	550.8	.80	1.07	.14	2.01	2.56
2" x 6" - 14' Avg.	Demo	LF	Lg	LB	.020	781.0	---	.60	---	.60	.84
	Demo	LF	Sm	LB	.024	663.9	---	.72	---	.72	1.01
2" x 6" - 14' Avg.	Inst	LF	Lg	2C	.022	721.0	.73	.81	.11	1.65	2.09
	Inst	LF	Sm	2C	.026	612.9	.80	.96	.13	1.89	2.40
2" x 6" - 16' Avg.	Demo	LF	Lg	LB	.019	855.0	---	.57	---	.57	.80
	Demo	LF	Sm	LB	.022	726.8	---	.66	---	.66	.92
2" x 6" - 16' Avg.	Inst	LF	Lg	2C	.020	789.0	.73	.74	.10	1.57	1.98
	Inst	LF	Sm	2C	.024	670.7	.80	.89	.12	1.81	2.28
2" x 6" - 18' Avg.	Demo	LF	Lg	LB	.017	923.0	---	.51	---	.51	.71
	Demo	LF	Sm	LB	.020	784.6	---	.60	---	.60	.84
2" x 6" - 18' Avg.	Inst	LF	Lg	2C	.019	853.0	.73	.70	.09	1.52	1.91
	Inst	LF	Sm	2C	.022	725.1	.80	.81	.11	1.72	2.17

Description	Oper	Unit	Vol	Crew Size	Man-hours per Unit	Crew Output per Day	Avg Mat'l Unit Cost	Avg Labor Unit Cost	Avg Equip Unit Cost	Avg Total Unit Cost	Avg Price Incl O&P
2" x 8" - 12' Avg.	Demo	LF	Lg	LB	.026	627.0	---	.78	---	.78	**1.09**
	Demo	LF	Sm	LB	.030	533.0	---	.90	---	.90	**1.26**
2" x 8" - 12' Avg.	Inst	LF	Lg	2C	.028	580.0	.95	1.04	.13	2.12	**2.67**
	Inst	LF	Sm	2C	.032	493.0	1.04	1.18	.16	2.38	**3.01**
2" x 8" - 14' Avg.	Demo	LF	Lg	LB	.023	691.0	---	.69	---	.69	**.97**
	Demo	LF	Sm	LB	.027	587.4	---	.81	---	.81	**1.13**
2" x 8" - 14' Avg.	Inst	LF	Lg	2C	.025	641.0	.95	.93	.12	2.00	**2.51**
	Inst	LF	Sm	2C	.029	544.9	1.04	1.07	.14	2.25	**2.84**
2" x 8" - 16' Avg.	Demo	LF	Lg	LB	.021	749.0	---	.63	---	.63	**.88**
	Demo	LF	Sm	LB	.025	636.7	---	.75	---	.75	**1.05**
2" x 8" - 16' Avg.	Inst	LF	Lg	2C	.023	695.0	.95	.85	.11	1.91	**2.39**
	Inst	LF	Sm	2C	.027	590.8	1.04	1.00	.13	2.17	**2.73**
2" x 8" - 18' Avg.	Demo	LF	Lg	LB	.020	802.0	---	.60	---	.60	**.84**
	Demo	LF	Sm	LB	.023	681.7	---	.69	---	.69	**.97**
2" x 8" - 18' Avg.	Inst	LF	Lg	2C	.021	745.0	.95	.78	.10	1.83	**2.28**
	Inst	LF	Sm	2C	.025	633.3	1.04	.93	.12	2.09	**2.61**
2" x 8" - 20' Avg.	Demo	LF	Lg	LB	.019	850.0	---	.57	---	.57	**.80**
	Demo	LF	Sm	LB	.022	722.5	---	.66	---	.66	**.92**
2" x 8" - 20' Avg.	Inst	LF	Lg	2C	.020	791.0	.95	.74	.10	1.79	**2.23**
	Inst	LF	Sm	2C	.024	672.4	1.04	.89	.12	2.05	**2.56**

Common, cut-up roofs, to 3/8-1/2 pitch

Description	Oper	Unit	Vol	Crew Size	Man-hours per Unit	Crew Output per Day	Avg Mat'l Unit Cost	Avg Labor Unit Cost	Avg Equip Unit Cost	Avg Total Unit Cost	Avg Price Incl O&P
2" x 4" - 8' Avg.	Demo	LF	Lg	LB	.031	516.0	---	.93	---	.93	**1.30**
	Demo	LF	Sm	LB	.036	438.6	---	1.08	---	1.08	**1.51**
2" x 4" - 8' Avg.	Inst	LF	Lg	2C	.034	473.0	.47	1.26	.16	1.89	**2.46**
	Inst	LF	Sm	2C	.040	402.1	.51	1.48	.19	2.18	**2.85**
2" x 4" - 10' Avg.	Demo	LF	Lg	LB	.026	612.0	---	.78	---	.78	**1.09**
	Demo	LF	Sm	LB	.031	520.2	---	.93	---	.93	**1.30**
2" x 4" - 10' Avg.	Inst	LF	Lg	2C	.028	562.0	.47	1.04	.14	1.65	**2.13**
	Inst	LF	Sm	2C	.033	477.7	.51	1.22	.16	1.89	**2.46**
2" x 4" - 12' Avg.	Demo	LF	Lg	LB	.023	697.0	---	.69	---	.69	**.97**
	Demo	LF	Sm	LB	.027	592.5	---	.81	---	.81	**1.13**
2" x 4" - 12' Avg.	Inst	LF	Lg	2C	.025	640.0	.47	.93	.12	1.52	**1.96**
	Inst	LF	Sm	2C	.029	544.0	.51	1.07	.14	1.72	**2.23**
2" x 4" - 14' Avg.	Demo	LF	Lg	LB	.021	777.0	---	.63	---	.63	**.88**
	Demo	LF	Sm	LB	.024	660.5	---	.72	---	.72	**1.01**
2" x 4" - 14' Avg.	Inst	LF	Lg	2C	.022	714.0	.47	.81	.11	1.39	**1.79**
	Inst	LF	Sm	2C	.026	606.9	.51	.96	.13	1.60	**2.06**
2" x 4" - 16' Avg.	Demo	LF	Lg	LB	.019	849.0	---	.57	---	.57	**.80**
	Demo	LF	Sm	LB	.022	721.7	---	.66	---	.66	**.92**
2" x 4" - 16' Avg.	Inst	LF	Lg	2C	.021	780.0	.47	.78	.10	1.35	**1.73**
	Inst	LF	Sm	2C	.024	663.0	.51	.89	.12	1.52	**1.95**

Description	Oper	Unit	Vol	Crew Size	Man-hours per Unit	Crew Output per Day	Avg Mat'l Unit Cost	Avg Labor Unit Cost	Avg Equip Unit Cost	Avg Total Unit Cost	Avg Price Incl O&P
2" x 6" - 10' Avg.	Demo	LF	Lg	LB	.029	552.0	---	.87	---	.87	**1.22**
	Demo	LF	Sm	LB	.034	469.2	---	1.02	---	1.02	**1.43**
2" x 6" - 10' Avg.	Inst	LF	Lg	2C	.031	508.0	.73	1.15	.15	2.03	**2.60**
	Inst	LF	Sm	2C	.037	431.8	.80	1.37	.18	2.35	**3.02**
2" x 6" - 12' Avg.	Demo	LF	Lg	LB	.025	633.0	---	.75	---	.75	**1.05**
	Demo	LF	Sm	LB	.030	538.1	---	.90	---	.90	**1.26**
2" x 6" - 12' Avg.	Inst	LF	Lg	2C	.027	583.0	.73	1.00	.13	1.86	**2.37**
	Inst	LF	Sm	2C	.032	495.6	.80	1.18	.16	2.14	**2.74**
2" x 6" - 14' Avg.	Demo	LF	Lg	LB	.023	706.0	---	.69	---	.69	**.97**
	Demo	LF	Sm	LB	.027	600.1	---	.81	---	.81	**1.13**
2" x 6" - 14' Avg.	Inst	LF	Lg	2C	.025	651.0	.73	.93	.12	1.78	**2.26**
	Inst	LF	Sm	2C	.029	553.4	.80	1.07	.14	2.01	**2.56**
2" x 6" - 16' Avg.	Demo	LF	Lg	LB	.021	776.0	---	.63	---	.63	**.88**
	Demo	LF	Sm	LB	.024	659.6	---	.72	---	.72	**1.01**
2" x 6" - 16' Avg.	Inst	LF	Lg	2C	.022	715.0	.73	.81	.11	1.65	**2.09**
	Inst	LF	Sm	2C	.026	607.8	.80	.96	.13	1.89	**2.40**
2" x 6" - 18' Avg.	Demo	LF	Lg	LB	.019	842.0	---	.57	---	.57	**.80**
	Demo	LF	Sm	LB	.022	715.7	---	.66	---	.66	**.92**
2" x 6" - 18' Avg.	Inst	LF	Lg	2C	.021	777.0	.73	.78	.10	1.61	**2.03**
	Inst	LF	Sm	2C	.024	660.5	.80	.89	.12	1.81	**2.28**
2" x 8" - 12' Avg.	Demo	LF	Lg	LB	.028	570.0	---	.84	---	.84	**1.18**
	Demo	LF	Sm	LB	.033	484.5	---	.99	---	.99	**1.39**
2" x 8" - 12' Avg.	Inst	LF	Lg	2C	.030	527.0	.95	1.11	.15	2.21	**2.80**
	Inst	LF	Sm	2C	.036	448.0	1.04	1.33	.17	2.54	**3.23**
2" x 8" - 14' Avg.	Demo	LF	Lg	LB	.025	632.0	---	.75	---	.75	**1.05**
	Demo	LF	Sm	LB	.030	537.2	---	.90	---	.90	**1.26**
2" x 8" - 14' Avg.	Inst	LF	Lg	2C	.027	585.0	.95	1.00	.13	2.08	**2.62**
	Inst	LF	Sm	2C	.032	497.3	1.04	1.18	.16	2.38	**3.01**
2" x 8" - 16' Avg.	Demo	LF	Lg	LB	.023	688.0	---	.69	---	.69	**.97**
	Demo	LF	Sm	LB	.027	584.8	---	.81	---	.81	**1.13**
2" x 8" - 16' Avg.	Inst	LF	Lg	2C	.025	638.0	.95	.93	.12	2.00	**2.51**
	Inst	LF	Sm	2C	.030	542.3	1.04	1.11	.14	2.29	**2.89**
2" x 8" - 18' Avg.	Demo	LF	Lg	LB	.022	739.0	---	.66	---	.66	**.92**
	Demo	LF	Sm	LB	.025	628.2	---	.75	---	.75	**1.05**
2" x 8" - 18' Avg.	Inst	LF	Lg	2C	.023	686.0	.95	.85	.11	1.91	**2.39**
	Inst	LF	Sm	2C	.027	583.1	1.04	1.00	.13	2.17	**2.73**
2" x 8" - 20' Avg.	Demo	LF	Lg	LB	.020	787.0	---	.60	---	.60	**.84**
	Demo	LF	Sm	LB	.024	669.0	---	.72	---	.72	**1.01**
2" x 8" - 20' Avg.	Inst	LF	Lg	2C	.022	731.0	.95	.81	.11	1.87	**2.34**
	Inst	LF	Sm	2C	.026	621.4	1.04	.96	.13	2.13	**2.67**

Description	Oper	Unit	Vol	Crew Size	Man-hours per Unit	Crew Output per Day	Avg Mat'l Unit Cost	Avg Labor Unit Cost	Avg Equip Unit Cost	Avg Total Unit Cost	Avg Price Incl O&P
Rafters, per SF of area											
Gable or hip, to 1/3 pitch											
2" x 4" - 12" oc	Demo	SF	Lg	LB	.019	840.0	---	.57	---	.57	**.80**
	Demo	SF	Sm	LB	.022	714.0	---	.66	---	.66	**.92**
2" x 4" - 12" oc	Inst	SF	Lg	2C	.021	774.0	.52	.78	.10	1.40	**1.79**
	Inst	SF	Sm	2C	.024	657.9	.57	.89	.12	1.58	**2.02**
2" x 4" - 16" oc	Demo	SF	Lg	LB	.016	1000	---	.48	---	.48	**.67**
	Demo	SF	Sm	LB	.019	850.0	---	.57	---	.57	**.80**
2" x 4" - 16" oc	Inst	SF	Lg	2C	.017	921.0	.40	.63	.08	1.11	**1.42**
	Inst	SF	Sm	2C	.020	782.9	.44	.74	.10	1.28	**1.64**
2" x 4" - 24" oc	Demo	SF	Lg	LB	.012	1312	---	.36	---	.36	**.50**
	Demo	SF	Sm	LB	.014	1115	---	.42	---	.42	**.59**
2" x 4" - 24" oc	Inst	SF	Lg	2C	.013	1208	.29	.48	.06	.83	**1.07**
	Inst	SF	Sm	2C	.016	1027	.32	.59	.08	.99	**1.28**
2" x 6" - 12" oc	Demo	SF	Lg	LB	.019	821.0	---	.57	---	.57	**.80**
	Demo	SF	Sm	LB	.023	697.9	---	.69	---	.69	**.97**
2" x 6" - 12" oc	Inst	SF	Lg	2C	.021	760.0	.78	.78	.10	1.66	**2.09**
	Inst	SF	Sm	2C	.025	646.0	.85	.93	.12	1.90	**2.39**
2" x 6" - 16" oc	Demo	SF	Lg	LB	.016	978.0	---	.48	---	.48	**.67**
	Demo	SF	Sm	LB	.019	831.3	---	.57	---	.57	**.80**
2" x 6" - 16" oc	Inst	SF	Lg	2C	.018	905.0	.60	.67	.09	1.36	**1.71**
	Inst	SF	Sm	2C	.021	769.3	.66	.78	.10	1.54	**1.95**
2" x 6" - 24" oc	Demo	SF	Lg	LB	.012	1284	---	.36	---	.36	**.50**
	Demo	SF	Sm	LB	.015	1091	---	.45	---	.45	**.63**
2" x 6" - 24" oc	Inst	SF	Lg	2C	.013	1187	.43	.48	.07	.98	**1.24**
	Inst	SF	Sm	2C	.016	1009	.47	.59	.08	1.14	**1.45**
2" x 8" - 12" oc	Demo	SF	Lg	LB	.020	785.0	---	.60	---	.60	**.84**
	Demo	SF	Sm	LB	.024	667.3	---	.72	---	.72	**1.01**
2" x 8" - 12" oc	Inst	SF	Lg	2C	.022	730.0	1.00	.81	.11	1.92	**2.40**
	Inst	SF	Sm	2C	.026	620.5	1.10	.96	.13	2.19	**2.74**
2" x 8" - 16" oc	Demo	SF	Lg	LB	.017	933.0	---	.51	---	.51	**.71**
	Demo	SF	Sm	LB	.020	793.1	---	.60	---	.60	**.84**
2" x 8" - 16" oc	Inst	SF	Lg	2C	.018	868.0	.77	.67	.09	1.53	**1.91**
	Inst	SF	Sm	2C	.022	737.8	.84	.81	.11	1.76	**2.22**
2" x 8" - 24" oc	Demo	SF	Lg	LB	.013	1225	---	.39	---	.39	**.55**
	Demo	SF	Sm	LB	.015	1041	---	.45	---	.45	**.63**
2" x 8" - 24" oc	Inst	SF	Lg	2C	.014	1140	.54	.52	.07	1.13	**1.42**
	Inst	SF	Sm	2C	.017	969.0	.59	.63	.08	1.30	**1.64**

Description	Oper	Unit	Vol	Crew Size	Man-hours per Unit	Crew Output per Day	Avg Mat'l Unit Cost	Avg Labor Unit Cost	Avg Equip Unit Cost	Avg Total Unit Cost	Avg Price Incl O&P
Gable or hip, to 3/8-1/2 pitch											
2" x 4" - 12" oc	Demo	SF	Lg	LB	.022	723.0	---	.66	---	.66	**.92**
	Demo	SF	Sm	LB	.026	614.6	---	.78	---	.78	**1.09**
2" x 4" - 12" oc	Inst	SF	Lg	2C	.024	664.0	.52	.89	.12	1.53	**1.96**
	Inst	SF	Sm	2C	.028	564.4	.57	1.04	.14	1.75	**2.25**
2" x 4" - 16" oc	Demo	SF	Lg	LB	.019	859.0	---	.57	---	.57	**.80**
	Demo	SF	Sm	LB	.022	730.2	---	.66	---	.66	**.92**
2" x 4" - 16" oc	Inst	SF	Lg	2C	.020	789.0	.40	.74	.10	1.24	**1.60**
	Inst	SF	Sm	2C	.024	670.7	.44	.89	.12	1.45	**1.87**
2" x 4" - 24" oc	Demo	SF	Lg	LB	.014	1127	---	.42	---	.42	**.59**
	Demo	SF	Sm	LB	.017	958.0	---	.51	---	.51	**.71**
2" x 4" - 24" oc	Inst	SF	Lg	2C	.015	1036	.29	.56	.08	.93	**1.19**
	Inst	SF	Sm	2C	.018	880.6	.32	.67	.09	1.08	**1.39**
2" x 6" - 12" oc	Demo	SF	Lg	LB	.022	725.0	---	.66	---	.66	**.92**
	Demo	SF	Sm	LB	.026	616.3	---	.78	---	.78	**1.09**
2" x 6" - 12" oc	Inst	SF	Lg	2C	.024	669.0	.78	.89	.12	1.79	**2.26**
	Inst	SF	Sm	2C	.028	568.7	.85	1.04	.14	2.03	**2.57**
2" x 6" - 16" oc	Demo	SF	Lg	LB	.019	862.0	---	.57	---	.57	**.80**
	Demo	SF	Sm	LB	.022	732.7	---	.66	---	.66	**.92**
2" x 6" - 16" oc	Inst	SF	Lg	2C	.020	796.0	.60	.74	.10	1.44	**1.83**
	Inst	SF	Sm	2C	.024	676.6	.66	.89	.12	1.67	**2.12**
2" x 6" - 24" oc	Demo	SF	Lg	LB	.014	1132	---	.42	---	.42	**.59**
	Demo	SF	Sm	LB	.017	962.2	---	.51	---	.51	**.71**
2" x 6" - 24" oc	Inst	SF	Lg	2C	.015	1045	.43	.56	.07	1.06	**1.34**
	Inst	SF	Sm	2C	.018	888.3	.47	.67	.09	1.23	**1.56**
2" x 8" - 12" oc	Demo	SF	Lg	LB	.023	708.0	---	.69	---	.69	**.97**
	Demo	SF	Sm	LB	.027	601.8	---	.81	---	.81	**1.13**
2" x 8" - 12" oc	Inst	SF	Lg	2C	.024	657.0	1.00	.89	.12	2.01	**2.51**
	Inst	SF	Sm	2C	.029	558.5	1.10	1.07	.14	2.31	**2.91**
2" x 8" - 16" oc	Demo	SF	Lg	LB	.019	841.0	---	.57	---	.57	**.80**
	Demo	SF	Sm	LB	.022	714.9	---	.66	---	.66	**.92**
2" x 8" - 16" oc	Inst	SF	Lg	2C	.020	781.0	.77	.74	.10	1.61	**2.02**
	Inst	SF	Sm	2C	.024	663.9	.84	.89	.12	1.85	**2.33**
2" x 8" - 24" oc	Demo	SF	Lg	LB	.012	1351	---	.36	---	.36	**.50**
	Demo	SF	Sm	LB	.014	1148	---	.42	---	.42	**.59**
2" x 8" - 24" oc	Inst	SF	Lg	2C	.013	1260	.54	.48	.06	1.08	**1.35**
	Inst	SF	Sm	2C	.015	1071	.59	.56	.07	1.22	**1.53**

Description	Oper	Unit	Vol	Crew Size	Man-hours per Unit	Crew Output per Day	Avg Mat'l Unit Cost	Avg Labor Unit Cost	Avg Equip Unit Cost	Avg Total Unit Cost	Avg Price Incl O&P
Cut-up roofs, to 1/3 pitch											
2" x 4" - 12" oc	Demo	SF	Lg	LB	.024	674.0	---	.72	---	.72	**1.01**
	Demo	SF	Sm	LB	.028	572.9	---	.84	---	.84	**1.18**
2" x 4" - 12" oc	Inst	SF	Lg	2C	.026	619.0	.53	.96	.13	1.62	**2.09**
	Inst	SF	Sm	2C	.030	526.2	.58	1.11	.15	1.84	**2.37**
2" x 4" - 16" oc	Demo	SF	Lg	LB	.020	804.0	---	.60	---	.60	**.84**
	Demo	SF	Sm	LB	.023	683.4	---	.69	---	.69	**.97**
2" x 4" - 16" oc	Inst	SF	Lg	2C	.022	738.0	.41	.81	.11	1.33	**1.72**
	Inst	SF	Sm	2C	.026	627.3	.45	.96	.12	1.53	**1.99**
2" x 4" - 24" oc	Demo	SF	Lg	LB	.015	1055	---	.45	---	.45	**.63**
	Demo	SF	Sm	LB	.018	896.8	---	.54	---	.54	**.76**
2" x 4" - 24" oc	Inst	SF	Lg	2C	.017	968.0	.29	.63	.08	1.00	**1.29**
	Inst	SF	Sm	2C	.019	822.8	.32	.70	.09	1.11	**1.44**
2" x 6" - 12" oc	Demo	SF	Lg	LB	.023	686.0	---	.69	---	.69	**.97**
	Demo	SF	Sm	LB	.027	583.1	---	.81	---	.81	**1.13**
2" x 6" - 12" oc	Inst	SF	Lg	2C	.025	633.0	.79	.93	.12	1.84	**2.32**
	Inst	SF	Sm	2C	.030	538.1	.87	1.11	.14	2.12	**2.70**
2" x 6" - 16" oc	Demo	SF	Lg	LB	.020	816.0	---	.60	---	.60	**.84**
	Demo	SF	Sm	LB	.023	693.6	---	.69	---	.69	**.97**
2" x 6" - 16" oc	Inst	SF	Lg	2C	.021	752.0	.61	.78	.10	1.49	**1.89**
	Inst	SF	Sm	2C	.025	639.2	.67	.93	.12	1.72	**2.19**
2" x 6" - 24" oc	Demo	SF	Lg	LB	.015	1070	---	.45	---	.45	**.63**
	Demo	SF	Sm	LB	.018	909.5	---	.54	---	.54	**.76**
2" x 6" - 24" oc	Inst	SF	Lg	2C	.016	987.0	.43	.59	.08	1.10	**1.40**
	Inst	SF	Sm	2C	.019	839.0	.48	.70	.09	1.27	**1.63**
2" x 8" - 12" oc	Demo	SF	Lg	LB	.024	674.0	---	.72	---	.72	**1.01**
	Demo	SF	Sm	LB	.028	572.9	---	.84	---	.84	**1.18**
2" x 8" - 12" oc	Inst	SF	Lg	2C	.026	625.0	1.02	.96	.12	2.10	**2.64**
	Inst	SF	Sm	2C	.030	531.3	1.12	1.11	.15	2.38	**2.99**
2" x 8" - 16" oc	Demo	SF	Lg	LB	.020	802.0	---	.60	---	.60	**.84**
	Demo	SF	Sm	LB	.023	681.7	---	.69	---	.69	**.97**
2" x 8" - 16" oc	Inst	SF	Lg	2C	.022	744.0	.78	.81	.10	1.69	**2.14**
	Inst	SF	Sm	2C	.025	632.4	.86	.93	.12	1.91	**2.40**
2" x 8" - 24" oc	Demo	SF	Lg	LB	.015	1053	---	.45	---	.45	**.63**
	Demo	SF	Sm	LB	.018	895.1	---	.54	---	.54	**.76**
2" x 8" - 24" oc	Inst	SF	Lg	2C	.016	976.0	.55	.59	.08	1.22	**1.54**
	Inst	SF	Sm	2C	.019	829.6	.60	.70	.09	1.39	**1.76**

Description	Oper	Unit	Vol	Crew Size	Man-hours per Unit	Crew Output per Day	Avg Mat'l Unit Cost	Avg Labor Unit Cost	Avg Equip Unit Cost	Avg Total Unit Cost	Avg Price Incl O&P
Cut-up roofs, to 3/8-1/2 pitch											
2" x 4" - 12" oc	Demo	SF	Lg	LB	.027	596.0	---	.81	---	.81	**1.13**
	Demo	SF	Sm	LB	.032	506.6	---	.96	---	.96	**1.34**
2" x 4" - 12" oc	Inst	SF	Lg	2C	.029	547.0	.53	1.07	.14	1.74	**2.25**
	Inst	SF	Sm	2C	.034	465.0	.58	1.26	.17	2.01	**2.60**
2" x 4" - 16" oc	Demo	SF	Lg	LB	.022	712.0	---	.66	---	.66	**.92**
	Demo	SF	Sm	LB	.026	605.2	---	.78	---	.78	**1.09**
2" x 4" - 16" oc	Inst	SF	Lg	2C	.025	653.0	.41	.93	.12	1.46	**1.89**
	Inst	SF	Sm	2C	.029	555.1	.45	1.07	.14	1.66	**2.16**
2" x 4" - 24" oc	Demo	SF	Lg	LB	.017	932.0	---	.51	---	.51	**.71**
	Demo	SF	Sm	LB	.020	792.2	---	.60	---	.60	**.84**
2" x 4" - 24" oc	Inst	SF	Lg	2C	.019	855.0	.29	.70	.09	1.08	**1.41**
	Inst	SF	Sm	2C	.022	726.8	.32	.81	.11	1.24	**1.62**
2" x 6" - 12" oc	Demo	SF	Lg	LB	.026	618.0	---	.78	---	.78	**1.09**
	Demo	SF	Sm	LB	.030	525.3	---	.90	---	.90	**1.26**
2" x 6" - 12" oc	Inst	SF	Lg	2C	.028	569.0	.79	1.04	.14	1.97	**2.50**
	Inst	SF	Sm	2C	.033	483.7	.87	1.22	.16	2.25	**2.87**
2" x 6" - 16" oc	Demo	SF	Lg	LB	.022	735.0	---	.66	---	.66	**.92**
	Demo	SF	Sm	LB	.026	624.8	---	.78	---	.78	**1.09**
2" x 6" - 16" oc	Inst	SF	Lg	2C	.024	677.0	.61	.89	.12	1.62	**2.07**
	Inst	SF	Sm	2C	.028	575.5	.67	1.04	.14	1.85	**2.36**
2" x 6" - 24" oc	Demo	SF	Lg	LB	.017	963.0	---	.51	---	.51	**.71**
	Demo	SF	Sm	LB	.020	818.6	---	.60	---	.60	**.84**
2" x 6" - 24" oc	Inst	SF	Lg	2C	.018	887.0	.43	.67	.09	1.19	**1.52**
	Inst	SF	Sm	2C	.021	754.0	.48	.78	.10	1.36	**1.74**
2" x 8" - 12" oc	Demo	SF	Lg	LB	.026	616.0	---	.78	---	.78	**1.09**
	Demo	SF	Sm	LB	.031	523.6	---	.93	---	.93	**1.30**
2" x 8" - 12" oc	Inst	SF	Lg	2C	.028	570.0	1.02	1.04	.14	2.20	**2.76**
	Inst	SF	Sm	2C	.033	484.5	1.12	1.22	.16	2.50	**3.16**
2" x 8" - 16" oc	Demo	SF	Lg	LB	.022	734.0	---	.66	---	.66	**.92**
	Demo	SF	Sm	LB	.026	623.9	---	.78	---	.78	**1.09**
2" x 8" - 16" oc	Inst	SF	Lg	2C	.024	679.0	.78	.89	.11	1.78	**2.25**
	Inst	SF	Sm	2C	.028	577.2	.86	1.04	.14	2.04	**2.58**
2" x 8" - 24" oc	Demo	SF	Lg	LB	.017	962.0	---	.51	---	.51	**.71**
	Demo	SF	Sm	LB	.020	817.7	---	.60	---	.60	**.84**
2" x 8" - 24" oc	Inst	SF	Lg	2C	.018	891.0	.55	.67	.09	1.31	**1.66**
	Inst	SF	Sm	2C	.021	757.4	.60	.78	.10	1.48	**1.88**

Description	Oper	Unit	Vol	Crew Size	Man-hours per Unit	Crew Output per Day	Avg Mat'l Unit Cost	Avg Labor Unit Cost	Avg Equip Unit Cost	Avg Total Unit Cost	Avg Price Incl O&P

Roof decking, solid, T&G, dry for plank-and-beam construction

Description	Oper	Unit	Vol	Crew Size	Man-hours per Unit	Crew Output per Day	Avg Mat'l Unit Cost	Avg Labor Unit Cost	Avg Equip Unit Cost	Avg Total Unit Cost	Avg Price Incl O&P
2" x 6" - 12'	Demo	SF	Lg	LB	.025	645.0	---	.75	---	.75	1.05
	Demo	SF	Sm	LB	.029	548.3	---	.87	---	.87	1.22
2" x 6" - 12'	Inst	SF	Lg	2C	.033	480.0	.11	1.22	.16	1.49	2.00
	Inst	SF	Sm	2C	.039	408.0	.12	1.44	.19	1.75	2.35
2" x 8" - 12'	Demo	SF	Lg	LB	.018	900.0	---	.54	---	.54	.76
	Demo	SF	Sm	LB	.021	765.0	---	.63	---	.63	.88
2" x 8" - 12'	Inst	SF	Lg	2C	.024	670.0	.08	.89	.12	1.09	1.46
	Inst	SF	Sm	2C	.028	569.5	.08	1.04	.14	1.26	1.68

Studs/plates, per LF of stick

Walls or partitions

Description	Oper	Unit	Vol	Crew Size	Man-hours per Unit	Crew Output per Day	Avg Mat'l Unit Cost	Avg Labor Unit Cost	Avg Equip Unit Cost	Avg Total Unit Cost	Avg Price Incl O&P
2" x 4" - 8' Avg.	Demo	LF	Lg	LB	.016	1031	---	.48	---	.48	.67
	Demo	LF	Sm	LB	.018	876.4	---	.54	---	.54	.76
2" x 4" - 8' Avg.	Inst	LF	Lg	2C	.019	848.0	.44	.70	.09	1.23	1.58
	Inst	LF	Sm	2C	.022	720.8	.48	.81	.11	1.40	1.80
2" x 4" - 10' Avg.	Demo	LF	Lg	LB	.014	1172	---	.42	---	.42	.59
	Demo	LF	Sm	LB	.016	996.2	---	.48	---	.48	.67
2" x 4" - 10' Avg.	Inst	LF	Lg	2C	.017	969.0	.44	.63	.08	1.15	1.47
	Inst	LF	Sm	2C	.019	823.7	.48	.70	.09	1.27	1.63
2" x 4" - 12' Avg.	Demo	LF	Lg	LB	.012	1308	---	.36	---	.36	.50
	Demo	LF	Sm	LB	.014	1112	---	.42	---	.42	.59
2" x 4" - 12' Avg.	Inst	LF	Lg	2C	.015	1082	.44	.56	.07	1.07	1.35
	Inst	LF	Sm	2C	.017	919.7	.48	.63	.08	1.19	1.51
2" x 6" - 8' Avg.	Demo	LF	Lg	LB	.018	904.0	---	.54	---	.54	.76
	Demo	LF	Sm	LB	.021	768.4	---	.63	---	.63	.88
2" x 6" - 8' Avg.	Inst	LF	Lg	2C	.021	752.0	.68	.78	.10	1.56	1.97
	Inst	LF	Sm	2C	.025	639.2	.75	.93	.12	1.80	2.28
2" x 6" - 10' Avg.	Demo	LF	Lg	LB	.016	1032	---	.48	---	.48	.67
	Demo	LF	Sm	LB	.018	877.2	---	.54	---	.54	.76
2" x 6" - 10' Avg.	Inst	LF	Lg	2C	.019	861.0	.68	.70	.09	1.47	1.86
	Inst	LF	Sm	2C	.022	731.9	.75	.81	.11	1.67	2.11
2" x 6" - 12' Avg.	Demo	LF	Lg	LB	.014	1142	---	.42	---	.42	.59
	Demo	LF	Sm	LB	.016	970.7	---	.48	---	.48	.67
2" x 6" - 12' Avg.	Inst	LF	Lg	2C	.017	956.0	.68	.63	.08	1.39	1.74
	Inst	LF	Sm	2C	.020	812.6	.75	.74	.10	1.59	2.00

Description	Oper	Unit	Vol	Crew Size	Man-hours per Unit	Crew Output per Day	Avg Mat'l Unit Cost	Avg Labor Unit Cost	Avg Equip Unit Cost	Avg Total Unit Cost	Avg Price Incl O&P
2" x 8" - 8' Avg.	Demo	LF	Lg	LB	.020	802.0	---	.60	---	.60	.84
	Demo	LF	Sm	LB	.023	681.7	---	.69	---	.69	.97
2" x 8" - 8' Avg.	Inst	LF	Lg	2C	.024	673.0	.89	.89	.12	1.90	2.39
	Inst	LF	Sm	2C	.028	572.1	.98	1.04	.14	2.16	2.72
2" x 8" - 10' Avg.	Demo	LF	Lg	LB	.017	915.0	---	.51	---	.51	.71
	Demo	LF	Sm	LB	.021	777.8	---	.63	---	.63	.88
2" x 8" - 10' Avg.	Inst	LF	Lg	2C	.021	771.0	.89	.78	.10	1.77	2.21
	Inst	LF	Sm	2C	.024	655.4	.98	.89	.12	1.99	2.49
2" x 8" - 12' Avg.	Demo	LF	Lg	LB	.016	1010	---	.48	---	.48	.67
	Demo	LF	Sm	LB	.019	858.5	---	.57	---	.57	.80
2" x 8" - 12' Avg.	Inst	LF	Lg	2C	.019	855.0	.89	.70	.09	1.68	2.10
	Inst	LF	Sm	2C	.022	726.8	.98	.81	.11	1.90	2.38

Gable ends

Description	Oper	Unit	Vol	Crew Size	Man-hours per Unit	Crew Output per Day	Avg Mat'l Unit Cost	Avg Labor Unit Cost	Avg Equip Unit Cost	Avg Total Unit Cost	Avg Price Incl O&P
2" x 4" - 3' Avg.	Demo	LF	Lg	LB	.024	660.0	---	.72	---	.72	1.01
	Demo	LF	Sm	LB	.029	561.0	---	.87	---	.87	1.22
2" x 4" - 3' Avg.	Inst	LF	Lg	2C	.047	344.0	.46	1.74	.23	2.43	3.20
	Inst	LF	Sm	2C	.055	292.4	.51	2.04	.27	2.82	3.71
2" x 4" - 4' Avg.	Demo	LF	Lg	LB	.020	818.0	---	.60	---	.60	.84
	Demo	LF	Sm	LB	.023	695.3	---	.69	---	.69	.97
2" x 4" - 4' Avg.	Inst	LF	Lg	2C	.037	431.0	.46	1.37	.18	2.01	2.63
	Inst	LF	Sm	2C	.044	366.4	.51	1.63	.21	2.35	3.08
2" x 4" - 5' Avg.	Demo	LF	Lg	LB	.017	960.0	---	.51	---	.51	.71
	Demo	LF	Sm	LB	.020	816.0	---	.60	---	.60	.84
2" x 4" - 5' Avg.	Inst	LF	Lg	2C	.031	511.0	.46	1.15	.15	1.76	2.29
	Inst	LF	Sm	2C	.037	434.4	.51	1.37	.18	2.06	2.68
2" x 4" - 6' Avg.	Demo	LF	Lg	LB	.015	1082	---	.45	---	.45	.63
	Demo	LF	Sm	LB	.017	919.7	---	.51	---	.51	.71
2" x 4" - 6' Avg.	Inst	LF	Lg	2C	.028	580.0	.46	1.04	.13	1.63	2.11
	Inst	LF	Sm	2C	.032	493.0	.51	1.18	.16	1.85	2.41
2" x 6" - 3' Avg.	Demo	LF	Lg	LB	.025	634.0	---	.75	---	.75	1.05
	Demo	LF	Sm	LB	.030	538.9	---	.90	---	.90	1.26
2" x 6" - 3' Avg.	Inst	LF	Lg	2C	.047	337.0	.72	1.74	.23	2.69	3.49
	Inst	LF	Sm	2C	.056	286.5	.78	2.07	.27	3.12	4.07
2" x 6" - 4' Avg.	Demo	LF	Lg	LB	.021	778.0	---	.63	---	.63	.88
	Demo	LF	Sm	LB	.024	661.3	---	.72	---	.72	1.01
2" x 6" - 4' Avg.	Inst	LF	Lg	2C	.038	420.0	.72	1.41	.19	2.32	2.99
	Inst	LF	Sm	2C	.045	357.0	.78	1.67	.22	2.67	3.45

Description	Oper	Unit	Vol	Crew Size	Man-hours per Unit	Crew Output per Day	Avg Mat'l Unit Cost	Avg Labor Unit Cost	Avg Equip Unit Cost	Avg Total Unit Cost	Avg Price Incl O&P
2" x 6" - 5' Avg.	Demo	LF	Lg	LB	.018	906.0	---	.54	---	.54	.76
	Demo	LF	Sm	LB	.021	770.1	---	.63	---	.63	.88
2" x 6" - 5' Avg.	Inst	LF	Lg	2C	.032	495.0	.72	1.18	.16	2.06	2.65
	Inst	LF	Sm	2C	.038	420.8	.78	1.41	.19	2.38	3.06
2" x 6" - 6' Avg.	Demo	LF	Lg	LB	.016	1013	---	.48	---	.48	.67
	Demo	LF	Sm	LB	.019	861.1	---	.57	---	.57	.80
2" x 6" - 6' Avg.	Inst	LF	Lg	2C	.029	560.0	.72	1.07	.14	1.93	2.47
	Inst	LF	Sm	2C	.034	476.0	.78	1.26	.16	2.20	2.82
2" x 8" - 3' Avg.	Demo	LF	Lg	LB	.026	610.0	---	.78	---	.78	1.09
	Demo	LF	Sm	LB	.031	518.5	---	.93	---	.93	1.30
2" x 8" - 3' Avg.	Inst	LF	Lg	2C	.048	330.0	.93	1.78	.24	2.95	3.80
	Inst	LF	Sm	2C	.057	280.5	1.02	2.11	.28	3.41	4.41
2" x 8" - 4' Avg.	Demo	LF	Lg	LB	.022	742.0	---	.66	---	.66	.92
	Demo	LF	Sm	LB	.025	630.7	---	.75	---	.75	1.05
2" x 8" - 4' Avg.	Inst	LF	Lg	2C	.039	409.0	.93	1.44	.19	2.56	3.28
	Inst	LF	Sm	2C	.046	347.7	1.02	1.70	.22	2.94	3.78
2" x 8" - 5' Avg.	Demo	LF	Lg	LB	.019	857.0	---	.57	---	.57	.80
	Demo	LF	Sm	LB	.022	728.5	---	.66	---	.66	.92
2" x 8" - 5' Avg.	Inst	LF	Lg	2C	.033	480.0	.93	1.22	.16	2.31	2.94
	Inst	LF	Sm	2C	.039	408.0	1.02	1.44	.19	2.65	3.38
2" x 8" - 6' Avg.	Demo	LF	Lg	LB	.017	953.0	---	.51	---	.51	.71
	Demo	LF	Sm	LB	.020	810.1	---	.60	---	.60	.84
2" x 8" - 6' Avg.	Inst	LF	Lg	2C	.030	541.0	.93	1.11	.14	2.18	2.76
	Inst	LF	Sm	2C	.035	459.9	1.02	1.30	.17	2.49	3.16

Studs/plates, per SF of area

Walls or partitions

Description	Oper	Unit	Vol	Crew Size	Man-hours per Unit	Crew Output per Day	Avg Mat'l Unit Cost	Avg Labor Unit Cost	Avg Equip Unit Cost	Avg Total Unit Cost	Avg Price Incl O&P
2" x 4" - 8', 12" oc	Demo	SF	Lg	LB	.027	601.0	---	.81	---	.81	1.13
	Demo	SF	Sm	LB	.031	510.9	---	.93	---	.93	1.30
2" x 4" - 8', 12" oc	Inst	SF	Lg	2C	.032	495.0	.76	1.18	.16	2.10	2.69
	Inst	SF	Sm	2C	.038	420.8	.84	1.41	.19	2.44	3.13
2" x 4" - 8', 16" oc	Demo	SF	Lg	LB	.024	674.0	---	.72	---	.72	1.01
	Demo	SF	Sm	LB	.028	572.9	---	.84	---	.84	1.18
2" x 4" - 8', 16" oc	Inst	SF	Lg	2C	.029	555.0	.62	1.07	.14	1.83	2.36
	Inst	SF	Sm	2C	.034	471.8	.68	1.26	.17	2.11	2.71
2" x 4" - 8', 24" oc	Demo	SF	Lg	LB	.020	793.0	---	.60	---	.60	.84
	Demo	SF	Sm	LB	.024	674.1	---	.72	---	.72	1.01
2" x 4" - 8', 24" oc	Inst	SF	Lg	2C	.025	652.0	.47	.93	.12	1.52	1.96
	Inst	SF	Sm	2C	.029	554.2	.52	1.07	.14	1.73	2.24

Description	Oper	Unit	Vol	Crew Size	Man-hours per Unit	Crew Output per Day	Avg Mat'l Unit Cost	Avg Labor Unit Cost	Avg Equip Unit Cost	Avg Total Unit Cost	Avg Price Incl O&P
2" x 4" - 10', 12" oc	Demo	SF	Lg	LB	.022	723.0	---	.66	---	.66	**.92**
	Demo	SF	Sm	LB	.026	614.6	---	.78	---	.78	**1.09**
2" x 4" - 10', 12" oc	Inst	SF	Lg	2C	.027	597.0	.73	1.00	.13	1.86	**2.37**
	Inst	SF	Sm	2C	.032	507.5	.80	1.18	.15	2.13	**2.73**
2" x 4" - 10', 16" oc	Demo	SF	Lg	LB	.020	816.0	---	.60	---	.60	**.84**
	Demo	SF	Sm	LB	.023	693.6	---	.69	---	.69	**.97**
2" x 4" - 10', 16" oc	Inst	SF	Lg	2C	.024	674.0	.59	.89	.12	1.60	**2.04**
	Inst	SF	Sm	2C	.028	572.9	.65	1.04	.14	1.83	**2.34**
2" x 4" - 10', 24" oc	Demo	SF	Lg	LB	.016	973.0	---	.48	---	.48	**.67**
	Demo	SF	Sm	LB	.019	827.1	---	.57	---	.57	**.80**
2" x 4" - 10', 24" oc	Inst	SF	Lg	2C	.020	803.0	.45	.74	.10	1.29	**1.65**
	Inst	SF	Sm	2C	.023	682.6	.49	.85	.11	1.45	**1.87**
2" x 4" - 12', 12" oc	Demo	SF	Lg	LB	.019	826.0	---	.57	---	.57	**.80**
	Demo	SF	Sm	LB	.023	702.1	---	.69	---	.69	**.97**
2" x 4" - 12', 12" oc	Inst	SF	Lg	2C	.023	683.0	.71	.85	.11	1.67	**2.12**
	Inst	SF	Sm	2C	.028	580.6	.78	1.04	.13	1.95	**2.48**
2" x 4" - 12', 16" oc	Demo	SF	Lg	LB	.017	941.0	---	.51	---	.51	**.71**
	Demo	SF	Sm	LB	.020	799.9	---	.60	---	.60	**.84**
2" x 4" - 12', 16" oc	Inst	SF	Lg	2C	.021	778.0	.56	.78	.10	1.44	**1.83**
	Inst	SF	Sm	2C	.024	661.3	.62	.89	.12	1.63	**2.08**
2" x 4" - 12', 24" oc	Demo	SF	Lg	LB	.014	1142	---	.42	---	.42	**.59**
	Demo	SF	Sm	LB	.016	970.7	---	.48	---	.48	**.67**
2" x 4" - 12', 24" oc	Inst	SF	Lg	2C	.017	944.0	.42	.63	.08	1.13	**1.44**
	Inst	SF	Sm	2C	.020	802.4	.47	.74	.10	1.31	**1.68**
2" x 6" - 8', 12" oc	Demo	SF	Lg	LB	.030	528.0	---	.90	---	.90	**1.26**
	Demo	SF	Sm	LB	.036	448.8	---	1.08	---	1.08	**1.51**
2" x 6" - 8', 12" oc	Inst	SF	Lg	2C	.036	439.0	1.18	1.33	.18	2.69	**3.40**
	Inst	SF	Sm	2C	.043	373.2	1.29	1.59	.21	3.09	**3.92**
2" x 6" - 8', 16" oc	Demo	SF	Lg	LB	.027	591.0	---	.81	---	.81	**1.13**
	Demo	SF	Sm	LB	.032	502.4	---	.96	---	.96	**1.34**
2" x 6" - 8', 16" oc	Inst	SF	Lg	2C	.033	491.0	.96	1.22	.16	2.34	**2.97**
	Inst	SF	Sm	2C	.038	417.4	1.05	1.41	.19	2.65	**3.37**
2" x 6" - 8', 24" oc	Demo	SF	Lg	LB	.023	696.0	---	.69	---	.69	**.97**
	Demo	SF	Sm	LB	.027	591.6	---	.81	---	.81	**1.13**
2" x 6" - 8', 24" oc	Inst	SF	Lg	2C	.028	579.0	.73	1.04	.13	1.90	**2.42**
	Inst	SF	Sm	2C	.033	492.2	.80	1.22	.16	2.18	**2.79**

Description	Oper	Unit	Vol	Crew Size	Man-hours per Unit	Crew Output per Day	Avg Mat'l Unit Cost	Avg Labor Unit Cost	Avg Equip Unit Cost	Avg Total Unit Cost	Avg Price Incl O&P
2" x 6" - 10', 12" oc	Demo	SF	Lg	LB	.025	632.0	---	.75	---	.75	**1.05**
	Demo	SF	Sm	LB	.030	537.2	---	.90	---	.90	**1.26**
2" x 6" - 10', 12" oc	Inst	SF	Lg	2C	.030	528.0	1.13	1.11	.15	2.39	**3.00**
	Inst	SF	Sm	2C	.036	448.8	1.23	1.33	.17	2.73	**3.45**
2" x 6" - 10', 16" oc	Demo	SF	Lg	LB	.022	714.0	---	.66	---	.66	**.92**
	Demo	SF	Sm	LB	.026	606.9	---	.78	---	.78	**1.09**
2" x 6" - 10', 16" oc	Inst	SF	Lg	2C	.027	596.0	.91	1.00	.13	2.04	**2.58**
	Inst	SF	Sm	2C	.032	506.6	.99	1.18	.15	2.32	**2.95**
2" x 6" - 10', 24" oc	Demo	SF	Lg	LB	.019	852.0	---	.57	---	.57	**.80**
	Demo	SF	Sm	LB	.022	724.2	---	.66	---	.66	**.92**
2" x 6" - 10', 24" oc	Inst	SF	Lg	2C	.023	711.0	.68	.85	.11	1.64	**2.08**
	Inst	SF	Sm	2C	.026	604.4	.75	.96	.13	1.84	**2.34**
2" x 6" - 12', 12" oc	Demo	SF	Lg	LB	.022	721.0	---	.66	---	.66	**.92**
	Demo	SF	Sm	LB	.026	612.9	---	.78	---	.78	**1.09**
2" x 6" - 12', 12" oc	Inst	SF	Lg	2C	.027	603.0	1.09	1.00	.13	2.22	**2.78**
	Inst	SF	Sm	2C	.031	512.6	1.20	1.15	.15	2.50	**3.14**
2" x 6" - 12', 16" oc	Demo	SF	Lg	LB	.019	822.0	---	.57	---	.57	**.80**
	Demo	SF	Sm	LB	.023	698.7	---	.69	---	.69	**.97**
2" x 6" - 12', 16" oc	Inst	SF	Lg	2C	.023	688.0	.87	.85	.11	1.83	**2.30**
	Inst	SF	Sm	2C	.027	584.8	.95	1.00	.13	2.08	**2.62**
2" x 6" - 12', 24" oc	Demo	SF	Lg	LB	.016	996.0	---	.48	---	.48	**.67**
	Demo	SF	Sm	LB	.019	846.6	---	.57	---	.57	**.80**
2" x 6" - 12', 24" oc	Inst	SF	Lg	2C	.019	834.0	.65	.70	.09	1.44	**1.82**
	Inst	SF	Sm	2C	.023	708.9	.71	.85	.11	1.67	**2.12**
2" x 8" - 8', 12" oc	Demo	SF	Lg	LB	.034	468.0	---	1.02	---	1.02	**1.43**
	Demo	SF	Sm	LB	.040	397.8	---	1.20	---	1.20	**1.68**
2" x 8" - 8', 12" oc	Inst	SF	Lg	2C	.041	392.0	1.54	1.52	.20	3.26	**4.10**
	Inst	SF	Sm	2C	.048	333.2	1.69	1.78	.23	3.70	**4.66**
2" x 8" - 8', 16" oc	Demo	SF	Lg	LB	.030	525.0	---	.90	---	.90	**1.26**
	Demo	SF	Sm	LB	.036	446.3	---	1.08	---	1.08	**1.51**
2" x 8" - 8', 16" oc	Inst	SF	Lg	2C	.036	441.0	1.24	1.33	.18	2.75	**3.47**
	Inst	SF	Sm	2C	.043	374.9	1.36	1.59	.21	3.16	**4.00**
2" x 8" - 8', 24" oc	Demo	SF	Lg	LB	.026	618.0	---	.78	---	.78	**1.09**
	Demo	SF	Sm	LB	.030	525.3	---	.90	---	.90	**1.26**
2" x 8" - 8', 24" oc	Inst	SF	Lg	2C	.031	518.0	.95	1.15	.15	2.25	**2.85**
	Inst	SF	Sm	2C	.036	440.3	1.04	1.33	.18	2.55	**3.24**

Description	Oper	Unit	Vol	Crew Size	Man-hours per Unit	Crew Output per Day	Avg Mat'l Unit Cost	Avg Labor Unit Cost	Avg Equip Unit Cost	Avg Total Unit Cost	Avg Price Incl O&P
2" x 8" - 10', 12" oc	Demo	SF	Lg	LB	.029	560.0	---	.87	---	.87	**1.22**
	Demo	SF	Sm	LB	.034	476.0	---	1.02	---	1.02	**1.43**
2" x 8" - 10', 12" oc	Inst	SF	Lg	2C	.034	472.0	1.47	1.26	.17	2.90	**3.62**
	Inst	SF	Sm	2C	.040	401.2	1.61	1.48	.19	3.28	**4.11**
2" x 8" - 10', 16" oc	Demo	SF	Lg	LB	.025	633.0	---	.75	---	.75	**1.05**
	Demo	SF	Sm	LB	.030	538.1	---	.90	---	.90	**1.26**
2" x 8" - 10', 16" oc	Inst	SF	Lg	2C	.030	533.0	1.18	1.11	.15	2.44	**3.06**
	Inst	SF	Sm	2C	.035	453.1	1.29	1.30	.17	2.76	**3.47**
2" x 8" - 10', 24" oc	Demo	SF	Lg	LB	.021	754.0	---	.63	---	.63	**.88**
	Demo	SF	Sm	LB	.025	640.9	---	.75	---	.75	**1.05**
2" x 8" - 10', 24" oc	Inst	SF	Lg	2C	.025	636.0	.89	.93	.12	1.94	**2.44**
	Inst	SF	Sm	2C	.030	540.6	.97	1.11	.14	2.22	**2.81**
2" x 8" - 12', 12" oc	Demo	SF	Lg	LB	.025	638.0	---	.75	---	.75	**1.05**
	Demo	SF	Sm	LB	.030	542.3	---	.90	---	.90	**1.26**
2" x 8" - 12', 12" oc	Inst	SF	Lg	2C	.030	540.0	1.43	1.11	.14	2.68	**3.34**
	Inst	SF	Sm	2C	.035	459.0	1.56	1.30	.17	3.03	**3.78**
2" x 8" - 12', 16" oc	Demo	SF	Lg	LB	.022	728.0	---	.66	---	.66	**.92**
	Demo	SF	Sm	LB	.026	618.8	---	.78	---	.78	**1.09**
2" x 8" - 12', 16" oc	Inst	SF	Lg	2C	.026	615.0	1.14	.96	.13	2.23	**2.79**
	Inst	SF	Sm	2C	.031	522.8	1.25	1.15	.15	2.55	**3.19**
2" x 8" - 12', 24" oc	Demo	SF	Lg	LB	.018	881.0	---	.54	---	.54	**.76**
	Demo	SF	Sm	LB	.021	748.9	---	.63	---	.63	**.88**
2" x 8" - 12', 24" oc	Inst	SF	Lg	2C	.021	745.0	.84	.78	.10	1.72	**2.15**
	Inst	SF	Sm	2C	.025	633.3	.92	.93	.12	1.97	**2.47**

Gable ends

Description	Oper	Unit	Vol	Crew Size	Man-hours per Unit	Crew Output per Day	Avg Mat'l Unit Cost	Avg Labor Unit Cost	Avg Equip Unit Cost	Avg Total Unit Cost	Avg Price Incl O&P
2" x 4" - 3' Avg., 12" oc	Demo	SF	Lg	LB	.074	216.0	---	2.22	---	2.22	**3.11**
	Demo	SF	Sm	LB	.087	183.6	---	2.61	---	2.61	**3.65**
2" x 4" - 3' Avg., 12" oc	Inst	SF	Lg	2C	.142	113.0	1.40	5.26	.69	7.35	**9.66**
	Inst	SF	Sm	2C	.167	96.05	1.54	6.18	.81	8.53	**11.20**
2" x 4" - 3' Avg., 16" oc	Demo	SF	Lg	LB	.069	231.0	---	2.07	---	2.07	**2.90**
	Demo	SF	Sm	LB	.081	196.4	---	2.43	---	2.43	**3.40**
2" x 4" - 3' Avg., 16" oc	Inst	SF	Lg	2C	.132	121.0	1.31	4.89	.64	6.84	**8.99**
	Inst	SF	Sm	2C	.156	102.9	1.44	5.78	.76	7.98	**10.50**
2" x 4" - 3' Avg., 24" oc	Demo	SF	Lg	LB	.063	253.0	---	1.89	---	1.89	**2.65**
	Demo	SF	Sm	LB	.074	215.1	---	2.22	---	2.22	**3.11**
2" x 4" - 3' Avg., 24" oc	Inst	SF	Lg	2C	.121	132.0	1.21	4.48	.59	6.28	**8.25**
	Inst	SF	Sm	2C	.143	112.2	1.33	5.29	.70	7.32	**9.64**

Description	Oper	Unit	Vol	Crew Size	Man-hours per Unit	Crew Output per Day	Avg Mat'l Unit Cost	Avg Labor Unit Cost	Avg Equip Unit Cost	Avg Total Unit Cost	Avg Price Incl O&P
2" x 4" - 4' Avg., 12" oc	Demo	SF	Lg	LB	.050	323.0	---	1.50	---	1.50	**2.10**
	Demo	SF	Sm	LB	.058	274.6	---	1.74	---	1.74	**2.44**
2" x 4" - 4' Avg., 12" oc	Inst	SF	Lg	2C	.094	170.0	1.17	3.48	.46	5.11	**6.68**
	Inst	SF	Sm	2C	.111	144.5	1.28	4.11	.54	5.93	**7.77**
2" x 4" - 4' Avg., 16" oc	Demo	SF	Lg	LB	.046	348.0	---	1.38	---	1.38	**1.93**
	Demo	SF	Sm	LB	.054	295.8	---	1.62	---	1.62	**2.27**
2" x 4" - 4' Avg., 16" oc	Inst	SF	Lg	2C	.087	183.0	1.09	3.22	.43	4.74	**6.19**
	Inst	SF	Sm	2C	.103	155.6	1.19	3.81	.50	5.50	**7.21**
2" x 4" - 4' Avg., 24" oc	Demo	SF	Lg	LB	.042	384.0	---	1.26	---	1.26	**1.76**
	Demo	SF	Sm	LB	.049	326.4	---	1.47	---	1.47	**2.06**
2" x 4" - 4' Avg., 24" oc	Inst	SF	Lg	2C	.079	202.0	.98	2.92	.39	4.29	**5.61**
	Inst	SF	Sm	2C	.093	171.7	1.08	3.44	.45	4.97	**6.51**
2" x 4" - 5' Avg., 12" oc	Demo	SF	Lg	LB	.039	412.0	---	1.17	---	1.17	**1.64**
	Demo	SF	Sm	LB	.046	350.2	---	1.38	---	1.38	**1.93**
2" x 4" - 5' Avg., 12" oc	Inst	SF	Lg	2C	.073	219.0	1.07	2.70	.36	4.13	**5.37**
	Inst	SF	Sm	2C	.086	186.2	1.18	3.18	.42	4.78	**6.23**
2" x 4" - 5' Avg., 16" oc	Demo	SF	Lg	LB	.035	454.0	---	1.05	---	1.05	**1.47**
	Demo	SF	Sm	LB	.041	385.9	---	1.23	---	1.23	**1.72**
2" x 4" - 5' Avg., 16" oc	Inst	SF	Lg	2C	.066	241.0	.98	2.44	.32	3.74	**4.87**
	Inst	SF	Sm	2C	.078	204.9	1.08	2.89	.38	4.35	**5.66**
2" x 4" - 5' Avg., 24" oc	Demo	SF	Lg	LB	.031	514.0	---	.93	---	.93	**1.30**
	Demo	SF	Sm	LB	.037	436.9	---	1.11	---	1.11	**1.55**
2" x 4" - 5' Avg., 24" oc	Inst	SF	Lg	2C	.059	273.0	.87	2.18	.29	3.34	**4.35**
	Inst	SF	Sm	2C	.069	232.1	.96	2.55	.34	3.85	**5.02**
2" x 4" - 6' Avg., 12" oc	Demo	SF	Lg	LB	.032	501.0	---	.96	---	.96	**1.34**
	Demo	SF	Sm	LB	.038	425.9	---	1.14	---	1.14	**1.60**
2" x 4" - 6' Avg., 12" oc	Inst	SF	Lg	2C	.059	269.0	1.00	2.18	.29	3.47	**4.50**
	Inst	SF	Sm	2C	.070	228.7	1.10	2.59	.34	4.03	**5.23**
2" x 4" - 6' Avg., 16" oc	Demo	SF	Lg	LB	.028	564.0	---	.84	---	.84	**1.18**
	Demo	SF	Sm	LB	.033	479.4	---	.99	---	.99	**1.39**
2" x 4" - 6' Avg., 16" oc	Inst	SF	Lg	2C	.053	302.0	.89	1.96	.26	3.11	**4.03**
	Inst	SF	Sm	2C	.062	256.7	.97	2.30	.30	3.57	**4.63**
2" x 4" - 6' Avg., 24" oc	Demo	SF	Lg	LB	.025	650.0	---	.75	---	.75	**1.05**
	Demo	SF	Sm	LB	.029	552.5	---	.87	---	.87	**1.22**
2" x 4" - 6' Avg., 24" oc	Inst	SF	Lg	2C	.046	349.0	.78	1.70	.22	2.70	**3.50**
	Inst	SF	Sm	2C	.054	296.7	.85	2.00	.26	3.11	**4.04**

Description	Oper	Unit	Vol	Crew Size	Man-hours per Unit	Crew Output per Day	Avg Mat'l Unit Cost	Avg Labor Unit Cost	Avg Equip Unit Cost	Avg Total Unit Cost	Avg Price Incl O&P
2" x 6" - 3' Avg., 12" oc	Demo	SF	Lg	LB	.077	208.0	---	2.31	---	2.31	**3.23**
	Demo	SF	Sm	LB	.090	176.8	---	2.70	---	2.70	**3.78**
2" x 6" - 3' Avg., 12" oc	Inst	SF	Lg	2C	.145	110.0	2.19	5.37	.71	8.27	**10.70**
	Inst	SF	Sm	2C	.171	93.50	2.39	6.33	.83	9.55	**12.40**
2" x 6" - 3' Avg., 16" oc	Demo	SF	Lg	LB	.072	222.0	---	2.16	---	2.16	**3.02**
	Demo	SF	Sm	LB	.085	188.7	---	2.55	---	2.55	**3.57**
2" x 6" - 3' Avg., 16" oc	Inst	SF	Lg	2C	.136	118.0	2.05	5.03	.66	7.74	**10.10**
	Inst	SF	Sm	2C	.160	100.3	2.25	5.92	.78	8.95	**11.70**
2" x 6" - 3' Avg., 24" oc	Demo	SF	Lg	LB	.066	243.0	---	1.98	---	1.98	**2.77**
	Demo	SF	Sm	LB	.077	206.6	---	2.31	---	2.31	**3.23**
2" x 6" - 3' Avg., 24" oc	Inst	SF	Lg	2C	.124	129.0	1.88	4.59	.60	7.07	**9.19**
	Inst	SF	Sm	2C	.146	109.7	2.06	5.40	.71	8.17	**10.70**
2" x 6" - 4' Avg., 12" oc	Demo	SF	Lg	LB	.052	307.0	---	1.56	---	1.56	**2.18**
	Demo	SF	Sm	LB	.061	261.0	---	1.83	---	1.83	**2.56**
2" x 6" - 4' Avg., 12" oc	Inst	SF	Lg	2C	.096	166.0	1.82	3.55	.47	5.84	**7.54**
	Inst	SF	Sm	2C	.113	141.1	1.99	4.18	.55	6.72	**8.70**
2" x 6" - 4' Avg., 16" oc	Demo	SF	Lg	LB	.048	331.0	---	1.44	---	1.44	**2.02**
	Demo	SF	Sm	LB	.057	281.4	---	1.71	---	1.71	**2.39**
2" x 6" - 4' Avg., 16" oc	Inst	SF	Lg	2C	.089	179.0	1.69	3.29	.44	5.42	**7.00**
	Inst	SF	Sm	2C	.105	152.2	1.85	3.89	.51	6.25	**8.08**
2" x 6" - 4' Avg., 24" oc	Demo	SF	Lg	LB	.044	366.0	---	1.32	---	1.32	**1.85**
	Demo	SF	Sm	LB	.051	311.1	---	1.53	---	1.53	**2.14**
2" x 6" - 4' Avg., 24" oc	Inst	SF	Lg	2C	.081	197.0	1.53	3.00	.40	4.93	**6.36**
	Inst	SF	Sm	2C	.096	167.5	1.67	3.55	.47	5.69	**7.37**
2" x 6" - 5' Avg., 12" oc	Demo	SF	Lg	LB	.041	389.0	---	1.23	---	1.23	**1.72**
	Demo	SF	Sm	LB	.048	330.7	---	1.44	---	1.44	**2.02**
2" x 6" - 5' Avg., 12" oc	Inst	SF	Lg	2C	.075	212.0	1.67	2.78	.37	4.82	**6.18**
	Inst	SF	Sm	2C	.089	180.2	1.82	3.29	.43	5.54	**7.14**
2" x 6" - 5' Avg., 16" oc	Demo	SF	Lg	LB	.037	428.0	---	1.11	---	1.11	**1.55**
	Demo	SF	Sm	LB	.044	363.8	---	1.32	---	1.32	**1.85**
2" x 6" - 5' Avg., 16" oc	Inst	SF	Lg	2C	.068	234.0	1.53	2.52	.33	4.38	**5.61**
	Inst	SF	Sm	2C	.080	198.9	1.67	2.96	.39	5.02	**6.46**
2" x 6" - 5' Avg., 24" oc	Demo	SF	Lg	LB	.033	484.0	---	.99	---	.99	**1.39**
	Demo	SF	Sm	LB	.039	411.4	---	1.17	---	1.17	**1.64**
2" x 6" - 5' Avg., 24" oc	Inst	SF	Lg	2C	.060	265.0	1.35	2.22	.29	3.86	**4.95**
	Inst	SF	Sm	2C	.071	225.3	1.48	2.63	.35	4.46	**5.73**

Framing, rough carpentry, studs/plates

Description	Oper	Unit	Vol	Crew Size	Man-hours per Unit	Crew Output per Day	Avg Mat'l Unit Cost	Avg Labor Unit Cost	Avg Equip Unit Cost	Avg Total Unit Cost	Avg Price Incl O&P
2" x 6" - 6' Avg., 12" oc	Demo	SF	Lg	LB	.034	469.0	---	1.02	---	1.02	**1.43**
	Demo	SF	Sm	LB	.040	398.7	---	1.20	---	1.20	**1.68**
2" x 6" - 6' Avg., 12" oc	Inst	SF	Lg	2C	.062	259.0	1.55	2.30	.30	4.15	**5.30**
	Inst	SF	Sm	2C	.073	220.2	1.70	2.70	.35	4.75	**6.09**
2" x 6" - 6' Avg., 16" oc	Demo	SF	Lg	LB	.030	528.0	---	.90	---	.90	**1.26**
	Demo	SF	Sm	LB	.036	448.8	---	1.08	---	1.08	**1.51**
2" x 6" - 6' Avg., 16" oc	Inst	SF	Lg	2C	.055	292.0	1.38	2.04	.27	3.69	**4.71**
	Inst	SF	Sm	2C	.064	248.2	1.51	2.37	.31	4.19	**5.36**
2" x 6" - 6' Avg., 24" oc	Demo	SF	Lg	LB	.026	609.0	---	.78	---	.78	**1.09**
	Demo	SF	Sm	LB	.031	517.7	---	.93	---	.93	**1.30**
2" x 6" - 6' Avg., 24" oc	Inst	SF	Lg	2C	.048	336.0	1.20	1.78	.23	3.21	**4.10**
	Inst	SF	Sm	2C	.056	285.6	1.31	2.07	.27	3.65	**4.68**
2" x 8" - 3' Avg., 12" oc	Demo	SF	Lg	LB	.080	200.0	---	2.40	---	2.40	**3.36**
	Demo	SF	Sm	LB	.094	170.0	---	2.82	---	2.82	**3.95**
2" x 8" - 3' Avg., 12" oc	Inst	SF	Lg	2C	.148	108.0	2.85	5.48	.72	9.05	**11.70**
	Inst	SF	Sm	2C	.174	91.80	3.13	6.44	.85	10.42	**13.50**
2" x 8" - 3' Avg., 16" oc	Demo	SF	Lg	LB	.075	213.0	---	2.25	---	2.25	**3.15**
	Demo	SF	Sm	LB	.088	181.1	---	2.64	---	2.64	**3.70**
2" x 8" - 3' Avg., 16" oc	Inst	SF	Lg	2C	.138	116.0	2.68	5.11	.67	8.46	**10.90**
	Inst	SF	Sm	2C	.162	98.60	2.94	6.00	.79	9.73	**12.60**
2" x 8" - 3' Avg., 24" oc	Demo	SF	Lg	LB	.068	234.0	---	2.04	---	2.04	**2.86**
	Demo	SF	Sm	LB	.080	198.9	---	2.40	---	2.40	**3.36**
2" x 8" - 3' Avg., 24" oc	Inst	SF	Lg	2C	.126	127.0	2.45	4.66	.61	7.72	**9.96**
	Inst	SF	Sm	2C	.148	108.0	2.68	5.48	.72	8.88	**11.50**
2" x 8" - 4' Avg., 12" oc	Demo	SF	Lg	LB	.055	293.0	---	1.65	---	1.65	**2.31**
	Demo	SF	Sm	LB	.064	249.1	---	1.92	---	1.92	**2.69**
2" x 8" - 4' Avg., 12" oc	Inst	SF	Lg	2C	.099	161.0	2.38	3.66	.48	6.52	**8.35**
	Inst	SF	Sm	2C	.117	136.9	2.60	4.33	.57	7.50	**9.62**
2" x 8" - 4' Avg., 16" oc	Demo	SF	Lg	LB	.051	316.0	---	1.53	---	1.53	**2.14**
	Demo	SF	Sm	LB	.060	268.6	---	1.80	---	1.80	**2.52**
2" x 8" - 4' Avg., 16" oc	Inst	SF	Lg	2C	.092	174.0	2.20	3.41	.45	6.06	**7.75**
	Inst	SF	Sm	2C	.108	147.9	2.41	4.00	.53	6.94	**8.90**
2" x 8" - 4' Avg., 24" oc	Demo	SF	Lg	LB	.046	349.0	---	1.38	---	1.38	**1.93**
	Demo	SF	Sm	LB	.054	296.7	---	1.62	---	1.62	**2.27**
2" x 8" - 4' Avg., 24" oc	Inst	SF	Lg	2C	.083	192.0	1.99	3.07	.41	5.47	**7.00**
	Inst	SF	Sm	2C	.098	163.2	2.18	3.63	.48	6.29	**8.07**

211

Description	Oper	Unit	Vol	Crew Size	Man-hours per Unit	Crew Output per Day	Avg Mat'l Unit Cost	Avg Labor Unit Cost	Avg Equip Unit Cost	Avg Total Unit Cost	Avg Price Incl O&P
2" x 8" - 5' Avg., 12" oc	Demo	SF	Lg	LB	.043	368.0	---	1.29	---	1.29	**1.81**
	Demo	SF	Sm	LB	.051	312.8	---	1.53	---	1.53	**2.14**
2" x 8" - 5' Avg., 12" oc	Inst	SF	Lg	2C	.078	206.0	2.17	2.89	.38	5.44	**6.92**
	Inst	SF	Sm	2C	.091	175.1	2.38	3.37	.45	6.20	**7.90**
2" x 8" - 5' Avg., 16" oc	Demo	SF	Lg	LB	.040	405.0	---	1.20	---	1.20	**1.68**
	Demo	SF	Sm	LB	.046	344.3	---	1.38	---	1.38	**1.93**
2" x 8" - 5' Avg., 16" oc	Inst	SF	Lg	2C	.070	227.0	1.95	2.59	.34	4.88	**6.21**
	Inst	SF	Sm	2C	.083	193.0	2.13	3.07	.40	5.60	**7.15**
2" x 8" - 5' Avg., 24" oc	Demo	SF	Lg	LB	.035	458.0	---	1.05	---	1.05	**1.47**
	Demo	SF	Sm	LB	.041	389.3	---	1.23	---	1.23	**1.72**
2" x 8" - 5' Avg., 24" oc	Inst	SF	Lg	2C	.062	257.0	1.72	2.30	.30	4.32	**5.49**
	Inst	SF	Sm	2C	.073	218.5	1.88	2.70	.36	4.94	**6.31**
2" x 8" - 6' Avg., 12" oc	Demo	SF	Lg	LB	.036	441.0	---	1.08	---	1.08	**1.51**
	Demo	SF	Sm	LB	.043	374.9	---	1.29	---	1.29	**1.81**
2" x 8" - 6' Avg., 12" oc	Inst	SF	Lg	2C	.064	251.0	2.02	2.37	.31	4.70	**5.95**
	Inst	SF	Sm	2C	.075	213.4	2.21	2.78	.37	5.36	**6.80**
2" x 8" - 6' Avg., 16" oc	Demo	SF	Lg	LB	.032	497.0	---	.96	---	.96	**1.34**
	Demo	SF	Sm	LB	.038	422.5	---	1.14	---	1.14	**1.60**
2" x 8" - 6' Avg., 16" oc	Inst	SF	Lg	2C	.057	282.0	1.79	2.11	.28	4.18	**5.29**
	Inst	SF	Sm	2C	.067	239.7	1.96	2.48	.33	4.77	**6.06**
2" x 8" - 6' Avg., 24" oc	Demo	SF	Lg	LB	.028	573.0	---	.84	---	.84	**1.18**
	Demo	SF	Sm	LB	.033	487.1	---	.99	---	.99	**1.39**
2" x 8" - 6' Avg., 24" oc	Inst	SF	Lg	2C	.049	325.0	1.56	1.81	.24	3.61	**4.57**
	Inst	SF	Sm	2C	.058	276.3	1.71	2.15	.28	4.14	**5.25**

Studs/plates, per LF of wall or partition

Walls or partitions

Description	Oper	Unit	Vol	Crew Size	Man-hours per Unit	Crew Output per Day	Avg Mat'l Unit Cost	Avg Labor Unit Cost	Avg Equip Unit Cost	Avg Total Unit Cost	Avg Price Incl O&P
2" x 4" - 8', 12" oc	Demo	LF	Lg	LB	.213	75.00	---	6.39	---	6.39	**8.95**
	Demo	LF	Sm	LB	.251	63.75	---	7.53	---	7.53	**10.50**
2" x 4" - 8', 12" oc	Inst	LF	Lg	2C	.258	62.00	5.87	9.55	1.26	16.68	**21.40**
	Inst	LF	Sm	2C	.304	52.70	6.45	11.30	1.48	19.23	**24.70**
2" x 4" - 10', 12" oc	Demo	LF	Lg	LB	.222	72.00	---	6.66	---	6.66	**9.32**
	Demo	LF	Sm	LB	.261	61.20	---	7.83	---	7.83	**11.00**
2" x 4" - 10', 12" oc	Inst	LF	Lg	2C	.271	59.00	7.01	10.00	1.32	18.33	**23.40**
	Inst	LF	Sm	2C	.319	50.15	7.70	11.80	1.56	21.06	**27.00**
2" x 4" - 12', 12" oc	Demo	LF	Lg	LB	.232	69.00	---	6.96	---	6.96	**9.74**
	Demo	LF	Sm	LB	.273	58.65	---	8.19	---	8.19	**11.50**
2" x 4" - 12', 12" oc	Inst	LF	Lg	2C	.281	57.00	8.18	10.40	1.37	19.95	**25.30**
	Inst	LF	Sm	2C	.330	48.45	8.98	12.20	1.61	22.79	**29.00**

Description	Oper	Unit	Vol	Crew Size	Man-hours per Unit	Crew Output per Day	Avg Mat'l Unit Cost	Avg Labor Unit Cost	Avg Equip Unit Cost	Avg Total Unit Cost	Avg Price Incl O&P
2" x 4" - 8', 16" oc	Demo	LF	Lg	LB	.188	85.00	---	5.64	---	5.64	7.90
	Demo	LF	Sm	LB	.221	72.25	---	6.63	---	6.63	9.28
2" x 4" - 8', 16" oc	Inst	LF	Lg	2C	.229	70.00	4.75	8.48	1.11	14.34	18.40
	Inst	LF	Sm	2C	.269	59.50	5.21	9.96	1.31	16.48	21.20
2" x 4" - 10', 16" oc	Demo	LF	Lg	LB	.198	81.00	---	5.94	---	5.94	8.32
	Demo	LF	Sm	LB	.232	68.85	---	6.96	---	6.96	9.74
2" x 4" - 10', 16" oc	Inst	LF	Lg	2C	.239	67.00	5.61	8.85	1.16	15.62	20.00
	Inst	LF	Sm	2C	.281	56.95	6.16	10.40	1.37	17.93	23.00
2" x 4" - 12', 16" oc	Demo	LF	Lg	LB	.205	78.00	---	6.15	---	6.15	8.61
	Demo	LF	Sm	LB	.241	66.30	---	7.23	---	7.23	10.10
2" x 4" - 12', 16" oc	Inst	LF	Lg	2C	.246	65.00	6.41	9.11	1.20	16.72	21.30
	Inst	LF	Sm	2C	.290	55.25	7.04	10.70	1.41	19.15	24.50
2" x 4" - 8', 24" oc	Demo	LF	Lg	LB	.162	99.00	---	4.86	---	4.86	6.80
	Demo	LF	Sm	LB	.190	84.15	---	5.70	---	5.70	7.98
2" x 4" - 8', 24" oc	Inst	LF	Lg	2C	.198	81.00	3.57	7.33	.96	11.86	15.30
	Inst	LF	Sm	2C	.232	68.85	3.92	8.59	1.13	13.64	17.70
2" x 4" - 10', 24" oc	Demo	LF	Lg	LB	.165	97.00	---	4.95	---	4.95	6.93
	Demo	LF	Sm	LB	.194	82.45	---	5.82	---	5.82	8.15
2" x 4" - 10', 24" oc	Inst	LF	Lg	2C	.200	80.00	4.20	7.40	.98	12.58	16.20
	Inst	LF	Sm	2C	.235	68.00	4.61	8.70	1.15	14.46	18.60
2" x 4" - 12', 24" oc	Demo	LF	Lg	LB	.168	95.00	---	5.04	---	5.04	7.06
	Demo	LF	Sm	LB	.198	80.75	---	5.94	---	5.94	8.32
2" x 4" - 12', 24" oc	Inst	LF	Lg	2C	.203	79.00	4.72	7.52	.99	13.23	16.90
	Inst	LF	Sm	2C	.238	67.15	5.19	8.81	1.16	15.16	19.50
2" x 6" - 8', 12" oc	Demo	LF	Lg	LB	.242	66.00	---	7.26	---	7.26	10.20
	Demo	LF	Sm	LB	.285	56.10	---	8.55	---	8.55	12.00
2" x 6" - 8', 12" oc	Inst	LF	Lg	2C	.291	55.00	9.23	10.80	1.42	21.45	27.10
	Inst	LF	Sm	2C	.342	46.75	10.10	12.70	1.67	24.47	31.00
2" x 6" - 10', 12" oc	Demo	LF	Lg	LB	.254	63.00	---	7.62	---	7.62	10.70
	Demo	LF	Sm	LB	.299	53.55	---	8.97	---	8.97	12.60
2" x 6" - 10', 12" oc	Inst	LF	Lg	2C	.302	53.00	11.00	11.20	1.47	23.67	29.80
	Inst	LF	Sm	2C	.355	45.05	12.00	13.10	1.73	26.83	34.00
2" x 6" - 12', 12" oc	Demo	LF	Lg	LB	.267	60.00	---	8.01	---	8.01	11.20
	Demo	LF	Sm	LB	.314	51.00	---	9.42	---	9.42	13.20
2" x 6" - 12', 12" oc	Inst	LF	Lg	2C	.320	50.00	12.80	11.90	1.56	26.26	32.80
	Inst	LF	Sm	2C	.376	42.50	14.00	13.90	1.84	29.74	37.40
2" x 6" - 8', 16" oc	Demo	LF	Lg	LB	.216	74.00	---	6.48	---	6.48	9.07
	Demo	LF	Sm	LB	.254	62.90	---	7.62	---	7.62	10.70
2" x 6" - 8', 16" oc	Inst	LF	Lg	2C	.262	61.00	7.45	9.70	1.28	18.43	23.40
	Inst	LF	Sm	2C	.309	51.85	8.15	11.40	1.50	21.05	26.90

Description	Oper	Unit	Vol	Crew Size	Man-hours per Unit	Crew Output per Day	Avg Mat'l Unit Cost	Avg Labor Unit Cost	Avg Equip Unit Cost	Avg Total Unit Cost	Avg Price Incl O&P
2" x 6" - 10', 16" oc	Demo	LF	Lg	LB	.225	71.00	---	6.75	---	6.75	**9.45**
	Demo	LF	Sm	LB	.265	60.35	---	7.95	---	7.95	**11.10**
2" x 6" - 10', 16" oc	Inst	LF	Lg	2C	.271	59.00	8.77	10.00	1.32	20.09	**25.50**
	Inst	LF	Sm	2C	.319	50.15	9.59	11.80	1.56	22.95	**29.10**
2" x 6" - 12', 16" oc	Demo	LF	Lg	LB	.232	69.00	---	6.96	---	6.96	**9.74**
	Demo	LF	Sm	LB	.273	58.65	---	8.19	---	8.19	**11.50**
2" x 6" - 12', 16" oc	Inst	LF	Lg	2C	.276	58.00	10.10	10.20	1.34	21.64	**27.30**
	Inst	LF	Sm	2C	.325	49.30	11.10	12.00	1.58	24.68	**31.10**
2" x 6" - 8', 24" oc	Demo	LF	Lg	LB	.184	87.00	---	5.52	---	5.52	**7.73**
	Demo	LF	Sm	LB	.216	73.95	---	6.48	---	6.48	**9.07**
2" x 6" - 8', 24" oc	Inst	LF	Lg	2C	.222	72.00	5.62	8.22	1.08	14.92	**19.10**
	Inst	LF	Sm	2C	.261	61.20	6.15	9.66	1.27	17.08	**21.90**
2" x 6" - 10', 24" oc	Demo	LF	Lg	LB	.188	85.00	---	5.64	---	5.64	**7.90**
	Demo	LF	Sm	LB	.221	72.25	---	6.63	---	6.63	**9.28**
2" x 6" - 10', 24" oc	Inst	LF	Lg	2C	.225	71.00	6.55	8.33	1.10	15.98	**20.30**
	Inst	LF	Sm	2C	.265	60.35	7.17	9.81	1.29	18.27	**23.30**
2" x 6" - 12', 24" oc	Demo	LF	Lg	LB	.190	84.00	---	5.70	---	5.70	**7.98**
	Demo	LF	Sm	LB	.224	71.40	---	6.72	---	6.72	**9.41**
2" x 6" - 12', 24" oc	Inst	LF	Lg	2C	.229	70.00	7.45	8.48	1.11	17.04	**21.60**
	Inst	LF	Sm	2C	.269	59.50	8.15	9.96	1.31	19.42	**24.60**
2" x 8" - 8', 12" oc	Demo	LF	Lg	LB	.271	59.00	---	8.13	---	8.13	**11.40**
	Demo	LF	Sm	LB	.319	50.15	---	9.57	---	9.57	**13.40**
2" x 8" - 8', 12" oc	Inst	LF	Lg	2C	.327	49.00	12.10	12.10	1.59	25.79	**32.50**
	Inst	LF	Sm	2C	.384	41.65	13.30	14.20	1.87	29.37	**37.00**
2" x 8" - 10', 12" oc	Demo	LF	Lg	LB	.286	56.00	---	8.58	---	8.58	**12.00**
	Demo	LF	Sm	LB	.336	47.60	---	10.10	---	10.10	**14.10**
2" x 8" - 10', 12" oc	Inst	LF	Lg	2C	.340	47.00	14.40	12.60	1.66	28.66	**35.80**
	Inst	LF	Sm	2C	.401	39.95	15.80	14.90	1.95	32.65	**40.90**
2" x 8" - 12', 12" oc	Demo	LF	Lg	LB	.302	53.00	---	9.06	---	9.06	**12.70**
	Demo	LF	Sm	LB	.355	45.05	---	10.70	---	10.70	**14.90**
2" x 8" - 12', 12" oc	Inst	LF	Lg	2C	.356	45.00	16.80	13.20	1.73	31.73	**39.50**
	Inst	LF	Sm	2C	.418	38.25	18.40	15.50	2.04	35.94	**44.80**
2" x 8" - 8', 16" oc	Demo	LF	Lg	LB	.242	66.00	---	7.26	---	7.26	**10.20**
	Demo	LF	Sm	LB	.285	56.10	---	8.55	---	8.55	**12.00**
2" x 8" - 8', 16" oc	Inst	LF	Lg	2C	.291	55.00	9.72	10.80	1.42	21.94	**27.70**
	Inst	LF	Sm	2C	.342	46.75	10.60	12.70	1.67	24.97	**31.60**
2" x 8" - 10', 16" oc	Demo	LF	Lg	LB	.254	63.00	---	7.62	---	7.62	**10.70**
	Demo	LF	Sm	LB	.299	53.55	---	8.97	---	8.97	**12.60**
2" x 8" - 10', 16" oc	Inst	LF	Lg	2C	.302	53.00	11.50	11.20	1.47	24.17	**30.30**
	Inst	LF	Sm	2C	.355	45.05	12.60	13.10	1.73	27.43	**34.60**
2" x 8" - 12', 16" oc	Demo	LF	Lg	LB	.262	61.00	---	7.86	---	7.86	**11.00**
	Demo	LF	Sm	LB	.309	51.85	---	9.27	---	9.27	**13.00**
2" x 8" - 12', 16" oc	Inst	LF	Lg	2C	.308	52.00	13.30	11.40	1.50	26.20	**32.80**
	Inst	LF	Sm	2C	.362	44.20	14.60	13.40	1.76	29.76	**37.30**

Description	Oper	Unit	Vol	Crew Size	Man-hours per Unit	Crew Output per Day	Avg Mat'l Unit Cost	Avg Labor Unit Cost	Avg Equip Unit Cost	Avg Total Unit Cost	Avg Price Incl O&P
2" x 8" - 8', 24" oc	Demo	LF	Lg	LB	.205	78.00	---	6.15	---	6.15	**8.61**
	Demo	LF	Sm	LB	.241	66.30	---	7.23	---	7.23	**10.10**
2" x 8" - 8', 24" oc	Inst	LF	Lg	2C	.246	65.00	7.39	9.11	1.20	17.70	**22.50**
	Inst	LF	Sm	2C	.290	55.25	8.09	10.70	1.41	20.20	**25.70**
2" x 8" - 10', 24" oc	Demo	LF	Lg	LB	.211	76.00	---	6.33	---	6.33	**8.86**
	Demo	LF	Sm	LB	.248	64.60	---	7.44	---	7.44	**10.40**
2" x 8" - 10', 24" oc	Inst	LF	Lg	2C	.250	64.00	8.57	9.26	1.22	19.05	**24.00**
	Inst	LF	Sm	2C	.294	54.40	9.38	10.90	1.43	21.71	**27.50**
2" x 8" - 12', 24" oc	Demo	LF	Lg	LB	.216	74.00	---	6.48	---	6.48	**9.07**
	Demo	LF	Sm	LB	.254	62.90	---	7.62	---	7.62	**10.70**
2" x 8" - 12', 24" oc	Inst	LF	Lg	2C	.258	62.00	9.72	9.55	1.26	20.53	**25.80**
	Inst	LF	Sm	2C	.304	52.70	10.60	11.30	1.48	23.38	**29.50**

Sheathing, walls

Boards, 1" x 8"

Description	Oper	Unit	Vol	Crew Size	Man-hours per Unit	Crew Output per Day	Avg Mat'l Unit Cost	Avg Labor Unit Cost	Avg Equip Unit Cost	Avg Total Unit Cost	Avg Price Incl O&P
Horizontal	Demo	SF	Lg	LB	.021	755.0	---	.63	---	.63	**.88**
	Demo	SF	Sm	LB	.025	641.8	---	.75	---	.75	**1.05**
Horizontal	Inst	SF	Lg	2C	.023	695.0	1.70	.85	.11	2.66	**3.26**
	Inst	SF	Sm	2C	.027	590.8	1.85	1.00	.13	2.98	**3.66**
Diagonal	Demo	SF	Lg	LB	.024	672.0	---	.72	---	.72	**1.01**
	Demo	SF	Sm	LB	.028	571.2	---	.84	---	.84	**1.18**
Diagonal	Inst	SF	Lg	2C	.026	618.0	1.87	.96	.13	2.96	**3.63**
	Inst	SF	Sm	2C	.030	525.3	2.03	1.11	.15	3.29	**4.04**

Plywood

Description	Oper	Unit	Vol	Crew Size	Man-hours per Unit	Crew Output per Day	Avg Mat'l Unit Cost	Avg Labor Unit Cost	Avg Equip Unit Cost	Avg Total Unit Cost	Avg Price Incl O&P
3/8"	Demo	SF	Lg	LB	.014	1145	---	.42	---	.42	**.59**
	Demo	SF	Sm	LB	.016	973.3	---	.48	---	.48	**.67**
3/8"	Inst	SF	Lg	2C	.015	1059	.48	.56	.07	1.11	**1.40**
	Inst	SF	Sm	2C	.018	900.2	.53	.67	.09	1.29	**1.63**
1/2"	Demo	SF	Lg	LB	.014	1145	---	.42	---	.42	**.59**
	Demo	SF	Sm	LB	.016	973.3	---	.48	---	.48	**.67**
1/2"	Inst	SF	Lg	2C	.015	1059	.57	.56	.07	1.20	**1.50**
	Inst	SF	Sm	2C	.018	900.2	.63	.67	.09	1.39	**1.75**
5/8"	Demo	SF	Lg	LB	.014	1145	---	.42	---	.42	**.59**
	Demo	SF	Sm	LB	.016	973.3	---	.48	---	.48	**.67**
5/8"	Inst	SF	Lg	2C	.015	1059	.66	.56	.07	1.29	**1.61**
	Inst	SF	Sm	2C	.018	900.2	.73	.67	.09	1.49	**1.86**

Particleboard

Description	Oper	Unit	Vol	Crew Size	Man-hours per Unit	Crew Output per Day	Avg Mat'l Unit Cost	Avg Labor Unit Cost	Avg Equip Unit Cost	Avg Total Unit Cost	Avg Price Incl O&P
1/2"	Demo	SF	Lg	LB	.014	1145	---	.42	---	.42	**.59**
	Demo	SF	Sm	LB	.016	973.3	---	.48	---	.48	**.67**
1/2"	Inst	SF	Lg	2C	.015	1059	.50	.56	.07	1.13	**1.42**
	Inst	SF	Sm	2C	.018	900.2	.54	.67	.09	1.30	**1.64**

Description	Oper	Unit	Vol	Crew Size	Man-hours per Unit	Crew Output per Day	Avg Mat'l Unit Cost	Avg Labor Unit Cost	Avg Equip Unit Cost	Avg Total Unit Cost	Avg Price Incl O&P
OSB strand board											
3/8"	Demo	SF	Lg	LB	.014	1145	---	.42	---	.42	.59
	Demo	SF	Sm	LB	.016	973.3	---	.48	---	.48	.67
3/8"	Inst	SF	Lg	2C	.015	1059	.34	.56	.07	.97	1.24
	Inst	SF	Sm	2C	.018	900.2	.38	.67	.09	1.14	1.46
1/2"	Demo	SF	Lg	LB	.014	1145	---	.42	---	.42	.59
	Demo	SF	Sm	LB	.016	973.3	---	.48	---	.48	.67
1/2"	Inst	SF	Lg	2C	.015	1059	.32	.56	.07	.95	1.22
	Inst	SF	Sm	2C	.018	900.2	.35	.67	.09	1.11	1.43
5/8"	Demo	SF	Lg	LB	.014	1145	---	.42	---	.42	.59
	Demo	SF	Sm	LB	.016	973.3	---	.48	---	.48	.67
5/8"	Inst	SF	Lg	2C	.015	1059	.42	.56	.07	1.05	1.33
	Inst	SF	Sm	2C	.018	900.2	.45	.67	.09	1.21	1.54
Sheathing, roof											
Boards, 1" x 8"											
Horizontal	Demo	SF	Lg	LB	.018	884.0	---	.54	---	.54	.76
	Demo	SF	Sm	LB	.021	751.4	---	.63	---	.63	.88
Horizontal	Inst	SF	Lg	2C	.020	819.0	1.70	.74	.10	2.54	3.09
	Inst	SF	Sm	2C	.023	696.2	1.85	.85	.11	2.81	3.43
Diagonal	Demo	SF	Lg	LB	.021	775.0	---	.63	---	.63	.88
	Demo	SF	Sm	LB	.024	658.8	---	.72	---	.72	1.01
Diagonal	Inst	SF	Lg	2C	.022	715.0	1.87	.81	.11	2.79	3.40
	Inst	SF	Sm	2C	.026	607.8	2.03	.96	.13	3.12	3.81
Plywood											
1/2"	Demo	SF	Lg	LB	.013	1277	---	.39	---	.39	.55
	Demo	SF	Sm	LB	.015	1085	---	.45	---	.45	.63
1/2"	Inst	SF	Lg	2C	.013	1187	.55	.48	.07	1.10	1.38
	Inst	SF	Sm	2C	.016	1009	.60	.59	.08	1.27	1.60
5/8"	Demo	SF	Lg	LB	.013	1277	---	.39	---	.39	.55
	Demo	SF	Sm	LB	.015	1085	---	.45	---	.45	.63
5/8"	Inst	SF	Lg	2C	.013	1187	.63	.48	.07	1.18	1.47
	Inst	SF	Sm	2C	.016	1009	.69	.59	.08	1.36	1.70
3/4"	Demo	SF	Lg	LB	.013	1187	---	.39	---	.39	.55
	Demo	SF	Sm	LB	.016	1009	---	.48	---	.48	.67
3/4"	Inst	SF	Lg	2C	.015	1102	.73	.56	.07	1.36	1.69
	Inst	SF	Sm	2C	.017	936.7	.79	.63	.08	1.50	1.87

Description	Oper	Unit	Vol	Crew Size	Man-hours per Unit	Crew Output per Day	Avg Mat'l Unit Cost	Avg Labor Unit Cost	Avg Equip Unit Cost	Avg Total Unit Cost	Avg Price Incl O&P
Sheathing, subfloor											
Boards, 1" x 8"											
Horizontal	Demo	SF	Lg	LB	.019	828.0	---	.57	---	.57	**.80**
	Demo	SF	Sm	LB	.023	703.8	---	.69	---	.69	**.97**
Horizontal	Inst	SF	Lg	2C	.021	764.0	1.75	.78	.10	2.63	**3.20**
	Inst	SF	Sm	2C	.025	649.4	1.90	.93	.12	2.95	**3.60**
Diagonal	Demo	SF	Lg	LB	.022	729.0	---	.66	---	.66	**.92**
	Demo	SF	Sm	LB	.026	619.7	---	.78	---	.78	**1.09**
Diagonal	Inst	SF	Lg	2C	.024	672.0	1.91	.89	.12	2.92	**3.56**
	Inst	SF	Sm	2C	.028	571.2	2.08	1.04	.14	3.26	**3.98**
Plywood											
5/8"	Demo	SF	Lg	LB	.013	1216	---	.39	---	.39	**.55**
	Demo	SF	Sm	LB	.015	1034	---	.45	---	.45	**.63**
5/8"	Inst	SF	Lg	2C	.014	1127	.66	.52	.07	1.25	**1.55**
	Inst	SF	Sm	2C	.017	958.0	.73	.63	.08	1.44	**1.80**
3/4"	Demo	SF	Lg	LB	.014	1134	---	.42	---	.42	**.59**
	Demo	SF	Sm	LB	.017	963.9	---	.51	---	.51	**.71**
3/4"	Inst	SF	Lg	2C	.015	1050	.76	.56	.07	1.39	**1.72**
	Inst	SF	Sm	2C	.018	892.5	.83	.67	.09	1.59	**1.98**
1-1/8"	Demo	SF	Lg	LB	.019	854.0	---	.57	---	.57	**.80**
	Demo	SF	Sm	LB	.022	725.9	---	.66	---	.66	**.92**
1-1/8"	Inst	SF	Lg	2C	.020	798.0	1.65	.74	.10	2.49	**3.03**
	Inst	SF	Sm	2C	.024	678.3	1.79	.89	.11	2.79	**3.41**
Particleboard											
5/8"	Demo	SF	Lg	LB	.013	1216	---	.39	---	.39	**.55**
	Demo	SF	Sm	LB	.015	1034	---	.45	---	.45	**.63**
5/8"	Inst	SF	Lg	2C	.014	1127	.62	.52	.07	1.21	**1.51**
	Inst	SF	Sm	2C	.017	958.0	.67	.63	.08	1.38	**1.73**
3/4"	Demo	SF	Lg	LB	.014	1134	---	.42	---	.42	**.59**
	Demo	SF	Sm	LB	.017	963.9	---	.51	---	.51	**.71**
3/4"	Inst	SF	Lg	2C	.015	1050	.74	.56	.07	1.37	**1.70**
	Inst	SF	Sm	2C	.018	892.5	.80	.67	.09	1.56	**1.94**
Underlayment											
Plywood, 3/8"	Demo	SF	Lg	LB	.013	1216	---	.39	---	.39	**.55**
	Demo	SF	Sm	LB	.015	1034	---	.45	---	.45	**.63**
Plywood, 3/8"	Inst	SF	Lg	2C	.014	1127	.68	.52	.07	1.27	**1.58**
	Inst	SF	Sm	2C	.017	958.0	.74	.63	.08	1.45	**1.81**
Hardboard, 0.215"	Demo	SF	Lg	LB	.013	1216	---	.39	---	.39	**.55**
	Demo	SF	Sm	LB	.015	1034	---	.45	---	.45	**.63**
Hardboard, 0.215"	Inst	SF	Lg	2C	.014	1127	.65	.52	.07	1.24	**1.54**
	Inst	SF	Sm	2C	.017	958.0	.72	.63	.08	1.43	**1.79**

Description	Oper	Unit	Vol	Crew Size	Man-hours per Unit	Crew Output per Day	Avg Mat'l Unit Cost	Avg Labor Unit Cost	Avg Equip Unit Cost	Avg Total Unit Cost	Avg Price Incl O&P

Trusses, shop fabricated, wood "W" type

1/8 pitch
3" rise in 12" run

Description	Oper	Unit	Vol	Crew Size	Man-hours per Unit	Crew Output per Day	Avg Mat'l Unit Cost	Avg Labor Unit Cost	Avg Equip Unit Cost	Avg Total Unit Cost	Avg Price Incl O&P
20' span	Demo	Ea	Lg	LJ	.865	37.00	---	26.00	---	26.00	**36.30**
	Demo	Ea	Sm	LJ	1.02	31.45	---	30.60	---	30.60	**42.80**
20' span	Inst	Ea	Lg	CX	.941	34.00	40.50	34.80	2.29	77.59	**97.70**
	Inst	Ea	Sm	CX	1.11	28.90	44.50	41.10	2.70	88.30	**111.00**
22' span	Demo	Ea	Lg	LJ	.865	37.00	---	26.00	---	26.00	**36.30**
	Demo	Ea	Sm	LJ	1.02	31.45	---	30.60	---	30.60	**42.80**
22' span	Inst	Ea	Lg	CX	.941	34.00	45.10	34.80	2.29	82.19	**103.00**
	Inst	Ea	Sm	CX	1.11	28.90	49.60	41.10	2.70	93.40	**117.00**
24' span	Demo	Ea	Lg	LJ	.865	37.00	---	26.00	---	26.00	**36.30**
	Demo	Ea	Sm	LJ	1.02	31.45	---	30.60	---	30.60	**42.80**
24' span	Inst	Ea	Lg	CX	.941	34.00	47.30	34.80	2.29	84.39	**105.00**
	Inst	Ea	Sm	CX	1.11	28.90	51.90	41.10	2.70	95.70	**120.00**
26' span	Demo	Ea	Lg	LJ	.865	37.00	---	26.00	---	26.00	**36.30**
	Demo	Ea	Sm	LJ	1.02	31.45	---	30.60	---	30.60	**42.80**
26' span	Inst	Ea	Lg	CX	.941	34.00	51.90	34.80	2.29	88.99	**111.00**
	Inst	Ea	Sm	CX	1.11	28.90	56.90	41.10	2.70	100.70	**126.00**
28' span	Demo	Ea	Lg	LJ	.865	37.00	---	26.00	---	26.00	**36.30**
	Demo	Ea	Sm	LJ	1.02	31.45	---	30.60	---	30.60	**42.80**
28' span	Inst	Ea	Lg	CX	.941	34.00	54.00	34.80	2.29	91.09	**113.00**
	Inst	Ea	Sm	CX	1.11	28.90	59.30	41.10	2.70	103.10	**128.00**
30' span	Demo	Ea	Lg	LJ	.914	35.00	---	27.40	---	27.40	**38.40**
	Demo	Ea	Sm	LJ	1.08	29.75	---	32.40	---	32.40	**45.40**
30' span	Inst	Ea	Lg	CX	1.00	32.00	58.60	37.00	2.44	98.04	**122.00**
	Inst	Ea	Sm	CX	1.18	27.20	64.30	43.70	2.87	110.87	**138.00**
32' span	Demo	Ea	Lg	LJ	.914	35.00	---	27.40	---	27.40	**38.40**
	Demo	Ea	Sm	LJ	1.08	29.75	---	32.40	---	32.40	**45.40**
32' span	Inst	Ea	Lg	CX	1.00	32.00	60.10	37.00	2.44	99.54	**123.00**
	Inst	Ea	Sm	CX	1.18	27.20	66.00	43.70	2.87	112.57	**140.00**
34' span	Demo	Ea	Lg	LJ	.914	35.00	---	27.40	---	27.40	**38.40**
	Demo	Ea	Sm	LJ	1.08	29.75	---	32.40	---	32.40	**45.40**
34' span	Inst	Ea	Lg	CX	1.00	32.00	62.90	37.00	2.44	102.34	**127.00**
	Inst	Ea	Sm	CX	1.18	27.20	69.00	43.70	2.87	115.57	**143.00**
36' span	Demo	Ea	Lg	LJ	.970	33.00	---	29.10	---	29.10	**40.70**
	Demo	Ea	Sm	LJ	1.14	28.05	---	34.20	---	34.20	**47.90**
36' span	Inst	Ea	Lg	CX	1.03	31.00	67.50	38.10	2.52	108.12	**133.00**
	Inst	Ea	Sm	CX	1.21	26.35	74.10	44.80	2.96	121.86	**151.00**

Description	Oper	Unit	Vol	Crew Size	Man-hours per Unit	Crew Output per Day	Avg Mat'l Unit Cost	Avg Labor Unit Cost	Avg Equip Unit Cost	Avg Total Unit Cost	Avg Price Incl O&P
5/24 pitch											
5" rise in 12" run											
20' span	Demo	Ea	Lg	LJ	.865	37.00	---	26.00	---	26.00	**36.30**
	Demo	Ea	Sm	LJ	1.02	31.45	---	30.60	---	30.60	**42.80**
20' span	Inst	Ea	Lg	CX	.941	34.00	32.30	34.80	2.29	69.39	**88.20**
	Inst	Ea	Sm	CX	1.11	28.90	35.50	41.10	2.70	79.30	**101.00**
22' span	Demo	Ea	Lg	LJ	.865	37.00	---	26.00	---	26.00	**36.30**
	Demo	Ea	Sm	LJ	1.02	31.45	---	30.60	---	30.60	**42.80**
22' span	Inst	Ea	Lg	CX	.941	34.00	36.20	34.80	2.29	73.29	**92.70**
	Inst	Ea	Sm	CX	1.11	28.90	39.80	41.10	2.70	83.60	**106.00**
24' span	Demo	Ea	Lg	LJ	.865	37.00	---	26.00	---	26.00	**36.30**
	Demo	Ea	Sm	LJ	1.02	31.45	---	30.60	---	30.60	**42.80**
24' span	Inst	Ea	Lg	CX	.941	34.00	38.30	34.80	2.29	75.39	**95.10**
	Inst	Ea	Sm	CX	1.11	28.90	42.00	41.10	2.70	85.80	**109.00**
26' span	Demo	Ea	Lg	LJ	.865	37.00	---	26.00	---	26.00	**36.30**
	Demo	Ea	Sm	LJ	1.02	31.45	---	30.60	---	30.60	**42.80**
26' span	Inst	Ea	Lg	CX	.941	34.00	42.80	34.80	2.29	79.89	**100.00**
	Inst	Ea	Sm	CX	1.11	28.90	47.00	41.10	2.70	90.80	**114.00**
28' span	Demo	Ea	Lg	LJ	.865	37.00	---	26.00	---	26.00	**36.30**
	Demo	Ea	Sm	LJ	1.02	31.45	---	30.60	---	30.60	**42.80**
28' span	Inst	Ea	Lg	CX	.941	34.00	51.10	34.80	2.29	88.19	**110.00**
	Inst	Ea	Sm	CX	1.11	28.90	56.10	41.10	2.70	99.90	**125.00**
30' span	Demo	Ea	Lg	LJ	.914	35.00	---	27.40	---	27.40	**38.40**
	Demo	Ea	Sm	LJ	1.08	29.75	---	32.40	---	32.40	**45.40**
30' span	Inst	Ea	Lg	CX	1.00	32.00	55.00	37.00	2.44	94.44	**118.00**
	Inst	Ea	Sm	CX	1.18	27.20	60.40	43.70	2.87	106.97	**134.00**
32' span	Demo	Ea	Lg	LJ	.914	35.00	---	27.40	---	27.40	**38.40**
	Demo	Ea	Sm	LJ	1.08	29.75	---	32.40	---	32.40	**45.40**
32' span	Inst	Ea	Lg	CX	1.00	32.00	56.50	37.00	2.44	95.94	**119.00**
	Inst	Ea	Sm	CX	1.18	27.20	62.00	43.70	2.87	108.57	**135.00**
34' span	Demo	Ea	Lg	LJ	.914	35.00	---	27.40	---	27.40	**38.40**
	Demo	Ea	Sm	LJ	1.08	29.75	---	32.40	---	32.40	**45.40**
34' span	Inst	Ea	Lg	CX	1.00	32.00	62.20	37.00	2.44	101.64	**126.00**
	Inst	Ea	Sm	CX	1.18	27.20	68.30	43.70	2.87	114.87	**143.00**
36' span	Demo	Ea	Lg	LJ	.970	33.00	---	29.10	---	29.10	**40.70**
	Demo	Ea	Sm	LJ	1.14	28.05	---	34.20	---	34.20	**47.90**
36' span	Inst	Ea	Lg	CX	1.03	31.00	64.30	38.10	2.52	104.92	**130.00**
	Inst	Ea	Sm	CX	1.21	26.35	70.60	44.80	2.96	118.36	**147.00**

Description	Oper	Unit	Vol	Crew Size	Man-hours per Unit	Crew Output per Day	Avg Mat'l Unit Cost	Avg Labor Unit Cost	Avg Equip Unit Cost	Avg Total Unit Cost	Avg Price Incl O&P
1/4 pitch											
6" rise in 12" run											
20' span	Demo	Ea	Lg	LJ	.865	37.00	---	26.00	---	26.00	**36.30**
	Demo	Ea	Sm	LJ	1.02	31.45	---	30.60	---	30.60	**42.80**
20' span	Inst	Ea	Lg	CX	.941	34.00	33.00	34.80	2.29	70.09	**89.00**
	Inst	Ea	Sm	CX	1.11	28.90	36.20	41.10	2.70	80.00	**102.00**
22' span	Demo	Ea	Lg	LJ	.865	37.00	---	26.00	---	26.00	**36.30**
	Demo	Ea	Sm	LJ	1.02	31.45	---	30.60	---	30.60	**42.80**
22' span	Inst	Ea	Lg	CX	.941	34.00	36.90	34.80	2.29	73.99	**93.50**
	Inst	Ea	Sm	CX	1.11	28.90	40.50	41.10	2.70	84.30	**107.00**
24' span	Demo	Ea	Lg	LJ	.865	37.00	---	26.00	---	26.00	**36.30**
	Demo	Ea	Sm	LJ	1.02	31.45	---	30.60	---	30.60	**42.80**
24' span	Inst	Ea	Lg	CX	.941	34.00	41.40	34.80	2.29	78.49	**98.70**
	Inst	Ea	Sm	CX	1.11	28.90	45.50	41.10	2.70	89.30	**113.00**
26' span	Demo	Ea	Lg	LJ	.865	37.00	---	26.00	---	26.00	**36.30**
	Demo	Ea	Sm	LJ	1.02	31.45	---	30.60	---	30.60	**42.80**
26' span	Inst	Ea	Lg	CX	.941	34.00	42.80	34.80	2.29	79.89	**100.00**
	Inst	Ea	Sm	CX	1.11	28.90	47.00	41.10	2.70	90.80	**114.00**
28' span	Demo	Ea	Lg	LJ	.865	37.00	---	26.00	---	26.00	**36.30**
	Demo	Ea	Sm	LJ	1.02	31.45	---	30.60	---	30.60	**42.80**
28' span	Inst	Ea	Lg	CX	.941	34.00	51.70	34.80	2.29	88.79	**111.00**
	Inst	Ea	Sm	CX	1.11	28.90	56.80	41.10	2.70	100.60	**126.00**
30' span	Demo	Ea	Lg	LJ	.914	35.00	---	27.40	---	27.40	**38.40**
	Demo	Ea	Sm	LJ	1.08	29.75	---	32.40	---	32.40	**45.40**
30' span	Inst	Ea	Lg	CX	1.00	32.00	53.80	37.00	2.44	93.24	**116.00**
	Inst	Ea	Sm	CX	1.18	27.20	59.00	43.70	2.87	105.57	**132.00**
32' span	Demo	Ea	Lg	LJ	.914	35.00	---	27.40	---	27.40	**38.40**
	Demo	Ea	Sm	LJ	1.08	29.75	---	32.40	---	32.40	**45.40**
32' span	Inst	Ea	Lg	CX	1.00	32.00	58.30	37.00	2.44	97.74	**121.00**
	Inst	Ea	Sm	CX	1.18	27.20	64.00	43.70	2.87	110.57	**138.00**
34' span	Demo	Ea	Lg	LJ	.914	35.00	---	27.40	---	27.40	**38.40**
	Demo	Ea	Sm	LJ	1.08	29.75	---	32.40	---	32.40	**45.40**
34' span	Inst	Ea	Lg	CX	1.00	32.00	62.80	37.00	2.44	102.24	**127.00**
	Inst	Ea	Sm	CX	1.18	27.20	69.00	43.70	2.87	115.57	**143.00**
36' span	Demo	Ea	Lg	LJ	.970	33.00	---	29.10	---	29.10	**40.70**
	Demo	Ea	Sm	LJ	1.14	28.05	---	34.20	---	34.20	**47.90**
36' span	Inst	Ea	Lg	CX	1.03	31.00	66.10	38.10	2.52	106.72	**132.00**
	Inst	Ea	Sm	CX	1.21	26.35	72.60	44.80	2.96	120.36	**149.00**

Description	Oper	Unit	Vol	Crew Size	Man-hours per Unit	Crew Output per Day	Avg Mat'l Unit Cost	Avg Labor Unit Cost	Avg Equip Unit Cost	Avg Total Unit Cost	Avg Price Incl O&P

Garage doors

Detach & reset operations

Wood, aluminum, or hardboard

Description	Oper	Unit	Vol	Crew Size	Man-hours per Unit	Crew Output per Day	Avg Mat'l Unit Cost	Avg Labor Unit Cost	Avg Equip Unit Cost	Avg Total Unit Cost	Avg Price Incl O&P
Single	Reset	Ea	Lg	LB	2.67	6.00	---	80.10	---	80.10	**112.00**
	Reset	Ea	Sm	LB	3.56	4.50	---	107.00	---	107.00	**150.00**
Double	Reset	Ea	Lg	LB	3.56	4.50	---	107.00	---	107.00	**150.00**
	Reset	Ea	Sm	LB	4.73	3.38	---	142.00	---	142.00	**199.00**

Steel

Description	Oper	Unit	Vol	Crew Size	Man-hours per Unit	Crew Output per Day	Avg Mat'l Unit Cost	Avg Labor Unit Cost	Avg Equip Unit Cost	Avg Total Unit Cost	Avg Price Incl O&P
Single	Reset	Ea	Lg	LB	3.20	5.00	---	96.00	---	96.00	**134.00**
	Reset	Ea	Sm	LB	4.27	3.75	---	128.00	---	128.00	**179.00**
Double	Reset	Ea	Lg	LB	4.00	4.00	---	120.00	---	120.00	**168.00**
	Reset	Ea	Sm	LB	4.92	3.25	---	148.00	---	148.00	**207.00**

Remove operations

Wood, aluminum, or hardboard

Description	Oper	Unit	Vol	Crew Size	Man-hours per Unit	Crew Output per Day	Avg Mat'l Unit Cost	Avg Labor Unit Cost	Avg Equip Unit Cost	Avg Total Unit Cost	Avg Price Incl O&P
Single	Demo	Ea	Lg	LB	2.00	8.00	---	60.00	---	60.00	**84.00**
	Demo	Ea	Sm	LB	3.08	5.20	---	92.40	---	92.40	**129.00**
Double	Demo	Ea	Lg	LB	2.67	6.00	---	80.10	---	80.10	**112.00**
	Demo	Ea	Sm	LB	4.10	3.90	---	123.00	---	123.00	**172.00**

Steel

Description	Oper	Unit	Vol	Crew Size	Man-hours per Unit	Crew Output per Day	Avg Mat'l Unit Cost	Avg Labor Unit Cost	Avg Equip Unit Cost	Avg Total Unit Cost	Avg Price Incl O&P
Single	Demo	Ea	Lg	LB	2.29	7.00	---	68.70	---	68.70	**96.20**
	Demo	Ea	Sm	LB	3.52	4.55	---	106.00	---	106.00	**148.00**
Double	Demo	Ea	Lg	LB	3.20	5.00	---	96.00	---	96.00	**134.00**
	Demo	Ea	Sm	LB	4.92	3.25	---	148.00	---	148.00	**207.00**

Replace operations

Aluminum frame with plastic skin bonded to polystyrene foam core

Jamb type with hardware and deluxe lock

Description	Oper	Unit	Vol	Crew Size	Man-hours per Unit	Crew Output per Day	Avg Mat'l Unit Cost	Avg Labor Unit Cost	Avg Equip Unit Cost	Avg Total Unit Cost	Avg Price Incl O&P
8' x 7', single	Inst	Ea	Lg	2C	4.00	4.00	507.00	148.00	---	655.00	**790.00**
	Inst	Ea	Sm	2C	5.71	2.80	557.00	211.00	---	768.00	**936.00**
8' x 8', single	Inst	Ea	Lg	2C	4.00	4.00	604.00	148.00	---	752.00	**902.00**
	Inst	Ea	Sm	2C	5.71	2.80	663.00	211.00	---	874.00	**1060.00**
9' x 7', single	Inst	Ea	Lg	2C	4.00	4.00	526.00	148.00	---	674.00	**813.00**
	Inst	Ea	Sm	2C	5.71	2.80	578.00	211.00	---	789.00	**961.00**
9' x 8', single	Inst	Ea	Lg	2C	4.00	4.00	630.00	148.00	---	778.00	**932.00**
	Inst	Ea	Sm	2C	5.71	2.80	692.00	211.00	---	903.00	**1090.00**
16' x 7', double	Inst	Ea	Lg	2C	5.33	3.00	739.00	197.00	---	936.00	**1130.00**
	Inst	Ea	Sm	2C	7.62	2.10	811.00	282.00	---	1093.00	**1330.00**
16' x 8', double	Inst	Ea	Lg	2C	5.33	3.00	848.00	197.00	---	1045.00	**1250.00**
	Inst	Ea	Sm	2C	7.62	2.10	931.00	282.00	---	1213.00	**1470.00**

Description	Oper	Unit	Vol	Crew Size	Man-hours per Unit	Crew Output per Day	Avg Mat'l Unit Cost	Avg Labor Unit Cost	Avg Equip Unit Cost	Avg Total Unit Cost	Avg Price Incl O&P
Track type with hardware and deluxe lock											
8' x 7', single	Inst	Ea	Lg	2C	4.00	4.00	230.00	148.00	---	378.00	**472.00**
	Inst	Ea	Sm	2C	5.71	2.80	252.00	211.00	---	463.00	**586.00**
9' x 7', single	Inst	Ea	Lg	2C	4.00	4.00	258.00	148.00	---	406.00	**504.00**
	Inst	Ea	Sm	2C	5.71	2.80	283.00	211.00	---	494.00	**621.00**
16' x 7', double	Inst	Ea	Lg	2C	5.33	3.00	542.00	197.00	---	739.00	**900.00**
	Inst	Ea	Sm	2C	7.62	2.10	595.00	282.00	---	877.00	**1080.00**
Sectional type with hardware and key lock											
8' x 7', single	Inst	Ea	Lg	2C	4.00	4.00	403.00	148.00	---	551.00	**670.00**
	Inst	Ea	Sm	2C	5.71	2.80	442.00	211.00	---	653.00	**804.00**
9' x 7', single	Inst	Ea	Lg	2C	4.00	4.00	416.00	148.00	---	564.00	**686.00**
	Inst	Ea	Sm	2C	5.71	2.80	457.00	211.00	---	668.00	**821.00**
16' x 7', double	Inst	Ea	Lg	2C	5.33	3.00	610.00	197.00	---	807.00	**978.00**
	Inst	Ea	Sm	2C	7.62	2.10	670.00	282.00	---	952.00	**1170.00**

Fiberglass

Description	Oper	Unit	Vol	Crew Size	Man-hours per Unit	Crew Output per Day	Avg Mat'l Unit Cost	Avg Labor Unit Cost	Avg Equip Unit Cost	Avg Total Unit Cost	Avg Price Incl O&P
Jamb type with hardware and deluxe lock											
8' x 7', single	Inst	Ea	Lg	2C	4.00	4.00	475.00	148.00	---	623.00	**754.00**
	Inst	Ea	Sm	2C	5.71	2.80	522.00	211.00	---	733.00	**896.00**
8' x 8', single	Inst	Ea	Lg	2C	4.00	4.00	566.00	148.00	---	714.00	**858.00**
	Inst	Ea	Sm	2C	5.71	2.80	621.00	211.00	---	832.00	**1010.00**
9' x 7', single	Inst	Ea	Lg	2C	4.00	4.00	493.00	148.00	---	641.00	**775.00**
	Inst	Ea	Sm	2C	5.71	2.80	542.00	211.00	---	753.00	**919.00**
9' x 8', single	Inst	Ea	Lg	2C	4.00	4.00	591.00	148.00	---	739.00	**887.00**
	Inst	Ea	Sm	2C	5.71	2.80	649.00	211.00	---	860.00	**1040.00**
16' x 7', double	Inst	Ea	Lg	2C	5.33	3.00	692.00	197.00	---	889.00	**1070.00**
	Inst	Ea	Sm	2C	7.62	2.10	760.00	282.00	---	1042.00	**1270.00**
16' x 8', double	Inst	Ea	Lg	2C	5.33	3.00	795.00	197.00	---	992.00	**1190.00**
	Inst	Ea	Sm	2C	7.62	2.10	873.00	282.00	---	1155.00	**1400.00**
Track type with hardware and deluxe lock											
8' x 7', single	Inst	Ea	Lg	2C	4.00	4.00	216.00	148.00	---	364.00	**455.00**
	Inst	Ea	Sm	2C	5.71	2.80	237.00	211.00	---	448.00	**568.00**
9' x 7', single	Inst	Ea	Lg	2C	4.00	4.00	242.00	148.00	---	390.00	**485.00**
	Inst	Ea	Sm	2C	5.71	2.80	265.00	211.00	---	476.00	**601.00**
16' x 7', double	Inst	Ea	Lg	2C	5.33	3.00	508.00	197.00	---	705.00	**861.00**
	Inst	Ea	Sm	2C	7.62	2.10	558.00	282.00	---	840.00	**1040.00**
Sectional type with hardware and key lock											
8' x 7', single	Inst	Ea	Lg	2C	4.00	4.00	378.00	148.00	---	526.00	**641.00**
	Inst	Ea	Sm	2C	5.71	2.80	415.00	211.00	---	626.00	**773.00**
9' x 7', single	Inst	Ea	Lg	2C	4.00	4.00	390.00	148.00	---	538.00	**656.00**
	Inst	Ea	Sm	2C	5.71	2.80	428.00	211.00	---	639.00	**788.00**
16' x 7', double	Inst	Ea	Lg	2C	5.33	3.00	572.00	197.00	---	769.00	**934.00**
	Inst	Ea	Sm	2C	7.62	2.10	628.00	282.00	---	910.00	**1120.00**

Description	Oper	Unit	Vol	Crew Size	Man-hours per Unit	Crew Output per Day	Avg Mat'l Unit Cost	Avg Labor Unit Cost	Avg Equip Unit Cost	Avg Total Unit Cost	Avg Price Incl O&P
Steel											
Jamb type with hardware and deluxe lock											
8' x 7', single	Inst	Ea	Lg	2C	4.00	4.00	634.00	148.00	---	782.00	**936.00**
	Inst	Ea	Sm	2C	5.71	2.80	696.00	211.00	---	907.00	**1100.00**
8' x 8', single	Inst	Ea	Lg	2C	4.00	4.00	755.00	148.00	---	903.00	**1080.00**
	Inst	Ea	Sm	2C	5.71	2.80	829.00	211.00	---	1040.00	**1250.00**
9' x 7', single	Inst	Ea	Lg	2C	4.00	4.00	658.00	148.00	---	806.00	**964.00**
	Inst	Ea	Sm	2C	5.71	2.80	722.00	211.00	---	933.00	**1130.00**
9' x 8', single	Inst	Ea	Lg	2C	4.00	4.00	788.00	148.00	---	936.00	**1110.00**
	Inst	Ea	Sm	2C	5.71	2.80	865.00	211.00	---	1076.00	**1290.00**
16' x 7', double	Inst	Ea	Lg	2C	5.33	3.00	923.00	197.00	---	1120.00	**1340.00**
	Inst	Ea	Sm	2C	7.62	2.10	1010.00	282.00	---	1292.00	**1560.00**
16' x 8', double	Inst	Ea	Lg	2C	5.33	3.00	1060.00	197.00	---	1257.00	**1500.00**
	Inst	Ea	Sm	2C	7.62	2.10	1160.00	282.00	---	1442.00	**1730.00**
Track type with hardware and deluxe lock											
8' x 7', single	Inst	Ea	Lg	2C	4.00	4.00	287.00	148.00	---	435.00	**538.00**
	Inst	Ea	Sm	2C	5.71	2.80	316.00	211.00	---	527.00	**659.00**
9' x 7', single	Inst	Ea	Lg	2C	4.00	4.00	322.00	148.00	---	470.00	**578.00**
	Inst	Ea	Sm	2C	5.71	2.80	354.00	211.00	---	565.00	**703.00**
16' x 7', double	Inst	Ea	Lg	2C	5.33	3.00	678.00	197.00	---	875.00	**1060.00**
	Inst	Ea	Sm	2C	7.62	2.10	744.00	282.00	---	1026.00	**1250.00**
Sectional type with hardware and key lock											
8' x 7', single	Inst	Ea	Lg	2C	4.00	4.00	503.00	148.00	---	651.00	**786.00**
	Inst	Ea	Sm	2C	5.71	2.80	553.00	211.00	---	764.00	**932.00**
9' x 7', single	Inst	Ea	Lg	2C	4.00	4.00	520.00	148.00	---	668.00	**805.00**
	Inst	Ea	Sm	2C	5.71	2.80	571.00	211.00	---	782.00	**952.00**
16' x 7', double	Inst	Ea	Lg	2C	5.33	3.00	763.00	197.00	---	960.00	**1150.00**
	Inst	Ea	Sm	2C	7.62	2.10	837.00	282.00	---	1119.00	**1360.00**
Wood											
Jamb type with hardware and deluxe lock											
8' x 7', single	Inst	Ea	Lg	2C	4.00	4.00	570.00	148.00	---	718.00	**863.00**
	Inst	Ea	Sm	2C	5.71	2.80	626.00	211.00	---	837.00	**1020.00**
8' x 8', single	Inst	Ea	Lg	2C	4.00	4.00	679.00	148.00	---	827.00	**988.00**
	Inst	Ea	Sm	2C	5.71	2.80	746.00	211.00	---	957.00	**1150.00**
9' x 7', single	Inst	Ea	Lg	2C	4.00	4.00	592.00	148.00	---	740.00	**888.00**
	Inst	Ea	Sm	2C	5.71	2.80	650.00	211.00	---	861.00	**1040.00**
9' x 8', single	Inst	Ea	Lg	2C	4.00	4.00	709.00	148.00	---	857.00	**1020.00**
	Inst	Ea	Sm	2C	5.71	2.80	779.00	211.00	---	990.00	**1190.00**
16' x 7', double	Inst	Ea	Lg	2C	5.33	3.00	831.00	197.00	---	1028.00	**1230.00**
	Inst	Ea	Sm	2C	7.62	2.10	912.00	282.00	---	1194.00	**1440.00**
16' x 8', double	Inst	Ea	Lg	2C	5.33	3.00	954.00	197.00	---	1151.00	**1370.00**
	Inst	Ea	Sm	2C	7.62	2.10	1050.00	282.00	---	1332.00	**1600.00**

Description	Oper	Unit	Vol	Crew Size	Man-hours per Unit	Crew Output per Day	Avg Mat'l Unit Cost	Avg Labor Unit Cost	Avg Equip Unit Cost	Avg Total Unit Cost	Avg Price Incl O&P
Track type with hardware and deluxe lock											
8' x 7', single	Inst	Ea	Lg	2C	4.00	4.00	259.00	148.00	---	407.00	**505.00**
	Inst	Ea	Sm	2C	5.71	2.80	284.00	211.00	---	495.00	**623.00**
9' x 7', single	Inst	Ea	Lg	2C	4.00	4.00	290.00	148.00	---	438.00	**541.00**
	Inst	Ea	Sm	2C	5.71	2.80	318.00	211.00	---	529.00	**662.00**
16' x 7', double	Inst	Ea	Lg	2C	5.33	3.00	610.00	197.00	---	807.00	**978.00**
	Inst	Ea	Sm	2C	7.62	2.10	670.00	282.00	---	952.00	**1170.00**
Sectional type with hardware and key lock											
8' x 7', single	Inst	Ea	Lg	2C	4.00	4.00	453.00	148.00	---	601.00	**728.00**
	Inst	Ea	Sm	2C	5.71	2.80	497.00	211.00	---	708.00	**868.00**
9' x 7', single	Inst	Ea	Lg	2C	4.00	4.00	468.00	148.00	---	616.00	**745.00**
	Inst	Ea	Sm	2C	5.71	2.80	514.00	211.00	---	725.00	**887.00**
16' x 7', double	Inst	Ea	Lg	2C	5.33	3.00	686.00	197.00	---	883.00	**1070.00**
	Inst	Ea	Sm	2C	7.62	2.10	754.00	282.00	---	1036.00	**1260.00**

Garage door operators

Radio controlled for single or double doors. Labor includes wiring, connection and installation.

Description	Oper	Unit	Vol	Crew Size	Man-hours per Unit	Crew Output per Day	Avg Mat'l Unit Cost	Avg Labor Unit Cost	Avg Equip Unit Cost	Avg Total Unit Cost	Avg Price Incl O&P
Belt drive, with receiver and 2 transmitters, time delay light											
1/2 HP	Inst	LS	Lg	ED	5.33	3.00	170.00	206.00	---	376.00	**494.00**
	Inst	LS	Sm	ED	7.11	2.25	195.00	275.00	---	470.00	**622.00**
3/4 HP	Inst	LS	Lg	ED	5.33	3.00	200.00	206.00	---	406.00	**528.00**
	Inst	LS	Sm	ED	7.11	2.25	230.00	275.00	---	505.00	**662.00**
Chain drive, with receiver and 2 transmitters, time delay light											
1/2 HP	Inst	LS	Lg	ED	5.33	3.00	170.00	206.00	---	376.00	**494.00**
	Inst	LS	Sm	ED	7.11	2.25	195.00	275.00	---	470.00	**622.00**
3/4 HP	Inst	LS	Lg	ED	5.33	3.00	181.00	206.00	---	387.00	**506.00**
	Inst	LS	Sm	ED	7.11	2.25	208.00	275.00	---	483.00	**637.00**
Screw-worm drive, with receiver and 2 transmitters, time delay light											
1/2 HP	Inst	LS	Lg	ED	5.33	3.00	176.00	206.00	---	382.00	**500.00**
	Inst	LS	Sm	ED	7.11	2.25	202.00	275.00	---	477.00	**630.00**
3/4 HP	Inst	LS	Lg	ED	5.33	3.00	217.00	206.00	---	423.00	**548.00**
	Inst	LS	Sm	ED	7.11	2.25	249.00	275.00	---	524.00	**685.00**
1 HP	Inst	LS	Lg	ED	5.33	3.00	230.00	206.00	---	436.00	**563.00**
	Inst	LS	Sm	ED	7.11	2.25	264.00	275.00	---	539.00	**702.00**
Additional transmitters, ADD											
	Inst	Ea	Lg	EA	---	---	32.30	---	---	32.30	**37.20**
	Inst	Ea	Sm	EA	---	---	37.10	---	---	37.10	**42.70**
Wired keyless entry pad	Inst	Ea	Lg	EA	.667	12.00	45.50	26.80	---	72.30	**91.10**
	Inst	Ea	Sm	EA	.889	9.00	52.20	35.70	---	87.90	**112.00**
Sensors only, per pair	Inst	Pr	Lg	EA	.667	12.00	37.90	26.80	---	64.70	**82.40**
	Inst	Pr	Sm	EA	.889	9.00	43.50	35.70	---	79.20	**102.00**
Detach & Reset unit and receiver											
	Inst	LS	Lg	2C	2.67	6.00	---	98.80	---	98.80	**138.00**
	Inst	LS	Sm	2C	3.56	4.50	---	132.00	---	132.00	**185.00**

Description	Oper	Unit	Vol	Crew Size	Man-hours per Unit	Crew Output per Day	Avg Mat'l Unit Cost	Avg Labor Unit Cost	Avg Equip Unit Cost	Avg Total Unit Cost	Avg Price Incl O&P

Garbage disposers

Includes wall switch and labor includes rough-in.
See also Trash compactors, page 448

Frequently encountered applications

Detach & reset operations

Description	Oper	Unit	Vol	Crew Size	Man-hours per Unit	Crew Output per Day	Avg Mat'l Unit Cost	Avg Labor Unit Cost	Avg Equip Unit Cost	Avg Total Unit Cost	Avg Price Incl O&P
Garbage disposer	Reset	Ea	Lg	SA	2.67	3.00	---	115.00	---	115.00	**167.00**
	Reset	Ea	Sm	SA	3.56	2.25	---	153.00	---	153.00	**222.00**

Remove operations

Garbage disposer	Demo	Ea	Lg	SA	2.67	3.00	---	115.00	---	115.00	**167.00**
	Demo	Ea	Sm	SA	3.56	2.25	---	153.00	---	153.00	**222.00**

Replace operations

Economy	Inst	Ea	Lg	SA	2.67	3.00	139.00	115.00	---	254.00	**326.00**
	Inst	Ea	Sm	SA	3.56	2.25	161.00	153.00	---	314.00	**407.00**
Standard	Inst	Ea	Lg	SA	2.67	3.00	160.00	115.00	---	275.00	**350.00**
	Inst	Ea	Sm	SA	3.56	2.25	186.00	153.00	---	339.00	**435.00**
Average	Inst	Ea	Lg	SA	2.67	3.00	212.00	115.00	---	327.00	**410.00**
	Inst	Ea	Sm	SA	3.56	2.25	247.00	153.00	---	400.00	**506.00**
High	Inst	Ea	Lg	SA	2.67	3.00	283.00	115.00	---	398.00	**492.00**
	Inst	Ea	Sm	SA	3.56	2.25	329.00	153.00	---	482.00	**600.00**
Premium	Inst	Ea	Lg	SA	2.67	3.00	348.00	115.00	---	463.00	**567.00**
	Inst	Ea	Sm	SA	3.56	2.25	405.00	153.00	---	558.00	**688.00**

In-Sink-Erator Products

Model Badger 1, 1/3 HP, continuous feed, 1 year parts protection

	Oper	Unit	Vol	Crew Size	Man-hours per Unit	Crew Output per Day	Avg Mat'l Unit Cost	Avg Labor Unit Cost	Avg Equip Unit Cost	Avg Total Unit Cost	Avg Price Incl O&P
	Inst	Ea	Lg	SA	2.67	3.00	139.00	115.00	---	254.00	**326.00**
	Inst	Ea	Sm	SA	3.56	2.25	161.00	153.00	---	314.00	**407.00**

Model Badger 5, 1/2 HP, continuous feed, 1 year parts protection

	Inst	Ea	Lg	SA	2.67	3.00	160.00	115.00	---	275.00	**350.00**
	Inst	Ea	Sm	SA	3.56	2.25	186.00	153.00	---	339.00	**435.00**

Model 444, 3/4 HP, continuous feed, 4 year parts protection

	Inst	Ea	Lg	SA	2.67	3.00	212.00	115.00	---	327.00	**410.00**
	Inst	Ea	Sm	SA	3.56	2.25	247.00	153.00	---	400.00	**506.00**

Model 555SS, 3/4 HP, automatic reversing feed, 5 year parts protection, stainless steel construction

	Inst	Ea	Lg	SA	2.67	3.00	283.00	115.00	---	398.00	**492.00**
	Inst	Ea	Sm	SA	3.56	2.25	329.00	153.00	---	482.00	**600.00**

Model 777SS 1 HP, continuous feed, 7 year parts protection, stainless steel construction

	Inst	Ea	Lg	SA	2.67	3.00	348.00	115.00	---	463.00	**567.00**
	Inst	Ea	Sm	SA	3.56	2.25	405.00	153.00	---	558.00	**688.00**

Model 17, 3/4 HP, batch feed, auto reversing, 5 year parts protection, stainless steel construction

	Inst	Ea	Lg	SA	2.67	3.00	453.00	115.00	---	568.00	**688.00**
	Inst	Ea	Sm	SA	3.56	2.25	527.00	153.00	---	680.00	**828.00**

Septic, 3 year parts protection, stainless steel grind elements

	Inst	Ea	Lg	SA	2.67	3.00	347.00	115.00	---	462.00	**566.00**
	Inst	Ea	Sm	SA	3.56	2.25	404.00	153.00	---	557.00	**686.00**

Description	Oper	Unit	Vol	Crew Size	Man-hours per Unit	Crew Output per Day	Avg Mat'l Unit Cost	Avg Labor Unit Cost	Avg Equip Unit Cost	Avg Total Unit Cost	Avg Price Incl O&P

Adjustments

To only remove and reset garbage disposer

Description	Oper	Unit	Vol	Crew Size	Man-hours per Unit	Crew Output per Day	Avg Mat'l Unit Cost	Avg Labor Unit Cost	Avg Equip Unit Cost	Avg Total Unit Cost	Avg Price Incl O&P
	Reset	Ea	Lg	SA	2.67	3.00	---	115.00	---	115.00	**167.00**
	Reset	Ea	Sm	SA	3.56	2.25	---	153.00	---	153.00	**222.00**

To only remove garbage disposer

Description	Oper	Unit	Vol	Crew Size	Man-hours per Unit	Crew Output per Day	Avg Mat'l Unit Cost	Avg Labor Unit Cost	Avg Equip Unit Cost	Avg Total Unit Cost	Avg Price Incl O&P
	Demo	Ea	Lg	SA	2.67	3.00	---	115.00	---	115.00	**167.00**
	Demo	Ea	Sm	SA	3.56	2.25	---	153.00	---	153.00	**222.00**

Parts and accessories

Description	Oper	Unit	Vol	Crew Size	Man-hours per Unit	Crew Output per Day	Avg Mat'l Unit Cost	Avg Labor Unit Cost	Avg Equip Unit Cost	Avg Total Unit Cost	Avg Price Incl O&P
Stainless steel stopper	Inst	Ea	Lg	---	---	---	13.00	---	---	13.00	**15.00**
	Inst	Ea	Sm	---	---	---	15.10	---	---	15.10	**17.40**
Dishwasher connector kit	Inst	Ea	Lg	---	---	---	11.30	---	---	11.30	**13.00**
	Inst	Ea	Sm	---	---	---	13.10	---	---	13.10	**15.10**
Flexible tail pipe	Inst	Ea	Lg	---	---	---	14.70	---	---	14.70	**14.70**
	Inst	Ea	Sm	---	---	---	17.10	---	---	17.10	**17.10**
Power cord accessory kit	Inst	Ea	Lg	---	---	---	12.50	---	---	12.50	**14.40**
	Inst	Ea	Sm	---	---	---	14.60	---	---	14.60	**16.80**
Service wrench	Inst	Ea	Lg	---	---	---	6.44	---	---	6.44	**6.44**
	Inst	Ea	Sm	---	---	---	7.49	---	---	7.49	**7.49**
Plastic stopper	Inst	Ea	Lg	---	---	---	6.44	---	---	6.44	**7.41**
	Inst	Ea	Sm	---	---	---	7.49	---	---	7.49	**8.61**
Deluxe mounting gasket	Inst	Ea	Lg	---	---	---	8.97	---	---	8.97	**10.30**
	Inst	Ea	Sm	---	---	---	10.40	---	---	10.40	**12.00**

Girders. See Framing, page 176

Description	Oper	Unit	Vol	Crew Size	Man-hours per Unit	Crew Output per Day	Avg Mat'l Unit Cost	Avg Labor Unit Cost	Avg Equip Unit Cost	Avg Total Unit Cost	Avg Price Incl O&P

Glass and glazing

3/16" T tempered with putty in wood sash

Description	Oper	Unit	Vol	Crew Size	Man-hours per Unit	Crew Output per Day	Avg Mat'l Unit Cost	Avg Labor Unit Cost	Avg Equip Unit Cost	Avg Total Unit Cost	Avg Price Incl O&P
8" x 12"	Demo	SF	Lg	GA	.320	25.00	---	11.50	---	11.50	**16.30**
	Demo	SF	Sm	GA	.457	17.50	---	16.40	---	16.40	**23.20**
8" x 12"	Inst	SF	Lg	GA	.267	30.00	7.61	9.55	---	17.16	**22.30**
	Inst	SF	Sm	GA	.381	21.00	8.35	13.60	---	21.95	**29.00**
12" x 16"	Demo	SF	Lg	GA	.178	45.00	---	6.37	---	6.37	**9.04**
	Demo	SF	Sm	GA	.254	31.50	---	9.09	---	9.09	**12.90**
12" x 16"	Inst	SF	Lg	GA	.145	55.00	7.00	5.19	---	12.19	**15.40**
	Inst	SF	Sm	GA	.208	38.50	7.68	7.44	---	15.12	**19.40**
14" x 20"	Demo	SF	Lg	GA	.145	55.00	---	5.19	---	5.19	**7.37**
	Demo	SF	Sm	GA	.208	38.50	---	7.44	---	7.44	**10.60**
14" x 20"	Inst	SF	Lg	GA	.114	70.00	6.40	4.08	---	10.48	**13.20**
	Inst	SF	Sm	GA	.163	49.00	7.02	5.83	---	12.85	**16.40**
16" x 24"	Demo	SF	Lg	GA	.114	70.00	---	4.08	---	4.08	**5.79**
	Demo	SF	Sm	GA	.163	49.00	---	5.83	---	5.83	**8.28**
16" x 24"	Inst	SF	Lg	GA	.089	90.00	5.79	3.18	---	8.97	**11.20**
	Inst	SF	Sm	GA	.127	63.00	6.35	4.54	---	10.89	**13.80**
24" x 26"	Demo	SF	Lg	GA	.084	95.00	---	3.01	---	3.01	**4.27**
	Demo	SF	Sm	GA	.120	66.50	---	4.29	---	4.29	**6.10**
24" x 26"	Inst	SF	Lg	GA	.067	120.0	5.18	2.40	---	7.58	**9.36**
	Inst	SF	Sm	GA	.095	84.00	5.68	3.40	---	9.08	**11.40**
36" x 24"	Demo	SF	Lg	GA	.064	125.0	---	2.29	---	2.29	**3.25**
	Demo	SF	Sm	GA	.091	87.50	---	3.26	---	3.26	**4.62**
36" x 24"	Inst	SF	Lg	GA	.052	155.0	4.56	1.86	---	6.42	**7.89**
	Inst	SF	Sm	GA	.074	108.5	5.01	2.65	---	7.66	**9.52**

1/8" T tempered with putty in steel sash

Description	Oper	Unit	Vol	Crew Size	Man-hours per Unit	Crew Output per Day	Avg Mat'l Unit Cost	Avg Labor Unit Cost	Avg Equip Unit Cost	Avg Total Unit Cost	Avg Price Incl O&P
12" x 16"	Demo	SF	Lg	GA	.178	45.00	---	6.37	---	6.37	**9.04**
	Demo	SF	Sm	GA	.254	31.50	---	9.09	---	9.09	**12.90**
12" x 16"	Inst	SF	Lg	GA	.145	55.00	7.21	5.19	---	12.40	**15.70**
	Inst	SF	Sm	GA	.208	38.50	7.91	7.44	---	15.35	**19.70**
16" x 20"	Demo	SF	Lg	GA	.123	65.00	---	4.40	---	4.40	**6.25**
	Demo	SF	Sm	GA	.176	45.50	---	6.30	---	6.30	**8.94**
16" x 20"	Inst	SF	Lg	GA	.100	80.00	6.63	3.58	---	10.21	**12.70**
	Inst	SF	Sm	GA	.143	56.00	7.28	5.12	---	12.40	**15.60**
16" x 24"	Demo	SF	Lg	GA	.114	70.00	---	4.08	---	4.08	**5.79**
	Demo	SF	Sm	GA	.163	49.00	---	5.83	---	5.83	**8.28**
16" x 24"	Inst	SF	Lg	GA	.089	90.00	6.06	3.18	---	9.24	**11.50**
	Inst	SF	Sm	GA	.127	63.00	6.64	4.54	---	11.18	**14.10**
24" x 24"	Demo	SF	Lg	GA	.084	95.00	---	3.01	---	3.01	**4.27**
	Demo	SF	Sm	GA	.120	66.50	---	4.29	---	4.29	**6.10**
24" x 24"	Inst	SF	Lg	GA	.067	120.0	5.48	2.40	---	7.88	**9.71**
	Inst	SF	Sm	GA	.095	84.00	6.01	3.40	---	9.41	**11.70**
28" x 32"	Demo	SF	Lg	GA	.062	130.0	---	2.22	---	2.22	**3.15**
	Demo	SF	Sm	GA	.088	91.00	---	3.15	---	3.15	**4.47**

Description	Oper	Unit	Vol	Crew Size	Man-hours per Unit	Crew Output per Day	Avg Mat'l Unit Cost	Avg Labor Unit Cost	Avg Equip Unit Cost	Avg Total Unit Cost	Avg Price Incl O&P
28" x 32"	Inst	SF	Lg	GA	.050	160.0	4.90	1.79	---	6.69	**8.18**
	Inst	SF	Sm	GA	.071	112.0	5.38	2.54	---	7.92	**9.79**
36" x 36"	Demo	SF	Lg	GA	.050	160.0	---	1.79	---	1.79	**2.54**
	Demo	SF	Sm	GA	.071	112.0	---	2.54	---	2.54	**3.61**
36" x 36"	Inst	SF	Lg	GA	.039	205.0	4.33	1.40	---	5.73	**6.96**
	Inst	SF	Sm	GA	.056	143.5	4.75	2.00	---	6.75	**8.31**
36" x 48"	Demo	SF	Lg	GA	.042	190.0	---	1.50	---	1.50	**2.13**
	Demo	SF	Sm	GA	.060	133.0	---	2.15	---	2.15	**3.05**
36" x 48"	Inst	SF	Lg	GA	.032	250.0	3.75	1.14	---	4.89	**5.94**
	Inst	SF	Sm	GA	.046	175.0	4.11	1.65	---	5.76	**7.06**

1/4" T tempered

With putty and points in wood sash

Description	Oper	Unit	Vol	Crew Size	Man-hours per Unit	Crew Output per Day	Avg Mat'l Unit Cost	Avg Labor Unit Cost	Avg Equip Unit Cost	Avg Total Unit Cost	Avg Price Incl O&P
72" x 48"	Demo	SF	Lg	GA	.043	185.0	---	1.54	---	1.54	**2.18**
	Demo	SF	Sm	GA	.062	129.5	---	2.22	---	2.22	**3.15**
72" x 48"	Inst	SF	Lg	GB	.052	305.0	2.78	1.86	---	4.64	**5.84**
	Inst	SF	Sm	GB	.075	213.5	3.05	2.68	---	5.73	**7.32**

With aluminum channel and rigid neoprene rubber in aluminum sash

Description	Oper	Unit	Vol	Crew Size	Man-hours per Unit	Crew Output per Day	Avg Mat'l Unit Cost	Avg Labor Unit Cost	Avg Equip Unit Cost	Avg Total Unit Cost	Avg Price Incl O&P
48" x 96"	Demo	SF	Lg	GA	.046	175.0	---	1.65	---	1.65	**2.34**
	Demo	SF	Sm	GA	.065	122.5	---	2.33	---	2.33	**3.30**
48" x 96"	Inst	SF	Lg	GB	.046	350.0	2.16	1.65	---	3.81	**4.82**
	Inst	SF	Sm	GB	.065	245.0	2.37	2.33	---	4.70	**6.03**
96" x 96"	Demo	SF	Lg	GA	.044	180.0	---	1.57	---	1.57	**2.24**
	Demo	SF	Sm	GA	.063	126.0	---	2.25	---	2.25	**3.20**
96" x 96"	Inst	SF	Lg	GC	.037	645.0	1.55	1.32	---	2.87	**3.66**
	Inst	SF	Sm	GC	.053	451.5	1.70	1.90	---	3.60	**4.65**

1" T insulating glass (2 pieces 1/4" T float with 1/2" air space) with putty and points in wood sash

Description	Oper	Unit	Vol	Crew Size	Man-hours per Unit	Crew Output per Day	Avg Mat'l Unit Cost	Avg Labor Unit Cost	Avg Equip Unit Cost	Avg Total Unit Cost	Avg Price Incl O&P
To 6.0 SF	Demo	SF	Lg	GA	.160	50.00	---	5.72	---	5.72	**8.13**
	Demo	SF	Sm	GA	.229	35.00	---	8.19	---	8.19	**11.60**
To 6.0 SF	Inst	SF	Lg	GA	.133	60.00	11.90	4.76	---	16.66	**20.50**
	Inst	SF	Sm	GA	.190	42.00	13.10	6.80	---	19.90	**24.70**
6.1 SF to 12.0 SF	Demo	SF	Lg	GA	.073	110.0	---	2.61	---	2.61	**3.71**
	Demo	SF	Sm	GA	.104	77.00	---	3.72	---	3.72	**5.28**
6.1 SF to 12.0 SF	Inst	SF	Lg	GA	.059	135.0	9.14	2.11	---	11.25	**13.50**
	Inst	SF	Sm	GA	.085	94.50	10.00	3.04	---	13.04	**15.80**
12.1 SF to 18.0 SF	Demo	SF	Lg	GA	.053	150.0	---	1.90	---	1.90	**2.69**
	Demo	SF	Sm	GA	.076	105.0	---	2.72	---	2.72	**3.86**
12.1 SF to 18.0 SF	Inst	SF	Lg	GA	.044	180.0	7.73	1.57	---	9.30	**11.10**
	Inst	SF	Sm	GA	.063	126.0	8.48	2.25	---	10.73	**13.00**
18.1 SF to 24.0 SF	Demo	SF	Lg	GA	.055	145.0	---	1.97	---	1.97	**2.79**
	Demo	SF	Sm	GA	.079	101.5	---	2.83	---	2.83	**4.01**
18.1 SF to 24.0 SF	Inst	SF	Lg	GB	.064	250.0	6.32	2.29	---	8.61	**10.50**
	Inst	SF	Sm	GB	.091	175.0	6.94	3.26	---	10.20	**12.60**

Description	Oper	Unit	Vol	Crew Size	Man-hours per Unit	Crew Output per Day	Avg Mat'l Unit Cost	Avg Labor Unit Cost	Avg Equip Unit Cost	Avg Total Unit Cost	Avg Price Incl O&P

Aluminum sliding door glass with aluminum channel and rigid neoprene rubber

3/16" T tempered glass

Description	Oper	Unit	Vol	Crew Size	MH	Output	Mat'l	Labor	Equip	Total	Price
34" W x 76" H	Demo	SF	Lg	GA	.041	195.0	---	1.47	---	1.47	**2.08**
	Demo	SF	Sm	GA	.059	136.5	---	2.11	---	2.11	**3.00**
34" W x 76" H	Inst	SF	Lg	GA	.033	245.0	3.35	1.18	---	4.53	**5.53**
	Inst	SF	Sm	GA	.047	171.5	3.67	1.68	---	5.35	**6.61**
46" W x 76" H	Demo	SF	Lg	GA	.033	245.0	---	1.18	---	1.18	**1.68**
	Demo	SF	Sm	GA	.047	171.5	---	1.68	---	1.68	**2.39**
46" W x 76" H	Inst	SF	Lg	GB	.048	330.0	2.74	1.72	---	4.46	**5.59**
	Inst	SF	Sm	GB	.069	231.0	3.01	2.47	---	5.48	**6.97**

5/8" T insulating glass (2 pieces 3/16" T tempered with 1/4" T air space)

Description	Oper	Unit	Vol	Crew Size	MH	Output	Mat'l	Labor	Equip	Total	Price
34" W x 76" H	Demo	SF	Lg	GA	.047	170.0	---	1.68	---	1.68	**2.39**
	Demo	SF	Sm	GA	.067	119.0	---	2.40	---	2.40	**3.40**
34" W x 76" H	Inst	SF	Lg	GA	.035	230.0	7.61	1.25	---	8.86	**10.50**
	Inst	SF	Sm	GA	.050	161.0	8.35	1.79	---	10.14	**12.10**
46" W x 76" H	Demo	SF	Lg	GA	.037	215.0	---	1.32	---	1.32	**1.88**
	Demo	SF	Sm	GA	.053	150.5	---	1.90	---	1.90	**2.69**
46" W x 76" H	Inst	SF	Lg	GB	.052	310.0	6.23	1.86	---	8.09	**9.81**
	Inst	SF	Sm	GB	.074	217.0	6.84	2.65	---	9.49	**11.60**

Grading. See Concrete, page 98

Glu-lam products

Beams

3-1/8" thick, SF pricing based on 16" oc

Description	Oper	Unit	Vol	Crew Size	Man-hours per Unit	Crew Output per Day	Avg Mat'l Unit Cost	Avg Labor Unit Cost	Avg Equip Unit Cost	Avg Total Unit Cost	Avg Price Incl O&P
9" deep, 20' long	Demo	LF	Lg	LK	.133	360.0	---	4.57	.72	5.29	7.12
	Demo	LF	Sm	LK	.190	252.0	---	6.53	1.03	7.56	10.20
9" deep, 20' long	Inst	LF	Lg	CY	.156	360.0	7.76	5.42	.72	13.90	17.20
	Inst	LF	Sm	CY	.222	252.0	9.08	7.72	1.03	17.83	22.30
9" deep, 20' long	Demo	BF	Lg	LK	.044	1080	---	1.51	.24	1.75	2.36
	Demo	BF	Sm	LK	.063	756.0	---	2.17	.34	2.51	3.37
9" deep, 20' long	Inst	BF	Lg	CY	.052	1080	2.59	1.81	.24	4.64	5.75
	Inst	BF	Sm	CY	.074	756.0	3.03	2.57	.34	5.94	7.43
9" deep, 20' long	Demo	SF	Lg	LK	.007	6545	---	.24	.04	.28	.38
	Demo	SF	Sm	LK	.010	4582	---	.34	.06	.40	.54
9" deep, 20' long	Inst	SF	Lg	CY	.009	6545	.43	.31	.04	.78	.97
	Inst	SF	Sm	CY	.012	4582	.50	.42	.06	.98	1.22
10-1/2" deep, 20' long	Demo	LF	Lg	LK	.133	360.0	---	4.57	.72	5.29	7.12
	Demo	LF	Sm	LK	.190	252.0	---	6.53	1.03	7.56	10.20
10-1/2" deep, 20' long	Inst	LF	Lg	CY	.156	360.0	9.04	5.42	.72	15.18	18.70
	Inst	LF	Sm	CY	.222	252.0	10.60	7.72	1.03	19.35	24.00
10-1/2" deep, 20' long	Demo	BF	Lg	LK	.038	1260	---	1.31	.21	1.52	2.04
	Demo	BF	Sm	LK	.054	882.0	---	1.86	.29	2.15	2.89
10-1/2" deep, 20' long	Inst	BF	Lg	CY	.044	1260	2.58	1.53	.21	4.32	5.32
	Inst	BF	Sm	CY	.063	882.0	3.03	2.19	.29	5.51	6.84
10-1/2" deep, 20' long	Demo	SF	Lg	LK	.007	6545	---	.24	.04	.28	.38
	Demo	SF	Sm	LK	.010	4582	---	.34	.06	.40	.54
10-1/2" deep, 20' long	Inst	SF	Lg	CY	.009	6545	.50	.31	.04	.85	1.05
	Inst	SF	Sm	CY	.012	4582	.58	.42	.06	1.06	1.31
12" deep, 20' long	Demo	LF	Lg	LK	.133	360.0	---	4.57	.72	5.29	7.12
	Demo	LF	Sm	LK	.190	252.0	---	6.53	1.03	7.56	10.20
12" deep, 20' long	Inst	LF	Lg	CY	.156	360.0	10.40	5.42	.72	16.54	20.20
	Inst	LF	Sm	CY	.222	252.0	12.10	7.72	1.03	20.85	25.80
12" deep, 20' long	Demo	BF	Lg	LK	.033	1440	---	1.13	.18	1.31	1.77
	Demo	BF	Sm	LK	.048	1008	---	1.65	.26	1.91	2.57
12" deep, 20' long	Inst	BF	Lg	CY	.039	1440	2.59	1.36	.18	4.13	5.06
	Inst	BF	Sm	CY	.056	1008	3.03	1.95	.26	5.24	6.47
12" deep, 20' long	Demo	SF	Lg	LK	.007	6545	---	.24	.04	.28	.38
	Demo	SF	Sm	LK	.010	4582	---	.34	.06	.40	.54
12" deep, 20' long	Inst	SF	Lg	CY	.009	6545	.57	.31	.04	.92	1.13
	Inst	SF	Sm	CY	.012	4582	.67	.42	.06	1.15	1.41
13-1/2" deep, 20' long	Demo	LF	Lg	LK	.133	360.0	---	4.57	.72	5.29	7.12
	Demo	LF	Sm	LK	.190	252.0	---	6.53	1.03	7.56	10.20
13-1/2" deep, 20' long	Inst	LF	Lg	CY	.156	360.0	11.60	5.42	.72	17.74	21.70
	Inst	LF	Sm	CY	.222	252.0	13.60	7.72	1.03	22.35	27.50
13-1/2" deep, 20' long	Demo	BF	Lg	LK	.030	1620	---	1.03	.16	1.19	1.60
	Demo	BF	Sm	LK	.042	1134	---	1.44	.23	1.67	2.25

Description	Oper	Unit	Vol	Crew Size	Man-hours per Unit	Crew Output per Day	Avg Mat'l Unit Cost	Avg Labor Unit Cost	Avg Equip Unit Cost	Avg Total Unit Cost	Avg Price Incl O&P
13-1/2" deep, 20' long	Inst	BF	Lg	CY	.035	1620	2.59	1.22	.16	3.97	**4.84**
	Inst	BF	Sm	CY	.049	1134	3.03	1.70	.23	4.96	**6.10**
13-1/2" deep, 20' long	Demo	SF	Lg	LK	.007	6545	---	.24	.04	.28	**.38**
	Demo	SF	Sm	LK	.010	4582	---	.34	.06	.40	**.54**
13-1/2" deep, 20' long	Inst	SF	Lg	CY	.009	6545	.64	.31	.04	.99	**1.21**
	Inst	SF	Sm	CY	.012	4582	.75	.42	.06	1.23	**1.51**
15" deep, 20' long	Demo	LF	Lg	LK	.133	360.0	---	4.57	.72	5.29	**7.12**
	Demo	LF	Sm	LK	.190	252.0	---	6.53	1.03	7.56	**10.20**
15" deep, 20' long	Inst	LF	Lg	CY	.156	360.0	12.90	5.42	.72	19.04	**23.20**
	Inst	LF	Sm	CY	.222	252.0	15.20	7.72	1.03	23.95	**29.30**
15" deep, 20' long	Demo	BF	Lg	LK	.027	1800	---	.93	.14	1.07	**1.44**
	Demo	BF	Sm	LK	.038	1260	---	1.31	.21	1.52	**2.04**
15" deep, 20' long	Inst	BF	Lg	CY	.031	1800	2.58	1.08	.14	3.80	**4.62**
	Inst	BF	Sm	CY	.044	1260	3.03	1.53	.21	4.77	**5.84**
15" deep, 20' long	Demo	SF	Lg	LK	.007	6545	---	.24	.04	.28	**.38**
	Demo	SF	Sm	LK	.010	4582	---	.34	.06	.40	**.54**
15" deep, 20' long	Inst	SF	Lg	CY	.009	6545	.71	.31	.04	1.06	**1.29**
	Inst	SF	Sm	CY	.012	4582	.83	.42	.06	1.31	**1.60**
16-1/2" deep, 20' long	Demo	LF	Lg	LK	.133	360.0	---	4.57	---	4.57	**6.40**
	Demo	LF	Sm	LK	.190	252.0	---	6.53	---	6.53	**9.15**
16-1/2" deep, 20' long	Inst	LF	Lg	CY	.156	360.0	14.20	5.42	---	19.62	**24.00**
	Inst	LF	Sm	CY	.222	252.0	16.70	7.72	---	24.42	**30.00**
16-1/2" deep, 20' long	Demo	BF	Lg	LK	.024	1980	---	.83	---	.83	**1.16**
	Demo	BF	Sm	LK	.035	1386	---	1.20	---	1.20	**1.68**
16-1/2" deep, 20' long	Inst	BF	Lg	CY	.028	1980	2.59	.97	---	3.56	**4.34**
	Inst	BF	Sm	CY	.040	1386	3.03	1.39	---	4.42	**5.43**
16-1/2" deep, 20' long	Demo	SF	Lg	LK	.007	6545	---	.24	---	.24	**.34**
	Demo	SF	Sm	LK	.010	4582	---	.34	---	.34	**.48**
16-1/2" deep, 20' long	Inst	SF	Lg	CY	.009	6545	.78	.31	---	1.09	**1.34**
	Inst	SF	Sm	CY	.012	4582	.92	.42	---	1.34	**1.64**
18" deep, 20' long	Demo	LF	Lg	LK	.133	360.0	---	4.57	.72	5.29	**7.12**
	Demo	LF	Sm	LK	.190	252.0	---	6.53	1.03	7.56	**10.20**
18" deep, 20' long	Inst	LF	Lg	CY	.156	360.0	15.50	5.42	.72	21.64	**26.20**
	Inst	LF	Sm	CY	.222	252.0	18.20	7.72	1.03	26.95	**32.80**
18" deep, 20' long	Demo	BF	Lg	LK	.022	2160	---	.76	.12	.88	**1.18**
	Demo	BF	Sm	LK	.032	1512	---	1.10	.17	1.27	**1.71**
18" deep, 20' long	Inst	BF	Lg	CY	.026	2160	2.59	.90	.12	3.61	**4.36**
	Inst	BF	Sm	CY	.037	1512	3.03	1.29	.17	4.49	**5.46**
18" deep, 20' long	Demo	SF	Lg	LK	.007	6545	---	.24	.04	.28	**.38**
	Demo	SF	Sm	LK	.010	4582	---	.34	.06	.40	**.54**
18" deep, 20' long	Inst	SF	Lg	CY	.009	6545	.85	.31	.04	1.20	**1.46**
	Inst	SF	Sm	CY	.012	4582	1.00	.42	.06	1.48	**1.79**

Description	Oper	Unit	Vol	Crew Size	Man-hours per Unit	Crew Output per Day	Avg Mat'l Unit Cost	Avg Labor Unit Cost	Avg Equip Unit Cost	Avg Total Unit Cost	Avg Price Incl O&P

3-1/8" thick beams, SF pricing based on 16" oc (continued)

Description	Oper	Unit	Vol	Crew Size	Man-hours per Unit	Crew Output per Day	Avg Mat'l Unit Cost	Avg Labor Unit Cost	Avg Equip Unit Cost	Avg Total Unit Cost	Avg Price Incl O&P
19-1/2" deep, 30' long	Demo	LF	Lg	LK	.133	360.0	---	4.57	.72	5.29	7.12
	Demo	LF	Sm	LK	.190	252.0	---	6.53	1.03	7.56	10.20
19-1/2" deep, 30' long	Inst	LF	Lg	CY	.156	360.0	16.80	5.42	.72	22.94	27.70
	Inst	LF	Sm	CY	.222	252.0	19.70	7.72	1.03	28.45	34.50
19-1/2" deep, 30' long	Demo	BF	Lg	LK	.021	2340	---	.72	.11	.83	1.12
	Demo	BF	Sm	LK	.029	1638	---	1.00	.16	1.16	1.56
19-1/2" deep, 30' long	Inst	BF	Lg	CY	.024	2340	2.59	.83	.11	3.53	4.26
	Inst	BF	Sm	CY	.034	1638	3.03	1.18	.16	4.37	5.30
19-1/2" deep, 30' long	Demo	SF	Lg	LK	.007	6545	---	.24	.04	.28	.38
	Demo	SF	Sm	LK	.010	4582	---	.34	.06	.40	.54
19-1/2" deep, 30' long	Inst	SF	Lg	CY	.009	6545	.93	.31	.04	1.28	1.55
	Inst	SF	Sm	CY	.012	4582	1.08	.42	.06	1.56	1.89
21" deep, 30' long	Demo	LF	Lg	LK	.133	360.0	---	4.57	.72	5.29	7.12
	Demo	LF	Sm	LK	.190	252.0	---	6.53	1.03	7.56	10.20
21" deep, 30' long	Inst	LF	Lg	CY	.156	360.0	18.10	5.42	.72	24.24	29.20
	Inst	LF	Sm	CY	.222	252.0	21.20	7.72	1.03	29.95	36.20
21" deep, 30' long	Demo	BF	Lg	LK	.019	2520	---	.65	.10	.75	1.01
	Demo	BF	Sm	LK	.027	1764	---	.93	.15	1.08	1.45
21" deep, 30' long	Inst	BF	Lg	CY	.022	2520	2.59	.76	.10	3.45	4.15
	Inst	BF	Sm	CY	.032	1764	3.03	1.11	.15	4.29	5.19
21" deep, 30' long	Demo	SF	Lg	LK	.007	6545	---	.24	.04	.28	.38
	Demo	SF	Sm	LK	.010	4582	---	.34	.06	.40	.54
21" deep, 30' long	Inst	SF	Lg	CY	.009	6545	1.00	.31	.04	1.35	1.63
	Inst	SF	Sm	CY	.012	4582	1.17	.42	.06	1.65	1.99
22-1/2" deep, 30' long	Demo	LF	Lg	LK	.133	360.0	---	4.57	.72	5.29	7.12
	Demo	LF	Sm	LK	.190	252.0	---	6.53	1.03	7.56	10.20
22-1/2" deep, 30' long	Inst	LF	Lg	CY	.156	360.0	19.40	5.42	.72	25.54	30.60
	Inst	LF	Sm	CY	.222	252.0	22.70	7.72	1.03	31.45	38.00
22-1/2" deep, 30' long	Demo	BF	Lg	LK	.018	2700	---	.62	.10	.72	.97
	Demo	BF	Sm	LK	.025	1890	---	.86	.14	1.00	1.34
22-1/2" deep, 30' long	Inst	BF	Lg	CY	.021	2700	2.59	.73	.10	3.42	4.10
	Inst	BF	Sm	CY	.030	1890	3.03	1.04	.14	4.21	5.08
22-1/2" deep, 30' long	Demo	SF	Lg	LK	.007	6545	---	.24	.04	.28	.38
	Demo	SF	Sm	LK	.010	4582	---	.34	.06	.40	.54
22-1/2" deep, 30' long	Inst	SF	Lg	CY	.009	6545	1.07	.31	.04	1.42	1.71
	Inst	SF	Sm	CY	.012	4582	1.25	.42	.06	1.73	2.08
24" deep, 30' long	Demo	LF	Lg	LK	.133	360.0	---	4.57	.72	5.29	7.12
	Demo	LF	Sm	LK	.190	252.0	---	6.53	1.03	7.56	10.20
24" deep, 30' long	Inst	LF	Lg	CY	.156	360.0	20.70	5.42	.72	26.84	32.10
	Inst	LF	Sm	CY	.222	252.0	24.20	7.72	1.03	32.95	39.70
24" deep, 30' long	Demo	BF	Lg	LK	.017	2880	---	.58	.09	.67	.91
	Demo	BF	Sm	LK	.024	2016	---	.83	.13	.96	1.29

Description	Oper	Unit	Vol	Crew Size	Man-hours per Unit	Crew Output per Day	Avg Mat'l Unit Cost	Avg Labor Unit Cost	Avg Equip Unit Cost	Avg Total Unit Cost	Avg Price Incl O&P
24" deep, 30' long	Inst	BF	Lg	CY	.019	2880	2.59	.66	.09	3.34	**3.99**
	Inst	BF	Sm	CY	.028	2016	3.03	.97	.13	4.13	**4.98**
24" deep, 30' long	Demo	SF	Lg	LK	.007	6545	---	.24	.04	.28	**.38**
	Demo	SF	Sm	LK	.010	4582	---	.34	.06	.40	**.54**
24" deep, 30' long	Inst	SF	Lg	CY	.009	6545	1.14	.31	.04	1.49	**1.79**
	Inst	SF	Sm	CY	.012	4582	1.33	.42	.06	1.81	**2.17**
25-1/2" deep, 30' long	Demo	LF	Lg	LK	.133	360.0	---	4.57	.72	5.29	**7.12**
	Demo	LF	Sm	LK	.190	252.0	---	6.53	1.03	7.56	**10.20**
25-1/2" deep, 30' long	Inst	LF	Lg	CY	.156	360.0	22.00	5.42	.72	28.14	**33.60**
	Inst	LF	Sm	CY	.222	252.0	25.80	7.72	1.03	34.55	**41.50**
25-1/2" deep, 30' long	Demo	BF	Lg	LK	.016	3060	---	.55	.08	.63	**.85**
	Demo	BF	Sm	LK	.022	2142	---	.76	.12	.88	**1.18**
25-1/2" deep, 30' long	Inst	BF	Lg	CY	.018	3060	2.59	.63	.08	3.30	**3.93**
	Inst	BF	Sm	CY	.026	2142	3.03	.90	.12	4.05	**4.87**
25-1/2" deep, 30' long	Demo	SF	Lg	LK	.007	6545	---	.24	.04	.28	**.38**
	Demo	SF	Sm	LK	.010	4582	---	.34	.06	.40	**.54**
25-1/2" deep, 30' long	Inst	SF	Lg	CY	.009	6545	1.21	.31	.04	1.56	**1.87**
	Inst	SF	Sm	CY	.012	4582	1.42	.42	.06	1.90	**2.28**
27" deep, 30' long	Demo	LF	Lg	LK	.133	360.0	---	4.57	.72	5.29	**7.12**
	Demo	LF	Sm	LK	.190	252.0	---	6.53	1.03	7.56	**10.20**
27" deep, 30' long	Inst	LF	Lg	CY	.156	360.0	23.30	5.42	.72	29.44	**35.10**
	Inst	LF	Sm	CY	.222	252.0	27.30	7.72	1.03	36.05	**43.20**
27" deep, 30' long	Demo	BF	Lg	LK	.015	3240	---	.52	.08	.60	**.80**
	Demo	BF	Sm	LK	.021	2268	---	.72	.11	.83	**1.12**
27" deep, 30' long	Inst	BF	Lg	CY	.017	3240	2.59	.59	.08	3.26	**3.89**
	Inst	BF	Sm	CY	.025	2268	3.03	.87	.11	4.01	**4.81**
27" deep, 30' long	Demo	SF	Lg	LK	.007	6545	---	.24	.04	.28	**.38**
	Demo	SF	Sm	LK	.010	4582	---	.34	.06	.40	**.54**
27" deep, 30' long	Inst	SF	Lg	CY	.009	6545	1.28	.31	.04	1.63	**1.95**
	Inst	SF	Sm	CY	.012	4582	1.50	.42	.06	1.98	**2.37**

5-1/8" thick, SF pricing based on 16" oc

Description	Oper	Unit	Vol	Crew Size	Man-hours per Unit	Crew Output per Day	Avg Mat'l Unit Cost	Avg Labor Unit Cost	Avg Equip Unit Cost	Avg Total Unit Cost	Avg Price Incl O&P
12" deep, 20' long	Demo	LF	Lg	LK	.133	360.0	---	4.57	.72	5.29	**7.12**
	Demo	LF	Sm	LK	.190	252.0	---	6.53	1.03	7.56	**10.20**
12" deep, 20' long	Inst	LF	Lg	CY	.156	360.0	16.10	5.42	.72	22.24	**26.90**
	Inst	LF	Sm	CY	.222	252.0	18.90	7.72	1.03	27.65	**33.60**
12" deep, 20' long	Demo	BF	Lg	LK	.022	2160	---	.76	.12	.88	**1.18**
	Demo	BF	Sm	LK	.032	1512	---	1.10	.17	1.27	**1.71**
12" deep, 20' long	Inst	BF	Lg	CY	.026	2160	2.69	.90	.12	3.71	**4.48**
	Inst	BF	Sm	CY	.037	1512	3.15	1.29	.17	4.61	**5.59**
12" deep, 20' long	Demo	SF	Lg	LK	.007	6545	---	.24	.04	.28	**.38**
	Demo	SF	Sm	LK	.010	4582	---	.34	.06	.40	**.54**
12" deep, 20' long	Inst	SF	Lg	CY	.009	6545	.89	.31	.04	1.24	**1.50**
	Inst	SF	Sm	CY	.012	4582	1.04	.42	.06	1.52	**1.84**

Description	Oper	Unit	Vol	Crew Size	Man-hours per Unit	Crew Output per Day	Avg Mat'l Unit Cost	Avg Labor Unit Cost	Avg Equip Unit Cost	Avg Total Unit Cost	Avg Price Incl O&P
5-1/8" thick beams, SF pricing based on 16" oc (continued)											
13-1/2" deep, 20' long	Demo	LF	Lg	LK	.133	360.0	---	4.57	.72	5.29	**7.12**
	Demo	LF	Sm	LK	.190	252.0	---	6.53	1.03	7.56	**10.20**
13-1/2" deep, 20' long	Inst	LF	Lg	CY	.156	360.0	18.20	5.42	.72	24.34	**29.20**
	Inst	LF	Sm	CY	.222	252.0	21.30	7.72	1.03	30.05	**36.30**
13-1/2" deep, 20' long	Demo	BF	Lg	LK	.020	2430	---	.69	.11	.80	**1.07**
	Demo	BF	Sm	LK	.028	1701	---	.96	.15	1.11	**1.50**
13-1/2" deep, 20' long	Inst	BF	Lg	CY	.023	2430	2.69	.80	.11	3.60	**4.32**
	Inst	BF	Sm	CY	.033	1701	3.15	1.15	.15	4.45	**5.38**
13-1/2" deep, 20' long	Demo	SF	Lg	LK	.007	6545	---	.24	.04	.28	**.38**
	Demo	SF	Sm	LK	.010	4582	---	.34	.06	.40	**.54**
13-1/2" deep, 20' long	Inst	SF	Lg	CY	.009	6545	1.00	.31	.04	1.35	**1.63**
	Inst	SF	Sm	CY	.012	4582	1.17	.42	.06	1.65	**1.99**
15" deep, 20' long	Demo	LF	Lg	LK	.133	360.0	---	4.57	.72	5.29	**7.12**
	Demo	LF	Sm	LK	.190	252.0	---	6.53	1.03	7.56	**10.20**
15" deep, 20' long	Inst	LF	Lg	CY	.156	360.0	20.20	5.42	.72	26.34	**31.50**
	Inst	LF	Sm	CY	.222	252.0	23.60	7.72	1.03	32.35	**39.00**
15" deep, 20' long	Demo	BF	Lg	LK	.018	2700	---	.62	.10	.72	**.97**
	Demo	BF	Sm	LK	.025	1890	---	.86	.14	1.00	**1.34**
15" deep, 20' long	Inst	BF	Lg	CY	.021	2700	2.69	.73	.10	3.52	**4.22**
	Inst	BF	Sm	CY	.030	1890	3.15	1.04	.14	4.33	**5.22**
15" deep, 20' long	Demo	SF	Lg	LK	.007	6545	---	.24	.04	.28	**.38**
	Demo	SF	Sm	LK	.010	4582	---	.34	.06	.40	**.54**
15" deep, 20' long	Inst	SF	Lg	CY	.009	6545	1.11	.31	.04	1.46	**1.75**
	Inst	SF	Sm	CY	.012	4582	1.30	.42	.06	1.78	**2.14**
16-1/2" deep, 20' long	Demo	LF	Lg	LK	.133	360.0	---	4.57	.72	5.29	**7.12**
	Demo	LF	Sm	LK	.190	252.0	---	6.53	1.03	7.56	**10.20**
16-1/2" deep, 20' long	Inst	LF	Lg	CY	.156	360.0	22.20	5.42	.72	28.34	**33.80**
	Inst	LF	Sm	CY	.222	252.0	26.00	7.72	1.03	34.75	**41.70**
16-1/2" deep, 20' long	Demo	BF	Lg	LK	.016	2970	---	.55	.09	.64	**.86**
	Demo	BF	Sm	LK	.023	2079	---	.79	.13	.92	**1.24**
16-1/2" deep, 20' long	Inst	BF	Lg	CY	.019	2970	2.69	.66	.09	3.44	**4.11**
	Inst	BF	Sm	CY	.027	2079	3.15	.94	.13	4.22	**5.07**
16-1/2" deep, 20' long	Demo	SF	Lg	LK	.007	6545	---	.24	.04	.28	**.38**
	Demo	SF	Sm	LK	.010	4582	---	.34	.06	.40	**.54**
16-1/2" deep, 20' long	Inst	SF	Lg	CY	.009	6545	1.22	.31	.04	1.57	**1.88**
	Inst	SF	Sm	CY	.012	4582	1.43	.42	.06	1.91	**2.29**
18" deep, 20' long	Demo	LF	Lg	LK	.133	360.0	---	4.57	.72	5.29	**7.12**
	Demo	LF	Sm	LK	.190	252.0	---	6.53	1.03	7.56	**10.20**
18" deep, 20' long	Inst	LF	Lg	CY	.156	360.0	24.20	5.42	.72	30.34	**36.10**
	Inst	LF	Sm	CY	.222	252.0	28.40	7.72	1.03	37.15	**44.50**
18" deep, 20' long	Demo	BF	Lg	LK	.015	3240	---	.52	.08	.60	**.80**
	Demo	BF	Sm	LK	.021	2268	---	.72	.11	.83	**1.12**

Description	Oper	Unit	Vol	Crew Size	Man-hours per Unit	Crew Output per Day	Avg Mat'l Unit Cost	Avg Labor Unit Cost	Avg Equip Unit Cost	Avg Total Unit Cost	Avg Price Incl O&P
18" deep, 20' long	Inst	BF	Lg	CY	.017	3240	2.69	.59	.08	3.36	**4.00**
	Inst	BF	Sm	CY	.025	2268	3.15	.87	.11	4.13	**4.95**
18" deep, 20' long	Demo	SF	Lg	LK	.007	6545	---	.24	.04	.28	**.38**
	Demo	SF	Sm	LK	.010	4582	---	.34	.06	.40	**.54**
18" deep, 20' long	Inst	SF	Lg	CY	.009	6545	1.33	.31	.04	1.68	**2.01**
	Inst	SF	Sm	CY	.012	4582	1.56	.42	.06	2.04	**2.44**
19-1/2" deep, 20' long	Demo	LF	Lg	LK	.133	360.0	---	4.57	.72	5.29	**7.12**
	Demo	LF	Sm	LK	.190	252.0	---	6.53	1.03	7.56	**10.20**
19-1/2" deep, 20' long	Inst	LF	Lg	CY	.156	360.0	26.20	5.42	.72	32.34	**38.40**
	Inst	LF	Sm	CY	.222	252.0	30.70	7.72	1.03	39.45	**47.20**
19-1/2" deep, 20' long	Demo	BF	Lg	LK	.014	3510	---	.48	.07	.55	**.74**
	Demo	BF	Sm	LK	.020	2457	---	.69	.11	.80	**1.07**
19-1/2" deep, 20' long	Inst	BF	Lg	CY	.016	3510	2.69	.56	.07	3.32	**3.94**
	Inst	BF	Sm	CY	.023	2457	3.15	.80	.11	4.06	**4.85**
19-1/2" deep, 20' long	Demo	SF	Lg	LK	.007	6545	---	.24	.04	.28	**.38**
	Demo	SF	Sm	LK	.010	4582	---	.34	.06	.40	**.54**
19-1/2" deep, 20' long	Inst	SF	Lg	CY	.009	6545	1.44	.31	.04	1.79	**2.13**
	Inst	SF	Sm	CY	.012	4582	1.69	.42	.06	2.17	**2.59**
21" deep, 30' long	Demo	LF	Lg	LK	.133	360.0	---	4.57	.72	5.29	**7.12**
	Demo	LF	Sm	LK	.190	252.0	---	6.53	1.03	7.56	**10.20**
21" deep, 30' long	Inst	LF	Lg	CY	.156	360.0	28.20	5.42	.72	34.34	**40.80**
	Inst	LF	Sm	CY	.222	252.0	33.10	7.72	1.03	41.85	**49.90**
21" deep, 30' long	Demo	BF	Lg	LK	.013	3780	---	.45	.07	.52	**.70**
	Demo	BF	Sm	LK	.018	2646	---	.62	.10	.72	**.97**
21" deep, 30' long	Inst	BF	Lg	CY	.015	3780	2.69	.52	.07	3.28	**3.89**
	Inst	BF	Sm	CY	.021	2646	3.15	.73	.10	3.98	**4.74**
21" deep, 30' long	Demo	SF	Lg	LK	.007	6545	---	.24	.04	.28	**.38**
	Demo	SF	Sm	LK	.010	4582	---	.34	.06	.40	**.54**
21" deep, 30' long	Inst	SF	Lg	CY	.009	6545	1.55	.31	.04	1.90	**2.26**
	Inst	SF	Sm	CY	.012	4582	1.82	.42	.06	2.30	**2.74**
22-1/2" deep, 30' long	Demo	LF	Lg	LK	.133	360.0	---	4.57	.72	5.29	**7.12**
	Demo	LF	Sm	LK	.190	252.0	---	6.53	1.03	7.56	**10.20**
22-1/2" deep, 30' long	Inst	LF	Lg	CY	.156	360.0	30.20	5.42	.72	36.34	**43.10**
	Inst	LF	Sm	CY	.222	252.0	35.50	7.72	1.03	44.25	**52.60**
22-1/2" deep, 30' long	Demo	BF	Lg	LK	.012	4050	---	.41	.06	.47	**.64**
	Demo	BF	Sm	LK	.017	2835	---	.58	.09	.67	**.91**
22-1/2" deep, 30' long	Inst	BF	Lg	CY	.014	4050	2.69	.49	.06	3.24	**3.83**
	Inst	BF	Sm	CY	.020	2835	3.15	.70	.09	3.94	**4.69**
22-1/2" deep, 30' long	Demo	SF	Lg	LK	.007	6545	---	.24	.04	.28	**.38**
	Demo	SF	Sm	LK	.010	4582	---	.34	.06	.40	**.54**
22-1/2" deep, 30' long	Inst	SF	Lg	CY	.009	6545	1.66	.31	.04	2.01	**2.39**
	Inst	SF	Sm	CY	.012	4582	1.95	.42	.06	2.43	**2.89**

Description	Oper	Unit	Vol	Crew Size	Man-hours per Unit	Crew Output per Day	Avg Mat'l Unit Cost	Avg Labor Unit Cost	Avg Equip Unit Cost	Avg Total Unit Cost	Avg Price Incl O&P

5-1/8" thick beams, SF pricing based on 16" oc (continued)

Description	Oper	Unit	Vol	Crew Size	Man-hours per Unit	Crew Output per Day	Avg Mat'l Unit Cost	Avg Labor Unit Cost	Avg Equip Unit Cost	Avg Total Unit Cost	Avg Price Incl O&P
24" deep, 30' long	Demo	LF	Lg	LK	.133	360.0	---	4.57	.72	5.29	**7.12**
	Demo	LF	Sm	LK	.190	252.0	---	6.53	1.03	7.56	**10.20**
24" deep, 30' long	Inst	LF	Lg	CY	.156	360.0	32.20	5.42	.72	38.34	**45.40**
	Inst	LF	Sm	CY	.222	252.0	37.80	7.72	1.03	46.55	**55.40**
24" deep, 30' long	Demo	BF	Lg	LK	.011	4320	---	.38	.06	.44	**.59**
	Demo	BF	Sm	LK	.016	3024	---	.55	.09	.64	**.86**
24" deep, 30' long	Inst	BF	Lg	CY	.013	4320	2.69	.45	.06	3.20	**3.79**
	Inst	BF	Sm	CY	.019	3024	3.15	.66	.09	3.90	**4.64**
24" deep, 30' long	Demo	SF	Lg	LK	.007	6545	---	.24	.04	.28	**.38**
	Demo	SF	Sm	LK	.010	4582	---	.34	.06	.40	**.54**
24" deep, 30' long	Inst	SF	Lg	CY	.009	6545	1.77	.31	.04	2.12	**2.51**
	Inst	SF	Sm	CY	.012	4582	2.08	.42	.06	2.56	**3.04**
25-1/2" deep, 30' long	Demo	LF	Lg	LK	.133	360.0	---	4.57	.72	5.29	**7.12**
	Demo	LF	Sm	LK	.190	252.0	---	6.53	1.03	7.56	**10.20**
25-1/2" deep, 30' long	Inst	LF	Lg	CY	.156	360.0	34.30	5.42	.72	40.44	**47.70**
	Inst	LF	Sm	CY	.222	252.0	40.20	7.72	1.03	48.95	**58.10**
25-1/2" deep, 30' long	Demo	BF	Lg	LK	.010	4590	---	.34	.06	.40	**.54**
	Demo	BF	Sm	LK	.015	3213	---	.52	.08	.60	**.80**
25-1/2" deep, 30' long	Inst	BF	Lg	CY	.012	4590	2.69	.42	.06	3.17	**3.74**
	Inst	BF	Sm	CY	.017	3213	3.15	.59	.08	3.82	**4.53**
25-1/2" deep, 30' long	Demo	SF	Lg	LK	.007	6545	---	.24	.04	.28	**.38**
	Demo	SF	Sm	LK	.010	4582	---	.34	.06	.40	**.54**
25-1/2" deep, 30' long	Inst	SF	Lg	CY	.009	6545	1.89	.31	.04	2.24	**2.65**
	Inst	SF	Sm	CY	.012	4582	2.21	.42	.06	2.69	**3.19**
27" deep, 40' long	Demo	LF	Lg	LK	.133	360.0	---	4.57	.72	5.29	**7.12**
	Demo	LF	Sm	LK	.190	252.0	---	6.53	1.03	7.56	**10.20**
27" deep, 40' long	Inst	LF	Lg	CY	.156	360.0	36.30	5.42	.72	42.44	**50.00**
	Inst	LF	Sm	CY	.222	252.0	42.60	7.72	1.03	51.35	**60.80**
27" deep, 40' long	Demo	BF	Lg	LK	.010	4860	---	.34	.05	.39	**.53**
	Demo	BF	Sm	LK	.014	3402	---	.48	.08	.56	**.75**
27" deep, 40' long	Inst	BF	Lg	CY	.012	4860	2.69	.42	.05	3.16	**3.73**
	Inst	BF	Sm	CY	.016	3402	3.15	.56	.08	3.79	**4.48**
27" deep, 40' long	Demo	SF	Lg	LK	.007	6545	---	.24	.04	.28	**.38**
	Demo	SF	Sm	LK	.010	4582	---	.34	.06	.40	**.54**
27" deep, 40' long	Inst	SF	Lg	CY	.009	6545	2.00	.31	.04	2.35	**2.78**
	Inst	SF	Sm	CY	.012	4582	2.34	.42	.06	2.82	**3.34**
28-1/2" deep, 40' long	Demo	LF	Lg	LK	.133	360.0	---	4.57	.72	5.29	**7.12**
	Demo	LF	Sm	LK	.190	252.0	---	6.53	1.03	7.56	**10.20**
28-1/2" deep, 40' long	Inst	LF	Lg	CY	.156	360.0	38.30	5.42	.72	44.44	**52.40**
	Inst	LF	Sm	CY	.222	252.0	44.90	7.72	1.03	53.65	**63.50**
28-1/2" deep, 40' long	Demo	BF	Lg	LK	.009	5130	---	.31	.05	.36	**.48**
	Demo	BF	Sm	LK	.013	3591	---	.45	.07	.52	**.70**
28-1/2" deep, 40' long	Inst	BF	Lg	CY	.011	5130	2.69	.38	.05	3.12	**3.68**
	Inst	BF	Sm	CY	.016	3591	3.15	.56	.07	3.78	**4.47**

Description	Oper	Unit	Vol	Crew Size	Man-hours per Unit	Crew Output per Day	Avg Mat'l Unit Cost	Avg Labor Unit Cost	Avg Equip Unit Cost	Avg Total Unit Cost	Avg Price Incl O&P
28-1/2" deep, 40' long	Demo	SF	Lg	LK	.007	6545	---	.24	.04	.28	.38
	Demo	SF	Sm	LK	.010	4582	---	.34	.06	.40	.54
28-1/2" deep, 40' long	Inst	SF	Lg	CY	.009	6545	2.11	.31	.04	2.46	2.90
	Inst	SF	Sm	CY	.012	4582	2.47	.42	.06	2.95	3.48
30" deep, 40' long	Demo	LF	Lg	LK	.133	360.0	---	4.57	.72	5.29	7.12
	Demo	LF	Sm	LK	.190	252.0	---	6.53	1.03	7.56	10.20
30" deep, 40' long	Inst	LF	Lg	CY	.156	360.0	40.30	5.42	.72	46.44	54.70
	Inst	LF	Sm	CY	.222	252.0	47.30	7.72	1.03	56.05	66.20
30" deep, 40' long	Demo	BF	Lg	LK	.009	5400	---	.31	.05	.36	.48
	Demo	BF	Sm	LK	.013	3780	---	.45	.07	.52	.70
30" deep, 40' long	Inst	BF	Lg	CY	.010	5400	2.69	.35	.05	3.09	3.63
	Inst	BF	Sm	CY	.015	3780	3.15	.52	.07	3.74	4.42
30" deep, 40' long	Demo	SF	Lg	LK	.007	6545	---	.24	.04	.28	.38
	Demo	SF	Sm	LK	.010	4582	---	.34	.06	.40	.54
30" deep, 40' long	Inst	SF	Lg	CY	.009	6545	2.22	.31	.04	2.57	3.03
	Inst	SF	Sm	CY	.012	4582	2.60	.42	.06	3.08	3.63
31-1/2" deep, 40' long	Demo	LF	Lg	LK	.133	360.0	---	4.57	.72	5.29	7.12
	Demo	LF	Sm	LK	.190	252.0	---	6.53	1.03	7.56	10.20
31-1/2" deep, 40' long	Inst	LF	Lg	CY	.156	360.0	42.30	5.42	.72	48.44	57.00
	Inst	LF	Sm	CY	.222	252.0	49.60	7.72	1.03	58.35	68.90
31-1/2" deep, 40' long	Demo	BF	Lg	LK	.008	5670	---	.28	.05	.33	.44
	Demo	BF	Sm	LK	.012	3969	---	.41	.07	.48	.65
31-1/2" deep, 40' long	Inst	BF	Lg	CY	.010	5670	2.69	.35	.05	3.09	3.63
	Inst	BF	Sm	CY	.014	3969	3.15	.49	.07	3.71	4.37
31-1/2" deep, 40' long	Demo	SF	Lg	LK	.007	6545	---	.24	.04	.28	.38
	Demo	SF	Sm	LK	.010	4582	---	.34	.06	.40	.54
31-1/2" deep, 40' long	Inst	SF	Lg	CY	.009	6545	2.33	.31	.04	2.68	3.16
	Inst	SF	Sm	CY	.012	4582	2.73	.42	.06	3.21	3.78
33" deep, 40' long	Demo	LF	Lg	LK	.133	360.0	---	4.57	.72	5.29	7.12
	Demo	LF	Sm	LK	.190	252.0	---	6.53	1.03	7.56	10.20
33" deep, 40' long	Inst	LF	Lg	CY	.156	360.0	44.40	5.42	.72	50.54	59.30
	Inst	LF	Sm	CY	.222	252.0	52.00	7.72	1.03	60.75	71.60
33" deep, 40' long	Demo	BF	Lg	LK	.008	5940	---	.28	.04	.32	.43
	Demo	BF	Sm	LK	.012	4158	---	.41	.06	.47	.64
33" deep, 40' long	Inst	BF	Lg	CY	.009	5940	2.69	.31	.04	3.04	3.57
	Inst	BF	Sm	CY	.013	4158	3.15	.45	.06	3.66	4.32
33" deep, 40' long	Demo	SF	Lg	LK	.007	6545	---	.24	.04	.28	.38
	Demo	SF	Sm	LK	.010	4582	---	.34	.06	.40	.54
33" deep, 40' long	Inst	SF	Lg	CY	.009	6545	2.44	.31	.04	2.79	3.28
	Inst	SF	Sm	CY	.012	4582	2.86	.42	.06	3.34	3.93
34-1/2" deep, 40' long	Demo	LF	Lg	LK	.133	360.0	---	4.57	.72	5.29	7.12
	Demo	LF	Sm	LK	.190	252.0	---	6.53	1.03	7.56	10.20
34-1/2" deep, 40' long	Inst	LF	Lg	CY	.156	360.0	46.40	5.42	.72	52.54	61.60
	Inst	LF	Sm	CY	.222	252.0	54.40	7.72	1.03	63.15	74.40
34-1/2" deep, 40' long	Demo	BF	Lg	LK	.008	6210	---	.28	.04	.32	.43
	Demo	BF	Sm	LK	.011	4347	---	.38	.06	.44	.59

National Repair & Remodeling Estimator

Description	Oper	Unit	Vol	Crew Size	Man-hours per Unit	Crew Output per Day	Avg Mat'l Unit Cost	Avg Labor Unit Cost	Avg Equip Unit Cost	Avg Total Unit Cost	Avg Price Incl O&P
34-1/2" deep, 40' long	Inst	BF	Lg	CY	.009	6210	2.69	.31	.04	3.04	3.57
	Inst	BF	Sm	CY	.013	4347	3.15	.45	.06	3.66	4.32
34-1/2" deep, 40' long	Demo	SF	Lg	LK	.007	6545	---	.24	.04	.28	.38
	Demo	SF	Sm	LK	.010	4582	---	.34	.06	.40	.54
34-1/2" deep, 40' long	Inst	SF	Lg	CY	.009	6545	2.55	.31	.04	2.90	3.41
	Inst	SF	Sm	CY	.012	4582	2.99	.42	.06	3.47	4.08
36" deep, 50' long	Demo	LF	Lg	LK	.133	360.0	---	4.57	.72	5.29	7.12
	Demo	LF	Sm	LK	.190	252.0	---	6.53	1.03	7.56	10.20
36" deep, 50' long	Inst	LF	Lg	CY	.156	360.0	48.40	5.42	.72	54.54	64.00
	Inst	LF	Sm	CY	.222	252.0	56.70	7.72	1.03	65.45	77.10
36" deep, 50' long	Demo	BF	Lg	LK	.007	6480	---	.24	.04	.28	.38
	Demo	BF	Sm	LK	.011	4536	---	.38	.06	.44	.59
36" deep, 50' long	Inst	BF	Lg	CY	.009	6480	2.69	.31	.04	3.04	3.57
	Inst	BF	Sm	CY	.012	4536	3.15	.42	.06	3.63	4.27
36" deep, 50' long	Demo	SF	Lg	LK	.007	6545	---	.24	.04	.28	.38
	Demo	SF	Sm	LK	.010	4582	---	.34	.06	.40	.54
36" deep, 50' long	Inst	SF	Lg	CY	.009	6545	2.66	.31	.04	3.01	3.54
	Inst	SF	Sm	CY	.012	4582	3.12	.42	.06	3.60	4.23
37-1/2" deep, 50' long	Demo	LF	Lg	LK	.133	360.0	---	4.57	.72	5.29	7.12
	Demo	LF	Sm	LK	.190	252.0	---	6.53	1.03	7.56	10.20
37-1/2" deep, 50' long	Inst	LF	Lg	CY	.156	360.0	50.40	5.42	.72	56.54	66.30
	Inst	LF	Sm	CY	.222	252.0	59.10	7.72	1.03	67.85	79.80
37-1/2" deep, 50' long	Demo	BF	Lg	LK	.007	6750	---	.24	.04	.28	.38
	Demo	BF	Sm	LK	.010	4725	---	.34	.06	.40	.54
37-1/2" deep, 50' long	Inst	BF	Lg	CY	.008	6750	2.69	.28	.04	3.01	3.52
	Inst	BF	Sm	CY	.012	4725	3.15	.42	.06	3.63	4.27
37-1/2" deep, 50' long	Demo	SF	Lg	LK	.007	6545	---	.24	.04	.28	.38
	Demo	SF	Sm	LK	.010	4582	---	.34	.06	.40	.54
37-1/2" deep, 50' long	Inst	SF	Lg	CY	.009	6545	2.77	.31	.04	3.12	3.66
	Inst	SF	Sm	CY	.012	4582	3.25	.42	.06	3.73	4.38
39" deep, 50' long	Demo	LF	Lg	LK	.133	360.0	---	4.57	.72	5.29	7.12
	Demo	LF	Sm	LK	.190	252.0	---	6.53	1.03	7.56	10.20
39" deep, 50' long	Inst	LF	Lg	CY	.156	360.0	52.40	5.42	.72	58.54	68.60
	Inst	LF	Sm	CY	.222	252.0	61.50	7.72	1.03	70.25	82.50
39" deep, 50' long	Demo	BF	Lg	LK	.007	7020	---	.24	.04	.28	.38
	Demo	BF	Sm	LK	.010	4914	---	.34	.05	.39	.53
39" deep, 50' long	Inst	BF	Lg	CY	.008	7020	2.69	.28	.04	3.01	3.52
	Inst	BF	Sm	CY	.011	4914	3.15	.38	.05	3.58	4.21
39" deep, 50' long	Demo	SF	Lg	LK	.007	6545	---	.24	.04	.28	.38
	Demo	SF	Sm	LK	.010	4582	---	.34	.06	.40	.54
39" deep, 50' long	Inst	SF	Lg	CY	.009	6545	2.88	.31	.04	3.23	3.79
	Inst	SF	Sm	CY	.012	4582	3.38	.42	.06	3.86	4.53

Description	Oper	Unit	Vol	Crew Size	Man-hours per Unit	Crew Output per Day	Avg Mat'l Unit Cost	Avg Labor Unit Cost	Avg Equip Unit Cost	Avg Total Unit Cost	Avg Price Incl O&P

6-3/4" thick, SF pricing based on 16" oc

Description	Oper	Unit	Vol	Crew Size	Man-hours per Unit	Crew Output per Day	Avg Mat'l Unit Cost	Avg Labor Unit Cost	Avg Equip Unit Cost	Avg Total Unit Cost	Avg Price Incl O&P
30" deep, 30' long	Demo	LF	Lg	LK	.133	360.0	---	4.57	.72	5.29	7.12
	Demo	LF	Sm	LK	.190	252.0	---	6.53	1.03	7.56	10.20
30" deep, 30' long	Inst	LF	Lg	CY	.156	360.0	53.40	5.42	.72	59.54	69.80
	Inst	LF	Sm	CY	.222	252.0	62.70	7.72	1.03	71.45	84.00
30" deep, 30' long	Demo	BF	Lg	LK	.007	7200	---	.24	.04	.28	.38
	Demo	BF	Sm	LK	.010	5040	---	.34	.05	.39	.53
30" deep, 30' long	Inst	BF	Lg	CY	.008	7200	2.67	.28	.04	2.99	3.50
	Inst	BF	Sm	CY	.011	5040	3.14	.38	.05	3.57	4.20
30" deep, 30' long	Demo	SF	Lg	LK	.007	6545	---	.24	.04	.28	.38
	Demo	SF	Sm	LK	.010	4582	---	.34	.06	.40	.54
30" deep, 30' long	Inst	SF	Lg	CY	.009	6545	2.94	.31	.04	3.29	3.86
	Inst	SF	Sm	CY	.012	4582	3.45	.42	.06	3.93	4.61
31-1/2" deep, 30' long	Demo	LF	Lg	LK	.133	360.0	---	4.57	.72	5.29	7.12
	Demo	LF	Sm	LK	.190	252.0	---	6.53	1.03	7.56	10.20
31-1/2" deep, 30' long	Inst	LF	Lg	CY	.156	360.0	56.10	5.42	.72	62.24	72.80
	Inst	LF	Sm	CY	.222	252.0	65.80	7.72	1.03	74.55	87.60
31-1/2" deep, 30' long	Demo	BF	Lg	LK	.006	7560	---	.21	.03	.24	.32
	Demo	BF	Sm	LK	.009	5292	---	.31	.05	.36	.48
31-1/2" deep, 30' long	Inst	BF	Lg	CY	.007	7560	2.67	.24	.03	2.94	3.44
	Inst	BF	Sm	CY	.011	5292	3.14	.38	.05	3.57	4.20
31-1/2" deep, 30' long	Demo	SF	Lg	LK	.007	6545	---	.24	.04	.28	.38
	Demo	SF	Sm	LK	.010	4582	---	.34	.06	.40	.54
31-1/2" deep, 30' long	Inst	SF	Lg	CY	.009	6545	3.08	.31	.04	3.43	4.02
	Inst	SF	Sm	CY	.012	4582	3.62	.42	.06	4.10	4.81
33" deep, 30' long	Demo	LF	Lg	LK	.133	360.0	---	4.57	.72	5.29	7.12
	Demo	LF	Sm	LK	.190	252.0	---	6.53	1.03	7.56	10.20
33" deep, 30' long	Inst	LF	Lg	CY	.156	360.0	58.80	5.42	.72	64.94	75.90
	Inst	LF	Sm	CY	.222	252.0	69.00	7.72	1.03	77.75	91.10
33" deep, 30' long	Demo	BF	Lg	LK	.006	7920	---	.21	.03	.24	.32
	Demo	BF	Sm	LK	.009	5544	---	.31	.05	.36	.48
33" deep, 30' long	Inst	BF	Lg	CY	.007	7920	2.67	.24	.03	2.94	3.44
	Inst	BF	Sm	CY	.010	5544	3.13	.35	.05	3.53	4.14
33" deep, 30' long	Demo	SF	Lg	LK	.007	6545	---	.24	.04	.28	.38
	Demo	SF	Sm	LK	.010	4582	---	.34	.06	.40	.54
33" deep, 30' long	Inst	SF	Lg	CY	.009	6545	3.23	.31	.04	3.58	4.19
	Inst	SF	Sm	CY	.012	4582	3.79	.42	.06	4.27	5.00
34-1/2" deep, 40' long	Demo	LF	Lg	LK	.133	360.0	---	4.57	.72	5.29	7.12
	Demo	LF	Sm	LK	.190	252.0	---	6.53	1.03	7.56	10.20
34-1/2" deep, 40' long	Inst	LF	Lg	CY	.156	360.0	61.40	5.42	.72	67.54	79.00
	Inst	LF	Sm	CY	.222	252.0	72.10	7.72	1.03	80.85	94.80
34-1/2" deep, 40' long	Demo	BF	Lg	LK	.006	8280	---	.21	.03	.24	.32
	Demo	BF	Sm	LK	.008	5796	---	.28	.04	.32	.43

Description	Oper	Unit	Vol	Crew Size	Man-hours per Unit	Crew Output per Day	Avg Mat'l Unit Cost	Avg Labor Unit Cost	Avg Equip Unit Cost	Avg Total Unit Cost	Avg Price Incl O&P
34-1/2" deep, 40' long	Inst	BF	Lg	CY	.007	8280	2.67	.24	.03	2.94	**3.44**
	Inst	BF	Sm	CY	.010	5796	3.14	.35	.04	3.53	**4.14**
34-1/2" deep, 40' long	Demo	SF	Lg	LK	.007	6545	---	.24	.04	.28	**.38**
	Demo	SF	Sm	LK	.010	4582	---	.34	.06	.40	**.54**
34-1/2" deep, 40' long	Inst	SF	Lg	CY	.009	6545	3.38	.31	.04	3.73	**4.37**
	Inst	SF	Sm	CY	.012	4582	3.97	.42	.06	4.45	**5.21**
36" deep, 40' long	Demo	LF	Lg	LK	.133	360.0	---	4.57	.72	5.29	**7.12**
	Demo	LF	Sm	LK	.190	252.0	---	6.53	1.03	7.56	**10.20**
36" deep, 40' long	Inst	LF	Lg	CY	.156	360.0	64.10	5.42	.72	70.24	**82.10**
	Inst	LF	Sm	CY	.222	252.0	75.20	7.72	1.03	83.95	**98.40**
36" deep, 40' long	Demo	BF	Lg	LK	.006	8640	---	.21	.03	.24	**.32**
	Demo	BF	Sm	LK	.008	6048	---	.28	.04	.32	**.43**
36" deep, 40' long	Inst	BF	Lg	CY	.006	8640	2.67	.21	.03	2.91	**3.39**
	Inst	BF	Sm	CY	.009	6048	3.14	.31	.04	3.49	**4.09**
36" deep, 40' long	Demo	SF	Lg	LK	.007	6545	---	.24	.04	.28	**.38**
	Demo	SF	Sm	LK	.010	4582	---	.34	.06	.40	**.54**
36" deep, 40' long	Inst	SF	Lg	CY	.009	6545	3.53	.31	.04	3.88	**4.54**
	Inst	SF	Sm	CY	.012	4582	4.14	.42	.06	4.62	**5.41**
37-1/2" deep, 40' long	Demo	LF	Lg	LK	.133	360.0	---	4.57	.72	5.29	**7.12**
	Demo	LF	Sm	LK	.190	252.0	---	6.53	1.03	7.56	**10.20**
37-1/2" deep, 40' long	Inst	LF	Lg	CY	.156	360.0	66.80	5.42	.72	72.94	**85.10**
	Inst	LF	Sm	CY	.222	252.0	78.40	7.72	1.03	87.15	**102.00**
37-1/2" deep, 40' long	Demo	BF	Lg	LK	.005	9000	---	.17	.03	.20	**.27**
	Demo	BF	Sm	LK	.008	6300	---	.28	.04	.32	**.43**
37-1/2" deep, 40' long	Inst	BF	Lg	CY	.006	9000	2.67	.21	.03	2.91	**3.39**
	Inst	BF	Sm	CY	.009	6300	3.14	.31	.04	3.49	**4.09**
37-1/2" deep, 40' long	Demo	SF	Lg	LK	.007	6545	---	.24	.04	.28	**.38**
	Demo	SF	Sm	LK	.010	4582	---	.34	.06	.40	**.54**
37-1/2" deep, 40' long	Inst	SF	Lg	CY	.009	6545	3.67	.31	.04	4.02	**4.70**
	Inst	SF	Sm	CY	.012	4582	4.31	.42	.06	4.79	**5.60**
39" deep, 50' long	Demo	LF	Lg	LK	.133	360.0	---	4.57	.72	5.29	**7.12**
	Demo	LF	Sm	LK	.190	252.0	---	6.53	1.03	7.56	**10.20**
39" deep, 50' long	Inst	LF	Lg	CY	.156	360.0	69.40	5.42	.72	75.54	**88.20**
	Inst	LF	Sm	CY	.222	252.0	81.50	7.72	1.03	90.25	**106.00**
39" deep, 50' long	Demo	BF	Lg	LK	.005	9360	---	.17	.03	.20	**.27**
	Demo	BF	Sm	LK	.007	6552	---	.24	.04	.28	**.38**
39" deep, 50' long	Inst	BF	Lg	CY	.006	9360	2.67	.21	.03	2.91	**3.39**
	Inst	BF	Sm	CY	.009	6552	3.14	.31	.04	3.49	**4.09**
39" deep, 50' long	Demo	SF	Lg	LK	.007	6545	---	.24	.04	.28	**.38**
	Demo	SF	Sm	LK	.010	4582	---	.34	.06	.40	**.54**
39" deep, 50' long	Inst	SF	Lg	CY	.009	6545	3.82	.31	.04	4.17	**4.87**
	Inst	SF	Sm	CY	.012	4582	4.48	.42	.06	4.96	**5.80**

Description	Oper	Unit	Vol	Crew Size	Man-hours per Unit	Crew Output per Day	Avg Mat'l Unit Cost	Avg Labor Unit Cost	Avg Equip Unit Cost	Avg Total Unit Cost	Avg Price Incl O&P
40-1/2" deep, 50' long	Demo	LF	Lg	LK	.133	360.0	---	4.57	.72	5.29	**7.12**
	Demo	LF	Sm	LK	.190	252.0	---	6.53	1.03	7.56	**10.20**
40-1/2" deep, 50' long	Inst	LF	Lg	CY	.156	360.0	72.10	5.42	.72	78.24	**91.30**
	Inst	LF	Sm	CY	.222	252.0	84.60	7.72	1.03	93.35	**109.00**
40-1/2" deep, 50' long	Demo	BF	Lg	LK	.005	9720	---	.17	.03	.20	**.27**
	Demo	BF	Sm	LK	.007	6804	---	.24	.04	.28	**.38**
40-1/2" deep, 50' long	Inst	BF	Lg	CY	.006	9720	2.67	.21	.03	2.91	**3.39**
	Inst	BF	Sm	CY	.008	6804	3.13	.28	.04	3.45	**4.03**
40-1/2" deep, 50' long	Demo	SF	Lg	LK	.007	6545	---	.24	.04	.28	**.38**
	Demo	SF	Sm	LK	.010	4582	---	.34	.06	.40	**.54**
40-1/2" deep, 50' long	Inst	SF	Lg	CY	.009	6545	3.97	.31	.04	4.32	**5.04**
	Inst	SF	Sm	CY	.012	4582	4.66	.42	.06	5.14	**6.00**
42" deep, 50' long	Demo	LF	Lg	LK	.133	360.0	---	4.57	.72	5.29	**7.12**
	Demo	LF	Sm	LK	.190	252.0	---	6.53	1.03	7.56	**10.20**
42" deep, 50' long	Inst	LF	Lg	CY	.156	360.0	74.80	5.42	.72	80.94	**94.30**
	Inst	LF	Sm	CY	.222	252.0	87.80	7.72	1.03	96.55	**113.00**
42" deep, 50' long	Demo	BF	Lg	LK	.005	10080	---	.17	.03	.20	**.27**
	Demo	BF	Sm	LK	.007	7056	---	.24	.04	.28	**.38**
42" deep, 50' long	Inst	BF	Lg	CY	.006	10080	2.67	.21	.03	2.91	**3.39**
	Inst	BF	Sm	CY	.008	7056	3.14	.28	.04	3.46	**4.04**
42" deep, 50' long	Demo	SF	Lg	LK	.007	6545	---	.24	.04	.28	**.38**
	Demo	SF	Sm	LK	.010	4582	---	.34	.06	.40	**.54**
42" deep, 50' long	Inst	SF	Lg	CY	.009	6545	4.11	.31	.04	4.46	**5.20**
	Inst	SF	Sm	CY	.012	4582	4.83	.42	.06	5.31	**6.20**
43-1/2" deep, 50' long	Demo	LF	Lg	LK	.133	360.0	---	4.57	.72	5.29	**7.12**
	Demo	LF	Sm	LK	.190	252.0	---	6.53	1.03	7.56	**10.20**
43-1/2" deep, 50' long	Inst	LF	Lg	CY	.156	360.0	77.50	5.42	.72	83.64	**97.40**
	Inst	LF	Sm	CY	.222	252.0	90.90	7.72	1.03	99.65	**116.00**
43-1/2" deep, 50' long	Demo	BF	Lg	LK	.005	10440	---	.17	.02	.19	**.26**
	Demo	BF	Sm	LK	.007	7308	---	.24	.04	.28	**.38**
43-1/2" deep, 50' long	Inst	BF	Lg	CY	.005	10440	2.67	.17	.02	2.86	**3.33**
	Inst	BF	Sm	CY	.008	7308	3.14	.28	.04	3.46	**4.04**
43-1/2" deep, 50' long	Demo	SF	Lg	LK	.007	6545	---	.24	.04	.28	**.38**
	Demo	SF	Sm	LK	.010	4582	---	.34	.06	.40	**.54**
43-1/2" deep, 50' long	Inst	SF	Lg	CY	.009	6545	4.26	.31	.04	4.61	**5.38**
	Inst	SF	Sm	CY	.012	4582	5.00	.42	.06	5.48	**6.39**
45" deep, 50' long	Demo	LF	Lg	LK	.133	360.0	---	4.57	.72	5.29	**7.12**
	Demo	LF	Sm	LK	.190	252.0	---	6.53	1.03	7.56	**10.20**
45" deep, 50' long	Inst	LF	Lg	CY	.156	360.0	80.10	5.42	.72	86.24	**100.00**
	Inst	LF	Sm	CY	.222	252.0	94.00	7.72	1.03	102.75	**120.00**
45" deep, 50' long	Demo	BF	Lg	LK	.004	10800	---	.14	.02	.16	**.21**
	Demo	BF	Sm	LK	.006	7560	---	.21	.03	.24	**.32**
45" deep, 50' long	Inst	BF	Lg	CY	.005	10800	2.67	.17	.02	2.86	**3.33**
	Inst	BF	Sm	CY	.007	7560	3.13	.24	.03	3.40	**3.97**
45" deep, 50' long	Demo	SF	Lg	LK	.007	6545	---	.24	.04	.28	**.38**
	Demo	SF	Sm	LK	.010	4582	---	.34	.06	.40	**.54**
45" deep, 50' long	Inst	SF	Lg	CY	.009	6545	4.41	.31	.04	4.76	**5.55**
	Inst	SF	Sm	CY	.012	4582	5.17	.42	.06	5.65	**6.59**

Description	Oper	Unit	Vol	Crew Size	Man-hours per Unit	Crew Output per Day	Avg Mat'l Unit Cost	Avg Labor Unit Cost	Avg Equip Unit Cost	Avg Total Unit Cost	Avg Price Incl O&P
8-3/4" thick, SF pricing based on 16" oc											
36" deep, 30' long	Demo	LF	Lg	LK	.133	360.0	---	4.57	.72	5.29	**7.12**
	Demo	LF	Sm	LK	.190	252.0	---	6.53	1.03	7.56	**10.20**
36" deep, 30' long	Inst	LF	Lg	CY	.156	360.0	86.70	5.42	.72	92.84	**108.00**
	Inst	LF	Sm	CY	.222	252.0	102.00	7.72	1.03	110.75	**129.00**
36" deep, 30' long	Demo	BF	Lg	LK	.004	10800	---	.14	.02	.16	**.21**
	Demo	BF	Sm	LK	.006	7560	---	.21	.03	.24	**.32**
36" deep, 30' long	Inst	BF	Lg	CY	.005	10800	2.89	.17	.02	3.08	**3.59**
	Inst	BF	Sm	CY	.007	7560	3.39	.24	.03	3.66	**4.27**
36" deep, 30' long	Demo	SF	Lg	LK	.007	6545	---	.24	.04	.28	**.38**
	Demo	SF	Sm	LK	.010	4582	---	.34	.06	.40	**.54**
36" deep, 30' long	Inst	SF	Lg	CY	.009	6545	4.77	.31	.04	5.12	**5.96**
	Inst	SF	Sm	CY	.012	4582	5.59	.42	.06	6.07	**7.07**
37-1/2" deep, 30' long	Demo	LF	Lg	LK	.133	360.0	---	4.57	.72	5.29	**7.12**
	Demo	LF	Sm	LK	.190	252.0	---	6.53	1.03	7.56	**10.20**
37-1/2" deep, 30' long	Inst	LF	Lg	CY	.156	360.0	90.40	5.42	.72	96.54	**112.00**
	Inst	LF	Sm	CY	.222	252.0	106.00	7.72	1.03	114.75	**134.00**
37-1/2" deep, 30' long	Demo	BF	Lg	LK	.004	11250	---	.14	.02	.16	**.21**
	Demo	BF	Sm	LK	.006	7875	---	.21	.03	.24	**.32**
37-1/2" deep, 30' long	Inst	BF	Lg	CY	.005	11250	2.89	.17	.02	3.08	**3.59**
	Inst	BF	Sm	CY	.007	7875	3.39	.24	.03	3.66	**4.27**
37-1/2" deep, 30' long	Demo	SF	Lg	LK	.007	6545	---	.24	.04	.28	**.38**
	Demo	SF	Sm	LK	.010	4582	---	.34	.06	.40	**.54**
37-1/2" deep, 30' long	Inst	SF	Lg	CY	.009	6545	4.97	.31	.04	5.32	**6.19**
	Inst	SF	Sm	CY	.012	4582	5.82	.42	.06	6.30	**7.34**
39" deep, 30' long	Demo	LF	Lg	LK	.133	360.0	---	4.57	.72	5.29	**7.12**
	Demo	LF	Sm	LK	.190	252.0	---	6.53	1.03	7.56	**10.20**
39" deep, 30' long	Inst	LF	Lg	CY	.156	360.0	94.00	5.42	.72	100.14	**116.00**
	Inst	LF	Sm	CY	.222	252.0	110.00	7.72	1.03	118.75	**138.00**
39" deep, 30' long	Demo	BF	Lg	LK	.004	11700	---	.14	.02	.16	**.21**
	Demo	BF	Sm	LK	.006	8190	---	.21	.03	.24	**.32**
39" deep, 30' long	Inst	BF	Lg	CY	.005	11700	2.89	.17	.02	3.08	**3.59**
	Inst	BF	Sm	CY	.007	8190	3.39	.24	.03	3.66	**4.27**
39" deep, 30' long	Demo	SF	Lg	LK	.007	6545	---	.24	.04	.28	**.38**
	Demo	SF	Sm	LK	.010	4582	---	.34	.06	.40	**.54**
39" deep, 30' long	Inst	SF	Lg	CY	.009	6545	5.17	.31	.04	5.52	**6.42**
	Inst	SF	Sm	CY	.012	4582	6.05	.42	.06	6.53	**7.60**
40-1/2" deep, 30' long	Demo	LF	Lg	LK	.133	360.0	---	4.57	.72	5.29	**7.12**
	Demo	LF	Sm	LK	.190	252.0	---	6.53	1.03	7.56	**10.20**
40-1/2" deep, 30' long	Inst	LF	Lg	CY	.156	360.0	97.60	5.42	.72	103.74	**121.00**
	Inst	LF	Sm	CY	.222	252.0	114.00	7.72	1.03	122.75	**143.00**
40-1/2" deep, 30' long	Demo	BF	Lg	LK	.004	12150	---	.14	.02	.16	**.21**
	Demo	BF	Sm	LK	.006	8505	---	.21	.03	.24	**.32**
40-1/2" deep, 30' long	Inst	BF	Lg	CY	.005	12150	2.89	.17	.02	3.08	**3.59**
	Inst	BF	Sm	CY	.007	8505	3.39	.24	.03	3.66	**4.27**
40-1/2" deep, 30' long	Demo	SF	Lg	LK	.007	6545	---	.24	.04	.28	**.38**
	Demo	SF	Sm	LK	.010	4582	---	.34	.06	.40	**.54**
40-1/2" deep, 30' long	Inst	SF	Lg	CY	.009	6545	5.37	.31	.04	5.72	**6.65**
	Inst	SF	Sm	CY	.012	4582	6.29	.42	.06	6.77	**7.88**

Description	Oper	Unit	Vol	Crew Size	Man-hours per Unit	Crew Output per Day	Avg Mat'l Unit Cost	Avg Labor Unit Cost	Avg Equip Unit Cost	Avg Total Unit Cost	Avg Price Incl O&P
42" deep, 30' long	Demo	LF	Lg	LK	.133	360.0	---	4.57	.72	5.29	**7.12**
	Demo	LF	Sm	LK	.190	252.0	---	6.53	1.03	7.56	**10.20**
42" deep, 30' long	Inst	LF	Lg	CY	.156	360.0	101.00	5.42	.72	107.14	**125.00**
	Inst	LF	Sm	CY	.222	252.0	119.00	7.72	1.03	127.75	**148.00**
42" deep, 30' long	Demo	BF	Lg	LK	.004	12600	---	.14	.02	.16	**.21**
	Demo	BF	Sm	LK	.005	8820	---	.17	.03	.20	**.27**
42" deep, 30' long	Inst	BF	Lg	CY	.004	12600	2.89	.14	.02	3.05	**3.54**
	Inst	BF	Sm	CY	.006	8820	3.39	.21	.03	3.63	**4.22**
42" deep, 30' long	Demo	SF	Lg	LK	.007	6545	---	.24	.04	.28	**.38**
	Demo	SF	Sm	LK	.010	4582	---	.34	.06	.40	**.54**
42" deep, 30' long	Inst	SF	Lg	CY	.009	6545	5.57	.31	.04	5.92	**6.88**
	Inst	SF	Sm	CY	.012	4582	6.52	.42	.06	7.00	**8.14**
43-1/2" deep, 40' long	Demo	LF	Lg	LK	.133	360.0	---	4.57	.72	5.29	**7.12**
	Demo	LF	Sm	LK	.190	252.0	---	6.53	1.03	7.56	**10.20**
43-1/2" deep, 40' long	Inst	LF	Lg	CY	.156	360.0	105.00	5.42	.72	111.14	**129.00**
	Inst	LF	Sm	CY	.222	252.0	123.00	7.72	1.03	131.75	**153.00**
43-1/2" deep, 40' long	Demo	BF	Lg	LK	.004	13050	---	.14	.02	.16	**.21**
	Demo	BF	Sm	LK	.005	9135	---	.17	.03	.20	**.27**
43-1/2" deep, 40' long	Inst	BF	Lg	CY	.004	13050	2.89	.14	.02	3.05	**3.54**
	Inst	BF	Sm	CY	.006	9135	3.39	.21	.03	3.63	**4.22**
43-1/2" deep, 40' long	Demo	SF	Lg	LK	.007	6545	---	.24	.04	.28	**.38**
	Demo	SF	Sm	LK	.010	4582	---	.34	.06	.40	**.54**
43-1/2" deep, 40' long	Inst	SF	Lg	CY	.009	6545	5.76	.31	.04	6.11	**7.10**
	Inst	SF	Sm	CY	.012	4582	6.75	.42	.06	7.23	**8.41**
45" deep, 40' long	Demo	LF	Lg	LK	.133	360.0	---	4.57	.72	5.29	**7.12**
	Demo	LF	Sm	LK	.190	252.0	---	6.53	1.03	7.56	**10.20**
45" deep, 40' long	Inst	LF	Lg	CY	.156	360.0	108.00	5.42	.72	114.14	**133.00**
	Inst	LF	Sm	CY	.222	252.0	127.00	7.72	1.03	135.75	**158.00**
45" deep, 40' long	Demo	BF	Lg	LK	.004	13500	---	.14	.02	.16	**.21**
	Demo	BF	Sm	LK	.005	9450	---	.17	.03	.20	**.27**
45" deep, 40' long	Inst	BF	Lg	CY	.004	13500	2.89	.14	.02	3.05	**3.54**
	Inst	BF	Sm	CY	.006	9450	3.39	.21	.03	3.63	**4.22**
45" deep, 40' long	Demo	SF	Lg	LK	.007	6545	---	.24	.04	.28	**.38**
	Demo	SF	Sm	LK	.010	4582	---	.34	.06	.40	**.54**
45" deep, 40' long	Inst	SF	Lg	CY	.009	6545	5.96	.31	.04	6.31	**7.33**
	Inst	SF	Sm	CY	.012	4582	6.99	.42	.06	7.47	**8.68**
46-1/2" deep, 40' long	Demo	LF	Lg	LK	.133	360.0	---	4.57	.72	5.29	**7.12**
	Demo	LF	Sm	LK	.190	252.0	---	6.53	1.03	7.56	**10.20**
46-1/2" deep, 40' long	Inst	LF	Lg	CY	.156	360.0	112.00	5.42	.72	118.14	**137.00**
	Inst	LF	Sm	CY	.222	252.0	131.00	7.72	1.03	139.75	**163.00**
46-1/2" deep, 40' long	Demo	BF	Lg	LK	.003	13950	---	.10	.02	.12	**.16**
	Demo	BF	Sm	LK	.005	9765	---	.17	.03	.20	**.27**

Description	Oper	Unit	Vol	Crew Size	Man-hours per Unit	Crew Output per Day	Avg Mat'l Unit Cost	Avg Labor Unit Cost	Avg Equip Unit Cost	Avg Total Unit Cost	Avg Price Incl O&P
8-3/4" thick beams, SF pricing based on 16" oc (continued)											
46-1/2" deep, 40' long	Inst	BF	Lg	CY	.004	13950	2.89	.14	.02	3.05	**3.54**
	Inst	BF	Sm	CY	.006	9765	3.39	.21	.03	3.63	**4.22**
46-1/2" deep, 40' long	Demo	SF	Lg	LK	.007	6545	---	.24	.04	.28	**.38**
	Demo	SF	Sm	LK	.010	4582	---	.34	.06	.40	**.54**
46-1/2" deep, 40' long	Inst	SF	Lg	CY	.009	6545	6.16	.31	.04	6.51	**7.56**
	Inst	SF	Sm	CY	.012	4582	7.22	.42	.06	7.70	**8.95**
48" deep, 50' long	Demo	LF	Lg	LK	.133	360.0	---	4.57	.72	5.29	**7.12**
	Demo	LF	Sm	LK	.190	252.0	---	6.53	1.03	7.56	**10.20**
48" deep, 50' long	Inst	LF	Lg	CY	.156	360.0	116.00	5.42	.72	122.14	**141.00**
	Inst	LF	Sm	CY	.222	252.0	135.00	7.72	1.03	143.75	**168.00**
48" deep, 50' long	Demo	BF	Lg	LK	.003	14400	---	.10	.02	.12	**.16**
	Demo	BF	Sm	LK	.005	10080	---	.17	.03	.20	**.27**
48" deep, 50' long	Inst	BF	Lg	CY	.004	14400	2.89	.14	.02	3.05	**3.54**
	Inst	BF	Sm	CY	.006	10080	3.39	.21	.03	3.63	**4.22**
48" deep, 50' long	Demo	SF	Lg	LK	.007	6545	---	.24	.04	.28	**.38**
	Demo	SF	Sm	LK	.010	4582	---	.34	.06	.40	**.54**
48" deep, 50' long	Inst	SF	Lg	CY	.009	6545	6.36	.31	.04	6.71	**7.79**
	Inst	SF	Sm	CY	.012	4582	7.45	.42	.06	7.93	**9.21**
49-1/2" deep, 50' long	Demo	LF	Lg	LK	.133	360.0	---	4.57	.72	5.29	**7.12**
	Demo	LF	Sm	LK	.190	252.0	---	6.53	1.03	7.56	**10.20**
49-1/2" deep, 50' long	Inst	LF	Lg	CY	.156	360.0	119.00	5.42	.72	125.14	**145.00**
	Inst	LF	Sm	CY	.222	252.0	140.00	7.72	1.03	148.75	**173.00**
49-1/2" deep, 50' long	Demo	BF	Lg	LK	.003	14850	---	.10	.02	.12	**.16**
	Demo	BF	Sm	LK	.005	10395	---	.17	.03	.20	**.27**
49-1/2" deep, 50' long	Inst	BF	Lg	CY	.004	14850	2.89	.14	.02	3.05	**3.54**
	Inst	BF	Sm	CY	.005	10395	3.39	.17	.03	3.59	**4.17**
49-1/2" deep, 50' long	Demo	SF	Lg	LK	.007	6545	---	.24	.04	.28	**.38**
	Demo	SF	Sm	LK	.010	4582	---	.34	.06	.40	**.54**
49-1/2" deep, 50' long	Inst	SF	Lg	CY	.009	6545	6.56	.31	.04	6.91	**8.02**
	Inst	SF	Sm	CY	.012	4582	7.68	.42	.06	8.16	**9.48**
51" deep, 50' long	Demo	LF	Lg	LK	.133	360.0	---	4.57	.72	5.29	**7.12**
	Demo	LF	Sm	LK	.190	252.0	---	6.53	1.03	7.56	**10.20**
51" deep, 50' long	Inst	LF	Lg	CY	.156	360.0	123.00	5.42	.72	129.14	**150.00**
	Inst	LF	Sm	CY	.222	252.0	144.00	7.72	1.03	152.75	**177.00**
51" deep, 50' long	Demo	BF	Lg	LK	.003	15300	---	.10	.02	.12	**.16**
	Demo	BF	Sm	LK	.004	10710	---	.14	.02	.16	**.21**
51" deep, 50' long	Inst	BF	Lg	CY	.004	15300	2.89	.14	.02	3.05	**3.54**
	Inst	BF	Sm	CY	.005	10710	3.39	.17	.02	3.58	**4.16**
51" deep, 50' long	Demo	SF	Lg	LK	.007	6545	---	.24	.04	.28	**.38**
	Demo	SF	Sm	LK	.010	4582	---	.34	.06	.40	**.54**
51" deep, 50' long	Inst	SF	Lg	CY	.009	6545	6.76	.31	.04	7.11	**8.25**
	Inst	SF	Sm	CY	.012	4582	7.92	.42	.06	8.40	**9.75**

Description	Oper	Unit	Vol	Crew Size	Man-hours per Unit	Crew Output per Day	Avg Mat'l Unit Cost	Avg Labor Unit Cost	Avg Equip Unit Cost	Avg Total Unit Cost	Avg Price Incl O&P
52-1/2" deep, 50' long	Demo	LF	Lg	LK	.133	360.0	---	4.57	.72	5.29	**7.12**
	Demo	LF	Sm	LK	.190	252.0	---	6.53	1.03	7.56	**10.20**
52-1/2" deep, 50' long	Inst	LF	Lg	CY	.156	360.0	126.00	5.42	.72	132.14	**154.00**
	Inst	LF	Sm	CY	.222	252.0	148.00	7.72	1.03	156.75	**182.00**
52-1/2" deep, 50' long	Demo	BF	Lg	LK	.003	15750	---	.10	.02	.12	**.16**
	Demo	BF	Sm	LK	.004	11025	---	.14	.02	.16	**.21**
52-1/2" deep, 50' long	Inst	BF	Lg	CY	.004	15750	2.89	.14	.02	3.05	**3.54**
	Inst	BF	Sm	CY	.005	11025	3.39	.17	.02	3.58	**4.16**
52-1/2" deep, 50' long	Demo	SF	Lg	LK	.007	6545	---	.24	.04	.28	**.38**
	Demo	SF	Sm	LK	.010	4582	---	.34	.06	.40	**.54**
52-1/2" deep, 50' long	Inst	SF	Lg	CY	.009	6545	6.96	.31	.04	7.31	**8.48**
	Inst	SF	Sm	CY	.012	4582	8.15	.42	.06	8.63	**10.00**
54" deep, 50' long	Demo	LF	Lg	LK	.133	360.0	---	4.57	.72	5.29	**7.12**
	Demo	LF	Sm	LK	.190	252.0	---	6.53	1.03	7.56	**10.20**
54" deep, 50' long	Inst	LF	Lg	CY	.156	360.0	130.00	5.42	.72	136.14	**158.00**
	Inst	LF	Sm	CY	.222	252.0	152.00	7.72	1.03	160.75	**187.00**
54" deep, 50' long	Demo	BF	Lg	LK	.003	16200	---	.10	.02	.12	**.16**
	Demo	BF	Sm	LK	.004	11340	---	.14	.02	.16	**.21**
54" deep, 50' long	Inst	BF	Lg	CY	.003	16200	2.89	.10	.02	3.01	**3.49**
	Inst	BF	Sm	CY	.005	11340	3.39	.17	.02	3.58	**4.16**
54" deep, 50' long	Demo	SF	Lg	LK	.007	6545	---	.24	.04	.28	**.38**
	Demo	SF	Sm	LK	.010	4582	---	.34	.06	.40	**.54**
54" deep, 50' long	Inst	SF	Lg	CY	.009	6545	7.16	.31	.04	7.51	**8.71**
	Inst	SF	Sm	CY	.012	4582	8.38	.42	.06	8.86	**10.30**
55-1/2" deep, 50' long	Demo	LF	Lg	LK	.133	360.0	---	4.57	.72	5.29	**7.12**
	Demo	LF	Sm	LK	.190	252.0	---	6.53	1.03	7.56	**10.20**
55-1/2" deep, 50' long	Inst	LF	Lg	CY	.156	360.0	134.00	5.42	.72	140.14	**162.00**
	Inst	LF	Sm	CY	.222	252.0	157.00	7.72	1.03	165.75	**192.00**
55-1/2" deep, 50' long	Demo	BF	Lg	LK	.003	16650	---	.10	.02	.12	**.16**
	Demo	BF	Sm	LK	.004	11655	---	.14	.02	.16	**.21**
55-1/2" deep, 50' long	Inst	BF	Lg	CY	.003	16650	2.89	.10	.02	3.01	**3.49**
	Inst	BF	Sm	CY	.005	11655	3.39	.17	.02	3.58	**4.16**
55-1/2" deep, 50' long	Demo	SF	Lg	LK	.007	6545	---	.24	.04	.28	**.38**
	Demo	SF	Sm	LK	.010	4582	---	.34	.06	.40	**.54**
55-1/2" deep, 50' long	Inst	SF	Lg	CY	.009	6545	7.35	.31	.04	7.70	**8.93**
	Inst	SF	Sm	CY	.012	4582	8.62	.42	.06	9.10	**10.60**
57" deep, 50' long	Demo	LF	Lg	LK	.133	360.0	---	4.57	.72	5.29	**7.12**
	Demo	LF	Sm	LK	.190	252.0	---	6.53	1.03	7.56	**10.20**
57" deep, 50' long	Inst	LF	Lg	CY	.156	360.0	137.00	5.42	.72	143.14	**166.00**
	Inst	LF	Sm	CY	.222	252.0	161.00	7.72	1.03	169.75	**197.00**
57" deep, 50' long	Demo	BF	Lg	LK	.003	17100	---	.10	.02	.12	**.16**
	Demo	BF	Sm	LK	.004	11970	---	.14	.02	.16	**.21**
57" deep, 50' long	Inst	BF	Lg	CY	.003	17100	2.89	.10	.02	3.01	**3.49**
	Inst	BF	Sm	CY	.005	11970	3.39	.17	.02	3.58	**4.16**
57" deep, 50' long	Demo	SF	Lg	LK	.007	6545	---	.24	.04	.28	**.38**
	Demo	SF	Sm	LK	.010	4582	---	.34	.06	.40	**.54**
57" deep, 50' long	Inst	SF	Lg	CY	.009	6545	7.55	.31	.04	7.90	**9.16**
	Inst	SF	Sm	CY	.012	4582	8.85	.42	.06	9.33	**10.80**

Description	Oper	Unit	Vol	Crew Size	Man-hours per Unit	Crew Output per Day	Avg Mat'l Unit Cost	Avg Labor Unit Cost	Avg Equip Unit Cost	Avg Total Unit Cost	Avg Price Incl O&P
10-3/4" thick, SF pricing based on 16' oc											
42" deep, 50' long	Demo	LF	Lg	LK	.133	360.0	---	4.57	.72	5.29	**7.12**
	Demo	LF	Sm	LK	.190	252.0	---	6.53	1.03	7.56	**10.20**
42" deep, 50' long	Inst	LF	Lg	CY	.156	360.0	118.00	5.42	.72	124.14	**144.00**
	Inst	LF	Sm	CY	.222	252.0	138.00	7.72	1.03	146.75	**171.00**
42" deep, 50' long	Demo	BF	Lg	LK	.003	15120	---	.10	.02	.12	**.16**
	Demo	BF	Sm	LK	.005	10584	---	.17	.02	.19	**.26**
42" deep, 50' long	Inst	BF	Lg	CY	.004	15120	2.81	.14	.02	2.97	**3.45**
	Inst	BF	Sm	CY	.005	10584	3.29	.17	.02	3.48	**4.05**
42" deep, 50' long	Demo	SF	Lg	LK	.007	6545	---	.24	.04	.28	**.38**
	Demo	SF	Sm	LK	.010	4582	---	.34	.06	.40	**.54**
42" deep, 50' long	Inst	SF	Lg	CY	.009	6545	6.48	.31	.04	6.83	**7.93**
	Inst	SF	Sm	CY	.012	4582	7.60	.42	.06	8.08	**9.38**
43-1/2" deep, 50' long	Demo	LF	Lg	LK	.133	360.0	---	4.57	.72	5.29	**7.12**
	Demo	LF	Sm	LK	.190	252.0	---	6.53	1.03	7.56	**10.20**
43-1/2" deep, 50' long	Inst	LF	Lg	CY	.156	360.0	122.00	5.42	.72	128.14	**149.00**
	Inst	LF	Sm	CY	.222	252.0	143.00	7.72	1.03	151.75	**176.00**
43-1/2" deep, 50' long	Demo	BF	Lg	LK	.003	15660	---	.10	.02	.12	**.16**
	Demo	BF	Sm	LK	.004	10962	---	.14	.02	.16	**.21**
43-1/2" deep, 50' long	Inst	BF	Lg	CY	.004	15660	2.81	.14	.02	2.97	**3.45**
	Inst	BF	Sm	CY	.005	10962	3.29	.17	.02	3.48	**4.05**
43-1/2" deep, 50' long	Demo	SF	Lg	LK	.007	6545	---	.24	.04	.28	**.38**
	Demo	SF	Sm	LK	.010	4582	---	.34	.06	.40	**.54**
43-1/2" deep, 50' long	Inst	SF	Lg	CY	.009	6545	6.71	.31	.04	7.06	**8.19**
	Inst	SF	Sm	CY	.012	4582	7.87	.42	.06	8.35	**9.69**
45" deep, 50' long	Demo	LF	Lg	LK	.133	360.0	---	4.57	.72	5.29	**7.12**
	Demo	LF	Sm	LK	.190	252.0	---	6.53	1.03	7.56	**10.20**
45" deep, 50' long	Inst	LF	Lg	CY	.156	360.0	126.00	5.42	.72	132.14	**153.00**
	Inst	LF	Sm	CY	.222	252.0	148.00	7.72	1.03	156.75	**182.00**
45" deep, 50' long	Demo	BF	Lg	LK	.003	16200	---	.10	.02	.12	**.16**
	Demo	BF	Sm	LK	.004	11340	---	.14	.02	.16	**.21**
45" deep, 50' long	Inst	BF	Lg	CY	.003	16200	2.81	.10	.02	2.93	**3.40**
	Inst	BF	Sm	CY	.005	11340	3.29	.17	.02	3.48	**4.05**
45" deep, 50' long	Demo	SF	Lg	LK	.007	6545	---	.24	.04	.28	**.38**
	Demo	SF	Sm	LK	.010	4582	---	.34	.06	.40	**.54**
45" deep, 50' long	Inst	SF	Lg	CY	.009	6545	6.94	.31	.04	7.29	**8.46**
	Inst	SF	Sm	CY	.012	4582	8.14	.42	.06	8.62	**10.00**
46-1/2" deep, 50' long	Demo	LF	Lg	LK	.133	360.0	---	4.57	.72	5.29	**7.12**
	Demo	LF	Sm	LK	.190	252.0	---	6.53	1.03	7.56	**10.20**
46-1/2" deep, 50' long	Inst	LF	Lg	CY	.156	360.0	130.00	5.42	.72	136.14	**158.00**
	Inst	LF	Sm	CY	.222	252.0	153.00	7.72	1.03	161.75	**188.00**
46-1/2" deep, 50' long	Demo	BF	Lg	LK	.003	16740	---	.10	.02	.12	**.16**
	Demo	BF	Sm	LK	.004	11718	---	.14	.02	.16	**.21**
46-1/2" deep, 50' long	Inst	BF	Lg	CY	.003	16740	2.81	.10	.02	2.93	**3.40**
	Inst	BF	Sm	CY	.005	11718	3.29	.17	.02	3.48	**4.05**
46-1/2" deep, 50' long	Demo	SF	Lg	LK	.007	6545	---	.24	.04	.28	**.38**
	Demo	SF	Sm	LK	.010	4582	---	.34	.06	.40	**.54**
46-1/2" deep, 50' long	Inst	SF	Lg	CY	.009	6545	7.17	.31	.04	7.52	**8.72**
	Inst	SF	Sm	CY	.012	4582	8.42	.42	.06	8.90	**10.30**

Description	Oper	Unit	Vol	Crew Size	Man-hours per Unit	Crew Output per Day	Avg Mat'l Unit Cost	Avg Labor Unit Cost	Avg Equip Unit Cost	Avg Total Unit Cost	Avg Price Incl O&P
48" deep, 50' long	Demo	LF	Lg	LK	.133	360.0	---	4.57	.72	5.29	7.12
	Demo	LF	Sm	LK	.190	252.0	---	6.53	1.03	7.56	10.20
48" deep, 50' long	Inst	LF	Lg	CY	.156	360.0	135.00	5.42	.72	141.14	163.00
	Inst	LF	Sm	CY	.222	252.0	158.00	7.72	1.03	166.75	193.00
48" deep, 50' long	Demo	BF	Lg	LK	.003	17280	---	.10	.02	.12	.16
	Demo	BF	Sm	LK	.004	12096	---	.14	.02	.16	.21
48" deep, 50' long	Inst	BF	Lg	CY	.003	17280	2.81	.10	.02	2.93	3.40
	Inst	BF	Sm	CY	.005	12096	3.29	.17	.02	3.48	4.05
48" deep, 50' long	Demo	SF	Lg	LK	.007	6545	---	.24	.04	.28	.38
	Demo	SF	Sm	LK	.010	4582	---	.34	.06	.40	.54
48" deep, 50' long	Inst	SF	Lg	CY	.009	6545	7.41	.31	.04	7.76	9.00
	Inst	SF	Sm	CY	.012	4582	8.69	.42	.06	9.17	10.60
49-1/2" deep, 50' long	Demo	LF	Lg	LK	.133	360.0	---	4.57	.72	5.29	7.12
	Demo	LF	Sm	LK	.190	252.0	---	6.53	1.03	7.56	10.20
49-1/2" deep, 50' long	Inst	LF	Lg	CY	.156	360.0	139.00	5.42	.72	145.14	168.00
	Inst	LF	Sm	CY	.222	252.0	163.00	7.72	1.03	171.75	199.00
49-1/2" deep, 50' long	Demo	BF	Lg	LK	.003	17820	---	.10	.01	.11	.15
	Demo	BF	Sm	LK	.004	12474	---	.14	.02	.16	.21
49-1/2" deep, 50' long	Inst	BF	Lg	CY	.003	17820	2.81	.10	.01	2.92	3.39
	Inst	BF	Sm	CY	.004	12474	3.29	.14	.02	3.45	4.00
49-1/2" deep, 50' long	Demo	SF	Lg	LK	.007	6545	---	.24	.04	.28	.38
	Demo	SF	Sm	LK	.010	4582	---	.34	.06	.40	.54
49-1/2" deep, 50' long	Inst	SF	Lg	CY	.009	6545	7.64	.31	.04	7.99	9.26
	Inst	SF	Sm	CY	.012	4582	8.96	.42	.06	9.44	11.00
51" deep, 50' long	Demo	LF	Lg	LK	.133	360.0	---	4.57	.72	5.29	7.12
	Demo	LF	Sm	LK	.190	252.0	---	6.53	1.03	7.56	10.20
51" deep, 50' long	Inst	LF	Lg	CY	.156	360.0	143.00	5.42	.72	149.14	173.00
	Inst	LF	Sm	CY	.222	252.0	168.00	7.72	1.03	176.75	205.00
51" deep, 50' long	Demo	BF	Lg	LK	.003	18360	---	.10	.01	.11	.15
	Demo	BF	Sm	LK	.004	12852	---	.14	.02	.16	.21
51" deep, 50' long	Inst	BF	Lg	CY	.003	18360	2.81	.10	.01	2.92	3.39
	Inst	BF	Sm	CY	.004	12852	3.29	.14	.02	3.45	4.00
51" deep, 50' long	Demo	SF	Lg	LK	.007	6545	---	.24	.04	.28	.38
	Demo	SF	Sm	LK	.010	4582	---	.34	.06	.40	.54
51" deep, 50' long	Inst	SF	Lg	CY	.009	6545	7.87	.31	.04	8.22	9.53
	Inst	SF	Sm	CY	.012	4582	9.23	.42	.06	9.71	11.30
52-1/2" deep, 60' long	Demo	LF	Lg	LK	.133	360.0	---	4.57	.72	5.29	7.12
	Demo	LF	Sm	LK	.190	252.0	---	6.53	1.03	7.56	10.20
52-1/2" deep, 60' long	Inst	LF	Lg	CY	.156	360.0	147.00	5.42	.72	153.14	178.00
	Inst	LF	Sm	CY	.222	252.0	173.00	7.72	1.03	181.75	211.00
52-1/2" deep, 60' long	Demo	BF	Lg	LK	.003	18900	---	.10	.01	.11	.15
	Demo	BF	Sm	LK	.004	13230	---	.14	.02	.16	.21
52-1/2" deep, 60' long	Inst	BF	Lg	CY	.003	18900	2.81	.10	.01	2.92	3.39
	Inst	BF	Sm	CY	.004	13230	3.29	.14	.02	3.45	4.00
52-1/2" deep, 60' long	Demo	SF	Lg	LK	.007	6545	---	.24	.04	.28	.38
	Demo	SF	Sm	LK	.010	4582	---	.34	.06	.40	.54
52-1/2" deep, 60' long	Inst	SF	Lg	CY	.009	6545	8.10	.31	.04	8.45	9.79
	Inst	SF	Sm	CY	.012	4582	9.50	.42	.06	9.98	11.60

Description	Oper	Unit	Vol	Crew Size	Man-hours per Unit	Crew Output per Day	Avg Mat'l Unit Cost	Avg Labor Unit Cost	Avg Equip Unit Cost	Avg Total Unit Cost	Avg Price Incl O&P

10-3/4" thick beams, SF pricing based on 16" oc (continued)

Description	Oper	Unit	Vol	Crew Size	Man-hours per Unit	Crew Output per Day	Avg Mat'l Unit Cost	Avg Labor Unit Cost	Avg Equip Unit Cost	Avg Total Unit Cost	Avg Price Incl O&P
54" deep, 60' long	Demo	LF	Lg	LK	.133	360.0	---	4.57	.72	5.29	**7.12**
	Demo	LF	Sm	LK	.190	252.0	---	6.53	1.03	7.56	**10.20**
54" deep, 60' long	Inst	LF	Lg	CY	.156	360.0	151.00	5.42	.72	157.14	**183.00**
	Inst	LF	Sm	CY	.222	252.0	178.00	7.72	1.03	186.75	**216.00**
54" deep, 60' long	Demo	BF	Lg	LK	.002	19440	---	.07	.01	.08	**.11**
	Demo	BF	Sm	LK	.004	13608	---	.14	.02	.16	**.21**
54" deep, 60' long	Inst	BF	Lg	CY	.003	19440	2.81	.10	.01	2.92	**3.39**
	Inst	BF	Sm	CY	.004	13608	3.29	.14	.02	3.45	**4.00**
54" deep, 60' long	Demo	SF	Lg	LK	.007	6545	---	.24	.04	.28	**.38**
	Demo	SF	Sm	LK	.010	4582	---	.34	.06	.40	**.54**
54" deep, 60' long	Inst	SF	Lg	CY	.009	6545	8.33	.31	.04	8.68	**10.10**
	Inst	SF	Sm	CY	.012	4582	9.77	.42	.06	10.25	**11.90**
55-1/2" deep, 60' long	Demo	LF	Lg	LK	.133	360.0	---	4.57	.72	5.29	**7.12**
	Demo	LF	Sm	LK	.190	252.0	---	6.53	1.03	7.56	**10.20**
55-1/2" deep, 60' long	Inst	LF	Lg	CY	.156	360.0	156.00	5.42	.72	162.14	**187.00**
	Inst	LF	Sm	CY	.222	252.0	183.00	7.72	1.03	191.75	**222.00**
55-1/2" deep, 60' long	Demo	BF	Lg	LK	.002	19980	---	.07	.01	.08	**.11**
	Demo	BF	Sm	LK	.003	13986	---	.10	.02	.12	**.16**
55-1/2" deep, 60' long	Inst	BF	Lg	CY	.003	19980	2.81	.10	.01	2.92	**3.39**
	Inst	BF	Sm	CY	.004	13986	3.29	.14	.02	3.45	**4.00**
55-1/2" deep, 60' long	Demo	SF	Lg	LK	.007	6545	---	.24	.04	.28	**.38**
	Demo	SF	Sm	LK	.010	4582	---	.34	.06	.40	**.54**
55-1/2" deep, 60' long	Inst	SF	Lg	CY	.009	6545	8.56	.31	.04	8.91	**10.30**
	Inst	SF	Sm	CY	.012	4582	10.10	.42	.06	10.58	**12.20**
57" deep, 60' long	Demo	LF	Lg	LK	.133	360.0	---	4.57	.72	5.29	**7.12**
	Demo	LF	Sm	LK	.190	252.0	---	6.53	1.03	7.56	**10.20**
57" deep, 60' long	Inst	LF	Lg	CY	.156	360.0	160.00	5.42	.72	166.14	**192.00**
	Inst	LF	Sm	CY	.222	252.0	188.00	7.72	1.03	196.75	**228.00**
57" deep, 60' long	Demo	BF	Lg	LK	.002	20520	---	.07	.01	.08	**.11**
	Demo	BF	Sm	LK	.003	14364	---	.10	.02	.12	**.16**
57" deep, 60' long	Inst	BF	Lg	CY	.003	20520	2.81	.10	.01	2.92	**3.39**
	Inst	BF	Sm	CY	.004	14364	3.29	.14	.02	3.45	**4.00**
57" deep, 60' long	Demo	SF	Lg	LK	.007	6545	---	.24	.04	.28	**.38**
	Demo	SF	Sm	LK	.010	4582	---	.34	.06	.40	**.54**
57" deep, 60' long	Inst	SF	Lg	CY	.009	6545	8.80	.31	.04	9.15	**10.60**
	Inst	SF	Sm	CY	.012	4582	10.30	.42	.06	10.78	**12.50**
58-1/2" deep, 60' long	Demo	LF	Lg	LK	.133	360.0	---	4.57	.72	5.29	**7.12**
	Demo	LF	Sm	LK	.190	252.0	---	6.53	1.03	7.56	**10.20**
58-1/2" deep, 60' long	Inst	LF	Lg	CY	.156	360.0	164.00	5.42	.72	170.14	**197.00**
	Inst	LF	Sm	CY	.222	252.0	193.00	7.72	1.03	201.75	**233.00**
58-1/2" deep, 60' long	Demo	BF	Lg	LK	.002	21060	---	.07	.01	.08	**.11**
	Demo	BF	Sm	LK	.003	14742	---	.10	.02	.12	**.16**
58-1/2" deep, 60' long	Inst	BF	Lg	CY	.003	21060	2.81	.10	.01	2.92	**3.39**
	Inst	BF	Sm	CY	.004	14742	3.29	.14	.02	3.45	**4.00**
58-1/2" deep, 60' long	Demo	SF	Lg	LK	.007	6545	---	.24	.04	.28	**.38**
	Demo	SF	Sm	LK	.010	4582	---	.34	.06	.40	**.54**
58-1/2" deep, 60' long	Inst	SF	Lg	CY	.009	6545	9.03	.31	.04	9.38	**10.90**
	Inst	SF	Sm	CY	.012	4582	10.60	.42	.06	11.08	**12.80**

Description	Oper	Unit	Vol	Crew Size	Man-hours per Unit	Crew Output per Day	Avg Mat'l Unit Cost	Avg Labor Unit Cost	Avg Equip Unit Cost	Avg Total Unit Cost	Avg Price Incl O&P
60" deep, 60' long	Demo	LF	Lg	LK	.133	360.0	---	4.57	.72	5.29	**7.12**
	Demo	LF	Sm	LK	.190	252.0	---	6.53	1.03	7.56	**10.20**
60" deep, 60' long	Inst	LF	Lg	CY	.156	360.0	168.00	5.42	.72	174.14	**202.00**
	Inst	LF	Sm	CY	.222	252.0	197.00	7.72	1.03	205.75	**239.00**
60" deep, 60' long	Demo	BF	Lg	LK	.002	21600	---	.07	.01	.08	**.11**
	Demo	BF	Sm	LK	.003	15120	---	.10	.02	.12	**.16**
60" deep, 60' long	Inst	BF	Lg	CY	.003	21600	2.81	.10	.01	2.92	**3.39**
	Inst	BF	Sm	CY	.004	15120	3.29	.14	.02	3.45	**4.00**
60" deep, 60' long	Demo	SF	Lg	LK	.007	6545	---	.24	.04	.28	**.38**
	Demo	SF	Sm	LK	.010	4582	---	.34	.06	.40	**.54**
60" deep, 60' long	Inst	SF	Lg	CY	.009	6545	9.26	.31	.04	9.61	**11.10**
	Inst	SF	Sm	CY	.012	4582	10.90	.42	.06	11.38	**13.10**

Purlins

16' long, STR #1, SF pricing based on 8' oc

Description	Oper	Unit	Vol	Crew Size	Man-hours per Unit	Crew Output per Day	Avg Mat'l Unit Cost	Avg Labor Unit Cost	Avg Equip Unit Cost	Avg Total Unit Cost	Avg Price Incl O&P
2" x 8"	Demo	LF	Lg	LL	.030	1620	---	1.00	.16	1.16	**1.56**
	Demo	LF	Sm	LL	.042	1134	---	1.40	.23	1.63	**2.18**
2" x 8"	Inst	LF	Lg	CZ	.067	1080	1.34	2.31	.24	3.89	**5.02**
	Inst	LF	Sm	CZ	.095	756	1.56	3.28	.34	5.18	**6.72**
2" x 8"	Demo	BF	Lg	LL	.022	2155	---	.73	.12	.85	**1.14**
	Demo	BF	Sm	LL	.032	1508	---	1.06	.17	1.23	**1.66**
2" x 8"	Inst	BF	Lg	CZ	.050	1436	1.01	1.72	.18	2.91	**3.76**
	Inst	BF	Sm	CZ	.072	1005	1.17	2.48	.26	3.91	**5.08**
2" x 8"	Demo	SF	Lg	LL	.003	14727	---	.10	.02	.12	**.16**
	Demo	SF	Sm	LL	.005	10309	---	.17	.03	.20	**.26**
2" x 8"	Inst	SF	Lg	CZ	.007	9818	.15	.24	.03	.42	**.54**
	Inst	SF	Sm	CZ	.010	6873	.17	.34	.04	.55	**.72**
2" x 10"	Demo	LF	Lg	LL	.030	1620	---	1.00	.16	1.16	**1.56**
	Demo	LF	Sm	LL	.042	1134	---	1.40	.23	1.63	**2.18**
2" x 10"	Inst	LF	Lg	CZ	.067	1080	1.80	2.31	.24	4.35	**5.54**
	Inst	LF	Sm	CZ	.095	756.0	2.12	3.28	.34	5.74	**7.36**
2" x 10"	Demo	BF	Lg	LL	.018	2705	---	.60	.10	.70	**.94**
	Demo	BF	Sm	LL	.025	1894	---	.83	.14	.97	**1.30**
2" x 10"	Inst	BF	Lg	CZ	.040	1804	1.08	1.38	.14	2.60	**3.31**
	Inst	BF	Sm	CZ	.057	1263	1.27	1.97	.21	3.45	**4.42**
2" x 10"	Demo	SF	Lg	LL	.003	14727	---	.10	.02	.12	**.16**
	Demo	SF	Sm	LL	.005	10309	---	.17	.03	.20	**.26**
2" x 10"	Inst	SF	Lg	CZ	.007	9818	.20	.24	.03	.47	**.60**
	Inst	SF	Sm	CZ	.010	6873	.23	.34	.04	.61	**.79**

Description	Oper	Unit	Vol	Crew Size	Man-hours per Unit	Crew Output per Day	Avg Mat'l Unit Cost	Avg Labor Unit Cost	Avg Equip Unit Cost	Avg Total Unit Cost	Avg Price Incl O&P
2" x 12"	Demo	LF	Lg	LL	.030	1620	---	1.00	.16	1.16	**1.56**
	Demo	LF	Sm	LL	.042	1134	---	1.40	.23	1.63	**2.18**
2" x 12"	Inst	LF	Lg	CZ	.067	1080	2.10	2.31	.24	4.65	**5.89**
	Inst	LF	Sm	CZ	.095	756.0	2.46	3.28	.34	6.08	**7.76**
2" x 12"	Demo	BF	Lg	LL	.015	3240	---	.50	.08	.58	**.78**
	Demo	BF	Sm	LL	.021	2268	---	.70	.11	.81	**1.09**
2" x 12"	Inst	BF	Lg	CZ	.033	2160	1.05	1.14	.12	2.31	**2.92**
	Inst	BF	Sm	CZ	.048	1512	1.23	1.66	.17	3.06	**3.90**
2" x 12"	Demo	SF	Lg	LL	.003	14727	---	.10	.02	.12	**.16**
	Demo	SF	Sm	LL	.005	10309	---	.17	.03	.20	**.26**
2" x 12"	Inst	SF	Lg	CZ	.007	9818	.23	.24	.03	.50	**.63**
	Inst	SF	Sm	CZ	.010	6873	.27	.34	.04	.65	**.83**
3" x 8"	Demo	LF	Lg	LL	.030	1620	---	1.00	.16	1.16	**1.56**
	Demo	LF	Sm	LL	.042	1134	---	1.40	.23	1.63	**2.18**
3" x 8"	Inst	LF	Lg	CZ	.067	1080	5.36	2.31	.24	7.91	**9.64**
	Inst	LF	Sm	CZ	.095	756.0	6.28	3.28	.34	9.90	**12.20**
3" x 8"	Demo	BF	Lg	LL	.015	3240	---	.50	.08	.58	**.78**
	Demo	BF	Sm	LL	.021	2268	---	.70	.11	.81	**1.09**
3" x 8"	Inst	BF	Lg	CZ	.033	2160	2.68	1.14	.12	3.94	**4.80**
	Inst	BF	Sm	CZ	.048	1512	3.14	1.66	.17	4.97	**6.10**
3" x 8"	Demo	SF	Lg	LL	.003	14727	---	.10	.02	.12	**.16**
	Demo	SF	Sm	LL	.005	10309	---	.17	.03	.20	**.26**
3" x 8"	Inst	SF	Lg	CZ	.007	9818	.59	.24	.03	.86	**1.05**
	Inst	SF	Sm	CZ	.010	6873	.69	.34	.04	1.07	**1.32**
3" x 10"	Demo	LF	Lg	LL	.030	1620	---	1.00	.16	1.16	**1.56**
	Demo	LF	Sm	LL	.042	1134	---	1.40	.23	1.63	**2.18**
3" x 10"	Inst	LF	Lg	CZ	.067	1080	7.24	2.31	.24	9.79	**11.80**
	Inst	LF	Sm	CZ	.095	756.0	8.48	3.28	.34	12.10	**14.70**
3" x 10"	Demo	BF	Lg	LL	.012	4050	---	.40	.06	.46	**.62**
	Demo	BF	Sm	LL	.017	2835	---	.56	.09	.65	**.88**
3" x 10"	Inst	BF	Lg	CZ	.027	2700	2.90	.93	.10	3.93	**4.74**
	Inst	BF	Sm	CZ	.038	1890	3.39	1.31	.14	4.84	**5.87**
3" x 10"	Demo	SF	Lg	LL	.003	14727	---	.10	.02	.12	**.16**
	Demo	SF	Sm	LL	.005	10309	---	.17	.03	.20	**.26**
3" x 10"	Inst	SF	Lg	CZ	.007	9818	.80	.24	.03	1.07	**1.29**
	Inst	SF	Sm	CZ	.010	6873	.93	.34	.04	1.31	**1.59**
3" x 12"	Demo	LF	Lg	LL	.030	1620	---	1.00	.16	1.16	**1.56**
	Demo	LF	Sm	LL	.042	1134	---	1.40	.23	1.63	**2.18**
3" x 12"	Inst	LF	Lg	CZ	.067	1080	8.40	2.31	.24	10.95	**13.10**
	Inst	LF	Sm	CZ	.095	756.0	9.88	3.28	.34	13.50	**16.30**
3" x 12"	Demo	BF	Lg	LL	.010	4860	---	.33	.05	.38	**.52**
	Demo	BF	Sm	LL	.014	3402	---	.47	.08	.55	**.73**
3" x 12"	Inst	BF	Lg	CZ	.022	3240	2.80	.76	.08	3.64	**4.36**
	Inst	BF	Sm	CZ	.032	2268	3.29	1.10	.11	4.50	**5.44**
3" x 12"	Demo	SF	Lg	LL	.003	14727	---	.10	.02	.12	**.16**
	Demo	SF	Sm	LL	.005	10309	---	.17	.03	.20	**.26**
3" x 12"	Inst	SF	Lg	CZ	.007	9818	.92	.24	.03	1.19	**1.43**
	Inst	SF	Sm	CZ	.010	6873	1.09	.34	.04	1.47	**1.78**

Description	Oper	Unit	Vol	Crew Size	Man-hours per Unit	Crew Output per Day	Avg Mat'l Unit Cost	Avg Labor Unit Cost	Avg Equip Unit Cost	Avg Total Unit Cost	Avg Price Incl O&P
3" x 14"	Demo	LF	Lg	LL	.030	1620	---	1.00	.16	1.16	**1.56**
	Demo	LF	Sm	LL	.042	1134	---	1.40	.23	1.63	**2.18**
3" x 14"	Inst	LF	Lg	CZ	.067	1080	10.90	2.31	.24	13.45	**16.00**
	Inst	LF	Sm	CZ	.095	756.0	12.80	3.28	.34	16.42	**19.60**
3" x 14"	Demo	BF	Lg	LL	.008	5670	---	.27	.05	.32	**.42**
	Demo	BF	Sm	LL	.012	3969	---	.40	.07	.47	**.63**
3" x 14"	Inst	BF	Lg	CZ	.019	3780	3.11	.66	.07	3.84	**4.56**
	Inst	BF	Sm	CZ	.027	2646	3.65	.93	.10	4.68	**5.60**
3" x 14"	Demo	SF	Lg	LL	.003	14727	---	.10	.02	.12	**.16**
	Demo	SF	Sm	LL	.005	10309	---	.17	.03	.20	**.26**
3" x 14"	Inst	SF	Lg	CZ	.007	9818	1.20	.24	.03	1.47	**1.75**
	Inst	SF	Sm	CZ	.010	6873	1.40	.34	.04	1.78	**2.13**

Sub-purlins

8' long, STR #1, SF pricing based on 2' oc

Description	Oper	Unit	Vol	Crew Size	Man-hours per Unit	Crew Output per Day	Avg Mat'l Unit Cost	Avg Labor Unit Cost	Avg Equip Unit Cost	Avg Total Unit Cost	Avg Price Incl O&P
2" x 4"	Demo	LF	Lg	LL	.013	3630	---	.43	.07	.50	**.67**
	Demo	LF	Sm	LL	.019	2541	---	.63	.10	.73	**.98**
2" x 4"	Inst	LF	Lg	CZ	.030	2420	.64	1.03	.11	1.78	**2.29**
	Inst	LF	Sm	CZ	.043	1694	.76	1.48	.15	2.39	**3.10**
2" x 4"	Demo	BF	Lg	LL	.020	2432	---	.66	.11	.77	**1.04**
	Demo	BF	Sm	LL	.028	1702	---	.93	.15	1.08	**1.45**
2" x 4"	Inst	BF	Lg	CZ	.044	1621	.96	1.52	.16	2.64	**3.39**
	Inst	BF	Sm	CZ	.063	1135	1.13	2.17	.23	3.53	**4.57**
2" x 4"	Demo	SF	Lg	LL	.006	8067	---	.20	.03	.23	**.31**
	Demo	SF	Sm	LL	.009	5647	---	.30	.05	.35	**.47**
2" x 4"	Inst	SF	Lg	CZ	.013	5378	.29	.45	.05	.79	**1.01**
	Inst	SF	Sm	CZ	.019	3764	.34	.66	.07	1.07	**1.38**
2" x 6"	Demo	LF	Lg	LL	.013	3630	---	.43	.07	.50	**.67**
	Demo	LF	Sm	LL	.019	2541	---	.63	.10	.73	**.98**
2" x 6"	Inst	LF	Lg	CZ	.030	2420	1.00	1.03	.11	2.14	**2.71**
	Inst	LF	Sm	CZ	.043	1694	1.18	1.48	.15	2.81	**3.58**
2" x 6"	Demo	BF	Lg	LL	.013	3630	---	.43	.07	.50	**.67**
	Demo	BF	Sm	LL	.019	2541	---	.63	.10	.73	**.98**
2" x 6"	Inst	BF	Lg	CZ	.030	2420	1.00	1.03	.11	2.14	**2.71**
	Inst	BF	Sm	CZ	.043	1694	1.18	1.48	.15	2.81	**3.58**
2" x 6"	Demo	SF	Lg	LL	.006	8067	---	.20	.03	.23	**.31**
	Demo	SF	Sm	LL	.009	5647	---	.30	.05	.35	**.47**
2" x 6"	Inst	SF	Lg	CZ	.013	5378	.45	.45	.05	.95	**1.20**
	Inst	SF	Sm	CZ	.019	3764	.53	.66	.07	1.26	**1.60**

Description	Oper	Unit	Vol	Crew Size	Man-hours per Unit	Crew Output per Day	Avg Mat'l Unit Cost	Avg Labor Unit Cost	Avg Equip Unit Cost	Avg Total Unit Cost	Avg Price Incl O&P
2" x 8"	Demo	LF	Lg	LL	.013	3630	---	.43	.07	.50	.67
	Demo	LF	Sm	LL	.019	2541	---	.63	.10	.73	.98
2" x 8"	Inst	LF	Lg	CZ	.030	2420	1.34	1.03	.11	2.48	3.10
	Inst	LF	Sm	CZ	.043	1694	1.56	1.48	.15	3.19	4.02
2" x 8"	Demo	BF	Lg	LL	.010	4828	---	.33	.05	.38	.52
	Demo	BF	Sm	LL	.014	3380	---	.47	.08	.55	.73
2" x 8"	Inst	BF	Lg	CZ	.022	3219	1.01	.76	.08	1.85	2.30
	Inst	BF	Sm	CZ	.032	2253	1.17	1.10	.12	2.39	3.01
2" x 8"	Demo	SF	Lg	LL	.006	8067	---	.20	.03	.23	.31
	Demo	SF	Sm	LL	.009	5647	---	.30	.05	.35	.47
2" x 8"	Inst	SF	Lg	CZ	.013	5378	.60	.45	.05	1.10	1.37
	Inst	SF	Sm	CZ	.019	3764	.70	.66	.07	1.43	1.79
3" x 4"	Demo	LF	Lg	LL	.013	3630	---	.43	.07	.50	.67
	Demo	LF	Sm	LL	.019	2541	---	.63	.10	.73	.98
3" x 4"	Inst	LF	Lg	CZ	.030	2420	1.30	1.03	.11	2.44	3.05
	Inst	LF	Sm	CZ	.043	1694	1.52	1.48	.15	3.15	3.97
3" x 4"	Demo	BF	Lg	LL	.013	3630	---	.43	.07	.50	.67
	Demo	BF	Sm	LL	.019	2541	---	.63	.10	.73	.98
3" x 4"	Inst	BF	Lg	CZ	.030	2420	1.30	1.03	.11	2.44	3.05
	Inst	BF	Sm	CZ	.043	1694	1.52	1.48	.15	3.15	3.97
3" x 4"	Demo	SF	Lg	LL	.006	8067	---	.20	.03	.23	.31
	Demo	SF	Sm	LL	.009	5647	---	.30	.05	.35	.47
3" x 4"	Inst	SF	Lg	CZ	.013	5378	.59	.45	.05	1.09	1.36
	Inst	SF	Sm	CZ	.019	3764	.68	.66	.07	1.41	1.77
3" x 6"	Demo	LF	Lg	LL	.013	3630	---	.43	.07	.50	.67
	Demo	LF	Sm	LL	.019	2541	---	.63	.10	.73	.98
3" x 6"	Inst	LF	Lg	CZ	.030	2420	2.02	1.03	.11	3.16	3.88
	Inst	LF	Sm	CZ	.043	1694	2.36	1.48	.15	3.99	4.94
3" x 6"	Demo	BF	Lg	LL	.009	5445	---	.30	.05	.35	.47
	Demo	BF	Sm	LL	.013	3812	---	.43	.07	.50	.67
3" x 6"	Inst	BF	Lg	CZ	.020	3630	1.35	.69	.07	2.11	2.59
	Inst	BF	Sm	CZ	.028	2541	1.57	.97	.10	2.64	3.26
3" x 6"	Demo	SF	Lg	LL	.006	8067	---	.20	.03	.23	.31
	Demo	SF	Sm	LL	.009	5647	---	.30	.05	.35	.47
3" x 6"	Inst	SF	Lg	CZ	.013	5378	.91	.45	.05	1.41	1.72
	Inst	SF	Sm	CZ	.019	3764	1.06	.66	.07	1.79	2.21
3" x 8"	Demo	LF	Lg	LL	.013	3630	---	.43	.07	.50	.67
	Demo	LF	Sm	LL	.019	2541	---	.63	.10	.73	.98
3" x 8"	Inst	LF	Lg	CZ	.030	2420	5.36	1.03	.11	6.50	7.72
	Inst	LF	Sm	CZ	.043	1694	6.28	1.48	.15	7.91	9.45
3" x 8"	Demo	BF	Lg	LL	.007	7260	---	.23	.04	.27	.37
	Demo	BF	Sm	LL	.009	5082	---	.30	.05	.35	.47
3" x 8"	Inst	BF	Lg	CZ	.015	4840	2.68	.52	.05	3.25	3.86
	Inst	BF	Sm	CZ	.021	3388	3.14	.72	.08	3.94	4.70
3" x 8"	Demo	SF	Lg	LL	.006	8067	---	.20	.03	.23	.31
	Demo	SF	Sm	LL	.009	5647	---	.30	.05	.35	.47
3" x 8"	Inst	SF	Lg	CZ	.013	5378	2.41	.45	.05	2.91	3.45
	Inst	SF	Sm	CZ	.019	3764	2.83	.66	.07	3.56	4.24

Description	Oper	Unit	Vol	Crew Size	Man-hours per Unit	Crew Output per Day	Avg Mat'l Unit Cost	Avg Labor Unit Cost	Avg Equip Unit Cost	Avg Total Unit Cost	Avg Price Incl O&P

Ledgers
Bolts 2' oc

Description	Oper	Unit	Vol	Crew	MH	Output	Mat'l	Labor	Equip	Total	Price
3" x 8"	Demo	LF	Lg	LC	.037	648.0	---	1.20	.40	1.60	**2.08**
	Demo	LF	Sm	LC	.053	453.6	---	1.71	.57	2.28	**2.97**
3" x 8"	Inst	LF	Lg	CS	.056	432.0	5.36	1.94	.60	7.90	**9.48**
	Inst	LF	Sm	CS	.079	302.4	6.28	2.74	.86	9.88	**11.90**
3" x 8"	Demo	BF	Lg	LC	.019	1296	---	.61	.20	.81	**1.06**
	Demo	BF	Sm	LC	.026	907.2	---	.84	.29	1.13	**1.47**
3" x 8"	Inst	BF	Lg	CS	.028	864.0	2.68	.97	.30	3.95	**4.74**
	Inst	BF	Sm	CS	.040	604.8	3.14	1.39	.43	4.96	**5.98**
3" x 8"	Demo	SF	Lg	LC	.002	12597	---	.06	.02	.08	**.11**
	Demo	SF	Sm	LC	.003	8818	---	.10	.03	.13	**.17**
3" x 8"	Inst	SF	Lg	CS	.003	8398	.28	.10	.03	.41	**.50**
	Inst	SF	Sm	CS	.004	5879	.32	.14	.04	.50	**.60**
3" x 10"	Demo	LF	Lg	LC	.037	648.0	---	1.20	.40	1.60	**2.08**
	Demo	LF	Sm	LC	.053	453.6	---	1.71	.57	2.28	**2.97**
3" x 10"	Inst	LF	Lg	CS	.056	432.0	7.24	1.94	.60	9.78	**11.60**
	Inst	LF	Sm	CS	.079	302.4	8.48	2.74	.86	12.08	**14.50**
3" x 10"	Demo	BF	Lg	LC	.015	1620	---	.49	.16	.65	**.84**
	Demo	BF	Sm	LC	.021	1134	---	.68	.23	.91	**1.18**
3" x 10"	Inst	BF	Lg	CS	.022	1080	2.90	.76	.24	3.90	**4.64**
	Inst	BF	Sm	CS	.032	756.0	3.39	1.11	.34	4.84	**5.79**
3" x 10"	Demo	SF	Lg	LC	.002	12597	---	.06	.02	.08	**.11**
	Demo	SF	Sm	LC	.003	8818	---	.10	.03	.13	**.17**
3" x 10"	Inst	SF	Lg	CS	.003	8398	.37	.10	.03	.50	**.60**
	Inst	SF	Sm	CS	.004	5879	.44	.14	.04	.62	**.74**
3" x 12"	Demo	LF	Lg	LC	.037	648.0	---	1.20	.40	1.60	**2.08**
	Demo	LF	Sm	LC	.053	453.6	---	1.71	.57	2.28	**2.97**
3" x 12"	Inst	LF	Lg	CS	.056	432.0	8.40	1.94	.60	10.94	**13.00**
	Inst	LF	Sm	CS	.079	302.4	9.88	2.74	.86	13.48	**16.10**
3" x 12"	Demo	BF	Lg	LC	.012	1944	---	.39	.13	.52	**.67**
	Demo	BF	Sm	LC	.018	1361	---	.58	.19	.77	**1.01**
3" x 12"	Inst	BF	Lg	CS	.019	1296	2.80	.66	.20	3.66	**4.34**
	Inst	BF	Sm	CS	.026	907.2	3.29	.90	.29	4.48	**5.34**
3" x 12"	Demo	SF	Lg	LC	.002	12597	---	.06	.02	.08	**.11**
	Demo	SF	Sm	LC	.003	8818	---	.10	.03	.13	**.17**
3" x 12"	Inst	SF	Lg	CS	.003	8398	.43	.10	.03	.56	**.67**
	Inst	SF	Sm	CS	.004	5879	.51	.14	.04	.69	**.82**

Description	Oper	Unit	Vol	Crew Size	Man-hours per Unit	Crew Output per Day	Avg Mat'l Unit Cost	Avg Labor Unit Cost	Avg Equip Unit Cost	Avg Total Unit Cost	Avg Price Incl O&P
4" x 8"	Demo	LF	Lg	LC	.037	648.0	---	1.20	.40	1.60	**2.08**
	Demo	LF	Sm	LC	.053	453.6	---	1.71	.57	2.28	**2.97**
4" x 8"	Inst	LF	Lg	CS	.056	432.0	4.58	1.94	.60	7.12	**8.59**
	Inst	LF	Sm	CS	.079	302.4	5.36	2.74	.86	8.96	**10.90**
4" x 8"	Demo	BF	Lg	LC	.014	1730	---	.45	.15	.60	**.78**
	Demo	BF	Sm	LC	.020	1211	---	.65	.21	.86	**1.12**
4" x 8"	Inst	BF	Lg	CS	.021	1153	1.72	.73	.23	2.68	**3.23**
	Inst	BF	Sm	CS	.030	807.4	2.01	1.04	.32	3.37	**4.09**
4" x 8"	Demo	SF	Lg	LC	.002	12597	---	.06	.02	.08	**.11**
	Demo	SF	Sm	LC	.003	8818	---	.10	.03	.13	**.17**
4" x 8"	Inst	SF	Lg	CS	.003	8398	.24	.10	.03	.37	**.45**
	Inst	SF	Sm	CS	.004	5879	.28	.14	.04	.46	**.56**
4" x 10"	Demo	LF	Lg	LC	.037	648.0	---	1.20	.40	1.60	**2.08**
	Demo	LF	Sm	LC	.053	453.6	---	1.71	.57	2.28	**2.97**
4" x 10"	Inst	LF	Lg	CS	.056	432.0	5.68	1.94	.60	8.22	**9.85**
	Inst	LF	Sm	CS	.079	302.4	6.64	2.74	.86	10.24	**12.30**
4" x 10"	Demo	BF	Lg	LC	.011	2158	---	.36	.12	.48	**.62**
	Demo	BF	Sm	LC	.016	1510	---	.52	.17	.69	**.89**
4" x 10"	Inst	BF	Lg	CS	.017	1439	1.71	.59	.18	2.48	**2.97**
	Inst	BF	Sm	CS	.024	1007	1.99	.83	.26	3.08	**3.71**
4" x 10"	Demo	SF	Lg	LC	.002	12597	---	.06	.02	.08	**.11**
	Demo	SF	Sm	LC	.003	8818	---	.10	.03	.13	**.17**
4" x 10"	Inst	SF	Lg	CS	.003	8398	.29	.10	.03	.42	**.51**
	Inst	SF	Sm	CS	.004	5879	.34	.14	.04	.52	**.63**
4" x 12"	Demo	LF	Lg	LC	.037	648.0	---	1.20	.40	1.60	**2.08**
	Demo	LF	Sm	LC	.053	453.6	---	1.71	.57	2.28	**2.97**
4" x 12"	Inst	LF	Lg	CS	.056	432.0	6.62	1.94	.60	9.16	**10.90**
	Inst	LF	Sm	CS	.079	302.4	7.76	2.74	.86	11.36	**13.60**
4" x 12"	Demo	BF	Lg	LC	.009	2592	---	.29	.10	.39	**.51**
	Demo	BF	Sm	LC	.013	1814	---	.42	.14	.56	**.73**
4" x 12"	Inst	BF	Lg	CS	.014	1728	1.66	.49	.15	2.30	**2.74**
	Inst	BF	Sm	CS	.020	1210	1.94	.69	.21	2.84	**3.41**
4" x 12"	Demo	SF	Lg	LC	.002	12597	---	.06	.02	.08	**.11**
	Demo	SF	Sm	LC	.003	8818	---	.10	.03	.13	**.17**
4" x 12"	Inst	SF	Lg	CS	.003	8398	.34	.10	.03	.47	**.57**
	Inst	SF	Sm	CS	.004	5879	.40	.14	.04	.58	**.69**

Description	Oper	Unit	Vol	Crew Size	Man-hours per Unit	Crew Output per Day	Avg Mat'l Unit Cost	Avg Labor Unit Cost	Avg Equip Unit Cost	Avg Total Unit Cost	Avg Price Incl O&P

Gutters and downspouts

Aluminum, baked on painted finish (white or brown)

Gutter, 5" box type

Description	Oper	Unit	Vol	Crew Size	Man-hours per Unit	Crew Output per Day	Avg Mat'l Unit Cost	Avg Labor Unit Cost	Avg Equip Unit Cost	Avg Total Unit Cost	Avg Price Incl O&P
Heavyweight gauge	Inst	LF	Lg	UB	.074	215.0	.87	3.09	---	3.96	**5.38**
	Inst	LF	Sm	UB	.106	150.5	.95	4.42	---	5.37	**7.37**
Standard weight gauge	Inst	LF	Lg	UB	.074	215.0	.69	3.09	---	3.78	**5.18**
	Inst	LF	Sm	UB	.106	150.5	.76	4.42	---	5.18	**7.15**
End cap	Inst	Ea	Lg	UB	---	---	1.60	---	---	1.60	**1.60**
	Inst	Ea	Sm	UB	---	---	1.76	---	---	1.76	**1.76**
Drop outlet for downspouts	Inst	Ea	Lg	UB	---	---	7.75	---	---	7.75	**7.75**
	Inst	Ea	Sm	UB	---	---	8.51	---	---	8.51	**8.51**
Inside/outside corner	Inst	Ea	Lg	UB	---	---	9.08	---	---	9.08	**9.08**
	Inst	Ea	Sm	UB	---	---	9.97	---	---	9.97	**9.97**
Joint connector											
	Inst	Ea	Lg	UB	---	---	4.69	---	---	4.69	**4.69**
	Inst	Ea	Sm	UB	---	---	5.15	---	---	5.15	**5.15**
Fascia support bracket											
	Inst	Ea	Lg	UB	---	---	2.53	---	---	2.53	**2.53**
	Inst	Ea	Sm	UB	---	---	2.78	---	---	2.78	**2.78**
Gutter hanger support											
	Inst	Ea	Lg	UB	---	---	1.75	---	---	1.75	**1.75**
	Inst	Ea	Sm	UB	---	---	1.93	---	---	1.93	**1.93**

Downspout, corrugated square

Description	Oper	Unit	Vol	Crew Size	Man-hours per Unit	Crew Output per Day	Avg Mat'l Unit Cost	Avg Labor Unit Cost	Avg Equip Unit Cost	Avg Total Unit Cost	Avg Price Incl O&P
Standard weight gauge	Inst	LF	Lg	UB	.064	250.0	3.48	2.67	---	6.15	**7.79**
	Inst	LF	Sm	UB	.091	175.0	3.82	3.80	---	7.62	**9.78**
Regular/side elbow	Inst	Ea	Lg	UB	---	---	2.96	---	---	2.96	**2.96**
	Inst	Ea	Sm	UB	---	---	3.25	---	---	3.25	**3.25**
Downspout holder											
	Inst	Ea	Lg	UB	---	---	1.70	---	---	1.70	**1.70**
	Inst	Ea	Sm	UB	---	---	1.87	---	---	1.87	**1.87**

Steel, natural finish

Gutter, 4" box type

Description	Oper	Unit	Vol	Crew Size	Man-hours per Unit	Crew Output per Day	Avg Mat'l Unit Cost	Avg Labor Unit Cost	Avg Equip Unit Cost	Avg Total Unit Cost	Avg Price Incl O&P
Heavyweight gauge	Inst	LF	Lg	UB	.074	215.0	.71	3.09	---	3.80	**5.20**
	Inst	LF	Sm	UB	.106	150.5	.78	4.42	---	5.20	**7.18**
End cap	Inst	Ea	Lg	UB	---	---	2.02	---	---	2.02	**2.02**
	Inst	Ea	Sm	UB	---	---	2.22	---	---	2.22	**2.22**
Drop outlet for downspouts	Inst	Ea	Lg	UB	---	---	9.41	---	---	9.41	**9.41**
	Inst	Ea	Sm	UB	---	---	10.30	---	---	10.30	**10.30**
Inside/outside corner	Inst	Ea	Lg	UB	---	---	9.16	---	---	9.16	**9.16**
	Inst	Ea	Sm	UB	---	---	10.10	---	---	10.10	**10.10**
Joint connector											
	Inst	Ea	Lg	UB	---	---	3.34	---	---	3.34	**3.34**
	Inst	Ea	Sm	UB	---	---	3.66	---	---	3.66	**3.66**
Strap hanger											
	Inst	Ea	Lg	UB	---	---	1.70	---	---	1.70	**1.70**
	Inst	Ea	Sm	UB	---	---	1.87	---	---	1.87	**1.87**

Description	Oper	Unit	Vol	Crew Size	Man-hours per Unit	Crew Output per Day	Avg Mat'l Unit Cost	Avg Labor Unit Cost	Avg Equip Unit Cost	Avg Total Unit Cost	Avg Price Incl O&P
Fascia support bracket											
	Inst	Ea	Lg	UB	---	---	3.09	---	---	3.09	**3.09**
	Inst	Ea	Sm	UB	---	---	3.39	---	---	3.39	**3.39**
Spike and ferrule support											
	Inst	Ea	Lg	UB	---	---	.91	---	---	.91	**.91**
	Inst	Ea	Sm	UB	---	---	1.00	---	---	1.00	**1.00**

Downspout, 30 gauge galvanized steel

Description	Oper	Unit	Vol	Crew Size	Man-hours per Unit	Crew Output per Day	Avg Mat'l Unit Cost	Avg Labor Unit Cost	Avg Equip Unit Cost	Avg Total Unit Cost	Avg Price Incl O&P
Standard weight gauge	Inst	LF	Lg	UB	.074	215.0	4.81	3.09	---	7.90	**9.92**
	Inst	LF	Sm	UB	.106	150.5	5.29	4.42	---	9.71	**12.40**
Regular/side elbow	Inst	Ea	Lg	UB	---	---	4.06	---	---	4.06	**4.06**
	Inst	Ea	Sm	UB	---	---	4.46	---	---	4.46	**4.46**
Downspout holder											
	Inst	Ea	Lg	UB	---	---	1.70	---	---	1.70	**1.70**
	Inst	Ea	Sm	UB	---	---	1.87	---	---	1.87	**1.87**

Vinyl, extruded 5" PVC
White

Description	Oper	Unit	Vol	Crew Size	Man-hours per Unit	Crew Output per Day	Avg Mat'l Unit Cost	Avg Labor Unit Cost	Avg Equip Unit Cost	Avg Total Unit Cost	Avg Price Incl O&P
Gutter	Inst	LF	Lg	UB	.074	215.0	1.38	3.09	---	4.47	**5.97**
	Inst	LF	Sm	UB	.106	150.5	1.51	4.42	---	5.93	**8.02**
End caps	Inst	Ea	Lg	UB	---	---	3.20	---	---	3.20	**3.20**
	Inst	Ea	Sm	UB	---	---	3.52	---	---	3.52	**3.52**
Drop outlet for downspouts	Inst	Ea	Lg	UB	---	---	8.97	---	---	8.97	**8.97**
	Inst	Ea	Sm	UB	---	---	9.84	---	---	9.84	**9.84**
Inside/outside corner	Inst	Ea	Lg	UB	---	---	7.15	---	---	7.15	**7.15**
	Inst	Ea	Sm	UB	---	---	7.85	---	---	7.85	**7.85**
Joint connector	Inst	Ea	Lg	UB	---	---	4.44	---	---	4.44	**4.44**
	Inst	Ea	Sm	UB	---	---	4.87	---	---	4.87	**4.87**
Fascia support bracket											
	Inst	Ea	Lg	UB	---	---	1.75	---	---	1.75	**1.75**
	Inst	Ea	Sm	UB	---	---	1.93	---	---	1.93	**1.93**
Downspout	Inst	LF	Lg	UB	.064	250.0	1.53	2.67	---	4.20	**5.55**
	Inst	LF	Sm	UB	.091	175.0	1.68	3.80	---	5.48	**7.32**
Downspout driplet	Inst	Ea	Lg	UB	---	---	6.12	---	---	6.12	**6.12**
	Inst	Ea	Sm	UB	---	---	6.72	---	---	6.72	**6.72**
Downspout joiner	Inst	Ea	Lg	UB	---	---	2.81	---	---	2.81	**2.81**
	Inst	Ea	Sm	UB	---	---	3.08	---	---	3.08	**3.08**
Downspout holder											
	Inst	Ea	Lg	UB	---	---	4.08	---	---	4.08	**4.08**
	Inst	Ea	Sm	UB	---	---	4.48	---	---	4.48	**4.48**
Regular elbow	Inst	Ea	Lg	UB	---	---	2.39	---	---	2.39	**2.39**
	Inst	Ea	Sm	UB	---	---	2.62	---	---	2.62	**2.62**
Well cap	Inst	Ea	Lg	UB	---	---	3.06	---	---	3.06	**3.06**
	Inst	Ea	Sm	UB	---	---	3.36	---	---	3.36	**3.36**
Well outlet	Inst	Ea	Lg	UB	---	---	4.08	---	---	4.08	**4.08**
	Inst	Ea	Sm	UB	---	---	4.48	---	---	4.48	**4.48**
Expansion joint connector	Inst	Ea	Lg	UB	---	---	6.63	---	---	6.63	**6.63**
	Inst	Ea	Sm	UB	---	---	7.28	---	---	7.28	**7.28**
Rafter adapter											
	Inst	Ea	Lg	UB	---	---	4.08	---	---	4.08	**4.08**
	Inst	Ea	Sm	UB	---	---	4.48	---	---	4.48	**4.48**

Description	Oper	Unit	Vol	Crew Size	Man-hours per Unit	Crew Output per Day	Avg Mat'l Unit Cost	Avg Labor Unit Cost	Avg Equip Unit Cost	Avg Total Unit Cost	Avg Price Incl O&P
Brown											
Gutter	Inst	LF	Lg	UB	.074	215.0	1.38	3.09	---	4.47	**5.97**
	Inst	LF	Sm	UB	.106	150.5	1.51	4.42	---	5.93	**8.02**
End caps	Inst	Ea	Lg	UB	---	---	3.20	---	---	3.20	**3.20**
	Inst	Ea	Sm	UB	---	---	3.52	---	---	3.52	**3.52**
Drop outlet for downspouts	Inst	Ea	Lg	UB	---	---	8.97	---	---	8.97	**8.97**
	Inst	Ea	Sm	UB	---	---	9.84	---	---	9.84	**9.84**
Inside/outside corner	Inst	Ea	Lg	UB	---	---	7.15	---	---	7.15	**7.15**
	Inst	Ea	Sm	UB	---	---	7.85	---	---	7.85	**7.85**
Joint connector	Inst	Ea	Lg	UB	---	---	4.44	---	---	4.44	**4.44**
	Inst	Ea	Sm	UB	---	---	4.87	---	---	4.87	**4.87**
Fascia support bracket											
	Inst	Ea	Lg	UB	---	---	1.75	---	---	1.75	**1.75**
	Inst	Ea	Sm	UB	---	---	1.93	---	---	1.93	**1.93**
Downspout	Inst	LF	Lg	UB	.064	250.0	1.53	2.67	---	4.20	**5.55**
	Inst	LF	Sm	UB	.091	175.0	1.68	3.80	---	5.48	**7.32**
Downspout driplet	Inst	Ea	Lg	UB	---	---	6.12	---	---	6.12	**6.12**
	Inst	Ea	Sm	UB	---	---	6.72	---	---	6.72	**6.72**
Downspout joiner	Inst	Ea	Lg	UB	---	---	2.81	---	---	2.81	**2.81**
	Inst	Ea	Sm	UB	---	---	3.08	---	---	3.08	**3.08**
Downspout holder											
	Inst	Ea	Lg	UB	---	---	4.08	---	---	4.08	**4.08**
	Inst	Ea	Sm	UB	---	---	4.48	---	---	4.48	**4.48**
Regular elbow	Inst	Ea	Lg	UB	---	---	2.39	---	---	2.39	**2.39**
	Inst	Ea	Sm	UB	---	---	2.62	---	---	2.62	**2.62**
Well cap	Inst	Ea	Lg	UB	---	---	3.06	---	---	3.06	**3.06**
	Inst	Ea	Sm	UB	---	---	3.36	---	---	3.36	**3.36**
Well outlet	Inst	Ea	Lg	UB	---	---	4.08	---	---	4.08	**4.08**
	Inst	Ea	Sm	UB	---	---	4.48	---	---	4.48	**4.48**
Expansion joint connector	Inst	Ea	Lg	UB	---	---	6.63	---	---	6.63	**6.63**
	Inst	Ea	Sm	UB	---	---	7.28	---	---	7.28	**7.28**
Rafter adapter											
	Inst	Ea	Lg	UB	---	---	4.08	---	---	4.08	**4.08**
	Inst	Ea	Sm	UB	---	---	4.48	---	---	4.48	**4.48**

Hardboard. See Paneling, page 340

Hardwood flooring

1. Strip flooring is nailed into place over wood sub-flooring or over wood sleeper strips. Using 3¼" W strips leaves 25% cutting and fitting waste; 2¼" W strips leave 33% waste. Nails and the respective cutting and fitting waste have been included in the unit costs.

2. Block flooring is laid in mastic applied to felt-covered wood subfloor. Mastic, 5% block waste and felt are included in material unit costs for block or parquet flooring.

Strip flooring:
A Side and end matched
B Side matched
C Square edged

Two types of wood block flooring

Installation of first strip of flooring

Nailing of flooring:
A Angle of nailing
B Setting the nail without damage to the flooring

Description	Oper	Unit	Vol	Crew Size	Man-hours per Unit	Crew Output per Day	Avg Mat'l Unit Cost	Avg Labor Unit Cost	Avg Equip Unit Cost	Avg Total Unit Cost	Avg Price Incl O&P

Hardwood flooring

Includes waste and nails

Strip; installed over wood subfloor

Prefinished oak, prime

25/32" x 3-1/4"

Description	Oper	Unit	Vol	Crew Size	Man-hours per Unit	Crew Output per Day	Avg Mat'l Unit Cost	Avg Labor Unit Cost	Avg Equip Unit Cost	Avg Total Unit Cost	Avg Price Incl O&P
Lay floor	Inst	SF	Lg	FD	.045	400.0	10.90	1.58	---	12.48	**14.80**
	Inst	SF	Sm	FD	.064	280.0	12.40	2.24	---	14.64	**17.40**
Wax, polish, machine buff	Inst	SF	Lg	FC	.009	860.0	.05	.32	.04	.41	**.55**
	Inst	SF	Sm	FC	.013	602.0	.05	.46	.05	.56	**.77**

25/32" x 2-1/4"

Description	Oper	Unit	Vol	Crew Size	Man-hours per Unit	Crew Output per Day	Avg Mat'l Unit Cost	Avg Labor Unit Cost	Avg Equip Unit Cost	Avg Total Unit Cost	Avg Price Incl O&P
Lay floor	Inst	SF	Lg	FD	.060	300.0	9.53	2.10	---	11.63	**13.90**
	Inst	SF	Sm	FD	.086	210.0	10.90	3.01	---	13.91	**16.80**
Wax, polish, machine buff	Inst	SF	Lg	FC	.009	860.0	.05	.32	.04	.41	**.55**
	Inst	SF	Sm	FC	.013	602.0	.05	.46	.05	.56	**.77**

Unfinished

25/32" x 3-1/4", lay floor only
Fir

Description	Oper	Unit	Vol	Crew Size	Man-hours per Unit	Crew Output per Day	Avg Mat'l Unit Cost	Avg Labor Unit Cost	Avg Equip Unit Cost	Avg Total Unit Cost	Avg Price Incl O&P
Vertical grain	Inst	SF	Lg	FD	.038	480.0	4.14	1.33	---	5.47	**6.65**
	Inst	SF	Sm	FD	.054	336.0	4.70	1.89	---	6.59	**8.09**
Flat grain	Inst	SF	Lg	FD	.038	480.0	3.46	1.33	---	4.79	**5.87**
	Inst	SF	Sm	FD	.054	336.0	3.94	1.89	---	5.83	**7.21**

Yellow pine

	Oper	Unit	Vol	Crew Size	Man-hours per Unit	Crew Output per Day	Avg Mat'l Unit Cost	Avg Labor Unit Cost	Avg Equip Unit Cost	Avg Total Unit Cost	Avg Price Incl O&P
	Inst	SF	Lg	FD	.038	480.0	3.12	1.33	---	4.45	**5.48**
	Inst	SF	Sm	FD	.054	336.0	3.55	1.89	---	5.44	**6.77**

25/32" x 2-1/4", lay floor only
Maple

	Oper	Unit	Vol	Crew Size	Man-hours per Unit	Crew Output per Day	Avg Mat'l Unit Cost	Avg Labor Unit Cost	Avg Equip Unit Cost	Avg Total Unit Cost	Avg Price Incl O&P
	Inst	SF	Lg	FD	.056	320.0	4.14	1.96	---	6.10	**7.54**
	Inst	SF	Sm	FD	.080	224.0	4.70	2.80	---	7.50	**9.38**

Oak

	Oper	Unit	Vol	Crew Size	Man-hours per Unit	Crew Output per Day	Avg Mat'l Unit Cost	Avg Labor Unit Cost	Avg Equip Unit Cost	Avg Total Unit Cost	Avg Price Incl O&P
	Inst	SF	Lg	FD	.056	320.0	4.50	1.96	---	6.46	**7.96**
	Inst	SF	Sm	FD	.080	224.0	5.12	2.80	---	7.92	**9.86**

Yellow pine

	Oper	Unit	Vol	Crew Size	Man-hours per Unit	Crew Output per Day	Avg Mat'l Unit Cost	Avg Labor Unit Cost	Avg Equip Unit Cost	Avg Total Unit Cost	Avg Price Incl O&P
	Inst	SF	Lg	FD	.047	385.0	3.07	1.65	---	4.72	**5.87**
	Inst	SF	Sm	FD	.067	269.5	3.48	2.35	---	5.83	**7.33**

Machine sand, fill and finish

Description	Oper	Unit	Vol	Crew Size	Man-hours per Unit	Crew Output per Day	Avg Mat'l Unit Cost	Avg Labor Unit Cost	Avg Equip Unit Cost	Avg Total Unit Cost	Avg Price Incl O&P
New floors	Inst	SF	Lg	FC	.019	430.0	.03	.68	.07	.78	**1.07**
	Inst	SF	Sm	FC	.027	301.0	.17	.96	.10	1.23	**1.66**
Damaged floors	Inst	SF	Lg	FC	.028	285.0	.08	1.00	.11	1.19	**1.62**
	Inst	SF	Sm	FC	.040	199.5	.22	1.42	.16	1.80	**2.44**
Wax, polish and machine buff	Inst	SF	Lg	FC	.009	860.0	.01	.32	.04	.37	**.51**
	Inst	SF	Sm	FC	.013	602.0	.05	.46	.05	.56	**.77**

Description	Oper	Unit	Vol	Crew Size	Man-hours per Unit	Crew Output per Day	Avg Mat'l Unit Cost	Avg Labor Unit Cost	Avg Equip Unit Cost	Avg Total Unit Cost	Avg Price Incl O&P

Block

Laid in mastic over wood subfloor covered with felt

Oak, 5/16" x 12" x 12"

Lay floor only

Description	Oper	Unit	Vol	Crew Size	Man-hours per Unit	Crew Output per Day	Avg Mat'l Unit Cost	Avg Labor Unit Cost	Avg Equip Unit Cost	Avg Total Unit Cost	Avg Price Incl O&P
Prefinished	Inst	SF	Lg	FD	.035	520.0	13.60	1.23	---	14.83	**17.40**
	Inst	SF	Sm	FD	.049	364.0	15.60	1.72	---	17.32	**20.40**
Unfinished	Inst	SF	Lg	FD	.033	550.0	7.94	1.16	---	9.10	**10.80**
	Inst	SF	Sm	FD	.047	385.0	9.13	1.65	---	10.78	**12.80**

Teak, 5/16" x 12" x 12"

Lay floor only

Description	Oper	Unit	Vol	Crew Size	Man-hours per Unit	Crew Output per Day	Avg Mat'l Unit Cost	Avg Labor Unit Cost	Avg Equip Unit Cost	Avg Total Unit Cost	Avg Price Incl O&P
Prefinished	Inst	SF	Lg	FD	.035	520.0	15.90	1.23	---	17.13	**20.00**
	Inst	SF	Sm	FD	.049	364.0	18.20	1.72	---	19.92	**23.30**
Unfinished	Inst	SF	Lg	FD	.033	550.0	10.20	1.16	---	11.36	**13.40**
	Inst	SF	Sm	FD	.047	385.0	11.70	1.65	---	13.35	**15.80**

Oak, 13/16" x 12" x 12"

Lay floor only

Description	Oper	Unit	Vol	Crew Size	Man-hours per Unit	Crew Output per Day	Avg Mat'l Unit Cost	Avg Labor Unit Cost	Avg Equip Unit Cost	Avg Total Unit Cost	Avg Price Incl O&P
Prefinished	Inst	SF	Lg	FD	.035	520.0	22.70	1.23	---	23.93	**27.80**
	Inst	SF	Sm	FD	.049	364.0	25.90	1.72	---	27.62	**32.20**
Unfinished	Inst	SF	Lg	FD	.036	500.0	17.00	1.26	---	18.26	**21.40**
	Inst	SF	Sm	FD	.051	350.0	19.50	1.79	---	21.29	**24.90**

Machine sand, fill and finish

Description	Oper	Unit	Vol	Crew Size	Man-hours per Unit	Crew Output per Day	Avg Mat'l Unit Cost	Avg Labor Unit Cost	Avg Equip Unit Cost	Avg Total Unit Cost	Avg Price Incl O&P
New floors	Inst	SF	Lg	FC	.019	430.0	.03	.68	.07	.78	**1.07**
	Inst	SF	Sm	FC	.027	301.0	.17	.96	.10	1.23	**1.66**
Damaged floors	Inst	SF	Lg	FC	.028	285.0	.08	1.00	.11	1.19	**1.62**
	Inst	SF	Sm	FC	.040	199.5	.22	1.42	.16	1.80	**2.44**
Wax, polish and machine buff											
	Inst	SF	Lg	FC	.009	860.0	.01	.32	.04	.37	**.51**
	Inst	SF	Sm	FC	.013	602.0	.05	.46	.05	.56	**.77**

Parquetry, 5/16" x 9" x 9"

Lay floor only

Description	Oper	Unit	Vol	Crew Size	Man-hours per Unit	Crew Output per Day	Avg Mat'l Unit Cost	Avg Labor Unit Cost	Avg Equip Unit Cost	Avg Total Unit Cost	Avg Price Incl O&P
Oak	Inst	SF	Lg	FD	.036	500.0	15.10	1.26	---	16.36	**19.10**
	Inst	SF	Sm	FD	.051	350.0	17.30	1.79	---	19.09	**22.40**
Walnut	Inst	SF	Lg	FD	.036	500.0	21.20	1.26	---	22.46	**26.20**
	Inst	SF	Sm	FD	.051	350.0	24.20	1.79	---	25.99	**30.40**
Teak	Inst	SF	Lg	FD	.036	500.0	18.60	1.26	---	19.86	**23.20**
	Inst	SF	Sm	FD	.051	350.0	21.30	1.79	---	23.09	**27.00**

Description	Oper	Unit	Vol	Crew Size	Man-hours per Unit	Crew Output per Day	Avg Mat'l Unit Cost	Avg Labor Unit Cost	Avg Equip Unit Cost	Avg Total Unit Cost	Avg Price Incl O&P
Machine sand, fill and finish											
New floors											
	Inst	SF	Lg	FC	.019	430.0	.03	.68	.07	.78	**1.07**
	Inst	SF	Sm	FC	.027	301.0	.17	.96	.10	1.23	**1.66**
Damaged floors											
	Inst	SF	Lg	FC	.028	285.0	.08	1.00	.11	1.19	**1.62**
	Inst	SF	Sm	FC	.040	199.5	.22	1.42	.16	1.80	**2.44**
Wax, polish and machine buff											
	Inst	SF	Lg	FC	.009	860.0	.01	.32	.04	.37	**.51**
	Inst	SF	Sm	FC	.013	602.0	.05	.46	.05	.56	**.77**
Acrylic wood parquet blocks											
5/16" x 12" x 12" set in epoxy											
	Inst	SF	Lg	FD	.036	500.0	6.80	1.26	---	8.06	**9.61**
	Inst	SF	Sm	FD	.051	350.0	7.83	1.79	---	9.62	**11.50**
Wax, polish and machine buff											
	Inst	SF	Lg	FC	.009	860.0	.05	.32	.04	.41	**.55**
	Inst	SF	Sm	FC	.013	602.0	.05	.46	.05	.56	**.77**

Heating

Boilers

Electric-fired heaters, includes standard controls and trim, ASME

Description	Oper	Unit	Vol	Crew Size	Man-hours per Unit	Crew Output per Day	Avg Mat'l Unit Cost	Avg Labor Unit Cost	Avg Equip Unit Cost	Avg Total Unit Cost	Avg Price Incl O&P
Hot water											
12 KW, 40 MBHP	Inst	Ea	Lg	SD	20.0	1.20	4560.00	755.00	---	5315.00	**6330.00**
	Inst	Ea	Sm	SD	26.7	0.90	5050.00	1010.00	---	6060.00	**7270.00**
24 KW, 82 MBHP	Inst	Ea	Lg	SD	20.9	1.15	4860.00	789.00	---	5649.00	**6740.00**
	Inst	Ea	Sm	SD	27.9	0.86	5400.00	1050.00	---	6450.00	**7730.00**
45 KW, 154 MBHP	Inst	Ea	Lg	SD	21.4	1.12	5340.00	808.00	---	6148.00	**7320.00**
	Inst	Ea	Sm	SD	28.6	0.84	5930.00	1080.00	---	7010.00	**8380.00**
60 KW, 205 MBHP	Inst	Ea	Lg	SD	21.8	1.10	6340.00	823.00	---	7163.00	**8480.00**
	Inst	Ea	Sm	SD	28.9	0.83	7030.00	1090.00	---	8120.00	**9670.00**
240 KW, 820 MBHP	Inst	Ea	Lg	SD	24.0	1.00	13700.00	906.00	---	14606.00	**17100.00**
	Inst	Ea	Sm	SD	32.0	0.75	15200.00	1210.00	---	16410.00	**19200.00**
480 KW, 1,635 MBHP	Inst	Ea	Lg	SD	25.3	0.95	23500.00	955.00	---	24455.00	**28500.00**
	Inst	Ea	Sm	SD	33.8	0.71	26100.00	1280.00	---	27380.00	**31900.00**
1,200 KW, 4,095 MBHP	Inst	Ea	Lg	SD	26.7	0.90	42900.00	1010.00	---	43910.00	**50800.00**
	Inst	Ea	Sm	SD	35.3	0.68	47600.00	1330.00	---	48930.00	**56700.00**
2,400 KW, 8,190 MBHP	Inst	Ea	Lg	SD	28.2	0.85	73200.00	1060.00	---	74260.00	**85700.00**
	Inst	Ea	Sm	SD	37.5	0.64	81200.00	1420.00	---	82620.00	**95500.00**
Steam											
6 KW, 20 MBHP	Inst	Ea	Lg	SD	21.8	1.10	10800.00	823.00	---	11623.00	**13600.00**
	Inst	Ea	Sm	SD	28.9	0.83	12000.00	1090.00	---	13090.00	**15400.00**
60 KW, 205 MBHP	Inst	Ea	Lg	SD	26.7	0.90	13100.00	1010.00	---	14110.00	**16500.00**
	Inst	Ea	Sm	SD	35.3	0.68	14600.00	1330.00	---	15930.00	**18700.00**
240 KW, 815 MBHP	Inst	Ea	Lg	SD	60.0	0.40	20700.00	2260.00	---	22960.00	**27100.00**
	Inst	Ea	Sm	SD	80.0	0.30	23000.00	3020.00	---	26020.00	**30800.00**
600 KW, 2,047 MBHP	Inst	Ea	Lg	SE	160	0.20	31900.00	6250.00	---	38150.00	**45800.00**
	Inst	Ea	Sm	SE	213	0.15	35400.00	8320.00	---	43720.00	**52800.00**
Minimum Job Charge											
	Inst	Job	Lg	SD	12.0	2.00	---	453.00	---	453.00	**657.00**
	Inst	Job	Sm	SD	17.1	1.40	---	645.00	---	645.00	**936.00**

Description	Oper	Unit	Vol	Crew Size	Man-hours per Unit	Crew Output per Day	Avg Mat'l Unit Cost	Avg Labor Unit Cost	Avg Equip Unit Cost	Avg Total Unit Cost	Avg Price Incl O&P

Gas-fired, natural or propane, heaters; includes standard controls;
MBHP gross output
Cast iron with insulated jacket
Hot water

Description	Oper	Unit	Vol	Crew Size	Man-hours per Unit	Crew Output per Day	Avg Mat'l Unit Cost	Avg Labor Unit Cost	Avg Equip Unit Cost	Avg Total Unit Cost	Avg Price Incl O&P
80 MBHP	Inst	Ea	Lg	SF	17.1	1.40	1440.00	661.00	---	2101.00	2610.00
	Inst	Ea	Sm	SF	22.9	1.05	1600.00	886.00	---	2486.00	3120.00
100 MBHP	Inst	Ea	Lg	SF	17.5	1.37	1640.00	677.00	---	2317.00	2870.00
	Inst	Ea	Sm	SF	23.3	1.03	1820.00	901.00	---	2721.00	3400.00
122 MBHP	Inst	Ea	Lg	SF	17.8	1.35	1820.00	689.00	---	2509.00	3090.00
	Inst	Ea	Sm	SF	23.8	1.01	2010.00	921.00	---	2931.00	3650.00
163 MBHP	Inst	Ea	Lg	SF	18.2	1.32	2230.00	704.00	---	2934.00	3580.00
	Inst	Ea	Sm	SF	24.2	0.99	2470.00	936.00	---	3406.00	4200.00
440 MBHP	Inst	Ea	Lg	SF	18.5	1.30	4350.00	716.00	---	5066.00	6040.00
	Inst	Ea	Sm	SF	24.5	0.98	4830.00	948.00	---	5778.00	6920.00
2,000 MBHP	Inst	Ea	Lg	SF	24.0	1.00	14100.00	928.00	---	15028.00	17600.00
	Inst	Ea	Sm	SF	32.0	0.75	15700.00	1240.00	---	16940.00	19800.00
6,970 MBHP	Inst	Ea	Lg	SF	60.0	0.40	95900.00	2320.00	---	98220.00	114000.00
	Inst	Ea	Sm	SF	80.0	0.30	106000.00	3090.00	---	109090.00	127000.00

Steam

Description	Oper	Unit	Vol	Crew Size	Man-hours per Unit	Crew Output per Day	Avg Mat'l Unit Cost	Avg Labor Unit Cost	Avg Equip Unit Cost	Avg Total Unit Cost	Avg Price Incl O&P
80 MBHP	Inst	Ea	Lg	SF	17.1	1.40	1440.00	661.00	---	2101.00	2610.00
	Inst	Ea	Sm	SF	22.9	1.05	1600.00	886.00	---	2486.00	3120.00
163 MBHP	Inst	Ea	Lg	SF	18.2	1.32	2230.00	704.00	---	2934.00	3580.00
	Inst	Ea	Sm	SF	24.2	0.99	2470.00	936.00	---	3406.00	4200.00
440 MBHP	Inst	Ea	Lg	SF	18.5	1.30	4350.00	716.00	---	5066.00	6040.00
	Inst	Ea	Sm	SF	24.5	0.98	4830.00	948.00	---	5778.00	6920.00
3,570 MBHP	Inst	Ea	Lg	SF	26.7	0.90	22200.00	1030.00	---	23230.00	27000.00
	Inst	Ea	Sm	SF	35.3	0.68	24600.00	1370.00	---	25970.00	30300.00
6,970 MBHP	Inst	Ea	Lg	SF	60.0	0.40	71900.00	2320.00	---	74220.00	86100.00
	Inst	Ea	Sm	SF	80.0	0.30	79800.00	3090.00	---	82890.00	96300.00

Steel with insulated jacket; includes burner and one zone valve
Hot water

Description	Oper	Unit	Vol	Crew Size	Man-hours per Unit	Crew Output per Day	Avg Mat'l Unit Cost	Avg Labor Unit Cost	Avg Equip Unit Cost	Avg Total Unit Cost	Avg Price Incl O&P
50 MBHP	Inst	Ea	Lg	SF	10.9	2.20	2160.00	422.00	---	2582.00	3090.00
	Inst	Ea	Sm	SF	14.5	1.65	2390.00	561.00	---	2951.00	3570.00
70 MBHP	Inst	Ea	Lg	SF	10.9	2.20	2400.00	422.00	---	2822.00	3370.00
	Inst	Ea	Sm	SF	14.5	1.65	2660.00	561.00	---	3221.00	3870.00
90 MBHP	Inst	Ea	Lg	SF	11.4	2.10	2430.00	441.00	---	2871.00	3440.00
	Inst	Ea	Sm	SF	15.2	1.58	2700.00	588.00	---	3288.00	3960.00
105 MBHP	Inst	Ea	Lg	SF	12.0	2.00	2740.00	464.00	---	3204.00	3820.00
	Inst	Ea	Sm	SF	16.0	1.50	3040.00	619.00	---	3659.00	4390.00
130 MBHP	Inst	Ea	Lg	SF	12.6	1.90	3120.00	487.00	---	3607.00	4290.00
	Inst	Ea	Sm	SF	16.8	1.43	3460.00	650.00	---	4110.00	4920.00

Description	Oper	Unit	Vol	Crew Size	Man-hours per Unit	Crew Output per Day	Avg Mat'l Unit Cost	Avg Labor Unit Cost	Avg Equip Unit Cost	Avg Total Unit Cost	Avg Price Incl O&P
150 MBHP	Inst	Ea	Lg	SF	13.3	1.80	3630.00	514.00	---	4144.00	**4920.00**
	Inst	Ea	Sm	SF	17.8	1.35	4030.00	689.00	---	4719.00	**5630.00**
185 MBHP	Inst	Ea	Lg	SF	14.5	1.65	4380.00	561.00	---	4941.00	**5850.00**
	Inst	Ea	Sm	SF	19.4	1.24	4860.00	750.00	---	5610.00	**6680.00**
235 MBHP	Inst	Ea	Lg	SF	16.0	1.50	5550.00	619.00	---	6169.00	**7280.00**
	Inst	Ea	Sm	SF	21.2	1.13	6160.00	820.00	---	6980.00	**8270.00**
290 MBHP	Inst	Ea	Lg	SF	17.1	1.40	6270.00	661.00	---	6931.00	**8170.00**
	Inst	Ea	Sm	SF	22.9	1.05	6950.00	886.00	---	7836.00	**9280.00**
480 MBHP	Inst	Ea	Lg	SF	26.7	0.90	9040.00	1030.00	---	10070.00	**11900.00**
	Inst	Ea	Sm	SF	35.3	0.68	10000.00	1370.00	---	11370.00	**13500.00**
640 MBHP	Inst	Ea	Lg	SF	34.3	0.70	10800.00	1330.00	---	12130.00	**14300.00**
	Inst	Ea	Sm	SF	45.3	0.53	11900.00	1750.00	---	13650.00	**16300.00**
800 MBHP	Inst	Ea	Lg	SF	41.4	0.58	12500.00	1600.00	---	14100.00	**16700.00**
	Inst	Ea	Sm	SF	54.5	0.44	13900.00	2110.00	---	16010.00	**19100.00**
960 MBHP	Inst	Ea	Lg	SF	43.6	0.55	15600.00	1690.00	---	17290.00	**20400.00**
	Inst	Ea	Sm	SF	58.5	0.41	17300.00	2260.00	---	19560.00	**23200.00**
Minimum Job Charge											
	Inst	Job	Lg	SF	12.0	2.00	---	464.00	---	464.00	**673.00**
	Inst	Job	Sm	SF	17.1	1.40	---	661.00	---	661.00	**959.00**

Oil-fired heaters; includes standard controls; flame retention burner; MBHP gross output

Cast iron with insulated jacket
Hot water

Description	Oper	Unit	Vol	Crew Size	Man-hours per Unit	Crew Output per Day	Avg Mat'l Unit Cost	Avg Labor Unit Cost	Avg Equip Unit Cost	Avg Total Unit Cost	Avg Price Incl O&P
110 MBHP	Inst	Ea	Lg	SF	24.0	1.00	1610.00	928.00	---	2538.00	**3200.00**
	Inst	Ea	Sm	SF	32.0	0.75	1790.00	1240.00	---	3030.00	**3850.00**
200 MBHP	Inst	Ea	Lg	SF	34.3	0.70	2230.00	1330.00	---	3560.00	**4480.00**
	Inst	Ea	Sm	SF	45.3	0.53	2470.00	1750.00	---	4220.00	**5380.00**
1,080 MBHP	Inst	Ea	Lg	SF	80.0	0.30	11400.00	3090.00	---	14490.00	**17600.00**
	Inst	Ea	Sm	SF	104	0.23	12600.00	4020.00	---	16620.00	**20300.00**
1,320 MBHP	Inst	Ea	Lg	SF	96.0	0.25	10300.00	3710.00	---	14010.00	**17200.00**
	Inst	Ea	Sm	SF	126	0.19	11400.00	4870.00	---	16270.00	**20200.00**
2,100 MBHP	Inst	Ea	Lg	SF	120	0.20	13700.00	4640.00	---	18340.00	**22400.00**
	Inst	Ea	Sm	SF	160	0.15	15200.00	6190.00	---	21390.00	**26400.00**
4,360 MBHP	Inst	Ea	Lg	SF	160	0.15	24500.00	6190.00	---	30690.00	**37200.00**
	Inst	Ea	Sm	SF	218	0.11	27200.00	8430.00	---	35630.00	**43500.00**
6,970 MBHP	Inst	Ea	Lg	SF	300	0.08	71200.00	11600.00	---	82800.00	**98800.00**
	Inst	Ea	Sm	SF	400	0.06	79000.00	15500.00	---	94500.00	**113000.00**
Steam											
110 MBHP	Inst	Ea	Lg	SF	24.0	1.00	1610.00	928.00	---	2538.00	**3200.00**
	Inst	Ea	Sm	SF	32.0	0.75	1790.00	1240.00	---	3030.00	**3850.00**
205 MBHP	Inst	Ea	Lg	SF	34.3	0.70	2230.00	1330.00	---	3560.00	**4480.00**
	Inst	Ea	Sm	SF	45.3	0.53	2470.00	1750.00	---	4220.00	**5380.00**
1,085 MBHP	Inst	Ea	Lg	SF	80.0	0.30	11400.00	3090.00	---	14490.00	**17600.00**
	Inst	Ea	Sm	SF	104	0.23	12600.00	4020.00	---	16620.00	**20300.00**

Description	Oper	Unit	Vol	Crew Size	Man-hours per Unit	Crew Output per Day	Avg Mat'l Unit Cost	Avg Labor Unit Cost	Avg Equip Unit Cost	Avg Total Unit Cost	Avg Price Incl O&P
1,360 MBHP	Inst	Ea	Lg	SF	96.0	0.25	10300.00	3710.00	---	14010.00	**17200.00**
	Inst	Ea	Sm	SF	126	0.19	11400.00	4870.00	---	16270.00	**20200.00**
2,175 MBHP	Inst	Ea	Lg	SF	120	0.20	13700.00	4640.00	---	18340.00	**22400.00**
	Inst	Ea	Sm	SF	160	0.15	15200.00	6190.00	---	21390.00	**26400.00**
4,360 MBHP	Inst	Ea	Lg	SF	160	0.15	24500.00	6190.00	---	30690.00	**37200.00**
	Inst	Ea	Sm	SF	218	0.11	27200.00	8430.00	---	35630.00	**43500.00**
6,970 MBHP	Inst	Ea	Lg	SF	300	0.08	71200.00	11600.00	---	82800.00	**98800.00**
	Inst	Ea	Sm	SF	400	0.06	79000.00	15500.00	---	94500.00	**113000.00**

Steel insulated jacket burner

Hot water

Description	Oper	Unit	Vol	Crew Size	Man-hours per Unit	Crew Output per Day	Avg Mat'l Unit Cost	Avg Labor Unit Cost	Avg Equip Unit Cost	Avg Total Unit Cost	Avg Price Incl O&P
105 MBHP	Inst	Ea	Lg	SF	13.3	1.80	2840.00	514.00	---	3354.00	**4020.00**
	Inst	Ea	Sm	SF	17.8	1.35	3150.00	689.00	---	3839.00	**4630.00**
120 MBHP	Inst	Ea	Lg	SF	15.0	1.60	2880.00	580.00	---	3460.00	**4150.00**
	Inst	Ea	Sm	SF	20.0	1.20	3190.00	774.00	---	3964.00	**4790.00**
140 MBHP	Inst	Ea	Lg	SF	17.1	1.40	3010.00	661.00	---	3671.00	**4430.00**
	Inst	Ea	Sm	SF	22.9	1.05	3340.00	886.00	---	4226.00	**5130.00**
170 MBHP	Inst	Ea	Lg	SF	20.0	1.20	3600.00	774.00	---	4374.00	**5260.00**
	Inst	Ea	Sm	SF	26.7	0.90	3990.00	1030.00	---	5020.00	**6090.00**
225 MBHP	Inst	Ea	Lg	SF	26.7	0.90	4280.00	1030.00	---	5310.00	**6420.00**
	Inst	Ea	Sm	SF	35.3	0.68	4750.00	1370.00	---	6120.00	**7440.00**
315 MBHP	Inst	Ea	Lg	SF	30.0	0.80	6300.00	1160.00	---	7460.00	**8930.00**
	Inst	Ea	Sm	SF	40.0	0.60	6990.00	1550.00	---	8540.00	**10300.00**
420 MBHP	Inst	Ea	Lg	SF	34.3	0.70	7090.00	1330.00	---	8420.00	**10100.00**
	Inst	Ea	Sm	SF	45.3	0.53	7870.00	1750.00	---	9620.00	**11600.00**
Minimum Job Charge											
	Inst	Job	Lg	SF	12.0	2.00	---	464.00	---	464.00	**673.00**
	Inst	Job	Sm	SF	17.1	1.40	---	661.00	---	661.00	**959.00**

Boiler accessories

Burners

Conversion, gas-fired, LP or natural

Residential, gun type, atmospheric input

Description	Oper	Unit	Vol	Crew Size	Man-hours per Unit	Crew Output per Day	Avg Mat'l Unit Cost	Avg Labor Unit Cost	Avg Equip Unit Cost	Avg Total Unit Cost	Avg Price Incl O&P
72 to 200 MBHP	Inst	Ea	Lg	SB	8.00	2.00	897.00	292.00	---	1189.00	**1460.00**
	Inst	Ea	Sm	SB	10.7	1.50	996.00	391.00	---	1387.00	**1710.00**
120 to 360 MBHP	Inst	Ea	Lg	SB	9.14	1.75	993.00	334.00	---	1327.00	**1630.00**
	Inst	Ea	Sm	SB	12.2	1.31	1100.00	445.00	---	1545.00	**1910.00**
280 to 800 MBHP	Inst	Ea	Lg	SB	10.7	1.50	1920.00	391.00	---	2311.00	**2770.00**
	Inst	Ea	Sm	SB	14.2	1.13	2130.00	518.00	---	2648.00	**3200.00**

Flame retention, oil fired assembly

Description	Oper	Unit	Vol	Crew Size	Man-hours per Unit	Crew Output per Day	Avg Mat'l Unit Cost	Avg Labor Unit Cost	Avg Equip Unit Cost	Avg Total Unit Cost	Avg Price Incl O&P
2.0 to 5.0 GPH	Inst	Ea	Lg	SB	9.14	1.75	685.00	334.00	---	1019.00	**1270.00**
	Inst	Ea	Sm	SB	12.2	1.31	760.00	445.00	---	1205.00	**1520.00**

Description	Oper	Unit	Vol	Crew Size	Man-hours per Unit	Crew Output per Day	Avg Mat'l Unit Cost	Avg Labor Unit Cost	Avg Equip Unit Cost	Avg Total Unit Cost	Avg Price Incl O&P

Forced warm air systems

Duct furnaces

Furnace includes burner, controls, stainless steel heat exchanger
Gas-fired with an electric ignition

Outdoor installation, includes vent cap

Description	Oper	Unit	Vol	Crew Size	Man-hours per Unit	Crew Output per Day	Avg Mat'l Unit Cost	Avg Labor Unit Cost	Avg Equip Unit Cost	Avg Total Unit Cost	Avg Price Incl O&P
225 MBHP output	Inst	Ea	Lg	SB	8.00	2.00	3840.00	292.00	---	4132.00	**4830.00**
	Inst	Ea	Sm	SB	10.7	1.50	4260.00	391.00	---	4651.00	**5460.00**
375 MBHP output	Inst	Ea	Lg	SB	10.7	1.50	5550.00	391.00	---	5941.00	**6950.00**
	Inst	Ea	Sm	SB	14.2	1.13	6160.00	518.00	---	6678.00	**7830.00**
450 MBHP output	Inst	Ea	Lg	SB	12.3	1.30	5820.00	449.00	---	6269.00	**7350.00**
	Inst	Ea	Sm	SB	16.3	0.98	6460.00	595.00	---	7055.00	**8290.00**

Furnaces, hot air heating with blowers and standard controls

Gas or oil lines and couplings not included (see below and next page), flue piping not included (see page 449)

Electric-fired, UL listed, heat staging, 240 volt run and connection

Description	Oper	Unit	Vol	Crew Size	Man-hours per Unit	Crew Output per Day	Avg Mat'l Unit Cost	Avg Labor Unit Cost	Avg Equip Unit Cost	Avg Total Unit Cost	Avg Price Incl O&P
30 MBHP	Inst	Ea	Lg	UE	5.56	3.60	555.00	204.00	---	759.00	**928.00**
	Inst	Ea	Sm	UE	7.41	2.70	616.00	272.00	---	888.00	**1090.00**
75 MBHP	Inst	Ea	Lg	UE	5.71	3.50	706.00	210.00	---	916.00	**1110.00**
	Inst	Ea	Sm	UE	7.60	2.63	783.00	279.00	---	1062.00	**1300.00**
85 MBHP	Inst	Ea	Lg	UE	6.25	3.20	788.00	230.00	---	1018.00	**1230.00**
	Inst	Ea	Sm	UE	8.33	2.40	874.00	306.00	---	1180.00	**1440.00**
90 MBHP	Inst	Ea	Lg	UE	6.67	3.00	986.00	245.00	---	1231.00	**1480.00**
	Inst	Ea	Sm	UE	8.89	2.25	1090.00	327.00	---	1417.00	**1720.00**
Minimum Job Charge											
	Inst	Job	Lg	UD	8.00	2.00	---	287.00	---	287.00	**407.00**
	Inst	Job	Sm	UD	11.4	1.40	---	409.00	---	409.00	**580.00**

Gas-fired, AGA certified, direct drive models

Description	Oper	Unit	Vol	Crew Size	Man-hours per Unit	Crew Output per Day	Avg Mat'l Unit Cost	Avg Labor Unit Cost	Avg Equip Unit Cost	Avg Total Unit Cost	Avg Price Incl O&P
40 MBHP	Inst	Ea	Lg	UD	4.44	3.60	596.00	159.00	---	755.00	**911.00**
	Inst	Ea	Sm	UD	5.93	2.70	661.00	213.00	---	874.00	**1060.00**
65 MBHP	Inst	Ea	Lg	UD	4.57	3.50	795.00	164.00	---	959.00	**1150.00**
	Inst	Ea	Sm	UD	6.08	2.63	882.00	218.00	---	1100.00	**1320.00**
80 MBHP	Inst	Ea	Lg	UD	4.71	3.40	843.00	169.00	---	1012.00	**1210.00**
	Inst	Ea	Sm	UD	6.27	2.55	935.00	225.00	---	1160.00	**1390.00**
85 MBHP	Inst	Ea	Lg	UD	5.00	3.20	870.00	179.00	---	1049.00	**1260.00**
	Inst	Ea	Sm	UD	6.67	2.40	965.00	239.00	---	1204.00	**1450.00**
105 MBHP	Inst	Ea	Lg	UD	5.33	3.00	897.00	191.00	---	1088.00	**1300.00**
	Inst	Ea	Sm	UD	7.11	2.25	996.00	255.00	---	1251.00	**1510.00**
125 MBHP	Inst	Ea	Lg	UD	5.71	2.80	1030.00	205.00	---	1235.00	**1480.00**
	Inst	Ea	Sm	UD	7.62	2.10	1150.00	273.00	---	1423.00	**1710.00**
160 MBHP	Inst	Ea	Lg	UD	6.15	2.60	1060.00	221.00	---	1281.00	**1530.00**
	Inst	Ea	Sm	UD	8.21	1.95	1180.00	294.00	---	1474.00	**1770.00**
200 MBHP	Inst	Ea	Lg	UD	6.67	2.40	2530.00	239.00	---	2769.00	**3250.00**
	Inst	Ea	Sm	UD	8.89	1.80	2810.00	319.00	---	3129.00	**3690.00**
Minimum Job Charge											
	Inst	Job	Lg	UD	8.00	2.00	---	287.00	---	287.00	**407.00**
	Inst	Job	Sm	UD	11.4	1.40	---	409.00	---	409.00	**580.00**

Gas line with couplings

Description	Oper	Unit	Vol	Crew Size	Man-hours per Unit	Crew Output per Day	Avg Mat'l Unit Cost	Avg Labor Unit Cost	Avg Equip Unit Cost	Avg Total Unit Cost	Avg Price Incl O&P
	Inst	LF	Lg	SB	.356	45.00	---	13.00	---	13.00	**18.90**
	Inst	LF	Sm	SB	.474	33.75	---	17.30	---	17.30	**25.10**

Description	Oper	Unit	Vol	Crew Size	Man-hours per Unit	Crew Output per Day	Avg Mat'l Unit Cost	Avg Labor Unit Cost	Avg Equip Unit Cost	Avg Total Unit Cost	Avg Price Incl O&P
Oil-fired, UL listed, gun-type burner											
55 MBHP	Inst	Ea	Lg	UD	4.57	3.50	1020.00	164.00	---	1184.00	**1410.00**
	Inst	Ea	Sm	UD	6.08	2.63	1130.00	218.00	---	1348.00	**1610.00**
100 MBHP	Inst	Ea	Lg	UD	5.33	3.00	1080.00	191.00	---	1271.00	**1520.00**
	Inst	Ea	Sm	UD	7.11	2.25	1200.00	255.00	---	1455.00	**1740.00**
125 MBHP	Inst	Ea	Lg	UD	5.71	2.80	1510.00	205.00	---	1715.00	**2020.00**
	Inst	Ea	Sm	UD	7.62	2.10	1670.00	273.00	---	1943.00	**2310.00**
150 MBHP	Inst	Ea	Lg	UD	6.15	2.60	1680.00	221.00	---	1901.00	**2240.00**
	Inst	Ea	Sm	UD	8.21	1.95	1860.00	294.00	---	2154.00	**2560.00**
200 MBHP	Inst	Ea	Lg	UD	6.67	2.40	2810.00	239.00	---	3049.00	**3570.00**
	Inst	Ea	Sm	UD	8.89	1.80	3120.00	319.00	---	3439.00	**4040.00**
Minimum Job Charge											
	Inst	Job	Lg	UD	8.00	2.00	---	287.00	---	287.00	**407.00**
	Inst	Job	Sm	UD	11.4	1.40	---	409.00	---	409.00	**580.00**
Oil line with couplings											
	Inst	LF	Lg	SB	.200	80.00	---	7.30	---	7.30	**10.60**
	Inst	LF	Sm	SB	.267	60.00	---	9.75	---	9.75	**14.10**
Combo fired (wood, coal, oil combination) complete with burner											
115 MBHP (based on oil)	Inst	Ea	Lg	UD	5.52	2.90	3050.00	198.00	---	3248.00	**3790.00**
	Inst	Ea	Sm	UD	7.34	2.18	3380.00	263.00	---	3643.00	**4260.00**
140 MBHP (based on oil)	Inst	Ea	Lg	UD	5.93	2.70	4900.00	213.00	---	5113.00	**5930.00**
	Inst	Ea	Sm	UD	7.88	2.03	5430.00	283.00	---	5713.00	**6650.00**
150 MBHP (based on oil)	Inst	Ea	Lg	UD	6.15	2.60	4900.00	221.00	---	5121.00	**5950.00**
	Inst	Ea	Sm	UD	8.21	1.95	5430.00	294.00	---	5724.00	**6670.00**
170 MBHP (based on oil)	Inst	Ea	Lg	UD	6.40	2.50	5170.00	230.00	---	5400.00	**6270.00**
	Inst	Ea	Sm	UD	8.51	1.88	5740.00	305.00	---	6045.00	**7030.00**
Minimum Job Charge											
	Inst	Job	Lg	UD	8.00	2.00	---	287.00	---	287.00	**407.00**
	Inst	Job	Sm	UD	11.4	1.40	---	409.00	---	409.00	**580.00**
Oil line with couplings											
	Inst	LF	Lg	SB	.200	80.00	---	7.30	---	7.30	**10.60**
	Inst	LF	Sm	SB	.267	60.00	---	9.75	---	9.75	**14.10**

Space heaters, gas-fired

Unit includes cabinet, grilles, fan, controls, burner and thermostat; no flue piping included (see page 449)

Floor mounted

Description	Oper	Unit	Vol	Crew Size	Man-hours per Unit	Crew Output per Day	Avg Mat'l Unit Cost	Avg Labor Unit Cost	Avg Equip Unit Cost	Avg Total Unit Cost	Avg Price Incl O&P
60 MBHP	Inst	Ea	Lg	SB	2.00	8.00	733.00	73.00	---	806.00	**949.00**
	Inst	Ea	Sm	SB	2.67	6.00	813.00	97.50	---	910.50	**1080.00**
180 MBHP	Inst	Ea	Lg	SB	4.00	4.00	1090.00	146.00	---	1236.00	**1460.00**
	Inst	Ea	Sm	SB	5.33	3.00	1210.00	195.00	---	1405.00	**1670.00**

Suspension mounted, propeller fan

Description	Oper	Unit	Vol	Crew Size	Man-hours per Unit	Crew Output per Day	Avg Mat'l Unit Cost	Avg Labor Unit Cost	Avg Equip Unit Cost	Avg Total Unit Cost	Avg Price Incl O&P
20 MBHP	Inst	Ea	Lg	SB	2.67	6.00	548.00	97.50	---	645.50	**772.00**
	Inst	Ea	Sm	SB	3.56	4.50	608.00	130.00	---	738.00	**888.00**
60 MBHP	Inst	Ea	Lg	SB	3.20	5.00	678.00	117.00	---	795.00	**949.00**
	Inst	Ea	Sm	SB	4.27	3.75	752.00	156.00	---	908.00	**1090.00**
130 MBHP	Inst	Ea	Lg	SB	4.00	4.00	1000.00	146.00	---	1146.00	**1360.00**
	Inst	Ea	Sm	SB	5.33	3.00	1110.00	195.00	---	1305.00	**1560.00**
320 MBHP	Inst	Ea	Lg	SB	8.00	2.00	2060.00	292.00	---	2352.00	**2790.00**
	Inst	Ea	Sm	SB	10.7	1.50	2280.00	391.00	---	2671.00	**3190.00**
Powered venter, adapter	ADD	Ea	Lg	SB	2.00	8.00	348.00	73.00	---	421.00	**506.00**
	ADD	Ea	Sm	SB	2.67	6.00	386.00	97.50	---	483.50	**585.00**

Description	Oper	Unit	Vol	Crew Size	Man-hours per Unit	Crew Output per Day	Avg Mat'l Unit Cost	Avg Labor Unit Cost	Avg Equip Unit Cost	Avg Total Unit Cost	Avg Price Incl O&P

Wall furnace, self-contained thermostat

Single capacity, recessed or surface mounted, 1-speed fan

Description	Oper	Unit	Vol	Crew Size	Man-hours per Unit	Crew Output per Day	Avg Mat'l Unit Cost	Avg Labor Unit Cost	Avg Equip Unit Cost	Avg Total Unit Cost	Avg Price Incl O&P
15 MBHP	Inst	Ea	Lg	SB	3.20	5.00	603.00	117.00	---	720.00	**863.00**
	Inst	Ea	Sm	SB	4.27	3.75	669.00	156.00	---	825.00	**995.00**
25 MBHP	Inst	Ea	Lg	SB	4.00	4.00	623.00	146.00	---	769.00	**929.00**
	Inst	Ea	Sm	SB	5.33	3.00	692.00	195.00	---	887.00	**1080.00**
35 MBHP	Inst	Ea	Lg	SB	5.33	3.00	836.00	195.00	---	1031.00	**1240.00**
	Inst	Ea	Sm	SB	7.11	2.25	927.00	260.00	---	1187.00	**1440.00**

Dual capacity, recessed or surface mounted, 2-speed blowers

Description	Oper	Unit	Vol	Crew Size	Man-hours per Unit	Crew Output per Day	Avg Mat'l Unit Cost	Avg Labor Unit Cost	Avg Equip Unit Cost	Avg Total Unit Cost	Avg Price Incl O&P
50 MBHP (direct vent)	Inst	Ea	Lg	SB	8.00	2.00	836.00	292.00	---	1128.00	**1380.00**
	Inst	Ea	Sm	SB	10.7	1.50	927.00	391.00	---	1318.00	**1630.00**
60 MBHP (up vent)	Inst	Ea	Lg	SB	8.00	2.00	740.00	292.00	---	1032.00	**1270.00**
	Inst	Ea	Sm	SB	10.7	1.50	821.00	391.00	---	1212.00	**1510.00**

Register kit for circulating heat to second room

Description	Oper	Unit	Vol	Crew Size	Man-hours per Unit	Crew Output per Day	Avg Mat'l Unit Cost	Avg Labor Unit Cost	Avg Equip Unit Cost	Avg Total Unit Cost	Avg Price Incl O&P
	Inst	Ea	Lg	SB	2.00	8.00	75.40	73.00	---	148.40	**193.00**
	Inst	Ea	Sm	SB	2.67	6.00	83.60	97.50	---	181.10	**237.00**

Minimum Job Charge

Description	Oper	Unit	Vol	Crew Size	Man-hours per Unit	Crew Output per Day	Avg Mat'l Unit Cost	Avg Labor Unit Cost	Avg Equip Unit Cost	Avg Total Unit Cost	Avg Price Incl O&P
	Inst	Job	Lg	SB	8.00	2.00	---	292.00	---	292.00	**424.00**
	Inst	Job	Sm	SB	11.4	1.40	---	416.00	---	416.00	**604.00**

Bathroom heaters, electric-fired

Ceiling Heat-A-Ventlite, includes grille, blower, 4" round duct 13" x 7" dia., 3-way switch

Description	Oper	Unit	Vol	Crew Size	Man-hours per Unit	Crew Output per Day	Avg Mat'l Unit Cost	Avg Labor Unit Cost	Avg Equip Unit Cost	Avg Total Unit Cost	Avg Price Incl O&P
1,500 watt	Inst	Ea	Lg	EA	4.00	2.00	325.00	161.00	---	486.00	**607.00**
	Inst	Ea	Sm	EA	5.33	1.50	360.00	214.00	---	574.00	**725.00**
1,800 watt	Inst	Ea	Lg	EA	4.00	2.00	360.00	161.00	---	521.00	**647.00**
	Inst	Ea	Sm	EA	5.33	1.50	400.00	214.00	---	614.00	**770.00**

Ceiling Heat-A-Lite, includes grille, airotor wheel, 13" x 7" dia., 2-way switch

Description	Oper	Unit	Vol	Crew Size	Man-hours per Unit	Crew Output per Day	Avg Mat'l Unit Cost	Avg Labor Unit Cost	Avg Equip Unit Cost	Avg Total Unit Cost	Avg Price Incl O&P
1,500 watt	Inst	Ea	Lg	EA	4.00	2.00	240.00	161.00	---	401.00	**509.00**
	Inst	Ea	Sm	EA	5.33	1.50	266.00	214.00	---	480.00	**617.00**

Ceiling radiant heating using infrared lamps

Recessed, Heat-A-Lamp

Description	Oper	Unit	Vol	Crew Size	Man-hours per Unit	Crew Output per Day	Avg Mat'l Unit Cost	Avg Labor Unit Cost	Avg Equip Unit Cost	Avg Total Unit Cost	Avg Price Incl O&P
One bulb, 250 watt lamp	Inst	Ea	Lg	EA	3.33	2.40	61.70	134.00	---	195.70	**265.00**
	Inst	Ea	Sm	EA	4.44	1.80	68.40	178.00	---	246.40	**337.00**
Two bulb, 500 watt lamp	Inst	Ea	Lg	EA	3.33	2.40	105.00	134.00	---	239.00	**315.00**
	Inst	Ea	Sm	EA	4.44	1.80	117.00	178.00	---	295.00	**393.00**
Three bulb, 750 watt lamp	Inst	Ea	Lg	EA	3.33	2.40	184.00	134.00	---	318.00	**405.00**
	Inst	Ea	Sm	EA	4.44	1.80	204.00	178.00	---	382.00	**493.00**

Recessed, Heat-A-Vent

Description	Oper	Unit	Vol	Crew Size	Man-hours per Unit	Crew Output per Day	Avg Mat'l Unit Cost	Avg Labor Unit Cost	Avg Equip Unit Cost	Avg Total Unit Cost	Avg Price Incl O&P
One bulb, 250 watt lamp	Inst	Ea	Lg	EA	3.33	2.40	127.00	134.00	---	261.00	**341.00**
	Inst	Ea	Sm	EA	4.44	1.80	141.00	178.00	---	319.00	**421.00**
Two bulb, 500 watt lamp	Inst	Ea	Lg	EA	3.33	2.40	148.00	134.00	---	282.00	**364.00**
	Inst	Ea	Sm	EA	4.44	1.80	164.00	178.00	---	342.00	**448.00**

Description	Oper	Unit	Vol	Crew Size	Man-hours per Unit	Crew Output per Day	Avg Mat'l Unit Cost	Avg Labor Unit Cost	Avg Equip Unit Cost	Avg Total Unit Cost	Avg Price Incl O&P
Wall heaters, recessed											
Fan forced											
1250 watt heating element	Inst	Ea	Lg	EA	2.50	3.20	170.00	100.00	---	270.00	**341.00**
	Inst	Ea	Sm	EA	3.33	2.40	188.00	134.00	---	322.00	**411.00**
Radiant heating											
1200 watt heating element	Inst	Ea	Lg	EA	2.50	3.20	134.00	100.00	---	234.00	**300.00**
	Inst	Ea	Sm	EA	3.33	2.40	149.00	134.00	---	283.00	**365.00**
1500 watt heating element	Inst	Ea	Lg	EA	2.50	3.20	141.00	100.00	---	241.00	**308.00**
	Inst	Ea	Sm	EA	3.33	2.40	157.00	134.00	---	291.00	**374.00**
Wiring, connection, and installation in closed wall or ceiling structure											
ADD	Inst	Ea	Lg	EA	2.42	3.30	---	97.30	---	97.30	**141.00**
	Inst	Ea	Sm	EA	3.46	2.31	---	139.00	---	139.00	**202.00**

Insulation

Batt or roll

With wall or ceiling finish already removed

Description	Oper	Unit	Vol	Crew Size	Man-hours per Unit	Crew Output per Day	Avg Mat'l Unit Cost	Avg Labor Unit Cost	Avg Equip Unit Cost	Avg Total Unit Cost	Avg Price Incl O&P
Joists, 16" or 24" oc	Demo	SF	Lg	LB	.005	2935	---	.15	---	.15	**.21**
	Demo	SF	Sm	LB	.007	2201	---	.21	---	.21	**.29**
Rafters, 16" or 24" oc	Demo	SF	Lg	LB	.006	2560	---	.18	---	.18	**.25**
	Demo	SF	Sm	LB	.008	1920	---	.24	---	.24	**.34**
Studs, 16" or 24" oc	Demo	SF	Lg	LB	.005	3285	---	.15	---	.15	**.21**
	Demo	SF	Sm	LB	.006	2464	---	.18	---	.18	**.25**

Place and/or staple, Johns-Manville and/or Owens Corning fiberglass
Allowance made for joists, rafters, studs

Joists
Unfaced
3-1/2" T (R-13)

Description	Oper	Unit	Vol	Crew Size	Man-hours per Unit	Crew Output per Day	Avg Mat'l Unit Cost	Avg Labor Unit Cost	Avg Equip Unit Cost	Avg Total Unit Cost	Avg Price Incl O&P
16" oc	Inst	SF	Lg	CA	.008	975.0	.31	.30	---	.61	**.77**
	Inst	SF	Sm	CA	.011	731.3	.34	.41	---	.75	**.96**
24" oc	Inst	SF	Lg	CA	.005	1460	.31	.19	---	.50	**.62**
	Inst	SF	Sm	CA	.007	1095	.34	.26	---	.60	**.75**
6-1/2" T (R-19)											
16" oc	Inst	SF	Lg	CA	.008	975.0	.34	.30	---	.64	**.81**
	Inst	SF	Sm	CA	.011	731.3	.37	.41	---	.78	**1.00**
24" oc	Inst	SF	Lg	CA	.005	1460	.34	.19	---	.53	**.65**
	Inst	SF	Sm	CA	.007	1095	.37	.26	---	.63	**.79**
7" T (R-22)											
16" oc	Inst	SF	Lg	CA	.008	975.0	.48	.30	---	.78	**.97**
	Inst	SF	Sm	CA	.011	731.3	.52	.41	---	.93	**1.17**
24" oc	Inst	SF	Lg	CA	.005	1460	.48	.19	---	.67	**.81**
	Inst	SF	Sm	CA	.007	1095	.52	.26	---	.78	**.96**

Description	Oper	Unit	Vol	Crew Size	Man-hours per Unit	Crew Output per Day	Avg Mat'l Unit Cost	Avg Labor Unit Cost	Avg Equip Unit Cost	Avg Total Unit Cost	Avg Price Incl O&P
9-1/4" T (R-30)											
16" oc	Inst	SF	Lg	CA	.008	975.0	.64	.30	---	.94	**1.15**
	Inst	SF	Sm	CA	.011	731.3	.70	.41	---	1.11	**1.38**
24" oc	Inst	SF	Lg	CA	.005	1460	.64	.19	---	.83	**1.00**
	Inst	SF	Sm	CA	.007	1095	.70	.26	---	.96	**1.17**
Kraft-faced											
3-1/2" T (R-11)											
16" oc	Inst	SF	Lg	CA	.008	975.0	.40	.30	---	.70	**.87**
	Inst	SF	Sm	CA	.011	731.3	.44	.41	---	.85	**1.08**
24" oc	Inst	SF	Lg	CA	.005	1460	.40	.19	---	.59	**.72**
	Inst	SF	Sm	CA	.007	1095	.44	.26	---	.70	**.87**
3-1/2" T (R-13)											
16" oc	Inst	SF	Lg	CA	.008	975.0	.45	.30	---	.75	**.93**
	Inst	SF	Sm	CA	.011	731.3	.49	.41	---	.90	**1.13**
24" oc	Inst	SF	Lg	CA	.005	1460	.45	.19	---	.64	**.78**
	Inst	SF	Sm	CA	.007	1095	.49	.26	---	.75	**.93**
6-1/2" T (R-19)											
16" oc	Inst	SF	Lg	CA	.008	975.0	.58	.30	---	.88	**1.08**
	Inst	SF	Sm	CA	.011	731.3	.64	.41	---	1.05	**1.31**
24" oc	Inst	SF	Lg	CA	.005	1460	.58	.19	---	.77	**.93**
	Inst	SF	Sm	CA	.007	1095	.64	.26	---	.90	**1.10**
7" T (R-22)											
16" oc	Inst	SF	Lg	CA	.008	975.0	.74	.30	---	1.04	**1.27**
	Inst	SF	Sm	CA	.011	731.3	.82	.41	---	1.23	**1.51**
24" oc	Inst	SF	Lg	CA	.005	1460	.74	.19	---	.93	**1.11**
	Inst	SF	Sm	CA	.007	1095	.82	.26	---	1.08	**1.31**
9-1/4" T (R-30)											
16" oc	Inst	SF	Lg	CA	.008	975.0	.95	.30	---	1.25	**1.51**
	Inst	SF	Sm	CA	.011	731.3	1.05	.41	---	1.46	**1.78**
24" oc	Inst	SF	Lg	CA	.005	1460	.95	.19	---	1.14	**1.35**
	Inst	SF	Sm	CA	.007	1095	1.05	.26	---	1.31	**1.57**
12" T (R-38)											
16" oc	Inst	SF	Lg	CA	.008	975.0	1.12	.30	---	1.42	**1.70**
	Inst	SF	Sm	CA	.011	731.3	1.24	.41	---	1.65	**2.00**
24" oc	Inst	SF	Lg	CA	.005	1460	1.12	.19	---	1.31	**1.55**
	Inst	SF	Sm	CA	.007	1095	1.24	.26	---	1.50	**1.79**

Description	Oper	Unit	Vol	Crew Size	Man-hours per Unit	Crew Output per Day	Avg Mat'l Unit Cost	Avg Labor Unit Cost	Avg Equip Unit Cost	Avg Total Unit Cost	Avg Price Incl O&P
Foil-faced											
4" T (R-11)											
16" oc	Inst	SF	Lg	CA	.008	975.0	.48	.30	---	.78	**.97**
	Inst	SF	Sm	CA	.011	731.3	.52	.41	---	.93	**1.17**
24" oc	Inst	SF	Lg	CA	.005	1460	.48	.19	---	.67	**.81**
	Inst	SF	Sm	CA	.007	1095	.52	.26	---	.78	**.96**
6-1/2" T (R-19)											
16" oc	Inst	SF	Lg	CA	.008	975.0	.64	.30	---	.94	**1.15**
	Inst	SF	Sm	CA	.011	731.3	.70	.41	---	1.11	**1.38**
24" oc	Inst	SF	Lg	CA	.005	1460	.64	.19	---	.83	**1.00**
	Inst	SF	Sm	CA	.007	1095	.70	.26	---	.96	**1.17**
Rafters											
Unfaced											
3-1/2" T (R-13)											
16" oc	Inst	SF	Lg	CA	.012	650.0	.31	.44	---	.75	**.98**
	Inst	SF	Sm	CA	.016	487.5	.34	.59	---	.93	**1.22**
24" oc	Inst	SF	Lg	CA	.008	975	.31	.30	---	.61	**.77**
	Inst	SF	Sm	CA	.011	731	.34	.41	---	.75	**.96**
6-1/2" T (R-19)											
16" oc	Inst	SF	Lg	CA	.012	650.0	.34	.44	---	.78	**1.01**
	Inst	SF	Sm	CA	.016	487.5	.37	.59	---	.96	**1.25**
24" oc	Inst	SF	Lg	CA	.008	975.0	.34	.30	---	.64	**.81**
	Inst	SF	Sm	CA	.011	731.3	.37	.41	---	.78	**1.00**
7" T (R-22)											
16" oc	Inst	SF	Lg	CA	.012	650.0	.48	.44	---	.92	**1.17**
	Inst	SF	Sm	CA	.016	487.5	.52	.59	---	1.11	**1.43**
24" oc	Inst	SF	Lg	CA	.008	975.0	.48	.30	---	.78	**.97**
	Inst	SF	Sm	CA	.011	731.3	.52	.41	---	.93	**1.17**
9-1/4" T (R-30)											
16" oc	Inst	SF	Lg	CA	.012	650.0	.64	.44	---	1.08	**1.36**
	Inst	SF	Sm	CA	.016	487.5	.70	.59	---	1.29	**1.63**
24" oc	Inst	SF	Lg	CA	.008	975.0	.64	.30	---	.94	**1.15**
	Inst	SF	Sm	CA	.011	731.3	.70	.41	---	1.11	**1.38**
Kraft-faced											
3-1/2" T (R-11)											
16" oc	Inst	SF	Lg	CA	.012	650.0	.40	.44	---	.84	**1.08**
	Inst	SF	Sm	CA	.016	487.5	.44	.59	---	1.03	**1.34**
24" oc	Inst	SF	Lg	CA	.008	975.0	.40	.30	---	.70	**.87**
	Inst	SF	Sm	CA	.011	731.3	.44	.41	---	.85	**1.08**

Description	Oper	Unit	Vol	Crew Size	Man-hours per Unit	Crew Output per Day	Avg Mat'l Unit Cost	Avg Labor Unit Cost	Avg Equip Unit Cost	Avg Total Unit Cost	Avg Price Incl O&P
3-1/2" T (R-13)											
16" oc	Inst	SF	Lg	CA	.012	650.0	.45	.44	---	.89	**1.14**
	Inst	SF	Sm	CA	.016	487.5	.49	.59	---	1.08	**1.39**
24" oc	Inst	SF	Lg	CA	.008	975.0	.45	.30	---	.75	**.93**
	Inst	SF	Sm	CA	.011	731.3	.49	.41	---	.90	**1.13**
6-1/2" T (R-19)											
16" oc	Inst	SF	Lg	CA	.012	650.0	.58	.44	---	1.02	**1.29**
	Inst	SF	Sm	CA	.016	487.5	.64	.59	---	1.23	**1.57**
24" oc	Inst	SF	Lg	CA	.008	975.0	.58	.30	---	.88	**1.08**
	Inst	SF	Sm	CA	.011	731.3	.64	.41	---	1.05	**1.31**
7" T (R-22)											
16" oc	Inst	SF	Lg	CA	.012	650.0	.74	.44	---	1.18	**1.47**
	Inst	SF	Sm	CA	.016	487.5	.82	.59	---	1.41	**1.77**
24" oc	Inst	SF	Lg	CA	.008	975.0	.74	.30	---	1.04	**1.27**
	Inst	SF	Sm	CA	.011	731.3	.82	.41	---	1.23	**1.51**
9-1/4" T (R-30)											
16" oc	Inst	SF	Lg	CA	.012	650.0	.95	.44	---	1.39	**1.71**
	Inst	SF	Sm	CA	.016	487.5	1.05	.59	---	1.64	**2.04**
24" oc	Inst	SF	Lg	CA	.008	975.0	.95	.30	---	1.25	**1.51**
	Inst	SF	Sm	CA	.011	731.3	1.05	.41	---	1.46	**1.78**
12" T (R-38)											
16" oc	Inst	SF	Lg	CA	.012	650.0	1.12	.44	---	1.56	**1.91**
	Inst	SF	Sm	CA	.016	487.5	1.24	.59	---	1.83	**2.26**
24" oc	Inst	SF	Lg	CA	.008	975	1.12	.30	---	1.42	**1.70**
	Inst	SF	Sm	CA	.011	731	1.24	.41	---	1.65	**2.00**
Foil-faced											
4" T (R-11)											
16" oc	Inst	SF	Lg	CA	.012	650.0	.48	.44	---	.92	**1.17**
	Inst	SF	Sm	CA	.016	487.5	.52	.59	---	1.11	**1.43**
24" oc	Inst	SF	Lg	CA	.008	975.0	.48	.30	---	.78	**.97**
	Inst	SF	Sm	CA	.011	731.3	.52	.41	---	.93	**1.17**
6-1/2" T (R-19)											
16" oc	Inst	SF	Lg	CA	.012	650.0	.64	.44	---	1.08	**1.36**
	Inst	SF	Sm	CA	.016	487.5	.70	.59	---	1.29	**1.63**
24" oc	Inst	SF	Lg	CA	.008	975.0	.64	.30	---	.94	**1.15**
	Inst	SF	Sm	CA	.011	731.3	.70	.41	---	1.11	**1.38**

Description	Oper	Unit	Vol	Crew Size	Man-hours per Unit	Crew Output per Day	Avg Mat'l Unit Cost	Avg Labor Unit Cost	Avg Equip Unit Cost	Avg Total Unit Cost	Avg Price Incl O&P
Studs											
Unfaced											
3-1/2" T (R-13)											
16" oc	Inst	SF	Lg	CA	.010	815.0	.31	.37	---	.68	**.87**
	Inst	SF	Sm	CA	.013	611.3	.34	.48	---	.82	**1.06**
24" oc	Inst	SF	Lg	CA	.007	1220	.31	.26	---	.57	**.72**
	Inst	SF	Sm	CA	.009	915	.34	.33	---	.67	**.86**
6-1/2" T (R-19)											
16" oc	Inst	SF	Lg	CA	.010	815.0	.34	.37	---	.71	**.91**
	Inst	SF	Sm	CA	.013	611.3	.37	.48	---	.85	**1.10**
24" oc	Inst	SF	Lg	CA	.007	1220	.34	.26	---	.60	**.75**
	Inst	SF	Sm	CA	.009	915.0	.37	.33	---	.70	**.89**
7" T (R-22)											
16" oc	Inst	SF	Lg	CA	.010	815.0	.48	.37	---	.85	**1.07**
	Inst	SF	Sm	CA	.013	611.3	.52	.48	---	1.00	**1.27**
24" oc	Inst	SF	Lg	CA	.007	1220	.48	.26	---	.74	**.91**
	Inst	SF	Sm	CA	.009	915.0	.52	.33	---	.85	**1.06**
9-1/4" T (R-30)											
16" oc	Inst	SF	Lg	CA	.010	815.0	.64	.37	---	1.01	**1.25**
	Inst	SF	Sm	CA	.013	611.3	.70	.48	---	1.18	**1.48**
24" oc	Inst	SF	Lg	CA	.007	1220	.64	.26	---	.90	**1.10**
	Inst	SF	Sm	CA	.009	915.0	.70	.33	---	1.03	**1.27**
Kraft-faced											
3-1/2" T (R-11)											
16" oc	Inst	SF	Lg	CA	.010	815.0	.40	.37	---	.77	**.98**
	Inst	SF	Sm	CA	.013	611.3	.44	.48	---	.92	**1.18**
24" oc	Inst	SF	Lg	CA	.007	1220	.40	.26	---	.66	**.82**
	Inst	SF	Sm	CA	.009	915.0	.44	.33	---	.77	**.97**
3-1/2" T (R-13)											
16" oc	Inst	SF	Lg	CA	.010	815.0	.45	.37	---	.82	**1.04**
	Inst	SF	Sm	CA	.013	611.3	.49	.48	---	.97	**1.24**
24" oc	Inst	SF	Lg	CA	.007	1220	.45	.26	---	.71	**.88**
	Inst	SF	Sm	CA	.009	915.0	.49	.33	---	.82	**1.03**
6-1/2" T (R-19)											
16" oc	Inst	SF	Lg	CA	.010	815.0	.58	.37	---	.95	**1.19**
	Inst	SF	Sm	CA	.013	611.3	.64	.48	---	1.12	**1.41**
24" oc	Inst	SF	Lg	CA	.007	1220	.58	.26	---	.84	**1.03**
	Inst	SF	Sm	CA	.009	915.0	.64	.33	---	.97	**1.20**

Description	Oper	Unit	Vol	Crew Size	Man-hours per Unit	Crew Output per Day	Avg Mat'l Unit Cost	Avg Labor Unit Cost	Avg Equip Unit Cost	Avg Total Unit Cost	Avg Price Incl O&P
7" T (R-22)											
16" oc	Inst	SF	Lg	CA	.010	815.0	.74	.37	---	1.11	**1.37**
	Inst	SF	Sm	CA	.013	611.3	.82	.48	---	1.30	**1.62**
24" oc	Inst	SF	Lg	CA	.007	1220	.74	.26	---	1.00	**1.21**
	Inst	SF	Sm	CA	.009	915.0	.82	.33	---	1.15	**1.41**
9-1/4" T (R-30)											
16" oc	Inst	SF	Lg	CA	.010	815.0	.95	.37	---	1.32	**1.61**
	Inst	SF	Sm	CA	.013	611.3	1.05	.48	---	1.53	**1.88**
24" oc	Inst	SF	Lg	CA	.007	1220	.95	.26	---	1.21	**1.46**
	Inst	SF	Sm	CA	.009	915.0	1.05	.33	---	1.38	**1.67**
12" T (R-38)											
16" oc	Inst	SF	Lg	CA	.010	815.0	1.12	.37	---	1.49	**1.81**
	Inst	SF	Sm	CA	.013	611.3	1.24	.48	---	1.72	**2.10**
24" oc	Inst	SF	Lg	CA	.007	1220	1.12	.26	---	1.38	**1.65**
	Inst	SF	Sm	CA	.009	915	1.24	.33	---	1.57	**1.89**
Foil-faced											
4" T (R-11)											
16" oc	Inst	SF	Lg	CA	.010	815.0	.48	.37	---	.85	**1.07**
	Inst	SF	Sm	CA	.013	611.3	.52	.48	---	1.00	**1.27**
24" oc	Inst	SF	Lg	CA	.007	1220	.48	.26	---	.74	**.91**
	Inst	SF	Sm	CA	.009	915.0	.52	.33	---	.85	**1.06**
6-1/2" T (R-19)											
16" oc	Inst	SF	Lg	CA	.010	815.0	.64	.37	---	1.01	**1.25**
	Inst	SF	Sm	CA	.013	611.3	.70	.48	---	1.18	**1.48**
24" oc	Inst	SF	Lg	CA	.007	1220	.64	.26	---	.90	**1.10**
	Inst	SF	Sm	CA	.009	915.0	.70	.33	---	1.03	**1.27**

Loose fill

With ceiling finish in place

Joists, 16" or 24" oc

Description	Oper	Unit	Vol	Crew Size	Man-hours per Unit	Crew Output per Day	Avg Mat'l Unit Cost	Avg Labor Unit Cost	Avg Equip Unit Cost	Avg Total Unit Cost	Avg Price Incl O&P
4-1/2" T	Demo	SF	Lg	LB	.005	3400	---	.15	.02	.17	**.23**
	Demo	SF	Sm	LB	.006	2550	---	.18	.03	.21	**.28**
6-1/2" T	Demo	SF	Lg	LB	.007	2380	---	.21	.03	.24	**.32**
	Demo	SF	Sm	LB	.009	1785	---	.27	.04	.31	**.42**
7-1/2" T	Demo	SF	Lg	LB	.008	2040	---	.24	.03	.27	**.37**
	Demo	SF	Sm	LB	.010	1530	---	.30	.05	.35	**.47**
8-3/4" T	Demo	SF	Lg	LB	.009	1700	---	.27	.04	.31	**.42**
	Demo	SF	Sm	LB	.013	1275	---	.39	.05	.44	**.60**
10-1/4" T	Demo	SF	Lg	LB	.011	1445	---	.33	.05	.38	**.51**
	Demo	SF	Sm	LB	.015	1084	---	.45	.06	.51	**.69**

Description	Oper	Unit	Vol	Crew Size	Man-hours per Unit	Crew Output per Day	Avg Mat'l Unit Cost	Avg Labor Unit Cost	Avg Equip Unit Cost	Avg Total Unit Cost	Avg Price Incl O&P

Allowance made for joists, cavities, and cores

Fiberglass Insulation (28.5 lbs/bag nominal weight)

Joists, @ 8.13 lbs/CF density, using appropriate machine with 2-1/2" hose

16" oc

Description	Oper	Unit	Vol	Crew Size	Man-hours per Unit	Crew Output per Day	Avg Mat'l Unit Cost	Avg Labor Unit Cost	Avg Equip Unit Cost	Avg Total Unit Cost	Avg Price Incl O&P
4-1/2" T, R-13, 6.6 bags/1,000 SF											
	Inst	SF	Lg	CH	.003	4000	.35	.10	.02	.47	.57
	Inst	SF	Sm	CH	.004	3000	.38	.14	.02	.54	.65
6-1/2" T, R-19, 9.4 bags/1,000 SF											
	Inst	SF	Lg	CH	.004	2800	.35	.14	.02	.51	.62
	Inst	SF	Sm	CH	.006	2100	.38	.21	.03	.62	.76
7-1/2" T, R-22, 11.1 bags/1,000 SF											
	Inst	SF	Lg	CH	.005	2400	.35	.17	.03	.55	.68
	Inst	SF	Sm	CH	.007	1800	.38	.24	.04	.66	.82
8-3/4" T, R-25, 13.3 bags/1,000 SF											
	Inst	SF	Lg	CH	.006	2000	.35	.21	.03	.59	.72
	Inst	SF	Sm	CH	.008	1500	.38	.28	.05	.71	.88
10-1/4" T, R-30, 15.3 bags/1,000 SF											
	Inst	SF	Lg	CH	.007	1700	.69	.24	.04	.97	1.17
	Inst	SF	Sm	CH	.009	1275	.76	.31	.05	1.12	1.36

24" oc

Description	Oper	Unit	Vol	Crew Size	Man-hours per Unit	Crew Output per Day	Avg Mat'l Unit Cost	Avg Labor Unit Cost	Avg Equip Unit Cost	Avg Total Unit Cost	Avg Price Incl O&P
4-1/2" T, R-13, 6.6 bags/1,000 SF											
	Inst	SF	Lg	CH	.003	3600	.35	.10	.02	.47	.57
	Inst	SF	Sm	CH	.004	2700	.38	.14	.03	.55	.66
6-1/2" T, R-19, 9.4 bags/1,000 SF											
	Inst	SF	Lg	CH	.005	2500	.35	.17	.03	.55	.68
	Inst	SF	Sm	CH	.006	1875	.38	.21	.04	.63	.77
7-1/2" T, R-22, 11.1 bags/1,000 SF											
	Inst	SF	Lg	CH	.006	2100	.35	.21	.03	.59	.72
	Inst	SF	Sm	CH	.008	1575	.38	.28	.04	.70	.87
8-3/4" T, R-25, 13.3 bags/1,000 SF											
	Inst	SF	Lg	CH	.007	1750	.35	.24	.04	.63	.78
	Inst	SF	Sm	CH	.009	1313	.38	.31	.05	.74	.92
10-1/4" T, R-30, 15.3 bags/1,000 SF											
	Inst	SF	Lg	CH	.008	1500	.69	.28	.05	1.02	1.23
	Inst	SF	Sm	CH	.011	1125	.76	.38	.06	1.20	1.47

Vermiculite/Perlite (approximately 10 lbs/bag, 4 CF/bag)

Joists

16" oc

Description	Oper	Unit	Vol	Crew Size	Man-hours per Unit	Crew Output per Day	Avg Mat'l Unit Cost	Avg Labor Unit Cost	Avg Equip Unit Cost	Avg Total Unit Cost	Avg Price Incl O&P
4" T	Inst	SF	Lg	CH	.006	2000	.88	.21	---	1.09	1.30
	Inst	SF	Sm	CH	.008	1500	.97	.28	---	1.25	1.50
6" T	Inst	SF	Lg	CH	.009	1400	1.43	.31	---	1.74	2.08
	Inst	SF	Sm	CH	.011	1050.0	1.57	.38	---	1.95	2.34

24" oc

Description	Oper	Unit	Vol	Crew Size	Man-hours per Unit	Crew Output per Day	Avg Mat'l Unit Cost	Avg Labor Unit Cost	Avg Equip Unit Cost	Avg Total Unit Cost	Avg Price Incl O&P
4" T	Inst	SF	Lg	CH	.007	1700	.99	.24	---	1.23	1.48
	Inst	SF	Sm	CH	.009	1275.0	1.09	.31	---	1.40	1.69
6" T	Inst	SF	Lg	CH	.010	1190.0	1.43	.35	---	1.78	2.13
	Inst	SF	Sm	CH	.013	892.5	1.57	.45	---	2.02	2.44

Description	Oper	Unit	Vol	Crew Size	Man-hours per Unit	Crew Output per Day	Avg Mat'l Unit Cost	Avg Labor Unit Cost	Avg Equip Unit Cost	Avg Total Unit Cost	Avg Price Incl O&P
Cavity walls											
1" T	Inst	SF	Lg	CH	.004	3070	.22	.14	---	.36	**.45**
	Inst	SF	Sm	CH	.005	2303	.24	.17	---	.41	**.52**
2" T	Inst	SF	Lg	CH	.007	1690	.44	.24	---	.68	**.85**
	Inst	SF	Sm	CH	.009	1268	.48	.31	---	.79	**.99**
Block walls (2 cores/block)											
8" T block	Inst	SF	Lg	CH	.015	815.0	.77	.52	---	1.29	**1.61**
	Inst	SF	Sm	CH	.020	611.3	.85	.69	---	1.54	**1.95**
12" T block	Inst	SF	Lg	CH	.020	610.0	1.43	.69	---	2.12	**2.62**
	Inst	SF	Sm	CH	.026	457.5	1.57	.90	---	2.47	**3.07**

Rigid insulating board (Demo)

Description	Oper	Unit	Vol	Crew Size	Man-hours per Unit	Crew Output per Day	Avg Mat'l Unit Cost	Avg Labor Unit Cost	Avg Equip Unit Cost	Avg Total Unit Cost	Avg Price Incl O&P
Roofs											
1/2" T	Demo	SQ	Lg	LB	.941	17.00	---	28.20	---	28.20	**39.50**
	Demo	SQ	Sm	LB	1.25	12.75	---	37.50	---	37.50	**52.50**
1" T	Demo	SQ	Lg	LB	1.07	15.00	---	32.10	---	32.10	**44.90**
	Demo	SQ	Sm	LB	1.42	11.25	---	42.60	---	42.60	**59.60**
Walls											
1/2" T	Demo	SF	Lg	LB	.007	2140	---	.21	---	.21	**.29**
	Demo	SF	Sm	LB	.010	1605	---	.30	---	.30	**.42**
3/4" T	Demo	SF	Lg	LB	.007	2140	---	.21	---	.21	**.29**
	Demo	SF	Sm	LB	.010	1605	---	.30	---	.30	**.42**
1" T	Demo	SF	Lg	LB	.009	1820	---	.27	---	.27	**.38**
	Demo	SF	Sm	LB	.012	1365	---	.36	---	.36	**.50**
2" T	Demo	SF	Lg	LB	.010	1550	---	.30	---	.30	**.42**
	Demo	SF	Sm	LB	.014	1163	---	.42	---	.42	**.59**

Rigid insulating board (Install)

Roofs, over wood decks, 5% waste included

Normal (dry) moisture conditions within building

Fasten one ply felt, then set and fasten:

Description	Oper	Unit	Vol	Crew Size	Man-hours per Unit	Crew Output per Day	Avg Mat'l Unit Cost	Avg Labor Unit Cost	Avg Equip Unit Cost	Avg Total Unit Cost	Avg Price Incl O&P
1" ISO board											
	Inst	SQ	Lg	RT	1.50	16.0	60.20	57.50	---	117.70	**154.00**
	Inst	SQ	Sm	RT	2.00	12.0	66.20	76.70	---	142.90	**189.00**
1" perlite board											
	Inst	SQ	Lg	RT	1.50	16.0	57.20	57.50	---	114.70	**150.00**
	Inst	SQ	Sm	RT	2.00	12.0	62.90	76.70	---	139.60	**185.00**
1" polystyrene board											
	Inst	SQ	Lg	RT	1.50	16.0	58.90	57.50	---	116.40	**152.00**
	Inst	SQ	Sm	RT	2.00	12.0	64.80	76.70	---	141.50	**187.00**
1" urethane board											
	Inst	SQ	Lg	RT	1.50	16.0	64.40	57.50	---	121.90	**159.00**
	Inst	SQ	Sm	RT	2.00	12.0	70.90	76.70	---	147.60	**194.00**

Description	Oper	Unit	Vol	Crew Size	Man-hours per Unit	Crew Output per Day	Avg Mat'l Unit Cost	Avg Labor Unit Cost	Avg Equip Unit Cost	Avg Total Unit Cost	Avg Price Incl O&P

Excessive (humid) moisture conditions within building

Nail and overlap three plies 15 lb felt, mop laps and surface one coat and embed:

1" ISO board

| | Inst | SQ | Lg | RT | 3.00 | 8.0 | 95.30 | 115.00 | --- | 210.30 | **279.00** |
| | Inst | SQ | Sm | RT | 4.00 | 6.0 | 105.00 | 153.00 | --- | 258.00 | **346.00** |

1" perlite board

| | Inst | SQ | Lg | RT | 3.00 | 8.0 | 92.30 | 115.00 | --- | 207.30 | **275.00** |
| | Inst | SQ | Sm | RT | 4.00 | 6.0 | 102.00 | 153.00 | --- | 255.00 | **342.00** |

1" polystyrene board

| | Inst | SQ | Lg | RT | 3.00 | 8.0 | 94.10 | 115.00 | --- | 209.10 | **277.00** |
| | Inst | SQ | Sm | RT | 4.00 | 6.0 | 103.00 | 153.00 | --- | 256.00 | **344.00** |

1" urethane board

| | Inst | SQ | Lg | RT | 3.00 | 8.0 | 99.60 | 115.00 | --- | 214.60 | **284.00** |
| | Inst | SQ | Sm | RT | 4.00 | 6.0 | 110.00 | 153.00 | --- | 263.00 | **351.00** |

Roofs, over noncombustible decks, 5% waste included

Normal (dry) moisture conditions within building

Mop one coat and embed:

1" ISO board

| | Inst | SQ | Lg | RT | 1.71 | 14.0 | 78.80 | 65.60 | --- | 144.40 | **187.00** |
| | Inst | SQ | Sm | RT | 2.29 | 10.5 | 86.60 | 87.80 | --- | 174.40 | **229.00** |

1" perlite board

| | Inst | SQ | Lg | RT | 1.71 | 14.0 | 75.80 | 65.60 | --- | 141.40 | **184.00** |
| | Inst | SQ | Sm | RT | 2.29 | 10.5 | 83.30 | 87.80 | --- | 171.10 | **225.00** |

1" polystyrene board

| | Inst | SQ | Lg | RT | 1.71 | 14.0 | 77.50 | 65.60 | --- | 143.10 | **186.00** |
| | Inst | SQ | Sm | RT | 2.29 | 10.5 | 85.20 | 87.80 | --- | 173.00 | **227.00** |

1" urethane board

| | Inst | SQ | Lg | RT | 1.71 | 14.0 | 83.00 | 65.60 | --- | 148.60 | **192.00** |
| | Inst | SQ | Sm | RT | 2.29 | 10.5 | 91.30 | 87.80 | --- | 179.10 | **234.00** |

Excessive (humid) moisture conditions within building

Mop one coat, embed two plies 15 lb felt, mop and embed:

1" ISO board

| | Inst | SQ | Lg | RT | 3.69 | 6.5 | 98.90 | 142.00 | --- | 240.90 | **322.00** |
| | Inst | SQ | Sm | RT | 4.92 | 4.9 | 109.00 | 189.00 | --- | 298.00 | **402.00** |

1" perlite board

| | Inst | SQ | Lg | RT | 3.69 | 6.5 | 95.90 | 142.00 | --- | 237.90 | **318.00** |
| | Inst | SQ | Sm | RT | 4.92 | 4.9 | 105.00 | 189.00 | --- | 294.00 | **399.00** |

1" polystyrene board

| | Inst | SQ | Lg | RT | 3.69 | 6.5 | 97.60 | 142.00 | --- | 239.60 | **320.00** |
| | Inst | SQ | Sm | RT | 4.92 | 4.9 | 107.00 | 189.00 | --- | 296.00 | **401.00** |

1" urethane board

| | Inst | SQ | Lg | RT | 3.69 | 6.5 | 103.00 | 142.00 | --- | 245.00 | **327.00** |
| | Inst | SQ | Sm | RT | 4.92 | 4.9 | 113.00 | 189.00 | --- | 302.00 | **408.00** |

Description	Oper	Unit	Vol	Crew Size	Man-hours per Unit	Crew Output per Day	Avg Mat'l Unit Cost	Avg Labor Unit Cost	Avg Equip Unit Cost	Avg Total Unit Cost	Avg Price Incl O&P
Walls, extruded polystyrene (XPS) rigid foam insulation, 5% waste included											
4' x 8' x 1/2", square edge											
Straight wall	Inst	SF	Lg	2C	.011	1440	.62	.41	---	1.03	**1.28**
	Inst	SF	Sm	2C	.015	1080	.68	.56	---	1.24	**1.56**
Cut-up wall	Inst	SF	Lg	2C	.013	1200	.62	.48	---	1.10	**1.39**
	Inst	SF	Sm	2C	.018	900.0	.68	.67	---	1.35	**1.71**
4' x 8' x 3/4", tongue-and-groove											
Straight wall	Inst	SF	Lg	2C	.011	1440	.69	.41	---	1.10	**1.36**
	Inst	SF	Sm	2C	.015	1080	.76	.56	---	1.32	**1.65**
Cut-up wall	Inst	SF	Lg	2C	.013	1200	.69	.48	---	1.17	**1.47**
	Inst	SF	Sm	2C	.018	900.0	.76	.67	---	1.43	**1.81**
4' x 8' x 1", tongue-and-groove											
Straight wall	Inst	SF	Lg	2C	.011	1440	.70	.41	---	1.11	**1.38**
	Inst	SF	Sm	2C	.015	1080	.77	.56	---	1.33	**1.66**
Cut-up wall	Inst	SF	Lg	2C	.013	1200	.70	.48	---	1.18	**1.48**
	Inst	SF	Sm	2C	.018	900.0	.77	.67	---	1.44	**1.82**
4' x 8' x 2", scored square edge											
Straight wall	Inst	SF	Lg	2C	.011	1440	1.09	.41	---	1.50	**1.82**
	Inst	SF	Sm	2C	.015	1080	1.20	.56	---	1.76	**2.16**
Cut-up wall	Inst	SF	Lg	2C	.013	1200	1.09	.48	---	1.57	**1.93**
	Inst	SF	Sm	2C	.018	900.0	1.20	.67	---	1.87	**2.31**

Intercom systems. See Electrical, page 159
Jacuzzi whirlpools. See Spas, page 431
Lath & plaster. See Plaster, page 345

Description	Oper	Unit	Vol	Crew Size	Man-hours per Unit	Crew Output per Day	Avg Mat'l Unit Cost	Avg Labor Unit Cost	Avg Equip Unit Cost	Avg Total Unit Cost	Avg Price Incl O&P

Lighting fixtures

Labor includes hanging and connecting fixtures

Indoor lighting

Fluorescent

Description	Oper	Unit	Vol	Crew Size	Man-hours per Unit	Crew Output per Day	Avg Mat'l Unit Cost	Avg Labor Unit Cost	Avg Equip Unit Cost	Avg Total Unit Cost	Avg Price Incl O&P
Pendent mounted worklights											
4' L, two 40 watt RS	Inst	Ea	Lg	EA	.800	10.00	55.90	32.20	---	88.10	**111.00**
	Inst	Ea	Sm	EA	1.14	7.00	62.40	45.80	---	108.20	**138.00**
4' L, two 60 watt RS	Inst	Ea	Lg	EA	.800	10.00	91.00	32.20	---	123.20	**151.00**
	Inst	Ea	Sm	EA	1.14	7.00	102.00	45.80	---	147.80	**183.00**
8' L, two 75 watt RS	Inst	Ea	Lg	EA	1.00	8.00	105.00	40.20	---	145.20	**179.00**
	Inst	Ea	Sm	EA	1.43	5.60	117.00	57.50	---	174.50	**218.00**
Recessed mounted light fixture with acrylic diffuser											
1' W x 4' L, two 40 watt RS	Inst	Ea	Lg	EA	.800	10.00	59.80	32.20	---	92.00	**115.00**
	Inst	Ea	Sm	EA	1.14	7.00	66.70	45.80	---	112.50	**143.00**
2' W x 2' L, two U 40 watt RS	Inst	Ea	Lg	EA	.800	10.00	65.00	32.20	---	97.20	**121.00**
	Inst	Ea	Sm	EA	1.14	7.00	72.50	45.80	---	118.30	**150.00**
2' W x 4' L, four 40 watt RS	Inst	Ea	Lg	EA	1.00	8.00	72.80	40.20	---	113.00	**142.00**
	Inst	Ea	Sm	EA	1.43	5.60	81.20	57.50	---	138.70	**177.00**
Strip lighting fixtures											
4' L, one 40 watt RS	Inst	Ea	Lg	EA	.800	10.00	33.80	32.20	---	66.00	**85.50**
	Inst	Ea	Sm	EA	1.14	7.00	37.70	45.80	---	83.50	**110.00**
4' L, two 40 watt RS	Inst	Ea	Lg	EA	.800	10.00	36.40	32.20	---	68.60	**88.50**
	Inst	Ea	Sm	EA	1.14	7.00	40.60	45.80	---	86.40	**113.00**
8' L, one 75 watt SL	Inst	Ea	Lg	EA	1.00	8.00	50.70	40.20	---	90.90	**117.00**
	Inst	Ea	Sm	EA	1.43	5.60	56.60	57.50	---	114.10	**148.00**
8' L, two 75 watt SL	Inst	Ea	Lg	EA	1.00	8.00	61.10	40.20	---	101.30	**129.00**
	Inst	Ea	Sm	EA	1.43	5.60	68.20	57.50	---	125.70	**162.00**
Surface mounted, acrylic diffuser											
1' W x 4' L, two 40 watt RS	Inst	Ea	Lg	EA	.800	10.00	88.40	32.20	---	120.60	**148.00**
	Inst	Ea	Sm	EA	1.14	7.00	98.60	45.80	---	144.40	**180.00**
2' W x 2' L, two U 40 watt RS	Inst	Ea	Lg	EA	.800	10.00	111.00	32.20	---	143.20	**174.00**
	Inst	Ea	Sm	EA	1.14	7.00	123.00	45.80	---	168.80	**208.00**
2' W x 4' L, four 40 watt RS	Inst	Ea	Lg	EA	1.00	8.00	113.00	40.20	---	153.20	**188.00**
	Inst	Ea	Sm	EA	1.43	5.60	126.00	57.50	---	183.50	**228.00**
White enameled circline steel ceiling fixtures											
8" W, 22 watt RS	Inst	Ea	Lg	EA	.667	12.00	31.70	26.80	---	58.50	**75.30**
	Inst	Ea	Sm	EA	.952	8.40	35.30	38.30	---	73.60	**96.10**
12" W, 22 to 32 watt RS	Inst	Ea	Lg	EA	.667	12.00	47.50	26.80	---	74.30	**93.50**
	Inst	Ea	Sm	EA	.952	8.40	53.00	38.30	---	91.30	**116.00**
16" W, 22 to 40 watt RS	Inst	Ea	Lg	EA	.667	12.00	63.30	26.80	---	90.10	**112.00**
	Inst	Ea	Sm	EA	0.95	8.40	70.60	38.20	---	108.80	**137.00**
Decorative circline fixtures											
12" W, 22 to 32 watt RS	Inst	Ea	Lg	EA	.667	12.00	124.00	26.80	---	150.80	**181.00**
	Inst	Ea	Sm	EA	.952	8.40	138.00	38.30	---	176.30	**214.00**
16" W, 22 to 40 watt RS	Inst	Ea	Lg	EA	.667	12.00	214.00	26.80	---	240.80	**285.00**
	Inst	Ea	Sm	EA	.952	8.40	238.00	38.30	---	276.30	**330.00**

Description	Oper	Unit	Vol	Crew Size	Man-hours per Unit	Crew Output per Day	Avg Mat'l Unit Cost	Avg Labor Unit Cost	Avg Equip Unit Cost	Avg Total Unit Cost	Avg Price Incl O&P

Incandescent

Ceiling fixture, surface mounted

Description	Oper	Unit	Vol	Crew Size	Man-hours per Unit	Crew Output per Day	Avg Mat'l Unit Cost	Avg Labor Unit Cost	Avg Equip Unit Cost	Avg Total Unit Cost	Avg Price Incl O&P
15" x 5", white bent glass	Inst	Ea	Lg	EA	.667	12.00	36.40	26.80	---	63.20	**80.70**
	Inst	Ea	Sm	EA	.952	8.40	40.60	38.30	---	78.90	**102.00**
10" x 7", two light, circular	Inst	Ea	Lg	EA	.667	12.00	45.90	26.80	---	72.70	**91.70**
	Inst	Ea	Sm	EA	.952	8.40	51.20	38.30	---	89.50	**114.00**
8" x 8", one light, screw-in	Inst	Ea	Lg	EA	.667	12.00	30.10	26.80	---	56.90	**73.50**
	Inst	Ea	Sm	EA	.952	8.40	33.60	38.30	---	71.90	**94.10**

Ceiling fixture, recessed
Square fixture, drop or flat lens

Description	Oper	Unit	Vol	Crew Size	Man-hours per Unit	Crew Output per Day	Avg Mat'l Unit Cost	Avg Labor Unit Cost	Avg Equip Unit Cost	Avg Total Unit Cost	Avg Price Incl O&P
8" frame	Inst	Ea	Lg	EA	1.00	8.00	45.90	40.20	---	86.10	**111.00**
	Inst	Ea	Sm	EA	1.43	5.60	51.20	57.50	---	108.70	**142.00**
10" frame	Inst	Ea	Lg	EA	1.00	8.00	52.30	40.20	---	92.50	**118.00**
	Inst	Ea	Sm	EA	1.43	5.60	58.30	57.50	---	115.80	**150.00**
12" frame	Inst	Ea	Lg	EA	1.00	8.00	55.40	40.20	---	95.60	**122.00**
	Inst	Ea	Sm	EA	1.43	5.60	61.80	57.50	---	119.30	**154.00**

Round fixture for concentrated light over small areas

Description	Oper	Unit	Vol	Crew Size	Man-hours per Unit	Crew Output per Day	Avg Mat'l Unit Cost	Avg Labor Unit Cost	Avg Equip Unit Cost	Avg Total Unit Cost	Avg Price Incl O&P
7" shower fixture frame	Inst	Ea	Lg	EA	1.00	8.00	45.90	40.20	---	86.10	**111.00**
	Inst	Ea	Sm	EA	1.43	5.60	51.20	57.50	---	108.70	**142.00**
8" spotlight fixture	Inst	Ea	Lg	EA	1.00	8.00	44.30	40.20	---	84.50	**109.00**
	Inst	Ea	Sm	EA	1.43	5.60	49.50	57.50	---	107.00	**140.00**
8" flat lens or stepped baffle frame											
	Inst	Ea	Lg	EA	1.00	8.00	45.90	40.20	---	86.10	**111.00**
	Inst	Ea	Sm	EA	1.43	5.60	51.20	57.50	---	108.70	**142.00**

Track lighting for highlighting effects from a ceiling or wall
Swivel track heads with the ability to slide head along track to a new position

Track heads

Description	Oper	Unit	Vol	Crew Size	Man-hours per Unit	Crew Output per Day	Avg Mat'l Unit Cost	Avg Labor Unit Cost	Avg Equip Unit Cost	Avg Total Unit Cost	Avg Price Incl O&P
Large cylinder	Inst	Ea	Lg	EA	---	---	53.80	---	---	53.80	**53.80**
	Inst	Ea	Sm	EA	---	---	60.00	---	---	60.00	**60.00**
Small cylinder	Inst	Ea	Lg	EA	---	---	44.30	---	---	44.30	**44.30**
	Inst	Ea	Sm	EA	---	---	49.50	---	---	49.50	**49.50**
Sphere cylinder	Inst	Ea	Lg	EA	---	---	53.80	---	---	53.80	**53.80**
	Inst	Ea	Sm	EA	---	---	60.00	---	---	60.00	**60.00**

Track, 1-7/16" W x 3/4" D

Description	Oper	Unit	Vol	Crew Size	Man-hours per Unit	Crew Output per Day	Avg Mat'l Unit Cost	Avg Labor Unit Cost	Avg Equip Unit Cost	Avg Total Unit Cost	Avg Price Incl O&P
2' track	Inst	Ea	Lg	EA	.333	24.00	22.20	13.40	---	35.60	**44.90**
	Inst	Ea	Sm	EA	.476	16.80	24.70	19.10	---	43.80	**56.20**
4' track	Inst	Ea	Lg	EA	.500	16.00	55.40	20.10	---	75.50	**92.90**
	Inst	Ea	Sm	EA	.714	11.20	61.80	28.70	---	90.50	**113.00**
8' track	Inst	Ea	Lg	EA	.667	12.00	82.30	26.80	---	109.10	**134.00**
	Inst	Ea	Sm	EA	.952	8.40	91.80	38.30	---	130.10	**161.00**

Straight connector; joins two track sections end to end

Description	Oper	Unit	Vol	Crew Size	Man-hours per Unit	Crew Output per Day	Avg Mat'l Unit Cost	Avg Labor Unit Cost	Avg Equip Unit Cost	Avg Total Unit Cost	Avg Price Incl O&P
7-5/8" L	Inst	Ea	Lg	EA	---	---	15.80	---	---	15.80	**15.80**
	Inst	Ea	Sm	EA	---	---	17.70	---	---	17.70	**17.70**

L - connector, joins two track sections for 90-degree angle turns

Description	Oper	Unit	Vol	Crew Size	Man-hours per Unit	Crew Output per Day	Avg Mat'l Unit Cost	Avg Labor Unit Cost	Avg Equip Unit Cost	Avg Total Unit Cost	Avg Price Incl O&P
7-5/8" L	Inst	Ea	Lg	EA	---	---	15.80	---	---	15.80	**15.80**
	Inst	Ea	Sm	EA	---	---	17.70	---	---	17.70	**17.70**

Feed in unit, attaches to ceiling or wall outlet box, supplies electrical current to all heads on track(s)

Description	Oper	Unit	Vol	Crew Size	Man-hours per Unit	Crew Output per Day	Avg Mat'l Unit Cost	Avg Labor Unit Cost	Avg Equip Unit Cost	Avg Total Unit Cost	Avg Price Incl O&P
	Inst	Ea	Lg	EA	.667	12.00	17.40	26.80	---	44.20	**58.90**
	Inst	Ea	Sm	EA	.952	8.40	19.40	38.30	---	57.70	**77.80**

Description	Oper	Unit	Vol	Crew Size	Man-hours per Unit	Crew Output per Day	Avg Mat'l Unit Cost	Avg Labor Unit Cost	Avg Equip Unit Cost	Avg Total Unit Cost	Avg Price Incl O&P
Wall fixtures											
White glass with on/off switch											
1 light, 5" W x 5" H	Inst	Ea	Lg	EA	.667	12.00	17.40	26.80	---	44.20	**58.90**
	Inst	Ea	Sm	EA	.952	8.40	19.40	38.30	---	57.70	**77.80**
2 light, 14" W x 5" H	Inst	Ea	Lg	EA	.667	12.00	26.90	26.80	---	53.70	**69.80**
	Inst	Ea	Sm	EA	.952	8.40	30.00	38.30	---	68.30	**90.00**
4 light, 24" W x 4" H	Inst	Ea	Lg	EA	.667	12.00	39.60	26.80	---	66.40	**84.40**
	Inst	Ea	Sm	EA	.952	8.40	44.20	38.30	---	82.50	**106.00**
Swivel wall fixture											
1 light, 4" W x 8" H	Inst	Ea	Lg	EA	.667	12.00	27.30	26.80	---	54.10	**70.30**
	Inst	Ea	Sm	EA	.952	8.40	30.50	38.30	---	68.80	**90.50**
2 light, 9" W x 9" H	Inst	Ea	Lg	EA	.667	12.00	47.50	26.80	---	74.30	**93.50**
	Inst	Ea	Sm	EA	.952	8.40	53.00	38.30	---	91.30	**116.00**

Outdoor lighting

Description	Oper	Unit	Vol	Crew Size	Man-hours per Unit	Crew Output per Day	Avg Mat'l Unit Cost	Avg Labor Unit Cost	Avg Equip Unit Cost	Avg Total Unit Cost	Avg Price Incl O&P
Ceiling fixture for porch											
7" W x 13" L, one 75 watt RS	Inst	Ea	Lg	EA	.667	12.00	57.00	26.80	---	83.80	**104.00**
	Inst	Ea	Sm	EA	.952	8.40	63.60	38.30	---	101.90	**129.00**
11" W x 4" L, two 60 watt RS	Inst	Ea	Lg	EA	.667	12.00	69.70	26.80	---	96.50	**119.00**
	Inst	Ea	Sm	EA	.952	8.40	77.70	38.30	---	116.00	**145.00**
15" W x 4" L, three 60 watt RS											
	Inst	Ea	Lg	EA	.667	12.00	71.30	26.80	---	98.10	**121.00**
	Inst	Ea	Sm	EA	.952	8.40	79.50	38.30	---	117.80	**147.00**
Wall fixture for porch											
6" W x 10" L, one 75 watt RS	Inst	Ea	Lg	EA	.667	12.00	61.80	26.80	---	88.60	**110.00**
	Inst	Ea	Sm	EA	.952	8.40	68.90	38.30	---	107.20	**135.00**
6" W x 16" L, one 75 watt RS	Inst	Ea	Lg	EA	.667	12.00	77.60	26.80	---	104.40	**128.00**
	Inst	Ea	Sm	EA	.952	8.40	86.50	38.30	---	124.80	**155.00**
Post lantern fixture											
Aluminum cast posts											
84" H post with lantern, set in concrete, includes 50' of conduit, circuit, and cement											
	Inst	Ea	Lg	EA	8.00	1.00	364.00	322.00	---	686.00	**885.00**
	Inst	Ea	Sm	EA	11.4	0.70	406.00	458.00	---	864.00	**1130.00**
Urethane (in form of simulated redwood) over steel post											
Post with matching lantern, set in concrete, includes 50' of conduit, circuit, and cement											
	Inst	Ea	Lg	EA	8.00	1.00	435.00	322.00	---	757.00	**967.00**
	Inst	Ea	Sm	EA	11.4	0.70	486.00	458.00	---	944.00	**1220.00**

Linoleum. See Resilient flooring, page 352

Lumber. See Framing, page 176

Description	Oper	Unit	Vol	Crew Size	Man-hours per Unit	Crew Output per Day	Avg Mat'l Unit Cost	Avg Labor Unit Cost	Avg Equip Unit Cost	Avg Total Unit Cost	Avg Price Incl O&P

Mantels, fireplace

Ponderosa pine, kiln-dried, unfinished, assembled

Versailles, ornate, French design

Description	Oper	Unit	Vol	Crew Size	Man-hours per Unit	Crew Output per Day	Avg Mat'l Unit Cost	Avg Labor Unit Cost	Avg Equip Unit Cost	Avg Total Unit Cost	Avg Price Incl O&P
59" W x 46" H	Inst	Ea	Lg	CJ	4.00	4.00	1220.00	134.00	---	1354.00	**1600.00**
	Inst	Ea	Sm	CJ	5.71	2.80	1340.00	191.00	---	1531.00	**1810.00**

Victorian, ornate, English design

Description	Oper	Unit	Vol	Crew Size	Man-hours per Unit	Crew Output per Day	Avg Mat'l Unit Cost	Avg Labor Unit Cost	Avg Equip Unit Cost	Avg Total Unit Cost	Avg Price Incl O&P
63" W x 52" H	Inst	Ea	Lg	CJ	4.00	4.00	1010.00	134.00	---	1144.00	**1350.00**
	Inst	Ea	Sm	CJ	5.71	2.80	1110.00	191.00	---	1301.00	**1540.00**

Chelsea, plain, English design

Description	Oper	Unit	Vol	Crew Size	Man-hours per Unit	Crew Output per Day	Avg Mat'l Unit Cost	Avg Labor Unit Cost	Avg Equip Unit Cost	Avg Total Unit Cost	Avg Price Incl O&P
70" W x 52" H	Inst	Ea	Lg	CJ	4.00	4.00	694.00	134.00	---	828.00	**985.00**
	Inst	Ea	Sm	CJ	5.71	2.80	762.00	191.00	---	953.00	**1140.00**

Jamestown, plain, Early American

Description	Oper	Unit	Vol	Crew Size	Man-hours per Unit	Crew Output per Day	Avg Mat'l Unit Cost	Avg Labor Unit Cost	Avg Equip Unit Cost	Avg Total Unit Cost	Avg Price Incl O&P
68" W x 53" H	Inst	Ea	Lg	CJ	4.00	4.00	469.00	134.00	---	603.00	**727.00**
	Inst	Ea	Sm	CJ	5.71	2.80	515.00	191.00	---	706.00	**860.00**

Marlite paneling

Panels, 4' x 8', adhesive set

Description	Oper	Unit	Vol	Crew Size	Man-hours per Unit	Crew Output per Day	Avg Mat'l Unit Cost	Avg Labor Unit Cost	Avg Equip Unit Cost	Avg Total Unit Cost	Avg Price Incl O&P
	Demo	SF	Lg	LB	.009	1850	---	.27	---	.27	**.38**
	Demo	SF	Sm	LB	.012	1295	---	.36	---	.36	**.50**

Plastic-coated masonite panels; 4' x 8', 5' x 5'; screw applied; channel molding around perimeter; 1/8" T

Description	Oper	Unit	Vol	Crew Size	Man-hours per Unit	Crew Output per Day	Avg Mat'l Unit Cost	Avg Labor Unit Cost	Avg Equip Unit Cost	Avg Total Unit Cost	Avg Price Incl O&P
Solid colors	Inst	SF	Lg	CJ	.047	340.0	2.70	1.57	---	4.27	**5.31**
	Inst	SF	Sm	CJ	.067	238.0	3.06	2.25	---	5.31	**6.66**
Patterned panels	Inst	SF	Lg	CJ	.047	340.0	2.95	1.57	---	4.52	**5.60**
	Inst	SF	Sm	CJ	.067	238.0	3.34	2.25	---	5.59	**6.98**

Molding, 1/8" panels; corners, divisions, or edging; nailed to framing or sheathing

Description	Oper	Unit	Vol	Crew Size	Man-hours per Unit	Crew Output per Day	Avg Mat'l Unit Cost	Avg Labor Unit Cost	Avg Equip Unit Cost	Avg Total Unit Cost	Avg Price Incl O&P
Bright anodized	Inst	LF	Lg	CJ	.063	255.0	.17	2.11	---	2.28	**3.15**
	Inst	LF	Sm	CJ	.090	178.5	.19	3.02	---	3.21	**4.44**
Gold anodized	Inst	LF	Lg	CJ	.063	255.0	.19	2.11	---	2.30	**3.17**
	Inst	LF	Sm	CJ	.090	178.5	.21	3.02	---	3.23	**4.46**
Colors	Inst	LF	Lg	CJ	.063	255.0	.23	2.11	---	2.34	**3.22**
	Inst	LF	Sm	CJ	.090	178.5	.26	3.02	---	3.28	**4.52**

Masonry

Brick. All material costs include mortar and waste, 5% on brick and 30% on mortar.

1. **Dimensions**

    a. Standard or regular: 8" L x 2$\frac{1}{4}$" H x 3$\frac{3}{4}$" W.

    b. Modular: 7$\frac{5}{8}$" L x 2$\frac{1}{4}$" H x 3$\frac{5}{8}$" W.

    c. Norman: 11$\frac{5}{8}$" L x 2$\frac{2}{3}$" H x 3$\frac{5}{8}$" W.

    d. Roman: 11$\frac{5}{8}$" L x 1$\frac{5}{8}$" H x 3$\frac{5}{8}$" W.

2. **Installation**

    a. Mortar joints are $\frac{3}{8}$" thick both horizontally and vertically.

    b. Mortar mix is 1:3, 1 part masonry cement and 3 parts sand.

    c. Galvanized, corrugated wall ties are used on veneers at 1 tie per SF wall area. The tie is $\frac{7}{8}$" x 7" x 16 ga.

    d. Running bond used on veneers and walls.

3. **Notes on Labor**. Output is based on a crew composed of bricklayers and bricktenders at a 1:1 ratio.

4. **Estimating Technique**. Chimneys and columns figured per vertical linear foot with allowances already made for brick waste and mortar waste. Veneers and walls are computed per square foot of wall area.

Concrete (Masonry) Block. All material costs include 3% block waste and 30% mortar waste.

1. **Dimension.** All blocks are two core.

    a. Heavyweight: 8" T blocks weigh approximately 46 lbs/block; 12" T blocks weigh approximately 65 lbs/block.

    b. Lightweight: Also known as haydite blocks. 8" T blocks weigh approximately 30 lbs/block; 12" T blocks weigh approximately 41 lbs/block.

2. **Installation**

    a. Mortar joints are $\frac{3}{8}$" T both horizontally and vertically.

    b. Mortar mix is 1:3, 1 part masonry cement and 3 parts sand.

    c. Reinforcing: Lateral metal is regular truss with 9 gauge sides and ties. Vertical steel is #4 ($\frac{1}{2}$" dia.) rods, at 0.668 lbs/LF.

3. **Notes on Labor**. Output is based on a crew composed of bricklayers and bricktenders.

4. **Estimating Technique.** Figure chimneys and columns per vertical linear foot, with allowances already made for block waste and mortar waste. Veneers and walls are computed per square foot of wall area.

Quarry Tile (on Floor). Includes 5% tile waste.

1. **Dimensions:** 6" square tile is $\frac{1}{2}$" T and 9" square tile is $\frac{3}{4}$" T.

2. **Installation**

    a. Conventional mortar set utilizes portland cement, mortar mix, sand, and water. The mortar dry-cures and bonds to tile.

    b. Dry-set mortar utilizes dry-set portland cement, mortar mix, sand, and water. The mortar dry-cures and bonds to tile.

3. **Notes on Labor.** Output is based on a crew composed of bricklayers and bricktenders.

4. **Estimating Technique.** Compute square feet of floor area.

Typical concrete block wall

4" wall thickness

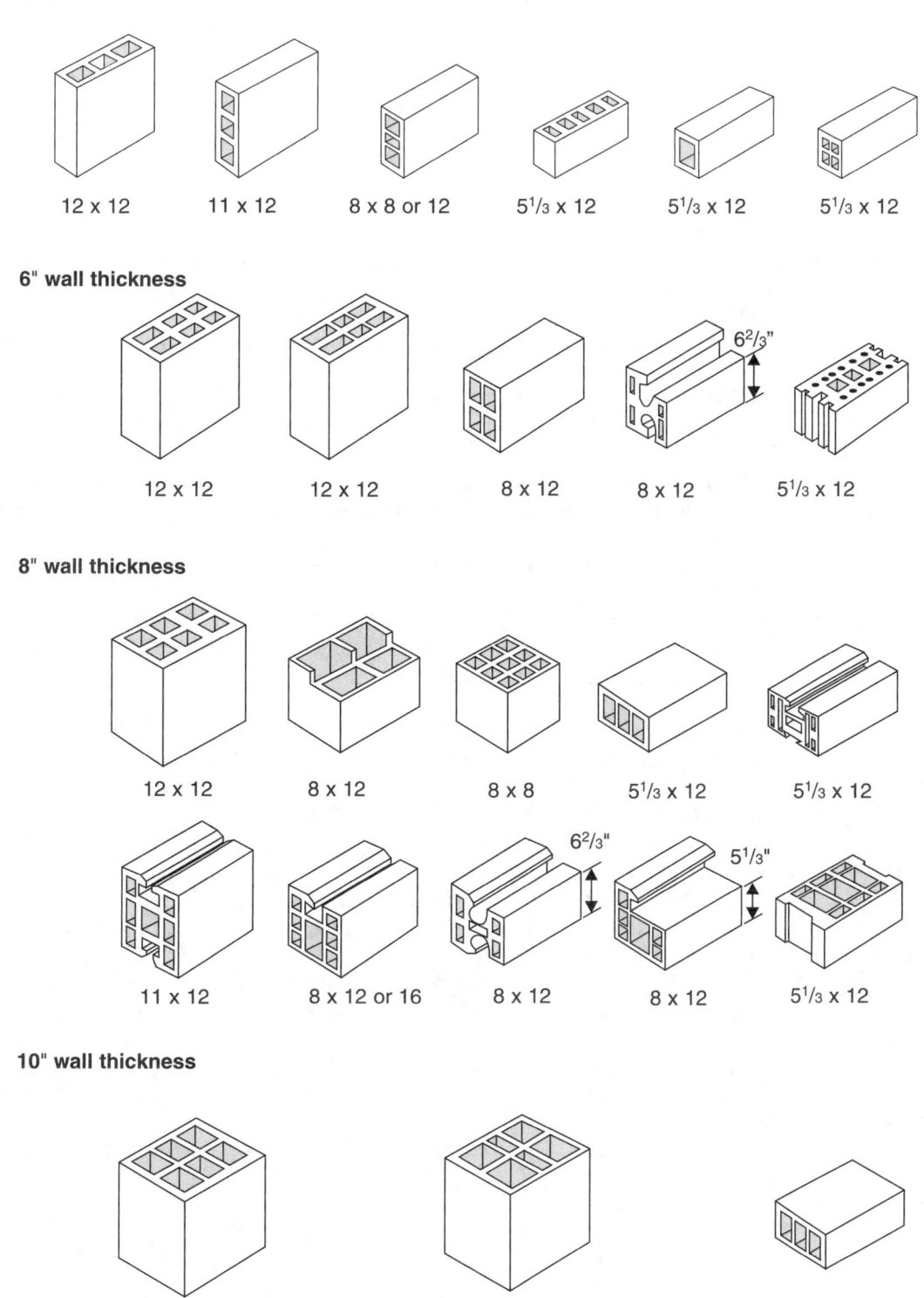

12 x 12   11 x 12   8 x 8 or 12 $5\frac{1}{3}$ x 12 $5\frac{1}{3}$ x 12 $5\frac{1}{3}$ x 12

6" wall thickness

12 x 12   12 x 12   8 x 12   8 x 12 $5\frac{1}{3}$ x 12

$6\frac{2}{3}$"

8" wall thickness

12 x 12   8 x 12   8 x 8 $5\frac{1}{3}$ x 12 $5\frac{1}{3}$ x 12

11 x 12   8 x 12 or 16   8 x 12   8 x 12 $5\frac{1}{3}$ x 12

$6\frac{2}{3}$" $5\frac{1}{3}$"

10" wall thickness

12 x 12   12 x 12 $5\frac{1}{3}$ or 8 x 12 or 16

Common sizes and shapes for clay tile

Description	Oper	Unit	Vol	Crew Size	Man-hours per Unit	Crew Output per Day	Avg Mat'l Unit Cost	Avg Labor Unit Cost	Avg Equip Unit Cost	Avg Total Unit Cost	Avg Price Incl O&P

Masonry

Brick, standard

Running bond, 3/8" mortar joints

Chimneys

Flue lining included; no scaffolding included

4" T wall with standard brick

Description	Oper	Unit	Vol	Crew Size	Man-hours per Unit	Crew Output per Day	Avg Mat'l Unit Cost	Avg Labor Unit Cost	Avg Equip Unit Cost	Avg Total Unit Cost	Avg Price Incl O&P
16" x 16" with one 8" x 8" flue											
	Demo	VLF	Lg	AB	1.04	15.40	---	38.30	10.10	48.40	**63.80**
	Demo	VLF	Sm	LB	1.48	10.78	---	44.40	14.50	58.90	**76.60**
20" x 16" with one 12" x 8" flue											
	Demo	VLF	Lg	AB	1.20	13.30	---	44.20	11.70	55.90	**73.60**
	Demo	VLF	Sm	LB	1.72	9.31	---	51.60	16.80	68.40	**89.00**
20" x 20" with one 12" x 12" flue											
	Demo	VLF	Lg	AB	1.31	12.20	---	48.30	12.80	61.10	**80.30**
	Demo	VLF	Sm	LB	1.87	8.54	---	56.10	18.30	74.40	**96.80**
28" x 16" with two 8" x 8" flues											
	Demo	VLF	Lg	AB	1.60	10.00	---	58.90	15.60	74.50	**98.10**
	Demo	VLF	Sm	LB	2.29	7.00	---	68.70	22.30	91.00	**118.00**
32" x 16" with one 8" x 8" and one 12" x 8" flue											
	Demo	VLF	Lg	AB	1.70	9.40	---	62.60	16.60	79.20	**104.00**
	Demo	VLF	Sm	LB	2.43	6.58	---	72.90	23.70	96.60	**126.00**
36" x 16" with two 12" x 8" flues											
	Demo	VLF	Lg	AB	1.82	8.80	---	67.00	17.70	84.70	**112.00**
	Demo	VLF	Sm	LB	2.60	6.16	---	78.00	25.30	103.30	**135.00**
36" x 20" with two 12" x 12" flues											
	Demo	VLF	Lg	AB	2.03	7.90	---	74.80	19.80	94.60	**124.00**
	Demo	VLF	Sm	LB	2.89	5.53	---	86.70	28.20	114.90	**150.00**
16" x 16" with one 8" x 8" flue											
	Inst	VLF	Lg	BK	1.12	14.30	31.20	36.70	6.06	73.96	**94.00**
	Inst	VLF	Sm	BK	1.60	10.01	35.40	52.40	8.66	96.46	**124.00**
20" x 16" with one 12" x 8" flue											
	Inst	VLF	Lg	BK	1.27	12.60	39.50	41.60	6.88	87.98	**111.00**
	Inst	VLF	Sm	BK	1.81	8.82	44.90	59.20	9.83	113.93	**146.00**
20" x 20" with one 12" x 12" flue											
	Inst	VLF	Lg	BK	1.42	11.30	43.90	46.50	7.67	98.07	**124.00**
	Inst	VLF	Sm	BK	2.02	7.91	49.80	66.10	11.00	126.90	**162.00**
28" x 16" with two 8" x 8" flues											
	Inst	VLF	Lg	BK	1.70	9.40	56.20	55.60	9.22	121.02	**153.00**
	Inst	VLF	Sm	BK	2.43	6.58	63.80	79.50	13.20	156.50	**199.00**
32" x 16" with one 8" x 8" and one 12" x 8" flue											
	Inst	VLF	Lg	BK	1.82	8.80	63.90	59.60	9.85	133.35	**168.00**
	Inst	VLF	Sm	BK	2.60	6.16	72.50	85.10	14.10	171.70	**218.00**
36" x 16" with two 12" x 8" flues											
	Inst	VLF	Lg	BK	1.95	8.20	72.20	63.80	10.60	146.60	**184.00**
	Inst	VLF	Sm	BK	2.79	5.74	82.00	91.30	15.10	188.40	**239.00**
36" x 20" with two 12" x 12" flues											
	Inst	VLF	Lg	BK	2.16	7.40	81.50	70.70	11.70	163.90	**206.00**
	Inst	VLF	Sm	BK	3.09	5.18	92.60	101.00	16.70	210.30	**267.00**

Description	Oper	Unit	Vol	Crew Size	Man-hours per Unit	Crew Output per Day	Avg Mat'l Unit Cost	Avg Labor Unit Cost	Avg Equip Unit Cost	Avg Total Unit Cost	Avg Price Incl O&P
8" T wall with standard brick											
24" x 24" with one 8" x 8" flue	Demo	VLF	Lg	AB	2.22	7.20	---	81.80	21.70	103.50	**136.00**
	Demo	VLF	Sm	LB	3.17	5.04	---	95.10	31.00	126.10	**164.00**
28" x 24" with one 12" x 8" flue	Demo	VLF	Lg	AB	2.39	6.70	---	88.00	23.30	111.30	**147.00**
	Demo	VLF	Sm	LB	3.41	4.69	---	102.00	33.30	135.30	**176.00**
28" x 28" with one 12" x 12" flue	Demo	VLF	Lg	AB	2.62	6.10	---	96.50	25.60	122.10	**161.00**
	Demo	VLF	Sm	LB	3.75	4.27	---	113.00	36.50	149.50	**194.00**
36" x 24" with two 8" x 8" flues	Demo	VLF	Lg	AB	2.91	5.50	---	107.00	28.40	135.40	**178.00**
	Demo	VLF	Sm	LB	4.16	3.85	---	125.00	40.50	165.50	**215.00**
40" x 24" with one 8" x 8" and one 12" x 8" flue											
	Demo	VLF	Lg	AB	3.20	5.00	---	118.00	31.20	149.20	**196.00**
	Demo	VLF	Sm	LB	4.57	3.50	---	137.00	44.60	181.60	**237.00**
44" x 24" with two 12" x 8" flues	Demo	VLF	Lg	AB	3.33	4.80	---	123.00	32.50	155.50	**204.00**
	Demo	VLF	Sm	LB	4.76	3.36	---	143.00	46.40	189.40	**246.00**
44" x 28" with two 12" x 12" flues	Demo	VLF	Lg	AB	3.56	4.50	---	131.00	34.70	165.70	**218.00**
	Demo	VLF	Sm	LB	5.08	3.15	---	152.00	49.50	201.50	**263.00**
24" x 24" with one 8" x 8" flue	Inst	VLF	Lg	BK	2.50	6.40	62.30	81.80	13.50	157.60	**201.00**
	Inst	VLF	Sm	BK	3.57	4.48	70.80	117.00	19.40	207.20	**267.00**
28" x 24" with one 12" x 8" flue	Inst	VLF	Lg	BK	2.76	5.80	73.30	90.30	14.90	178.50	**227.00**
	Inst	VLF	Sm	BK	3.94	4.06	83.20	129.00	21.40	233.60	**300.00**
28" x 28" with one 12" x 12" flue	Inst	VLF	Lg	BK	2.96	5.40	80.90	96.90	16.10	193.90	**247.00**
	Inst	VLF	Sm	BK	4.23	3.78	91.90	138.00	22.90	252.80	**325.00**
36" x 24" with two 8" x 8" flues	Inst	VLF	Lg	BK	3.33	4.80	96.10	109.00	18.10	223.20	**283.00**
	Inst	VLF	Sm	BK	4.76	3.36	109.00	156.00	25.80	290.80	**372.00**
40" x 24" with one 8" x 8" and one 12" x 8" flue											
	Inst	VLF	Lg	BK	3.72	4.30	110.00	122.00	20.20	252.20	**320.00**
	Inst	VLF	Sm	BK	5.32	3.01	125.00	174.00	28.80	327.80	**420.00**
44" x 24" with two 12" x 8" flues	Inst	VLF	Lg	BK	3.81	4.20	119.00	125.00	20.60	264.60	**334.00**
	Inst	VLF	Sm	BK	5.44	2.94	135.00	178.00	29.50	342.50	**437.00**
44" x 28" with two 12" x 12" flues	Inst	VLF	Lg	BK	4.10	3.90	132.00	134.00	22.20	288.20	**364.00**
	Inst	VLF	Sm	BK	5.86	2.73	149.00	192.00	31.80	372.80	**476.00**

Columns

Outside dimension; no shoring; solid centers; no scaffolding included

Description	Oper	Unit	Vol	Crew Size	Man-hours per Unit	Crew Output per Day	Avg Mat'l Unit Cost	Avg Labor Unit Cost	Avg Equip Unit Cost	Avg Total Unit Cost	Avg Price Incl O&P
8" x 8"	Demo	VLF	Lg	AB	.331	48.30	---	12.20	3.23	15.43	**20.30**
	Demo	VLF	Sm	LB	.473	33.81	---	14.20	4.61	18.81	**24.50**
12" x 8"	Demo	VLF	Lg	AB	.546	29.30	---	20.10	5.32	25.42	**33.50**
	Demo	VLF	Sm	LB	.780	20.51	---	23.40	7.61	31.01	**40.40**
16" x 8"	Demo	VLF	Lg	AB	.711	22.50	---	26.20	6.93	33.13	**43.60**
	Demo	VLF	Sm	LB	1.02	15.75	---	30.60	9.90	40.50	**52.70**
20" x 8"	Demo	VLF	Lg	AB	.870	18.40	---	32.00	8.48	40.48	**53.30**
	Demo	VLF	Sm	LB	1.24	12.88	---	37.20	12.10	49.30	**64.20**
24" x 8"	Demo	VLF	Lg	AB	1.02	15.70	---	37.60	9.94	47.54	**62.50**
	Demo	VLF	Sm	LB	1.46	10.99	---	43.80	14.20	58.00	**75.50**

Description	Oper	Unit	Vol	Crew Size	Man-hours per Unit	Crew Output per Day	Avg Mat'l Unit Cost	Avg Labor Unit Cost	Avg Equip Unit Cost	Avg Total Unit Cost	Avg Price Incl O&P
Columns (continued)											
12" x 12"	Demo	VLF	Lg	AB	.792	20.20	---	29.20	7.72	36.92	**48.60**
	Demo	VLF	Sm	LB	1.13	14.14	---	33.90	11.00	44.90	**58.50**
16" x 12"	Demo	VLF	Lg	AB	1.02	15.70	---	37.60	9.94	47.54	**62.50**
	Demo	VLF	Sm	LB	1.46	10.99	---	43.80	14.20	58.00	**75.50**
20" x 12"	Demo	VLF	Lg	AB	1.23	13.00	---	45.30	12.00	57.30	**75.40**
	Demo	VLF	Sm	LB	1.76	9.10	---	52.80	17.10	69.90	**91.10**
24" x 12"	Demo	VLF	Lg	AB	1.43	11.20	---	52.70	13.90	66.60	**87.70**
	Demo	VLF	Sm	LB	2.04	7.84	---	61.20	19.90	81.10	**106.00**
28" x 12"	Demo	VLF	Lg	AB	1.62	9.90	---	59.70	15.80	75.50	**99.30**
	Demo	VLF	Sm	LB	2.31	6.93	---	69.30	22.50	91.80	**120.00**
32" x 12"	Demo	VLF	Lg	AB	1.80	8.90	---	66.30	17.50	83.80	**110.00**
	Demo	VLF	Sm	LB	2.57	6.23	---	77.10	25.00	102.10	**133.00**
16" x 16"	Demo	VLF	Lg	AB	1.30	12.30	---	47.90	12.70	60.60	**79.70**
	Demo	VLF	Sm	AB	1.86	8.61	---	68.50	18.10	86.60	**114.00**
20" x 16"	Demo	VLF	Lg	AB	1.55	10.30	---	57.10	15.20	72.30	**95.10**
	Demo	VLF	Sm	AB	2.22	7.21	---	81.80	21.60	103.40	**136.00**
24" x 16"	Demo	VLF	Lg	AB	1.80	8.90	---	66.30	17.50	83.80	**110.00**
	Demo	VLF	Sm	AB	2.57	6.23	---	94.70	25.00	119.70	**158.00**
28" x 16"	Demo	VLF	Lg	AB	2.00	8.00	---	73.70	19.50	93.20	**123.00**
	Demo	VLF	Sm	AB	2.86	5.60	---	105.00	27.90	132.90	**175.00**
32" x 16"	Demo	VLF	Lg	AB	2.22	7.20	---	81.80	21.70	103.50	**136.00**
	Demo	VLF	Sm	AB	3.17	5.04	---	117.00	31.00	148.00	**194.00**
36" x 16"	Demo	VLF	Lg	AB	2.39	6.70	---	88.00	23.30	111.30	**147.00**
	Demo	VLF	Sm	AB	3.41	4.69	---	126.00	33.30	159.30	**209.00**
20" x 20"	Demo	VLF	Lg	AB	1.84	8.70	---	67.80	17.90	85.70	**113.00**
	Demo	VLF	Sm	AB	2.63	6.09	---	96.90	25.60	122.50	**161.00**
24" x 20"	Demo	VLF	Lg	AB	2.16	7.40	---	79.60	21.10	100.70	**132.00**
	Demo	VLF	Sm	AB	3.09	5.18	---	114.00	30.10	144.10	**189.00**
28" x 20"	Demo	VLF	Lg	AB	2.39	6.70	---	88.00	23.30	111.30	**147.00**
	Demo	VLF	Sm	AB	3.41	4.69	---	126.00	33.30	159.30	**209.00**
32" x 20"	Demo	VLF	Lg	AB	2.62	6.10	---	96.50	25.60	122.10	**161.00**
	Demo	VLF	Sm	AB	3.75	4.27	---	138.00	36.50	174.50	**230.00**
36" x 20"	Demo	VLF	Lg	AB	2.81	5.70	---	103.00	27.40	130.40	**172.00**
	Demo	VLF	Sm	AB	4.01	3.99	---	148.00	39.10	187.10	**246.00**
24" x 24"	Demo	VLF	Lg	AB	2.39	6.70	---	88.00	23.30	111.30	**147.00**
	Demo	VLF	Sm	AB	3.41	4.69	---	126.00	33.30	159.30	**209.00**
28" x 24"	Demo	VLF	Lg	AB	2.67	6.00	---	98.30	26.00	124.30	**164.00**
	Demo	VLF	Sm	AB	3.81	4.20	---	140.00	37.10	177.10	**234.00**
32" x 24"	Demo	VLF	Lg	AB	2.91	5.50	---	107.00	28.40	135.40	**178.00**
	Demo	VLF	Sm	AB	4.16	3.85	---	153.00	40.50	193.50	**255.00**
36" x 24"	Demo	VLF	Lg	AB	3.14	5.10	---	116.00	30.60	146.60	**192.00**
	Demo	VLF	Sm	AB	4.48	3.57	---	165.00	43.70	208.70	**275.00**

Description	Oper	Unit	Vol	Crew Size	Man-hours per Unit	Crew Output per Day	Avg Mat'l Unit Cost	Avg Labor Unit Cost	Avg Equip Unit Cost	Avg Total Unit Cost	Avg Price Incl O&P
28" x 28"	Demo	VLF	Lg	AB	2.96	5.40	---	109.00	28.90	137.90	**182.00**
	Demo	VLF	Sm	AB	4.23	3.78	---	156.00	41.30	197.30	**259.00**
32" x 28"	Demo	VLF	Lg	AB	3.27	4.90	---	120.00	31.80	151.80	**200.00**
	Demo	VLF	Sm	AB	4.66	3.43	---	172.00	45.50	217.50	**286.00**
36" x 28"	Demo	VLF	Lg	AB	3.56	4.50	---	131.00	34.70	165.70	**218.00**
	Demo	VLF	Sm	AB	5.08	3.15	---	187.00	49.50	236.50	**311.00**
32" x 32"	Demo	VLF	Lg	AB	3.56	4.50	---	131.00	34.70	165.70	**218.00**
	Demo	VLF	Sm	AB	5.08	3.15	---	187.00	49.50	236.50	**311.00**
36" x 32"	Demo	VLF	Lg	AB	3.90	4.10	---	144.00	38.10	182.10	**239.00**
	Demo	VLF	Sm	AB	5.57	2.87	---	205.00	54.40	259.40	**342.00**
36" x 36"	Demo	VLF	Lg	AB	4.21	3.80	---	155.00	41.10	196.10	**258.00**
	Demo	VLF	Sm	AB	6.02	2.66	---	222.00	58.70	280.70	**369.00**
8" x 8" (9.33 Brick/VLF)	Inst	VLF	Lg	BK	.415	38.60	6.11	13.60	2.25	21.96	**28.60**
	Inst	VLF	Sm	BK	.592	27.02	6.94	19.40	3.21	29.55	**38.70**
12" x 8" (14.00 Brick/VLF)	Inst	VLF	Lg	BK	.606	26.40	9.21	19.80	3.28	32.29	**42.00**
	Inst	VLF	Sm	BK	.866	18.48	10.50	28.30	4.69	43.49	**56.90**
16" x 8" (18.67 Brick/VLF)	Inst	VLF	Lg	BK	.784	20.40	12.30	25.70	4.25	42.25	**54.90**
	Inst	VLF	Sm	BK	1.12	14.28	14.00	36.70	6.07	56.77	**74.20**
20" x 8" (23.33 Brick/VLF)	Inst	VLF	Lg	BK	.958	16.70	15.30	31.40	5.19	51.89	**67.30**
	Inst	VLF	Sm	BK	1.37	11.69	17.40	44.80	7.41	69.61	**91.10**
24" x 8" (28.00 Brick/VLF)	Inst	VLF	Lg	BK	1.12	14.30	18.50	36.70	6.06	61.26	**79.30**
	Inst	VLF	Sm	BK	1.60	10.01	21.00	52.40	8.66	82.06	**107.00**
12" x 12" (21.00 Brick/VLF)	Inst	VLF	Lg	BK	.874	18.30	13.90	28.60	4.74	47.24	**61.30**
	Inst	VLF	Sm	BK	1.25	12.81	15.70	40.90	6.77	63.37	**82.90**
16" x 12" (28.00 Brick/VLF)	Inst	VLF	Lg	BK	1.12	14.30	18.50	36.70	6.06	61.26	**79.30**
	Inst	VLF	Sm	BK	1.60	10.01	21.00	52.40	8.66	82.06	**107.00**
20" x 12" (35.00 Brick/VLF)	Inst	VLF	Lg	BK	1.34	11.90	23.10	43.80	7.28	74.18	**96.10**
	Inst	VLF	Sm	BK	1.92	8.33	26.20	62.80	10.40	99.40	**130.00**
24" x 12" (42.00 Brick/VLF)	Inst	VLF	Lg	BK	1.57	10.20	27.60	51.40	8.50	87.50	**113.00**
	Inst	VLF	Sm	BK	2.24	7.14	31.30	73.30	12.10	116.70	**152.00**
28" x 12" (49.00 Brick/VLF)	Inst	VLF	Lg	BK	1.76	9.10	32.30	57.60	9.52	99.42	**128.00**
	Inst	VLF	Sm	BK	2.51	6.37	36.70	82.10	13.60	132.40	**172.00**
32" x 12" (56.00 Brick/VLF)	Inst	VLF	Lg	BK	1.95	8.20	36.90	63.80	10.60	111.30	**144.00**
	Inst	VLF	Sm	BK	2.79	5.74	41.90	91.30	15.10	148.30	**193.00**
16" x 16" (37.33 Brick/VLF)	Inst	VLF	Lg	BK	1.42	11.30	24.60	46.50	7.67	78.77	**102.00**
	Inst	VLF	Sm	BK	2.02	7.91	27.90	66.10	11.00	105.00	**137.00**
20" x 16" (46.67 Brick/VLF)	Inst	VLF	Lg	BK	1.70	9.40	30.80	55.60	9.22	95.62	**124.00**
	Inst	VLF	Sm	BK	2.43	6.58	35.00	79.50	13.20	127.70	**166.00**
24" x 16" (56.00 Brick/VLF)	Inst	VLF	Lg	BK	1.95	8.20	36.90	63.80	10.60	111.30	**144.00**
	Inst	VLF	Sm	BK	2.79	5.74	41.90	91.30	15.10	148.30	**193.00**
28" x 16" (65.33 Brick/VLF)	Inst	VLF	Lg	BK	2.16	7.40	43.00	70.70	11.70	125.40	**162.00**
	Inst	VLF	Sm	BK	3.09	5.18	48.80	101.00	16.70	166.50	**216.00**
32" x 16" (74.67 Brick/VLF)	Inst	VLF	Lg	BK	2.39	6.70	49.30	78.20	12.90	140.40	**181.00**
	Inst	VLF	Sm	BK	3.41	4.69	55.90	112.00	18.50	186.40	**241.00**
36" x 16" (84.00 Brick/VLF)	Inst	VLF	Lg	BK	2.58	6.20	55.40	84.40	14.00	153.80	**198.00**
	Inst	VLF	Sm	BK	3.69	4.34	62.90	121.00	20.00	203.90	**264.00**

Description	Oper	Unit	Vol	Crew Size	Man-hours per Unit	Crew Output per Day	Avg Mat'l Unit Cost	Avg Labor Unit Cost	Avg Equip Unit Cost	Avg Total Unit Cost	Avg Price Incl O&P
20" x 20" (58.33 Brick/VLF)	Inst	VLF	Lg	BK	2.00	8.00	38.50	65.40	10.80	114.70	**148.00**
	Inst	VLF	Sm	BK	2.86	5.60	43.70	93.60	15.50	152.80	**199.00**
24" x 20" (70.00 Brick/VLF)	Inst	VLF	Lg	BK	2.32	6.90	46.00	75.90	12.60	134.50	**173.00**
	Inst	VLF	Sm	BK	3.31	4.83	52.20	108.00	17.90	178.10	**232.00**
28" x 20" (81.67 Brick/VLF)	Inst	VLF	Lg	BK	2.58	6.20	53.80	84.40	14.00	152.20	**196.00**
	Inst	VLF	Sm	BK	3.69	4.34	61.00	121.00	20.00	202.00	**262.00**
32" x 20" (93.33 Brick/VLF)	Inst	VLF	Lg	BK	2.81	5.70	61.50	91.90	15.20	168.60	**216.00**
	Inst	VLF	Sm	BK	4.01	3.99	69.80	131.00	21.70	222.50	**288.00**
36" x 20" (105.00 Brick/VLF)	Inst	VLF	Lg	BK	3.02	5.30	69.20	98.80	16.40	184.40	**236.00**
	Inst	VLF	Sm	BK	4.31	3.71	78.60	141.00	23.40	243.00	**314.00**
24" x 24" (84.00 Brick/VLF)	Inst	VLF	Lg	BK	2.58	6.20	55.40	84.40	14.00	153.80	**198.00**
	Inst	VLF	Sm	BK	3.69	4.34	62.90	121.00	20.00	203.90	**264.00**
28" x 24" (98.00 Brick/VLF)	Inst	VLF	Lg	BK	2.86	5.60	64.50	93.60	15.50	173.60	**223.00**
	Inst	VLF	Sm	BK	4.08	3.92	73.20	134.00	22.10	229.30	**296.00**
32" x 24" (112.00 Brick/VLF)	Inst	VLF	Lg	BK	3.08	5.20	73.80	101.00	16.70	191.50	**245.00**
	Inst	VLF	Sm	BK	4.40	3.64	83.80	144.00	23.80	251.60	**325.00**
36" x 24" (126.00 Brick/VLF)	Inst	VLF	Lg	BK	3.33	4.80	82.90	109.00	18.10	210.00	**268.00**
	Inst	VLF	Sm	BK	4.76	3.36	94.10	156.00	25.80	275.90	**355.00**
28" x 28" (114.33 Brick/VLF)	Inst	VLF	Lg	BK	3.20	5.00	75.40	105.00	17.30	197.70	**253.00**
	Inst	VLF	Sm	BK	4.57	3.50	85.60	150.00	24.80	260.40	**336.00**
32" x 28" (130.67 Brick/VLF)	Inst	VLF	Lg	BK	3.48	4.60	86.20	114.00	18.80	219.00	**280.00**
	Inst	VLF	Sm	BK	4.97	3.22	97.80	163.00	26.90	287.70	**370.00**
36" x 28" (147.00 Brick/VLF)	Inst	VLF	Lg	BK	3.90	4.10	96.90	128.00	21.10	246.00	**314.00**
	Inst	VLF	Sm	BK	5.57	2.87	110.00	182.00	30.20	322.20	**415.00**
32" x 32" (149.33 Brick/VLF)	Inst	VLF	Lg	BK	4.00	4.00	98.40	131.00	21.70	251.10	**321.00**
	Inst	VLF	Sm	BK	5.71	2.80	112.00	187.00	31.00	330.00	**425.00**
36" x 32" (168.00 Brick/VLF)	Inst	VLF	Lg	BK	4.44	3.60	111.00	145.00	24.10	280.10	**358.00**
	Inst	VLF	Sm	BK	6.35	2.52	126.00	208.00	34.40	368.40	**474.00**
36" x 36" (189.00 Brick/VLF)	Inst	VLF	Lg	BK	5.00	3.20	124.00	164.00	27.10	315.10	**402.00**
	Inst	VLF	Sm	BK	7.14	2.24	141.00	234.00	38.70	413.70	**533.00**

Veneers

4" T, with air tools

Description	Oper	Unit	Vol	Crew Size	Man-hours per Unit	Crew Output per Day	Avg Mat'l Unit Cost	Avg Labor Unit Cost	Avg Equip Unit Cost	Avg Total Unit Cost	Avg Price Incl O&P
	Demo	SF	Lg	AB	.049	325.0	---	1.80	.48	2.28	**3.01**
	Demo	SF	Sm	AB	.070	227.5	---	2.58	.69	3.27	**4.30**

4" T, with wall ties; no scaffolding included

Description	Oper	Unit	Vol	Crew Size	Man-hours per Unit	Crew Output per Day	Avg Mat'l Unit Cost	Avg Labor Unit Cost	Avg Equip Unit Cost	Avg Total Unit Cost	Avg Price Incl O&P
Common, 8" x 2-2/3" x 4"	Inst	SF	Lg	BD	.170	235.0	3.60	5.73	.37	9.70	**12.60**
	Inst	SF	Sm	BO	.195	164.5	4.07	6.38	.53	10.98	**14.30**
Standard face, 8" x 2-2/3" x 4'	Inst	SF	Lg	BD	.182	220.0	4.47	6.13	.39	10.99	**14.20**
	Inst	SF	Sm	BO	.208	154.0	5.08	6.81	.56	12.45	**16.10**
Glazed, 8" x 2-2/3" x 4"	Inst	SF	Lg	BD	.190	210.0	8.39	6.40	.41	15.20	**19.20**
	Inst	SF	Sm	BO	.218	147.0	9.53	7.13	.59	17.25	**21.70**

Description	Oper	Unit	Vol	Crew Size	Man-hours per Unit	Crew Output per Day	Avg Mat'l Unit Cost	Avg Labor Unit Cost	Avg Equip Unit Cost	Avg Total Unit Cost	Avg Price Incl O&P
Other brick types/sizes											
8" x 3-1/5" x 4"	Inst	SF	Lg	BD	.151	265.0	4.42	5.09	.33	9.84	**12.60**
	Inst	SF	Sm	BO	.173	185.5	5.02	5.66	.47	11.15	**14.30**
8" x 4" x 4"	Inst	SF	Lg	BD	.127	315.0	3.03	4.28	.28	7.59	**9.84**
	Inst	SF	Sm	BO	.145	220.5	3.47	4.74	.39	8.60	**11.10**
12" x 4" x 6"	Inst	SF	Lg	BD	.091	440.0	4.58	3.07	.20	7.85	**9.82**
	Inst	SF	Sm	BO	.104	308.0	5.20	3.40	.28	8.88	**11.10**
12" x 2-2/3" x 4"	Inst	SF	Lg	BD	.123	325.0	5.37	4.14	.27	9.78	**12.30**
	Inst	SF	Sm	BO	.141	227.5	6.08	4.61	.38	11.07	**13.90**
12" x 3-1/5" x 4"	Inst	SF	Lg	BD	.107	375.0	3.26	3.60	.23	7.09	**9.10**
	Inst	SF	Sm	BO	.122	262.5	3.67	3.99	.33	7.99	**10.20**
12" x 2" x 4"	Inst	SF	Lg	BD	.160	250.0	5.58	5.39	.35	11.32	**14.40**
	Inst	SF	Sm	BO	.183	175.0	6.38	5.99	.50	12.87	**16.30**
12" x 2-2/3" x 6"	Inst	SF	Lg	BD	.127	315.0	4.52	4.28	.28	9.08	**11.60**
	Inst	SF	Sm	BO	.145	220.5	5.13	4.74	.39	10.26	**13.00**
12" x 4" x 4"	Inst	SF	Lg	BD	.089	450.0	3.56	3.00	.19	6.75	**8.54**
	Inst	SF	Sm	BO	.102	315.0	4.03	3.34	.28	7.65	**9.65**

Walls

With air tools

Description	Oper	Unit	Vol	Crew Size	Man-hours per Unit	Crew Output per Day	Avg Mat'l Unit Cost	Avg Labor Unit Cost	Avg Equip Unit Cost	Avg Total Unit Cost	Avg Price Incl O&P
8" T	Demo	SF	Lg	AB	.086	185.0	---	3.17	.84	4.01	**5.27**
	Demo	SF	Sm	AB	.124	129.5	---	4.57	1.20	5.77	**7.59**
12" T	Demo	SF	Lg	AB	.123	130.0	---	4.53	1.20	5.73	**7.54**
	Demo	SF	Sm	AB	.176	91.00	---	6.48	1.71	8.19	**10.80**
16" T	Demo	SF	Lg	AB	.160	100.0	---	5.89	1.56	7.45	**9.81**
	Demo	SF	Sm	AB	.229	70.00	---	8.43	2.23	10.66	**14.00**
24" T	Demo	SF	Lg	AB	.188	85.00	---	6.92	1.84	8.76	**11.50**
	Demo	SF	Sm	AB	.269	59.50	---	9.91	2.62	12.53	**16.50**

With common brick; no scaffolding included

Description	Oper	Unit	Vol	Crew Size	Man-hours per Unit	Crew Output per Day	Avg Mat'l Unit Cost	Avg Labor Unit Cost	Avg Equip Unit Cost	Avg Total Unit Cost	Avg Price Incl O&P
8" T (13.50 Brick/SF)	Inst	SF	Lg	BO	.337	95.00	7.08	11.00	.91	18.99	**24.70**
	Inst	SF	Sm	ML	.361	66.50	8.01	12.40	1.30	21.71	**28.10**
12" T (20.25 Brick/SF)	Inst	SF	Lg	BO	.457	70.00	10.80	15.00	1.24	27.04	**34.90**
	Inst	SF	Sm	ML	.490	49.00	12.20	16.80	1.77	30.77	**39.70**
16" T (27.00 Brick/SF)	Inst	SF	Lg	BO	.582	55.00	14.40	19.00	1.58	34.98	**45.20**
	Inst	SF	Sm	ML	.623	38.50	16.30	21.40	2.25	39.95	**51.40**
24" T (40.50 Brick/SF)	Inst	SF	Lg	BO	.800	40.00	21.50	26.20	2.17	49.87	**64.10**
	Inst	SF	Sm	ML	.857	28.00	24.30	29.40	3.10	56.80	**72.90**

Description	Oper	Unit	Vol	Crew Size	Man-hours per Unit	Crew Output per Day	Avg Mat'l Unit Cost	Avg Labor Unit Cost	Avg Equip Unit Cost	Avg Total Unit Cost	Avg Price Incl O&P

Brick, adobe

Running bond, 3/8" mortar joints

Walls, with air tools

Description	Oper	Unit	Vol	Crew Size	Man-hours per Unit	Crew Output per Day	Avg Mat'l Unit Cost	Avg Labor Unit Cost	Avg Equip Unit Cost	Avg Total Unit Cost	Avg Price Incl O&P
4" T	Demo	SF	Lg	AB	.041	390.0	---	1.51	.40	1.91	**2.51**
	Demo	SF	Sm	AB	.059	273.0	---	2.17	.57	2.74	**3.61**
6" T	Demo	SF	Lg	AB	.042	380.0	---	1.55	.41	1.96	**2.58**
	Demo	SF	Sm	AB	.060	266.0	---	2.21	.59	2.80	**3.68**
8" T	Demo	SF	Lg	AB	.043	370.0	---	1.58	.42	2.00	**2.64**
	Demo	SF	Sm	AB	.062	259.0	---	2.28	.60	2.88	**3.80**
12" T	Demo	SF	Lg	AB	.046	350.0	---	1.69	.45	2.14	**2.82**
	Demo	SF	Sm	AB	.065	245.0	---	2.39	.64	3.03	**3.99**

Walls, no scaffolding included

Description	Oper	Unit	Vol	Crew Size	Man-hours per Unit	Crew Output per Day	Avg Mat'l Unit Cost	Avg Labor Unit Cost	Avg Equip Unit Cost	Avg Total Unit Cost	Avg Price Incl O&P
4" x 4" x 16"	Inst	SF	Lg	BO	.139	230.0	4.71	4.55	.38	9.64	**12.30**
	Inst	SF	Sm	ML	.149	161.0	5.35	5.12	.54	11.01	**14.00**
6" x 4" x 16"	Inst	SF	Lg	BO	.145	220.0	5.44	4.74	.39	10.57	**13.40**
	Inst	SF	Sm	ML	.156	154.0	5.35	5.36	.56	11.27	**14.30**
8" x 4" x 16"	Inst	SF	Lg	BO	.152	210.0	6.54	4.97	.41	11.92	**15.00**
	Inst	SF	Sm	ML	.163	147.0	7.43	5.60	.59	13.62	**17.10**
12" x 4" x 16"	Inst	SF	Lg	BO	.168	190.0	9.87	5.50	.46	15.83	**19.60**
	Inst	SF	Sm	ML	.180	133.0	11.20	6.18	.65	18.03	**22.30**

Concrete block

Lightweight (haydite) or heavyweight blocks; 2 cores/block, solid face; includes allowances for lintels, bond beams

Foundations and retaining walls

No excavation included

Without reinforcing or with lateral reinforcing only

With air tools

Description	Oper	Unit	Vol	Crew Size	Man-hours per Unit	Crew Output per Day	Avg Mat'l Unit Cost	Avg Labor Unit Cost	Avg Equip Unit Cost	Avg Total Unit Cost	Avg Price Incl O&P
8" W x 8" H x 16" L	Demo	SF	Lg	AB	.048	335.0	---	1.77	.47	2.24	**2.94**
	Demo	SF	Sm	AB	.068	234.5	---	2.50	.67	3.17	**4.18**
10" W x 8" H x 16" L	Demo	SF	Lg	AB	.052	310.0	---	1.92	.50	2.42	**3.18**
	Demo	SF	Sm	AB	.074	217.0	---	2.73	.72	3.45	**4.54**
12" W x 8" H x 16" L	Demo	SF	Lg	AB	.055	290.0	---	2.03	.54	2.57	**3.38**
	Demo	SF	Sm	AB	.079	203.0	---	2.91	.77	3.68	**4.84**

Without air tools

Description	Oper	Unit	Vol	Crew Size	Man-hours per Unit	Crew Output per Day	Avg Mat'l Unit Cost	Avg Labor Unit Cost	Avg Equip Unit Cost	Avg Total Unit Cost	Avg Price Incl O&P
8" W x 8" H x 16" L	Demo	SF	Lg	LB	.059	270.0	---	1.77	---	1.77	**2.48**
	Demo	SF	Sm	LB	.085	189.0	---	2.55	---	2.55	**3.57**
10" W x 8" H x 16" L	Demo	SF	Lg	LB	.064	250.0	---	1.92	---	1.92	**2.69**
	Demo	SF	Sm	LB	.091	175.0	---	2.73	---	2.73	**3.82**
12" W x 8" H x 16" L	Demo	SF	Lg	LB	.070	230.0	---	2.10	---	2.10	**2.94**
	Demo	SF	Sm	LB	.099	161.0	---	2.97	---	2.97	**4.16**

With vertical reinforcing in every other core (2 core blocks) with core concrete filled

With air tools

Description	Oper	Unit	Vol	Crew Size	Man-hours per Unit	Crew Output per Day	Avg Mat'l Unit Cost	Avg Labor Unit Cost	Avg Equip Unit Cost	Avg Total Unit Cost	Avg Price Incl O&P
8" W x 8" H x 16" L	Demo	SF	Lg	AB	.078	205.0	---	2.87	.76	3.63	**4.78**
	Demo	SF	Sm	AB	.111	143.5	---	4.09	1.09	5.18	**6.81**
10" W x 8" H x 16" L	Demo	SF	Lg	AB	.084	190.0	---	3.09	.82	3.91	**5.15**
	Demo	SF	Sm	AB	.120	133.0	---	4.42	1.17	5.59	**7.36**
12" W x 8" H x 16" L	Demo	SF	Lg	AB	.091	175.0	---	3.35	.89	4.24	**5.58**
	Demo	SF	Sm	AB	.131	122.5	---	4.82	1.27	6.09	**8.02**

Description	Oper	Unit	Vol	Crew Size	Man-hours per Unit	Crew Output per Day	Avg Mat'l Unit Cost	Avg Labor Unit Cost	Avg Equip Unit Cost	Avg Total Unit Cost	Avg Price Incl O&P
No reinforcing											
Heavyweight blocks											
8" x 8" x 16"	Inst	SF	Lg	BD	.127	315.0	3.00	4.28	.28	7.56	**9.81**
	Inst	SF	Sm	BO	.145	220.5	3.41	4.74	.39	8.54	**11.10**
10" x 8" x 16"	Inst	SF	Lg	BD	.138	290.0	4.22	4.65	.30	9.17	**11.80**
	Inst	SF	Sm	BO	.158	203.0	4.79	5.17	.43	10.39	**13.30**
12" x 8" x 16"	Inst	SF	Lg	BD	.151	265.0	4.15	5.09	.33	9.57	**12.30**
	Inst	SF	Sm	BO	.173	185.5	4.73	5.66	.47	10.86	**14.00**
Lightweight blocks											
8" x 8" x 16"	Inst	SF	Lg	BD	.114	350.0	3.13	3.84	.25	7.22	**9.30**
	Inst	SF	Sm	BO	.131	245.0	3.56	4.29	.35	8.20	**10.50**
10" x 8" x 16"	Inst	SF	Lg	BD	.125	320.0	4.53	4.21	.27	9.01	**11.50**
	Inst	SF	Sm	BO	.143	224.0	5.15	4.68	.39	10.22	**13.00**
12" x 8" x 16"	Inst	SF	Lg	BD	.136	295.0	4.53	4.58	.29	9.40	**12.00**
	Inst	SF	Sm	BO	.155	206.5	5.15	5.07	.42	10.64	**13.50**
Lateral reinforcing every second course											
Heavyweight blocks											
8" x 8" x 16"	Inst	SF	Lg	BD	.133	300.0	3.00	4.48	.29	7.77	**10.10**
	Inst	SF	Sm	BO	.152	210.0	3.41	4.97	.41	8.79	**11.40**
10" x 8" x 16"	Inst	SF	Lg	BD	.145	275.0	4.22	4.89	.32	9.43	**12.10**
	Inst	SF	Sm	BO	.166	192.5	4.79	5.43	.45	10.67	**13.70**
12" x 8" x 16"	Inst	SF	Lg	BD	.160	250.0	4.15	5.39	.35	9.89	**12.80**
	Inst	SF	Sm	BO	.183	175.0	4.73	5.99	.50	11.22	**14.40**
Lightweight blocks											
8" x 8" x 16"	Inst	SF	Lg	BD	.119	335.0	3.13	4.01	.26	7.40	**9.55**
	Inst	SF	Sm	BO	.136	234.5	3.56	4.45	.37	8.38	**10.80**
10" x 8" x 16"	Inst	SF	Lg	BD	.131	305.0	4.53	4.41	.28	9.22	**11.80**
	Inst	SF	Sm	BO	.150	213.5	5.15	4.91	.41	10.47	**13.30**
12" x 8" x 16"	Inst	SF	Lg	BD	.143	280.0	4.53	4.82	.31	9.66	**12.40**
	Inst	SF	Sm	BO	.163	196.0	5.15	5.33	.44	10.92	**13.90**
Vertical reinforcing (No. 4 rod) every second core with core concrete filled											
Heavyweight blocks											
8" x 8" x 16"	Inst	SF	Lg	BD	.182	220.0	6.38	6.13	.39	12.90	**16.40**
	Inst	SF	Sm	BD	.260	154.0	7.25	8.76	.56	16.57	**21.30**
10" x 8" x 16"	Inst	SF	Lg	BD	.200	200.0	7.71	6.74	.43	14.88	**18.90**
	Inst	SF	Sm	BD	.286	140.0	8.76	9.64	.62	19.02	**24.40**
12" x 8" x 16"	Inst	SF	Lg	BD	.216	185.0	8.79	7.28	.47	16.54	**20.90**
	Inst	SF	Sm	BD	.309	129.5	10.00	10.40	.67	21.07	**27.00**
Lightweight blocks											
8" x 8" x 16"	Inst	SF	Lg	BD	.167	240.0	6.51	5.63	.36	12.50	**15.80**
	Inst	SF	Sm	BD	.238	168.0	7.40	8.02	.52	15.94	**20.40**
10" x 8" x 16"	Inst	SF	Lg	BD	.182	220.0	8.02	6.13	.39	14.54	**18.30**
	Inst	SF	Sm	BD	.260	154.0	9.12	8.76	.56	18.44	**23.50**
12" x 8" x 16"	Inst	SF	Lg	BD	.200	200.0	9.16	6.74	.43	16.33	**20.50**
	Inst	SF	Sm	BD	.286	140.0	10.40	9.64	.62	20.66	**26.30**

Description	Oper	Unit	Vol	Crew Size	Man-hours per Unit	Crew Output per Day	Avg Mat'l Unit Cost	Avg Labor Unit Cost	Avg Equip Unit Cost	Avg Total Unit Cost	Avg Price Incl O&P

Exterior walls (above grade)

No bracing or shoring included
Without reinforcing or with lateral reinforcing only

With air tools

Description	Oper	Unit	Vol	Crew Size	Man-hours per Unit	Crew Output per Day	Avg Mat'l Unit Cost	Avg Labor Unit Cost	Avg Equip Unit Cost	Avg Total Unit Cost	Avg Price Incl O&P
8" W x 8" H x 16" L	Demo	SF	Lg	AB	.048	335.0	---	1.77	.47	2.24	**2.94**
	Demo	SF	Sm	AB	.068	234.5	---	2.50	.67	3.17	**4.18**
10" W x 8" H x 16" L	Demo	SF	Lg	AB	.052	305.0	---	1.92	.51	2.43	**3.19**
	Demo	SF	Sm	AB	.075	213.5	---	2.76	.73	3.49	**4.60**
12" W x 8" H x 16" L	Demo	SF	Lg	AB	.058	275.0	---	2.14	.57	2.71	**3.56**
	Demo	SF	Sm	AB	.083	192.5	---	3.06	.81	3.87	**5.09**

Without air tools

Description	Oper	Unit	Vol	Crew Size	Man-hours per Unit	Crew Output per Day	Avg Mat'l Unit Cost	Avg Labor Unit Cost	Avg Equip Unit Cost	Avg Total Unit Cost	Avg Price Incl O&P
8" W x 8" H x 16" L	Demo	SF	Lg	LB	.060	265.0	---	1.80	---	1.80	**2.52**
	Demo	SF	Sm	LB	.086	185.5	---	2.58	---	2.58	**3.61**
10" W x 8" H x 16" L	Demo	SF	Lg	LB	.067	240.0	---	2.01	---	2.01	**2.81**
	Demo	SF	Sm	LB	.095	168.0	---	2.85	---	2.85	**3.99**
12" W x 8" H x 16" L	Demo	SF	Lg	LB	.073	220.0	---	2.19	---	2.19	**3.07**
	Demo	SF	Sm	LB	.104	154.0	---	3.12	---	3.12	**4.37**

No reinforcing
Heavyweight blocks

Description	Oper	Unit	Vol	Crew Size	Man-hours per Unit	Crew Output per Day	Avg Mat'l Unit Cost	Avg Labor Unit Cost	Avg Equip Unit Cost	Avg Total Unit Cost	Avg Price Incl O&P
8" x 8" x 16"	Inst	SF	Lg	BD	.136	295.0	3.00	4.58	.29	7.87	**10.30**
	Inst	SF	Sm	BO	.155	206.5	3.41	5.07	.42	8.90	**11.50**
10" x 8" x 16"	Inst	SF	Lg	BD	.148	270.0	4.22	4.99	.32	9.53	**12.30**
	Inst	SF	Sm	BO	.169	189.0	4.79	5.53	.46	10.78	**13.80**
12" x 8" x 16"	Inst	SF	Lg	BD	.160	250.0	4.15	5.39	.35	9.89	**12.80**
	Inst	SF	Sm	BO	.183	175.0	4.73	5.99	.50	11.22	**14.40**

Lightweight blocks

Description	Oper	Unit	Vol	Crew Size	Man-hours per Unit	Crew Output per Day	Avg Mat'l Unit Cost	Avg Labor Unit Cost	Avg Equip Unit Cost	Avg Total Unit Cost	Avg Price Incl O&P
8" x 8" x 16"	Inst	SF	Lg	BD	.121	330.0	3.13	4.08	.26	7.47	**9.65**
	Inst	SF	Sm	BO	.139	231.0	3.56	4.55	.38	8.49	**10.90**
10" x 8" x 16"	Inst	SF	Lg	BD	.131	305.0	4.53	4.41	.28	9.22	**11.80**
	Inst	SF	Sm	BO	.150	213.5	4.63	4.91	.41	9.95	**12.70**
12" x 8" x 16"	Inst	SF	Lg	BD	.143	280.0	4.53	4.82	.31	9.66	**12.40**
	Inst	SF	Sm	BO	.163	196.0	5.15	5.33	.44	10.92	**13.90**

Lateral reinforcing every second course
Heavyweight blocks

Description	Oper	Unit	Vol	Crew Size	Man-hours per Unit	Crew Output per Day	Avg Mat'l Unit Cost	Avg Labor Unit Cost	Avg Equip Unit Cost	Avg Total Unit Cost	Avg Price Incl O&P
8" x 8" x 16"	Inst	SF	Lg	BD	.143	280.0	3.00	4.82	.31	8.13	**10.60**
	Inst	SF	Sm	BO	.163	196.0	3.41	5.33	.44	9.18	**11.90**
10" x 8" x 16"	Inst	SF	Lg	BD	.154	260.0	4.22	5.19	.33	9.74	**12.60**
	Inst	SF	Sm	BO	.176	182.0	4.79	5.76	.48	11.03	**14.20**
12" x 8" x 16"	Inst	SF	Lg	BD	.167	240.0	4.15	5.63	.36	10.14	**13.10**
	Inst	SF	Sm	BO	.190	168.0	4.73	6.22	.52	11.47	**14.80**

Lightweight blocks

Description	Oper	Unit	Vol	Crew Size	Man-hours per Unit	Crew Output per Day	Avg Mat'l Unit Cost	Avg Labor Unit Cost	Avg Equip Unit Cost	Avg Total Unit Cost	Avg Price Incl O&P
8" x 8" x 16"	Inst	SF	Lg	BD	.127	315.0	3.13	4.28	.28	7.69	**9.96**
	Inst	SF	Sm	BO	.145	220.5	3.56	4.74	.39	8.69	**11.20**
10" x 8" x 16"	Inst	SF	Lg	BD	.138	290.0	4.27	4.65	.30	9.22	**11.80**
	Inst	SF	Sm	BO	.158	203.0	4.63	5.17	.43	10.23	**13.10**
12" x 8" x 16"	Inst	SF	Lg	BD	.151	265.0	4.53	5.09	.33	9.95	**12.80**
	Inst	SF	Sm	BO	.173	185.5	5.15	5.66	.47	11.28	**14.40**

Description	Oper	Unit	Vol	Crew Size	Man-hours per Unit	Crew Output per Day	Avg Mat'l Unit Cost	Avg Labor Unit Cost	Avg Equip Unit Cost	Avg Total Unit Cost	Avg Price Incl O&P
Partitions (above grade)											
No bracing or shoring included											
Without reinforcing or with lateral reinforcing only											
With air tools											
4" W x 8" H x 16" L	Demo	SF	Lg	AB	.048	330.0	---	1.77	.47	2.24	**2.94**
	Demo	SF	Sm	AB	.069	231.0	---	2.54	.68	3.22	**4.24**
6" W x 8" H x 16" L	Demo	SF	Lg	AB	.052	310.0	---	1.92	.50	2.42	**3.18**
	Demo	SF	Sm	AB	.074	217.0	---	2.73	.72	3.45	**4.54**
8" W x 8" H x 16" L	Demo	SF	Lg	AB	.054	295.0	---	1.99	.53	2.52	**3.31**
	Demo	SF	Sm	AB	.077	206.5	---	2.84	.76	3.60	**4.73**
10" W x 8" H x 16" L	Demo	SF	Lg	AB	.060	265.0	---	2.21	.59	2.80	**3.68**
	Demo	SF	Sm	AB	.086	185.5	---	3.17	.84	4.01	**5.27**
12" W x 8" H x 16" L	Demo	SF	Lg	AB	.068	235.0	---	2.50	.66	3.16	**4.17**
	Demo	SF	Sm	AB	.097	164.5	---	3.57	.95	4.52	**5.95**
No reinforcing											
Heavyweight blocks											
4" W x 8" H x 16" L	Inst	SF	Lg	BD	.129	310.0	1.90	4.35	.28	6.53	**8.64**
	Inst	SF	Sm	BO	.147	217.0	2.15	4.81	.40	7.36	**9.70**
6" W x 8" H x 16" L	Inst	SF	Lg	BD	.138	290.0	2.33	4.65	.30	7.28	**9.58**
	Inst	SF	Sm	BO	.158	203.0	2.65	5.17	.43	8.25	**10.80**
8" W x 8" H x 16" L	Inst	SF	Lg	BD	.151	265.0	3.00	5.09	.33	8.42	**11.00**
	Inst	SF	Sm	BO	.173	185.5	3.41	5.66	.47	9.54	**12.40**
10" W x 8" H x 16" L	Inst	SF	Lg	BD	.163	245.0	4.22	5.49	.35	10.06	**13.00**
	Inst	SF	Sm	BO	.187	171.5	4.79	6.12	.51	11.42	**14.70**
12" W x 8" H x 16" L	Inst	SF	Lg	BD	.178	225.0	4.15	6.00	.39	10.54	**13.70**
	Inst	SF	Sm	BO	.203	157.5	4.73	6.64	.55	11.92	**15.40**
Lightweight blocks											
4" W x 8" H x 16" L	Inst	SF	Lg	BD	.119	335.0	1.90	4.01	.26	6.17	**8.14**
	Inst	SF	Sm	BO	.136	234.5	2.15	4.45	.37	6.97	**9.16**
6" W x 8" H x 16" L	Inst	SF	Lg	BD	.127	315.0	2.46	4.28	.28	7.02	**9.18**
	Inst	SF	Sm	BO	.145	220.5	2.79	4.74	.39	7.92	**10.30**
8" W x 8" H x 16" L	Inst	SF	Lg	BD	.136	295.0	3.13	4.58	.29	8.00	**10.40**
	Inst	SF	Sm	BO	.155	206.5	3.56	5.07	.42	9.05	**11.70**
10" W x 8" H x 16" L	Inst	SF	Lg	BD	.148	270.0	4.53	4.99	.32	9.84	**12.60**
	Inst	SF	Sm	BO	.169	189.0	4.63	5.53	.46	10.62	**13.60**
12" W x 8" H x 16" L	Inst	SF	Lg	BD	.160	250.0	4.53	5.39	.35	10.27	**13.20**
	Inst	SF	Sm	BO	.183	175.0	5.15	5.99	.50	11.64	**14.90**
Lateral reinforcing every second course											
Heavyweight blocks											
4" W x 8" H x 16" L	Inst	SF	Lg	BD	.136	295.0	1.90	4.58	.29	6.77	**8.98**
	Inst	SF	Sm	BO	.155	206.5	2.15	5.07	.42	7.64	**10.10**
6" W x 8" H x 16" L	Inst	SF	Lg	BD	.145	275.0	2.33	4.89	.32	7.54	**9.94**
	Inst	SF	Sm	BO	.166	192.5	2.65	5.43	.45	8.53	**11.20**

Description	Oper	Unit	Vol	Crew Size	Man-hours per Unit	Crew Output per Day	Avg Mat'l Unit Cost	Avg Labor Unit Cost	Avg Equip Unit Cost	Avg Total Unit Cost	Avg Price Incl O&P
8" W x 8" H x 16" L	Inst	SF	Lg	BD	.160	250.0	3.00	5.39	.35	8.74	**11.50**
	Inst	SF	Sm	BO	.183	175.0	3.41	5.99	.50	9.90	**12.90**
10" W x 8" H x 16" L	Inst	SF	Lg	BD	.174	230.0	4.22	5.86	.38	10.46	**13.60**
	Inst	SF	Sm	BO	.199	161.0	4.79	6.51	.54	11.84	**15.30**
12" W x 8" H x 16" L	Inst	SF	Lg	BD	.190	210.0	4.15	6.40	.41	10.96	**14.30**
	Inst	SF	Sm	BO	.218	147.0	4.73	7.13	.59	12.45	**16.20**
Lightweight blocks											
4" W x 8" H x 16" L	Inst	SF	Lg	BD	.125	320.0	1.90	4.21	.27	6.38	**8.44**
	Inst	SF	Sm	BO	.143	224.0	2.15	4.68	.39	7.22	**9.51**
6" W x 8" H x 16" L	Inst	SF	Lg	BD	.133	300.0	2.46	4.48	.29	7.23	**9.48**
	Inst	SF	Sm	BO	.152	210.0	2.79	4.97	.41	8.17	**10.70**
8" W x 8" H x 16" L	Inst	SF	Lg	BD	.143	280.0	3.13	4.82	.31	8.26	**10.80**
	Inst	SF	Sm	BO	.163	196.0	3.56	5.33	.44	9.33	**12.10**
10" W x 8" H x 16" L	Inst	SF	Lg	BD	.154	260.0	4.53	5.19	.33	10.05	**12.90**
	Inst	SF	Sm	BO	.176	182.0	4.63	5.76	.48	10.87	**14.00**
12" W x 8" H x 16" L	Inst	SF	Lg	BD	.167	240.0	4.53	5.63	.36	10.52	**13.60**
	Inst	SF	Sm	BO	.190	168.0	5.15	6.22	.52	11.89	**15.30**

Fences

Without reinforcing or with lateral reinforcing only

With air tools

Description	Oper	Unit	Vol	Crew Size	Man-hours per Unit	Crew Output per Day	Avg Mat'l Unit Cost	Avg Labor Unit Cost	Avg Equip Unit Cost	Avg Total Unit Cost	Avg Price Incl O&P
6" W x 4" H x 16" L	Demo	SF	Lg	AB	.041	390.0	---	1.51	.40	1.91	**2.51**
	Demo	SF	Sm	AB	.059	273.0	---	2.17	.57	2.74	**3.61**
6" W x 6" H x 16" L	Demo	SF	Lg	AB	.043	370.0	---	1.58	.42	2.00	**2.64**
	Demo	SF	Sm	AB	.062	259.0	---	2.28	.60	2.88	**3.80**
8" W x 8" H x 16" L	Demo	SF	Lg	AB	.046	350.0	---	1.69	.45	2.14	**2.82**
	Demo	SF	Sm	AB	.065	245.0	---	2.39	.64	3.03	**3.99**
10" W x 8" H x 16" L	Demo	SF	Lg	AB	.049	325.0	---	1.80	.48	2.28	**3.01**
	Demo	SF	Sm	AB	.070	227.5	---	2.58	.69	3.27	**4.30**
12" W x 8" H x 16" L	Demo	SF	Lg	AB	.053	300.0	---	1.95	.52	2.47	**3.25**
	Demo	SF	Sm	AB	.076	210.0	---	2.80	.74	3.54	**4.66**

Without air tools

Description	Oper	Unit	Vol	Crew Size	Man-hours per Unit	Crew Output per Day	Avg Mat'l Unit Cost	Avg Labor Unit Cost	Avg Equip Unit Cost	Avg Total Unit Cost	Avg Price Incl O&P
6" W x 4" H x 16" L	Demo	SF	Lg	LB	.052	310.0	---	1.56	---	1.56	**2.18**
	Demo	SF	Sm	LB	.074	217.0	---	2.22	---	2.22	**3.11**
6" W x 6" H x 16" L	Demo	SF	Lg	LB	.054	295.0	---	1.62	---	1.62	**2.27**
	Demo	SF	Sm	LB	.077	206.5	---	2.31	---	2.31	**3.23**
8" W x 8" H x 16" L	Demo	SF	Lg	LB	.057	280.0	---	1.71	---	1.71	**2.39**
	Demo	SF	Sm	LB	.082	196.0	---	2.46	---	2.46	**3.44**
10" W x 8" H x 16" L	Demo	SF	Lg	LB	.073	220.0	---	2.19	---	2.19	**3.07**
	Demo	SF	Sm	LB	.104	154.0	---	3.12	---	3.12	**4.37**
12" W x 8" H x 16" L	Demo	SF	Lg	LB	.067	240.0	---	2.01	---	2.01	**2.81**
	Demo	SF	Sm	LB	.095	168.0	---	2.85	---	2.85	**3.99**

Description	Oper	Unit	Vol	Crew Size	Man-hours per Unit	Crew Output per Day	Avg Mat'l Unit Cost	Avg Labor Unit Cost	Avg Equip Unit Cost	Avg Total Unit Cost	Avg Price Incl O&P
Fences, lightweight blocks											
No reinforcing											
4" W x 8" H x 16" L	Inst	SF	Lg	BD	.108	370.0	1.90	3.64	.23	5.77	**7.58**
	Inst	SF	Sm	BO	.124	259.0	2.15	4.06	.33	6.54	**8.56**
6" W x 4" H x 16" L	Inst	SF	Lg	BD	.222	180.0	4.51	7.48	.48	12.47	**16.30**
	Inst	SF	Sm	BO	.254	126.0	5.13	8.31	.69	14.13	**18.40**
6" W x 6" H x 16" L	Inst	SF	Lg	BD	.154	260.0	3.44	5.19	.33	8.96	**11.70**
	Inst	SF	Sm	BO	.176	182.0	3.91	5.76	.48	10.15	**13.20**
6" W x 8" H x 16" L	Inst	SF	Lg	BD	.114	350.0	2.46	3.84	.25	6.55	**8.53**
	Inst	SF	Sm	BO	.131	245.0	2.79	4.29	.35	7.43	**9.64**
8" W x 8" H x 16" L	Inst	SF	Lg	BD	.121	330.0	3.13	4.08	.26	7.47	**9.65**
	Inst	SF	Sm	BO	.139	231.0	3.56	4.55	.38	8.49	**10.90**
10" W x 8" H x 16" L	Inst	SF	Lg	BD	.131	305.0	4.53	4.41	.28	9.22	**11.80**
	Inst	SF	Sm	BO	.150	213.5	4.63	4.91	.41	9.95	**12.70**
12" W x 8" H x 16" L	Inst	SF	Lg	BD	.143	280.0	4.53	4.82	.31	9.66	**12.40**
	Inst	SF	Sm	BO	.163	196.0	5.15	5.33	.44	10.92	**13.90**
Lateral reinforcing every third course											
4" W x 8" H x 16" L	Inst	SF	Lg	BD	.113	355.0	1.90	3.81	.24	5.95	**7.83**
	Inst	SF	Sm	BO	.129	248.5	2.15	4.22	.35	6.72	**8.82**
6" W x 4" H x 16" L	Inst	SF	Lg	BD	.229	175.0	4.51	7.72	.50	12.73	**16.60**
	Inst	SF	Sm	BO	.261	122.5	5.13	8.54	.71	14.38	**18.70**
6" W x 6" H x 16" L	Inst	SF	Lg	BD	.163	245.0	3.44	5.49	.35	9.28	**12.10**
	Inst	SF	Sm	BO	.187	171.5	3.91	6.12	.51	10.54	**13.70**
6" W x 8" H x 16" L	Inst	SF	Lg	BD	.119	335.0	2.46	4.01	.26	6.73	**8.78**
	Inst	SF	Sm	BO	.136	234.5	2.79	4.45	.37	7.61	**9.90**
8" W x 8" H x 16" L	Inst	SF	Lg	BD	.127	315.0	3.13	4.28	.28	7.69	**9.96**
	Inst	SF	Sm	BO	.145	220.5	3.56	4.74	.39	8.69	**11.20**
10" W x 8" H x 16" L	Inst	SF	Lg	BD	.138	290.0	4.53	4.65	.30	9.48	**12.10**
	Inst	SF	Sm	BO	.158	203.0	4.63	5.17	.43	10.23	**13.10**
12" W x 8" H x 16" L	Inst	SF	Lg	BD	.151	265.0	4.53	5.09	.33	9.95	**12.80**
	Inst	SF	Sm	BO	.173	185.5	5.15	5.66	.47	11.28	**14.40**

Concrete slump block

Running bond, 3/8" mortar joints

Walls, with air tools

Description	Oper	Unit	Vol	Crew Size	Man-hours per Unit	Crew Output per Day	Avg Mat'l Unit Cost	Avg Labor Unit Cost	Avg Equip Unit Cost	Avg Total Unit Cost	Avg Price Incl O&P
4" T	Demo	SF	Lg	AB	.043	370.0	---	1.58	.42	2.00	**2.64**
	Demo	SF	Sm	AB	.062	259.0	---	2.28	.60	2.88	**3.80**
6" T	Demo	SF	Lg	AB	.046	350.0	---	1.69	.45	2.14	**2.82**
	Demo	SF	Sm	AB	.065	245.0	---	2.39	.64	3.03	**3.99**
8" T	Demo	SF	Lg	AB	.048	335.0	---	1.77	.47	2.24	**2.94**
	Demo	SF	Sm	AB	.068	234.5	---	2.50	.67	3.17	**4.18**
12" T	Demo	SF	Lg	AB	.058	275.0	---	2.14	.57	2.71	**3.56**
	Demo	SF	Sm	AB	.083	192.5	---	3.06	.81	3.87	**5.09**

Description	Oper	Unit	Vol	Crew Size	Man-hours per Unit	Crew Output per Day	Avg Mat'l Unit Cost	Avg Labor Unit Cost	Avg Equip Unit Cost	Avg Total Unit Cost	Avg Price Incl O&P
Walls, no scaffolding included											
4" x 4" x 16"	Inst	SF	Lg	BO	.128	250.0	4.22	4.19	.35	8.76	**11.20**
	Inst	SF	Sm	ML	.137	175.0	4.79	4.70	.50	9.99	**12.70**
6" x 4" x 16"	Inst	SF	Lg	BO	.133	240.0	4.87	4.35	.36	9.58	**12.10**
	Inst	SF	Sm	ML	.143	168.0	5.53	4.91	.52	10.96	**13.90**
6" x 6" x 16"	Inst	SF	Lg	BO	.119	270.0	3.80	3.89	.32	8.01	**10.20**
	Inst	SF	Sm	ML	.127	189.0	4.32	4.36	.46	9.14	**11.60**
8" x 4" x 16"	Inst	SF	Lg	BO	.139	230.0	5.95	4.55	.38	10.88	**13.70**
	Inst	SF	Sm	ML	.149	161.0	6.77	5.12	.54	12.43	**15.60**
8" x 6" x 16"	Inst	SF	Lg	BO	.123	260.0	4.79	4.02	.33	9.14	**11.60**
	Inst	SF	Sm	ML	.132	182.0	5.45	4.53	.48	10.46	**13.20**
12" x 4" x 16"	Inst	SF	Lg	BO	.152	210.0	9.17	4.97	.41	14.55	**18.00**
	Inst	SF	Sm	ML	.163	147.0	10.40	5.60	.59	16.59	**20.50**
12" x 6" x 16"	Inst	SF	Lg	BO	.133	240.0	6.97	4.35	.36	11.68	**14.60**
	Inst	SF	Sm	ML	.143	168.0	7.92	4.91	.52	13.35	**16.60**

Concrete slump brick

Running bond, 3/8" mortar joints

Walls, with air tools

Description	Oper	Unit	Vol	Crew Size	Man-hours per Unit	Crew Output per Day	Avg Mat'l Unit Cost	Avg Labor Unit Cost	Avg Equip Unit Cost	Avg Total Unit Cost	Avg Price Incl O&P
4" T	Demo	SF	Lg	AB	.043	370.0	---	1.58	.42	2.00	**2.64**
	Demo	SF	Sm	AB	.062	259.0	---	2.28	.60	2.88	**3.80**

Walls, no scaffolding included

Description	Oper	Unit	Vol	Crew Size	Man-hours per Unit	Crew Output per Day	Avg Mat'l Unit Cost	Avg Labor Unit Cost	Avg Equip Unit Cost	Avg Total Unit Cost	Avg Price Incl O&P
4" x 4" x 8"	Inst	SF	Lg	BO	.145	220.0	13.90	4.74	.39	19.03	**23.10**
	Inst	SF	Sm	ML	.156	154.0	15.80	5.36	.56	21.72	**26.40**
4" x 4" x 12"	Inst	SF	Lg	BO	.133	240.0	8.12	4.35	.36	12.83	**15.90**
	Inst	SF	Sm	ML	.143	168.0	9.23	4.91	.52	14.66	**18.10**

Concrete textured screen block

Running bond, 3/8" mortar joints

Walls, with air tools

Description	Oper	Unit	Vol	Crew Size	Man-hours per Unit	Crew Output per Day	Avg Mat'l Unit Cost	Avg Labor Unit Cost	Avg Equip Unit Cost	Avg Total Unit Cost	Avg Price Incl O&P
4" T	Demo	SF	Lg	AB	.033	480.0	---	1.22	.33	1.55	**2.03**
	Demo	SF	Sm	AB	.048	336.0	---	1.77	.46	2.23	**2.93**

Walls, no scaffolding included

Description	Oper	Unit	Vol	Crew Size	Man-hours per Unit	Crew Output per Day	Avg Mat'l Unit Cost	Avg Labor Unit Cost	Avg Equip Unit Cost	Avg Total Unit Cost	Avg Price Incl O&P
4" x 6" x 6"	Inst	SF	Lg	BO	.200	160.0	15.00	6.54	.54	22.08	**27.10**
	Inst	SF	Sm	ML	.214	112.0	17.10	7.35	.77	25.22	**30.80**
4" x 8" x 8"	Inst	SF	Lg	BO	.133	240.0	12.60	4.35	.36	17.31	**21.00**
	Inst	SF	Sm	ML	.143	168.0	14.30	4.91	.52	19.73	**23.90**
4" x 12" x 12"	Inst	SF	Lg	BO	.089	360.0	4.41	2.91	.24	7.56	**9.45**
	Inst	SF	Sm	ML	.095	252.0	5.02	3.26	.34	8.62	**10.80**

Description	Oper	Unit	Vol	Crew Size	Man-hours per Unit	Crew Output per Day	Avg Mat'l Unit Cost	Avg Labor Unit Cost	Avg Equip Unit Cost	Avg Total Unit Cost	Avg Price Incl O&P
Glass block											
Plain, 4" thick											
6" x 6"	Demo	SF	Lg	LB	.064	250.0	---	1.92	---	1.92	**2.69**
	Demo	SF	Sm	LB	.091	175.0	---	2.73	---	2.73	**3.82**
8" x 8"	Demo	SF	Lg	LB	.057	280.0	---	1.71	---	1.71	**2.39**
	Demo	SF	Sm	LB	.082	196.0	---	2.46	---	2.46	**3.44**
12" x 12"	Demo	SF	Lg	LB	.052	310.0	---	1.56	---	1.56	**2.18**
	Demo	SF	Sm	LB	.074	217.0	---	2.22	---	2.22	**3.11**
6" x 6"	Inst	SF	Lg	ML	.320	75.00	22.80	11.00	---	33.80	**41.80**
	Inst	SF	Sm	BK	.305	52.50	25.90	9.98	---	35.88	**44.00**
8" x 8"	Inst	SF	Lg	ML	.218	110.0	13.50	7.49	---	20.99	**26.10**
	Inst	SF	Sm	BK	.208	77.00	15.30	6.81	---	22.11	**27.30**
12" x 12"	Inst	SF	Lg	ML	.145	165.0	16.90	4.98	---	21.88	**26.50**
	Inst	SF	Sm	BK	.139	115.5	19.20	4.55	---	23.75	**28.60**
Glazed tile											
6-T Series. Includes normal allowance for special shapes											
All sizes	Demo	SF	Lg	LB	.052	310.0	---	1.56	---	1.56	**2.18**
Glazed 1 side	Demo	SF	Sm	LB	.074	217.0	---	2.22	---	2.22	**3.11**
2" x 5-1/3" x 12"	Inst	SF	Lg	ML	.286	84.00	3.89	9.82	---	13.71	**18.40**
	Inst	SF	Sm	BK	.379	42.22	4.14	12.40	---	16.54	**22.40**
4" x 5-1/3" x 12"	Inst	SF	Lg	ML	.300	80.00	6.03	10.30	---	16.33	**21.60**
	Inst	SF	Sm	BK	.398	40.20	6.31	13.00	---	19.31	**25.80**
6" x 5-1/3" x 12"	Inst	SF	Lg	ML	.316	76.00	7.81	10.90	---	18.71	**24.40**
	Inst	SF	Sm	BK	.419	38.19	8.06	13.70	---	21.76	**28.70**
8" x 5-1/3" x 12"	Inst	SF	Lg	ML	.353	68.00	9.35	12.10	---	21.45	**28.00**
	Inst	SF	Sm	BK	.468	34.19	9.54	15.30	---	24.84	**32.70**
Glazed 2 sides											
4" x 5-1/3" x 12"	Inst	SF	Lg	ML	.375	64.00	8.64	12.90	---	21.54	**28.20**
	Inst	SF	Sm	BK	.498	32.13	9.26	16.30	---	25.56	**33.80**
6" x 5-1/3" x 12"	Inst	SF	Lg	ML	.400	60.00	10.80	13.70	---	24.50	**31.90**
	Inst	SF	Sm	BK	.531	30.13	11.40	17.40	---	28.80	**37.80**
8" x 5-1/3" x 12"	Inst	SF	Lg	ML	.462	52.00	13.10	15.90	---	29.00	**37.60**
	Inst	SF	Sm	BK	.612	26.14	13.80	20.00	---	33.80	**44.30**
Quarry tile											
Floors											
Conventional mortar set	Demo	SF	Lg	LB	.030	535.0	---	.90	---	.90	**1.26**
	Demo	SF	Sm	LB	.043	372.1	---	1.29	---	1.29	**1.81**
Dry-set mortar	Demo	SF	Lg	LB	.026	620.0	---	.78	---	.78	**1.09**
	Demo	SF	Sm	LB	.037	432.4	---	1.11	---	1.11	**1.55**
Conventional mortar set with unmounted tile											
6" x 6" x 1/2" T	Inst	SF	Lg	BO	.123	260.0	2.27	4.02	.23	6.52	**8.56**
	Inst	SF	Sm	ML	.164	146.3	2.58	5.63	.41	8.62	**11.40**
9" x 9" x 3/4" T	Inst	SF	Lg	BO	.103	310.0	2.85	3.37	.20	6.42	**8.26**
	Inst	SF	Sm	ML	.138	173.9	3.24	4.74	.35	8.33	**10.80**
Dry-set mortar with unmounted tile											
6" x 6" x 1/2" T	Inst	SF	Lg	BO	.102	315.0	5.34	3.34	.19	8.87	**11.10**
	Inst	SF	Sm	ML	.135	177.8	6.07	4.64	.34	11.05	**13.90**
9" x 9" x 3/4" T	Inst	SF	Lg	BO	.082	390.0	5.92	2.68	.16	8.76	**10.80**
	Inst	SF	Sm	ML	.109	220.2	6.73	3.74	.28	10.75	**13.30**

Molding

Base shoe

Rounded edge stop

Bed mold

Stops

Base

Casings

Astragal

Corner mold

Cove

Chair rail

Crown

Brick mold

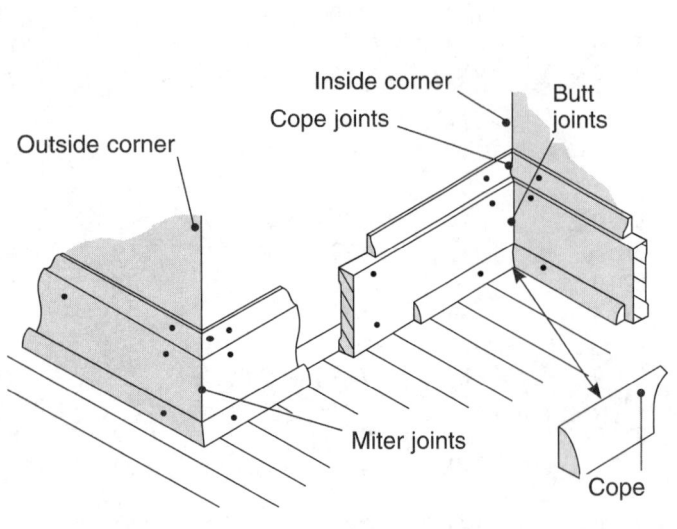

Outside corner

Inside corner

Cope joints

Butt joints

Miter joints

Cope

Base molding installation

Cope

Butt first piece against wall

Inside corner

Ceiling molding installation

Description	Oper	Unit	Vol	Crew Size	Man-hours per Unit	Crew Output per Day	Avg Mat'l Unit Cost	Avg Labor Unit Cost	Avg Equip Unit Cost	Avg Total Unit Cost	Avg Price Incl O&P
Molding and trim											
Removal											
At base (floor)	Demo	LF	Lg	LB	.015	1060	---	.45	---	.45	**.63**
	Demo	LF	Sm	LB	.022	742.0	---	.66	---	.66	**.92**
At ceiling	Demo	LF	Lg	LB	.013	1200	---	.39	---	.39	**.55**
	Demo	LF	Sm	LB	.019	840.0	---	.57	---	.57	**.80**
On wall or cabinets	Demo	LF	Lg	LB	.010	1600	---	.30	---	.30	**.42**
	Demo	LF	Sm	LB	.014	1120	---	.42	---	.42	**.59**
Solid pine											
Unfinished											
Casing											
Flat streamline											
1/2" x 1-5/8"	Inst	LF	Lg	CA	.030	266.0	1.10	1.11	---	2.21	**2.82**
	Inst	LF	Sm	CA	.043	186.2	1.25	1.59	---	2.84	**3.67**
5/8" x 1-5/8"	Inst	LF	Lg	CA	.030	266.0	1.20	1.11	---	2.31	**2.93**
	Inst	LF	Sm	CA	.043	186.2	1.35	1.59	---	2.94	**3.78**
5/8" x 2-1/2"	Inst	LF	Lg	CA	.030	266.0	1.54	1.11	---	2.65	**3.33**
	Inst	LF	Sm	CA	.043	186.2	1.74	1.59	---	3.33	**4.23**
Oval streamline											
1/2" x 1-5/8"	Inst	LF	Lg	CA	.030	266.0	1.13	1.11	---	2.24	**2.85**
	Inst	LF	Sm	CA	.043	186.2	1.27	1.59	---	2.86	**3.69**
5/8" x 1-5/8"	Inst	LF	Lg	CA	.030	266.0	1.20	1.11	---	2.31	**2.93**
	Inst	LF	Sm	CA	.043	186.2	1.35	1.59	---	2.94	**3.78**
5/8" x 2-1/2"	Inst	LF	Lg	CA	.030	266.0	1.76	1.11	---	2.87	**3.58**
	Inst	LF	Sm	CA	.043	186.2	1.99	1.59	---	3.58	**4.52**
711											
5/8" x 1-5/8"	Inst	LF	Lg	CA	.030	266.0	1.20	1.11	---	2.31	**2.93**
	Inst	LF	Sm	CA	.043	186.2	1.35	1.59	---	2.94	**3.78**
5/8" x 2-1/2"	Inst	LF	Lg	CA	.030	266.0	1.76	1.11	---	2.87	**3.58**
	Inst	LF	Sm	CA	.043	186.2	1.99	1.59	---	3.58	**4.52**
3 step											
5/8" x 1-5/8"	Inst	LF	Lg	CA	.030	266.0	1.07	1.11	---	2.18	**2.79**
	Inst	LF	Sm	CA	.043	186.2	1.21	1.59	---	2.80	**3.62**
5/8" x 2-1/2"	Inst	LF	Lg	CA	.030	266.0	1.58	1.11	---	2.69	**3.37**
	Inst	LF	Sm	CA	.043	186.2	1.78	1.59	---	3.37	**4.28**
2 round edge											
5/8" x 2-1/2"	Inst	LF	Lg	CA	.030	266.0	1.16	1.11	---	2.27	**2.89**
	Inst	LF	Sm	CA	.043	186.2	1.31	1.59	---	2.90	**3.74**
B & B											
1/2" x 1-5/8"	Inst	LF	Lg	CA	.030	266.0	1.07	1.11	---	2.18	**2.79**
	Inst	LF	Sm	CA	.043	186.2	1.21	1.59	---	2.80	**3.62**
4 bead											
1/2" x 1-5/8"	Inst	LF	Lg	CA	.030	266.0	1.01	1.11	---	2.12	**2.72**
	Inst	LF	Sm	CA	.043	186.2	1.14	1.59	---	2.73	**3.54**

Description	Oper	Unit	Vol	Crew Size	Man-hours per Unit	Crew Output per Day	Avg Mat'l Unit Cost	Avg Labor Unit Cost	Avg Equip Unit Cost	Avg Total Unit Cost	Avg Price Incl O&P
1550											
1/2" x 1-5/8"	Inst	LF	Lg	CA	.030	266.0	.89	1.11	---	2.00	**2.58**
	Inst	LF	Sm	CA	.043	186.2	1.00	1.59	---	2.59	**3.38**
Mullion											
1/4" x 3-1/2"	Inst	LF	Lg	CA	.030	266.0	1.13	1.11	---	2.24	**2.85**
	Inst	LF	Sm	CA	.043	186.2	1.27	1.59	---	2.86	**3.69**
Universal											
5/8" x 2-1/2"	Inst	LF	Lg	CA	.030	266.0	1.25	1.11	---	2.36	**2.99**
	Inst	LF	Sm	CA	.043	186.2	1.42	1.59	---	3.01	**3.86**
Colonial											
11/16" x 2-1/2"	Inst	LF	Lg	CA	.030	266.0	1.43	1.11	---	2.54	**3.20**
	Inst	LF	Sm	CA	.043	186.2	1.61	1.59	---	3.20	**4.08**
11/16" x 3-1/2"	Inst	LF	Lg	CA	.030	266.0	1.79	1.11	---	2.90	**3.61**
	Inst	LF	Sm	CA	.043	186.2	2.03	1.59	---	3.62	**4.56**
11/16" x 4-1/2"	Inst	LF	Lg	CA	.030	266.0	3.30	1.11	---	4.41	**5.35**
	Inst	LF	Sm	CA	.043	186.2	3.73	1.59	---	5.32	**6.52**
11/16" x 2-7/8"	Inst	LF	Lg	CA	.030	266.0	1.77	1.11	---	2.88	**3.59**
	Inst	LF	Sm	CA	.043	186.2	2.00	1.59	---	3.59	**4.53**
356											
11/16" x 2-1/4"	Inst	LF	Lg	CA	.030	266.0	1.45	1.11	---	2.56	**3.22**
	Inst	LF	Sm	CA	.043	186.2	1.64	1.59	---	3.23	**4.11**
Back band											
11/16" x 1-1/8"	Inst	LF	Lg	CA	.030	266.0	.82	1.11	---	1.93	**2.50**
	Inst	LF	Sm	CA	.043	186.2	.92	1.59	---	2.51	**3.29**
Cape Cod											
5/8" x 2-1/2"	Inst	LF	Lg	CA	.030	266.0	1.58	1.11	---	2.69	**3.37**
	Inst	LF	Sm	CA	.043	186.2	1.78	1.59	---	3.37	**4.28**
11/16" x 3-1/2"	Inst	LF	Lg	CA	.030	266.0	2.44	1.11	---	3.55	**4.36**
	Inst	LF	Sm	CA	.043	186.2	2.76	1.59	---	4.35	**5.40**
Rosette plinth block w/ edge detail											
3/4" x 2-3/4"	Inst	Ea	Lg	CA	.250	32.00	4.28	9.26	---	13.54	**17.90**
	Inst	Ea	Sm	CA	.357	22.40	4.84	13.20	---	18.04	**24.10**
3/4" x 3-1/2"	Inst	Ea	Lg	CA	.250	32.00	4.73	9.26	---	13.99	**18.40**
	Inst	Ea	Sm	CA	.357	22.40	5.34	13.20	---	18.54	**24.60**
3/4" x 3-3/4"	Inst	Ea	Lg	CA	.250	32.00	5.47	9.26	---	14.73	**19.30**
	Inst	Ea	Sm	CA	.357	22.40	6.19	13.20	---	19.39	**25.60**

Description	Oper	Unit	Vol	Crew Size	Man-hours per Unit	Crew Output per Day	Avg Mat'l Unit Cost	Avg Labor Unit Cost	Avg Equip Unit Cost	Avg Total Unit Cost	Avg Price Incl O&P
Base & base shoe											
Shoe											
3/8" x 3/4"	Inst	LF	Lg	CA	.030	266.0	.62	1.11	---	1.73	**2.27**
	Inst	LF	Sm	CA	.043	186.2	.70	1.59	---	2.29	**3.03**
Flat streamline											
7/16" x 1-1/2"	Inst	LF	Lg	CA	.030	266.0	.72	1.11	---	1.83	**2.38**
	Inst	LF	Sm	CA	.043	186.2	.82	1.59	---	2.41	**3.17**
Streamline											
7/16" x 1-5/8"	Inst	LF	Lg	CA	.030	266.0	.84	1.11	---	1.95	**2.52**
	Inst	LF	Sm	CA	.043	186.2	.95	1.59	---	2.54	**3.32**
1/2" x 1-5/8"	Inst	LF	Lg	CA	.030	266.0	.91	1.11	---	2.02	**2.60**
	Inst	LF	Sm	CA	.043	186.2	1.03	1.59	---	2.62	**3.41**
3/8" x 2-1/4"	Inst	LF	Lg	CA	.030	266.0	1.10	1.11	---	2.21	**2.82**
	Inst	LF	Sm	CA	.043	186.2	1.25	1.59	---	2.84	**3.67**
7/16" x 2-1/2"	Inst	LF	Lg	CA	.030	266.0	1.54	1.11	---	2.65	**3.33**
	Inst	LF	Sm	CA	.043	186.2	1.74	1.59	---	3.33	**4.23**
7/16" x 3-1/2"	Inst	LF	Lg	CA	.030	266.0	1.86	1.11	---	2.97	**3.69**
	Inst	LF	Sm	CA	.043	186.2	2.11	1.59	---	3.70	**4.66**
1/2" x 2-1/2"	Inst	LF	Lg	CA	.030	266.0	1.51	1.11	---	2.62	**3.29**
	Inst	LF	Sm	CA	.043	186.2	1.70	1.59	---	3.29	**4.18**
Combination											
1/2" x 1-5/8"	Inst	LF	Lg	CA	.030	266.0	.84	1.11	---	1.95	**2.52**
	Inst	LF	Sm	CA	.043	186.2	.95	1.59	---	2.54	**3.32**
1/2" x 2-1/2"	Inst	LF	Lg	CA	.030	266.0	1.24	1.11	---	2.35	**2.98**
	Inst	LF	Sm	CA	.043	186.2	1.40	1.59	---	2.99	**3.84**
711											
1/2" x 2-1/2"	Inst	LF	Lg	CA	.030	266.0	1.21	1.11	---	2.32	**2.95**
	Inst	LF	Sm	CA	.043	186.2	1.37	1.59	---	2.96	**3.80**
7/16" x 3-1/2"	Inst	LF	Lg	CA	.030	266.0	1.32	1.11	---	2.43	**3.07**
	Inst	LF	Sm	CA	.043	186.2	1.50	1.59	---	3.09	**3.95**
3 step											
1/2" x 2-1/2"	Inst	LF	Lg	CA	.030	266.0	.98	1.11	---	2.09	**2.68**
	Inst	LF	Sm	CA	.043	186.2	1.11	1.59	---	2.70	**3.51**
1/2" x 3-1/2"	Inst	LF	Lg	CA	.030	266.0	1.41	1.11	---	2.52	**3.18**
	Inst	LF	Sm	CA	.043	186.2	1.60	1.59	---	3.19	**4.07**
1550											
7/16" x 2-1/2"	Inst	LF	Lg	CA	.030	266.0	1.54	1.11	---	2.65	**3.33**
	Inst	LF	Sm	CA	.043	186.2	1.74	1.59	---	3.33	**4.23**
Cape Cod											
9/16" x 4"	Inst	LF	Lg	CA	.030	266.0	1.61	1.11	---	2.72	**3.41**
	Inst	LF	Sm	CA	.043	186.2	1.82	1.59	---	3.41	**4.32**

Description	Oper	Unit	Vol	Crew Size	Man-hours per Unit	Crew Output per Day	Avg Mat'l Unit Cost	Avg Labor Unit Cost	Avg Equip Unit Cost	Avg Total Unit Cost	Avg Price Incl O&P
Colonial											
11/16" x 3-1/2"	Inst	LF	Lg	CA	.030	266.0	1.98	1.11	---	3.09	**3.83**
	Inst	LF	Sm	CA	.043	186.2	2.24	1.59	---	3.83	**4.80**
11/16" x 4-1/2"	Inst	LF	Lg	CA	.030	266.0	2.24	1.11	---	3.35	**4.13**
	Inst	LF	Sm	CA	.043	186.2	2.54	1.59	---	4.13	**5.15**
Base cap											
11/16" x 1-3/8"	Inst	LF	Lg	CA	.030	266.0	.93	1.11	---	2.04	**2.62**
	Inst	LF	Sm	CA	.043	186.2	1.05	1.59	---	2.64	**3.44**
Rosette plinth block w/ edge detail											
3/4" x 2-3/4" x 6"	Inst	Ea	Lg	CA	.250	32.00	3.51	9.26	---	12.77	**17.00**
	Inst	Ea	Sm	CA	.357	22.40	3.97	13.20	---	17.17	**23.10**
3/4" x 3-1/2" x 6"	Inst	Ea	Lg	CA	.250	32.00	3.88	9.26	---	13.14	**17.40**
	Inst	Ea	Sm	CA	.357	22.40	4.38	13.20	---	17.58	**23.50**
3/4" x 3-3/4" x 6"	Inst	Ea	Lg	CA	.250	32.00	4.49	9.26	---	13.75	**18.10**
	Inst	Ea	Sm	CA	.357	22.40	5.07	13.20	---	18.27	**24.30**
Colonial plinth block w/ edge detail											
1" x 2-3/4" x 6"	Inst	Ea	Lg	CA	.250	32.00	3.51	9.26	---	12.77	**17.00**
	Inst	Ea	Sm	CA	.357	22.40	3.97	13.20	---	17.17	**23.10**
1" x 3-3/4" x 6"	Inst	Ea	Lg	CA	.250	32.00	4.49	9.26	---	13.75	**18.10**
	Inst	Ea	Sm	CA	.357	22.40	5.07	13.20	---	18.27	**24.30**

Stops

Description	Oper	Unit	Vol	Crew Size	Man-hours per Unit	Crew Output per Day	Avg Mat'l Unit Cost	Avg Labor Unit Cost	Avg Equip Unit Cost	Avg Total Unit Cost	Avg Price Incl O&P
Round edge											
3/8" x 1/2"	Inst	LF	Lg	CA	.030	266.0	.64	1.11	---	1.75	**2.29**
	Inst	LF	Sm	CA	.043	186.2	.73	1.59	---	2.32	**3.07**
3/8" x 3/4"	Inst	LF	Lg	CA	.030	266.0	.68	1.11	---	1.79	**2.34**
	Inst	LF	Sm	CA	.043	186.2	.77	1.59	---	2.36	**3.11**
3/8" x 1"	Inst	LF	Lg	CA	.030	266.0	.84	1.11	---	1.95	**2.52**
	Inst	LF	Sm	CA	.043	186.2	.95	1.59	---	2.54	**3.32**
3/8" x 1-1/4"	Inst	LF	Lg	CA	.030	266.0	1.00	1.11	---	2.11	**2.70**
	Inst	LF	Sm	CA	.043	186.2	1.13	1.59	---	2.72	**3.53**
3/8" x 1-5/8"	Inst	LF	Lg	CA	.030	266.0	1.02	1.11	---	2.13	**2.73**
	Inst	LF	Sm	CA	.043	186.2	1.16	1.59	---	2.75	**3.56**
1/2" x 3/4"	Inst	LF	Lg	CA	.030	266.0	.79	1.11	---	1.90	**2.46**
	Inst	LF	Sm	CA	.043	186.2	.90	1.59	---	2.49	**3.26**
1/2" x 1"	Inst	LF	Lg	CA	.030	266.0	.82	1.11	---	1.93	**2.50**
	Inst	LF	Sm	CA	.043	186.2	.92	1.59	---	2.51	**3.29**
1/2" x 1-1/4"	Inst	LF	Lg	CA	.030	266.0	.99	1.11	---	2.10	**2.69**
	Inst	LF	Sm	CA	.043	186.2	1.12	1.59	---	2.71	**3.52**
1/2" x 1-5/8"	Inst	LF	Lg	CA	.030	266.0	1.14	1.11	---	2.25	**2.87**
	Inst	LF	Sm	CA	.043	186.2	1.29	1.59	---	2.88	**3.71**
Ogee stop											
7/16" x 1-5/8"	Inst	LF	Lg	CA	.030	266.0	.71	1.11	---	1.82	**2.37**
	Inst	LF	Sm	CA	.043	186.2	.81	1.59	---	2.40	**3.16**

Description	Oper	Unit	Vol	Crew Size	Man-hours per Unit	Crew Output per Day	Avg Mat'l Unit Cost	Avg Labor Unit Cost	Avg Equip Unit Cost	Avg Total Unit Cost	Avg Price Incl O&P
Crown & cornice											
Crown											
9/16" x 1-5/8"	Inst	LF	Lg	CA	.040	200.0	1.55	1.48	---	3.03	**3.86**
	Inst	LF	Sm	CA	.057	140.0	1.76	2.11	---	3.87	**4.98**
9/16" x 2-1/4"	Inst	LF	Lg	CA	.040	200.0	1.73	1.48	---	3.21	**4.06**
	Inst	LF	Sm	CA	.057	140.0	1.95	2.11	---	4.06	**5.20**
9/16" x 3-1/2"	Inst	LF	Lg	CA	.040	200.0	1.90	1.48	---	3.38	**4.26**
	Inst	LF	Sm	CA	.057	140.0	2.15	2.11	---	4.26	**5.43**
9/16" x 4-1/4"	Inst	LF	Lg	CA	.040	200.0	2.13	1.48	---	3.61	**4.52**
	Inst	LF	Sm	CA	.057	140.0	2.41	2.11	---	4.52	**5.73**
9/16" x 5-1/2"	Inst	LF	Lg	CA	.040	200.0	2.40	1.48	---	3.88	**4.83**
	Inst	LF	Sm	CA	.057	140.0	2.72	2.11	---	4.83	**6.08**
Colonial crown											
9/16" x 3-3/8"	Inst	LF	Lg	CA	.040	200.0	1.66	1.48	---	3.14	**3.98**
	Inst	LF	Sm	CA	.057	140.0	1.87	2.11	---	3.98	**5.10**
9/16" x 4-1/2"	Inst	LF	Lg	CA	.040	200.0	2.13	1.48	---	3.61	**4.52**
	Inst	LF	Sm	CA	.057	140.0	2.41	2.11	---	4.52	**5.73**
Cornice											
1-1/8" x 4-1/2"	Inst	LF	Lg	CA	.040	200.0	8.82	1.48	---	10.30	**12.20**
	Inst	LF	Sm	CA	.057	140.0	9.97	2.11	---	12.08	**14.40**
1-1/4" x 6"	Inst	LF	Lg	CA	.040	200.0	9.63	1.48	---	11.11	**13.20**
	Inst	LF	Sm	CA	.057	140.0	10.90	2.11	---	13.01	**15.50**
Chair rail											
Chair rail											
1/2" x 1-1/2"	Inst	LF	Lg	CA	.030	266.0	.82	1.11	---	1.93	**2.50**
	Inst	LF	Sm	CA	.043	186.2	.92	1.59	---	2.51	**3.29**
9/16" x 2-1/2"	Inst	LF	Lg	CA	.030	266.0	1.79	1.11	---	2.90	**3.61**
	Inst	LF	Sm	CA	.043	186.2	2.03	1.59	---	3.62	**4.56**
Colonial chair rail											
11/16" x 2-1/2"	Inst	LF	Lg	CA	.030	266.0	1.38	1.11	---	2.49	**3.14**
	Inst	LF	Sm	CA	.043	186.2	1.56	1.59	---	3.15	**4.02**
Outside corner guard											
3/4" x 3/4"	Inst	LF	Lg	CA	.030	266.0	.83	1.11	---	1.94	**2.51**
	Inst	LF	Sm	CA	.043	186.2	.94	1.59	---	2.53	**3.31**
1" x 1"	Inst	LF	Lg	CA	.030	266.0	1.54	1.11	---	2.65	**3.33**
	Inst	LF	Sm	CA	.043	186.2	1.74	1.59	---	3.33	**4.23**
1-1/8" x 1-1/8"	Inst	LF	Lg	CA	.030	266.0	2.12	1.11	---	3.23	**3.99**
	Inst	LF	Sm	CA	.043	186.2	2.39	1.59	---	3.98	**4.98**
1-3/8" x 1-3/8"	Inst	LF	Lg	CA	.030	266.0	2.31	1.11	---	3.42	**4.21**
	Inst	LF	Sm	CA	.043	186.2	2.61	1.59	---	4.20	**5.23**

Description	Oper	Unit	Vol	Crew Size	Man-hours per Unit	Crew Output per Day	Avg Mat'l Unit Cost	Avg Labor Unit Cost	Avg Equip Unit Cost	Avg Total Unit Cost	Avg Price Incl O&P
Astragal											
Flat astragal											
3/4" x 1-5/8"	Inst	LF	Lg	CA	.030	266.0	2.05	1.11	---	3.16	**3.91**
	Inst	LF	Sm	CA	.043	186.2	2.31	1.59	---	3.90	**4.89**
T astragal											
1-1/4" x 2-1/4"	Inst	LF	Lg	CA	.030	266.0	3.32	1.11	---	4.43	**5.37**
	Inst	LF	Sm	CA	.043	186.2	3.76	1.59	---	5.35	**6.55**
Cap											
Panel cap											
1/2" x 1-1/2"	Inst	LF	Lg	CA	.030	266.0	1.25	1.11	---	2.36	**2.99**
	Inst	LF	Sm	CA	.043	186.2	1.42	1.59	---	3.01	**3.86**
Wainscot cap											
5/8" x 1-1/4"	Inst	LF	Lg	CA	.030	266.0	1.25	1.11	---	2.36	**2.99**
	Inst	LF	Sm	CA	.043	186.2	1.42	1.59	---	3.01	**3.86**
Glass bead & screen											
Insert											
3/16" x 1/2"	Inst	LF	Lg	CA	.030	266.0	.60	1.11	---	1.71	**2.24**
	Inst	LF	Sm	CA	.043	186.2	.68	1.59	---	2.27	**3.01**
Flat											
1/4" x 3/4"	Inst	LF	Lg	CA	.030	266.0	.60	1.11	---	1.71	**2.24**
	Inst	LF	Sm	CA	.043	186.2	.68	1.59	---	2.27	**3.01**
Beaded											
1/4" x 3/4"	Inst	LF	Lg	CA	.030	266.0	.60	1.11	---	1.71	**2.24**
	Inst	LF	Sm	CA	.043	186.2	.68	1.59	---	2.27	**3.01**
Scribe											
3/16" x 3/4"	Inst	LF	Lg	CA	.030	266.0	.37	1.11	---	1.48	**1.98**
	Inst	LF	Sm	CA	.043	186.2	.42	1.59	---	2.01	**2.71**
Cloverleaf											
3/8" x 3/4"	Inst	LF	Lg	CA	.030	266.0	.71	1.11	---	1.82	**2.37**
	Inst	LF	Sm	CA	.043	186.2	.81	1.59	---	2.40	**3.16**
Glass bead											
1/4" x 7/16"	Inst	LF	Lg	CA	.030	266.0	.55	1.11	---	1.66	**2.19**
	Inst	LF	Sm	CA	.043	186.2	.62	1.59	---	2.21	**2.94**
3/8" x 3/8"	Inst	LF	Lg	CA	.030	266.0	.55	1.11	---	1.66	**2.19**
	Inst	LF	Sm	CA	.043	186.2	.62	1.59	---	2.21	**2.94**
Quarter round											
1/4" x 1/4"	Inst	LF	Lg	CA	.030	266.0	.40	1.11	---	1.51	**2.01**
	Inst	LF	Sm	CA	.043	186.2	.46	1.59	---	2.05	**2.76**
3/8" x 3/8"	Inst	LF	Lg	CA	.030	266.0	.49	1.11	---	1.60	**2.12**
	Inst	LF	Sm	CA	.043	186.2	.56	1.59	---	2.15	**2.87**
1/2" x 1/2"	Inst	LF	Lg	CA	.030	266.0	.60	1.11	---	1.71	**2.24**
	Inst	LF	Sm	CA	.043	186.2	.68	1.59	---	2.27	**3.01**
5/8" x 5/8"	Inst	LF	Lg	CA	.030	266.0	.64	1.11	---	1.75	**2.29**
	Inst	LF	Sm	CA	.043	186.2	.73	1.59	---	2.32	**3.07**
3/4" x 3/4"	Inst	LF	Lg	CA	.030	266.0	.83	1.11	---	1.94	**2.51**
	Inst	LF	Sm	CA	.043	186.2	.94	1.59	---	2.53	**3.31**
1" x 1"	Inst	LF	Lg	CA	.030	266.0	1.66	1.11	---	2.77	**3.46**
	Inst	LF	Sm	CA	.043	186.2	1.87	1.59	---	3.46	**4.38**

Description	Oper	Unit	Vol	Crew Size	Man-hours per Unit	Crew Output per Day	Avg Mat'l Unit Cost	Avg Labor Unit Cost	Avg Equip Unit Cost	Avg Total Unit Cost	Avg Price Incl O&P
Cove											
Cove											
3/8" x 3/8"	Inst	LF	Lg	CA	.040	200.0	.46	1.48	---	1.94	**2.60**
	Inst	LF	Sm	CA	.057	140.0	.52	2.11	---	2.63	**3.55**
1/2" x 1/2"	Inst	LF	Lg	CA	.040	200.0	.55	1.48	---	2.03	**2.71**
	Inst	LF	Sm	CA	.057	140.0	.62	2.11	---	2.73	**3.67**
5/8" x 5/8"	Inst	LF	Lg	CA	.040	200.0	.83	1.48	---	2.31	**3.03**
	Inst	LF	Sm	CA	.057	140.0	.94	2.11	---	3.05	**4.04**
3/4" x 3/4"	Inst	LF	Lg	CA	.040	200.0	.83	1.48	---	2.31	**3.03**
	Inst	LF	Sm	CA	.057	140.0	.94	2.11	---	3.05	**4.04**
1" x 1"	Inst	LF	Lg	CA	.040	200.0	1.66	1.48	---	3.14	**3.98**
	Inst	LF	Sm	CA	.057	140.0	1.87	2.11	---	3.98	**5.10**
Sprung cove											
5/8" x 1-5/8"	Inst	LF	Lg	CA	.040	200.0	1.60	1.48	---	3.08	**3.91**
	Inst	LF	Sm	CA	.057	140.0	1.81	2.11	---	3.92	**5.04**
5/8" x 2-1/4"	Inst	LF	Lg	CA	.040	200.0	1.96	1.48	---	3.44	**4.33**
	Inst	LF	Sm	CA	.057	140.0	2.21	2.11	---	4.32	**5.50**
Linoleum cove											
7/16" x 1-1/4"	Inst	LF	Lg	CA	.040	200.0	.94	1.48	---	2.42	**3.15**
	Inst	LF	Sm	CA	.057	140.0	1.07	2.11	---	3.18	**4.18**
Half round											
1/4" x 1/2"	Inst	LF	Lg	CA	.030	266.0	.46	1.11	---	1.57	**2.08**
	Inst	LF	Sm	CA	.043	186.2	.52	1.59	---	2.11	**2.83**
1/4" x 5/8"	Inst	LF	Lg	CA	.030	266.0	.46	1.11	---	1.57	**2.08**
	Inst	LF	Sm	CA	.043	186.2	.52	1.59	---	2.11	**2.83**
3/8" x 3/4"	Inst	LF	Lg	CA	.030	266.0	.55	1.11	---	1.66	**2.19**
	Inst	LF	Sm	CA	.043	186.2	.62	1.59	---	2.21	**2.94**
1/2" x 1"	Inst	LF	Lg	CA	.030	266.0	1.01	1.11	---	2.12	**2.72**
	Inst	LF	Sm	CA	.043	186.2	1.14	1.59	---	2.73	**3.54**
Lattice - batts - S4S											
Lattice											
5/16" x 1-1/4"	Inst	LF	Lg	CA	.030	266.0	.66	1.11	---	1.77	**2.31**
	Inst	LF	Sm	CA	.043	186.2	.74	1.59	---	2.33	**3.08**
5/16" x 1-5/8"	Inst	LF	Lg	CA	.030	266.0	.87	1.11	---	1.98	**2.56**
	Inst	LF	Sm	CA	.043	186.2	.99	1.59	---	2.58	**3.37**
5/16" x 2-1/2"	Inst	LF	Lg	CA	.030	266.0	1.25	1.11	---	2.36	**2.99**
	Inst	LF	Sm	CA	.043	186.2	1.42	1.59	---	3.01	**3.86**
Batts											
5/16" x 2-1/2"	Inst	LF	Lg	CA	.030	266.0	.91	1.11	---	2.02	**2.60**
	Inst	LF	Sm	CA	.043	186.2	1.03	1.59	---	2.62	**3.41**
5/16" x 3-1/2"	Inst	LF	Lg	CA	.030	266.0	1.33	1.11	---	2.44	**3.08**
	Inst	LF	Sm	CA	.043	186.2	1.51	1.59	---	3.10	**3.97**

Description	Oper	Unit	Vol	Crew Size	Man-hours per Unit	Crew Output per Day	Avg Mat'l Unit Cost	Avg Labor Unit Cost	Avg Equip Unit Cost	Avg Total Unit Cost	Avg Price Incl O&P
S4S											
1/2" x 1/2"	Inst	LF	Lg	CA	.030	266.0	.43	1.11	---	1.54	**2.05**
	Inst	LF	Sm	CA	.043	186.2	.48	1.59	---	2.07	**2.78**
1/2" x 3/4"	Inst	LF	Lg	CA	.030	266.0	.49	1.11	---	1.60	**2.12**
	Inst	LF	Sm	CA	.043	186.2	.56	1.59	---	2.15	**2.87**
1/2" x 1-1/2"	Inst	LF	Lg	CA	.030	266.0	1.01	1.11	---	2.12	**2.72**
	Inst	LF	Sm	CA	.043	186.2	1.14	1.59	---	2.73	**3.54**
1/2" x 2-1/2"	Inst	LF	Lg	CA	.030	266.0	1.43	1.11	---	2.54	**3.20**
	Inst	LF	Sm	CA	.043	186.2	1.61	1.59	---	3.20	**4.08**
1/2" x 3-1/2"	Inst	LF	Lg	CA	.030	266.0	1.94	1.11	---	3.05	**3.79**
	Inst	LF	Sm	CA	.043	186.2	2.20	1.59	---	3.79	**4.76**
1/2" x 5-1/2"	Inst	LF	Lg	CA	.030	266.0	3.46	1.11	---	4.57	**5.53**
	Inst	LF	Sm	CA	.043	186.2	3.91	1.59	---	5.50	**6.73**
11/16" x 1-1/4"	Inst	LF	Lg	CA	.030	266.0	1.45	1.11	---	2.56	**3.22**
	Inst	LF	Sm	CA	.043	186.2	1.64	1.59	---	3.23	**4.11**
11/16" x 1-5/8"	Inst	LF	Lg	CA	.030	266.0	1.79	1.11	---	2.90	**3.61**
	Inst	LF	Sm	CA	.043	186.2	2.03	1.59	---	3.62	**4.56**
11/16" x 2-1/2"	Inst	LF	Lg	CA	.030	266.0	2.31	1.11	---	3.42	**4.21**
	Inst	LF	Sm	CA	.043	186.2	2.61	1.59	---	4.20	**5.23**
11/16" x 3-1/2"	Inst	LF	Lg	CA	.030	266.0	3.16	1.11	---	4.27	**5.19**
	Inst	LF	Sm	CA	.043	186.2	3.58	1.59	---	5.17	**6.35**
3/4" x 3/4"	Inst	LF	Lg	CA	.030	266.0	.91	1.11	---	2.02	**2.60**
	Inst	LF	Sm	CA	.043	186.2	1.03	1.59	---	2.62	**3.41**
1" x 1"	Inst	LF	Lg	CA	.030	266.0	1.63	1.11	---	2.74	**3.43**
	Inst	LF	Sm	CA	.043	186.2	1.85	1.59	---	3.44	**4.36**
1-9/16" x 1-9/16"	Inst	LF	Lg	CA	.030	266.0	3.11	1.11	---	4.22	**5.13**
	Inst	LF	Sm	CA	.043	186.2	3.51	1.59	---	5.10	**6.27**
S4S 4EE											
1-1/2" x 1-1/2"	Inst	LF	Lg	CA	.030	266.0	3.01	1.11	---	4.12	**5.02**
	Inst	LF	Sm	CA	.043	186.2	3.41	1.59	---	5.00	**6.15**

Window stool

Flat stool

Description	Oper	Unit	Vol	Crew Size	Man-hours per Unit	Crew Output per Day	Avg Mat'l Unit Cost	Avg Labor Unit Cost	Avg Equip Unit Cost	Avg Total Unit Cost	Avg Price Incl O&P
11/16" x 4-3/4"	Inst	LF	Lg	CA	.030	266.0	5.18	1.11	---	6.29	**7.51**
	Inst	LF	Sm	CA	.043	186.2	5.85	1.59	---	7.44	**8.96**
11/16" x 5-1/2"	Inst	LF	Lg	CA	.030	266.0	5.64	1.11	---	6.75	**8.04**
	Inst	LF	Sm	CA	.043	186.2	6.37	1.59	---	7.96	**9.55**
11/16" x 7-1/4"	Inst	LF	Lg	CA	.030	266.0	8.40	1.11	---	9.51	**11.20**
	Inst	LF	Sm	CA	.043	186.2	9.49	1.59	---	11.08	**13.10**

Rabbeted stool

Description	Oper	Unit	Vol	Crew Size	Man-hours per Unit	Crew Output per Day	Avg Mat'l Unit Cost	Avg Labor Unit Cost	Avg Equip Unit Cost	Avg Total Unit Cost	Avg Price Incl O&P
7/8" x 2-1/2"	Inst	LF	Lg	CA	.030	266.0	4.04	1.11	---	5.15	**6.20**
	Inst	LF	Sm	CA	.043	186.2	4.56	1.59	---	6.15	**7.47**
7/8" x 3-1/2"	Inst	LF	Lg	CA	.030	266.0	5.64	1.11	---	6.75	**8.04**
	Inst	LF	Sm	CA	.043	186.2	6.37	1.59	---	7.96	**9.55**
7/8" x 5-1/2"	Inst	LF	Lg	CA	.030	266.0	6.82	1.11	---	7.93	**9.40**
	Inst	LF	Sm	CA	.043	186.2	7.71	1.59	---	9.30	**11.10**

Description	Oper	Unit	Vol	Crew Size	Man-hours per Unit	Crew Output per Day	Avg Mat'l Unit Cost	Avg Labor Unit Cost	Avg Equip Unit Cost	Avg Total Unit Cost	Avg Price Incl O&P
Panel & decorative molds											
Panel											
3/8" x 5/8"	Inst	LF	Lg	CA	.030	266.0	.78	1.11	---	1.89	**2.45**
	Inst	LF	Sm	CA	.043	186.2	.88	1.59	---	2.47	**3.24**
5/8" x 3/4"	Inst	LF	Lg	CA	.030	266.0	1.16	1.11	---	2.27	**2.89**
	Inst	LF	Sm	CA	.043	186.2	1.31	1.59	---	2.90	**3.74**
3/4" x 1"	Inst	LF	Lg	CA	.030	266.0	1.68	1.11	---	2.79	**3.49**
	Inst	LF	Sm	CA	.043	186.2	1.90	1.59	---	3.49	**4.41**
Panel or brick											
1-1/16" x 1-1/2"	Inst	LF	Lg	CA	.030	266.0	2.17	1.11	---	3.28	**4.05**
	Inst	LF	Sm	CA	.043	186.2	2.46	1.59	---	4.05	**5.06**
Panel											
3/8" x 1-1/8"	Inst	LF	Lg	CA	.030	266.0	1.16	1.11	---	2.27	**2.89**
	Inst	LF	Sm	CA	.043	186.2	1.31	1.59	---	2.90	**3.74**
9/16" x 1-3/8"	Inst	LF	Lg	CA	.030	266.0	1.10	1.11	---	2.21	**2.82**
	Inst	LF	Sm	CA	.043	186.2	1.25	1.59	---	2.84	**3.67**
3/4" x 1-5/8"	Inst	LF	Lg	CA	.030	266.0	2.20	1.11	---	3.31	**4.08**
	Inst	LF	Sm	CA	.043	186.2	2.48	1.59	---	4.07	**5.08**
Beauty M-340											
3/4" x 1-5/8"	Inst	LF	Lg	CA	.030	266.0	1.66	1.11	---	2.77	**3.46**
	Inst	LF	Sm	CA	.043	186.2	1.87	1.59	---	3.46	**4.38**
Beauty M-400											
3/4" x 1-7/8"	Inst	LF	Lg	CA	.030	266.0	2.61	1.11	---	3.72	**4.56**
	Inst	LF	Sm	CA	.043	186.2	2.95	1.59	---	4.54	**5.62**
Decorative											
1-3/8" x 3-1/4"	Inst	LF	Lg	CA	.030	266.0	6.54	1.11	---	7.65	**9.08**
	Inst	LF	Sm	CA	.043	186.2	7.40	1.59	---	8.99	**10.70**
Base cap											
11/16" x 1-3/8"	Inst	LF	Lg	CA	.030	266.0	1.90	1.11	---	3.01	**3.74**
	Inst	LF	Sm	CA	.043	186.2	2.15	1.59	---	3.74	**4.70**
M340 corner arcs											
3/4" x 1-5/8"	Inst	LF	Lg	CA	.250	32.00	4.14	9.26	---	13.40	**17.70**
	Inst	LF	Sm	CA	.357	22.40	4.68	13.20	---	17.88	**23.90**
Miscellaneous											
Band mold											
3/4" x 1-5/8"	Inst	LF	Lg	CA	.030	266.0	1.47	1.11	---	2.58	**3.25**
	Inst	LF	Sm	CA	.043	186.2	1.66	1.59	---	3.25	**4.14**
Parting bead											
3/8" x 3/4"	Inst	LF	Lg	CA	.030	266.0	2.02	1.11	---	3.13	**3.88**
	Inst	LF	Sm	CA	.043	186.2	2.29	1.59	---	3.88	**4.86**

Description	Oper	Unit	Vol	Crew Size	Man-hours per Unit	Crew Output per Day	Avg Mat'l Unit Cost	Avg Labor Unit Cost	Avg Equip Unit Cost	Avg Total Unit Cost	Avg Price Incl O&P
Apron											
3/8" x 1-1/2"	Inst	LF	Lg	CA	.030	266.0	1.04	1.11	---	2.15	**2.75**
	Inst	LF	Sm	CA	.043	186.2	1.17	1.59	---	2.76	**3.57**
Flat Hoffco											
3/8" x 1"	Inst	LF	Lg	CA	.030	266.0	.72	1.11	---	1.83	**2.38**
	Inst	LF	Sm	CA	.043	186.2	.82	1.59	---	2.41	**3.17**
Drip											
3/4" x 1-1/4"	Inst	LF	Lg	CA	.030	266.0	1.51	1.11	---	2.62	**3.29**
	Inst	LF	Sm	CA	.043	186.2	1.70	1.59	---	3.29	**4.18**
1139 picture											
3/4" x 1-5/8"	Inst	LF	Lg	CA	.030	266.0	1.61	1.11	---	2.72	**3.41**
	Inst	LF	Sm	CA	.043	186.2	1.82	1.59	---	3.41	**4.32**
Chamfer											
1/2" x 1/2"	Inst	LF	Lg	CA	.030	266.0	.40	1.11	---	1.51	**2.01**
	Inst	LF	Sm	CA	.043	186.2	.46	1.59	---	2.05	**2.76**
3/4" x 3/4"	Inst	LF	Lg	CA	.030	266.0	.52	1.11	---	1.63	**2.15**
	Inst	LF	Sm	CA	.043	186.2	.59	1.59	---	2.18	**2.91**
1" x 1"	Inst	LF	Lg	CA	.030	266.0	1.14	1.11	---	2.25	**2.87**
	Inst	LF	Sm	CA	.043	186.2	1.29	1.59	---	2.88	**3.71**
Nose & cove											
1" x 1-5/8"	Inst	LF	Lg	CA	.030	266.0	2.69	1.11	---	3.80	**4.65**
	Inst	LF	Sm	CA	.043	186.2	3.04	1.59	---	4.63	**5.72**
Cabinet crown											
5/16" x 1-1/4"	Inst	LF	Lg	CA	.030	266.0	.58	1.11	---	1.69	**2.22**
	Inst	LF	Sm	CA	.043	186.2	.65	1.59	---	2.24	**2.98**

Finger joint pine

Paint grade

Casing

Prefit

Description	Oper	Unit	Vol	Crew Size	Man-hours per Unit	Crew Output per Day	Avg Mat'l Unit Cost	Avg Labor Unit Cost	Avg Equip Unit Cost	Avg Total Unit Cost	Avg Price Incl O&P
9/16" x 1-1/2"	Inst	LF	Lg	CA	.030	266.0	.58	1.11	---	1.69	**2.22**
	Inst	LF	Sm	CA	.043	186.2	.65	1.59	---	2.24	**2.98**
Flat streamline											
1/2" x 1-5/8"	Inst	LF	Lg	CA	.030	266.0	.76	1.11	---	1.87	**2.43**
	Inst	LF	Sm	CA	.043	186.2	.86	1.59	---	2.45	**3.22**
5/8" x 1-5/8"	Inst	LF	Lg	CA	.030	266.0	.78	1.11	---	1.89	**2.45**
	Inst	LF	Sm	CA	.043	186.2	.88	1.59	---	2.47	**3.24**
11/16" x 2-1/4"	Inst	LF	Lg	CA	.030	266.0	1.10	1.11	---	2.21	**2.82**
	Inst	LF	Sm	CA	.043	186.2	1.25	1.59	---	2.84	**3.67**
711											
5/8" x 1-5/8"	Inst	LF	Lg	CA	.030	266.0	.79	1.11	---	1.90	**2.46**
	Inst	LF	Sm	CA	.043	186.2	.90	1.59	---	2.49	**3.26**
5/8" x 2-1/2"	Inst	LF	Lg	CA	.030	266.0	1.20	1.11	---	2.31	**2.93**
	Inst	LF	Sm	CA	.043	186.2	1.35	1.59	---	2.94	**3.78**

Description	Oper	Unit	Vol	Crew Size	Man-hours per Unit	Crew Output per Day	Avg Mat'l Unit Cost	Avg Labor Unit Cost	Avg Equip Unit Cost	Avg Total Unit Cost	Avg Price Incl O&P
Monterey											
5/8" x 2-1/2"	Inst	LF	Lg	CA	.030	266.0	1.28	1.11	---	2.39	**3.03**
	Inst	LF	Sm	CA	.043	186.2	1.44	1.59	---	3.03	**3.88**
3 step											
5/8" x 2-1/2"	Inst	LF	Lg	CA	.030	266.0	1.20	1.11	---	2.31	**2.93**
	Inst	LF	Sm	CA	.043	186.2	1.35	1.59	---	2.94	**3.78**
Universal											
5/8" x 2-1/2"	Inst	LF	Lg	CA	.030	266.0	1.21	1.11	---	2.32	**2.95**
	Inst	LF	Sm	CA	.043	186.2	1.37	1.59	---	2.96	**3.80**
Colonial											
9/16" x 4-1/4"	Inst	LF	Lg	CA	.030	266.0	2.00	1.11	---	3.11	**3.85**
	Inst	LF	Sm	CA	.043	186.2	2.26	1.59	---	3.85	**4.83**
11/16" x 2-7/8"	Inst	LF	Lg	CA	.030	266.0	1.44	1.11	---	2.55	**3.21**
	Inst	LF	Sm	CA	.043	186.2	1.63	1.59	---	3.22	**4.10**
Clam shell											
11/16" x 2"	Inst	LF	Lg	CA	.030	266.0	.97	1.11	---	2.08	**2.67**
	Inst	LF	Sm	CA	.043	186.2	1.09	1.59	---	2.68	**3.48**
356											
9/16" x 2"	Inst	LF	Lg	CA	.030	266.0	.97	1.11	---	2.08	**2.67**
	Inst	LF	Sm	CA	.043	186.2	1.09	1.59	---	2.68	**3.48**
11/16" x 2-1/4"	Inst	LF	Lg	CA	.030	266.0	1.06	1.11	---	2.17	**2.77**
	Inst	LF	Sm	CA	.043	186.2	1.20	1.59	---	2.79	**3.61**
WM 366											
11/16" x 2-1/4"	Inst	LF	Lg	CA	.030	266.0	1.06	1.11	---	2.17	**2.77**
	Inst	LF	Sm	CA	.043	186.2	1.20	1.59	---	2.79	**3.61**
3 fluted											
1/2" x 3-1/4"	Inst	LF	Lg	CA	.030	266.0	1.52	1.11	---	2.63	**3.30**
	Inst	LF	Sm	CA	.043	186.2	1.72	1.59	---	3.31	**4.21**
5 fluted											
1/2" x 3-1/2"	Inst	LF	Lg	CA	.030	266.0	1.62	1.11	---	2.73	**3.42**
	Inst	LF	Sm	CA	.043	186.2	1.83	1.59	---	3.42	**4.33**
Cape Cod											
5/8" x 2-1/2"	Inst	LF	Lg	CA	.030	266.0	1.27	1.11	---	2.38	**3.02**
	Inst	LF	Sm	CA	.043	186.2	1.43	1.59	---	3.02	**3.87**
11/16" x 3-1/2"	Inst	LF	Lg	CA	.030	266.0	2.10	1.11	---	3.21	**3.97**
	Inst	LF	Sm	CA	.043	186.2	2.38	1.59	---	3.97	**4.97**
Chesapeake											
3/4" x 3-1/2"	Inst	LF	Lg	CA	.030	266.0	2.13	1.11	---	3.24	**4.00**
	Inst	LF	Sm	CA	.043	186.2	2.41	1.59	---	4.00	**5.00**
Coronado											
1-1/4" x 2-1/2"	Inst	LF	Lg	CA	.030	266.0	2.48	1.11	---	3.59	**4.41**
	Inst	LF	Sm	CA	.043	186.2	2.81	1.59	---	4.40	**5.46**

Description	Oper	Unit	Vol	Crew Size	Man-hours per Unit	Crew Output per Day	Avg Mat'l Unit Cost	Avg Labor Unit Cost	Avg Equip Unit Cost	Avg Total Unit Cost	Avg Price Incl O&P
Bell court											
1-1/4" x 2-1/2"	Inst	LF	Lg	CA	.030	266.0	2.48	1.11	---	3.59	**4.41**
	Inst	LF	Sm	CA	.043	186.2	2.81	1.59	---	4.40	**5.46**
Hermosa											
1-1/4" x 3-1/4"	Inst	LF	Lg	CA	.030	266.0	3.37	1.11	---	4.48	**5.43**
	Inst	LF	Sm	CA	.043	186.2	3.81	1.59	---	5.40	**6.61**
Cambridge											
11/16" x 3-1/4"	Inst	LF	Lg	CA	.030	266.0	2.07	1.11	---	3.18	**3.94**
	Inst	LF	Sm	CA	.043	186.2	2.34	1.59	---	3.93	**4.92**
275											
5/8" x 3"	Inst	LF	Lg	CA	.030	266.0	1.55	1.11	---	2.66	**3.34**
	Inst	LF	Sm	CA	.043	186.2	1.76	1.59	---	3.35	**4.25**

Stops

Description	Oper	Unit	Vol	Crew Size	Man-hours per Unit	Crew Output per Day	Avg Mat'l Unit Cost	Avg Labor Unit Cost	Avg Equip Unit Cost	Avg Total Unit Cost	Avg Price Incl O&P
2 round edge											
3/8" x 1-1/4"	Inst	LF	Lg	CA	.030	266.0	.45	1.11	---	1.56	**2.07**
	Inst	LF	Sm	CA	.043	186.2	.51	1.59	---	2.10	**2.82**
Round edge											
1/2" x 1-1/4"	Inst	LF	Lg	CA	.030	266.0	.64	1.11	---	1.75	**2.29**
	Inst	LF	Sm	CA	.043	186.2	.73	1.59	---	2.32	**3.07**
1/2" x 1-1/2"	Inst	LF	Lg	CA	.030	266.0	.83	1.11	---	1.94	**2.51**
	Inst	LF	Sm	CA	.043	186.2	.94	1.59	---	2.53	**3.31**
Ogee											
1/2" x 1-3/4"	Inst	LF	Lg	CA	.030	266.0	.89	1.11	---	2.00	**2.58**
	Inst	LF	Sm	CA	.043	186.2	1.00	1.59	---	2.59	**3.38**

Base

Description	Oper	Unit	Vol	Crew Size	Man-hours per Unit	Crew Output per Day	Avg Mat'l Unit Cost	Avg Labor Unit Cost	Avg Equip Unit Cost	Avg Total Unit Cost	Avg Price Incl O&P
Base shoe											
3/8" x 3/4"	Inst	LF	Lg	CA	.030	266.0	.41	1.11	---	1.52	**2.03**
	Inst	LF	Sm	CA	.043	186.2	.47	1.59	---	2.06	**2.77**
Flat											
7/16" x 1-1/2"	Inst	LF	Lg	CA	.030	266.0	.52	1.11	---	1.63	**2.15**
	Inst	LF	Sm	CA	.043	186.2	.59	1.59	---	2.18	**2.91**
Streamline or reversible											
3/8" x 2-1/4"	Inst	LF	Lg	CA	.030	266.0	.69	1.11	---	1.80	**2.35**
	Inst	LF	Sm	CA	.043	186.2	.78	1.59	---	2.37	**3.13**
Streamline											
7/16" x 2-1/2"	Inst	LF	Lg	CA	.030	266.0	.85	1.11	---	1.96	**2.53**
	Inst	LF	Sm	CA	.043	186.2	.96	1.59	---	2.55	**3.33**
7/16" x 3-1/2"	Inst	LF	Lg	CA	.030	266.0	1.30	1.11	---	2.41	**3.05**
	Inst	LF	Sm	CA	.043	186.2	1.47	1.59	---	3.06	**3.92**

Description	Oper	Unit	Vol	Crew Size	Man-hours per Unit	Crew Output per Day	Avg Mat'l Unit Cost	Avg Labor Unit Cost	Avg Equip Unit Cost	Avg Total Unit Cost	Avg Price Incl O&P
711											
7/16" x 2-1/2"	Inst	LF	Lg	CA	.040	200.0	.90	1.48	---	2.38	**3.11**
	Inst	LF	Sm	CA	.057	140.0	1.01	2.11	---	3.12	**4.12**
7/16" x 3-1/2"	Inst	LF	Lg	CA	.040	200.0	1.21	1.48	---	2.69	**3.46**
	Inst	LF	Sm	CA	.057	140.0	1.37	2.11	---	3.48	**4.53**
3 step											
7/16" x 2-1/2"	Inst	LF	Lg	CA	.040	200.0	.99	1.48	---	2.47	**3.21**
	Inst	LF	Sm	CA	.057	140.0	1.12	2.11	---	3.23	**4.24**
3 step base											
1/2" x 4-1/2"	Inst	LF	Lg	CA	.040	200.0	2.23	1.48	---	3.71	**4.64**
	Inst	LF	Sm	CA	.057	140.0	2.52	2.11	---	4.63	**5.85**
WM 623											
9/16" x 3-1/4"	Inst	LF	Lg	CA	.040	200.0	1.58	1.48	---	3.06	**3.89**
	Inst	LF	Sm	CA	.057	140.0	1.78	2.11	---	3.89	**5.00**
WM 618											
9/16" x 5-1/4"	Inst	LF	Lg	CA	.040	200.0	2.44	1.48	---	3.92	**4.88**
	Inst	LF	Sm	CA	.057	140.0	2.76	2.11	---	4.87	**6.13**
Monterey											
7/16" x 4-1/4"	Inst	LF	Lg	CA	.040	200.0	1.61	1.48	---	3.09	**3.92**
	Inst	LF	Sm	CA	.057	140.0	1.82	2.11	---	3.93	**5.05**
Cape Cod											
9/16" x 4"	Inst	LF	Lg	CA	.040	200.0	2.02	1.48	---	3.50	**4.40**
	Inst	LF	Sm	CA	.057	140.0	2.29	2.11	---	4.40	**5.59**
9/16" x 5-1/4"	Inst	LF	Lg	CA	.040	200.0	2.85	1.48	---	4.33	**5.35**
	Inst	LF	Sm	CA	.057	140.0	3.22	2.11	---	5.33	**6.66**
"B" Cape Cod base											
9/16" x 5-1/4"	Inst	LF	Lg	CA	.040	200.0	2.85	1.48	---	4.33	**5.35**
	Inst	LF	Sm	CA	.057	140.0	3.22	2.11	---	5.33	**6.66**
356 base											
1/2" x 2-1/2"	Inst	LF	Lg	CA	.030	266.0	1.14	1.11	---	2.25	**2.87**
	Inst	LF	Sm	CA	.043	186.2	1.29	1.59	---	2.88	**3.71**
1/2" x 3-1/4"	Inst	LF	Lg	CA	.030	266.0	1.48	1.11	---	2.59	**3.26**
	Inst	LF	Sm	CA	.043	186.2	1.68	1.59	---	3.27	**4.16**
175 base											
9/16" x 4-1/4"	Inst	LF	Lg	CA	.040	200.0	2.09	1.48	---	3.57	**4.48**
	Inst	LF	Sm	CA	.057	140.0	2.37	2.11	---	4.48	**5.68**
Colonial											
9/16" x 4-1/4"	Inst	LF	Lg	CA	.040	200.0	3.06	1.48	---	4.54	**5.59**
	Inst	LF	Sm	CA	.057	140.0	3.46	2.11	---	5.57	**6.93**

Description	Oper	Unit	Vol	Crew Size	Man-hours per Unit	Crew Output per Day	Avg Mat'l Unit Cost	Avg Labor Unit Cost	Avg Equip Unit Cost	Avg Total Unit Cost	Avg Price Incl O&P
Crown & cornice											
Colonial crown											
9/16" x 2-1/4"	Inst	LF	Lg	CA	.040	200.0	1.10	1.48	---	2.58	**3.34**
	Inst	LF	Sm	CA	.057	140.0	1.25	2.11	---	3.36	**4.39**
9/16" x 3-3/8"	Inst	LF	Lg	CA	.040	200.0	1.78	1.48	---	3.26	**4.12**
	Inst	LF	Sm	CA	.057	140.0	2.02	2.11	---	4.13	**5.28**
9/16" x 4-1/2"	Inst	LF	Lg	CA	.040	200.0	2.44	1.48	---	3.92	**4.88**
	Inst	LF	Sm	CA	.057	140.0	2.76	2.11	---	4.87	**6.13**
Cornice											
13/16" x 4-5/8"	Inst	LF	Lg	CA	.040	200.0	4.45	1.48	---	5.93	**7.19**
	Inst	LF	Sm	CA	.057	140.0	5.03	2.11	---	7.14	**8.74**
1-1/4" x 5-7/8"	Inst	LF	Lg	CA	.040	200.0	6.85	1.48	---	8.33	**9.95**
	Inst	LF	Sm	CA	.057	140.0	7.75	2.11	---	9.86	**11.90**
Crown											
3/4" x 6"	Inst	LF	Lg	CA	.040	200.0	4.66	1.48	---	6.14	**7.43**
	Inst	LF	Sm	CA	.057	140.0	5.27	2.11	---	7.38	**9.01**
Cornice											
1-1/8" x 3-1/2"	Inst	LF	Lg	CA	.040	200.0	3.37	1.48	---	4.85	**5.95**
	Inst	LF	Sm	CA	.057	140.0	3.81	2.11	---	5.92	**7.34**
Georgian crown											
11/16" x 4-1/4"	Inst	LF	Lg	CA	.040	200.0	2.71	1.48	---	4.19	**5.19**
	Inst	LF	Sm	CA	.057	140.0	3.07	2.11	---	5.18	**6.48**
Cove											
11/16" x 11/16"	Inst	LF	Lg	CA	.030	266.0	.54	1.11	---	1.65	**2.18**
	Inst	LF	Sm	CA	.043	186.2	.61	1.59	---	2.20	**2.93**
Chair rail											
Chair rail											
9/16" x 2-1/2"	Inst	LF	Lg	CA	.030	266.0	1.24	1.11	---	2.35	**2.98**
	Inst	LF	Sm	CA	.043	186.2	1.40	1.59	---	2.99	**3.84**
Colonial chair rail											
3/4" x 3"	Inst	LF	Lg	CA	.030	266.0	1.89	1.11	---	3.00	**3.73**
	Inst	LF	Sm	CA	.043	186.2	2.13	1.59	---	3.72	**4.68**
Exterior mold											
Stucco mold											
7/8" x 1-1/4"	Inst	LF	Lg	CA	.030	266.0	.99	1.11	---	2.10	**2.69**
	Inst	LF	Sm	CA	.043	186.2	1.12	1.59	---	2.71	**3.52**
WM 180 eastern brick											
1-1/4" x 2"	Inst	LF	Lg	CA	.030	266.0	2.13	1.11	---	3.24	**4.00**
	Inst	LF	Sm	CA	.043	186.2	2.41	1.59	---	4.00	**5.00**

Description	Oper	Unit	Vol	Crew Size	Man-hours per Unit	Crew Output per Day	Avg Mat'l Unit Cost	Avg Labor Unit Cost	Avg Equip Unit Cost	Avg Total Unit Cost	Avg Price Incl O&P
Stool & apron											
Flat stool											
11/16" x 4-3/4"	Inst	LF	Lg	CA	.030	266.0	3.11	1.11	---	4.22	**5.13**
	Inst	LF	Sm	CA	.043	186.2	3.51	1.59	---	5.10	**6.27**
11/16" x 5-1/2"	Inst	LF	Lg	CA	.030	266.0	4.14	1.11	---	5.25	**6.32**
	Inst	LF	Sm	CA	.043	186.2	4.68	1.59	---	6.27	**7.61**
11/16" x 7-1/4"	Inst	LF	Lg	CA	.030	266.0	5.18	1.11	---	6.29	**7.51**
	Inst	LF	Sm	CA	.043	186.2	5.85	1.59	---	7.44	**8.96**
Apron											
3/8" x 1-1/2"	Inst	LF	Lg	CA	.030	266.0	.64	1.11	---	1.75	**2.29**
	Inst	LF	Sm	CA	.043	186.2	.73	1.59	---	2.32	**3.07**

Oak

Hardwood

Casing

Description	Oper	Unit	Vol	Crew Size	Man-hours per Unit	Crew Output per Day	Avg Mat'l Unit Cost	Avg Labor Unit Cost	Avg Equip Unit Cost	Avg Total Unit Cost	Avg Price Incl O&P
Streamline											
5/8" x 1-5/8"	Inst	LF	Lg	CA	.030	266.0	1.52	1.11	---	2.63	**3.30**
	Inst	LF	Sm	CA	.043	186.2	1.72	1.59	---	3.31	**4.21**
711											
1/2" x 1-5/8"	Inst	LF	Lg	CA	.030	266.0	1.44	1.11	---	2.55	**3.21**
	Inst	LF	Sm	CA	.043	186.2	1.63	1.59	---	3.22	**4.10**
5/8" x 2-3/8"	Inst	LF	Lg	CA	.030	266.0	1.79	1.11	---	2.90	**3.61**
	Inst	LF	Sm	CA	.043	186.2	2.03	1.59	---	3.62	**4.56**
Universal											
5/8" x 2-1/2"	Inst	LF	Lg	CA	.030	266.0	2.16	1.11	---	3.27	**4.04**
	Inst	LF	Sm	CA	.043	186.2	2.44	1.59	---	4.03	**5.03**
Colonial											
11/16" x 2-7/8"	Inst	LF	Lg	CA	.030	266.0	1.67	1.11	---	2.78	**3.48**
	Inst	LF	Sm	CA	.043	186.2	1.89	1.59	---	3.48	**4.40**
11/16" x 3-1/2"	Inst	LF	Lg	CA	.030	266.0	2.33	1.11	---	3.44	**4.23**
	Inst	LF	Sm	CA	.043	186.2	2.64	1.59	---	4.23	**5.26**
11/16" x 4-1/4"	Inst	LF	Lg	CA	.030	266.0	2.58	1.11	---	3.69	**4.52**
	Inst	LF	Sm	CA	.043	186.2	2.91	1.59	---	4.50	**5.58**
Mull											
5/16" x 3-1/4"	Inst	LF	Lg	CA	.030	266.0	1.98	1.11	---	3.09	**3.83**
	Inst	LF	Sm	CA	.043	186.2	2.24	1.59	---	3.83	**4.80**
356											
9/16" x 2-1/4"	Inst	LF	Lg	CA	.030	266.0	1.21	1.11	---	2.32	**2.95**
	Inst	LF	Sm	CA	.043	186.2	1.37	1.59	---	2.96	**3.80**
Cape Cod											
5/8" x 2-1/2"	Inst	LF	Lg	CA	.030	266.0	1.28	1.11	---	2.39	**3.03**
	Inst	LF	Sm	CA	.043	186.2	1.44	1.59	---	3.03	**3.88**

Description	Oper	Unit	Vol	Crew Size	Man-hours per Unit	Crew Output per Day	Avg Mat'l Unit Cost	Avg Labor Unit Cost	Avg Equip Unit Cost	Avg Total Unit Cost	Avg Price Incl O&P
Fluted											
1/2" x 3-1/2"	Inst	LF	Lg	CA	.030	266.0	1.82	1.11	---	2.93	**3.65**
	Inst	LF	Sm	CA	.043	186.2	2.05	1.59	---	3.64	**4.59**
Victorian											
11/16" x 4-1/4"	Inst	LF	Lg	CA	.030	266.0	5.00	1.11	---	6.11	**7.30**
	Inst	LF	Sm	CA	.043	186.2	5.66	1.59	---	7.25	**8.74**
Cambridge											
11/16" x 3-1/4"	Inst	LF	Lg	CA	.030	266.0	2.93	1.11	---	4.04	**4.92**
	Inst	LF	Sm	CA	.043	186.2	3.32	1.59	---	4.91	**6.05**
Rosette plinth block w/ edge detail											
3/4" x 2-3/4"	Inst	Ea	Lg	CA	.250	32.00	4.31	9.26	---	13.57	**17.90**
	Inst	Ea	Sm	CA	.357	22.40	4.88	13.20	---	18.08	**24.10**
3/4" x 3-3/4"	Inst	Ea	Lg	CA	.250	32.00	5.18	9.26	---	14.44	**18.90**
	Inst	Ea	Sm	CA	.357	22.40	5.85	13.20	---	19.05	**25.20**

Base

Description	Oper	Unit	Vol	Crew Size	Man-hours per Unit	Crew Output per Day	Avg Mat'l Unit Cost	Avg Labor Unit Cost	Avg Equip Unit Cost	Avg Total Unit Cost	Avg Price Incl O&P
Base shoe											
1/2" x 3/4"	Inst	LF	Lg	CA	.030	266.0	.79	1.11	---	1.90	**2.46**
	Inst	LF	Sm	CA	.043	186.2	.90	1.59	---	2.49	**3.26**
Colonial											
11/16" x 4-1/4"	Inst	LF	Lg	CA	.030	266.0	3.05	1.11	---	4.16	**5.06**
	Inst	LF	Sm	CA	.043	186.2	3.45	1.59	---	5.04	**6.20**
Streamline											
1/2" x 2-1/2"	Inst	LF	Lg	CA	.030	266.0	1.60	1.11	---	2.71	**3.39**
	Inst	LF	Sm	CA	.043	186.2	1.81	1.59	---	3.40	**4.31**
1/2" x 3-1/2"	Inst	LF	Lg	CA	.030	266.0	1.82	1.11	---	2.93	**3.65**
	Inst	LF	Sm	CA	.043	186.2	2.05	1.59	---	3.64	**4.59**
711											
1/2" x 2-1/2"	Inst	LF	Lg	CA	.030	266.0	1.68	1.11	---	2.79	**3.49**
	Inst	LF	Sm	CA	.043	186.2	1.90	1.59	---	3.49	**4.41**
1/2" x 3-1/2"	Inst	LF	Lg	CA	.030	266.0	2.23	1.11	---	3.34	**4.12**
	Inst	LF	Sm	CA	.043	186.2	2.52	1.59	---	4.11	**5.13**
Cape Cod											
7/16" x 4-1/4"	Inst	LF	Lg	CA	.030	266.0	2.83	1.11	---	3.94	**4.81**
	Inst	LF	Sm	CA	.043	186.2	3.20	1.59	---	4.79	**5.91**
Monterey											
7/16" x 4-1/4"	Inst	LF	Lg	CA	.030	266.0	2.83	1.11	---	3.94	**4.81**
	Inst	LF	Sm	CA	.043	186.2	3.20	1.59	---	4.79	**5.91**
Rosette plinth block w/ edge detail											
3/4" x 2-3/4"	Inst	Ea	Lg	CA	.250	32.00	6.64	9.26	---	15.90	**20.60**
	Inst	Ea	Sm	CA	.357	22.40	7.50	13.20	---	20.70	**27.10**
3/4" x 3-1/2"	Inst	Ea	Lg	CA	.250	32.00	7.94	9.26	---	17.20	**22.10**
	Inst	Ea	Sm	CA	.357	22.40	8.97	13.20	---	22.17	**28.80**
Colonial plinth block w/ edge detail											
1" x 2-3/4" x 6"	Inst	Ea	Lg	CA	.250	32.00	5.00	9.26	---	14.26	**18.70**
	Inst	Ea	Sm	CA	.357	22.40	5.66	13.20	---	18.86	**25.00**
1" x 3-3/4" x 6"	Inst	Ea	Lg	CA	.250	32.00	6.12	9.26	---	15.38	**20.00**
	Inst	Ea	Sm	CA	.357	22.40	6.92	13.20	---	20.12	**26.50**

Description	Oper	Unit	Vol	Crew Size	Man-hours per Unit	Crew Output per Day	Avg Mat'l Unit Cost	Avg Labor Unit Cost	Avg Equip Unit Cost	Avg Total Unit Cost	Avg Price Incl O&P
Stops											
Round edge											
3/8" x 1-1/4"	Inst	LF	Lg	CA	.030	266.0	1.12	1.11	---	2.23	**2.84**
	Inst	LF	Sm	CA	.043	186.2	1.26	1.59	---	2.85	**3.68**
Ogee											
1/2" x 1-3/4"	Inst	LF	Lg	CA	.030	266.0	2.07	1.11	---	3.18	**3.94**
	Inst	LF	Sm	CA	.043	186.2	2.34	1.59	---	3.93	**4.92**
Crown & cornice											
Crown											
1/2" x 1-5/8"	Inst	LF	Lg	CA	.040	200.0	1.41	1.48	---	2.89	**3.69**
	Inst	LF	Sm	CA	.057	140.0	1.60	2.11	---	3.71	**4.79**
1/2" x 2-1/4"	Inst	LF	Lg	CA	.040	200.0	1.98	1.48	---	3.46	**4.35**
	Inst	LF	Sm	CA	.057	140.0	2.24	2.11	---	4.35	**5.53**
1/2" x 3-1/2"	Inst	LF	Lg	CA	.040	200.0	2.84	1.48	---	4.32	**5.34**
	Inst	LF	Sm	CA	.057	140.0	3.21	2.11	---	5.32	**6.65**
Colonial crown											
5/8" x 3-1/2"	Inst	LF	Lg	CA	.040	200.0	2.93	1.48	---	4.41	**5.44**
	Inst	LF	Sm	CA	.057	140.0	3.32	2.11	---	5.43	**6.77**
5/8" x 4-1/2"	Inst	LF	Lg	CA	.040	200.0	4.49	1.48	---	5.97	**7.24**
	Inst	LF	Sm	CA	.057	140.0	5.07	2.11	---	7.18	**8.78**
Cornice											
13/16" x 4-5/8"	Inst	LF	Lg	CA	.040	200.0	4.57	1.48	---	6.05	**7.33**
	Inst	LF	Lg	CA	.057	140.0	5.16	2.11	---	7.27	**8.89**
1-1/4" x 6"	Inst	LF	Lg	CA	.040	200.0	9.14	1.48	---	10.62	**12.60**
	Inst	LF	Sm	CA	.057	140.0	10.30	2.11	---	12.41	**14.90**
Quarter round											
1/2" x 1/2"	Inst	LF	Lg	CA	.030	266.0	.72	1.11	---	1.83	**2.38**
	Inst	LF	Sm	CA	.043	186.2	.82	1.59	---	2.41	**3.17**
3/4 x 3/4"	Inst	LF	Lg	CA	.030	266.0	1.28	1.11	---	2.39	**3.03**
	Inst	LF	Sm	CA	.043	186.2	1.44	1.59	---	3.03	**3.88**
Cove											
1/2" x 1/2"	Inst	LF	Lg	CA	.040	200.0	.72	1.48	---	2.20	**2.90**
	Inst	LF	Sm	CA	.057	140.0	.82	2.11	---	2.93	**3.90**
3/4 x 3/4"	Inst	LF	Lg	CA	.040	200.0	1.28	1.48	---	2.76	**3.55**
	Inst	LF	Sm	CA	.057	140.0	1.44	2.11	---	3.55	**4.61**
Half round											
3/8" x 3/4"	Inst	LF	Lg	CA	.030	266.0	.77	1.11	---	1.88	**2.44**
	Inst	LF	Sm	CA	.043	186.2	.87	1.59	---	2.46	**3.23**

Description	Oper	Unit	Vol	Crew Size	Man-hours per Unit	Crew Output per Day	Avg Mat'l Unit Cost	Avg Labor Unit Cost	Avg Equip Unit Cost	Avg Total Unit Cost	Avg Price Incl O&P
Screen mold											
Flat screen											
3/8" x 3/4"	Inst	LF	Lg	CA	.030	266.0	.81	1.11	---	1.92	**2.49**
	Inst	LF	Sm	CA	.043	186.2	.91	1.59	---	2.50	**3.28**
Scribe											
3/16" x 3/4"	Inst	LF	Lg	CA	.030	266.0	.70	1.11	---	1.81	**2.36**
	Inst	LF	Sm	CA	.043	186.2	.79	1.59	---	2.38	**3.14**
Cloverleaf											
3/8" x 3/4"	Inst	LF	Lg	CA	.030	266.0	.97	1.11	---	2.08	**2.67**
	Inst	LF	Sm	CA	.043	186.2	1.09	1.59	---	2.68	**3.48**
Outside corner guard											
3/4" x 3/4"	Inst	LF	Lg	CA	.030	266.0	1.29	1.11	---	2.40	**3.04**
	Inst	LF	Sm	CA	.043	186.2	1.46	1.59	---	3.05	**3.91**
1" x 1"	Inst	LF	Lg	CA	.030	266.0	1.48	1.11	---	2.59	**3.26**
	Inst	LF	Sm	CA	.043	186.2	1.68	1.59	---	3.27	**4.16**
1-1/8" x 1-1/8"	Inst	LF	Lg	CA	.030	266.0	2.21	1.11	---	3.32	**4.10**
	Inst	LF	Sm	CA	.043	186.2	2.50	1.59	---	4.09	**5.10**
Chair rail											
Chair rail											
5/8" x 2-1/2"	Inst	LF	Lg	CA	.030	266.0	2.32	1.11	---	3.43	**4.22**
	Inst	LF	Sm	CA	.043	186.2	2.63	1.59	---	4.22	**5.25**
Colonial chair rail											
5/8" x 2-1/2"	Inst	LF	Lg	CA	.030	266.0	2.76	1.11	---	3.87	**4.73**
	Inst	LF	Sm	CA	.043	186.2	3.12	1.59	---	4.71	**5.82**
Victorian											
11/16" x 4-1/4"	Inst	LF	Lg	CA	.030	266.0	6.18	1.11	---	7.29	**8.66**
	Inst	LF	Sm	CA	.043	186.2	6.98	1.59	---	8.57	**10.30**
Panel cap											
1/2" x 1-1/2"	Inst	LF	Lg	CA	.030	266.0	1.59	1.11	---	2.70	**3.38**
	Inst	LF	Sm	CA	.043	186.2	1.79	1.59	---	3.38	**4.29**
Astragal											
Flat astragal											
3/4" x 1-5/8"	Inst	LF	Lg	CA	.030	266.0	2.31	1.11	---	3.42	**4.21**
	Inst	LF	Sm	CA	.043	186.2	2.61	1.59	---	4.20	**5.23**
1-3/4 T astragal											
1-1/4" x 2-1/4"	Inst	LF	Lg	CA	.030	266.0	8.45	1.11	---	9.56	**11.30**
	Inst	LF	Sm	CA	.043	186.2	9.56	1.59	---	11.15	**13.20**
T astragal mahogany											
1-1/4" x 2-1/4" (1-3/8" door)	Inst	LF	Lg	CA	.030	266.0	4.30	1.11	---	5.41	**6.50**
	Inst	LF	Sm	CA	.043	186.2	4.86	1.59	---	6.45	**7.82**

Description	Oper	Unit	Vol	Crew Size	Man-hours per Unit	Crew Output per Day	Avg Mat'l Unit Cost	Avg Labor Unit Cost	Avg Equip Unit Cost	Avg Total Unit Cost	Avg Price Incl O&P
Nose & cove											
1" x 1-5/8"	Inst	LF	Lg	CA	.040	200.0	2.84	1.48	---	4.32	**5.34**
	Inst	LF	Sm	CA	.057	140.0	3.21	2.11	---	5.32	**6.65**
Hand rail											
Hand rail											
1-1/2" x 2-1/2"	Inst	LF	Lg	CA	.030	266.0	5.00	1.11	---	6.11	**7.30**
	Inst	LF	Sm	CA	.043	186.2	5.66	1.59	---	7.25	**8.74**
Plowed											
1-1/2" x 2-1/2"	Inst	LF	Lg	CA	.030	266.0	5.52	1.11	---	6.63	**7.90**
	Inst	LF	Sm	CA	.043	186.2	6.24	1.59	---	7.83	**9.40**
Panel mold											
Panel mold											
3/8" x 5/8"	Inst	LF	Lg	CA	.030	266.0	.83	1.11	---	1.94	**2.51**
	Inst	LF	Sm	CA	.043	186.2	.94	1.59	---	2.53	**3.31**
5/8" x 3/4"	Inst	LF	Lg	CA	.030	266.0	1.18	1.11	---	2.29	**2.91**
	Inst	LF	Sm	CA	.043	186.2	1.34	1.59	---	2.93	**3.77**
3/4" x 1"	Inst	LF	Lg	CA	.030	266.0	1.63	1.11	---	2.74	**3.43**
	Inst	LF	Sm	CA	.043	186.2	1.85	1.59	---	3.44	**4.36**
3/4" x 1-5/8"	Inst	LF	Lg	CA	.030	266.0	2.38	1.11	---	3.49	**4.29**
	Inst	LF	Sm	CA	.043	186.2	2.69	1.59	---	4.28	**5.32**
Beauty mold											
9/16" x 1-3/8"	Inst	LF	Lg	CA	.030	266.0	1.98	1.11	---	3.09	**3.83**
	Inst	LF	Sm	CA	.043	186.2	2.24	1.59	---	3.83	**4.80**
3/4" x 1-7/8"	Inst	LF	Lg	CA	.030	266.0	3.04	1.11	---	4.15	**5.05**
	Inst	LF	Sm	CA	.043	186.2	3.43	1.59	---	5.02	**6.17**
Raised panel											
1-1/8" x 1-1/4"	Inst	LF	Lg	CA	.030	266.0	2.38	1.11	---	3.49	**4.29**
	Inst	LF	Sm	CA	.043	186.2	2.69	1.59	---	4.28	**5.32**
Full round											
1-3/8"	Inst	LF	Lg	CA	.030	266.0	3.36	1.11	---	4.47	**5.42**
	Inst	LF	Sm	CA	.043	186.2	3.80	1.59	---	5.39	**6.60**
S4S											
1" x 4"	Inst	LF	Lg	CA	.040	200.0	4.57	1.48	---	6.05	**7.33**
	Inst	LF	Sm	CA	.057	140.0	5.16	2.11	---	7.27	**8.89**
1" x 6"	Inst	LF	Lg	CA	.040	200.0	6.90	1.48	---	8.38	**10.00**
	Inst	LF	Sm	CA	.057	140.0	7.80	2.11	---	9.91	**11.90**
1" x 8"	Inst	LF	Lg	CA	.040	200.0	9.14	1.48	---	10.62	**12.60**
	Inst	LF	Sm	CA	.057	140.0	10.30	2.11	---	12.41	**14.90**
1" x 10"	Inst	LF	Lg	CA	.040	200.0	11.80	1.48	---	13.28	**15.70**
	Inst	LF	Sm	CA	.057	140.0	13.40	2.11	---	15.51	**18.30**
1" x 12"	Inst	LF	Lg	CA	.040	200.0	14.70	1.48	---	16.18	**18.90**
	Inst	LF	Sm	CA	.057	140.0	16.60	2.11	---	18.71	**22.00**

Description	Oper	Unit	Vol	Crew Size	Man-hours per Unit	Crew Output per Day	Avg Mat'l Unit Cost	Avg Labor Unit Cost	Avg Equip Unit Cost	Avg Total Unit Cost	Avg Price Incl O&P
Oak bar nosing											
1-1/4" x 3-1/2"	Inst	LF	Lg	CA	.030	266.0	8.28	1.11	---	9.39	**11.10**
	Inst	LF	Sm	CA	.043	186.2	9.36	1.59	---	10.95	**13.00**
1-5/8" x 5"	Inst	LF	Lg	CA	.030	266.0	11.80	1.11	---	12.91	**15.10**
	Inst	LF	Sm	CA	.043	186.2	13.40	1.59	---	14.99	**17.60**

Redwood
Lattice
Lattice

Description	Oper	Unit	Vol	Crew Size	Man-hours per Unit	Crew Output per Day	Avg Mat'l Unit Cost	Avg Labor Unit Cost	Avg Equip Unit Cost	Avg Total Unit Cost	Avg Price Incl O&P
5/16" x 1-1/4"	Inst	LF	Lg	CA	.030	266.0	.38	1.11	---	1.49	**1.99**
	Inst	LF	Sm	CA	.043	186.2	.43	1.59	---	2.02	**2.72**
5/16" x 1-5/8"	Inst	LF	Lg	CA	.030	266.0	.45	1.11	---	1.56	**2.07**
	Inst	LF	Sm	CA	.043	186.2	.51	1.59	---	2.10	**2.82**

Batts

Description	Oper	Unit	Vol	Crew Size	Man-hours per Unit	Crew Output per Day	Avg Mat'l Unit Cost	Avg Labor Unit Cost	Avg Equip Unit Cost	Avg Total Unit Cost	Avg Price Incl O&P
5/16" x 2-1/2"	Inst	LF	Lg	CA	.030	266.0	.70	1.11	---	1.81	**2.36**
	Inst	LF	Sm	CA	.043	186.2	.79	1.59	---	2.38	**3.14**
5/16" x 3-1/2"	Inst	LF	Lg	CA	.030	266.0	.98	1.11	---	2.09	**2.68**
	Inst	LF	Sm	CA	.043	186.2	1.11	1.59	---	2.70	**3.51**
5/16" x 5-1/2"	Inst	LF	Lg	CA	.030	266.0	1.67	1.11	---	2.78	**3.48**
	Inst	LF	Sm	CA	.043	186.2	1.89	1.59	---	3.48	**4.40**

Miscellaneous exterior molds
Bricks

Description	Oper	Unit	Vol	Crew Size	Man-hours per Unit	Crew Output per Day	Avg Mat'l Unit Cost	Avg Labor Unit Cost	Avg Equip Unit Cost	Avg Total Unit Cost	Avg Price Incl O&P
1-1/2" x 1-1/2"	Inst	LF	Lg	CA	.040	200.0	1.70	1.48	---	3.18	**4.03**
	Inst	LF	Sm	CA	.057	140.0	1.92	2.11	---	4.03	**5.16**

Siding

Description	Oper	Unit	Vol	Crew Size	Man-hours per Unit	Crew Output per Day	Avg Mat'l Unit Cost	Avg Labor Unit Cost	Avg Equip Unit Cost	Avg Total Unit Cost	Avg Price Incl O&P
7/8" x 1-5/8"	Inst	LF	Lg	CA	.040	200.0	1.25	1.48	---	2.73	**3.51**
	Inst	LF	Sm	CA	.057	140.0	1.42	2.11	---	3.53	**4.59**

Stucco

Description	Oper	Unit	Vol	Crew Size	Man-hours per Unit	Crew Output per Day	Avg Mat'l Unit Cost	Avg Labor Unit Cost	Avg Equip Unit Cost	Avg Total Unit Cost	Avg Price Incl O&P
7/8" x 1-1/2"	Inst	LF	Lg	CA	.040	200.0	.74	1.48	---	2.22	**2.92**
	Inst	LF	Sm	CA	.057	140.0	.83	2.11	---	2.94	**3.91**

Watertable without lip

Description	Oper	Unit	Vol	Crew Size	Man-hours per Unit	Crew Output per Day	Avg Mat'l Unit Cost	Avg Labor Unit Cost	Avg Equip Unit Cost	Avg Total Unit Cost	Avg Price Incl O&P
1-1/2" x 2-3/8"	Inst	LF	Lg	CA	.040	200.0	2.73	1.48	---	4.21	**5.21**
	Inst	LF	Sm	CA	.057	140.0	3.08	2.11	---	5.19	**6.50**

Watertable with lip

Description	Oper	Unit	Vol	Crew Size	Man-hours per Unit	Crew Output per Day	Avg Mat'l Unit Cost	Avg Labor Unit Cost	Avg Equip Unit Cost	Avg Total Unit Cost	Avg Price Incl O&P
1-1/2" x 2-3/8"	Inst	LF	Lg	CA	.040	200.0	2.73	1.48	---	4.21	**5.21**
	Inst	LF	Sm	CA	.057	140.0	3.08	2.11	---	5.19	**6.50**

Corrugated

Description	Oper	Unit	Vol	Crew Size	Man-hours per Unit	Crew Output per Day	Avg Mat'l Unit Cost	Avg Labor Unit Cost	Avg Equip Unit Cost	Avg Total Unit Cost	Avg Price Incl O&P
3/4" x 1-5/8"	Inst	LF	Lg	CA	.040	200.0	.52	1.48	---	2.00	**2.67**
	Inst	LF	Sm	CA	.057	140.0	.59	2.11	---	2.70	**3.63**

Crest

Description	Oper	Unit	Vol	Crew Size	Man-hours per Unit	Crew Output per Day	Avg Mat'l Unit Cost	Avg Labor Unit Cost	Avg Equip Unit Cost	Avg Total Unit Cost	Avg Price Incl O&P
3/4" x 1-5/8"	Inst	LF	Lg	CA	.040	200.0	.52	1.48	---	2.00	**2.67**
	Inst	LF	Sm	CA	.057	140.0	.59	2.11	---	2.70	**3.63**

Description	Oper	Unit	Vol	Crew Size	Man-hours per Unit	Crew Output per Day	Avg Mat'l Unit Cost	Avg Labor Unit Cost	Avg Equip Unit Cost	Avg Total Unit Cost	Avg Price Incl O&P

Resin flexible molding
Primed paint grade

Diameter casing
711

Description	Oper	Unit	Vol	Crew Size	Man-hours per Unit	Crew Output per Day	Avg Mat'l Unit Cost	Avg Labor Unit Cost	Avg Equip Unit Cost	Avg Total Unit Cost	Avg Price Incl O&P
5/8" x 2-1/2"	Inst	LF	Lg	CA	.030	266.0	12.20	1.11	---	13.31	**15.60**
	Inst	LF	Sm	CA	.043	186.2	13.80	1.59	---	15.39	**18.10**

Universal

Description	Oper	Unit	Vol	Crew Size	Man-hours per Unit	Crew Output per Day	Avg Mat'l Unit Cost	Avg Labor Unit Cost	Avg Equip Unit Cost	Avg Total Unit Cost	Avg Price Incl O&P
5/8" x 2-1/2"	Inst	LF	Lg	CA	.030	266.0	12.20	1.11	---	13.31	**15.60**
	Inst	LF	Sm	CA	.043	186.2	13.80	1.59	---	15.39	**18.10**

356

Description	Oper	Unit	Vol	Crew Size	Man-hours per Unit	Crew Output per Day	Avg Mat'l Unit Cost	Avg Labor Unit Cost	Avg Equip Unit Cost	Avg Total Unit Cost	Avg Price Incl O&P
5/8" x 2-1/2"	Inst	LF	Lg	CA	.030	266.0	12.20	1.11	---	13.31	**15.60**
	Inst	LF	Sm	CA	.043	186.2	13.80	1.59	---	15.39	**18.10**

Cape Cod

Description	Oper	Unit	Vol	Crew Size	Man-hours per Unit	Crew Output per Day	Avg Mat'l Unit Cost	Avg Labor Unit Cost	Avg Equip Unit Cost	Avg Total Unit Cost	Avg Price Incl O&P
5/8" x 2-1/2"	Inst	LF	Lg	CA	.030	266.0	12.20	1.11	---	13.31	**15.60**
	Inst	LF	Sm	CA	.043	186.2	13.80	1.59	---	15.39	**18.10**

Bases & round corner blocks
Base shoe

Description	Oper	Unit	Vol	Crew Size	Man-hours per Unit	Crew Output per Day	Avg Mat'l Unit Cost	Avg Labor Unit Cost	Avg Equip Unit Cost	Avg Total Unit Cost	Avg Price Incl O&P
3/8" x 3/4"	Inst	LF	Lg	CA	.030	266.0	2.31	1.11	---	3.42	**4.21**
	Inst	LF	Sm	CA	.043	186.2	2.61	1.59	---	4.20	**5.23**

Streamline

Description	Oper	Unit	Vol	Crew Size	Man-hours per Unit	Crew Output per Day	Avg Mat'l Unit Cost	Avg Labor Unit Cost	Avg Equip Unit Cost	Avg Total Unit Cost	Avg Price Incl O&P
3/8" x 2-1/4"	Inst	LF	Lg	CA	.030	266.0	3.77	1.11	---	4.88	**5.89**
	Inst	LF	Sm	CA	.043	186.2	4.26	1.59	---	5.85	**7.13**
7/16" x 3-1/2"	Inst	LF	Lg	CA	.030	266.0	6.08	1.11	---	7.19	**8.55**
	Inst	LF	Sm	CA	.043	186.2	6.88	1.59	---	8.47	**10.10**

711

Description	Oper	Unit	Vol	Crew Size	Man-hours per Unit	Crew Output per Day	Avg Mat'l Unit Cost	Avg Labor Unit Cost	Avg Equip Unit Cost	Avg Total Unit Cost	Avg Price Incl O&P
7/16" x 2-1/2"	Inst	LF	Lg	CA	.030	266.0	3.63	1.11	---	4.74	**5.73**
	Inst	LF	Sm	CA	.043	186.2	4.11	1.59	---	5.70	**6.96**
7/16" x 3-1/2"	Inst	LF	Lg	CA	.030	266.0	5.49	1.11	---	6.60	**7.87**
	Inst	LF	Sm	CA	.043	186.2	6.20	1.59	---	7.79	**9.36**

WM 623

Description	Oper	Unit	Vol	Crew Size	Man-hours per Unit	Crew Output per Day	Avg Mat'l Unit Cost	Avg Labor Unit Cost	Avg Equip Unit Cost	Avg Total Unit Cost	Avg Price Incl O&P
9/16" x 3-1/4"	Inst	LF	Lg	CA	.030	266.0	5.03	1.11	---	6.14	**7.34**
	Inst	LF	Sm	CA	.043	186.2	5.68	1.59	---	7.27	**8.76**

WM 618

Description	Oper	Unit	Vol	Crew Size	Man-hours per Unit	Crew Output per Day	Avg Mat'l Unit Cost	Avg Labor Unit Cost	Avg Equip Unit Cost	Avg Total Unit Cost	Avg Price Incl O&P
9/16" x 5-1/4"	Inst	LF	Lg	CA	.030	266.0	11.60	1.11	---	12.71	**14.90**
	Inst	LF	Sm	CA	.043	186.2	13.20	1.59	---	14.79	**17.40**

Cape Cod

Description	Oper	Unit	Vol	Crew Size	Man-hours per Unit	Crew Output per Day	Avg Mat'l Unit Cost	Avg Labor Unit Cost	Avg Equip Unit Cost	Avg Total Unit Cost	Avg Price Incl O&P
9/16" x 5-1/4"	Inst	LF	Lg	CA	.030	266.0	9.26	1.11	---	10.37	**12.20**
	Inst	LF	Sm	CA	.043	186.2	10.50	1.59	---	12.09	**14.30**
9/16" x 4"	Inst	LF	Lg	CA	.030	266.0	6.61	1.11	---	7.72	**9.16**
	Inst	LF	Sm	CA	.043	186.2	7.48	1.59	---	9.07	**10.80**

Description	Oper	Unit	Vol	Crew Size	Man-hours per Unit	Crew Output per Day	Avg Mat'l Unit Cost	Avg Labor Unit Cost	Avg Equip Unit Cost	Avg Total Unit Cost	Avg Price Incl O&P
"B" Cape Cod											
9/16" x 5-1/4"	Inst	LF	Lg	CA	.030	266.0	10.60	1.11	---	11.71	**13.70**
	Inst	LF	Sm	CA	.043	186.2	12.00	1.59	---	13.59	**16.00**
Colonial											
11/16" x 4-1/4"	Inst	LF	Lg	CA	.030	266.0	7.94	1.11	---	9.05	**10.70**
	Inst	LF	Sm	CA	.043	186.2	8.97	1.59	---	10.56	**12.50**
Monterey											
7/16" x 4-1/4"	Inst	LF	Lg	CA	.030	266.0	7.94	1.11	---	9.05	**10.70**
	Inst	LF	Sm	CA	.043	186.2	8.97	1.59	---	10.56	**12.50**
356											
1-1/2" x 2-1/2"	Inst	LF	Lg	CA	.030	266.0	3.97	1.11	---	5.08	**6.12**
	Inst	LF	Sm	CA	.043	186.2	4.49	1.59	---	6.08	**7.39**
1-1/2" x 3-1/4"	Inst	LF	Lg	CA	.030	266.0	6.08	1.11	---	7.19	**8.55**
	Inst	LF	Sm	CA	.043	186.2	6.88	1.59	---	8.47	**10.10**
Step											
7/16" x 2-1/2"	Inst	LF	Lg	CA	.030	266.0	4.23	1.11	---	5.34	**6.42**
	Inst	LF	Sm	CA	.043	186.2	4.78	1.59	---	6.37	**7.73**
1/2" x 4-1/2"	Inst	LF	Lg	CA	.030	266.0	8.34	1.11	---	9.45	**11.20**
	Inst	LF	Sm	CA	.043	186.2	9.43	1.59	---	11.02	**13.10**

Oak grain

Diameter casing
711

Description	Oper	Unit	Vol	Crew Size	Man-hours per Unit	Crew Output per Day	Avg Mat'l Unit Cost	Avg Labor Unit Cost	Avg Equip Unit Cost	Avg Total Unit Cost	Avg Price Incl O&P
5/8" x 2-1/2"	Inst	LF	Lg	CA	.030	266.0	13.20	1.11	---	14.31	**16.80**
	Inst	LF	Sm	CA	.043	186.2	15.00	1.59	---	16.59	**19.40**
356											
11/16" x 2-1/2"	Inst	LF	Lg	CA	.030	266.0	13.20	1.11	---	14.31	**16.80**
	Inst	LF	Sm	CA	.043	186.2	15.00	1.59	---	16.59	**19.40**

Bases & base shoe
711 base

Description	Oper	Unit	Vol	Crew Size	Man-hours per Unit	Crew Output per Day	Avg Mat'l Unit Cost	Avg Labor Unit Cost	Avg Equip Unit Cost	Avg Total Unit Cost	Avg Price Incl O&P
3/8" x 2-1/2"	Inst	LF	Lg	CA	.030	266.0	5.29	1.11	---	6.40	**7.64**
	Inst	LF	Sm	CA	.043	186.2	5.98	1.59	---	7.57	**9.11**
3/8" x 3-1/2"	Inst	LF	Lg	CA	.030	266.0	7.94	1.11	---	9.05	**10.70**
	Inst	LF	Sm	CA	.043	186.2	8.97	1.59	---	10.56	**12.50**
Base shoe											
3/8" x 3/4"	Inst	LF	Lg	CA	.030	266.0	2.65	1.11	---	3.76	**4.60**
	Inst	LF	Sm	CA	.043	186.2	2.99	1.59	---	4.58	**5.67**

Description	Oper	Unit	Vol	Crew Size	Man-hours per Unit	Crew Output per Day	Avg Mat'l Unit Cost	Avg Labor Unit Cost	Avg Equip Unit Cost	Avg Total Unit Cost	Avg Price Incl O&P

Spindles

Western hemlock, clear, kiln dried, turned for decorative applications

Planter design

1-11/16" x 1-11/16"

Description	Oper	Unit	Vol	Crew Size	Man-hours per Unit	Crew Output per Day	Avg Mat'l Unit Cost	Avg Labor Unit Cost	Avg Equip Unit Cost	Avg Total Unit Cost	Avg Price Incl O&P
3'-0" H	Inst	Ea	Lg	CA	.333	24.00	4.90	12.30	---	17.20	**22.90**
	Inst	Ea	Sm	CA	.476	16.80	5.54	17.60	---	23.14	**31.00**
4'-0" H	Inst	Ea	Lg	CA	.333	24.00	6.28	12.30	---	18.58	**24.50**
	Inst	Ea	Sm	CA	.476	16.80	7.10	17.60	---	24.70	**32.80**

2-3/8" x 2-3/8"

Description	Oper	Unit	Vol	Crew Size	Man-hours per Unit	Crew Output per Day	Avg Mat'l Unit Cost	Avg Labor Unit Cost	Avg Equip Unit Cost	Avg Total Unit Cost	Avg Price Incl O&P
3'-0" H	Inst	Ea	Lg	CA	.333	24.00	10.20	12.30	---	22.50	**29.00**
	Inst	Ea	Sm	CA	.476	16.80	11.50	17.60	---	29.10	**37.90**
4'-0" H	Inst	Ea	Lg	CA	.333	24.00	14.00	12.30	---	26.30	**33.30**
	Inst	Ea	Sm	CA	.476	16.80	15.80	17.60	---	33.40	**42.80**
5'-0" H	Inst	Ea	Lg	CA	.333	24.00	16.90	12.30	---	29.20	**36.70**
	Inst	Ea	Sm	CA	.476	16.80	19.10	17.60	---	36.70	**46.70**
6'-0" H	Inst	Ea	Lg	CA	.400	20.00	21.60	14.80	---	36.40	**45.50**
	Inst	Ea	Sm	CA	.571	14.00	24.40	21.10	---	45.50	**57.60**
8'-0" H	Inst	Ea	Lg	CA	.400	20.00	41.90	14.80	---	56.70	**69.00**
	Inst	Ea	Sm	CA	.571	14.00	47.40	21.10	---	68.50	**84.10**

3-1/4" x 3-1/4"

Description	Oper	Unit	Vol	Crew Size	Man-hours per Unit	Crew Output per Day	Avg Mat'l Unit Cost	Avg Labor Unit Cost	Avg Equip Unit Cost	Avg Total Unit Cost	Avg Price Incl O&P
3'-0" H	Inst	Ea	Lg	CA	.333	24.00	19.30	12.30	---	31.60	**39.50**
	Inst	Ea	Sm	CA	.476	16.80	21.80	17.60	---	39.40	**49.80**
4'-0" H	Inst	Ea	Lg	CA	.333	24.00	25.80	12.30	---	38.10	**46.90**
	Inst	Ea	Sm	CA	.476	16.80	29.20	17.60	---	46.80	**58.20**
5'-0" H	Inst	Ea	Lg	CA	.333	24.00	32.70	12.30	---	45.00	**54.80**
	Inst	Ea	Sm	CA	.476	16.80	36.90	17.60	---	54.50	**67.10**
6'-0" H	Inst	Ea	Lg	CA	.400	20.00	39.10	14.80	---	53.90	**65.70**
	Inst	Ea	Sm	CA	.571	14.00	44.20	21.10	---	65.30	**80.40**
8'-0" H	Inst	Ea	Lg	CA	.400	20.00	56.40	14.80	---	71.20	**85.60**
	Inst	Ea	Sm	CA	.571	14.00	63.80	21.10	---	84.90	**103.00**

Colonial design

1-11/16" x 1-11/16"

Description	Oper	Unit	Vol	Crew Size	Man-hours per Unit	Crew Output per Day	Avg Mat'l Unit Cost	Avg Labor Unit Cost	Avg Equip Unit Cost	Avg Total Unit Cost	Avg Price Incl O&P
1'-0" H	Inst	Ea	Lg	CA	.286	28.00	1.59	10.60	---	12.19	**16.70**
	Inst	Ea	Sm	CA	.408	19.60	1.79	15.10	---	16.89	**23.20**
1'-6" H	Inst	Ea	Lg	CA	.286	28.00	2.84	10.60	---	13.44	**18.10**
	Inst	Ea	Sm	CA	.408	19.60	3.21	15.10	---	18.31	**24.80**
2'-0" H	Inst	Ea	Lg	CA	.286	28.00	3.63	10.60	---	14.23	**19.00**
	Inst	Ea	Sm	CA	.408	19.60	4.11	15.10	---	19.21	**25.90**
2'-4" H	Inst	Ea	Lg	CA	.333	24.00	3.77	12.30	---	16.07	**21.60**
	Inst	Ea	Sm	CA	.476	16.80	4.26	17.60	---	21.86	**29.60**
2'-8" H	Inst	Ea	Lg	CA	.333	24.00	4.23	12.30	---	16.53	**22.10**
	Inst	Ea	Sm	CA	.476	16.80	4.78	17.60	---	22.38	**30.20**
3'-0" H	Inst	Ea	Lg	CA	.333	24.00	5.03	12.30	---	17.33	**23.00**
	Inst	Ea	Sm	CA	.476	16.80	5.68	17.60	---	23.28	**31.20**

Description	Oper	Unit	Vol	Crew Size	Man-hours per Unit	Crew Output per Day	Avg Mat'l Unit Cost	Avg Labor Unit Cost	Avg Equip Unit Cost	Avg Total Unit Cost	Avg Price Incl O&P
2-3/8" x 2-3/8"											
1'-0" H	Inst	Ea	Lg	CA	.286	28.00	3.24	10.60	---	13.84	**18.60**
	Inst	Ea	Sm	CA	.408	19.60	3.67	15.10	---	18.77	**25.40**
1'-6" H	Inst	Ea	Lg	CA	.286	28.00	4.50	10.60	---	15.10	**20.00**
	Inst	Ea	Sm	CA	.408	19.60	5.08	15.10	---	20.18	**27.00**
2'-0" H	Inst	Ea	Lg	CA	.286	28.00	6.81	10.60	---	17.41	**22.70**
	Inst	Ea	Sm	CA	.408	19.60	7.70	15.10	---	22.80	**30.00**
2'-4" H	Inst	Ea	Lg	CA	.333	24.00	7.28	12.30	---	19.58	**25.60**
	Inst	Ea	Sm	CA	.476	16.80	8.23	17.60	---	25.83	**34.10**
2'-8" H	Inst	Ea	Lg	CA	.333	24.00	9.26	12.30	---	21.56	**27.90**
	Inst	Ea	Sm	CA	.476	16.80	10.50	17.60	---	28.10	**36.70**
3'-0" H	Inst	Ea	Lg	CA	.333	24.00	10.20	12.30	---	22.50	**29.00**
	Inst	Ea	Sm	CA	.476	16.80	11.50	17.60	---	29.10	**37.90**
3-1/4" x 3-1/4"											
1'-6" H	Inst	Ea	Lg	CA	.286	28.00	7.60	10.60	---	18.20	**23.60**
	Inst	Ea	Sm	CA	.408	19.60	8.59	15.10	---	23.69	**31.00**
2'-0" H	Inst	Ea	Lg	CA	.286	28.00	10.30	10.60	---	20.90	**26.70**
	Inst	Ea	Sm	CA	.408	19.60	11.70	15.10	---	26.80	**34.60**
2'-4" H	Inst	Ea	Lg	CA	.333	24.00	12.10	12.30	---	24.40	**31.20**
	Inst	Ea	Sm	CA	.476	16.80	13.70	17.60	---	31.30	**40.40**
2'-8" H	Inst	Ea	Lg	CA	.333	24.00	13.70	12.30	---	26.00	**33.00**
	Inst	Ea	Sm	CA	.476	16.80	15.50	17.60	---	33.10	**42.50**
3'-0" H	Inst	Ea	Lg	CA	.333	24.00	19.30	12.30	---	31.60	**39.50**
	Inst	Ea	Sm	CA	.476	16.80	21.80	17.60	---	39.40	**49.80**
8'-0" H	Inst	Ea	Lg	CA	.400	20.00	56.40	14.80	---	71.20	**85.60**
	Inst	Ea	Sm	CA	.571	14.00	63.80	21.10	---	84.90	**103.00**

Mediterranean design

Description	Oper	Unit	Vol	Crew Size	Man-hours per Unit	Crew Output per Day	Avg Mat'l Unit Cost	Avg Labor Unit Cost	Avg Equip Unit Cost	Avg Total Unit Cost	Avg Price Incl O&P
1-11/16" x 1-11/16"											
1'-0" H	Inst	Ea	Lg	CA	.286	28.00	1.66	10.60	---	12.26	**16.70**
	Inst	Ea	Sm	CA	.408	19.60	1.87	15.10	---	16.97	**23.30**
1'-6" H	Inst	Ea	Lg	CA	.286	28.00	2.71	10.60	---	13.31	**17.90**
	Inst	Ea	Sm	CA	.408	19.60	3.07	15.10	---	18.17	**24.70**
2'-0" H	Inst	Ea	Lg	CA	.286	28.00	2.98	10.60	---	13.58	**18.30**
	Inst	Ea	Sm	CA	.408	19.60	3.37	15.10	---	18.47	**25.00**
2'-4" H	Inst	Ea	Lg	CA	.333	24.00	3.51	12.30	---	15.81	**21.30**
	Inst	Ea	Sm	CA	.476	16.80	3.97	17.60	---	21.57	**29.20**
2'-8" H	Inst	Ea	Lg	CA	.333	24.00	3.90	12.30	---	16.20	**21.70**
	Inst	Ea	Sm	CA	.476	16.80	4.41	17.60	---	22.01	**29.70**
3'-0" H	Inst	Ea	Lg	CA	.333	24.00	4.90	12.30	---	17.20	**22.90**
	Inst	Ea	Sm	CA	.476	16.80	5.54	17.60	---	23.14	**31.00**
4'-0" H	Inst	Ea	Lg	CA	.333	24.00	6.28	12.30	---	18.58	**24.50**
	Inst	Ea	Sm	CA	.476	16.80	7.10	17.60	---	24.70	**32.80**
5'-0" H	Inst	Ea	Lg	CA	.333	24.00	11.30	12.30	---	23.60	**30.30**
	Inst	Ea	Sm	CA	.476	16.80	12.80	17.60	---	30.40	**39.40**

Description	Oper	Unit	Vol	Crew Size	Man-hours per Unit	Crew Output per Day	Avg Mat'l Unit Cost	Avg Labor Unit Cost	Avg Equip Unit Cost	Avg Total Unit Cost	Avg Price Incl O&P
2-3/8" x 2-3/8"											
1'-0" H	Inst	Ea	Lg	CA	.286	28.00	2.98	10.60	---	13.58	**18.30**
	Inst	Ea	Sm	CA	.408	19.60	3.37	15.10	---	18.47	**25.00**
1'-6" H	Inst	Ea	Lg	CA	.286	28.00	4.30	10.60	---	14.90	**19.80**
	Inst	Ea	Sm	CA	.408	19.60	4.86	15.10	---	19.96	**26.70**
2'-0" H	Inst	Ea	Lg	CA	.286	28.00	5.43	10.60	---	16.03	**21.10**
	Inst	Ea	Sm	CA	.408	19.60	6.14	15.10	---	21.24	**28.20**
2'-4" H	Inst	Ea	Lg	CA	.333	24.00	6.95	12.30	---	19.25	**25.30**
	Inst	Ea	Sm	CA	.476	16.80	7.85	17.60	---	25.45	**33.70**
2'-8" H	Inst	Ea	Lg	CA	.333	24.00	8.66	12.30	---	20.96	**27.20**
	Inst	Ea	Sm	CA	.476	16.80	9.79	17.60	---	27.39	**35.90**
3'-0" H	Inst	Ea	Lg	CA	.333	24.00	9.92	12.30	---	22.22	**28.70**
	Inst	Ea	Sm	CA	.476	16.80	11.20	17.60	---	28.80	**37.60**
4'-0" H	Inst	Ea	Lg	CA	.333	24.00	11.80	12.30	---	24.10	**30.80**
	Inst	Ea	Sm	CA	.476	16.80	13.30	17.60	---	30.90	**40.00**
5'-0" H	Inst	Ea	Lg	CA	.333	24.00	16.20	12.30	---	28.50	**35.90**
	Inst	Ea	Sm	CA	.476	16.80	18.30	17.60	---	35.90	**45.70**
6'-0" H	Inst	Ea	Lg	CA	.400	20.00	22.80	14.80	---	37.60	**46.90**
	Inst	Ea	Sm	CA	.571	14.00	25.70	21.10	---	46.80	**59.20**
8'-0" H	Inst	Ea	Lg	CA	.400	20.00	41.90	14.80	---	56.70	**69.00**
	Inst	Ea	Sm	CA	.571	14.00	47.40	21.10	---	68.50	**84.10**
3-1/4" x 3-1/4"											
3'-0" H	Inst	Ea	Lg	CA	.333	24.00	18.70	12.30	---	31.00	**38.80**
	Inst	Ea	Sm	CA	.476	16.80	21.20	17.60	---	38.80	**49.00**
4'-0" H	Inst	Ea	Lg	CA	.333	24.00	22.00	12.30	---	34.30	**42.60**
	Inst	Ea	Sm	CA	.476	16.80	24.90	17.60	---	42.50	**53.30**
5'-0" H	Inst	Ea	Lg	CA	.333	24.00	29.60	12.30	---	41.90	**51.30**
	Inst	Ea	Sm	CA	.476	16.80	33.50	17.60	---	51.10	**63.20**
6'-0" H	Inst	Ea	Lg	CA	.400	20.00	41.70	14.80	---	56.50	**68.60**
	Inst	Ea	Sm	CA	.571	14.00	47.10	21.10	---	68.20	**83.80**
8'-0" H	Inst	Ea	Lg	CA	.400	20.00	65.70	14.80	---	80.50	**96.30**
	Inst	Ea	Sm	CA	.571	14.00	74.30	21.10	---	95.40	**115.00**

Spindle rails, 8'-0" H pieces
For 1-11/16" spindles

	Oper	Unit	Vol	Crew Size			Avg Mat'l			Avg Total	Avg Price
	Inst	Ea	Lg	CA	---	---	16.70	---	---	16.70	**19.20**
	Inst	Ea	Sm	CA	---	---	18.80	---	---	18.80	**21.70**
For 2-3/8" spindles											
	Inst	Ea	Lg	CA	---	---	24.10	---	---	24.10	**27.70**
	Inst	Ea	Sm	CA	---	---	27.20	---	---	27.20	**31.30**
For 3-1/4" spindles											
	Inst	Ea	Lg	CA	---	---	28.00	---	---	28.00	**32.20**
	Inst	Ea	Sm	CA	---	---	31.60	---	---	31.60	**36.40**

Description	Oper	Unit	Vol	Crew Size	Man-hours per Unit	Crew Output per Day	Avg Mat'l Unit Cost	Avg Labor Unit Cost	Avg Equip Unit Cost	Avg Total Unit Cost	Avg Price Incl O&P

Wood bullnose round corners

Pine base R/C

Colonial

Description	Oper	Unit	Vol	Crew Size	Man-hours per Unit	Crew Output per Day	Avg Mat'l Unit Cost	Avg Labor Unit Cost	Avg Equip Unit Cost	Avg Total Unit Cost	Avg Price Incl O&P
11/16" x 4-1/4"	Inst	LF	Lg	CA	.030	266.0	1.35	1.11	---	2.46	**3.11**
	Inst	LF	Sm	CA	.043	186.2	1.52	1.59	---	3.11	**3.98**

Streamline

Description	Oper	Unit	Vol	Crew Size	Man-hours per Unit	Crew Output per Day	Avg Mat'l Unit Cost	Avg Labor Unit Cost	Avg Equip Unit Cost	Avg Total Unit Cost	Avg Price Incl O&P
3/8" x 2-1/4"	Inst	LF	Lg	CA	.030	266.0	.70	1.11	---	1.81	**2.36**
	Inst	LF	Sm	CA	.043	186.2	.79	1.59	---	2.38	**3.14**
7/16" x 3-1/2"	Inst	LF	Lg	CA	.030	266.0	1.00	1.11	---	2.11	**2.70**
	Inst	LF	Sm	CA	.043	186.2	1.13	1.59	---	2.72	**3.53**

711

Description	Oper	Unit	Vol	Crew Size	Man-hours per Unit	Crew Output per Day	Avg Mat'l Unit Cost	Avg Labor Unit Cost	Avg Equip Unit Cost	Avg Total Unit Cost	Avg Price Incl O&P
7/16" x 2-1/2"	Inst	LF	Lg	CA	.030	266.0	.83	1.11	---	1.94	**2.51**
	Inst	LF	Sm	CA	.043	186.2	.94	1.59	---	2.53	**3.31**
7/16" x 3-1/2"	Inst	LF	Lg	CA	.030	266.0	1.17	1.11	---	2.28	**2.90**
	Inst	LF	Sm	CA	.043	186.2	1.33	1.59	---	2.92	**3.76**

3 step

Description	Oper	Unit	Vol	Crew Size	Man-hours per Unit	Crew Output per Day	Avg Mat'l Unit Cost	Avg Labor Unit Cost	Avg Equip Unit Cost	Avg Total Unit Cost	Avg Price Incl O&P
7/16" x 2-1/2"	Inst	LF	Lg	CA	.030	266.0	.74	1.11	---	1.85	**2.41**
	Inst	LF	Sm	CA	.043	186.2	.83	1.59	---	2.42	**3.18**
1/2" x 4-1/2"	Inst	LF	Lg	CA	.030	266.0	2.17	1.11	---	3.28	**4.05**
	Inst	LF	Sm	CA	.043	186.2	2.46	1.59	---	4.05	**5.06**

WM 623

Description	Oper	Unit	Vol	Crew Size	Man-hours per Unit	Crew Output per Day	Avg Mat'l Unit Cost	Avg Labor Unit Cost	Avg Equip Unit Cost	Avg Total Unit Cost	Avg Price Incl O&P
9/16" x 3-1/4"	Inst	LF	Lg	CA	.030	266.0	1.02	1.11	---	2.13	**2.73**
	Inst	LF	Sm	CA	.043	186.2	1.16	1.59	---	2.75	**3.56**

WM 618

Description	Oper	Unit	Vol	Crew Size	Man-hours per Unit	Crew Output per Day	Avg Mat'l Unit Cost	Avg Labor Unit Cost	Avg Equip Unit Cost	Avg Total Unit Cost	Avg Price Incl O&P
9/16" x 5-1/4"	Inst	LF	Lg	CA	.030	266.0	1.58	1.11	---	2.69	**3.37**
	Inst	LF	Sm	CA	.043	186.2	1.78	1.59	---	3.37	**4.28**

Monterey

Description	Oper	Unit	Vol	Crew Size	Man-hours per Unit	Crew Output per Day	Avg Mat'l Unit Cost	Avg Labor Unit Cost	Avg Equip Unit Cost	Avg Total Unit Cost	Avg Price Incl O&P
7/16" x 4-1/4"	Inst	LF	Lg	CA	.030	266.0	1.09	1.11	---	2.20	**2.81**
	Inst	LF	Sm	CA	.043	186.2	1.24	1.59	---	2.83	**3.65**

Cape Cod

Description	Oper	Unit	Vol	Crew Size	Man-hours per Unit	Crew Output per Day	Avg Mat'l Unit Cost	Avg Labor Unit Cost	Avg Equip Unit Cost	Avg Total Unit Cost	Avg Price Incl O&P
9/16" x 4"	Inst	LF	Lg	CA	.030	266.0	1.32	1.11	---	2.43	**3.07**
	Inst	LF	Sm	CA	.043	186.2	1.50	1.59	---	3.09	**3.95**
9/16" x 5-1/4"	Inst	LF	Lg	CA	.030	266.0	1.59	1.11	---	2.70	**3.38**
	Inst	LF	Sm	CA	.043	186.2	1.79	1.59	---	3.38	**4.29**

"B" Cape Cod

Description	Oper	Unit	Vol	Crew Size	Man-hours per Unit	Crew Output per Day	Avg Mat'l Unit Cost	Avg Labor Unit Cost	Avg Equip Unit Cost	Avg Total Unit Cost	Avg Price Incl O&P
9/16" x 5-1/4"	Inst	LF	Lg	CA	.030	266.0	1.59	1.11	---	2.70	**3.38**
	Inst	LF	Sm	CA	.043	186.2	1.79	1.59	---	3.38	**4.29**

356

Description	Oper	Unit	Vol	Crew Size	Man-hours per Unit	Crew Output per Day	Avg Mat'l Unit Cost	Avg Labor Unit Cost	Avg Equip Unit Cost	Avg Total Unit Cost	Avg Price Incl O&P
1/2" x 2-1/4"	Inst	LF	Lg	CA	.030	266.0	.97	1.11	---	2.08	**2.67**
	Inst	LF	Sm	CA	.043	186.2	1.09	1.59	---	2.68	**3.48**
1/2" x 3-1/4"	Inst	LF	Lg	CA	.030	266.0	1.22	1.11	---	2.33	**2.96**
	Inst	LF	Sm	CA	.043	186.2	1.38	1.59	---	2.97	**3.82**

Base shoe

Description	Oper	Unit	Vol	Crew Size	Man-hours per Unit	Crew Output per Day	Avg Mat'l Unit Cost	Avg Labor Unit Cost	Avg Equip Unit Cost	Avg Total Unit Cost	Avg Price Incl O&P
3/8" x 3/4"	Inst	LF	Lg	CA	.030	266.0	.25	1.11	---	1.36	**1.84**
	Inst	LF	Sm	CA	.043	186.2	.29	1.59	---	1.88	**2.56**

Description	Oper	Unit	Vol	Crew Size	Man-hours per Unit	Crew Output per Day	Avg Mat'l Unit Cost	Avg Labor Unit Cost	Avg Equip Unit Cost	Avg Total Unit Cost	Avg Price Incl O&P
Oak base R/C											
Base shoe											
3/8" x 3/4"	Inst	LF	Lg	CA	.030	266.0	.41	1.11	---	1.52	**2.03**
	Inst	LF	Sm	CA	.043	186.2	.47	1.59	---	2.06	**2.77**
711											
3/8" x 2-1/2"	Inst	LF	Lg	CA	.030	266.0	1.21	1.11	---	2.32	**2.95**
	Inst	LF	Sm	CA	.043	186.2	1.37	1.59	---	2.96	**3.80**
3/8" x 3-1/2"	Inst	LF	Lg	CA	.030	266.0	1.52	1.11	---	2.63	**3.30**
	Inst	LF	Sm	CA	.043	186.2	1.72	1.59	---	3.31	**4.21**
Pine chair rail R/C											
Chair rail											
9/16" x 2-1/2"	Inst	LF	Lg	CA	.030	266.0	1.07	1.11	---	2.18	**2.79**
	Inst	LF	Sm	CA	.043	186.2	1.21	1.59	---	2.80	**3.62**
Colonial chair rail											
11/16" x 2-1/2"	Inst	LF	Lg	CA	.030	266.0	1.08	1.11	---	2.19	**2.80**
	Inst	LF	Sm	CA	.043	186.2	1.22	1.59	---	2.81	**3.63**
3/4" x 3"	Inst	LF	Lg	CA	.030	266.0	1.24	1.11	---	2.35	**2.98**
	Inst	LF	Sm	CA	.043	186.2	1.40	1.59	---	2.99	**3.84**
Pine crown & cornice R/C											
Colonial crown											
9/16" x 2-1/4"	Inst	LF	Lg	CA	.030	266.0	.97	1.11	---	2.08	**2.67**
	Inst	LF	Sm	CA	.043	186.2	1.09	1.59	---	2.68	**3.48**
11/16" x 3-3/8"	Inst	LF	Lg	CA	.030	266.0	1.30	1.11	---	2.41	**3.05**
	Inst	LF	Sm	CA	.043	186.2	1.47	1.59	---	3.06	**3.92**
11/16" x 4-1/2"	Inst	LF	Lg	CA	.030	266.0	2.27	1.11	---	3.38	**4.17**
	Inst	LF	Sm	CA	.043	186.2	2.56	1.59	---	4.15	**5.17**
Cornice											
13/16" x 4-5/8"	Inst	LF	Lg	CA	.030	266.0	2.56	1.11	---	3.67	**4.50**
	Inst	LF	Sm	CA	.043	186.2	2.90	1.59	---	4.49	**5.56**
Georgian crown											
11/16" x 4-1/4"	Inst	LF	Lg	CA	.030	266.0	2.81	1.11	---	3.92	**4.79**
	Inst	LF	Sm	CA	.043	186.2	3.17	1.59	---	4.76	**5.87**

Painting

Interior and Exterior. There is a paint for almost every type of surface and surface condition. The large variety makes it impractical to consider each paint individually. For this reason, average output and average material cost/unit are based on the paints and prices listed below.

1. **Installation.** Paint can be applied by brush, roller or spray gun. Only application by brush or roller is considered in this section.

2. **Notes on Labor.** Average Manhours per Unit, for both roller and brush, is based on what one painter can do in one day. The output for cleaning is also based on what one painter can do in one day.

3. **Estimating Technique.** Use these techniques to determine quantities for interior and exterior painting before you apply unit costs.

Interior

a. Floors, walls and ceilings. Figure actual area. No deductions for openings.

b. Doors and windows. **Only openings to be painted:** Figure 36 SF or 4 SY for each side of each door and 27 SF for each side of each window. Based on doors 3'-0" x 7'-0" or smaller and windows 3'-0" x 4'-0" or smaller. **Openings to be painted with walls:** Figure wall area plus 27 SF or 3 SY for each side of each door and 18 SF or 2 SY for each side of each window. Based on doors 3'-0" x 7'-0" or smaller and windows 3'-0" x 4'-0" or smaller.

For larger doors and windows, add 1'-0" to height and width and figure area.

c. Base or picture moldings and chair rails. Less than 1'-0" wide, figure one SF/LF. On 1'-0" or larger, figure actual area.

d. Stairs (including treads, risers, cove and stringers). Add 2'-0" width (for treads, risers, etc.) times length plus 2'-0".

e. Balustrades. Add 1'-0" to height, figure two times area to paint two sides.

Exterior

a. Walls. (No deductions for openings.)

Siding. Figure actual area plus 10%.

Shingles. Figure actual area plus 40%.

Characteristics - Interior			Characteristics - Exterior		
Type	Coverage SF/Gal.	Surface	Type	Coverage SF/Gal.	Surface
Latex, flat	450	Plaster/drywall	Oil base*	300	Plain siding & stucco
Latex, enamel	450	Doors, windows, trim	Oil base*	450	Door, windows, trim
Shellac	500	Woodwork	Oil base*	300	Shingle siding
Varnish	500	Woodwork	Stain	200	Shingle siding
Stain	500	Woodwork	Latex, masonry	400	Stucco & masonry

*Certain latex paints may also be used on exterior work.

Brick, stucco, concrete and smooth wood surfaces. Figure actual area.

b. Doors and windows. See Interior, doors and windows.

c. Eaves (including soffit or exposed rafter ends and fascia). **Enclosed.** If sidewalls are to be painted the same color, figure 1.5 times actual area. If sidewalls are to be painted a different color, figure 2.0 times actual area. If sidewalls are not to be painted, figure 2.5 times actual area. **Rafter ends exposed:** If sidewalls are to be painted same color, figure 2.5 times actual area. If sidewalls are to be painted a different color, figure 3.0 times actual area. If sidewalls are not to be painted, figure 4.0 times actual area.

d. Porch rails. See Interior, balustrades (previous page).

e. Gutters and downspouts. Figure 2.0 SF/LF or $^2/_9$ SY/LF.

f. Latticework. Figure 2.0 times actual area for each side.

g. Fences. **Solid fence:** Figure actual area of each side to be painted. **Basketweave:** Figure 1.5 times actual area for each side to be painted.

Calculating Square Foot Coverage

Triangle

To find the number of square feet in any shape triangle or 3 sided surface, multiply the height by the width and divide the total by 2.

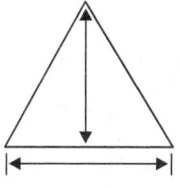

Square

Multiply the base measurement in feet times the height in feet.

Rectangle

Multiply the base measurement in feet times the height in feet.

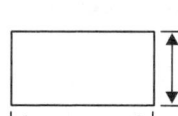

Arch Roof

Multiply length (B) by width (A) and add one-half the total.

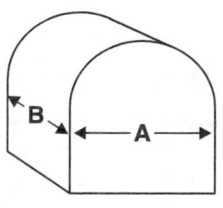

Circle

To find the number of square feet in a circle multiply the diameter (distance across) by itself and them multiply this total by .7854.

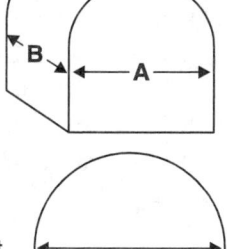

Cylinder

When the circumference (distance around the cylinder) is known, multiply height by circumference. When the diameter (distance across) is known, multiply diameter by 3.1416. This gives circumference. Then multiply by height.

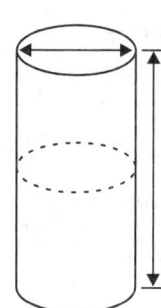

Gambrel Roof

Multiply length (B) by width (A) and add one-third of the total.

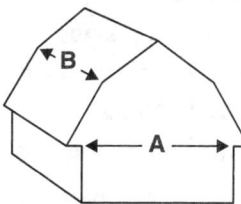

Cone

Determine area of base by multiplying 3.1416 times radius (A) in feet.

Determine the surface area of a cone by multiplying circumference of base (in feet) times one-half of the slant height (B) in feet.

Add the square foot area of the base to the square foot area of the cone for total square foot area.

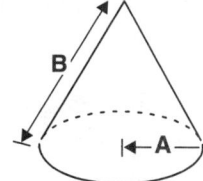

Description	Oper	Unit	Vol	Crew Size	Man-hours per Unit	Crew Output per Day	Avg Mat'l Unit Cost	Avg Labor Unit Cost	Avg Equip Unit Cost	Avg Total Unit Cost	Avg Price Incl O&P

Painting and cleaning

Frequently encountered applications

Interior

Description	Oper	Unit	Vol	Crew Size	Man-hours per Unit	Crew Output per Day	Avg Mat'l Unit Cost	Avg Labor Unit Cost	Avg Equip Unit Cost	Avg Total Unit Cost	Avg Price Incl O&P
Wet clean, walls	Inst	SF	Lg	NA	.005	1680	.02	.19	---	.21	.29
	Inst	SF	Sm	NA	.006	1260	.02	.23	---	.25	.34
Wet clean, floors	Inst	SF	Lg	NA	.004	2240	.02	.15	---	.17	.23
	Inst	SF	Sm	NA	.005	1680	.02	.19	---	.21	.29
Wet clean, millwork and trim	Inst	SF	Lg	NA	.005	1600	.02	.19	---	.21	.29
	Inst	SF	Sm	NA	.007	1200	.03	.26	---	.29	.40
Prime or seal, one coat	Inst	SF	Lg	NA	.004	1840	.07	.15	---	.22	.29
	Inst	SF	Sm	NA	.006	1380	.08	.23	---	.31	.41
Paint, one coat	Inst	SF	Lg	NA	.005	1680	.12	.19	---	.31	.40
	Inst	SF	Sm	NA	.006	1260	.13	.23	---	.36	.46
Paint, two coats	Inst	SF	Lg	NA	.008	1040	.21	.30	---	.51	.65
	Inst	SF	Sm	NA	.010	780.0	.24	.38	---	.62	.79

Exterior

Description	Oper	Unit	Vol	Crew Size	Man-hours per Unit	Crew Output per Day	Avg Mat'l Unit Cost	Avg Labor Unit Cost	Avg Equip Unit Cost	Avg Total Unit Cost	Avg Price Incl O&P
Wet clean, walls	Inst	SF	Lg	NA	.005	1480	.03	.19	---	.22	.30
	Inst	SF	Sm	NA	.007	1110	.03	.26	---	.29	.40
Paint, one coat	Inst	SF	Lg	NA	.007	1200	.27	.26	---	.53	.67
	Inst	SF	Sm	NA	.009	900.0	.30	.34	---	.64	.81
Paint, two coats	Inst	SF	Lg	NA	.012	680.0	.40	.45	---	.85	1.08
	Inst	SF	Sm	NA	.016	510.0	.44	.61	---	1.05	1.33

Interior

Time calculations include normal materials handling and protection of furniture and other property not to be painted

Preparation

Excluding openings, unless otherwise indicated

Cleaning, wet

Smooth finishes

Description	Oper	Unit	Vol	Crew Size	Man-hours per Unit	Crew Output per Day	Avg Mat'l Unit Cost	Avg Labor Unit Cost	Avg Equip Unit Cost	Avg Total Unit Cost	Avg Price Incl O&P
Plaster and drywall	Inst	SF	Lg	NA	.005	1680	.02	.19	---	.21	.29
	Inst	SF	Sm	NA	.006	1260	.02	.23	---	.25	.34
Paneling	Inst	SF	Lg	NA	.004	1800	.02	.15	---	.17	.23
	Inst	SF	Sm	NA	.006	1350	.03	.23	---	.26	.35
Millwork and trim	Inst	SF	Lg	NA	.005	1600	.02	.19	---	.21	.29
	Inst	SF	Sm	NA	.007	1200	.03	.26	---	.29	.40
Floors	Inst	SF	Lg	NA	.004	2240	.02	.15	---	.17	.23
	Inst	SF	Sm	NA	.005	1680	.02	.19	---	.21	.29

Sand finishes

Description	Oper	Unit	Vol	Crew Size	Man-hours per Unit	Crew Output per Day	Avg Mat'l Unit Cost	Avg Labor Unit Cost	Avg Equip Unit Cost	Avg Total Unit Cost	Avg Price Incl O&P
	Inst	SF	Lg	NA	.007	1160	.02	.26	---	.28	.39
	Inst	SF	Sm	NA	.009	870.0	.02	.34	---	.36	.50

Description	Oper	Unit	Vol	Crew Size	Man-hours per Unit	Crew Output per Day	Avg Mat'l Unit Cost	Avg Labor Unit Cost	Avg Equip Unit Cost	Avg Total Unit Cost	Avg Price Incl O&P
Sheetrock or drywall, repair joints and cracks or pops											
Tape, fill, and finish	Inst	SF	Lg	NA	.009	880.0	.05	.34	---	.39	.53
	Inst	SF	Sm	NA	.012	660.0	.06	.45	---	.51	.70
Sheetrock or drywall, repair											
Thin coat plaster in lieu of taping											
	Inst	SF	Lg	NA	.012	680.0	.10	.45	---	.55	.75
	Inst	SF	Sm	NA	.016	510.0	.11	.61	---	.72	.97
Light sanding											
Before first coat	Inst	SF	Lg	NA	.005	1600	.01	.19	---	.20	.28
	Inst	SF	Sm	NA	.007	1200	.01	.26	---	.27	.38
Before second coat	Inst	SF	Lg	NA	.005	1760	.01	.19	---	.20	.28
	Inst	SF	Sm	NA	.006	1320	.01	.23	---	.24	.33
Before third coat	Inst	SF	Lg	NA	.004	1920	.01	.15	---	.16	.22
	Inst	SF	Sm	NA	.006	1440	.01	.23	---	.24	.33
Liquid removal of paint or varnish											
Paneling (170 SF/gal)	Inst	SF	Lg	NA	.025	320.0	.20	.95	---	1.15	1.54
	Inst	SF	Sm	NA	.033	240.0	.22	1.25	---	1.47	1.99
Millwork & trim (170 SF/gal)	Inst	SF	Lg	NA	.029	280.0	.20	1.10	---	1.30	1.76
	Inst	SF	Sm	NA	.038	210.0	.22	1.44	---	1.66	2.25
Floors (170 SF/gal)	Inst	SF	Lg	NA	.017	480.0	.20	.64	---	.84	1.12
	Inst	SF	Sm	NA	.022	360.0	.22	.83	---	1.05	1.41
Burning off paint											
	Inst	SF	Lg	NA	.040	200.0	.04	1.51	---	1.55	2.16
	Inst	SF	Sm	NA	.053	150.0	.04	2.00	---	2.04	2.85

One coat application

Excluding openings unless otherwise indicated

Sizing, on sheetrock or plaster

Smooth finish

Description	Oper	Unit	Vol	Crew Size	Man-hours per Unit	Crew Output per Day	Avg Mat'l Unit Cost	Avg Labor Unit Cost	Avg Equip Unit Cost	Avg Total Unit Cost	Avg Price Incl O&P
Brush (650 SF/gal)	Inst	SF	Lg	NA	.003	2400	.04	.11	---	.15	.20
	Inst	SF	Sm	NA	.004	1800	.04	.15	---	.19	.26
Roller (625 SF/gal)	Inst	SF	Lg	NA	.003	3200	.04	.11	---	.15	.20
	Inst	SF	Sm	NA	.003	2400	.04	.11	---	.15	.20

Sand finish

Description	Oper	Unit	Vol	Crew Size	Man-hours per Unit	Crew Output per Day	Avg Mat'l Unit Cost	Avg Labor Unit Cost	Avg Equip Unit Cost	Avg Total Unit Cost	Avg Price Incl O&P
Brush (550 SF/gal)	Inst	SF	Lg	NA	.005	1720	.05	.19	---	.24	.32
	Inst	SF	Sm	NA	.006	1290	.05	.23	---	.28	.37
Roller (525 SF/gal)	Inst	SF	Lg	NA	.003	2320	.05	.11	---	.16	.21
	Inst	SF	Sm	NA	.005	1740	.05	.19	---	.24	.32

Description	Oper	Unit	Vol	Crew Size	Man-hours per Unit	Crew Output per Day	Avg Mat'l Unit Cost	Avg Labor Unit Cost	Avg Equip Unit Cost	Avg Total Unit Cost	Avg Price Incl O&P
Sealer											
Sheetrock or plaster											
Smooth finish											
Brush (300 SF/gal)	Inst	SF	Lg	NA	.006	1440	.07	.23	---	.30	.39
	Inst	SF	Sm	NA	.007	1080	.08	.26	---	.34	.46
Roller (285 SF/gal)	Inst	SF	Lg	NA	.004	1840	.07	.15	---	.22	.29
	Inst	SF	Sm	NA	.006	1380	.08	.23	---	.31	.41
Spray (250 SF/gal)	Inst	SF	Lg	NC	.003	2600	.08	.12	.02	.22	.27
	Inst	SF	Sm	NC	.004	1950	.09	.16	.03	.28	.35
Sand finish											
Brush (250 SF/gal)	Inst	SF	Lg	NA	.008	1040	.08	.30	---	.38	.51
	Inst	SF	Sm	NA	.010	780.00	.09	.38	---	.47	.63
Roller (235 SF/gal)	Inst	SF	Lg	NA	.006	1360	.09	.23	---	.32	.42
	Inst	SF	Sm	NA	.008	1020	.10	.30	---	.40	.53
Spray (210 SF/gal)	Inst	SF	Lg	NC	.003	2600	.10	.12	.02	.24	.29
	Inst	SF	Sm	NC	.004	1950	.11	.16	.03	.30	.37
Acoustical tile or panels											
Brush (225 SF/gal)	Inst	SF	Lg	NA	.006	1240	.09	.23	---	.32	.42
	Inst	SF	Sm	NA	.009	930.0	.10	.34	---	.44	.59
Roller (200 SF/gal)	Inst	SF	Lg	NA	.005	1600	.10	.19	---	.29	.37
	Inst	SF	Sm	NA	.007	1200	.11	.26	---	.37	.49
Spray (160 SF/gal)	Inst	SF	Lg	NC	.004	2200	.13	.16	.02	.31	.38
	Inst	SF	Sm	NC	.005	1650	.14	.19	.03	.36	.46
Latex											
Drywall or plaster, latex flat											
Smooth finish											
Brush (300 SF/gal)	Inst	SF	Lg	NA	.006	1320	.11	.23	---	.34	.44
	Inst	SF	Sm	NA	.008	990.0	.13	.30	---	.43	.57
Roller (285 SF/gal)	Inst	SF	Lg	NA	.005	1680	.12	.19	---	.31	.40
	Inst	SF	Sm	NA	.006	1260	.13	.23	---	.36	.46
Spray (260 SF/gal)	Inst	SF	Lg	NC	.003	2400	.13	.12	.02	.27	.33
	Inst	SF	Sm	NC	.004	1800	.15	.16	.03	.34	.41
Sand finish											
Brush (250 SF/gal)	Inst	SF	Lg	NA	.008	960.0	.14	.30	---	.44	.58
	Inst	SF	Sm	NA	.011	720.0	.15	.42	---	.57	.75
Roller (235 SF/gal)	Inst	SF	Lg	NA	.007	1200	.15	.26	---	.41	.54
	Inst	SF	Sm	NA	.009	900.0	.16	.34	---	.50	.65
Spray (210 SF/gal)	Inst	SF	Lg	NC	.003	2400	.16	.12	.02	.30	.36
	Inst	SF	Sm	NC	.004	1800	.18	.16	.03	.37	.45
Texture or stipple applied to drywall, one coat											
Brush (125 SF/gal)	Inst	SF	Lg	NA	.007	1200	.27	.26	---	.53	.67
	Inst	SF	Sm	NA	.009	900.0	.30	.34	---	.64	.81
Roller (120 SF/gal)	Inst	SF	Lg	NA	.005	1600	.29	.19	---	.48	.58
	Inst	SF	Sm	NA	.007	1200	.31	.26	---	.57	.71

Description	Oper	Unit	Vol	Crew Size	Man-hours per Unit	Crew Output per Day	Avg Mat'l Unit Cost	Avg Labor Unit Cost	Avg Equip Unit Cost	Avg Total Unit Cost	Avg Price Incl O&P
Paneling, latex enamel											
Brush (300 SF/gal)	Inst	SF	Lg	NA	.006	1320	.11	.23	---	.34	**.44**
	Inst	SF	Sm	NA	.008	990.0	.13	.30	---	.43	**.57**
Roller (285 SF/gal)	Inst	SF	Lg	NA	.005	1680	.12	.19	---	.31	**.40**
	Inst	SF	Sm	NA	.006	1260	.13	.23	---	.36	**.46**
Spray (260 SF/gal)	Inst	SF	Lg	NC	.003	2400	.13	.12	.02	.27	**.33**
	Inst	SF	Sm	NC	.004	1800	.15	.16	.03	.34	**.41**
Acoustical tile or panels, latex flat											
Brush (225 SF/gal)	Inst	SF	Lg	NA	.007	1120	.15	.26	---	.41	**.54**
	Inst	SF	Sm	NA	.010	840.0	.17	.38	---	.55	**.72**
Roller (210 SF/gal)	Inst	SF	Lg	NA	.006	1440	.16	.23	---	.39	**.49**
	Inst	SF	Sm	NA	.007	1080	.18	.26	---	.44	**.57**
Spray (185 SF/gal)	Inst	SF	Lg	NC	.004	2000	.19	.16	.03	.38	**.46**
	Inst	SF	Sm	NC	.005	1500	.20	.19	.03	.42	**.52**
Millwork and trim, latex enamel											
Doors and windows											
Roller and/or brush (360 SF/gal)	Inst	SF	Lg	NA	.013	640.0	.10	.49	---	.59	**.80**
	Inst	SF	Sm	NA	.017	480.0	.10	.64	---	.74	**1.01**
Spray, doors only (325 SF / gal)	Inst	SF	Lg	NC	.006	1360	.11	.23	.04	.38	**.49**
	Inst	SF	Sm	NC	.008	1020	.12	.31	.05	.48	**.62**
Cabinets											
Roller and/or brush (360 SF/gal)	Inst	SF	Lg	NA	.013	600.0	.10	.49	---	.59	**.80**
	Inst	SF	Sm	NA	.018	450.0	.10	.68	---	.78	**1.06**
Spray, doors only (325 SF / gal)	Inst	SF	Lg	NC	.006	1300	.11	.23	.04	.38	**.49**
	Inst	SF	Sm	NC	.008	975.0	.12	.31	.05	.48	**.62**
Louvers, spray (300 SF/gal)											
	Inst	SF	Lg	NC	.018	440.0	.11	.70	.12	.93	**1.22**
	Inst	SF	Sm	NC	.024	330.0	.13	.94	.16	1.23	**1.61**
Picture molding, chair rail, base, ceiling mold etc., less than 6" high											
Note: SF equals LF on trim less than 6" high											
Brush (900 SF/gal)	Inst	SF	Lg	NA	.008	960.0	.04	.30	---	.34	**.47**
	Inst	SF	Sm	NA	.011	720.0	.04	.42	---	.46	**.63**
Floors, wood											
Brush (405 SF/gal)	Inst	SF	Lg	NA	.004	2000	.08	.15	---	.23	**.30**
	Inst	SF	Sm	NA	.005	1500	.09	.19	---	.28	**.36**
Roller (385 SF/gal)	Inst	SF	Lg	NA	.003	2400	.09	.11	---	.20	**.26**
	Inst	SF	Sm	NA	.004	1800	.10	.15	---	.25	**.32**
For custom colors, ADD	Inst	%	Lg	---	---	---	10.0	---	---	---	**---**
	Inst	%	Sm	---	---	---	10.0	---	---	---	**---**
Floor seal											
Brush (450 SF/gal)	Inst	SF	Lg	NA	.003	2800	.07	.11	---	.18	**.24**
	Inst	SF	Sm	NA	.004	2100	.08	.15	---	.23	**.30**
Roller (430 SF/gal)	Inst	SF	Lg	NA	.003	3200	.08	.11	---	.19	**.25**
	Inst	SF	Sm	NA	.003	2400	.08	.11	---	.19	**.25**
Penetrating stainwax (hardwood floors)											
Brush (450 SF/gal)	Inst	SF	Lg	NA	.004	2000	.07	.15	---	.22	**.29**
	Inst	SF	Sm	NA	.005	1500	.08	.19	---	.27	**.35**
Roller (425 SF/gal)	Inst	SF	Lg	NA	.003	2400	.08	.11	---	.19	**.25**
	Inst	SF	Sm	NA	.004	1800	.09	.15	---	.24	**.31**

Description	Oper	Unit	Vol	Crew Size	Man-hours per Unit	Crew Output per Day	Avg Mat'l Unit Cost	Avg Labor Unit Cost	Avg Equip Unit Cost	Avg Total Unit Cost	Avg Price Incl O&P
Natural finishes											
Paneling, brush work unless otherwise indicated											
Stain, brush on - wipe off (360 SF/gal)											
	Inst	SF	Lg	NA	.014	560.0	.09	.53	---	.62	**.84**
	Inst	SF	Sm	NA	.019	420.0	.10	.72	---	.82	**1.12**
Varnish (380 SF/gal)											
	Inst	SF	Lg	NA	.006	1360	.12	.23	---	.35	**.45**
	Inst	SF	Sm	NA	.008	1020	.13	.30	---	.43	**.57**
Shellac (630 SF/gal)											
	Inst	SF	Lg	NA	.005	1600	.07	.19	---	.26	**.34**
	Inst	SF	Sm	NA	.007	1200	.08	.26	---	.34	**.46**
Lacquer											
Brush (450 SF/gal)											
	Inst	SF	Lg	NA	.004	1920	.07	.15	---	.22	**.29**
	Inst	SF	Sm	NA	.006	1440	.08	.23	---	.31	**.41**
Spray (300 SF/gal)	Inst	SF	Lg	NC	.003	2400	.11	.12	.02	.25	**.30**
	Inst	SF	Sm	NC	.004	1800	.12	.16	.03	.31	**.38**
Doors and windows, brush work unless otherwise indicated											
Stain, brush on - wipe off (450 SF/gal)											
	Inst	SF	Lg	NA	.032	250.0	.07	1.21	---	1.28	**1.77**
	Inst	SF	Sm	NA	.043	187.5	.08	1.63	---	1.71	**2.36**
Varnish (550 SF/gal)											
	Inst	SF	Lg	NA	.024	340.0	.08	.91	---	.99	**1.36**
	Inst	SF	Sm	NA	.031	255.0	.09	1.17	---	1.26	**1.74**
Shellac (550 SF/gal)											
	Inst	SF	Lg	NA	.022	365.0	.08	.83	---	.91	**1.25**
	Inst	SF	Sm	NA	.029	273.8	.09	1.10	---	1.19	**1.63**
Lacquer											
Brush (550 SF/gal)											
	Inst	SF	Lg	NA	.020	405.0	.06	.76	---	.82	**1.13**
	Inst	SF	Sm	NA	.026	303.8	.06	.98	---	1.04	**1.44**
Spray doors (300 SF/gal)	Inst	SF	Lg	NC	.010	800.0	.11	.39	.07	.57	**.74**
	Inst	SF	Sm	NC	.013	600.0	.12	.51	.09	.72	**.93**
Cabinets, brush work unless otherwise indicated											
Stain, brush on - wipe off (450 SF/gal)											
	Inst	SF	Lg	NA	.034	235.0	.07	1.29	---	1.36	**1.88**
	Inst	SF	Sm	NA	.045	176.3	.08	1.70	---	1.78	**2.47**
Varnish (550 SF/gal)											
	Inst	SF	Lg	NA	.025	320.0	.08	.95	---	1.03	**1.41**
	Inst	SF	Sm	NA	.033	240.0	.09	1.25	---	1.34	**1.85**
Shellac (550 SF/gal)											
	Inst	SF	Lg	NA	.023	345.0	.08	.87	---	.95	**1.31**
	Inst	SF	Sm	NA	.031	258.8	.09	1.17	---	1.26	**1.74**
Lacquer											
Brush (550 SF/gal)											
	Inst	SF	Lg	NA	.021	385.0	.06	.79	---	.85	**1.18**
	Inst	SF	Sm	NA	.028	288.8	.06	1.06	---	1.12	**1.55**
Spray (300 SF/gal)	Inst	SF	Lg	NC	.011	750.0	.11	.43	.07	.61	**.79**
	Inst	SF	Sm	NC	.014	562.5	.12	.55	.09	.76	**.99**
Louvers, lacquer, spray											
(300 SF/gal)	Inst	SF	Lg	NC	.017	480.0	.11	.66	.11	.88	**1.16**
	Inst	SF	Sm	NC	.022	360.0	.12	.86	.14	1.12	**1.47**

Description	Oper	Unit	Vol	Crew Size	Man-hours per Unit	Crew Output per Day	Avg Mat'l Unit Cost	Avg Labor Unit Cost	Avg Equip Unit Cost	Avg Total Unit Cost	Avg Price Incl O&P
Picture molding, chair rail, base, ceiling mold etc., less than 6" high											
Note: SF equals LF on trim less than 6" high											
Varnish, brush (900 SF/gal)											
	Inst	SF	Lg	NA	.008	1040	.05	.30	---	.35	.48
	Inst	SF	Sm	NA	.010	780.0	.06	.38	---	.44	.60
Shellac, brush (900 SF/gal)											
	Inst	SF	Lg	NA	.008	1040	.05	.30	---	.35	.48
	Inst	SF	Sm	NA	.010	780.0	.06	.38	---	.44	.60
Lacquer, spray (700 SF/gal)											
	Inst	SF	Lg	NA	.006	1280	.05	.23	.04	.32	.41
	Inst	SF	Sm	NA	.008	960.0	.05	.30	.05	.40	.53
Floors, wood, brush work unless otherwise indicated											
Shellac (450 SF/gal)											
	Inst	SF	Lg	NA	.004	2000	.10	.15	---	.25	.32
	Inst	SF	Sm	NA	.005	1500	.11	.19	---	.30	.39
Varnish (500 SF/gal)											
	Inst	SF	Lg	NA	.004	2000	.09	.15	---	.24	.31
	Inst	SF	Sm	NA	.005	1500	.10	.19	---	.29	.37
Buffing, by machine											
	Inst	SF	Lg	NA	.003	2800	.02	.11	---	.13	.18
	Inst	SF	Sm	NA	.004	2100	.03	.15	---	.18	.24
Waxing and polishing, by hand (1,000 SF/gal)											
	Inst	SF	Lg	NA	.005	1520	.04	.19	---	.23	.31
	Inst	SF	Sm	NA	.007	1140	.05	.26	---	.31	.43

Two coat application

Excluding openings, unless otherwise indicated
For sizing or sealer, see One coat application, page 329

Latex

No spray work included, see One coat application, page 330

Description	Oper	Unit	Vol	Crew Size	Man-hours per Unit	Crew Output per Day	Avg Mat'l Unit Cost	Avg Labor Unit Cost	Avg Equip Unit Cost	Avg Total Unit Cost	Avg Price Incl O&P
Drywall or plaster, latex flat											
Smooth finish											
Brush (170 SF/gal)	Inst	SF	Lg	NA	.009	880.0	.20	.34	---	.54	.70
	Inst	SF	Sm	NA	.012	660.0	.22	.45	---	.67	.88
Roller (160 SF/gal)	Inst	SF	Lg	NA	.008	1040	.21	.30	---	.51	.65
	Inst	SF	Sm	NA	.010	780.0	.24	.38	---	.62	.79
Sand finish											
Brush (170 SF/gal)	Inst	SF	Lg	NA	.013	600.0	.20	.49	---	.69	.91
	Inst	SF	Sm	NA	.018	450.0	.22	.68	---	.90	1.20
Roller (160 SF/gal)	Inst	SF	Lg	NA	.011	760.0	.21	.42	---	.63	.81
	Inst	SF	Sm	NA	.014	570.0	.24	.53	---	.77	1.01
Paneling, latex enamel											
Brush (170 SF/gal)	Inst	SF	Lg	NA	.009	880.0	.20	.34	---	.54	.70
	Inst	SF	Sm	NA	.012	660.0	.22	.45	---	.67	.88
Roller (160 SF/gal)	Inst	SF	Lg	NA	.008	1040	.21	.30	---	.51	.65
	Inst	SF	Sm	NA	.010	780.0	.24	.38	---	.62	.79
Acoustical tile or panels, latex flat											
Brush (130 SF/gal)	Inst	SF	Lg	NA	.012	680.0	.26	.45	---	.71	.92
	Inst	SF	Sm	NA	.016	510.0	.29	.61	---	.90	1.17
Roller (120 SF/gal)	Inst	SF	Lg	NA	.009	880.0	.29	.34	---	.63	.80
	Inst	SF	Sm	NA	.012	660.0	.31	.45	---	.76	.98

Description	Oper	Unit	Vol	Crew Size	Man-hours per Unit	Crew Output per Day	Avg Mat'l Unit Cost	Avg Labor Unit Cost	Avg Equip Unit Cost	Avg Total Unit Cost	Avg Price Incl O&P
Millwork and trim, enamel											
Doors and windows											
Roller and/or brush (200 SF/gal)											
	Inst	SF	Lg	NA	.024	335.0	.17	.91	---	1.08	**1.46**
	Inst	SF	Sm	NA	.032	251.3	.19	1.21	---	1.40	**1.90**
Cabinets											
Roller and/or brush (200 SF/gal)											
	Inst	SF	Lg	NA	.025	315.0	.17	.95	---	1.12	**1.51**
	Inst	SF	Sm	NA	.034	236.3	.19	1.29	---	1.48	**2.01**

Louvers, see One coat application, page 331

Picture molding, chair rail, base, ceiling mold etc., less than 6" high

Note: SF equals LF on trim less than 6" high

Description	Oper	Unit	Vol	Crew Size	Man-hours per Unit	Crew Output per Day	Avg Mat'l Unit Cost	Avg Labor Unit Cost	Avg Equip Unit Cost	Avg Total Unit Cost	Avg Price Incl O&P
Brush (510 SF/gal)											
	Inst	SF	Lg	NA	.016	500.0	.07	.61	---	.68	**.92**
	Inst	SF	Sm	NA	.021	375.0	.07	.79	---	.86	**1.19**
Floors, wood											
Brush (230 SF/gal)											
	Inst	SF	Lg	NA	.007	1120	.15	.26	---	.41	**.54**
	Inst	SF	Sm	NA	.010	840.0	.16	.38	---	.54	**.71**
Roller (220 SF/gal)											
	Inst	SF	Lg	NA	.006	1280	.16	.23	---	.39	**.49**
	Inst	SF	Sm	NA	.008	960.0	.17	.30	---	.47	**.61**
For custom colors, ADD											
	Inst	%	Lg	---	---	---	10.0	---	---	---	---
	Inst	%	Sm	---	---	---	10.0	---	---	---	---

For wood floor seal, penetrating stainwax, or natural finish, see One coat application, page 331

Exterior

Time calculations include normal materials handling and protection of property not to be painted

Preparation

Excluding openings, unless otherwise indicated

Cleaning, wet

Description	Oper	Unit	Vol	Crew Size	Man-hours per Unit	Crew Output per Day	Avg Mat'l Unit Cost	Avg Labor Unit Cost	Avg Equip Unit Cost	Avg Total Unit Cost	Avg Price Incl O&P
Plain siding	Inst	SF	Lg	NA	.005	1480	.03	.19	---	.22	**.30**
	Inst	SF	Sm	NA	.007	1110	.03	.26	---	.29	**.40**
Exterior doors and trim											

Note: SF equals LF on trim less than 6" high

Description	Oper	Unit	Vol	Crew Size	Man-hours per Unit	Crew Output per Day	Avg Mat'l Unit Cost	Avg Labor Unit Cost	Avg Equip Unit Cost	Avg Total Unit Cost	Avg Price Incl O&P
	Inst	SF	Lg	NA	.006	1400	.03	.23	---	.26	**.35**
	Inst	SF	Sm	NA	.008	1050	.03	.30	---	.33	**.46**
Windows, wash and clean glass											
	Inst	SF	Lg	NA	.006	1280	.02	.23	---	.25	**.34**
	Inst	SF	Sm	NA	.008	960.0	.02	.30	---	.32	**.45**
Porch floors and steps	Inst	SF	Lg	NA	.004	2240	.02	.15	---	.17	**.23**
	Inst	SF	Sm	NA	.005	1680	.03	.19	---	.22	**.30**
Acid wash											
Gutters and downspouts	Inst	SF	Lg	NA	.008	1040	.02	.30	---	.32	**.45**
	Inst	SF	Sm	NA	.010	780.0	.02	.38	---	.40	**.55**
Sanding, light											
Porch floors and steps	Inst	SF	Lg	NA	.005	1760	.02	.19	---	.21	**.29**
	Inst	SF	Sm	NA	.006	1320	.02	.23	---	.25	**.34**

Description	Oper	Unit	Vol	Crew Size	Man-hours per Unit	Crew Output per Day	Avg Mat'l Unit Cost	Avg Labor Unit Cost	Avg Equip Unit Cost	Avg Total Unit Cost	Avg Price Incl O&P
Sanding and puttying											
Plain siding	Inst	SF	Lg	NA	.006	1440	.02	.23	---	.25	.34
	Inst	SF	Sm	NA	.007	1080	.02	.26	---	.28	.39
Exterior doors and trim											
Note: SF equals LF on trim less than 6" high											
	Inst	SF	Lg	NA	.011	720.0	.02	.42	---	.44	.60
	Inst	SF	Sm	NA	.015	540.0	.02	.57	---	.59	.82
Puttying sash or reglazing -- Windows (30 SF glass/lb glazing compound)											
	Inst	SF	Lg	NA	.033	240.0	.65	1.25	---	1.90	2.46
	Inst	SF	Sm	NA	.044	180.0	.72	1.66	---	2.38	3.12

One coat application
Excluding openings, unless otherwise indicated

Latex, flat (unless otherwise indicated)

Description	Oper	Unit	Vol	Crew Size	Man-hours per Unit	Crew Output per Day	Avg Mat'l Unit Cost	Avg Labor Unit Cost	Avg Equip Unit Cost	Avg Total Unit Cost	Avg Price Incl O&P
Plain siding											
Brush (300 SF/gal)	Inst	SF	Lg	NA	.010	800.0	.11	.38	---	.49	.65
	Inst	SF	Sm	NA	.013	600.0	.13	.49	---	.62	.83
Roller (275 SF/gal)	Inst	SF	Lg	NA	.008	1040	.12	.30	---	.42	.56
	Inst	SF	Sm	NA	.010	780.0	.14	.38	---	.52	.68
Spray (325 SF/gal)	Inst	SF	Lg	NC	.005	1750	.11	.19	.03	.33	.42
	Inst	SF	Sm	NC	.006	1313	.12	.23	.04	.39	.50
Shingle siding											
Brush (270 SF/gal)	Inst	SF	Lg	NA	.009	880.0	.13	.34	---	.47	.62
	Inst	SF	Sm	NA	.012	660.0	.14	.45	---	.59	.79
Roller (260 SF/gal)	Inst	SF	Lg	NA	.007	1200	.13	.26	---	.39	.51
	Inst	SF	Sm	NA	.009	900.0	.15	.34	---	.49	.64
Spray (300 SF/gal)	Inst	SF	Lg	NC	.005	1600	.11	.19	.03	.33	.42
	Inst	SF	Sm	NC	.007	1200	.13	.27	.04	.44	.56
Stucco											
Brush (135 SF/gal)	Inst	SF	Lg	NA	.010	800.0	.25	.38	---	.63	.80
	Inst	SF	Sm	NA	.013	600.0	.28	.49	---	.77	1.00
Roller (125 SF/gal)	Inst	SF	Lg	NA	.007	1200	.27	.26	---	.53	.67
	Inst	SF	Sm	NA	.009	900.0	.30	.34	---	.64	.81
Spray (150 SF/gal)	Inst	SF	Lg	NC	.005	1600	.23	.19	.03	.45	.56
	Inst	SF	Sm	NC	.007	1200	.25	.27	.04	.56	.70

Cement walls, see Cement base paint, page 337

Description	Oper	Unit	Vol	Crew Size	Man-hours per Unit	Crew Output per Day	Avg Mat'l Unit Cost	Avg Labor Unit Cost	Avg Equip Unit Cost	Avg Total Unit Cost	Avg Price Incl O&P
Masonry block, brick, tile; masonry latex											
Brush (180 SF/gal)	Inst	SF	Lg	NA	.009	880.0	.19	.34	---	.53	.69
	Inst	SF	Sm	NA	.012	660.0	.21	.45	---	.66	.87
Roller (125 SF/gal)	Inst	SF	Lg	NA	.006	1440	.27	.23	---	.50	.61
	Inst	SF	Sm	NA	.007	1080	.30	.26	---	.56	.70
Spray (160 SF/gal)	Inst	SF	Lg	NC	.004	1840	.21	.16	.03	.40	.48
	Inst	SF	Sm	NC	.006	1380	.24	.23	.04	.51	.63

Description	Oper	Unit	Vol	Crew Size	Man-hours per Unit	Crew Output per Day	Avg Mat'l Unit Cost	Avg Labor Unit Cost	Avg Equip Unit Cost	Avg Total Unit Cost	Avg Price Incl O&P
Doors, exterior side only											
Brush (375 SF/gal)	Inst	SF	Lg	NA	.013	640.0	.09	.49	---	.58	**.79**
	Inst	SF	Sm	NA	.017	480.0	.10	.64	---	.74	**1.01**
Roller (375 SF/gal)	Inst	SF	Lg	NA	.009	865.0	.09	.34	---	.43	**.58**
	Inst	SF	Sm	NA	.012	648.8	.10	.45	---	.55	**.75**
Windows, exterior side only, brush work											
(450 SF/gal)	Inst	SF	Lg	NA	.013	640.0	.08	.49	---	.57	**.78**
	Inst	SF	Sm	NA	.017	480.0	.08	.64	---	.72	**.99**
Trim, less than 6" high, brush											
Note: SF equals LF on trim less than 6" high											
High gloss (300 SF/gal)	Inst	SF	Lg	NA	.009	900.0	.11	.34	---	.45	**.60**
	Inst	SF	Sm	NA	.012	675.0	.13	.45	---	.58	**.78**
Screens, full; high gloss											
Paint applied to wood only, brush work											
(700 SF/gal)	Inst	SF	Lg	NA	.015	540.0	.05	.57	---	.62	**.85**
	Inst	SF	Sm	NA	.020	405.0	.05	.76	---	.81	**1.11**
Paint applied to wood (brush) and wire (spray)											
(475 SF/gal)	Inst	SF	Lg	NC	.018	450.0	.07	.70	---	.77	**1.06**
	Inst	SF	Sm	NC	.024	337.5	.08	.94	---	1.02	**1.40**
Storm windows and doors, 2 lites, brush work											
(340 SF/gal)	Inst	SF	Lg	NA	.024	340.0	.10	.91	---	1.01	**1.38**
	Inst	SF	Sm	NA	.031	255.0	.11	1.17	---	1.28	**1.76**
Blinds or shutters											
Brush (120 SF/gal)	Inst	SF	Lg	NA	.062	130.0	.29	2.34	---	2.63	**3.60**
	Inst	SF	Sm	NA	.082	97.50	.31	3.10	---	3.41	**4.68**
Spray (300 SF/gal)	Inst	SF	Lg	NC	.020	400.0	.11	.78	---	.89	**1.21**
	Inst	SF	Sm	NC	.027	300.0	.13	1.05	---	1.18	**1.62**
Gutters and downspouts, brush work											
(225 LF/gal), galvanized	Inst	SF	Lg	NA	.013	600.0	.15	.49	---	.64	**.85**
	Inst	SF	Sm	NA	.018	450.0	.17	.68	---	.85	**1.14**
Porch floors and steps, wood											
Brush (340 SF/gal)	Inst	SF	Lg	NA	.005	1520	.10	.19	---	.29	**.37**
	Inst	SF	Sm	NA	.007	1140	.11	.26	---	.37	**.49**
Roller (325 SF/gal)	Inst	SF	Lg	NA	.004	1920	.11	.15	---	.26	**.33**
	Inst	SF	Sm	NA	.006	1440	.12	.23	---	.35	**.45**
Shingle roofs											
Brush (135 SF/gal)	Inst	SF	Lg	NA	.008	1040	.25	.30	---	.55	**.70**
	Inst	SF	Sm	NA	.010	780.0	.28	.38	---	.66	**.84**
Roller (125 SF/gal)	Inst	SF	Lg	NA	.006	1360	.27	.23	---	.50	**.61**
	Inst	SF	Sm	NA	.008	1020	.30	.30	---	.60	**.75**
Spray (150 SF/gal)	Inst	SF	Lg	NC	.004	2080	.23	.16	.03	.42	**.50**
	Inst	SF	Sm	NC	.005	1560	.25	.19	.03	.47	**.58**
For custom colors, ADD	Inst	%	Lg	---	---	---	10.0	---	---	---	---
	Inst	%	Sm	---	---	---	10.0	---	---	---	---

Description	Oper	Unit	Vol	Crew Size	Man-hours per Unit	Crew Output per Day	Avg Mat'l Unit Cost	Avg Labor Unit Cost	Avg Equip Unit Cost	Avg Total Unit Cost	Avg Price Incl O&P
Cement base paint (epoxy concrete enamel)											
Cement walls, smooth finish											
Brush (120 SF/gal)	Inst	SF	Lg	NA	.006	1320	.68	.23	---	.91	**1.07**
	Inst	SF	Sm	NA	.008	990.0	.75	.30	---	1.05	**1.25**
Roller (110 SF/gal)	Inst	SF	Lg	NA	.004	1920	.74	.15	---	.89	**1.03**
	Inst	SF	Sm	NA	.006	1440	.81	.23	---	1.04	**1.21**
Concrete porch floors and steps											
Brush (400 SF/gal)	Inst	SF	Lg	NA	.004	2000	.20	.15	---	.35	**.43**
	Inst	SF	Sm	NA	.005	1500	.22	.19	---	.41	**.51**
Roller (375 SF/gal)	Inst	SF	Lg	NA	.003	2400	.22	.11	---	.33	**.40**
	Inst	SF	Sm	NA	.004	1800	.24	.15	---	.39	**.48**
Stain											
Shingle siding											
Brush (180 SF/gal)	Inst	SF	Lg	NA	.010	800.0	.18	.38	---	.56	**.73**
	Inst	SF	Sm	NA	.013	600.0	.20	.49	---	.69	**.91**
Roller (170 SF/gal)	Inst	SF	Lg	NA	.007	1120	.19	.26	---	.45	**.58**
	Inst	SF	Sm	NA	.010	840.0	.21	.38	---	.59	**.76**
Spray (200 SF/gal)	Inst	SF	Lg	NC	.005	1520	.17	.19	.03	.39	**.49**
	Inst	SF	Sm	NC	.007	1140	.18	.27	.05	.50	**.63**
Shingle roofs											
Brush (180 SF/gal)	Inst	SF	Lg	NA	.008	960.0	.18	.30	---	.48	**.62**
	Inst	SF	Sm	NA	.011	720.0	.20	.42	---	.62	**.80**
Roller (170 SF/gal)	Inst	SF	Lg	NA	.006	1280	.19	.23	---	.42	**.53**
	Inst	SF	Sm	NA	.008	960.0	.21	.30	---	.51	**.65**
Spray (200 SF/gal)	Inst	SF	Lg	NC	.004	1920	.17	.16	.03	.36	**.44**
	Inst	SF	Sm	NC	.006	1440	.18	.23	.04	.45	**.57**

Two coat application

Excluding openings, unless otherwise indicated

Latex, flat (unless otherwise indicated)

Description	Oper	Unit	Vol	Crew Size	Man-hours per Unit	Crew Output per Day	Avg Mat'l Unit Cost	Avg Labor Unit Cost	Avg Equip Unit Cost	Avg Total Unit Cost	Avg Price Incl O&P
Plain siding											
Brush (170 SF/gal)	Inst	SF	Lg	NA	.018	440.0	.20	.68	---	.88	**1.17**
	Inst	SF	Sm	NA	.024	330.0	.22	.91	---	1.13	**1.51**
Roller (155 SF/gal)	Inst	SF	Lg	NA	.014	560.0	.22	.53	---	.75	**.98**
	Inst	SF	Sm	NA	.019	420.0	.24	.72	---	.96	**1.27**
Spray (185 SF/gal)	Inst	SF	Lg	NC	.008	960.0	.19	.31	.05	.55	**.70**
	Inst	SF	Sm	NC	.011	720.0	.20	.43	.07	.70	**.89**
Shingle siding											
Brush (150 SF/gal)	Inst	SF	Lg	NA	.017	480.0	.23	.64	---	.87	**1.15**
	Inst	SF	Sm	NA	.022	360.0	.25	.83	---	1.08	**1.44**
Roller (150 SF/gal)	Inst	SF	Lg	NA	.013	640.0	.23	.49	---	.72	**.94**
	Inst	SF	Sm	NA	.017	480.0	.25	.64	---	.89	**1.18**
Spray (170 SF/gal)	Inst	SF	Lg	NC	.009	880.0	.20	.35	.06	.61	**.77**
	Inst	SF	Sm	NC	.012	660.0	.22	.47	.08	.77	**.98**

Description	Oper	Unit	Vol	Crew Size	Man-hours per Unit	Crew Output per Day	Avg Mat'l Unit Cost	Avg Labor Unit Cost	Avg Equip Unit Cost	Avg Total Unit Cost	Avg Price Incl O&P
Stucco											
Brush (90 SF/gal)	Inst	SF	Lg	NA	.017	480.0	.38	.64	---	1.02	**1.32**
	Inst	SF	Sm	NA	.022	360.0	.42	.83	---	1.25	**1.63**
Roller (85 SF/gal)	Inst	SF	Lg	NA	.012	680.0	.40	.45	---	.85	**1.08**
	Inst	SF	Sm	NA	.016	510.0	.44	.61	---	1.05	**1.33**
Spray (100 SF/gal)	Inst	SF	Lg	NC	.009	880.0	.34	.35	.06	.75	**.92**
	Inst	SF	Sm	NC	.012	660.0	.38	.47	.08	.93	**1.15**

Cement wall, see Cement base paint, page 339

Masonry block, brick, tile; masonry latex

Description	Oper	Unit	Vol	Crew Size	Man-hours per Unit	Crew Output per Day	Avg Mat'l Unit Cost	Avg Labor Unit Cost	Avg Equip Unit Cost	Avg Total Unit Cost	Avg Price Incl O&P
Brush (120 SF/gal)	Inst	SF	Lg	NA	.015	520.0	.29	.57	---	.86	**1.11**
	Inst	SF	Sm	NA	.021	390.0	.31	.79	---	1.10	**1.45**
Roller (85 SF/gal)	Inst	SF	Lg	NA	.011	760.0	.40	.42	---	.82	**1.02**
	Inst	SF	Sm	NA	.014	570.0	.44	.53	---	.97	**1.23**
Spray (105 SF/gal)	Inst	SF	Lg	NC	.008	1000	.33	.31	.05	.69	**.85**
	Inst	SF	Sm	NC	.011	750.0	.36	.43	.07	.86	**1.07**
Doors, exterior side only											
Brush (215 SF/gal)	Inst	SF	Lg	NA	.024	335.0	.16	.91	---	1.07	**1.45**
	Inst	SF	Sm	NA	.032	251.3	.18	1.21	---	1.39	**1.89**
Roller (215 SF/gal)	Inst	SF	Lg	NA	.018	455.0	.16	.68	---	.84	**1.13**
	Inst	SF	Sm	NA	.023	341.3	.18	.87	---	1.05	**1.42**
Windows, exterior side only, brush work (255 SF/gal)											
	Inst	SF	Lg	NA	.024	335.0	.13	.91	---	1.04	**1.41**
	Inst	SF	Sm	NA	.032	251.3	.15	1.21	---	1.36	**1.86**
Trim, less than 6" high, brush. High gloss (230 SF/gal)											

Note: SF equals LF on trim less than 6" high

Description	Oper	Unit	Vol	Crew Size	Man-hours per Unit	Crew Output per Day	Avg Mat'l Unit Cost	Avg Labor Unit Cost	Avg Equip Unit Cost	Avg Total Unit Cost	Avg Price Incl O&P
	Inst	SF	Lg	NA	.017	480.0	.15	.64	---	.79	**1.07**
	Inst	SF	Sm	NA	.022	360.0	.16	.83	---	.99	**1.34**
Screens, full; high gloss											
Paint applied to wood only, brush work (400 SF/gal)											
	Inst	SF	Lg	NA	.028	285.0	.09	1.06	---	1.15	**1.58**
	Inst	SF	Sm	NA	.037	213.8	.09	1.40	---	1.49	**2.06**
Paint applied to wood (brush) and wire (spray) (270 SF/gal)											
	Inst	SF	Lg	NC	.033	240.0	.13	1.29	---	1.42	**1.94**
	Inst	SF	Sm	NC	.044	180.0	.14	1.71	---	1.85	**2.55**
Blinds or shutters											
Brush (65 SF/gal)	Inst	SF	Lg	NA	.114	70.00	.53	4.31	---	4.84	**6.62**
	Inst	SF	Sm	NA	.152	52.50	.58	5.75	---	6.33	**8.69**
Spray (170 SF/gal)	Inst	SF	Lg	NC	.038	210.0	.20	1.48	.25	1.93	**2.54**
	Inst	SF	Sm	NC	.051	157.5	.22	1.99	.33	2.54	**3.35**
Gutters and downspouts, brush work (130 LF/gal), galvanized											
	Inst	SF	Lg	NA	.025	315.0	.26	.95	---	1.21	**1.61**
	Inst	SF	Sm	NA	.034	236.3	.29	1.29	---	1.58	**2.12**

Description	Oper	Unit	Vol	Crew Size	Man-hours per Unit	Crew Output per Day	Avg Mat'l Unit Cost	Avg Labor Unit Cost	Avg Equip Unit Cost	Avg Total Unit Cost	Avg Price Incl O&P
Porch floors and steps, wood											
Brush (195 SF/gal)	Inst	SF	Lg	NA	.010	800.0	.18	.38	---	.56	**.73**
	Inst	SF	Sm	NA	.013	600.0	.19	.49	---	.68	**.90**
Roller (185 SF/gal)	Inst	SF	Lg	NA	.008	1000	.19	.30	---	.49	**.63**
	Inst	SF	Sm	NA	.011	750.0	.20	.42	---	.62	**.80**
Shingle roofs											
Brush (75 SF/gal)	Inst	SF	Lg	NA	.013	640.0	.46	.49	---	.95	**1.19**
	Inst	SF	Sm	NA	.017	480.0	.50	.64	---	1.14	**1.45**
Roller (70 SF/gal)	Inst	SF	Lg	NA	.010	800.0	.49	.38	---	.87	**1.07**
	Inst	SF	Sm	NA	.013	600.0	.54	.49	---	1.03	**1.28**
Spray (85 SF/gal)	Inst	SF	Lg	NC	.008	1000	.40	.31	.05	.76	**.93**
	Inst	SF	Sm	NC	.011	750.0	.44	.43	.07	.94	**1.15**
For custom colors, ADD	Inst	%	Lg	---	---	---	10.0	---	---	---	---
	Inst	%	Sm	---	---	---	10.0	---	---	---	---

Cement base paint (epoxy concrete enamel)

Cement walls, smooth finish

Description	Oper	Unit	Vol	Crew Size	Man-hours per Unit	Crew Output per Day	Avg Mat'l Unit Cost	Avg Labor Unit Cost	Avg Equip Unit Cost	Avg Total Unit Cost	Avg Price Incl O&P
Brush (80 SF/gal)	Inst	SF	Lg	NA	.011	720.0	1.02	.42	---	1.44	**1.70**
	Inst	SF	Sm	NA	.015	540.0	1.12	.57	---	1.69	**2.03**
Roller (75 SF/gal)	Inst	SF	Lg	NA	.008	1040	1.08	.30	---	1.38	**1.61**
	Inst	SF	Sm	NA	.010	780.0	1.20	.38	---	1.58	**1.85**

Concrete porch floors and steps

Description	Oper	Unit	Vol	Crew Size	Man-hours per Unit	Crew Output per Day	Avg Mat'l Unit Cost	Avg Labor Unit Cost	Avg Equip Unit Cost	Avg Total Unit Cost	Avg Price Incl O&P
Brush (225 SF/gal)	Inst	SF	Lg	NA	.008	1040	.36	.30	---	.66	**.82**
	Inst	SF	Sm	NA	.010	780.0	.40	.38	---	.78	**.97**
Roller (210 SF/gal)	Inst	SF	Lg	NA	.008	1000	.39	.30	---	.69	**.85**
	Inst	SF	Sm	NA	.011	750.0	.43	.42	---	.85	**1.06**

Stain

Shingle siding

Description	Oper	Unit	Vol	Crew Size	Man-hours per Unit	Crew Output per Day	Avg Mat'l Unit Cost	Avg Labor Unit Cost	Avg Equip Unit Cost	Avg Total Unit Cost	Avg Price Incl O&P
Brush (105 SF/gal)	Inst	SF	Lg	NA	.017	480.0	.31	.64	---	.95	**1.24**
	Inst	SF	Sm	NA	.022	360.0	.35	.83	---	1.18	**1.55**
Roller (100 SF/gal)	Inst	SF	Lg	NA	.013	600.0	.33	.49	---	.82	**1.05**
	Inst	SF	Sm	NA	.018	450.0	.36	.68	---	1.04	**1.35**
Spray (115 SF/gal)	Inst	SF	Lg	NC	.009	880.0	.29	.35	.06	.70	**.87**
	Inst	SF	Sm	NC	.012	660.0	.32	.47	.08	.87	**1.09**

Shingle roofs

Description	Oper	Unit	Vol	Crew Size	Man-hours per Unit	Crew Output per Day	Avg Mat'l Unit Cost	Avg Labor Unit Cost	Avg Equip Unit Cost	Avg Total Unit Cost	Avg Price Incl O&P
Brush (105 SF/gal)	Inst	SF	Lg	NA	.014	560.0	.31	.53	---	.84	**1.08**
	Inst	SF	Sm	NA	.019	420.0	.35	.72	---	1.07	**1.39**
Roller (100 SF/gal)	Inst	SF	Lg	NA	.011	760.0	.33	.42	---	.75	**.95**
	Inst	SF	Sm	NA	.014	570.0	.36	.53	---	.89	**1.14**
Spray (115 SF/gal)	Inst	SF	Lg	NC	.007	1120	.29	.27	.05	.61	**.75**
	Inst	SF	Sm	NC	.010	840.0	.32	.39	.06	.77	**.96**

Description	Oper	Unit	Vol	Crew Size	Man-hours per Unit	Crew Output per Day	Avg Mat'l Unit Cost	Avg Labor Unit Cost	Avg Equip Unit Cost	Avg Total Unit Cost	Avg Price Incl O&P

Paneling
Hardboard and plywood

Demolition

Description	Oper	Unit	Vol	Crew Size	Man-hours per Unit	Crew Output per Day	Avg Mat'l Unit Cost	Avg Labor Unit Cost	Avg Equip Unit Cost	Avg Total Unit Cost	Avg Price Incl O&P
Sheets, plywood or hardboard	Demo	SF	Lg	LB	.009	1850	---	.27	---	.27	**.38**
	Demo	SF	Sm	LB	.012	1295	---	.36	---	.36	**.50**
Boards, wood	Demo	SF	Lg	LB	.010	1650	---	.30	---	.30	**.42**
	Demo	SF	Sm	LB	.014	1155	---	.42	---	.42	**.59**

Installation
Waste, nails, and adhesives not included

Economy hardboard

Presdwood, 4' x 8' sheets
Standard

Description	Oper	Unit	Vol	Crew Size	Man-hours per Unit	Crew Output per Day	Avg Mat'l Unit Cost	Avg Labor Unit Cost	Avg Equip Unit Cost	Avg Total Unit Cost	Avg Price Incl O&P
1/8" T	Inst	SF	Lg	2C	.016	1025	.26	.59	---	.85	**1.13**
	Inst	SF	Sm	2C	.022	717.5	.28	.81	---	1.09	**1.46**
1/4" T	Inst	SF	Lg	2C	.016	1025	.39	.59	---	.98	**1.28**
	Inst	SF	Sm	2C	.022	717.5	.44	.81	---	1.25	**1.65**

Tempered

Description	Oper	Unit	Vol	Crew Size	Man-hours per Unit	Crew Output per Day	Avg Mat'l Unit Cost	Avg Labor Unit Cost	Avg Equip Unit Cost	Avg Total Unit Cost	Avg Price Incl O&P
1/8" T	Inst	SF	Lg	2C	.016	1025	.43	.59	---	1.02	**1.32**
	Inst	SF	Sm	2C	.022	717.5	.49	.81	---	1.30	**1.70**
1/4" T	Inst	SF	Lg	2C	.016	1025	.71	.59	---	1.30	**1.65**
	Inst	SF	Sm	2C	.022	717.5	.78	.81	---	1.59	**2.04**

Duolux, 4' x 8' sheets
Standard

Description	Oper	Unit	Vol	Crew Size	Man-hours per Unit	Crew Output per Day	Avg Mat'l Unit Cost	Avg Labor Unit Cost	Avg Equip Unit Cost	Avg Total Unit Cost	Avg Price Incl O&P
1/8" T	Inst	SF	Lg	2C	.016	1025	.27	.59	---	.86	**1.14**
	Inst	SF	Sm	2C	.022	717.5	.30	.81	---	1.11	**1.49**
1/4" T	Inst	SF	Lg	2C	.016	1025	.41	.59	---	1.00	**1.30**
	Inst	SF	Sm	2C	.022	717.5	.46	.81	---	1.27	**1.67**

Tempered

Description	Oper	Unit	Vol	Crew Size	Man-hours per Unit	Crew Output per Day	Avg Mat'l Unit Cost	Avg Labor Unit Cost	Avg Equip Unit Cost	Avg Total Unit Cost	Avg Price Incl O&P
1/8" T	Inst	SF	Lg	2C	.016	1025	.48	.59	---	1.07	**1.38**
	Inst	SF	Sm	2C	.022	717.5	.53	.81	---	1.34	**1.75**
1/4" T	Inst	SF	Lg	2C	.016	1025	.54	.59	---	1.13	**1.45**
	Inst	SF	Sm	2C	.022	717.5	.59	.81	---	1.40	**1.82**

Particleboard, 40 lb interior underlayment

Nailed to floors

Description	Oper	Unit	Vol	Crew Size	Man-hours per Unit	Crew Output per Day	Avg Mat'l Unit Cost	Avg Labor Unit Cost	Avg Equip Unit Cost	Avg Total Unit Cost	Avg Price Incl O&P
3/8" T	Inst	SF	Lg	2C	.010	1535	.48	.37	---	.85	**1.07**
	Inst	SF	Sm	2C	.015	1075	.53	.56	---	1.09	**1.39**
1/2" T	Inst	SF	Lg	2C	.010	1535	.56	.37	---	.93	**1.16**
	Inst	SF	Sm	2C	.015	1075	.63	.56	---	1.19	**1.50**
5/8" T	Inst	SF	Lg	2C	.010	1535	.63	.37	---	1.00	**1.24**
	Inst	SF	Sm	2C	.015	1075	.71	.56	---	1.27	**1.59**
3/4" T	Inst	SF	Lg	2C	.010	1535	.72	.37	---	1.09	**1.35**
	Inst	SF	Sm	2C	.015	1075	.80	.56	---	1.36	**1.70**

Nailed to walls

Description	Oper	Unit	Vol	Crew Size	Man-hours per Unit	Crew Output per Day	Avg Mat'l Unit Cost	Avg Labor Unit Cost	Avg Equip Unit Cost	Avg Total Unit Cost	Avg Price Incl O&P
3/8" T	Inst	SF	Lg	2C	.011	1440	.48	.41	---	.89	**1.12**
	Inst	SF	Sm	2C	.016	1008	.53	.59	---	1.12	**1.44**
1/2" T	Inst	SF	Lg	2C	.011	1440	.56	.41	---	.97	**1.21**
	Inst	SF	Sm	2C	.016	1008	.63	.59	---	1.22	**1.55**
5/8" T	Inst	SF	Lg	2C	.011	1440	.63	.41	---	1.04	**1.29**
	Inst	SF	Sm	2C	.016	1008	.71	.59	---	1.30	**1.65**
3/4" T	Inst	SF	Lg	2C	.011	1440	.72	.41	---	1.13	**1.40**
	Inst	SF	Sm	2C	.016	1008	.80	.59	---	1.39	**1.75**

Description	Oper	Unit	Vol	Crew Size	Man-hours per Unit	Crew Output per Day	Avg Mat'l Unit Cost	Avg Labor Unit Cost	Avg Equip Unit Cost	Avg Total Unit Cost	Avg Price Incl O&P

Masonite prefinished 4' x 8' panels

1/4" T, oak and maple designs	Inst	SF	Lg	2C	.020	800.0	.64	.74	---	1.38	**1.77**
	Inst	SF	Sm	2C	.029	560.0	.72	1.07	---	1.79	**2.33**
1/4" T, nutwood designs	Inst	SF	Lg	2C	.020	800.0	.75	.74	---	1.49	**1.90**
	Inst	SF	Sm	2C	.029	560.0	.83	1.07	---	1.90	**2.46**
1/4" T, weathered white	Inst	SF	Lg	2C	.020	800.0	.75	.74	---	1.49	**1.90**
	Inst	SF	Sm	2C	.029	560.0	.83	1.07	---	1.90	**2.46**
1/4" T, brick or stone designs	Inst	SF	Lg	2C	.020	800.0	1.04	.74	---	1.78	**2.23**
	Inst	SF	Sm	2C	.029	560.0	1.17	1.07	---	2.24	**2.85**

Pegboard, 4' x 8' sheets

Presdwood, tempered

1/8" T	Inst	SF	Lg	2C	.016	1025	.56	.59	---	1.15	**1.47**
	Inst	SF	Sm	2C	.022	717.5	.63	.81	---	1.44	**1.86**
1/4" T	Inst	SF	Lg	2C	.016	1025	.75	.59	---	1.34	**1.69**
	Inst	SF	Sm	2C	.022	717.5	.82	.81	---	1.63	**2.08**

Duolux, tempered

1/8" T	Inst	SF	Lg	2C	.016	1025	.81	.59	---	1.40	**1.76**
	Inst	SF	Sm	2C	.022	717.5	.91	.81	---	1.72	**2.19**
1/4" T	Inst	SF	Lg	2C	.016	1025	1.18	.59	---	1.77	**2.19**
	Inst	SF	Sm	2C	.022	717.5	1.32	.81	---	2.13	**2.66**

Unfinished hardwood plywood, applied with nails (nail heads filled)

Ash, flush face

1/8" x 4' x 7', 8'	Inst	SF	Lg	CS	.027	900.0	1.24	.94	---	2.18	**2.74**
	Inst	SF	Sm	CS	.038	630.0	1.38	1.32	---	2.70	**3.43**
3/16" x 4' x 8'	Inst	SF	Lg	CS	.027	900.0	1.50	.94	---	2.44	**3.04**
	Inst	SF	Sm	CS	.038	630.0	1.65	1.32	---	2.97	**3.74**
1/4" x 4' x 8'	Inst	SF	Lg	CS	.027	900.0	1.75	.94	---	2.69	**3.32**
	Inst	SF	Sm	CS	.038	630.0	1.94	1.32	---	3.26	**4.08**
1/4" x 4' x 10'	Inst	SF	Lg	CS	.027	900.0	1.97	.94	---	2.91	**3.58**
	Inst	SF	Sm	CS	.038	630.0	2.19	1.32	---	3.51	**4.36**
1/2" x 4' x 10'	Inst	SF	Lg	CS	.027	900.0	2.24	.94	---	3.18	**3.89**
	Inst	SF	Sm	CS	.038	630.0	2.48	1.32	---	3.80	**4.70**
3/4" x 4' x 8' vertical core	Inst	SF	Lg	CS	.027	900.0	2.45	.94	---	3.39	**4.13**
	Inst	SF	Sm	CS	.038	630.0	2.73	1.32	---	4.05	**4.98**
3/4" x 4' x 8' lumber core	Inst	SF	Lg	CS	.027	900.0	3.48	.94	---	4.42	**5.31**
	Inst	SF	Sm	CS	.038	630.0	3.87	1.32	---	5.19	**6.30**

Ash, V-grooved

3/16" x 4' x 8'	Inst	SF	Lg	CS	.027	900.0	1.35	.94	---	2.29	**2.86**
	Inst	SF	Sm	CS	.038	630.0	1.51	1.32	---	2.83	**3.58**
1/4" x 4' x 8'	Inst	SF	Lg	CS	.027	900.0	1.66	.94	---	2.60	**3.22**
	Inst	SF	Sm	CS	.038	630.0	1.84	1.32	---	3.16	**3.96**
1/4" x 4' x 10'	Inst	SF	Lg	CS	.027	900.0	1.92	.94	---	2.86	**3.52**
	Inst	SF	Sm	CS	.038	630.0	2.13	1.32	---	3.45	**4.29**

Description	Oper	Unit	Vol	Crew Size	Man-hours per Unit	Crew Output per Day	Avg Mat'l Unit Cost	Avg Labor Unit Cost	Avg Equip Unit Cost	Avg Total Unit Cost	Avg Price Incl O&P
Birch, natural, "A" grade face											
Flush face											
1/8" x 4' x 8'	Inst	SF	Lg	CS	.027	900.0	.96	.94	---	1.90	**2.41**
	Inst	SF	Sm	CS	.038	630.0	1.07	1.32	---	2.39	**3.08**
3/16" x 4' x 8'	Inst	SF	Lg	CS	.027	900.0	1.50	.94	---	2.44	**3.04**
	Inst	SF	Sm	CS	.038	630.0	1.65	1.32	---	2.97	**3.74**
1/4" x 4' x 8'	Inst	SF	Lg	CS	.027	900.0	1.51	.94	---	2.45	**3.05**
	Inst	SF	Sm	CS	.038	630.0	1.68	1.32	---	3.00	**3.78**
1/4" x 4' x 10'	Inst	SF	Lg	CS	.027	900.0	1.97	.94	---	2.91	**3.58**
	Inst	SF	Sm	CS	.038	630.0	2.19	1.32	---	3.51	**4.36**
3/8" x 4' x 8'	Inst	SF	Lg	CS	.027	900.0	2.17	.94	---	3.11	**3.81**
	Inst	SF	Sm	CS	.038	630.0	2.41	1.32	---	3.73	**4.62**
1/2" x 4' x 8'	Inst	SF	Lg	CS	.027	900.0	2.50	.94	---	3.44	**4.19**
	Inst	SF	Sm	CS	.038	630.0	2.79	1.32	---	4.11	**5.05**
3/4" x 4' x 8' lumber core	Inst	SF	Lg	CS	.027	900.0	3.42	.94	---	4.36	**5.24**
	Inst	SF	Sm	CS	.038	630.0	3.81	1.32	---	5.13	**6.23**
V-grooved											
1/4" x 4' x 8', mismatched	Inst	SF	Lg	CS	.027	900.0	1.87	.94	---	2.81	**3.46**
	Inst	SF	Sm	CS	.038	630.0	2.08	1.32	---	3.40	**4.24**
1/4" x 4' x 8'	Inst	SF	Lg	CS	.027	900.0	1.88	.94	---	2.82	**3.47**
	Inst	SF	Sm	CS	.038	630.0	2.10	1.32	---	3.42	**4.26**
1/4" x 4' x 10'	Inst	SF	Lg	CS	.027	900.0	2.14	.94	---	3.08	**3.77**
	Inst	SF	Sm	CS	.038	630.0	2.38	1.32	---	3.70	**4.58**
Birch, select red											
1/4" x 4' x 8'	Inst	SF	Lg	CS	.027	900.0	1.88	.94	---	2.82	**3.47**
	Inst	SF	Sm	CS	.038	630.0	2.10	1.32	---	3.42	**4.26**
Birch, select white											
1/4" x 4' x 8'	Inst	SF	Lg	CS	.027	900.0	1.88	.94	---	2.82	**3.47**
	Inst	SF	Sm	CS	.038	630.0	2.10	1.32	---	3.42	**4.26**
Oak, flush face											
1/8" x 4' x 8'	Inst	SF	Lg	CS	.027	900.0	.94	.94	---	1.88	**2.39**
	Inst	SF	Sm	CS	.038	630.0	1.05	1.32	---	2.37	**3.05**
1/4" x 4' x 8'	Inst	SF	Lg	CS	.027	900.0	1.20	.94	---	2.14	**2.69**
	Inst	SF	Sm	CS	.038	630.0	1.33	1.32	---	2.65	**3.37**
1/2" x 4' x 8'	Inst	SF	Lg	CS	.027	900.0	2.32	.94	---	3.26	**3.98**
	Inst	SF	Sm	CS	.038	630.0	2.58	1.32	---	3.90	**4.81**

Description	Oper	Unit	Vol	Crew Size	Man-hours per Unit	Crew Output per Day	Avg Mat'l Unit Cost	Avg Labor Unit Cost	Avg Equip Unit Cost	Avg Total Unit Cost	Avg Price Incl O&P
Philippine mahogany											
Rotary cut											
1/8" x 4' x 8'	Inst	SF	Lg	CS	.027	900.0	.46	.94	---	1.40	**1.84**
	Inst	SF	Sm	CS	.038	630.0	.50	1.32	---	1.82	**2.42**
3/16" x 4' x 8'	Inst	SF	Lg	CS	.027	900.0	.67	.94	---	1.61	**2.08**
	Inst	SF	Sm	CS	.038	630.0	.74	1.32	---	2.06	**2.70**
1/4" x 4' x 8'	Inst	SF	Lg	CS	.027	900.0	.67	.94	---	1.61	**2.08**
	Inst	SF	Sm	CS	.038	630.0	.74	1.32	---	2.06	**2.70**
1/4" x 4' x 10'	Inst	SF	Lg	CS	.027	900.0	1.16	.94	---	2.10	**2.64**
	Inst	SF	Sm	CS	.038	630.0	1.29	1.32	---	2.61	**3.33**
1/2" x 4' x 8'	Inst	SF	Lg	CS	.027	900.0	1.34	.94	---	2.28	**2.85**
	Inst	SF	Sm	CS	.038	630.0	1.49	1.32	---	2.81	**3.56**
3/4" x 4' x 8' vert. core	Inst	SF	Lg	CS	.027	900.0	2.04	.94	---	2.98	**3.66**
	Inst	SF	Sm	CS	.038	630.0	2.27	1.32	---	3.59	**4.46**
V-grooved											
3/16" x 4' x 8'	Inst	SF	Lg	CS	.027	900.0	.71	.94	---	1.65	**2.13**
	Inst	SF	Sm	CS	.038	630.0	.78	1.32	---	2.10	**2.74**
1/4" x 4' x 8'	Inst	SF	Lg	CS	.027	900.0	.79	.94	---	1.73	**2.22**
	Inst	SF	Sm	CS	.038	630.0	.88	1.32	---	2.20	**2.86**
1/4" x 4' x 10'	Inst	SF	Lg	CS	.027	900.0	1.22	.94	---	2.16	**2.71**
	Inst	SF	Sm	CS	.038	630.0	1.36	1.32	---	2.68	**3.41**

Plaster & Stucco

1. Dimensions (Lath)

a. Gypsum. Plain, perforated and insulating. Normally, each lath is 16" x 48" in $3/8$" or $1/2$" thicknesses; a five-piece bundle covers 3 SY.

b. Wire. Only diamond and riblash are discussed here. Diamond lath is furnished in 27" x 96"-wide sheets covering 16 SY and 20 SY respectively.

c. Wood. Can be fir, pine, redwood, spruce, etc. Bundles may consist of 50 or 100 pieces of $3/8$" x $1\,1/2$" x 48" lath covering 3.4 SY and 6.8 SY respectively. There is usually a $3/8$" gap between lath.

2. Dimensions (Plaster)

Only two and three coat gypsum cement plaster are discussed here.

3. Installation (Lath)

Laths are nailed. The types and size of nails vary with the type and thickness of lath. Quantity will vary with oc spacing of studs or joists. Only lath applied to wood will be considered here.

a. Nails for gypsum lath. Common type is 13 gauge blued $19/64$" flathead, $1\,1/8$" long, spaced approximately 4" oc, and $1\,1/4$" long spaced approximately 5" oc for $3/8$" and $1/2$" lath respectively.

b. Nails for wire lath. For ceiling, common is $1\,1/2$" long 11 gauge barbed galvanized with a $7/16$" head diameter.

c. Nails for wood lath. 3d fine common.

d. Gypsum lath may be attached by the use of air-driven staples. Wire lath may be tied to support, usually with 18 gauge wire.

4. Installation (Plaster)

Quantities of materials used to plaster vary with the type of lath and thickness of plaster.

a. Two coat. Brown and finish coat.

b. Three coat. Scratch, brown and finish coat.

For types and quantities of material used, see cost tables under **Plaster**.

5. Notes on Labor

a. Lath. Average Manhour per Unit is based on what one lather can do in one day.

b. Plaster. Average Manhour per Unit is based on what two plasterers and one laborer can do in one day.

Stucco

1. Dimensions

a. 18 gauge wire

b. 15 lb. felt paper

c. 1" x 18 gauge galvanized netting

d. Mortar of 1:3 mix

2. Installation (Lathing)

a. 18 gauge wire stretched taut horizontally across studs at approximately 8" oc.

b. 15 lb. felt paper placed over wire.

c. 1" x 18 gauge galvanized netting placed over felt.

3. Installation (Mortar)

a. The mortar mix used in this section is a 1:3 mix.

b. One CY of mortar is comprised of 1 CY sand, 9 CF portland cement and 100 lbs. hydrated lime.

c. For mortar requirements for 100 SY of stucco, see table below.

4. Estimating Technique

Determine area and deduct area of window and door openings. No waste has been included in the following figures unless otherwise noted. For waste, add 10% to total area.

	Cubic Yards Per CSY	
Stucco Thickness	On Masonry	On Netting
1/2"	1.50	1.75
5/8"	1.90	2.20
3/4"	2.20	2.60
1"	2.90	3.40

Description	Oper	Unit	Vol	Crew Size	Man-hours per Unit	Crew Output per Day	Avg Mat'l Unit Cost	Avg Labor Unit Cost	Avg Equip Unit Cost	Avg Total Unit Cost	Avg Price Incl O&P

Plaster and stucco
Remove both plaster or stucco and lath or netting to studs or sheathing
Lath (wood or metal) and plaster, walls and ceilings

2 coats	Demo	SY	Lg	LB	.123	130.00	---	3.69	---	3.69	**5.17**
	Demo	SY	Sm	LB	.176	91.00	---	5.28	---	5.28	**7.39**
3 coats	Demo	SY	Lg	LB	.133	120.00	---	3.99	---	3.99	**5.59**
	Demo	SY	Sm	LB	.190	84.00	---	5.70	---	5.70	**7.98**

Lath (only), nails included
Gypsum lath, 16" x 48", applied with nails to ceilings or walls, 5% waste included, nails included (.067 lbs per CY)

3/8" T, perforated or plain	Inst	SY	Lg	LR	.100	80.00	2.94	3.56	---	6.50	**8.43**
	Inst	SY	Sm	LR	.143	56.00	3.59	5.09	---	8.68	**11.40**
1/2" T, perforated or plain	Inst	SY	Lg	LR	.100	80.00	3.48	3.56	---	7.04	**9.05**
	Inst	SY	Sm	LR	.143	56.00	4.24	5.09	---	9.33	**12.10**
3/8" T, insulating, aluminum foil back											
	Inst	SY	Lg	LR	.100	80.00	3.79	3.56	---	7.35	**9.41**
	Inst	SY	Sm	LR	.143	56.00	4.63	5.09	---	9.72	**12.60**
1/2" T, insulating, aluminum foil back											
	Inst	SY	Lg	LR	.100	80.00	4.09	3.56	---	7.65	**9.76**
	Inst	SY	Sm	LR	.143	56.00	4.99	5.09	---	10.08	**13.00**
For installation with staples,											
DEDUCT	Inst	SY	Lg	LR	-.025	-325.0	---	.89	---	.89	---
	Inst	SY	Sm	LR	-.035	-227.5	---	1.25	---	1.25	---

Metal lath, nailed to ceilings or walls, 5% waste and nails (0.067 lbs per SY) included
Diamond lath (junior mesh), 27" x 96" sheets, nailed to wood members @ 16" oc

3.4 lb black painted	Inst	SY	Lg	LR	.067	120.0	4.08	2.38	---	6.46	**8.08**
	Inst	SY	Sm	LR	.095	84.00	4.97	3.38	---	8.35	**10.50**
3.4 lb galvanized	Inst	SY	Lg	LR	.067	120.0	4.43	2.38	---	6.81	**8.48**
	Inst	SY	Sm	LR	.095	84.00	5.41	3.38	---	8.79	**11.00**

Riblath, 3/8" high rib, 27" x 96" sheets, nailed to wood members @ 24" oc

3.4 lb painted	Inst	SY	Lg	LR	.050	160.00	4.55	1.78	---	6.33	**7.76**
	Inst	SY	Sm	LR	.071	112.00	5.55	2.53	---	8.08	**9.97**
3.4 lb galvanized	Inst	SY	Lg	LR	.050	160.00	5.36	1.78	---	7.14	**8.69**
	Inst	SY	Sm	LR	.071	112.00	6.54	2.53	---	9.07	**11.10**

Wood lath, nailed to ceilings or walls, 5% waste and nails included, redwood, "A" grade and better
3/8" x 1-1/2" x 48" @ 3/8" spacing

	Inst	SY	Lg	LR	.100	80.00	6.82	3.56	---	10.38	**12.90**
	Inst	SY	Sm	LR	.143	56.00	8.33	5.09	---	13.42	**16.80**

Description	Oper	Unit	Vol	Crew Size	Man-hours per Unit	Crew Output per Day	Avg Mat'l Unit Cost	Avg Labor Unit Cost	Avg Equip Unit Cost	Avg Total Unit Cost	Avg Price Incl O&P

Labor adjustments, lath

For gypsum or wood lath above second floor

ADD	Inst	SY	Lg	LR	.007	1140	---	.25	---	.25	**.35**
	Inst	SY	Sm	LR	.010	798.0	---	.36	---	.36	**.51**

For metal lath above second floor

ADD	Inst	SY	Lg	LR	.017	475.0	---	.60	---	.60	**.86**
	Inst	SY	Sm	LR	.024	332.5	---	.85	---	.85	**1.21**

Plaster (only), applied to ceilings and walls, 10% waste included

Material price includes gypsum plaster, sand, hydrated lime and gauging plaster

Two coats gypsum plaster

On gypsum lath	Inst	SY	Lg	PD	.209	115.0	5.02	7.19	.53	12.74	**16.50**
	Inst	SY	Sm	PD	.298	80.50	6.11	10.30	.75	17.16	**22.30**
On unit masonry, no lath	Inst	SY	Lg	PD	.214	112.0	5.43	7.36	.54	13.33	**17.20**
	Inst	SY	Sm	PD	.306	78.40	6.61	10.50	.77	17.88	**23.30**

Three coats gypsum plaster

On gypsum lath	Inst	SY	Lg	PD	.289	83.00	5.40	9.94	.73	16.07	**21.10**
	Inst	SY	Sm	PD	.413	58.10	6.57	14.20	1.04	21.81	**28.80**
On unit masonry, no lath	Inst	SY	Lg	PD	.289	83.00	5.85	9.94	.73	16.52	**21.60**
	Inst	SY	Sm	PD	.413	58.10	7.13	14.20	1.04	22.37	**29.40**
On wire lath	Inst	SY	Lg	PD	.300	80.00	8.74	10.30	.76	19.80	**25.50**
	Inst	SY	Sm	PD	.429	56.00	10.60	14.80	1.08	26.48	**34.30**
On wood lath	Inst	SY	Lg	PD	.300	80.00	5.75	10.30	.76	16.81	**22.00**
	Inst	SY	Sm	PD	.429	56.00	7.01	14.80	1.08	22.89	**30.10**

Labor adjustments, plaster

For plaster above second floor

ADD	Inst	SY	Lg	PD	.063	384.0	---	2.17	---	2.17	**3.08**
	Inst	SY	Sm	PD	.089	268.8	---	3.06	---	3.06	**4.35**

Thin coat plaster over sheetrock (in lieu of taping)

	Inst	SY	Lg	PD	.192	125.0	1.31	6.60	---	7.91	**10.90**
	Inst	SY	Sm	PD	.274	87.50	1.59	9.43	---	11.02	**15.20**

Description	Oper	Unit	Vol	Crew Size	Man-hours per Unit	Crew Output per Day	Avg Mat'l Unit Cost	Avg Labor Unit Cost	Avg Equip Unit Cost	Avg Total Unit Cost	Avg Price Incl O&P

Stucco, exterior walls

Netting, galvanized, 1" x 18 ga x 48", with 18 ga wire and 15 lb felt

| | Inst | SY | Lg | LR | .133 | 60.00 | 3.72 | 4.73 | --- | 8.45 | **11.00** |
| | Inst | SY | Sm | LR | .190 | 42.00 | 4.55 | 6.76 | --- | 11.31 | **14.80** |

Steel-Tex, 49" W x 11-1/2' L rolls, with felt backing

| | Inst | SY | Lg | LR | .100 | 80.00 | 5.96 | 3.56 | --- | 9.52 | **11.90** |
| | Inst | SY | Sm | LR | .143 | 56.00 | 7.25 | 5.09 | --- | 12.34 | **15.60** |

1 coat work with float finish
Over masonry

| | Inst | SY | Lg | PD | .209 | 115.00 | .72 | 7.19 | .53 | 8.44 | **11.60** |
| | Inst | SY | Sm | PD | .298 | 80.50 | .88 | 10.30 | .75 | 11.93 | **16.30** |

2 coat work with float finish
Over masonry

| | Inst | SY | Lg | PD | .400 | 60.00 | 2.16 | 13.80 | 1.01 | 16.97 | **23.00** |
| | Inst | SY | Sm | PD | .571 | 42.00 | 2.63 | 19.60 | 1.44 | 23.67 | **32.40** |

Over metal netting

| | Inst | SY | Lg | PE | .471 | 85.00 | 3.05 | 16.00 | .71 | 19.76 | **26.90** |
| | Inst | SY | Sm | PE | .672 | 59.50 | 3.72 | 22.80 | 1.02 | 27.54 | **37.60** |

3 coat work with float finish
Over metal netting

| | Inst | SY | Lg | PE | .615 | 65.00 | 4.12 | 20.80 | .93 | 25.85 | **35.30** |
| | Inst | SY | Sm | PE | .879 | 45.50 | 5.03 | 29.80 | 1.33 | 36.16 | **49.40** |

Plumbing. See individual items

Description	Oper	Unit	Vol	Crew Size	Man-hours per Unit	Crew Output per Day	Avg Mat'l Unit Cost	Avg Labor Unit Cost	Avg Equip Unit Cost	Avg Total Unit Cost	Avg Price Incl O&P

Range hoods

Metal finishes

Labor includes wiring and connection by electrician and installation by carpenter in stud-exposed structure only

Economy model, UL approved; mitered, welded construction; completely assembled and wired; includes fan, motor, washable aluminum filter, and light

24" wide

Description	Oper	Unit	Vol	Crew Size	Man-hours per Unit	Crew Output per Day	Avg Mat'l Unit Cost	Avg Labor Unit Cost	Avg Equip Unit Cost	Avg Total Unit Cost	Avg Price Incl O&P
3-1/4" x 10" duct, 160 CFM	Inst	Ea	Lg	ED	4.00	4.00	68.50	154.00	---	222.50	**303.00**
	Inst	Ea	Sm	ED	5.71	2.80	74.90	220.00	---	294.90	**406.00**
Non-ducted, 160 CFM	Inst	Ea	Lg	ED	4.00	4.00	74.40	154.00	---	228.40	**309.00**
	Inst	Ea	Sm	ED	5.71	2.80	81.30	220.00	---	301.30	**413.00**

30" wide

Description	Oper	Unit	Vol	Crew Size	Man-hours per Unit	Crew Output per Day	Avg Mat'l Unit Cost	Avg Labor Unit Cost	Avg Equip Unit Cost	Avg Total Unit Cost	Avg Price Incl O&P
7" round duct, 240 CFM	Inst	Ea	Lg	ED	4.00	4.00	74.90	154.00	---	228.90	**310.00**
	Inst	Ea	Sm	ED	5.71	2.80	81.90	220.00	---	301.90	**414.00**
3-1/4" x 10" duct, 160 CFM	Inst	Ea	Lg	ED	4.00	4.00	80.30	154.00	---	234.30	**316.00**
	Inst	Ea	Sm	ED	5.71	2.80	87.80	220.00	---	307.80	**421.00**
Non-ducted, 160 CFM	Inst	Ea	Lg	ED	4.00	4.00	91.00	154.00	---	245.00	**329.00**
	Inst	Ea	Sm	ED	5.71	2.80	99.50	220.00	---	319.50	**434.00**

36" wide

Description	Oper	Unit	Vol	Crew Size	Man-hours per Unit	Crew Output per Day	Avg Mat'l Unit Cost	Avg Labor Unit Cost	Avg Equip Unit Cost	Avg Total Unit Cost	Avg Price Incl O&P
7" round duct, 240 CFM	Inst	Ea	Lg	ED	4.00	4.00	109.00	154.00	---	263.00	**349.00**
	Inst	Ea	Sm	ED	5.71	2.80	119.00	220.00	---	339.00	**457.00**
3-1/4" x 10" duct, 160 CFM	Inst	Ea	Lg	ED	4.00	4.00	114.00	154.00	---	268.00	**356.00**
	Inst	Ea	Sm	ED	5.71	2.80	125.00	220.00	---	345.00	**464.00**
Non-ducted, 160 CFM	Inst	Ea	Lg	ED	4.00	4.00	131.00	154.00	---	285.00	**374.00**
	Inst	Ea	Sm	ED	5.71	2.80	143.00	220.00	---	363.00	**484.00**

Standard model, UL approved; deluxe mitered wrap-around styling; solid state fan control, infinite speed settings; removable filter; built-in damper and dual light assembly

30" wide x 9" deep

Description	Oper	Unit	Vol	Crew Size	Man-hours per Unit	Crew Output per Day	Avg Mat'l Unit Cost	Avg Labor Unit Cost	Avg Equip Unit Cost	Avg Total Unit Cost	Avg Price Incl O&P
3-1/4" x 10" duct	Inst	Ea	Lg	ED	4.00	4.00	118.00	154.00	---	272.00	**359.00**
	Inst	Ea	Sm	ED	5.71	2.80	129.00	220.00	---	349.00	**468.00**
Non-ducted	Inst	Ea	Lg	ED	4.00	4.00	134.00	154.00	---	288.00	**378.00**
	Inst	Ea	Sm	ED	5.71	2.80	146.00	220.00	---	366.00	**488.00**

36" wide x 9" deep

Description	Oper	Unit	Vol	Crew Size	Man-hours per Unit	Crew Output per Day	Avg Mat'l Unit Cost	Avg Labor Unit Cost	Avg Equip Unit Cost	Avg Total Unit Cost	Avg Price Incl O&P
3-1/4" x 10" duct	Inst	Ea	Lg	ED	4.00	4.00	155.00	154.00	---	309.00	**402.00**
	Inst	Ea	Sm	ED	5.71	2.80	170.00	220.00	---	390.00	**515.00**
Non-ducted	Inst	Ea	Lg	ED	4.00	4.00	166.00	154.00	---	320.00	**415.00**
	Inst	Ea	Sm	ED	5.71	2.80	181.00	220.00	---	401.00	**528.00**

42" wide x 9" deep

Description	Oper	Unit	Vol	Crew Size	Man-hours per Unit	Crew Output per Day	Avg Mat'l Unit Cost	Avg Labor Unit Cost	Avg Equip Unit Cost	Avg Total Unit Cost	Avg Price Incl O&P
3-1/4" x 10" duct	Inst	Ea	Lg	ED	5.33	3.00	214.00	206.00	---	420.00	**544.00**
	Inst	Ea	Sm	ED	7.62	2.10	234.00	294.00	---	528.00	**696.00**
Non-ducted	Inst	Ea	Lg	ED	5.33	3.00	230.00	206.00	---	436.00	**563.00**
	Inst	Ea	Sm	ED	7.62	2.10	252.00	294.00	---	546.00	**716.00**

Description	Oper	Unit	Vol	Crew Size	Man-hours per Unit	Crew Output per Day	Avg Mat'l Unit Cost	Avg Labor Unit Cost	Avg Equip Unit Cost	Avg Total Unit Cost	Avg Price Incl O&P

Decorator/designer model; solid state fan control, infinite speed settings; easy clean aluminum mesh grease filters; enclosed light assembly and switches

Single faced hood - fan exhausts horizontally or vertically, 24" D canopy x 21" front to back

Description	Oper	Unit	Vol	Crew Size	Man-hours per Unit	Crew Output per Day	Avg Mat'l	Avg Labor	Avg Equip	Avg Total	Avg Price O&P
30" wide	Inst	Ea	Lg	ED	5.33	3.00	182.00	206.00	---	388.00	**508.00**
	Inst	Ea	Sm	ED	7.62	2.10	199.00	294.00	---	493.00	**655.00**
36" wide	Inst	Ea	Lg	ED	5.33	3.00	198.00	206.00	---	404.00	**526.00**
	Inst	Ea	Sm	ED	7.62	2.10	216.00	294.00	---	510.00	**675.00**

Single faced, contemporary style, duct horizontally or vertically, 9" D canopy
30" wide

Description	Oper	Unit	Vol	Crew Size	Man-hours per Unit	Crew Output per Day	Avg Mat'l	Avg Labor	Avg Equip	Avg Total	Avg Price O&P
With 330 cfm power unit	Inst	Ea	Lg	ED	5.33	3.00	268.00	206.00	---	474.00	**606.00**
	Inst	Ea	Sm	ED	7.62	2.10	293.00	294.00	---	587.00	**763.00**
With 410 cfm power unit	Inst	Ea	Lg	ED	5.33	3.00	284.00	206.00	---	490.00	**624.00**
	Inst	Ea	Sm	ED	7.62	2.10	310.00	294.00	---	604.00	**783.00**

36" wide

Description	Oper	Unit	Vol	Crew Size	Man-hours per Unit	Crew Output per Day	Avg Mat'l	Avg Labor	Avg Equip	Avg Total	Avg Price O&P
With 330 cfm power unit	Inst	Ea	Lg	ED	5.33	3.00	332.00	206.00	---	538.00	**680.00**
	Inst	Ea	Sm	ED	7.62	2.10	363.00	294.00	---	657.00	**844.00**
With 410 cfm power unit	Inst	Ea	Lg	ED	5.33	3.00	348.00	206.00	---	554.00	**698.00**
	Inst	Ea	Sm	ED	7.62	2.10	380.00	294.00	---	674.00	**864.00**

Material adjustments

Description	Oper	Unit	Vol	Crew Size	Man-hours per Unit	Crew Output per Day	Avg Mat'l	Avg Labor	Avg Equip	Avg Total	Avg Price O&P
Stainless steel, ADD	Inst	%	Lg	---	---	---	33.0	---	---	---	---
	Inst	%	Sm	---	---	---	33.0	---	---	---	---

Reinforcing steel. See Concrete, page 99

Resilient flooring

Sheet Products

Linoleum or vinyl sheet are normally installed either over a wood subfloor or a smooth concrete subfloor. When laid over wood, a layer of felt must first be laid in paste. This keeps irregularities in the wood from showing through. The amount of paste required to bond both felt and sheet is approximately 16 gallons (5% waste included) per 100 SY. When laid over smooth concrete subfloor, the sheet products can be bonded directly to the floor. However, the concrete subfloor should not be in direct contact with the ground because of excessive moisture. For bonding to concrete, 8 gallons of paste is required (5% waste included) per 100 SY. After laying the flooring over concrete or wood, wax is applied using 0.5 gallon per 100 SY. Paste, wax, felt (as needed), and 10% sheet waste are included in material costs.

Tile Products

All resilient tile can be bonded the same way as sheet products, either to smooth concrete or to felt over wood subfloor. When bonded to smooth concrete, a concrete primer (0.5 gal/100 SF) is first applied to seal the concrete. The tiles are then bonded to the sealed floor with resilient tile cement (0.6 gal/100 SF). On wood subfloors, felt is first laid in paste (0.9 gal/100 SF) and then the tiles are bonded to the felt with resilient tile emulsion (0.7 gal/100 SF). Bonding materials, felt (as needed), and 10% tile waste are included in material costs.

Description	Oper	Unit	Vol	Crew Size	Man-hours per Unit	Crew Output per Day	Avg Mat'l Unit Cost	Avg Labor Unit Cost	Avg Equip Unit Cost	Avg Total Unit Cost	Avg Price Incl O&P
Resilient flooring											
Adhesive set sheet products											
	Demo	SY	Lg	LB	.100	160.0	---	3.00	---	3.00	**4.20**
	Demo	SY	Sm	LB	.133	120.0	---	3.99	---	3.99	**5.59**
Adhesive set tile products											
	Demo	SF	Lg	LB	.011	1500	---	.33	---	.33	**.46**
	Demo	SF	Sm	LB	.014	1125	---	.42	---	.42	**.59**

Install over smooth concrete subfloor
Tile

Asphalt, 9" x 9", 1/8" thick, marbleized

Description	Oper	Unit	Vol	Crew Size	Man-hours per Unit	Crew Output per Day	Avg Mat'l Unit Cost	Avg Labor Unit Cost	Avg Equip Unit Cost	Avg Total Unit Cost	Avg Price Incl O&P
Group B colors, dark	Inst	SF	Lg	FB	.020	896.0	1.17	.67	---	1.84	**2.28**
	Inst	SF	Sm	FB	.027	672.0	1.29	.90	---	2.19	**2.75**
Group C colors, medium	Inst	SF	Lg	FB	.020	896.0	1.32	.67	---	1.99	**2.46**
	Inst	SF	Sm	FB	.027	672.0	1.46	.90	---	2.36	**2.95**
Group D colors, light	Inst	SF	Lg	FB	.020	896.0	1.32	.67	---	1.99	**2.46**
	Inst	SF	Sm	FB	.027	672.0	1.46	.90	---	2.36	**2.95**

Vinyl tile, 12" x 12", including adhesive
1/16" thick

Description	Oper	Unit	Vol	Crew Size	Man-hours per Unit	Crew Output per Day	Avg Mat'l Unit Cost	Avg Labor Unit Cost	Avg Equip Unit Cost	Avg Total Unit Cost	Avg Price Incl O&P
Vega II	Inst	SF	Lg	FB	.013	1344.0	1.06	.44	---	1.50	**1.83**
	Inst	SF	Sm	FB	.018	1008.0	1.17	.60	---	1.77	**2.19**

.080" thick

Description	Oper	Unit	Vol	Crew Size	Man-hours per Unit	Crew Output per Day	Avg Mat'l Unit Cost	Avg Labor Unit Cost	Avg Equip Unit Cost	Avg Total Unit Cost	Avg Price Incl O&P
Designer slate	Inst	SF	Lg	FB	.013	1344.0	2.27	.44	---	2.71	**3.22**
	Inst	SF	Sm	FB	.018	1008.0	2.51	.60	---	3.11	**3.73**

1/8" thick

Description	Oper	Unit	Vol	Crew Size	Man-hours per Unit	Crew Output per Day	Avg Mat'l Unit Cost	Avg Labor Unit Cost	Avg Equip Unit Cost	Avg Total Unit Cost	Avg Price Incl O&P
Embassy oak	Inst	SF	Lg	FB	.013	1344.0	2.80	.44	---	3.24	**3.83**
	Inst	SF	Sm	FB	.018	1008.0	3.09	.60	---	3.69	**4.40**
Majestic slate	Inst	SF	Lg	FB	.013	1344.0	2.27	.44	---	2.71	**3.22**
	Inst	SF	Sm	FB	.018	1008.0	2.51	.60	---	3.11	**3.73**
Mediterranean marble	Inst	SF	Lg	FB	.013	1344.0	2.49	.44	---	2.93	**3.47**
	Inst	SF	Sm	FB	.018	1008.0	2.74	.60	---	3.34	**4.00**
Pecan	Inst	SF	Lg	FB	.013	1344.0	2.91	.44	---	3.35	**3.96**
	Inst	SF	Sm	FB	.018	1008.0	3.21	.60	---	3.81	**4.54**
Plaza brick	Inst	SF	Lg	FB	.013	1344.0	4.39	.44	---	4.83	**5.66**
	Inst	SF	Sm	FB	.018	1008.0	4.84	.60	---	5.44	**6.41**
Plymouth plank	Inst	SF	Lg	FB	.013	1344.0	3.18	.44	---	3.62	**4.27**
	Inst	SF	Sm	FB	.018	1008.0	3.50	.60	---	4.10	**4.87**
Teak	Inst	SF	Lg	FB	.013	1344.0	2.70	.44	---	3.14	**3.71**
	Inst	SF	Sm	FB	.018	1008.0	2.97	.60	---	3.57	**4.26**
Terrazzo	Inst	SF	Lg	FB	.013	1344.0	2.17	.44	---	2.61	**3.11**
	Inst	SF	Sm	FB	.018	1008.0	2.39	.60	---	2.99	**3.59**

Vinyl tile, 12" x 12", self-stick
.080" thick

Description	Oper	Unit	Vol	Crew Size	Man-hours per Unit	Crew Output per Day	Avg Mat'l Unit Cost	Avg Labor Unit Cost	Avg Equip Unit Cost	Avg Total Unit Cost	Avg Price Incl O&P
Elite	Inst	SF	Lg	FB	.016	1120.0	1.70	.54	---	2.24	**2.71**
	Inst	SF	Sm	FB	.021	840.0	1.87	.70	---	2.57	**3.14**
Stylglo	Inst	SF	Lg	FB	.016	1120.0	1.27	.54	---	1.81	**2.21**
	Inst	SF	Sm	FB	.021	840.0	1.40	.70	---	2.10	**2.59**

1/16" thick

Description	Oper	Unit	Vol	Crew Size	Man-hours per Unit	Crew Output per Day	Avg Mat'l Unit Cost	Avg Labor Unit Cost	Avg Equip Unit Cost	Avg Total Unit Cost	Avg Price Incl O&P
Decorator	Inst	SF	Lg	FB	.016	1120.0	.84	.54	---	1.38	**1.72**
	Inst	SF	Sm	FB	.021	840.0	.93	.70	---	1.63	**2.05**
Proclaim	Inst	SF	Lg	FB	.016	1120.0	1.11	.54	---	1.65	**2.03**
	Inst	SF	Sm	FB	.021	840.0	1.22	.70	---	1.92	**2.39**

Description	Oper	Unit	Vol	Crew Size	Man-hours per Unit	Crew Output per Day	Avg Mat'l Unit Cost	Avg Labor Unit Cost	Avg Equip Unit Cost	Avg Total Unit Cost	Avg Price Incl O&P
Composition vinyl tile, 12" x 12"											
3/32" thick											
Designer colors	Inst	SF	Lg	FB	.013	1344.0	.95	.44	---	1.39	**1.70**
	Inst	SF	Sm	FB	.018	1008.0	1.05	.60	---	1.65	**2.05**
Standard colors (marbleized)	Inst	SF	Lg	FB	.013	1344.0	1.22	.44	---	1.66	**2.01**
	Inst	SF	Sm	FB	.018	1008.0	1.34	.60	---	1.94	**2.39**
1/8" thick											
Designer colors, pebbled	Inst	SF	Lg	FB	.013	1344.0	1.80	.44	---	2.24	**2.68**
	Inst	SF	Sm	FB	.018	1008.0	1.99	.60	---	2.59	**3.13**
Standard colors (marbleized)	Inst	SF	Lg	FB	.013	1344.0	1.06	.44	---	1.50	**1.83**
	Inst	SF	Sm	FB	.018	1008.0	1.17	.60	---	1.77	**2.19**
Solid black or white	Inst	SF	Lg	FB	.013	1344.0	1.70	.44	---	2.14	**2.56**
	Inst	SF	Sm	FB	.018	1008.0	1.87	.60	---	2.47	**2.99**
Solid colors	Inst	SF	Lg	FB	.013	1344.0	1.85	.44	---	2.29	**2.74**
	Inst	SF	Sm	FB	.018	1008.0	2.04	.60	---	2.64	**3.19**

Sheet vinyl

Description	Oper	Unit	Vol	Crew Size	Man-hours per Unit	Crew Output per Day	Avg Mat'l Unit Cost	Avg Labor Unit Cost	Avg Equip Unit Cost	Avg Total Unit Cost	Avg Price Incl O&P
Armstrong, no-wax, 6' wide											
Designer Solarian (.070")	Inst	SY	Lg	FB	.145	124.44	29.60	4.86	---	34.46	**40.90**
	Inst	SY	Sm	FB	.193	93.33	32.70	6.46	---	39.16	**46.60**
Designer Solarian II (.090")	Inst	SY	Lg	FB	.145	124.44	38.10	4.86	---	42.96	**50.60**
	Inst	SY	Sm	FB	.193	93.33	42.00	6.46	---	48.46	**57.30**
Imperial Accotone (.065")	Inst	SY	Lg	FB	.145	124.44	9.53	4.86	---	14.39	**17.80**
	Inst	SY	Sm	FB	.193	93.33	10.50	6.46	---	16.96	**21.10**
Solarian Supreme (.090")	Inst	SY	Lg	FB	.145	124.44	40.20	4.86	---	45.06	**53.10**
	Inst	SY	Sm	FB	.193	93.33	44.30	6.46	---	50.76	**60.00**
Sundial Solarian (.077")	Inst	SY	Lg	FB	.145	124.44	14.80	4.86	---	19.66	**23.80**
	Inst	SY	Sm	FB	.193	93.33	16.30	6.46	---	22.76	**27.80**
Mannington, 6' wide											
Vega (.080")	Inst	SY	Lg	FB	.145	124.44	8.47	4.86	---	13.33	**16.50**
	Inst	SY	Sm	FB	.193	93.33	9.33	6.46	---	15.79	**19.80**
Vinyl Ease (.073")	Inst	SY	Lg	FB	.145	124.44	7.41	4.86	---	12.27	**15.30**
	Inst	SY	Sm	FB	.193	93.33	8.16	6.46	---	14.62	**18.40**
Tarkett, 6' wide											
Preference (.065")	Inst	SY	Lg	FB	.145	124.44	6.88	4.86	---	11.74	**14.70**
	Inst	SY	Sm	FB	.193	93.33	7.58	6.46	---	14.04	**17.80**
Softred (.062")	Inst	SY	Lg	FB	.145	124.44	8.47	4.86	---	13.33	**16.50**
	Inst	SY	Sm	FB	.193	93.33	9.33	6.46	---	15.79	**19.80**

Description	Oper	Unit	Vol	Crew Size	Man- hours per Unit	Crew Output per Day	Avg Mat'l Unit Cost	Avg Labor Unit Cost	Avg Equip Unit Cost	Avg Total Unit Cost	Avg Price Incl O&P

Install over wood subfloor

Tile

Asphalt, 9" x 9", 1/8" thick, marbleized

Description	Oper	Unit	Vol	Crew Size	Man-hours per Unit	Crew Output per Day	Avg Mat'l Unit Cost	Avg Labor Unit Cost	Avg Equip Unit Cost	Avg Total Unit Cost	Avg Price Incl O&P
Group B colors, dark	Inst	SF	Lg	FB	.027	672.0	1.17	.90	---	2.07	**2.61**
	Inst	SF	Sm	FB	.036	504.0	1.29	1.21	---	2.50	**3.17**
Group C colors, medium	Inst	SF	Lg	FB	.027	672.0	1.32	.90	---	2.22	**2.78**
	Inst	SF	Sm	FB	.036	504.0	1.46	1.21	---	2.67	**3.37**
Group D colors, light	Inst	SF	Lg	FB	.027	672.0	1.32	.90	---	2.22	**2.78**
	Inst	SF	Sm	FB	.036	504.0	1.46	1.21	---	2.67	**3.37**

Vinyl tile, 12" x 12", including adhesive
1/16" thick

Description	Oper	Unit	Vol	Crew Size	Man-hours per Unit	Crew Output per Day	Avg Mat'l Unit Cost	Avg Labor Unit Cost	Avg Equip Unit Cost	Avg Total Unit Cost	Avg Price Incl O&P
Vega II	Inst	SF	Lg	FB	.016	1120.0	1.06	.54	---	1.60	**1.97**
	Inst	SF	Sm	FB	.021	840.0	1.17	.70	---	1.87	**2.33**

.080" thick

Description	Oper	Unit	Vol	Crew Size	Man-hours per Unit	Crew Output per Day	Avg Mat'l Unit Cost	Avg Labor Unit Cost	Avg Equip Unit Cost	Avg Total Unit Cost	Avg Price Incl O&P
Designer slate	Inst	SF	Lg	FB	.016	1120.0	2.27	.54	---	2.81	**3.36**
	Inst	SF	Sm	FB	.021	840.0	2.51	.70	---	3.21	**3.87**

1/8" thick

Description	Oper	Unit	Vol	Crew Size	Man-hours per Unit	Crew Output per Day	Avg Mat'l Unit Cost	Avg Labor Unit Cost	Avg Equip Unit Cost	Avg Total Unit Cost	Avg Price Incl O&P
Embassy oak	Inst	SF	Lg	FB	.016	1120.0	2.80	.54	---	3.34	**3.97**
	Inst	SF	Sm	FB	.021	840.0	3.09	.70	---	3.79	**4.54**
Majestic slate	Inst	SF	Lg	FB	.016	1120.0	2.27	.54	---	2.81	**3.36**
	Inst	SF	Sm	FB	.021	840.0	2.51	.70	---	3.21	**3.87**
Mediterranean marble	Inst	SF	Lg	FB	.016	1120.0	2.49	.54	---	3.03	**3.61**
	Inst	SF	Sm	FB	.021	840.0	2.74	.70	---	3.44	**4.14**
Pecan	Inst	SF	Lg	FB	.016	1120.0	2.91	.54	---	3.45	**4.10**
	Inst	SF	Sm	FB	.021	840.0	3.21	.70	---	3.91	**4.68**
Plaza brick	Inst	SF	Lg	FB	.016	1120.0	4.39	.54	---	4.93	**5.80**
	Inst	SF	Sm	FB	.021	840.0	4.84	.70	---	5.54	**6.55**
Plymouth plank	Inst	SF	Lg	FB	.016	1120.0	3.18	.54	---	3.72	**4.41**
	Inst	SF	Sm	FB	.021	840.0	3.50	.70	---	4.20	**5.01**
Teak	Inst	SF	Lg	FB	.016	1120.0	2.70	.54	---	3.24	**3.86**
	Inst	SF	Sm	FB	.021	840.0	2.97	.70	---	3.67	**4.40**
Terrazzo	Inst	SF	Lg	FB	.016	1120.0	2.17	.54	---	2.71	**3.25**
	Inst	SF	Sm	FB	.021	840.0	2.39	.70	---	3.09	**3.73**

Vinyl tile, 12" x 12", self-stick
.080" thick

Description	Oper	Unit	Vol	Crew Size	Man-hours per Unit	Crew Output per Day	Avg Mat'l Unit Cost	Avg Labor Unit Cost	Avg Equip Unit Cost	Avg Total Unit Cost	Avg Price Incl O&P
Elite	Inst	SF	Lg	FB	.020	896.0	1.70	.67	---	2.37	**2.89**
	Inst	SF	Sm	FB	.027	672.0	1.87	.90	---	2.77	**3.42**
Stylglo	Inst	SF	Lg	FB	.020	896.0	1.27	.67	---	1.94	**2.40**
	Inst	SF	Sm	FB	.027	672.0	1.40	.90	---	2.30	**2.88**

1/16" thick

Description	Oper	Unit	Vol	Crew Size	Man-hours per Unit	Crew Output per Day	Avg Mat'l Unit Cost	Avg Labor Unit Cost	Avg Equip Unit Cost	Avg Total Unit Cost	Avg Price Incl O&P
Decorator	Inst	SF	Lg	FB	.020	896.0	.84	.67	---	1.51	**1.90**
	Inst	SF	Sm	FB	.027	672.0	.93	.90	---	1.83	**2.34**
Proclaim	Inst	SF	Lg	FB	.020	896.0	1.11	.67	---	1.78	**2.21**
	Inst	SF	Sm	FB	.027	672.0	1.22	.90	---	2.12	**2.67**

Description	Oper	Unit	Vol	Crew Size	Man-hours per Unit	Crew Output per Day	Avg Mat'l Unit Cost	Avg Labor Unit Cost	Avg Equip Unit Cost	Avg Total Unit Cost	Avg Price Incl O&P
Composition vinyl tile, 12" x 12"											
3/32" thick											
Designer colors	Inst	SF	Lg	FB	.016	1120.0	.95	.54	---	1.49	**1.84**
	Inst	SF	Sm	FB	.021	840.0	1.05	.70	---	1.75	**2.19**
Standard colors (marbleized)	Inst	SF	Lg	FB	.016	1120.0	1.22	.54	---	1.76	**2.15**
	Inst	SF	Sm	FB	.021	840.0	1.34	.70	---	2.04	**2.53**
1/8" thick											
Designer colors, pebbled	Inst	SF	Lg	FB	.016	1120.0	1.80	.54	---	2.34	**2.82**
	Inst	SF	Sm	FB	.021	840.0	1.99	.70	---	2.69	**3.27**
Standard colors (marbleized)	Inst	SF	Lg	FB	.016	1120.0	1.06	.54	---	1.60	**1.97**
	Inst	SF	Sm	FB	.021	840.0	1.17	.70	---	1.87	**2.33**
Solid black or white	Inst	SF	Lg	FB	.016	1120.0	1.70	.54	---	2.24	**2.71**
	Inst	SF	Sm	FB	.021	840.0	1.87	.70	---	2.57	**3.14**
Solid colors	Inst	SF	Lg	FB	.016	1120.0	1.85	.54	---	2.39	**2.88**
	Inst	SF	Sm	FB	.021	840.0	2.04	.70	---	2.74	**3.33**

Sheet vinyl

Description	Oper	Unit	Vol	Crew Size	Man-hours per Unit	Crew Output per Day	Avg Mat'l Unit Cost	Avg Labor Unit Cost	Avg Equip Unit Cost	Avg Total Unit Cost	Avg Price Incl O&P
Armstrong, no-wax, 6' wide											
Designer Solarian (.070")	Inst	SY	Lg	FB	.181	99.56	29.60	6.06	---	35.66	**42.60**
	Inst	SY	Sm	FB	.241	74.67	32.70	8.07	---	40.77	**48.90**
Designer Solarian II (.090")	Inst	SY	Lg	FB	.181	99.56	38.10	6.06	---	44.16	**52.30**
	Inst	SY	Sm	FB	.241	74.67	42.00	8.07	---	50.07	**59.60**
Imperial Accotone (.065")	Inst	SY	Lg	FB	.181	99.56	9.53	6.06	---	15.59	**19.50**
	Inst	SY	Sm	FB	.241	74.67	10.50	8.07	---	18.57	**23.40**
Solarian Supreme (.090")	Inst	SY	Lg	FB	.181	99.56	40.20	6.06	---	46.26	**54.70**
	Inst	SY	Sm	FB	.241	74.67	44.30	8.07	---	52.37	**62.30**
Sundial Solarian (.077")	Inst	SY	Lg	FB	.181	99.56	14.80	6.06	---	20.86	**25.50**
	Inst	SY	Sm	FB	.241	74.67	16.30	8.07	---	24.37	**30.10**
Mannington, 6' wide											
Vega (.080")	Inst	SY	Lg	FB	.181	99.56	8.47	6.06	---	14.53	**18.20**
	Inst	SY	Sm	FB	.241	74.67	9.33	8.07	---	17.40	**22.00**
Vinyl Ease (.073")	Inst	SY	Lg	FB	.181	99.56	7.41	6.06	---	13.47	**17.00**
	Inst	SY	Sm	FB	.241	74.67	8.16	8.07	---	16.23	**20.70**
Tarkett, 6' wide											
Preference (.065")	Inst	SY	Lg	FB	.181	99.56	6.88	6.06	---	12.94	**16.40**
	Inst	SY	Sm	FB	.241	74.67	7.58	8.07	---	15.65	**20.00**
Softred (.062")	Inst	SY	Lg	FB	.181	99.56	8.47	6.06	---	14.53	**18.20**
	Inst	SY	Sm	FB	.241	74.67	9.33	8.07	---	17.40	**22.00**

Description	Oper	Unit	Vol	Crew Size	Man-hours per Unit	Crew Output per Day	Avg Mat'l Unit Cost	Avg Labor Unit Cost	Avg Equip Unit Cost	Avg Total Unit Cost	Avg Price Incl O&P

Related materials and operations

Top set base
Vinyl
2-1/2" H

Description	Oper	Unit	Vol	Crew Size	Man-hours per Unit	Crew Output per Day	Avg Mat'l Unit Cost	Avg Labor Unit Cost	Avg Equip Unit Cost	Avg Total Unit Cost	Avg Price Incl O&P
Colors	Inst	LF	Lg	FB	.036	500.0	.40	1.21	---	1.61	**2.15**
	Inst	LF	Sm	FB	.048	375.0	.44	1.61	---	2.05	**2.76**
Wood grain	Inst	LF	Lg	FB	.036	500.0	.54	1.21	---	1.75	**2.31**
	Inst	LF	Sm	FB	.048	375.0	.59	1.61	---	2.20	**2.93**

4" H

Description	Oper	Unit	Vol	Crew Size	Man-hours per Unit	Crew Output per Day	Avg Mat'l Unit Cost	Avg Labor Unit Cost	Avg Equip Unit Cost	Avg Total Unit Cost	Avg Price Incl O&P
Colors	Inst	LF	Lg	FB	.036	500.0	.47	1.21	---	1.68	**2.23**
	Inst	LF	Sm	FB	.048	375.0	.52	1.61	---	2.13	**2.85**
Wood grain	Inst	LF	Lg	FB	.036	500.0	.64	1.21	---	1.85	**2.42**
	Inst	LF	Sm	FB	.048	375.0	.70	1.61	---	2.31	**3.06**

Linoleum cove, 7/16" x 1-1/4"

Description	Oper	Unit	Vol	Crew Size	Man-hours per Unit	Crew Output per Day	Avg Mat'l Unit Cost	Avg Labor Unit Cost	Avg Equip Unit Cost	Avg Total Unit Cost	Avg Price Incl O&P
Softwood	Inst	LF	Lg	FB	.051	350.0	.47	1.71	---	2.18	**2.93**
	Inst	LF	Sm	FB	.069	262.5	.52	2.31	---	2.83	**3.83**

Retaining walls, see Concrete, page 100, or Masonry, page 290

Roofing

Fiberglass Shingles, 225 lb., three tab strip. Three bundle/square; 20 year

1. **Dimensions**. Each shingle is 12" x 36". With a 5" exposure to the weather, 80 shingles are required to cover one square (100 SF).

2. **Installation**

   a. Over wood. After scatter-nailing one ply of 15 lb. felt, the shingles are installed. Four nails per shingle is customary.

   b. Over existing roofing. 15 lb. felt is not required. Shingles are installed the same as over wood, except longer nails are used, i.e., 1¼" in lieu of 1".

3. **Estimating Technique.** Determine roof area and add a percentage for starters, ridge, and valleys. The percent to be added varies, but generally:

   a. For plain gable and hip – add 10%.

   b. For gable or hip with dormers or intersecting roof(s) – add 15%.

   c. For gable or hip with dormers and intersecting roof(s) – add 20%.

When ridge or hip shingles are special ordered, reduce the above percentages by approximately 50%. Then apply unit costs to the area calculated (including the allowance above).

Mineral Surfaced Roll Roofing, 90 lb.

1. **Dimensions.** A roll is 36" wide x 36'-0" long, or 108 SF. It covers one square (100 SF), after including 8 SF for head and end laps.

2. **Installation.** Usually, lap cement and ⁷⁄₈" galvanized nails are furnished with each roll.

   a. Over wood. Roll roofing is usually applied directly to sheathing with ⁷⁄₈" galvanized nails. End and head laps are normally 6" and 2" or 3" respectively.

   b. Over existing roofing. Applied the same as over wood, except nails are not less than 1¼" long.

   c. Roll roofing may be installed by the exposed nail or the concealed nail method. In the exposed nail method, nails are visible at laps, and head laps are usually 2". In the concealed nail method, no nails are visible, the head lap is a minimum of 3", and there is a 9"-wide strip of roll installed along rakes and eaves.

3. **Estimating Technique.** Determine the area and add a percentage for hip and/or ridge. The percentage to be added varies, but generally:

   a. For plain gable or hip — add 5%.

   b. For cut-up roof – add 10%.

If metal ridge and/or hip are used, reduce the above percentages by approximately 50%. Then apply unit costs to the area calculated (including the allowance above).

Wood Shingles

1. **Dimensions.** Shingles are available in 16", 18", and 24" lengths and in uniform widths of 4", 5", or 6". But they are commonly furnished in random widths averaging 4" wide.

2. **Installation.** The normal exposure to weather for 16", 18" and 24" shingles on roofs with ¼ or steeper pitch is 5", 5½", and 7½" respectively. Where the slope is less than ¼, the exposure is usually reduced. Generally, 3d commons are used when shingles are applied to strip sheathing. 5d commons are used when shingles are applied over existing shingles. Two nails per shingle is the general rule, but on some roofs, one nail per shingle is used.

3. **Estimating Technique.** Determine the roof area and add a percentage for waste, starters, ridge, and hip shingles.

   a. Wood shingles. The amount of exposure determines the percentage of 1 square of shingles required to cover 100 SF of roof. Multiply the material cost per square of shingles by the appropriate percent (from the table on the next page) to determine the cost to cover 100 SF of roof with wood shingles. The table does not include cutting waste. NOTE: Nails and the exposure factors in this table have already been calculated into the Average Unit Material Costs.

   b. Nails. The weight of nails required per square varies with the size of the nail and with the shingle exposure. Multiply cost per pound of nails by the appropriate pounds per square. In the table on the next page, pounds of nails per square are based on two nails per shingle. For one nail per shingle, deduct 50%.

   c. The percentage to be added for starters, hip, and ridge shingles varies, but generally:

   1) Plain gable and hip — add 10%.

   2) Gable or hip with dormers or intersecting roof(s) — add 15%.

   3) Gable or hip with dormers and intersecting roof(s) — add 20%.

When ridge and/or hip shingles are special ordered, reduce these percentages by 50%. Then

Shingle Length	Exposure	% of Sq. Required to Cover 100 SF	Lbs of Nails per Square (2 Nails/Shingle)	
			3d	5d
24"	7½"	100	2.3	2.7
24"	7"	107	2.4	2.9
24"	6½"	115	2.6	3.2
24"	6"	125	2.8	3.4
24"	5¾"	130	2.9	3.6
18"	5½"	100	3.1	3.7
18"	5"	110	3.4	4.1
18"	4½"	122	3.8	4.6
16"	5"	100	3.4	4.1
16"	4½"	111	3.8	4.6
16"	4"	125	4.2	5.1
16"	3¾"	133	4.5	5.5

apply unit costs to the area calculated (including the allowance above).

Built-Up Roofing

1. **Dimensions**

   a. 15 lb. felt. Rolls are 36" wide x 144'-0" long or 432 SF – 4 squares per roll. 32 SF (or 8 SF/sq) is for laps.

   b. 30 lb. felt. Rolls are 36" wide x 72'-0" long or 216 SF – 2 squares per roll. 16 SF (or 8 SF/sq) is for laps.

   c. Asphalt. Available in 100 lb. cartons. Average asphalt usage is:

      1) Top coat without gravel – 35 lbs. per square.

      2) Top coat with gravel – 60 lbs. per square.

      3) Each coat (except top coat) – 25 lbs. per square.

   d. Tar. Available in 550 lb. kegs. Average tar usage is:

      1) Top coat without gravel – 40 lbs. per square.

      2) Top coat without gravel – 75 lbs. per square.

      3) Each coat (except top coat) – 30 lbs. per square.

   e. Gravel or slag. Normally, 400 lbs. of gravel or 275 lbs. of slag are used to cover one square.

2. **Installation**

   a. Over wood. Normally, one or two plies of felt are applied by scatter nailing before hot mopping is commenced. Subsequent plies of felt and gravel or slag are imbedded in hot asphalt or tar.

   b. Over concrete. Every ply of felt and gravel or slag is imbedded in hot asphalt or tar.

3. **Estimating Technique**

   a. For buildings with parapet walls, use the outside dimensions of the building to determine the area. This area is usually sufficient to include the flashing.

   b. For buildings without parapet walls, determine the area.

   c. Don't deduct any opening less than 10'-0" x 10'-0" (100 SF). Deduct 50% of the opening for openings larger than 100 SF but smaller than 300 SF, and 100% of the openings exceeding 300 SF.

Roll roofing for ice-dam protection

Project shingles for drip

$^{3}/_{4}$" edge distance

Space $^{1}/_{8}$"-$^{1}/_{4}$"

Roof boards

2 nails per shingle

$1^{1}/_{2}$"

Wood shingles

Exposure

Fascia board

First shingle course (double)

5" to the weather

4" lap

Starter course

Guide line or chalk line

Roofing felt underlay

30 lb. saturated felt (nail dry)

15 lb. saturated felt

Roof sheathing

Mop coat

Gravel

Mop each layer

Gravel stop

Siding

Block

Flashing

Cant strip

Built-up roof

Roof sheathing

Description	Oper	Unit	Vol	Crew Size	Man-hours per Unit	Crew Output per Day	Avg Mat'l Unit Cost	Avg Labor Unit Cost	Avg Equip Unit Cost	Avg Total Unit Cost	Avg Price Incl O&P

Roofing

Aluminum, nailed to wood

Corrugated (2-1/2"), 26" W, with 3-3/4" side lap and 6" end lap

| | Demo | Sq | Lg | LB | 1.36 | 11.80 | --- | 40.80 | --- | 40.80 | **57.10** |
| | Demo | Sq | Sm | LB | 1.60 | 10.00 | --- | 48.00 | --- | 48.00 | **67.20** |

Corrugated (2-1/2"), 26" W, with 3-3/4" side lap and 6" end lap
0.0175" thick

Natural	Inst	Sq	Lg	UC	1.81	17.70	162.00	64.90	---	226.90	**279.00**
	Inst	Sq	Sm	UC	2.13	15.00	187.00	76.40	---	263.40	**323.00**
Painted	Inst	Sq	Lg	UC	1.81	17.70	209.00	64.90	---	273.90	**333.00**
	Inst	Sq	Sm	UC	2.13	15.00	240.00	76.40	---	316.40	**385.00**

0.019" thick

Natural	Inst	Sq	Lg	UC	1.81	17.70	162.00	64.90	---	226.90	**279.00**
	Inst	Sq	Sm	UC	2.13	15.00	187.00	76.40	---	263.40	**323.00**
Painted	Inst	Sq	Lg	UC	1.81	17.70	209.00	64.90	---	273.90	**333.00**
	Inst	Sq	Sm	UC	2.13	15.00	240.00	76.40	---	316.40	**385.00**

Composition shingle roofing, 3 tab strip, 12" x 36", nailed, seal down

Demo Shingle, to deck

| 5" exposure | Demo | Sq | Lg | LB | 0.85 | 18.88 | --- | 25.50 | --- | 25.50 | **35.70** |
| | Demo | Sq | Sm | LB | 1.00 | 16.00 | --- | 30.00 | --- | 30.00 | **42.00** |

Install 25-year shingles, 240 lb/sq

Over existing roofing

Gable, plain	Inst	Sq	Lg	RL	1.13	17.70	83.60	44.10	---	127.70	**161.00**
	Inst	Sq	Sm	RL	1.33	15.00	96.20	51.90	---	148.10	**187.00**
Gable with dormers	Inst	Sq	Lg	RL	1.26	15.93	84.40	49.20	---	133.60	**169.00**
	Inst	Sq	Sm	RL	1.48	13.50	97.10	57.80	---	154.90	**196.00**
Gable with intersecting roofs	Inst	Sq	Lg	RL	1.26	15.93	85.20	49.20	---	134.40	**170.00**
	Inst	Sq	Sm	RL	1.48	13.50	97.90	57.80	---	155.70	**198.00**
Gable w/dormers & intersections											
	Inst	Sq	Lg	RL	1.41	14.16	85.90	55.00	---	140.90	**180.00**
	Inst	Sq	Sm	RL	1.67	12.00	98.80	65.20	---	164.00	**209.00**
Hip, plain	Inst	Sq	Lg	RL	1.18	16.91	84.40	46.00	---	130.40	**165.00**
	Inst	Sq	Sm	RL	1.40	14.33	97.10	54.60	---	151.70	**192.00**
Hip with dormers	Inst	Sq	Lg	RL	1.32	15.10	85.20	51.50	---	136.70	**174.00**
	Inst	Sq	Sm	RL	1.56	12.80	97.90	60.90	---	158.80	**202.00**
Hip with intersecting roofs	Inst	Sq	Lg	RL	1.32	15.10	85.90	51.50	---	137.40	**175.00**
	Inst	Sq	Sm	RL	1.56	12.80	98.80	60.90	---	159.70	**203.00**
Hip with dormers & intersections											
	Inst	Sq	Lg	RL	1.50	13.33	86.70	58.50	---	145.20	**186.00**
	Inst	Sq	Sm	RL	1.77	11.30	99.70	69.10	---	168.80	**216.00**

Description	Oper	Unit	Vol	Crew Size	Man-hours per Unit	Crew Output per Day	Avg Mat'l Unit Cost	Avg Labor Unit Cost	Avg Equip Unit Cost	Avg Total Unit Cost	Avg Price Incl O&P

Over wood decks, includes felt

Gable, plain	Inst	Sq	Lg	RL	1.21	16.52	87.20	47.20	---	134.40	**170.00**
	Inst	Sq	Sm	RL	1.43	14.00	100.00	55.80	---	155.80	**197.00**
Gable with dormers	Inst	Sq	Lg	RL	1.36	14.75	88.00	53.10	---	141.10	**179.00**
	Inst	Sq	Sm	RL	1.60	12.50	101.00	62.40	---	163.40	**208.00**
Gable with intersecting roofs	Inst	Sq	Lg	RL	1.36	14.75	88.80	53.10	---	141.90	**180.00**
	Inst	Sq	Sm	RL	1.60	12.50	102.00	62.40	---	164.40	**209.00**
Gable w/dormers & intersections											
	Inst	Sq	Lg	RL	1.54	12.98	89.50	60.10	---	149.60	**191.00**
	Inst	Sq	Sm	RL	1.82	11.00	103.00	71.00	---	174.00	**223.00**
Hip, plain	Inst	Sq	Lg	RL	1.27	15.73	88.00	49.60	---	137.60	**174.00**
	Inst	Sq	Sm	RL	1.50	13.33	101.00	58.50	---	159.50	**202.00**
Hip with dormers	Inst	Sq	Lg	RL	1.44	13.92	88.80	56.20	---	145.00	**185.00**
	Inst	Sq	Sm	RL	1.69	11.80	102.00	65.90	---	167.90	**214.00**
Hip with intersecting roofs	Inst	Sq	Lg	RL	1.44	13.92	89.50	56.20	---	145.70	**186.00**
	Inst	Sq	Sm	RL	1.69	11.80	103.00	65.90	---	168.90	**215.00**
Hip with dormers & intersections											
	Inst	Sq	Lg	RL	1.65	12.15	90.30	64.40	---	154.70	**198.00**
	Inst	Sq	Sm	RL	1.94	10.30	104.00	75.70	---	179.70	**231.00**

Install 30-year laminated shingles

Over existing roofing

Gable, plain	Inst	Sq	Lg	RL	1.13	17.70	92.00	44.10	---	136.10	**171.00**
	Inst	Sq	Sm	RL	1.33	15.00	106.00	51.90	---	157.90	**198.00**
Gable with dormers	Inst	Sq	Lg	RL	1.26	15.93	92.90	49.20	---	142.10	**179.00**
	Inst	Sq	Sm	RL	1.48	13.50	107.00	57.80	---	164.80	**208.00**
Gable with intersecting roofs	Inst	Sq	Lg	RL	1.26	15.93	93.80	49.20	---	143.00	**180.00**
	Inst	Sq	Sm	RL	1.48	13.50	108.00	57.80	---	165.80	**209.00**
Gable w/dormers & intersections											
	Inst	Sq	Lg	RL	1.41	14.16	94.60	55.00	---	149.60	**190.00**
	Inst	Sq	Sm	RL	1.67	12.00	109.00	65.20	---	174.20	**221.00**
Hip, plain	Inst	Sq	Lg	RL	1.18	16.91	92.90	46.00	---	138.90	**175.00**
	Inst	Sq	Sm	RL	1.40	14.33	107.00	54.60	---	161.60	**203.00**
Hip with dormers	Inst	Sq	Lg	RL	1.32	15.10	93.80	51.50	---	145.30	**184.00**
	Inst	Sq	Sm	RL	1.56	12.80	108.00	60.90	---	168.90	**213.00**
Hip with intersecting roofs	Inst	Sq	Lg	RL	1.32	15.10	94.60	51.50	---	146.10	**185.00**
	Inst	Sq	Sm	RL	1.56	12.80	109.00	60.90	---	169.90	**215.00**
Hip with dormers & intersections											
	Inst	Sq	Lg	RL	1.50	13.33	95.50	58.50	---	154.00	**196.00**
	Inst	Sq	Sm	RL	1.77	11.30	110.00	69.10	---	179.10	**228.00**

Over wood decks, includes felt

Gable, plain	Inst	Sq	Lg	RL	1.21	16.52	95.60	47.20	---	142.80	**179.00**
	Inst	Sq	Sm	RL	1.43	14.00	110.00	55.80	---	165.80	**208.00**
Gable with dormers	Inst	Sq	Lg	RL	1.36	14.75	96.50	53.10	---	149.60	**189.00**
	Inst	Sq	Sm	RL	1.60	12.50	111.00	62.40	---	173.40	**219.00**
Gable with intersecting roofs	Inst	Sq	Lg	RL	1.36	14.75	97.30	53.10	---	150.40	**190.00**
	Inst	Sq	Sm	RL	1.60	12.50	112.00	62.40	---	174.40	**220.00**
Gable w/dormers & intersections											
	Inst	Sq	Lg	RL	1.54	12.98	98.20	60.10	---	158.30	**201.00**
	Inst	Sq	Sm	RL	1.82	11.00	113.00	71.00	---	184.00	**234.00**
Hip, plain	Inst	Sq	Lg	RL	1.27	15.73	96.50	49.60	---	146.10	**184.00**
	Inst	Sq	Sm	RL	1.50	13.33	111.00	58.50	---	169.50	**214.00**

Description	Oper	Unit	Vol	Crew Size	Man-hours per Unit	Crew Output per Day	Avg Mat'l Unit Cost	Avg Labor Unit Cost	Avg Equip Unit Cost	Avg Total Unit Cost	Avg Price Incl O&P
Hip with dormers	Inst	Sq	Lg	RL	1.44	13.92	97.30	56.20	---	153.50	**195.00**
	Inst	Sq	Sm	RL	1.69	11.80	112.00	65.90	---	177.90	**226.00**
Hip with intersecting roofs	Inst	Sq	Lg	RL	1.44	13.92	98.20	56.20	---	154.40	**196.00**
	Inst	Sq	Sm	RL	1.69	11.80	113.00	65.90	---	178.90	**227.00**
Hip with dormers & intersections											
	Inst	Sq	Lg	RL	1.65	12.15	99.00	64.40	---	163.40	**209.00**
	Inst	Sq	Sm	RL	1.94	10.30	114.00	75.70	---	189.70	**242.00**

Install 40-year laminated shingles

Over existing roofing

Description	Oper	Unit	Vol	Crew Size	Man-hours per Unit	Crew Output per Day	Avg Mat'l Unit Cost	Avg Labor Unit Cost	Avg Equip Unit Cost	Avg Total Unit Cost	Avg Price Incl O&P
Gable, plain	Inst	Sq	Lg	RL	1.13	17.70	95.20	44.10	---	139.30	**174.00**
	Inst	Sq	Sm	RL	1.33	15.00	110.00	51.90	---	161.90	**202.00**
Gable with dormers	Inst	Sq	Lg	RL	1.26	15.93	96.10	49.20	---	145.30	**183.00**
	Inst	Sq	Sm	RL	1.48	13.50	111.00	57.80	---	168.80	**212.00**
Gable with intersecting roofs	Inst	Sq	Lg	RL	1.26	15.93	97.00	49.20	---	146.20	**184.00**
	Inst	Sq	Sm	RL	1.48	13.50	112.00	57.80	---	169.80	**213.00**
Gable w/dormers & intersections											
	Inst	Sq	Lg	RL	1.41	14.16	97.90	55.00	---	152.90	**193.00**
	Inst	Sq	Sm	RL	1.67	12.00	113.00	65.20	---	178.20	**225.00**
Hip, plain	Inst	Sq	Lg	RL	1.18	16.91	96.10	46.00	---	142.10	**178.00**
	Inst	Sq	Sm	RL	1.40	14.33	111.00	54.60	---	165.60	**207.00**
Hip with dormers	Inst	Sq	Lg	RL	1.32	15.10	97.00	51.50	---	148.50	**187.00**
	Inst	Sq	Sm	RL	1.56	12.80	112.00	60.90	---	172.90	**218.00**
Hip with intersecting roofs	Inst	Sq	Lg	RL	1.32	15.10	97.90	51.50	---	149.40	**188.00**
	Inst	Sq	Sm	RL	1.56	12.80	113.00	60.90	---	173.90	**219.00**
Hip with dormers & intersections											
	Inst	Sq	Lg	RL	1.50	13.33	98.80	58.50	---	157.30	**200.00**
	Inst	Sq	Sm	RL	1.77	11.30	114.00	69.10	---	183.10	**232.00**

Over wood decks, includes felt

Description	Oper	Unit	Vol	Crew Size	Man-hours per Unit	Crew Output per Day	Avg Mat'l Unit Cost	Avg Labor Unit Cost	Avg Equip Unit Cost	Avg Total Unit Cost	Avg Price Incl O&P
Gable, plain	Inst	Sq	Lg	RL	1.21	16.52	98.80	47.20	---	146.00	**183.00**
	Inst	Sq	Sm	RL	1.43	14.00	114.00	55.80	---	169.80	**213.00**
Gable with dormers	Inst	Sq	Lg	RL	1.36	14.75	99.70	53.10	---	152.80	**193.00**
	Inst	Sq	Sm	RL	1.60	12.50	115.00	62.40	---	177.40	**224.00**
Gable with intersecting roofs	Inst	Sq	Lg	RL	1.36	14.75	101.00	53.10	---	154.10	**194.00**
	Inst	Sq	Sm	RL	1.60	12.50	116.00	62.40	---	178.40	**225.00**
Gable w/dormers & intersections											
	Inst	Sq	Lg	RL	1.54	12.98	101.00	60.10	---	161.10	**205.00**
	Inst	Sq	Sm	RL	1.82	11.00	117.00	71.00	---	188.00	**239.00**
Hip, plain	Inst	Sq	Lg	RL	1.27	15.73	99.70	49.60	---	149.30	**187.00**
	Inst	Sq	Sm	RL	1.50	13.33	115.00	58.50	---	173.50	**218.00**
Hip with dormers	Inst	Sq	Lg	RL	1.44	13.92	101.00	56.20	---	157.20	**198.00**
	Inst	Sq	Sm	RL	1.69	11.80	116.00	65.90	---	181.90	**230.00**
Hip with intersecting roofs	Inst	Sq	Lg	RL	1.44	13.92	101.00	56.20	---	157.20	**199.00**
	Inst	Sq	Sm	RL	1.69	11.80	117.00	65.90	---	182.90	**231.00**
Hip with dormers & intersections											
	Inst	Sq	Lg	RL	1.65	12.15	102.00	64.40	---	166.40	**212.00**
	Inst	Sq	Sm	RL	1.94	10.30	118.00	75.70	---	193.70	**247.00**

Description	Oper	Unit	Vol	Crew Size	Man-hours per Unit	Crew Output per Day	Avg Mat'l Unit Cost	Avg Labor Unit Cost	Avg Equip Unit Cost	Avg Total Unit Cost	Avg Price Incl O&P

Install 50-year lifetime laminated shingles

Over existing roofing

Description	Oper	Unit	Vol	Crew Size	Man-hours per Unit	Crew Output per Day	Avg Mat'l Unit Cost	Avg Labor Unit Cost	Avg Equip Unit Cost	Avg Total Unit Cost	Avg Price Incl O&P
Gable, plain	Inst	Sq	Lg	RL	1.13	17.70	98.40	44.10	---	142.50	**178.00**
	Inst	Sq	Sm	RL	1.33	15.00	113.00	51.90	---	164.90	**206.00**
Gable with dormers	Inst	Sq	Lg	RL	1.26	15.93	99.30	49.20	---	148.50	**186.00**
	Inst	Sq	Sm	RL	1.48	13.50	114.00	57.80	---	171.80	**216.00**
Gable with intersecting roofs	Inst	Sq	Lg	RL	1.26	15.93	100.00	49.20	---	149.20	**188.00**
	Inst	Sq	Sm	RL	1.48	13.50	115.00	57.80	---	172.80	**217.00**
Gable w/dormers & intersections											
	Inst	Sq	Lg	RL	1.41	14.16	101.00	55.00	---	156.00	**197.00**
	Inst	Sq	Sm	RL	1.67	12.00	116.00	65.20	---	181.20	**230.00**
Hip, plain	Inst	Sq	Lg	RL	1.18	16.91	99.30	46.00	---	145.30	**182.00**
	Inst	Sq	Sm	RL	1.40	14.33	114.00	54.60	---	168.60	**212.00**
Hip with dormers	Inst	Sq	Lg	RL	1.32	15.10	100.00	51.50	---	151.50	**191.00**
	Inst	Sq	Sm	RL	1.56	12.80	115.00	60.90	---	175.90	**222.00**
Hip with intersecting roofs	Inst	Sq	Lg	RL	1.32	15.10	101.00	51.50	---	152.50	**192.00**
	Inst	Sq	Sm	RL	1.56	12.80	116.00	60.90	---	176.90	**223.00**
Hip with dormers & intersections											
	Inst	Sq	Lg	RL	1.50	13.33	102.00	58.50	---	160.50	**203.00**
	Inst	Sq	Sm	RL	1.77	11.30	117.00	69.10	---	186.10	**237.00**

Over wood decks, includes felt

Description	Oper	Unit	Vol	Crew Size	Man-hours per Unit	Crew Output per Day	Avg Mat'l Unit Cost	Avg Labor Unit Cost	Avg Equip Unit Cost	Avg Total Unit Cost	Avg Price Incl O&P
Gable, plain	Inst	Sq	Lg	RL	1.21	16.52	102.00	47.20	---	149.20	**187.00**
	Inst	Sq	Sm	RL	1.43	14.00	117.00	55.80	---	172.80	**217.00**
Gable with dormers	Inst	Sq	Lg	RL	1.36	14.75	103.00	53.10	---	156.10	**196.00**
	Inst	Sq	Sm	RL	1.60	12.50	118.00	62.40	---	180.40	**228.00**
Gable with intersecting roofs	Inst	Sq	Lg	RL	1.36	14.75	104.00	53.10	---	157.10	**197.00**
	Inst	Sq	Sm	RL	1.60	12.50	119.00	62.40	---	181.40	**229.00**
Gable w/dormers & intersections											
	Inst	Sq	Lg	RL	1.54	12.98	105.00	60.10	---	165.10	**209.00**
	Inst	Sq	Sm	RL	1.82	11.00	120.00	71.00	---	191.00	**243.00**
Hip, plain	Inst	Sq	Lg	RL	1.27	15.73	103.00	49.60	---	152.60	**191.00**
	Inst	Sq	Sm	RL	1.50	13.33	118.00	58.50	---	176.50	**222.00**
Hip with dormers	Inst	Sq	Lg	RL	1.44	13.92	104.00	56.20	---	160.20	**202.00**
	Inst	Sq	Sm	RL	1.69	11.80	119.00	65.90	---	184.90	**234.00**
Hip with intersecting roofs	Inst	Sq	Lg	RL	1.44	13.92	105.00	56.20	---	161.20	**203.00**
	Inst	Sq	Sm	RL	1.69	11.80	120.00	65.90	---	185.90	**235.00**
Hip with dormers & intersections											
	Inst	Sq	Lg	RL	1.65	12.15	106.00	64.40	---	170.40	**216.00**
	Inst	Sq	Sm	RL	1.94	10.30	122.00	75.70	---	197.70	**251.00**

Related materials and operations

Ridge or hip roll

Description	Oper	Unit	Vol	Crew Size	Man-hours per Unit	Crew Output per Day	Avg Mat'l Unit Cost	Avg Labor Unit Cost	Avg Equip Unit Cost	Avg Total Unit Cost	Avg Price Incl O&P
90 lb mineral surfaced	Inst	LF	Lg	2R	.017	944.0	.45	.70	---	1.15	**1.55**
	Inst	LF	Sm	2R	.020	800.0	.51	.83	---	1.34	**1.80**

Valley roll

Description	Oper	Unit	Vol	Crew Size	Man-hours per Unit	Crew Output per Day	Avg Mat'l Unit Cost	Avg Labor Unit Cost	Avg Equip Unit Cost	Avg Total Unit Cost	Avg Price Incl O&P
90 lb mineral surfaced	Inst	LF	Lg	2R	.017	944.0	.45	.70	---	1.15	**1.55**
	Inst	LF	Sm	2R	.020	800.0	.51	.83	---	1.34	**1.80**

Description	Oper	Unit	Vol	Crew Size	Man-hours per Unit	Crew Output per Day	Avg Mat'l Unit Cost	Avg Labor Unit Cost	Avg Equip Unit Cost	Avg Total Unit Cost	Avg Price Incl O&P
Ridge / hip units, 9" x 12" with 5" exp.; 80 pcs / bdle @ 33.3 LF/bdle											
Standard											
Over existing roofing	Inst	LF	Lg	2R	.019	826.0	1.35	.78	---	2.13	**2.71**
	Inst	LF	Sm	2R	.023	700.0	1.56	.95	---	2.51	**3.19**
Over wood decks	Inst	LF	Lg	2R	.021	778.8	1.35	.87	---	2.22	**2.83**
	Inst	LF	Sm	2R	.024	660.0	1.56	.99	---	2.55	**3.25**
Architectural											
Over existing roofing	Inst	LF	Lg	2R	.019	826.0	1.47	.78	---	2.25	**2.84**
	Inst	LF	Sm	2R	.023	700.0	1.69	.95	---	2.64	**3.34**
Over wood decks	Inst	LF	Lg	2R	.021	778.8	1.47	.87	---	2.34	**2.96**
	Inst	LF	Sm	2R	.024	660.0	1.69	.99	---	2.68	**3.40**

Built-up or membrane roofing

Install over existing roofing

Description	Oper	Unit	Vol	Crew Size	Man-hours per Unit	Crew Output per Day	Avg Mat'l Unit Cost	Avg Labor Unit Cost	Avg Equip Unit Cost	Avg Total Unit Cost	Avg Price Incl O&P
One mop coat over smooth surface											
With asphalt	Inst	Sq	Lg	RS	.301	159.3	45.00	11.70	---	56.70	**68.90**
	Inst	Sq	Sm	RS	.356	135.0	51.80	13.80	---	65.60	**79.80**
With tar	Inst	Sq	Lg	RS	.301	159.3	77.00	11.70	---	88.70	**106.00**
	Inst	Sq	Sm	RS	.356	135.0	88.40	13.80	---	102.20	**122.00**
Remove gravel, mop one coat, redistribute old gravel											
With asphalt	Inst	Sq	Lg	RS	.768	62.54	70.00	29.80	---	99.80	**124.00**
	Inst	Sq	Sm	RS	0.91	53.00	80.50	35.30	---	115.80	**145.00**
With tar	Inst	Sq	Lg	RS	.768	62.54	119.00	29.80	---	148.80	**180.00**
	Inst	Sq	Sm	RS	0.91	53.00	136.00	35.30	---	171.30	**209.00**
Mop in one 30 lb cap sheet, plus smooth top mop coat											
With asphalt	Inst	Sq	Lg	RS	.714	67.26	77.70	27.70	---	105.40	**130.00**
	Inst	Sq	Sm	RS	0.84	57.00	89.40	32.60	---	122.00	**151.00**
With tar	Inst	Sq	Lg	RS	.714	67.26	128.00	27.70	---	155.70	**188.00**
	Inst	Sq	Sm	RS	0.84	57.00	147.00	32.60	---	179.60	**217.00**
Remove gravel, mop in one 30 lb cap sheet, mop in and redistribute old gravel											
With asphalt	Inst	Sq	Lg	RS	1.23	38.94	103.00	47.80	---	150.80	**188.00**
	Inst	Sq	Sm	RS	1.45	33.00	118.00	56.30	---	174.30	**219.00**
With tar	Inst	Sq	Lg	RS	1.23	38.94	170.00	47.80	---	217.80	**265.00**
	Inst	Sq	Sm	RS	1.45	33.00	195.00	56.30	---	251.30	**307.00**
Mop in two 15 lb felt plies, plus smooth top mop coat											
With asphalt	Inst	Sq	Lg	RS	1.13	42.48	103.00	43.90	---	146.90	**183.00**
	Inst	Sq	Sm	RS	1.33	36.00	118.00	51.60	---	169.60	**212.00**
With tar	Inst	Sq	Lg	RS	1.13	42.48	171.00	43.90	---	214.90	**261.00**
	Inst	Sq	Sm	RS	1.33	36.00	196.00	51.60	---	247.60	**302.00**
Remove gravel, mop in two 15 lb felt plies, mop in and redistribute old gravel											
With asphalt	Inst	Sq	Lg	RS	1.63	29.50	128.00	63.30	---	191.30	**240.00**
	Inst	Sq	Sm	RS	1.92	25.00	147.00	74.60	---	221.60	**279.00**
With tar	Inst	Sq	Lg	RS	1.63	29.50	213.00	63.30	---	276.30	**338.00**
	Inst	Sq	Sm	RS	1.92	25.00	244.00	74.60	---	318.60	**391.00**

Description	Oper	Unit	Vol	Crew Size	Man-hours per Unit	Crew Output per Day	Avg Mat'l Unit Cost	Avg Labor Unit Cost	Avg Equip Unit Cost	Avg Total Unit Cost	Avg Price Incl O&P

Demo over smooth wood or concrete deck

3 ply

Description	Oper	Unit	Vol	Crew Size	Man-hours per Unit	Crew Output per Day	Avg Mat'l Unit Cost	Avg Labor Unit Cost	Avg Equip Unit Cost	Avg Total Unit Cost	Avg Price Incl O&P
With gravel	Demo	Sq	Lg	LB	1.23	12.98	---	36.90	---	36.90	**51.70**
	Demo	Sq	Sm	LB	1.45	11.00	---	43.50	---	43.50	**60.90**
Without gravel	Demo	Sq	Lg	LB	0.97	16.52	---	29.10	---	29.10	**40.70**
	Demo	Sq	Sm	LB	1.14	14.00	---	34.20	---	34.20	**47.90**

5 ply

Description	Oper	Unit	Vol	Crew Size	Man-hours per Unit	Crew Output per Day	Avg Mat'l Unit Cost	Avg Labor Unit Cost	Avg Equip Unit Cost	Avg Total Unit Cost	Avg Price Incl O&P
With gravel	Demo	Sq	Lg	LB	1.36	11.80	---	40.80	---	40.80	**57.10**
	Demo	Sq	Sm	LB	1.60	10.00	---	48.00	---	48.00	**67.20**
Without gravel	Demo	Sq	Lg	LB	1.04	15.34	---	31.20	---	31.20	**43.70**
	Demo	Sq	Sm	LB	1.23	13.00	---	36.90	---	36.90	**51.70**

Install over smooth wood decks

Nail one 15 lb felt ply, plus mop in one 90 lb mineral surfaced ply

Description	Oper	Unit	Vol	Crew Size	Man-hours per Unit	Crew Output per Day	Avg Mat'l Unit Cost	Avg Labor Unit Cost	Avg Equip Unit Cost	Avg Total Unit Cost	Avg Price Incl O&P
With asphalt	Inst	Sq	Lg	RS	.508	94.40	76.40	19.70	---	96.10	**117.00**
	Inst	Sq	Sm	RS	.600	80.00	87.80	23.30	---	111.10	**135.00**
With tar	Inst	Sq	Lg	RS	.508	94.40	97.70	19.70	---	117.40	**141.00**
	Inst	Sq	Sm	RS	.600	80.00	112.00	23.30	---	135.30	**163.00**

Nail one and mop in two 15 lb felt plies, plus smooth top mop coat

Description	Oper	Unit	Vol	Crew Size	Man-hours per Unit	Crew Output per Day	Avg Mat'l Unit Cost	Avg Labor Unit Cost	Avg Equip Unit Cost	Avg Total Unit Cost	Avg Price Incl O&P
With asphalt	Inst	Sq	Lg	RS	1.23	38.94	108.00	47.80	---	155.80	**194.00**
	Inst	Sq	Sm	RS	1.45	33.00	124.00	56.30	---	180.30	**225.00**
With tar	Inst	Sq	Lg	RS	1.23	38.94	176.00	47.80	---	223.80	**273.00**
	Inst	Sq	Sm	RS	1.45	33.00	202.00	56.30	---	258.30	**315.00**

Nail one and mop in two 15 lb felt plies, plus mop in and distribute gravel

Description	Oper	Unit	Vol	Crew Size	Man-hours per Unit	Crew Output per Day	Avg Mat'l Unit Cost	Avg Labor Unit Cost	Avg Equip Unit Cost	Avg Total Unit Cost	Avg Price Incl O&P
With asphalt	Inst	Sq	Lg	RS	1.63	29.50	161.00	63.30	---	224.30	**278.00**
	Inst	Sq	Sm	RS	1.92	25.00	185.00	74.60	---	259.60	**322.00**
With tar	Inst	Sq	Lg	RS	1.63	29.50	246.00	63.30	---	309.30	**376.00**
	Inst	Sq	Sm	RS	1.92	25.00	282.00	74.60	---	356.60	**434.00**

Nail one and mop in three 15 lb felt plies, plus mop in and distribute gravel

Description	Oper	Unit	Vol	Crew Size	Man-hours per Unit	Crew Output per Day	Avg Mat'l Unit Cost	Avg Labor Unit Cost	Avg Equip Unit Cost	Avg Total Unit Cost	Avg Price Incl O&P
With asphalt	Inst	Sq	Lg	RS	2.03	23.60	190.00	78.80	---	268.80	**334.00**
	Inst	Sq	Sm	RS	2.40	20.00	218.00	93.20	---	311.20	**387.00**
With tar	Inst	Sq	Lg	RS	2.03	23.60	293.00	78.80	---	371.80	**453.00**
	Inst	Sq	Sm	RS	2.40	20.00	336.00	93.20	---	429.20	**524.00**

Nail one and mop in four 15 lb plies, plus mop in and distribute gravel

Description	Oper	Unit	Vol	Crew Size	Man-hours per Unit	Crew Output per Day	Avg Mat'l Unit Cost	Avg Labor Unit Cost	Avg Equip Unit Cost	Avg Total Unit Cost	Avg Price Incl O&P
With asphalt	Inst	Sq	Lg	RS	2.54	18.88	218.00	98.60	---	316.60	**396.00**
	Inst	Sq	Sm	RS	3.00	16.00	251.00	116.00	---	367.00	**460.00**
With tar	Inst	Sq	Lg	RS	2.54	18.88	340.00	98.60	---	438.60	**536.00**
	Inst	Sq	Sm	RS	3.00	16.00	390.00	116.00	---	506.00	**620.00**

Description	Oper	Unit	Vol	Crew Size	Man-hours per Unit	Crew Output per Day	Avg Mat'l Unit Cost	Avg Labor Unit Cost	Avg Equip Unit Cost	Avg Total Unit Cost	Avg Price Incl O&P

Install over smooth concrete decks

Nail one 15 lb felt ply, plus mop in one 90 lb mineral surfaced ply

Description	Oper	Unit	Vol	Crew Size	Man-hours per Unit	Crew Output per Day	Avg Mat'l Unit Cost	Avg Labor Unit Cost	Avg Equip Unit Cost	Avg Total Unit Cost	Avg Price Incl O&P
With asphalt	Inst	Sq	Lg	RS	.656	73.16	101.00	25.50	---	126.50	**154.00**
	Inst	Sq	Sm	RS	.774	62.00	117.00	30.10	---	147.10	**178.00**
With tar	Inst	Sq	Lg	RS	.656	73.16	140.00	25.50	---	165.50	**198.00**
	Inst	Sq	Sm	RS	.774	62.00	160.00	30.10	---	190.10	**228.00**

Nail one and mop in two 15 lb felt plies, plus smooth top mop coat

Description	Oper	Unit	Vol	Crew Size	Man-hours per Unit	Crew Output per Day	Avg Mat'l Unit Cost	Avg Labor Unit Cost	Avg Equip Unit Cost	Avg Total Unit Cost	Avg Price Incl O&P
With asphalt	Inst	Sq	Lg	RS	1.51	31.86	132.00	58.60	---	190.60	**238.00**
	Inst	Sq	Sm	RS	1.78	27.00	151.00	69.10	---	220.10	**276.00**
With tar	Inst	Sq	Lg	RS	1.51	31.86	218.00	58.60	---	276.60	**337.00**
	Inst	Sq	Sm	RS	1.78	27.00	250.00	69.10	---	319.10	**390.00**

Nail one and mop in two 15 lb felt plies, plus mop in and distribute gravel

Description	Oper	Unit	Vol	Crew Size	Man-hours per Unit	Crew Output per Day	Avg Mat'l Unit Cost	Avg Labor Unit Cost	Avg Equip Unit Cost	Avg Total Unit Cost	Avg Price Incl O&P
With asphalt	Inst	Sq	Lg	RS	1.94	24.78	185.00	75.30	---	260.30	**323.00**
	Inst	Sq	Sm	RS	2.29	21.00	212.00	88.90	---	300.90	**375.00**
With tar	Inst	Sq	Lg	RS	1.94	24.78	288.00	75.30	---	363.30	**442.00**
	Inst	Sq	Sm	RS	2.29	21.00	331.00	88.90	---	419.90	**511.00**

Nail one and mop in three 15 lb felt plies, plus mop in and distribute gravel

Description	Oper	Unit	Vol	Crew Size	Man-hours per Unit	Crew Output per Day	Avg Mat'l Unit Cost	Avg Labor Unit Cost	Avg Equip Unit Cost	Avg Total Unit Cost	Avg Price Incl O&P
With asphalt	Inst	Sq	Lg	RS	2.39	20.06	213.00	92.80	---	305.80	**382.00**
	Inst	Sq	Sm	RS	2.82	17.00	245.00	110.00	---	355.00	**443.00**
With tar	Inst	Sq	Lg	RS	2.39	20.06	335.00	92.80	---	427.80	**522.00**
	Inst	Sq	Sm	RS	2.82	17.00	385.00	110.00	---	495.00	**603.00**

Nail one and mop in four 15 lb plies, plus mop in and distribute gravel

Description	Oper	Unit	Vol	Crew Size	Man-hours per Unit	Crew Output per Day	Avg Mat'l Unit Cost	Avg Labor Unit Cost	Avg Equip Unit Cost	Avg Total Unit Cost	Avg Price Incl O&P
With asphalt	Inst	Sq	Lg	RS	2.71	17.70	242.00	105.00	---	347.00	**433.00**
	Inst	Sq	Sm	RS	3.20	15.00	278.00	124.00	---	402.00	**503.00**
With tar	Inst	Sq	Lg	RS	2.71	17.70	382.00	105.00	---	487.00	**594.00**
	Inst	Sq	Sm	RS	3.20	15.00	439.00	124.00	---	563.00	**687.00**

Tile, clay or concrete
Demo tile over wood

Description	Oper	Unit	Vol	Crew Size	Man-hours per Unit	Crew Output per Day	Avg Mat'l Unit Cost	Avg Labor Unit Cost	Avg Equip Unit Cost	Avg Total Unit Cost	Avg Price Incl O&P
2 piece (interlocking)	Demo	Sq	Lg	LB	1.69	9.44	---	50.70	---	50.70	**71.00**
	Demo	Sq	Sm	LB	2.00	8.00	---	60.00	---	60.00	**84.00**
1 piece	Demo	Sq	Lg	LB	1.51	10.62	---	45.30	---	45.30	**63.40**
	Demo	Sq	Sm	LB	1.78	9.00	---	53.40	---	53.40	**74.80**

Install tile over wood; includes felt

2 piece (interlocking)

Description	Oper	Unit	Vol	Crew Size	Man-hours per Unit	Crew Output per Day	Avg Mat'l Unit Cost	Avg Labor Unit Cost	Avg Equip Unit Cost	Avg Total Unit Cost	Avg Price Incl O&P
Red	Inst	Sq	Lg	RG	5.08	4.72	444.00	191.00	---	635.00	**791.00**
	Inst	Sq	Sm	RG	6.00	4.00	511.00	225.00	---	736.00	**918.00**
Other colors	Inst	Sq	Lg	RG	5.08	4.72	553.00	191.00	---	744.00	**916.00**
	Inst	Sq	Sm	RG	6.00	4.00	635.00	225.00	---	860.00	**1060.00**

Tile shingles

Description	Oper	Unit	Vol	Crew Size	Man-hours per Unit	Crew Output per Day	Avg Mat'l Unit Cost	Avg Labor Unit Cost	Avg Equip Unit Cost	Avg Total Unit Cost	Avg Price Incl O&P
Mission	Inst	Sq	Lg	RG	4.07	5.90	317.00	153.00	---	470.00	**589.00**
	Inst	Sq	Sm	RG	4.8	5.00	365.00	180.00	---	545.00	**684.00**
Spanish	Inst	Sq	Lg	RG	4.07	5.90	394.00	153.00	---	547.00	**677.00**
	Inst	Sq	Sm	RG	4.8	5.00	453.00	180.00	---	633.00	**785.00**

Description	Oper	Unit	Vol	Crew Size	Man-hours per Unit	Crew Output per Day	Avg Mat'l Unit Cost	Avg Labor Unit Cost	Avg Equip Unit Cost	Avg Total Unit Cost	Avg Price Incl O&P

Mineral surfaced roll

Single coverage 90 lb/sq roll, with 6" end lap and 2" head lap

	Oper	Unit	Vol	Crew Size	Man-hours per Unit	Crew Output per Day	Avg Mat'l Unit Cost	Avg Labor Unit Cost	Avg Equip Unit Cost	Avg Total Unit Cost	Avg Price Incl O&P
	Demo	Sq	Lg	LB	.424	37.76	---	12.70	---	12.70	**17.80**
	Demo	Sq	Sm	LB	.500	32.00	---	15.00	---	15.00	**21.00**

Single coverage roll on

Plain gable over

Existing roofing with

	Oper	Unit	Vol	Crew Size	Man-hours per Unit	Crew Output per Day	Avg Mat'l Unit Cost	Avg Labor Unit Cost	Avg Equip Unit Cost	Avg Total Unit Cost	Avg Price Incl O&P
Nails concealed	Inst	Sq	Lg	2R	.590	27.14	49.10	24.40	---	73.50	**92.30**
	Inst	Sq	Sm	2R	.696	23.00	56.50	28.70	---	85.20	**107.00**
Nails exposed	Inst	Sq	Lg	2R	.542	29.50	44.60	22.40	---	67.00	**84.20**
	Inst	Sq	Sm	2R	.640	25.00	51.30	26.40	---	77.70	**97.90**

Wood deck with

	Oper	Unit	Vol	Crew Size	Man-hours per Unit	Crew Output per Day	Avg Mat'l Unit Cost	Avg Labor Unit Cost	Avg Equip Unit Cost	Avg Total Unit Cost	Avg Price Incl O&P
Nails concealed	Inst	Sq	Lg	2R	.616	25.96	50.50	25.40	---	75.90	**95.40**
	Inst	Sq	Sm	2R	.727	22.00	58.10	30.00	---	88.10	**111.00**
Nails exposed	Inst	Sq	Lg	2R	.565	28.32	45.90	23.30	---	69.20	**87.10**
	Inst	Sq	Sm	2R	.667	24.00	52.80	27.50	---	80.30	**101.00**

Plain hip over

Existing roofing with

	Oper	Unit	Vol	Crew Size	Man-hours per Unit	Crew Output per Day	Avg Mat'l Unit Cost	Avg Labor Unit Cost	Avg Equip Unit Cost	Avg Total Unit Cost	Avg Price Incl O&P
Nails concealed	Inst	Sq	Lg	2R	.616	25.96	50.50	25.40	---	75.90	**95.40**
	Inst	Sq	Sm	2R	.727	22.00	58.10	30.00	---	88.10	**111.00**
Nails exposed	Inst	Sq	Lg	2R	.565	28.32	45.90	23.30	---	69.20	**87.10**
	Inst	Sq	Sm	2R	.667	24.00	52.80	27.50	---	80.30	**101.00**

Wood deck with

	Oper	Unit	Vol	Crew Size	Man-hours per Unit	Crew Output per Day	Avg Mat'l Unit Cost	Avg Labor Unit Cost	Avg Equip Unit Cost	Avg Total Unit Cost	Avg Price Incl O&P
Nails concealed	Inst	Sq	Lg	2R	.678	23.60	51.40	28.00	---	79.40	**100.00**
	Inst	Sq	Sm	2R	.80	20.00	59.10	33.00	---	92.10	**117.00**
Nails exposed	Inst	Sq	Lg	2R	.590	27.14	46.80	24.40	---	71.20	**89.60**
	Inst	Sq	Sm	2R	.696	23.00	53.80	28.70	---	82.50	**104.00**

Double coverage selvage roll, with 19" lap and 17" exposure

	Oper	Unit	Vol	Crew Size	Man-hours per Unit	Crew Output per Day	Avg Mat'l Unit Cost	Avg Labor Unit Cost	Avg Equip Unit Cost	Avg Total Unit Cost	Avg Price Incl O&P
	Demo	Sq	Lg	LB	.616	25.96	---	18.50	---	18.50	**25.90**
	Demo	Sq	Sm	LB	.727	22.00	---	21.80	---	21.80	**30.50**

Double coverage selvage roll, with 19" lap and 17" exposure (2 rolls/sq)

Plain gable over

Wood deck with nails exposed

	Oper	Unit	Vol	Crew Size	Man-hours per Unit	Crew Output per Day	Avg Mat'l Unit Cost	Avg Labor Unit Cost	Avg Equip Unit Cost	Avg Total Unit Cost	Avg Price Incl O&P
	Inst	Sq	Lg	2R	0.97	16.52	103.00	40.00	---	143.00	**177.00**
	Inst	Sq	Sm	2R	1.14	14.00	118.00	47.10	---	165.10	**205.00**

Related materials and operations

Starter strips (36' L rolls) along eaves and up rakes and gable ends on new roofing over wood decks

	Oper	Unit	Vol	Crew Size	Man-hours per Unit	Crew Output per Day	Avg Mat'l Unit Cost	Avg Labor Unit Cost	Avg Equip Unit Cost	Avg Total Unit Cost	Avg Price Incl O&P
9" W	Inst	LF	Lg	---	---	---	.48	---	---	.48	**.55**
	Inst	LF	Sm	---	---	---	.55	---	---	.55	**.63**
12" W	Inst	LF	Lg	---	---	---	.60	---	---	.60	**.69**
	Inst	LF	Sm	---	---	---	.69	---	---	.69	**.79**
18" W	Inst	LF	Lg	---	---	---	.78	---	---	.78	**.90**
	Inst	LF	Sm	---	---	---	.90	---	---	.90	**1.04**
24" W	Inst	LF	Lg	---	---	---	.96	---	---	.96	**1.10**
	Inst	LF	Sm	---	---	---	1.10	---	---	1.10	**1.27**

Description	Oper	Unit	Vol	Crew Size	Man-hours per Unit	Crew Output per Day	Avg Mat'l Unit Cost	Avg Labor Unit Cost	Avg Equip Unit Cost	Avg Total Unit Cost	Avg Price Incl O&P

Wood
Shakes
24" L with 10" exposure

Description	Oper	Unit	Vol	Crew Size	Man-hours per Unit	Crew Output per Day	Avg Mat'l Unit Cost	Avg Labor Unit Cost	Avg Equip Unit Cost	Avg Total Unit Cost	Avg Price Incl O&P
1/2" to 3/4" T	Demo	Sq	Lg	LB	.542	29.50	---	16.30	---	16.30	**22.80**
	Demo	Sq	Sm	LB	.640	25.00	---	19.20	---	19.20	**26.90**
3/4" to 5/4" T	Demo	Sq	Lg	LB	.603	26.55	---	18.10	---	18.10	**25.30**
	Demo	Sq	Sm	LB	.711	22.50	---	21.30	---	21.30	**29.90**

Shakes, over wood deck; 2 nails/shake, 24" L with 10" exp., 6" W (avg.), red cedar, sawn one side
Gable

Description	Oper	Unit	Vol	Crew Size	Man-hours per Unit	Crew Output per Day	Avg Mat'l Unit Cost	Avg Labor Unit Cost	Avg Equip Unit Cost	Avg Total Unit Cost	Avg Price Incl O&P
1/2" to 3/4" T	Inst	Sq	Lg	RQ	1.55	14.87	192.00	60.90	---	252.90	**310.00**
	Inst	Sq	Sm	RQ	1.83	12.60	221.00	71.90	---	292.90	**359.00**
3/4" to 5/4" T	Inst	Sq	Lg	RQ	1.73	13.33	277.00	68.00	---	345.00	**419.00**
	Inst	Sq	Sm	RQ	2.04	11.30	319.00	80.10	---	399.10	**485.00**

Gable with dormers

Description	Oper	Unit	Vol	Crew Size	Man-hours per Unit	Crew Output per Day	Avg Mat'l Unit Cost	Avg Labor Unit Cost	Avg Equip Unit Cost	Avg Total Unit Cost	Avg Price Incl O&P
1/2" to 3/4" T	Inst	Sq	Lg	RQ	1.62	14.16	195.00	63.60	---	258.60	**318.00**
	Inst	Sq	Sm	RQ	1.92	12.00	225.00	75.40	---	300.40	**369.00**
3/4" to 5/4" T	Inst	Sq	Lg	RQ	1.82	12.63	283.00	71.50	---	354.50	**430.00**
	Inst	Sq	Sm	RQ	2.15	10.70	325.00	84.50	---	409.50	**498.00**

Gable with valleys

Description	Oper	Unit	Vol	Crew Size	Man-hours per Unit	Crew Output per Day	Avg Mat'l Unit Cost	Avg Labor Unit Cost	Avg Equip Unit Cost	Avg Total Unit Cost	Avg Price Incl O&P
1/2" to 3/4" T	Inst	Sq	Lg	RQ	1.62	14.16	195.00	63.60	---	258.60	**318.00**
	Inst	Sq	Sm	RQ	1.92	12.00	225.00	75.40	---	300.40	**369.00**
3/4" to 5/4" T	Inst	Sq	Lg	RQ	1.82	12.63	283.00	71.50	---	354.50	**430.00**
	Inst	Sq	Sm	RQ	2.15	10.70	325.00	84.50	---	409.50	**498.00**

Hip

Description	Oper	Unit	Vol	Crew Size	Man-hours per Unit	Crew Output per Day	Avg Mat'l Unit Cost	Avg Labor Unit Cost	Avg Equip Unit Cost	Avg Total Unit Cost	Avg Price Incl O&P
1/2" to 3/4" T	Inst	Sq	Lg	RQ	1.62	14.16	195.00	63.60	---	258.60	**318.00**
	Inst	Sq	Sm	RQ	1.92	12.00	225.00	75.40	---	300.40	**369.00**
3/4" to 5/4" T	Inst	Sq	Lg	RQ	1.82	12.63	283.00	71.50	---	354.50	**430.00**
	Inst	Sq	Sm	RQ	2.15	10.70	325.00	84.50	---	409.50	**498.00**

Hip with valleys

Description	Oper	Unit	Vol	Crew Size	Man-hours per Unit	Crew Output per Day	Avg Mat'l Unit Cost	Avg Labor Unit Cost	Avg Equip Unit Cost	Avg Total Unit Cost	Avg Price Incl O&P
1/2" to 3/4" T	Inst	Sq	Lg	RQ	1.73	13.33	199.00	68.00	---	267.00	**329.00**
	Inst	Sq	Sm	RQ	2.04	11.30	229.00	80.10	---	309.10	**381.00**
3/4" to 5/4" T	Inst	Sq	Lg	RQ	1.91	12.04	288.00	75.00	---	363.00	**441.00**
	Inst	Sq	Sm	RQ	2.25	10.20	331.00	88.40	---	419.40	**511.00**

Related materials and operations
Ridge/hip units, 10" W with 10" exp., 20 pieces / bundle

Description	Oper	Unit	Vol	Crew Size	Man-hours per Unit	Crew Output per Day	Avg Mat'l Unit Cost	Avg Labor Unit Cost	Avg Equip Unit Cost	Avg Total Unit Cost	Avg Price Incl O&P
	Inst	LF	Lg	RJ	.015	1062.0	3.56	.65	---	4.21	**5.05**
	Inst	LF	Sm	RJ	.018	900.0	4.10	.78	---	4.88	**5.86**

Roll valley, galvanized, unpainted, 28 gauge, 50' L rolls

Description	Oper	Unit	Vol	Crew Size	Man-hours per Unit	Crew Output per Day	Avg Mat'l Unit Cost	Avg Labor Unit Cost	Avg Equip Unit Cost	Avg Total Unit Cost	Avg Price Incl O&P
14" W	Inst	LF	Lg	UA	.056	141.6	.73	2.34	---	3.07	**4.16**
	Inst	LF	Sm	UA	.067	120.00	.84	2.80	---	3.64	**4.94**
20" W	Inst	LF	Lg	UA	.056	141.6	1.21	2.34	---	3.55	**4.71**
	Inst	LF	Sm	UA	.067	120.00	1.39	2.80	---	4.19	**5.57**

Rosin sized sheathing paper 36" W, 500 SF/roll; nailed

Description	Oper	Unit	Vol	Crew Size	Man-hours per Unit	Crew Output per Day	Avg Mat'l Unit Cost	Avg Labor Unit Cost	Avg Equip Unit Cost	Avg Total Unit Cost	Avg Price Incl O&P
Over open sheathing	Inst	Sq	Lg	RJ	.143	112.10	2.63	6.20	---	8.83	**12.10**
	Inst	Sq	Sm	RJ	.168	95.00	3.02	7.28	---	10.30	**14.20**
Over solid sheathing	Inst	Sq	Lg	RJ	.097	165.2	2.63	4.20	---	6.83	**9.20**
	Inst	Sq	Sm	RJ	.114	140.0	3.02	4.94	---	7.96	**10.70**

Description	Oper	Unit	Vol	Crew Size	Man-hours per Unit	Crew Output per Day	Avg Mat'l Unit Cost	Avg Labor Unit Cost	Avg Equip Unit Cost	Avg Total Unit Cost	Avg Price Incl O&P
Shingles											
16" L with 5" exposure	Demo	Sq	Lg	LB	1.13	14.16	---	33.90	---	33.90	**47.50**
	Demo	Sq	Sm	LB	1.33	12.00	---	39.90	---	39.90	**55.90**
18" L with 5-1/2" exposure	Demo	Sq	Lg	LB	1.08	14.87	---	32.40	---	32.40	**45.40**
	Demo	Sq	Sm	LB	1.27	12.60	---	38.10	---	38.10	**53.30**
24" L with 7-1/2" exposure	Demo	Sq	Lg	LB	.753	21.24	---	22.60	---	22.60	**31.60**
	Demo	Sq	Sm	LB	0.89	18.00	---	26.70	---	26.70	**37.40**

Shingles, red cedar, No. 1 perfect, 4" W (avg.), 2 nails per shingle

Over existing roofing materials on

Gable, plain

Description	Oper	Unit	Vol	Crew Size	Man-hours per Unit	Crew Output per Day	Avg Mat'l Unit Cost	Avg Labor Unit Cost	Avg Equip Unit Cost	Avg Total Unit Cost	Avg Price Incl O&P
16" L with 5" exposure	Inst	Sq	Lg	RM	3.03	6.61	279.00	123.00	---	402.00	**502.00**
	Inst	Sq	Sm	RM	3.57	5.60	321.00	145.00	---	466.00	**583.00**
18" L with 5-1/2" exposure	Inst	Sq	Lg	RM	2.73	7.32	311.00	111.00	---	422.00	**521.00**
	Inst	Sq	Sm	RM	3.23	6.20	358.00	131.00	---	489.00	**605.00**
24" L with 7-1/2" exposure	Inst	Sq	Lg	RM	1.97	10.15	291.00	80.10	---	371.10	**452.00**
	Inst	Sq	Sm	RM	2.33	8.60	334.00	94.80	---	428.80	**524.00**

Gable with dormers

Description	Oper	Unit	Vol	Crew Size	Man-hours per Unit	Crew Output per Day	Avg Mat'l Unit Cost	Avg Labor Unit Cost	Avg Equip Unit Cost	Avg Total Unit Cost	Avg Price Incl O&P
16" L with 5" exposure	Inst	Sq	Lg	RM	3.14	6.37	282.00	128.00	---	410.00	**512.00**
	Inst	Sq	Sm	RM	3.70	5.40	324.00	150.00	---	474.00	**594.00**
18" L with 5-1/2" exposure	Inst	Sq	Lg	RM	2.82	7.08	314.00	115.00	---	429.00	**530.00**
	Inst	Sq	Sm	RM	3.33	6.00	361.00	135.00	---	496.00	**615.00**
24" L with 7-1/2" exposure	Inst	Sq	Lg	RM	2.69	7.43	293.00	109.00	---	402.00	**498.00**
	Inst	Sq	Sm	RM	3.17	6.30	337.00	129.00	---	466.00	**577.00**

Gable with intersecting roofs

Description	Oper	Unit	Vol	Crew Size	Man-hours per Unit	Crew Output per Day	Avg Mat'l Unit Cost	Avg Labor Unit Cost	Avg Equip Unit Cost	Avg Total Unit Cost	Avg Price Incl O&P
16" L with 5" exposure	Inst	Sq	Lg	RM	3.14	6.37	282.00	128.00	---	410.00	**512.00**
	Inst	Sq	Sm	RM	3.70	5.40	324.00	150.00	---	474.00	**594.00**
18" L with 5-1/2" exposure	Inst	Sq	Lg	RM	2.82	7.08	314.00	115.00	---	429.00	**530.00**
	Inst	Sq	Sm	RM	3.33	6.00	361.00	135.00	---	496.00	**615.00**
24" L with 7-1/2" exposure	Inst	Sq	Lg	RM	2.69	7.43	293.00	109.00	---	402.00	**498.00**
	Inst	Sq	Sm	RM	3.17	6.30	337.00	129.00	---	466.00	**577.00**

Gable with dormers & intersecting roofs

Description	Oper	Unit	Vol	Crew Size	Man-hours per Unit	Crew Output per Day	Avg Mat'l Unit Cost	Avg Labor Unit Cost	Avg Equip Unit Cost	Avg Total Unit Cost	Avg Price Incl O&P
16" L with 5" exposure	Inst	Sq	Lg	RM	3.26	6.14	287.00	133.00	---	420.00	**525.00**
	Inst	Sq	Sm	RM	3.85	5.20	330.00	157.00	---	487.00	**610.00**
18" L with 5-1/2" exposure	Inst	Sq	Lg	RM	2.92	6.84	320.00	119.00	---	439.00	**542.00**
	Inst	Sq	Sm	RM	3.45	5.80	368.00	140.00	---	508.00	**629.00**
24" L with 7-1/2" exposure	Inst	Sq	Lg	RM	2.09	9.56	298.00	85.00	---	383.00	**468.00**
	Inst	Sq	Sm	RM	2.47	8.10	343.00	100.00	---	443.00	**542.00**

Hip, plain

Description	Oper	Unit	Vol	Crew Size	Man-hours per Unit	Crew Output per Day	Avg Mat'l Unit Cost	Avg Labor Unit Cost	Avg Equip Unit Cost	Avg Total Unit Cost	Avg Price Incl O&P
16" L with 5" exposure	Inst	Sq	Lg	RM	3.14	6.37	282.00	128.00	---	410.00	**512.00**
	Inst	Sq	Sm	RM	3.70	5.40	324.00	150.00	---	474.00	**594.00**
18" L with 5-1/2" exposure	Inst	Sq	Lg	RM	2.82	7.08	314.00	115.00	---	429.00	**530.00**
	Inst	Sq	Sm	RM	3.33	6.00	361.00	135.00	---	496.00	**615.00**
24" L with 7-1/2" exposure	Inst	Sq	Lg	RM	2.04	9.79	293.00	83.00	---	376.00	**459.00**
	Inst	Sq	Sm	RM	2.41	8.30	337.00	98.00	---	435.00	**532.00**

Description	Oper	Unit	Vol	Crew Size	Man-hours per Unit	Crew Output per Day	Avg Mat'l Unit Cost	Avg Labor Unit Cost	Avg Equip Unit Cost	Avg Total Unit Cost	Avg Price Incl O&P
Hip with dormers											
16" L with 5" exposure	Inst	Sq	Lg	RM	3.26	6.14	284.00	133.00	---	417.00	**522.00**
	Inst	Sq	Sm	RM	3.85	5.20	327.00	157.00	---	484.00	**606.00**
18" L with 5-1/2" exposure	Inst	Sq	Lg	RM	2.97	6.73	317.00	121.00	---	438.00	**542.00**
	Inst	Sq	Sm	RM	3.51	5.70	364.00	143.00	---	507.00	**629.00**
24" L with 7-1/2" exposure	Inst	Sq	Lg	RM	2.15	9.32	296.00	87.40	---	383.40	**469.00**
	Inst	Sq	Sm	RM	2.53	7.90	340.00	103.00	---	443.00	**543.00**
Hip with intersecting roofs											
16" L with 5" exposure	Inst	Sq	Lg	RM	3.26	6.14	284.00	133.00	---	417.00	**522.00**
	Inst	Sq	Sm	RM	3.85	5.20	327.00	157.00	---	484.00	**606.00**
18" L with 5-1/2" exposure	Inst	Sq	Lg	RM	2.97	6.73	317.00	121.00	---	438.00	**542.00**
	Inst	Sq	Sm	RM	3.51	5.70	364.00	143.00	---	507.00	**629.00**
24" L with 7-1/2" exposure	Inst	Sq	Lg	RM	2.15	9.32	296.00	87.40	---	383.40	**469.00**
	Inst	Sq	Sm	RM	2.53	7.90	340.00	103.00	---	443.00	**543.00**
Hip with dormers & intersecting roofs											
16" L with 5" exposure	Inst	Sq	Lg	RM	3.39	5.90	289.00	138.00	---	427.00	**535.00**
	Inst	Sq	Sm	RM	4.00	5.00	333.00	163.00	---	496.00	**622.00**
18" L with 5-1/2" exposure	Inst	Sq	Lg	RM	3.08	6.49	322.00	125.00	---	447.00	**555.00**
	Inst	Sq	Sm	RM	3.64	5.50	371.00	148.00	---	519.00	**644.00**
24" L with 7-1/2" exposure	Inst	Sq	Lg	RM	2.20	9.09	301.00	89.50	---	390.50	**478.00**
	Inst	Sq	Sm	RM	2.60	7.70	346.00	106.00	---	452.00	**554.00**
Over wood decks on											
Gable, plain											
16" L with 5" exposure	Inst	Sq	Lg	RM	2.82	7.08	276.00	115.00	---	391.00	**486.00**
	Inst	Sq	Sm	RM	3.33	6.00	317.00	135.00	---	452.00	**564.00**
18" L with 5-1/2" exposure	Inst	Sq	Lg	RM	2.57	7.79	308.00	105.00	---	413.00	**508.00**
	Inst	Sq	Sm	RM	3.03	6.60	354.00	123.00	---	477.00	**589.00**
24" L with 7-1/2" exposure	Inst	Sq	Lg	RM	1.88	10.62	288.00	76.50	---	364.50	**443.00**
	Inst	Sq	Sm	RM	2.22	9.00	331.00	90.30	---	421.30	**513.00**
Gable with dormers											
16" L with 5" exposure	Inst	Sq	Lg	RM	2.92	6.84	278.00	119.00	---	397.00	**495.00**
	Inst	Sq	Sm	RM	3.45	5.80	320.00	140.00	---	460.00	**575.00**
18" L with 5-1/2" exposure	Inst	Sq	Lg	RM	2.65	7.55	311.00	108.00	---	419.00	**516.00**
	Inst	Sq	Sm	RM	3.13	6.40	358.00	127.00	---	485.00	**598.00**
24" L with 7-1/2" exposure	Inst	Sq	Lg	RM	1.95	10.27	290.00	79.30	---	369.30	**451.00**
	Inst	Sq	Sm	RM	2.30	8.70	334.00	93.50	---	427.50	**522.00**
Gable with intersecting roofs											
16" L with 5" exposure	Inst	Sq	Lg	RM	2.92	6.84	278.00	119.00	---	397.00	**495.00**
	Inst	Sq	Sm	RM	3.45	5.80	320.00	140.00	---	460.00	**575.00**
18" L with 5-1/2" exposure	Inst	Sq	Lg	RM	2.65	7.55	311.00	108.00	---	419.00	**516.00**
	Inst	Sq	Sm	RM	3.13	6.40	358.00	127.00	---	485.00	**598.00**
24" L with 7-1/2" exposure	Inst	Sq	Lg	RM	1.95	10.27	290.00	79.30	---	369.30	**451.00**
	Inst	Sq	Sm	RM	2.30	8.70	334.00	93.50	---	427.50	**522.00**

Description	Oper	Unit	Vol	Crew Size	Man-hours per Unit	Crew Output per Day	Avg Mat'l Unit Cost	Avg Labor Unit Cost	Avg Equip Unit Cost	Avg Total Unit Cost	Avg Price Incl O&P
Gable with dormers & intersecting roofs											
16" L with 5" exposure	Inst	Sq	Lg	RM	3.03	6.61	283.00	123.00	---	406.00	**507.00**
	Inst	Sq	Sm	RM	3.57	5.60	326.00	145.00	---	471.00	**588.00**
18" L with 5-1/2" exposure	Inst	Sq	Lg	RM	2.73	7.32	317.00	111.00	---	428.00	**527.00**
	Inst	Sq	Sm	RM	3.23	6.20	364.00	131.00	---	495.00	**612.00**
24" L with 7-1/2" exposure	Inst	Sq	Lg	RM	1.99	10.03	296.00	80.90	---	376.90	**459.00**
	Inst	Sq	Sm	RM	2.35	8.50	340.00	95.60	---	435.60	**531.00**
Hip, plain											
16" L with 5" exposure	Inst	Sq	Lg	RM	2.92	6.84	278.00	119.00	---	397.00	**495.00**
	Inst	Sq	Sm	RM	3.45	5.80	320.00	140.00	---	460.00	**575.00**
18" L with 5-1/2" exposure	Inst	Sq	Lg	RM	2.65	7.55	311.00	108.00	---	419.00	**516.00**
	Inst	Sq	Sm	RM	3.13	6.40	358.00	127.00	---	485.00	**598.00**
24" L with 7-1/2" exposure	Inst	Sq	Lg	RM	1.95	10.27	290.00	79.30	---	369.30	**451.00**
	Inst	Sq	Sm	RM	2.30	8.70	334.00	93.50	---	427.50	**522.00**
Hip with dormers											
16" L with 5" exposure	Inst	Sq	Lg	RM	3.03	6.61	281.00	123.00	---	404.00	**504.00**
	Inst	Sq	Sm	RM	3.57	5.60	323.00	145.00	---	468.00	**585.00**
18" L with 5-1/2" exposure	Inst	Sq	Lg	RM	2.78	7.20	314.00	113.00	---	427.00	**527.00**
	Inst	Sq	Sm	RM	3.28	6.10	361.00	133.00	---	494.00	**611.00**
24" L with 7-1/2" exposure	Inst	Sq	Lg	RM	2.04	9.79	293.00	83.00	---	376.00	**459.00**
	Inst	Sq	Sm	RM	2.41	8.30	337.00	98.00	---	435.00	**532.00**
Hip with intersecting roofs											
16" L with 5" exposure	Inst	Sq	Lg	RM	3.03	6.61	281.00	123.00	---	404.00	**504.00**
	Inst	Sq	Sm	RM	3.57	5.60	323.00	145.00	---	468.00	**585.00**
18" L with 5-1/2" exposure	Inst	Sq	Lg	RM	2.78	7.20	314.00	113.00	---	427.00	**527.00**
	Inst	Sq	Sm	RM	3.28	6.10	361.00	133.00	---	494.00	**611.00**
24" L with 7-1/2" exposure	Inst	Sq	Lg	RM	2.04	9.79	293.00	83.00	---	376.00	**459.00**
	Inst	Sq	Sm	RM	2.41	8.30	337.00	98.00	---	435.00	**532.00**
Hip with dormers & intersecting roofs											
16" L with 5" exposure	Inst	Sq	Lg	RM	3.14	6.37	286.00	128.00	---	414.00	**516.00**
	Inst	Sq	Sm	RM	3.70	5.40	329.00	150.00	---	479.00	**599.00**
18" L with 5-1/2" exposure	Inst	Sq	Lg	RM	2.87	6.96	319.00	117.00	---	436.00	**539.00**
	Inst	Sq	Sm	RM	3.39	5.90	367.00	138.00	---	505.00	**625.00**
24" L with 7-1/2" exposure	Inst	Sq	Lg	RM	2.09	9.56	298.00	85.00	---	383.00	**468.00**
	Inst	Sq	Sm	RM	2.47	8.10	343.00	100.00	---	443.00	**542.00**

Description	Oper	Unit	Vol	Crew Size	Man-hours per Unit	Crew Output per Day	Avg Mat'l Unit Cost	Avg Labor Unit Cost	Avg Equip Unit Cost	Avg Total Unit Cost	Avg Price Incl O&P
Related materials and operations											
Ridge/hip units, 40 pieces / bundle											
Over existing roofing											
5" exposure	Inst	LF	Lg	RJ	.024	660.8	3.06	1.04	---	4.10	**5.05**
	Inst	LF	Sm	RJ	.029	560.0	3.51	1.26	---	4.77	**5.88**
5-1/2" exposure	Inst	LF	Lg	RJ	.023	696.2	3.06	1.00	---	4.06	**4.98**
	Inst	LF	Sm	RJ	.027	590.0	3.51	1.17	---	4.68	**5.76**
7-1/2" exposure	Inst	LF	Lg	RJ	.019	826.0	2.04	.82	---	2.86	**3.56**
	Inst	LF	Sm	RJ	.023	700.0	2.35	1.00	---	3.35	**4.17**
Over wood decks											
5" exposure	Inst	LF	Lg	RJ	.023	708.0	3.06	1.00	---	4.06	**4.98**
	Inst	LF	Sm	RJ	.027	600.0	3.51	1.17	---	4.68	**5.76**
5-1/2" exposure	Inst	LF	Lg	RJ	.022	743.4	3.06	.95	---	4.01	**4.92**
	Inst	LF	Sm	RJ	.025	630.0	3.51	1.08	---	4.59	**5.63**
7-1/2" exposure	Inst	LF	Lg	RJ	.018	885.0	2.04	.78	---	2.82	**3.49**
	Inst	LF	Sm	RJ	.021	750.0	2.35	.91	---	3.26	**4.04**
Roll valley, galvanized, 28 gauge 50' L rolls, unpainted											
18" W	Inst	LF	Lg	UA	.056	141.6	.73	2.34	---	3.07	**4.16**
	Inst	LF	Sm	UA	.067	120.00	.84	2.80	---	3.64	**4.94**
24" W	Inst	LF	Lg	UA	.056	141.6	1.21	2.34	---	3.55	**4.71**
	Inst	LF	Sm	UA	.067	120.00	1.39	2.80	---	4.19	**5.57**
Rosin sized sheathing paper, 36" W, 500 SF/roll; nailed											
Over open sheathing	Inst	Sq	Lg	RJ	.143	112.10	2.63	6.20	---	8.83	**12.10**
	Inst	Sq	Sm	RJ	.168	95.00	3.02	7.28	---	10.30	**14.20**
Over solid sheathing	Inst	Sq	Lg	RJ	.097	165.2	2.63	4.20	---	6.83	**9.20**
	Inst	Sq	Sm	RJ	.114	140.0	3.02	4.94	---	7.96	**10.70**
For No. 2 (red label) grade											
DEDUCT	Inst	%	Lg	---	---	---	-10.0	---	---	---	---
	Inst	%	Sm	---	---	---	-10.0	---	---	---	---

Sheathing. See Framing, page 215

Description	Oper	Unit	Vol	Crew Size	Man-hours per Unit	Crew Output per Day	Avg Mat'l Unit Cost	Avg Labor Unit Cost	Avg Equip Unit Cost	Avg Total Unit Cost	Avg Price Incl O&P

Sheet metal

Flashing, general; galvanized

Vertical chimney flashing

Description	Oper	Unit	Vol	Crew Size	Man-hours per Unit	Crew Output per Day	Avg Mat'l Unit Cost	Avg Labor Unit Cost	Avg Equip Unit Cost	Avg Total Unit Cost	Avg Price Incl O&P
	Inst	LF	Lg	UA	.059	135.0	.43	2.46	---	2.89	**3.99**
	Inst	LF	Sm	UA	.079	101.3	.50	3.30	---	3.80	**5.25**

"Z" bar flashing

Description	Oper	Unit	Vol	Crew Size	Man-hours per Unit	Crew Output per Day	Avg Mat'l Unit Cost	Avg Labor Unit Cost	Avg Equip Unit Cost	Avg Total Unit Cost	Avg Price Incl O&P
Standard	Inst	LF	Lg	UA	.019	420.0	.43	.79	---	1.22	**1.62**
	Inst	LF	Sm	UA	.025	315.0	.50	1.04	---	1.54	**2.06**
Old style	Inst	LF	Lg	UA	.019	420.0	.43	.79	---	1.22	**1.62**
	Inst	LF	Sm	UA	.025	315.0	.50	1.04	---	1.54	**2.06**
For plywood siding	Inst	LF	Lg	UA	.019	420.0	.32	.79	---	1.11	**1.49**
	Inst	LF	Sm	UA	.025	315.0	.37	1.04	---	1.41	**1.91**

Rain diverter, 1" x 3"

Description	Oper	Unit	Vol	Crew Size	Man-hours per Unit	Crew Output per Day	Avg Mat'l Unit Cost	Avg Labor Unit Cost	Avg Equip Unit Cost	Avg Total Unit Cost	Avg Price Incl O&P
4' long	Inst	Ea	Lg	UA	.160	50.0	2.46	6.68	---	9.14	**12.30**
	Inst	Ea	Sm	UA	.213	37.5	2.82	8.89	---	11.71	**15.90**
5' long	Inst	Ea	Lg	UA	.160	50.0	2.77	6.68	---	9.45	**12.70**
	Inst	Ea	Sm	UA	.213	37.5	3.17	8.89	---	12.06	**16.30**
10' long	Inst	Ea	Lg	UA	.229	35.0	4.66	9.55	---	14.21	**18.90**
	Inst	Ea	Sm	UA	.305	26.3	5.33	12.70	---	18.03	**24.20**

Roof flashing

Nosing, roof edging at 90-degree angle or open at 105-degree; galvanized

Description	Oper	Unit	Vol	Crew Size	Man-hours per Unit	Crew Output per Day	Avg Mat'l Unit Cost	Avg Labor Unit Cost	Avg Equip Unit Cost	Avg Total Unit Cost	Avg Price Incl O&P
3/4" x 3/4"	Inst	LF	Lg	UA	.016	500.0	.20	.67	---	.87	**1.18**
	Inst	LF	Sm	UA	.021	375.0	.22	.88	---	1.10	**1.50**
1" x 1"	Inst	LF	Lg	UA	.016	500.0	.20	.67	---	.87	**1.18**
	Inst	LF	Sm	UA	.021	375.0	.22	.88	---	1.10	**1.50**
1" x 2"	Inst	LF	Lg	UA	.016	500.0	.24	.67	---	.91	**1.22**
	Inst	LF	Sm	UA	.021	375.0	.27	.88	---	1.15	**1.55**
1-1/2" x 1-1/2"	Inst	LF	Lg	UA	.016	500.0	.24	.67	---	.91	**1.22**
	Inst	LF	Sm	UA	.021	375.0	.27	.88	---	1.15	**1.55**
2" x 2"	Inst	LF	Lg	UA	.016	500.0	.29	.67	---	.96	**1.28**
	Inst	LF	Sm	UA	.021	375.0	.34	.88	---	1.22	**1.64**
2" x 3"	Inst	LF	Lg	UA	.016	500.0	.36	.67	---	1.03	**1.36**
	Inst	LF	Sm	UA	.021	375.0	.42	.88	---	1.30	**1.73**
2" x 4"	Inst	LF	Lg	UA	.016	500.0	.50	.67	---	1.17	**1.52**
	Inst	LF	Sm	UA	.021	375.0	.58	.88	---	1.46	**1.91**
3" x 3"	Inst	LF	Lg	UA	.020	400.0	.50	.83	---	1.33	**1.76**
	Inst	LF	Sm	UA	.027	300.0	.58	1.13	---	1.71	**2.27**
3" x 4"	Inst	LF	Lg	UA	.020	400.0	.59	.83	---	1.42	**1.86**
	Inst	LF	Sm	UA	.027	300.0	.67	1.13	---	1.80	**2.37**
3" x 5"	Inst	LF	Lg	UA	.027	300.0	.70	1.13	---	1.83	**2.40**
	Inst	LF	Sm	UA	.036	225.0	.80	1.50	---	2.30	**3.05**
4" x 4"	Inst	LF	Lg	UA	.027	300.0	.70	1.13	---	1.83	**2.40**
	Inst	LF	Sm	UA	.036	225.0	.80	1.50	---	2.30	**3.05**
4" x 6"	Inst	LF	Lg	UA	.027	300.0	.88	1.13	---	2.01	**2.61**
	Inst	LF	Sm	UA	.036	225.0	1.01	1.50	---	2.51	**3.29**
5" x 5"	Inst	LF	Lg	UA	.027	300.0	.88	1.13	---	2.01	**2.61**
	Inst	LF	Sm	UA	.036	225.0	1.01	1.50	---	2.51	**3.29**
6" x 6"	Inst	LF	Lg	UA	.027	300.0	1.04	1.13	---	2.17	**2.80**
	Inst	LF	Sm	UA	.036	225.0	1.18	1.50	---	2.68	**3.49**

Description	Oper	Unit	Vol	Crew Size	Man-hours per Unit	Crew Output per Day	Avg Mat'l Unit Cost	Avg Labor Unit Cost	Avg Equip Unit Cost	Avg Total Unit Cost	Avg Price Incl O&P
Roll valley, 50' rolls											
Galvanized, 28 gauge, unpainted											
8" wide	Inst	LF	Lg	UA	.027	300.0	.57	1.13	---	1.70	**2.25**
	Inst	LF	Sm	UA	.036	225.0	.66	1.50	---	2.16	**2.89**
10" wide	Inst	LF	Lg	UA	.027	300.0	.94	1.13	---	2.07	**2.68**
	Inst	LF	Sm	UA	.036	225.0	1.07	1.50	---	2.57	**3.36**
20" wide	Inst	LF	Lg	UA	.027	300.0	1.32	1.13	---	2.45	**3.12**
	Inst	LF	Sm	UA	.036	225.0	1.50	1.50	---	3.00	**3.86**
Tin seamless, painted											
8" wide	Inst	LF	Lg	UA	.027	300.0	.45	1.13	---	1.58	**2.12**
	Inst	LF	Sm	UA	.036	225.0	.51	1.50	---	2.01	**2.72**
10" wide	Inst	LF	Lg	UA	.027	300.0	.70	1.13	---	1.83	**2.40**
	Inst	LF	Sm	UA	.036	225.0	.80	1.50	---	2.30	**3.05**
20" wide	Inst	LF	Lg	UA	.027	300.0	.98	1.13	---	2.11	**2.73**
	Inst	LF	Sm	UA	.036	225.0	1.12	1.50	---	2.62	**3.42**
Aluminum seamless, .016 gauge											
8" wide	Inst	LF	Lg	UA	.027	300.0	.53	1.13	---	1.66	**2.21**
	Inst	LF	Sm	UA	.036	225.0	.61	1.50	---	2.11	**2.83**
10" wide	Inst	LF	Lg	UA	.027	300.0	.90	1.13	---	2.03	**2.63**
	Inst	LF	Sm	UA	.036	225.0	1.02	1.50	---	2.52	**3.31**
20" wide	Inst	LF	Lg	UA	.027	300.0	1.27	1.13	---	2.40	**3.06**
	Inst	LF	Sm	UA	.036	225.0	1.46	1.50	---	2.96	**3.81**
"W" valley											
Galvanized hemmed tin											
18" girth	Inst	LF	Lg	UA	.027	300.0	1.39	1.13	---	2.52	**3.20**
	Inst	LF	Sm	UA	.036	225.0	1.58	1.50	---	3.08	**3.95**
24" girth	Inst	LF	Lg	UA	.027	300.0	1.83	1.13	---	2.96	**3.70**
	Inst	LF	Sm	UA	.036	225.0	2.10	1.50	---	3.60	**4.55**

Gravel stop

Description	Oper	Unit	Vol	Crew Size	Man-hours per Unit	Crew Output per Day	Avg Mat'l Unit Cost	Avg Labor Unit Cost	Avg Equip Unit Cost	Avg Total Unit Cost	Avg Price Incl O&P
4-1/2" galvanized	Inst	LF	Lg	UA	.020	400.0	.32	.83	---	1.15	**1.55**
	Inst	LF	Sm	UA	.027	300.0	.37	1.13	---	1.50	**2.02**
6" galvanized	Inst	LF	Lg	UA	.023	350.0	.42	.96	---	1.38	**1.85**
	Inst	LF	Sm	UA	.030	262.5	.48	1.25	---	1.73	**2.33**
7-1/4" galvanized	Inst	LF	Lg	UA	.027	300.0	.46	1.13	---	1.59	**2.13**
	Inst	LF	Sm	UA	.036	225.0	.53	1.50	---	2.03	**2.74**
4-1/2" bonderized	Inst	LF	Lg	UA	.020	400.0	.41	.83	---	1.24	**1.66**
	Inst	LF	Sm	UA	.027	300.0	.46	1.13	---	1.59	**2.13**
6" bonderized	Inst	LF	Lg	UA	.023	350.0	.55	.96	---	1.51	**2.00**
	Inst	LF	Sm	UA	.030	262.5	.62	1.25	---	1.87	**2.49**
7-1/4" bonderized	Inst	LF	Lg	UA	.027	300.0	.60	1.13	---	1.73	**2.29**
	Inst	LF	Sm	UA	.036	225.0	.69	1.50	---	2.19	**2.93**

Gutters and downspouts. See page 255

Description	Oper	Unit	Vol	Crew Size	Man-hours per Unit	Crew Output per Day	Avg Mat'l Unit Cost	Avg Labor Unit Cost	Avg Equip Unit Cost	Avg Total Unit Cost	Avg Price Incl O&P

Roof edging (drip edge) with 1/4" kickout, galvanized

Description	Oper	Unit	Vol	Crew Size	Man-hours per Unit	Crew Output per Day	Avg Mat'l Unit Cost	Avg Labor Unit Cost	Avg Equip Unit Cost	Avg Total Unit Cost	Avg Price Incl O&P
1" x 1-1/2"	Inst	LF	Lg	UA	.016	500.0	.25	.67	---	.92	**1.24**
	Inst	LF	Sm	UA	.021	375.0	.29	.88	---	1.17	**1.58**
1-1/2" x 1-1/2"	Inst	LF	Lg	UA	.016	500.0	.25	.67	---	.92	**1.24**
	Inst	LF	Sm	UA	.021	375.0	.29	.88	---	1.17	**1.58**
2" x 2"	Inst	LF	Lg	UA	.016	500.0	.31	.67	---	.98	**1.30**
	Inst	LF	Sm	UA	.021	375.0	.35	.88	---	1.23	**1.65**

Vents

Clothes dryer vent set, aluminum, hood, duct, inside plate

Description	Oper	Unit	Vol	Crew Size	Man-hours per Unit	Crew Output per Day	Avg Mat'l Unit Cost	Avg Labor Unit Cost	Avg Equip Unit Cost	Avg Total Unit Cost	Avg Price Incl O&P
3" diameter	Inst	Set	Lg	UA	.500	16.00	3.43	20.90	---	24.33	**33.60**
	Inst	Set	Sm	UA	.667	12.00	3.92	27.80	---	31.72	**44.00**
4" diameter	Inst	Set	Lg	UA	.500	16.00	3.78	20.90	---	24.68	**34.00**
	Inst	Set	Sm	UA	.667	12.00	4.32	27.80	---	32.12	**44.50**

Dormer louvers, half round, 1/8" or 1/4" mesh

18" x 9"

Description	Oper	Unit	Vol	Crew Size	Man-hours per Unit	Crew Output per Day	Avg Mat'l Unit Cost	Avg Labor Unit Cost	Avg Equip Unit Cost	Avg Total Unit Cost	Avg Price Incl O&P
Galvanized, 5-12 pitch	Inst	Ea	Lg	UA	.667	12.00	21.40	27.80	---	49.20	**64.10**
	Inst	Ea	Sm	UA	0.89	9.00	24.40	37.10	---	61.50	**80.80**
Painted, 3-12 pitch	Inst	Ea	Lg	UA	.667	12.00	25.20	27.80	---	53.00	**68.50**
	Inst	Ea	Sm	UA	0.89	9.00	28.80	37.10	---	65.90	**85.80**

24" x 12"

Description	Oper	Unit	Vol	Crew Size	Man-hours per Unit	Crew Output per Day	Avg Mat'l Unit Cost	Avg Labor Unit Cost	Avg Equip Unit Cost	Avg Total Unit Cost	Avg Price Incl O&P
Galvanized, 5-12 pitch	Inst	Ea	Lg	UA	.667	12.00	26.80	27.80	---	54.60	**70.30**
	Inst	Ea	Sm	UA	0.89	9.00	30.60	37.10	---	67.70	**87.90**
Painted, 3-12 pitch	Inst	Ea	Lg	UA	.667	12.00	30.40	27.80	---	58.20	**74.40**
	Inst	Ea	Sm	UA	0.89	9.00	34.70	37.10	---	71.80	**92.60**

Foundation vents, galvanized, 1/4" mesh

Description	Oper	Unit	Vol	Crew Size	Man-hours per Unit	Crew Output per Day	Avg Mat'l Unit Cost	Avg Labor Unit Cost	Avg Equip Unit Cost	Avg Total Unit Cost	Avg Price Incl O&P
6" x 14", stucco	Inst	Ea	Lg	UA	.333	24.00	1.64	13.90	---	15.54	**21.60**
	Inst	Ea	Sm	UA	.444	18.00	1.87	18.50	---	20.37	**28.50**
8" x 14", stucco	Inst	Ea	Lg	UA	.333	24.00	1.96	13.90	---	15.86	**22.00**
	Inst	Ea	Sm	UA	.444	18.00	2.24	18.50	---	20.74	**28.90**
6" x 14", two-way	Inst	Ea	Lg	UA	.333	24.00	1.96	13.90	---	15.86	**22.00**
	Inst	Ea	Sm	UA	.444	18.00	2.24	18.50	---	20.74	**28.90**
6" x 14", for siding (flat type)	Inst	Ea	Lg	UA	.333	24.00	1.64	13.90	---	15.54	**21.60**
	Inst	Ea	Sm	UA	.444	18.00	1.87	18.50	---	20.37	**28.50**
6" x 14", louver type	Inst	Ea	Lg	UA	.333	24.00	1.89	13.90	---	15.79	**21.90**
	Inst	Ea	Sm	UA	.444	18.00	2.16	18.50	---	20.66	**28.80**
6" x 14", foundation insert	Inst	Ea	Lg	UA	.333	24.00	1.64	13.90	---	15.54	**21.60**
	Inst	Ea	Sm	UA	.444	18.00	1.87	18.50	---	20.37	**28.50**

Description	Oper	Unit	Vol	Crew Size	Man-hours per Unit	Crew Output per Day	Avg Mat'l Unit Cost	Avg Labor Unit Cost	Avg Equip Unit Cost	Avg Total Unit Cost	Avg Price Incl O&P
Louver vents, round, 1/8" or 1/4" mesh, galvanized											
12" diameter	Inst	Ea	Lg	UA	.500	16.00	21.80	20.90	---	42.70	**54.70**
	Inst	Ea	Sm	UA	.667	12.00	25.00	27.80	---	52.80	**68.20**
14" diameter	Inst	Ea	Lg	UA	.500	16.00	23.20	20.90	---	44.10	**56.30**
	Inst	Ea	Sm	UA	.667	12.00	26.50	27.80	---	54.30	**70.00**
16" diameter	Inst	Ea	Lg	UA	.500	16.00	25.10	20.90	---	46.00	**58.50**
	Inst	Ea	Sm	UA	.667	12.00	28.70	27.80	---	56.50	**72.60**
18" diameter	Inst	Ea	Lg	UA	.500	16.00	28.90	20.90	---	49.80	**62.80**
	Inst	Ea	Sm	UA	.667	12.00	33.00	27.80	---	60.80	**77.40**
24" diameter	Inst	Ea	Lg	UA	.500	16.00	49.00	20.90	---	69.90	**86.00**
	Inst	Ea	Sm	UA	.667	12.00	56.00	27.80	---	83.80	**104.00**
Access doors											
Multi-purpose, galvanized											
24" x 18", nail-on type	Inst	Ea	Lg	UA	.500	16.00	13.90	20.90	---	34.80	**45.60**
	Inst	Ea	Sm	UA	.667	12.00	15.80	27.80	---	43.60	**57.70**
24" x 24", nail-on type	Inst	Ea	Lg	UA	.500	16.00	15.60	20.90	---	36.50	**47.60**
	Inst	Ea	Sm	UA	.667	12.00	17.90	27.80	---	45.70	**60.10**
24" x 18" x 6" deep box type	Inst	Ea	Lg	UA	.500	16.00	18.90	20.90	---	39.80	**51.40**
	Inst	Ea	Sm	UA	.667	12.00	21.60	27.80	---	49.40	**64.40**
Attic access doors, galvanized											
22" x 22"	Inst	Ea	Lg	UA	.667	12.00	19.60	27.80	---	47.40	**62.10**
	Inst	Ea	Sm	UA	0.89	9.00	22.40	37.10	---	59.50	**78.50**
22" x 30"	Inst	Ea	Lg	UA	.667	12.00	22.70	27.80	---	50.50	**65.60**
	Inst	Ea	Sm	UA	0.89	9.00	25.90	37.10	---	63.00	**82.50**
30" x 30"	Inst	Ea	Lg	UA	.667	12.00	23.90	27.80	---	51.70	**67.00**
	Inst	Ea	Sm	UA	0.89	9.00	27.40	37.10	---	64.50	**84.20**
Tub access doors, galvanized											
14" x 12"	Inst	Ea	Lg	UA	.500	16.00	9.73	20.90	---	30.63	**40.80**
	Inst	Ea	Sm	UA	.667	12.00	11.10	27.80	---	38.90	**52.30**
14" x 15"	Inst	Ea	Lg	UA	.500	16.00	10.10	20.90	---	31.00	**41.20**
	Inst	Ea	Sm	UA	.667	12.00	11.50	27.80	---	39.30	**52.80**
Utility louvers, aluminum or galvanized											
4" x 6"	Inst	Ea	Lg	UA	.200	40.00	1.16	8.34	---	9.50	**13.20**
	Inst	Ea	Sm	UA	.267	30.00	1.33	11.10	---	12.43	**17.40**
8" x 6"	Inst	Ea	Lg	UA	.200	40.00	1.64	8.34	---	9.98	**13.70**
	Inst	Ea	Sm	UA	.267	30.00	1.87	11.10	---	12.97	**18.00**
8" x 8"	Inst	Ea	Lg	UA	.200	40.00	1.89	8.34	---	10.23	**14.00**
	Inst	Ea	Sm	UA	.267	30.00	2.16	11.10	---	13.26	**18.30**
8" x 12"	Inst	Ea	Lg	UA	.200	40.00	2.21	8.34	---	10.55	**14.40**
	Inst	Ea	Sm	UA	.267	30.00	2.53	11.10	---	13.63	**18.70**
8" x 18"	Inst	Ea	Lg	UA	.200	40.00	2.65	8.34	---	10.99	**14.90**
	Inst	Ea	Sm	UA	.267	30.00	3.02	11.10	---	14.12	**19.30**
12" x 12"	Inst	Ea	Lg	UA	.200	40.00	2.65	8.34	---	10.99	**14.90**
	Inst	Ea	Sm	UA	.267	30.00	3.02	11.10	---	14.12	**19.30**
14" x 14"	Inst	Ea	Lg	UA	.200	40.00	3.35	8.34	---	11.69	**15.70**
	Inst	Ea	Sm	UA	.267	30.00	3.82	11.10	---	14.92	**20.20**

Description	Oper	Unit	Vol	Crew Size	Man-hours per Unit	Crew Output per Day	Avg Mat'l Unit Cost	Avg Labor Unit Cost	Avg Equip Unit Cost	Avg Total Unit Cost	Avg Price Incl O&P

Shower and tub doors

Shower doors

Hinged shower doors, anodized aluminum frame, tempered hammered glass, hardware included

67" H door, adjustable
29-3/4" to 31-1/2"

Obscure glass

Description	Oper	Unit	Vol	Crew Size	Man-hours per Unit	Crew Output per Day	Avg Mat'l Unit Cost	Avg Labor Unit Cost	Avg Equip Unit Cost	Avg Total Unit Cost	Avg Price Incl O&P
Chrome	Inst	Ea	Lg	CA	1.33	6.00	337.00	49.20	---	386.20	**456.00**
	Inst	Ea	Sm	CA	1.78	4.50	392.00	65.90	---	457.90	**543.00**
Polished brass	Inst	Ea	Lg	CA	1.33	6.00	377.00	49.20	---	426.20	**503.00**
	Inst	Ea	Sm	CA	1.78	4.50	439.00	65.90	---	504.90	**597.00**
White	Inst	Ea	Lg	CA	1.33	6.00	481.00	49.20	---	530.20	**622.00**
	Inst	Ea	Sm	CA	1.78	4.50	560.00	65.90	---	625.90	**736.00**
Bone	Inst	Ea	Lg	CA	1.33	6.00	481.00	49.20	---	530.20	**622.00**
	Inst	Ea	Sm	CA	1.78	4.50	560.00	65.90	---	625.90	**736.00**

Clear glass

Description	Oper	Unit	Vol	Crew Size	Man-hours per Unit	Crew Output per Day	Avg Mat'l Unit Cost	Avg Labor Unit Cost	Avg Equip Unit Cost	Avg Total Unit Cost	Avg Price Incl O&P
Chrome	Inst	Ea	Lg	CA	1.33	6.00	385.00	49.20	---	434.20	**512.00**
	Inst	Ea	Sm	CA	1.78	4.50	448.00	65.90	---	513.90	**608.00**
Polished brass	Inst	Ea	Lg	CA	1.33	6.00	421.00	49.20	---	470.20	**554.00**
	Inst	Ea	Sm	CA	1.78	4.50	490.00	65.90	---	555.90	**656.00**
White	Inst	Ea	Lg	CA	1.33	6.00	524.00	49.20	---	573.20	**672.00**
	Inst	Ea	Sm	CA	1.78	4.50	610.00	65.90	---	675.90	**794.00**
Bone	Inst	Ea	Lg	CA	1.33	6.00	524.00	49.20	---	573.20	**672.00**
	Inst	Ea	Sm	CA	1.78	4.50	610.00	65.90	---	675.90	**794.00**

Etched glass

Description	Oper	Unit	Vol	Crew Size	Man-hours per Unit	Crew Output per Day	Avg Mat'l Unit Cost	Avg Labor Unit Cost	Avg Equip Unit Cost	Avg Total Unit Cost	Avg Price Incl O&P
Chrome	Inst	Ea	Lg	CA	1.33	6.00	412.00	49.20	---	461.20	**543.00**
	Inst	Ea	Sm	CA	1.78	4.50	479.00	65.90	---	544.90	**644.00**
Polished brass	Inst	Ea	Lg	CA	1.33	6.00	451.00	49.20	---	500.20	**587.00**
	Inst	Ea	Sm	CA	1.78	4.50	524.00	65.90	---	589.90	**695.0**
White	Inst	Ea	Lg	CA	1.33	6.00	556.00	49.20	---	605.20	**708.00**
	Inst	Ea	Sm	CA	1.78	4.50	646.00	65.90	---	711.90	**835.00**
Bone	Inst	Ea	Lg	CA	1.33	6.00	556.00	49.20	---	605.20	**708.00**
	Inst	Ea	Sm	CA	1.78	4.50	646.00	65.90	---	711.90	**835.00**

Fluted

Description	Oper	Unit	Vol	Crew Size	Man-hours per Unit	Crew Output per Day	Avg Mat'l Unit Cost	Avg Labor Unit Cost	Avg Equip Unit Cost	Avg Total Unit Cost	Avg Price Incl O&P
Chrome	Inst	Ea	Lg	CA	1.33	6.00	527.00	49.20	---	576.20	**675.00**
	Inst	Ea	Sm	CA	1.78	4.50	613.00	65.90	---	678.90	**797.00**
Polished brass	Inst	Ea	Lg	CA	1.33	6.00	569.00	49.20	---	618.20	**723.00**
	Inst	Ea	Sm	CA	1.78	4.50	661.00	65.90	---	726.90	**853.00**
White	Inst	Ea	Lg	CA	1.33	6.00	671.00	49.20	---	720.20	**840.00**
	Inst	Ea	Sm	CA	1.78	4.50	780.00	65.90	---	845.90	**989.00**
Bone	Inst	Ea	Lg	CA	1.33	6.00	671.00	49.20	---	720.20	**840.00**
	Inst	Ea	Sm	CA	1.78	4.50	780.00	65.90	---	845.90	**989.00**

Description	Oper	Unit	Vol	Crew Size	Man-hours per Unit	Crew Output per Day	Avg Mat'l Unit Cost	Avg Labor Unit Cost	Avg Equip Unit Cost	Avg Total Unit Cost	Avg Price Incl O&P
33-1/8" to 34-7/8"											
Obscure glass											
Chrome	Inst	Ea	Lg	CA	1.33	6.00	337.00	49.20	---	386.20	**456.00**
	Inst	Ea	Sm	CA	1.78	4.50	392.00	65.90	---	457.90	**543.00**
Polished brass	Inst	Ea	Lg	CA	1.33	6.00	377.00	49.20	---	426.20	**503.00**
	Inst	Ea	Sm	CA	1.78	4.50	439.00	65.90	---	504.90	**597.00**
White	Inst	Ea	Lg	CA	1.33	6.00	481.00	49.20	---	530.20	**622.00**
	Inst	Ea	Sm	CA	1.78	4.50	560.00	65.90	---	625.90	**736.00**
Bone	Inst	Ea	Lg	CA	1.33	6.00	524.00	49.20	---	573.20	**672.00**
	Inst	Ea	Sm	CA	1.78	4.50	610.00	65.90	---	675.90	**794.00**
Clear glass											
Chrome	Inst	Ea	Lg	CA	1.33	6.00	385.00	49.20	---	434.20	**512.00**
	Inst	Ea	Sm	CA	1.78	4.50	448.00	65.90	---	513.90	**608.00**
Polished brass	Inst	Ea	Lg	CA	1.33	6.00	430.00	49.20	---	479.20	**563.00**
	Inst	Ea	Sm	CA	1.78	4.50	500.00	65.90	---	565.90	**667.00**
White	Inst	Ea	Lg	CA	1.33	6.00	524.00	49.20	---	573.20	**672.00**
	Inst	Ea	Sm	CA	1.78	4.50	610.00	65.90	---	675.90	**794.00**
Bone	Inst	Ea	Lg	CA	1.33	6.00	524.00	49.20	---	573.20	**672.00**
	Inst	Ea	Sm	CA	1.78	4.50	610.00	65.90	---	675.90	**794.00**
Etched glass											
Chrome	Inst	Ea	Lg	CA	1.33	6.00	412.00	49.20	---	461.20	**543.00**
	Inst	Ea	Sm	CA	1.78	4.50	479.00	65.90	---	544.90	**644.00**
Polished brass	Inst	Ea	Lg	CA	1.33	6.00	451.00	49.20	---	500.20	**587.00**
	Inst	Ea	Sm	CA	1.78	4.50	524.00	65.90	---	589.90	**695.00**
White	Inst	Ea	Lg	CA	1.33	6.00	556.00	49.20	---	605.20	**708.00**
	Inst	Ea	Sm	CA	1.78	4.50	646.00	65.90	---	711.90	**835.00**
Bone	Inst	Ea	Lg	CA	1.33	6.00	556.00	49.20	---	605.20	**708.00**
	Inst	Ea	Sm	CA	1.78	4.50	646.00	65.90	---	711.90	**835.00**
Fluted											
Chrome	Inst	Ea	Lg	CA	1.33	6.00	527.00	49.20	---	576.20	**675.00**
	Inst	Ea	Sm	CA	1.78	4.50	613.00	65.90	---	678.90	**797.00**
Polished brass	Inst	Ea	Lg	CA	1.33	6.00	569.00	49.20	---	618.20	**723.00**
	Inst	Ea	Sm	CA	1.78	4.50	661.00	65.90	---	726.90	**853.00**
White	Inst	Ea	Lg	CA	1.33	6.00	671.00	49.20	---	720.20	**840.00**
	Inst	Ea	Sm	CA	1.78	4.50	780.00	65.90	---	845.90	**989.00**
Bone	Inst	Ea	Lg	CA	1.33	6.00	671.00	49.20	---	720.20	**840.00**
	Inst	Ea	Sm	CA	1.78	4.50	780.00	65.90	---	845.90	**989.00**
23" x 24-1/2" x 23 x 72" Neo Angle											
Obscure glass											
Chrome	Inst	Ea	Lg	CA	1.33	6.00	698.00	49.20	---	747.20	**872.00**
	Inst	Ea	Sm	CA	1.78	4.50	812.00	65.90	---	877.90	**1030.00**
Polished brass	Inst	Ea	Lg	CA	1.33	6.00	856.00	49.20	---	905.20	**1050.00**
	Inst	Ea	Sm	CA	1.78	4.50	995.00	65.90	---	1060.90	**1240.00**
White	Inst	Ea	Lg	CA	1.33	6.00	1060.00	49.20	---	1109.20	**1290.00**
	Inst	Ea	Sm	CA	1.78	4.50	1230.00	65.90	---	1295.90	**1510.00**
Bone	Inst	Ea	Lg	CA	1.33	6.00	1060.00	49.20	---	1109.20	**1290.00**
	Inst	Ea	Sm	CA	1.78	4.50	1230.00	65.90	---	1295.90	**1510.00**

Description	Oper	Unit	Vol	Crew Size	Man-hours per Unit	Crew Output per Day	Avg Mat'l Unit Cost	Avg Labor Unit Cost	Avg Equip Unit Cost	Avg Total Unit Cost	Avg Price Incl O&P
Clear glass											
Chrome	Inst	Ea	Lg	CA	1.33	6.00	774.00	49.20	---	823.20	**959.00**
	Inst	Ea	Sm	CA	1.78	4.50	900.00	65.90	---	965.90	**1130.00**
Polished brass	Inst	Ea	Lg	CA	1.33	6.00	932.00	49.20	---	981.20	**1140.00**
	Inst	Ea	Sm	CA	1.78	4.50	1080.00	65.90	---	1145.90	**1340.00**
White	Inst	Ea	Lg	CA	1.33	6.00	1120.00	49.20	---	1169.20	**1350.00**
	Inst	Ea	Sm	CA	1.78	4.50	1300.00	65.90	---	1365.90	**1590.00**
Bone	Inst	Ea	Lg	CA	1.33	6.00	1120.00	49.20	---	1169.20	**1350.00**
	Inst	Ea	Sm	CA	1.78	4.50	1300.00	65.90	---	1365.90	**1590.00**
Etched glass											
Chrome	Inst	Ea	Lg	CA	1.33	6.00	788.00	49.20	---	837.20	**976.00**
	Inst	Ea	Sm	CA	1.78	4.50	917.00	65.90	---	982.90	**1150.00**
Polished brass	Inst	Ea	Lg	CA	1.33	6.00	945.00	49.20	---	994.20	**1160.00**
	Inst	Ea	Sm	CA	1.78	4.50	1100.00	65.90	---	1165.90	**1360.00**
White	Inst	Ea	Lg	CA	1.33	6.00	1150.00	49.20	---	1199.20	**1390.00**
	Inst	Ea	Sm	CA	1.78	4.50	1330.00	65.90	---	1395.90	**1630.00**
Bone	Inst	Ea	Lg	CA	1.33	6.00	1150.00	49.20	---	1199.20	**1390.00**
	Inst	Ea	Sm	CA	1.78	4.50	1330.00	65.90	---	1395.90	**1630.00**
Fluted											
Chrome	Inst	Ea	Lg	CA	1.33	6.00	1160.00	49.20	---	1209.20	**1400.00**
	Inst	Ea	Sm	CA	1.78	4.50	1350.00	65.90	---	1415.90	**1640.00**
Polished brass	Inst	Ea	Lg	CA	1.33	6.00	1310.00	49.20	---	1359.20	**1580.00**
	Inst	Ea	Sm	CA	1.78	4.50	1530.00	65.90	---	1595.90	**1850.00**
White	Inst	Ea	Lg	CA	1.33	6.00	1520.00	49.20	---	1569.20	**1810.00**
	Inst	Ea	Sm	CA	1.78	4.50	1770.00	65.90	---	1835.90	**2120.00**
Bone	Inst	Ea	Lg	CA	1.33	6.00	1520.00	49.20	---	1569.20	**1810.00**
	Inst	Ea	Sm	CA	1.78	4.50	1770.00	65.90	---	1835.90	**2120.00**

Sliding shower doors, 2 bypassing panels, anodized aluminum frame, tempered hammered glass, hardware included

71-1/2" H doors

40" to 42" wide opening

Description	Oper	Unit	Vol	Crew Size	Man-hours per Unit	Crew Output per Day	Avg Mat'l Unit Cost	Avg Labor Unit Cost	Avg Equip Unit Cost	Avg Total Unit Cost	Avg Price Incl O&P
Obscure glass											
Chrome	Inst	Ea	Lg	CA	1.45	5.50	395.00	53.70	---	448.70	**529.00**
	Inst	Ea	Sm	CA	1.94	4.13	459.00	71.80	---	530.80	**628.00**
Polished brass	Inst	Ea	Lg	CA	1.45	5.50	444.00	53.70	---	497.70	**586.00**
	Inst	Ea	Sm	CA	1.94	4.13	517.00	71.80	---	588.80	**695.00**
White	Inst	Ea	Lg	CA	1.45	5.50	596.00	53.70	---	649.70	**761.00**
	Inst	Ea	Sm	CA	1.94	4.13	693.00	71.80	---	764.80	**898.00**
Bone	Inst	Ea	Lg	CA	1.45	5.50	596.00	53.70	---	649.70	**761.00**
	Inst	Ea	Sm	CA	1.94	4.13	693.00	71.80	---	764.80	**898.00**
Clear glass											
Chrome	Inst	Ea	Lg	CA	1.45	5.50	456.00	53.70	---	509.70	**600.00**
	Inst	Ea	Sm	CA	1.94	4.13	531.00	71.80	---	602.80	**711.00**
Polished brass	Inst	Ea	Lg	CA	1.45	5.50	509.00	53.70	---	562.70	**660.00**
	Inst	Ea	Sm	CA	1.94	4.13	592.00	71.80	---	663.80	**781.00**
White	Inst	Ea	Lg	CA	1.45	5.50	659.00	53.70	---	712.70	**833.00**
	Inst	Ea	Sm	CA	1.94	4.13	766.00	71.80	---	837.80	**982.00**
Bone	Inst	Ea	Lg	CA	1.45	5.50	659.00	53.70	---	712.70	**833.00**
	Inst	Ea	Sm	CA	1.94	4.13	766.00	71.80	---	837.80	**982.00**

Description	Oper	Unit	Vol	Crew Size	Man-hours per Unit	Crew Output per Day	Avg Mat'l Unit Cost	Avg Labor Unit Cost	Avg Equip Unit Cost	Avg Total Unit Cost	Avg Price Incl O&P
Etched glass											
Chrome	Inst	Ea	Lg	CA	1.45	5.50	477.00	53.70	---	530.70	**624.00**
	Inst	Ea	Sm	CA	1.94	4.13	555.00	71.80	---	626.80	**739.00**
Polished brass	Inst	Ea	Lg	CA	1.45	5.50	525.00	53.70	---	578.70	**679.00**
	Inst	Ea	Sm	CA	1.94	4.13	611.00	71.80	---	682.80	**803.00**
White	Inst	Ea	Lg	CA	1.45	5.50	684.00	53.70	---	737.70	**861.00**
	Inst	Ea	Sm	CA	1.94	4.13	795.00	71.80	---	866.80	**1010.00**
Bone	Inst	Ea	Lg	CA	1.45	5.50	684.00	53.70	---	737.70	**861.00**
	Inst	Ea	Sm	CA	1.94	4.13	795.00	71.80	---	866.80	**1010.00**
Fluted											
Chrome	Inst	Ea	Lg	CA	1.45	5.50	701.00	53.70	---	754.70	**881.00**
	Inst	Ea	Sm	CA	1.94	4.13	815.00	71.80	---	886.80	**1040.00**
Polished brass	Inst	Ea	Lg	CA	1.45	5.50	750.00	53.70	---	803.70	**937.00**
	Inst	Ea	Sm	CA	1.94	4.13	872.00	71.80	---	943.80	**1100.00**
White	Inst	Ea	Lg	CA	1.45	5.50	908.00	53.70	---	961.70	**1120.00**
	Inst	Ea	Sm	CA	1.94	4.13	1060.00	71.80	---	1131.80	**1320.00**
Bone	Inst	Ea	Lg	CA	1.45	5.50	908.00	53.70	---	961.70	**1120.00**
	Inst	Ea	Sm	CA	1.94	4.13	1060.00	71.80	---	1131.80	**1320.00**
44" to 48" wide opening											
Obscure glass											
Chrome	Inst	Ea	Lg	CA	1.45	5.50	395.00	53.70	---	448.70	**529.00**
	Inst	Ea	Sm	CA	1.94	4.13	459.00	71.80	---	530.80	**628.00**
Polished brass	Inst	Ea	Lg	CA	1.45	5.50	444.00	53.70	---	497.70	**586.00**
	Inst	Ea	Sm	CA	1.94	4.13	517.00	71.80	---	588.80	**695.00**
White	Inst	Ea	Lg	CA	1.45	5.50	596.00	53.70	---	649.70	**761.00**
	Inst	Ea	Sm	CA	1.94	4.13	693.00	71.80	---	764.80	**898.00**
Bone	Inst	Ea	Lg	CA	1.45	5.50	596.00	53.70	---	649.70	**761.00**
	Inst	Ea	Sm	CA	1.94	4.13	693.00	71.80	---	764.80	**898.00**
Clear glass											
Chrome	Inst	Ea	Lg	CA	1.45	5.50	456.00	53.70	---	509.70	**600.00**
	Inst	Ea	Sm	CA	1.94	4.13	531.00	71.80	---	602.80	**711.00**
Polished brass	Inst	Ea	Lg	CA	1.45	5.50	509.00	53.70	---	562.70	**660.00**
	Inst	Ea	Sm	CA	1.94	4.13	592.00	71.80	---	663.80	**781.00**
White	Inst	Ea	Lg	CA	1.45	5.50	659.00	53.70	---	712.70	**833.00**
	Inst	Ea	Sm	CA	1.94	4.13	766.00	71.80	---	837.80	**982.00**
Bone	Inst	Ea	Lg	CA	1.45	5.50	659.00	53.70	---	712.70	**833.00**
	Inst	Ea	Sm	CA	1.94	4.13	766.00	71.80	---	837.80	**982.00**
Etched glass											
Chrome	Inst	Ea	Lg	CA	1.45	5.50	477.00	53.70	---	530.70	**624.00**
	Inst	Ea	Sm	CA	1.94	4.13	555.00	71.80	---	626.80	**739.00**
Polished brass	Inst	Ea	Lg	CA	1.45	5.50	525.00	53.70	---	578.70	**679.00**
	Inst	Ea	Sm	CA	1.94	4.13	611.00	71.80	---	682.80	**803.00**
White	Inst	Ea	Lg	CA	1.45	5.50	684.00	53.70	---	737.70	**861.00**
	Inst	Ea	Sm	CA	1.94	4.13	795.00	71.80	---	866.80	**1010.00**
Bone	Inst	Ea	Lg	CA	1.45	5.50	684.00	53.70	---	737.70	**861.00**
	Inst	Ea	Sm	CA	1.94	4.13	795.00	71.80	---	866.80	**1010.00**

Description	Oper	Unit	Vol	Crew Size	Man-hours per Unit	Crew Output per Day	Avg Mat'l Unit Cost	Avg Labor Unit Cost	Avg Equip Unit Cost	Avg Total Unit Cost	Avg Price Incl O&P
Fluted											
Chrome	Inst	Ea	Lg	CA	1.45	5.50	701.00	53.70	---	754.70	**881.00**
	Inst	Ea	Sm	CA	1.94	4.13	815.00	71.80	---	886.80	**1040.00**
Polished brass	Inst	Ea	Lg	CA	1.45	5.50	750.00	53.70	---	803.70	**937.00**
	Inst	Ea	Sm	CA	1.94	4.13	872.00	71.80	---	943.80	**1100.00**
White	Inst	Ea	Lg	CA	1.45	5.50	908.00	53.70	---	961.70	**1120.00**
	Inst	Ea	Sm	CA	1.94	4.13	1060.00	71.80	---	1131.80	**1320.00**
Bone	Inst	Ea	Lg	CA	1.45	5.50	908.00	53.70	---	961.70	**1120.00**
	Inst	Ea	Sm	CA	1.94	4.13	1060.00	71.80	---	1131.80	**1320.00**
56" to 60" wide opening											
Obscure glass											
Chrome	Inst	Ea	Lg	CA	1.45	5.50	462.00	53.70	---	515.70	**606.00**
	Inst	Ea	Sm	CA	1.94	4.13	537.00	71.80	---	608.80	**718.00**
Polished brass	Inst	Ea	Lg	CA	1.45	5.50	510.00	53.70	---	563.70	**661.00**
	Inst	Ea	Sm	CA	1.94	4.13	593.00	71.80	---	664.80	**782.00**
White	Inst	Ea	Lg	CA	1.45	5.50	620.00	53.70	---	673.70	**788.00**
	Inst	Ea	Sm	CA	1.94	4.13	721.00	71.80	---	792.80	**930.00**
Bone	Inst	Ea	Lg	CA	1.45	5.50	620.00	53.70	---	673.70	**788.00**
	Inst	Ea	Sm	CA	1.94	4.13	721.00	71.80	---	792.80	**930.00**
Clear glass											
Chrome	Inst	Ea	Lg	CA	1.45	5.50	525.00	53.70	---	578.70	**679.00**
	Inst	Ea	Sm	CA	1.94	4.13	611.00	71.80	---	682.80	**803.00**
Polished brass	Inst	Ea	Lg	CA	1.45	5.50	574.00	53.70	---	627.70	**735.00**
	Inst	Ea	Sm	CA	1.94	4.13	668.00	71.80	---	739.80	**868.00**
White	Inst	Ea	Lg	CA	1.45	5.50	722.00	53.70	---	775.70	**906.00**
	Inst	Ea	Sm	CA	1.94	4.13	840.00	71.80	---	911.80	**1070.00**
Bone	Inst	Ea	Lg	CA	1.45	5.50	722.00	53.70	---	775.70	**906.00**
	Inst	Ea	Sm	CA	1.94	4.13	840.00	71.80	---	911.80	**1070.00**
Etched glass											
Chrome	Inst	Ea	Lg	CA	1.45	5.50	543.00	53.70	---	596.70	**699.00**
	Inst	Ea	Sm	CA	1.94	4.13	631.00	71.80	---	702.80	**827.00**
Polished brass	Inst	Ea	Lg	CA	1.45	5.50	591.00	53.70	---	644.70	**754.00**
	Inst	Ea	Sm	CA	1.94	4.13	687.00	71.80	---	758.80	**891.00**
White	Inst	Ea	Lg	CA	1.45	5.50	751.00	53.70	---	804.70	**938.00**
	Inst	Ea	Sm	CA	1.94	4.13	873.00	71.80	---	944.80	**1100.00**
Bone	Inst	Ea	Lg	CA	1.45	5.50	751.00	53.70	---	804.70	**938.00**
	Inst	Ea	Sm	CA	1.94	4.13	873.00	71.80	---	944.80	**1100.00**
Fluted											
Chrome	Inst	Ea	Lg	CA	1.45	5.50	748.00	53.70	---	801.70	**935.00**
	Inst	Ea	Sm	CA	1.94	4.13	870.00	71.80	---	941.80	**1100.00**
Polished brass	Inst	Ea	Lg	CA	1.45	5.50	840.00	53.70	---	893.70	**1040.00**
	Inst	Ea	Sm	CA	1.94	4.13	977.00	71.80	---	1048.80	**1220.00**
White	Inst	Ea	Lg	CA	1.45	5.50	972.00	53.70	---	1025.70	**1190.00**
	Inst	Ea	Sm	CA	1.94	4.13	1130.00	71.80	---	1201.80	**1400.00**
Bone	Inst	Ea	Lg	CA	1.45	5.50	972.00	53.70	---	1025.70	**1190.00**
	Inst	Ea	Sm	CA	1.94	4.13	1130.00	71.80	---	1201.80	**1400.00**

Description	Oper	Unit	Vol	Crew Size	Man-hours per Unit	Crew Output per Day	Avg Mat'l Unit Cost	Avg Labor Unit Cost	Avg Equip Unit Cost	Avg Total Unit Cost	Avg Price Incl O&P

Tub doors

Sliding tub doors, 2 bypassing panels

60" W x 58-1/4" H

Obscure glass

Description	Oper	Unit	Vol	Crew Size	Man-hours per Unit	Crew Output per Day	Avg Mat'l Unit Cost	Avg Labor Unit Cost	Avg Equip Unit Cost	Avg Total Unit Cost	Avg Price Incl O&P
Chrome	Inst	Ea	Lg	CA	1.45	5.50	373.00	53.70	---	426.70	**504.00**
	Inst	Ea	Sm	CA	1.94	4.13	433.00	71.80	---	504.80	**599.00**
Polished brass	Inst	Ea	Lg	CA	1.45	5.50	412.00	53.70	---	465.70	**549.00**
	Inst	Ea	Sm	CA	1.94	4.13	479.00	71.80	---	550.80	**652.00**

Clear glass

Description	Oper	Unit	Vol	Crew Size	Man-hours per Unit	Crew Output per Day	Avg Mat'l Unit Cost	Avg Labor Unit Cost	Avg Equip Unit Cost	Avg Total Unit Cost	Avg Price Incl O&P
Chrome	Inst	Ea	Lg	CA	1.45	5.50	425.00	53.70	---	478.70	**564.00**
	Inst	Ea	Sm	CA	1.94	4.13	494.00	71.80	---	565.80	**669.00**
Polished brass	Inst	Ea	Lg	CA	1.45	5.50	465.00	53.70	---	518.70	**609.00**
	Inst	Ea	Sm	CA	1.94	4.13	540.00	71.80	---	611.80	**722.00**

Shower bases or receptors

American Standard Products, acrylic, includes drain strainer

Detach & reset operations

Description	Oper	Unit	Vol	Crew Size	Man-hours per Unit	Crew Output per Day	Avg Mat'l Unit Cost	Avg Labor Unit Cost	Avg Equip Unit Cost	Avg Total Unit Cost	Avg Price Incl O&P
Any size	Reset	Ea	Lg	SB	2.67	6.00	32.20	97.50	---	129.70	**178.00**
	Reset	Ea	Sm	SB	3.56	4.50	37.50	130.00	---	167.50	**232.00**

Remove operations

Description	Oper	Unit	Vol	Crew Size	Man-hours per Unit	Crew Output per Day	Avg Mat'l Unit Cost	Avg Labor Unit Cost	Avg Equip Unit Cost	Avg Total Unit Cost	Avg Price Incl O&P
Any size	Demo	Ea	Lg	SB	1.60	10.00	---	58.40	---	58.40	**84.70**
	Demo	Ea	Sm	SB	2.13	7.50	---	77.80	---	77.80	**113.00**

Install rough-in

Shower base

Description	Oper	Unit	Vol	Crew Size	Man-hours per Unit	Crew Output per Day	Avg Mat'l Unit Cost	Avg Labor Unit Cost	Avg Equip Unit Cost	Avg Total Unit Cost	Avg Price Incl O&P
Any size	Inst	Ea	Lg	SB	13.3	1.20	92.00	486.00	---	578.00	**810.00**
	Inst	Ea	Sm	SB	17.8	0.90	107.00	650.00	---	757.00	**1070.00**

Replace operations

32" x 32" x 6-5/8" H, single threshold

Description	Oper	Unit	Vol	Crew Size	Man-hours per Unit	Crew Output per Day	Avg Mat'l Unit Cost	Avg Labor Unit Cost	Avg Equip Unit Cost	Avg Total Unit Cost	Avg Price Incl O&P
White	Inst	Ea	Lg	SB	4.00	4.00	454.00	146.00	---	600.00	**733.00**
	Inst	Ea	Sm	SB	5.33	3.00	528.00	195.00	---	723.00	**889.00**
Colors	Inst	Ea	Lg	SB	4.00	4.00	491.00	146.00	---	637.00	**777.00**
	Inst	Ea	Sm	SB	5.33	3.00	571.00	195.00	---	766.00	**939.00**
Premium colors	Inst	Ea	Lg	SB	4.00	4.00	521.00	146.00	---	667.00	**811.00**
	Inst	Ea	Sm	SB	5.33	3.00	606.00	195.00	---	801.00	**979.00**

36" x 36-3/16" x 6-5/8" H, single threshold

Description	Oper	Unit	Vol	Crew Size	Man-hours per Unit	Crew Output per Day	Avg Mat'l Unit Cost	Avg Labor Unit Cost	Avg Equip Unit Cost	Avg Total Unit Cost	Avg Price Incl O&P
White	Inst	Ea	Lg	SB	4.00	4.00	466.00	146.00	---	612.00	**748.00**
	Inst	Ea	Sm	SB	5.33	3.00	542.00	195.00	---	737.00	**906.00**
Colors	Inst	Ea	Lg	SB	4.00	4.00	505.00	146.00	---	651.00	**793.00**
	Inst	Ea	Sm	SB	5.33	3.00	587.00	195.00	---	782.00	**958.00**
Premium colors	Inst	Ea	Lg	SB	4.00	4.00	535.00	146.00	---	681.00	**828.00**
	Inst	Ea	Sm	SB	5.33	3.00	623.00	195.00	---	818.00	**998.00**

Description	Oper	Unit	Vol	Crew Size	Man-hours per Unit	Crew Output per Day	Avg Mat'l Unit Cost	Avg Labor Unit Cost	Avg Equip Unit Cost	Avg Total Unit Cost	Avg Price Incl O&P
42-1/8" x 42-1/8" x 6-5/8" H, single threshold											
White	Inst	Ea	Lg	SB	4.00	4.00	740.00	146.00	---	886.00	1060.00
	Inst	Ea	Sm	SB	5.33	3.00	860.00	195.00	---	1055.00	1270.00
Colors	Inst	Ea	Lg	SB	4.00	4.00	787.00	146.00	---	933.00	1120.00
	Inst	Ea	Sm	SB	5.33	3.00	915.00	195.00	---	1110.00	1330.00
Premium colors	Inst	Ea	Lg	SB	4.00	4.00	814.00	146.00	---	960.00	1150.00
	Inst	Ea	Sm	SB	5.33	3.00	947.00	195.00	---	1142.00	1370.00
48-1/8" x 34-1/4" x 6-5/8" H, single threshold											
White	Inst	Ea	Lg	SB	4.00	4.00	627.00	146.00	---	773.00	933.00
	Inst	Ea	Sm	SB	5.33	3.00	730.00	195.00	---	925.00	1120.00
Colors	Inst	Ea	Lg	SB	4.00	4.00	673.00	146.00	---	819.00	985.00
	Inst	Ea	Sm	SB	5.33	3.00	782.00	195.00	---	977.00	1180.00
Premium colors	Inst	Ea	Lg	SB	4.00	4.00	699.00	146.00	---	845.00	1020.00
	Inst	Ea	Sm	SB	5.33	3.00	813.00	195.00	---	1008.00	1220.00
60-1/8" x 34-1/8" x 6-5/8" H, single threshold											
White	Inst	Ea	Lg	SB	4.00	4.00	776.00	146.00	---	922.00	1100.00
	Inst	Ea	Sm	SB	5.33	3.00	902.00	195.00	---	1097.00	1320.00
Colors	Inst	Ea	Lg	SB	4.00	4.00	822.00	146.00	---	968.00	1160.00
	Inst	Ea	Sm	SB	5.33	3.00	957.00	195.00	---	1152.00	1380.00
Premium colors	Inst	Ea	Lg	SB	4.00	4.00	853.00	146.00	---	999.00	1190.00
	Inst	Ea	Sm	SB	5.33	3.00	992.00	195.00	---	1187.00	1420.00
36-1/4" x 36-1/8" x 6-5/8" H, neo angle											
White	Inst	Ea	Lg	SB	4.00	4.00	484.00	146.00	---	630.00	768.00
	Inst	Ea	Sm	SB	5.33	3.00	563.00	195.00	---	758.00	929.00
Colors	Inst	Ea	Lg	SB	4.00	4.00	524.00	146.00	---	670.00	815.00
	Inst	Ea	Sm	SB	5.33	3.00	610.00	195.00	---	805.00	984.00
Premium colors	Inst	Ea	Lg	SB	4.00	4.00	554.00	146.00	---	700.00	849.00
	Inst	Ea	Sm	SB	5.33	3.00	644.00	195.00	---	839.00	1020.00
38-1/8" x 38-1/16" x 6-5/8" H, neo angle											
White	Inst	Ea	Lg	SB	4.00	4.00	507.00	146.00	---	653.00	795.00
	Inst	Ea	Sm	SB	5.33	3.00	590.00	195.00	---	785.00	960.00
Colors	Inst	Ea	Lg	SB	4.00	4.00	547.00	146.00	---	693.00	841.00
	Inst	Ea	Sm	SB	5.33	3.00	637.00	195.00	---	832.00	1010.00
Premium colors	Inst	Ea	Lg	SB	4.00	4.00	577.00	146.00	---	723.00	875.00
	Inst	Ea	Sm	SB	5.33	3.00	671.00	195.00	---	866.00	1050.00
42-1/4" x 42-1/8" x 6-5/8" H, neo angle											
White	Inst	Ea	Lg	SB	4.00	4.00	776.00	146.00	---	922.00	1100.00
	Inst	Ea	Sm	SB	5.33	3.00	902.00	195.00	---	1097.00	1320.00
Colors	Inst	Ea	Lg	SB	4.00	4.00	822.00	146.00	---	968.00	1160.00
	Inst	Ea	Sm	SB	5.33	3.00	957.00	195.00	---	1152.00	1380.00
Premium colors	Inst	Ea	Lg	SB	4.00	4.00	853.00	146.00	---	999.00	1190.00
	Inst	Ea	Sm	SB	5.33	3.00	992.00	195.00	---	1187.00	1420.00

Description	Oper	Unit	Vol	Crew Size	Man-hours per Unit	Crew Output per Day	Avg Mat'l Unit Cost	Avg Labor Unit Cost	Avg Equip Unit Cost	Avg Total Unit Cost	Avg Price Incl O&P

Shower stalls

Shower stall units with slip-resistant fiberglass floors, and reinforced plastic integral wall surrounds (Aqua Glass), available in white or color, with good quality fittings, single control faucets, and shower head sprayer

Detach & reset operations

Description	Oper	Unit	Vol	Crew Size	Man-hours per Unit	Crew Output per Day	Avg Mat'l Unit Cost	Avg Labor Unit Cost	Avg Equip Unit Cost	Avg Total Unit Cost	Avg Price Incl O&P
Single integral piece	Reset	Ea	Lg	SB	5.33	3.00	69.00	195.00	---	264.00	**362.00**
	Reset	Ea	Sm	SB	7.11	2.25	80.30	260.00	---	340.30	**469.00**
Multi-piece, non-integral	Reset	Ea	Lg	SB	4.00	4.00	69.00	146.00	---	215.00	**291.00**
	Reset	Ea	Sm	SB	5.33	3.00	80.30	195.00	---	275.30	**374.00**

Remove operations

Description	Oper	Unit	Vol	Crew Size	Man-hours per Unit	Crew Output per Day	Avg Mat'l Unit Cost	Avg Labor Unit Cost	Avg Equip Unit Cost	Avg Total Unit Cost	Avg Price Incl O&P
Single integral piece	Demo	Ea	Lg	SB	2.67	6.00	46.00	97.50	---	143.50	**194.00**
	Demo	Ea	Sm	SB	3.56	4.50	53.50	130.00	---	183.50	**250.00**
Multi-piece, non-integral	Demo	Ea	Lg	SB	2.00	8.00	46.00	73.00	---	119.00	**159.00**
	Demo	Ea	Sm	SB	2.67	6.00	53.50	97.50	---	151.00	**203.00**

Install rough-in

Description	Oper	Unit	Vol	Crew Size	Man-hours per Unit	Crew Output per Day	Avg Mat'l Unit Cost	Avg Labor Unit Cost	Avg Equip Unit Cost	Avg Total Unit Cost	Avg Price Incl O&P
Shower stall, any size	Inst	Ea	Lg	SB	10.0	1.60	92.00	365.00	---	457.00	**635.00**
	Inst	Ea	Sm	SB	13.3	1.20	107.00	486.00	---	593.00	**827.00**

Replace operations

Three-wall stall, one integral piece, no door, with plastic drain

Lasco Compact, Paloma-I
32" x 32" x 72" H

Description	Oper	Unit	Vol	Crew Size	Man-hours per Unit	Crew Output per Day	Avg Mat'l Unit Cost	Avg Labor Unit Cost	Avg Equip Unit Cost	Avg Total Unit Cost	Avg Price Incl O&P
Stock color	Inst	Ea	Lg	SB	8.00	2.00	702.00	292.00	---	994.00	**1230.00**
	Inst	Ea	Sm	SB	10.7	1.50	816.00	391.00	---	1207.00	**1510.00**

Lasco Compact, Paloma-II
34" x 34" x 72" H

Description	Oper	Unit	Vol	Crew Size	Man-hours per Unit	Crew Output per Day	Avg Mat'l Unit Cost	Avg Labor Unit Cost	Avg Equip Unit Cost	Avg Total Unit Cost	Avg Price Incl O&P
Stock color	Inst	Ea	Lg	SB	8.00	2.00	784.00	292.00	---	1076.00	**1320.00**
	Inst	Ea	Sm	SB	10.7	1.50	912.00	391.00	---	1303.00	**1610.00**

Lasco Compact, Paloma-III
36" x 36" x 72" H

Description	Oper	Unit	Vol	Crew Size	Man-hours per Unit	Crew Output per Day	Avg Mat'l Unit Cost	Avg Labor Unit Cost	Avg Equip Unit Cost	Avg Total Unit Cost	Avg Price Incl O&P
Stock color	Inst	Ea	Lg	SB	8.00	2.00	755.00	292.00	---	1047.00	**1290.00**
	Inst	Ea	Sm	SB	10.7	1.50	878.00	391.00	---	1269.00	**1580.00**

Lasco Compact, Paloma-IV
42" x 34" x 72" H

Description	Oper	Unit	Vol	Crew Size	Man-hours per Unit	Crew Output per Day	Avg Mat'l Unit Cost	Avg Labor Unit Cost	Avg Equip Unit Cost	Avg Total Unit Cost	Avg Price Incl O&P
Stock color	Inst	Ea	Lg	SB	8.00	2.00	798.00	292.00	---	1090.00	**1340.00**
	Inst	Ea	Sm	SB	10.7	1.50	928.00	391.00	---	1319.00	**1630.00**

Lasco Deluxe, Larissa, 1 seat
47-3/4" x 33-1/2" x 72" H

Description	Oper	Unit	Vol	Crew Size	Man-hours per Unit	Crew Output per Day	Avg Mat'l Unit Cost	Avg Labor Unit Cost	Avg Equip Unit Cost	Avg Total Unit Cost	Avg Price Incl O&P
Stock color	Inst	Ea	Lg	SB	8.00	2.00	866.00	292.00	---	1158.00	**1420.00**
	Inst	Ea	Sm	SB	10.7	1.50	1010.00	391.00	---	1401.00	**1720.00**

Description	Oper	Unit	Vol	Crew Size	Man-hours per Unit	Crew Output per Day	Avg Mat'l Unit Cost	Avg Labor Unit Cost	Avg Equip Unit Cost	Avg Total Unit Cost	Avg Price Incl O&P
Lasco Deluxe, Camila-I, 2 seat 48" x 35" x 72" H											
Stock color	Inst	Ea	Lg	SB	8.00	2.00	833.00	292.00	---	1125.00	**1380.00**
	Inst	Ea	Sm	SB	10.7	1.50	968.00	391.00	---	1359.00	**1680.00**
Lasco Deluxe, Camila-II, 2 seat 54" x 35" x 72" H											
Stock color	Inst	Ea	Lg	SB	8.89	1.80	857.00	325.00	---	1182.00	**1460.00**
	Inst	Ea	Sm	SB	11.9	1.35	996.00	434.00	---	1430.00	**1780.00**
Lasco Deluxe, Camila-III, 2 seat 60" x 35" x 72" H											
Stock color	Inst	Ea	Lg	SB	8.89	1.80	866.00	325.00	---	1191.00	**1470.00**
	Inst	Ea	Sm	SB	11.9	1.35	1010.00	434.00	---	1444.00	**1790.00**

Two-wall stall, one integral piece, no door, with plastic drain

Description	Oper	Unit	Vol	Crew Size	Man-hours per Unit	Crew Output per Day	Avg Mat'l Unit Cost	Avg Labor Unit Cost	Avg Equip Unit Cost	Avg Total Unit Cost	Avg Price Incl O&P
Lasco Varina, space saver 36" x 36" x 72" H											
Stock color	Inst	Ea	Lg	SB	8.00	2.00	791.00	292.00	---	1083.00	**1330.00**
	Inst	Ea	Sm	SB	10.7	1.50	920.00	391.00	---	1311.00	**1620.00**
Lasco Galina-I, space saver, neo angle 38" x 38" x 72" H											
Stock color	Inst	Ea	Lg	SB	8.00	2.00	745.00	292.00	---	1037.00	**1280.00**
	Inst	Ea	Sm	SB	10.7	1.50	867.00	391.00	---	1258.00	**1560.00**
Lasco Galina-II, space saver, neo angle 38" x 38" x 80" H											
Stock color	Inst	Ea	Lg	SB	8.00	2.00	802.00	292.00	---	1094.00	**1350.00**
	Inst	Ea	Sm	SB	10.7	1.50	933.00	391.00	---	1324.00	**1640.00**
Lasco Galina-III, space saver, neo angle 36" x 36" x 77" H											
Stock color	Inst	Ea	Lg	SB	8.00	2.00	1070.00	292.00	---	1362.00	**1660.00**
	Inst	Ea	Sm	SB	10.7	1.50	1250.00	391.00	---	1641.00	**2000.00**
Lasco Neopolitan-I, space saver, neo angle 38" x 38" x 72" H											
Stock color	Inst	Ea	Lg	SB	8.00	2.00	849.00	292.00	---	1141.00	**1400.00**
	Inst	Ea	Sm	SB	10.7	1.50	988.00	391.00	---	1379.00	**1700.00**

Description	Oper	Unit	Vol	Crew Size	Man-hours per Unit	Crew Output per Day	Avg Mat'l Unit Cost	Avg Labor Unit Cost	Avg Equip Unit Cost	Avg Total Unit Cost	Avg Price Incl O&P

Multi-piece, nonintegral, nonassembled units with drain

Lasco Caledon-I, 2-piece
32" x 32" x 72-3/4" H

Description	Oper	Unit	Vol	Crew Size	Man-hours per Unit	Crew Output per Day	Avg Mat'l Unit Cost	Avg Labor Unit Cost	Avg Equip Unit Cost	Avg Total Unit Cost	Avg Price Incl O&P
Stock color	Inst	Ea	Lg	SB	8.00	2.00	735.00	292.00	---	1027.00	**1270.00**
	Inst	Ea	Sm	SB	10.7	1.50	855.00	391.00	---	1246.00	**1550.00**

Lasco Caledon-II, 3-piece
36" x 36" x 72-3/4" H

| Stock color | Inst | Ea | Lg | SB | 8.00 | 2.00 | 833.00 | 292.00 | --- | 1125.00 | **1380.00** |
| | Inst | Ea | Sm | SB | 10.7 | 1.50 | 968.00 | 391.00 | --- | 1359.00 | **1680.00** |

Lasco Caledon-III, 2-piece
48" x 34" x 72" H

| Stock color | Inst | Ea | Lg | SB | 8.89 | 1.80 | 862.00 | 325.00 | --- | 1187.00 | **1460.00** |
| | Inst | Ea | Sm | SB | 11.9 | 1.35 | 1000.00 | 434.00 | --- | 1434.00 | **1780.00** |

Lasco Caledon-III, 3-piece
48" x 34" x 72-3/4" H

| Stock color | Inst | Ea | Lg | SB | 8.89 | 1.80 | 808.00 | 325.00 | --- | 1133.00 | **1400.00** |
| | Inst | Ea | Sm | SB | 11.9 | 1.35 | 939.00 | 434.00 | --- | 1373.00 | **1710.00** |

Lasco Talia-II, 2-piece
36" x 36" x 72" H

| Stock color | Inst | Ea | Lg | SB | 8.00 | 2.00 | 813.00 | 292.00 | --- | 1105.00 | **1360.00** |
| | Inst | Ea | Sm | SB | 10.7 | 1.50 | 946.00 | 391.00 | --- | 1337.00 | **1650.00** |

Description	Oper	Unit	Vol	Crew Size	Man-hours per Unit	Crew Output per Day	Avg Mat'l Unit Cost	Avg Labor Unit Cost	Avg Equip Unit Cost	Avg Total Unit Cost	Avg Price Incl O&P

Shower tub units

Shower tub three-wall stall combinations are fiberglass reinforced plastic with integral bath/shower and wall surrounds; includes good quality fittings, single control faucets, and shower head sprayer

Detach & reset operations

Description	Oper	Unit	Vol	Crew Size	Man-hours per Unit	Crew Output per Day	Avg Mat'l Unit Cost	Avg Labor Unit Cost	Avg Equip Unit Cost	Avg Total Unit Cost	Avg Price Incl O&P
Single integral piece	Reset	Ea	Lg	SB	5.33	3.00	69.00	195.00	---	264.00	**362.00**
	Reset	Ea	Sm	SB	7.11	2.25	80.30	260.00	---	340.30	**469.00**
Multi-piece, non-integral	Reset	Ea	Lg	SB	4.00	4.00	69.00	146.00	---	215.00	**291.00**
	Reset	Ea	Sm	SB	5.33	3.00	80.30	195.00	---	275.30	**374.00**

Remove operations

Description	Oper	Unit	Vol	Crew Size	Man-hours per Unit	Crew Output per Day	Avg Mat'l Unit Cost	Avg Labor Unit Cost	Avg Equip Unit Cost	Avg Total Unit Cost	Avg Price Incl O&P
Single integral piece	Demo	Ea	Lg	SB	2.67	6.00	46.00	97.50	---	143.50	**194.00**
	Demo	Ea	Sm	SB	3.56	4.50	53.50	130.00	---	183.50	**250.00**
Multi-piece, non-integral	Demo	Ea	Lg	SB	2.00	8.00	46.00	73.00	---	119.00	**159.00**
	Demo	Ea	Sm	SB	2.67	6.00	53.50	97.50	---	151.00	**203.00**

Install rough-in

Description	Oper	Unit	Vol	Crew Size	Man-hours per Unit	Crew Output per Day	Avg Mat'l Unit Cost	Avg Labor Unit Cost	Avg Equip Unit Cost	Avg Total Unit Cost	Avg Price Incl O&P
Shower tub	Inst	Ea	Lg	SB	11.4	1.40	92.00	416.00	---	508.00	**709.00**
	Inst	Ea	Sm	SB	15.2	1.05	107.00	555.00	---	662.00	**928.00**

Replace operations

One-piece combination (unitized), no door

Lasco Kassia, with grab bar
54-1/2" x 29" x 72" H

Description	Oper	Unit	Vol	Crew Size	Man-hours per Unit	Crew Output per Day	Avg Mat'l Unit Cost	Avg Labor Unit Cost	Avg Equip Unit Cost	Avg Total Unit Cost	Avg Price Incl O&P
Stock color	Inst	Ea	Lg	SB	8.00	2.00	738.00	292.00	---	1030.00	**1270.00**
	Inst	Ea	Sm	SB	10.7	1.50	858.00	391.00	---	1249.00	**1550.00**

Lasco Capriel-I, with grab bar
60" x 30" x 72" H

Description	Oper	Unit	Vol	Crew Size	Man-hours per Unit	Crew Output per Day	Avg Mat'l Unit Cost	Avg Labor Unit Cost	Avg Equip Unit Cost	Avg Total Unit Cost	Avg Price Incl O&P
Stock color	Inst	Ea	Lg	SB	8.00	2.00	849.00	292.00	---	1141.00	**1400.00**
	Inst	Ea	Sm	SB	10.7	1.50	988.00	391.00	---	1379.00	**1700.00**

Lasco Capriel-II, with grab bar
60" x 32" x 74" H

Description	Oper	Unit	Vol	Crew Size	Man-hours per Unit	Crew Output per Day	Avg Mat'l Unit Cost	Avg Labor Unit Cost	Avg Equip Unit Cost	Avg Total Unit Cost	Avg Price Incl O&P
Stock color	Inst	Ea	Lg	SB	8.00	2.00	867.00	292.00	---	1159.00	**1420.00**
	Inst	Ea	Sm	SB	10.7	1.50	1010.00	391.00	---	1401.00	**1730.00**

Lasco Capriel-III, with grab bar
60" x 32" x 78" H

Description	Oper	Unit	Vol	Crew Size	Man-hours per Unit	Crew Output per Day	Avg Mat'l Unit Cost	Avg Labor Unit Cost	Avg Equip Unit Cost	Avg Total Unit Cost	Avg Price Incl O&P
Stock color	Inst	Ea	Lg	SB	8.00	2.00	944.00	292.00	---	1236.00	**1510.00**
	Inst	Ea	Sm	SB	10.7	1.50	1100.00	391.00	---	1491.00	**1830.00**

Multi-piece combination, no door

Lasco Mali, 3-piece
60" x 30" x 72" H

Description	Oper	Unit	Vol	Crew Size	Man-hours per Unit	Crew Output per Day	Avg Mat'l Unit Cost	Avg Labor Unit Cost	Avg Equip Unit Cost	Avg Total Unit Cost	Avg Price Incl O&P
Stock color	Inst	Ea	Lg	SB	8.00	2.00	868.00	292.00	---	1160.00	**1420.00**
	Inst	Ea	Sm	SB	10.7	1.50	1010.00	391.00	---	1401.00	**1730.00**

Lasco Oriana, 2-piece
60" x 30" x 72" H

Description	Oper	Unit	Vol	Crew Size	Man-hours per Unit	Crew Output per Day	Avg Mat'l Unit Cost	Avg Labor Unit Cost	Avg Equip Unit Cost	Avg Total Unit Cost	Avg Price Incl O&P
Stock color	Inst	Ea	Lg	SB	8.00	2.00	812.00	292.00	---	1104.00	**1360.00**
	Inst	Ea	Sm	SB	10.7	1.50	945.00	391.00	---	1336.00	**1650.00**

Description	Oper	Unit	Vol	Crew Size	Man-hours per Unit	Crew Output per Day	Avg Mat'l Unit Cost	Avg Labor Unit Cost	Avg Equip Unit Cost	Avg Total Unit Cost	Avg Price Incl O&P

Shutters

Aluminum, louvered, 14" W

Description	Oper	Unit	Vol	Crew Size	Man-hours per Unit	Crew Output per Day	Avg Mat'l Unit Cost	Avg Labor Unit Cost	Avg Equip Unit Cost	Avg Total Unit Cost	Avg Price Incl O&P
3'-0" long	Inst	Pair	Lg	CA	1.00	8.00	157.00	37.00	---	194.00	**232.00**
	Inst	Pair	Sm	CA	1.33	6.00	182.00	49.20	---	231.20	**278.00**
6'-8" long	Inst	Pair	Lg	CA	1.00	8.00	311.00	37.00	---	348.00	**409.00**
	Inst	Pair	Sm	CA	1.33	6.00	360.00	49.20	---	409.20	**483.00**

Pine or fir, provincial raised panel, primed, in stock, 1-1/16" T

12" W

Description	Oper	Unit	Vol	Crew Size	Man-hours per Unit	Crew Output per Day	Avg Mat'l Unit Cost	Avg Labor Unit Cost	Avg Equip Unit Cost	Avg Total Unit Cost	Avg Price Incl O&P
2'-1" long	Inst	Pair	Lg	CA	1.00	8.00	97.30	37.00	---	134.30	**164.00**
	Inst	Pair	Sm	CA	1.33	6.00	113.00	49.20	---	162.20	**198.00**
3'-1" long	Inst	Pair	Lg	CA	1.00	8.00	107.00	37.00	---	144.00	**175.00**
	Inst	Pair	Sm	CA	1.33	6.00	124.00	49.20	---	173.20	**211.00**
4'-1" long	Inst	Pair	Lg	CA	1.00	8.00	124.00	37.00	---	161.00	**194.00**
	Inst	Pair	Sm	CA	1.33	6.00	143.00	49.20	---	192.20	**234.00**
5'-1" long	Inst	Pair	Lg	CA	1.00	8.00	198.00	37.00	---	235.00	**279.00**
	Inst	Pair	Sm	CA	1.33	6.00	229.00	49.20	---	278.20	**332.00**
6'-1" long	Inst	Pair	Lg	CA	1.00	8.00	237.00	37.00	---	274.00	**325.00**
	Inst	Pair	Sm	CA	1.33	6.00	275.00	49.20	---	324.20	**385.00**

18" W

Description	Oper	Unit	Vol	Crew Size	Man-hours per Unit	Crew Output per Day	Avg Mat'l Unit Cost	Avg Labor Unit Cost	Avg Equip Unit Cost	Avg Total Unit Cost	Avg Price Incl O&P
2'-1" long	Inst	Pair	Lg	CA	1.00	8.00	122.00	37.00	---	159.00	**192.00**
	Inst	Pair	Sm	CA	1.33	6.00	141.00	49.20	---	190.20	**231.00**
3'-1" long	Inst	Pair	Lg	CA	1.00	8.00	134.00	37.00	---	171.00	**206.00**
	Inst	Pair	Sm	CA	1.33	6.00	155.00	49.20	---	204.20	**247.00**
4'-1" long	Inst	Pair	Lg	CA	1.00	8.00	155.00	37.00	---	192.00	**230.00**
	Inst	Pair	Sm	CA	1.33	6.00	179.00	49.20	---	228.20	**275.00**
5'-1" long	Inst	Pair	Lg	CA	1.00	8.00	247.00	37.00	---	284.00	**336.00**
	Inst	Pair	Sm	CA	1.33	6.00	286.00	49.20	---	335.20	**398.00**
6'-1" long	Inst	Pair	Lg	CA	1.00	8.00	296.00	37.00	---	333.00	**393.00**
	Inst	Pair	Sm	CA	1.33	6.00	343.00	49.20	---	392.20	**464.00**

Door blinds, 6'-9" long

Description	Oper	Unit	Vol	Crew Size	Man-hours per Unit	Crew Output per Day	Avg Mat'l Unit Cost	Avg Labor Unit Cost	Avg Equip Unit Cost	Avg Total Unit Cost	Avg Price Incl O&P
1'-3" wide	Inst	Pair	Lg	CA	1.00	8.00	308.00	37.00	---	345.00	**406.00**
	Inst	Pair	Sm	CA	1.33	6.00	357.00	49.20	---	406.20	**479.00**
1'-6" wide	Inst	Pair	Lg	CA	1.00	8.00	385.00	37.00	---	422.00	**495.00**
	Inst	Pair	Sm	CA	1.33	6.00	446.00	49.20	---	495.20	**582.00**

Description	Oper	Unit	Vol	Crew Size	Man-hours per Unit	Crew Output per Day	Avg Mat'l Unit Cost	Avg Labor Unit Cost	Avg Equip Unit Cost	Avg Total Unit Cost	Avg Price Incl O&P

Birch, special order stationary slat blinds, 1-1/16" T

12" W

Description	Oper	Unit	Vol	Crew Size	Man-hours per Unit	Crew Output per Day	Avg Mat'l Unit Cost	Avg Labor Unit Cost	Avg Equip Unit Cost	Avg Total Unit Cost	Avg Price Incl O&P
2'-1" long	Inst	Pair	Lg	CA	1.00	8.00	146.00	37.00	---	183.00	**220.00**
	Inst	Pair	Sm	CA	1.33	6.00	169.00	49.20	---	218.20	**263.00**
3'-1" long	Inst	Pair	Lg	CA	1.00	8.00	161.00	37.00	---	198.00	**236.00**
	Inst	Pair	Sm	CA	1.33	6.00	186.00	49.20	---	235.20	**283.00**
4'-1" long	Inst	Pair	Lg	CA	1.00	8.00	186.00	37.00	---	223.00	**266.00**
	Inst	Pair	Sm	CA	1.33	6.00	215.00	49.20	---	264.20	**316.00**
5'-1" long	Inst	Pair	Lg	CA	1.00	8.00	296.00	37.00	---	333.00	**393.00**
	Inst	Pair	Sm	CA	1.33	6.00	343.00	49.20	---	392.20	**464.00**
6'-1" long	Inst	Pair	Lg	CA	1.00	8.00	356.00	37.00	---	393.00	**461.00**
	Inst	Pair	Sm	CA	1.33	6.00	412.00	49.20	---	461.20	**543.00**

18" W

Description	Oper	Unit	Vol	Crew Size	Man-hours per Unit	Crew Output per Day	Avg Mat'l Unit Cost	Avg Labor Unit Cost	Avg Equip Unit Cost	Avg Total Unit Cost	Avg Price Incl O&P
2'-1" long	Inst	Pair	Lg	CA	1.00	8.00	182.00	37.00	---	219.00	**262.00**
	Inst	Pair	Sm	CA	1.33	6.00	211.00	49.20	---	260.20	**312.00**
3'-1" long	Inst	Pair	Lg	CA	1.00	8.00	201.00	37.00	---	238.00	**283.00**
	Inst	Pair	Sm	CA	1.33	6.00	232.00	49.20	---	281.20	**336.00**
4'-1" long	Inst	Pair	Lg	CA	1.00	8.00	232.00	37.00	---	269.00	**319.00**
	Inst	Pair	Sm	CA	1.33	6.00	269.00	49.20	---	318.20	**378.00**
5'-1" long	Inst	Pair	Lg	CA	1.00	8.00	371.00	37.00	---	408.00	**478.00**
	Inst	Pair	Sm	CA	1.33	6.00	429.00	49.20	---	478.20	**562.00**
6'-1" long	Inst	Pair	Lg	CA	1.00	8.00	445.00	37.00	---	482.00	**563.00**
	Inst	Pair	Sm	CA	1.33	6.00	515.00	49.20	---	564.20	**661.00**

Western hemlock, colonial style, primed, 1-1/8" T

14" wide

Description	Oper	Unit	Vol	Crew Size	Man-hours per Unit	Crew Output per Day	Avg Mat'l Unit Cost	Avg Labor Unit Cost	Avg Equip Unit Cost	Avg Total Unit Cost	Avg Price Incl O&P
5'-7" long	Inst	Pair	Lg	CA	1.00	8.00	243.00	37.00	---	280.00	**332.00**
	Inst	Pair	Sm	CA	1.33	6.00	282.00	49.20	---	331.20	**393.00**

16" wide

Description	Oper	Unit	Vol	Crew Size	Man-hours per Unit	Crew Output per Day	Avg Mat'l Unit Cost	Avg Labor Unit Cost	Avg Equip Unit Cost	Avg Total Unit Cost	Avg Price Incl O&P
3'-0" long	Inst	Pair	Lg	CA	1.00	8.00	188.00	37.00	---	225.00	**268.00**
	Inst	Pair	Sm	CA	1.33	6.00	218.00	49.20	---	267.20	**319.00**
4'-3" long	Inst	Pair	Lg	CA	1.00	8.00	263.00	37.00	---	300.00	**354.00**
	Inst	Pair	Sm	CA	1.33	6.00	305.00	49.20	---	354.20	**419.00**
5'-0" long	Inst	Pair	Lg	CA	1.00	8.00	304.00	37.00	---	341.00	**401.00**
	Inst	Pair	Sm	CA	1.33	6.00	352.00	49.20	---	401.20	**474.00**
6'-0" long	Inst	Pair	Lg	CA	1.00	8.00	365.00	37.00	---	402.00	**471.00**
	Inst	Pair	Sm	CA	1.33	6.00	422.00	49.20	---	471.20	**555.00**

Door blinds, 6'-9" long

Description	Oper	Unit	Vol	Crew Size	Man-hours per Unit	Crew Output per Day	Avg Mat'l Unit Cost	Avg Labor Unit Cost	Avg Equip Unit Cost	Avg Total Unit Cost	Avg Price Incl O&P
1'-3" wide	Inst	Pair	Lg	CA	1.00	8.00	462.00	37.00	---	499.00	**584.00**
	Inst	Pair	Sm	CA	1.33	6.00	535.00	49.20	---	584.20	**685.00**
1'-6" wide	Inst	Pair	Lg	CA	1.00	8.00	578.00	37.00	---	615.00	**717.00**
	Inst	Pair	Sm	CA	1.33	6.00	669.00	49.20	---	718.20	**839.00**

Description	Oper	Unit	Vol	Crew Size	Man-hours per Unit	Crew Output per Day	Avg Mat'l Unit Cost	Avg Labor Unit Cost	Avg Equip Unit Cost	Avg Total Unit Cost	Avg Price Incl O&P
Cellwood shutters, molded structural foam polystyrene											
Prefinished louver, 16" wide											
3'-3" long	Inst	Pair	Lg	CA	1.00	8.00	24.70	37.00	---	61.70	**80.20**
	Inst	Pair	Sm	CA	1.33	6.00	28.60	49.20	---	77.80	**102.00**
4'-7" long	Inst	Pair	Lg	CA	1.00	8.00	37.10	37.00	---	74.10	**94.40**
	Inst	Pair	Sm	CA	1.33	6.00	42.90	49.20	---	92.10	**118.00**
5'-3" long	Inst	Pair	Lg	CA	1.00	8.00	45.60	37.00	---	82.60	**104.00**
	Inst	Pair	Sm	CA	1.33	6.00	52.80	49.20	---	102.00	**130.00**
6'-3" long	Inst	Pair	Lg	CA	1.00	8.00	54.70	37.00	---	91.70	**115.00**
	Inst	Pair	Sm	CA	1.33	6.00	63.40	49.20	---	112.60	**142.00**
Door blinds											
16" wide x 6'-9" long	Inst	Pair	Lg	CA	1.00	8.00	63.80	37.00	---	100.80	**125.00**
	Inst	Pair	Sm	CA	1.33	6.00	73.90	49.20	---	123.10	**154.00**
Prefinished panel, 16" wide											
3'-3" long	Inst	Pair	Lg	CA	1.00	8.00	27.20	37.00	---	64.20	**83.10**
	Inst	Pair	Sm	CA	1.33	6.00	31.50	49.20	---	80.70	**105.00**
4'-7" long	Inst	Pair	Lg	CA	1.00	8.00	40.80	37.00	---	77.80	**98.70**
	Inst	Pair	Sm	CA	1.33	6.00	47.20	49.20	---	96.40	**123.00**
5'-3" long	Inst	Pair	Lg	CA	1.00	8.00	50.20	37.00	---	87.20	**110.00**
	Inst	Pair	Sm	CA	1.33	6.00	58.10	49.20	---	107.30	**136.00**
6'-3" long	Inst	Pair	Lg	CA	1.00	8.00	60.20	37.00	---	97.20	**121.00**
	Inst	Pair	Sm	CA	1.33	6.00	69.70	49.20	---	118.90	**149.00**
Door blinds											
16" wide x 6'-9" long	Inst	Pair	Lg	CA	1.00	8.00	70.20	37.00	---	107.20	**133.00**
	Inst	Pair	Sm	CA	1.33	6.00	81.30	49.20	---	130.50	**162.00**

Siding

Aluminum Siding

1. **Dimensions and Descriptions.** The types of aluminum siding discussed are: (1) painted (2) available in various colors, (3) either 0.024" gauge or 0.019" gauge. The types of aluminum siding discussed in this section are:

   a. Clapboard: 12'-6" long; 8" exposure; $5/8$" butt; 0.024" gauge.

   b. Board and batten: 10'-0" long; 10" exposure; 1/2" butt; 0.024" gauge.

   c. "Double-five-inch" clapboard: 12'-0" long; 10" exposure; $1/2$" butt; 0.024" gauge.

   d. Sculpture clapboard: 12'-6" long; 8" exposure; $1/2$" butt; 0.024" gauge.

   e. Shingle siding: 24" long; 12" exposure; $1^1/8$" butt; 0.019" gauge.

Most types of aluminum siding may be available in a smooth or rough texture.

2. **Installation.** Applied horizontally with nails. See chart below.

3. **Estimating Technique.** Determine area and deduct area of window and door openings then add for cutting and fitting waste. In the figures on aluminum siding, no waste has been included.

Wood Siding

The types of wood exterior finishes covered in this section are:

    a. Bevel siding

    b. Drop siding

    c. Vertical siding

    d. Batten siding

    e. Plywood siding with battens

    f. Wood shingle siding

Bevel Siding

1. **Dimension.** Boards are 4", 6", 8", or 12" wide with a thickness of the top edge of $3/16$". The thickness of the bottom edge is $9/16$" for 4" and 6" widths and $11/16$" for 8", 10", 12" widths.

2. **Installation.** Applied horizontally with 6d or 8d common nails. See exposure and waste table below.

3. **Estimating Technique.** Determine area and deduct area of window and door openings, then add for lap, exposure, and cutting and fitting waste. In the figures on bevel siding, waste has been included, unless otherwise noted.

Type	Exposure	Butt	Normal Range of Cut & Fit Waste*
Clapboard	8"	$5/8$"	6% - 10%
Board & Batten	10"	$1/2$"	4% - 8%
Double-Five-Inch	10"	$1/2$"	6% - 10%
Sculptured	8"	$1/2$"	6% - 10%
Shingle Siding	12"	$1^1/8$"	4% - 6%

*The amount of waste will vary with the methods of installing siding and can be affected by dimension of the area to be covered.

Board Size	Actual Width	Lap	Exposure	Milling & Lap Waste	Normal Range of Cut & Fit Waste*
$1/2$" x 4"	$3^1/4$"	$1/2$"	$2^3/4$"	31.25%	19% - 23%
$1/2$" x 6"	$5^1/4$"	$1/2$"	$4^3/4$"	21.00%	10% - 13%
$1/2$" x 8"	$7^1/4$"	$1/2$"	$6^3/4$"	15.75%	7% - 10%
$5/8$" x 4"	$3^1/4$"	$1/2$"	$2^3/4$"	31.25%	19% - 23%
$5/8$" x 6"	$5^1/4$"	$1/2$"	$4^3/4$"	21.00%	10% - 13%
$5/8$" x 8"	$7^1/4$"	$1/2$"	$6^3/4$"	15.75%	7% - 10%
$5/8$" x 10"	$9^1/4$"	$1/2$"	$8^3/4$"	12.50%	6% - 10%
$3/4$" x 6"	$5^1/4$"	$1/2$"	$4^3/4$"	21.00%	10% - 13%
$3/4$" x 8"	$7^1/4$"	$1/2$"	$6^3/4$"	15.75%	7% - 10%
$3/4$" x 10"	$9^1/4$"	$1/2$"	$8^3/4$"	12.50%	6% - 10%
$3/4$" x 12"	$11^1/4$"	$1/2$"	$10^3/4$"	10.50%	6% - 10%

*The amount of waste will vary with the methods of installing siding and can be affected by dimension of the area to be covered.

Drop Siding, Tongue-and-Groove

1. **Dimension.** The boards are 4", 6", 8", 10", or 12" wide, and all boards are ³/₄" thick at both edges.

2. **Installation.** Applied horizontally, usually with 8d common nails. See exposure and waste table below:

Board Size	Actual Width	Lap +1/16"	Exposure	Milling & Lap Waste	Normal Range of Cut & Waste*
1" x 4"	3¹/₄"	³/₁₆"	3¹/₁₆"	23.50%	7% - 10%
1" x 6"	5¹/₄"	³/₁₆"	5¹/₁₆"	15.75%	6% - 8%
1" x 8"	7¹/₄"	³/₁₆"	7¹/₁₆"	11.75%	5% - 6%
1" x 10"	9¹/₄"	³/₁₆"	9¹/₁₆"	9.50%	4% - 5%
1" x 12"	11¹/₄"	³/₁₆"	11¹/₁₆"	8.00%	4% - 5%

*The amount of waste will vary with the methods of installing siding and can be affected by dimensions of the area to be covered.

3. **Estimating Technique.** Determine area and deduct area of window and door openings; then add for lap, exposure, butting and fitting waste. In the figures on drop siding, waste has been included, unless otherwise noted.

Vertical Siding, Tongue-and-Groove

1. **Dimensions.** Boards are 8", 10", or 12" wide, and all boards are ³/₄" thick at both top and bottom edges.

2. **Installation.** Applied vertically over horizontal furring strips usually with 8d common nails. See exposure and waste table below:

Board Size	Actual Width	Lap ¹/₁₆"	Exposure	Milling & Lap Waste	Normal Range of Cut & Fit Waste
1" x 8"	7¹/₄"	³/₁₆"	7¹/₁₆"	11.75%	5% - 7%
1" x 10"	9¹/₄"	³/₁₆"	9¹/₁₆"	9.50%	4% - 5%
1" x 12"	11¹/₄"	³/₁₆"	11¹/₁₆"	8.00%	4% - 5%

3. **Estimating Technique.** Determine area and deduct area of window and door openings; then add for lap, exposure, cutting and fitting waste. In the figures on vertical siding, waste has been included, unless otherwise noted.

Batten Siding

1. **Dimension.** The boards are 8", 10", or 12" wide. If the boards are rough, they are 1" thick; if the boards are dressed, then they are ²⁵/₃₂" thick. The battens are 1" thick and 2" wide.

2. **Installation.** The 8", 10", or 12"-wide boards are installed vertically over 1" x 3" or 1" x 4" horizontal furring strips. The battens are then installed over the seams of the vertical boards. See exposure and waste table below:

Board Size & Type		Actual Width & Exposure	Milling Waste	Normal Range of Cut & Fit Waste*
1" x 8"	rough sawn	8"	—	3% - 5%
	dressed	7¹/₂"	6.25%	3% - 5%
1" x 10"	rough sawn	10"	—	3% - 5%
	dressed	9¹/₂"	5.00%	3% - 5%
1" x 12"	rough sawn	12"	—	3% - 5%
	dressed	11¹/₂"	4.25%	3% - 5%

*The amount of waste will vary with the methods of installing siding and can be affected by dimension of the area to be covered.

3. **Estimating Technique.** Determine area and deduct area of window and door openings; then add for exposure, cutting and fitting waste. In the figures on batten siding, waste has been included, unless otherwise noted.

Quantity of Battens - No Cut and Fit Waste Included		
Board Size and Type		**LF per SF or BF**
1" x 6"	rough sawn	2.00
	dressed	2.25
1" x 8"	rough sawn	1.55
	dressed	1.60
1" x 10"	rough sawn	1.20
	dressed	1.30
1" x 12"	rough sawn	1.00
	dressed	1.05

Plywood Siding with Battens

1. **Dimensions.** The plywood panels are 4' wide and 8', 9', or 10' long. The panels are $^3/_8$", $^1/_2$" or $^5/_8$" thick. The battens are 1" thick and 2" wide.

2. **Installation.** The panels are applied directly to the studs with the 4'-0" width parallel to the plate. Nails used are 6d commons. The waste will normally range from 3% to 5%.

Quantity of Battens - No Cut and Fit Waste Included	
Spacing	LF per SF or BF
16" oc	.75
24" oc	.50

3. **Estimating Technique.** Determine area and deduct area of window and door openings; then add for cutting and fitting waste. In the figures on plywood siding with battens, waste has been included, unless otherwise noted.

Wood Shingle Siding

1. **Dimension.** The wood shingles have an average width of 4" and length of 16", 18" or 24". The thickness may vary in all cases.

2. **Installation.** On roofs with wood shingles, there should be three thicknesses of wood shingle at every point on the roof. But on exterior walls with wood shingles, only two thicknesses of wood siding shingles are needed. Nail to 1" x 3" or 1" x 4" furring strips using 3d rust-resistant nails. Use 5d rust-resistant nails when applying new shingles over old shingles. See table below:

Shingle Length	Exposure	Shingles per Square, No Waste Included	Lbs. of Nails at Two Nails per Shingle	
			3d	5d
16"	7$^1/_2$"	480	2.3	2.7
18"	8$^1/_2$"	424	2.0	2.4
24"	11$^1/_2$"	313	1.5	1.8

3. **Estimating Technique.** Determine the area and deduct the area of window and door openings. Then add approximately 10% for waste. In the figures on wood shingle siding, waste has been included, unless otherwise noted. In the above table, pounds of nails per square are based on two nails per shingle. For one nail per shingle, deduct 50%.

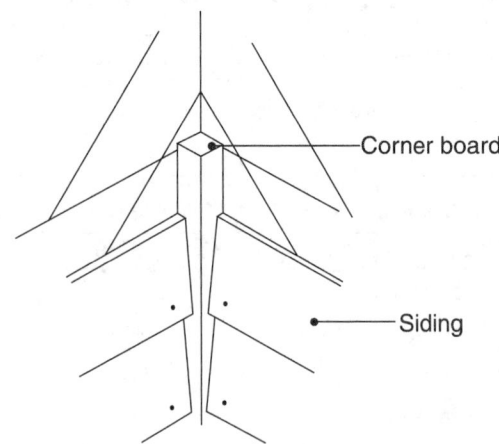

Corner board for application of horizontal siding at interior corner

Corner boards for application of horizontal siding at exterior corner

Description	Oper	Unit	Vol	Crew Size	Man-hours per Unit	Crew Output per Day	Avg Mat'l Unit Cost	Avg Labor Unit Cost	Avg Equip Unit Cost	Avg Total Unit Cost	Avg Price Incl O&P

Siding
Aluminum, nailed to wood
Clapboard (i.e. lap, drop)

Description	Oper	Unit	Vol	Crew Size	Man-hours per Unit	Crew Output per Day	Avg Mat'l Unit Cost	Avg Labor Unit Cost	Avg Equip Unit Cost	Avg Total Unit Cost	Avg Price Incl O&P
8" exposure	Demo	SF	Lg	LB	.016	1025	---	.48	---	.48	.67
	Demo	SF	Sm	LB	.022	717.5	---	.66	---	.66	.92
10" exposure	Demo	SF	Lg	LB	.013	1280	---	.39	---	.39	.55
	Demo	SF	Sm	LB	.018	896.0	---	.54	---	.54	.76

Clapboard, horizontal, 1/2" butt
Straight wall

Description	Oper	Unit	Vol	Crew Size	Man-hours per Unit	Crew Output per Day	Avg Mat'l Unit Cost	Avg Labor Unit Cost	Avg Equip Unit Cost	Avg Total Unit Cost	Avg Price Incl O&P
8" exposure	Inst	SF	Lg	2C	.026	620.0	1.97	.96	---	2.93	3.61
	Inst	SF	Sm	2C	.037	434.0	2.23	1.37	---	3.60	4.48
10" exposure	Inst	SF	Lg	2C	.021	770.0	1.63	.78	---	2.41	2.96
	Inst	SF	Sm	2C	.030	539.0	1.85	1.11	---	2.96	3.68

Cut-up wall

Description	Oper	Unit	Vol	Crew Size	Man-hours per Unit	Crew Output per Day	Avg Mat'l Unit Cost	Avg Labor Unit Cost	Avg Equip Unit Cost	Avg Total Unit Cost	Avg Price Incl O&P
8" exposure	Inst	SF	Lg	2C	.031	520.0	2.59	1.15	---	3.74	4.59
	Inst	SF	Sm	2C	.044	364.0	2.93	1.63	---	4.56	5.65
10" exposure	Inst	SF	Lg	2C	.025	640.0	2.24	.93	---	3.17	3.87
	Inst	SF	Sm	2C	.036	448.0	2.54	1.33	---	3.87	4.79

Corrugated (2-1/2"), 26" W, 2-1/2" side lap, 4" end lap

Description	Oper	Unit	Vol	Crew Size	Man-hours per Unit	Crew Output per Day	Avg Mat'l Unit Cost	Avg Labor Unit Cost	Avg Equip Unit Cost	Avg Total Unit Cost	Avg Price Incl O&P
	Demo	SF	Lg	LB	.013	1200	---	.39	---	.39	.55
	Demo	SF	Sm	LB	.019	840.0	---	.57	---	.57	.80

0.0175" thick

Description	Oper	Unit	Vol	Crew Size	Man-hours per Unit	Crew Output per Day	Avg Mat'l Unit Cost	Avg Labor Unit Cost	Avg Equip Unit Cost	Avg Total Unit Cost	Avg Price Incl O&P
Natural	Inst	SF	Lg	UC	.019	1660	2.26	.68	---	2.94	3.57
	Inst	SF	Sm	UC	.028	1162	2.56	1.00	---	3.56	4.37
Painted	Inst	SF	Lg	UC	.019	1660	2.46	.68	---	3.14	3.80
	Inst	SF	Sm	UC	.028	1162	2.78	1.00	---	3.78	4.62

0.019" thick

Description	Oper	Unit	Vol	Crew Size	Man-hours per Unit	Crew Output per Day	Avg Mat'l Unit Cost	Avg Labor Unit Cost	Avg Equip Unit Cost	Avg Total Unit Cost	Avg Price Incl O&P
Natural	Inst	SF	Lg	UC	.019	1660	2.30	.68	---	2.98	3.61
	Inst	SF	Sm	UC	.028	1162	2.61	1.00	---	3.61	4.43
Painted	Inst	SF	Lg	UC	.019	1660	2.50	.68	---	3.18	3.84
	Inst	SF	Sm	UC	.028	1162	2.82	1.00	---	3.82	4.67

Panels, 4' x 8' board and batten (12" oc)

Description	Oper	Unit	Vol	Crew Size	Man-hours per Unit	Crew Output per Day	Avg Mat'l Unit Cost	Avg Labor Unit Cost	Avg Equip Unit Cost	Avg Total Unit Cost	Avg Price Incl O&P
	Demo	SF	Lg	LB	.007	2400	---	.21	---	.21	.29
	Demo	SF	Sm	LB	.010	1680	---	.30	---	.30	.42

Straight wall

Description	Oper	Unit	Vol	Crew Size	Man-hours per Unit	Crew Output per Day	Avg Mat'l Unit Cost	Avg Labor Unit Cost	Avg Equip Unit Cost	Avg Total Unit Cost	Avg Price Incl O&P
Smooth	Inst	SF	Lg	2C	.013	1220	2.02	.48	---	2.50	3.00
	Inst	SF	Sm	2C	.019	854.0	2.29	.70	---	2.99	3.62
Rough sawn	Inst	SF	Lg	2C	.013	1220	2.23	.48	---	2.71	3.24
	Inst	SF	Sm	2C	.019	854.0	2.52	.70	---	3.22	3.88

Description	Oper	Unit	Vol	Crew Size	Man-hours per Unit	Crew Output per Day	Avg Mat'l Unit Cost	Avg Labor Unit Cost	Avg Equip Unit Cost	Avg Total Unit Cost	Avg Price Incl O&P
Cut-up wall											
Smooth	Inst	SF	Lg	2C	.016	1025	2.65	.59	---	3.24	**3.88**
	Inst	SF	Sm	2C	.022	717.5	2.99	.81	---	3.80	**4.58**
Rough sawn	Inst	SF	Lg	2C	.016	1025	2.85	.59	---	3.44	**4.11**
	Inst	SF	Sm	2C	.022	717.5	3.23	.81	---	4.04	**4.85**

Shingle, 24" L with 12" exposure

Description	Oper	Unit	Vol	Crew Size	Man-hours per Unit	Crew Output per Day	Avg Mat'l Unit Cost	Avg Labor Unit Cost	Avg Equip Unit Cost	Avg Total Unit Cost	Avg Price Incl O&P
	Demo	SF	Lg	LB	.011	1450	---	.33	---	.33	**.46**
	Demo	SF	Sm	LB	.016	1015	---	.48	---	.48	**.67**
Straight wall	Inst	SF	Lg	2C	.018	890.0	.04	.67	---	.71	**.98**
	Inst	SF	Sm	2C	.026	623.0	.05	.96	---	1.01	**1.41**
Cut-up wall	Inst	SF	Lg	2C	.023	710.0	.05	.85	---	.90	**1.25**
	Inst	SF	Sm	2C	.032	497.0	.05	1.18	---	1.23	**1.72**

Hardboard siding, Masonite

Lap, 1/2" T x 12" W x 16' L, with 11" exposure

Description	Oper	Unit	Vol	Crew Size	Man-hours per Unit	Crew Output per Day	Avg Mat'l Unit Cost	Avg Labor Unit Cost	Avg Equip Unit Cost	Avg Total Unit Cost	Avg Price Incl O&P
	Demo	SF	Lg	LB	.012	1345	---	.36	---	.36	**.50**
	Demo	SF	Sm	LB	.017	941.5	---	.51	---	.51	**.71**
Straight wall											
Smooth finish	Inst	SF	Lg	2C	.023	700.0	1.28	.85	---	2.13	**2.66**
	Inst	SF	Sm	2C	.033	490.0	1.45	1.22	---	2.67	**3.38**
Textured finish	Inst	SF	Lg	2C	.023	700.0	1.52	.85	---	2.37	**2.94**
	Inst	SF	Sm	2C	.033	490.0	1.72	1.22	---	2.94	**3.69**
Wood-like finish	Inst	SF	Lg	2C	.023	700.0	1.62	.85	---	2.47	**3.06**
	Inst	SF	Sm	2C	.033	490.0	1.83	1.22	---	3.05	**3.81**
Cut-up wall											
Smooth finish	Inst	SF	Lg	2C	.027	585.0	1.32	1.00	---	2.32	**2.92**
	Inst	SF	Sm	2C	.039	409.5	1.49	1.44	---	2.93	**3.73**
Textured finish	Inst	SF	Lg	2C	.027	585.0	1.56	1.00	---	2.56	**3.19**
	Inst	SF	Sm	2C	.039	409.5	1.76	1.44	---	3.20	**4.05**
Wood-like finish	Inst	SF	Lg	2C	.027	585.0	1.67	1.00	---	2.67	**3.32**
	Inst	SF	Sm	2C	.039	409.5	1.88	1.44	---	3.32	**4.18**

Description	Oper	Unit	Vol	Crew Size	Man-hours per Unit	Crew Output per Day	Avg Mat'l Unit Cost	Avg Labor Unit Cost	Avg Equip Unit Cost	Avg Total Unit Cost	Avg Price Incl O&P
Panels, 7/16" T x 4' W x 8' H											
	Demo	SF	Lg	LB	.006	2520	---	.18	---	.18	.25
	Demo	SF	Sm	LB	.009	1764	---	.27	---	.27	.38
Grooved/planked panels, textured or wood-like finish											
Primecote	Inst	SF	Lg	2C	.013	1215	1.22	.48	---	1.70	2.08
	Inst	SF	Sm	2C	.019	850.5	1.37	.70	---	2.07	2.56
Unprimed	Inst	SF	Lg	2C	.013	1215	1.32	.48	---	1.80	2.19
	Inst	SF	Sm	2C	.019	850.5	1.48	.70	---	2.18	2.69
Panel with batten preattached											
Unprimed	Inst	SF	Lg	2C	.013	1215	1.38	.48	---	1.86	2.26
	Inst	SF	Sm	2C	.019	850.5	1.56	.70	---	2.26	2.78
Stucco textured panel											
Primecote	Inst	SF	Lg	2C	.013	1215	1.42	.48	---	1.90	2.31
	Inst	SF	Sm	2C	.019	850.5	1.61	.70	---	2.31	2.84

Vinyl

Solid vinyl panels .024 gauge, woodgrained or colors

Description	Oper	Unit	Vol	Crew Size	Man-hours per Unit	Crew Output per Day	Avg Mat'l Unit Cost	Avg Labor Unit Cost	Avg Equip Unit Cost	Avg Total Unit Cost	Avg Price Incl O&P
10" or double 5" panels	Demo	SF	Lg	LB	.012	1345	---	.36	---	.36	.50
	Demo	SF	Sm	LB	.017	941.5	---	.51	---	.51	.71
10" or double 5" panels, standard											
	Inst	SF	Lg	2C	.032	500.0	1.46	1.18	---	2.64	3.34
	Inst	SF	Sm	2C	.046	350.0	1.65	1.70	---	3.35	4.28
10" or double 5" panels, insulated											
	Inst	SF	Lg	2C	.032	500.0	1.82	1.18	---	3.00	3.75
	Inst	SF	Sm	2C	.046	350.0	2.06	1.70	---	3.76	4.75
Starter strip	Inst	LF	Lg	2C	.040	400.0	.30	1.48	---	1.78	2.42
	Inst	LF	Sm	2C	.057	280.0	.34	2.11	---	2.45	3.35
J channel for corners	Inst	LF	Lg	2C	.036	450.0	.71	1.33	---	2.04	2.68
	Inst	LF	Sm	2C	.051	315.0	.81	1.89	---	2.70	3.57
Outside corner and corner post											
	Inst	LF	Lg	2C	.040	400.0	1.05	1.48	---	2.53	3.28
	Inst	LF	Sm	2C	.057	280.0	1.19	2.11	---	3.30	4.32
Casing and trim	Inst	LF	Lg	2C	.046	350.0	.55	1.70	---	2.25	3.02
	Inst	LF	Sm	2C	.065	245.0	.62	2.41	---	3.03	4.08
Soffit and fascia	Inst	LF	Lg	2C	.040	400.0	.78	1.48	---	2.26	2.97
	Inst	LF	Sm	2C	.057	280.0	.88	2.11	---	2.99	3.97

Wood

Bevel

Description	Oper	Unit	Vol	Crew Size	Man-hours per Unit	Crew Output per Day	Avg Mat'l Unit Cost	Avg Labor Unit Cost	Avg Equip Unit Cost	Avg Total Unit Cost	Avg Price Incl O&P
1/2" x 8" with 6-3/4" exp.	Demo	SF	Lg	LB	.018	910.0	---	.54	---	.54	.76
	Demo	SF	Sm	LB	.025	637.0	---	.75	---	.75	1.05
5/8" x 10" with 8-3/4" exp.	Demo	SF	Lg	LB	.014	1180	---	.42	---	.42	.59
	Demo	SF	Sm	LB	.019	826.0	---	.57	---	.57	.80
3/4" x 12" with 10-3/4" exp.	Demo	SF	Lg	LB	.011	1450	---	.33	---	.33	.46
	Demo	SF	Sm	LB	.016	1015	---	.48	---	.48	.67

Description	Oper	Unit	Vol	Crew Size	Man-hours per Unit	Crew Output per Day	Avg Mat'l Unit Cost	Avg Labor Unit Cost	Avg Equip Unit Cost	Avg Total Unit Cost	Avg Price Incl O&P

Bevel (horizontal), 1/2" lap, 10' L

Redwood, kiln-dried, clear VG, pattern

1/2" x 8", with 6-3/4" exp.

Description	Oper	Unit	Vol	Crew Size	Man-hours per Unit	Crew Output per Day	Avg Mat'l Unit Cost	Avg Labor Unit Cost	Avg Equip Unit Cost	Avg Total Unit Cost	Avg Price Incl O&P
Rough ends	Inst	SF	Lg	2C	.037	435.0	2.40	1.37	---	3.77	**4.68**
	Inst	SF	Sm	2C	.053	304.5	2.71	1.96	---	4.67	**5.86**
Fitted ends	Inst	SF	Lg	2C	.048	335.0	2.46	1.78	---	4.24	**5.32**
	Inst	SF	Sm	2C	.068	234.5	2.77	2.52	---	5.29	**6.71**
Mitered ends	Inst	SF	Lg	2C	.056	285.0	2.52	2.07	---	4.59	**5.80**
	Inst	SF	Sm	2C	.080	199.5	2.84	2.96	---	5.80	**7.41**

5/8" x 10", with 8-3/4" exp.

Description	Oper	Unit	Vol	Crew Size	Man-hours per Unit	Crew Output per Day	Avg Mat'l Unit Cost	Avg Labor Unit Cost	Avg Equip Unit Cost	Avg Total Unit Cost	Avg Price Incl O&P
Rough ends	Inst	SF	Lg	2C	.029	560.0	2.35	1.07	---	3.42	**4.21**
	Inst	SF	Sm	2C	.041	392.0	2.64	1.52	---	4.16	**5.16**
Fitted ends	Inst	SF	Lg	2C	.037	430.0	2.40	1.37	---	3.77	**4.68**
	Inst	SF	Sm	2C	.053	301.0	2.71	1.96	---	4.67	**5.86**
Mitered ends	Inst	SF	Lg	2C	.043	370.0	2.46	1.59	---	4.05	**5.06**
	Inst	SF	Sm	2C	.062	259.0	2.77	2.30	---	5.07	**6.40**

3/4" x 12", with 10-3/4" exp.

Description	Oper	Unit	Vol	Crew Size	Man-hours per Unit	Crew Output per Day	Avg Mat'l Unit Cost	Avg Labor Unit Cost	Avg Equip Unit Cost	Avg Total Unit Cost	Avg Price Incl O&P
Rough ends	Inst	SF	Lg	2C	.023	690.0	4.06	.85	---	4.91	**5.86**
	Inst	SF	Sm	2C	.033	483.0	4.58	1.22	---	5.80	**6.98**
Fitted ends	Inst	SF	Lg	2C	.030	530.0	4.17	1.11	---	5.28	**6.35**
	Inst	SF	Sm	2C	.043	371.0	4.70	1.59	---	6.29	**7.63**
Mitered ends	Inst	SF	Lg	2C	.035	455.0	4.27	1.30	---	5.57	**6.72**
	Inst	SF	Sm	2C	.050	318.5	4.82	1.85	---	6.67	**8.13**

Red cedar, clear, kiln-dried

1/2" x 8", with 6-3/4" exp.

Description	Oper	Unit	Vol	Crew Size	Man-hours per Unit	Crew Output per Day	Avg Mat'l Unit Cost	Avg Labor Unit Cost	Avg Equip Unit Cost	Avg Total Unit Cost	Avg Price Incl O&P
Rough ends	Inst	SF	Lg	2C	.037	435.0	2.12	1.37	---	3.49	**4.36**
	Inst	SF	Sm	2C	.053	304.5	2.39	1.96	---	4.35	**5.50**
Fitted ends	Inst	SF	Lg	2C	.048	335.0	2.17	1.78	---	3.95	**4.98**
	Inst	SF	Sm	2C	.068	234.5	2.45	2.52	---	4.97	**6.34**
Mitered ends	Inst	SF	Lg	2C	.056	285.0	2.22	2.07	---	4.29	**5.46**
	Inst	SF	Sm	2C	.080	199.5	2.50	2.96	---	5.46	**7.02**

5/8" x 10", with 8-3/4" exp.

Description	Oper	Unit	Vol	Crew Size	Man-hours per Unit	Crew Output per Day	Avg Mat'l Unit Cost	Avg Labor Unit Cost	Avg Equip Unit Cost	Avg Total Unit Cost	Avg Price Incl O&P
Rough ends	Inst	SF	Lg	2C	.029	560.0	2.22	1.07	---	3.29	**4.06**
	Inst	SF	Sm	2C	.041	392.0	2.52	1.52	---	4.04	**5.02**
Fitted ends	Inst	SF	Lg	2C	.037	430.0	2.28	1.37	---	3.65	**4.54**
	Inst	SF	Sm	2C	.053	301.0	2.58	1.96	---	4.54	**5.71**
Mitered ends	Inst	SF	Lg	2C	.043	370.0	2.33	1.59	---	3.92	**4.91**
	Inst	SF	Sm	2C	.062	259.0	2.64	2.30	---	4.94	**6.25**

3/4" x 12", with 10-3/4" exp.

Description	Oper	Unit	Vol	Crew Size	Man-hours per Unit	Crew Output per Day	Avg Mat'l Unit Cost	Avg Labor Unit Cost	Avg Equip Unit Cost	Avg Total Unit Cost	Avg Price Incl O&P
Rough ends	Inst	SF	Lg	2C	.023	690.0	3.67	.85	---	4.52	**5.41**
	Inst	SF	Sm	2C	.033	483.0	4.15	1.22	---	5.37	**6.48**
Fitted ends	Inst	SF	Lg	2C	.030	530.0	3.77	1.11	---	4.88	**5.89**
	Inst	SF	Sm	2C	.043	371.0	4.25	1.59	---	5.84	**7.12**
Mitered ends	Inst	SF	Lg	2C	.035	455.0	3.86	1.30	---	5.16	**6.25**
	Inst	SF	Sm	2C	.050	318.5	4.36	1.85	---	6.21	**7.61**

Description	Oper	Unit	Vol	Crew Size	Man-hours per Unit	Crew Output per Day	Avg Mat'l Unit Cost	Avg Labor Unit Cost	Avg Equip Unit Cost	Avg Total Unit Cost	Avg Price Incl O&P

Drop (horizontal) T&G, 1/4" lap

Description	Oper	Unit	Vol	Crew Size	Man-hours per Unit	Crew Output per Day	Avg Mat'l Unit Cost	Avg Labor Unit Cost	Avg Equip Unit Cost	Avg Total Unit Cost	Avg Price Incl O&P
1" x 8" with 7" exp.	Demo	SF	Lg	LB	.017	945.0	---	.51	---	.51	.71
	Demo	SF	Sm	LB	.024	661.5	---	.72	---	.72	1.01
1" x 10" with 9" exp.	Demo	SF	Lg	LB	.013	1215	---	.39	---	.39	.55
	Demo	SF	Sm	LB	.019	850.5	---	.57	---	.57	.80

Drop (horizontal) T&G, 1/4" lap, 10' L (avg.)

Redwood, kiln-dried, clear VG, patterns

1" x 8", with 7" exp.

Description	Oper	Unit	Vol	Crew Size	Man-hours per Unit	Crew Output per Day	Avg Mat'l Unit Cost	Avg Labor Unit Cost	Avg Equip Unit Cost	Avg Total Unit Cost	Avg Price Incl O&P
Rough ends	Inst	SF	Lg	2C	.034	465.0	3.94	1.26	---	5.20	6.29
	Inst	SF	Sm	2C	.049	325.5	4.44	1.81	---	6.25	7.65
Fitted ends	Inst	SF	Lg	2C	.044	360.0	4.03	1.63	---	5.66	6.92
	Inst	SF	Sm	2C	.063	252.0	4.54	2.33	---	6.87	8.49
Mitered ends	Inst	SF	Lg	2C	.051	315.0	4.13	1.89	---	6.02	7.39
	Inst	SF	Sm	2C	.073	220.5	4.65	2.70	---	7.35	9.13

1" x 10", with 9" exp.

Description	Oper	Unit	Vol	Crew Size	Man-hours per Unit	Crew Output per Day	Avg Mat'l Unit Cost	Avg Labor Unit Cost	Avg Equip Unit Cost	Avg Total Unit Cost	Avg Price Incl O&P
Rough ends	Inst	SF	Lg	2C	.027	600.0	4.13	1.00	---	5.13	6.15
	Inst	SF	Sm	2C	.038	420.0	4.66	1.41	---	6.07	7.33
Fitted ends	Inst	SF	Lg	2C	.034	465.0	4.23	1.26	---	5.49	6.63
	Inst	SF	Sm	2C	.049	325.5	4.77	1.81	---	6.58	8.03
Mitered ends	Inst	SF	Lg	2C	.040	405.0	4.33	1.48	---	5.81	7.05
	Inst	SF	Sm	2C	.056	283.5	4.89	2.07	---	6.96	8.53

1" x 8", with 7-3/4" exp.

Description	Oper	Unit	Vol	Crew Size	Man-hours per Unit	Crew Output per Day	Avg Mat'l Unit Cost	Avg Labor Unit Cost	Avg Equip Unit Cost	Avg Total Unit Cost	Avg Price Incl O&P
Rough ends	Inst	SF	Lg	2C	.031	515.0	3.57	1.15	---	4.72	5.71
	Inst	SF	Sm	2C	.044	360.5	4.03	1.63	---	5.66	6.92
Fitted ends	Inst	SF	Lg	2C	.040	400.0	3.67	1.48	---	5.15	6.29
	Inst	SF	Sm	2C	.057	280.0	4.13	2.11	---	6.24	7.70
Mitered ends	Inst	SF	Lg	2C	.046	350.0	3.76	1.70	---	5.46	6.71
	Inst	SF	Sm	2C	.065	245.0	4.24	2.41	---	6.65	8.24

1" x 10", with 9-3/4" exp.

Description	Oper	Unit	Vol	Crew Size	Man-hours per Unit	Crew Output per Day	Avg Mat'l Unit Cost	Avg Labor Unit Cost	Avg Equip Unit Cost	Avg Total Unit Cost	Avg Price Incl O&P
Rough ends	Inst	SF	Lg	2C	.025	650.0	3.84	.93	---	4.77	5.71
	Inst	SF	Sm	2C	.035	455.0	4.33	1.30	---	5.63	6.79
Fitted ends	Inst	SF	Lg	2C	.032	505.0	3.94	1.18	---	5.12	6.19
	Inst	SF	Sm	2C	.045	353.5	4.44	1.67	---	6.11	7.44
Mitered ends	Inst	SF	Lg	2C	.036	440.0	4.04	1.33	---	5.37	6.51
	Inst	SF	Sm	2C	.052	308.0	4.56	1.93	---	6.49	7.94

Description	Oper	Unit	Vol	Crew Size	Man-hours per Unit	Crew Output per Day	Avg Mat'l Unit Cost	Avg Labor Unit Cost	Avg Equip Unit Cost	Avg Total Unit Cost	Avg Price Incl O&P
Red cedar, clear, kiln-dried											
1" x 8", with 7" exp.											
Rough ends	Inst	SF	Lg	2C	.034	465.0	3.59	1.26	---	4.85	**5.89**
	Inst	SF	Sm	2C	.049	325.5	4.06	1.81	---	5.87	**7.21**
Fitted ends	Inst	SF	Lg	2C	.044	360.0	3.68	1.63	---	5.31	**6.51**
	Inst	SF	Sm	2C	.063	252.0	4.15	2.33	---	6.48	**8.04**
Mitered ends	Inst	SF	Lg	2C	.051	315.0	3.76	1.89	---	5.65	**6.97**
	Inst	SF	Sm	2C	.073	220.5	4.25	2.70	---	6.95	**8.67**
1" x 10", with 9" exp.											
Rough ends	Inst	SF	Lg	2C	.027	600.0	3.71	1.00	---	4.71	**5.67**
	Inst	SF	Sm	2C	.038	420.0	4.19	1.41	---	5.60	**6.79**
Fitted ends	Inst	SF	Lg	2C	.034	465.0	3.80	1.26	---	5.06	**6.13**
	Inst	SF	Sm	2C	.049	325.5	4.30	1.81	---	6.11	**7.48**
Mitered ends	Inst	SF	Lg	2C	.040	405.0	3.90	1.48	---	5.38	**6.56**
	Inst	SF	Sm	2C	.056	283.5	4.40	2.07	---	6.47	**7.96**
Pine, kiln-dried, select (Rough sawn)											
1" x 8", with 7-3/4" exp.											
Rough ends	Inst	SF	Lg	2C	.031	515.0	2.51	1.15	---	3.66	**4.49**
	Inst	SF	Sm	2C	.044	360.5	2.83	1.63	---	4.46	**5.54**
Fitted ends	Inst	SF	Lg	2C	.040	400.0	2.57	1.48	---	4.05	**5.03**
	Inst	SF	Sm	2C	.057	280.0	2.90	2.11	---	5.01	**6.29**
Mitered ends	Inst	SF	Lg	2C	.046	350.0	2.64	1.70	---	4.34	**5.42**
	Inst	SF	Sm	2C	.065	245.0	2.98	2.41	---	5.39	**6.80**
1" x 10", with 9-3/4" exp.											
Rough ends	Inst	SF	Lg	2C	.025	650.0	3.16	.93	---	4.09	**4.93**
	Inst	SF	Sm	2C	.035	455.0	3.58	1.30	---	4.88	**5.93**
Fitted ends	Inst	SF	Lg	2C	.032	505.0	3.25	1.18	---	4.43	**5.40**
	Inst	SF	Sm	2C	.045	353.5	3.67	1.67	---	5.34	**6.55**
Mitered ends	Inst	SF	Lg	2C	.036	440.0	3.33	1.33	---	4.66	**5.70**
	Inst	SF	Sm	2C	.052	308.0	3.77	1.93	---	5.70	**7.03**
(Dressed/milled)											
1" x 8", with 7" exp.											
Rough ends	Inst	SF	Lg	2C	.034	465.0	3.00	1.26	---	4.26	**5.21**
	Inst	SF	Sm	2C	.049	325.5	3.39	1.81	---	5.20	**6.44**
Fitted ends	Inst	SF	Lg	2C	.044	360.0	3.07	1.63	---	4.70	**5.81**
	Inst	SF	Sm	2C	.063	252.0	3.47	2.33	---	5.80	**7.26**
Mitered ends	Inst	SF	Lg	2C	.051	315.0	3.15	1.89	---	5.04	**6.27**
	Inst	SF	Sm	2C	.073	220.5	3.55	2.70	---	6.25	**7.87**
1" x 10", with 9" exp.											
Rough ends	Inst	SF	Lg	2C	.027	600.0	3.74	1.00	---	4.74	**5.70**
	Inst	SF	Sm	2C	.038	420.0	4.22	1.41	---	5.63	**6.82**
Fitted ends	Inst	SF	Lg	2C	.034	465.0	3.83	1.26	---	5.09	**6.17**
	Inst	SF	Sm	2C	.049	325.5	4.32	1.81	---	6.13	**7.51**
Mitered ends	Inst	SF	Lg	2C	.040	405.0	3.92	1.48	---	5.40	**6.58**
	Inst	SF	Sm	2C	.056	283.5	4.43	2.07	---	6.50	**8.00**

Description	Oper	Unit	Vol	Crew Size	Man-hours per Unit	Crew Output per Day	Avg Mat'l Unit Cost	Avg Labor Unit Cost	Avg Equip Unit Cost	Avg Total Unit Cost	Avg Price Incl O&P

Board (1" x 12") and batten (1" x 2", 12" oc)

Horizontal

| | Demo | SF | Lg | LB | .013 | 1280 | --- | .39 | --- | .39 | .55 |
| | Demo | SF | Sm | LB | .018 | 896.0 | --- | .54 | --- | .54 | .76 |

Vertical

Standard

| | Demo | SF | Lg | LB | .016 | 1025 | --- | .48 | --- | .48 | .67 |
| | Demo | SF | Sm | LB | .022 | 717.5 | --- | .66 | --- | .66 | .92 |

Reverse

| | Demo | SF | Lg | LB | .015 | 1065 | --- | .45 | --- | .45 | .63 |
| | Demo | SF | Sm | LB | .021 | 745.5 | --- | .63 | --- | .63 | .88 |

Board (1" x 12") and batten (1" x 2", 12" oc); rough sawn, common, standard and better, green

Horizontal application, @ 10' L

Redwood	Inst	SF	Lg	2C	.029	560.0	1.85	1.07	---	2.92	3.63
	Inst	SF	Sm	2C	.041	392.0	2.08	1.52	---	3.60	4.52
Red cedar	Inst	SF	Lg	2C	.029	560.0	1.40	1.07	---	2.47	3.11
	Inst	SF	Sm	2C	.041	392.0	1.70	1.52	---	3.22	4.08
Pine	Inst	SF	Lg	2C	.029	560.0	1.83	1.07	---	2.90	3.61
	Inst	SF	Sm	2C	.041	392.0	2.07	1.52	---	3.59	4.51

Vertical, std. (batten on board), @ 8' L

Redwood	Inst	SF	Lg	2C	.036	450.0	1.85	1.33	---	3.18	3.99
	Inst	SF	Sm	2C	.051	315.0	2.08	1.89	---	3.97	5.04
Red cedar	Inst	SF	Lg	2C	.036	450.0	1.40	1.33	---	2.73	3.48
	Inst	SF	Sm	2C	.051	315.0	1.70	1.89	---	3.59	4.60
Pine	Inst	SF	Lg	2C	.036	450.0	1.83	1.33	---	3.16	3.97
	Inst	SF	Sm	2C	.051	315.0	2.07	1.89	---	3.96	5.02

Vertical, reverse (board on batten), @ 8' L

Redwood	Inst	SF	Lg	2C	.036	440.0	1.85	1.33	---	3.18	3.99
	Inst	SF	Sm	2C	.052	308.0	2.08	1.93	---	4.01	5.09
Red cedar	Inst	SF	Lg	2C	.036	440.0	1.40	1.33	---	2.73	3.48
	Inst	SF	Sm	2C	.052	308.0	1.70	1.93	---	3.63	4.65
Pine	Inst	SF	Lg	2C	.036	440.0	1.83	1.33	---	3.16	3.97
	Inst	SF	Sm	2C	.052	308.0	2.07	1.93	---	4.00	5.08

Board on board (1" x 12" with 1-1/2" overlap), vertical

| | Demo | SF | Lg | LB | .017 | 950.0 | --- | .51 | --- | .51 | .71 |
| | Demo | SF | Sm | LB | .024 | 665.0 | --- | .72 | --- | .72 | 1.01 |

Board on board (1" x 12" with 1-1/2" overlap) rough sawn common, standard & better green, 8' L; vertica

Redwood	Inst	SF	Lg	2C	.027	590.0	1.78	1.00	---	2.78	3.45
	Inst	SF	Sm	2C	.039	413.0	2.00	1.44	---	3.44	4.32
Red cedar	Inst	SF	Lg	2C	.027	590.0	1.38	1.00	---	2.38	2.99
	Inst	SF	Sm	2C	.039	413.0	1.69	1.44	---	3.13	3.96
Pine	Inst	SF	Lg	2C	.027	590.0	1.86	1.00	---	2.86	3.54
	Inst	SF	Sm	2C	.039	413.0	2.11	1.44	---	3.55	4.45

Description	Oper	Unit	Vol	Crew Size	Man-hours per Unit	Crew Output per Day	Avg Mat'l Unit Cost	Avg Labor Unit Cost	Avg Equip Unit Cost	Avg Total Unit Cost	Avg Price Incl O&P

Plywood (1/2" T) with battens (1" x 2")

Description	Oper	Unit	Vol	Crew Size	Man-hours per Unit	Crew Output per Day	Avg Mat'l Unit Cost	Avg Labor Unit Cost	Avg Equip Unit Cost	Avg Total Unit Cost	Avg Price Incl O&P
16" oc battens	Demo	SF	Lg	LB	.007	2255	---	.21	---	.21	**.29**
	Demo	SF	Sm	LB	.010	1579	---	.30	---	.30	**.42**
24" oc battens	Demo	SF	Lg	LB	.007	2365	---	.21	---	.21	**.29**
	Demo	SF	Sm	LB	.010	1656	---	.30	---	.30	**.42**

Plywood (1/2" T) sanded exterior, AB grade with battens (1" x 2") S4S, common, standard & better green

16" oc

Description	Oper	Unit	Vol	Crew Size	Man-hours per Unit	Crew Output per Day	Avg Mat'l Unit Cost	Avg Labor Unit Cost	Avg Equip Unit Cost	Avg Total Unit Cost	Avg Price Incl O&P
Fir	Inst	SF	Lg	2C	.022	735.0	1.33	.81	---	2.14	**2.67**
	Inst	SF	Sm	2C	.031	514.5	1.49	1.15	---	2.64	**3.32**
Pine	Inst	SF	Lg	2C	.022	735.0	1.36	.81	---	2.17	**2.70**
	Inst	SF	Sm	2C	.031	514.5	1.53	1.15	---	2.68	**3.37**

24" oc

Description	Oper	Unit	Vol	Crew Size	Man-hours per Unit	Crew Output per Day	Avg Mat'l Unit Cost	Avg Labor Unit Cost	Avg Equip Unit Cost	Avg Total Unit Cost	Avg Price Incl O&P
Fir	Inst	SF	Lg	2C	.018	865.0	1.29	.67	---	1.96	**2.42**
	Inst	SF	Sm	2C	.026	605.5	1.45	.96	---	2.41	**3.02**
Pine	Inst	SF	Lg	2C	.018	865.0	1.31	.67	---	1.98	**2.44**
	Inst	SF	Sm	2C	.026	605.5	1.47	.96	---	2.43	**3.04**

Shakes only, no sheathing included

24" L with 11-1/2" exposure

Description	Oper	Unit	Vol	Crew Size	Man-hours per Unit	Crew Output per Day	Avg Mat'l Unit Cost	Avg Labor Unit Cost	Avg Equip Unit Cost	Avg Total Unit Cost	Avg Price Incl O&P
1/2" to 3/4" T	Demo	SF	Lg	LB	.010	1600	---	.30	---	.30	**.42**
	Demo	SF	Sm	LB	.014	1120	---	.42	---	.42	**.59**
3/4" to 5/4" T	Demo	SF	Lg	LB	.011	1440	---	.33	---	.33	**.46**
	Demo	SF	Sm	LB	.016	1008	---	.48	---	.48	**.67**

Shakes only, over sheathing, 2 nails/shake

24" L with 11-1/2" exp., @ 6" W, red cedar, sawn one side
Straight wall

Description	Oper	Unit	Vol	Crew Size	Man-hours per Unit	Crew Output per Day	Avg Mat'l Unit Cost	Avg Labor Unit Cost	Avg Equip Unit Cost	Avg Total Unit Cost	Avg Price Incl O&P
1/2" to 3/4" T	Inst	SF	Lg	CN	.021	940.0	2.02	.75	---	2.77	**3.37**
	Inst	SF	Sm	CN	.030	658.0	2.29	1.07	---	3.36	**4.13**
3/4" to 5/4" T	Inst	SF	Lg	CN	.024	850.0	2.69	.85	---	3.54	**4.29**
	Inst	SF	Sm	CN	.034	595.0	3.04	1.21	---	4.25	**5.19**

Cut-up wall

Description	Oper	Unit	Vol	Crew Size	Man-hours per Unit	Crew Output per Day	Avg Mat'l Unit Cost	Avg Labor Unit Cost	Avg Equip Unit Cost	Avg Total Unit Cost	Avg Price Incl O&P
1/2" to 3/4" T	Inst	SF	Lg	CN	.027	750.0	2.06	.96	---	3.02	**3.72**
	Inst	SF	Sm	CN	.038	525.0	2.33	1.35	---	3.68	**4.57**
3/4" to 5/4" T	Inst	SF	Lg	CN	.029	680.0	2.74	1.03	---	3.77	**4.60**
	Inst	SF	Sm	CN	.042	476.0	3.10	1.50	---	4.60	**5.66**

Related materials and operations
Rosin sized sheathing paper, 36" W 500 SF/roll; nailed

Description	Oper	Unit	Vol	Crew Size	Man-hours per Unit	Crew Output per Day	Avg Mat'l Unit Cost	Avg Labor Unit Cost	Avg Equip Unit Cost	Avg Total Unit Cost	Avg Price Incl O&P
Over solid sheathing	Inst	SF	Lg	2C	.001	12500	.21	.04	---	.25	**.29**
	Inst	SF	Sm	2C	.002	8750	.24	.07	---	.31	**.38**

Description	Oper	Unit	Vol	Crew Size	Man-hours per Unit	Crew Output per Day	Avg Mat'l Unit Cost	Avg Labor Unit Cost	Avg Equip Unit Cost	Avg Total Unit Cost	Avg Price Incl O&P
Shingles only, no sheathing included											
16" L with 7-1/2" exposure	Demo	SF	Lg	LB	.016	1000	---	.48	---	.48	**.67**
	Demo	SF	Sm	LB	.023	700.0	---	.69	---	.69	**.97**
18" L with 8-1/2" exposure	Demo	SF	Lg	LB	.014	1130	---	.42	---	.42	**.59**
	Demo	SF	Sm	LB	.020	791.0	---	.60	---	.60	**.84**
24" L with 11-1/2" exposure	Demo	SF	Lg	LB	.010	1530	---	.30	---	.30	**.42**
	Demo	SF	Sm	LB	.015	1071	---	.45	---	.45	**.63**
Shingles only, red cedar, No 1. perfect, @ 4" W, 2 nails/shake, over sheathing											
Straight wall											
16" L with 7-1/2" exposure	Inst	SF	Lg	2C	.027	585.0	2.59	1.00	---	3.59	**4.38**
	Inst	SF	Sm	2C	.039	409.5	2.92	1.44	---	4.36	**5.38**
18" L with 8-1/2" exposure	Inst	SF	Lg	2C	.024	660.0	2.08	.89	---	2.97	**3.64**
	Inst	SF	Sm	2C	.035	462.0	2.35	1.30	---	3.65	**4.52**
24" L with 11-1/2" exposure	Inst	SF	Lg	2C	.018	895.0	2.42	.67	---	3.09	**3.72**
	Inst	SF	Sm	2C	.026	626.5	2.73	.96	---	3.69	**4.49**
Cut-up wall											
16" L with 7-1/2" exposure	Inst	SF	Lg	2C	.034	470.0	2.64	1.26	---	3.90	**4.80**
	Inst	SF	Sm	2C	.049	329.0	2.98	1.81	---	4.79	**5.97**
18" L with 8-1/2" exposure	Inst	SF	Lg	2C	.030	530.0	2.11	1.11	---	3.22	**3.98**
	Inst	SF	Sm	2C	.043	371.0	2.39	1.59	---	3.98	**4.98**
24" L with 11-1/2" exposure	Inst	SF	Lg	2C	.022	715.0	2.46	.81	---	3.27	**3.97**
	Inst	SF	Sm	2C	.032	500.5	2.78	1.18	---	3.96	**4.86**
Related materials and operations											
Rosin sized sheathing paper, 36" W 500 SF/roll; nailed											
Over solid sheathing	Inst	SF	Lg	2C	.001	12500	.21	.04	---	.25	**.29**
	Inst	SF	Sm	2C	.002	8750	.24	.07	---	.31	**.38**

Description	Oper	Unit	Vol	Crew Size	Man-hours per Unit	Crew Output per Day	Avg Mat'l Unit Cost	Avg Labor Unit Cost	Avg Equip Unit Cost	Avg Total Unit Cost	Avg Price Incl O&P

Sinks

Frequently encountered applications

Bathroom Sinks or Lavatories

To only remove and reset lavatory

| | Reset | Ea | Lg | SA | 2.00 | 4.00 | 23.00 | 86.00 | --- | 109.00 | **151.00** |
| | Reset | Ea | Sm | SA | 2.67 | 3.00 | 26.80 | 115.00 | --- | 141.80 | **197.00** |

To install lavatory rough-in

| | Inst | Ea | Lg | SA | 6.67 | 1.20 | 170.00 | 287.00 | --- | 457.00 | **612.00** |
| | Inst | Ea | Sm | SA | 8.89 | 0.90 | 198.00 | 382.00 | --- | 580.00 | **782.00** |

To install lavatory (material + labor), see Sections below

Kitchen / Bar / Utility Sinks

To only remove and reset sink

Single bowl	Reset	Ea	Lg	SA	2.00	4.00	23.00	86.00	---	109.00	**151.00**
	Reset	Ea	Sm	SA	2.67	3.00	26.80	115.00	---	141.80	**197.00**
Double bowl	Reset	Ea	Lg	SA	2.11	3.80	27.60	90.80	---	118.40	**163.00**
	Reset	Ea	Sm	SA	2.81	2.85	32.10	121.00	---	153.10	**212.00**
Triple bowl	Reset	Ea	Lg	SA	2.29	3.50	32.20	98.50	---	130.70	**180.00**
	Reset	Ea	Sm	SA	3.04	2.63	37.50	131.00	---	168.50	**233.00**

To install sink rough-in

| | Inst | Ea | Lg | SA | 6.67 | 1.20 | 170.00 | 287.00 | --- | 457.00 | **612.00** |
| | Inst | Ea | Sm | SA | 8.89 | 0.90 | 198.00 | 382.00 | --- | 580.00 | **782.00** |

To install sink (material + labor), see Sections below

For 18 gauge steel, ADD	Inst	%	Lg	---	---	---	50.0	---	---	---	---
	Inst	%	Sm	---	---	---	50.0	---	---	---	---

Bathroom

Lavatories (bathroom sinks), with good quality fittings and faucets, concealed overflow

Vitreous china

Countertop units, with self rim (American Standard Products)

Antiquity
24-1/2" x 18" with 8" or 4" cc

White	Inst	Ea	Lg	SA	2.67	3.00	349.00	115.00	---	464.00	**568.00**
	Inst	Ea	Sm	SA	3.56	2.25	406.00	153.00	---	559.00	**688.00**
Color	Inst	Ea	Lg	SA	2.67	3.00	391.00	115.00	---	506.00	**616.00**
	Inst	Ea	Sm	SA	3.56	2.25	455.00	153.00	---	608.00	**745.00**

Aqualyn
20" x 17" with 8" or 4" cc

White	Inst	Ea	Lg	SA	2.67	3.00	266.00	115.00	---	381.00	**472.00**
	Inst	Ea	Sm	SA	3.56	2.25	309.00	153.00	---	462.00	**578.00**
Color	Inst	Ea	Lg	SA	2.67	3.00	288.00	115.00	---	403.00	**498.00**
	Inst	Ea	Sm	SA	3.56	2.25	335.00	153.00	---	488.00	**607.00**
Premium Color	Inst	Ea	Lg	SA	2.67	3.00	300.00	115.00	---	415.00	**511.00**
	Inst	Ea	Sm	SA	3.56	2.25	349.00	153.00	---	502.00	**623.00**

Description	Oper	Unit	Vol	Crew Size	Man-hours per Unit	Crew Output per Day	Avg Mat'l Unit Cost	Avg Labor Unit Cost	Avg Equip Unit Cost	Avg Total Unit Cost	Avg Price Incl O&P
Cadet											
17" diameter with 8" or 4" cc											
White	Inst	Ea	Lg	SA	2.67	3.00	285.00	115.00	---	400.00	**495.00**
	Inst	Ea	Sm	SA	3.56	2.25	332.00	153.00	---	485.00	**604.00**
Color	Inst	Ea	Lg	SA	2.67	3.00	312.00	115.00	---	427.00	**525.00**
	Inst	Ea	Sm	SA	3.56	2.25	363.00	153.00	---	516.00	**639.00**
Premium Color	Inst	Ea	Lg	SA	2.67	3.00	327.00	115.00	---	442.00	**542.00**
	Inst	Ea	Sm	SA	3.56	2.25	380.00	153.00	---	533.00	**659.00**
Ellisse Petite											
24" x 19" with 8" or 4" cc											
White	Inst	Ea	Lg	SA	2.67	3.00	367.00	115.00	---	482.00	**588.00**
	Inst	Ea	Sm	SA	3.56	2.25	427.00	153.00	---	580.00	**713.00**
Color	Inst	Ea	Lg	SA	2.67	3.00	405.00	115.00	---	520.00	**633.00**
	Inst	Ea	Sm	SA	3.56	2.25	472.00	153.00	---	625.00	**764.00**
Premium Color	Inst	Ea	Lg	SA	2.67	3.00	439.00	115.00	---	554.00	**672.00**
	Inst	Ea	Sm	SA	3.56	2.25	511.00	153.00	---	664.00	**810.00**
Enfield											
16-5/8" diameter											
White	Inst	Ea	Lg	SA	2.67	3.00	347.00	115.00	---	462.00	**565.00**
	Inst	Ea	Sm	SA	3.56	2.25	403.00	153.00	---	556.00	**686.00**
Color	Inst	Ea	Lg	SA	2.67	3.00	388.00	115.00	---	503.00	**613.00**
	Inst	Ea	Sm	SA	3.56	2.25	452.00	153.00	---	605.00	**741.00**
Premium Color	Inst	Ea	Lg	SA	2.67	3.00	413.00	115.00	---	528.00	**642.00**
	Inst	Ea	Sm	SA	3.56	2.25	480.00	153.00	---	633.00	**775.00**
Heritage											
26" x 20" with 8" or 4" cc											
White	Inst	Ea	Lg	SA	2.67	3.00	499.00	115.00	---	614.00	**740.00**
	Inst	Ea	Sm	SA	3.56	2.25	580.00	153.00	---	733.00	**889.00**
Color	Inst	Ea	Lg	SA	2.67	3.00	665.00	115.00	---	780.00	**931.00**
	Inst	Ea	Sm	SA	3.56	2.25	774.00	153.00	---	927.00	**1110.00**
Hexalyn											
22" x 19" with 8" or 4" cc											
White	Inst	Ea	Lg	SA	2.67	3.00	345.00	115.00	---	460.00	**563.00**
	Inst	Ea	Sm	SA	3.56	2.25	401.00	153.00	---	554.00	**684.00**
Color	Inst	Ea	Lg	SA	2.67	3.00	386.00	115.00	---	501.00	**611.00**
	Inst	Ea	Sm	SA	3.56	2.25	449.00	153.00	---	602.00	**739.00**
Premium Color	Inst	Ea	Lg	SA	2.67	3.00	410.00	115.00	---	525.00	**638.00**
	Inst	Ea	Sm	SA	3.56	2.25	477.00	153.00	---	630.00	**771.00**
Mezzo, space-saving design											
23-1/2" x 22" with 8" or 4" cc w/ sealant											
White	Inst	Ea	Lg	SA	2.67	3.00	361.00	115.00	---	476.00	**581.00**
	Inst	Ea	Sm	SA	3.56	2.25	419.00	153.00	---	572.00	**704.00**
Color	Inst	Ea	Lg	SA	2.67	3.00	404.00	115.00	---	519.00	**631.00**
	Inst	Ea	Sm	SA	3.56	2.25	470.00	153.00	---	623.00	**762.00**
Premium Color	Inst	Ea	Lg	SA	2.67	3.00	431.00	115.00	---	546.00	**662.00**
	Inst	Ea	Sm	SA	3.56	2.25	501.00	153.00	---	654.00	**798.00**

Description	Oper	Unit	Vol	Crew Size	Man-hours per Unit	Crew Output per Day	Avg Mat'l Unit Cost	Avg Labor Unit Cost	Avg Equip Unit Cost	Avg Total Unit Cost	Avg Price Incl O&P
Reminiscence											
22-1/4" x 18" with 8" or 4" cc w/ sealant											
White	Inst	Ea	Lg	SA	2.67	3.00	419.00	115.00	---	534.00	**648.00**
	Inst	Ea	Sm	SA	3.56	2.25	487.00	153.00	---	640.00	**782.00**
Color	Inst	Ea	Lg	SA	2.67	3.00	477.00	115.00	---	592.00	**716.00**
	Inst	Ea	Sm	SA	3.56	2.25	555.00	153.00	---	708.00	**861.00**
Premium Color	Inst	Ea	Lg	SA	2.67	3.00	513.00	115.00	---	628.00	**757.00**
	Inst	Ea	Sm	SA	3.56	2.25	597.00	153.00	---	750.00	**909.00**
Rondalyn											
19" diameter with 8" or 4" cc											
White	Inst	Ea	Lg	SA	2.67	3.00	266.00	115.00	---	381.00	**472.00**
	Inst	Ea	Sm	SA	3.56	2.25	309.00	153.00	---	462.00	**578.00**
Color	Inst	Ea	Lg	SA	2.67	3.00	288.00	115.00	---	403.00	**498.00**
	Inst	Ea	Sm	SA	3.56	2.25	335.00	153.00	---	488.00	**607.00**
Premium Color	Inst	Ea	Lg	SA	2.67	3.00	300.00	115.00	---	415.00	**511.00**
	Inst	Ea	Sm	SA	3.56	2.25	349.00	153.00	---	502.00	**623.00**
Savona											
22" x 17" with 8" or 4" cc											
White	Inst	Ea	Lg	SA	2.67	3.00	399.00	115.00	---	514.00	**626.00**
	Inst	Ea	Sm	SA	3.56	2.25	464.00	153.00	---	617.00	**756.00**
Color	Inst	Ea	Lg	SA	2.67	3.00	454.00	115.00	---	569.00	**689.00**
	Inst	Ea	Sm	SA	3.56	2.25	529.00	153.00	---	682.00	**830.00**
Premium Color	Inst	Ea	Lg	SA	2.67	3.00	487.00	115.00	---	602.00	**726.00**
	Inst	Ea	Sm	SA	3.56	2.25	566.00	153.00	---	719.00	**873.00**
Town Square											
23" x 18-1/2" with 8" or 4" cc w/ sealant											
White	Inst	Ea	Lg	SA	2.67	3.00	371.00	115.00	---	486.00	**593.00**
	Inst	Ea	Sm	SA	3.56	2.25	431.00	153.00	---	584.00	**718.00**
Color	Inst	Ea	Lg	SA	2.67	3.00	417.00	115.00	---	532.00	**646.00**
	Inst	Ea	Sm	SA	3.56	2.25	485.00	153.00	---	638.00	**779.00**
Premium Color	Inst	Ea	Lg	SA	2.67	3.00	444.00	115.00	---	559.00	**678.00**
	Inst	Ea	Sm	SA	3.56	2.25	517.00	153.00	---	670.00	**816.00**

Counter and undercounter units (Kohler Products, Artists Edition)

Ankara, 17" x 14"

Description	Oper	Unit	Vol	Crew Size	Man-hours per Unit	Crew Output per Day	Avg Mat'l Unit Cost	Avg Labor Unit Cost	Avg Equip Unit Cost	Avg Total Unit Cost	Avg Price Incl O&P
Self-Rimming	Inst	Ea	Lg	SA	2.67	3.00	1570.00	115.00	---	1685.00	**1980.00**
	Inst	Ea	Sm	SA	3.56	2.25	1830.00	153.00	---	1983.00	**2330.00**
Undercounter	Inst	Ea	Lg	SA	2.67	3.00	1360.00	115.00	---	1475.00	**1730.00**
	Inst	Ea	Sm	SA	3.56	2.25	1580.00	153.00	---	1733.00	**2040.00**
Briar Rose, 17" x 14"											
Self-Rimming	Inst	Ea	Lg	SA	2.67	3.00	1500.00	115.00	---	1615.00	**1890.00**
	Inst	Ea	Sm	SA	3.56	2.25	1740.00	153.00	---	1893.00	**2220.00**
Undercounter	Inst	Ea	Lg	SA	2.67	3.00	1360.00	115.00	---	1475.00	**1730.00**
	Inst	Ea	Sm	SA	3.56	2.25	1580.00	153.00	---	1733.00	**2040.00**
Crimson Topaz, 17" x 14"											
Self-Rimming	Inst	Ea	Lg	SA	2.67	3.00	1320.00	115.00	---	1435.00	**1680.00**
	Inst	Ea	Sm	SA	3.56	2.25	1530.00	153.00	---	1683.00	**1990.00**
Undercounter	Inst	Ea	Lg	SA	2.67	3.00	1320.00	115.00	---	1435.00	**1680.00**
	Inst	Ea	Sm	SA	3.56	2.25	1530.00	153.00	---	1683.00	**1990.00**

Description	Oper	Unit	Vol	Crew Size	Man-hours per Unit	Crew Output per Day	Avg Mat'l Unit Cost	Avg Labor Unit Cost	Avg Equip Unit Cost	Avg Total Unit Cost	Avg Price Incl O&P
English Trellis, 17" x 14"											
Self-Rimming	Inst	Ea	Lg	SA	2.67	3.00	1500.00	115.00	---	1615.00	**1890.00**
	Inst	Ea	Sm	SA	3.56	2.25	1740.00	153.00	---	1893.00	**2220.00**
Undercounter	Inst	Ea	Lg	SA	2.67	3.00	1360.00	115.00	---	1475.00	**1730.00**
	Inst	Ea	Sm	SA	3.56	2.25	1580.00	153.00	---	1733.00	**2040.00**
Peonies and Ivy, 17" x 14"											
Self-Rimming	Inst	Ea	Lg	SA	2.67	3.00	1570.00	115.00	---	1685.00	**1980.00**
	Inst	Ea	Sm	SA	3.56	2.25	1830.00	153.00	---	1983.00	**2330.00**
Undercounter	Inst	Ea	Lg	SA	2.67	3.00	1360.00	115.00	---	1475.00	**1730.00**
	Inst	Ea	Sm	SA	3.56	2.25	1580.00	153.00	---	1733.00	**2040.00**
Provencial, 17" x 14"											
Self-Rimming	Inst	Ea	Lg	SA	2.67	3.00	1990.00	115.00	---	2105.00	**2460.00**
	Inst	Ea	Sm	SA	3.56	2.25	2320.00	153.00	---	2473.00	**2890.00**
Undercounter	Inst	Ea	Lg	SA	2.67	3.00	1360.00	115.00	---	1475.00	**1730.00**
	Inst	Ea	Sm	SA	3.56	2.25	1580.00	153.00	---	1733.00	**2040.00**

Pedestal sinks (American Standard Products)

Adjustments

Description	Oper	Unit	Vol	Crew Size	Man-hours per Unit	Crew Output per Day	Avg Mat'l Unit Cost	Avg Labor Unit Cost	Avg Equip Unit Cost	Avg Total Unit Cost	Avg Price Incl O&P
For two 15" L towel bars, ADD											
	Inst	Pr	Lg	---	---	---	55.20	---	---	55.20	**63.50**
	Inst	Pr	Sm	---	---	---	64.20	---	---	64.20	**73.80**
Antiquity w/ pedestal											
24-1/2" x 19" with 8" or 4" cc											
White	Inst	Ea	Lg	SA	2.67	3.00	300.00	115.00	---	415.00	**511.00**
	Inst	Ea	Sm	SA	3.56	2.25	349.00	153.00	---	502.00	**623.00**
Color	Inst	Ea	Lg	SA	2.67	3.00	559.00	115.00	---	674.00	**810.00**
	Inst	Ea	Sm	SA	3.56	2.25	651.00	153.00	---	804.00	**970.00**
Lavatory slab only											
White	Inst	Ea	Lg	SA	1.60	5.00	180.00	68.80	---	248.80	**307.00**
	Inst	Ea	Sm	SA	2.13	3.75	210.00	91.60	---	301.60	**374.00**
Color	Inst	Ea	Lg	SA	1.60	5.00	224.00	68.80	---	292.80	**358.00**
	Inst	Ea	Sm	SA	2.13	3.75	261.00	91.60	---	352.60	**433.00**
Pedestal only											
White	Inst	Ea	Lg	SA	1.60	5.00	120.00	68.80	---	188.80	**237.00**
	Inst	Ea	Sm	SA	2.13	3.75	139.00	91.60	---	230.60	**293.00**
Color	Inst	Ea	Lg	SA	1.60	5.00	151.00	68.80	---	219.80	**273.00**
	Inst	Ea	Sm	SA	2.13	3.75	175.00	91.60	---	266.60	**335.00**
Cadet w/ pedestal											
24" x 20" with 8" or 4" cc											
White	Inst	Ea	Lg	SA	2.67	3.00	386.00	115.00	---	501.00	**611.00**
	Inst	Ea	Sm	SA	3.56	2.25	449.00	153.00	---	602.00	**739.00**
Color	Inst	Ea	Lg	SA	2.67	3.00	437.00	115.00	---	552.00	**669.00**
	Inst	Ea	Sm	SA	3.56	2.25	508.00	153.00	---	661.00	**807.00**
Premium Color	Inst	Ea	Lg	SA	2.67	3.00	467.00	115.00	---	582.00	**704.00**
	Inst	Ea	Sm	SA	3.56	2.25	544.00	153.00	---	697.00	**847.00**

Description	Oper	Unit	Vol	Crew Size	Man-hours per Unit	Crew Output per Day	Avg Mat'l Unit Cost	Avg Labor Unit Cost	Avg Equip Unit Cost	Avg Total Unit Cost	Avg Price Incl O&P
Lavatory slab only											
White	Inst	Ea	Lg	SA	1.60	5.00	148.00	68.80	---	216.80	**270.00**
	Inst	Ea	Sm	SA	2.13	3.75	172.00	91.60	---	263.60	**331.00**
Color	Inst	Ea	Lg	SA	1.60	5.00	190.00	68.80	---	258.80	**318.00**
	Inst	Ea	Sm	SA	2.13	3.75	220.00	91.60	---	311.60	**386.00**
Premium Color	Inst	Ea	Lg	SA	1.60	5.00	207.00	68.80	---	275.80	**338.00**
	Inst	Ea	Sm	SA	2.13	3.75	241.00	91.60	---	332.60	**410.00**
Pedestal only											
White	Inst	Ea	Lg	SA	1.60	5.00	54.30	68.80	---	123.10	**162.00**
	Inst	Ea	Sm	SA	2.13	3.75	63.10	91.60	---	154.70	**205.00**
Color	Inst	Ea	Lg	SA	1.60	5.00	63.50	68.80	---	132.30	**173.00**
	Inst	Ea	Sm	SA	2.13	3.75	73.80	91.60	---	165.40	**218.00**
Premium Color	Inst	Ea	Lg	SA	1.60	5.00	76.40	68.80	---	145.20	**188.00**
	Inst	Ea	Sm	SA	2.13	3.75	88.80	91.60	---	180.40	**235.00**
Heritage w/ pedestal											
30" x 20" with 8" or 4" cc											
White	Inst	Ea	Lg	SA	2.67	3.00	667.00	115.00	---	782.00	**934.00**
	Inst	Ea	Sm	SA	3.56	2.25	776.00	153.00	---	929.00	**1110.00**
Color	Inst	Ea	Lg	SA	2.67	3.00	791.00	115.00	---	906.00	**1080.00**
	Inst	Ea	Sm	SA	3.56	2.25	920.00	153.00	---	1073.00	**1280.00**
Lavatory slab only											
White	Inst	Ea	Lg	SA	1.60	5.00	338.00	68.80	---	406.80	**488.00**
	Inst	Ea	Sm	SA	2.13	3.75	393.00	91.60	---	484.60	**584.00**
Color	Inst	Ea	Lg	SA	1.60	5.00	425.00	68.80	---	493.80	**589.00**
	Inst	Ea	Sm	SA	2.13	3.75	494.00	91.60	---	585.60	**701.00**
Pedestal only											
White	Inst	Ea	Lg	SA	1.60	5.00	145.00	68.80	---	213.80	**267.00**
	Inst	Ea	Sm	SA	2.13	3.75	169.00	91.60	---	260.60	**327.00**
Color	Inst	Ea	Lg	SA	1.60	5.00	182.00	68.80	---	250.80	**309.00**
	Inst	Ea	Sm	SA	2.13	3.75	212.00	91.60	---	303.60	**377.00**
Lexington w/ pedestal											
24" x 18" with 8" or 4" cc											
White	Inst	Ea	Lg	SA	2.67	3.00	630.00	115.00	---	745.00	**891.00**
	Inst	Ea	Sm	SA	3.56	2.25	733.00	153.00	---	886.00	**1060.00**
Color	Inst	Ea	Lg	SA	2.67	3.00	742.00	115.00	---	857.00	**1020.00**
	Inst	Ea	Sm	SA	3.56	2.25	862.00	153.00	---	1015.00	**1210.00**
Premium Color	Inst	Ea	Lg	SA	2.67	3.00	809.00	115.00	---	924.00	**1100.00**
	Inst	Ea	Sm	SA	3.56	2.25	941.00	153.00	---	1094.00	**1300.00**
Lavatory slab only											
White	Inst	Ea	Lg	SA	1.60	5.00	309.00	68.80	---	377.80	**455.00**
	Inst	Ea	Sm	SA	2.13	3.75	360.00	91.60	---	451.60	**546.00**
Color	Inst	Ea	Lg	SA	1.60	5.00	351.00	68.80	---	419.80	**503.00**
	Inst	Ea	Sm	SA	2.13	3.75	408.00	91.60	---	499.60	**602.00**
Premium Color	Inst	Ea	Lg	SA	1.60	5.00	433.00	68.80	---	501.80	**598.00**
	Inst	Ea	Sm	SA	2.13	3.75	504.00	91.60	---	595.60	**712.00**

Description	Oper	Unit	Vol	Crew Size	Man-hours per Unit	Crew Output per Day	Avg Mat'l Unit Cost	Avg Labor Unit Cost	Avg Equip Unit Cost	Avg Total Unit Cost	Avg Price Incl O&P
Pedestal only											
White	Inst	Ea	Lg	SA	1.60	5.00	137.00	68.80	---	205.80	**257.00**
	Inst	Ea	Sm	SA	2.13	3.75	159.00	91.60	---	250.60	**316.00**
Color	Inst	Ea	Lg	SA	1.60	5.00	171.00	68.80	---	239.80	**297.00**
	Inst	Ea	Sm	SA	2.13	3.75	199.00	91.60	---	290.60	**362.00**
Premium Color	Inst	Ea	Lg	SA	1.60	5.00	191.00	68.80	---	259.80	**320.00**
	Inst	Ea	Sm	SA	2.13	3.75	223.00	91.60	---	314.60	**389.00**
Repertoire w/ pedestal											
23" x 18-1/4" with 8" or 4" cc											
White	Inst	Ea	Lg	SA	2.67	3.00	533.00	115.00	---	648.00	**779.00**
	Inst	Ea	Sm	SA	3.56	2.25	620.00	153.00	---	773.00	**935.00**
Color	Inst	Ea	Lg	SA	2.67	3.00	620.00	115.00	---	735.00	**880.00**
	Inst	Ea	Sm	SA	3.56	2.25	721.00	153.00	---	874.00	**1050.00**
Premium Color	Inst	Ea	Lg	SA	2.67	3.00	672.00	115.00	---	787.00	**939.00**
	Inst	Ea	Sm	SA	3.56	2.25	781.00	153.00	---	934.00	**1120.00**
Lavatory slab only											
White	Inst	Ea	Lg	SA	1.60	5.00	253.00	68.80	---	321.80	**391.00**
	Inst	Ea	Sm	SA	2.13	3.75	294.00	91.60	---	385.60	**471.00**
Color	Inst	Ea	Lg	SA	1.60	5.00	316.00	68.80	---	384.80	**464.00**
	Inst	Ea	Sm	SA	2.13	3.75	368.00	91.60	---	459.60	**556.00**
Premium Color	Inst	Ea	Lg	SA	1.60	5.00	354.00	68.80	---	422.80	**507.00**
	Inst	Ea	Sm	SA	2.13	3.75	412.00	91.60	---	503.60	**607.00**
Pedestal only											
White	Inst	Ea	Lg	SA	1.60	5.00	95.70	68.80	---	164.50	**210.00**
	Inst	Ea	Sm	SA	2.13	3.75	111.00	91.60	---	202.60	**261.00**
Color	Inst	Ea	Lg	SA	1.60	5.00	120.00	68.80	---	188.80	**237.00**
	Inst	Ea	Sm	SA	2.13	3.75	139.00	91.60	---	230.60	**293.00**
Premium Color	Inst	Ea	Lg	SA	1.60	5.00	133.00	68.80	---	201.80	**253.00**
	Inst	Ea	Sm	SA	2.13	3.75	155.00	91.60	---	246.60	**311.00**

Pedestal sinks (Kohler Products)

Adjustments

Description	Oper	Unit	Vol	Crew Size	Man-hours per Unit	Crew Output per Day	Avg Mat'l Unit Cost	Avg Labor Unit Cost	Avg Equip Unit Cost	Avg Total Unit Cost	Avg Price Incl O&P
For two 15" L towel bars, ADD											
	Inst	Pr	Lg	---	---	---	55.20	---	---	55.20	**63.50**
	Inst	Pr	Sm	---	---	---	64.20	---	---	64.20	**73.80**
Anatole											
22" x 18" x 32" with 8" or 4" cc											
White	Inst	Ea	Lg	SA	2.67	3.00	947.00	115.00	---	1062.00	**1260.00**
	Inst	Ea	Sm	SA	3.56	2.25	1100.00	153.00	---	1253.00	**1490.00**
Color	Inst	Ea	Lg	SA	2.67	3.00	1180.00	115.00	---	1295.00	**1520.00**
	Inst	Ea	Sm	SA	3.56	2.25	1370.00	153.00	---	1523.00	**1790.00**
Premium Color	Inst	Ea	Lg	SA	2.67	3.00	1320.00	115.00	---	1435.00	**1690.00**
	Inst	Ea	Sm	SA	3.56	2.25	1540.00	153.00	---	1693.00	**1990.00**

Description	Oper	Unit	Vol	Crew Size	Man-hours per Unit	Crew Output per Day	Avg Mat'l Unit Cost	Avg Labor Unit Cost	Avg Equip Unit Cost	Avg Total Unit Cost	Avg Price Incl O&P
Lavatory slab only											
White	Inst	Ea	Lg	SA	1.60	5.00	495.00	68.80	---	563.80	**670.00**
	Inst	Ea	Sm	SA	2.13	3.75	576.00	91.60	---	667.60	**796.00**
Color	Inst	Ea	Lg	SA	1.60	5.00	644.00	68.80	---	712.80	**840.00**
	Inst	Ea	Sm	SA	2.13	3.75	749.00	91.60	---	840.60	**994.00**
Premium Color	Inst	Ea	Lg	SA	1.60	5.00	741.00	68.80	---	809.80	**951.00**
	Inst	Ea	Sm	SA	2.13	3.75	861.00	91.60	---	952.60	**1120.00**
Pedestal only											
White	Inst	Ea	Lg	SA	1.60	5.00	267.00	68.80	---	335.80	**407.00**
	Inst	Ea	Sm	SA	2.13	3.75	311.00	91.60	---	402.60	**490.00**
Color	Inst	Ea	Lg	SA	1.60	5.00	347.00	68.80	---	415.80	**499.00**
	Inst	Ea	Sm	SA	2.13	3.75	404.00	91.60	---	495.60	**597.00**
Premium Color	Inst	Ea	Lg	SA	1.60	5.00	399.00	68.80	---	467.80	**559.00**
	Inst	Ea	Sm	SA	2.13	3.75	464.00	91.60	---	555.60	**667.00**

Cabernet
22" x 18" x 33" with 8" or 4" cc

Description	Oper	Unit	Vol	Crew Size	Man-hours per Unit	Crew Output per Day	Avg Mat'l Unit Cost	Avg Labor Unit Cost	Avg Equip Unit Cost	Avg Total Unit Cost	Avg Price Incl O&P
White	Inst	Ea	Lg	SA	2.67	3.00	597.00	115.00	---	712.00	**853.00**
	Inst	Ea	Sm	SA	3.56	2.25	694.00	153.00	---	847.00	**1020.00**
Color	Inst	Ea	Lg	SA	2.67	3.00	720.00	115.00	---	835.00	**995.00**
	Inst	Ea	Sm	SA	3.56	2.25	838.00	153.00	---	991.00	**1190.00**
Premium Color	Inst	Ea	Lg	SA	2.67	3.00	800.00	115.00	---	915.00	**1090.00**
	Inst	Ea	Sm	SA	3.56	2.25	931.00	153.00	---	1084.00	**1290.00**
Lavatory slab only											
White	Inst	Ea	Lg	SA	1.60	5.00	268.00	68.80	---	336.80	**408.00**
	Inst	Ea	Sm	SA	2.13	3.75	312.00	91.60	---	403.60	**491.00**
Color	Inst	Ea	Lg	SA	1.60	5.00	348.00	68.80	---	416.80	**500.00**
	Inst	Ea	Sm	SA	2.13	3.75	405.00	91.60	---	496.60	**599.00**
Premium Color	Inst	Ea	Lg	SA	1.60	5.00	401.00	68.80	---	469.80	**561.00**
	Inst	Ea	Sm	SA	2.13	3.75	466.00	91.60	---	557.60	**669.00**
Pedestal only											
White	Inst	Ea	Lg	SA	1.60	5.00	145.00	68.80	---	213.80	**266.00**
	Inst	Ea	Sm	SA	2.13	3.75	168.00	91.60	---	259.60	**326.00**
Color	Inst	Ea	Lg	SA	1.60	5.00	188.00	68.80	---	256.80	**316.00**
	Inst	Ea	Sm	SA	2.13	3.75	218.00	91.60	---	309.60	**384.00**
Premium Color	Inst	Ea	Lg	SA	1.60	5.00	216.00	68.80	---	284.80	**348.00**
	Inst	Ea	Sm	SA	2.13	3.75	251.00	91.60	---	342.60	**422.00**

Chablis
24" x 19" x 32" with 8" or 4" cc

Description	Oper	Unit	Vol	Crew Size	Man-hours per Unit	Crew Output per Day	Avg Mat'l Unit Cost	Avg Labor Unit Cost	Avg Equip Unit Cost	Avg Total Unit Cost	Avg Price Incl O&P
White	Inst	Ea	Lg	SA	2.67	3.00	571.00	115.00	---	686.00	**823.00**
	Inst	Ea	Sm	SA	3.56	2.25	664.00	153.00	---	817.00	**985.00**
Color	Inst	Ea	Lg	SA	2.67	3.00	687.00	115.00	---	802.00	**956.00**
	Inst	Ea	Sm	SA	3.56	2.25	798.00	153.00	---	951.00	**1140.00**
Premium Color	Inst	Ea	Lg	SA	2.67	3.00	761.00	115.00	---	876.00	**1040.00**
	Inst	Ea	Sm	SA	3.56	2.25	886.00	153.00	---	1039.00	**1240.00**

Description	Oper	Unit	Vol	Crew Size	Man-hours per Unit	Crew Output per Day	Avg Mat'l Unit Cost	Avg Labor Unit Cost	Avg Equip Unit Cost	Avg Total Unit Cost	Avg Price Incl O&P
Lavatory slab only											
White	Inst	Ea	Lg	SA	1.60	5.00	251.00	68.80	---	319.80	**389.00**
	Inst	Ea	Sm	SA	2.13	3.75	292.00	91.60	---	383.60	**469.00**
Color	Inst	Ea	Lg	SA	1.60	5.00	326.00	68.80	---	394.80	**475.00**
	Inst	Ea	Sm	SA	2.13	3.75	380.00	91.60	---	471.60	**569.00**
Premium Color	Inst	Ea	Lg	SA	1.60	5.00	375.00	68.80	---	443.80	**531.00**
	Inst	Ea	Sm	SA	2.13	3.75	436.00	91.60	---	527.60	**634.00**
Pedestal only											
White	Inst	Ea	Lg	SA	1.60	5.00	136.00	68.80	---	204.80	**256.00**
	Inst	Ea	Sm	SA	2.13	3.75	158.00	91.60	---	249.60	**314.00**
Color	Inst	Ea	Lg	SA	1.60	5.00	176.00	68.80	---	244.80	**302.00**
	Inst	Ea	Sm	SA	2.13	3.75	205.00	91.60	---	296.60	**368.00**
Premium Color	Inst	Ea	Lg	SA	1.60	5.00	202.00	68.80	---	270.80	**333.00**
	Inst	Ea	Sm	SA	2.13	3.75	236.00	91.60	---	327.60	**404.00**
Devonshire											
27-1/2" x 20" x 33-1/2" with 8" or 4" cc											
White	Inst	Ea	Lg	SA	2.67	3.00	632.00	115.00	---	747.00	**893.00**
	Inst	Ea	Sm	SA	3.56	2.25	735.00	153.00	---	888.00	**1070.00**
Color	Inst	Ea	Lg	SA	2.67	3.00	766.00	115.00	---	881.00	**1050.00**
	Inst	Ea	Sm	SA	3.56	2.25	891.00	153.00	---	1044.00	**1250.00**
Premium Color	Inst	Ea	Lg	SA	2.67	3.00	853.00	115.00	---	968.00	**1150.00**
	Inst	Ea	Sm	SA	3.56	2.25	993.00	153.00	---	1146.00	**1360.00**
Lavatory slab only											
White	Inst	Ea	Lg	SA	1.60	5.00	328.00	68.80	---	396.80	**477.00**
	Inst	Ea	Sm	SA	2.13	3.75	382.00	91.60	---	473.60	**572.00**
Color	Inst	Ea	Lg	SA	1.60	5.00	427.00	68.80	---	495.80	**591.00**
	Inst	Ea	Sm	SA	2.13	3.75	496.00	91.60	---	587.60	**704.00**
Premium Color	Inst	Ea	Lg	SA	1.60	5.00	491.00	68.80	---	559.80	**664.00**
	Inst	Ea	Sm	SA	2.13	3.75	571.00	91.60	---	662.60	**789.00**
Pedestal only											
White	Inst	Ea	Lg	SA	1.60	5.00	120.00	68.80	---	188.80	**237.00**
	Inst	Ea	Sm	SA	2.13	3.75	139.00	91.60	---	230.60	**293.00**
Color	Inst	Ea	Lg	SA	1.60	5.00	155.00	68.80	---	223.80	**279.00**
	Inst	Ea	Sm	SA	2.13	3.75	181.00	91.60	---	272.60	**341.00**
Premium Color	Inst	Ea	Lg	SA	1.60	5.00	179.00	68.80	---	247.80	**305.00**
	Inst	Ea	Sm	SA	2.13	3.75	208.00	91.60	---	299.60	**372.00**
Parigi											
20" x 14" x 33" with 4" cc											
White	Inst	Ea	Lg	SA	2.67	3.00	776.00	115.00	---	891.00	**1060.00**
	Inst	Ea	Sm	SA	3.56	2.25	902.00	153.00	---	1055.00	**1260.00**
Color	Inst	Ea	Lg	SA	2.67	3.00	953.00	115.00	---	1068.00	**1260.00**
	Inst	Ea	Sm	SA	3.56	2.25	1110.00	153.00	---	1263.00	**1500.00**
Premium Color	Inst	Ea	Lg	SA	2.67	3.00	1070.00	115.00	---	1185.00	**1400.00**
	Inst	Ea	Sm	SA	3.56	2.25	1240.00	153.00	---	1393.00	**1650.00**

Description	Oper	Unit	Vol	Crew Size	Man-hours per Unit	Crew Output per Day	Avg Mat'l Unit Cost	Avg Labor Unit Cost	Avg Equip Unit Cost	Avg Total Unit Cost	Avg Price Incl O&P
Lavatory slab only											
White	Inst	Ea	Lg	SA	1.60	5.00	414.00	68.80	---	482.80	**576.00**
	Inst	Ea	Sm	SA	2.13	3.75	482.00	91.60	---	573.60	**687.00**
Color	Inst	Ea	Lg	SA	1.60	5.00	538.00	68.80	---	606.80	**719.00**
	Inst	Ea	Sm	SA	2.13	3.75	626.00	91.60	---	717.60	**853.00**
Premium Color	Inst	Ea	Lg	SA	1.60	5.00	619.00	68.80	---	687.80	**812.00**
	Inst	Ea	Sm	SA	2.13	3.75	720.00	91.60	---	811.60	**961.00**
Pedestal only											
White	Inst	Ea	Lg	SA	1.60	5.00	178.00	68.80	---	246.80	**304.00**
	Inst	Ea	Sm	SA	2.13	3.75	207.00	91.60	---	298.60	**371.00**
Color	Inst	Ea	Lg	SA	1.60	5.00	231.00	68.80	---	299.80	**365.00**
	Inst	Ea	Sm	SA	2.13	3.75	269.00	91.60	---	360.60	**442.00**
Premium Color	Inst	Ea	Lg	SA	1.60	5.00	266.00	68.80	---	334.80	**405.00**
	Inst	Ea	Sm	SA	2.13	3.75	309.00	91.60	---	400.60	**488.00**

Pinoir
22" x 18" x 33" with 8" or 4" cc

Description	Oper	Unit	Vol	Crew Size	Man-hours per Unit	Crew Output per Day	Avg Mat'l Unit Cost	Avg Labor Unit Cost	Avg Equip Unit Cost	Avg Total Unit Cost	Avg Price Incl O&P
White	Inst	Ea	Lg	SA	2.67	3.00	457.00	115.00	---	572.00	**692.00**
	Inst	Ea	Sm	SA	3.56	2.25	531.00	153.00	---	684.00	**833.00**
Color	Inst	Ea	Lg	SA	2.67	3.00	538.00	115.00	---	653.00	**785.00**
	Inst	Ea	Sm	SA	3.56	2.25	626.00	153.00	---	779.00	**942.00**
Premium Color	Inst	Ea	Lg	SA	2.67	3.00	591.00	115.00	---	706.00	**847.00**
	Inst	Ea	Sm	SA	3.56	2.25	688.00	153.00	---	841.00	**1010.00**
Lavatory slab only											
White	Inst	Ea	Lg	SA	1.60	5.00	182.00	68.80	---	250.80	**309.00**
	Inst	Ea	Sm	SA	2.13	3.75	212.00	91.60	---	303.60	**377.00**
Color	Inst	Ea	Lg	SA	1.60	5.00	237.00	68.80	---	305.80	**373.00**
	Inst	Ea	Sm	SA	2.13	3.75	276.00	91.60	---	367.60	**450.00**
Premium Color	Inst	Ea	Lg	SA	1.60	5.00	273.00	68.80	---	341.80	**414.00**
	Inst	Ea	Sm	SA	2.13	3.75	318.00	91.60	---	409.60	**498.00**
Pedestal only											
White	Inst	Ea	Lg	SA	1.60	5.00	90.30	68.80	---	159.10	**204.00**
	Inst	Ea	Sm	SA	2.13	3.75	105.00	91.60	---	196.60	**254.00**
Color	Inst	Ea	Lg	SA	1.60	5.00	117.00	68.80	---	185.80	**234.00**
	Inst	Ea	Sm	SA	2.13	3.75	136.00	91.60	---	227.60	**289.00**
Premium Color	Inst	Ea	Lg	SA	1.60	5.00	134.00	68.80	---	202.80	**254.00**
	Inst	Ea	Sm	SA	2.13	3.75	156.00	91.60	---	247.60	**313.00**

Portrait
27" x 19" x 34" with 8" or 4" cc

Description	Oper	Unit	Vol	Crew Size	Man-hours per Unit	Crew Output per Day	Avg Mat'l Unit Cost	Avg Labor Unit Cost	Avg Equip Unit Cost	Avg Total Unit Cost	Avg Price Incl O&P
White	Inst	Ea	Lg	SA	2.67	3.00	727.00	115.00	---	842.00	**1000.00**
	Inst	Ea	Sm	SA	3.56	2.25	846.00	153.00	---	999.00	**1190.00**
Color	Inst	Ea	Lg	SA	2.67	3.00	890.00	115.00	---	1005.00	**1190.00**
	Inst	Ea	Sm	SA	3.56	2.25	1040.00	153.00	---	1193.00	**1410.00**
Premium Color	Inst	Ea	Lg	SA	2.67	3.00	996.00	115.00	---	1111.00	**1310.00**
	Inst	Ea	Sm	SA	3.56	2.25	1160.00	153.00	---	1313.00	**1550.00**

Description	Oper	Unit	Vol	Crew Size	Man-hours per Unit	Crew Output per Day	Avg Mat'l Unit Cost	Avg Labor Unit Cost	Avg Equip Unit Cost	Avg Total Unit Cost	Avg Price Incl O&P
Lavatory slab only											
White	Inst	Ea	Lg	SA	1.60	5.00	373.00	68.80	---	441.80	**529.00**
	Inst	Ea	Sm	SA	2.13	3.75	434.00	91.60	---	525.60	**632.00**
Color	Inst	Ea	Lg	SA	1.60	5.00	485.00	68.80	---	553.80	**658.00**
	Inst	Ea	Sm	SA	2.13	3.75	564.00	91.60	---	655.60	**782.00**
Premium Color	Inst	Ea	Lg	SA	1.60	5.00	558.00	68.80	---	626.80	**741.00**
	Inst	Ea	Sm	SA	2.13	3.75	649.00	91.60	---	740.60	**879.00**
Pedestal only											
White	Inst	Ea	Lg	SA	1.60	5.00	170.00	68.80	---	238.80	**295.00**
	Inst	Ea	Sm	SA	2.13	3.75	198.00	91.60	---	289.60	**360.00**
Color	Inst	Ea	Lg	SA	1.60	5.00	221.00	68.80	---	289.80	**354.00**
	Inst	Ea	Sm	SA	2.13	3.75	257.00	91.60	---	348.60	**429.00**
Premium Color	Inst	Ea	Lg	SA	1.60	5.00	254.00	68.80	---	322.80	**392.00**
	Inst	Ea	Sm	SA	2.13	3.75	296.00	91.60	---	387.60	**473.00**
Revival											
24" x 18" x 34" with 8" or 4" cc											
White	Inst	Ea	Lg	SA	2.67	3.00	910.00	115.00	---	1025.00	**1210.00**
	Inst	Ea	Sm	SA	3.56	2.25	1060.00	153.00	---	1213.00	**1440.00**
Color	Inst	Ea	Lg	SA	2.67	3.00	1130.00	115.00	---	1245.00	**1460.00**
	Inst	Ea	Sm	SA	3.56	2.25	1310.00	153.00	---	1463.00	**1730.00**
Premium Color	Inst	Ea	Lg	SA	2.67	3.00	1270.00	115.00	---	1385.00	**1630.00**
	Inst	Ea	Sm	SA	3.56	2.25	1480.00	153.00	---	1633.00	**1920.00**
Lavatory slab only											
White	Inst	Ea	Lg	SA	1.60	5.00	489.00	68.80	---	557.80	**662.00**
	Inst	Ea	Sm	SA	2.13	3.75	569.00	91.60	---	660.60	**787.00**
Color	Inst	Ea	Lg	SA	1.60	5.00	636.00	68.80	---	704.80	**832.00**
	Inst	Ea	Sm	SA	2.13	3.75	740.00	91.60	---	831.60	**984.00**
Premium Color	Inst	Ea	Lg	SA	1.60	5.00	731.00	68.80	---	799.80	**941.00**
	Inst	Ea	Sm	SA	2.13	3.75	851.00	91.60	---	942.60	**1110.00**
Pedestal only											
White	Inst	Ea	Lg	SA	1.60	5.00	237.00	68.80	---	305.80	**373.00**
	Inst	Ea	Sm	SA	2.13	3.75	276.00	91.60	---	367.60	**450.00**
Color	Inst	Ea	Lg	SA	1.60	5.00	308.00	68.80	---	376.80	**454.00**
	Inst	Ea	Sm	SA	2.13	3.75	358.00	91.60	---	449.60	**545.00**
Premium Color	Inst	Ea	Lg	SA	1.60	5.00	354.00	68.80	---	422.80	**507.00**
	Inst	Ea	Sm	SA	2.13	3.75	412.00	91.60	---	503.60	**607.00**

Wall-hung units (American Standard Products)

Adjustments

Description	Oper	Unit	Vol	Crew Size	Man-hours per Unit	Crew Output per Day	Avg Mat'l Unit Cost	Avg Labor Unit Cost	Avg Equip Unit Cost	Avg Total Unit Cost	Avg Price Incl O&P
For two 15" L towel bars, ADD											
	Inst	Pr	Lg	---	---	---	55.20	---	---	55.20	**63.50**
	Inst	Pr	Sm	---	---	---	64.20	---	---	64.20	**73.80**
Comrade											
20" x 18" with 4" cc											
White	Inst	Ea	Lg	SA	2.67	3.00	294.00	115.00	---	409.00	**505.00**
	Inst	Ea	Sm	SA	3.56	2.25	342.00	153.00	---	495.00	**616.00**
Color	Inst	Ea	Lg	SA	2.67	3.00	322.00	115.00	---	437.00	**537.00**
	Inst	Ea	Sm	SA	3.56	2.25	375.00	153.00	---	528.00	**653.00**

Description	Oper	Unit	Vol	Crew Size	Man-hours per Unit	Crew Output per Day	Avg Mat'l Unit Cost	Avg Labor Unit Cost	Avg Equip Unit Cost	Avg Total Unit Cost	Avg Price Incl O&P
Corner Minette											
11" x 16" with 4" cc											
White	Inst	Ea	Lg	SA	2.00	4.00	434.00	86.00	---	520.00	**624.00**
	Inst	Ea	Sm	SA	2.67	3.00	505.00	115.00	---	620.00	**747.00**
Color	Inst	Ea	Lg	SA	2.00	4.00	493.00	86.00	---	579.00	**692.00**
	Inst	Ea	Sm	SA	2.67	3.00	574.00	115.00	---	689.00	**826.00**
Declyn											
19" x 17" with 4" cc											
White	Inst	Ea	Lg	SA	2.67	3.00	285.00	115.00	---	400.00	**495.00**
	Inst	Ea	Sm	SA	3.56	2.25	332.00	153.00	---	485.00	**604.00**
Color	Inst	Ea	Lg	SA	2.67	3.00	316.00	115.00	---	431.00	**529.00**
	Inst	Ea	Sm	SA	3.56	2.25	367.00	153.00	---	520.00	**644.00**
Lucerne											
20" x 18" with 8" or 4" cc											
White	Inst	Ea	Lg	SA	2.67	3.00	312.00	115.00	---	427.00	**525.00**
	Inst	Ea	Sm	SA	3.56	2.25	363.00	153.00	---	516.00	**639.00**
Color	Inst	Ea	Lg	SA	2.67	3.00	343.00	115.00	---	458.00	**561.00**
	Inst	Ea	Sm	SA	3.56	2.25	399.00	153.00	---	552.00	**681.00**
Penlyn											
18" x 16" with 4" cc											
White	Inst	Ea	Lg	SA	2.67	3.00	366.00	115.00	---	481.00	**588.00**
	Inst	Ea	Sm	SA	3.56	2.25	426.00	153.00	---	579.00	**712.00**
Roxalyn											
20" x 18" with 8" or 4" cc											
White	Inst	Ea	Lg	SA	2.67	3.00	363.00	115.00	---	478.00	**584.00**
	Inst	Ea	Sm	SA	3.56	2.25	423.00	153.00	---	576.00	**708.00**
Color	Inst	Ea	Lg	SA	2.67	3.00	408.00	115.00	---	523.00	**636.00**
	Inst	Ea	Sm	SA	3.56	2.25	475.00	153.00	---	628.00	**768.00**
Wheelchair, meets ADA requirements											
20" x 27" with 8" or 4" cc											
White	Inst	Ea	Lg	SA	2.67	3.00	513.00	115.00	---	628.00	**757.00**
	Inst	Ea	Sm	SA	3.56	2.25	597.00	153.00	---	750.00	**909.00**
Color	Inst	Ea	Lg	SA	2.67	3.00	595.00	115.00	---	710.00	**851.00**
	Inst	Ea	Sm	SA	3.56	2.25	692.00	153.00	---	845.00	**1020.00**

Wall-hung units (Kohler Products)

Adjustments

Description	Oper	Unit	Vol	Crew Size	Man-hours per Unit	Crew Output per Day	Avg Mat'l Unit Cost	Avg Labor Unit Cost	Avg Equip Unit Cost	Avg Total Unit Cost	Avg Price Incl O&P
For two 15" L towel bars, ADD											
	Inst	Pr	Lg	---	---	---	55.20	---	---	55.20	**63.50**
	Inst	Pr	Sm	---	---	---	64.20	---	---	64.20	**73.80**
Chablis, with shroud											
24" x 19" with 8" or 4" cc											
White	Inst	Ea	Lg	SA	2.67	3.00	596.00	115.00	---	711.00	**852.00**
	Inst	Ea	Sm	SA	3.56	2.25	693.00	153.00	---	846.00	**1020.00**
Color	Inst	Ea	Lg	SA	2.67	3.00	719.00	115.00	---	834.00	**994.00**
	Inst	Ea	Sm	SA	3.56	2.25	837.00	153.00	---	990.00	**1180.00**
Premium Color	Inst	Ea	Lg	SA	2.67	3.00	799.00	115.00	---	914.00	**1090.00**
	Inst	Ea	Sm	SA	3.56	2.25	930.00	153.00	---	1083.00	**1290.00**

Description	Oper	Unit	Vol	Crew Size	Man-hours per Unit	Crew Output per Day	Avg Mat'l Unit Cost	Avg Labor Unit Cost	Avg Equip Unit Cost	Avg Total Unit Cost	Avg Price Incl O&P
Lavatory slab only											
White	Inst	Ea	Lg	SA	1.60	5.00	251.00	68.80	---	319.80	**389.00**
	Inst	Ea	Sm	SA	2.13	3.75	292.00	91.60	---	383.60	**469.00**
Color	Inst	Ea	Lg	SA	1.60	5.00	326.00	68.80	---	394.80	**475.00**
	Inst	Ea	Sm	SA	2.13	3.75	380.00	91.60	---	471.60	**569.00**
Premium Color	Inst	Ea	Lg	SA	1.60	5.00	375.00	68.80	---	443.80	**531.00**
	Inst	Ea	Sm	SA	2.13	3.75	436.00	91.60	---	527.60	**634.00**
Shroud only											
White	Inst	Ea	Lg	SA	1.60	5.00	161.00	68.80	---	229.80	**285.00**
	Inst	Ea	Sm	SA	2.13	3.75	187.00	91.60	---	278.60	**348.00**
Color	Inst	Ea	Lg	SA	1.60	5.00	209.00	68.80	---	277.80	**340.00**
	Inst	Ea	Sm	SA	2.13	3.75	243.00	91.60	---	334.60	**412.00**
Premium Color	Inst	Ea	Lg	SA	1.60	5.00	240.00	68.80	---	308.80	**376.00**
	Inst	Ea	Sm	SA	2.13	3.75	279.00	91.60	---	370.60	**454.00**
Chesapeake											
19" x 17" with 4" cc											
White	Inst	Ea	Lg	SA	2.67	3.00	296.00	115.00	---	411.00	**507.00**
	Inst	Ea	Sm	SA	3.56	2.25	344.00	153.00	---	497.00	**618.00**
Color	Inst	Ea	Lg	SA	2.67	3.00	270.00	115.00	---	385.00	**477.00**
	Inst	Ea	Sm	SA	3.56	2.25	314.00	153.00	---	467.00	**584.00**
20" x 18" with 4" cc											
White	Inst	Ea	Lg	SA	2.67	3.00	296.00	115.00	---	411.00	**507.00**
	Inst	Ea	Sm	SA	3.56	2.25	344.00	153.00	---	497.00	**618.00**
Color	Inst	Ea	Lg	SA	2.67	3.00	270.00	115.00	---	385.00	**477.00**
	Inst	Ea	Sm	SA	3.56	2.25	314.00	153.00	---	467.00	**584.00**
Fleur, with shroud											
19-7/8" x 14-3/8" with single hole											
White	Inst	Ea	Lg	SA	2.67	3.00	749.00	115.00	---	864.00	**1030.00**
	Inst	Ea	Sm	SA	3.56	2.25	872.00	153.00	---	1025.00	**1220.00**
Color	Inst	Ea	Lg	SA	2.67	3.00	919.00	115.00	---	1034.00	**1220.00**
	Inst	Ea	Sm	SA	3.56	2.25	1070.00	153.00	---	1223.00	**1450.00**
Lavatory slab only											
White	Inst	Ea	Lg	SA	1.60	5.00	367.00	68.80	---	435.80	**522.00**
	Inst	Ea	Sm	SA	2.13	3.75	427.00	91.60	---	518.60	**624.00**
Color	Inst	Ea	Lg	SA	1.60	5.00	478.00	68.80	---	546.80	**649.00**
	Inst	Ea	Sm	SA	2.13	3.75	555.00	91.60	---	646.60	**772.00**
Shroud only											
White	Inst	Ea	Lg	SA	1.60	5.00	198.00	68.80	---	266.80	**328.00**
	Inst	Ea	Sm	SA	2.13	3.75	230.00	91.60	---	321.60	**398.00**
Color	Inst	Ea	Lg	SA	1.60	5.00	258.00	68.80	---	326.80	**396.00**
	Inst	Ea	Sm	SA	2.13	3.75	299.00	91.60	---	390.60	**477.00**

Description	Oper	Unit	Vol	Crew Size	Man-hours per Unit	Crew Output per Day	Avg Mat'l Unit Cost	Avg Labor Unit Cost	Avg Equip Unit Cost	Avg Total Unit Cost	Avg Price Incl O&P
Pinoir, with shroud											
22" x 18" with 8" or 4" cc											
White	Inst	Ea	Lg	SA	2.67	3.00	450.00	115.00	---	565.00	**684.00**
	Inst	Ea	Sm	SA	3.56	2.25	524.00	153.00	---	677.00	**824.00**
Color	Inst	Ea	Lg	SA	2.67	3.00	530.00	115.00	---	645.00	**776.00**
	Inst	Ea	Sm	SA	3.56	2.25	616.00	153.00	---	769.00	**931.00**
Premium Color	Inst	Ea	Lg	SA	2.67	3.00	582.00	115.00	---	697.00	**836.00**
	Inst	Ea	Sm	SA	3.56	2.25	677.00	153.00	---	830.00	**1000.00**
Lavatory slab only											
White	Inst	Ea	Lg	SA	1.60	5.00	182.00	68.80	---	250.80	**309.00**
	Inst	Ea	Sm	SA	2.13	3.75	212.00	91.60	---	303.60	**377.00**
Color	Inst	Ea	Lg	SA	1.60	5.00	237.00	68.80	---	305.80	**373.00**
	Inst	Ea	Sm	SA	2.13	3.75	276.00	91.60	---	367.60	**450.00**
Premium Color	Inst	Ea	Lg	SA	1.60	5.00	273.00	68.80	---	341.80	**414.00**
	Inst	Ea	Sm	SA	2.13	3.75	318.00	91.60	---	409.60	**498.00**
Shroud only											
White	Inst	Ea	Lg	SA	1.60	5.00	84.00	68.80	---	152.80	**196.00**
	Inst	Ea	Sm	SA	2.13	3.75	97.70	91.60	---	189.30	**245.00**
Color	Inst	Ea	Lg	SA	1.60	5.00	109.00	68.80	---	177.80	**225.00**
	Inst	Ea	Sm	SA	2.13	3.75	127.00	91.60	---	218.60	**279.00**
Premium Color	Inst	Ea	Lg	SA	1.60	5.00	125.00	68.80	---	193.80	**244.00**
	Inst	Ea	Sm	SA	2.13	3.75	146.00	91.60	---	237.60	**300.00**
Portrait, with shroud											
20" x 15" (shroud not available in this size)											
White	Inst	Ea	Lg	SA	2.67	3.00	658.00	115.00	---	773.00	**924.00**
	Inst	Ea	Sm	SA	3.56	2.25	766.00	153.00	---	919.00	**1100.00**
Color	Inst	Ea	Lg	SA	2.67	3.00	801.00	115.00	---	916.00	**1090.00**
	Inst	Ea	Sm	SA	3.56	2.25	931.00	153.00	---	1084.00	**1290.00**
27" x 19-3/8" with 8" cc											
White	Inst	Ea	Lg	SA	2.67	3.00	733.00	115.00	---	848.00	**1010.00**
	Inst	Ea	Sm	SA	3.56	2.25	852.00	153.00	---	1005.00	**1200.00**
Color	Inst	Ea	Lg	SA	2.67	3.00	897.00	115.00	---	1012.00	**1200.00**
	Inst	Ea	Sm	SA	3.56	2.25	1040.00	153.00	---	1193.00	**1420.00**
Premium Color	Inst	Ea	Lg	SA	2.67	3.00	1010.00	115.00	---	1125.00	**1330.00**
	Inst	Ea	Sm	SA	3.56	2.25	1170.00	153.00	---	1323.00	**1570.00**
Lavatory slab only											
White	Inst	Ea	Lg	SA	1.60	5.00	373.00	68.80	---	441.80	**529.00**
	Inst	Ea	Sm	SA	2.13	3.75	434.00	91.60	---	525.60	**632.00**
Color	Inst	Ea	Lg	SA	1.60	5.00	485.00	68.80	---	553.80	**658.00**
	Inst	Ea	Sm	SA	2.13	3.75	564.00	91.60	---	655.60	**782.00**
Premium Color	Inst	Ea	Lg	SA	1.60	5.00	558.00	68.80	---	626.80	**741.00**
	Inst	Ea	Sm	SA	2.13	3.75	649.00	91.60	---	740.60	**879.00**

Description	Oper	Unit	Vol	Crew Size	Man-hours per Unit	Crew Output per Day	Avg Mat'l Unit Cost	Avg Labor Unit Cost	Avg Equip Unit Cost	Avg Total Unit Cost	Avg Price Incl O&P
Shroud only											
White	Inst	Ea	Lg	SA	1.60	5.00	176.00	68.80	---	244.80	**302.00**
	Inst	Ea	Sm	SA	2.13	3.75	204.00	91.60	---	295.60	**368.00**
Color	Inst	Ea	Lg	SA	1.60	5.00	228.00	68.80	---	296.80	**362.00**
	Inst	Ea	Sm	SA	2.13	3.75	265.00	91.60	---	356.60	**438.00**
Premium Color	Inst	Ea	Lg	SA	1.60	5.00	262.00	68.80	---	330.80	**401.00**
	Inst	Ea	Sm	SA	2.13	3.75	305.00	91.60	---	396.60	**484.00**
Wheelchair, meets ADA requirements											
20" x 27" with 8" or 4" cc											
White	Inst	Ea	Lg	SA	2.67	3.00	505.00	115.00	---	620.00	**747.00**
	Inst	Ea	Sm	SA	3.56	2.25	587.00	153.00	---	740.00	**897.00**
Color	Inst	Ea	Lg	SA	2.67	3.00	601.00	115.00	---	716.00	**858.00**
	Inst	Ea	Sm	SA	3.56	2.25	699.00	153.00	---	852.00	**1030.00**

Enameled cast iron

Countertop units (Kohler Products)

Farmington
19" x 16" with 8" or 4" cc

Description	Oper	Unit	Vol	Crew Size	Man-hours per Unit	Crew Output per Day	Avg Mat'l Unit Cost	Avg Labor Unit Cost	Avg Equip Unit Cost	Avg Total Unit Cost	Avg Price Incl O&P
White	Inst	Ea	Lg	SA	2.67	3.00	307.00	115.00	---	422.00	**520.00**
	Inst	Ea	Sm	SA	3.56	2.25	357.00	153.00	---	510.00	**633.00**
Color	Inst	Ea	Lg	SA	2.67	3.00	344.00	115.00	---	459.00	**562.00**
	Inst	Ea	Sm	SA	3.56	2.25	400.00	153.00	---	553.00	**682.00**
Premium Color	Inst	Ea	Lg	SA	2.67	3.00	368.00	115.00	---	483.00	**590.00**
	Inst	Ea	Sm	SA	3.56	2.25	428.00	153.00	---	581.00	**714.00**

Radiant
19" diameter with 4" cc

Description	Oper	Unit	Vol	Crew Size	Man-hours per Unit	Crew Output per Day	Avg Mat'l Unit Cost	Avg Labor Unit Cost	Avg Equip Unit Cost	Avg Total Unit Cost	Avg Price Incl O&P
White	Inst	Ea	Lg	SA	2.67	3.00	312.00	115.00	---	427.00	**526.00**
	Inst	Ea	Sm	SA	3.56	2.25	363.00	153.00	---	516.00	**640.00**
Color	Inst	Ea	Lg	SA	2.67	3.00	351.00	115.00	---	466.00	**570.00**
	Inst	Ea	Sm	SA	3.56	2.25	408.00	153.00	---	561.00	**691.00**
Premium Color	Inst	Ea	Lg	SA	2.67	3.00	376.00	115.00	---	491.00	**598.00**
	Inst	Ea	Sm	SA	3.56	2.25	437.00	153.00	---	590.00	**724.00**

Tahoe
21" x 19" with 8" or 4" cc

Description	Oper	Unit	Vol	Crew Size	Man-hours per Unit	Crew Output per Day	Avg Mat'l Unit Cost	Avg Labor Unit Cost	Avg Equip Unit Cost	Avg Total Unit Cost	Avg Price Incl O&P
White	Inst	Ea	Lg	SA	2.67	3.00	450.00	115.00	---	565.00	**684.00**
	Inst	Ea	Sm	SA	3.56	2.25	523.00	153.00	---	676.00	**823.00**
Color	Inst	Ea	Lg	SA	2.67	3.00	529.00	115.00	---	644.00	**775.00**
	Inst	Ea	Sm	SA	3.56	2.25	615.00	153.00	---	768.00	**930.00**

Description	Oper	Unit	Vol	Crew Size	Man-hours per Unit	Crew Output per Day	Avg Mat'l Unit Cost	Avg Labor Unit Cost	Avg Equip Unit Cost	Avg Total Unit Cost	Avg Price Incl O&P

Countertop units, with self rim (Kohler Products)

Ellington
19-1/4" x 16-1/4" with 8" or 4" cc

Description	Oper	Unit	Vol	Crew Size	Man-hours per Unit	Crew Output per Day	Avg Mat'l Unit Cost	Avg Labor Unit Cost	Avg Equip Unit Cost	Avg Total Unit Cost	Avg Price Incl O&P
White	Inst	Ea	Lg	SA	2.67	3.00	332.00	115.00	---	447.00	**548.00**
	Inst	Ea	Sm	SA	3.56	2.25	386.00	153.00	---	539.00	**666.00**
Color	Inst	Ea	Lg	SA	2.67	3.00	376.00	115.00	---	491.00	**599.00**
	Inst	Ea	Sm	SA	3.56	2.25	437.00	153.00	---	590.00	**725.00**
Premium Color	Inst	Ea	Lg	SA	2.67	3.00	405.00	115.00	---	520.00	**632.00**
	Inst	Ea	Sm	SA	3.56	2.25	471.00	153.00	---	624.00	**763.00**

Ellipse
33" x 19" with 8" cc

Description	Oper	Unit	Vol	Crew Size	Man-hours per Unit	Crew Output per Day	Avg Mat'l Unit Cost	Avg Labor Unit Cost	Avg Equip Unit Cost	Avg Total Unit Cost	Avg Price Incl O&P
White	Inst	Ea	Lg	SA	2.67	3.00	656.00	115.00	---	771.00	**920.00**
	Inst	Ea	Sm	SA	3.56	2.25	762.00	153.00	---	915.00	**1100.00**
Color	Inst	Ea	Lg	SA	2.67	3.00	797.00	115.00	---	912.00	**1080.00**
	Inst	Ea	Sm	SA	3.56	2.25	927.00	153.00	---	1080.00	**1290.00**
Premium Color	Inst	Ea	Lg	SA	2.67	3.00	889.00	115.00	---	1004.00	**1190.00**
	Inst	Ea	Sm	SA	3.56	2.25	1030.00	153.00	---	1183.00	**1410.00**

Farmington
19-1/4" x 16-1/4" with 8" or 4" cc

Description	Oper	Unit	Vol	Crew Size	Man-hours per Unit	Crew Output per Day	Avg Mat'l Unit Cost	Avg Labor Unit Cost	Avg Equip Unit Cost	Avg Total Unit Cost	Avg Price Incl O&P
White	Inst	Ea	Lg	SA	2.67	3.00	307.00	115.00	---	422.00	**520.00**
	Inst	Ea	Sm	SA	3.56	2.25	357.00	153.00	---	510.00	**633.00**
Color	Inst	Ea	Lg	SA	2.67	3.00	344.00	115.00	---	459.00	**562.00**
	Inst	Ea	Sm	SA	3.56	2.25	400.00	153.00	---	553.00	**682.00**
Premium Color	Inst	Ea	Lg	SA	2.67	3.00	368.00	115.00	---	483.00	**590.00**
	Inst	Ea	Sm	SA	3.56	2.25	428.00	153.00	---	581.00	**714.00**

Larkspur (scalloped oval)
28" x 19" with 8" cc

Description	Oper	Unit	Vol	Crew Size	Man-hours per Unit	Crew Output per Day	Avg Mat'l Unit Cost	Avg Labor Unit Cost	Avg Equip Unit Cost	Avg Total Unit Cost	Avg Price Incl O&P
White	Inst	Ea	Lg	SA	2.67	3.00	520.00	115.00	---	635.00	**765.00**
	Inst	Ea	Sm	SA	3.56	2.25	605.00	153.00	---	758.00	**918.00**
Color	Inst	Ea	Lg	SA	2.67	3.00	621.00	115.00	---	736.00	**881.00**
	Inst	Ea	Sm	SA	3.56	2.25	722.00	153.00	---	875.00	**1050.00**
Premium Color	Inst	Ea	Lg	SA	2.67	3.00	686.00	115.00	---	801.00	**956.00**
	Inst	Ea	Sm	SA	3.56	2.25	798.00	153.00	---	951.00	**1140.00**

Man's
28" x 19" with 8" cc

Description	Oper	Unit	Vol	Crew Size	Man-hours per Unit	Crew Output per Day	Avg Mat'l Unit Cost	Avg Labor Unit Cost	Avg Equip Unit Cost	Avg Total Unit Cost	Avg Price Incl O&P
White	Inst	Ea	Lg	SA	2.67	3.00	683.00	115.00	---	798.00	**952.00**
	Inst	Ea	Sm	SA	3.56	2.25	794.00	153.00	---	947.00	**1140.00**
Color	Inst	Ea	Lg	SA	2.67	3.00	832.00	115.00	---	947.00	**1120.00**
	Inst	Ea	Sm	SA	3.56	2.25	968.00	153.00	---	1121.00	**1340.00**
Premium Color	Inst	Ea	Lg	SA	2.67	3.00	929.00	115.00	---	1044.00	**1240.00**
	Inst	Ea	Sm	SA	3.56	2.25	1080.00	153.00	---	1233.00	**1470.00**

Description	Oper	Unit	Vol	Crew Size	Man-hours per Unit	Crew Output per Day	Avg Mat'l Unit Cost	Avg Labor Unit Cost	Avg Equip Unit Cost	Avg Total Unit Cost	Avg Price Incl O&P
Providence											
22" x 19" with 8" or 4" cc											
White	Inst	Ea	Lg	SA	2.67	3.00	439.00	115.00	---	554.00	**671.00**
	Inst	Ea	Sm	SA	3.56	2.25	510.00	153.00	---	663.00	**809.00**
Color	Inst	Ea	Lg	SA	2.67	3.00	515.00	115.00	---	630.00	**758.00**
	Inst	Ea	Sm	SA	3.56	2.25	599.00	153.00	---	752.00	**910.00**
Premium Color	Inst	Ea	Lg	SA	2.67	3.00	564.00	115.00	---	679.00	**815.00**
	Inst	Ea	Sm	SA	3.56	2.25	656.00	153.00	---	809.00	**977.00**
Revival											
28" x 19" with 8" or 4" cc											
White	Inst	Ea	Lg	SA	2.67	3.00	500.00	115.00	---	615.00	**742.00**
	Inst	Ea	Sm	SA	3.56	2.25	582.00	153.00	---	735.00	**891.00**
Color	Inst	Ea	Lg	SA	2.67	3.00	595.00	115.00	---	710.00	**851.00**
	Inst	Ea	Sm	SA	3.56	2.25	692.00	153.00	---	845.00	**1020.00**
Premium Color	Inst	Ea	Lg	SA	2.67	3.00	656.00	115.00	---	771.00	**921.00**
	Inst	Ea	Sm	SA	3.56	2.25	763.00	153.00	---	916.00	**1100.00**
Thoreau											
24" x 18" oval											
White	Inst	Ea	Lg	SA	2.67	3.00	467.00	115.00	---	582.00	**704.00**
	Inst	Ea	Sm	SA	3.56	2.25	544.00	153.00	---	697.00	**847.00**
Color	Inst	Ea	Lg	SA	2.67	3.00	552.00	115.00	---	667.00	**802.00**
	Inst	Ea	Sm	SA	3.56	2.25	642.00	153.00	---	795.00	**961.00**
Premium Color	Inst	Ea	Lg	SA	2.67	3.00	608.00	115.00	---	723.00	**865.00**
	Inst	Ea	Sm	SA	3.56	2.25	707.00	153.00	---	860.00	**1030.00**

Wall-hung units, with shelf back (Kohler Products)
Adjustments

Description	Oper	Unit	Vol	Crew Size	Man-hours per Unit	Crew Output per Day	Avg Mat'l Unit Cost	Avg Labor Unit Cost	Avg Equip Unit Cost	Avg Total Unit Cost	Avg Price Incl O&P
For two 15" L towel bars, ADD											
	Inst	Pr	Lg	---	---	---	55.20	---	---	55.20	**63.50**
	Inst	Pr	Sm	---	---	---	64.20	---	---	64.20	**73.80**
Hampton											
19" x 17"											
White	Inst	Ea	Lg	SA	2.67	3.00	518.00	115.00	---	633.00	**762.00**
	Inst	Ea	Sm	SA	3.56	2.25	602.00	153.00	---	755.00	**915.00**
Color	Inst	Ea	Lg	SA	2.67	3.00	618.00	115.00	---	733.00	**877.00**
	Inst	Ea	Sm	SA	3.56	2.25	719.00	153.00	---	872.00	**1050.00**
22" x 19"											
White	Inst	Ea	Lg	SA	2.67	3.00	578.00	115.00	---	693.00	**832.00**
	Inst	Ea	Sm	SA	3.56	2.25	673.00	153.00	---	826.00	**996.00**
Color	Inst	Ea	Lg	SA	2.67	3.00	695.00	115.00	---	810.00	**966.00**
	Inst	Ea	Sm	SA	3.56	2.25	808.00	153.00	---	961.00	**1150.00**
Marston, corner unit											
16" x 16"											
White	Inst	Ea	Lg	SA	2.67	3.00	652.00	115.00	---	767.00	**916.00**
	Inst	Ea	Sm	SA	3.56	2.25	758.00	153.00	---	911.00	**1090.00**
Color	Inst	Ea	Lg	SA	2.67	3.00	792.00	115.00	---	907.00	**1080.00**
	Inst	Ea	Sm	SA	3.56	2.25	921.00	153.00	---	1074.00	**1280.00**

Description	Oper	Unit	Vol	Crew Size	Man-hours per Unit	Crew Output per Day	Avg Mat'l Unit Cost	Avg Labor Unit Cost	Avg Equip Unit Cost	Avg Total Unit Cost	Avg Price Incl O&P
Taunton											
16" x 14"											
White	Inst	Ea	Lg	SA	2.67	3.00	612.00	115.00	---	727.00	**871.00**
	Inst	Ea	Sm	SA	3.56	2.25	712.00	153.00	---	865.00	**1040.00**
Trailer											
13" x 13"											
White	Inst	Ea	Lg	SA	2.00	4.00	618.00	86.00	---	704.00	**836.00**
	Inst	Ea	Sm	SA	2.67	3.00	719.00	115.00	---	834.00	**993.00**

Americast - Porcelain enameled finish over steel composite material
Countertop units, with self rim (American Standard Products)

Description	Oper	Unit	Vol	Crew Size	Man-hours per Unit	Crew Output per Day	Avg Mat'l Unit Cost	Avg Labor Unit Cost	Avg Equip Unit Cost	Avg Total Unit Cost	Avg Price Incl O&P
Acclivity											
19" diameter with 8" or 4" cc											
White	Inst	Ea	Lg	SA	2.67	3.00	275.00	115.00	---	390.00	**483.00**
	Inst	Ea	Sm	SA	3.56	2.25	320.00	153.00	---	473.00	**590.00**
Color	Inst	Ea	Lg	SA	2.67	3.00	307.00	115.00	---	422.00	**520.00**
	Inst	Ea	Sm	SA	3.56	2.25	357.00	153.00	---	510.00	**633.00**
Premium Color	Inst	Ea	Lg	SA	2.67	3.00	404.00	115.00	---	519.00	**631.00**
	Inst	Ea	Sm	SA	3.56	2.25	470.00	153.00	---	623.00	**762.0**
Affinity											
20" x 17" with 8" or 4" cc											
White	Inst	Ea	Lg	SA	2.67	3.00	293.00	115.00	---	408.00	**504.00**
	Inst	Ea	Sm	SA	3.56	2.25	341.00	153.00	---	494.00	**615.00**
Color	Inst	Ea	Lg	SA	2.67	3.00	334.00	115.00	---	449.00	**551.00**
	Inst	Ea	Sm	SA	3.56	2.25	388.00	153.00	---	541.00	**669.00**
Premium Color	Inst	Ea	Lg	SA	2.67	3.00	432.00	115.00	---	547.00	**664.00**
	Inst	Ea	Sm	SA	3.56	2.25	503.00	153.00	---	656.00	**800.00**

Kitchen

Kitchen and utility, with good quality fittings, faucets, and sprayer

Americast - Porcelain enameled finish over steel composite material (American Standard)

Description	Oper	Unit	Vol	Crew Size	Man-hours per Unit	Crew Output per Day	Avg Mat'l Unit Cost	Avg Labor Unit Cost	Avg Equip Unit Cost	Avg Total Unit Cost	Avg Price Incl O&P
Silhouette, triple bowl (2 large ends / 1 small center) with self rim											
41-1/2" x 22" x 9-1/2"											
White	Inst	Ea	Lg	SA	5.71	1.40	737.00	246.00	---	983.00	**1200.00**
	Inst	Ea	Sm	SA	7.62	1.05	857.00	328.00	---	1185.00	**1460.00**
Color	Inst	Ea	Lg	SA	5.71	1.40	878.00	246.00	---	1124.00	**1370.00**
	Inst	Ea	Sm	SA	7.62	1.05	1020.00	328.00	---	1348.00	**1650.00**
Premium Color	Inst	Ea	Lg	SA	5.71	1.40	969.00	246.00	---	1215.00	**1470.00**
	Inst	Ea	Sm	SA	7.62	1.05	1130.00	328.00	---	1458.00	**1770.00**
Silhouette, double bowl with self rim											
33" x 22" x 9-1/2"											
White	Inst	Ea	Lg	SA	5.00	1.60	481.00	215.00	---	696.00	**865.00**
	Inst	Ea	Sm	SA	6.67	1.20	560.00	287.00	---	847.00	**1060.00**
Color	Inst	Ea	Lg	SA	5.00	1.60	558.00	215.00	---	773.00	**954.00**
	Inst	Ea	Sm	SA	6.67	1.20	649.00	287.00	---	936.00	**1160.00**
Premium Color	Inst	Ea	Lg	SA	5.00	1.60	615.00	215.00	---	830.00	**1020.00**
	Inst	Ea	Sm	SA	6.67	1.20	715.00	287.00	---	1002.00	**1240.00**

Description	Oper	Unit	Vol	Crew Size	Man-hours per Unit	Crew Output per Day	Avg Mat'l Unit Cost	Avg Labor Unit Cost	Avg Equip Unit Cost	Avg Total Unit Cost	Avg Price Incl O&P
Silhouette, double bowl with tile edge											
33" x 22" x 9-1/2"											
White	Inst	Ea	Lg	SA	5.00	1.60	499.00	215.00	---	714.00	**885.00**
	Inst	Ea	Sm	SA	6.67	1.20	580.00	287.00	---	867.00	**1080.00**
Color	Inst	Ea	Lg	SA	5.00	1.60	583.00	215.00	---	798.00	**983.00**
	Inst	Ea	Sm	SA	6.67	1.20	678.00	287.00	---	965.00	**1200.00**
Premium Color	Inst	Ea	Lg	SA	5.00	1.60	639.00	215.00	---	854.00	**1050.00**
	Inst	Ea	Sm	SA	6.67	1.20	744.00	287.00	---	1031.00	**1270.00**
Silhouette, dual level double bowl with self rim											
33" x 22" x 9-1/2"											
White	Inst	Ea	Lg	SA	5.00	1.60	495.00	215.00	---	710.00	**881.00**
	Inst	Ea	Sm	SA	6.67	1.20	576.00	287.00	---	863.00	**1080.00**
Color	Inst	Ea	Lg	SA	5.00	1.60	588.00	215.00	---	803.00	**988.00**
	Inst	Ea	Sm	SA	6.67	1.20	684.00	287.00	---	971.00	**1200.00**
Premium Color	Inst	Ea	Lg	SA	5.00	1.60	643.00	215.00	---	858.00	**1050.00**
	Inst	Ea	Sm	SA	6.67	1.20	748.00	287.00	---	1035.00	**1280.00**
Silhouette, dual level double bowl with tile edge											
33" x 22" x 9-1/2"											
White	Inst	Ea	Lg	SA	5.00	1.60	522.00	215.00	---	737.00	**912.00**
	Inst	Ea	Sm	SA	6.67	1.20	607.00	287.00	---	894.00	**1110.00**
Color	Inst	Ea	Lg	SA	5.00	1.60	610.00	215.00	---	825.00	**1010.00**
	Inst	Ea	Sm	SA	6.67	1.20	709.00	287.00	---	996.00	**1230.00**
Premium Color	Inst	Ea	Lg	SA	5.00	1.60	670.00	215.00	---	885.00	**1080.00**
	Inst	Ea	Sm	SA	6.67	1.20	779.00	287.00	---	1066.00	**1310.00**
Silhouette, dual level double bowl with self rim											
38" x 22" x 9-1/2"											
White	Inst	Ea	Lg	SA	5.00	1.60	615.00	215.00	---	830.00	**1020.00**
	Inst	Ea	Sm	SA	6.67	1.20	716.00	287.00	---	1003.00	**1240.00**
Color	Inst	Ea	Lg	SA	5.00	1.60	727.00	215.00	---	942.00	**1150.00**
	Inst	Ea	Sm	SA	6.67	1.20	845.00	287.00	---	1132.00	**1390.00**
Premium Color	Inst	Ea	Lg	SA	5.00	1.60	800.00	215.00	---	1015.00	**1230.00**
	Inst	Ea	Sm	SA	6.67	1.20	931.00	287.00	---	1218.00	**1490.00**
Silhouette, dual level double bowl with tile edge											
38" x 22" x 9-1/2"											
White	Inst	Ea	Lg	SA	5.00	1.60	633.00	215.00	---	848.00	**1040.00**
	Inst	Ea	Sm	SA	6.67	1.20	736.00	287.00	---	1023.00	**1260.00**
Color	Inst	Ea	Lg	SA	5.00	1.60	748.00	215.00	---	963.00	**1170.00**
	Inst	Ea	Sm	SA	6.67	1.20	870.00	287.00	---	1157.00	**1420.00**
Premium Color	Inst	Ea	Lg	SA	5.00	1.60	826.00	215.00	---	1041.00	**1260.00**
	Inst	Ea	Sm	SA	6.67	1.20	961.00	287.00	---	1248.00	**1520.00**
Silhouette, single bowl with self rim											
25" x 22" x 9-1/2"											
White	Inst	Ea	Lg	SA	4.00	2.00	377.00	172.00	---	549.00	**683.00**
	Inst	Ea	Sm	SA	5.33	1.50	439.00	229.00	---	668.00	**837.00**
Color	Inst	Ea	Lg	SA	4.00	2.00	432.00	172.00	---	604.00	**747.00**
	Inst	Ea	Sm	SA	5.33	1.50	503.00	229.00	---	732.00	**911.00**
Premium Color	Inst	Ea	Lg	SA	4.00	2.00	469.00	172.00	---	641.00	**789.00**
	Inst	Ea	Sm	SA	5.33	1.50	546.00	229.00	---	775.00	**960.00**

Description	Oper	Unit	Vol	Crew Size	Man-hours per Unit	Crew Output per Day	Avg Mat'l Unit Cost	Avg Labor Unit Cost	Avg Equip Unit Cost	Avg Total Unit Cost	Avg Price Incl O&P
Silhouette, single bowl with tile edge											
25" x 22" x 9-1/2"											
White	Inst	Ea	Lg	SA	4.00	2.00	396.00	172.00	---	568.00	**704.00**
	Inst	Ea	Sm	SA	5.33	1.50	460.00	229.00	---	689.00	**862.00**
Color	Inst	Ea	Lg	SA	4.00	2.00	456.00	172.00	---	628.00	**774.00**
	Inst	Ea	Sm	SA	5.33	1.50	531.00	229.00	---	760.00	**943.00**
Premium Color	Inst	Ea	Lg	SA	4.00	2.00	495.00	172.00	---	667.00	**819.00**
	Inst	Ea	Sm	SA	5.33	1.50	576.00	229.00	---	805.00	**994.00**
Silhouette, single bowl (island) with self rim											
18" x 18" x 8-1/2"											
White	Inst	Ea	Lg	SA	2.67	3.00	342.00	115.00	---	457.00	**560.00**
	Inst	Ea	Sm	SA	3.56	2.25	398.00	153.00	---	551.00	**680.00**
Color	Inst	Ea	Lg	SA	2.67	3.00	389.00	115.00	---	504.00	**614.00**
	Inst	Ea	Sm	SA	3.56	2.25	453.00	153.00	---	606.00	**743.00**
Premium Color	Inst	Ea	Lg	SA	2.67	3.00	420.00	115.00	---	535.00	**649.00**
	Inst	Ea	Sm	SA	3.56	2.25	488.00	153.00	---	641.00	**783.00**
Silhouette, shallow, double bowl with self rim											
33" x 22" x 6-1/2"											
White	Inst	Ea	Lg	SA	5.00	1.60	469.00	215.00	---	684.00	**851.00**
	Inst	Ea	Sm	SA	6.67	1.20	546.00	287.00	---	833.00	**1040.00**
Color	Inst	Ea	Lg	SA	5.00	1.60	546.00	215.00	---	761.00	**940.00**
	Inst	Ea	Sm	SA	6.67	1.20	636.00	287.00	---	923.00	**1150.00**
Premium Color	Inst	Ea	Lg	SA	5.00	1.60	597.00	215.00	---	812.00	**999.00**
	Inst	Ea	Sm	SA	6.67	1.20	694.00	287.00	---	981.00	**1210.00**

Enameled cast iron (Kohler Products)

Description	Oper	Unit	Vol	Crew Size	Man-hours per Unit	Crew Output per Day	Avg Mat'l Unit Cost	Avg Labor Unit Cost	Avg Equip Unit Cost	Avg Total Unit Cost	Avg Price Incl O&P
Bakersfield, single bowl with self rim											
31" x 22"											
White	Inst	Ea	Lg	SA	4.00	2.00	542.00	172.00	---	714.00	**873.00**
	Inst	Ea	Sm	SA	5.33	1.50	630.00	229.00	---	859.00	**1060.00**
Color	Inst	Ea	Lg	SA	4.00	2.00	644.00	172.00	---	816.00	**990.00**
	Inst	Ea	Sm	SA	5.33	1.50	749.00	229.00	---	978.00	**1190.00**
Premium Color	Inst	Ea	Lg	SA	4.00	2.00	721.00	172.00	---	893.00	**1080.00**
	Inst	Ea	Sm	SA	5.33	1.50	838.00	229.00	---	1067.00	**1300.00**
Bon Vivant, triple bowl (2 large / 1 small) with tile edge or self rim											
48" x 22"											
White	Inst	Ea	Lg	SA	5.71	1.40	941.00	246.00	---	1187.00	**1440.00**
	Inst	Ea	Sm	SA	7.62	1.05	1090.00	328.00	---	1418.00	**1730.00**
Color	Inst	Ea	Lg	SA	5.71	1.40	1140.00	246.00	---	1386.00	**1670.00**
	Inst	Ea	Sm	SA	7.62	1.05	1330.00	328.00	---	1658.00	**2000.00**
Premium Color	Inst	Ea	Lg	SA	5.71	1.40	1290.00	246.00	---	1536.00	**1850.00**
	Inst	Ea	Sm	SA	7.62	1.05	1510.00	328.00	---	1838.00	**2210.00**
Brookfield, double bowl with tile edge or self rim											
33" x 22"											
White	Inst	Ea	Lg	SA	5.00	1.60	483.00	215.00	---	698.00	**868.00**
	Inst	Ea	Sm	SA	6.67	1.20	562.00	287.00	---	849.00	**1060.00**
Color	Inst	Ea	Lg	SA	5.00	1.60	571.00	215.00	---	786.00	**968.00**
	Inst	Ea	Sm	SA	6.67	1.20	664.00	287.00	---	951.00	**1180.00**
Premium Color	Inst	Ea	Lg	SA	5.00	1.60	636.00	215.00	---	851.00	**1040.00**
	Inst	Ea	Sm	SA	6.67	1.20	740.00	287.00	---	1027.00	**1270.00**

Description	Oper	Unit	Vol	Crew Size	Man-hours per Unit	Crew Output per Day	Avg Mat'l Unit Cost	Avg Labor Unit Cost	Avg Equip Unit Cost	Avg Total Unit Cost	Avg Price Incl O&P
Cilantro, double bowl with tile edge or self rim											
36" x 22"											
White	Inst	Ea	Lg	SA	5.00	1.60	637.00	215.00	---	852.00	**1040.00**
	Inst	Ea	Sm	SA	6.67	1.20	740.00	287.00	---	1027.00	**1270.00**
Color	Inst	Ea	Lg	SA	5.00	1.60	762.00	215.00	---	977.00	**1190.00**
	Inst	Ea	Sm	SA	6.67	1.20	886.00	287.00	---	1173.00	**1440.00**
Premium Color	Inst	Ea	Lg	SA	5.00	1.60	856.00	215.00	---	1071.00	**1300.00**
	Inst	Ea	Sm	SA	6.67	1.20	996.00	287.00	---	1283.00	**1560.00**
Entrée, single bowl, undercounter											
33" x 22"											
White	Inst	Ea	Lg	SA	4.00	2.00	798.00	172.00	---	970.00	**1170.00**
	Inst	Ea	Sm	SA	5.33	1.50	928.00	229.00	---	1157.00	**1400.00**
Color	Inst	Ea	Lg	SA	4.00	2.00	964.00	172.00	---	1136.00	**1360.00**
	Inst	Ea	Sm	SA	5.33	1.50	1120.00	229.00	---	1349.00	**1620.00**
Premium Color	Inst	Ea	Lg	SA	4.00	2.00	1090.00	172.00	---	1262.00	**1500.00**
	Inst	Ea	Sm	SA	5.33	1.50	1270.00	229.00	---	1499.00	**1790.00**
Executive Chef, double bowl (1 large / 1 medium), undercounter											
33" x 22"											
White	Inst	Ea	Lg	SA	5.00	1.60	712.00	215.00	---	927.00	**1130.00**
	Inst	Ea	Sm	SA	6.67	1.20	829.00	287.00	---	1116.00	**1370.00**
Color	Inst	Ea	Lg	SA	5.00	1.60	857.00	215.00	---	1072.00	**1300.00**
	Inst	Ea	Sm	SA	6.67	1.20	997.00	287.00	---	1284.00	**1560.00**
Premium Color	Inst	Ea	Lg	SA	5.00	1.60	966.00	215.00	---	1181.00	**1420.00**
	Inst	Ea	Sm	SA	6.67	1.20	1120.00	287.00	---	1407.00	**1710.00**
Lakefield High / Low, double bowl (1 large / 1 small), undercounter											
33" x 22"											
White	Inst	Ea	Lg	SA	5.00	1.60	604.00	215.00	---	819.00	**1010.00**
	Inst	Ea	Sm	SA	6.67	1.20	702.00	287.00	---	989.00	**1220.00**
Color	Inst	Ea	Lg	SA	5.00	1.60	721.00	215.00	---	936.00	**1140.00**
	Inst	Ea	Sm	SA	6.67	1.20	839.00	287.00	---	1126.00	**1380.00**
Premium Color	Inst	Ea	Lg	SA	5.00	1.60	810.00	215.00	---	1025.00	**1240.00**
	Inst	Ea	Sm	SA	6.67	1.20	942.00	287.00	---	1229.00	**1500.00**
Marsala, double bowl (1 large / 1 medium) with tile edge or self rim											
33" x 22"											
White	Inst	Ea	Lg	SA	5.00	1.60	740.00	215.00	---	955.00	**1160.00**
	Inst	Ea	Sm	SA	6.67	1.20	861.00	287.00	---	1148.00	**1410.00**
Color	Inst	Ea	Lg	SA	5.00	1.60	859.00	215.00	---	1074.00	**1300.00**
	Inst	Ea	Sm	SA	6.67	1.20	1000.00	287.00	---	1287.00	**1570.00**
Premium Color	Inst	Ea	Lg	SA	5.00	1.60	968.00	215.00	---	1183.00	**1430.00**
	Inst	Ea	Sm	SA	6.67	1.20	1130.00	287.00	---	1417.00	**1710.00**
Mayfield, single bowl with self rim											
25" x 22"											
White	Inst	Ea	Lg	SA	4.00	2.00	383.00	172.00	---	555.00	**689.00**
	Inst	Ea	Sm	SA	5.33	1.50	445.00	229.00	---	674.00	**844.00**
Color	Inst	Ea	Lg	SA	4.00	2.00	445.00	172.00	---	617.00	**761.00**
	Inst	Ea	Sm	SA	5.33	1.50	517.00	229.00	---	746.00	**927.00**
Premium Color	Inst	Ea	Lg	SA	4.00	2.00	492.00	172.00	---	664.00	**815.00**
	Inst	Ea	Sm	SA	5.33	1.50	572.00	229.00	---	801.00	**990.00**

Description	Oper	Unit	Vol	Crew Size	Man-hours per Unit	Crew Output per Day	Avg Mat'l Unit Cost	Avg Labor Unit Cost	Avg Equip Unit Cost	Avg Total Unit Cost	Avg Price Incl O&P

Porcelain on steel (American Standard)

Double bowl, with self rim
33" x 22"

Description	Oper	Unit	Vol	Crew Size	Man-hours per Unit	Crew Output per Day	Avg Mat'l Unit Cost	Avg Labor Unit Cost	Avg Equip Unit Cost	Avg Total Unit Cost	Avg Price Incl O&P
White	Inst	Ea	Lg	SA	5.00	1.60	279.00	215.00	---	494.00	**632.00**
	Inst	Ea	Sm	SA	6.67	1.20	324.00	287.00	---	611.00	**789.00**
Color	Inst	Ea	Lg	SA	5.00	1.60	293.00	215.00	---	508.00	**648.00**
	Inst	Ea	Sm	SA	6.67	1.20	340.00	287.00	---	627.00	**807.00**

Double bowl, dual level with self rim
33" x 22"

Description	Oper	Unit	Vol	Crew Size	Man-hours per Unit	Crew Output per Day	Avg Mat'l Unit Cost	Avg Labor Unit Cost	Avg Equip Unit Cost	Avg Total Unit Cost	Avg Price Incl O&P
White	Inst	Ea	Lg	SA	5.00	1.60	282.00	215.00	---	497.00	**636.00**
	Inst	Ea	Sm	SA	6.67	1.20	327.00	287.00	---	614.00	**793.00**
Color	Inst	Ea	Lg	SA	5.00	1.60	294.00	215.00	---	509.00	**650.00**
	Inst	Ea	Sm	SA	6.67	1.20	342.00	287.00	---	629.00	**810.00**

Single bowl
25" x 22"

Description	Oper	Unit	Vol	Crew Size	Man-hours per Unit	Crew Output per Day	Avg Mat'l Unit Cost	Avg Labor Unit Cost	Avg Equip Unit Cost	Avg Total Unit Cost	Avg Price Incl O&P
White	Inst	Ea	Lg	SA	4.00	2.00	255.00	172.00	---	427.00	**543.00**
	Inst	Ea	Sm	SA	5.33	1.50	296.00	229.00	---	525.00	**673.00**
Color	Inst	Ea	Lg	SA	4.00	2.00	269.00	172.00	---	441.00	**558.00**
	Inst	Ea	Sm	SA	5.33	1.50	312.00	229.00	---	541.00	**692.00**

Stainless steel (Kohler)

Triple bowl, flat rim, undercounter

Description	Oper	Unit	Vol	Crew Size	Man-hours per Unit	Crew Output per Day	Avg Mat'l Unit Cost	Avg Labor Unit Cost	Avg Equip Unit Cost	Avg Total Unit Cost	Avg Price Incl O&P
43" x 22"	Inst	Ea	Lg	SA	5.71	1.40	1570.00	246.00	---	1816.00	**2170.00**
	Inst	Ea	Sm	SA	7.62	1.05	1830.00	328.00	---	2158.00	**2580.00**

Double bowl, flat rim, undercounter

Description	Oper	Unit	Vol	Crew Size	Man-hours per Unit	Crew Output per Day	Avg Mat'l Unit Cost	Avg Labor Unit Cost	Avg Equip Unit Cost	Avg Total Unit Cost	Avg Price Incl O&P
29" x 16" (equal)	Inst	Ea	Lg	SA	5.00	1.60	1040.00	215.00	---	1255.00	**1510.00**
	Inst	Ea	Sm	SA	6.67	1.20	1210.00	287.00	---	1497.00	**1810.00**
29" x 16" (high / low)	Inst	Ea	Lg	SA	5.00	1.60	1040.00	215.00	---	1255.00	**1510.00**
	Inst	Ea	Sm	SA	6.67	1.20	1210.00	287.00	---	1497.00	**1810.00**
29" x 19" (large / medium)	Inst	Ea	Lg	SA	5.00	1.60	1060.00	215.00	---	1275.00	**1540.00**
	Inst	Ea	Sm	SA	6.67	1.20	1240.00	287.00	---	1527.00	**1840.00**
37" x 19" (xtra lge / med)	Inst	Ea	Lg	SA	5.00	1.60	1230.00	215.00	---	1445.00	**1720.00**
	Inst	Ea	Sm	SA	6.67	1.20	1430.00	287.00	---	1717.00	**2060.00**

Single bowl, flat rim, undercounter

Description	Oper	Unit	Vol	Crew Size	Man-hours per Unit	Crew Output per Day	Avg Mat'l Unit Cost	Avg Labor Unit Cost	Avg Equip Unit Cost	Avg Total Unit Cost	Avg Price Incl O&P
14" x 16" x 9-1/2"	Inst	Ea	Lg	SA	4.00	2.00	639.00	172.00	---	811.00	**985.00**
	Inst	Ea	Sm	SA	5.33	1.50	744.00	229.00	---	973.00	**1190.00**
16" x 16" x 9-1/2"	Inst	Ea	Lg	SA	4.00	2.00	721.00	172.00	---	893.00	**1080.00**
	Inst	Ea	Sm	SA	5.33	1.50	838.00	229.00	---	1067.00	**1300.00**
18" x 18" x 9-1/2"	Inst	Ea	Lg	SA	4.00	2.00	771.00	172.00	---	943.00	**1140.00**
	Inst	Ea	Sm	SA	5.33	1.50	896.00	229.00	---	1125.00	**1360.00**
35" x 16" x 9-1/2"	Inst	Ea	Lg	SA	4.00	2.00	1090.00	172.00	---	1262.00	**1500.00**
	Inst	Ea	Sm	SA	5.33	1.50	1270.00	229.00	---	1499.00	**1790.00**

Description	Oper	Unit	Vol	Crew Size	Man-hours per Unit	Crew Output per Day	Avg Mat'l Unit Cost	Avg Labor Unit Cost	Avg Equip Unit Cost	Avg Total Unit Cost	Avg Price Incl O&P

Bar

Enameled cast iron (Kohler)

Addison
13" x 13"

Description	Oper	Unit	Vol	Crew Size	Man-hours per Unit	Crew Output per Day	Avg Mat'l Unit Cost	Avg Labor Unit Cost	Avg Equip Unit Cost	Avg Total Unit Cost	Avg Price Incl O&P
White	Inst	Ea	Lg	SA	4.00	2.00	345.00	172.00	---	517.00	**646.00**
	Inst	Ea	Sm	SA	5.33	1.50	401.00	229.00	---	630.00	**794.00**
Color	Inst	Ea	Lg	SA	4.00	2.00	398.00	172.00	---	570.00	**707.00**
	Inst	Ea	Sm	SA	5.33	1.50	463.00	229.00	---	692.00	**865.00**
Premium Color	Inst	Ea	Lg	SA	4.00	2.00	437.00	172.00	---	609.00	**753.00**
	Inst	Ea	Sm	SA	5.33	1.50	509.00	229.00	---	738.00	**917.00**

Apertif with tile edge or self rim
16" x 19"

Description	Oper	Unit	Vol	Crew Size	Man-hours per Unit	Crew Output per Day	Avg Mat'l Unit Cost	Avg Labor Unit Cost	Avg Equip Unit Cost	Avg Total Unit Cost	Avg Price Incl O&P
White	Inst	Ea	Lg	SA	4.00	2.00	428.00	172.00	---	600.00	**742.00**
	Inst	Ea	Sm	SA	5.33	1.50	498.00	229.00	---	727.00	**906.00**
Color	Inst	Ea	Lg	SA	4.00	2.00	502.00	172.00	---	674.00	**827.00**
	Inst	Ea	Sm	SA	5.33	1.50	584.00	229.00	---	813.00	**1000.00**
Premium Color	Inst	Ea	Lg	SA	4.00	2.00	558.00	172.00	---	730.00	**891.00**
	Inst	Ea	Sm	SA	5.33	1.50	649.00	229.00	---	878.00	**1080.00**

Entertainer, semicircular with self rim or undercounter self rim
22" x 18"

Description	Oper	Unit	Vol	Crew Size	Man-hours per Unit	Crew Output per Day	Avg Mat'l Unit Cost	Avg Labor Unit Cost	Avg Equip Unit Cost	Avg Total Unit Cost	Avg Price Incl O&P
White	Inst	Ea	Lg	SA	4.00	2.00	460.00	172.00	---	632.00	**779.00**
	Inst	Ea	Sm	SA	5.33	1.50	535.00	229.00	---	764.00	**948.00**
Color	Inst	Ea	Lg	SA	4.00	2.00	542.00	172.00	---	714.00	**873.00**
	Inst	Ea	Sm	SA	5.33	1.50	630.00	229.00	---	859.00	**1060.00**
Premium Color	Inst	Ea	Lg	SA	4.00	2.00	603.00	172.00	---	775.00	**943.00**
	Inst	Ea	Sm	SA	5.33	1.50	701.00	229.00	---	930.00	**1140.00**

Sorbet with tile edge or self rim
15" x 15"

Description	Oper	Unit	Vol	Crew Size	Man-hours per Unit	Crew Output per Day	Avg Mat'l Unit Cost	Avg Labor Unit Cost	Avg Equip Unit Cost	Avg Total Unit Cost	Avg Price Incl O&P
White	Inst	Ea	Lg	SA	4.00	2.00	391.00	172.00	---	563.00	**699.00**
	Inst	Ea	Sm	SA	5.33	1.50	455.00	229.00	---	684.00	**856.00**
Color	Inst	Ea	Lg	SA	4.00	2.00	455.00	172.00	---	627.00	**773.00**
	Inst	Ea	Sm	SA	5.33	1.50	529.00	229.00	---	758.00	**941.00**
Premium Color	Inst	Ea	Lg	SA	4.00	2.00	504.00	172.00	---	676.00	**829.00**
	Inst	Ea	Sm	SA	5.33	1.50	586.00	229.00	---	815.00	**1010.00**

Stainless steel (Kohler)

Lyric, single bowl with self rim
15" x 15"

Description	Oper	Unit	Vol	Crew Size	Man-hours per Unit	Crew Output per Day	Avg Mat'l Unit Cost	Avg Labor Unit Cost	Avg Equip Unit Cost	Avg Total Unit Cost	Avg Price Incl O&P
	Inst	Ea	Lg	SA	4.00	2.00	348.00	172.00	---	520.00	**649.00**
	Inst	Ea	Sm	SA	5.33	1.50	404.00	229.00	---	633.00	**797.00**

Description	Oper	Unit	Vol	Crew Size	Man-hours per Unit	Crew Output per Day	Avg Mat'l Unit Cost	Avg Labor Unit Cost	Avg Equip Unit Cost	Avg Total Unit Cost	Avg Price Incl O&P

Utility/service

Enameled cast iron (Kohler)

Sutton high back

24" x 18", 8" high back	Inst	Ea	Lg	SA	4.00	2.00	818.00	172.00	---	990.00	**1190.00**
	Inst	Ea	Sm	SA	5.33	1.50	951.00	229.00	---	1180.00	**1430.00**

Tech

24" x 18", bubbler mound	Inst	Ea	Lg	SA	4.00	2.00	497.00	172.00	---	669.00	**821.00**
	Inst	Ea	Sm	SA	5.33	1.50	578.00	229.00	---	807.00	**997.00**

Whitby

28" x 28" corner	Inst	Ea	Lg	SA	4.00	2.00	1030.00	172.00	---	1202.00	**1430.00**
	Inst	Ea	Sm	SA	5.33	1.50	1200.00	229.00	---	1429.00	**1710.00**

Glen Falls, laundry sink
25" x 22"

White	Inst	Ea	Lg	SA	4.00	2.00	572.00	172.00	---	744.00	**907.00**
	Inst	Ea	Sm	SA	5.33	1.50	665.00	229.00	---	894.00	**1100.00**
Color	Inst	Ea	Lg	SA	4.00	2.00	686.00	172.00	---	858.00	**1040.00**
	Inst	Ea	Sm	SA	5.33	1.50	798.00	229.00	---	1027.00	**1250.00**

River Falls, laundry sink
25" x 22"

White	Inst	Ea	Lg	SA	4.00	2.00	627.00	172.00	---	799.00	**970.00**
	Inst	Ea	Sm	SA	5.33	1.50	729.00	229.00	---	958.00	**1170.00**
Color	Inst	Ea	Lg	SA	4.00	2.00	755.00	172.00	---	927.00	**1120.00**
	Inst	Ea	Sm	SA	5.33	1.50	878.00	229.00	---	1107.00	**1340.00**

Westover, double deep, laundry sink
42" x 21"

White	Inst	Ea	Lg	SA	5.00	1.60	1010.00	215.00	---	1225.00	**1470.00**
	Inst	Ea	Sm	SA	6.67	1.20	1170.00	287.00	---	1457.00	**1760.00**
Color	Inst	Ea	Lg	SA	5.00	1.60	1230.00	215.00	---	1445.00	**1720.00**
	Inst	Ea	Sm	SA	6.67	1.20	1430.00	287.00	---	1717.00	**2060.00**

Stainless steel (Kohler)

Ballad, single bowl with self rim

19" x 19" x 9-1/2"	Inst	Ea	Lg	SA	4.00	2.00	919.00	172.00	---	1091.00	**1310.00**
	Inst	Ea	Sm	SA	5.33	1.50	1070.00	229.00	---	1299.00	**1560.00**
25" x 22" x 10"	Inst	Ea	Lg	SA	4.00	2.00	1040.00	172.00	---	1212.00	**1450.00**
	Inst	Ea	Sm	SA	5.33	1.50	1210.00	229.00	---	1439.00	**1730.00**
25" x 22" x 12"	Inst	Ea	Lg	SA	4.00	2.00	1110.00	172.00	---	1282.00	**1530.00**
	Inst	Ea	Sm	SA	5.33	1.50	1290.00	229.00	---	1519.00	**1820.00**

Vitreous china (Kohler)

Hollister

28" x 22"	Inst	Ea	Lg	SA	4.00	2.00	1090.00	172.00	---	1262.00	**1500.00**
	Inst	Ea	Sm	SA	5.33	1.50	1270.00	229.00	---	1499.00	**1790.00**

Sudbury

22" x 20"	Inst	Ea	Lg	SA	4.00	2.00	630.00	172.00	---	802.00	**974.00**
	Inst	Ea	Sm	SA	5.33	1.50	733.00	229.00	---	962.00	**1180.00**

Tyrrell

21" x 27" w/ siphon jet	Inst	Ea	Lg	SA	5.00	1.60	1160.00	215.00	---	1375.00	**1650.00**
	Inst	Ea	Sm	SA	6.67	1.20	1350.00	287.00	---	1637.00	**1970.00**

Description	Oper	Unit	Vol	Crew Size	Man-hours per Unit	Crew Output per Day	Avg Mat'l Unit Cost	Avg Labor Unit Cost	Avg Equip Unit Cost	Avg Total Unit Cost	Avg Price Incl O&P

Skylights, skywindows, roof windows

Labor costs are for installation of skylight, flashing and roller shade only; no carpentry or roofing work included

Polycarbonate dome, clear transparent or tinted, roof opening sizes, curb or flush mount, self-flashing

Description	Oper	Unit	Vol	Crew Size	Man-hours per Unit	Crew Output per Day	Avg Mat'l Unit Cost	Avg Labor Unit Cost	Avg Equip Unit Cost	Avg Total Unit Cost	Avg Price Incl O&P
Fixed, single dome											
22" x 22"	Inst	Ea	Lg	CA	1.90	4.20	140.00	70.30	---	210.30	**259.00**
	Inst	Ea	Sm	CA	2.93	2.73	154.00	108.00	---	262.00	**329.00**
22" x 46"	Inst	Ea	Lg	CA	2.58	3.10	160.00	95.50	---	255.50	**318.00**
	Inst	Ea	Sm	CA	3.96	2.02	176.00	147.00	---	323.00	**408.00**
30" x 30"	Inst	Ea	Lg	CA	2.58	3.10	194.00	95.50	---	289.50	**357.00**
	Inst	Ea	Sm	CA	3.96	2.02	213.00	147.00	---	360.00	**451.00**
30" x 46"	Inst	Ea	Lg	CA	2.96	2.70	231.00	110.00	---	341.00	**419.00**
	Inst	Ea	Sm	CA	4.55	1.76	254.00	168.00	---	422.00	**528.00**
46" x 46"	Inst	Ea	Lg	CA	3.48	2.30	276.00	129.00	---	405.00	**498.00**
	Inst	Ea	Sm	CA	5.33	1.50	304.00	197.00	---	501.00	**625.00**
Fixed, double dome											
22" x 22"	Inst	Ea	Lg	CA	1.90	4.20	170.00	70.30	---	240.30	**294.00**
	Inst	Ea	Sm	CA	2.93	2.73	187.00	108.00	---	295.00	**367.00**
22" x 46"	Inst	Ea	Lg	CA	2.58	3.10	190.00	95.50	---	285.50	**352.00**
	Inst	Ea	Sm	CA	3.96	2.02	209.00	147.00	---	356.00	**446.00**
30" x 30"	Inst	Ea	Lg	CA	2.58	3.10	225.00	95.50	---	320.50	**392.00**
	Inst	Ea	Sm	CA	3.96	2.02	248.00	147.00	---	395.00	**490.00**
30" x 46"	Inst	Ea	Lg	CA	2.96	2.70	265.00	110.00	---	375.00	**458.00**
	Inst	Ea	Sm	CA	4.55	1.76	292.00	168.00	---	460.00	**571.00**
46" x 46"	Inst	Ea	Lg	CA	3.48	2.30	345.00	129.00	---	474.00	**577.00**
	Inst	Ea	Sm	CA	5.33	1.50	380.00	197.00	---	577.00	**713.00**
Fixed, triple dome											
22" x 22"	Inst	Ea	Lg	CA	1.90	4.20	230.00	70.30	---	300.30	**362.00**
	Inst	Ea	Sm	CA	2.93	2.73	252.00	108.00	---	360.00	**442.00**
22" x 46"	Inst	Ea	Lg	CA	2.58	3.10	257.00	95.50	---	352.50	**429.00**
	Inst	Ea	Sm	CA	3.96	2.02	282.00	147.00	---	429.00	**530.00**
30" x 30"	Inst	Ea	Lg	CA	2.58	3.10	304.00	95.50	---	399.50	**483.00**
	Inst	Ea	Sm	CA	3.96	2.02	334.00	147.00	---	481.00	**590.00**
30" x 46"	Inst	Ea	Lg	CA	2.96	2.70	358.00	110.00	---	468.00	**565.00**
	Inst	Ea	Sm	CA	4.55	1.76	394.00	168.00	---	562.00	**688.00**
46" x 46"	Inst	Ea	Lg	CA	3.48	2.30	466.00	129.00	---	595.00	**716.00**
	Inst	Ea	Sm	CA	5.33	1.50	512.00	197.00	---	709.00	**865.00**

Description	Oper	Unit	Vol	Crew Size	Man-hours per Unit	Crew Output per Day	Avg Mat'l Unit Cost	Avg Labor Unit Cost	Avg Equip Unit Cost	Avg Total Unit Cost	Avg Price Incl O&P
Operable, single dome											
22" x 22"	Inst	Ea	Lg	CA	2.00	4.00	295.00	74.00	---	369.00	**443.00**
	Inst	Ea	Sm	CA	3.08	2.60	325.00	114.00	---	439.00	**533.00**
22" x 46"	Inst	Ea	Lg	CA	2.76	2.90	315.00	102.00	---	417.00	**505.00**
	Inst	Ea	Sm	CA	4.23	1.89	347.00	157.00	---	504.00	**618.00**
30" x 30"	Inst	Ea	Lg	CA	2.76	2.90	372.00	102.00	---	474.00	**571.00**
	Inst	Ea	Sm	CA	4.23	1.89	409.00	157.00	---	566.00	**690.00**
30" x 46"	Inst	Ea	Lg	CA	3.20	2.50	421.00	118.00	---	539.00	**650.00**
	Inst	Ea	Sm	CA	4.91	1.63	463.00	182.00	---	645.00	**787.00**
46" x 46"	Inst	Ea	Lg	CA	3.81	2.10	542.00	141.00	---	683.00	**821.00**
	Inst	Ea	Sm	CA	5.84	1.37	596.00	216.00	---	812.00	**988.00**
Operable, double dome											
22" x 22"	Inst	Ea	Lg	CA	2.00	4.00	370.00	74.00	---	444.00	**529.00**
	Inst	Ea	Sm	CA	3.08	2.60	407.00	114.00	---	521.00	**628.00**
22" x 46"	Inst	Ea	Lg	CA	2.76	2.90	390.00	102.00	---	492.00	**592.00**
	Inst	Ea	Sm	CA	4.23	1.89	429.00	157.00	---	586.00	**713.00**
30" x 30"	Inst	Ea	Lg	CA	2.76	2.90	463.00	102.00	---	565.00	**676.00**
	Inst	Ea	Sm	CA	4.23	1.89	509.00	157.00	---	666.00	**805.00**
30" x 46"	Inst	Ea	Lg	CA	3.20	2.50	531.00	118.00	---	649.00	**777.00**
	Inst	Ea	Sm	CA	4.91	1.63	584.00	182.00	---	766.00	**926.00**
46" x 46"	Inst	Ea	Lg	CA	3.81	2.10	650.00	141.00	---	791.00	**945.00**
	Inst	Ea	Sm	CA	5.84	1.37	715.00	216.00	---	931.00	**1120.00**
Operable, triple dome											
22" x 22"	Inst	Ea	Lg	CA	2.00	4.00	500.00	74.00	---	574.00	**678.00**
	Inst	Ea	Sm	CA	3.08	2.60	549.00	114.00	---	663.00	**792.00**
22" x 46"	Inst	Ea	Lg	CA	2.76	2.90	527.00	102.00	---	629.00	**749.00**
	Inst	Ea	Sm	CA	4.23	1.89	579.00	157.00	---	736.00	**885.00**
30" x 30"	Inst	Ea	Lg	CA	2.76	2.90	625.00	102.00	---	727.00	**862.00**
	Inst	Ea	Sm	CA	4.23	1.89	688.00	157.00	---	845.00	**1010.00**
30" x 46"	Inst	Ea	Lg	CA	3.20	2.50	717.00	118.00	---	835.00	**990.00**
	Inst	Ea	Sm	CA	4.91	1.63	789.00	182.00	---	971.00	**1160.00**
46" x 46"	Inst	Ea	Lg	CA	3.81	2.10	878.00	141.00	---	1019.00	**1210.00**
	Inst	Ea	Sm	CA	5.84	1.37	965.00	216.00	---	1181.00	**1410.00**

Description	Oper	Unit	Vol	Crew Size	Man-hours per Unit	Crew Output per Day	Avg Mat'l Unit Cost	Avg Labor Unit Cost	Avg Equip Unit Cost	Avg Total Unit Cost	Avg Price Incl O&P

Low profile, acrylic double domes with molded edge. Preassembled units include plywood curb-liner, 16 oz. copper flashing for pitched or flat roof, screen, and all hardware

Ventarama

Ventilating type

Description	Oper	Unit	Vol	Crew Size	Man-hours per Unit	Crew Output per Day	Avg Mat'l Unit Cost	Avg Labor Unit Cost	Avg Equip Unit Cost	Avg Total Unit Cost	Avg Price Incl O&P
22" x 30"	Inst	Ea	Lg	CA	2.07	3.87	319.00	76.60	---	395.60	**474.00**
	Inst	Ea	Sm	CA	3.17	2.52	350.00	117.00	---	467.00	**567.00**
22" x 45-1/2"	Inst	Ea	Lg	CA	2.07	3.87	384.00	76.60	---	460.60	**548.00**
	Inst	Ea	Sm	CA	3.17	2.52	422.00	117.00	---	539.00	**649.00**
30" x 22"	Inst	Ea	Lg	CA	2.07	3.87	319.00	76.60	---	395.60	**474.00**
	Inst	Ea	Sm	CA	3.17	2.52	350.00	117.00	---	467.00	**567.00**
30" x 30"	Inst	Ea	Lg	CA	2.07	3.87	351.00	76.60	---	427.60	**511.00**
	Inst	Ea	Sm	CA	3.17	2.52	386.00	117.00	---	503.00	**608.00**
30" x 45-1/2"	Inst	Ea	Lg	CA	2.58	3.10	429.00	95.50	---	524.50	**627.00**
	Inst	Ea	Sm	CA	3.96	2.02	472.00	147.00	---	619.00	**748.00**
30" x 72"	Inst	Ea	Lg	CA	2.58	3.10	579.00	95.50	---	674.50	**799.00**
	Inst	Ea	Sm	CA	3.96	2.02	636.00	147.00	---	783.00	**937.00**
45-1/2" x 30"	Inst	Ea	Lg	CA	2.58	3.10	429.00	95.50	---	524.50	**627.00**
	Inst	Ea	Sm	CA	3.96	2.02	472.00	147.00	---	619.00	**748.00**
45-1/2" x 45-1/2"	Inst	Ea	Lg	CA	2.58	3.10	520.00	95.50	---	615.50	**732.00**
	Inst	Ea	Sm	CA	3.96	2.02	572.00	147.00	---	719.00	**863.00**
Add for insulated glass											
	Inst	%	Lg	---	---	---	30.0	---	---	---	---
	Inst	%	Sm	---	---	---	30.0	---	---	---	---
Add for bronze tinted outer dome											
	Inst	Ea	Lg	---	---	---	45.50	---	---	---	**52.30**
	Inst	Ea	Sm	---	---	---	50.10	---	---	---	**57.60**
Add for white inner dome											
	Inst	Ea	Lg	---	---	---	22.10	---	---	---	**25.40**
	Inst	Ea	Sm	---	---	---	24.30	---	---	---	**28.00**
Add for roll shade											
22" width	Inst	Ea	Lg	---	---	---	130.00	---	---	---	**150.00**
	Inst	Ea	Sm	---	---	---	143.00	---	---	---	**164.00**
30" width	Inst	Ea	Lg	---	---	---	140.00	---	---	---	**161.00**
	Inst	Ea	Sm	---	---	---	154.00	---	---	---	**178.00**
45-1/2" width	Inst	Ea	Lg	---	---	---	150.00	---	---	---	**172.00**
	Inst	Ea	Sm	---	---	---	164.00	---	---	---	**189.00**

Description	Oper	Unit	Vol	Crew Size	Man-hours per Unit	Crew Output per Day	Avg Mat'l Unit Cost	Avg Labor Unit Cost	Avg Equip Unit Cost	Avg Total Unit Cost	Avg Price Incl O&P
Add for storm panel with weatherstripping											
30" x 30"	Inst	Ea	Lg	---	---	---	65.00	---	---	---	**74.80**
	Inst	Ea	Sm	---	---	---	71.50	---	---	---	**82.20**
45-1/2" x 45-1/2"	Inst	Ea	Lg	---	---	---	89.70	---	---	---	**103.00**
	Inst	Ea	Sm	---	---	---	98.70	---	---	---	**113.00**
Add for motorization											
	Inst	Ea	Lg	CA	3.23	2.48	260.00	120.00	---	380.00	**466.00**
	Inst	Ea	Sm	CA	4.97	1.61	286.00	184.00	---	470.00	**587.00**
Fixed type											
22" x 30"	Inst	Ea	Lg	CA	2.07	3.87	247.00	76.60	---	323.60	**391.00**
	Inst	Ea	Sm	CA	3.17	2.52	272.00	117.00	---	389.00	**477.00**
22" x 45-1/2"	Inst	Ea	Lg	CA	2.07	3.87	312.00	76.60	---	388.60	**466.00**
	Inst	Ea	Sm	CA	3.17	2.52	343.00	117.00	---	460.00	**559.00**
30" x 22"	Inst	Ea	Lg	CA	2.07	3.87	247.00	76.60	---	323.60	**391.00**
	Inst	Ea	Sm	CA	3.17	2.52	272.00	117.00	---	389.00	**477.00**
30" x 30"	Inst	Ea	Lg	CA	2.07	3.87	280.00	76.60	---	356.60	**429.00**
	Inst	Ea	Sm	CA	3.17	2.52	307.00	117.00	---	424.00	**518.00**
30" x 45-1/2"	Inst	Ea	Lg	CA	2.58	3.10	345.00	95.50	---	440.50	**530.00**
	Inst	Ea	Sm	CA	3.96	2.02	379.00	147.00	---	526.00	**641.00**
30" x 72"	Inst	Ea	Lg	CA	2.58	3.10	455.00	95.50	---	550.50	**657.00**
	Inst	Ea	Sm	CA	3.96	2.02	501.00	147.00	---	648.00	**781.00**
45-1/2" x 30"	Inst	Ea	Lg	CA	2.58	3.10	345.00	95.50	---	440.50	**530.00**
	Inst	Ea	Sm	CA	3.96	2.02	379.00	147.00	---	526.00	**641.00**
45-1/2" x 45-1/2"	Inst	Ea	Lg	CA	2.58	3.10	390.00	95.50	---	485.50	**582.00**
	Inst	Ea	Sm	CA	3.96	2.02	429.00	147.00	---	576.00	**699.00**
Add for insulated laminated glass											
	Inst	%	Lg	---	---	---	30.0	---	---	---	---
	Inst	%	Sm	---	---	---	30.0	---	---	---	---

Description	Oper	Unit	Vol	Crew Size	Man-hours per Unit	Crew Output per Day	Avg Mat'l Unit Cost	Avg Labor Unit Cost	Avg Equip Unit Cost	Avg Total Unit Cost	Avg Price Incl O&P

Skywindows

Labor costs are for installation of skywindows only, no carpentry or roofing work included

Ultraseal self-flashing units. Clear insulated glass, flexible flange, no mastic or step flashing required. Other glazings available

Skywindow E-Class

Description	Oper	Unit	Vol	Crew Size	Man-hours per Unit	Crew Output per Day	Avg Mat'l Unit Cost	Avg Labor Unit Cost	Avg Equip Unit Cost	Avg Total Unit Cost	Avg Price Incl O&P
22-1/2" x 22-1/2" fixed	Inst	Ea	Lg	CA	.800	10.00	281.00	29.60	---	310.60	**364.00**
	Inst	Ea	Sm	CA	1.23	6.50	309.00	45.50	---	354.50	**419.00**
22-1/2" x 38-1/2" fixed	Inst	Ea	Lg	CA	.800	10.00	322.00	29.60	---	351.60	**412.00**
	Inst	Ea	Sm	CA	1.23	6.50	355.00	45.50	---	400.50	**472.00**
22-1/2" x 46-1/2" fixed	Inst	Ea	Lg	CA	.800	10.00	380.00	29.60	---	409.60	**478.00**
	Inst	Ea	Sm	CA	1.23	6.50	418.00	45.50	---	463.50	**544.00**
22-1/2" x 70-1/2" fixed	Inst	Ea	Lg	CA	.800	10.00	416.00	29.60	---	445.60	**520.00**
	Inst	Ea	Sm	CA	1.23	6.50	458.00	45.50	---	503.50	**590.00**
30-1/2" x 30-1/2" fixed	Inst	Ea	Lg	CA	.800	10.00	380.00	29.60	---	409.60	**478.00**
	Inst	Ea	Sm	CA	1.23	6.50	418.00	45.50	---	463.50	**544.00**
30-1/2" x 46-1/2" fixed	Inst	Ea	Lg	CA	.800	10.00	463.00	29.60	---	492.60	**574.00**
	Inst	Ea	Sm	CA	1.23	6.50	509.00	45.50	---	554.50	**649.00**
46-1/2" x 46-1/2" fixed	Inst	Ea	Lg	CA	.800	10.00	520.00	29.60	---	549.60	**639.00**
	Inst	Ea	Sm	CA	1.23	6.50	572.00	45.50	---	617.50	**722.00**
22-1/2" x 22-1/2" venting	Inst	Ea	Lg	CA	.800	10.00	532.00	29.60	---	561.60	**653.00**
	Inst	Ea	Sm	CA	1.23	6.50	585.00	45.50	---	630.50	**736.00**
22-1/2" x 30-1/2" venting	Inst	Ea	Lg	CA	.800	10.00	576.00	29.60	---	605.60	**704.00**
	Inst	Ea	Sm	CA	1.23	6.50	633.00	45.50	---	678.50	**792.00**
22-1/2" x 46-1/2" venting	Inst	Ea	Lg	CA	.800	10.00	651.00	29.60	---	680.60	**790.00**
	Inst	Ea	Sm	CA	1.23	6.50	716.00	45.50	---	761.50	**888.00**
30-1/2" x 30-1/2" venting	Inst	Ea	Lg	CA	.800	10.00	616.00	29.60	---	645.60	**750.00**
	Inst	Ea	Sm	CA	1.23	6.50	678.00	45.50	---	723.50	**843.00**
30-1/2" x 46-1/2" venting	Inst	Ea	Lg	CA	.800	10.00	707.00	29.60	---	736.60	**855.00**
	Inst	Ea	Sm	CA	1.23	6.50	778.00	45.50	---	823.50	**958.00**

Step flash-pan flashed units. Insulated clear tempered glass. Deck-mounted step flash unit. Other glazings available

Skywindow Excel-10

Description	Oper	Unit	Vol	Crew Size	Man-hours per Unit	Crew Output per Day	Avg Mat'l Unit Cost	Avg Labor Unit Cost	Avg Equip Unit Cost	Avg Total Unit Cost	Avg Price Incl O&P
22-1/2" x 22-1/2" fixed	Inst	Ea	Lg	CA	2.58	3.10	260.00	95.50	---	355.50	**433.00**
	Inst	Ea	Sm	CA	3.96	2.02	286.00	147.00	---	433.00	**534.00**
22-1/2" x 38-1/2" fixed	Inst	Ea	Lg	CA	2.58	3.10	273.00	95.50	---	368.50	**448.00**
	Inst	Ea	Sm	CA	3.96	2.02	300.00	147.00	---	447.00	**551.00**
22-1/2" x 46-1/2" fixed	Inst	Ea	Lg	CA	2.58	3.10	287.00	95.50	---	382.50	**464.00**
	Inst	Ea	Sm	CA	3.96	2.02	316.00	147.00	---	463.00	**569.00**
22-1/2" x 70-1/2" fixed	Inst	Ea	Lg	CA	2.58	3.10	333.00	95.50	---	428.50	**516.00**
	Inst	Ea	Sm	CA	3.96	2.02	366.00	147.00	---	513.00	**626.00**
30-1/2" x 30-1/2" fixed	Inst	Ea	Lg	CA	2.58	3.10	308.00	95.50	---	403.50	**488.00**
	Inst	Ea	Sm	CA	3.96	2.02	339.00	147.00	---	486.00	**595.00**

Description	Oper	Unit	Vol	Crew Size	Man-hours per Unit	Crew Output per Day	Avg Mat'l Unit Cost	Avg Labor Unit Cost	Avg Equip Unit Cost	Avg Total Unit Cost	Avg Price Incl O&P
30-1/2" x 46-1/2" fixed	Inst	Ea	Lg	CA	2.58	3.10	372.00	95.50	---	467.50	**561.00**
	Inst	Ea	Sm	CA	3.96	2.02	409.00	147.00	---	556.00	**676.00**
22-1/2" x 22-1/2" vented	Inst	Ea	Lg	CA	2.58	3.10	436.00	95.50	---	531.50	**635.00**
	Inst	Ea	Sm	CA	3.96	2.02	479.00	147.00	---	626.00	**756.00**
22-1/2" x 30-1/2" vented	Inst	Ea	Lg	CA	2.58	3.10	469.00	95.50	---	564.50	**673.00**
	Inst	Ea	Sm	CA	3.96	2.02	516.00	147.00	---	663.00	**799.00**
22-1/2" x 46-1/2" vented	Inst	Ea	Lg	CA	2.58	3.10	560.00	95.50	---	655.50	**778.00**
	Inst	Ea	Sm	CA	3.96	2.02	616.00	147.00	---	763.00	**914.00**
30-1/2" x 30-1/2" vented	Inst	Ea	Lg	CA	2.58	3.10	540.00	95.50	---	635.50	**754.00**
	Inst	Ea	Sm	CA	3.96	2.02	593.00	147.00	---	740.00	**888.00**
30-1/2" x 46-1/2" vented	Inst	Ea	Lg	CA	2.58	3.10	602.00	95.50	---	697.50	**826.00**
	Inst	Ea	Sm	CA	3.96	2.02	662.00	147.00	---	809.00	**967.00**
Add for flashing kit	Inst	Ea	Lg	---	---	---	60.00	---	---	---	**60.00**
	Inst	Ea	Sm	---	---	---	60.00	---	---	---	**60.00**

Low-profile insulated glass skywindow. Deck mount, clear tempered glass, self-flashing models. Other glazings available

Skywindow Genra-1

Description	Oper	Unit	Vol	Crew Size	Man-hours per Unit	Crew Output per Day	Avg Mat'l Unit Cost	Avg Labor Unit Cost	Avg Equip Unit Cost	Avg Total Unit Cost	Avg Price Incl O&P
22-1/2" x 22-1/2" fixed	Inst	Ea	Lg	CA	2.58	3.10	231.00	95.50	---	326.50	**400.00**
	Inst	Ea	Sm	CA	3.96	2.02	255.00	147.00	---	402.00	**498.00**
22-1/2" x 30-1/2" fixed	Inst	Ea	Lg	CA	2.58	3.10	273.00	95.50	---	368.50	**448.00**
	Inst	Ea	Sm	CA	3.96	2.02	300.00	147.00	---	447.00	**551.00**
22-1/2" x 46-1/2" fixed	Inst	Ea	Lg	CA	2.58	3.10	335.00	95.50	---	430.50	**519.00**
	Inst	Ea	Sm	CA	3.96	2.02	369.00	147.00	---	516.00	**630.00**
22-1/2" x 70-1/2" fixed	Inst	Ea	Lg	CA	2.58	3.10	442.00	95.50	---	537.50	**642.00**
	Inst	Ea	Sm	CA	3.96	2.02	486.00	147.00	---	633.00	**764.00**
30-1/2" x 30-1/2" fixed	Inst	Ea	Lg	CA	2.58	3.10	316.00	95.50	---	411.50	**497.00**
	Inst	Ea	Sm	CA	3.96	2.02	347.00	147.00	---	494.00	**605.00**
30-1/2" x 46-1/2" fixed	Inst	Ea	Lg	CA	2.58	3.10	385.00	95.50	---	480.50	**576.00**
	Inst	Ea	Sm	CA	3.96	2.02	423.00	147.00	---	570.00	**692.00**
46-1/2" x 46-1/2" fixed	Inst	Ea	Lg	CA	2.58	3.10	491.00	95.50	---	586.50	**699.00**
	Inst	Ea	Sm	CA	3.96	2.02	541.00	147.00	---	688.00	**827.00**
22-1/2" x 22-1/2" vented	Inst	Ea	Lg	CA	2.58	3.10	454.00	95.50	---	549.50	**655.00**
	Inst	Ea	Sm	CA	3.96	2.02	499.00	147.00	---	646.00	**779.00**
22-1/2" x 30-1/2" vented	Inst	Ea	Lg	CA	2.58	3.10	481.00	95.50	---	576.50	**687.00**
	Inst	Ea	Sm	CA	3.96	2.02	529.00	147.00	---	676.00	**814.00**
22-1/2" x 46-1/2" vented	Inst	Ea	Lg	CA	2.58	3.10	572.00	95.50	---	667.50	**792.00**
	Inst	Ea	Sm	CA	3.96	2.02	629.00	147.00	---	776.00	**929.00**
30-1/2" x 30-1/2" vented	Inst	Ea	Lg	CA	2.58	3.10	533.00	95.50	---	628.50	**747.00**
	Inst	Ea	Sm	CA	3.96	2.02	586.00	147.00	---	733.00	**879.00**
30-1/2" x 46-1/2" vented	Inst	Ea	Lg	CA	2.58	3.10	624.00	95.50	---	719.50	**851.00**
	Inst	Ea	Sm	CA	3.96	2.02	686.00	147.00	---	833.00	**995.00**
46-1/2" x 46-1/2" vented	Inst	Ea	Lg	CA	2.58	3.10	767.00	95.50	---	862.50	**1020.00**
	Inst	Ea	Sm	CA	3.96	2.02	844.00	147.00	---	991.00	**1180.00**

Description	Oper	Unit	Vol	Crew Size	Man-hours per Unit	Crew Output per Day	Avg Mat'l Unit Cost	Avg Labor Unit Cost	Avg Equip Unit Cost	Avg Total Unit Cost	Avg Price Incl O&P

Roof windows

Includes prefabricated flashing, exterior awning, interior rollerblind and insect screen. Sash rotates 180 degrees. Labor costs are for installation on roofs with 10- to 85-degree slope and include installation of roof window, flashing and sun screen accessories. Labor costs do not include carpentry or roofing work other than curb. Add for interior trim. Listed by actual dimensions, top hung

Aluminum-clad wood frame, double-insulated tempered glass

Description	Oper	Unit	Vol	Crew Size	Man-hrs	Output	Mat'l	Labor	Equip	Total	Price O&P
30-1/2" x 46-1/2" fixed	Inst	Ea	Lg	CA	3.56	2.25	767.00	132.00	---	899.00	**1070.00**
	Inst	Ea	Sm	CA	5.48	1.46	844.00	203.00	---	1047.00	**1250.00**
46-1/2" x 46-1/2" fixed	Inst	Ea	Lg	CA	3.56	2.25	858.00	132.00	---	990.00	**1170.00**
	Inst	Ea	Sm	CA	5.48	1.46	944.00	203.00	---	1147.00	**1370.00**

Spas

Spas, with good quality fittings and faucets
Also see Bathtubs

Detach & reset operations

Description	Oper	Unit	Vol	Crew Size	Man-hrs	Output	Mat'l	Labor	Equip	Total	Price O&P
Whirlpool spa	Reset	Ea	Lg	SB	5.33	3.00	69.00	195.00	---	264.00	**362.00**
	Reset	Ea	Sm	SB	7.11	2.25	80.30	260.00	---	340.30	**469.00**

Remove operations

Description	Oper	Unit	Vol	Crew Size	Man-hrs	Output	Mat'l	Labor	Equip	Total	Price O&P
Whirlpool spa	Demo	Ea	Lg	SB	2.67	6.00	46.00	97.50	---	143.50	**194.00**
	Demo	Ea	Sm	SB	3.56	4.50	53.50	130.00	---	183.50	**250.00**

Install rough-in

Description	Oper	Unit	Vol	Crew Size	Man-hrs	Output	Mat'l	Labor	Equip	Total	Price O&P
Whirlpool spa	Inst	Ea	Lg	SB	10.0	1.60	92.00	365.00	---	457.00	**635.00**
	Inst	Ea	Sm	SB	13.3	1.20	107.00	486.00	---	593.00	**827.00**

Replace operations
Jacuzzi Products, whirlpools and baths with color matched trim on jets and suction

Builder Series

Nova model, oval tub, with ledge
60" x 42" x 18-1/2" H

Description	Oper	Unit	Vol	Crew Size	Man-hrs	Output	Mat'l	Labor	Equip	Total	Price O&P
White / stock color	Inst	Ea	Lg	SB	8.00	2.00	1880.00	292.00	---	2172.00	**2580.00**
	Inst	Ea	Sm	SB	10.7	1.50	2180.00	391.00	---	2571.00	**3080.00**
Premium color	Inst	Ea	Lg	SB	8.00	2.00	2040.00	292.00	---	2332.00	**2760.00**
	Inst	Ea	Sm	SB	10.7	1.50	2370.00	391.00	---	2761.00	**3290.00**

72" x 42" x 20-1/2" H

Description	Oper	Unit	Vol	Crew Size	Man-hrs	Output	Mat'l	Labor	Equip	Total	Price O&P
White / stock color	Inst	Ea	Lg	SB	8.00	2.00	2330.00	292.00	---	2622.00	**3100.00**
	Inst	Ea	Sm	SB	10.7	1.50	2710.00	391.00	---	3101.00	**3680.00**
Premium color	Inst	Ea	Lg	SB	8.00	2.00	2360.00	292.00	---	2652.00	**3140.00**
	Inst	Ea	Sm	SB	10.7	1.50	2750.00	391.00	---	3141.00	**3730.00**

Description	Oper	Unit	Vol	Crew Size	Man-hours per Unit	Crew Output per Day	Avg Mat'l Unit Cost	Avg Labor Unit Cost	Avg Equip Unit Cost	Avg Total Unit Cost	Avg Price Incl O&P
Riva model, oval tub											
62" x 43" x 18-1/2" H											
White / stock color	Inst	Ea	Lg	SB	8.00	2.00	1920.00	292.00	---	2212.00	**2630.00**
	Inst	Ea	Sm	SB	10.7	1.50	2230.00	391.00	---	2621.00	**3130.00**
Premium color	Inst	Ea	Lg	SB	8.00	2.00	2070.00	292.00	---	2362.00	**2800.00**
	Inst	Ea	Sm	SB	10.7	1.50	2410.00	391.00	---	2801.00	**3330.00**
72" x 42" x 20-1/2" H											
White / stock color	Inst	Ea	Lg	SB	8.00	2.00	2330.00	292.00	---	2622.00	**3100.00**
	Inst	Ea	Sm	SB	10.7	1.50	2710.00	391.00	---	3101.00	**3680.00**
Premium color	Inst	Ea	Lg	SB	8.00	2.00	2370.00	292.00	---	2662.00	**3150.00**
	Inst	Ea	Sm	SB	10.7	1.50	2760.00	391.00	---	3151.00	**3740.00**
Tara model, corner unit, angled tub											
60" x 60" x 20-3/4" H											
White / stock color	Inst	Ea	Lg	SB	8.00	2.00	1920.00	292.00	---	2212.00	**2630.00**
	Inst	Ea	Sm	SB	10.7	1.50	2230.00	391.00	---	2621.00	**3130.00**
Premium color	Inst	Ea	Lg	SB	8.00	2.00	2070.00	292.00	---	2362.00	**2800.00**
	Inst	Ea	Sm	SB	10.7	1.50	2410.00	391.00	---	2801.00	**3330.00**
Torino model, rectangle tub											
66" x 42" x 20-1/2" H											
White / stock color	Inst	Ea	Lg	SB	8.00	2.00	1920.00	292.00	---	2212.00	**2630.00**
	Inst	Ea	Sm	SB	10.7	1.50	2230.00	391.00	---	2621.00	**3130.00**
Premium color	Inst	Ea	Lg	SB	8.00	2.00	2070.00	292.00	---	2362.00	**2800.00**
	Inst	Ea	Sm	SB	10.7	1.50	2410.00	391.00	---	2801.00	**3330.00**

Designer Collection

Description	Oper	Unit	Vol	Crew Size	Man-hours per Unit	Crew Output per Day	Avg Mat'l Unit Cost	Avg Labor Unit Cost	Avg Equip Unit Cost	Avg Total Unit Cost	Avg Price Incl O&P
Allusion model, rectangle tub											
66" x 36" x 26" H											
White / stock color	Inst	Ea	Lg	SB	8.00	2.00	3810.00	292.00	---	4102.00	**4810.00**
	Inst	Ea	Sm	SB	10.7	1.50	4440.00	391.00	---	4831.00	**5670.00**
Premium color	Inst	Ea	Lg	SB	8.00	2.00	3860.00	292.00	---	4152.00	**4860.00**
	Inst	Ea	Sm	SB	10.7	1.50	4490.00	391.00	---	4881.00	**5730.00**
72" x 36" x 26" H											
White / stock color	Inst	Ea	Lg	SB	8.00	2.00	4020.00	292.00	---	4312.00	**5050.00**
	Inst	Ea	Sm	SB	10.7	1.50	4680.00	391.00	---	5071.00	**5940.00**
Premium color	Inst	Ea	Lg	SB	8.00	2.00	4070.00	292.00	---	4362.00	**5100.00**
	Inst	Ea	Sm	SB	10.7	1.50	4730.00	391.00	---	5121.00	**6010.00**
72" x 42" x 26" H											
White / stock color	Inst	Ea	Lg	SB	8.00	2.00	4220.00	292.00	---	4512.00	**5280.00**
	Inst	Ea	Sm	SB	10.7	1.50	4910.00	391.00	---	5301.00	**6210.00**
Premium color	Inst	Ea	Lg	SB	8.00	2.00	4270.00	292.00	---	4562.00	**5330.00**
	Inst	Ea	Sm	SB	10.7	1.50	4960.00	391.00	---	5351.00	**6270.00**
Aura model											
72" x 60" x 20-1/2"											
White / stock color	Inst	Ea	Lg	SB	8.00	2.00	7320.00	292.00	---	7612.00	**8850.00**
	Inst	Ea	Sm	SB	10.7	1.50	8520.00	391.00	---	8911.00	**10400.00**
Premium color	Inst	Ea	Lg	SB	8.00	2.00	7370.00	292.00	---	7662.00	**8900.00**
	Inst	Ea	Sm	SB	10.7	1.50	8570.00	391.00	---	8961.00	**10400.00**

Description	Oper	Unit	Vol	Crew Size	Man-hours per Unit	Crew Output per Day	Avg Mat'l Unit Cost	Avg Labor Unit Cost	Avg Equip Unit Cost	Avg Total Unit Cost	Avg Price Incl O&P
Ciprea model, with removable skirt											
72" x 48" x 20-1/2"											
White / stock color	Inst	Ea	Lg	SB	8.00	2.00	6520.00	292.00	---	6812.00	**7920.00**
	Inst	Ea	Sm	SB	10.7	1.50	7590.00	391.00	---	7981.00	**9290.00**
Premium color	Inst	Ea	Lg	SB	8.00	2.00	6720.00	292.00	---	7012.00	**8160.00**
	Inst	Ea	Sm	SB	10.7	1.50	7820.00	391.00	---	8211.00	**9560.00**
Fiore model, with removable skirt											
66" x 66" x 27-1/4"											
White / stock color	Inst	Ea	Lg	SB	8.00	2.00	8470.00	292.00	---	8762.00	**10200.00**
	Inst	Ea	Sm	SB	10.7	1.50	9850.00	391.00	---	10241.00	**11900.00**
Premium color	Inst	Ea	Lg	SB	8.00	2.00	8650.00	292.00	---	8942.00	**10400.00**
	Inst	Ea	Sm	SB	10.7	1.50	10100.00	391.00	---	10491.00	**12100.00**
Fontana model											
72" x 54" x 28" H, angled back, with RapidHeat											
White / stock color	Inst	Ea	Lg	SB	8.00	2.00	7710.00	292.00	---	8002.00	**9290.00**
	Inst	Ea	Sm	SB	10.7	1.50	8970.00	391.00	---	9361.00	**10900.00**
Premium color	Inst	Ea	Lg	SB	8.00	2.00	7760.00	292.00	---	8052.00	**9340.00**
	Inst	Ea	Sm	SB	10.7	1.50	9020.00	391.00	---	9411.00	**10900.00**

Options for whirlpool baths and spas

Description	Oper	Unit	Vol	Crew Size	Man-hours per Unit	Crew Output per Day	Avg Mat'l Unit Cost	Avg Labor Unit Cost	Avg Equip Unit Cost	Avg Total Unit Cost	Avg Price Incl O&P
Timer kit, 30 min, wall mount											
Polished chrome	Inst	Ea	Lg	---	---	---	83.70	---	---	83.70	**96.30**
	Inst	Ea	Sm	---	---	---	97.40	---	---	97.40	**112.00**
Gold	Inst	Ea	Lg	---	---	---	97.50	---	---	97.50	**112.00**
	Inst	Ea	Sm	---	---	---	113.00	---	---	113.00	**130.00**
Trim kit											
Polished chrome	Inst	Ea	Lg	---	---	---	146.00	---	---	146.00	**168.00**
	Inst	Ea	Sm	---	---	---	170.00	---	---	170.00	**196.00**
Bright brass	Inst	Ea	Lg	---	---	---	192.00	---	---	192.00	**221.00**
	Inst	Ea	Sm	---	---	---	224.00	---	---	224.00	**257.00**
Trip lever drain with vent											
Polished chrome	Inst	Ea	Lg	---	---	---	124.00	---	---	124.00	**143.00**
	Inst	Ea	Sm	---	---	---	144.00	---	---	144.00	**166.00**
Bright brass	Inst	Ea	Lg	---	---	---	167.00	---	---	167.00	**193.00**
	Inst	Ea	Sm	---	---	---	195.00	---	---	195.00	**224.00**
Gold	Inst	Ea	Lg	---	---	---	184.00	---	---	184.00	**212.00**
	Inst	Ea	Sm	---	---	---	214.00	---	---	214.00	**246.00**
Turn drain with vent											
Polished chrome	Inst	Ea	Lg	---	---	---	171.00	---	---	171.00	**197.00**
	Inst	Ea	Sm	---	---	---	199.00	---	---	199.00	**229.00**
Bright brass	Inst	Ea	Lg	---	---	---	217.00	---	---	217.00	**250.00**
	Inst	Ea	Sm	---	---	---	253.00	---	---	253.00	**290.00**
Gold	Inst	Ea	Lg	---	---	---	199.00	---	---	199.00	**229.00**
	Inst	Ea	Sm	---	---	---	231.00	---	---	231.00	**266.00**

Description	Oper	Unit	Vol	Crew Size	Man-hours per Unit	Crew Output per Day	Avg Mat'l Unit Cost	Avg Labor Unit Cost	Avg Equip Unit Cost	Avg Total Unit Cost	Avg Price Incl O&P

Stairs

Stair parts

Balusters, stock pine

Description	Oper	Unit	Vol	Crew Size	Man-hours per Unit	Crew Output per Day	Avg Mat'l Unit Cost	Avg Labor Unit Cost	Avg Equip Unit Cost	Avg Total Unit Cost	Avg Price Incl O&P
1-1/16" x 1-1/16"	Inst	LF	Lg	CA	.040	200.0	2.76	1.48	---	4.24	**5.25**
	Inst	LF	Sm	CA	.062	130.0	2.96	2.30	---	5.26	**6.62**
1-5/8" x 1-5/8"	Inst	LF	Lg	CA	.050	160.0	2.55	1.85	---	4.40	**5.52**
	Inst	LF	Sm	CA	.077	104.0	2.73	2.85	---	5.58	**7.13**

Balusters, turned

30" high

Description	Oper	Unit	Vol	Crew Size	Man-hours per Unit	Crew Output per Day	Avg Mat'l Unit Cost	Avg Labor Unit Cost	Avg Equip Unit Cost	Avg Total Unit Cost	Avg Price Incl O&P
Pine	Inst	Ea	Lg	CA	.333	24.00	10.40	12.30	---	22.70	**29.20**
	Inst	Ea	Sm	CA	.513	15.60	11.10	19.00	---	30.10	**39.40**
Birch	Inst	Ea	Lg	CA	.333	24.00	12.10	12.30	---	24.40	**31.20**
	Inst	Ea	Sm	CA	.513	15.60	13.00	19.00	---	32.00	**41.50**

42" high

Description	Oper	Unit	Vol	Crew Size	Man-hours per Unit	Crew Output per Day	Avg Mat'l Unit Cost	Avg Labor Unit Cost	Avg Equip Unit Cost	Avg Total Unit Cost	Avg Price Incl O&P
Pine	Inst	Ea	Lg	CA	.400	20.00	12.10	14.80	---	26.90	**34.70**
	Inst	Ea	Sm	CA	.615	13.00	13.00	22.80	---	35.80	**46.80**
Birch	Inst	Ea	Lg	CA	.400	20.00	15.60	14.80	---	30.40	**38.70**
	Inst	Ea	Sm	CA	.615	13.00	16.70	22.80	---	39.50	**51.10**

Newels, 3-1/4" wide

Description	Oper	Unit	Vol	Crew Size	Man-hours per Unit	Crew Output per Day	Avg Mat'l Unit Cost	Avg Labor Unit Cost	Avg Equip Unit Cost	Avg Total Unit Cost	Avg Price Incl O&P
Starting	Inst	Ea	Lg	CA	1.33	6.00	168.00	49.20	---	217.20	**262.00**
	Inst	Ea	Sm	CA	2.05	3.90	180.00	75.90	---	255.90	**313.00**
Landing	Inst	Ea	Lg	CA	2.00	4.00	238.00	74.00	---	312.00	**377.00**
	Inst	Ea	Sm	CA	3.08	2.60	255.00	114.00	---	369.00	**453.00**

Railings, built-up

Description	Oper	Unit	Vol	Crew Size	Man-hours per Unit	Crew Output per Day	Avg Mat'l Unit Cost	Avg Labor Unit Cost	Avg Equip Unit Cost	Avg Total Unit Cost	Avg Price Incl O&P
Oak	Inst	LF	Lg	CA	.160	50.00	16.80	5.92	---	22.72	**27.60**
	Inst	LF	Sm	CA	.246	32.50	18.00	9.11	---	27.11	**33.50**

Railings, subrail

Description	Oper	Unit	Vol	Crew Size	Man-hours per Unit	Crew Output per Day	Avg Mat'l Unit Cost	Avg Labor Unit Cost	Avg Equip Unit Cost	Avg Total Unit Cost	Avg Price Incl O&P
Oak	Inst	LF	Lg	CA	.080	100.0	22.40	2.96	---	25.36	**29.90**
	Inst	LF	Sm	CA	.123	65.00	24.00	4.55	---	28.55	**34.00**

Risers, 3/4" x 7-1/2" high

Description	Oper	Unit	Vol	Crew Size	Man-hours per Unit	Crew Output per Day	Avg Mat'l Unit Cost	Avg Labor Unit Cost	Avg Equip Unit Cost	Avg Total Unit Cost	Avg Price Incl O&P
Beech	Inst	LF	Lg	CA	.133	60.00	7.28	4.92	---	12.20	**15.30**
	Inst	LF	Sm	CA	.205	39.00	7.80	7.59	---	15.39	**19.60**
Fir	Inst	LF	Lg	CA	.133	60.00	2.10	4.92	---	7.02	**9.31**
	Inst	LF	Sm	CA	.205	39.00	2.25	7.59	---	9.84	**13.20**
Oak	Inst	LF	Lg	CA	.133	60.00	6.65	4.92	---	11.57	**14.50**
	Inst	LF	Sm	CA	.205	39.00	7.13	7.59	---	14.72	**18.80**
Pine	Inst	LF	Lg	CA	.133	60.00	2.10	4.92	---	7.02	**9.31**
	Inst	LF	Sm	CA	.205	39.00	2.25	7.59	---	9.84	**13.20**

Description	Oper	Unit	Vol	Crew Size	Man-hours per Unit	Crew Output per Day	Avg Mat'l Unit Cost	Avg Labor Unit Cost	Avg Equip Unit Cost	Avg Total Unit Cost	Avg Price Incl O&P
Skirt board, pine											
1" x 10"	Inst	LF	Lg	CA	.160	50.00	2.31	5.92	---	8.23	**11.00**
	Inst	LF	Sm	CA	.246	32.50	2.48	9.11	---	11.59	**15.60**
1" x 12"	Inst	LF	Lg	CA	.178	45.00	2.80	6.59	---	9.39	**12.50**
	Inst	LF	Sm	CA	.274	29.25	3.00	10.10	---	13.10	**17.70**
Treads, oak											
1-16" x 9-1/2" wide											
3' long	Inst	Ea	Lg	CA	.500	16.00	30.80	18.50	---	49.30	**61.30**
	Inst	Ea	Sm	CA	.769	10.40	33.00	28.50	---	61.50	**77.80**
4' long	Inst	Ea	Lg	CA	.533	15.00	40.60	19.70	---	60.30	**74.30**
	Inst	Ea	Sm	CA	.821	9.75	43.50	30.40	---	73.90	**92.60**
1-1/16" x 11-1/2" wide											
3' long	Inst	Ea	Lg	CA	.500	16.00	32.90	18.50	---	51.40	**63.80**
	Inst	Ea	Sm	CA	.769	10.40	35.30	28.50	---	63.80	**80.40**
6' long	Inst	Ea	Lg	CA	.667	12.00	78.40	24.70	---	103.10	**125.00**
	Inst	Ea	Sm	CA	1.03	7.80	84.00	38.10	---	122.10	**150.00**
For beech treads, ADD	Inst	%	Lg	---	---	---	40.0	---	---	---	---
	Inst	%	Sm	---	---	---	40.0	---	---	---	---
For mitered return nosings, ADD											
	Inst	LF	Lg	CA	.133	60.00	11.80	4.92	---	16.72	**20.40**
	Inst	LF	Sm	CA	.205	39.00	12.60	7.59	---	20.19	**25.10**

Stairs, pre-manufactured, folding / disapperaring, attic access, ladder type

Description	Oper	Unit	Vol	Crew Size	Man-hours per Unit	Crew Output per Day	Avg Mat'l Unit Cost	Avg Labor Unit Cost	Avg Equip Unit Cost	Avg Total Unit Cost	Avg Price Incl O&P
Average grade	Inst	Flt	Lg	2C	2.29	7.00	203.00	84.80	---	287.80	**352.00**
	Inst	Flt	Sm	2C	3.52	4.55	218.00	130.00	---	348.00	**433.00**
High grade	Inst	Flt	Lg	2C	2.29	7.00	259.00	84.80	---	343.80	**417.00**
	Inst	Flt	Sm	2C	3.52	4.55	278.00	130.00	---	408.00	**502.00**

Stairs, shop fabricated, per flight

Basement stairs, soft wood, open risers

Description	Oper	Unit	Vol	Crew Size	Man-hours per Unit	Crew Output per Day	Avg Mat'l Unit Cost	Avg Labor Unit Cost	Avg Equip Unit Cost	Avg Total Unit Cost	Avg Price Incl O&P
3' wide, 8' high	Inst	Flt	Lg	2C	4.00	4.00	525.00	148.00	---	673.00	**811.00**
	Inst	Flt	Sm	2C	6.15	2.60	563.00	228.00	---	791.00	**966.00**

Box stairs, no handrails, 3'-wide

Oak treads

Description	Oper	Unit	Vol	Crew Size	Man-hours per Unit	Crew Output per Day	Avg Mat'l Unit Cost	Avg Labor Unit Cost	Avg Equip Unit Cost	Avg Total Unit Cost	Avg Price Incl O&P
2' high	Inst	Flt	Lg	2C	3.20	5.00	209.00	118.00	---	327.00	**406.00**
	Inst	Flt	Sm	2C	4.92	3.25	224.00	182.00	---	406.00	**512.00**
4' high	Inst	Flt	Lg	2C	4.00	4.00	448.00	148.00	---	596.00	**723.00**
	Inst	Flt	Sm	2C	6.15	2.60	480.00	228.00	---	708.00	**871.00**
6' high	Inst	Flt	Lg	2C	4.57	3.50	728.00	169.00	---	897.00	**1070.00**
	Inst	Flt	Sm	2C	7.02	2.28	780.00	260.00	---	1040.00	**1260.00**
8' high	Inst	Flt	Lg	2C	5.33	3.00	910.00	197.00	---	1107.00	**1320.00**
	Inst	Flt	Sm	2C	8.21	1.95	975.00	304.00	---	1279.00	**1550.00**

Description	Oper	Unit	Vol	Crew Size	Man-hours per Unit	Crew Output per Day	Avg Mat'l Unit Cost	Avg Labor Unit Cost	Avg Equip Unit Cost	Avg Total Unit Cost	Avg Price Incl O&P
Pine treads for carpet											
2' high	Inst	Flt	Lg	2C	3.20	5.00	165.00	118.00	---	283.00	**356.00**
	Inst	Flt	Sm	2C	4.92	3.25	177.00	182.00	---	359.00	**459.00**
4' high	Inst	Flt	Lg	2C	4.00	4.00	281.00	148.00	---	429.00	**531.00**
	Inst	Flt	Sm	2C	6.15	2.60	302.00	228.00	---	530.00	**665.00**
6' high	Inst	Flt	Lg	2C	4.57	3.50	427.00	169.00	---	596.00	**728.00**
	Inst	Flt	Sm	2C	7.02	2.28	458.00	260.00	---	718.00	**890.00**
8' high	Inst	Flt	Lg	2C	5.33	3.00	532.00	197.00	---	729.00	**888.00**
	Inst	Flt	Sm	2C	8.21	1.95	570.00	304.00	---	874.00	**1080.00**
Stair rail with balusters, 5 risers											
	Inst	Ea	Lg	2C	1.07	15.00	245.00	39.60	---	284.60	**337.00**
	Inst	Ea	Sm	2C	1.64	9.75	263.00	60.70	---	323.70	**387.00**
For 4' wide stairs, ADD											
	Inst	%	Lg	2C	---	---	25.0	5.0	---	---	---
	Inst	%	Sm	2C	---	---	25.0	5.0	---	---	---

Open stairs, prefinished, metal stringers, 3'-6"-wide treads, no railings

Description	Oper	Unit	Vol	Crew Size	Man-hours per Unit	Crew Output per Day	Avg Mat'l Unit Cost	Avg Labor Unit Cost	Avg Equip Unit Cost	Avg Total Unit Cost	Avg Price Incl O&P
3' high	Inst	Flt	Lg	2C	3.20	5.00	609.00	118.00	---	727.00	**866.00**
	Inst	Flt	Sm	2C	4.92	3.25	653.00	182.00	---	835.00	**1010.00**
4' high	Inst	Flt	Lg	2C	4.00	4.00	763.00	148.00	---	911.00	**1080.00**
	Inst	Flt	Sm	2C	6.15	2.60	818.00	228.00	---	1046.00	**1260.00**
6' high	Inst	Flt	Lg	2C	4.57	3.50	1330.00	169.00	---	1499.00	**1770.00**
	Inst	Flt	Sm	2C	7.02	2.28	1430.00	260.00	---	1690.00	**2000.00**
8' high	Inst	Flt	Lg	2C	5.33	3.00	2140.00	197.00	---	2337.00	**2730.00**
	Inst	Flt	Sm	2C	8.21	1.95	2290.00	304.00	---	2594.00	**3060.00**

Adjustments

For 3-piece wood railings and balusters, ADD

Description	Oper	Unit	Vol	Crew Size	Man-hours per Unit	Crew Output per Day	Avg Mat'l Unit Cost	Avg Labor Unit Cost	Avg Equip Unit Cost	Avg Total Unit Cost	Avg Price Incl O&P
3' high	Inst	Ea	Lg	2C	1.07	15.00	209.00	39.60	---	248.60	**295.00**
	Inst	Ea	Sm	2C	1.64	9.75	224.00	60.70	---	284.70	**342.00**
4' high	Inst	Ea	Lg	2C	1.14	14.00	267.00	42.20	---	309.20	**367.00**
	Inst	Ea	Sm	2C	1.76	9.10	287.00	65.20	---	352.20	**421.00**
6' high	Inst	Ea	Lg	2C	1.23	13.00	412.00	45.50	---	457.50	**537.00**
	Inst	Ea	Sm	2C	1.89	8.45	441.00	70.00	---	511.00	**605.00**
8' high	Inst	Ea	Lg	2C	1.33	12.00	511.00	49.20	---	560.20	**657.00**
	Inst	Ea	Sm	2C	2.05	7.80	548.00	75.90	---	623.90	**736.00**
For 3'-6" x 3'-6" platform, ADD											
	Inst	Ea	Lg	2C	4.00	4.00	238.00	148.00	---	386.00	**481.00**
	Inst	Ea	Sm	2C	6.15	2.60	255.00	228.00	---	483.00	**612.00**

Description	Oper	Unit	Vol	Crew Size	Man-hours per Unit	Crew Output per Day	Avg Mat'l Unit Cost	Avg Labor Unit Cost	Avg Equip Unit Cost	Avg Total Unit Cost	Avg Price Incl O&P
Curved stairways, oak, unfinished, curved balustrade											
Open one side											
9' high	Inst	Flt	Lg	2C	22.9	.700	8930.00	848.00	---	9778.00	**11500.00**
	Inst	Flt	Sm	2C	34.8	.460	9560.00	1290.00	---	10850.00	**12800.00**
10' high	Inst	Flt	Lg	2C	22.9	.700	10100.00	848.00	---	10948.00	**12800.00**
	Inst	Flt	Sm	2C	34.8	.460	10800.00	1290.00	---	12090.00	**14200.00**
Open both sides											
9' high	Inst	Flt	Lg	2C	32.0	.500	14000.00	1180.00	---	15180.00	**17800.00**
	Inst	Flt	Sm	2C	48.5	.330	15000.00	1800.00	---	16800.00	**19800.00**
10' high	Inst	Flt	Lg	2C	32.0	.500	15100.00	1180.00	---	16280.00	**19000.00**
	Inst	Flt	Sm	2C	48.5	.330	16200.00	1800.00	---	18000.00	**21100.00**

Steel, reinforcing. See Concrete, page 99

Stucco. See Plaster, page 345

Studs. See Framing, page 203

Subflooring. See Framing, page 217

Suspended Ceilings

Suspended ceilings consist of a grid of small metal hangers which are hung from the ceiling framing with wire or strap, and drop-in panels sized to fit the grid system. The main advantage to this type of ceiling finish is that it can be adjusted to any height desired. It can cover a lot of flaws and obstructions (uneven plaster, pipes, wiring, and ductwork). With a high ceiling, the suspended ceiling reduces the sound transfer from the floor above and increases the ceiling's insulating value. One great advantage of suspended ceilings is that the area directly above the tiles is readily accessible for repair and maintenance work; the tiles merely have to be lifted out from the grid. This system also eliminates the need for any other ceiling finish.

1. **Installation Procedure**

    a. Decide on ceiling height. It must clear the lowest obstacles but remain above windows and doors. Snap a chalk line around walls at the new height. Check it with a carpenter's level.

    b. Install wall molding/angle at the marked line; this supports the tiles around the room's perimeter. Check with a level. Use nails (6d) or screws to fasten molding to studs (16" or 24" oc); on masonry, use concrete nails 24" oc. The molding should be flush along the chalk line with the bottom leg of the L-angle facing into the room.

    c. Fit wall molding at inside corners by straight cutting (90 degrees) and overlapping; for outside corners, miter cut corner (45 degrees) and butt together. Cut the molding to required lengths with tin snips or a hacksaw.

    d. Mark center line of room above the wall molding. Decide where the first main runner should be to get the desired border width. Position main runners by running taut string lines across room. Repeat for the first row of cross tees closest to one wall. Then attach hanger wires with screw eyes to the joists at 4' intervals.

    e. Trim main runners at wall to line up the slot with cross tee string. Rest trimmed end on wall molding; insert wire through holes; recheck with level; twist wire several times.

    f. Insert cross tee and tabs into main runner's slots; push down to lock. Check with level. Repeat.

    g. Drop 2' x 4' panels into place.

2. **Estimating Materials**

    a. Measure the ceiling and plot it on graph paper. Mark the direction of ceiling joists. On the ceiling itself, snap chalk lines along the joist lines.

    b. Draw ceiling layout for grid system onto graph paper. Plan the ceiling layout, figuring full panels across the main ceiling and evenly trimmed partial panels at the edges. To calculate the width of border panels in each direction, determine the width of the gap left after full panels are placed all across the dimension; then divide by 2.

    c. For purposes of ordering material, determine the room size in even number of feet. If the room length or width is not divisible by 2 feet, increase the dimension to the next larger unit divisible by 2. For example, a room that measured 11'-6" x 14'-4" would be considered a 12' x 16' room. This allows for waste and/or breakage. In this example, you would order 192 SF of material.

    d. Main runners and tees must run perpendicular to ceiling joists. For a 2' x 2' grid, cross and main tees are 2' apart. For a 2' x 4' grid, main tees are 4' apart and 4' cross tees connect the main tees; then 2' cross tees can be used to connect the 4' cross tees. The long panels of the grid are set parallel to the ceiling joists, so the T-shaped main runner is attached perpendicular to joists at 4' oc.

    e. Wall molding/angle is manufactured in 10' lengths. Main runners and tees are manufactured in 12' lengths. Cross tees are either 2' long or 4' long. Hanger wire is 12 gauge, and attached to joists with either screw eyes or hook-and-nail. Drop-in panels are either 8 SF (2' x 4') or 4 SF (2' x 2').

    f. To find the number of drop-in panels required, divide the nominal room size in square feet (e.g., 192 SF in above example) by square feet of panel to be used.

    g. The quantity of 12 gauge wire depends on the "drop" distance of the ceiling. Figure one suspension wire and screw eye for each 4' of main runner; if any main run is longer than 12' then splice plates are needed, with a wire and screw eye on each side of the splice. The length of each wire should be at least 2" longer than the "drop" distance, to allow for a twist after passing through runner or tee.

Description	Oper	Unit	Vol	Crew Size	Man-hours per Unit	Crew Output per Day	Avg Mat'l Unit Cost	Avg Labor Unit Cost	Avg Equip Unit Cost	Avg Total Unit Cost	Avg Price Incl O&P

Suspended ceilings

Suspended ceiling panels and grid system

| | Demo | SF | Lg | LB | .009 | 1780 | --- | .27 | --- | .27 | .38 |
| | Demo | SF | Sm | LB | .013 | 1246 | --- | .39 | --- | .39 | .55 |

Complete 2' x 4' slide lock grid system (baked enamel)
Labor includes installing grid and laying in panels

Luminous panels

	Oper	Unit	Vol	Crew Size	MH/Unit	Output/Day	Mat'l	Labor	Equip	Total	Price O&P
Average grade	Inst	SF	Lg	CA	.021	380.0	1.45	.78	---	2.23	**2.76**
	Inst	SF	Sm	CA	.030	266.0	1.60	1.11	---	2.71	**3.39**
High grade	Inst	SF	Lg	CA	.021	380.0	1.70	.78	---	2.48	**3.04**
	Inst	SF	Sm	CA	.030	266.0	1.87	1.11	---	2.98	**3.71**
Premium grade	Inst	SF	Lg	CA	.021	380.0	1.95	.78	---	2.73	**3.33**
	Inst	SF	Sm	CA	.030	266.0	2.15	1.11	---	3.26	**4.03**

Acoustical rated panels

	Oper	Unit	Vol	Crew Size	MH/Unit	Output/Day	Mat'l	Labor	Equip	Total	Price O&P
Average grade	Inst	SF	Lg	CA	.020	405.0	1.95	.74	---	2.69	**3.28**
	Inst	SF	Sm	CA	.028	283.5	2.15	1.04	---	3.19	**3.92**
High grade	Inst	SF	Lg	CA	.020	405.0	2.70	.74	---	3.44	**4.14**
	Inst	SF	Sm	CA	.028	283.5	2.97	1.04	---	4.01	**4.87**
Premium grade	Inst	SF	Lg	CA	.020	405.0	3.20	.74	---	3.94	**4.72**
	Inst	SF	Sm	CA	.028	283.5	3.52	1.04	---	4.56	**5.50**

Non-acoustical rated panels

	Oper	Unit	Vol	Crew Size	MH/Unit	Output/Day	Mat'l	Labor	Equip	Total	Price O&P
Standard grade	Inst	SF	Lg	CA	.020	405.0	1.17	.74	---	1.91	**2.38**
	Inst	SF	Sm	CA	.028	283.5	1.29	1.04	---	2.33	**2.93**
Average grade	Inst	SF	Lg	CA	.020	405.0	1.39	.74	---	2.13	**2.64**
	Inst	SF	Sm	CA	.028	283.5	1.53	1.04	---	2.57	**3.21**
High grade	Inst	SF	Lg	CA	.020	405.0	1.58	.74	---	2.32	**2.85**
	Inst	SF	Sm	CA	.028	283.5	1.74	1.04	---	2.78	**3.45**
Premium grade	Inst	SF	Lg	CA	.020	405.0	2.01	.74	---	2.75	**3.35**
	Inst	SF	Sm	CA	.028	283.5	2.21	1.04	---	3.25	**3.99**

For wood grained grid

	Oper	Unit	Vol	Crew Size	MH/Unit	Output/Day	Mat'l	Labor	Equip	Total	Price O&P
ADD	Inst	%	Lg	---	---	---	7.0	---	---	---	---
	Inst	%	Sm	---	---	---	7.0	---	---	---	---

Description	Oper	Unit	Vol	Crew Size	Man-hours per Unit	Crew Output per Day	Avg Mat'l Unit Cost	Avg Labor Unit Cost	Avg Equip Unit Cost	Avg Total Unit Cost	Avg Price Incl O&P

Panels only (labor to lay panels in pre-existing grid system)

Luminous panels

Description	Oper	Unit	Vol	Crew Size	Man-hours per Unit	Crew Output per Day	Avg Mat'l Unit Cost	Avg Labor Unit Cost	Avg Equip Unit Cost	Avg Total Unit Cost	Avg Price Incl O&P
Average grade	Inst	SF	Lg	CA	.008	1020	1.00	.30	---	1.30	**1.56**
	Inst	SF	Sm	CA	.011	714.0	1.10	.41	---	1.51	**1.84**
High grade	Inst	SF	Lg	CA	.008	1020	1.25	.30	---	1.55	**1.85**
	Inst	SF	Sm	CA	.011	714.0	1.38	.41	---	1.79	**2.16**
Premium grade	Inst	SF	Lg	CA	.008	1020	1.50	.30	---	1.80	**2.14**
	Inst	SF	Sm	CA	.011	714.0	1.65	.41	---	2.06	**2.47**

Acoustical rated panels

Description	Oper	Unit	Vol	Crew Size	Man-hours per Unit	Crew Output per Day	Avg Mat'l Unit Cost	Avg Labor Unit Cost	Avg Equip Unit Cost	Avg Total Unit Cost	Avg Price Incl O&P
Average grade	Inst	SF	Lg	CA	.007	1220	1.50	.26	---	1.76	**2.09**
	Inst	SF	Sm	CA	.009	854.0	1.65	.33	---	1.98	**2.36**
High grade	Inst	SF	Lg	CA	.007	1220	2.25	.26	---	2.51	**2.95**
	Inst	SF	Sm	CA	.009	854.0	2.48	.33	---	2.81	**3.32**
Premium grade	Inst	SF	Lg	CA	.007	1220	2.75	.26	---	3.01	**3.53**
	Inst	SF	Sm	CA	.009	854.0	3.03	.33	---	3.36	**3.95**

Non-acoustical rated panels

Description	Oper	Unit	Vol	Crew Size	Man-hours per Unit	Crew Output per Day	Avg Mat'l Unit Cost	Avg Labor Unit Cost	Avg Equip Unit Cost	Avg Total Unit Cost	Avg Price Incl O&P
Standard grade	Inst	SF	Lg	CA	.007	1220	.72	.26	---	.98	**1.19**
	Inst	SF	Sm	CA	.009	854.0	.79	.33	---	1.12	**1.37**
Average grade	Inst	SF	Lg	CA	.007	1220	.94	.26	---	1.20	**1.44**
	Inst	SF	Sm	CA	.009	854.0	1.03	.33	---	1.36	**1.65**
High grade	Inst	SF	Lg	CA	.007	1220	1.13	.26	---	1.39	**1.66**
	Inst	SF	Sm	CA	.009	854.0	1.24	.33	---	1.57	**1.89**
Premium grade	Inst	SF	Lg	CA	.007	1220	1.56	.26	---	1.82	**2.16**
	Inst	SF	Sm	CA	.009	854.0	1.72	.33	---	2.05	**2.44**

Description	Oper	Unit	Vol	Crew Size	Man-hours per Unit	Crew Output per Day	Avg Mat'l Unit Cost	Avg Labor Unit Cost	Avg Equip Unit Cost	Avg Total Unit Cost	Avg Price Incl O&P
Grid system components											
Main runner, 12' L pieces											
Enamel	Inst	Ea	Lg	---	---	---	6.04	---	---	6.04	**6.95**
	Inst	Ea	Sm	---	---	---	6.64	---	---	6.64	**7.64**
Wood grain	Inst	Ea	Lg	---	---	---	7.85	---	---	7.85	**9.03**
	Inst	Ea	Sm	---	---	---	8.64	---	---	8.64	**9.94**
Cross tees											
2' L pieces											
Enamel	Inst	Ea	Lg	---	---	---	1.43	---	---	1.43	**1.64**
	Inst	Ea	Sm	---	---	---	1.57	---	---	1.57	**1.81**
Wood grain	Inst	Ea	Lg	---	---	---	1.86	---	---	1.86	**2.14**
	Inst	Ea	Sm	---	---	---	2.05	---	---	2.05	**2.36**
4' L pieces											
Enamel	Inst	Ea	Lg	---	---	---	2.58	---	---	2.58	**2.97**
	Inst	Ea	Sm	---	---	---	2.84	---	---	2.84	**3.27**
Wood grain	Inst	Ea	Lg	---	---	---	3.35	---	---	3.35	**3.85**
	Inst	Ea	Sm	---	---	---	3.69	---	---	3.69	**4.24**
Wall molding, 12' L pieces											
Enamel	Inst	Ea	Lg	---	---	---	3.74	---	---	3.74	**4.30**
	Inst	Ea	Sm	---	---	---	4.11	---	---	4.11	**4.73**
Wood grain	Inst	Ea	Lg	---	---	---	4.86	---	---	4.86	**5.59**
	Inst	Ea	Sm	---	---	---	5.35	---	---	5.35	**6.15**
Main runner hold-down clips											
1/2" T panels (1000/carton)											
	Inst	Ctn	Lg	---	---	---	9.00	---	---	9.00	**10.40**
	Inst	Ctn	Sm	---	---	---	9.90	---	---	9.90	**11.40**
5/8" T panels (1000/carton)											
	Inst	Ctn	Lg	---	---	---	10.00	---	---	10.00	**11.50**
	Inst	Ctn	Sm	---	---	---	11.00	---	---	11.00	**12.70**

Telephone prewiring. See Electrical, page 159

Television antenna. See Electrical, page 159

Thermostat. See Electrical, page 159

Tile, ceiling. See Acoustical treatment, page 22

Tile, ceramic. See Ceramic tile, page 84

Tile, quarry. See Masonry, page 297

Tile, vinyl or asphalt. See Resilient flooring, page 351

Description	Oper	Unit	Vol	Crew Size	Man-hours per Unit	Crew Output per Day	Avg Mat'l Unit Cost	Avg Labor Unit Cost	Avg Equip Unit Cost	Avg Total Unit Cost	Avg Price Incl O&P

Toilets, bidets, urinals

Toilets (water closets), vitreous china, 1.6 GPF, includes seat, shut-off valve, connectors, flanges, water supply valve

Frequently encountered applications

Detach & reset operations

Description	Oper	Unit	Vol	Crew Size	Man-hours per Unit	Crew Output per Day	Avg Mat'l Unit Cost	Avg Labor Unit Cost	Avg Equip Unit Cost	Avg Total Unit Cost	Avg Price Incl O&P
Toilet	Reset	Ea	Lg	SA	1.33	6.00	46.00	57.20	---	103.20	**136.00**
	Reset	Ea	Sm	SA	1.78	4.50	53.50	76.60	---	130.10	**173.00**
Bidet	Reset	Ea	Lg	SA	1.33	6.00	46.00	57.20	---	103.20	**136.00**
	Reset	Ea	Sm	SA	1.78	4.50	53.50	76.60	---	130.10	**173.00**
Urinal	Reset	Ea	Lg	SA	1.33	6.00	46.00	57.20	---	103.20	**136.00**
	Reset	Ea	Sm	SA	1.78	4.50	53.50	76.60	---	130.10	**173.00**

Remove operations

Description	Oper	Unit	Vol	Crew Size	Man-hours per Unit	Crew Output per Day	Avg Mat'l Unit Cost	Avg Labor Unit Cost	Avg Equip Unit Cost	Avg Total Unit Cost	Avg Price Incl O&P
Toilet	Demo	Ea	Lg	SA	0.67	12.00	13.80	28.80	---	42.60	**57.70**
	Demo	Ea	Sm	SA	0.89	9.00	16.10	38.30	---	54.40	**74.00**
Bidet	Demo	Ea	Lg	SA	0.67	12.00	13.80	28.80	---	42.60	**57.70**
	Demo	Ea	Sm	SA	0.89	9.00	16.10	38.30	---	54.40	**74.00**
Urinal	Demo	Ea	Lg	SA	0.67	12.00	13.80	28.80	---	42.60	**57.70**
	Demo	Ea	Sm	SA	0.89	9.00	16.10	38.30	---	54.40	**74.00**

Install rough-in

Description	Oper	Unit	Vol	Crew Size	Man-hours per Unit	Crew Output per Day	Avg Mat'l Unit Cost	Avg Labor Unit Cost	Avg Equip Unit Cost	Avg Total Unit Cost	Avg Price Incl O&P
Toilet	Inst	Ea	Lg	SA	8.00	1.00	184.00	344.00	---	528.00	**711.00**
	Inst	Ea	Sm	SA	10.7	0.75	214.00	460.00	---	674.00	**914.00**
Bidet	Inst	Ea	Lg	SA	8.00	1.00	161.00	344.00	---	505.00	**684.00**
	Inst	Ea	Sm	SA	10.7	0.75	187.00	460.00	---	647.00	**883.00**

Replace operations

Toilet/water closet

Description	Oper	Unit	Vol	Crew Size	Man-hours per Unit	Crew Output per Day	Avg Mat'l Unit Cost	Avg Labor Unit Cost	Avg Equip Unit Cost	Avg Total Unit Cost	Avg Price Incl O&P
One piece, floor mounted	Inst	Ea	Lg	SA	2.00	4.00	469.00	86.00	---	555.00	**664.00**
	Inst	Ea	Sm	SA	2.67	3.00	546.00	115.00	---	661.00	**794.00**
Two piece, floor mounted	Inst	Ea	Lg	SA	2.00	4.00	371.00	86.00	---	457.00	**551.00**
	Inst	Ea	Sm	SA	2.67	3.00	431.00	115.00	---	546.00	**662.00**
Two piece, wall mounted	Inst	Ea	Lg	SA	2.00	4.00	912.00	86.00	---	998.00	**1170.00**
	Inst	Ea	Sm	SA	2.67	3.00	1060.00	115.00	---	1175.00	**1390.00**

Bidet

Description	Oper	Unit	Vol	Crew Size	Man-hours per Unit	Crew Output per Day	Avg Mat'l Unit Cost	Avg Labor Unit Cost	Avg Equip Unit Cost	Avg Total Unit Cost	Avg Price Incl O&P
Deck-mounted fittings	Inst	Ea	Lg	SA	1.60	5.00	1520.00	68.80	---	1588.80	**1840.00**
	Inst	Ea	Sm	SA	2.13	3.75	1760.00	91.60	---	1851.60	**2160.00**

Urinal

Description	Oper	Unit	Vol	Crew Size	Man-hours per Unit	Crew Output per Day	Avg Mat'l Unit Cost	Avg Labor Unit Cost	Avg Equip Unit Cost	Avg Total Unit Cost	Avg Price Incl O&P
Wall mounted	Inst	Ea	Lg	SA	2.67	3.00	979.00	115.00	---	1094.00	**1290.00**
	Inst	Ea	Sm	SA	3.56	2.25	1140.00	153.00	---	1293.00	**1530.00**

Description	Oper	Unit	Vol	Crew Size	Man-hours per Unit	Crew Output per Day	Avg Mat'l Unit Cost	Avg Labor Unit Cost	Avg Equip Unit Cost	Avg Total Unit Cost	Avg Price Incl O&P

One piece, floor mounted
American Standard Products

Cadet, round

Description	Oper	Unit	Vol	Crew Size	Man-hours per Unit	Crew Output per Day	Avg Mat'l Unit Cost	Avg Labor Unit Cost	Avg Equip Unit Cost	Avg Total Unit Cost	Avg Price Incl O&P
White	Inst	Ea	Lg	SA	2.00	4.00	378.00	86.00	---	464.00	**560.00**
	Inst	Ea	Sm	SA	2.67	3.00	440.00	115.00	---	555.00	**672.00**
Color	Inst	Ea	Lg	SA	2.00	4.00	443.00	86.00	---	529.00	**634.00**
	Inst	Ea	Sm	SA	2.67	3.00	515.00	115.00	---	630.00	**758.00**
Premium color	Inst	Ea	Lg	SA	2.00	4.00	521.00	86.00	---	607.00	**724.00**
	Inst	Ea	Sm	SA	2.67	3.00	606.00	115.00	---	721.00	**863.00**

Cadet, elongated

Description	Oper	Unit	Vol	Crew Size	Man-hours per Unit	Crew Output per Day	Avg Mat'l Unit Cost	Avg Labor Unit Cost	Avg Equip Unit Cost	Avg Total Unit Cost	Avg Price Incl O&P
White	Inst	Ea	Lg	SA	2.00	4.00	443.00	86.00	---	529.00	**634.00**
	Inst	Ea	Sm	SA	2.67	3.00	515.00	115.00	---	630.00	**758.00**
Color	Inst	Ea	Lg	SA	2.00	4.00	525.00	86.00	---	611.00	**729.00**
	Inst	Ea	Sm	SA	2.67	3.00	611.00	115.00	---	726.00	**869.00**
Premium color	Inst	Ea	Lg	SA	2.00	4.00	607.00	86.00	---	693.00	**823.00**
	Inst	Ea	Sm	SA	2.67	3.00	706.00	115.00	---	821.00	**979.00**

Hamilton, elongated, space saving

Description	Oper	Unit	Vol	Crew Size	Man-hours per Unit	Crew Output per Day	Avg Mat'l Unit Cost	Avg Labor Unit Cost	Avg Equip Unit Cost	Avg Total Unit Cost	Avg Price Incl O&P
White	Inst	Ea	Lg	SA	2.00	4.00	365.00	86.00	---	451.00	**545.00**
	Inst	Ea	Sm	SA	2.67	3.00	425.00	115.00	---	540.00	**655.00**
Color	Inst	Ea	Lg	SA	2.00	4.00	469.00	86.00	---	555.00	**664.00**
	Inst	Ea	Sm	SA	2.67	3.00	546.00	115.00	---	661.00	**794.00**
Premium color	Inst	Ea	Lg	SA	2.00	4.00	544.00	86.00	---	630.00	**750.00**
	Inst	Ea	Sm	SA	2.67	3.00	632.00	115.00	---	747.00	**894.00**

Savona, elongated

Description	Oper	Unit	Vol	Crew Size	Man-hours per Unit	Crew Output per Day	Avg Mat'l Unit Cost	Avg Labor Unit Cost	Avg Equip Unit Cost	Avg Total Unit Cost	Avg Price Incl O&P
White	Inst	Ea	Lg	SA	2.00	4.00	664.00	86.00	---	750.00	**889.00**
	Inst	Ea	Sm	SA	2.67	3.00	773.00	115.00	---	888.00	**1050.00**
Color	Inst	Ea	Lg	SA	2.00	4.00	827.00	86.00	---	913.00	**1080.00**
	Inst	Ea	Sm	SA	2.67	3.00	962.00	115.00	---	1077.00	**1270.00**
Premium color	Inst	Ea	Lg	SA	2.00	4.00	924.00	86.00	---	1010.00	**1190.00**
	Inst	Ea	Sm	SA	2.67	3.00	1070.00	115.00	---	1185.00	**1400.00**

Lexington, elongated, low profile model

Description	Oper	Unit	Vol	Crew Size	Man-hours per Unit	Crew Output per Day	Avg Mat'l Unit Cost	Avg Labor Unit Cost	Avg Equip Unit Cost	Avg Total Unit Cost	Avg Price Incl O&P
White	Inst	Ea	Lg	SA	2.00	4.00	740.00	86.00	---	826.00	**975.00**
	Inst	Ea	Sm	SA	2.67	3.00	860.00	115.00	---	975.00	**1160.00**
Color	Inst	Ea	Lg	SA	2.00	4.00	917.00	86.00	---	1003.00	**1180.00**
	Inst	Ea	Sm	SA	2.67	3.00	1070.00	115.00	---	1185.00	**1390.00**
Premium color	Inst	Ea	Lg	SA	2.00	4.00	1030.00	86.00	---	1116.00	**1310.00**
	Inst	Ea	Sm	SA	2.67	3.00	1200.00	115.00	---	1315.00	**1540.00**

Champion, elongated

Description	Oper	Unit	Vol	Crew Size	Man-hours per Unit	Crew Output per Day	Avg Mat'l Unit Cost	Avg Labor Unit Cost	Avg Equip Unit Cost	Avg Total Unit Cost	Avg Price Incl O&P
White	Inst	Ea	Lg	SA	2.00	4.00	676.00	86.00	---	762.00	**902.00**
	Inst	Ea	Sm	SA	2.67	3.00	786.00	115.00	---	901.00	**1070.00**
Color	Inst	Ea	Lg	SA	2.00	4.00	760.00	86.00	---	846.00	**999.00**
	Inst	Ea	Sm	SA	2.67	3.00	884.00	115.00	---	999.00	**1180.00**
Premium color	Inst	Ea	Lg	SA	2.00	4.00	903.00	86.00	---	989.00	**1160.00**
	Inst	Ea	Sm	SA	2.67	3.00	1050.00	115.00	---	1165.00	**1370.00**

Description	Oper	Unit	Vol	Crew Size	Man-hours per Unit	Crew Output per Day	Avg Mat'l Unit Cost	Avg Labor Unit Cost	Avg Equip Unit Cost	Avg Total Unit Cost	Avg Price Incl O&P
Kohler Products											
Rialto, round											
White	Inst	Ea	Lg	SA	2.00	4.00	436.00	86.00	---	522.00	**626.00**
	Inst	Ea	Sm	SA	2.67	3.00	507.00	115.00	---	622.00	**749.00**
Color	Inst	Ea	Lg	SA	2.00	4.00	559.00	86.00	---	645.00	**768.00**
	Inst	Ea	Sm	SA	2.67	3.00	651.00	115.00	---	766.00	**915.00**
Premium color	Inst	Ea	Lg	SA	2.00	4.00	640.00	86.00	---	726.00	**861.00**
	Inst	Ea	Sm	SA	2.67	3.00	744.00	115.00	---	859.00	**1020.00**
Gabrielle, elongated											
White	Inst	Ea	Lg	SA	2.00	4.00	432.00	86.00	---	518.00	**621.00**
	Inst	Ea	Sm	SA	2.67	3.00	502.00	115.00	---	617.00	**744.00**
Color	Inst	Ea	Lg	SA	2.00	4.00	554.00	86.00	---	640.00	**762.00**
	Inst	Ea	Sm	SA	2.67	3.00	645.00	115.00	---	760.00	**908.00**
Premium color	Inst	Ea	Lg	SA	2.00	4.00	634.00	86.00	---	720.00	**854.00**
	Inst	Ea	Sm	SA	2.67	3.00	737.00	115.00	---	852.00	**1010.00**
San Martine, elongated											
White	Inst	Ea	Lg	SA	2.00	4.00	789.00	86.00	---	875.00	**1030.00**
	Inst	Ea	Sm	SA	2.67	3.00	917.00	115.00	---	1032.00	**1220.00**
Color	Inst	Ea	Lg	SA	2.00	4.00	1020.00	86.00	---	1106.00	**1300.00**
	Inst	Ea	Sm	SA	2.67	3.00	1180.00	115.00	---	1295.00	**1530.00**
Premium color	Inst	Ea	Lg	SA	2.00	4.00	1170.00	86.00	---	1256.00	**1470.00**
	Inst	Ea	Sm	SA	2.67	3.00	1360.00	115.00	---	1475.00	**1730.00**
Revival, elongated, with lift knob											
White	Inst	Ea	Lg	SA	2.00	4.00	1230.00	86.00	---	1316.00	**1540.00**
	Inst	Ea	Sm	SA	2.67	3.00	1430.00	115.00	---	1545.00	**1810.00**
Color	Inst	Ea	Lg	SA	2.00	4.00	1610.00	86.00	---	1696.00	**1970.00**
	Inst	Ea	Sm	SA	2.67	3.00	1870.00	115.00	---	1985.00	**2320.00**
Premium color	Inst	Ea	Lg	SA	2.00	4.00	1800.00	86.00	---	1886.00	**2200.00**
	Inst	Ea	Sm	SA	2.67	3.00	2100.00	115.00	---	2215.00	**2580.00**

Two piece, floor mounted
American Standard Products

Description	Oper	Unit	Vol	Crew Size	Man-hours per Unit	Crew Output per Day	Avg Mat'l Unit Cost	Avg Labor Unit Cost	Avg Equip Unit Cost	Avg Total Unit Cost	Avg Price Incl O&P
Cadet, elongated											
White	Inst	Ea	Lg	SA	2.00	4.00	314.00	86.00	---	400.00	**486.00**
	Inst	Ea	Sm	SA	2.67	3.00	365.00	115.00	---	480.00	**586.00**
Color	Inst	Ea	Lg	SA	2.00	4.00	371.00	86.00	---	457.00	**551.00**
	Inst	Ea	Sm	SA	2.67	3.00	431.00	115.00	---	546.00	**662.00**
Premium color	Inst	Ea	Lg	SA	2.00	4.00	403.00	86.00	---	489.00	**588.00**
	Inst	Ea	Sm	SA	2.67	3.00	469.00	115.00	---	584.00	**706.00**
Cadet, elongated, pressure assisted											
White	Inst	Ea	Lg	SA	2.00	4.00	535.00	86.00	---	621.00	**739.00**
	Inst	Ea	Sm	SA	2.67	3.00	622.00	115.00	---	737.00	**881.00**
Color	Inst	Ea	Lg	SA	2.00	4.00	641.00	86.00	---	727.00	**862.00**
	Inst	Ea	Sm	SA	2.67	3.00	746.00	115.00	---	861.00	**1020.00**
Premium color	Inst	Ea	Lg	SA	2.00	4.00	686.00	86.00	---	772.00	**914.00**
	Inst	Ea	Sm	SA	2.67	3.00	798.00	115.00	---	913.00	**1080.00**

Description	Oper	Unit	Vol	Crew Size	Man-hours per Unit	Crew Output per Day	Avg Mat'l Unit Cost	Avg Labor Unit Cost	Avg Equip Unit Cost	Avg Total Unit Cost	Avg Price Incl O&P
Cadet, elongated, hi-boy,16-1/2" H											
White	Inst	Ea	Lg	SA	2.00	4.00	408.00	86.00	---	494.00	**595.00**
	Inst	Ea	Sm	SA	2.67	3.00	475.00	115.00	---	590.00	**713.00**
Color	Inst	Ea	Lg	SA	2.00	4.00	490.00	86.00	---	576.00	**689.00**
	Inst	Ea	Sm	SA	2.67	3.00	570.00	115.00	---	685.00	**822.00**
Premium color	Inst	Ea	Lg	SA	2.00	4.00	534.00	86.00	---	620.00	**738.00**
	Inst	Ea	Sm	SA	2.67	3.00	621.00	115.00	---	736.00	**880.00**
Repertoire											
Round											
White	Inst	Ea	Lg	SA	2.00	4.00	449.00	86.00	---	535.00	**641.00**
	Inst	Ea	Sm	SA	2.67	3.00	522.00	115.00	---	637.00	**767.00**
Color	Inst	Ea	Lg	SA	2.00	4.00	540.00	86.00	---	626.00	**746.00**
	Inst	Ea	Sm	SA	2.67	3.00	628.00	115.00	---	743.00	**889.00**
Premium color	Inst	Ea	Lg	SA	2.00	4.00	600.00	86.00	---	686.00	**815.00**
	Inst	Ea	Sm	SA	2.67	3.00	698.00	115.00	---	813.00	**969.00**
Elongated											
White	Inst	Ea	Lg	SA	2.00	4.00	521.00	86.00	---	607.00	**724.00**
	Inst	Ea	Sm	SA	2.67	3.00	606.00	115.00	---	721.00	**863.00**
Color	Inst	Ea	Lg	SA	2.00	4.00	625.00	86.00	---	711.00	**843.00**
	Inst	Ea	Sm	SA	2.67	3.00	727.00	115.00	---	842.00	**1000.00**
Premium color	Inst	Ea	Lg	SA	2.00	4.00	690.00	86.00	---	776.00	**918.00**
	Inst	Ea	Sm	SA	2.67	3.00	803.00	115.00	---	918.00	**1090.00**
Town Square											
Round											
White	Inst	Ea	Lg	SA	2.00	4.00	389.00	86.00	---	475.00	**572.00**
	Inst	Ea	Sm	SA	2.67	3.00	453.00	115.00	---	568.00	**687.00**
Color	Inst	Ea	Lg	SA	2.00	4.00	498.00	86.00	---	584.00	**697.00**
	Inst	Ea	Sm	SA	2.67	3.00	579.00	115.00	---	694.00	**832.00**
Premium color	Inst	Ea	Lg	SA	2.00	4.00	571.00	86.00	---	657.00	**782.00**
	Inst	Ea	Sm	SA	2.67	3.00	664.00	115.00	---	779.00	**931.00**
Elongated											
White	Inst	Ea	Lg	SA	2.00	4.00	445.00	86.00	---	531.00	**637.00**
	Inst	Ea	Sm	SA	2.67	3.00	518.00	115.00	---	633.00	**762.00**
Color	Inst	Ea	Lg	SA	2.00	4.00	571.00	86.00	---	657.00	**782.00**
	Inst	Ea	Sm	SA	2.67	3.00	664.00	115.00	---	779.00	**931.00**
Premium color	Inst	Ea	Lg	SA	2.00	4.00	656.00	86.00	---	742.00	**879.00**
	Inst	Ea	Sm	SA	2.67	3.00	763.00	115.00	---	878.00	**1040.00**
Yorkville, elongated, pressure assisted											
White	Inst	Ea	Lg	SA	2.00	4.00	715.00	86.00	---	801.00	**947.00**
	Inst	Ea	Sm	SA	2.67	3.00	831.00	115.00	---	946.00	**1120.00**
Color	Inst	Ea	Lg	SA	2.00	4.00	882.00	86.00	---	968.00	**1140.00**
	Inst	Ea	Sm	SA	2.67	3.00	1030.00	115.00	---	1145.00	**1350.00**
Premium color	Inst	Ea	Lg	SA	2.00	4.00	975.00	86.00	---	1061.00	**1250.00**
	Inst	Ea	Sm	SA	2.67	3.00	1130.00	115.00	---	1245.00	**1470.00**

Description	Oper	Unit	Vol	Crew Size	Man-hours per Unit	Crew Output per Day	Avg Mat'l Unit Cost	Avg Labor Unit Cost	Avg Equip Unit Cost	Avg Total Unit Cost	Avg Price Incl O&P
Kohler Products											
Memoirs, round											
White	Inst	Ea	Lg	SA	2.00	4.00	437.00	86.00	---	523.00	**628.00**
	Inst	Ea	Sm	SA	2.67	3.00	509.00	115.00	---	624.00	**751.00**
Color	Inst	Ea	Lg	SA	2.00	4.00	546.00	86.00	---	632.00	**752.00**
	Inst	Ea	Sm	SA	2.67	3.00	635.00	115.00	---	750.00	**896.00**
Premium color	Inst	Ea	Lg	SA	2.00	4.00	616.00	86.00	---	702.00	**833.00**
	Inst	Ea	Sm	SA	2.67	3.00	716.00	115.00	---	831.00	**991.00**
Memoirs, elongated											
White	Inst	Ea	Lg	SA	2.00	4.00	507.00	86.00	---	593.00	**708.00**
	Inst	Ea	Sm	SA	2.67	3.00	590.00	115.00	---	705.00	**845.00**
Color	Inst	Ea	Lg	SA	2.00	4.00	633.00	86.00	---	719.00	**853.00**
	Inst	Ea	Sm	SA	2.67	3.00	737.00	115.00	---	852.00	**1010.00**
Premium color	Inst	Ea	Lg	SA	2.00	4.00	715.00	86.00	---	801.00	**948.00**
	Inst	Ea	Sm	SA	2.67	3.00	832.00	115.00	---	947.00	**1120.00**
Highline, elongated											
White	Inst	Ea	Lg	SA	2.00	4.00	350.00	86.00	---	436.00	**527.00**
	Inst	Ea	Sm	SA	2.67	3.00	407.00	115.00	---	522.00	**634.00**
Color	Inst	Ea	Lg	SA	2.00	4.00	424.00	86.00	---	510.00	**612.00**
	Inst	Ea	Sm	SA	2.67	3.00	493.00	115.00	---	608.00	**734.00**
Premium color	Inst	Ea	Lg	SA	2.00	4.00	475.00	86.00	---	561.00	**671.00**
	Inst	Ea	Sm	SA	2.67	3.00	552.00	115.00	---	667.00	**801.00**
Revival, elongated, with lift knob											
White	Inst	Ea	Lg	SA	2.00	4.00	665.00	86.00	---	751.00	**889.00**
	Inst	Ea	Sm	SA	2.67	3.00	773.00	115.00	---	888.00	**1060.00**
Color	Inst	Ea	Lg	SA	2.00	4.00	876.00	86.00	---	962.00	**1130.00**
	Inst	Ea	Sm	SA	2.67	3.00	1020.00	115.00	---	1135.00	**1340.00**
Premium color	Inst	Ea	Lg	SA	2.00	4.00	1020.00	86.00	---	1106.00	**1290.00**
	Inst	Ea	Sm	SA	2.67	3.00	1180.00	115.00	---	1295.00	**1530.00**

Two piece, wall mounted
American Standard Products

Description	Oper	Unit	Vol	Crew Size	Man-hours per Unit	Crew Output per Day	Avg Mat'l Unit Cost	Avg Labor Unit Cost	Avg Equip Unit Cost	Avg Total Unit Cost	Avg Price Incl O&P
Glenwall, elongated											
White	Inst	Ea	Lg	SA	2.00	4.00	758.00	86.00	---	844.00	**997.00**
	Inst	Ea	Sm	SA	2.67	3.00	882.00	115.00	---	997.00	**1180.00**
Color	Inst	Ea	Lg	SA	2.00	4.00	912.00	86.00	---	998.00	**1170.00**
	Inst	Ea	Sm	SA	2.67	3.00	1060.00	115.00	---	1175.00	**1390.00**
Premium color	Inst	Ea	Lg	SA	2.00	4.00	1010.00	86.00	---	1096.00	**1280.00**
	Inst	Ea	Sm	SA	2.67	3.00	1170.00	115.00	---	1285.00	**1520.00**

Description	Oper	Unit	Vol	Crew Size	Man-hours per Unit	Crew Output per Day	Avg Mat'l Unit Cost	Avg Labor Unit Cost	Avg Equip Unit Cost	Avg Total Unit Cost	Avg Price Incl O&P
Bidet, deck-mounted fitting											
American Standard Products											
Cadet											
White	Inst	Ea	Lg	SA	1.60	5.00	1240.00	68.80	---	1308.80	**1520.00**
	Inst	Ea	Sm	SA	2.13	3.75	1440.00	91.60	---	1531.60	**1790.00**
Color	Inst	Ea	Lg	SA	1.60	5.00	1350.00	68.80	---	1418.80	**1650.00**
	Inst	Ea	Sm	SA	2.13	3.75	1570.00	91.60	---	1661.60	**1940.00**
Premium Color	Inst	Ea	Lg	SA	1.60	5.00	1420.00	68.80	---	1488.80	**1730.00**
	Inst	Ea	Sm	SA	2.13	3.75	1650.00	91.60	---	1741.60	**2030.00**
Heritage											
White	Inst	Ea	Lg	SA	1.60	5.00	1460.00	68.80	---	1528.80	**1770.00**
	Inst	Ea	Sm	SA	2.13	3.75	1690.00	91.60	---	1781.60	**2080.00**
Color	Inst	Ea	Lg	SA	1.60	5.00	1620.00	68.80	---	1688.80	**1970.00**
	Inst	Ea	Sm	SA	2.13	3.75	1890.00	91.60	---	1981.60	**2310.00**
Savona											
White	Inst	Ea	Lg	SA	1.60	5.00	1250.00	68.80	---	1318.80	**1530.00**
	Inst	Ea	Sm	SA	2.13	3.75	1450.00	91.60	---	1541.60	**1800.00**
Color	Inst	Ea	Lg	SA	1.60	5.00	1360.00	68.80	---	1428.80	**1670.00**
	Inst	Ea	Sm	SA	2.13	3.75	1580.00	91.60	---	1671.60	**1950.00**
Premium color	Inst	Ea	Lg	SA	1.60	5.00	1420.00	68.80	---	1488.80	**1740.00**
	Inst	Ea	Sm	SA	2.13	3.75	1660.00	91.60	---	1751.60	**2040.00**
Kohler Products											
Portrait											
White	Inst	Ea	Lg	SA	1.60	5.00	1350.00	68.80	---	1418.80	**1650.00**
	Inst	Ea	Sm	SA	2.13	3.75	1570.00	91.60	---	1661.60	**1930.00**
Color	Inst	Ea	Lg	SA	1.60	5.00	1520.00	68.80	---	1588.80	**1840.00**
	Inst	Ea	Sm	SA	2.13	3.75	1760.00	91.60	---	1851.60	**2160.00**
Premium Color	Inst	Ea	Lg	SA	1.60	5.00	1620.00	68.80	---	1688.80	**1970.00**
	Inst	Ea	Sm	SA	2.13	3.75	1890.00	91.60	---	1981.60	**2310.00**
Revival											
White	Inst	Ea	Lg	SA	1.60	5.00	1440.00	68.80	---	1508.80	**1750.00**
	Inst	Ea	Sm	SA	2.13	3.75	1670.00	91.60	---	1761.60	**2060.00**
Color	Inst	Ea	Lg	SA	1.60	5.00	1630.00	68.80	---	1698.80	**1980.00**
	Inst	Ea	Sm	SA	2.13	3.75	1900.00	91.60	---	1991.60	**2320.00**
Premium color	Inst	Ea	Lg	SA	1.60	5.00	1760.00	68.80	---	1828.80	**2120.00**
	Inst	Ea	Sm	SA	2.13	3.75	2050.00	91.60	---	2141.60	**2490.00**

Description	Oper	Unit	Vol	Crew Size	Man-hours per Unit	Crew Output per Day	Avg Mat'l Unit Cost	Avg Labor Unit Cost	Avg Equip Unit Cost	Avg Total Unit Cost	Avg Price Incl O&P
Urinal, wall mounted, 1.0 GPF											
American Standard Products											
Lynnbrook											
White	Inst	Ea	Lg	SA	2.67	3.00	423.00	115.00	---	538.00	**653.00**
	Inst	Ea	Sm	SA	3.56	2.25	492.00	153.00	---	645.00	**788.00**
Color	Inst	Ea	Lg	SA	2.67	3.00	524.00	115.00	---	639.00	**770.00**
	Inst	Ea	Sm	SA	3.56	2.25	610.00	153.00	---	763.00	**923.00**
Innsbrook											
White	Inst	Ea	Lg	SA	2.67	3.00	799.00	115.00	---	914.00	**1080.00**
	Inst	Ea	Sm	SA	3.56	2.25	929.00	153.00	---	1082.00	**1290.00**
Color	Inst	Ea	Lg	SA	2.67	3.00	979.00	115.00	---	1094.00	**1290.00**

Trash compactors

Includes wiring, connection, and installation in a pre-cutout area

Description	Oper	Unit	Vol	Crew Size	Man-hours per Unit	Crew Output per Day	Avg Mat'l Unit Cost	Avg Labor Unit Cost	Avg Equip Unit Cost	Avg Total Unit Cost	Avg Price Incl O&P
White	Inst	Ea	Lg	EA	2.00	4.00	575.00	80.40	---	655.40	**778.00**
	Inst	Ea	Sm	EA	2.67	3.00	669.00	107.00	---	776.00	**925.00**
Colors	Inst	Ea	Lg	EA	2.00	4.00	621.00	80.40	---	701.40	**831.00**
	Inst	Ea	Sm	EA	2.67	3.00	722.00	107.00	---	829.00	**986.00**
To remove and reset											
	Reset	Ea	Lg	EA	.727	11.00	---	29.20	---	29.20	**42.40**
	Reset	Ea	Sm	EA	.970	8.25	---	39.00	---	39.00	**56.50**
Material adjustments											
Stainless steel trim	R&R	LS	Lg	---	---	---	32.20	---	---	32.20	**37.00**
	R&R	LS	Sm	---	---	---	37.50	---	---	37.50	**43.10**
Stainless steel panel / trim	R&R	LS	Lg	---	---	---	69.00	---	---	69.00	**79.40**
	R&R	LS	Sm	---	---	---	80.30	---	---	80.30	**92.30**
"Black Glas" acrylic front panel / trim											
	R&R	LS	Lg	---	---	---	69.00	---	---	69.00	**79.40**
	R&R	LS	Sm	---	---	---	80.30	---	---	80.30	**92.30**
Hardwood top	R&R	LS	Lg	---	---	---	46.00	---	---	46.00	**52.90**
	R&R	LS	Sm	---	---	---	53.50	---	---	53.50	**61.50**

Trim. See Molding, page 299

Trusses. See Framing, page 218

Vanity units. See Cabinets, page 72

Description	Oper	Unit	Vol	Crew Size	Man-hours per Unit	Crew Output per Day	Avg Mat'l Unit Cost	Avg Labor Unit Cost	Avg Equip Unit Cost	Avg Total Unit Cost	Avg Price Incl O&P

Ventilation

Flue piping or vent chimney

Prefabricated metal, UL listed

Gas, double wall, galv. steel

Description	Oper	Unit	Vol	Crew Size	Man-hours per Unit	Crew Output per Day	Avg Mat'l Unit Cost	Avg Labor Unit Cost	Avg Equip Unit Cost	Avg Total Unit Cost	Avg Price Incl O&P
3" diameter	Inst	VLF	Lg	UB	.229	70.00	3.72	9.55	---	13.27	17.80
	Inst	VLF	Sm	UB	.286	56.00	4.56	11.90	---	16.46	22.20
4" diameter	Inst	VLF	Lg	UB	.242	66.00	4.55	10.10	---	14.65	19.60
	Inst	VLF	Sm	UB	.303	52.80	5.59	12.60	---	18.19	24.40
5" diameter	Inst	VLF	Lg	UB	.258	62.00	5.40	10.80	---	16.20	21.50
	Inst	VLF	Sm	UB	.323	49.60	6.63	13.50	---	20.13	26.80
6" diameter	Inst	VLF	Lg	UB	.276	58.00	6.27	11.50	---	17.77	23.60
	Inst	VLF	Sm	UB	.345	46.40	7.70	14.40	---	22.10	29.30
7" diameter	Inst	VLF	Lg	UB	.296	54.00	9.24	12.40	---	21.64	28.20
	Inst	VLF	Sm	UB	.370	43.20	11.30	15.40	---	26.70	35.00
8" diameter	Inst	VLF	Lg	UB	.320	50.00	10.30	13.40	---	23.70	30.80
	Inst	VLF	Sm	UB	.400	40.00	12.60	16.70	---	29.30	38.20
10" diameter	Inst	VLF	Lg	UB	.348	46.00	21.70	14.50	---	36.20	45.60
	Inst	VLF	Sm	UB	.435	36.80	26.70	18.20	---	44.90	56.40
12" diameter	Inst	VLF	Lg	UB	.381	42.00	29.20	15.90	---	45.10	56.10
	Inst	VLF	Sm	UB	.476	33.60	35.80	19.90	---	55.70	69.40
16" diameter	Inst	VLF	Lg	UB	.421	38.00	66.00	17.60	---	83.60	101.00
	Inst	VLF	Sm	UB	.526	30.40	81.00	21.90	---	102.90	124.00
20" diameter	Inst	VLF	Lg	UB	.471	34.00	101.00	19.70	---	120.70	144.00
	Inst	VLF	Sm	UB	.588	27.20	124.00	24.50	---	148.50	178.00
24" diameter	Inst	VLF	Lg	UB	.533	30.00	157.00	22.20	---	179.20	212.00
	Inst	VLF	Sm	UB	.667	24.00	193.00	27.80	---	220.80	262.00

Vent damper, bi-metal, 6" flue

Description	Oper	Unit	Vol	Crew Size	Man-hours per Unit	Crew Output per Day	Avg Mat'l Unit Cost	Avg Labor Unit Cost	Avg Equip Unit Cost	Avg Total Unit Cost	Avg Price Incl O&P
Gas, auto., electric	Inst	Ea	Lg	UB	2.67	6.00	143.00	111.00	---	254.00	323.00
	Inst	Ea	Sm	UB	3.33	4.80	176.00	139.00	---	315.00	399.00
Oil, auto., electric	Inst	Ea	Lg	UB	2.67	6.00	172.00	111.00	---	283.00	356.00
	Inst	Ea	Sm	UB	3.33	4.80	211.00	139.00	---	350.00	439.00

All fuel, double wall, stainless steel

Description	Oper	Unit	Vol	Crew Size	Man-hours per Unit	Crew Output per Day	Avg Mat'l Unit Cost	Avg Labor Unit Cost	Avg Equip Unit Cost	Avg Total Unit Cost	Avg Price Incl O&P
6" diameter	Inst	VLF	Lg	UB	.267	60.00	30.80	11.10	---	41.90	51.20
	Inst	VLF	Sm	UB	.333	48.00	37.80	13.90	---	51.70	63.20
7" diameter	Inst	VLF	Lg	UB	.286	56.00	39.60	11.90	---	51.50	62.50
	Inst	VLF	Sm	UB	.357	44.80	48.60	14.90	---	63.50	77.00
8" diameter	Inst	VLF	Lg	UB	.308	52.00	46.20	12.90	---	59.10	71.40
	Inst	VLF	Sm	UB	.385	41.60	56.70	16.10	---	72.80	88.00
10" diameter	Inst	VLF	Lg	UB	.333	48.00	67.10	13.90	---	81.00	96.90
	Inst	VLF	Sm	UB	.417	38.40	82.40	17.40	---	99.80	119.00
12" diameter	Inst	VLF	Lg	UB	.364	44.00	90.20	15.20	---	105.40	125.00
	Inst	VLF	Sm	UB	.455	35.20	111.00	19.00	---	130.00	154.00
14" diameter	Inst	VLF	Lg	UB	.400	40.00	119.00	16.70	---	135.70	160.00
	Inst	VLF	Sm	UB	.500	32.00	146.00	20.90	---	166.90	197.00

Description	Oper	Unit	Vol	Crew Size	Man-hours per Unit	Crew Output per Day	Avg Mat'l Unit Cost	Avg Labor Unit Cost	Avg Equip Unit Cost	Avg Total Unit Cost	Avg Price Incl O&P
All fuel, double wall, stainless steel fittings											
Roof support											
6" diameter	Inst	Ea	Lg	UB	.533	30.00	78.70	22.20	---	100.90	**122.00**
	Inst	Ea	Sm	UB	.667	24.00	96.50	27.80	---	124.30	**151.00**
7" diameter	Inst	Ea	Lg	UB	.571	28.00	88.60	23.80	---	112.40	**136.00**
	Inst	Ea	Sm	UB	.714	22.40	109.00	29.80	---	138.80	**167.00**
8" diameter	Inst	Ea	Lg	UB	.615	26.00	96.30	25.70	---	122.00	**147.00**
	Inst	Ea	Sm	UB	.769	20.80	118.00	32.10	---	150.10	**181.00**
10" diameter	Inst	Ea	Lg	UB	.667	24.00	127.00	27.80	---	154.80	**185.00**
	Inst	Ea	Sm	UB	.833	19.20	155.00	34.80	---	189.80	**228.00**
12" diameter	Inst	Ea	Lg	UB	.727	22.00	153.00	30.30	---	183.30	**219.00**
	Inst	Ea	Sm	UB	.909	17.60	188.00	37.90	---	225.90	**270.00**
14" diameter	Inst	Ea	Lg	UB	.800	20.00	194.00	33.40	---	227.40	**270.00**
	Inst	Ea	Sm	UB	1.00	16.00	238.00	41.70	---	279.70	**332.00**
Elbow, 15 degree											
6" diameter	Inst	Ea	Lg	UB	.533	30.00	68.80	22.20	---	91.00	**111.00**
	Inst	Ea	Sm	UB	.667	24.00	84.40	27.80	---	112.20	**137.00**
7" diameter	Inst	Ea	Lg	UB	.571	28.00	77.00	23.80	---	100.80	**122.00**
	Inst	Ea	Sm	UB	.714	22.40	94.50	29.80	---	124.30	**151.00**
8" diameter	Inst	Ea	Lg	UB	.615	26.00	88.00	25.70	---	113.70	**138.00**
	Inst	Ea	Sm	UB	.769	20.80	108.00	32.10	---	140.10	**170.00**
10" diameter	Inst	Ea	Lg	UB	.667	24.00	114.00	27.80	---	141.80	**171.00**
	Inst	Ea	Sm	UB	.833	19.20	140.00	34.80	---	174.80	**211.00**
12" diameter	Inst	Ea	Lg	UB	.727	22.00	140.00	30.30	---	170.30	**204.00**
	Inst	Ea	Sm	UB	.909	17.60	171.00	37.90	---	208.90	**251.00**
14" diameter	Inst	Ea	Lg	UB	.800	20.00	167.00	33.40	---	200.40	**240.00**
	Inst	Ea	Sm	UB	1.00	16.00	205.00	41.70	---	246.70	**295.00**
Insulated tee with insulated tee cap											
6" diameter	Inst	Ea	Lg	UB	.533	30.00	130.00	22.20	---	152.20	**181.00**
	Inst	Ea	Sm	UB	.667	24.00	159.00	27.80	---	186.80	**223.00**
7" diameter	Inst	Ea	Lg	UB	.571	28.00	169.00	23.80	---	192.80	**229.00**
	Inst	Ea	Sm	UB	.714	22.40	208.00	29.80	---	237.80	**281.00**
8" diameter	Inst	Ea	Lg	UB	.615	26.00	191.00	25.70	---	216.70	**257.00**
	Inst	Ea	Sm	UB	.769	20.80	235.00	32.10	---	267.10	**316.00**
10" diameter	Inst	Ea	Lg	UB	.667	24.00	270.00	27.80	---	297.80	**349.00**
	Inst	Ea	Sm	UB	.833	19.20	331.00	34.80	---	365.80	**430.00**
12" diameter	Inst	Ea	Lg	UB	.727	22.00	380.00	30.30	---	410.30	**479.00**
	Inst	Ea	Sm	UB	.909	17.60	466.00	37.90	---	503.90	**589.00**
14" diameter	Inst	Ea	Lg	UB	.800	20.00	495.00	33.40	---	528.40	**617.00**
	Inst	Ea	Sm	UB	1.00	16.00	608.00	41.70	---	649.70	**758.00**

Description	Oper	Unit	Vol	Crew Size	Man-hours per Unit	Crew Output per Day	Avg Mat'l Unit Cost	Avg Labor Unit Cost	Avg Equip Unit Cost	Avg Total Unit Cost	Avg Price Incl O&P
Joist shield											
6" diameter	Inst	Ea	Lg	UB	.533	30.00	39.60	22.20	---	61.80	**77.10**
	Inst	Ea	Sm	UB	.667	24.00	48.60	27.80	---	76.40	**95.40**
7" diameter	Inst	Ea	Lg	UB	.571	28.00	42.90	23.80	---	66.70	**83.20**
	Inst	Ea	Sm	UB	.714	22.40	52.70	29.80	---	82.50	**103.00**
8" diameter	Inst	Ea	Lg	UB	.615	26.00	52.80	25.70	---	78.50	**97.20**
	Inst	Ea	Sm	UB	.769	20.80	64.80	32.10	---	96.90	**120.00**
10" diameter	Inst	Ea	Lg	UB	.667	24.00	60.00	27.80	---	87.80	**108.00**
	Inst	Ea	Sm	UB	.833	19.20	73.60	34.80	---	108.40	**134.00**
12" diameter	Inst	Ea	Lg	UB	.727	22.00	88.60	30.30	---	118.90	**145.00**
	Inst	Ea	Sm	UB	.909	17.60	109.00	37.90	---	146.90	**179.00**
14" diameter	Inst	Ea	Lg	UB	.800	20.00	110.00	33.40	---	143.40	**174.00**
	Inst	Ea	Sm	UB	1.00	16.00	135.00	41.70	---	176.70	**214.00**
Round top											
6" diameter	Inst	Ea	Lg	UB	.533	30.00	44.00	22.20	---	66.20	**82.20**
	Inst	Ea	Sm	UB	.667	24.00	54.00	27.80	---	81.80	**102.00**
7" diameter	Inst	Ea	Lg	UB	.571	28.00	60.00	23.80	---	83.80	**103.00**
	Inst	Ea	Sm	UB	.714	22.40	73.60	29.80	---	103.40	**127.00**
8" diameter	Inst	Ea	Lg	UB	.615	26.00	80.30	25.70	---	106.00	**129.00**
	Inst	Ea	Sm	UB	.769	20.80	98.60	32.10	---	130.70	**159.00**
10" diameter	Inst	Ea	Lg	UB	.667	24.00	144.00	27.80	---	171.80	**205.00**
	Inst	Ea	Sm	UB	.833	19.20	177.00	34.80	---	211.80	**253.00**
12" diameter	Inst	Ea	Lg	UB	.727	22.00	206.00	30.30	---	236.30	**280.00**
	Inst	Ea	Sm	UB	.909	17.60	252.00	37.90	---	289.90	**344.00**
14" diameter	Inst	Ea	Lg	UB	.800	20.00	271.00	33.40	---	304.40	**359.00**
	Inst	Ea	Sm	UB	1.00	16.00	332.00	41.70	---	373.70	**441.00**
Adjustable roof flashing											
6" diameter	Inst	Ea	Lg	UB	.533	30.00	52.30	22.20	---	74.50	**91.70**
	Inst	Ea	Sm	UB	.667	24.00	64.10	27.80	---	91.90	**113.00**
7" diameter	Inst	Ea	Lg	UB	.571	28.00	59.40	23.80	---	83.20	**102.00**
	Inst	Ea	Sm	UB	.714	22.40	72.90	29.80	---	102.70	**126.00**
8" diameter	Inst	Ea	Lg	UB	.615	26.00	64.90	25.70	---	90.60	**111.00**
	Inst	Ea	Sm	UB	.769	20.80	79.70	32.10	---	111.80	**137.00**
10" diameter	Inst	Ea	Lg	UB	.667	24.00	83.10	27.80	---	110.90	**135.00**
	Inst	Ea	Sm	UB	.833	19.20	102.00	34.80	---	136.80	**167.00**
12" diameter	Inst	Ea	Lg	UB	.727	22.00	107.00	30.30	---	137.30	**166.00**
	Inst	Ea	Sm	UB	.909	17.60	132.00	37.90	---	169.90	**205.00**
14" diameter	Inst	Ea	Lg	UB	.800	20.00	134.00	33.40	---	167.40	**202.00**
	Inst	Ea	Sm	UB	1.00	16.00	165.00	41.70	---	206.70	**249.00**
Minimum Job Charge											
	Inst	Job	Lg	UB	5.33	3.00	---	222.00	---	222.00	**316.00**
	Inst	Job	Sm	UB	6.67	2.40	---	278.00	---	278.00	**395.00**

Wallpaper

Most wall coverings today are really not wallpapers in the technical sense. Wallpaper is a paper material (which may or not be coated with washable plastic). Most of today's products, though still called wallpaper, are actually composed of a vinyl on a fabric, not a paper, backing. Some vinyl/fabric coverings come prepasted.

Vinyl coverings with non-woven fabric, woven fabric or synthetic fiber backing are fire, mildew and fade resistant, and they can be stripped from plaster walls. Coverings with paper backing must be steamed or scraped from the walls. Vinyl coverings may also be stripped from gypsum wallboard, but unless the vinyl covering has a synthetic fiber backing, it's likely to damage the wallboard paper surface.

One gallon of paste (approximately two-thirds pound of dry paste and water) should adequately cover 12 rolls with paper backing and 6 rolls with fabric backing. The rougher the texture of the surface to be pasted, the greater the quantity of wet paste needed.

1. **Dimensions**

    a. Single roll is 36 SF. The paper is 18" wide x 24'-0" long.

    b. Double roll is 72 SF. The paper is 18" wide x 48'-0" long.

2. **Installation.** New paper may be applied over existing paper if the existing paper has butt joints, a smooth surface, and is tight to the wall. When new paper is applied direct to plaster or drywall, the wall should receive a coat of glue size before the paper is applied.

3. **Estimating Technique.** Determine the gross area, deduct openings and other areas not to be papered, and add 20% to the net area for waste. To find the number of rolls needed, divide the net area plus 20% by the number of SF per roll.

The steps in wallpapering

Description	Oper	Unit	Vol	Crew Size	Man-hours per Unit	Crew Output per Day	Avg Mat'l Unit Cost	Avg Labor Unit Cost	Avg Equip Unit Cost	Avg Total Unit Cost	Avg Price Incl O&P

Wallpaper

Butt joint

Includes application of glue sizing. Material prices are not given because they vary radically

Description	Oper	Unit	Vol	Crew Size	Man-hours per Unit	Crew Output per Day	Avg Mat'l Unit Cost	Avg Labor Unit Cost	Avg Equip Unit Cost	Avg Total Unit Cost	Avg Price Incl O&P
Paper, single rolls, 36 SF/roll	Inst	Roll	Lg	QA	.357	22.40	28.50	14.20	2.32	45.02	**55.70**
	Inst	Roll	Sm	QA	.549	14.56	31.40	21.80	3.57	56.77	**71.30**
Vinyl, with fabric backing (prepasted), single rolls, 36 SF/roll											
	Inst	Roll	Lg	QA	.400	20.00	39.90	15.90	2.60	58.40	**71.60**
	Inst	Roll	Sm	QA	.615	13.00	44.00	24.40	4.00	72.40	**90.10**
Vinyl, with fabric backing (not prepasted), single rolls, 36 SF/roll											
	Inst	Roll	Lg	QA	.435	18.40	47.10	17.30	2.83	67.23	**82.00**
	Inst	Roll	Sm	QA	.669	11.96	51.90	26.60	4.35	82.85	**103.00**

Labor adjustments

ADD

Description	Oper	Unit	Vol	Crew Size	Man-hours per Unit	Crew Output per Day	Avg Mat'l Unit Cost	Avg Labor Unit Cost	Avg Equip Unit Cost	Avg Total Unit Cost	Avg Price Incl O&P
For ceiling 9'-0" high or more											
	Inst	%	Lg	QA	20.0	---	---	---	---	---	---
	Inst	%	Sm	QA	20.0	---	---	---	---	---	---
For kitchens, baths, and other rooms where floor area is less than 50.0 SF											
	Inst	%	Lg	QA	32.0	---	---	---	---	---	---
	Inst	%	Sm	QA	32.0	---	---	---	---	---	---

Water closets. See Toilets, page 442

Water filters

Automatic setup

Backwashing

Description	Oper	Unit	Vol	Crew Size	Man-hours per Unit	Crew Output per Day	Avg Mat'l Unit Cost	Avg Labor Unit Cost	Avg Equip Unit Cost	Avg Total Unit Cost	Avg Price Incl O&P
1.0 CF, 5-layer sediment											
	---	Ea	Lg	---	---	---	551.00	---	---	551.00	**634.00**
	---	Ea	Sm	---	---	---	641.00	---	---	641.00	**737.00**
1.0 CF, taste and odor, activated carbon											
	---	Ea	Lg	---	---	---	581.00	---	---	581.00	**668.00**
	---	Ea	Sm	---	---	---	675.00	---	---	675.00	**776.00**
1.5 CF, acid neutralizing, calcite											
	---	Ea	Lg	---	---	---	635.00	---	---	635.00	**730.00**
	---	Ea	Sm	---	---	---	738.00	---	---	738.00	**849.00**
1.0 CF, chem-free iron reduction											
	---	Ea	Lg	---	---	---	804.00	---	---	804.00	**924.00**
	---	Ea	Sm	---	---	---	935.00	---	---	935.00	**1070.00**

Description	Oper	Unit	Vol	Crew Size	Man-hours per Unit	Crew Output per Day	Avg Mat'l Unit Cost	Avg Labor Unit Cost	Avg Equip Unit Cost	Avg Total Unit Cost	Avg Price Incl O&P

On Demand setup

Iron & Sulphur filter, with mechanical meter

1.0 CF, manganese greensand

Description	Oper	Unit	Vol	Crew Size	Man-hours per Unit	Crew Output per Day	Avg Mat'l Unit Cost	Avg Labor Unit Cost	Avg Equip Unit Cost	Avg Total Unit Cost	Avg Price Incl O&P
	---	Ea	Lg	---	---	---	818.00	---	---	818.00	**941.00**
	---	Ea	Sm	---	---	---	951.00	---	---	951.00	**1090.00**

Water heaters

(A.O. Smith Products)

Detach & reset operations

Description	Oper	Unit	Vol	Crew Size	Man-hours per Unit	Crew Output per Day	Avg Mat'l Unit Cost	Avg Labor Unit Cost	Avg Equip Unit Cost	Avg Total Unit Cost	Avg Price Incl O&P
Water heater	Inst	Ea	Lg	SA	1.33	6.00	---	57.20	---	57.20	**83.00**
	Inst	Ea	Sm	SA	1.78	4.50	---	76.60	---	76.60	**111.00**

Remove operations

Description	Oper	Unit	Vol	Crew Size	Man-hours per Unit	Crew Output per Day	Avg Mat'l Unit Cost	Avg Labor Unit Cost	Avg Equip Unit Cost	Avg Total Unit Cost	Avg Price Incl O&P
Water heater	Demo	Ea	Lg	SA	1.00	8.00	---	43.00	---	43.00	**62.40**
	Demo	Ea	Sm	SA	1.33	6.00	---	57.20	---	57.20	**83.00**

Replace operations

Electric

Standard model, tall

6-year Energy Saver, foam insulated

Description	Oper	Unit	Vol	Crew Size	Man-hours per Unit	Crew Output per Day	Avg Mat'l Unit Cost	Avg Labor Unit Cost	Avg Equip Unit Cost	Avg Total Unit Cost	Avg Price Incl O&P
30 gal round	Inst	Ea	Lg	SA	2.00	4.00	673.00	86.00	---	759.00	**899.00**
	Inst	Ea	Sm	SA	2.67	3.00	783.00	115.00	---	898.00	**1070.00**
40 gal round	Inst	Ea	Lg	SA	2.00	4.00	716.00	86.00	---	802.00	**948.00**
	Inst	Ea	Sm	SA	2.67	3.00	832.00	115.00	---	947.00	**1120.00**
50 gal round	Inst	Ea	Lg	SA	2.00	4.00	799.00	86.00	---	885.00	**1040.00**
	Inst	Ea	Sm	SA	2.67	3.00	929.00	115.00	---	1044.00	**1230.00**
55 gal round	Inst	Ea	Lg	SA	2.00	4.00	799.00	86.00	---	885.00	**1040.00**
	Inst	Ea	Sm	SA	2.67	3.00	929.00	115.00	---	1044.00	**1230.00**
65 gal round	Inst	Ea	Lg	SA	2.67	3.00	1070.00	115.00	---	1185.00	**1400.00**
	Inst	Ea	Sm	SA	3.56	2.25	1250.00	153.00	---	1403.00	**1660.00**
80 gal round	Inst	Ea	Lg	SA	2.67	3.00	1190.00	115.00	---	1305.00	**1540.00**
	Inst	Ea	Sm	SA	3.56	2.25	1390.00	153.00	---	1543.00	**1820.00**
120 gal round	Inst	Ea	Lg	SA	2.67	3.00	1690.00	115.00	---	1805.00	**2100.00**
	Inst	Ea	Sm	SA	3.56	2.25	1960.00	153.00	---	2113.00	**2480.00**

Description	Oper	Unit	Vol	Crew Size	Man-hours per Unit	Crew Output per Day	Avg Mat'l Unit Cost	Avg Labor Unit Cost	Avg Equip Unit Cost	Avg Total Unit Cost	Avg Price Incl O&P
Standard model, short											
6-year Energy Saver, foam insulated											
30 gal round	Inst	Ea	Lg	SA	2.00	4.00	673.00	86.00	---	759.00	**899.00**
	Inst	Ea	Sm	SA	2.67	3.00	783.00	115.00	---	898.00	**1070.00**
40 gal round	Inst	Ea	Lg	SA	2.00	4.00	716.00	86.00	---	802.00	**948.00**
	Inst	Ea	Sm	SA	2.67	3.00	832.00	115.00	---	947.00	**1120.00**
50 gal round	Inst	Ea	Lg	SA	2.00	4.00	572.00	86.00	---	658.00	**783.00**
	Inst	Ea	Sm	SA	2.67	3.00	666.00	115.00	---	781.00	**932.00**
Standard model, low boy, top connection											
6-year Energy Saver, foam insulated											
6 gal round	Inst	Ea	Lg	SA	1.60	5.00	484.00	68.80	---	552.80	**656.00**
	Inst	Ea	Sm	SA	2.13	3.75	563.00	91.60	---	654.60	**780.00**
15 gal round	Inst	Ea	Lg	SA	1.60	5.00	517.00	68.80	---	585.80	**694.00**
	Inst	Ea	Sm	SA	2.13	3.75	601.00	91.60	---	692.60	**824.00**
19.9 gal round	Inst	Ea	Lg	SA	1.60	5.00	618.00	68.80	---	686.80	**811.00**
	Inst	Ea	Sm	SA	2.13	3.75	719.00	91.60	---	810.60	**960.00**
29 gal round	Inst	Ea	Lg	SA	2.00	4.00	703.00	86.00	---	789.00	**933.00**
	Inst	Ea	Sm	SA	2.67	3.00	817.00	115.00	---	932.00	**1110.00**
40 gal round	Inst	Ea	Lg	SA	2.00	4.00	745.00	86.00	---	831.00	**982.00**
	Inst	Ea	Sm	SA	2.67	3.00	867.00	115.00	---	982.00	**1160.00**
50 gal round	Inst	Ea	Lg	SA	2.00	4.00	826.00	86.00	---	912.00	**1070.00**
	Inst	Ea	Sm	SA	2.67	3.00	961.00	115.00	---	1076.00	**1270.00**
Standard model, low boy, side connection											
6-year Energy Saver, foam insulated											
10 gal round	Inst	Ea	Lg	SA	1.60	5.00	480.00	68.80	---	548.80	**652.00**
	Inst	Ea	Sm	SA	2.13	3.75	559.00	91.60	---	650.60	**775.00**
15 gal round	Inst	Ea	Lg	SA	1.60	5.00	464.00	68.80	---	532.80	**633.00**
	Inst	Ea	Sm	SA	2.13	3.75	539.00	91.60	---	630.60	**753.00**
20 gal round	Inst	Ea	Lg	SA	1.60	5.00	548.00	68.80	---	616.80	**730.00**
	Inst	Ea	Sm	SA	2.13	3.75	638.00	91.60	---	729.60	**866.00**
29 gal round	Inst	Ea	Lg	SA	2.00	4.00	594.00	86.00	---	680.00	**808.00**
	Inst	Ea	Sm	SA	2.67	3.00	691.00	115.00	---	806.00	**961.00**
40 gal round	Inst	Ea	Lg	SA	2.00	4.00	631.00	86.00	---	717.00	**851.00**
	Inst	Ea	Sm	SA	2.67	3.00	734.00	115.00	---	849.00	**1010.00**

Description	Oper	Unit	Vol	Crew Size	Man-hours per Unit	Crew Output per Day	Avg Mat'l Unit Cost	Avg Labor Unit Cost	Avg Equip Unit Cost	Avg Total Unit Cost	Avg Price Incl O&P

Deluxe model, tall

10-year Energy Saver, foam insulated

Description	Oper	Unit	Vol	Crew Size	Man-hours per Unit	Crew Output per Day	Avg Mat'l Unit Cost	Avg Labor Unit Cost	Avg Equip Unit Cost	Avg Total Unit Cost	Avg Price Incl O&P
30 gal round	Inst	Ea	Lg	SA	2.00	4.00	839.00	86.00	---	925.00	**1090.00**
	Inst	Ea	Sm	SA	2.67	3.00	976.00	115.00	---	1091.00	**1290.00**
40 gal round	Inst	Ea	Lg	SA	2.00	4.00	881.00	86.00	---	967.00	**1140.00**
	Inst	Ea	Sm	SA	2.67	3.00	1030.00	115.00	---	1145.00	**1350.00**
50 gal round	Inst	Ea	Lg	SA	2.00	4.00	964.00	86.00	---	1050.00	**1230.00**
	Inst	Ea	Sm	SA	2.67	3.00	1120.00	115.00	---	1235.00	**1460.00**
55 gal round	Inst	Ea	Lg	SA	2.00	4.00	856.00	86.00	---	942.00	**1110.00**
	Inst	Ea	Sm	SA	2.67	3.00	995.00	115.00	---	1110.00	**1310.00**
66 gal round	Inst	Ea	Lg	SA	2.67	3.00	1240.00	115.00	---	1355.00	**1590.00**
	Inst	Ea	Sm	SA	3.56	2.25	1440.00	153.00	---	1593.00	**1880.00**
80 gal round	Inst	Ea	Lg	SA	2.67	3.00	1360.00	115.00	---	1475.00	**1730.00**
	Inst	Ea	Sm	SA	3.56	2.25	1580.00	153.00	---	1733.00	**2040.00**
119 gal round	Inst	Ea	Lg	SA	2.67	3.00	1850.00	115.00	---	1965.00	**2300.00**
	Inst	Ea	Sm	SA	3.56	2.25	2150.00	153.00	---	2303.00	**2700.00**

Deluxe model, short

10-year Energy Saver, foam insulated

Description	Oper	Unit	Vol	Crew Size	Man-hours per Unit	Crew Output per Day	Avg Mat'l Unit Cost	Avg Labor Unit Cost	Avg Equip Unit Cost	Avg Total Unit Cost	Avg Price Incl O&P
30 gal round	Inst	Ea	Lg	SA	2.00	4.00	839.00	86.00	---	925.00	**1090.00**
	Inst	Ea	Sm	SA	2.67	3.00	976.00	115.00	---	1091.00	**1290.00**
40 gal round	Inst	Ea	Lg	SA	2.00	4.00	881.00	86.00	---	967.00	**1140.00**
	Inst	Ea	Sm	SA	2.67	3.00	1030.00	115.00	---	1145.00	**1350.00**

Deluxe model, low boy, top connection

10-year Energy Saver, foam insulated

Description	Oper	Unit	Vol	Crew Size	Man-hours per Unit	Crew Output per Day	Avg Mat'l Unit Cost	Avg Labor Unit Cost	Avg Equip Unit Cost	Avg Total Unit Cost	Avg Price Incl O&P
6 gal round	Inst	Ea	Lg	SA	1.60	5.00	591.00	68.80	---	659.80	**779.00**
	Inst	Ea	Sm	SA	2.13	3.75	687.00	91.60	---	778.60	**923.00**
15 gal round	Inst	Ea	Lg	SA	1.60	5.00	620.00	68.80	---	688.80	**813.00**
	Inst	Ea	Sm	SA	2.13	3.75	721.00	91.60	---	812.60	**962.00**
19.9 gal round	Inst	Ea	Lg	SA	1.60	5.00	714.00	68.80	---	782.80	**921.00**
	Inst	Ea	Sm	SA	2.13	3.75	830.00	91.60	---	921.60	**1090.00**
29 gal round	Inst	Ea	Lg	SA	2.00	4.00	868.00	86.00	---	954.00	**1120.00**
	Inst	Ea	Sm	SA	2.67	3.00	1010.00	115.00	---	1125.00	**1330.00**
40 gal round	Inst	Ea	Lg	SA	2.00	4.00	911.00	86.00	---	997.00	**1170.00**
	Inst	Ea	Sm	SA	2.67	3.00	1060.00	115.00	---	1175.00	**1380.00**
50 gal round	Inst	Ea	Lg	SA	2.00	4.00	992.00	86.00	---	1078.00	**1270.00**
	Inst	Ea	Sm	SA	2.67	3.00	1150.00	115.00	---	1265.00	**1490.00**

Description	Oper	Unit	Vol	Crew Size	Man-hours per Unit	Crew Output per Day	Avg Mat'l Unit Cost	Avg Labor Unit Cost	Avg Equip Unit Cost	Avg Total Unit Cost	Avg Price Incl O&P

Deluxe model, low boy, side connection

10-year Energy Saver, foam insulated

Description	Oper	Unit	Vol	Crew Size	Man-hours per Unit	Crew Output per Day	Avg Mat'l Unit Cost	Avg Labor Unit Cost	Avg Equip Unit Cost	Avg Total Unit Cost	Avg Price Incl O&P
10 gal round	Inst	Ea	Lg	SA	1.60	5.00	466.00	68.80	---	534.80	**635.00**
	Inst	Ea	Sm	SA	2.13	3.75	541.00	91.60	---	632.60	**756.00**
15 gal round	Inst	Ea	Lg	SA	1.60	5.00	484.00	68.80	---	552.80	**656.00**
	Inst	Ea	Sm	SA	2.13	3.75	563.00	91.60	---	654.60	**780.00**
20 gal round	Inst	Ea	Lg	SA	1.60	5.00	515.00	68.80	---	583.80	**692.00**
	Inst	Ea	Sm	SA	2.13	3.75	599.00	91.60	---	690.60	**822.00**
29 gal round	Inst	Ea	Lg	SA	2.00	4.00	591.00	86.00	---	677.00	**804.00**
	Inst	Ea	Sm	SA	2.67	3.00	687.00	115.00	---	802.00	**957.00**
40 gal round	Inst	Ea	Lg	SA	2.00	4.00	620.00	86.00	---	706.00	**838.00**
	Inst	Ea	Sm	SA	2.67	3.00	721.00	115.00	---	836.00	**996.00**

Gas

Standard model, high recovery, tall

6-year Energy Saver

Description	Oper	Unit	Vol	Crew Size	Man-hours per Unit	Crew Output per Day	Avg Mat'l Unit Cost	Avg Labor Unit Cost	Avg Equip Unit Cost	Avg Total Unit Cost	Avg Price Incl O&P
38 gal round, 50,000 btu	Inst	Ea	Lg	SA	4.44	1.80	887.00	191.00	---	1078.00	**1300.00**
	Inst	Ea	Sm	SA	6.15	1.30	1030.00	265.00	---	1295.00	**1570.00**
48 gal round, 50,000 btu	Inst	Ea	Lg	SA	4.44	1.80	940.00	191.00	---	1131.00	**1360.00**
	Inst	Ea	Sm	SA	6.15	1.30	1090.00	265.00	---	1355.00	**1640.00**
50 gal round, 65,000 btu	Inst	Ea	Lg	SA	4.71	1.70	988.00	203.00	---	1191.00	**1430.00**
	Inst	Ea	Sm	SA	6.67	1.20	1150.00	287.00	---	1437.00	**1740.00**
65 gal round, 65,000 btu	Inst	Ea	Lg	SA	4.71	1.70	1110.00	203.00	---	1313.00	**1570.00**
	Inst	Ea	Sm	SA	6.67	1.20	1290.00	287.00	---	1577.00	**1900.00**
74 gal round, 75,100 btu	Inst	Ea	Lg	SA	4.71	1.70	1460.00	203.00	---	1663.00	**1970.00**
	Inst	Ea	Sm	SA	6.67	1.20	1690.00	287.00	---	1977.00	**2360.00**
98 gal round, 75,100 btu	Inst	Ea	Lg	SA	4.71	1.70	2300.00	203.00	---	2503.00	**2940.00**
	Inst	Ea	Sm	SA	6.67	1.20	2680.00	287.00	---	2967.00	**3500.00**

Standard model, tall

6-year Energy Saver

Description	Oper	Unit	Vol	Crew Size	Man-hours per Unit	Crew Output per Day	Avg Mat'l Unit Cost	Avg Labor Unit Cost	Avg Equip Unit Cost	Avg Total Unit Cost	Avg Price Incl O&P
28 gal round, 40,000 btu	Inst	Ea	Lg	SA	4.44	1.80	808.00	191.00	---	999.00	**1210.00**
	Inst	Ea	Sm	SA	6.15	1.30	939.00	265.00	---	1204.00	**1460.00**
38 gal round, 40,000 btu	Inst	Ea	Lg	SA	4.44	1.80	841.00	191.00	---	1032.00	**1240.00**
	Inst	Ea	Sm	SA	6.15	1.30	978.00	265.00	---	1243.00	**1510.00**
50 gal round, 40,000 btu	Inst	Ea	Lg	SA	4.71	1.70	896.00	203.00	---	1099.00	**1320.00**
	Inst	Ea	Sm	SA	6.67	1.20	1040.00	287.00	---	1327.00	**1610.00**

Standard model, short

6-year Energy Saver

Description	Oper	Unit	Vol	Crew Size	Man-hours per Unit	Crew Output per Day	Avg Mat'l Unit Cost	Avg Labor Unit Cost	Avg Equip Unit Cost	Avg Total Unit Cost	Avg Price Incl O&P
30 gal round, 40,000 btu	Inst	Ea	Lg	SA	4.44	1.80	808.00	191.00	---	999.00	**1210.00**
	Inst	Ea	Sm	SA	6.15	1.30	939.00	265.00	---	1204.00	**1460.00**
40 gal round, 40,000 btu	Inst	Ea	Lg	SA	4.44	1.80	841.00	191.00	---	1032.00	**1240.00**
	Inst	Ea	Sm	SA	6.15	1.30	978.00	265.00	---	1243.00	**1510.00**
50 gal round, 40,000 btu	Inst	Ea	Lg	SA	4.71	1.70	896.00	203.00	---	1099.00	**1320.00**
	Inst	Ea	Sm	SA	6.67	1.20	1040.00	287.00	---	1327.00	**1610.00**

Description	Oper	Unit	Vol	Crew Size	Man-hours per Unit	Crew Output per Day	Avg Mat'l Unit Cost	Avg Labor Unit Cost	Avg Equip Unit Cost	Avg Total Unit Cost	Avg Price Incl O&P

Deluxe model, high recovery, tall

10-year Energy Saver

Description	Oper	Unit	Vol	Crew Size	Man-hours per Unit	Crew Output per Day	Avg Mat'l Unit Cost	Avg Labor Unit Cost	Avg Equip Unit Cost	Avg Total Unit Cost	Avg Price Incl O&P
38 gal round, 50,000 btu	Inst	Ea	Lg	SA	4.44	1.80	1030.00	191.00	---	1221.00	**1470.00**
	Inst	Ea	Sm	SA	6.15	1.30	1200.00	265.00	---	1465.00	**1770.00**
48 gal round, 50,000 btu	Inst	Ea	Lg	SA	4.44	1.80	1090.00	191.00	---	1281.00	**1530.00**
	Inst	Ea	Sm	SA	6.15	1.30	1260.00	265.00	---	1525.00	**1840.00**
50 gal round, 65,000 btu	Inst	Ea	Lg	SA	4.71	1.70	1140.00	203.00	---	1343.00	**1600.00**
	Inst	Ea	Sm	SA	6.67	1.20	1320.00	287.00	---	1607.00	**1930.00**
65 gal round, 65,000 btu	Inst	Ea	Lg	SA	4.71	1.70	1160.00	203.00	---	1363.00	**1630.00**
	Inst	Ea	Sm	SA	6.67	1.20	1350.00	287.00	---	1637.00	**1970.00**
74 gal round, 75,100 btu	Inst	Ea	Lg	SA	4.71	1.70	1420.00	203.00	---	1623.00	**1930.00**
	Inst	Ea	Sm	SA	6.67	1.20	1660.00	287.00	---	1947.00	**2320.00**
98 gal round, 75,100 btu	Inst	Ea	Lg	SA	4.71	1.70	2230.00	203.00	---	2433.00	**2860.00**
	Inst	Ea	Sm	SA	6.67	1.20	2590.00	287.00	---	2877.00	**3400.00**

Deluxe model, tall

10-year Energy Saver

Description	Oper	Unit	Vol	Crew Size	Man-hours per Unit	Crew Output per Day	Avg Mat'l Unit Cost	Avg Labor Unit Cost	Avg Equip Unit Cost	Avg Total Unit Cost	Avg Price Incl O&P
28 gal round, 40,000 btu	Inst	Ea	Lg	SA	4.44	1.80	955.00	191.00	---	1146.00	**1380.00**
	Inst	Ea	Sm	SA	6.15	1.30	1110.00	265.00	---	1375.00	**1660.00**
38 gal round, 40,000 btu	Inst	Ea	Lg	SA	4.44	1.80	988.00	191.00	---	1179.00	**1410.00**
	Inst	Ea	Sm	SA	6.15	1.30	1150.00	265.00	---	1415.00	**1710.00**
50 gal round, 40,000 btu	Inst	Ea	Lg	SA	4.71	1.70	1040.00	203.00	---	1243.00	**1490.00**
	Inst	Ea	Sm	SA	6.67	1.20	1210.00	287.00	---	1497.00	**1810.00**

Deluxe model, short

10-year Energy Saver

Description	Oper	Unit	Vol	Crew Size	Man-hours per Unit	Crew Output per Day	Avg Mat'l Unit Cost	Avg Labor Unit Cost	Avg Equip Unit Cost	Avg Total Unit Cost	Avg Price Incl O&P
30 gal round, 40,000 btu	Inst	Ea	Lg	SA	4.44	1.80	955.00	191.00	---	1146.00	**1380.00**
	Inst	Ea	Sm	SA	6.15	1.30	1110.00	265.00	---	1375.00	**1660.00**
40 gal round, 40,000 btu	Inst	Ea	Lg	SA	4.44	1.80	988.00	191.00	---	1179.00	**1410.00**
	Inst	Ea	Sm	SA	6.15	1.30	1150.00	265.00	---	1415.00	**1710.00**
50 gal round, 40,000 btu	Inst	Ea	Lg	SA	4.71	1.70	1040.00	203.00	---	1243.00	**1490.00**
	Inst	Ea	Sm	SA	6.67	1.20	1210.00	287.00	---	1497.00	**1810.00**

Optional accessories

Water heater cabinets

24" x 24" x 72"

Description	Oper	Unit	Vol	Crew Size	Man-hours per Unit	Crew Output per Day	Avg Mat'l Unit Cost	Avg Labor Unit Cost	Avg Equip Unit Cost	Avg Total Unit Cost	Avg Price Incl O&P
heaters up to 40 gal	---	Ea	Lg	---	---	---	161.00	---	---	161.00	**185.00**
	---	Ea	Sm	---	---	---	187.00	---	---	187.00	**215.00**

30" x 30" x 72"

Description	Oper	Unit	Vol	Crew Size	Man-hours per Unit	Crew Output per Day	Avg Mat'l Unit Cost	Avg Labor Unit Cost	Avg Equip Unit Cost	Avg Total Unit Cost	Avg Price Incl O&P
heaters up to 75 gal	---	Ea	Lg	---	---	---	183.00	---	---	183.00	**210.00**
	---	Ea	Sm	---	---	---	212.00	---	---	212.00	**244.00**

36" x 36" x 83"

Description	Oper	Unit	Vol	Crew Size	Man-hours per Unit	Crew Output per Day	Avg Mat'l Unit Cost	Avg Labor Unit Cost	Avg Equip Unit Cost	Avg Total Unit Cost	Avg Price Incl O&P
heaters up to 100 gal	---	Ea	Lg	---	---	---	364.00	---	---	364.00	**418.00**
	---	Ea	Sm	---	---	---	423.00	---	---	423.00	**486.00**

Description	Oper	Unit	Vol	Crew Size	Man-hours per Unit	Crew Output per Day	Avg Mat'l Unit Cost	Avg Labor Unit Cost	Avg Equip Unit Cost	Avg Total Unit Cost	Avg Price Incl O&P
Water heater pans, by diameter											
20" pan (up to 18" unit)	---	Ea	Lg	---	---	---	19.10	---	---	19.10	**22.00**
	---	Ea	Sm	---	---	---	22.30	---	---	22.30	**25.60**
24" pan (up to 22" unit)	---	Ea	Lg	---	---	---	22.80	---	---	22.80	**26.20**
	---	Ea	Sm	---	---	---	26.50	---	---	26.50	**30.50**
26" pan (up to 24" unit)	---	Ea	Lg	---	---	---	27.80	---	---	27.80	**32.00**
	---	Ea	Sm	---	---	---	32.30	---	---	32.30	**37.20**
28" pan (up to 26" unit)	---	Ea	Lg	---	---	---	32.20	---	---	32.20	**37.00**
	---	Ea	Sm	---	---	---	37.50	---	---	37.50	**43.10**
Water heater stands											
22" x 22", heaters up to 52 ga	---	Ea	Lg	---	---	---	78.00	---	---	78.00	**89.70**
	---	Ea	Sm	---	---	---	90.70	---	---	90.70	**104.00**
26" x 26", heaters up to 75 ga	---	Ea	Lg	---	---	---	107.00	---	---	107.00	**123.00**
	---	Ea	Sm	---	---	---	124.00	---	---	124.00	**143.00**
Free-standing restraint system											
75 gal capacity	---	Ea	Lg	---	---	---	316.00	---	---	316.00	**363.00**
	---	Ea	Sm	---	---	---	367.00	---	---	367.00	**422.00**
100 gal capacity	---	Ea	Lg	---	---	---	336.00	---	---	336.00	**386.00**
	---	Ea	Sm	---	---	---	391.00	---	---	391.00	**449.00**
Wall mount platform restraint system											
75 gal capacity	---	Ea	Lg	---	---	---	272.00	---	---	272.00	**313.00**
	---	Ea	Sm	---	---	---	316.00	---	---	316.00	**364.00**
100 gal capacity	---	Ea	Lg	---	---	---	301.00	---	---	301.00	**347.00**
	---	Ea	Sm	---	---	---	351.00	---	---	351.00	**403.00**

Solar water heating systems

Complete closed loop solar system with solar electric water heater with exchanger, differential control, heating element, circulator, collector and tank, and panel sensors. The material costs given include the subcontractor's overhead and profit

82-gallon capacity collector

Description	Oper	Unit	Vol	Crew Size	Man-hours per Unit	Crew Output per Day	Avg Mat'l Unit Cost	Avg Labor Unit Cost	Avg Equip Unit Cost	Avg Total Unit Cost	Avg Price Incl O&P
One deluxe collector											
	---	LS	Lg	---	---	---	3320.00	---	---	3320.00	**3810.00**
	---	LS	Sm	---	---	---	3570.00	---	---	3570.00	**4110.00**
Two deluxe collectors											
Standard collectors	---	LS	Lg	---	---	---	4100.00	---	---	4100.00	**4720.00**
	---	LS	Sm	---	---	---	4420.00	---	---	4420.00	**5080.00**
Deluxe collectors	---	LS	Lg	---	---	---	4230.00	---	---	4230.00	**4860.00**
	---	LS	Sm	---	---	---	4550.00	---	---	4550.00	**5230.00**
Three collectors											
Economy collectors	---	LS	Lg	---	---	---	4820.00	---	---	4820.00	**5540.00**
	---	LS	Sm	---	---	---	5190.00	---	---	5190.00	**5970.00**
Standard collectors	---	LS	Lg	---	---	---	4940.00	---	---	4940.00	**5680.00**
	---	LS	Sm	---	---	---	5320.00	---	---	5320.00	**6120.00**
Four collectors											
Economy collectors	---	LS	Lg	---	---	---	5200.00	---	---	5200.00	**5980.00**
	---	LS	Sm	---	---	---	5600.00	---	---	5600.00	**6440.00**
Standard collectors	---	LS	Lg	---	---	---	5330.00	---	---	5330.00	**6130.00**
	---	LS	Sm	---	---	---	5740.00	---	---	5740.00	**6600.00**

Description	Oper	Unit	Vol	Crew Size	Man-hours per Unit	Crew Output per Day	Avg Mat'l Unit Cost	Avg Labor Unit Cost	Avg Equip Unit Cost	Avg Total Unit Cost	Avg Price Incl O&P

120-gallon capacity system

Three collectors

Description	Oper	Unit	Vol	Crew Size	Man-hours per Unit	Crew Output per Day	Avg Mat'l Unit Cost	Avg Labor Unit Cost	Avg Equip Unit Cost	Avg Total Unit Cost	Avg Price Incl O&P
Economy collectors	---	LS	Lg	---	---	---	5970.00	---	---	5970.00	**6870.00**
	---	LS	Sm	---	---	---	6430.00	---	---	6430.00	**7400.00**
Standard collectors	---	LS	Lg	---	---	---	6110.00	---	---	6110.00	**7030.00**
	---	LS	Sm	---	---	---	6580.00	---	---	6580.00	**7570.00**

Four standard collectors

Description	Oper	Unit	Vol	Crew Size	Man-hours per Unit	Crew Output per Day	Avg Mat'l Unit Cost	Avg Labor Unit Cost	Avg Equip Unit Cost	Avg Total Unit Cost	Avg Price Incl O&P
	---	LS	Lg	---	---	---	7150.00	---	---	7150.00	**8220.00**
	---	LS	Sm	---	---	---	7700.00	---	---	7700.00	**8860.00**

Five collectors

Description	Oper	Unit	Vol	Crew Size	Man-hours per Unit	Crew Output per Day	Avg Mat'l Unit Cost	Avg Labor Unit Cost	Avg Equip Unit Cost	Avg Total Unit Cost	Avg Price Incl O&P
Economy collectors	---	LS	Lg	---	---	---	7800.00	---	---	7800.00	**8970.00**
	---	LS	Sm	---	---	---	8400.00	---	---	8400.00	**9660.00**
Standard collectors	---	LS	Lg	---	---	---	7930.00	---	---	7930.00	**9120.00**
	---	LS	Sm	---	---	---	8540.00	---	---	8540.00	**9820.00**

Six collectors

Description	Oper	Unit	Vol	Crew Size	Man-hours per Unit	Crew Output per Day	Avg Mat'l Unit Cost	Avg Labor Unit Cost	Avg Equip Unit Cost	Avg Total Unit Cost	Avg Price Incl O&P
Economy collectors	---	LS	Lg	---	---	---	8450.00	---	---	8450.00	**9720.00**
	---	LS	Sm	---	---	---	9100.00	---	---	9100.00	**10500.00**
Standard collectors	---	LS	Lg	---	---	---	8580.00	---	---	8580.00	**9870.00**
	---	LS	Sm	---	---	---	9240.00	---	---	9240.00	**10600.00**

Material adjustments

Collector mounting kits, one required per collector panel

Description	Oper	Unit	Vol	Crew Size	Man-hours per Unit	Crew Output per Day	Avg Mat'l Unit Cost	Avg Labor Unit Cost	Avg Equip Unit Cost	Avg Total Unit Cost	Avg Price Incl O&P
Adjustable position hinge	---	Ea	Lg	---	---	---	74.10	---	---	74.10	**85.20**
	---	Ea	Sm	---	---	---	79.80	---	---	79.80	**91.80**
Integral flange	---	Ea	Lg	---	---	---	6.50	---	---	6.50	**7.48**
	---	Ea	Sm	---	---	---	7.00	---	---	7.00	**8.05**

Additional panels

Description	Oper	Unit	Vol	Crew Size	Man-hours per Unit	Crew Output per Day	Avg Mat'l Unit Cost	Avg Labor Unit Cost	Avg Equip Unit Cost	Avg Total Unit Cost	Avg Price Incl O&P
Economy collectors	---	Ea	Lg	---	---	---	650.00	---	---	650.00	**748.00**
	---	Ea	Sm	---	---	---	700.00	---	---	700.00	**805.0**
Standard collectors	---	Ea	Lg	---	---	---	780.00	---	---	780.00	**897.00**
	---	Ea	Sm	---	---	---	840.00	---	---	840.00	**966.00**
Deluxe collectors	---	Ea	Lg	---	---	---	910.00	---	---	910.00	**1050.00**
	---	Ea	Sm	---	---	---	980.00	---	---	980.00	**1130.00**

Description	Oper	Unit	Vol	Crew Size	Man-hours per Unit	Crew Output per Day	Avg Mat'l Unit Cost	Avg Labor Unit Cost	Avg Equip Unit Cost	Avg Total Unit Cost	Avg Price Incl O&P

Individual components

Solar storage tanks, glass lined with fiberglass insulation

Description	Oper	Unit	Vol	Crew Size	Man-hours per Unit	Crew Output per Day	Avg Mat'l Unit Cost	Avg Labor Unit Cost	Avg Equip Unit Cost	Avg Total Unit Cost	Avg Price Incl O&P
66 gallon	---	Ea	Lg	---	---	---	774.00	---	---	774.00	**890.00**
	---	Ea	Sm	---	---	---	833.00	---	---	833.00	**958.00**
82 gallon	---	Ea	Lg	---	---	---	878.00	---	---	878.00	**1010.00**
	---	Ea	Sm	---	---	---	945.00	---	---	945.00	**1090.00**
120 gallon	---	Ea	Lg	---	---	---	1330.00	---	---	1330.00	**1530.00**
	---	Ea	Sm	---	---	---	1430.00	---	---	1430.00	**1650.00**

Solar electric water heaters, glass lined with fiberglass insulation, heating element with thermostat

Description	Oper	Unit	Vol	Crew Size	Man-hours per Unit	Crew Output per Day	Avg Mat'l Unit Cost	Avg Labor Unit Cost	Avg Equip Unit Cost	Avg Total Unit Cost	Avg Price Incl O&P
66 gallon, 4.5 KW	---	Ea	Lg	---	---	---	772.00	---	---	772.00	**888.00**
	---	Ea	Sm	---	---	---	832.00	---	---	832.00	**956.00**
82 gallon, 4.5 KW	---	Ea	Lg	---	---	---	888.00	---	---	888.00	**1020.00**
	---	Ea	Sm	---	---	---	956.00	---	---	956.00	**1100.00**
120 gallon, 4.5 KW	---	Ea	Lg	---	---	---	1060.00	---	---	1060.00	**1220.00**
	---	Ea	Sm	---	---	---	1140.00	---	---	1140.00	**1310.00**
Additional element	---	Ea	Lg	---	---	---	42.90	---	---	42.90	**49.30**
	---	Ea	Sm	---	---	---	46.20	---	---	46.20	**53.10**

Solar electric water heaters with heat exchangers, glass lined with fiberglass insulation, two copper exchangers, powered circulator, differential control, adjustable thermostat

Description	Oper	Unit	Vol	Crew Size	Man-hours per Unit	Crew Output per Day	Avg Mat'l Unit Cost	Avg Labor Unit Cost	Avg Equip Unit Cost	Avg Total Unit Cost	Avg Price Incl O&P
82 gallon, 4.5 KW, 1/20 HP	---	Ea	Lg	---	---	---	1150.00	---	---	1150.00	**1330.00**
	---	Ea	Sm	---	---	---	1240.00	---	---	1240.00	**1430.00**
120 gallon, 4.5 KW, 1/20 HP	---	Ea	Lg	---	---	---	1520.00	---	---	1520.00	**1740.00**
	---	Ea	Sm	---	---	---	1630.00	---	---	1630.00	**1880.00**

Description	Oper	Unit	Vol	Crew Size	Man-hours per Unit	Crew Output per Day	Avg Mat'l Unit Cost	Avg Labor Unit Cost	Avg Equip Unit Cost	Avg Total Unit Cost	Avg Price Incl O&P

Water softeners

Time Clock setup

Cabinet style

Description	Oper	Unit	Vol	Crew Size	Man-hours per Unit	Crew Output per Day	Avg Mat'l Unit Cost	Avg Labor Unit Cost	Avg Equip Unit Cost	Avg Total Unit Cost	Avg Price Incl O&P
18,600 grains, 0.75 CF	---	Ea	Lg	---	---	---	685.00	---	---	685.00	**787.00**
	---	Ea	Sm	---	---	---	796.00	---	---	796.00	**916.00**
24,800 grains, 1.0 CF	---	Ea	Lg	---	---	---	753.00	---	---	753.00	**866.00**
	---	Ea	Sm	---	---	---	876.00	---	---	876.00	**1010.00**

Two-tank style

Description	Oper	Unit	Vol	Crew Size	Man-hours per Unit	Crew Output per Day	Avg Mat'l Unit Cost	Avg Labor Unit Cost	Avg Equip Unit Cost	Avg Total Unit Cost	Avg Price Incl O&P
24,800 grains, 1.0 CF											
	---	Ea	Lg	---	---	---	712.00	---	---	712.00	**819.00**
	---	Ea	Sm	---	---	---	829.00	---	---	829.00	**953.00**
39,960 grains, 1.5 CF											
	---	Ea	Lg	---	---	---	763.00	---	---	763.00	**877.00**
	---	Ea	Sm	---	---	---	887.00	---	---	887.00	**1020.00**

On Demand setup

Cabinet style, with mechanical meter

Description	Oper	Unit	Vol	Crew Size	Man-hours per Unit	Crew Output per Day	Avg Mat'l Unit Cost	Avg Labor Unit Cost	Avg Equip Unit Cost	Avg Total Unit Cost	Avg Price Incl O&P
18,600 grains, 0.75 CF											
	---	Ea	Lg	---	---	---	726.00	---	---	726.00	**835.00**
	---	Ea	Sm	---	---	---	845.00	---	---	845.00	**971.00**
24,800 grains, 1.0 CF											
	---	Ea	Lg	---	---	---	797.00	---	---	797.00	**917.00**
	---	Ea	Sm	---	---	---	927.00	---	---	927.00	**1070.00**

Description	Oper	Unit	Vol	Crew Size	Man-hours per Unit	Crew Output per Day	Avg Mat'l Unit Cost	Avg Labor Unit Cost	Avg Equip Unit Cost	Avg Total Unit Cost	Avg Price Incl O&P
Two-tank style, with mechanical meter											
18,600 grains, 0.75 CF	---	Ea	Lg	---	---	---	795.00	---	---	795.00	**914.00**
	---	Ea	Sm	---	---	---	924.00	---	---	924.00	**1060.00**
24,800 grains, 1.0 CF	---	Ea	Lg	---	---	---	812.00	---	---	812.00	**933.00**
	---	Ea	Sm	---	---	---	944.00	---	---	944.00	**1090.00**
39,960 grains, 1.5 CF	---	Ea	Lg	---	---	---	875.00	---	---	875.00	**1010.00**
	---	Ea	Sm	---	---	---	1020.00	---	---	1020.00	**1170.00**
49,600 grains, 2.0 CF	---	Ea	Lg	---	---	---	1040.00	---	---	1040.00	**1200.00**
	---	Ea	Sm	---	---	---	1210.00	---	---	1210.00	**1390.00**
99,900 grains, 3.0 CF	---	Ea	Lg	---	---	---	1350.00	---	---	1350.00	**1550.00**
	---	Ea	Sm	---	---	---	1570.00	---	---	1570.00	**1800.00**

Weathervanes. See Cupolas, page 113

Windows

Windows, with related trim and frame

Description	Oper	Unit	Vol	Crew Size	Man-hours per Unit	Crew Output per Day	Avg Mat'l Unit Cost	Avg Labor Unit Cost	Avg Equip Unit Cost	Avg Total Unit Cost	Avg Price Incl O&P
To 12 SF											
Aluminum	Demo	Ea	Lg	LB	.762	21.00	---	22.90	---	22.90	**32.00**
	Demo	Ea	Sm	LB	1.17	13.65	---	35.10	---	35.10	**49.10**
Wood	Demo	Ea	Lg	LB	1.00	16.00	---	30.00	---	30.00	**42.00**
	Demo	Ea	Sm	LB	1.54	10.40	---	46.20	---	46.20	**64.70**
13 SF to 50 SF											
Aluminum	Demo	Ea	Lg	LB	1.23	13.00	---	36.90	---	36.90	**51.70**
	Demo	Ea	Sm	LB	1.89	8.45	---	56.70	---	56.70	**79.40**
Wood	Demo	Ea	Lg	LB	1.60	10.00	---	48.00	---	48.00	**67.20**
	Demo	Ea	Sm	LB	2.46	6.50	---	73.80	---	73.80	**103.00**

Aluminum

Vertical slide, satin anodized finish, includes screen and hardware

Description	Oper	Unit	Vol	Crew Size	Man-hours per Unit	Crew Output per Day	Avg Mat'l Unit Cost	Avg Labor Unit Cost	Avg Equip Unit Cost	Avg Total Unit Cost	Avg Price Incl O&P
Single glazed											
1'-6" x 3'-0" H	Inst	Set	Lg	CA	1.14	7.00	99.00	42.20	---	141.20	**173.00**
	Inst	Set	Sm	CA	1.76	4.55	106.00	65.20	---	171.20	**213.00**
2'-0" x 2'-0" H	Inst	Set	Lg	CA	1.14	7.00	90.00	42.20	---	132.20	**163.00**
	Inst	Set	Sm	CA	1.76	4.55	96.00	65.20	---	161.20	**202.00**
2'-0" x 2'-6" H	Inst	Set	Lg	CA	1.14	7.00	102.00	42.20	---	144.20	**176.00**
	Inst	Set	Sm	CA	1.76	4.55	109.00	65.20	---	174.20	**216.00**
2'-0" x 3'-0" H	Inst	Set	Lg	CA	1.23	6.50	110.00	45.50	---	155.50	**190.00**
	Inst	Set	Sm	CA	1.89	4.23	117.00	70.00	---	187.00	**232.00**
2'-0" x 3'-6" H	Inst	Set	Lg	CA	1.23	6.50	117.00	45.50	---	162.50	**198.00**
	Inst	Set	Sm	CA	1.89	4.23	125.00	70.00	---	195.00	**241.00**
2'-0" x 4'-0" H	Inst	Set	Lg	CA	1.23	6.50	123.00	45.50	---	168.50	**205.00**
	Inst	Set	Sm	CA	1.89	4.23	131.00	70.00	---	201.00	**249.00**

Description	Oper	Unit	Vol	Crew Size	Man-hours per Unit	Crew Output per Day	Avg Mat'l Unit Cost	Avg Labor Unit Cost	Avg Equip Unit Cost	Avg Total Unit Cost	Avg Price Incl O&P
2'-0" x 4'-6" H	Inst	Set	Lg	CA	1.23	6.50	132.00	45.50	---	177.50	**216.00**
	Inst	Set	Sm	CA	1.89	4.23	141.00	70.00	---	211.00	**260.00**
2'-0" x 5'-0" H	Inst	Set	Lg	CA	1.33	6.00	138.00	49.20	---	187.20	**228.00**
	Inst	Set	Sm	CA	2.05	3.90	147.00	75.90	---	222.90	**276.00**
2'-0" x 6'-0" H	Inst	Set	Lg	CA	1.33	6.00	152.00	49.20	---	201.20	**243.00**
	Inst	Set	Sm	CA	2.05	3.90	162.00	75.90	---	237.90	**292.00**
2'-6" x 3'-0" H	Inst	Set	Lg	CA	1.23	6.50	120.00	45.50	---	165.50	**202.00**
	Inst	Set	Sm	CA	1.89	4.23	128.00	70.00	---	198.00	**245.00**
2'-6" x 3'-6" H	Inst	Set	Lg	CA	1.23	6.50	128.00	45.50	---	173.50	**210.00**
	Inst	Set	Sm	CA	1.89	4.23	136.00	70.00	---	206.00	**254.00**
2'-6" x 4'-0" H	Inst	Set	Lg	CA	1.23	6.50	135.00	45.50	---	180.50	**219.00**
	Inst	Set	Sm	CA	1.89	4.23	144.00	70.00	---	214.00	**264.00**
2'-6" x 4'-6" H	Inst	Set	Lg	CA	1.23	6.50	146.00	45.50	---	191.50	**231.00**
	Inst	Set	Sm	CA	1.89	4.23	155.00	70.00	---	225.00	**276.00**
2'-6" x 5'-0" H	Inst	Set	Lg	CA	1.33	6.00	152.00	49.20	---	201.20	**243.00**
	Inst	Set	Sm	CA	2.05	3.90	162.00	75.90	---	237.90	**292.00**
2'-6" x 6'-0" H	Inst	Set	Lg	CA	1.33	6.00	167.00	49.20	---	216.20	**260.00**
	Inst	Set	Sm	CA	2.05	3.90	178.00	75.90	---	253.90	**310.00**
3'-0" x 2'-0" H	Inst	Set	Lg	CA	1.23	6.50	116.00	45.50	---	161.50	**197.00**
	Inst	Set	Sm	CA	1.89	4.23	123.00	70.00	---	193.00	**240.00**
3'-0" x 3'-0" H	Inst	Set	Lg	CA	1.23	6.50	129.00	45.50	---	174.50	**212.00**
	Inst	Set	Sm	CA	1.89	4.23	138.00	70.00	---	208.00	**256.00**
3'-0" x 3'-6" H	Inst	Set	Lg	CA	1.23	6.50	138.00	45.50	---	183.50	**222.00**
	Inst	Set	Sm	CA	1.89	4.23	147.00	70.00	---	217.00	**267.00**
3'-0" x 4'-0" H	Inst	Set	Lg	CA	1.23	6.50	147.00	45.50	---	192.50	**233.00**
	Inst	Set	Sm	CA	1.89	4.23	157.00	70.00	---	227.00	**278.00**
3'-0" x 4'-6" H	Inst	Set	Lg	CA	1.23	6.50	159.00	45.50	---	204.50	**247.00**
	Inst	Set	Sm	CA	1.89	4.23	170.00	70.00	---	240.00	**293.00**
3'-0" x 5'-0" H	Inst	Set	Lg	CJ	2.76	5.80	165.00	92.50	---	257.50	**319.00**
	Inst	Set	Sm	CJ	4.24	3.77	176.00	142.00	---	318.00	**401.00**
3'-0" x 6'-0" H	Inst	Set	Lg	CJ	3.08	5.20	182.00	103.00	---	285.00	**353.00**
	Inst	Set	Sm	CJ	4.73	3.38	194.00	159.00	---	353.00	**445.00**
3'-6" x 3'-6" H	Inst	Set	Lg	CA	1.23	6.50	149.00	45.50	---	194.50	**235.00**
	Inst	Set	Sm	CA	1.89	4.23	158.00	70.00	---	228.00	**280.00**
3'-6" x 4'-0" H	Inst	Set	Lg	CA	1.45	5.50	159.00	53.70	---	212.70	**258.00**
	Inst	Set	Sm	CA	2.23	3.58	170.00	82.60	---	252.60	**311.00**
3'-6" x 4'-6" H	Inst	Set	Lg	CA	1.78	4.50	174.00	65.90	---	239.90	**292.00**
	Inst	Set	Sm	CA	2.73	2.93	186.00	101.00	---	287.00	**355.00**
3'-6" x 5'-0" H	Inst	Set	Lg	CJ	3.08	5.20	179.00	103.00	---	282.00	**350.00**
	Inst	Set	Sm	CJ	4.73	3.38	190.00	159.00	---	349.00	**441.00**
4'-0" x 3'-0" H	Inst	Set	Lg	CA	1.23	6.50	149.00	45.50	---	194.50	**235.00**
	Inst	Set	Sm	CA	1.89	4.23	158.00	70.00	---	228.00	**280.00**
4'-0" x 3'-6" H	Inst	Set	Lg	CA	1.45	5.50	159.00	53.70	---	212.70	**258.00**
	Inst	Set	Sm	CA	2.23	3.58	170.00	82.60	---	252.60	**311.00**
4'-0" x 4'-0" H	Inst	Set	Lg	CJ	2.76	5.80	170.00	92.50	---	262.50	**324.00**
	Inst	Set	Sm	CJ	4.24	3.77	181.00	142.00	---	323.00	**407.00**
4'-0" x 4'-6" H	Inst	Set	Lg	CJ	2.76	5.80	180.00	92.50	---	272.50	**336.00**
	Inst	Set	Sm	CJ	4.24	3.77	192.00	142.00	---	334.00	**420.00**
4'-0" x 5'-0" H	Inst	Set	Lg	CJ	3.08	5.20	192.00	103.00	---	295.00	**365.00**
	Inst	Set	Sm	CJ	4.73	3.38	205.00	159.00	---	364.00	**457.00**

Description	Oper	Unit	Vol	Crew Size	Man-hours per Unit	Crew Output per Day	Avg Mat'l Unit Cost	Avg Labor Unit Cost	Avg Equip Unit Cost	Avg Total Unit Cost	Avg Price Incl O&P
Dual glazed											
1'-6" x 3'-0" H	Inst	Set	Lg	CA	1.18	6.80	134.00	43.70	---	177.70	**215.00**
	Inst	Set	Sm	CA	1.81	4.42	142.00	67.00	---	209.00	**258.00**
2'-0" x 2'-6" H	Inst	Set	Lg	CA	1.18	6.80	138.00	43.70	---	181.70	**220.00**
	Inst	Set	Sm	CA	1.81	4.42	147.00	67.00	---	214.00	**263.00**
2'-0" x 3'-0" H	Inst	Set	Lg	CA	1.27	6.30	147.00	47.00	---	194.00	**235.00**
	Inst	Set	Sm	CA	1.95	4.10	157.00	72.20	---	229.20	**281.00**
2'-0" x 3'-6" H	Inst	Set	Lg	CA	1.27	6.30	158.00	47.00	---	205.00	**247.00**
	Inst	Set	Sm	CA	1.95	4.10	168.00	72.20	---	240.20	**294.00**
2'-0" x 4'-0" H	Inst	Set	Lg	CA	1.27	6.30	167.00	47.00	---	214.00	**257.00**
	Inst	Set	Sm	CA	1.95	4.10	178.00	72.20	---	250.20	**305.00**
2'-0" x 4'-6" H	Inst	Set	Lg	CA	1.27	6.30	183.00	47.00	---	230.00	**276.00**
	Inst	Set	Sm	CA	1.95	4.10	195.00	72.20	---	267.20	**326.00**
2'-0" x 5'-0" H	Inst	Set	Lg	CA	1.38	5.80	197.00	51.10	---	248.10	**298.00**
	Inst	Set	Sm	CA	2.12	3.77	210.00	78.50	---	288.50	**351.00**
2'-0" x 6'-0" H	Inst	Set	Lg	CA	1.38	5.80	216.00	51.10	---	267.10	**320.00**
	Inst	Set	Sm	CA	2.12	3.77	230.00	78.50	---	308.50	**375.00**
2'-6" x 3'-0" H	Inst	Set	Lg	CA	1.27	6.30	162.00	47.00	---	209.00	**252.00**
	Inst	Set	Sm	CA	1.95	4.10	173.00	72.20	---	245.20	**300.00**
2'-6" x 3'-6" H	Inst	Set	Lg	CA	1.27	6.30	173.00	47.00	---	220.00	**264.00**
	Inst	Set	Sm	CA	1.95	4.10	184.00	72.20	---	256.20	**313.00**
2'-6" x 4'-0" H	Inst	Set	Lg	CA	1.27	6.30	185.00	47.00	---	232.00	**278.00**
	Inst	Set	Sm	CA	1.95	4.10	197.00	72.20	---	269.20	**327.00**
2'-6" x 4'-6" H	Inst	Set	Lg	CA	1.27	6.30	201.00	47.00	---	248.00	**297.00**
	Inst	Set	Sm	CA	1.95	4.10	214.00	72.20	---	286.20	**348.00**
2'-6" x 5'-0" H	Inst	Set	Lg	CA	1.38	5.80	216.00	51.10	---	267.10	**320.00**
	Inst	Set	Sm	CA	2.12	3.77	230.00	78.50	---	308.50	**375.00**
2'-6" x 6'-0" H	Inst	Set	Lg	CA	1.38	5.80	239.00	51.10	---	290.10	**346.00**
	Inst	Set	Sm	CA	2.12	3.77	254.00	78.50	---	332.50	**402.00**
3'-0" x 3'-0" H	Inst	Set	Lg	CA	1.27	6.30	176.00	47.00	---	223.00	**268.00**
	Inst	Set	Sm	CA	1.95	4.10	187.00	72.20	---	259.20	**316.00**
3'-0" x 3'-6" H	Inst	Set	Lg	CA	1.27	6.30	189.00	47.00	---	236.00	**283.00**
	Inst	Set	Sm	CA	1.95	4.10	202.00	72.20	---	274.20	**333.00**
3'-0" x 4'-0" H	Inst	Set	Lg	CA	1.27	6.30	201.00	47.00	---	248.00	**297.00**
	Inst	Set	Sm	CA	1.95	4.10	214.00	72.20	---	286.20	**348.00**
3'-0" x 4'-6" H	Inst	Set	Lg	CA	1.27	6.30	221.00	47.00	---	268.00	**319.00**
	Inst	Set	Sm	CA	1.95	4.10	235.00	72.20	---	307.20	**372.00**
3'-0" x 5'-0" H	Inst	Set	Lg	CJ	2.86	5.60	236.00	95.80	---	331.80	**405.00**
	Inst	Set	Sm	CJ	4.40	3.64	251.00	147.00	---	398.00	**495.00**
3'-0" x 6'-0" H	Inst	Set	Lg	CJ	3.20	5.00	260.00	107.00	---	367.00	**449.00**
	Inst	Set	Sm	CJ	4.92	3.25	277.00	165.00	---	442.00	**549.00**
3'-6" x 3'-6" H	Inst	Set	Lg	CA	1.27	6.30	212.00	47.00	---	259.00	**309.00**
	Inst	Set	Sm	CA	1.95	4.10	226.00	72.20	---	298.20	**361.00**
3'-6" x 4'-0" H	Inst	Set	Lg	CA	1.51	5.30	219.00	55.90	---	274.90	**330.00**
	Inst	Set	Sm	CA	2.32	3.45	234.00	85.90	---	319.90	**389.00**
3'-6" x 4'-6" H	Inst	Set	Lg	CA	1.86	4.30	240.00	68.90	---	308.90	**372.00**
	Inst	Set	Sm	CA	2.86	2.80	256.00	106.00	---	362.00	**443.00**
3'-6" x 5'-0" H	Inst	Set	Lg	CJ	3.20	5.00	254.00	107.00	---	361.00	**442.00**
	Inst	Set	Sm	CJ	4.92	3.25	270.00	165.00	---	435.00	**542.00**

Description	Oper	Unit	Vol	Crew Size	Man-hours per Unit	Crew Output per Day	Avg Mat'l Unit Cost	Avg Labor Unit Cost	Avg Equip Unit Cost	Avg Total Unit Cost	Avg Price Incl O&P
4'-0" x 3'-0" H	Inst	Set	Lg	CA	1.27	6.30	204.00	47.00	---	251.00	**300.00**
	Inst	Set	Sm	CA	1.95	4.10	218.00	72.20	---	290.20	**351.00**
4'-0" x 3'-6" H	Inst	Set	Lg	CA	1.51	5.30	221.00	55.90	---	276.90	**332.00**
	Inst	Set	Sm	CA	2.32	3.45	235.00	85.90	---	320.90	**391.00**
4'-0" x 4'-0" H	Inst	Set	Lg	CJ	2.86	5.60	236.00	95.80	---	331.80	**405.00**
	Inst	Set	Sm	CJ	4.40	3.64	251.00	147.00	---	398.00	**495.00**
4'-0" x 4'-6" H	Inst	Set	Lg	CJ	2.86	5.60	263.00	95.80	---	358.80	**436.00**
	Inst	Set	Sm	CJ	4.40	3.64	280.00	147.00	---	427.00	**528.00**
4'-0" x 5'-0" H	Inst	Set	Lg	CJ	3.20	5.00	285.00	107.00	---	392.00	**478.00**
	Inst	Set	Sm	CJ	4.92	3.25	304.00	165.00	---	469.00	**580.00**
For bronze finish ADD	Inst	%	Lg	---	---	---	12.0	---	---	12.0	---
	Inst	%	Sm	---	---	---	12.0	---	---	12.0	---

Horizontal slide, satin anodized finish, includes screen and hardware

1 sliding lite, 1 fixed lite
Single glazed

Description	Oper	Unit	Vol	Crew Size	Man-hours per Unit	Crew Output per Day	Avg Mat'l Unit Cost	Avg Labor Unit Cost	Avg Equip Unit Cost	Avg Total Unit Cost	Avg Price Incl O&P
2'-0" x 2'-0" H	Inst	Set	Lg	CA	1.23	6.50	66.00	45.50	---	111.50	**140.00**
	Inst	Set	Sm	CA	1.89	4.23	70.40	70.00	---	140.40	**179.00**
2'-0" x 3'-0" H	Inst	Set	Lg	CA	1.23	6.50	79.50	45.50	---	125.00	**155.00**
	Inst	Set	Sm	CA	1.89	4.23	84.80	70.00	---	154.80	**195.00**
2'-6" x 3'-0" H	Inst	Set	Lg	CA	1.23	6.50	85.50	45.50	---	131.00	**162.00**
	Inst	Set	Sm	CA	1.89	4.23	91.20	70.00	---	161.20	**203.00**
3'-0" x 1'-0" H	Inst	Set	Lg	CA	1.23	6.50	61.50	45.50	---	107.00	**134.00**
	Inst	Set	Sm	CA	1.89	4.23	65.60	70.00	---	135.60	**173.00**
3'-0" x 1'-6" H	Inst	Set	Lg	CA	1.23	6.50	69.00	45.50	---	114.50	**143.00**
	Inst	Set	Sm	CA	1.89	4.23	73.60	70.00	---	143.60	**183.00**
3'-0" x 2'-0" H	Inst	Set	Lg	CA	1.23	6.50	78.00	45.50	---	123.50	**153.00**
	Inst	Set	Sm	CA	1.89	4.23	83.20	70.00	---	153.20	**194.00**
3'-0" x 2'-6" H	Inst	Set	Lg	CA	1.23	6.50	85.50	45.50	---	131.00	**162.00**
	Inst	Set	Sm	CA	1.89	4.23	91.20	70.00	---	161.20	**203.00**
3'-0" x 3'-0" H	Inst	Set	Lg	CA	1.23	6.50	93.00	45.50	---	138.50	**171.00**
	Inst	Set	Sm	CA	1.89	4.23	99.20	70.00	---	169.20	**212.0**
3'-0" x 3'-6" H	Inst	Set	Lg	CA	1.45	5.50	101.00	53.70	---	154.70	**191.00**
	Inst	Set	Sm	CA	2.23	3.58	107.00	82.60	---	189.60	**239.00**
3'-0" x 4'-0" H	Inst	Set	Lg	CA	1.78	4.50	108.00	65.90	---	173.90	**216.00**
	Inst	Set	Sm	CA	2.73	2.93	115.00	101.00	---	216.00	**274.00**
3'-0" x 5'-0" H	Inst	Set	Lg	CJ	4.10	3.90	125.00	137.00	---	262.00	**336.00**
	Inst	Set	Sm	CJ	6.30	2.54	133.00	211.00	---	344.00	**448.00**
3'-6" x 2'-0" H	Inst	Set	Lg	CA	1.23	6.50	82.50	45.50	---	128.00	**159.00**
	Inst	Set	Sm	CA	1.89	4.23	88.00	70.00	---	158.00	**199.00**
3'-6" x 2'-6" H	Inst	Set	Lg	CA	1.23	6.50	91.50	45.50	---	137.00	**169.00**
	Inst	Set	Sm	CA	1.89	4.23	97.60	70.00	---	167.60	**210.00**
3'-6" x 3'-0" H	Inst	Set	Lg	CA	1.45	5.50	99.00	53.70	---	152.70	**189.00**
	Inst	Set	Sm	CA	2.23	3.58	106.00	82.60	---	188.60	**237.00**
3'-6" x 3'-6" H	Inst	Set	Lg	CA	1.45	5.50	108.00	53.70	---	161.70	**199.00**
	Inst	Set	Sm	CA	2.23	3.58	115.00	82.60	---	197.60	**248.00**
3'-6" x 4'-0" H	Inst	Set	Lg	CA	1.78	4.50	116.00	65.90	---	181.90	**225.00**
	Inst	Set	Sm	CA	2.73	2.93	123.00	101.00	---	224.00	**283.00**

Description	Oper	Unit	Vol	Crew Size	Man-hours per Unit	Crew Output per Day	Avg Mat'l Unit Cost	Avg Labor Unit Cost	Avg Equip Unit Cost	Avg Total Unit Cost	Avg Price Incl O&P
4'-0" x 1'-0" H	Inst	Set	Lg	CA	1.45	5.50	70.50	53.70	---	124.20	**156.00**
	Inst	Set	Sm	CA	2.23	3.58	75.20	82.60	---	157.80	**202.00**
4'-0" x 1'-6" H	Inst	Set	Lg	CA	1.45	5.50	78.00	53.70	---	131.70	**165.00**
	Inst	Set	Sm	CA	2.23	3.58	83.20	82.60	---	165.80	**211.00**
4'-0" x 2'-0" H	Inst	Set	Lg	CA	1.78	4.50	88.50	65.90	---	154.40	**194.00**
	Inst	Set	Sm	CA	2.73	2.93	94.40	101.00	---	195.40	**250.00**
4'-0" x 2'-6" H	Inst	Set	Lg	CA	1.78	4.50	97.50	65.90	---	163.40	**204.00**
	Inst	Set	Sm	CA	2.73	2.93	104.00	101.00	---	205.00	**261.00**
4'-0" x 3'-0" H	Inst	Set	Lg	CA	1.78	4.50	107.00	65.90	---	172.90	**215.00**
	Inst	Set	Sm	CA	2.73	2.93	114.00	101.00	---	215.00	**272.00**
4'-0" x 3'-6" H	Inst	Set	Lg	CA	1.90	4.20	116.00	70.30	---	186.30	**231.00**
	Inst	Set	Sm	CA	2.93	2.73	123.00	108.00	---	231.00	**294.00**
4'-0" x 4'-0" H	Inst	Set	Lg	CA	1.90	4.20	125.00	70.30	---	195.30	**242.00**
	Inst	Set	Sm	CA	2.93	2.73	133.00	108.00	---	241.00	**305.00**
4'-0" x 5'-0" H	Inst	Set	Lg	CJ	4.57	3.50	143.00	153.00	---	296.00	**378.00**
	Inst	Set	Sm	CJ	7.02	2.28	152.00	235.00	---	387.00	**504.00**
5'-0" x 2'-0" H	Inst	Set	Lg	CJ	3.81	4.20	99.00	128.00	---	227.00	**293.00**
	Inst	Set	Sm	CJ	5.86	2.73	106.00	196.00	---	302.00	**396.00**
5'-0" x 2'-6" H	Inst	Set	Lg	CJ	3.81	4.20	110.00	128.00	---	238.00	**305.00**
	Inst	Set	Sm	CJ	5.86	2.73	117.00	196.00	---	313.00	**409.00**
5'-0" x 3'-0" H	Inst	Set	Lg	CJ	4.10	3.90	119.00	137.00	---	256.00	**329.00**
	Inst	Set	Sm	CJ	6.30	2.54	126.00	211.00	---	337.00	**441.00**
5'-0" x 3'-6" H	Inst	Set	Lg	CJ	4.10	3.90	129.00	137.00	---	266.00	**341.00**
	Inst	Set	Sm	CJ	6.30	2.54	138.00	211.00	---	349.00	**454.00**
5'-0" x 4'-0" H	Inst	Set	Lg	CJ	4.57	3.50	140.00	153.00	---	293.00	**375.00**
	Inst	Set	Sm	CJ	7.02	2.28	149.00	235.00	---	384.00	**500.00**
5'-0" x 5'-0" H	Inst	Set	Lg	CJ	4.57	3.50	168.00	153.00	---	321.00	**408.00**
	Inst	Set	Sm	CJ	7.02	2.28	179.00	235.00	---	414.00	**535.00**
6'-0" x 2'-0" H	Inst	Set	Lg	CJ	3.90	4.10	110.00	131.00	---	241.00	**309.00**
	Inst	Set	Sm	CJ	5.99	2.67	117.00	201.00	---	318.00	**415.00**
6'-0" x 2'-6" H	Inst	Set	Lg	CJ	3.90	4.10	120.00	131.00	---	251.00	**321.00**
	Inst	Set	Sm	CJ	5.99	2.67	128.00	201.00	---	329.00	**428.00**
6'-0" x 3'-0" H	Inst	Set	Lg	CJ	4.10	3.90	132.00	137.00	---	269.00	**344.00**
	Inst	Set	Sm	CJ	6.30	2.54	141.00	211.00	---	352.00	**457.00**
8'-0" x 2'-0" H	Inst	Set	Lg	CJ	4.10	3.90	137.00	137.00	---	274.00	**349.00**
	Inst	Set	Sm	CJ	6.30	2.54	146.00	211.00	---	357.00	**463.00**
8'-0" x 2'-6" H	Inst	Set	Lg	CJ	4.10	3.90	152.00	137.00	---	289.00	**367.00**
	Inst	Set	Sm	CJ	6.30	2.54	162.00	211.00	---	373.00	**481.00**
8'-0" x 3'-0" H	Inst	Set	Lg	CJ	4.57	3.50	167.00	153.00	---	320.00	**406.00**
	Inst	Set	Sm	CJ	7.02	2.28	178.00	235.00	---	413.00	**534.00**
8'-0" x 4'-0" H	Inst	Set	Lg	CJ	5.00	3.20	210.00	168.00	---	378.00	**476.00**
	Inst	Set	Sm	CJ	7.69	2.08	224.00	258.00	---	482.00	**618.00**
8'-0" x 5'-0" H	Inst	Set	Lg	CJ	5.33	3.00	254.00	179.00	---	433.00	**542.00**
	Inst	Set	Sm	CJ	8.21	1.95	270.00	275.00	---	545.00	**696.00**
For bronze finish, ADD	Inst	%	Lg	---	---	---	20.0	---	---	20.0	---
	Inst	%	Sm	---	---	---	20.0	---	---	20.0	---

Description	Oper	Unit	Vol	Crew Size	Man-hours per Unit	Crew Output per Day	Avg Mat'l Unit Cost	Avg Labor Unit Cost	Avg Equip Unit Cost	Avg Total Unit Cost	Avg Price Incl O&P
Dual glazed											
2'-0" x 2'-0" H	Inst	Set	Lg	CA	1.27	6.30	107.00	47.00	---	154.00	**188.00**
	Inst	Set	Sm	CA	1.95	4.10	114.00	72.20	---	186.20	**232.00**
2'-0" x 2'-6" H	Inst	Set	Lg	CA	1.27	6.30	117.00	47.00	---	164.00	**200.00**
	Inst	Set	Sm	CA	1.95	4.10	125.00	72.20	---	197.20	**245.00**
2'-0" x 3'-0" H	Inst	Set	Lg	CA	1.27	6.30	128.00	47.00	---	175.00	**212.00**
	Inst	Set	Sm	CA	1.95	4.10	136.00	72.20	---	208.20	**257.00**
2'-0" x 3'-6" H	Inst	Set	Lg	CA	1.27	6.30	138.00	47.00	---	185.00	**225.00**
	Inst	Set	Sm	CA	1.95	4.10	147.00	72.20	---	219.20	**270.00**
2'-0" x 4'-0" H	Inst	Set	Lg	CA	1.27	6.30	149.00	47.00	---	196.00	**237.00**
	Inst	Set	Sm	CA	1.95	4.10	158.00	72.20	---	230.20	**283.00**
2'-6" x 2'-0" H	Inst	Set	Lg	CA	1.27	6.30	114.00	47.00	---	161.00	**197.00**
	Inst	Set	Sm	CA	1.95	4.10	122.00	72.20	---	194.20	**241.00**
2'-6" x 2'-6" H	Inst	Set	Lg	CA	1.27	6.30	128.00	47.00	---	175.00	**212.00**
	Inst	Set	Sm	CA	1.95	4.10	136.00	72.20	---	208.20	**257.00**
2'-6" x 3'-0" H	Inst	Set	Lg	CA	1.31	6.10	138.00	48.50	---	186.50	**227.00**
	Inst	Set	Sm	CA	2.02	3.97	147.00	74.80	---	221.80	**274.00**
2'-6" x 3'-6" H	Inst	Set	Lg	CA	1.31	6.10	150.00	48.50	---	198.50	**240.00**
	Inst	Set	Sm	CA	2.02	3.97	160.00	74.80	---	234.80	**289.00**
2'-6" x 4'-0" H	Inst	Set	Lg	CA	1.38	5.80	162.00	51.10	---	213.10	**258.00**
	Inst	Set	Sm	CA	2.12	3.77	173.00	78.50	---	251.50	**309.00**
3'-0" x 2'-0" H	Inst	Set	Lg	CA	1.27	6.30	123.00	47.00	---	170.00	**207.00**
	Inst	Set	Sm	CA	1.95	4.10	131.00	72.20	---	203.20	**252.00**
3'-0" x 2'-6" H	Inst	Set	Lg	CA	1.27	6.30	137.00	47.00	---	184.00	**223.00**
	Inst	Set	Sm	CA	1.95	4.10	146.00	72.20	---	218.20	**269.00**
3'-0" x 3'-0" H	Inst	Set	Lg	CA	1.27	6.30	149.00	47.00	---	196.00	**237.00**
	Inst	Set	Sm	CA	1.95	4.10	158.00	72.20	---	230.20	**283.00**
3'-0" x 3'-6" H	Inst	Set	Lg	CA	1.51	5.30	162.00	55.90	---	217.90	**265.00**
	Inst	Set	Sm	CA	2.32	3.45	173.00	85.90	---	258.90	**319.00**
3'-0" x 4'-0" H	Inst	Set	Lg	CA	1.86	4.30	176.00	68.90	---	244.90	**298.00**
	Inst	Set	Sm	CA	2.86	2.80	187.00	106.00	---	293.00	**364.00**
3'-0" x 5'-0" H	Inst	Set	Lg	CA	2.16	3.70	203.00	80.00	---	283.00	**345.00**
	Inst	Set	Sm	CA	3.32	2.41	216.00	123.00	---	339.00	**420.00**
3'-6" x 2'-0" H	Inst	Set	Lg	CA	1.27	6.30	132.00	47.00	---	179.00	**218.00**
	Inst	Set	Sm	CA	1.95	4.10	141.00	72.20	---	213.20	**263.00**
3'-6" x 2'-6" H	Inst	Set	Lg	CA	1.27	6.30	146.00	47.00	---	193.00	**233.00**
	Inst	Set	Sm	CA	1.95	4.10	155.00	72.20	---	227.20	**280.00**
3'-6" x 3'-0" H	Inst	Set	Lg	CA	1.51	5.30	161.00	55.90	---	216.90	**263.00**
	Inst	Set	Sm	CA	2.32	3.45	171.00	85.90	---	256.90	**317.00**
3'-6" x 3'-6" H	Inst	Set	Lg	CA	1.51	5.30	174.00	55.90	---	229.90	**278.00**
	Inst	Set	Sm	CA	2.32	3.45	186.00	85.90	---	271.90	**334.00**
3'-6" x 4'-0" H	Inst	Set	Lg	CA	1.86	4.30	189.00	68.90	---	257.90	**314.00**
	Inst	Set	Sm	CA	2.86	2.80	202.00	106.00	---	308.00	**380.00**
3'-6" x 5'-0" H	Inst	Set	Lg	CA	1.86	4.30	221.00	68.90	---	289.90	**350.00**
	Inst	Set	Sm	CA	2.86	2.80	235.00	106.00	---	341.00	**419.00**
4'-0" x 2'-0" H	Inst	Set	Lg	CA	1.86	4.30	140.00	68.90	---	208.90	**257.00**
	Inst	Set	Sm	CA	2.86	2.80	149.00	106.00	---	255.00	**319.00**
4'-0" x 2'-6" H	Inst	Set	Lg	CA	1.86	4.30	156.00	68.90	---	224.90	**276.00**
	Inst	Set	Sm	CA	2.86	2.80	166.00	106.00	---	272.00	**340.00**

Description	Oper	Unit	Vol	Crew Size	Man-hours per Unit	Crew Output per Day	Avg Mat'l Unit Cost	Avg Labor Unit Cost	Avg Equip Unit Cost	Avg Total Unit Cost	Avg Price Incl O&P
4'-0" x 3'-0" H	Inst	Set	Lg	CA	1.86	4.30	171.00	68.90	---	239.90	**293.00**
	Inst	Set	Sm	CA	2.86	2.80	182.00	106.00	---	288.00	**358.00**
4'-0" x 3'-6" H	Inst	Set	Lg	CA	2.00	4.00	186.00	74.00	---	260.00	**318.00**
	Inst	Set	Sm	CA	3.08	2.60	198.00	114.00	---	312.00	**388.00**
4'-0" x 4'-0" H	Inst	Set	Lg	CA	2.00	4.00	203.00	74.00	---	277.00	**337.00**
	Inst	Set	Sm	CA	3.08	2.60	216.00	114.00	---	330.00	**408.00**
4'-0" x 5'-0" H	Inst	Set	Lg	CA	2.42	3.30	236.00	89.60	---	325.60	**396.00**
	Inst	Set	Sm	CA	3.72	2.15	251.00	138.00	---	389.00	**482.00**
5'-0" x 2'-0" H	Inst	Set	Lg	CA	2.00	4.00	158.00	74.00	---	232.00	**285.00**
	Inst	Set	Sm	CA	3.08	2.60	168.00	114.00	---	282.00	**353.00**
5'-0" x 2'-6" H	Inst	Set	Lg	CA	2.00	4.00	176.00	74.00	---	250.00	**305.00**
	Inst	Set	Sm	CA	3.08	2.60	187.00	114.00	---	301.00	**375.00**
5'-0" x 3'-0" H	Inst	Set	Lg	CJ	4.32	3.70	194.00	145.00	---	339.00	**425.00**
	Inst	Set	Sm	CJ	6.64	2.41	206.00	223.00	---	429.00	**549.00**
5'-0" x 3'-6" H	Inst	Set	Lg	CJ	4.32	3.70	212.00	145.00	---	357.00	**446.00**
	Inst	Set	Sm	CJ	6.64	2.41	226.00	223.00	---	449.00	**571.00**
5'-0" x 4'-0" H	Inst	Set	Lg	CJ	4.85	3.30	230.00	163.00	---	393.00	**491.00**
	Inst	Set	Sm	CJ	7.44	2.15	245.00	249.00	---	494.00	**631.00**
5'-0" x 5'-0" H	Inst	Set	Lg	CJ	4.85	3.30	287.00	163.00	---	450.00	**557.00**
	Inst	Set	Sm	CJ	7.44	2.15	306.00	249.00	---	555.00	**700.00**
6'-0" x 2'-0" H	Inst	Set	Lg	CJ	4.10	3.90	174.00	137.00	---	311.00	**392.00**
	Inst	Set	Sm	CJ	6.30	2.54	186.00	211.00	---	397.00	**509.00**
6'-0" x 2'-6" H	Inst	Set	Lg	CJ	4.10	3.90	195.00	137.00	---	332.00	**417.00**
	Inst	Set	Sm	CJ	6.30	2.54	208.00	211.00	---	419.00	**535.00**
6'-0" x 3'-0" H	Inst	Set	Lg	CJ	4.32	3.70	215.00	145.00	---	360.00	**449.00**
	Inst	Set	Sm	CJ	6.64	2.41	229.00	223.00	---	452.00	**575.00**
6'-0" x 3'-6" H	Inst	Set	Lg	CJ	4.85	3.30	233.00	163.00	---	396.00	**495.00**
	Inst	Set	Sm	CJ	7.44	2.15	248.00	249.00	---	497.00	**634.00**
6'-0" x 4'-0" H	Inst	Set	Lg	CJ	4.85	3.30	257.00	163.00	---	420.00	**522.00**
	Inst	Set	Sm	CJ	7.44	2.15	274.00	249.00	---	523.00	**664.00**
6'-0" x 5'-0" H	Inst	Set	Lg	CJ	4.85	3.30	324.00	163.00	---	487.00	**600.00**
	Inst	Set	Sm	CJ	7.44	2.15	346.00	249.00	---	595.00	**746.00**
For bronze finish, ADD	Inst	%	Lg	---	---	---	15.0	---	---	15.0	---
	Inst	%	Sm	---	---	---	15.0	---	---	15.0	---

2 sliding lites, 1 fixed lite
Single glazed

Description	Oper	Unit	Vol	Crew Size	Man-hours per Unit	Crew Output per Day	Avg Mat'l Unit Cost	Avg Labor Unit Cost	Avg Equip Unit Cost	Avg Total Unit Cost	Avg Price Incl O&P
6'-0" x 2'-0" H	Inst	Set	Lg	CJ	4.32	3.70	138.00	145.00	---	283.00	**361.00**
	Inst	Set	Sm	CJ	6.64	2.41	147.00	223.00	---	370.00	**481.00**
6'-0" x 2'-6" H	Inst	Set	Lg	CJ	4.32	3.70	152.00	145.00	---	297.00	**377.00**
	Inst	Set	Sm	CJ	6.64	2.41	162.00	223.00	---	385.00	**497.00**
6'-0" x 3'-0" H	Inst	Set	Lg	CJ	4.57	3.50	165.00	153.00	---	318.00	**404.00**
	Inst	Set	Sm	CJ	7.02	2.28	176.00	235.00	---	411.00	**532.00**
6'-0" x 4'-0" H	Inst	Set	Lg	CJ	4.57	3.50	197.00	153.00	---	350.00	**440.00**
	Inst	Set	Sm	CJ	7.02	2.28	210.00	235.00	---	445.00	**570.00**
6'-0" x 5'-0" H	Inst	Set	Lg	CJ	4.57	3.50	228.00	153.00	---	381.00	**477.00**
	Inst	Set	Sm	CJ	7.02	2.28	243.00	235.00	---	478.00	**609.00**

Description	Oper	Unit	Vol	Crew Size	Man-hours per Unit	Crew Output per Day	Avg Mat'l Unit Cost	Avg Labor Unit Cost	Avg Equip Unit Cost	Avg Total Unit Cost	Avg Price Incl O&P
7'-0" x 2'-0" H	Inst	Set	Lg	CJ	4.32	3.70	146.00	145.00	---	291.00	**370.00**
	Inst	Set	Sm	CJ	6.64	2.41	155.00	223.00	---	378.00	**490.00**
7'-0" x 2'-6" H	Inst	Set	Lg	CJ	4.32	3.70	162.00	145.00	---	307.00	**389.00**
	Inst	Set	Sm	CJ	6.64	2.41	173.00	223.00	---	396.00	**510.00**
7'-0" x 3'-0" H	Inst	Set	Lg	CJ	4.57	3.50	179.00	153.00	---	332.00	**420.00**
	Inst	Set	Sm	CJ	7.02	2.28	190.00	235.00	---	425.00	**548.00**
7'-0" x 4'-0" H	Inst	Set	Lg	CJ	4.57	3.50	227.00	153.00	---	380.00	**475.00**
	Inst	Set	Sm	CJ	7.02	2.28	242.00	235.00	---	477.00	**607.00**
7'-0" x 5'-0" H	Inst	Set	Lg	CJ	5.71	2.80	287.00	191.00	---	478.00	**597.00**
	Inst	Set	Sm	CJ	8.79	1.82	306.00	295.00	---	601.00	**764.00**
8'-0" x 2'-0" H	Inst	Set	Lg	CJ	4.57	3.50	161.00	153.00	---	314.00	**399.00**
	Inst	Set	Sm	CJ	7.02	2.28	171.00	235.00	---	406.00	**526.00**
8'-0" x 2'-6" H	Inst	Set	Lg	CJ	4.57	3.50	177.00	153.00	---	330.00	**418.00**
	Inst	Set	Sm	CJ	7.02	2.28	189.00	235.00	---	424.00	**546.00**
8'-0" x 3'-0" H	Inst	Set	Lg	CJ	4.57	3.50	197.00	153.00	---	350.00	**440.00**
	Inst	Set	Sm	CJ	7.02	2.28	210.00	235.00	---	445.00	**570.00**
8'-0" x 3'-6" H	Inst	Set	Lg	CJ	4.57	3.50	213.00	153.00	---	366.00	**459.00**
	Inst	Set	Sm	CJ	7.02	2.28	227.00	235.00	---	462.00	**591.00**
8'-0" x 4'-0" H	Inst	Set	Lg	CJ	5.71	2.80	231.00	191.00	---	422.00	**534.00**
	Inst	Set	Sm	CJ	8.79	1.82	246.00	295.00	---	541.00	**696.00**
8'-0" x 5'-0" H	Inst	Set	Lg	CJ	5.71	2.80	290.00	191.00	---	481.00	**601.00**
	Inst	Set	Sm	CJ	8.79	1.82	309.00	295.00	---	604.00	**767.00**
10'-0" x 2'-0" H	Inst	Set	Lg	CJ	4.57	3.50	207.00	153.00	---	360.00	**452.00**
	Inst	Set	Sm	CJ	7.02	2.28	221.00	235.00	---	456.00	**583.00**
10'-0" x 3'-0" H	Inst	Set	Lg	CJ	4.57	3.50	237.00	153.00	---	390.00	**487.00**
	Inst	Set	Sm	CJ	7.02	2.28	253.00	235.00	---	488.00	**620.00**
10'-0" x 3'-6" H	Inst	Set	Lg	CJ	5.71	2.80	272.00	191.00	---	463.00	**580.00**
	Inst	Set	Sm	CJ	8.79	1.82	290.00	295.00	---	585.00	**745.00**
10'-0" x 4'-0" H	Inst	Set	Lg	CJ	5.71	2.80	285.00	191.00	---	476.00	**596.00**
	Inst	Set	Sm	CJ	8.79	1.82	304.00	295.00	---	599.00	**762.00**
10'-0" x 5'-0" H	Inst	Set	Lg	CJ	5.71	2.80	401.00	191.00	---	592.00	**728.00**
	Inst	Set	Sm	CJ	8.79	1.82	427.00	295.00	---	722.00	**904.00**
For bronze finish, ADD	Inst	%	Lg	---	---	---	13.5	---	---	13.5	---
	Inst	%	Sm	---	---	---	13.5	---	---	13.5	---

Description	Oper	Unit	Vol	Crew Size	Man-hours per Unit	Crew Output per Day	Avg Mat'l Unit Cost	Avg Labor Unit Cost	Avg Equip Unit Cost	Avg Total Unit Cost	Avg Price Incl O&P
Dual glazed											
6'-0" x 2'-0" H	Inst	Set	Lg	CJ	4.57	3.50	216.00	153.00	---	369.00	**463.00**
	Inst	Set	Sm	CJ	7.02	2.28	230.00	235.00	---	465.00	**594.00**
6'-0" x 2'-6" H	Inst	Set	Lg	CJ	4.57	3.50	240.00	153.00	---	393.00	**490.00**
	Inst	Set	Sm	CJ	7.02	2.28	256.00	235.00	---	491.00	**624.00**
6'-0" x 3'-0" H	Inst	Set	Lg	CJ	4.85	3.30	264.00	163.00	---	427.00	**531.00**
	Inst	Set	Sm	CJ	7.44	2.15	282.00	249.00	---	531.00	**673.00**
6'-0" x 3'-6" H	Inst	Set	Lg	CJ	4.85	3.30	288.00	163.00	---	451.00	**559.00**
	Inst	Set	Sm	CJ	7.44	2.15	307.00	249.00	---	556.00	**702.00**
6'-0" x 4'-0" H	Inst	Set	Lg	CJ	4.85	3.30	326.00	163.00	---	489.00	**602.00**
	Inst	Set	Sm	CJ	7.44	2.15	347.00	249.00	---	596.00	**748.00**
6'-0" x 5'-0" H	Inst	Set	Lg	CJ	4.85	3.30	377.00	163.00	---	540.00	**660.00**
	Inst	Set	Sm	CJ	7.44	2.15	402.00	249.00	---	651.00	**811.00**
7'-0" x 2'-0" H	Inst	Set	Lg	CJ	4.32	3.70	239.00	145.00	---	384.00	**477.00**
	Inst	Set	Sm	CJ	6.64	2.41	254.00	223.00	---	477.00	**604.00**
7'-0" x 2'-6" H	Inst	Set	Lg	CJ	4.32	3.70	263.00	145.00	---	408.00	**505.00**
	Inst	Set	Sm	CJ	6.64	2.41	280.00	223.00	---	503.00	**633.00**
7'-0" x 3'-0" H	Inst	Set	Lg	CJ	4.57	3.50	290.00	153.00	---	443.00	**547.00**
	Inst	Set	Sm	CJ	7.02	2.28	309.00	235.00	---	544.00	**684.00**
7'-0" x 3'-6" H	Inst	Set	Lg	CJ	4.85	3.30	332.00	163.00	---	495.00	**609.00**
	Inst	Set	Sm	CJ	7.44	2.15	354.00	249.00	---	603.00	**756.00**
7'-0" x 4'-0" H	Inst	Set	Lg	CJ	4.85	3.30	362.00	163.00	---	525.00	**643.00**
	Inst	Set	Sm	CJ	7.44	2.15	386.00	249.00	---	635.00	**792.00**
7'-0" x 5'-0" H	Inst	Set	Lg	CJ	6.15	2.60	444.00	206.00	---	650.00	**799.00**
	Inst	Set	Sm	CJ	9.47	1.69	474.00	317.00	---	791.00	**989.00**
8'-0" x 2'-0" H	Inst	Set	Lg	CJ	4.85	3.30	252.00	163.00	---	415.00	**517.00**
	Inst	Set	Sm	CJ	7.44	2.15	269.00	249.00	---	518.00	**658.00**
8'-0" x 2'-6" H	Inst	Set	Lg	CJ	4.85	3.30	281.00	163.00	---	444.00	**550.00**
	Inst	Set	Sm	CJ	7.44	2.15	299.00	249.00	---	548.00	**693.00**
8'-0" x 3'-0" H	Inst	Set	Lg	CJ	4.85	3.30	324.00	163.00	---	487.00	**600.00**
	Inst	Set	Sm	CJ	7.44	2.15	346.00	249.00	---	595.00	**746.00**
8'-0" x 3'-6" H	Inst	Set	Lg	CJ	4.85	3.30	353.00	163.00	---	516.00	**633.00**
	Inst	Set	Sm	CJ	7.44	2.15	376.00	249.00	---	625.00	**781.00**
8'-0" x 4'-0" H	Inst	Set	Lg	CJ	6.15	2.60	383.00	206.00	---	589.00	**728.00**
	Inst	Set	Sm	CJ	9.47	1.69	408.00	317.00	---	725.00	**913.00**
8'-0" x 5'-0" H	Inst	Set	Lg	CJ	6.15	2.60	455.00	206.00	---	661.00	**811.00**
	Inst	Set	Sm	CJ	9.47	1.69	485.00	317.00	---	802.00	**1000.00**
10'-0" x 2'-0" H	Inst	Set	Lg	CJ	4.57	3.50	354.00	153.00	---	507.00	**621.00**
	Inst	Set	Sm	CJ	7.02	2.28	378.00	235.00	---	613.00	**764.00**
10'-0" x 3'-0" H	Inst	Set	Lg	CJ	4.57	3.50	435.00	153.00	---	588.00	**715.00**
	Inst	Set	Sm	CJ	7.02	2.28	464.00	235.00	---	699.00	**863.00**
10'-0" x 3'-6" H	Inst	Set	Lg	CJ	5.71	2.80	495.00	191.00	---	686.00	**837.00**
	Inst	Set	Sm	CJ	8.79	1.82	528.00	295.00	---	823.00	**1020.00**
10'-0" x 4'-0" H	Inst	Set	Lg	CJ	5.71	2.80	536.00	191.00	---	727.00	**884.00**
	Inst	Set	Sm	CJ	8.79	1.82	571.00	295.00	---	866.00	**1070.00**
10'-0" x 5'-0" H	Inst	Set	Lg	CJ	5.71	2.80	650.00	191.00	---	841.00	**1010.00**
	Inst	Set	Sm	CJ	8.79	1.82	693.00	295.00	---	988.00	**1210.00**
For bronze finish, ADD	Inst	%	Lg	---	---	---	15.0	---	---	15.0	---
	Inst	%	Sm	---	---	---	15.0	---	---	15.0	---

Description	Oper	Unit	Vol	Crew Size	Man-hours per Unit	Crew Output per Day	Avg Mat'l Unit Cost	Avg Labor Unit Cost	Avg Equip Unit Cost	Avg Total Unit Cost	Avg Price Incl O&P

Wood

Awning windows; pine frames, exterior treated and primed, interior natural finish; glazed 1/2" T insulating glass; unit includes weatherstripping and exterior trim

Unit is one ventilating lite wide

20", 24" x 32" W

Description	Oper	Unit	Vol	Crew Size	Man-hours per Unit	Crew Output per Day	Avg Mat'l Unit Cost	Avg Labor Unit Cost	Avg Equip Unit Cost	Avg Total Unit Cost	Avg Price Incl O&P
High quality workmanship	Inst	Set	Lg	CA	1.25	6.40	345.00	46.30	---	391.30	**462.00**
	Inst	Set	Sm	CA	1.92	4.16	368.00	71.10	---	439.10	**523.00**
Good quality workmanship	Inst	Set	Lg	CA	1.00	8.00	308.00	37.00	---	345.00	**405.00**
	Inst	Set	Sm	CA	1.54	5.20	328.00	57.00	---	385.00	**457.00**
Average quality workmanship	Inst	Set	Lg	CA	.833	9.60	255.00	30.80	---	285.80	**336.00**
	Inst	Set	Sm	CA	1.28	6.24	272.00	47.40	---	319.40	**379.00**

32", 36" x 32" W

Description	Oper	Unit	Vol	Crew Size	Man-hours per Unit	Crew Output per Day	Avg Mat'l Unit Cost	Avg Labor Unit Cost	Avg Equip Unit Cost	Avg Total Unit Cost	Avg Price Incl O&P
High quality workmanship	Inst	Set	Lg	CA	1.25	6.40	458.00	46.30	---	504.30	**591.00**
	Inst	Set	Sm	CA	1.92	4.16	488.00	71.10	---	559.10	**661.00**
Good quality workmanship	Inst	Set	Lg	CA	1.00	8.00	405.00	37.00	---	442.00	**518.00**
	Inst	Set	Sm	CA	1.54	5.20	432.00	57.00	---	489.00	**577.00**
Average quality workmanship	Inst	Set	Lg	CA	.833	9.60	338.00	30.80	---	368.80	**431.00**
	Inst	Set	Sm	CA	1.28	6.24	360.00	47.40	---	407.40	**480.00**

20", 24" x 40" W

Description	Oper	Unit	Vol	Crew Size	Man-hours per Unit	Crew Output per Day	Avg Mat'l Unit Cost	Avg Labor Unit Cost	Avg Equip Unit Cost	Avg Total Unit Cost	Avg Price Incl O&P
High quality workmanship	Inst	Set	Lg	CA	1.25	6.40	375.00	46.30	---	421.30	**496.00**
	Inst	Set	Sm	CA	1.92	4.16	400.00	71.10	---	471.10	**560.00**
Good quality workmanship	Inst	Set	Lg	CA	1.00	8.00	360.00	37.00	---	397.00	**466.00**
	Inst	Set	Sm	CA	1.54	5.20	384.00	57.00	---	441.00	**521.00**
Average quality workmanship	Inst	Set	Lg	CA	.833	9.60	300.00	30.80	---	330.80	**388.00**
	Inst	Set	Sm	CA	1.28	6.24	320.00	47.40	---	367.40	**434.00**

32", 36" x 40" W

Description	Oper	Unit	Vol	Crew Size	Man-hours per Unit	Crew Output per Day	Avg Mat'l Unit Cost	Avg Labor Unit Cost	Avg Equip Unit Cost	Avg Total Unit Cost	Avg Price Incl O&P
High quality workmanship	Inst	Set	Lg	CA	1.25	6.40	473.00	46.30	---	519.30	**608.00**
	Inst	Set	Sm	CA	1.92	4.16	504.00	71.10	---	575.10	**679.00**
Good quality workmanship	Inst	Set	Lg	CA	1.00	8.00	398.00	37.00	---	435.00	**509.00**
	Inst	Set	Sm	CA	1.54	5.20	424.00	57.00	---	481.00	**567.00**
Average quality workmanship	Inst	Set	Lg	CA	.833	9.60	330.00	30.80	---	360.80	**423.00**
	Inst	Set	Sm	CA	1.28	6.24	352.00	47.40	---	399.40	**471.00**

20", 24" x 48" W

Description	Oper	Unit	Vol	Crew Size	Man-hours per Unit	Crew Output per Day	Avg Mat'l Unit Cost	Avg Labor Unit Cost	Avg Equip Unit Cost	Avg Total Unit Cost	Avg Price Incl O&P
High quality workmanship	Inst	Set	Lg	CA	1.25	6.40	473.00	46.30	---	519.30	**608.00**
	Inst	Set	Sm	CA	1.92	4.16	504.00	71.10	---	575.10	**679.00**
Good quality workmanship	Inst	Set	Lg	CA	1.00	8.00	390.00	37.00	---	427.00	**500.00**
	Inst	Set	Sm	CA	1.54	5.20	416.00	57.00	---	473.00	**558.00**
Average quality workmanship	Inst	Set	Lg	CA	.833	9.60	324.00	30.80	---	354.80	**416.00**
	Inst	Set	Sm	CA	1.28	6.24	346.00	47.40	---	393.40	**464.00**

32", 36" x 48" W

Description	Oper	Unit	Vol	Crew Size	Man-hours per Unit	Crew Output per Day	Avg Mat'l Unit Cost	Avg Labor Unit Cost	Avg Equip Unit Cost	Avg Total Unit Cost	Avg Price Incl O&P
High quality workmanship	Inst	Set	Lg	CA	1.25	6.40	713.00	46.30	---	759.30	**884.00**
	Inst	Set	Sm	CA	1.92	4.16	760.00	71.10	---	831.10	**974.00**
Good quality workmanship	Inst	Set	Lg	CA	1.00	8.00	443.00	37.00	---	480.00	**561.00**
	Inst	Set	Sm	CA	1.54	5.20	472.00	57.00	---	529.00	**623.00**
Average quality workmanship	Inst	Set	Lg	CA	.833	9.60	368.00	30.80	---	398.80	**466.00**
	Inst	Set	Sm	CA	1.28	6.24	392.00	47.40	---	439.40	**517.00**

Description	Oper	Unit	Vol	Crew Size	Man-hours per Unit	Crew Output per Day	Avg Mat'l Unit Cost	Avg Labor Unit Cost	Avg Equip Unit Cost	Avg Total Unit Cost	Avg Price Incl O&P
Unit is two ventilating lites wide											
20", 24" x 48" W											
High quality workmanship	Inst	Set	Lg	CJ	3.33	4.80	585.00	112.00	---	697.00	**829.00**
	Inst	Set	Sm	CJ	5.13	3.12	624.00	172.00	---	796.00	**958.00**
Good quality workmanship	Inst	Set	Lg	CJ	2.67	6.00	540.00	89.50	---	629.50	**746.00**
	Inst	Set	Sm	CJ	4.10	3.90	576.00	137.00	---	713.00	**855.00**
Average quality workmanship	Inst	Set	Lg	CJ	2.22	7.20	450.00	74.40	---	524.40	**622.00**
	Inst	Set	Sm	CJ	3.42	4.68	480.00	115.00	---	595.00	**712.00**
32", 36" x 48" W											
High quality workmanship	Inst	Set	Lg	CJ	3.33	4.80	645.00	112.00	---	757.00	**898.00**
	Inst	Set	Sm	CJ	5.13	3.12	688.00	172.00	---	860.00	**1030.00**
Good quality workmanship	Inst	Set	Lg	CJ	2.67	6.00	615.00	89.50	---	704.50	**833.00**
	Inst	Set	Sm	CJ	4.10	3.90	656.00	137.00	---	793.00	**947.00**
Average quality workmanship	Inst	Set	Lg	CJ	2.22	7.20	512.00	74.40	---	586.40	**692.00**
	Inst	Set	Sm	CJ	3.42	4.68	546.00	115.00	---	661.00	**788.00**
20", 24" x 72" W											
High quality workmanship	Inst	Set	Lg	CJ	3.33	4.80	638.00	112.00	---	750.00	**889.00**
	Inst	Set	Sm	CJ	5.13	3.12	680.00	172.00	---	852.00	**1020.00**
Good quality workmanship	Inst	Set	Lg	CJ	2.67	6.00	600.00	89.50	---	689.50	**815.00**
	Inst	Set	Sm	CJ	4.10	3.90	640.00	137.00	---	777.00	**928.00**
Average quality workmanship	Inst	Set	Lg	CJ	2.22	7.20	500.00	74.40	---	574.40	**679.00**
	Inst	Set	Sm	CJ	3.42	4.68	533.00	115.00	---	648.00	**773.00**
32", 36" x 72" W											
High quality workmanship	Inst	Set	Lg	CJ	3.33	4.80	750.00	112.00	---	862.00	**1020.00**
	Inst	Set	Sm	CJ	5.13	3.12	800.00	172.00	---	972.00	**1160.00**
Good quality workmanship	Inst	Set	Lg	CJ	2.67	6.00	713.00	89.50	---	802.50	**945.00**
	Inst	Set	Sm	CJ	4.10	3.90	760.00	137.00	---	897.00	**1070.00**
Average quality workmanship	Inst	Set	Lg	CJ	2.22	7.20	593.00	74.40	---	667.40	**786.00**
	Inst	Set	Sm	CJ	3.42	4.68	632.00	115.00	---	747.00	**887.00**
20", 24" x 80" W											
High quality workmanship	Inst	Set	Lg	CJ	3.33	4.80	690.00	112.00	---	802.00	**950.00**
	Inst	Set	Sm	CJ	5.13	3.12	736.00	172.00	---	908.00	**1090.00**
Good quality workmanship	Inst	Set	Lg	CJ	2.67	6.00	650.00	89.50	---	739.50	**872.00**
	Inst	Set	Sm	CJ	4.10	3.90	693.00	137.00	---	830.00	**989.00**
Average quality workmanship	Inst	Set	Lg	CJ	2.22	7.20	542.00	74.40	---	616.40	**727.00**
	Inst	Set	Sm	CJ	3.42	4.68	578.00	115.00	---	693.00	**825.00**
32", 36" x 80" W											
High quality workmanship	Inst	Set	Lg	CJ	3.33	4.80	795.00	112.00	---	907.00	**1070.00**
	Inst	Set	Sm	CJ	5.13	3.12	848.00	172.00	---	1020.00	**1220.00**
Good quality workmanship	Inst	Set	Lg	CJ	2.67	6.00	750.00	89.50	---	839.50	**988.00**
	Inst	Set	Sm	CJ	4.10	3.90	800.00	137.00	---	937.00	**1110.00**
Average quality workmanship	Inst	Set	Lg	CJ	2.22	7.20	624.00	74.40	---	698.40	**822.00**
	Inst	Set	Sm	CJ	3.42	4.68	666.00	115.00	---	781.00	**926.00**

Description	Oper	Unit	Vol	Crew Size	Man-hours per Unit	Crew Output per Day	Avg Mat'l Unit Cost	Avg Labor Unit Cost	Avg Equip Unit Cost	Avg Total Unit Cost	Avg Price Incl O&P
20", 24" x 96" W											
High quality workmanship	Inst	Set	Lg	CJ	3.33	4.80	750.00	112.00	---	862.00	**1020.00**
	Inst	Set	Sm	CJ	5.13	3.12	800.00	172.00	---	972.00	**1160.00**
Good quality workmanship	Inst	Set	Lg	CJ	2.67	6.00	705.00	89.50	---	794.50	**936.00**
	Inst	Set	Sm	CJ	4.10	3.90	752.00	137.00	---	889.00	**1060.00**
Average quality workmanship	Inst	Set	Lg	CJ	2.22	7.20	590.00	74.40	---	664.40	**782.00**
	Inst	Set	Sm	CJ	3.42	4.68	629.00	115.00	---	744.00	**884.00**
32", 36" x 96" W											
High quality workmanship	Inst	Set	Lg	CJ	3.33	4.80	885.00	112.00	---	997.00	**1170.00**
	Inst	Set	Sm	CJ	5.13	3.12	944.00	172.00	---	1116.00	**1330.00**
Good quality workmanship	Inst	Set	Lg	CJ	2.67	6.00	833.00	89.50	---	922.50	**1080.00**
	Inst	Set	Sm	CJ	4.10	3.90	888.00	137.00	---	1025.00	**1210.00**
Average quality workmanship	Inst	Set	Lg	CJ	2.22	7.20	695.00	74.40	---	769.40	**903.00**
	Inst	Set	Sm	CJ	3.42	4.68	741.00	115.00	---	856.00	**1010.00**

Unit is three ventilating lites wide
20", 24" x 72" W

Description	Oper	Unit	Vol	Crew Size	Man-hours per Unit	Crew Output per Day	Avg Mat'l Unit Cost	Avg Labor Unit Cost	Avg Equip Unit Cost	Avg Total Unit Cost	Avg Price Incl O&P
High quality workmanship	Inst	Set	Lg	CJ	4.44	3.60	885.00	149.00	---	1034.00	**1230.00**
	Inst	Set	Sm	CJ	6.84	2.34	944.00	229.00	---	1173.00	**1410.00**
Good quality workmanship	Inst	Set	Lg	CJ	3.56	4.50	825.00	119.00	---	944.00	**1120.00**
	Inst	Set	Sm	CJ	5.46	2.93	880.00	183.00	---	1063.00	**1270.00**
Average quality workmanship	Inst	Set	Lg	CJ	2.96	5.40	687.00	99.20	---	786.20	**929.00**
	Inst	Set	Sm	CJ	4.56	3.51	733.00	153.00	---	886.00	**1060.00**
32", 36" x 72" W											
High quality workmanship	Inst	Set	Lg	CJ	4.44	3.60	975.00	149.00	---	1124.00	**1330.00**
	Inst	Set	Sm	CJ	6.84	2.34	1040.00	229.00	---	1269.00	**1520.00**
Good quality workmanship	Inst	Set	Lg	CJ	3.56	4.50	915.00	119.00	---	1034.00	**1220.00**
	Inst	Set	Sm	CJ	5.46	2.93	976.00	183.00	---	1159.00	**1380.00**
Average quality workmanship	Inst	Set	Lg	CJ	2.96	5.40	765.00	99.20	---	864.20	**1020.00**
	Inst	Set	Sm	CJ	4.56	3.51	816.00	153.00	---	969.00	**1150.00**
20", 24" x 108" W											
High quality workmanship	Inst	Set	Lg	CJ	4.44	3.60	960.00	149.00	---	1109.00	**1310.00**
	Inst	Set	Sm	CJ	6.84	2.34	1020.00	229.00	---	1249.00	**1500.00**
Good quality workmanship	Inst	Set	Lg	CJ	3.56	4.50	900.00	119.00	---	1019.00	**1200.00**
	Inst	Set	Sm	CJ	5.46	2.93	960.00	183.00	---	1143.00	**1360.00**
Average quality workmanship	Inst	Set	Lg	CJ	2.96	5.40	750.00	99.20	---	849.20	**1000.00**
	Inst	Set	Sm	CJ	4.56	3.51	800.00	153.00	---	953.00	**1130.00**
32", 36" x 108" W											
High quality workmanship	Inst	Set	Lg	CJ	4.44	3.60	1140.00	149.00	---	1289.00	**1520.00**
	Inst	Set	Sm	CJ	6.84	2.34	1220.00	229.00	---	1449.00	**1720.00**
Good quality workmanship	Inst	Set	Lg	CJ	3.56	4.50	1070.00	119.00	---	1189.00	**1400.00**
	Inst	Set	Sm	CJ	5.46	2.93	1140.00	183.00	---	1323.00	**1570.00**
Average quality workmanship	Inst	Set	Lg	CJ	2.96	5.40	900.00	99.20	---	999.20	**1170.00**
	Inst	Set	Sm	CJ	4.56	3.51	960.00	153.00	---	1113.00	**1320.00**

Description	Oper	Unit	Vol	Crew Size	Man-hours per Unit	Crew Output per Day	Avg Mat'l Unit Cost	Avg Labor Unit Cost	Avg Equip Unit Cost	Avg Total Unit Cost	Avg Price Incl O&P
20", 24" x 120" W											
High quality workmanship	Inst	Set	Lg	CJ	4.44	3.60	1050.00	149.00	---	1199.00	**1420.00**
	Inst	Set	Sm	CJ	6.84	2.34	1120.00	229.00	---	1349.00	**1610.00**
Good quality workmanship	Inst	Set	Lg	CJ	3.56	4.50	990.00	119.00	---	1109.00	**1310.00**
	Inst	Set	Sm	CJ	5.46	2.93	1060.00	183.00	---	1243.00	**1470.00**
Average quality workmanship	Inst	Set	Lg	CJ	2.96	5.40	825.00	99.20	---	924.20	**1090.00**
	Inst	Set	Sm	CJ	4.56	3.51	880.00	153.00	---	1033.00	**1230.00**
32", 36" x 120" W											
High quality workmanship	Inst	Set	Lg	CJ	4.44	3.60	1210.00	149.00	---	1359.00	**1600.00**
	Inst	Set	Sm	CJ	6.84	2.34	1290.00	229.00	---	1519.00	**1800.00**
Good quality workmanship	Inst	Set	Lg	CJ	3.56	4.50	1130.00	119.00	---	1249.00	**1470.00**
	Inst	Set	Sm	CJ	5.46	2.93	1210.00	183.00	---	1393.00	**1650.00**
Average quality workmanship	Inst	Set	Lg	CJ	2.96	5.40	945.00	99.20	---	1044.20	**1230.00**
	Inst	Set	Sm	CJ	4.56	3.51	1010.00	153.00	---	1163.00	**1370.00**
20", 24" x 144" W											
High quality workmanship	Inst	Set	Lg	CJ	4.44	3.60	1140.00	149.00	---	1289.00	**1520.00**
	Inst	Set	Sm	CJ	6.84	2.34	1220.00	229.00	---	1449.00	**1720.00**
Good quality workmanship	Inst	Set	Lg	CJ	3.56	4.50	1070.00	119.00	---	1189.00	**1400.00**
	Inst	Set	Sm	CJ	5.46	2.93	1140.00	183.00	---	1323.00	**1570.00**
Average quality workmanship	Inst	Set	Lg	CJ	2.96	5.40	893.00	99.20	---	992.20	**1170.00**
	Inst	Set	Sm	CJ	4.56	3.51	952.00	153.00	---	1105.00	**1310.00**
32", 36" x 144" W											
High quality workmanship	Inst	Set	Lg	CJ	4.44	3.60	1340.00	149.00	---	1489.00	**1740.00**
	Inst	Set	Sm	CJ	6.84	2.34	1420.00	229.00	---	1649.00	**1960.00**
Good quality workmanship	Inst	Set	Lg	CJ	3.56	4.50	1250.00	119.00	---	1369.00	**1610.00**
	Inst	Set	Sm	CJ	5.46	2.93	1340.00	183.00	---	1523.00	**1790.00**
Average quality workmanship	Inst	Set	Lg	CJ	2.96	5.40	1050.00	99.20	---	1149.20	**1350.00**
	Inst	Set	Sm	CJ	4.56	3.51	1120.00	153.00	---	1273.00	**1500.00**
For aluminum clad (baked white enamel exterior)											
ADD	Inst	%	Lg	---	---	---	12.0	---	---	12.0	---
	Inst	%	Sm	---	---	---	12.0	---	---	12.0	---

Casement windows; glazed 1/2" T insulating glass; unit includes: hardware, drip cap and weatherstripping; does not include screens; rough opening sizes

1 ventilating lite, no fixed lites; 20", 24", 28" W

Description	Oper	Unit	Vol	Crew Size	Man-hours per Unit	Crew Output per Day	Avg Mat'l Unit Cost	Avg Labor Unit Cost	Avg Equip Unit Cost	Avg Total Unit Cost	Avg Price Incl O&P
36" H											
High quality workmanship	Inst	Set	Lg	CJ	2.00	8.00	345.00	67.00	---	412.00	**491.00**
	Inst	Set	Sm	CJ	3.08	5.20	368.00	103.00	---	471.00	**568.00**
Good quality workmanship	Inst	Set	Lg	CJ	1.60	10.00	318.00	53.60	---	371.60	**441.00**
	Inst	Set	Sm	CJ	2.46	6.50	339.00	82.40	---	421.40	**505.00**
Average quality workmanship	Inst	Set	Lg	CJ	1.33	12.00	266.00	44.60	---	310.60	**368.00**
	Inst	Set	Sm	CJ	2.05	7.80	283.00	68.70	---	351.70	**422.00**
41" H											
High quality workmanship	Inst	Set	Lg	CJ	2.11	7.60	368.00	70.70	---	438.70	**522.00**
	Inst	Set	Sm	CJ	3.24	4.94	392.00	109.00	---	501.00	**603.00**
Good quality workmanship	Inst	Set	Lg	CJ	1.68	9.50	341.00	56.30	---	397.30	**470.00**
	Inst	Set	Sm	CJ	2.59	6.18	363.00	86.80	---	449.80	**539.00**
Average quality workmanship	Inst	Set	Lg	CJ	1.40	11.40	284.00	46.90	---	330.90	**392.00**
	Inst	Set	Sm	CJ	2.16	7.41	302.00	72.40	---	374.40	**449.00**

Description	Oper	Unit	Vol	Crew Size	Man-hours per Unit	Crew Output per Day	Avg Mat'l Unit Cost	Avg Labor Unit Cost	Avg Equip Unit Cost	Avg Total Unit Cost	Avg Price Incl O&P
48" H											
High quality workmanship	Inst	Set	Lg	CJ	2.22	7.20	420.00	74.40	---	494.40	**587.00**
	Inst	Set	Sm	CJ	3.42	4.68	448.00	115.00	---	563.00	**676.00**
Good quality workmanship	Inst	Set	Lg	CJ	1.78	9.00	389.00	59.70	---	448.70	**530.00**
	Inst	Set	Sm	CJ	2.74	5.85	414.00	91.80	---	505.80	**605.00**
Average quality workmanship	Inst	Set	Lg	CJ	1.48	10.80	324.00	49.60	---	373.60	**442.00**
	Inst	Set	Sm	CJ	2.28	7.02	346.00	76.40	---	422.40	**504.00**
53" H											
High quality workmanship	Inst	Set	Lg	CJ	2.35	6.80	458.00	78.80	---	536.80	**636.00**
	Inst	Set	Sm	CJ	3.62	4.42	488.00	121.00	---	609.00	**731.00**
Good quality workmanship	Inst	Set	Lg	CJ	1.88	8.50	423.00	63.00	---	486.00	**575.00**
	Inst	Set	Sm	CJ	2.89	5.53	451.00	96.80	---	547.80	**654.00**
Average quality workmanship	Inst	Set	Lg	CJ	1.57	10.20	353.00	52.60	---	405.60	**479.00**
	Inst	Set	Sm	CJ	2.41	6.63	376.00	80.80	---	456.80	**545.00**
60" H											
High quality workmanship	Inst	Set	Lg	CJ	2.50	6.40	503.00	83.80	---	586.80	**695.00**
	Inst	Set	Sm	CJ	3.85	4.16	536.00	129.00	---	665.00	**797.00**
Good quality workmanship	Inst	Set	Lg	CJ	2.00	8.00	465.00	67.00	---	532.00	**629.00**
	Inst	Set	Sm	CJ	3.08	5.20	496.00	103.00	---	599.00	**715.00**
Average quality workmanship	Inst	Set	Lg	CJ	1.67	9.60	387.00	56.00	---	443.00	**523.00**
	Inst	Set	Sm	CJ	2.56	6.24	413.00	85.80	---	498.80	**595.00**
66" H											
High quality workmanship	Inst	Set	Lg	CJ	2.50	6.40	540.00	83.80	---	623.80	**738.00**
	Inst	Set	Sm	CJ	3.85	4.16	576.00	129.00	---	705.00	**843.00**
Good quality workmanship	Inst	Set	Lg	CJ	2.00	8.00	500.00	67.00	---	567.00	**668.00**
	Inst	Set	Sm	CJ	3.08	5.20	533.00	103.00	---	636.00	**757.00**
Average quality workmanship	Inst	Set	Lg	CJ	1.67	9.60	416.00	56.00	---	472.00	**556.00**
	Inst	Set	Sm	CJ	2.56	6.24	443.00	85.80	---	528.80	**630.00**
72" H											
High quality workmanship	Inst	Set	Lg	CJ	2.67	6.00	578.00	89.50	---	667.50	**789.00**
	Inst	Set	Sm	CJ	4.10	3.90	616.00	137.00	---	753.00	**901.00**
Good quality workmanship	Inst	Set	Lg	CJ	2.13	7.50	534.00	71.40	---	605.40	**714.00**
	Inst	Set	Sm	CJ	3.28	4.88	570.00	110.00	---	680.00	**809.00**
Average quality workmanship	Inst	Set	Lg	CJ	1.78	9.00	446.00	59.70	---	505.70	**596.00**
	Inst	Set	Sm	CJ	2.74	5.85	475.00	91.80	---	566.80	**675.00**

2 ventilating lites, no fixed lites; 40" W

Description	Oper	Unit	Vol	Crew Size	Man-hours per Unit	Crew Output per Day	Avg Mat'l Unit Cost	Avg Labor Unit Cost	Avg Equip Unit Cost	Avg Total Unit Cost	Avg Price Incl O&P
36" H											
High quality workmanship	Inst	Set	Lg	CJ	2.50	6.40	570.00	83.80	---	653.80	**773.00**
	Inst	Set	Sm	CJ	3.85	4.16	608.00	129.00	---	737.00	**880.00**
Good quality workmanship	Inst	Set	Lg	CJ	2.00	8.00	527.00	67.00	---	594.00	**699.00**
	Inst	Set	Sm	CJ	3.08	5.20	562.00	103.00	---	665.00	**790.00**
Average quality workmanship	Inst	Set	Lg	CJ	1.67	9.60	440.00	56.00	---	496.00	**584.00**
	Inst	Set	Sm	CJ	2.56	6.24	469.00	85.80	---	554.80	**659.00**

Description	Oper	Unit	Vol	Crew Size	Man-hours per Unit	Crew Output per Day	Avg Mat'l Unit Cost	Avg Labor Unit Cost	Avg Equip Unit Cost	Avg Total Unit Cost	Avg Price Incl O&P
41" H											
High quality workmanship	Inst	Set	Lg	CJ	2.67	6.00	600.00	89.50	---	689.50	**815.00**
	Inst	Set	Sm	CJ	4.10	3.90	640.00	137.00	---	777.00	**928.00**
Good quality workmanship	Inst	Set	Lg	CJ	2.13	7.50	555.00	71.40	---	626.40	**738.00**
	Inst	Set	Sm	CJ	3.28	4.88	592.00	110.00	---	702.00	**835.00**
Average quality workmanship	Inst	Set	Lg	CJ	1.78	9.00	462.00	59.70	---	521.70	**615.00**
	Inst	Set	Sm	CJ	2.74	5.85	493.00	91.80	---	584.80	**695.00**
48" H											
High quality workmanship	Inst	Set	Lg	CJ	2.86	5.60	690.00	95.80	---	785.80	**928.00**
	Inst	Set	Sm	CJ	4.40	3.64	736.00	147.00	---	883.00	**1050.00**
Good quality workmanship	Inst	Set	Lg	CJ	2.29	7.00	638.00	76.70	---	714.70	**841.00**
	Inst	Set	Sm	CJ	3.52	4.55	680.00	118.00	---	798.00	**947.00**
Average quality workmanship	Inst	Set	Lg	CJ	1.90	8.40	531.00	63.70	---	594.70	**700.00**
	Inst	Set	Sm	CJ	2.93	5.46	566.00	98.20	---	664.20	**789.00**
53" H											
High quality workmanship	Inst	Set	Lg	CJ	3.08	5.20	750.00	103.00	---	853.00	**1010.00**
	Inst	Set	Sm	CJ	4.73	3.38	800.00	159.00	---	959.00	**1140.00**
Good quality workmanship	Inst	Set	Lg	CJ	2.46	6.50	695.00	82.40	---	777.40	**914.00**
	Inst	Set	Sm	CJ	3.78	4.23	741.00	127.00	---	868.00	**1030.00**
Average quality workmanship	Inst	Set	Lg	CJ	2.05	7.80	578.00	68.70	---	646.70	**760.00**
	Inst	Set	Sm	CJ	3.16	5.07	616.00	106.00	---	722.00	**857.00**
60" H											
High quality workmanship	Inst	Set	Lg	CJ	3.33	4.80	833.00	112.00	---	945.00	**1110.00**
	Inst	Set	Sm	CJ	5.13	3.12	888.00	172.00	---	1060.00	**1260.00**
Good quality workmanship	Inst	Set	Lg	CJ	2.67	6.00	770.00	89.50	---	859.50	**1010.00**
	Inst	Set	Sm	CJ	4.10	3.90	821.00	137.00	---	958.00	**1140.00**
Average quality workmanship	Inst	Set	Lg	CJ	2.22	7.20	642.00	74.40	---	716.40	**842.00**
	Inst	Set	Sm	CJ	3.42	4.68	685.00	115.00	---	800.00	**948.00**
66" H											
High quality workmanship	Inst	Set	Lg	CJ	3.33	4.80	870.00	112.00	---	982.00	**1160.00**
	Inst	Set	Sm	CJ	5.13	3.12	928.00	172.00	---	1100.00	**1310.00**
Good quality workmanship	Inst	Set	Lg	CJ	2.67	6.00	806.00	89.50	---	895.50	**1050.00**
	Inst	Set	Sm	CJ	4.10	3.90	859.00	137.00	---	996.00	**1180.00**
Average quality workmanship	Inst	Set	Lg	CJ	2.22	7.20	671.00	74.40	---	745.40	**875.00**
	Inst	Set	Sm	CJ	3.42	4.68	715.00	115.00	---	830.00	**983.00**
72" H											
High quality workmanship	Inst	Set	Lg	CJ	3.64	4.40	908.00	122.00	---	1030.00	**1210.00**
	Inst	Set	Sm	CJ	5.59	2.86	968.00	187.00	---	1155.00	**1380.00**
Good quality workmanship	Inst	Set	Lg	CJ	2.91	5.50	840.00	97.50	---	937.50	**1100.00**
	Inst	Set	Sm	CJ	4.47	3.58	896.00	150.00	---	1046.00	**1240.00**
Average quality workmanship	Inst	Set	Lg	CJ	2.42	6.60	699.00	81.10	---	780.10	**917.00**
	Inst	Set	Sm	CJ	3.73	4.29	746.00	125.00	---	871.00	**1030.00**

Description	Oper	Unit	Vol	Crew Size	Man-hours per Unit	Crew Output per Day	Avg Mat'l Unit Cost	Avg Labor Unit Cost	Avg Equip Unit Cost	Avg Total Unit Cost	Avg Price Incl O&P
2 ventilating lites, no fixed lites; 48" W											
36" H											
High quality workmanship	Inst	Set	Lg	CJ	2.50	6.40	615.00	83.80	---	698.80	**825.00**
	Inst	Set	Sm	CJ	3.85	4.16	656.00	129.00	---	785.00	**935.00**
Good quality workmanship	Inst	Set	Lg	CJ	2.00	8.00	570.00	67.00	---	637.00	**749.00**
	Inst	Set	Sm	CJ	3.08	5.20	608.00	103.00	---	711.00	**844.00**
Average quality workmanship	Inst	Set	Lg	CJ	1.67	9.60	474.00	56.00	---	530.00	**623.00**
	Inst	Set	Sm	CJ	2.56	6.24	506.00	85.80	---	591.80	**702.00**
41" H											
High quality workmanship	Inst	Set	Lg	CJ	2.67	6.00	668.00	89.50	---	757.50	**893.00**
	Inst	Set	Sm	CJ	4.10	3.90	712.00	137.00	---	849.00	**1010.00**
Good quality workmanship	Inst	Set	Lg	CJ	2.13	7.50	618.00	71.40	---	689.40	**811.00**
	Inst	Set	Sm	CJ	3.28	4.88	659.00	110.00	---	769.00	**912.00**
Average quality workmanship	Inst	Set	Lg	CJ	1.78	9.00	515.00	59.70	---	574.70	**675.00**
	Inst	Set	Sm	CJ	2.74	5.85	549.00	91.80	---	640.80	**760.00**
48" H											
High quality workmanship	Inst	Set	Lg	CJ	3.33	4.80	735.00	112.00	---	847.00	**1000.00**
	Inst	Set	Sm	CJ	5.13	3.12	784.00	172.00	---	956.00	**1140.00**
Good quality workmanship	Inst	Set	Lg	CJ	2.67	6.00	680.00	89.50	---	769.50	**907.00**
	Inst	Set	Sm	CJ	4.10	3.90	725.00	137.00	---	862.00	**1030.00**
Average quality workmanship	Inst	Set	Lg	CJ	2.22	7.20	567.00	74.40	---	641.40	**756.00**
	Inst	Set	Sm	CJ	3.42	4.68	605.00	115.00	---	720.00	**856.00**
53" H											
High quality workmanship	Inst	Set	Lg	CJ	3.08	5.20	803.00	103.00	---	906.00	**1070.00**
	Inst	Set	Sm	CJ	4.73	3.38	856.00	159.00	---	1015.00	**1210.00**
Good quality workmanship	Inst	Set	Lg	CJ	2.46	6.50	743.00	82.40	---	825.40	**969.00**
	Inst	Set	Sm	CJ	3.78	4.23	792.00	127.00	---	919.00	**1090.00**
Average quality workmanship	Inst	Set	Lg	CJ	2.05	7.80	618.00	68.70	---	686.70	**807.00**
	Inst	Set	Sm	CJ	3.16	5.07	659.00	106.00	---	765.00	**906.00**
60" H											
High quality workmanship	Inst	Set	Lg	CJ	3.33	4.80	848.00	112.00	---	960.00	**1130.00**
	Inst	Set	Sm	CJ	5.13	3.12	904.00	172.00	---	1076.00	**1280.00**
Good quality workmanship	Inst	Set	Lg	CJ	2.67	6.00	785.00	89.50	---	874.50	**1030.00**
	Inst	Set	Sm	CJ	4.10	3.90	837.00	137.00	---	974.00	**1150.00**
Average quality workmanship	Inst	Set	Lg	CJ	2.22	7.20	653.00	74.40	---	727.40	**855.00**
	Inst	Set	Sm	CJ	3.42	4.68	696.00	115.00	---	811.00	**961.00**
66" H											
High quality workmanship	Inst	Set	Lg	CJ	3.33	4.80	908.00	112.00	---	1020.00	**1200.00**
	Inst	Set	Sm	CJ	5.13	3.12	968.00	172.00	---	1140.00	**1350.00**
Good quality workmanship	Inst	Set	Lg	CJ	2.67	6.00	840.00	89.50	---	929.50	**1090.00**
	Inst	Set	Sm	CJ	4.10	3.90	896.00	137.00	---	1033.00	**1220.00**
Average quality workmanship	Inst	Set	Lg	CJ	2.22	7.20	699.00	74.40	---	773.40	**908.00**
	Inst	Set	Sm	CJ	3.42	4.68	746.00	115.00	---	861.00	**1020.00**
72" H											
High quality workmanship	Inst	Set	Lg	CJ	3.64	4.40	968.00	122.00	---	1090.00	**1280.00**
	Inst	Set	Sm	CJ	5.59	2.86	1030.00	187.00	---	1217.00	**1450.00**
Good quality workmanship	Inst	Set	Lg	CJ	2.91	5.50	896.00	97.50	---	993.50	**1170.00**
	Inst	Set	Sm	CJ	4.47	3.58	955.00	150.00	---	1105.00	**1310.00**
Average quality workmanship	Inst	Set	Lg	CJ	2.42	6.60	746.00	81.10	---	827.10	**971.00**
	Inst	Set	Sm	CJ	3.73	4.29	795.00	125.00	---	920.00	**1090.00**

Description	Oper	Unit	Vol	Crew Size	Man-hours per Unit	Crew Output per Day	Avg Mat'l Unit Cost	Avg Labor Unit Cost	Avg Equip Unit Cost	Avg Total Unit Cost	Avg Price Incl O&P

2 ventilating lites, no fixed lites; 56" W

36" H

Description	Oper	Unit	Vol	Crew Size	Man-hours per Unit	Crew Output per Day	Avg Mat'l Unit Cost	Avg Labor Unit Cost	Avg Equip Unit Cost	Avg Total Unit Cost	Avg Price Incl O&P
High quality workmanship	Inst	Set	Lg	CJ	2.50	6.40	668.00	83.80	---	751.80	**885.00**
	Inst	Set	Sm	CJ	3.85	4.16	712.00	129.00	---	841.00	**999.00**
Good quality workmanship	Inst	Set	Lg	CJ	2.00	8.00	618.00	67.00	---	685.00	**805.00**
	Inst	Set	Sm	CJ	3.08	5.20	659.00	103.00	---	762.00	**903.00**
Average quality workmanship	Inst	Set	Lg	CJ	1.67	9.60	515.00	56.00	---	571.00	**670.00**
	Inst	Set	Sm	CJ	2.56	6.24	549.00	85.80	---	634.80	**751.00**

41" H

Description	Oper	Unit	Vol	Crew Size	Man-hours per Unit	Crew Output per Day	Avg Mat'l Unit Cost	Avg Labor Unit Cost	Avg Equip Unit Cost	Avg Total Unit Cost	Avg Price Incl O&P
High quality workmanship	Inst	Set	Lg	CJ	2.67	6.00	735.00	89.50	---	824.50	**971.00**
	Inst	Set	Sm	CJ	4.10	3.90	784.00	137.00	---	921.00	**1090.00**
Good quality workmanship	Inst	Set	Lg	CJ	2.13	7.50	680.00	71.40	---	751.40	**881.00**
	Inst	Set	Sm	CJ	3.28	4.88	725.00	110.00	---	835.00	**987.00**
Average quality workmanship	Inst	Set	Lg	CJ	1.78	9.00	567.00	59.70	---	626.70	**736.00**
	Inst	Set	Sm	CJ	2.74	5.85	605.00	91.80	---	696.80	**824.00**

48" H

Description	Oper	Unit	Vol	Crew Size	Man-hours per Unit	Crew Output per Day	Avg Mat'l Unit Cost	Avg Labor Unit Cost	Avg Equip Unit Cost	Avg Total Unit Cost	Avg Price Incl O&P
High quality workmanship	Inst	Set	Lg	CJ	2.86	5.60	818.00	95.80	---	913.80	**1070.00**
	Inst	Set	Sm	CJ	4.40	3.64	872.00	147.00	---	1019.00	**1210.00**
Good quality workmanship	Inst	Set	Lg	CJ	2.29	7.00	756.00	76.70	---	832.70	**977.00**
	Inst	Set	Sm	CJ	3.52	4.55	806.00	118.00	---	924.00	**1090.00**
Average quality workmanship	Inst	Set	Lg	CJ	1.90	8.40	630.00	63.70	---	693.70	**814.00**
	Inst	Set	Sm	CJ	2.93	5.46	672.00	98.20	---	770.20	**910.00**

53" H

Description	Oper	Unit	Vol	Crew Size	Man-hours per Unit	Crew Output per Day	Avg Mat'l Unit Cost	Avg Labor Unit Cost	Avg Equip Unit Cost	Avg Total Unit Cost	Avg Price Incl O&P
High quality workmanship	Inst	Set	Lg	CJ	3.08	5.20	897.00	103.00	---	1000.00	**1180.00**
	Inst	Set	Sm	CJ	4.73	3.38	957.00	159.00	---	1116.00	**1320.00**
Good quality workmanship	Inst	Set	Lg	CJ	2.46	6.50	830.00	82.40	---	912.40	**1070.00**
	Inst	Set	Sm	CJ	3.78	4.23	885.00	127.00	---	1012.00	**1190.00**
Average quality workmanship	Inst	Set	Lg	CJ	2.05	7.80	692.00	68.70	---	760.70	**891.00**
	Inst	Set	Sm	CJ	3.16	5.07	738.00	106.00	---	844.00	**996.00**

60" H

Description	Oper	Unit	Vol	Crew Size	Man-hours per Unit	Crew Output per Day	Avg Mat'l Unit Cost	Avg Labor Unit Cost	Avg Equip Unit Cost	Avg Total Unit Cost	Avg Price Incl O&P
High quality workmanship	Inst	Set	Lg	CJ	3.33	4.80	975.00	112.00	---	1087.00	**1280.00**
	Inst	Set	Sm	CJ	5.13	3.12	1040.00	172.00	---	1212.00	**1440.00**
Good quality workmanship	Inst	Set	Lg	CJ	2.67	6.00	903.00	89.50	---	992.50	**1160.00**
	Inst	Set	Sm	CJ	4.10	3.90	963.00	137.00	---	1100.00	**1300.00**
Average quality workmanship	Inst	Set	Lg	CJ	2.22	7.20	752.00	74.40	---	826.40	**968.00**
	Inst	Set	Sm	CJ	3.42	4.68	802.00	115.00	---	917.00	**1080.00**

66" H

Description	Oper	Unit	Vol	Crew Size	Man-hours per Unit	Crew Output per Day	Avg Mat'l Unit Cost	Avg Labor Unit Cost	Avg Equip Unit Cost	Avg Total Unit Cost	Avg Price Incl O&P
High quality workmanship	Inst	Set	Lg	CJ	3.33	4.80	1040.00	112.00	---	1152.00	**1360.00**
	Inst	Set	Sm	CJ	5.13	3.12	1110.00	172.00	---	1282.00	**1520.00**
Good quality workmanship	Inst	Set	Lg	CJ	2.67	6.00	966.00	89.50	---	1055.50	**1240.00**
	Inst	Set	Sm	CJ	4.10	3.90	1030.00	137.00	---	1167.00	**1380.00**
Average quality workmanship	Inst	Set	Lg	CJ	2.22	7.20	804.00	74.40	---	878.40	**1030.00**
	Inst	Set	Sm	CJ	3.42	4.68	858.00	115.00	---	973.00	**1150.00**

72" H

Description	Oper	Unit	Vol	Crew Size	Man-hours per Unit	Crew Output per Day	Avg Mat'l Unit Cost	Avg Labor Unit Cost	Avg Equip Unit Cost	Avg Total Unit Cost	Avg Price Incl O&P
High quality workmanship	Inst	Set	Lg	CJ	3.64	4.40	1110.00	122.00	---	1232.00	**1450.00**
	Inst	Set	Sm	CJ	5.59	2.86	1180.00	187.00	---	1367.00	**1620.00**
Good quality workmanship	Inst	Set	Lg	CJ	2.91	5.50	1030.00	97.50	---	1127.50	**1320.00**
	Inst	Set	Sm	CJ	4.47	3.58	1100.00	150.00	---	1250.00	**1470.00**
Average quality workmanship	Inst	Set	Lg	CJ	2.42	6.60	855.00	81.10	---	936.10	**1100.00**
	Inst	Set	Sm	CJ	3.73	4.29	912.00	125.00	---	1037.00	**1220.00**

Description	Oper	Unit	Vol	Crew Size	Man-hours per Unit	Crew Output per Day	Avg Mat'l Unit Cost	Avg Labor Unit Cost	Avg Equip Unit Cost	Avg Total Unit Cost	Avg Price Incl O&P
2 ventilating lites, no fixed lites; 72" W											
36" H											
High quality workmanship	Inst	Set	Lg	CJ	2.86	5.60	870.00	95.80	---	965.80	**1130.00**
	Inst	Set	Sm	CJ	4.40	3.64	928.00	147.00	---	1075.00	**1270.00**
Good quality workmanship	Inst	Set	Lg	CJ	2.29	7.00	806.00	76.70	---	882.70	**1030.00**
	Inst	Set	Sm	CJ	3.52	4.55	859.00	118.00	---	977.00	**1150.00**
Average quality workmanship	Inst	Set	Lg	CJ	1.90	8.40	671.00	63.70	---	734.70	**860.00**
	Inst	Set	Sm	CJ	2.93	5.46	715.00	98.20	---	813.20	**960.00**
41" H											
High quality workmanship	Inst	Set	Lg	CJ	3.08	5.20	960.00	103.00	---	1063.00	**1250.00**
	Inst	Set	Sm	CJ	4.73	3.38	1020.00	159.00	---	1179.00	**1400.00**
Good quality workmanship	Inst	Set	Lg	CJ	2.46	6.50	888.00	82.40	---	970.40	**1140.00**
	Inst	Set	Sm	CJ	3.78	4.23	947.00	127.00	---	1074.00	**1270.00**
Average quality workmanship	Inst	Set	Lg	CJ	2.05	7.80	740.00	68.70	---	808.70	**947.00**
	Inst	Set	Sm	CJ	3.16	5.07	789.00	106.00	---	895.00	**1060.00**
48" H											
High quality workmanship	Inst	Set	Lg	CJ	3.33	4.80	1040.00	112.00	---	1152.00	**1360.00**
	Inst	Set	Sm	CJ	5.13	3.12	1110.00	172.00	---	1282.00	**1520.00**
Good quality workmanship	Inst	Set	Lg	CJ	2.67	6.00	965.00	89.50	---	1054.50	**1230.00**
	Inst	Set	Sm	CJ	4.10	3.90	1030.00	137.00	---	1167.00	**1380.00**
Average quality workmanship	Inst	Set	Lg	CJ	2.22	7.20	804.00	74.40	---	878.40	**1030.00**
	Inst	Set	Sm	CJ	3.42	4.68	858.00	115.00	---	973.00	**1150.00**
60" H											
High quality workmanship	Inst	Set	Lg	CJ	3.33	4.80	1190.00	112.00	---	1302.00	**1520.00**
	Inst	Set	Sm	CJ	5.13	3.12	1260.00	172.00	---	1432.00	**1690.00**
Good quality workmanship	Inst	Set	Lg	CJ	2.67	6.00	1100.00	89.50	---	1189.50	**1390.00**
	Inst	Set	Sm	CJ	4.10	3.90	1170.00	137.00	---	1307.00	**1540.00**
Average quality workmanship	Inst	Set	Lg	CJ	2.22	7.20	914.00	74.40	---	988.40	**1150.00**
	Inst	Set	Sm	CJ	3.42	4.68	974.00	115.00	---	1089.00	**1280.00**
4 ventilating lites, no fixed lites; 68" W											
36" H											
High quality workmanship	Inst	Set	Lg	CJ	3.33	4.80	1110.00	112.00	---	1222.00	**1430.00**
	Inst	Set	Sm	CJ	5.13	3.12	1180.00	172.00	---	1352.00	**1600.00**
Good quality workmanship	Inst	Set	Lg	CJ	2.67	6.00	1030.00	89.50	---	1119.50	**1310.00**
	Inst	Set	Sm	CJ	4.10	3.90	1100.00	137.00	---	1237.00	**1450.00**
Average quality workmanship	Inst	Set	Lg	CJ	2.22	7.20	855.00	74.40	---	929.40	**1090.00**
	Inst	Set	Sm	CJ	3.42	4.68	912.00	115.00	---	1027.00	**1210.00**
41" H											
High quality workmanship	Inst	Set	Lg	CJ	3.64	4.40	1250.00	122.00	---	1372.00	**1600.00**
	Inst	Set	Sm	CJ	5.59	2.86	1330.00	187.00	---	1517.00	**1790.00**
Good quality workmanship	Inst	Set	Lg	CJ	2.91	5.50	1150.00	97.50	---	1247.50	**1460.00**
	Inst	Set	Sm	CJ	4.47	3.58	1230.00	150.00	---	1380.00	**1620.00**
Average quality workmanship	Inst	Set	Lg	CJ	2.42	6.60	960.00	81.10	---	1041.10	**1220.00**
	Inst	Set	Sm	CJ	3.73	4.29	1020.00	125.00	---	1145.00	**1350.00**

Description	Oper	Unit	Vol	Crew Size	Man-hours per Unit	Crew Output per Day	Avg Mat'l Unit Cost	Avg Labor Unit Cost	Avg Equip Unit Cost	Avg Total Unit Cost	Avg Price Incl O&P
48" H											
High quality workmanship	Inst	Set	Lg	CJ	4.00	4.00	1430.00	134.00	---	1564.00	**1830.00**
	Inst	Set	Sm	CJ	6.15	2.60	1520.00	206.00	---	1726.00	**2040.00**
Good quality workmanship	Inst	Set	Lg	CJ	3.20	5.00	1320.00	107.00	---	1427.00	**1670.00**
	Inst	Set	Sm	CJ	4.92	3.25	1410.00	165.00	---	1575.00	**1850.00**
Average quality workmanship	Inst	Set	Lg	CJ	2.67	6.00	1100.00	89.50	---	1189.50	**1390.00**
	Inst	Set	Sm	CJ	4.10	3.90	1170.00	137.00	---	1307.00	**1540.00**
60" H											
High quality workmanship	Inst	Set	Lg	CJ	4.44	3.60	1760.00	149.00	---	1909.00	**2240.00**
	Inst	Set	Sm	CJ	6.84	2.34	1880.00	229.00	---	2109.00	**2480.00**
Good quality workmanship	Inst	Set	Lg	CJ	3.56	4.50	1630.00	119.00	---	1749.00	**2040.00**
	Inst	Set	Sm	CJ	5.46	2.93	1740.00	183.00	---	1923.00	**2250.00**
Average quality workmanship	Inst	Set	Lg	CJ	2.96	5.40	1360.00	99.20	---	1459.20	**1700.00**
	Inst	Set	Sm	CJ	4.56	3.51	1450.00	153.00	---	1603.00	**1880.00**
72" H											
High quality workmanship	Inst	Set	Lg	CJ	5.00	3.20	1940.00	168.00	---	2108.00	**2460.00**
	Inst	Set	Sm	CJ	7.69	2.08	2060.00	258.00	---	2318.00	**2730.00**
Good quality workmanship	Inst	Set	Lg	CJ	4.00	4.00	1790.00	134.00	---	1924.00	**2250.00**
	Inst	Set	Sm	CJ	6.15	2.60	1910.00	206.00	---	2116.00	**2490.00**
Average quality workmanship	Inst	Set	Lg	CJ	3.33	4.80	1490.00	112.00	---	1602.00	**1870.00**
	Inst	Set	Sm	CJ	5.13	3.12	1590.00	172.00	---	1762.00	**2070.00**

4 ventilating lites, no fixed lites; 82" W

Description	Oper	Unit	Vol	Crew Size	Man-hours per Unit	Crew Output per Day	Avg Mat'l Unit Cost	Avg Labor Unit Cost	Avg Equip Unit Cost	Avg Total Unit Cost	Avg Price Incl O&P
36" H											
High quality workmanship	Inst	Set	Lg	CJ	3.33	4.80	1210.00	112.00	---	1322.00	**1540.00**
	Inst	Set	Sm	CJ	5.13	3.12	1290.00	172.00	---	1462.00	**1720.00**
Good quality workmanship	Inst	Set	Lg	CJ	2.67	6.00	1120.00	89.50	---	1209.50	**1410.00**
	Inst	Set	Sm	CJ	4.10	3.90	1190.00	137.00	---	1327.00	**1560.00**
Average quality workmanship	Inst	Set	Lg	CJ	2.22	7.20	932.00	74.40	---	1006.40	**1180.00**
	Inst	Set	Sm	CJ	3.42	4.68	994.00	115.00	---	1109.00	**1300.00**
41" H											
High quality workmanship	Inst	Set	Lg	CJ	3.64	4.40	1280.00	122.00	---	1402.00	**1640.00**
	Inst	Set	Sm	CJ	5.59	2.86	1360.00	187.00	---	1547.00	**1830.00**
Good quality workmanship	Inst	Set	Lg	CJ	2.91	5.50	1180.00	97.50	---	1277.50	**1490.00**
	Inst	Set	Sm	CJ	4.47	3.58	1260.00	150.00	---	1410.00	**1660.00**
Average quality workmanship	Inst	Set	Lg	CJ	2.42	6.60	983.00	81.10	---	1064.10	**1240.00**
	Inst	Set	Sm	CJ	3.73	4.29	1050.00	125.00	---	1175.00	**1380.00**
48" H											
High quality workmanship	Inst	Set	Lg	CJ	4.00	4.00	1460.00	134.00	---	1594.00	**1870.00**
	Inst	Set	Sm	CJ	6.15	2.60	1560.00	206.00	---	1766.00	**2080.00**
Good quality workmanship	Inst	Set	Lg	CJ	3.20	5.00	1350.00	107.00	---	1457.00	**1710.00**
	Inst	Set	Sm	CJ	4.92	3.25	1440.00	165.00	---	1605.00	**1890.00**
Average quality workmanship	Inst	Set	Lg	CJ	2.67	6.00	1130.00	89.50	---	1219.50	**1420.00**
	Inst	Set	Sm	CJ	4.10	3.90	1200.00	137.00	---	1337.00	**1580.00**

Description	Oper	Unit	Vol	Crew Size	Man-hours per Unit	Crew Output per Day	Avg Mat'l Unit Cost	Avg Labor Unit Cost	Avg Equip Unit Cost	Avg Total Unit Cost	Avg Price Incl O&P
60" H											
High quality workmanship	Inst	Set	Lg	CJ	4.44	3.60	1790.00	149.00	---	1939.00	**2260.00**
	Inst	Set	Sm	CJ	6.84	2.34	1900.00	229.00	---	2129.00	**2510.00**
Good quality workmanship	Inst	Set	Lg	CJ	3.56	4.50	1650.00	119.00	---	1769.00	**2070.00**
	Inst	Set	Sm	CJ	5.46	2.93	1760.00	183.00	---	1943.00	**2280.00**
Average quality workmanship	Inst	Set	Lg	CJ	2.96	5.40	1380.00	99.20	---	1479.20	**1720.00**
	Inst	Set	Sm	CJ	4.56	3.51	1470.00	153.00	---	1623.00	**1900.00**
72" H											
High quality workmanship	Inst	Set	Lg	CJ	5.00	3.20	2050.00	168.00	---	2218.00	**2590.00**
	Inst	Set	Sm	CJ	7.69	2.08	2180.00	258.00	---	2438.00	**2870.00**
Good quality workmanship	Inst	Set	Lg	CJ	4.00	4.00	1890.00	134.00	---	2024.00	**2370.00**
	Inst	Set	Sm	CJ	6.15	2.60	2020.00	206.00	---	2226.00	**2610.00**
Average quality workmanship	Inst	Set	Lg	CJ	3.33	4.80	1580.00	112.00	---	1692.00	**1970.00**
	Inst	Set	Sm	CJ	5.13	3.12	1680.00	172.00	---	1852.00	**2180.00**

4 ventilating lites, no fixed lites; 96" W

Description	Oper	Unit	Vol	Crew Size	Man-hours per Unit	Crew Output per Day	Avg Mat'l Unit Cost	Avg Labor Unit Cost	Avg Equip Unit Cost	Avg Total Unit Cost	Avg Price Incl O&P
36" H											
High quality workmanship	Inst	Set	Lg	CJ	3.33	4.80	1290.00	112.00	---	1402.00	**1640.00**
	Inst	Set	Sm	CJ	5.13	3.12	1380.00	172.00	---	1552.00	**1820.00**
Good quality workmanship	Inst	Set	Lg	CJ	2.67	6.00	1190.00	89.50	---	1279.50	**1500.00**
	Inst	Set	Sm	CJ	4.10	3.90	1270.00	137.00	---	1407.00	**1660.00**
Average quality workmanship	Inst	Set	Lg	CJ	2.22	7.20	995.00	74.40	---	1069.40	**1250.00**
	Inst	Set	Sm	CJ	3.42	4.68	1060.00	115.00	---	1175.00	**1380.00**
41" H											
High quality workmanship	Inst	Set	Lg	CJ	3.64	4.40	1410.00	122.00	---	1532.00	**1790.00**
	Inst	Set	Sm	CJ	5.59	2.86	1500.00	187.00	---	1687.00	**1990.00**
Good quality workmanship	Inst	Set	Lg	CJ	2.91	5.50	1310.00	97.50	---	1407.50	**1640.00**
	Inst	Set	Sm	CJ	4.47	3.58	1390.00	150.00	---	1540.00	**1810.00**
Average quality workmanship	Inst	Set	Lg	CJ	2.42	6.60	1090.00	81.10	---	1171.10	**1360.00**
	Inst	Set	Sm	CJ	3.73	4.29	1160.00	125.00	---	1285.00	**1510.00**
48" H											
High quality workmanship	Inst	Set	Lg	CJ	4.00	4.00	1550.00	134.00	---	1684.00	**1960.00**
	Inst	Set	Sm	CJ	6.15	2.60	1650.00	206.00	---	1856.00	**2180.00**
Good quality workmanship	Inst	Set	Lg	CJ	3.20	5.00	1430.00	107.00	---	1537.00	**1800.00**
	Inst	Set	Sm	CJ	4.92	3.25	1530.00	165.00	---	1695.00	**1990.00**
Average quality workmanship	Inst	Set	Lg	CJ	2.67	6.00	1190.00	89.50	---	1279.50	**1500.00**
	Inst	Set	Sm	CJ	4.10	3.90	1270.00	137.00	---	1407.00	**1660.00**
60" H											
High quality workmanship	Inst	Set	Lg	CJ	4.44	3.60	1940.00	149.00	---	2089.00	**2440.00**
	Inst	Set	Sm	CJ	6.84	2.34	2070.00	229.00	---	2299.00	**2700.00**
Good quality workmanship	Inst	Set	Lg	CJ	3.56	4.50	1800.00	119.00	---	1919.00	**2240.00**
	Inst	Set	Sm	CJ	5.46	2.93	1920.00	183.00	---	2103.00	**2460.00**
Average quality workmanship	Inst	Set	Lg	CJ	2.96	5.40	1500.00	99.20	---	1599.20	**1860.00**
	Inst	Set	Sm	CJ	4.56	3.51	1600.00	153.00	---	1753.00	**2050.00**
72" H											
High quality workmanship	Inst	Set	Lg	CJ	5.00	3.20	2140.00	168.00	---	2308.00	**2690.00**
	Inst	Set	Sm	CJ	7.69	2.08	2280.00	258.00	---	2538.00	**2980.00**
Good quality workmanship	Inst	Set	Lg	CJ	4.00	4.00	1980.00	134.00	---	2114.00	**2460.00**
	Inst	Set	Sm	CJ	6.15	2.60	2110.00	206.00	---	2316.00	**2720.00**
Average quality workmanship	Inst	Set	Lg	CJ	3.33	4.80	1650.00	112.00	---	1762.00	**2050.00**
	Inst	Set	Sm	CJ	5.13	3.12	1760.00	172.00	---	1932.00	**2260.00**

Description	Oper	Unit	Vol	Crew Size	Man-hours per Unit	Crew Output per Day	Avg Mat'l Unit Cost	Avg Labor Unit Cost	Avg Equip Unit Cost	Avg Total Unit Cost	Avg Price Incl O&P

4 ventilating lites, no fixed lites; 114" W
36" H

Description	Oper	Unit	Vol	Crew Size	Man-hours per Unit	Crew Output per Day	Avg Mat'l Unit Cost	Avg Labor Unit Cost	Avg Equip Unit Cost	Avg Total Unit Cost	Avg Price Incl O&P
High quality workmanship	Inst	Set	Lg	CJ	3.33	4.80	1400.00	112.00	---	1512.00	**1770.00**
	Inst	Set	Sm	CJ	5.13	3.12	1500.00	172.00	---	1672.00	**1960.00**
Good quality workmanship	Inst	Set	Lg	CJ	2.67	6.00	1300.00	89.50	---	1389.50	**1620.00**
	Inst	Set	Sm	CJ	4.10	3.90	1390.00	137.00	---	1527.00	**1790.00**
Average quality workmanship	Inst	Set	Lg	CJ	2.22	7.20	1080.00	74.40	---	1154.40	**1350.00**
	Inst	Set	Sm	CJ	3.42	4.68	1150.00	115.00	---	1265.00	**1490.00**

41" H

Description	Oper	Unit	Vol	Crew Size	Man-hours per Unit	Crew Output per Day	Avg Mat'l Unit Cost	Avg Labor Unit Cost	Avg Equip Unit Cost	Avg Total Unit Cost	Avg Price Incl O&P
High quality workmanship	Inst	Set	Lg	CJ	3.64	4.40	1510.00	122.00	---	1632.00	**1900.00**
	Inst	Set	Sm	CJ	5.59	2.86	1610.00	187.00	---	1797.00	**2110.00**
Good quality workmanship	Inst	Set	Lg	CJ	2.91	5.50	1400.00	97.50	---	1497.50	**1740.00**
	Inst	Set	Sm	CJ	4.47	3.58	1490.00	150.00	---	1640.00	**1920.00**
Average quality workmanship	Inst	Set	Lg	CJ	2.42	6.60	1160.00	81.10	---	1241.10	**1450.00**
	Inst	Set	Sm	CJ	3.73	4.29	1240.00	125.00	---	1365.00	**1600.00**

48" H

Description	Oper	Unit	Vol	Crew Size	Man-hours per Unit	Crew Output per Day	Avg Mat'l Unit Cost	Avg Labor Unit Cost	Avg Equip Unit Cost	Avg Total Unit Cost	Avg Price Incl O&P
High quality workmanship	Inst	Set	Lg	CJ	4.00	4.00	1720.00	134.00	---	1854.00	**2160.00**
	Inst	Set	Sm	CJ	6.15	2.60	1830.00	206.00	---	2036.00	**2400.00**
Good quality workmanship	Inst	Set	Lg	CJ	3.20	5.00	1590.00	107.00	---	1697.00	**1980.00**
	Inst	Set	Sm	CJ	4.92	3.25	1700.00	165.00	---	1865.00	**2180.00**
Average quality workmanship	Inst	Set	Lg	CJ	2.67	6.00	1320.00	89.50	---	1409.50	**1650.00**
	Inst	Set	Sm	CJ	4.10	3.90	1410.00	137.00	---	1547.00	**1820.00**

60" H

Description	Oper	Unit	Vol	Crew Size	Man-hours per Unit	Crew Output per Day	Avg Mat'l Unit Cost	Avg Labor Unit Cost	Avg Equip Unit Cost	Avg Total Unit Cost	Avg Price Incl O&P
High quality workmanship	Inst	Set	Lg	CJ	4.44	3.60	2050.00	149.00	---	2199.00	**2560.00**
	Inst	Set	Sm	CJ	6.84	2.34	2180.00	229.00	---	2409.00	**2830.00**
Good quality workmanship	Inst	Set	Lg	CJ	3.56	4.50	1890.00	119.00	---	2009.00	**2350.00**
	Inst	Set	Sm	CJ	5.46	2.93	2020.00	183.00	---	2203.00	**2580.00**
Average quality workmanship	Inst	Set	Lg	CJ	2.96	5.40	1580.00	99.20	---	1679.20	**1960.00**
	Inst	Set	Sm	CJ	4.56	3.51	1680.00	153.00	---	1833.00	**2150.00**

72" H

Description	Oper	Unit	Vol	Crew Size	Man-hours per Unit	Crew Output per Day	Avg Mat'l Unit Cost	Avg Labor Unit Cost	Avg Equip Unit Cost	Avg Total Unit Cost	Avg Price Incl O&P
High quality workmanship	Inst	Set	Lg	CJ	5.00	3.20	2330.00	168.00	---	2498.00	**2920.00**
	Inst	Set	Sm	CJ	7.69	2.08	2490.00	258.00	---	2748.00	**3220.00**
Good quality workmanship	Inst	Set	Lg	CJ	4.00	4.00	2160.00	134.00	---	2294.00	**2670.00**
	Inst	Set	Sm	CJ	6.15	2.60	2300.00	206.00	---	2506.00	**2940.00**
Average quality workmanship	Inst	Set	Lg	CJ	3.33	4.80	1800.00	112.00	---	1912.00	**2220.00**
	Inst	Set	Sm	CJ	5.13	3.12	1920.00	172.00	---	2092.00	**2450.00**

4 ventilating lites, 1 fixed lite; 86" W
36" H

Description	Oper	Unit	Vol	Crew Size	Man-hours per Unit	Crew Output per Day	Avg Mat'l Unit Cost	Avg Labor Unit Cost	Avg Equip Unit Cost	Avg Total Unit Cost	Avg Price Incl O&P
High quality workmanship	Inst	Set	Lg	CJ	4.00	4.00	1400.00	134.00	---	1534.00	**1800.00**
	Inst	Set	Sm	CJ	6.15	2.60	1500.00	206.00	---	1706.00	**2010.00**
Good quality workmanship	Inst	Set	Lg	CJ	3.20	5.00	1300.00	107.00	---	1407.00	**1640.00**
	Inst	Set	Sm	CJ	4.92	3.25	1380.00	165.00	---	1545.00	**1820.00**
Average quality workmanship	Inst	Set	Lg	CJ	2.67	6.00	1080.00	89.50	---	1169.50	**1370.00**
	Inst	Set	Sm	CJ	4.10	3.90	1150.00	137.00	---	1287.00	**1520.00**

41" H

Description	Oper	Unit	Vol	Crew Size	Man-hours per Unit	Crew Output per Day	Avg Mat'l Unit Cost	Avg Labor Unit Cost	Avg Equip Unit Cost	Avg Total Unit Cost	Avg Price Incl O&P
High quality workmanship	Inst	Set	Lg	CJ	4.44	3.60	1580.00	149.00	---	1729.00	**2020.00**
	Inst	Set	Sm	CJ	6.84	2.34	1680.00	229.00	---	1909.00	**2250.00**
Good quality workmanship	Inst	Set	Lg	CJ	3.56	4.50	1460.00	119.00	---	1579.00	**1840.00**
	Inst	Set	Sm	CJ	5.46	2.93	1560.00	183.00	---	1743.00	**2040.00**
Average quality workmanship	Inst	Set	Lg	CJ	2.96	5.40	1220.00	99.20	---	1319.20	**1540.00**
	Inst	Set	Sm	CJ	4.56	3.51	1300.00	153.00	---	1453.00	**1700.00**

Description	Oper	Unit	Vol	Crew Size	Man-hours per Unit	Crew Output per Day	Avg Mat'l Unit Cost	Avg Labor Unit Cost	Avg Equip Unit Cost	Avg Total Unit Cost	Avg Price Incl O&P
48" H											
High quality workmanship	Inst	Set	Lg	CJ	5.00	3.20	1790.00	168.00	---	1958.00	**2290.00**
	Inst	Set	Sm	CJ	7.69	2.08	1900.00	258.00	---	2158.00	**2550.00**
Good quality workmanship	Inst	Set	Lg	CJ	4.00	4.00	1380.00	134.00	---	1514.00	**1770.00**
	Inst	Set	Sm	CJ	6.15	2.60	1470.00	206.00	---	1676.00	**1980.00**
Average quality workmanship	Inst	Set	Lg	CJ	3.33	4.80	1150.00	112.00	---	1262.00	**1480.00**
	Inst	Set	Sm	CJ	5.13	3.12	1220.00	172.00	---	1392.00	**1650.00**
64" H											
High quality workmanship	Inst	Set	Lg	CJ	5.71	2.80	2410.00	191.00	---	2601.00	**3040.00**
	Inst	Set	Sm	CJ	8.79	1.82	2570.00	295.00	---	2865.00	**3370.00**
Good quality workmanship	Inst	Set	Lg	CJ	4.57	3.50	2230.00	153.00	---	2383.00	**2780.00**
	Inst	Set	Sm	CJ	7.02	2.28	2380.00	235.00	---	2615.00	**3060.00**
Average quality workmanship	Inst	Set	Lg	CJ	3.81	4.20	1860.00	128.00	---	1988.00	**2310.00**
	Inst	Set	Sm	CJ	5.86	2.73	1980.00	196.00	---	2176.00	**2550.00**
72" H											
High quality workmanship	Inst	Set	Lg	CJ	6.67	2.40	2650.00	224.00	---	2874.00	**3360.00**
	Inst	Set	Sm	CJ	10.3	1.56	2820.00	345.00	---	3165.00	**3730.00**
Good quality workmanship	Inst	Set	Lg	CJ	5.33	3.00	2450.00	179.00	---	2629.00	**3070.00**
	Inst	Set	Sm	CJ	8.21	1.95	2610.00	275.00	---	2885.00	**3390.00**
Average quality workmanship	Inst	Set	Lg	CJ	4.44	3.60	2040.00	149.00	---	2189.00	**2560.00**
	Inst	Set	Sm	CJ	6.84	2.34	2180.00	229.00	---	2409.00	**2830.00**

4 ventilating lites, 1 fixed lite; 112" W

Description	Oper	Unit	Vol	Crew Size	Man-hours per Unit	Crew Output per Day	Avg Mat'l Unit Cost	Avg Labor Unit Cost	Avg Equip Unit Cost	Avg Total Unit Cost	Avg Price Incl O&P
36" H											
High quality workmanship	Inst	Set	Lg	CJ	4.00	4.00	1510.00	134.00	---	1644.00	**1920.00**
	Inst	Set	Sm	CJ	6.15	2.60	1610.00	206.00	---	1816.00	**2140.00**
Good quality workmanship	Inst	Set	Lg	CJ	3.20	5.00	1400.00	107.00	---	1507.00	**1750.00**
	Inst	Set	Sm	CJ	4.92	3.25	1490.00	165.00	---	1655.00	**1940.00**
Average quality workmanship	Inst	Set	Lg	CJ	2.67	6.00	1160.00	89.50	---	1249.50	**1460.00**
	Inst	Set	Sm	CJ	4.10	3.90	1240.00	137.00	---	1377.00	**1620.00**
41" H											
High quality workmanship	Inst	Set	Lg	CJ	4.44	3.60	1610.00	149.00	---	1759.00	**2050.00**
	Inst	Set	Sm	CJ	6.84	2.34	1710.00	229.00	---	1939.00	**2290.00**
Good quality workmanship	Inst	Set	Lg	CJ	3.56	4.50	1490.00	119.00	---	1609.00	**1870.00**
	Inst	Set	Sm	CJ	5.46	2.93	1580.00	183.00	---	1763.00	**2080.00**
Average quality workmanship	Inst	Set	Lg	CJ	2.96	5.40	1240.00	99.20	---	1339.20	**1560.00**
	Inst	Set	Sm	CJ	4.56	3.51	1320.00	153.00	---	1473.00	**1730.00**
48" H											
High quality workmanship	Inst	Set	Lg	CJ	5.00	3.20	1820.00	168.00	---	1988.00	**2330.00**
	Inst	Set	Sm	CJ	7.69	2.08	1940.00	258.00	---	2198.00	**2600.00**
Good quality workmanship	Inst	Set	Lg	CJ	4.00	4.00	1690.00	134.00	---	1824.00	**2130.00**
	Inst	Set	Sm	CJ	6.15	2.60	1800.00	206.00	---	2006.00	**2360.00**
Average quality workmanship	Inst	Set	Lg	CJ	3.33	4.80	1410.00	112.00	---	1522.00	**1770.00**
	Inst	Set	Sm	CJ	5.13	3.12	1500.00	172.00	---	1672.00	**1960.00**

Description	Oper	Unit	Vol	Crew Size	Man-hours per Unit	Crew Output per Day	Avg Mat'l Unit Cost	Avg Labor Unit Cost	Avg Equip Unit Cost	Avg Total Unit Cost	Avg Price Incl O&P
60" H											
High quality workmanship	Inst	Set	Lg	CJ	5.71	2.80	2210.00	191.00	---	2401.00	**2810.00**
	Inst	Set	Sm	CJ	8.79	1.82	2360.00	295.00	---	2655.00	**3130.00**
Good quality workmanship	Inst	Set	Lg	CJ	4.57	3.50	2050.00	153.00	---	2203.00	**2570.00**
	Inst	Set	Sm	CJ	7.02	2.28	2180.00	235.00	---	2415.00	**2840.00**
Average quality workmanship	Inst	Set	Lg	CJ	3.81	4.20	1710.00	128.00	---	1838.00	**2140.00**
	Inst	Set	Sm	CJ	5.86	2.73	1820.00	196.00	---	2016.00	**2370.00**
72" H											
High quality workmanship	Inst	Set	Lg	CJ	6.67	2.40	2440.00	224.00	---	2664.00	**3120.00**
	Inst	Set	Sm	CJ	10.3	1.56	2600.00	345.00	---	2945.00	**3470.00**
Good quality workmanship	Inst	Set	Lg	CJ	5.33	3.00	2260.00	179.00	---	2439.00	**2840.00**
	Inst	Set	Sm	CJ	8.21	1.95	2410.00	275.00	---	2685.00	**3150.00**
Average quality workmanship	Inst	Set	Lg	CJ	4.44	3.60	1880.00	149.00	---	2029.00	**2370.00**
	Inst	Set	Sm	CJ	6.84	2.34	2000.00	229.00	---	2229.00	**2630.00**

4 ventilating lites, 1 fixed lite; 120" W

Description	Oper	Unit	Vol	Crew Size	Man-hours per Unit	Crew Output per Day	Avg Mat'l Unit Cost	Avg Labor Unit Cost	Avg Equip Unit Cost	Avg Total Unit Cost	Avg Price Incl O&P
36" H											
High quality workmanship	Inst	Set	Lg	CJ	4.00	4.00	1610.00	134.00	---	1744.00	**2030.00**
	Inst	Set	Sm	CJ	6.15	2.60	1710.00	206.00	---	1916.00	**2260.00**
Good quality workmanship	Inst	Set	Lg	CJ	3.20	5.00	1490.00	107.00	---	1597.00	**1860.00**
	Inst	Set	Sm	CJ	4.92	3.25	1590.00	165.00	---	1755.00	**2050.00**
Average quality workmanship	Inst	Set	Lg	CJ	2.67	6.00	1240.00	89.50	---	1329.50	**1550.00**
	Inst	Set	Sm	CJ	4.10	3.90	1320.00	137.00	---	1457.00	**1710.00**
41" H											
High quality workmanship	Inst	Set	Lg	CJ	4.44	3.60	1770.00	149.00	---	1919.00	**2240.00**
	Inst	Set	Sm	CJ	6.84	2.34	1890.00	229.00	---	2119.00	**2490.00**
Good quality workmanship	Inst	Set	Lg	CJ	3.56	4.50	1640.00	119.00	---	1759.00	**2050.00**
	Inst	Set	Sm	CJ	5.46	2.93	1750.00	183.00	---	1933.00	**2270.00**
Average quality workmanship	Inst	Set	Lg	CJ	2.96	5.40	1370.00	99.20	---	1469.20	**1710.00**
	Inst	Set	Sm	CJ	4.56	3.51	1460.00	153.00	---	1613.00	**1890.00**
48" H											
High quality workmanship	Inst	Set	Lg	CJ	5.00	3.20	1940.00	168.00	---	2108.00	**2460.00**
	Inst	Set	Sm	CJ	7.69	2.08	2060.00	258.00	---	2318.00	**2730.00**
Good quality workmanship	Inst	Set	Lg	CJ	4.00	4.00	1790.00	134.00	---	1924.00	**2250.00**
	Inst	Set	Sm	CJ	6.15	2.60	1910.00	206.00	---	2116.00	**2490.00**
Average quality workmanship	Inst	Set	Lg	CJ	3.33	4.80	1490.00	112.00	---	1602.00	**1870.00**
	Inst	Set	Sm	CJ	5.13	3.12	1590.00	172.00	---	1762.00	**2070.00**
60" H											
High quality workmanship	Inst	Set	Lg	CJ	5.71	2.80	2230.00	191.00	---	2421.00	**2830.00**
	Inst	Set	Sm	CJ	8.79	1.82	2380.00	295.00	---	2675.00	**3140.00**
Good quality workmanship	Inst	Set	Lg	CJ	4.57	3.50	2060.00	153.00	---	2213.00	**2590.00**
	Inst	Set	Sm	CJ	7.02	2.28	2200.00	235.00	---	2435.00	**2860.00**
Average quality workmanship	Inst	Set	Lg	CJ	3.81	4.20	1720.00	128.00	---	1848.00	**2150.00**
	Inst	Set	Sm	CJ	5.86	2.73	1830.00	196.00	---	2026.00	**2380.00**
72" H											
High quality workmanship	Inst	Set	Lg	CJ	6.67	2.40	2600.00	224.00	---	2824.00	**3310.00**
	Inst	Set	Sm	CJ	10.3	1.56	2780.00	345.00	---	3125.00	**3680.00**
Good quality workmanship	Inst	Set	Lg	CJ	5.33	3.00	2410.00	179.00	---	2589.00	**3020.00**
	Inst	Set	Sm	CJ	8.21	1.95	2570.00	275.00	---	2845.00	**3340.00**
Average quality workmanship	Inst	Set	Lg	CJ	4.44	3.60	2010.00	149.00	---	2159.00	**2520.00**
	Inst	Set	Sm	CJ	6.84	2.34	2140.00	229.00	---	2369.00	**2780.00**

Description	Oper	Unit	Vol	Crew Size	Man-hours per Unit	Crew Output per Day	Avg Mat'l Unit Cost	Avg Labor Unit Cost	Avg Equip Unit Cost	Avg Total Unit Cost	Avg Price Incl O&P

4 ventilating lites, 1 fixed lite; 142" W

36" H

Description	Oper	Unit	Vol	Crew Size	Man-hours per Unit	Crew Output per Day	Avg Mat'l Unit Cost	Avg Labor Unit Cost	Avg Equip Unit Cost	Avg Total Unit Cost	Avg Price Incl O&P
High quality workmanship	Inst	Set	Lg	CJ	4.00	4.00	1760.00	134.00	---	1894.00	**2210.00**
	Inst	Set	Sm	CJ	6.15	2.60	1870.00	206.00	---	2076.00	**2440.00**
Good quality workmanship	Inst	Set	Lg	CJ	3.20	5.00	1620.00	107.00	---	1727.00	**2020.00**
	Inst	Set	Sm	CJ	4.92	3.25	1730.00	165.00	---	1895.00	**2220.00**
Average quality workmanship	Inst	Set	Lg	CJ	2.67	6.00	1350.00	89.50	---	1439.50	**1680.00**
	Inst	Set	Sm	CJ	4.10	3.90	1440.00	137.00	---	1577.00	**1850.00**

41" H

Description	Oper	Unit	Vol	Crew Size	Man-hours per Unit	Crew Output per Day	Avg Mat'l Unit Cost	Avg Labor Unit Cost	Avg Equip Unit Cost	Avg Total Unit Cost	Avg Price Incl O&P
High quality workmanship	Inst	Set	Lg	CJ	4.00	4.00	1890.00	134.00	---	2024.00	**2360.00**
	Inst	Set	Sm	CJ	6.15	2.60	2020.00	206.00	---	2226.00	**2610.00**
Good quality workmanship	Inst	Set	Lg	CJ	3.20	5.00	1750.00	107.00	---	1857.00	**2160.00**
	Inst	Set	Sm	CJ	4.92	3.25	1870.00	165.00	---	2035.00	**2380.00**
Average quality workmanship	Inst	Set	Lg	CJ	2.67	6.00	1460.00	89.50	---	1549.50	**1800.00**
	Inst	Set	Sm	CJ	4.10	3.90	1560.00	137.00	---	1697.00	**1980.00**

48" H

Description	Oper	Unit	Vol	Crew Size	Man-hours per Unit	Crew Output per Day	Avg Mat'l Unit Cost	Avg Labor Unit Cost	Avg Equip Unit Cost	Avg Total Unit Cost	Avg Price Incl O&P
High quality workmanship	Inst	Set	Lg	CJ	5.00	3.20	2150.00	168.00	---	2318.00	**2710.00**
	Inst	Set	Sm	CJ	7.69	2.08	2300.00	258.00	---	2558.00	**3000.00**
Good quality workmanship	Inst	Set	Lg	CJ	4.00	4.00	1990.00	134.00	---	2124.00	**2480.00**
	Inst	Set	Sm	CJ	6.15	2.60	2120.00	206.00	---	2326.00	**2730.00**
Average quality workmanship	Inst	Set	Lg	CJ	3.33	4.80	1660.00	112.00	---	1772.00	**2070.00**
	Inst	Set	Sm	CJ	5.13	3.12	1770.00	172.00	---	1942.00	**2280.00**

60" H

Description	Oper	Unit	Vol	Crew Size	Man-hours per Unit	Crew Output per Day	Avg Mat'l Unit Cost	Avg Labor Unit Cost	Avg Equip Unit Cost	Avg Total Unit Cost	Avg Price Incl O&P
High quality workmanship	Inst	Set	Lg	CJ	5.71	2.80	2580.00	191.00	---	2771.00	**3230.00**
	Inst	Set	Sm	CJ	8.79	1.82	2750.00	295.00	---	3045.00	**3580.00**
Good quality workmanship	Inst	Set	Lg	CJ	4.57	3.50	2390.00	153.00	---	2543.00	**2960.00**
	Inst	Set	Sm	CJ	7.02	2.28	2550.00	235.00	---	2785.00	**3260.00**
Average quality workmanship	Inst	Set	Lg	CJ	3.81	4.20	1990.00	128.00	---	2118.00	**2470.00**
	Inst	Set	Sm	CJ	5.86	2.73	2120.00	196.00	---	2316.00	**2720.00**

72" H

Description	Oper	Unit	Vol	Crew Size	Man-hours per Unit	Crew Output per Day	Avg Mat'l Unit Cost	Avg Labor Unit Cost	Avg Equip Unit Cost	Avg Total Unit Cost	Avg Price Incl O&P
High quality workmanship	Inst	Set	Lg	CJ	6.67	2.40	2960.00	224.00	---	3184.00	**3710.00**
	Inst	Set	Sm	CJ	10.3	1.56	3150.00	345.00	---	3495.00	**4110.00**
Good quality workmanship	Inst	Set	Lg	CJ	5.33	3.00	2740.00	179.00	---	2919.00	**3400.00**
	Inst	Set	Sm	CJ	8.21	1.95	2920.00	275.00	---	3195.00	**3740.00**
Average quality workmanship	Inst	Set	Lg	CJ	4.44	3.60	2280.00	149.00	---	2429.00	**2830.00**
	Inst	Set	Sm	CJ	6.84	2.34	2430.00	229.00	---	2659.00	**3120.00**

For aluminum clad (baked white enamel) exterior

Description	Oper	Unit	Vol	Crew Size	Man-hours per Unit	Crew Output per Day	Avg Mat'l Unit Cost	Avg Labor Unit Cost	Avg Equip Unit Cost	Avg Total Unit Cost	Avg Price Incl O&P
ADD	Inst	%	Lg	---	---	---	20.0	---	---	20.0	---
	Inst	%	Sm	---	---	---	20.0	---	---	20.0	---

Description	Oper	Unit	Vol	Crew Size	Man-hours per Unit	Crew Output per Day	Avg Mat'l Unit Cost	Avg Labor Unit Cost	Avg Equip Unit Cost	Avg Total Unit Cost	Avg Price Incl O&P
Double hung windows; glazed 7/16" T insulating glass; two lites per unit; unit includes screens and weatherstripping; rough opening sizes											
1'-6" x 2'-0", 2'-6", 3'-0", 3'-6"											
High quality workmanship	Inst	Set	Lg	CA	2.50	3.20	360.00	92.60	---	452.60	**544.00**
	Inst	Set	Sm	CA	3.85	2.08	384.00	143.00	---	527.00	**641.00**
Good quality workmanship	Inst	Set	Lg	CA	2.00	4.00	332.00	74.00	---	406.00	**485.00**
	Inst	Set	Sm	CA	3.08	2.60	354.00	114.00	---	468.00	**566.00**
Average quality workmanship	Inst	Set	Lg	CA	1.67	4.80	294.00	61.80	---	355.80	**425.00**
	Inst	Set	Sm	CA	2.56	3.12	314.00	94.80	---	408.80	**493.00**
1'-6" x 4'-0", 4'-6", 5'-0", 5'-6"											
High quality workmanship	Inst	Set	Lg	CA	2.50	3.20	516.00	92.60	---	608.60	**723.00**
	Inst	Set	Sm	CA	3.85	2.08	550.00	143.00	---	693.00	**833.00**
Good quality workmanship	Inst	Set	Lg	CA	2.00	4.00	470.00	74.00	---	544.00	**644.00**
	Inst	Set	Sm	CA	3.08	2.60	501.00	114.00	---	615.00	**736.00**
Average quality workmanship	Inst	Set	Lg	CA	1.67	4.80	408.00	61.80	---	469.80	**556.00**
	Inst	Set	Sm	CA	2.56	3.12	435.00	94.80	---	529.80	**633.00**
2'-0" x 2'-0", 2'-6", 3'-0", 3'-6"											
High quality workmanship	Inst	Set	Lg	CA	2.50	3.20	372.00	92.60	---	464.60	**557.00**
	Inst	Set	Sm	CA	3.85	2.08	397.00	143.00	---	540.00	**656.00**
Good quality workmanship	Inst	Set	Lg	CA	2.00	4.00	329.00	74.00	---	403.00	**481.00**
	Inst	Set	Sm	CA	3.08	2.60	350.00	114.00	---	464.00	**563.00**
Average quality workmanship	Inst	Set	Lg	CA	1.67	4.80	308.00	61.80	---	369.80	**440.00**
	Inst	Set	Sm	CA	2.56	3.12	328.00	94.80	---	422.80	**510.00**
2'-0" x 4'-0", 4'-6", 5'-0", 6'-0"											
High quality workmanship	Inst	Set	Lg	CA	2.50	3.20	489.00	92.60	---	581.60	**692.00**
	Inst	Set	Sm	CA	3.85	2.08	522.00	143.00	---	665.00	**799.00**
Good quality workmanship	Inst	Set	Lg	CA	2.00	4.00	453.00	74.00	---	527.00	**625.00**
	Inst	Set	Sm	CA	3.08	2.60	483.00	114.00	---	597.00	**715.00**
Average quality workmanship	Inst	Set	Lg	CA	1.67	4.80	420.00	61.80	---	481.80	**570.00**
	Inst	Set	Sm	CA	2.56	3.12	448.00	94.80	---	542.80	**648.00**
2'-6" x 2'-0", 2'-6", 3'-0", 3'-6"											
High quality workmanship	Inst	Set	Lg	CA	2.50	3.20	387.00	92.60	---	479.60	**575.00**
	Inst	Set	Sm	CA	3.85	2.08	413.00	143.00	---	556.00	**674.00**
Good quality workmanship	Inst	Set	Lg	CA	2.00	4.00	359.00	74.00	---	433.00	**516.00**
	Inst	Set	Sm	CA	3.08	2.60	382.00	114.00	---	496.00	**599.00**
Average quality workmanship	Inst	Set	Lg	CA	1.67	4.80	318.00	61.80	---	379.80	**452.00**
	Inst	Set	Sm	CA	2.56	3.12	339.00	94.80	---	433.80	**523.00**
2'-6" x 4'-0", 4'-6", 5'-0", 6'-0"											
High quality workmanship	Inst	Set	Lg	CA	2.50	3.20	546.00	92.60	---	638.60	**757.00**
	Inst	Set	Sm	CA	3.85	2.08	582.00	143.00	---	725.00	**869.00**
Good quality workmanship	Inst	Set	Lg	CA	2.00	4.00	489.00	74.00	---	563.00	**666.00**
	Inst	Set	Sm	CA	3.08	2.60	522.00	114.00	---	636.00	**759.00**
Average quality workmanship	Inst	Set	Lg	CA	1.67	4.80	458.00	61.80	---	519.80	**613.00**
	Inst	Set	Sm	CA	2.56	3.12	488.00	94.80	---	582.80	**694.00**

Description	Oper	Unit	Vol	Crew Size	Man-hours per Unit	Crew Output per Day	Avg Mat'l Unit Cost	Avg Labor Unit Cost	Avg Equip Unit Cost	Avg Total Unit Cost	Avg Price Incl O&P
3'-0" x 2'-0", 2'-6", 3'-0", 3'-6"											
High quality workmanship	Inst	Set	Lg	CA	2.50	3.20	449.00	92.60	---	541.60	**645.00**
	Inst	Set	Sm	CA	3.85	2.08	478.00	143.00	---	621.00	**750.00**
Good quality workmanship	Inst	Set	Lg	CA	2.00	4.00	378.00	74.00	---	452.00	**538.00**
	Inst	Set	Sm	CA	3.08	2.60	403.00	114.00	---	517.00	**623.00**
Average quality workmanship	Inst	Set	Lg	CA	1.67	4.80	345.00	61.80	---	406.80	**483.00**
	Inst	Set	Sm	CA	2.56	3.12	368.00	94.80	---	462.80	**556.00**
3'-0" x 4'-0", 4'-6", 5'-0", 6'-0"											
High quality workmanship	Inst	Set	Lg	CA	2.50	3.20	602.00	92.60	---	694.60	**821.00**
	Inst	Set	Sm	CA	3.85	2.08	642.00	143.00	---	785.00	**937.00**
Good quality workmanship	Inst	Set	Lg	CA	2.00	4.00	564.00	74.00	---	638.00	**752.00**
	Inst	Set	Sm	CA	3.08	2.60	602.00	114.00	---	716.00	**851.00**
Average quality workmanship	Inst	Set	Lg	CA	1.67	4.80	498.00	61.80	---	559.80	**659.00**
	Inst	Set	Sm	CA	2.56	3.12	531.00	94.80	---	625.80	**744.00**
3'-6" x 3'-0", 3'-6", 4'-0"											
High quality workmanship	Inst	Set	Lg	CA	2.50	3.20	537.00	92.60	---	629.60	**747.00**
	Inst	Set	Sm	CA	3.85	2.08	573.00	143.00	---	716.00	**858.00**
Good quality workmanship	Inst	Set	Lg	CA	2.00	4.00	456.00	74.00	---	530.00	**628.00**
	Inst	Set	Sm	CA	3.08	2.60	486.00	114.00	---	600.00	**719.00**
Average quality workmanship	Inst	Set	Lg	CA	1.67	4.80	404.00	61.80	---	465.80	**551.00**
	Inst	Set	Sm	CA	2.56	3.12	430.00	94.80	---	524.80	**628.00**
3'-6" x 4'-6", 5'-0", 6'-0"											
High quality workmanship	Inst	Set	Lg	CA	2.50	3.20	738.00	92.60	---	830.60	**978.00**
	Inst	Set	Sm	CA	3.85	2.08	787.00	143.00	---	930.00	**1100.00**
Good quality workmanship	Inst	Set	Lg	CA	2.00	4.00	677.00	74.00	---	751.00	**882.00**
	Inst	Set	Sm	CA	3.08	2.60	722.00	114.00	---	836.00	**989.00**
Average quality workmanship	Inst	Set	Lg	CA	1.67	4.80	605.00	61.80	---	666.80	**782.00**
	Inst	Set	Sm	CA	2.56	3.12	645.00	94.80	---	739.80	**874.00**
4'-0" x 3'-0", 3'-6", 4'-0"											
High quality workmanship	Inst	Set	Lg	CA	2.50	3.20	783.00	92.60	---	875.60	**1030.00**
	Inst	Set	Sm	CA	3.85	2.08	835.00	143.00	---	978.00	**1160.00**
Good quality workmanship	Inst	Set	Lg	CA	2.00	4.00	630.00	74.00	---	704.00	**828.00**
	Inst	Set	Sm	CA	3.08	2.60	672.00	114.00	---	786.00	**932.00**
Average quality workmanship	Inst	Set	Lg	CA	1.67	4.80	471.00	61.80	---	532.80	**628.00**
	Inst	Set	Sm	CA	2.56	3.12	502.00	94.80	---	596.80	**710.00**
4'-0" x 4'-6", 5'-0", 6'-0"											
High quality workmanship	Inst	Set	Lg	CA	2.50	3.20	825.00	92.60	---	917.60	**1080.00**
	Inst	Set	Sm	CA	3.85	2.08	880.00	143.00	---	1023.00	**1210.00**
Good quality workmanship	Inst	Set	Lg	CA	2.00	4.00	750.00	74.00	---	824.00	**966.00**
	Inst	Set	Sm	CA	3.08	2.60	800.00	114.00	---	914.00	**1080.00**
Average quality workmanship	Inst	Set	Lg	CA	1.67	4.80	659.00	61.80	---	720.80	**844.00**
	Inst	Set	Sm	CA	2.56	3.12	702.00	94.80	---	796.80	**940.00**

Description	Oper	Unit	Vol	Crew Size	Man-hours per Unit	Crew Output per Day	Avg Mat'l Unit Cost	Avg Labor Unit Cost	Avg Equip Unit Cost	Avg Total Unit Cost	Avg Price Incl O&P
4'-6" x 4'-0", 4'-6											
High quality workmanship	Inst	Set	Lg	CA	2.50	3.20	870.00	92.60	---	962.60	**1130.00**
	Inst	Set	Sm	CA	3.85	2.08	928.00	143.00	---	1071.00	**1270.00**
Good quality workmanship	Inst	Set	Lg	CA	2.00	4.00	675.00	74.00	---	749.00	**880.00**
	Inst	Set	Sm	CA	3.08	2.60	720.00	114.00	---	834.00	**988.00**
Average quality workmanship	Inst	Set	Lg	CA	1.67	4.80	567.00	61.80	---	628.80	**739.00**
	Inst	Set	Sm	CA	2.56	3.12	605.00	94.80	---	699.80	**828.00**
4'-6" x 5'-0", 6'-0"											
High quality workmanship	Inst	Set	Lg	CA	2.50	3.20	945.00	92.60	---	1037.60	**1220.00**
	Inst	Set	Sm	CA	3.85	2.08	1010.00	143.00	---	1153.00	**1360.00**
Good quality workmanship	Inst	Set	Lg	CA	2.00	4.00	780.00	74.00	---	854.00	**1000.00**
	Inst	Set	Sm	CA	3.08	2.60	832.00	114.00	---	946.00	**1120.00**
Average quality workmanship	Inst	Set	Lg	CA	1.67	4.80	701.00	61.80	---	762.80	**892.00**
	Inst	Set	Sm	CA	2.56	3.12	747.00	94.80	---	841.80	**992.00**
5'-0" x 4'-0", 4'-6											
High quality workmanship	Inst	Set	Lg	CA	2.50	3.20	1020.00	92.60	---	1112.60	**1300.00**
	Inst	Set	Sm	CA	3.85	2.08	1090.00	143.00	---	1233.00	**1450.00**
Good quality workmanship	Inst	Set	Lg	CA	2.00	4.00	885.00	74.00	---	959.00	**1120.00**
	Inst	Set	Sm	CA	3.08	2.60	944.00	114.00	---	1058.00	**1250.00**
Average quality workmanship	Inst	Set	Lg	CA	1.67	4.80	612.00	61.80	---	673.80	**790.00**
	Inst	Set	Sm	CA	2.56	3.12	653.00	94.80	---	747.80	**883.00**
5'-0" x 5'-0", 6'-0"											
High quality workmanship	Inst	Set	Lg	CA	2.50	3.20	1100.00	92.60	---	1192.60	**1390.00**
	Inst	Set	Sm	CA	3.85	2.08	1170.00	143.00	---	1313.00	**1540.00**
Good quality workmanship	Inst	Set	Lg	CA	2.00	4.00	945.00	74.00	---	1019.00	**1190.00**
	Inst	Set	Sm	CA	3.08	2.60	1010.00	114.00	---	1124.00	**1320.00**
Average quality workmanship	Inst	Set	Lg	CA	1.67	4.80	746.00	61.80	---	807.80	**944.00**
	Inst	Set	Sm	CA	2.56	3.12	795.00	94.80	---	889.80	**1050.00**

Picture windows

Unit with one fixed lite, 3/4" T insulating glass, frame sizes

Description	Oper	Unit	Vol	Crew Size	Man-hours per Unit	Crew Output per Day	Avg Mat'l Unit Cost	Avg Labor Unit Cost	Avg Equip Unit Cost	Avg Total Unit Cost	Avg Price Incl O&P
4'-0" W x 3'-6" H; 3'-6" W x 4'-0" H											
High quality workmanship	Inst	Ea	Lg	CJ	1.82	8.80	456.00	61.00	---	517.00	**610.00**
	Inst	Ea	Sm	CJ	2.80	5.72	486.00	93.80	---	579.80	**691.00**
Good quality workmanship	Inst	Ea	Lg	CJ	1.45	11.00	420.00	48.60	---	468.60	**551.00**
	Inst	Ea	Sm	CJ	2.24	7.15	448.00	75.10	---	523.10	**620.00**
Average quality workmanship	Inst	Ea	Lg	CJ	1.21	13.20	351.00	40.60	---	391.60	**460.00**
	Inst	Ea	Sm	CJ	1.86	8.58	374.00	62.30	---	436.30	**518.00**
4'-8" W x 3'-6" H; 4'-0" W x 4'-0" H; 3'-6" W x 4'-8"H											
High quality workmanship	Inst	Ea	Lg	CJ	1.82	8.80	525.00	61.00	---	586.00	**689.00**
	Inst	Ea	Sm	CJ	2.80	5.72	560.00	93.80	---	653.80	**775.00**
Good quality workmanship	Inst	Ea	Lg	CJ	1.45	11.00	486.00	48.60	---	534.60	**627.00**
	Inst	Ea	Sm	CJ	2.24	7.15	518.00	75.10	---	593.10	**701.00**
Average quality workmanship	Inst	Ea	Lg	CJ	1.21	13.20	405.00	40.60	---	445.60	**523.00**
	Inst	Ea	Sm	CJ	1.86	8.58	432.00	62.30	---	494.30	**584.00**

Description	Oper	Unit	Vol	Crew Size	Man-hours per Unit	Crew Output per Day	Avg Mat'l Unit Cost	Avg Labor Unit Cost	Avg Equip Unit Cost	Avg Total Unit Cost	Avg Price Incl O&P
4'-8" W x 4'-0" H; 4'-0" W x 4'-10" H											
High quality workmanship	Inst	Ea	Lg	CJ	1.82	8.80	578.00	61.00	---	639.00	**750.00**
	Inst	Ea	Sm	CJ	2.80	5.72	616.00	93.80	---	709.80	**840.00**
Good quality workmanship	Inst	Ea	Lg	CJ	1.45	11.00	534.00	48.60	---	582.60	**682.00**
	Inst	Ea	Sm	CJ	2.24	7.15	570.00	75.10	---	645.10	**760.00**
Average quality workmanship	Inst	Ea	Lg	CJ	1.21	13.20	446.00	40.60	---	486.60	**569.00**
	Inst	Ea	Sm	CJ	1.86	8.58	475.00	62.30	---	537.30	**634.00**
4'-8" W x 4'-8" H											
High quality workmanship	Inst	Ea	Lg	CJ	2.00	8.00	630.00	67.00	---	697.00	**818.00**
	Inst	Ea	Sm	CJ	3.08	5.20	672.00	103.00	---	775.00	**917.00**
Good quality workmanship	Inst	Ea	Lg	CJ	1.60	10.00	582.00	53.60	---	635.60	**744.00**
	Inst	Ea	Sm	CJ	2.46	6.50	621.00	82.40	---	703.40	**829.00**
Average quality workmanship	Inst	Ea	Lg	CJ	1.33	12.00	486.00	44.60	---	530.60	**621.00**
	Inst	Ea	Sm	CJ	2.05	7.80	518.00	68.70	---	586.70	**692.00**
4'-8" W x 5'-6" H; 5'-4" W x 4'-8" H											
High quality workmanship	Inst	Ea	Lg	CJ	2.00	8.00	795.00	67.00	---	862.00	**1010.00**
	Inst	Ea	Sm	CJ	3.08	5.20	848.00	103.00	---	951.00	**1120.00**
Good quality workmanship	Inst	Ea	Lg	CJ	1.60	10.00	735.00	53.60	---	788.60	**920.00**
	Inst	Ea	Sm	CJ	2.46	6.50	784.00	82.40	---	866.40	**1020.00**
Average quality workmanship	Inst	Ea	Lg	CJ	1.33	12.00	612.00	44.60	---	656.60	**766.00**
	Inst	Ea	Sm	CJ	2.05	7.80	653.00	68.70	---	721.70	**847.00**
5'-4" W x 5'-6" H											
High quality workmanship	Inst	Ea	Lg	CJ	2.00	8.00	900.00	67.00	---	967.00	**1130.00**
	Inst	Ea	Sm	CJ	3.08	5.20	960.00	103.00	---	1063.00	**1250.00**
Good quality workmanship	Inst	Ea	Lg	CJ	1.60	10.00	833.00	53.60	---	886.60	**1030.00**
	Inst	Ea	Sm	CJ	2.46	6.50	888.00	82.40	---	970.40	**1140.00**
Average quality workmanship	Inst	Ea	Lg	CJ	1.33	12.00	693.00	44.60	---	737.60	**859.00**
	Inst	Ea	Sm	CJ	2.05	7.80	739.00	68.70	---	807.70	**946.00**

Unit with one fixed lite, glazed 3/4" T insulating glass and two glazed S.S.B. casement flankers, 15", 19" or 23" W; unit includes: hardware, casing and molding; rough opening sizes

40" H

88" W

Description	Oper	Unit	Vol	Crew Size	Man-hours per Unit	Crew Output per Day	Avg Mat'l Unit Cost	Avg Labor Unit Cost	Avg Equip Unit Cost	Avg Total Unit Cost	Avg Price Incl O&P
High quality workmanship	Inst	Set	Lg	CJ	2.50	6.40	1220.00	83.80	---	1303.80	**1520.00**
	Inst	Set	Sm	CJ	3.85	4.16	1300.00	129.00	---	1429.00	**1680.00**
Good quality workmanship	Inst	Set	Lg	CJ	2.00	8.00	1130.00	67.00	---	1197.00	**1390.00**
	Inst	Set	Sm	CJ	3.08	5.20	1210.00	103.00	---	1313.00	**1530.00**
Average quality workmanship	Inst	Set	Lg	CJ	1.67	9.60	942.00	56.00	---	998.00	**1160.00**
	Inst	Set	Sm	CJ	2.56	6.24	1000.00	85.80	---	1085.80	**1280.00**
96" W											
High quality workmanship	Inst	Set	Lg	CJ	2.50	6.40	1240.00	83.80	---	1323.80	**1540.00**
	Inst	Set	Sm	CJ	3.85	4.16	1320.00	129.00	---	1449.00	**1700.00**
Good quality workmanship	Inst	Set	Lg	CJ	2.00	8.00	1140.00	67.00	---	1207.00	**1410.00**
	Inst	Set	Sm	CJ	3.08	5.20	1220.00	103.00	---	1323.00	**1550.00**
Average quality workmanship	Inst	Set	Lg	CJ	1.67	9.60	954.00	56.00	---	1010.00	**1180.00**
	Inst	Set	Sm	CJ	2.56	6.24	1020.00	85.80	---	1105.80	**1290.00**

Description	Oper	Unit	Vol	Crew Size	Man-hours per Unit	Crew Output per Day	Avg Mat'l Unit Cost	Avg Labor Unit Cost	Avg Equip Unit Cost	Avg Total Unit Cost	Avg Price Incl O&P
104" W											
High quality workmanship	Inst	Set	Lg	CJ	2.50	6.40	1410.00	83.80	---	1493.80	**1740.00**
	Inst	Set	Sm	CJ	3.85	4.16	1500.00	129.00	---	1629.00	**1910.00**
Good quality workmanship	Inst	Set	Lg	CJ	2.00	8.00	1310.00	67.00	---	1377.00	**1590.00**
	Inst	Set	Sm	CJ	3.08	5.20	1390.00	103.00	---	1493.00	**1750.00**
Average quality workmanship	Inst	Set	Lg	CJ	1.67	9.60	1090.00	56.00	---	1146.00	**1330.00**
	Inst	Set	Sm	CJ	2.56	6.24	1160.00	85.80	---	1245.80	**1450.00**
112" W											
High quality workmanship	Inst	Set	Lg	CJ	2.50	6.40	1430.00	83.80	---	1513.80	**1760.00**
	Inst	Set	Sm	CJ	3.85	4.16	1520.00	129.00	---	1649.00	**1930.00**
Good quality workmanship	Inst	Set	Lg	CJ	2.00	8.00	1320.00	67.00	---	1387.00	**1610.00**
	Inst	Set	Sm	CJ	3.08	5.20	1410.00	103.00	---	1513.00	**1760.00**
Average quality workmanship	Inst	Set	Lg	CJ	1.67	9.60	1100.00	56.00	---	1156.00	**1340.00**
	Inst	Set	Sm	CJ	2.56	6.24	1170.00	85.80	---	1255.80	**1460.00**
48" H											
88" W											
High quality workmanship	Inst	Set	Lg	CJ	2.50	6.40	1360.00	83.80	---	1443.80	**1680.00**
	Inst	Set	Sm	CJ	3.85	4.16	1450.00	129.00	---	1579.00	**1850.00**
Good quality workmanship	Inst	Set	Lg	CJ	2.00	8.00	1260.00	67.00	---	1327.00	**1540.00**
	Inst	Set	Sm	CJ	3.08	5.20	1340.00	103.00	---	1443.00	**1680.00**
Average quality workmanship	Inst	Set	Lg	CJ	1.67	9.60	1050.00	56.00	---	1106.00	**1280.00**
	Inst	Set	Sm	CJ	2.56	6.24	1120.00	85.80	---	1205.80	**1400.00**
96" W											
High quality workmanship	Inst	Set	Lg	CJ	2.86	5.60	1370.00	95.80	---	1465.80	**1710.00**
	Inst	Set	Sm	CJ	4.40	3.64	1460.00	147.00	---	1607.00	**1890.00**
Good quality workmanship	Inst	Set	Lg	CJ	2.29	7.00	1270.00	76.70	---	1346.70	**1570.00**
	Inst	Set	Sm	CJ	3.52	4.55	1360.00	118.00	---	1478.00	**1720.00**
Average quality workmanship	Inst	Set	Lg	CJ	1.90	8.40	1060.00	63.70	---	1123.70	**1310.00**
	Inst	Set	Sm	CJ	2.93	5.46	1130.00	98.20	---	1228.20	**1440.00**
104" W											
High quality workmanship	Inst	Set	Lg	CJ	2.86	5.60	1600.00	95.80	---	1695.80	**1970.00**
	Inst	Set	Sm	CJ	4.40	3.64	1700.00	147.00	---	1847.00	**2170.00**
Good quality workmanship	Inst	Set	Lg	CJ	2.29	7.00	1480.00	76.70	---	1556.70	**1810.00**
	Inst	Set	Sm	CJ	3.52	4.55	1580.00	118.00	---	1698.00	**1980.00**
Average quality workmanship	Inst	Set	Lg	CJ	1.90	8.40	1230.00	63.70	---	1293.70	**1510.00**
	Inst	Set	Sm	CJ	2.93	5.46	1310.00	98.20	---	1408.20	**1650.00**
112" W											
High quality workmanship	Inst	Set	Lg	CJ	2.86	5.60	1610.00	95.80	---	1705.80	**1990.00**
	Inst	Set	Sm	CJ	4.40	3.64	1720.00	147.00	---	1867.00	**2180.00**
Good quality workmanship	Inst	Set	Lg	CJ	2.29	7.00	1490.00	76.70	---	1566.70	**1820.00**
	Inst	Set	Sm	CJ	3.52	4.55	1590.00	118.00	---	1708.00	**2000.00**
Average quality workmanship	Inst	Set	Lg	CJ	1.90	8.40	1240.00	63.70	---	1303.70	**1520.00**
	Inst	Set	Sm	CJ	2.93	5.46	1330.00	98.20	---	1428.20	**1660.00**

Description	Oper	Unit	Vol	Crew Size	Man-hours per Unit	Crew Output per Day	Avg Mat'l Unit Cost	Avg Labor Unit Cost	Avg Equip Unit Cost	Avg Total Unit Cost	Avg Price Incl O&P
60" H											
88" W											
High quality workmanship	Inst	Set	Lg	CJ	2.86	5.60	1610.00	95.80	---	1705.80	**1980.00**
	Inst	Set	Sm	CJ	4.40	3.64	1710.00	147.00	---	1857.00	**2180.00**
Good quality workmanship	Inst	Set	Lg	CJ	2.29	7.00	1490.00	76.70	---	1566.70	**1820.00**
	Inst	Set	Sm	CJ	3.52	4.55	1580.00	118.00	---	1698.00	**1990.00**
Average quality workmanship	Inst	Set	Lg	CJ	1.90	8.40	1240.00	63.70	---	1303.70	**1510.00**
	Inst	Set	Sm	CJ	2.93	5.46	1320.00	98.20	---	1418.20	**1660.00**
96" W											
High quality workmanship	Inst	Set	Lg	CJ	2.86	5.60	1620.00	95.80	---	1715.80	**2000.00**
	Inst	Set	Sm	CJ	4.40	3.64	1730.00	147.00	---	1877.00	**2190.00**
Good quality workmanship	Inst	Set	Lg	CJ	2.29	7.00	1500.00	76.70	---	1576.70	**1830.00**
	Inst	Set	Sm	CJ	3.52	4.55	1600.00	118.00	---	1718.00	**2010.00**
Average quality workmanship	Inst	Set	Lg	CJ	1.90	8.40	1250.00	63.70	---	1313.70	**1530.00**
	Inst	Set	Sm	CJ	2.93	5.46	1330.00	98.20	---	1428.20	**1670.00**
104" W											
High quality workmanship	Inst	Set	Lg	CJ	3.33	4.80	2030.00	112.00	---	2142.00	**2490.00**
	Inst	Set	Sm	CJ	5.13	3.12	2170.00	172.00	---	2342.00	**2730.00**
Good quality workmanship	Inst	Set	Lg	CJ	2.67	6.00	1880.00	89.50	---	1969.50	**2290.00**
	Inst	Set	Sm	CJ	4.10	3.90	2010.00	137.00	---	2147.00	**2500.00**
Average quality workmanship	Inst	Set	Lg	CJ	2.22	7.20	1570.00	74.40	---	1644.40	**1910.00**
	Inst	Set	Sm	CJ	3.42	4.68	1670.00	115.00	---	1785.00	**2080.00**
112" W											
High quality workmanship	Inst	Set	Lg	CJ	3.33	4.80	2050.00	112.00	---	2162.00	**2510.00**
	Inst	Set	Sm	CJ	5.13	3.12	2180.00	172.00	---	2352.00	**2750.00**
Good quality workmanship	Inst	Set	Lg	CJ	2.67	6.00	1890.00	89.50	---	1979.50	**2300.00**
	Inst	Set	Sm	CJ	4.10	3.90	2020.00	137.00	---	2157.00	**2520.00**
Average quality workmanship	Inst	Set	Lg	CJ	2.22	7.20	1580.00	74.40	---	1654.40	**1920.00**
	Inst	Set	Sm	CJ	3.42	4.68	1680.00	115.00	---	1795.00	**2100.00**
72" H											
88" W											
High quality workmanship	Inst	Set	Lg	CJ	3.33	4.80	1890.00	112.00	---	2002.00	**2330.00**
	Inst	Set	Sm	CJ	5.13	3.12	2020.00	172.00	---	2192.00	**2560.00**
Good quality workmanship	Inst	Set	Lg	CJ	2.67	6.00	1750.00	89.50	---	1839.50	**2140.00**
	Inst	Set	Sm	CJ	4.10	3.90	1870.00	137.00	---	2007.00	**2340.00**
Average quality workmanship	Inst	Set	Lg	CJ	2.22	7.20	1460.00	74.40	---	1534.40	**1780.00**
	Inst	Set	Sm	CJ	3.42	4.68	1560.00	115.00	---	1675.00	**1950.00**
96" W											
High quality workmanship	Inst	Set	Lg	CJ	3.33	4.80	1910.00	112.00	---	2022.00	**2350.00**
	Inst	Set	Sm	CJ	5.13	3.12	2030.00	172.00	---	2202.00	**2580.00**
Good quality workmanship	Inst	Set	Lg	CJ	2.67	6.00	1760.00	89.50	---	1849.50	**2150.00**
	Inst	Set	Sm	CJ	4.10	3.90	1880.00	137.00	---	2017.00	**2350.00**
Average quality workmanship	Inst	Set	Lg	CJ	2.22	7.20	1470.00	74.40	---	1544.40	**1790.00**
	Inst	Set	Sm	CJ	3.42	4.68	1570.00	115.00	---	1685.00	**1960.00**
Material adjustments											
For glazed 1/2" insulated flankers,											
ADD	Inst	%	Lg	---	---	---	15.0	---	---	---	---
	Inst	%	Sm	---	---	---	15.0	---	---	---	---
For screen per flanker,											
ADD	Inst	Ea	Lg	---	---	---	7.50	---	---	7.50	**8.63**
	Inst	Ea	Sm	---	---	---	8.00	---	---	8.00	**9.20**

Description	Oper	Unit	Vol	Crew Size	Man-hours per Unit	Crew Output per Day	Avg Mat'l Unit Cost	Avg Labor Unit Cost	Avg Equip Unit Cost	Avg Total Unit Cost	Avg Price Incl O&P

Garden windows, unit extends out 13-1/4" from wall, bronze tempered glass in top panels of all units, wood shelves included

1 fixed lite
Single glazed
3'-0" x 3'-0" H

Description	Oper	Unit	Vol	Crew Size	Man-hours per Unit	Crew Output per Day	Avg Mat'l Unit Cost	Avg Labor Unit Cost	Avg Equip Unit Cost	Avg Total Unit Cost	Avg Price Incl O&P
High quality workmanship	Inst	Ea	Lg	CJ	4.44	3.60	626.00	149.00	---	775.00	**928.00**
	Inst	Ea	Sm	CJ	6.84	2.34	667.00	229.00	---	896.00	**1090.00**
Good quality workmanship	Inst	Ea	Lg	CJ	3.56	4.50	573.00	119.00	---	692.00	**826.00**
	Inst	Ea	Sm	CJ	5.46	2.93	611.00	183.00	---	794.00	**959.00**
Average quality workmanship	Inst	Ea	Lg	CJ	2.96	5.40	479.00	99.20	---	578.20	**689.00**
	Inst	Ea	Sm	CJ	4.56	3.51	510.00	153.00	---	663.00	**801.00**

3'-0" x 4'-0" H

Description	Oper	Unit	Vol	Crew Size	Man-hours per Unit	Crew Output per Day	Avg Mat'l Unit Cost	Avg Labor Unit Cost	Avg Equip Unit Cost	Avg Total Unit Cost	Avg Price Incl O&P
High quality workmanship	Inst	Ea	Lg	CJ	4.44	3.60	678.00	149.00	---	827.00	**988.00**
	Inst	Ea	Sm	CJ	6.84	2.34	723.00	229.00	---	952.00	**1150.00**
Good quality workmanship	Inst	Ea	Lg	CJ	3.56	4.50	623.00	119.00	---	742.00	**883.00**
	Inst	Ea	Sm	CJ	5.46	2.93	664.00	183.00	---	847.00	**1020.00**
Average quality workmanship	Inst	Ea	Lg	CJ	2.96	5.40	521.00	99.20	---	620.20	**737.00**
	Inst	Ea	Sm	CJ	4.56	3.51	555.00	153.00	---	708.00	**852.00**

4'-0" x 3'-0" H

Description	Oper	Unit	Vol	Crew Size	Man-hours per Unit	Crew Output per Day	Avg Mat'l Unit Cost	Avg Labor Unit Cost	Avg Equip Unit Cost	Avg Total Unit Cost	Avg Price Incl O&P
High quality workmanship	Inst	Ea	Lg	CJ	4.44	3.60	708.00	149.00	---	857.00	**1020.00**
	Inst	Ea	Sm	CJ	6.84	2.34	755.00	229.00	---	984.00	**1190.00**
Good quality workmanship	Inst	Ea	Lg	CJ	3.56	4.50	650.00	119.00	---	769.00	**914.00**
	Inst	Ea	Sm	CJ	5.46	2.93	693.00	183.00	---	876.00	**1050.00**
Average quality workmanship	Inst	Ea	Lg	CJ	2.96	5.40	542.00	99.20	---	641.20	**762.00**
	Inst	Ea	Sm	CJ	4.56	3.51	578.00	153.00	---	731.00	**878.00**

4'-0" x 4'-0" H

Description	Oper	Unit	Vol	Crew Size	Man-hours per Unit	Crew Output per Day	Avg Mat'l Unit Cost	Avg Labor Unit Cost	Avg Equip Unit Cost	Avg Total Unit Cost	Avg Price Incl O&P
High quality workmanship	Inst	Ea	Lg	CJ	5.00	3.20	726.00	168.00	---	894.00	**1070.00**
	Inst	Ea	Sm	CJ	7.69	2.08	774.00	258.00	---	1032.00	**1250.00**
Good quality workmanship	Inst	Ea	Lg	CJ	4.00	4.00	666.00	134.00	---	800.00	**954.00**
	Inst	Ea	Sm	CJ	6.15	2.60	710.00	206.00	---	916.00	**1110.00**
Average quality workmanship	Inst	Ea	Lg	CJ	3.33	4.80	555.00	112.00	---	667.00	**794.00**
	Inst	Ea	Sm	CJ	5.13	3.12	592.00	172.00	---	764.00	**921.00**

4'-0" x 5'-0" H

Description	Oper	Unit	Vol	Crew Size	Man-hours per Unit	Crew Output per Day	Avg Mat'l Unit Cost	Avg Labor Unit Cost	Avg Equip Unit Cost	Avg Total Unit Cost	Avg Price Incl O&P
High quality workmanship	Inst	Ea	Lg	CJ	5.71	2.80	779.00	191.00	---	970.00	**1160.00**
	Inst	Ea	Sm	CJ	8.79	1.82	830.00	295.00	---	1125.00	**1370.00**
Good quality workmanship	Inst	Ea	Lg	CJ	4.57	3.50	714.00	153.00	---	867.00	**1040.00**
	Inst	Ea	Sm	CJ	7.02	2.28	762.00	235.00	---	997.00	**1210.00**
Average quality workmanship	Inst	Ea	Lg	CJ	3.81	4.20	596.00	128.00	---	724.00	**864.00**
	Inst	Ea	Sm	CJ	5.86	2.73	635.00	196.00	---	831.00	**1010.00**

5'-0" x 3'-0" H

Description	Oper	Unit	Vol	Crew Size	Man-hours per Unit	Crew Output per Day	Avg Mat'l Unit Cost	Avg Labor Unit Cost	Avg Equip Unit Cost	Avg Total Unit Cost	Avg Price Incl O&P
High quality workmanship	Inst	Ea	Lg	CJ	5.00	3.20	723.00	168.00	---	891.00	**1070.00**
	Inst	Ea	Sm	CJ	7.69	2.08	771.00	258.00	---	1029.00	**1250.00**
Good quality workmanship	Inst	Ea	Lg	CJ	4.00	4.00	663.00	134.00	---	797.00	**950.00**
	Inst	Ea	Sm	CJ	6.15	2.60	707.00	206.00	---	913.00	**1100.00**
Average quality workmanship	Inst	Ea	Lg	CJ	3.33	4.80	554.00	112.00	---	666.00	**793.00**
	Inst	Ea	Sm	CJ	5.13	3.12	590.00	172.00	---	762.00	**920.00**

Description	Oper	Unit	Vol	Crew Size	Man-hours per Unit	Crew Output per Day	Avg Mat'l Unit Cost	Avg Labor Unit Cost	Avg Equip Unit Cost	Avg Total Unit Cost	Avg Price Incl O&P
5'-0" x 3'-8" H											
High quality workmanship	Inst	Ea	Lg	CJ	5.71	2.80	767.00	191.00	---	958.00	**1150.00**
	Inst	Ea	Sm	CJ	8.79	1.82	818.00	295.00	---	1113.00	**1350.00**
Good quality workmanship	Inst	Ea	Lg	CJ	4.57	3.50	704.00	153.00	---	857.00	**1020.00**
	Inst	Ea	Sm	CJ	7.02	2.28	750.00	235.00	---	985.00	**1190.00**
Average quality workmanship	Inst	Ea	Lg	CJ	3.81	4.20	587.00	128.00	---	715.00	**853.00**
	Inst	Ea	Sm	CJ	5.86	2.73	626.00	196.00	---	822.00	**994.00**
5'-0" x 4'-0" H											
High quality workmanship	Inst	Ea	Lg	CJ	5.71	2.80	779.00	191.00	---	970.00	**1160.00**
	Inst	Ea	Sm	CJ	8.79	1.82	830.00	295.00	---	1125.00	**1370.00**
Good quality workmanship	Inst	Ea	Lg	CJ	4.57	3.50	714.00	153.00	---	867.00	**1040.00**
	Inst	Ea	Sm	CJ	7.02	2.28	762.00	235.00	---	997.00	**1210.00**
Average quality workmanship	Inst	Ea	Lg	CJ	3.81	4.20	596.00	128.00	---	724.00	**864.00**
	Inst	Ea	Sm	CJ	5.86	2.73	635.00	196.00	---	831.00	**1010.00**
5'-0" x 5'-0" H											
High quality workmanship	Inst	Ea	Lg	CJ	6.67	2.40	848.00	224.00	---	1072.00	**1290.00**
	Inst	Ea	Sm	CJ	10.3	1.56	904.00	345.00	---	1249.00	**1520.00**
Good quality workmanship	Inst	Ea	Lg	CJ	5.33	3.00	777.00	179.00	---	956.00	**1140.00**
	Inst	Ea	Sm	CJ	8.21	1.95	829.00	275.00	---	1104.00	**1340.00**
Average quality workmanship	Inst	Ea	Lg	CJ	4.44	3.60	648.00	149.00	---	797.00	**953.00**
	Inst	Ea	Sm	CJ	6.84	2.34	691.00	229.00	---	920.00	**1120.00**
6'-0" x 3'-0" H											
High quality workmanship	Inst	Ea	Lg	CJ	5.71	2.80	773.00	191.00	---	964.00	**1160.00**
	Inst	Ea	Sm	CJ	8.79	1.82	824.00	295.00	---	1119.00	**1360.00**
Good quality workmanship	Inst	Ea	Lg	CJ	4.57	3.50	708.00	153.00	---	861.00	**1030.00**
	Inst	Ea	Sm	CJ	7.02	2.28	755.00	235.00	---	990.00	**1200.00**
Average quality workmanship	Inst	Ea	Lg	CJ	3.81	4.20	591.00	128.00	---	719.00	**858.00**
	Inst	Ea	Sm	CJ	5.86	2.73	630.00	196.00	---	826.00	**1000.00**
6'-0" x 3'-8" H											
High quality workmanship	Inst	Ea	Lg	CJ	6.15	2.60	807.00	206.00	---	1013.00	**1220.00**
	Inst	Ea	Sm	CJ	9.47	1.69	861.00	317.00	---	1178.00	**1430.00**
Good quality workmanship	Inst	Ea	Lg	CJ	5.00	3.20	741.00	168.00	---	909.00	**1090.00**
	Inst	Ea	Sm	CJ	7.69	2.08	790.00	258.00	---	1048.00	**1270.00**
Average quality workmanship	Inst	Ea	Lg	CJ	4.21	3.80	618.00	141.00	---	759.00	**908.00**
	Inst	Ea	Sm	CJ	6.48	2.47	659.00	217.00	---	876.00	**1060.00**
6'-0" x 4'-0" H											
High quality workmanship	Inst	Ea	Lg	CJ	6.67	2.40	842.00	224.00	---	1066.00	**1280.00**
	Inst	Ea	Sm	CJ	10.3	1.56	898.00	345.00	---	1243.00	**1520.00**
Good quality workmanship	Inst	Ea	Lg	CJ	5.33	3.00	771.00	179.00	---	950.00	**1140.00**
	Inst	Ea	Sm	CJ	8.21	1.95	822.00	275.00	---	1097.00	**1330.00**
Average quality workmanship	Inst	Ea	Lg	CJ	4.44	3.60	644.00	149.00	---	793.00	**948.00**
	Inst	Ea	Sm	CJ	6.84	2.34	686.00	229.00	---	915.00	**1110.00**

Description	Oper	Unit	Vol	Crew Size	Man-hours per Unit	Crew Output per Day	Avg Mat'l Unit Cost	Avg Labor Unit Cost	Avg Equip Unit Cost	Avg Total Unit Cost	Avg Price Incl O&P
Dual glazed											
3'-0" x 3'-0" H											
High quality workmanship	Inst	Ea	Lg	CJ	4.44	3.60	857.00	149.00	---	1006.00	**1190.00**
	Inst	Ea	Sm	CJ	6.84	2.34	914.00	229.00	---	1143.00	**1370.00**
Good quality workmanship	Inst	Ea	Lg	CJ	3.56	4.50	786.00	119.00	---	905.00	**1070.00**
	Inst	Ea	Sm	CJ	5.46	2.93	838.00	183.00	---	1021.00	**1220.00**
Average quality workmanship	Inst	Ea	Lg	CJ	2.96	5.40	656.00	99.20	---	755.20	**893.00**
	Inst	Ea	Sm	CJ	4.56	3.51	699.00	153.00	---	852.00	**1020.00**
3'-0" x 4'-0" H											
High quality workmanship	Inst	Ea	Lg	CJ	4.44	3.60	944.00	149.00	---	1093.00	**1290.00**
	Inst	Ea	Sm	CJ	6.84	2.34	1010.00	229.00	---	1239.00	**1480.00**
Good quality workmanship	Inst	Ea	Lg	CJ	3.56	4.50	866.00	119.00	---	985.00	**1160.00**
	Inst	Ea	Sm	CJ	5.46	2.93	923.00	183.00	---	1106.00	**1320.00**
Average quality workmanship	Inst	Ea	Lg	CJ	2.96	5.40	722.00	99.20	---	821.20	**969.00**
	Inst	Ea	Sm	CJ	4.56	3.51	770.00	153.00	---	923.00	**1100.00**
4'-0" x 3'-0" H											
High quality workmanship	Inst	Ea	Lg	CJ	4.44	3.60	935.00	149.00	---	1084.00	**1280.00**
	Inst	Ea	Sm	CJ	6.84	2.34	997.00	229.00	---	1226.00	**1470.00**
Good quality workmanship	Inst	Ea	Lg	CJ	3.56	4.50	858.00	119.00	---	977.00	**1150.00**
	Inst	Ea	Sm	CJ	5.46	2.93	915.00	183.00	---	1098.00	**1310.00**
Average quality workmanship	Inst	Ea	Lg	CJ	2.96	5.40	716.00	99.20	---	815.20	**962.00**
	Inst	Ea	Sm	CJ	4.56	3.51	763.00	153.00	---	916.00	**1090.00**
4'-0" x 4'-0" H											
High quality workmanship	Inst	Ea	Lg	CJ	5.00	3.20	1010.00	168.00	---	1178.00	**1400.00**
	Inst	Ea	Sm	CJ	7.69	2.08	1080.00	258.00	---	1338.00	**1600.00**
Good quality workmanship	Inst	Ea	Lg	CJ	4.00	4.00	930.00	134.00	---	1064.00	**1260.00**
	Inst	Ea	Sm	CJ	6.15	2.60	992.00	206.00	---	1198.00	**1430.00**
Average quality workmanship	Inst	Ea	Lg	CJ	3.33	4.80	776.00	112.00	---	888.00	**1050.00**
	Inst	Ea	Sm	CJ	5.13	3.12	827.00	172.00	---	999.00	**1190.00**
4'-0" x 5'-0" H											
High quality workmanship	Inst	Ea	Lg	CJ	5.71	2.80	1110.00	191.00	---	1301.00	**1550.00**
	Inst	Ea	Sm	CJ	8.79	1.82	1190.00	295.00	---	1485.00	**1780.00**
Good quality workmanship	Inst	Ea	Lg	CJ	4.57	3.50	1020.00	153.00	---	1173.00	**1390.00**
	Inst	Ea	Sm	CJ	7.02	2.28	1090.00	235.00	---	1325.00	**1580.00**
Average quality workmanship	Inst	Ea	Lg	CJ	3.81	4.20	852.00	128.00	---	980.00	**1160.00**
	Inst	Ea	Sm	CJ	5.86	2.73	909.00	196.00	---	1105.00	**1320.00**
5'-0" x 3'-0" H											
High quality workmanship	Inst	Ea	Lg	CJ	5.00	3.20	1010.00	168.00	---	1178.00	**1390.00**
	Inst	Ea	Sm	CJ	7.69	2.08	1070.00	258.00	---	1328.00	**1590.00**
Good quality workmanship	Inst	Ea	Lg	CJ	4.00	4.00	921.00	134.00	---	1055.00	**1250.00**
	Inst	Ea	Sm	CJ	6.15	2.60	982.00	206.00	---	1188.00	**1420.00**
Average quality workmanship	Inst	Ea	Lg	CJ	3.33	4.80	768.00	112.00	---	880.00	**1040.00**
	Inst	Ea	Sm	CJ	5.13	3.12	819.00	172.00	---	991.00	**1180.00**

Description	Oper	Unit	Vol	Crew Size	Man-hours per Unit	Crew Output per Day	Avg Mat'l Unit Cost	Avg Labor Unit Cost	Avg Equip Unit Cost	Avg Total Unit Cost	Avg Price Incl O&P
5'-0" x 3'-8" H											
High quality workmanship	Inst	Ea	Lg	CJ	5.71	2.80	1070.00	191.00	---	1261.00	**1500.00**
	Inst	Ea	Sm	CJ	8.79	1.82	1140.00	295.00	---	1435.00	**1730.00**
Good quality workmanship	Inst	Ea	Lg	CJ	4.57	3.50	984.00	153.00	---	1137.00	**1350.00**
	Inst	Ea	Sm	CJ	7.02	2.28	1050.00	235.00	---	1285.00	**1540.00**
Average quality workmanship	Inst	Ea	Lg	CJ	3.81	4.20	821.00	128.00	---	949.00	**1120.00**
	Inst	Ea	Sm	CJ	5.86	2.73	875.00	196.00	---	1071.00	**1280.00**
5'-0" x 4'-0" H											
High quality workmanship	Inst	Ea	Lg	CJ	5.71	2.80	1100.00	191.00	---	1291.00	**1530.00**
	Inst	Ea	Sm	CJ	8.79	1.82	1170.00	295.00	---	1465.00	**1760.00**
Good quality workmanship	Inst	Ea	Lg	CJ	4.57	3.50	1010.00	153.00	---	1163.00	**1370.00**
	Inst	Ea	Sm	CJ	7.02	2.28	1070.00	235.00	---	1305.00	**1560.00**
Average quality workmanship	Inst	Ea	Lg	CJ	3.81	4.20	837.00	128.00	---	965.00	**1140.00**
	Inst	Ea	Sm	CJ	5.86	2.73	893.00	196.00	---	1089.00	**1300.00**
5'-0" x 5'-0" H											
High quality workmanship	Inst	Ea	Lg	CJ	6.67	2.40	1220.00	224.00	---	1444.00	**1710.00**
	Inst	Ea	Sm	CJ	10.3	1.56	1300.00	345.00	---	1645.00	**1980.00**
Good quality workmanship	Inst	Ea	Lg	CJ	5.33	3.00	1120.00	179.00	---	1299.00	**1540.00**
	Inst	Ea	Sm	CJ	8.21	1.95	1190.00	275.00	---	1465.00	**1760.00**
Average quality workmanship	Inst	Ea	Lg	CJ	4.44	3.60	932.00	149.00	---	1081.00	**1280.00**
	Inst	Ea	Sm	CJ	6.84	2.34	994.00	229.00	---	1223.00	**1460.00**
6'-0" x 3'-0" H											
High quality workmanship	Inst	Ea	Lg	CJ	5.71	2.80	1100.00	191.00	---	1291.00	**1530.00**
	Inst	Ea	Sm	CJ	8.79	1.82	1170.00	295.00	---	1465.00	**1760.00**
Good quality workmanship	Inst	Ea	Lg	CJ	4.57	3.50	1010.00	153.00	---	1163.00	**1370.00**
	Inst	Ea	Sm	CJ	7.02	2.28	1070.00	235.00	---	1305.00	**1560.00**
Average quality workmanship	Inst	Ea	Lg	CJ	3.81	4.20	837.00	128.00	---	965.00	**1140.00**
	Inst	Ea	Sm	CJ	5.86	2.73	893.00	196.00	---	1089.00	**1300.00**
6'-0" x 3'-8" H											
High quality workmanship	Inst	Ea	Lg	CJ	6.15	2.60	1160.00	206.00	---	1366.00	**1620.00**
	Inst	Ea	Sm	CJ	9.47	1.69	1230.00	317.00	---	1547.00	**1860.00**
Good quality workmanship	Inst	Ea	Lg	CJ	5.00	3.20	1060.00	168.00	---	1228.00	**1450.00**
	Inst	Ea	Sm	CJ	7.69	2.08	1130.00	258.00	---	1388.00	**1660.00**
Average quality workmanship	Inst	Ea	Lg	CJ	4.21	3.80	884.00	141.00	---	1025.00	**1210.00**
	Inst	Ea	Sm	CJ	6.48	2.47	942.00	217.00	---	1159.00	**1390.00**
6'-0" x 4'-0" H											
High quality workmanship	Inst	Ea	Lg	CJ	6.67	2.40	1220.00	224.00	---	1444.00	**1710.00**
	Inst	Ea	Sm	CJ	10.3	1.56	1300.00	345.00	---	1645.00	**1970.00**
Good quality workmanship	Inst	Ea	Lg	CJ	5.33	3.00	1110.00	179.00	---	1289.00	**1530.00**
	Inst	Ea	Sm	CJ	8.21	1.95	1190.00	275.00	---	1465.00	**1750.00**
Average quality workmanship	Inst	Ea	Lg	CJ	4.44	3.60	929.00	149.00	---	1078.00	**1280.00**
	Inst	Ea	Sm	CJ	6.84	2.34	990.00	229.00	---	1219.00	**1460.00**

Description	Oper	Unit	Vol	Crew Size	Man-hours per Unit	Crew Output per Day	Avg Mat'l Unit Cost	Avg Labor Unit Cost	Avg Equip Unit Cost	Avg Total Unit Cost	Avg Price Incl O&P

1 fixed lite, 1 sliding lite

Single glazed

3'-0" x 3'-0" H

Description	Oper	Unit	Vol	Crew Size	Man-hours per Unit	Crew Output per Day	Avg Mat'l Unit Cost	Avg Labor Unit Cost	Avg Equip Unit Cost	Avg Total Unit Cost	Avg Price Incl O&P
High quality workmanship	Inst	Ea	Lg	CJ	4.44	3.60	798.00	149.00	---	947.00	**1130.00**
	Inst	Ea	Sm	CJ	6.84	2.34	851.00	229.00	---	1080.00	**1300.00**
Good quality workmanship	Inst	Ea	Lg	CJ	3.56	4.50	732.00	119.00	---	851.00	**1010.00**
	Inst	Ea	Sm	CJ	5.46	2.93	781.00	183.00	---	964.00	**1150.00**
Average quality workmanship	Inst	Ea	Lg	CJ	2.96	5.40	611.00	99.20	---	710.20	**841.00**
	Inst	Ea	Sm	CJ	4.56	3.51	651.00	153.00	---	804.00	**963.00**

3'-0" x 4'-0" H

Description	Oper	Unit	Vol	Crew Size	Man-hours per Unit	Crew Output per Day	Avg Mat'l Unit Cost	Avg Labor Unit Cost	Avg Equip Unit Cost	Avg Total Unit Cost	Avg Price Incl O&P
High quality workmanship	Inst	Ea	Lg	CJ	4.44	3.60	878.00	149.00	---	1027.00	**1220.00**
	Inst	Ea	Sm	CJ	6.84	2.34	936.00	229.00	---	1165.00	**1400.00**
Good quality workmanship	Inst	Ea	Lg	CJ	3.56	4.50	804.00	119.00	---	923.00	**1090.00**
	Inst	Ea	Sm	CJ	5.46	2.93	858.00	183.00	---	1041.00	**1240.00**
Average quality workmanship	Inst	Ea	Lg	CJ	2.96	5.40	671.00	99.20	---	770.20	**910.00**
	Inst	Ea	Sm	CJ	4.56	3.51	715.00	153.00	---	868.00	**1040.00**

4'-0" x 3'-0" H

Description	Oper	Unit	Vol	Crew Size	Man-hours per Unit	Crew Output per Day	Avg Mat'l Unit Cost	Avg Labor Unit Cost	Avg Equip Unit Cost	Avg Total Unit Cost	Avg Price Incl O&P
High quality workmanship	Inst	Ea	Lg	CJ	4.44	3.60	858.00	149.00	---	1007.00	**1190.00**
	Inst	Ea	Sm	CJ	6.84	2.34	915.00	229.00	---	1144.00	**1370.00**
Good quality workmanship	Inst	Ea	Lg	CJ	3.56	4.50	786.00	119.00	---	905.00	**1070.00**
	Inst	Ea	Sm	CJ	5.46	2.93	838.00	183.00	---	1021.00	**1220.00**
Average quality workmanship	Inst	Ea	Lg	CJ	2.96	5.40	656.00	99.20	---	755.20	**893.00**
	Inst	Ea	Sm	CJ	4.56	3.51	699.00	153.00	---	852.00	**1020.00**

4'-0" x 4'-0" H

Description	Oper	Unit	Vol	Crew Size	Man-hours per Unit	Crew Output per Day	Avg Mat'l Unit Cost	Avg Labor Unit Cost	Avg Equip Unit Cost	Avg Total Unit Cost	Avg Price Incl O&P
High quality workmanship	Inst	Ea	Lg	CJ	5.00	3.20	929.00	168.00	---	1097.00	**1300.00**
	Inst	Ea	Sm	CJ	7.69	2.08	990.00	258.00	---	1248.00	**1500.00**
Good quality workmanship	Inst	Ea	Lg	CJ	4.00	4.00	854.00	134.00	---	988.00	**1170.00**
	Inst	Ea	Sm	CJ	6.15	2.60	910.00	206.00	---	1116.00	**1340.00**
Average quality workmanship	Inst	Ea	Lg	CJ	3.33	4.80	711.00	112.00	---	823.00	**974.00**
	Inst	Ea	Sm	CJ	5.13	3.12	758.00	172.00	---	930.00	**1110.00**

4'-0" x 5'-0" H

Description	Oper	Unit	Vol	Crew Size	Man-hours per Unit	Crew Output per Day	Avg Mat'l Unit Cost	Avg Labor Unit Cost	Avg Equip Unit Cost	Avg Total Unit Cost	Avg Price Incl O&P
High quality workmanship	Inst	Ea	Lg	CJ	5.71	2.80	1020.00	191.00	---	1211.00	**1440.00**
	Inst	Ea	Sm	CJ	8.79	1.82	1090.00	295.00	---	1385.00	**1670.00**
Good quality workmanship	Inst	Ea	Lg	CJ	4.57	3.50	938.00	153.00	---	1091.00	**1290.00**
	Inst	Ea	Sm	CJ	7.02	2.28	1000.00	235.00	---	1235.00	**1480.00**
Average quality workmanship	Inst	Ea	Lg	CJ	3.81	4.20	782.00	128.00	---	910.00	**1080.00**
	Inst	Ea	Sm	CJ	5.86	2.73	834.00	196.00	---	1030.00	**1230.00**

5'-0" x 3'-0" H

Description	Oper	Unit	Vol	Crew Size	Man-hours per Unit	Crew Output per Day	Avg Mat'l Unit Cost	Avg Labor Unit Cost	Avg Equip Unit Cost	Avg Total Unit Cost	Avg Price Incl O&P
High quality workmanship	Inst	Ea	Lg	CJ	5.00	3.20	917.00	168.00	---	1085.00	**1290.00**
	Inst	Ea	Sm	CJ	7.69	2.08	978.00	258.00	---	1236.00	**1480.00**
Good quality workmanship	Inst	Ea	Lg	CJ	4.00	4.00	840.00	134.00	---	974.00	**1150.00**
	Inst	Ea	Sm	CJ	6.15	2.60	896.00	206.00	---	1102.00	**1320.00**
Average quality workmanship	Inst	Ea	Lg	CJ	3.33	4.80	701.00	112.00	---	813.00	**962.00**
	Inst	Ea	Sm	CJ	5.13	3.12	747.00	172.00	---	919.00	**1100.00**

Description	Oper	Unit	Vol	Crew Size	Man-hours per Unit	Crew Output per Day	Avg Mat'l Unit Cost	Avg Labor Unit Cost	Avg Equip Unit Cost	Avg Total Unit Cost	Avg Price Incl O&P
5'-0" x 3'-8" H											
High quality workmanship	Inst	Ea	Lg	CJ	5.71	2.80	983.00	191.00	---	1174.00	**1400.00**
	Inst	Ea	Sm	CJ	8.79	1.82	1050.00	295.00	---	1345.00	**1620.00**
Good quality workmanship	Inst	Ea	Lg	CJ	4.57	3.50	902.00	153.00	---	1055.00	**1250.00**
	Inst	Ea	Sm	CJ	7.02	2.28	962.00	235.00	---	1197.00	**1440.00**
Average quality workmanship	Inst	Ea	Lg	CJ	3.81	4.20	752.00	128.00	---	880.00	**1040.00**
	Inst	Ea	Sm	CJ	5.86	2.73	802.00	196.00	---	998.00	**1200.00**
5'-0" x 4'-0" H											
High quality workmanship	Inst	Ea	Lg	CJ	5.71	2.80	993.00	191.00	---	1184.00	**1410.00**
	Inst	Ea	Sm	CJ	8.79	1.82	1060.00	295.00	---	1355.00	**1630.00**
Good quality workmanship	Inst	Ea	Lg	CJ	4.57	3.50	911.00	153.00	---	1064.00	**1260.00**
	Inst	Ea	Sm	CJ	7.02	2.28	971.00	235.00	---	1206.00	**1450.00**
Average quality workmanship	Inst	Ea	Lg	CJ	3.81	4.20	759.00	128.00	---	887.00	**1050.00**
	Inst	Ea	Sm	CJ	5.86	2.73	810.00	196.00	---	1006.00	**1210.00**
5'-0" x 5'-0" H											
High quality workmanship	Inst	Ea	Lg	CJ	6.67	2.40	1120.00	224.00	---	1344.00	**1600.00**
	Inst	Ea	Sm	CJ	10.3	1.56	1190.00	345.00	---	1535.00	**1850.00**
Good quality workmanship	Inst	Ea	Lg	CJ	5.33	3.00	1020.00	179.00	---	1199.00	**1430.00**
	Inst	Ea	Sm	CJ	8.21	1.95	1090.00	275.00	---	1365.00	**1640.00**
Average quality workmanship	Inst	Ea	Lg	CJ	4.44	3.60	828.00	149.00	---	977.00	**1160.00**
	Inst	Ea	Sm	CJ	6.84	2.34	883.00	229.00	---	1112.00	**1340.00**
6'-0" x 3'-0" H											
High quality workmanship	Inst	Ea	Lg	CJ	5.71	2.80	963.00	191.00	---	1154.00	**1380.00**
	Inst	Ea	Sm	CJ	8.79	1.82	1030.00	295.00	---	1325.00	**1590.00**
Good quality workmanship	Inst	Ea	Lg	CJ	4.57	3.50	884.00	153.00	---	1037.00	**1230.00**
	Inst	Ea	Sm	CJ	7.02	2.28	942.00	235.00	---	1177.00	**1410.00**
Average quality workmanship	Inst	Ea	Lg	CJ	3.81	4.20	737.00	128.00	---	865.00	**1030.00**
	Inst	Ea	Sm	CJ	5.86	2.73	786.00	196.00	---	982.00	**1180.00**
6'-0" x 3'-8" H											
High quality workmanship	Inst	Ea	Lg	CJ	6.67	2.40	1020.00	224.00	---	1244.00	**1490.00**
	Inst	Ea	Sm	CJ	10.3	1.56	1090.00	345.00	---	1435.00	**1740.00**
Good quality workmanship	Inst	Ea	Lg	CJ	5.33	3.00	938.00	179.00	---	1117.00	**1330.00**
	Inst	Ea	Sm	CJ	8.21	1.95	1000.00	275.00	---	1275.00	**1540.00**
Average quality workmanship	Inst	Ea	Lg	CJ	4.44	3.60	782.00	149.00	---	931.00	**1110.00**
	Inst	Ea	Sm	CJ	6.84	2.34	834.00	229.00	---	1063.00	**1280.00**
6'-0" x 4'-0" H											
High quality workmanship	Inst	Ea	Lg	CJ	6.67	2.40	1050.00	224.00	---	1274.00	**1520.00**
	Inst	Ea	Sm	CJ	10.3	1.56	1120.00	345.00	---	1465.00	**1770.00**
Good quality workmanship	Inst	Ea	Lg	CJ	5.33	3.00	960.00	179.00	---	1139.00	**1350.00**
	Inst	Ea	Sm	CJ	8.21	1.95	1020.00	275.00	---	1295.00	**1560.00**
Average quality workmanship	Inst	Ea	Lg	CJ	4.44	3.60	801.00	149.00	---	950.00	**1130.00**
	Inst	Ea	Sm	CJ	6.84	2.34	854.00	229.00	---	1083.00	**1300.00**

Wiring. See Electrical, page 156

Index

Practical References for Builders

Renovating & Restyling Older Homes

Any builder can turn a run-down old house into a showcase of perfection — if the customer has unlimited funds to spend. Unfortunately, most customers are on a tight budget. They usually want more improvements than they can afford — and they expect you to deliver. This book shows how to add economical improvements that can increase the property value by two, five or even ten times the cost of the remodel. Sound impossible? Here you'll find the secrets of a builder who has been putting these techniques to work on Victorian and Craftsman-style houses for twenty years. You'll see what to repair, what to replace and what to leave, so you can remodel or restyle older homes for the least amount of money and the greatest increase in value. **416 pages, 8½ x 11, $33.50**

CD Estimator

CD Estimator (for *Windows*™) puts at your fingertips over 135,000 construction costs for new construction, remodeling, renovation & insurance repair, home improvement, framing & finish carpentry, electrical, concrete & masonry, painting, and plumbing & HVAC. Quarterly cost updates are available at no charge on the Internet. You'll also have the National Estimator program — a stand-alone estimating program for *Windows*™ that Remodeling magazine called a "computer wiz," and *Job Cost Wizard*, a program that lets you export your estimates to QuickBooks Pro for actual job costing. A 60-minute interactive video teaches you how to use this CD-ROM to estimate construction costs. And to top it off, to help you create professional-looking estimates, the disk includes over 40 construction estimating and bidding forms. **CD Estimator is $133.50**

National Renovation & Insurance Repair Estimator

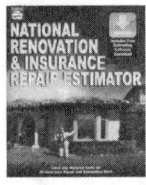

Current prices in dollars and cents for hard-to-find items needed on most insurance, repair, remodeling, and renovation jobs. All price items include labor, material, and equipment breakouts, plus spe- cial charts that tell you exactly how these costs are calculated. Includes a free download of an electron-ic version of the book with *National Estimator*, a stand-alone *Windows*™ estimating program. An interactive multimedia video that shows how to use the software to compile renovation and repair cost estimates is free at www.craftsman-book.com. **488 pages, 8½ x 11, $89.50. Revised annually**
Also available as an eBook (PDF), $44.75 at www.craftsman-book.com

Markup & Profit: A Contractor's Guide, Revisited

In order to succeed in a construction business, you have to be able to price your jobs to cover all labor, material and overhead expenses, and make a decent profit. But calculating markup is only part of the picture. If you're going to beat the odds and stay in business – profitably, you also need to know how to write good contracts, manage your crews, work with subcontractors and collect on your work. This book covers the business basics of running a construction company, whether you're a general or specialty contractor working in remodeling, new construction or commercial work. The principles outlined here apply to all construction-related businesses. You'll find tried and tested formulas to guarantee profits, with step-by-step instructions and easy-to-follow examples to help you learn how to operate your business successfully. Includes a link to free downloads of blank forms and checklists used in this book. **336 pages, 8½ x 11, $52.50**
Also available as an eBook (ePub, mobi for Kindle), $39.95 at www.craftsman-book.com

Construction Forms for Contractors

This practical guide contains 78 practical forms, letters and checklists, guaranteed to help you streamline your office, organize your jobsites, gather and organize records and documents, keep a handle on your subs, reduce estimating errors, administer change orders and lien issues, monitor crew productivity, track your equipment use, and more. Includes accounting forms, change order forms, forms for customers, estimating forms, field work forms, HR forms, lien forms, office forms, bids and proposals, subcontracts, and more. All are also on the CD-ROM included, in Excel spreadsheets, as formatted Rich Text that you can fill out on your computer, and as PDFs. **360 pages, 8½ x 11, $48.50**
eBook (PDF) also available; $24.25 at www.craftsman-book.com

Paper Contracting: The How-To of Construction Management Contracting

Risk, and the headaches that go with it, have always been a major part of any construction project — risk of loss, negative cash flow, construction claims, regulations, excessive changes, disputes, slow pay — sometimes you'll make money, and often you won't. But many contractors today are avoiding almost all of that risk by working under a construction management contract, where they are simply a paid consultant to the owner, running the job, but leaving him the risk. This manual is the how-to of construction management contracting. You'll learn how the process works, how to get started as a CM contractor, what the job entails, how to deal with the issues that come up, when to step back, and how to get the job completed on time and on budget. Includes a link to free downloads of CM contracts legal in each state. **272 pages, 8½ x 11, $55.50**
eBook (PDF) also available; $27.75 at www.craftsman-book.com

National Appraisal Estimator

An Online Appraisal Estimating Service. Produce credible single-family residence appraisals – in as little as five minutes. A smart resource for appraisers using the cost approach. Reports consider all significant cost variables and both physical and functional depreciation. For more information, visit
www.craftsman-book.com/national-appraisal-estimator-online-software

Insurance Replacement Estimator

Insurance underwriters demand detailed, accurate valuation data. There's no better authority on replacement cost for single-family homes than the *Insurance Replacement Estimator*. In minutes you get an insurance-to-value report showing the cost of re-construction based on your specification. You can generate and save unlimited reports. For more details, visit
www.craftsman-book.com/insurance-replacement-estimator-online-software

National Home Improvement Estimator

Current labor and material prices for home improvement projects. Provides manhours for each job, recommended crew size, and the labor cost for removal and installation work. Material prices are current, with location adjustment factors and free monthly updates on the Web. Gives step-by-step instructions for the work, with helpful diagrams, and home improvement shortcuts and tips from experts. Includes a free download of an electronic version of the book, and *National Estimator*, a stand-alone *Windows*™ estimating program. An interactive multimedia tutorial that shows how to use the software to compile home improvement cost estimates is free at www.craftsman-book.com. **568 pages, 8½ x 11, $88.75. Revised annually**
Also available as an eBook (PDF), $44.38 at www.craftsman-book.com

Construction Contract Writer

Relying on a "one-size-fits-all" construction contract to fit your jobs can be dangerous — almost as dangerous as a handshake agreement. *Construction Contract Writer* lets you draft a con-tract in minutes that precisely fits your needs and the particular job, and meets state and federal requirements. You answer a series of questions — like an interview – to construct a legal contract for each project you take on. Anticipate where disputes could arise and settle them in the contract before they happen. Include the warranty protection you intend, the payment schedule, and create subcontracts from the prime contract by just clicking a box. Includes a feedback button to an attorney on the Craftsman staff to help should you need it — *No extra charge*. **$149.95.** Download *Construction Contract Writer* at http://www.constructioncontractwriter.com

Contractor's Guide to *QuickBooks* 2015

QuickBooks 2015 has many new features that simplify a building contractor's bookkeeping work. You'll wonder how you managed without them. To help you make the most of these new features, or to make getting set up with *QuickBooks* almost painless, this user-friendly manual walks you through *QuickBooks'* detailed setup procedure and explains step-by-step how to create a first-rate accounting system. You'll learn in days, rather than weeks, how to use *QuickBooks* to get your contracting business organized, with simple, fast accounting procedures. But setting up *QuickBooks* from scratch can be time-consuming. On the free download included with purchase of the book you'll find a *QuickBooks* file preconfigured for a construction company. Open it, enter your company's data, add info on your suppliers, subs and customers, and you're up and running. The setup's done for you. **280 pages, 8½ x 11, $68.50**

See checklist for other available editions.

eBook (PDF) also available; **$34.25** at www.craftsman-book.com
eBooks also available for **2007, 2008, 2009, 2010 and 2012**

Profits in Buying & Renovating Homes

Step-by-step instructions for selecting, repairing, improving, and selling highly profitable "fixer-uppers." Shows which price ranges offer the highest profit-to-investment ratios, which neighborhoods offer the best return, practical directions for repairs, and tips on dealing with buyers, sellers, and real estate agents. Shows you how to determine your profit before you buy, what "bargains" to avoid, and how to make simple, profitable, inexpensive upgrades. **304 pages, 8½ x 11, $24.75**

Craftsman eLibrary

Craftsman's eLibrary license gives you immediate access to 60+ PDF eBooks in our bookstore for 12 full months!
You pay only one low price. $129.99.
Visit www.craftsman-book.com **for more details.**

Insurance Restoration Contracting: Startup to Success

Insurance restoration — the repair of buildings damaged by water, fire, smoke, storms, vandalism and other disasters — is an exciting field of construction that provides lucrative work that's immune to economic downturns. And, with insurance companies funding the repairs, your payment is virtually guaranteed. But this type of work requires special knowledge and equipment, and that's what you'll learn about in this book. It covers fire repairs and smoke damage, water losses and specialized drying methods, mold remediation, content restoration, even damage to mobile and manufactured homes. You'll also find information on equipment needs, training classes, estimating books and software, and how restoration leads to lucrative remodeling jobs. It covers all you need to know to start and succeed as the restoration contractor that both homeowners and insurance companies call on first for the best jobs. **640 pages, 8½ x 11, $69.00**

eBook (PDF) also available; **$34.50** at www.craftsman-book.com

Home Building Mistakes & Fixes

This is an encyclopedia of practical fixes for real-world home building and repair problems. There's never an end to "surprises" when you're in the business of building and fixing homes, yet there's little published on how to deal with construction that went wrong — where out-of-square or non-standard or jerry-rigged turns what should be a simple job into a nightmare. This manual describes jaw-dropping building mistakes that actually occurred, from disastrous misunderstandings over property lines, through basement floors leveled with an out-of-level instrument, to a house collapse when a siding crew removed the old siding. You'll learn the pitfalls the painless way, and real-world working solutions for the problems every contractor finds in a home building or repair jobsite. Includes dozens of those "surprises" and the author's step-by-step, clearly illustrated tips, tricks and workarounds for dealing with them.
384 pages, 8½ x 11, $52.50

eBook (PDF) also available; **$26.25** at www.craftsman-book.com

Contractor's Survival Manual Revised

The "real skinny" on the down-and-dirty survival skills that no one likes to talk about — unique, unconventional ways to get through a debt crisis: what to do when the bills can't be paid, finding money and buying time, conserving income, transferring debt, setting payment priorities, cash float techniques, dealing with judgments and liens, and laying the foundation for recovery. Here you'll find out how to survive a downturn and the key things you can do to pave the road to success. Have this book as your insurance policy; when hard times come to your business it will be your guide. **336 pages, 8½ x 11, $38.00**

eBook (PDF) also available; **$19.00** at www.craftsman-book.com

National Construction Estimator

Current building costs for residential, commercial, and industrial construction. Estimated prices for every common building material. Provides manhours, recommended crew, and gives the labor cost for installation. Includes a free download of an electronic version of the book with *National Estimator*, a stand-alone *Windows*™ estimating program. An interactive multimedia video that shows how to use the software to compile construction cost estimates is free at www.craftsman-book.com.
672 pages, 8½ x 11, $87.50. Revised annually

Also available as an eBook (PDF), **$43.75** at www.craftsman-book.com

Building Code Compliance for Contractors & Inspectors

An answer book for both contractors and building inspectors, this manual explains what it takes to pass inspections under the 2009 *International Residential Code*. It includes a code checklist for every trade, covering some of the most common reasons why inspectors reject residential work – footings, foundations, slabs, framing, sheathing, plumbing, electrical, HVAC, energy conservation and final inspection. The requirement for each item on the checklist is explained, and the code section cited so you can look it up or show it to the inspector. Knowing in advance what the inspector wants to see gives you an (almost unfair) advantage. To pass inspection, do your own pre-inspection before the inspector arrives. If your work requires getting permits and passing inspections, put this manual to work on your next job. If you're considering a career in code enforcement, this can be your guidebook. **8½ x 11, 232 pages, $32.50**

eBook (PDF) also available; **$16.25** at www.craftsman-book.com

Estimating Home Building Costs, Revised

Estimate every phase of residential construction from site costs to the profit margin you include in your bid. Shows how to keep track of manhours and make accurate labor cost estimates for site clearing and excavation, footings, foundations, framing and sheathing finishes, electrical, plumbing, and more. Provides and explains sample cost estimate worksheets with complete instructions for each job phase. This practical guide to estimating home construction costs has been updated with digital *Excel* estimating forms and worksheets that ensure accurate and complete estimates for your residential projects. Enter your project information on the worksheets and *Excel* automatically totals each material and labor cost from every stage of construction to a final cost estimate worksheet. Load the enclosed CD-ROM into your computer and create your own estimate as you follow along with the step-by-step techniques in this book.
336 pages, 8½ x 11, $38.00

eBook (PDF) also available; **$19.00** at www.craftsman-book.com

Home Inspection Handbook

Every area you need to check in a home inspection – especially in older homes. Twenty complete inspection checklists: building site, foundation and basement, structural, bathrooms, chimneys and flues, ceilings, interior & exterior finishes, electrical, plumbing, HVAC, insects, vermin and decay, and more. Also includes information on starting and running your own home inspection business. **324 pages, 5½ x 8½, $29.95**

Builder's Guide to Room Additions

How to tackle problems that are unique to additions, such as requirements for basement conversions, reinforcing ceiling joists for second-story con-versions, handling problems in attic conversions, what's required for foot- ings, foundations, and slabs, how to design the best bathroom for the space, and much more. Besides actual construction, you'll even find help in designing, planning, and estimating your room addition jobs. **352 pages, 8½ x 11, $34.95**

Construction Spanish

Carry in your pocket over 1000 words and terms and 15 commonly-used phrases in both English to Spanish and Spanish to English for job use on residential, commercial and heavy commercial projects. If you want an inexpensive English-Spanish dictionary that fits in your shirt pocket, you should have a copy of this book. **120 pages, 3½ x 5, $6.00**

Drafting House Plans

Here you'll find step-by-step instructions for drawing a complete set of house plans for a one-story house, an addition to an existing house, or a remodeling project. This book shows how to visualize spatial relationships, use architectural scales and symbols, sketch preliminary drawings, develop detailed floor plans and exterior elevations, and prepare a final plot plan. It even includes code-approved joist and rafter spans and how to make sure that drawings meet code requirements. **188 pages, 8½ x 11, $34.95**

How to Succeed With Your Own Construction Business

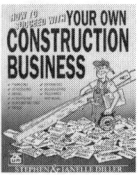

Everything you need to start your own construction business: setting up the paperwork, finding the jobs, advertising, using contracts, dealing with lenders, estimating, scheduling, finding and keeping good employees, keeping the books, and coping with success. If you're considering starting your own construction business, all the knowledge, tips, and blank forms you need are here. **336 pages, 8½ x 11, $28.50**

eBook (PDF) also available, **$14.25** at www.craftsman-book.com

Rough Framing Carpentry

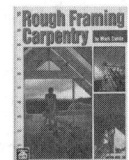

If you'd like to make good money working outdoors as a framer, this is the book for you. Here you'll find shortcuts to laying out studs; speed cutting blocks, trimmers and plates by eye; quickly building and blocking rake walls; installing ceiling backing, ceiling joists, and truss joists; cutting and assembling hip trusses and California fills; arches and drop ceilings — all with production line procedures that save you time and help you make more money. Over 100 on-the-job photos of how to do it right and what can go wrong. **304 pages, 8½ x 11, $26.50**

Download all of Craftsman's most popular costbooks for one low price with the Craftsman Site License. www.craftsmansitelicense.com

---

Craftsman Book Company
6058 Corte del Cedro
Carlsbad, CA 92011

☎ **Call me.**
1-800-829-8123
Fax (760) 438-0398

Name _____

e-mail address (for order tracking and special offers) _____

Company _____

Address _____

City/State/Zip _____ ○ This is a residence

Total enclosed _____ (In California add 7.5% tax)

Free Media Mail shipping, within the US when your check covers your order in full.

In A Hurry?
We accept phone orders charged to your
○ Visa, ○ MasterCard, ○ Discover or ○ American Express

Card _____

Exp. date _____ CVV# _____ Initials _____

Order online http://www.craftsman-book.com
Free on the Internet! Download any of Craftsman's estimating costbooks for a 30-day free trial! www.craftsman-book.com

Tax Deductible: Treasury regulations make these references tax deductible when used in your work. Save the canceled check or charge card statement as your receipt.

10-Day Money Back Guarantee

○ 34.95 Builder's Guide to Room Additions
○ 32.50 Building Code Compliance for Contractors & Inspectors
○ 133.50 CD Estimator
○ 48.50 Construction Forms for Contractors
○ 6.00 Construction Spanish
○ 68.50 Contractor's Guide to *QuickBooks* 2015
○ 57.00 Contractor's Guide to *QuickBooks Pro* 2010
○ 56.50 Contractor's Guide to *QuickBooks Pro* 2009
○ 54.75 Contractor's Guide to *QuickBooks Pro* 2008
○ 53.00 Contractor's Guide to *QuickBooks Pro* 2007
○ 49.75 Contractor's Guide to *QuickBooks Pro* 2005
○ 48.50 Contractor's Guide to *QuickBooks Pro* 2004
○ 47.75 Contractor's Guide to *QuickBooks Pro* 2003
○ 46.50 Contractor's Guide to *QuickBooks Pro* 2002
○ 45.25 Contractor's Guide to *QuickBooks Pro* 2001
○ 38.00 Contractor's Survival Manual Revised

○ 34.95 Drafting House Plans
○ 38.00 Estimating Home Building Costs, Revised
○ 52.50 Home Building Mistakes & Fixes
○ 29.95 Home Inspection Handbook
○ 28.50 How to Succeed With Your Own Construction Business
○ 69.00 Insurance Restoration Contracting: Startup to Success
○ 52.50 Markup & Profit: A Contractor's Guide, Revisited
○ 87.50 Natl. Construction Estimator w/FREE Natl. Est. Download
○ 88.75 Natl. Home Improvement Est. w/FREE Natl. Est. Download
○ 89.50 Natl. Renovation & Ins. Repair Est. w/FREE Natl. Est. Download
○ 55.50 Paper Contracting: The How-To of Constr Mgmt Contracting
○ 24.75 Profits in Buying & Renovating Homes
○ 33.50 Renovating & Restyling Older Homes
○ 26.50 Rough Framing Carpentry
○ 88.50 Natl. Repair & Remodeling Est. w/FREE Natl. Est. Download
○ FREE Full Color Catalog

Prices subject to change without notice